Frederick Douglass

SELECTED SPEECHES AND WRITINGS

EDITED BY
Philip S. Foner

ABRIDGED AND ADAPTED BY
Yuval Taylor

Lawrence Hill Books

Library of Congress Cataloging-in-Publication Data

Douglass, Frederick, 1817?–1895. Selections. 1999.
  Frederick Douglass : selected speeches and writings / edited by
Philip S. Foner / abridged and adapted by Yuval Taylor.
     p.   cm.
  Includes bibliographical references and index.
  ISBN 1–55652–349-1 (cloth).—ISBN 1–55652–352-1 (paper)
  1. Antislavery movements—United States—History—19th century.
2. Slaves—United States—Social conditions—19th century. 3. Afro-
Americans—Civil rights—History—19th century. 4. Speeches,
addresses, etc., American. I. Foner, Philip Sheldon, 1910–1994.
II. Taylor, Yuval. III. Title.
E449.D7345 1999
973.8'092—dc21
                                                          99-23180
                                                             CIP

This book is an abridgement and adaptation of Philip S. Foner's *The Life and Writings of Frederick Douglass,* originally published in New York in five volumes, 1950–1975. It is published by arrangement with Elizabeth Foner Vandepaer and Laura Foner.

Published by Lawrence Hill Books
An imprint of Chicago Review Press, Incorporated
814 North Franklin Street
Chicago, Illinois 60610

ISBN 1–55652–349-1 (cloth)
1–55652–352-1 (paper)

Printed in the United States of America

5 4 3 2 1

CONTENTS

Part Four: From the Kansas-Nebraska Act to the Election of Abraham Lincoln 273

Part Five: From Secession to the Emancipation Proclamation 423

Part Six: From the Emancipation Proclamation
to the Eve of Appomattox 515

In a fifty-four-year career as the preeminent spokesman for African Americans, Frederick Douglass gave over 2,000 speeches; wrote thousands of editorials, articles, and letters; and, not incidentally, published three autobiographies, the first two of which are now commonly acknowledged as masterpieces transcending their genre. Although most students of African American history and literature study the latter, during his life Douglass was mainly known as an orator, not an autobiographer; and it was through his speeches and writings that Douglass changed American history. For, more than any other African American, it was he who was responsible for the downfall of slavery, for the enlistment of men of his race in the Union army, and, in the last few years of his life, for the awakening of the American people to the realization that, through disenfranchisement, slavery-like practices, and wholesale slaughter, Southern blacks had lost almost every gain they had made during the Civil War and Reconstruction.

The power of oratory in the formation of public opinion in nineteenth-century America was as great as that of television today, for political culture had inherited from the Revolutionary period a classical, oratorical, consensus-based model. With his combination of rhetorical power, intellectual acumen, classical eloquence, and physical presence, Douglass may well rank as the greatest American orator of his time. The testimony of his contemporaries helps explain why. Only four months after his first speech at a Nantucket anti-slavery meeting in 1841, N. P. Rogers, a New Hampshire editor, wrote:

> As a speaker he has few equals. It is not declamation—but oratory, power of debate. He watches the tide of discussion with the eye of the veteran, and dashes into it at once with all the tact of the forum or the bar. He has wit, argument, sarcasm, pathos—all that first-rate men show in their master efforts. His voice is highly melodious and rich, and his enunciation quite elegant, and yet he has been but two or three years out of the house of bondage. . . . The brotherhood of thieves, the *posse comitatus* of divines, we wish a hecatomb or two of the proudest and flintiest of them, were obliged to hear him thunder for human liberty, and lay the enslavement of his people at their doors. They would tremble like Belshazzar.

And in 1852, William G. Allen, a professor of rhetoric and belles lettres, wrote:

> In versatility of oratorical power, I know of no one who can begin to approach the celebrated Frederick Douglass. He, in very deed, sways a magic wand. In the ability to imitate, he stands almost alone and unapproachable; and there is no actor living, whether he be tragedian or comedian, who would not give the world for such a face as his. His slaveholder's sermon is a masterpiece in its line [see the first speech in this collection, "The Church and Prejudice"]. When he rises to speak there is a slight hesitancy in his manner, which disappears as he warms up to the subject. He works with the power of a mighty intellect, and in the vast audiences which he never fails to assemble, touches chords in the inner chambers thereof which vibrate music now sweet,

now sad, now lightsome, now solemn, now startling, now grand, now majestic, now sublime. He has a voice of terrific power, of great compass, and under most admirable control. Douglass is not only great in oratory, tongue-wise, but, considering his circumstances in early life, still more marvelous in composition, pen-wise. . . . Long may he live—an honor to his age, his race, his country and the world.

Douglass clearly drew from African American rhetorical traditions—storytelling, trickster tales, black preaching, and "signifying." But his speeches and writings for the most part confirm, rather than challenge, the American rhetorical practice of his time. For example, his apocalyptic visions of America's future were usually counterbalanced by an offer of hope that the true American values embodied in the Declaration of Independence could be sustained. Douglass' mixture of doomsaying with affirmation of America's potential for greatness fits well into a long tradition of American jeremiads stretching from the seventeenth century to the present day. Also typical were his rhetorical crescendoes from a plain style at the beginning of a speech to a grand style at the end; his skillful deployment of a host of rhetorical devices such as anaphora, personification, wordplay, antithesis, and hyperbole; his citations from the Bible, Shakespeare, and eighteenth- and nineteenth-century writers; his extended use of irony and sarcasm when denouncing wrongdoing; and, as the century progressed, his increasing reliance on documentation to verify his points.

However fully Douglass fit into the American rhetorical tradition, though, his race—at least at first—effectively excluded him from it. At the time of his entry into the field of oratory, African Americans were almost universally regarded as culturally inferior, and a black orator would far sooner be judged an oddity than a leader. What enabled Douglass to overcome this handicap and break down these prejudices—and what helped distinguish him from contemporaneous orators such as Wendell Phillips, Edward Everett, and Ralph Waldo Emerson—was not only his remarkable rhetorical skill, but his inventiveness, militancy, breadth of knowledge, sense of humor, skill at mimicry, vivid language, and emotional investment in every word he spoke. Considering that the vast majority of his arguments concern only one broad topic—the conditions and rights of African Americans—the variety of his approaches and ideas is all the more astonishing. But Douglass did not like to repeat himself. He makes this clear in his account of his growth as an orator in his second autobiography, *My Bondage and My Freedom*:

> During the first three or four months, my speeches were almost exclusively made up of narrations of my own personal experience as a slave. "Let us have the facts," said the people. So also said Friend George Foster, who always wished to pin me down to my simple narrative. "Give us the facts," said Collins, "we will take care of the philosophy." Just here arose some embarrassment. It was impossible for me to repeat the same old story month after month, and to keep up my interest in it. It was new to the people, it is true, but it was an old story to me; and to go through with it night after night, was a task altogether too mechanical for my nature. "Tell your story, Frederick," would whisper my then revered friend, William Lloyd Garrison, as I stepped upon the platform. I could not always obey, for I was now reading and thinking. New views of the subject were presented to my mind. It did not entirely sat-

isfy me to *narrate* wrongs; I felt like *denouncing* them. I could not always curb my moral indignation for the perpetrators of slaveholding villainy, long enough for a circumstantial statement of the facts which I felt almost everybody must know. Besides, I was growing, and needed room. "People won't believe you ever was a slave, Frederick, if you keep on this way," said Friend Foster. "Be yourself," said Collins, "and tell your story." It was said to me, "Better have a *little* of the plantation manner of speech than not; 'tis not best that you seem too learned." These excellent friends were actuated by the best of motives, and were not altogether wrong in their advice; and still I must speak just the word that seemed to *me* the word to be spoken *by* me.

In his first autobiography, *The Narrative of the Life of Frederick Douglass, an American Slave,* Douglass transformed his "story" into the story of *all* slaves by making himself their exemplar; similarly, in his speeches and writings, he transformed his concern for his race into a concern for all America by making the "Negro question" an "American question." In doing so—and because he never gave up hope, no matter how dire the outlook—Frederick Douglass was perhaps the most significant motivator of America's long (and as yet unfinished) transformation from a land of oppression into the land of the free.

The Life and Writings of Frederick Douglass, edited by Philip S. Foner—the primary source for the present collection—was originally published in four volumes between 1950 and 1955; a fifth volume supplementing the first two was published in 1975, and a sixth supplementing volumes three and four was at least partially prepared but never published. The published volumes included approximately 2,000 pages of material written by Douglass as well as a 400-page biography of Douglass written by Foner.

Philip S. Foner (1910–1994) was one of the outstanding historians and editors of our time. His over 100 books include *The History of the Labor Movement in the United States* (ten volumes, 1947–1994), *A History of Cuba and Its Relations with the United States* (two volumes, 1962–1963), *The Voice of Black America: Major Speeches by Negroes in the United States* (1972), *Organized Labor and the Black Worker* (1974), *The History of Black Americans* (three volumes, 1975–1983), *The Black Worker: A Documentary History* (eight volumes, 1978–1984), and collections of writings and speeches by Thomas Paine, W. E. B. DuBois, Paul Robeson, George Washington Woodbey, the Black Panthers, Carl Liebknecht, Clara Zetkin, José Martí, and many others.

When *The Life and Writings* was first published, Frederick Douglass was a nearly forgotten figure in American history. As Foner pointed out, in John B. McMaster's ten-volume *History of the People of the United States* (1883–1919), Douglass was referred to only once, and was not even mentioned in Dwight L. Dumond's *Anti-Slavery Origins of the Civil War* (1939). Foner apparently had difficulty finding a publisher, for he later wrote:

> No commercial publisher or even university press displayed the slightest interest in making available the letters, editorials, and speeches of this man of towering dimen-

sions. (Indeed, the vast majority of the editors in these publishing houses had never even heard of Frederick Douglass.) The miracle was that even though harassed and financially hard-pressed during these years of McCarthyism—Alexander Trachtenberg, the publisher, even went to prison under the viciously un-American Smith Act—International Publishers undertook the expensive task of publishing the four volumes.

Doubtless it is not entirely coincidental that shortly after the publication of Foner's four volumes, Douglass began to gain widespread acceptance as *the* outstanding African American of the nineteenth century, for the books garnered overwhelming praise from prominent intellectuals:

> The Life and Writings of Frederick Douglass puts all America under deep obligation. . . . The figure of a great man rises from these volumes (W. E. B. DuBois).

> Dr. Foner has made an outstanding contribution to the social history of the Negro in the United States (E. Franklin Frazier).

> Dr. Foner's work, evident outcome of great labor and love, is a monumental piece of historical scholarship, contributing as much to vital aspects of American history as to the documentary portraiture of the nineteenth century's greatest American Negro (Alain Locke).

> A veritable treasurehouse of historical information. . . . Many of Douglass' speeches and writings have a contemporary ring (Benjamin Quarles).

> The Life and Writings of Frederick Douglass is not alone a contribution of inestimable value to the Negro people. It is of incalculable value to all Americans (William L. Patterson).

> These volumes . . . will force future historians to give Frederick Douglass the recognition he deserves. Foner, through his tireless industry in gathering this material from various libraries, and by his able job of editing, has made a major contribution to nineteenth-century political and social history (Kenneth M. Stampp).

The *Philadelphia Tribune* even went so far as to call it "one of the most important books ever published in America. It should occupy a prominent place on the bookshelf of every American home."

Unfortunately, Foner's five volumes are out of print. Five volumes of Douglass' speeches were subsequently published by Yale University Press, but at $475 for the set, they are beyond the means of most bookbuyers, and they include none of Douglass' hundreds of surviving letters, articles, and editorials. Although Douglass is undoubtedly one of America's greatest orators, political thinkers, and writers, no substantial one-volume collection of his speeches and writings has ever been published before now.

In aiming to fill that gap, I have collected from Foner's five volumes well over one-third of Douglass' material included therein. In doing so, I have attempted to balance what I think would be Foner's own wishes in compiling such a volume with the requirements of the contemporary reader; and in choosing what to include or exclude, I was concerned not only with the historical significance of each selection, but its literary merit. Foner's biography of Douglass is excellent, but to abridge it would have made it far less so, and to include it *in toto* would have filled up half this volume. I have therefore omitted it, only including, as headnotes, sections of it that pertain to particular speeches or writings. Like Foner, I have not included selections from Douglass' autobiographies, which are readily available, and which should be read as companions to this collection. I have added eight additional speeches and one article, most of which Foner would have probably included in his projected sixth volume. (They are: "My Slave Experience in Maryland," May 6, 1845; "The War and How to End It," March 25, 1862; "The Unknown Loyal Dead," May 30, 1871; "There Was a Right Side in the Late War," May 30, 1878; "John Brown," May 30, 1881; "I Denounce the So-Called Emancipation as a Stupendous Fraud," April 16, 1888, which Foner included in his collection *The Voice of Black America;* "The Bloody Shirt," June 19, 1888; "The Nation's Problem," April 16, 1889; and "Lynch Law in the South," *The North American Review,* July, 1892.) In addition, I have emended typographical errors and incorrect dates.

I would like to thank Henry Foner, Elizabeth Foner Vandepaer, and Laura Foner for their cooperation and the staff at Chicago Review Press for their support.

Benjamin Quarles once noted, "Douglass' own writings are models of clarity and good literary form. He never wrote an article or gave a speech without careful preparation. . . . Incapable of writing a dull line, Douglass invests his sentences with an almost poetic cadence, compelling the reader to turn the page." I hope that this selection—representing only a small fraction of Douglass' monumental output—convinces the reader of the truth of Quarles' remarks; and I would like to believe that, had they lived to see it, this book would have made its authors, Frederick Douglass and Philip S. Foner, proud.

YUVAL TAYLOR

BIBLIOGRAPHY

Bercovitch, Sacvan. *The American Jeremiad.* Madison, WI: University of Wisconsin Press, 1978.

Blassingame, John W., ed. *The Frederick Douglass Papers, Series One: Speeches, Debates, and Interviews.* 5 vols. New Haven, CT: Yale University Press, 1979–1992.

Chesebrough, David B. *Frederick Douglass: Oratory from Slavery.* Westport, CT: Greenwood Press, 1998.

Clark, Gregory, and Halloran, S. Michael, eds. *Oratorical Culture in Nineteenth-Century America: Transformations in the Theory and Practice of Rhetoric.* Carbondale, IL: Southern Illinois University Press, 1993.

Douglass, Frederick. *Life and Times of Frederick Douglass.* New rev. ed. Boston: De Wolfe, Fisk, & Co., [1892].

———. *My Bondage and My Freedom.* New York and Auburn, NY: Miller, Orton & Mulligan, 1855.

———. *Narrative of the Life of Frederick Douglass, an American Slave.* Boston: Anti-Slavery Office, 1845.

Fishkin, Shelley Fisher, and Peterson, Carla L. "'We Hold These Truths to Be Self-Evident': The Rhetoric of Frederick Douglass's Journalism." In *Frederick Douglass: New Literary and Historical Essays,* ed. by Eric J. Sundquist. Cambridge: Cambridge University Press, 1990.

Foner, Philip S., ed. *The Life and Writings of Frederick Douglass.* 5 vols. New York: International Publishers, 1950–1975.

————, ed. *The Voice of Black America: Major Speeches by Negroes in the United States, 1797–1971.* New York: Simon & Schuster, 1972.

Fulkerson, Gerald. "Frederick Douglass (1818–1895), Abolitionist, Reformer." In *African-American Orators: A Bio-Critical Sourcebook,* ed. by Richard W. Leeman. Westport, CT: Greenwood Press, 1996.

Gates, Henry Louis, Jr. *The Signifying Monkey: A Theory of Afro-American Literary Criticism.* New York: Oxford University Press, 1988.

————, ed. *The Classic Slave Narratives.* New York: Mentor, 1987.

Holland, Frederic May. *Frederick Douglass: The Colored Orator.* New York: Funk & Wagnalls, 1891.

Martin, Waldo E., Jr. "Frederick Douglass (1818–1895), Race Statesman, Abolitionist, Republican." In *American Orators Before 1900: Critical Sources and Studies,* ed. by Bernard K. Duffy and Halford R. Ryan. Westport, CT: Greenwood Press, 1987.

McFeely, William S. *Frederick Douglass.* New York: W. W. Norton, 1991.

Quarles, Benjamin. *Frederick Douglass.* Washington, DC: Associated Publishers, 1948.

————, ed. *Frederick Douglass.* Englewood Cliffs, NJ: Prentice-Hall, 1968.

In February, 1818, a Negro child was born in Maryland who was destined to become one of the nation's most distinguished citizens. Born a slave, he lifted himself up from bondage by his own efforts, taught himself to read and write, developed a great talent as lecturer, editor, and organizer, became a noted figure in American life, and gained world-wide recognition as the foremost spokesman for his oppressed people and courageous champion of many other progressive causes of his time.

The name of this man is Frederick Douglass. . . .

No biography by itself can do the man full justice. For this we still have to read Douglass himself. Fortunately, this is no chore. These writings of a man whom slavery deprived of formal education constitute an important and distinctive contribution to our literature. Here is the clearest articulation of discontent, protest, militant action, and hope of the American Negro. Here one of the most brilliant minds of his time, constantly responsive to the great forces of his day, analyzes every important issue confronting the Negro and the American people generally during fifty crucial years in our history. Here are the eloquent words and penetrating thoughts that exerted a decisive influence on the course of national affairs for half a century and moved countless men and women to action in behalf of freedom. Most important of all, here are the militant principles of the outstanding leader of the Negro people whose ideas have remained vital and valid down to the present day.

Emphasis has been placed throughout these volumes on presenting Douglass' writings and speeches as they appeared in their original form. . . . There have been a few editorial alterations in the selections to correct obvious misprints. Moreover, the writer has deemed it advisable to change the lower-case spelling of the word Negro to the upper-case spelling. . . . Towards the end of his career Douglass began to use the upper-case spelling in his writings. It was the judgment of the writer that the upper case spelling of the word Negro should be used throughout these volumes.

Occasionally, too, the reader will come upon words in Douglass' speeches and writings which are correctly considered scurrilous and part of the parlance of the adherents of "white supremacy." In using them Douglass made it clear that he was doing so only to indicate the contempt expressed by the pro-slavery apologists for the Negro people. These words have not been fully spelled out in the present edition. By presenting these words in this form the writer believes that he best expresses the deepest indignation of all decent people at the slanderous attacks on the Negro people revealed in these epithets.

In all of Douglass' editorials and in most of his speeches, the original titles have been retained. The writer has supplied titles where they were missing or where more descriptive titles were considered advisable. The source of the originals of Douglass' writings and speeches has been placed at the end of each speech or article. . . .

In the preparation of these volumes I have had the generous assistance and cooperation of the following: the libraries and personnel of the American Antiquarian Society, American Philosophical Library, the Frederick Douglass Memorial Association, Henry E. Huntington Library, the Historical Society of Pennsylvania, the Library Company of Philadelphia, the Library of Congress, New York Historical Society, Ohio State Archeological and Historical Society, Rutherford B. Hayes Memorial Association, the Schomburg Collection, New York, and the Wisconsin State Historical Society; the libraries of Fisk University, Harvard University, Moorland Foundation of Howard University, New York University, Oberlin College, Syracuse University, University of Rochester, and Yale University; the public libraries of Boston, New York City, and Rochester.

I also wish to thank Mr. Arthur B. Spingarn, Dr. Carter G. Woodson, and Mr. Henry P. Slaughter for making available to me writings and speeches of Frederick Douglass in their personal collections.

Mr. Doxey A. Wilkerson, Dr. Herbert Aptheker, and Elizabeth Lawson have kindly read this manuscript and offered valuable suggestions. . . .

PHILIP S. FONER

PART ONE

From 1841 to the Founding of *The North Star*

From the beginning of his career as a lecturer, Douglass moved beyond the narrow limits prescribed for him by the Garrisonians. He had been hired to tell the story of his slave experiences, and in his first public addresses he discussed nothing else. But within two months, he was discussing the "progress of the cause." . . . [In this early speech,] Douglass struck the central theme of his career as an Abolitionist—the twin battle against slavery in the South and prejudice in the North. . . .

Here was no mere copy of other Abolitionist lecturers. Here was a spokesman for his people who experienced their degradation every day of his life, and who could express in vivid burning language the pent-up indignation of the American Negro. [I:48–49]

THE CHURCH AND PREJUDICE, speech delivered at the Plymouth Church Anti-Slavery Society, December 23, 1841

At the South I was a member of the Methodist Church. When I came north, I thought one Sunday I would attend communion, at one of the churches of my denomination, in the town I was staying. The white people gathered round the altar, the blacks clustered by the door. After the good minister had served out the bread and wine to one portion of those near him, he said, "These may withdraw, and others come forward"; thus he proceeded till all the white members had been served. Then he drew a long breath, and looking out towards the door, exclaimed, "Come up, colored friends, come up! for you know *God is no respecter of persons!*" I haven't been there to see the sacraments taken since.

At New Bedford, where I live, there was a great revival of religion not long ago—many were converted and "received" as they said, "into the kingdom of heaven." But it seems, the kingdom of heaven is like a net; at least so it was according to the practice of these pious Christians; and when the net was drawn ashore, they had to set down and cull out the fish. Well, it happened now that some of the fish had rather black scales; so these were sorted out and packed by themselves. But among those who experienced religion at this time was a colored girl; she was baptised in the same water as the rest; so she thought she might sit at the Lord's table and partake of the same sacramental elements with the others. The deacon handed round the cup, and when he came to the black girl, he could not pass her, for there was the minister looking right at him, and as he was a kind of abolitionist, the deacon was rather afraid of giving him offence; so he handed the girl the cup, and she tasted. Now it so happened that next to her sat a young lady who had been converted at the same time, baptised in the same water, and put her trust in the same blessed Saviour; yet when the cup, containing the precious blood which had been shed for all, came to her, she rose in disdain, and walked out of the church. Such was the religion *she* had experienced!

Another young lady fell into a trance. When she awoke, she declared she had been to heaven. Her friends were all anxious to know what and whom she had seen there; so she told the whole story. But there was one good old lady whose curiosity went beyond that of all the others—and she inquired of the girl that had the vision, if she saw any black folks in heaven? After some hesitation, the reply was, "*Oh! I didn't go into the kitchen!*"

Thus you see, my hearers, this prejudice goes even into the church of God. And there are those who carry it so far that it is disagreeable to them even to think of going to heaven, if colored people are going there too. And whence comes it? The

3

grand cause is slavery; but there are others less prominent; one of them is the way in which children in this part of the country are instructed to regard the blacks.

"Yes!" exclaimed an old gentleman, interrupting him—"when they behave wrong, they are told, 'black man come catch you.'"

Yet people in general will say they like colored men as well as any other, *but in their proper place!* They assign us that place; they don't let us do it for ourselves, nor will they allow us a voice in the decision. They will not allow that we have a head to think, and a heart to feel, and a soul to aspire. They treat us not as men, but as dogs—they cry "Stu-boy!" and expect us to run and do their bidding. That's the way we are liked. You degrade us, and then ask why we are degraded—you shut our mouths, and then ask why we don't speak—you close your colleges and seminaries against us, and then ask why we don't know more.

But all this prejudice sinks into insignificance in *my* mind, when compared with the enormous iniquity of the system which is its cause—the system that sold my four sisters and my brothers into bondage—and which calls in its priests to defend it even from the Bible! The slaveholding ministers preach up the divine right of the slaveholders to property in their fellow-men. The southern preachers say to the poor slave, "Oh! if you wish to be happy in time, happy in eternity, you must be obedient to your masters; their interest is yours. God made one portion of men to do the working, and another to do the thinking; how good God is! Now, you have no trouble or anxiety; but ah! you can't imagine how perplexing it is to your masters and mistresses to have so much thinking to do in your behalf! You cannot appreciate your blessings; you know not how happy a thing it is for you, that you were born of that portion of the human family which has the working, instead of the thinking to do! Oh! how grateful and obedient you ought to be to your masters! How beautiful are the arrangements of Providence! Look at your hard, horny hands—see how nicely they are adapted to the labor you have to perform! Look at our delicate fingers, so exactly fitted for our station, and see how manifest it is that God designed us to be His thinkers, and you the workers— Oh! the wisdom of God!"—I used to attend a Methodist church, in which my master was a class-leader; he would talk most sanctimoniously about the dear Redeemer, who was sent "to preach deliverance to the captives, and set at liberty them that are bruised"—he could pray at morning, pray at noon, and pray at night; yet he could lash up my poor cousin by his two thumbs, and inflict stripes and blows upon his bare back, till the blood streamed to the ground! all the time quoting scripture, for his authority, and appealing to that passage of the Holy Bible which says, "He that knoweth his master's will, and doeth it not, shall be beaten with many stripes!" Such was the amount of this good Methodist's piety.

National Anti-Slavery Standard, December 23, 1841

George Latimer, a fugitive slave, had fled to Boston from Norfolk, Virginia, in October, 1842. He was arrested without a warrant and thrown into a Boston jail solely on a warrant order to the jailer of Suffolk County from James B. Gray who claimed to be his owner. Friends rallied to the slave's side and demanded a trial by jury. When Chief Justice Shaw denied the demand and refused to grant a writ of habeas corpus, the movement to save Latimer gained tremendous momentum.

Boston was wild with excitement. Placards were distributed and handbills posted throughout the city denouncing the outrage, and summoning the citizens to a meeting in Faneuil Hall "For the Rescue of Liberty!" "Agitate! Agitate!" cried the *Liberator* of November 11, 1842. "Latimer *shall go free!* . . . Be vigilant, firm, uncompromising, friends of freedom! friends of God!" . . .

In mid-November Latimer was purchased from Gray for four hundred dollars, and then set free. Around this event, the Abolitionists organized a series of celebrations with Latimer as the central figure. Douglass, a prominent speaker at the celebrations, was moved by Latimer's freedom to unusual brilliance.[1]

[This is the first public letter Douglass ever wrote.] [I:54]

TO WILLIAM LLOYD GARRISON

Lynn, November 8th, 1842

Dear Friend Garrison:

The date of this letter finds me quite unwell. I have for a week past been laboring, in company with bro[ther] Charles Remond, in New Bedford, with special reference to the case of our outraged brother, George Latimer, and speaking almost day and night, in public and in private; and for the reward of our labor, I have the best evidence that a great good has been done. It is said by many residents, that New Bedford has never been so favorably aroused to her anti-slavery responsibility as at present. Our meetings were characterized by that deep and solemn feeling which the importance of the cause, when properly set forth, is always calculated to awaken. On Sunday, we held three meetings in the new town hall, at the usual meeting hours, morning, afternoon, and evening. In the morning, we had quite a large meeting, at the opening of which, I occupied about an hour, on the question as to whether a man is better than a sheep. Mr. Dean then made a few remarks, and after him, Mr. Clapp of Nantucket arose and gave his testimony to the truth, as it is in anti-slavery. The meeting then adjourned, to meet again in the afternoon. I said that we held our meetings at the regular meeting hours. Truth requires me to make our afternoon meeting an exception to this remark. For long before the drawling, lazy church bells commenced sounding their deathly notes, mighty crowds were making their way to the town hall. . . . After a short space, allotted to secret or public prayer, bro[ther] J. B. Sanderson arose and requested the attention of the audience to the reading of a few passages of scripture, selected by yourself in the editorial of last week. They did give their attention, and as he read the solemn and soul-stirring denunciations of Jehovah, by the mouth of his prophets and apostles, against oppressors, the deep stillness that pervaded that magnificent hall was a brilliant demonstration that the audience felt that what was read was but the reiteration of words which had fallen from the great Judge of the universe. After reading, he proceeded to make some remarks on the general question of human rights. These, too, seemed to sink deep into the hearts of the gathered multitude. Not a word was lost; it was good seed, sown in good ground, by a careful hand; it must, it will bring forth fruit.

After him, rose bro[ther] Remond, who addressed the meeting in his usual happy and deeply affecting style. When he had concluded his remarks, the meeting adjourned to meet again at an early hour in the evening. . . .

The meeting met according to adjournment, at an early hour. The splendid hall was brilliantly lighted, and crowded with an earnest, listening audience, and notwithstanding the efforts of our friends before named to have them seated, a large number had to stand during the meeting, which lasted about three hours; where the standing part of the audience were, at the commencement of the meeting, there they were at the conclusion of it; no moving about with them; any place was good enough, so they could but hear. From the eminence which I occupied, I could see the entire audience; and from its appearance, I should conclude that prejudice against color was not there, at any rate, it was not to be seen by me; we were all on a level, every one took a seat just where they chose; there were neither men's side, nor women's side; white pew, nor black pew; but all seats were free, and all sides free. When the meeting was fully gathered, I had something to say, and was followed by bro[thers] Sanderson and Remond. When they had concluded their remarks, I again took the stand, and called the attention of the meeting to the case of bro[ther] George Latimer, which proved the finishing stroke of my present public speaking. On taking my seat, I was seized with a violent pain in my breast, which continued till morning, and with occasional raising of blood; this past off in about two hours, after which, weakness of breast, a cough, and shortness of breath ensued, so that now such is the state of my lungs, that I am unfit for public speaking, for the present. My condition goes harder with me, much harder than it would at ordinary times. These are certainly extraordinary times; times that demand the efforts of the humblest of our most humble advocates of our perishing and dying fellow-countrymen. Those that can but whisper freedom, should be doing even that, though they can only be heard from one side of their short fire place to the other. It is a struggle of life and death with us just now. No sword that can be used, be it never so rusty, should lay idle in its scabbard. Slavery, our enemy, has landed in our very midst, and commenced its bloody work. Just look at it; here is George Latimer a man—a brother—a husband—a father, stamped with the likeness of the eternal God, and redeemed by the blood of Jesus Christ, out-lawed, hunted down like a wild beast, and ferociously dragged through the streets of Boston, and incarcerated within the walls of Leverett-st. jail. And all this is done in Boston—liberty-loving, slavery-hating Boston—intellectual, moral, and religious Boston. And why was this—what crime had George Latimer committed? He had committed the crime of availing himself of his natural rights, in defence of which the founders of this very Boston enveloped her in midnight darkness, with the smoke proceeding from their thundering artillery. What a horrible state of things is here presented. Boston has become the hunting-ground of merciless men-hunters, and man-stealers. Henceforth we need not portray to the imagination of northern people, the flying slave making his way through thick and dark woods of the South, with white fanged blood-hounds yelping on his blood-stained track; but refer to the streets of Boston, made dark and dense by crowds of professed Christians. Take a look at James B. Gray's new pack, turned loose on the track of poor Latimer. I see the blood-thirsty animals, smelling at every corner, part with each other, and meet again; they seem to be consulting as to the best mode of coming upon their victim. Now they look sad, discouraged;—tired, they drag along, as if they were ashamed of their business, and about to give up the chase; but presently they get a sight of their prey, their eyes brighten, they become more courageous, they approach their victim unlike the common hound. They come upon him softly, wagging their tails, pretending friendship, and do not pounce upon him, until they have secured him beyond possible escape. Such is the character of James B. Gray's new pack of two-legged blood-hounds that hunted down George Latimer, and dragged him away to the Leverett-street slave prison but a few days since. We need not point to the sugar fields of Louisiana, or to the rice swamps of Alabama, for the bloody deeds of this soul-crushing system, but to the city of the pilgrims. In future, we need not uncap the bloody cells of the horrible slave prisons of Norfolk, Richmond, Mobile, and New-Orleans, and depict the wretched and forlorn condition of their miserable inmates, whose groans rend the air, pierce heaven, and disturb the Almighty; listen no longer at the snappings of the bloody slavedrivers' lash. Withdraw your attention, for a moment, from the agonizing cries coming from hearts bursting with the keenest anguish at the South, gaze no longer upon the base, cold-blooded, heartless slave-dealer of the South, who lays his iron clutch upon the hearts of husband and wife, and, with one mighty effort, tears the bleeding ligaments apart which before constituted the twain one flesh. I say, turn your attention from all this cruelty abroad, look now at home—follow me to your courts of justice—mark him who sits upon the bench. He may, or he may not—God grant he may not—tear George Latimer from a beloved wife and tender infant. But let us take a walk to the prison in which George Latimer is confined, inquire for the turn-key; let him open the large iron-barred door that leads you to the inner prison. You need go no further. Hark! Listen! hear the groans and cries of George Latimer, mingling with which may be heard the cry—my wife, my child—and all is still again.

A moment of reflection ensues—I am to be taken back to Norfolk—must be torn from a wife and tender babe, with the threat from Mr. Gray that I am to be murdered, though not in the ordinary way—not to have my head severed from my shoulders, not to be hanged—not to have my heart pierced through with a dagger—not to have my brains blown out. No, no, all these are too good for me. No: I am to be killed by inches. I know not how; perhaps by cat-hauling until my back is torn all to pieces, my flesh is to be cut with the rugged lash, and I faint; warm brine must now be poured into my bleeding wounds, and through this process I must pass, until death shall end my sufferings. Good God! save me from a fate so horrible. Hark! hear him roll in his chains; "I can die, I had rather, than go back. O, my wife! O, my child!" You have heard enough. What man, what Christian can look upon this bloody state of things without his soul swelling big with indignation on the guilty perpetrators of it, and without re-solving to cast in his influence with those who are collecting the elements which are to come down in ten-fold thunder, and dash this state of things into atoms?

Men, husbands and fathers of Massachusetts—put yourselves in the place of George Latimer; feel his pain and anxiety of mind; give vent to the groans that are breaking through his fever-parched lips, from a heart emersed in the deepest agony and suffering; rattle his chains; let his prospects be yours, for the space of a few moments. Remember George Latimer in bonds as bound with him; keep in view the golden rule—"All things whatsoever ye would that men should do unto you, do ye even so to them." "In as much as ye did it unto the least of these my brethren ye have done it unto me."

Now make up your minds to what your duty is to George Latimer, and when you have made your minds up, prepare to do it and take the consequences, and I have no fears of George Latimer going back. I can sympathize with George Latimer, having myself been cast into a miserable jail, on suspicion of my intending to do what he is said to have done, viz., appropriating my own body to my use.

My heart is full, and had I my voice, I should be doing all that I am capable of, for Latimer's redemption. I can do but little in any department; but if one department is more the place for me than another, that one is before the people.

I can't write to much advantage, having never had a day's schooling in my life, nor have I ever ventured to give publicity to any of my scribbling before; nor would I now, but for my peculiar circumstances.

Your grateful friend,
Frederick Douglass

The *Liberator,* November 18, 1842

1. *The Latimer Journal and North Star,* Nov. 26, 1842. After Latimer's purchase, the Abolitionists presented a petition to the State Legislature praying that fugitive slaves should never again be arrested by town or city officials, nor held as prisoners in the jails of Massachusetts, and that the State Constitution should be "so amended as shall forever separate the people of Massachusetts from all connection with slavery." The petition, signed by 60,000 persons headed by George Latimer himself, was presented on February 17, 1843, to the Massachusetts House of Representatives. It resulted in the passage of a law, with very few dissenting votes, making it a penal offense for any magistrate or executive officer of the state to assist in the arrest or delivery of any person claimed as a fugitive slave and prohibiting those having charge of the jails and other places of confinement to use them for his detention. (See *The Latimer Journal and North Star,* Nov. 23, 1842; *Twelfth Annual Report of the Massachusetts Anti-Slavery Society,* Boston, 1844, p. 45.)

THE FOLLY OF OUR OPPONENTS

In a note enclosing this article, Mr. Douglass says:—"It was intended for a place in The Liberty Bell, *but my literary advantages have been so limited, that I am ill prepared to decide what is, and what is not, appropriate for such a collection. I looked exceedingly strange in my own eyes, as I sat writing. The thought of writing for a book!—and only six years since a fugitive from a Southern cornfield—caused a singular jingle in my mind."*

Dr. Dewey, in his somewhat notorious defence of American Morals, published soon after his return to this country from Europe, where he had witnessed those morals subjected to a most rigid examination, treats of the conduct of the American people with regard to prejudice and Slavery; and, in extenuation of their conduct, speaks of the existence of an "*impassable barrier*" between the white and colored people of this country, and proceeds to draw a most odious picture of the character of his colored fellow-countrymen. Mean and wicked as is this position, the Doctor assumes it; and in so doing, becomes the favorite representative of a large class of his divine order, as well as of his white fellow citizens, who, like himself, being stung to very shame by the exposures abroad of their naked inhumanity at home, strive, with fig-leaf sophistry, to cover their guilt from the penetrating eye and scorching rebukes of the Christian world.

Fortunately for the cause of truth and human brotherhood, it has reached a period, when such mean-spirited efforts tend more to advance than retard its progress. Ingenious as are the arguments of its foes, they but defeat the object they are intended to promote. Their authors, in seeking thus to cover their sins, succeed only in lighting the lamp of investigation by which their guilt is more completely exposed. It is the decree of the Supreme Ruler of the universe, that he will confound the wisdom of the crafty, and bring to naught the counsels of the ungodly; and how faithfully is his decree executed upon those who bring their worldly wisdom to cover up the guilt of the American people! Their iniquity has grown too large for its robe. When one part is covered, another, equally odious and revolting, is made to appear. The efforts of priests and politicians to stretch the garment, to suit the dimensions of this giant sin, has resulted in tearing it asunder, and leaving the monster revealed as perhaps it never was before.

When they tell the world that the Negro is ignorant, and naturally and intellectually incapacitated to appreciate and enjoy freedom, they also publish their own condemnation, by bringing to light those infamous Laws by which the Slave is compelled to live in the grossest ignorance. When they tell the world that the Slave is immoral, vicious and degraded, they but invite attention to their own depravity: for the world sees the Slave stripped, *by his accusers,* of every safeguard to virtue, even of that purest and most sacred institution of marriage. When they represent the Slave as being destitute of religious principle—as in the preceding cases—they profit nothing by the plea. In addition to their moral condemnation they brand themselves with bold and daring impiety, in making it an offence punishable with fine and imprisonment, and even death, to teach a Slave to read the will of God. When they pretend that they hold the Slave out of actual regard to the Slave's welfare, and not because of any profit which accrues to themselves, as owners, they are covered with confusion by the single fact that Virginia alone has realized, in one short year, eighteen millions of dollars from the sale of human flesh. When they attempt to shield themselves by the grossly absurd and wicked pretence that the Slave is contented and happy, and, therefore, "better off" in Slavery than he could be possessed of freedom, their shield is broken by that long and bloody list of advertisements for runaway Slaves who have left their happy homes, and sought for freedom, even at the hazard of losing their lives in the attempt to gain it. When it is most foolishly asserted by Henry Clay, and those he represents, that the freedom of the colored is incompatible with the liberty of the white people of this country, the wicked intent of its author, and the barefaced absurdity of the proposition, are equally manifest. And when John C. Calhoun and Senator Walker attempt to prove that freedom is fraught with deafness, insanity and blindness to the people of color, their whole refuge of lies is swept away by the palpable inaccuracy of the last United States Census. And when, to cap the climax, Dr. Dewey tells the people of England that the white and colored people in this country are separated by an "impassable barrier," the hundreds of thousands of mulattoes, quadroons, &c. in this country, silently but unequivocally brand him with the guilt of having uttered a most egregious falsehood.

Bad, however, as are the apologies which the American people make in defence of themselves and their "peculiar institution," I am always glad to see them. I prize them very highly, as indications of a living sense of shame, which renders them susceptible of outward influences, and which shall one day bring them to repentance. Men seldom sink so deep in sin as to rid themselves of all disposition to apologize for their iniquity;—when they do, it is quite idle to labor for their reformation. Fortunately for our brethren under the accursed yoke, the American people have not yet reached that depth; and whilst there is a sense of shame left, there is strong ground for hope. The year eighteen hundred and forty-four has produced an abundant harvest of anti-slavery discussion. Slavery and prejudice cannot endure discussion, even though such discussion be had in its favor. The light necessary to reason by, is at once too painful to the eyes of these twin-monsters of darkness to be endured. Their motto is, "Put out the light!" Thanks to Heaven, "the morning light is breaking"; our cause is onward; the efforts of our enemies, not less than the efforts of our friends, are contributing to increase the strength of that sentiment at home, as well as abroad, which is very soon to dash down the bloody altar of Slavery, and "proclaim liberty through all the land, unto all the inhabitants thereof."

Lynn, Massachusetts, U.S.

The Liberty Bell, 1845, pp. 166–172

Pleased though they were with Douglass' effectiveness on the platform, his associates were becoming convinced that his development had been too rapid. As early as 1841 Stephen S. Foster had warned Douglass, "People won't believe that you were ever a slave, Frederick, if you keep on in this way." [John A.] Collins had added, "Better have a little of the plantation speech than not; it is not best that you seem too learned." But Douglass refused to be stereotyped and stunted, and despite repeated exhortations to "give us the facts, we will take care of the philosophy," he refused to confine himself to repeating the story of his life over and over again. "I could not always follow the injunction," he wrote later, "for I was now reading and thinking. New views of the subject were being presented to my mind. It did not entirely satisfy me to narrate wrongs; I felt like denouncing them. . . . Besides I was growing and needed room."[1]

The conflict on this issue was inevitable. Many middle and upperclass white Abolitionists would not see the former Negro slave as anything but an exhibit. The white antislavery leaders would be the main actors; the Negroes would be the extras or only part of the stage props. Some white Abolitionists were sorry to see Douglass' rapid development as a brilliant thinker and orator. Instead of being proud that this former Negro slave had been able in such a short time to equal and even surpass many of the white spokesmen against slavery, they were worried by it and even resented it.

Yet Douglass was soon to discover that the fears of his advisers were not entirely groundless. He began to hear and read statements expressing doubt as to his ever having seen slavery. "Many persons in the audience," wrote a Philadelphia correspondent in the *Liberator* of August 30, 1844, "seemed unable to credit the statements which he gave of himself, and could not believe that he was actually a slave. How a man, only six years out of bondage, and who had never gone to school a day in his life, could speak with such eloquence—with such precision of language and power of thought—they were utterly at a loss to devise."

Douglass was aware that if such reports continued, they would be fatal to his effectiveness as an Abolitionist agent. So he resolved to throw caution to the winds and write the story of his life. During the winter months of 1844–1845 he was busily engaged in setting down an account of his slave experiences. His *Narrative of the Life of Frederick Douglass,* a small volume of 125 pages selling for fifty cents, with introductions by Garrison and Phillips, came off the press in May, 1845. [I:59]

MY SLAVE EXPERIENCE IN MARYLAND, speech before the American Anti-Slavery Society, May 6, 1845

I do not know that I can say anything to the point. My habits and early life have done much to unfit me for public speaking, and I fear that your patience has already been wearied by the lengthened remarks of other speakers, more eloquent than I can possibly be, and better prepared to command the attention of the audience. And I can scarcely hope to get your attention even for a longer period than fifteen minutes.

Before coming to this meeting, I had a sort of desire—I don't know but it was vanity—to stand before a New-York audience in the Tabernacle. But when I came in this morning, and looked at those massive pillars, and saw the vast throng which had assembled, I got a little frightened, and was afraid that I could not speak; but now that the audience is not so large and I have recovered from my fright, I will venture to say a word on Slavery.

I ran away from the South seven years ago—passing through this city in no little hurry, I assure you—and lived about three years in New Bedford, Massachusetts, before I became publicly known to the anti-slavery people. Since then I have been engaged for three years in telling the people what I know of it. I have come to this meeting to throw in my mite, and since no fugitive slave has preceded me, I am encouraged to say a word about the sunny South. I thought, when the eloquent female who addressed this audience a while ago, was speaking of the horrors of Slavery, that many an honest man would doubt the truth of the picture which she drew; and I can unite with the gentleman from Kentucky in saying, that she came far short of describing them.

I can tell you what I have seen with my own eyes, felt on my own person, and know to have occurred in my own neighborhood. I am not from any of those States where the slaves are said to be in their most degraded condition; but from Maryland, where Slavery is said to exist in its mildest form; yet I can stand here and relate atrocities which would make your blood to boil at the statement of them. I lived on the plantation of Col. Lloyd, on the eastern shore of Maryland, and belonged to that gentleman's clerk. He owned, probably, not less than a thousand slaves.

I mention the name of this man, and also of the persons who perpetrated the deeds which I am about to relate, running the risk of being hurled back into interminable bondage—for I am yet a slave;—yet for the sake of the cause—for the sake of humanity, I will mention the names, and glory in running the risk. I have the gratification to know that if I fall by the utterance of truth in this matter, that if I shall be hurled back into bondage to gratify the slaveholder—to be killed by inches—that every drop of blood which I shall shed, every groan which I shall utter, every pain which shall rack my frame, every sob in which I shall indulge, shall be the instrument, under God, of tearing down the bloody pillar of Slavery, and of hastening the day of deliverance for three millions of my brethren in bondage.

I therefore tell the names of these bloody men, not because they are worse than other men would have been in their circumstances. No, they are bloody from necessity. Slavery makes it necessary for the slaveholder to commit all conceivable outrages upon the miserable slave. It is impossible to hold the slaves in bondage without this.

We had on the plantation an overseer, by the name of Austin Gore, a man who was highly respected as an overseer—proud, ambitious, cruel, artful, obdurate. Nearly every slave stood in the utmost dread and horror of that man. His eye flashed confusion amongst them. He never spoke but to command, nor commanded but to be obeyed. He was lavish with the whip, sparing with his word. I have seen that man tie up men by the two hands, and for two hours, at intervals, ply the lash. I have seen women stretched up on the limbs of trees, and their bare backs made bloody with the lash. One slave refused to be whipped by him— I need not tell you that he was a man, though black his features, degraded his condition. He had committed some trifling offence—for they whip for trifling offences—the slave refused to be whipped, and ran—he did not stand to and fight his master as I did once, and might do again—though I hope I shall not have occasion to do so—he ran and stood in a creek, and refused to come out. At length his master told him he would shoot him if he did not come out. Three calls were to be given him. The first, second, and third, were given, at each of which the slave stood his ground. Gore, equally determined and firm, raised his musket, and in an instant poor Derby was no more. He sank beneath the waves, and naught but the crimsoned waters marked the spot. Then a general outcry might be heard amongst us. Mr. Lloyd asked Gore why he had resorted to such a cruel measure. He replied, coolly, that he had done it from necessity; that the slave was setting a dangerous example, and that if he was permitted to be corrected and yet save his life, that the slaves would effectually rise and be freemen, and their masters be slaves. His defence was satisfactory. He remained on the plantation, and his fame went abroad. He still lives in St. Michaels, Talbot county, Maryland, and is now, I presume, as much respected, as though his guilty soul had never been stained with his brother's blood.

I might go on and mention other facts if time would permit. My own wife had a dear cousin who was terribly mangled in her sleep, while nursing the child of a Mrs. Hicks. Finding the girl asleep, Mrs. Hicks beat her to death with a billet of wood, and the woman has never been brought to justice." It is not a crime to kill a negro in Talbot county, Maryland, farther than it is a deprivation of a man's property. I used to know of one who boasted that he had killed two slaves, and with an oath would say, "I'm the only benefactor in the country."

Now, my friends, pardon me for having detained you so long; but let me tell you with regard to the feelings of the slave. The people at the North say—"Why don't you rise? If we were thus treated we would rise and throw off the yoke. We would wade knee deep in blood before we would endure the bondage." You'd rise up! Who are these that are asking for manhood in the slave, and who say that he has it not, because he does not rise? The very men who are ready by the Constitution to bring the strength of the nation to put us down! You, the people of New-York, the people of Massachusetts, of New England, of the whole Northern States, have sworn under God that we shall be slaves or die! And shall we three millions be taunted with a want of the love of freedom, by the very men who stand upon us and say, submit, or be crushed?

We don't ask you to engage in any physical warfare against the slaveholder. We only ask that in Massachusetts, and the several non-slaveholding States which maintain a union with the slaveholder—who stand with your heavy heels on the quivering heart-strings of the slave, that you will stand off. Leave us to take care of our masters. But here you come up to our masters and tell them that they ought to shoot us—to take away our wives and little ones—to sell our mothers into interminable bondage, and sever the tenderest ties. You say to us, if you dare to carry out the principles of our fathers, we'll shoot you down. Others may tamely submit; not I. You may put the chains upon me and fetter me, but I am not a slave, for my master who puts the chains upon me, shall stand in as much dread of me as I do of him. I ask you in the name of my three millions of brethren at the South. We know that we are unable to cope with you in numbers; you are numerically stronger, politically stronger, than we are—but we ask you if you will rend asunder the heart and [crush] the body of the slave? If so, you must do it at your own expense.

While you continue in the Union, you are as bad as the slaveholder. If you have thus wronged the poor black man, by stripping him of his freedom, how are you going to give evidence of your repentance? Undo what you have done. Do you say that the slave ought not to be free? These hands—are they not mine? This body—is it not mine? Again, I am your brother, white as you are. I'm your blood-kin. You don't get rid of me so easily. I mean to hold on to you. And in this land of liberty, I'm a slave. The twenty-six States that blaze forth on your flag, proclaim a compact to return me to bondage if I run away, and keep me in bondage if I submit. Wherever I go, under the aegis of your liberty, there I'm a slave. If I go to Lexington or Bunker Hill, there I'm a slave, chained in perpetual servitude. I may go to your deepest valley, to your highest mountain, I'm still a slave, and the bloodhound may chase me down.

Now I ask you if you are willing to have your country the hunting-ground of the slave. God says thou shalt not oppress: the Constitution says oppress: which will you serve, God or man? The American Anti-Slavery Society says God, and I am thankful for it. In the name of my brethren, to you, Mr. President, and the noble band who cluster around you, to you, who are scouted on every hand by priest, people, politician, Church, and State, to you I bring a thankful heart, and in the name of three millions of slaves, I offer you their gratitude for your faithful advocacy in behalf of the slave.

National Anti-Slavery Standard, May 22, 1845

1. *Life and Times of Frederick Douglass,* p. 242.

On August 16, 1845, accompanied by the Hutchinsons and James N. Buffum, Douglass sailed for Liverpool on the Cunard steamer *Cambria.* Buffum's efforts to get first-class passage for Douglass had failed for what was politely referred to as "complexional reasons," and Douglass was forced to travel steerage. Every morning during the eleven-day trip, however, he joined his colleagues on the promenade deck, mingled with the passengers, and sold copies of the *Narrative.* The captain of the steamer was disposed to be friendly to his Negro passenger and ignored the protests of southerners on board. But the night before the *Cambria* docked at Liverpool, the explosion came. [I:62]

TO WILLIAM LLOYD GARRISON

Dublin, Sept. 1, 1845

Dear Friend Garrison:

Thanks to a kind Providence, I am now safe in old Ireland, in the beautiful city of Dublin, surrounded by the kind family, and seated at the table of our mutual friend, James H. Webb, brother of the well-known Richard D. Webb. . . . I know it will gladden your heart to hear, that from the moment we first lost sight of the American shore, till we landed at Liverpool, our gallant steam-ship was the theatre of an almost constant discussion of the subject of slavery—commencing cool, but growing hotter every moment as it advanced. It was a great time for anti-slavery, and a hard time for slavery;—the one delighting in the sunshine of free discussion, and the other horror-stricken at its God-like approach. The discussion was general. If suppressed in the saloon, it broke out in the steerage; and if it ceased in the steerage, it was renewed in the saloon; and if suppressed in both, it broke out with redoubled energy, high upon the saloon deck, in the open, refreshing, free ocean air. I was happy. Every thing went on nobly. The truth was being told, and having its legitimate effect upon the hearts of those who heard it. At last, the evening previous to our arrival at Liverpool, the slaveholders, convinced that reason, morality, common honesty, humanity, and

Christianity, were all against them, and that argument was no longer any means of defence, or at least but a poor means, abandoned their post in debate, and resorted to their old and natural mode of defending their morality by brute force.

Yes, they actually got up a *mob*—a real American, republican, democratic, Christian mob,—and that, too, on the deck of a British steamer, and in sight of the beautiful high lands of Dungarvan! I declare, it is enough to make a slave ashamed of the country that enslaved him, to think of it. Without the slightest pretensions to patriotism, as the phrase goes, the conduct of the mobocratic Americans on board the Cambria almost made me ashamed to say I *had run away* from such a country. It was decidedly the most daring and disgraceful, as well as wicked exhibition of depravity, I ever witnessed, North or South; and the actors in it showed themselves to be as hard in heart, as venomous in spirit, and as bloody in design, as the infuriated men who bathed their hands in the warm blood of the noble Lovejoy.[1]

The facts connected with, and the circumstances leading to, this most disgraceful transaction, I will now give, with some minuteness, though I may border, at times, a little on the ludicrous.

In the first place, our passengers were made up of nearly all sorts of people, from different countries, of the most opposite modes of thinking on all subjects. We had nearly all sorts of parties in morals, religion, and politics, as well as trades, callings, and professions. The doctor and the lawyer, the soldier and the sailor, were there. The scheming Connecticut wooden clock-maker, the large, surly, New-York lion-tamer, the solemn Roman Catholic bishop, and the Orthodox Quaker were there. A minister of the Free Church of Scotland, and a minister of the Church of England—the established Christian and the wandering Jew, the Whig and the Democrat, the white and the black—were there. There was the dark-visaged Spaniard, and the light-visaged Englishman—the man from Montreal, and the man from Mexico. There were slaveholders from Cuba, and slaveholders from Georgia. We had anti-slavery singing and pro-slavery grumbling; and at the same time that Governor Hammond's Letters were being read,[2] my Narrative was being circulated.

In the midst of the debate going on, there sprang up quite a desire, on the part of a number on board, to have me lecture to them on slavery. I was first requested to do so by one of the passengers, who had become quite interested. I, of course, declined, well knowing that that was a privilege which the captain alone had a right to give, and intimated as much to the friend who invited me. I told him I should not feel at liberty to lecture, unless the captain should personally invite me to speak. Things went on as usual till between five and six o'clock in the afternoon of Wednesday, when I received an invitation from the captain to deliver an address upon the saloon deck. I signified my willingness to do so, and he at once ordered the bell to be rung and the meeting cried. This was the signal for a general excitement. Some swore I should not speak, and others that I should. Bloody threats were being made against me, if I attempted it. At the hour appointed, I went upon the saloon deck, where I was expected to speak. There was much noise going on among the passengers, evidently intended to make it impossible for me to proceed. At length, our Hutchinson friends broke forth in one of their unrivalled songs, which, like the angel of old, closed the lions' mouths, so that, for a time, silence prevailed. The captain, taking advantage of this silence, now introduced me, and expressed the hope that the audience would hear me with attention. I then commenced speaking; and, after expressing my gratitude to a kind Providence that had brought us safely across the sea, I proceeded to portray the condition of my brethren in bonds. I had not uttered five words, when a Mr. Hazzard, from Connecticut, called out, in a loud voice, "That's a lie!" I went on, taking no notice of him, though he was murmuring nearly all the while, backed up by a man from New-Jersey. I continued till I said something which seemed to cut to the quick, when out bawled Hazzard, "That's a lie!" and appeared anxious to strike me. I then said to the audience that I would explain to them the reason of Hazzard's conduct. The colored man, in our country, was treated as a being without rights. "That's a lie!" said Hazzard. I then told the audience that as almost every thing I said was pronounced lies, I would endeavor to substantiate them by reading a few extracts from slave laws. The slavocrats, finding they were now to be fully exposed, rushed up about me, with hands clenched, and swore I should not speak. They were ashamed to have American laws read before an English audience. Silence was restored by the interference of the captain, who took a noble stand in regard to my speaking. He said he had tried to please all of his passengers—and a part of them had expressed to him a desire to hear me lecture to them, and in obedience to their wishes he had invited me to speak; and those who did not wish to hear, might go to some other part of the ship. He then turned, and requested me to proceed. I again commenced, but was again interrupted—more violently than before. One slaveholder from Cuba shook his fist in my face, and said, "O, I wish I had you in Cuba!" "Ah!" said another, "I wish I had him in Savannah! We would use him up!" Said another, "I will be one of a number to throw him overboard!"

We were now fully divided into two distinct parties—those in favor of my speaking, and those against me. A noble-spirited Irish gentleman assured the man who proposed to throw me overboard, that two could play at that game, and that, in the end, he might be thrown overboard himself. The clamor went on, waxing hotter and hotter, till it was quite impossible for me to proceed. I was stopped, but the cause went on. Anti-slavery was uppermost, and the mob was never of more service to the cause against which it was directed. The clamor went on long after I ceased speaking, and was only silenced by the captain, who told the mobocrats if they did not cease their clamor, he would have them put in irons; and he actually sent for the irons, and doubtless would have made use of them, had not the rioters become orderly.

Such is but a faint outline of an AMERICAN MOB ON BOARD OF A BRITISH STEAM PACKET.

Yours, to the end of the race,

Frederick Douglass

The *Liberator*, September 26, 1845

1. In 1837, Elijah P. Lovejoy (1802–1837), a clergyman who had edited an anti-slavery paper in St. Louis, was forced to leave that city and to carry on his work in Alton, Illinois. Here

he organized the Illinois Anti-Slavery Society and edited the *Alton Observer*. Pro-slavery mobs destroyed one printing press after another, and, on November 7, 1837, the night after the third press was installed, the printing office was attacked and Lovejoy was killed while defending his property. Thereafter he was referred to as the "martyr abolitionist."

2. John L. Brown of Fairfield, South Carolina, was convicted in the fall of 1843 of aiding a slave to escape, and was sentenced to be hanged. Petitions poured in to Governor James Henry Hammond (1810–1864) demanding that he reprieve the sentence. To one of the Memorials, that from the Free Church of Glasgow, Hammond replied, defending slavery. He also sent two letters to Thomas Clarkson, elaborating his pro-slavery arguments. The Free Church and Clarkson letters were published in pamphlet form in late May and June, 1845, by the Charleston *Mercury;* were translated and circulated all over Europe. They were republished in 1853 in the *Pro-Slavery Argument,* and again in 1860 in *Cotton is King and Pro-Slavery Arguments.*

TO WILLIAM LLOYD GARRISON

Victoria Hotel, Belfast,
January 1, 1846

My Dear Friend Garrison:

I am now about to take leave of the Emerald Isle, for Glasgow, Scotland. I have been here a little more than four months. Up to this time, I have given no direct expression of the views, feelings and opinions which I have formed, respecting the character and condition of the people in this land. I have refrained thus purposely. I wish to speak advisedly, and in order to do this, I have waited till I trust experience has brought my opinions to an intelligent maturity. I have been thus careful, not because I think what I may say will have much effect in shaping the opinions of the world, but because whatever of influence I may possess, whether little or much, I wish it to go in the right direction, and according to truth. I hardly need say that, in speaking of Ireland, I shall be influenced by prejudices in favor of America. I think my circumstances all forbid that. I have no end to serve, no creed to uphold, no government to defend; and as to nation, I belong to none. I have no protection at home, or resting-place abroad. The land of my birth welcomes me to her shores only as a slave, and spurns with contempt the idea of treating me differently. So that I am an outcast from the society of my childhood, and an outlaw in the land of my birth. "I am a stranger with thee, and a sojourner as all my fathers were." That men should be patriotic is to me perfectly natural; and as a philosophical fact, I am able to give it an *intellectual* recognition. But no further can I go. If ever I had any patriotism, or any capacity for the feeling, it was whipt out of me long since by the lash of the American soul-drivers.

In thinking of America, I sometimes find myself admiring her bright blue sky— her grand old woods—her fertile fields—her beautiful rivers—her mighty lakes, and star-crowned mountains. But my rapture is soon checked, my joy is soon turned to mourning. When I remember that all is cursed with the infernal spirit of slaveholding, robbery and wrong,—when I remember that with the waters of her noblest rivers, the tears of my brethren are borne to the ocean, disregarded and forgotten, and that her most fertile fields drink daily of the warm blood of my outraged sisters, I am filled with unutterable loathing, and led to reproach myself that any thing could fall from my lips in praise of such a land. America will not allow her children to love her. She seems bent on compelling those who would be her warmest friends, to be her worst enemies. May God give her repentance before it is too late, is the ardent prayer of my heart. I will continue to pray, labor and wait, believing that she cannot always be insensible to the dictates of justice, or deaf to the voice of humanity.

My opportunities for learning the character and condition of the people of this land have been very great. I have travelled almost from the hill of "Howth" to the Giant's Causeway, and from the Giant's Causeway to Cape Clear. During these travels, I have met with much in the character and condition of the people to approve, and much to condemn—much that has thrilled me with pleasure—and very much that has filled me with pain. I will not, in this letter, attempt to give any description of those scenes which have given me pain. This I will do hereafter. I have enough, and more than your subscribers will be disposed to read at one time, of the bright side of the picture. I can truly say, I have spent some of the happiest moments of my life since landing in this country. I seem to have undergone a transformation. I live a new life. The warm and generous co-operation extended to me by the friends of my despised race—the prompt and liberal manner with which the press has rendered me its aid—the glorious enthusiasm with which thousands have flocked to hear the cruel wrongs of my down-trodden and long-enslaved fellow-countrymen portrayed—the deep sympathy for the slave, and the strong abhorrence of the slaveholder, everywhere evinced—the cordiality with which members and ministers of various religious bodies, and of various shades of religious opinion, have embraced me, and lent me their aid—the kind hospitality constantly proffered to me by persons of the highest rank in society—the spirit of freedom that seems to animate all with whom I come in contact—and the entire absence of every thing that looked like prejudice against me, on account of the color of my skin—contrasted so strongly with my long and bitter experience in the United States, that I look with wonder and amazement on the transition. In the Southern part of the United States, I was a slave, thought of and spoken of as property. In the language of the LAW, "*held, taken, reputed and adjudged to be a chattel in the hands of my owners and possessors, and their executors, administrators, and assigns, to all intents, constructions, and purposes whatsoever.*"—Brev. Digest, 224. In the Northern States, a fugitive slave, liable to be hunted at any moment like a felon, and to be hurled into the terrible jaws of slavery—doomed by an inveterate prejudice against color to insult and outrage on every hand, (Massachusetts out of the question)—denied the privileges and courtesies common to others in the use of the most humble means of conveyance—shut out from the cabins on steamboats—refused admission to respectable hotels—caricatured, scorned, scoffed, mocked and maltreated with impunity by any one, (no matter how black his heart,) so he has a white skin. But now behold the change! Eleven days and a half gone, and I have crossed three thousand miles of the perilous deep. Instead of a democratic government, I am under a monarchical government. Instead of the bright blue sky of America, I am covered with the soft grey fog of the Emerald Isle. I breathe, and lo! the chattel becomes a man. I gaze around in vain for one who will question my equal humanity, claim me as his slave, or offer me an insult. I employ a cab—I am seated beside white people—I reach the hotel—I enter the same door—I am shown into the same parlor—I dine at the same table—and no one is offended. No delicate nose grows deformed in my presence. I find no difficulty here in obtaining admission into any place of worship, instruction or amusement, on equal terms with people as white as any I ever saw in the United States. I meet nothing to remind me of my complexion. I find myself regarded and treated at every turn with the kindness and deference paid to white people. When I go to church, I am met by no upturned nose and scornful lip to tell me, "*We don't allow n——rs in here*"!

I remember, about two years ago, there was in Boston, near the southwest corner of Boston Common, a menagerie. I had long desired to see such a collection as I understood were being exhibited there. Never having had an opportunity while a slave, I resolved to seize this, my first, since my escape. I went, and as I approached the entrance to gain admission, I was met and told by the door-keeper, in a harsh and contemptuous tone, "*We don't allow n——rs in here.*" I also remember attending a revival meeting in the Rev. Henry Jackson's meeting-house, at New-Bedford, and going up the broad aisle to find a seat. I was met by a good deacon, who told me, in a pious tone, "*We don't allow n——rs in here*"! Soon after my arrival in New-Bedford from the South, I had a strong desire to attend the Lyceum, but was told, "*They don't allow n——rs in here*"! While passing from New York to Boston on the steamer Massachusetts, on the night of 9th Dec. 1843, when chilled almost through with the cold, I went into the cabin to get a little warm. I was soon touched upon the shoulder, and told, "*We don't allow n——rs in here*"! On arriving in Boston from an anti-slavery tour, hungry and tired, I went into an eating-house near my friend Mr. Campbell's, to get some refreshments. I was met by a lad in a white apron, "*We don't allow n——rs in here*"! A week or two before leaving the United States, I had a meeting appointed at Weymouth, the home of that glorious band of true abolitionists, the Weston family, and others. On attempting to take a seat in the Omnibus to that place, I was told by the driver, (and I never shall forget his fiendish hate,) "*I don't allow n——rs in here*"! Thank heaven for the respite I now enjoy! I had been in Dublin but a few days, when a gentleman of great respectability kindly offered to conduct me through all the public buildings of that beautiful city; and a little afterwards, I found myself dining with the Lord Mayor of Dublin. What a pity there was not some American democratic Christian at the door of his splendid mansion, to bark out at my approach, "*They don't allow n——rs in here*"! The truth is, the people here know nothing of the republican Negro hate prevalent in our glorious land. They measure and esteem men according to their moral and intellectual worth, and not according to the color of their skin. Whatever may be said of the aristocracies here, there is none based on the color of a man's skin. This species of aristocracy belongs pre-eminently to "the land of the free, and the home of the brave." I have never found it abroad, in any but Americans. It sticks to them wherever they go. They find it almost as hard to get rid of it as to get rid of their skins.

The second day after my arrival at Liverpool, in company with my friend Buffum, and several other friends, I went to Eaton Hall, the residence of the Marquis of Westminster, one of the most splendid buildings in England. On approaching the door, I found several of our American passengers, who came out with us in the Cambria, waiting at the door for admission, as but one party was allowed in the house at a time. We all had to wait till the company within came out. And of all the faces, expressive of chagrin, those of the Americans were pre-eminent. They looked as sour as vinegar, and bitter as gall, when they found I was to be admitted on equal terms with themselves. When the door was opened, I walked in, on an equal footing with my white fellow-citizens, and from all I could see, I had as much attention paid me by the servants that showed us through the house, as any with a paler skin. As I walked through the building, the statuary did not fall down, the pictures did not leap from their places, the doors did not refuse to open, and the servants did not say, "*We don't allow n——rs in here*"!

A happy new year to you, and all the friends of freedom.

Excuse this imperfect scrawl, and believe me to be ever and always yours,

Frederick Douglass

The *Liberator,* January 30, 1846

TO WILLIAM LLOYD GARRISON

Perth, (Scotland), 27th Jan. 1846

Dear Friend:

For the sake of our righteous cause, I was delighted to see, by an extract copied into the Liberator of 12th Dec. 1845, from the Delaware Republican, that Mr. A. C. C. Thompson, No. 101, Market-street, Wilmington, has undertaken to invalidate my testimony against the slaveholders, whose names I have made prominent in the narrative of my experience while in slavery.[1]

Slaveholders and slave-traders never betray greater indiscretion, than when they venture to defend themselves, or their system of plunder, in any other community than a slaveholding one. Slavery has its own standards of morality, humanity, justice, and Christianity. Tried by that standard, it is a system of the greatest kindness to the slave—sanctioned by the purest morality—in perfect agreement with justice—and, of course, not inconsistent with Christianity. But, tried by any other, it is doomed to condemnation. The naked relation of master and slave is one of those monsters of darkness, to whom the light of truth is death! The wise ones among the slaveholders know this, and they studiously avoid doing anything, which, in their judgment, tends to elicit truth. They seem fully to understand, that their safety is in their silence. They may have learned this Wisdom from Junius, who counselled his opponent, Sir William Draper, when defending Lord Granby, never to attract attention to a character, which would only pass without condemnation, when it passed without observation.

I am now almost too far away to answer this attempted refutation by Mr. Thompson. I fear his article will be forgotten, before you get my reply. I, however, think the whole thing worth reviving, as it is seldom we have so good a case for dissection. In any country but the United States, I might hope to get a hearing through the columns of the paper in which I was attacked. But this would be inconsistent with American usage and magnanimity. It would be folly to expect such a hearing. They might possibly advertise me as a runaway slave, and share the reward of my apprehension; but on no other condition would they allow my reply a place in their columns.

In this, however, I may judge the "Republican" harshly. It may be that, having admitted Mr. Thompson's article, the editor will think it but fair—Negro though I am—to allow my reply an insertion.

In replying to Mr. Thompson, I shall proceed as I usually do in preaching the slaveholders' sermon,—dividing the subject under two general heads, as follows:—

1st. The statement of Mr. Thompson, in confirmation of the truth of my narrative.

2ndly. His denials of its truthfulness.

Under the first, I beg Mr. Thompson to accept my thanks for his full, free and unsolicited testimony, in regard to my identity. There now need be no doubt on that point, however much there might have been before. Your testimony, Mr. Thompson, has settled the question forever. I give you the fullest credit for the deed, saying nothing of the motive. But for you, sir, the pro-slavery people in the North might have persisted, with some show of reason, in representing me as being an imposter—a free Negro who had never been south of Mason & Dixon's line—one whom the abolitionists, acting on the jesuitical principle, that the end justifies the means, had educated and sent forth to attract attention to their faltering cause. I am greatly indebted to you, sir, for silencing those truly prejudicial insinuations. I wish I could make you understand the amount of service you have done me. You have completely tripped up the heels of your pro-slavery friends, and laid them flat at my feet. You have done a piece of anti-slavery work, which no anti-slavery man could do. Our cautious and truth-loving people in New England would never have believed this testimony, in proof of my identity, had it been borne by an abolitionist. Not that they really think an abolitionist capable of bearing false witness intentionally; but such persons are thought fanatical, and to look at every thing through a distorted medium. They will believe you—they will believe a slaveholder. They have, some how or other, imbibed (and I confess strangely enough) the idea that persons such as yourself are dispassionate, impartial and disinterested, and therefore capable of giving a fair representation of things connected with slavery. Now, under these circumstances, your testimony is of the utmost importance. It will serve to give effect to my exposures of slavery, both at home and abroad. I hope I shall not administer to your vanity when I tell you that you seem to have been raised up for this purpose! I came to this land with the highest testimonials from some of the most intelligent and distinguished abolitionists in the United States; yet some here have entertained and expressed doubt as to whether I have ever been a slave. You may easily imagine the perplexing and embarrassing nature of my situation, and how anxious I must have been to be relieved from it. You, sir, have relieved me. I now stand before both the American and British public, endorsed by you as being just what I have ever represented myself to be—to wit, an *American slave.*

You say, "I knew this recreant slave by the name of Frederick Bailey" (instead of Douglass). Yes, that was my name; and leaving out the term recreant, which savors a little of bitterness, your testimony is direct and perfect—just what I have long wanted. But you are not yet satisfied. You seem determined to bear the most ample testimony in my favor. You say you knew me when I lived with Mr. Covey.—"And with most of the persons" mentioned in my narrative, "you are intimately acquainted." This is excellent. Then Mr. Edward Covey is not a creature of my imagination, but really did, and may yet exist.[2]

You thus brush away the miserable insinuation of my northern pro-slavery enemies, that I have used fictitious not real names. You say—"Col. Lloyd was a wealthy planter. Mr. Gore was once an overseer for Col. Lloyd, but is now living near St. Michael's, is respected, and [you] believe he is a member of the Methodist Episcopal Church. Mr. Thomas Auld is an honorable and worthy member of the Methodist Episcopal Church. Mr. Covey, too, is a member of the Methodist Church, and all that can be said of him is, that he is a good Christian," &c., &c. Do allow me, once more, to thank you for this triumphant vindication of the truth of my statements; and to show you how highly I value your testimony, I will inform you that I am now publishing a second edition of my narrative in this country, having already disposed of the first. I will insert your article with my reply as an appendix to the edition now in progress. If you find any fault with my frequent thanks, you may find some excuse for me in the fact, that I have serious fears that you will be but poorly thanked by those whose characters you have felt it your duty to defend. I am almost certain they will regard you as running before you were sent, and as having spoken when you should have been silent. Under these trying circumstances, it is evidently the duty of those interested in your welfare to extend to you such words of consolation as may ease, if not remove, the pain of your sad disappointment. But enough of this.

Now, then, to the second part—or your denials. You are confident I did not write the book; and the reason of your confidence is, that when you knew me, I was an unlearned and rather an ordinary Negro. Well, I have to admit I was rather an ordinary Negro when you knew me, and I do not claim to be a very extraordinary one now. But you knew me under very unfavorable circumstances. It was when I lived with Mr. Covey, the Negro-breaker, *and member of the Methodist Church.* I had just been living with master Thomas Auld, where I had been reduced by hunger. Master Thomas did not allow me enough to eat. Well, when I lived with Mr. Covey, I was driven so hard, and whipt so often, that my soul was crushed and my spirits broken. I was a mere wreck. The degradation to which I was then subjected, as I now look back to it, seems more like a dream than a horrible reality. I can scarcely realize how I ever passed through it, without quite losing all my moral and intellectual energies. I can easily understand that you sincerely doubt if I wrote the narrative; for if any one had told me, seven years ago, I should ever be able to write such a one, I should have doubted as strongly as you now do. You must not judge me now by what I then was—a change of circumstances has made a surprising change in me. Frederick Douglass, the *freeman,* is a very different person from Frederick Bailey, (my former name), the *slave.* I feel myself almost a new man—freedom has given me new life. I fancy you would scarcely know me. I think I have altered very much in my general appearance, and know I have in my manners. You remember when I used to meet you on the road to St. Michaels, or near Mr. Covey's lane gate, I hardly dared to lift my head, and look up at you. If I should meet you now, amid the free hills of old Scotland, where the ancient "black Douglass" once met his foes,[3] I presume I might summon sufficient fortitude to look you full in the face; and were you to attempt to make a slave of me, it is possible you might find me almost as disagreeable a subject, as was the Douglass to whom I have just referred. Of one thing, I am certain—you would see *a great change* in me!

I trust I have now explained away your reason for thinking I did not write the narrative in question.

You next deny the existence of such cruelty in Maryland as I reveal in my narrative; and ask, with truly marvellous simplicity, "could it be possible that charitable, feeling men could murder human beings with as little remorse as the narrative of this infamous libeller would make us believe; and that the laws of Maryland, which operate alike upon black and white, bond and free, could permit such foul murders to pass unnoticed?" "No," you say, "it is impossible." I am not to determine what charitable, feeling men can do; but, to show what Maryland slaveholders actually do, their charitable feeling is to be determined by their deeds, and not their deeds by their charitable feelings. The cowskin makes as deep a gash in my flesh, when wielded by a professed saint, as it does when wielded by an open sinner. The deadly musket does as fatal execution when its trigger is pulled by Austin Gore, the Christian, as when the same is done by Beal Bondly, the infidel. The best way to ascertain what those charitable, feeling men can do, will be to point you to the laws made by them, and which you say operate alike upon the white and the black, the bond and the free. By consulting the statute laws of Maryland, you will find the following:—"Any slave for rambling in the night, or riding horses in the day time without leave, or running away, may be punished by whipping, cropping, branding in the cheek, or otherwise—not rendering him unfit for labor."—p. 337.

Then another:—"Any slave convicted of petty treason, murder, or wilful burning of dwelling-houses, may be sentenced to have the right hand cut off, to be hanged in the usual way—his head severed from his body—the body divided into four quarters, and the head and quarters set up in the most public place where such act was committed."—page 190.

Now, Mr. Thompson, when you consider with what ease a slave may be convicted of any one or all of these crimes, how bloody and atrocious do these laws appear! Yet, sir, they are but the breath of those pious and charitable feeling men, whom you would defend. I am sure I have recorded in my narrative, nothing so revolting cruel, murderous, and infernal, as may be found in your own statute book.

You say that the laws of Maryland operate alike upon the white and black, the bond and free. If you mean by this, that the parties named are all equally protected by law, you perpetrate a falsehood as big as that told by President Polk in his inaugural address.[4] It is a notorious fact, even on this side the Atlantic, that a black man cannot testify against a white in any court in Maryland, or any other slave State. If you do not know this, you are more than ordinarily ignorant, and are to be pitied rather than censured. I will not say "that the detection of this falsehood proves all you have said to be false"—for I wish to avail myself of your testimony, in regard to my identity,—but I will say, you have made yourself very liable to suspicion.

I will close these remarks by saying, your positive opposition to slavery is fully explained, and will be well understood by anti-slavery men, when you say the evil of the system does not fall upon the slave, but the slaveholder. This is like saying that the evil of being burnt is not felt by the person burnt, but by him who kindles up the fire about him.

Frederick Douglass.

The *Liberator,* February 27, 1846

1. "I shall . . . briefly notice some of the most glaring falsehoods contained in the aforesaid Narrative," Thompson introduced his testimony, "and give a true representation of the character or those gentlemen who have been censured in such an uncharitable manner, as murderers, hypocrites, and everything else that is vile." Thompson characterized Douglass' *Narrative* as "a budget of falsehood, from beginning to end."

2. Edward Covey was a "breaker" of slaves, and at Covey's farm, Douglass was "made to drink the bitterest dregs of slavery." In his *Narrative,* Douglass described that not only was he pushed beyond the limits of human endurance by the physical requirements imposed upon him by Covey, but he was virtually destroyed also in soul and spirit: "My natural elasticity was crushed, my intellect languished, the disposition to read departed . . . the dark night of slavery closed in upon me; and behold a man transformed into a brute."

3. The "black Douglass" was a character in Sir Walter Scott's *Lady of the Lake,* and it was suggested as the name Frederick Bailey should assume in freedom by Nathan Johnson, a free Negro of New Bedford, Massachusetts.

4. Douglass may have been referring to the assertion by Polk in his inaugural address in March; 1845, that "the right of the United States to that portion of our territory which lies beyond the Rocky Mountains . . . to the country of the Oregon, is 'clear and unquestionable.' . . . "

After more than fifty lectures in Ireland, Douglass went to Scotland which he found "in a blaze of anti-slavery agitation." Here he and Buffum, who had rejoined him, became involved in the exciting battle to compel the Free Church of Scotland to return contributions made by American slaveholders. The Free Church (an organization based on the right of congregations to control the appointment of their own ministers) had sent a deputation to the United States in 1844 to form an alliance with churches in this country and to solicit funds to build Free Churches and pay Free ministers in Scotland. An outburst of indignation arose from American Abolitionists when the delegation announced its intention of visiting the southern states, but, ignoring these protests, the delegates raised £3,000 from slaveholders, entering into an alliance with southern churches. They justified their action by denouncing the Abolitionists as belonging to the tradition of "the infidels and anarchists of the French Revolution," asserting that the slaveholders were "entitled to be regarded as respectable, useful, honoured Christians, living under the power of the truth, labouring faithfully, and serving God in the Gospel of His Son." Most members of the Free Church in Scotland were not impressed either by the diatribe against the American Abolitionists or by the eulogy of the slaveholders, and a loud cry arose that the money collected in the South was tainted and should be returned. Douglass added his voice to this demand, speaking in halls decorated with posters proclaiming the slogan of the day—"*Send Back the Money.*"[1] [I:64–65]

TO FRANCIS JACKSON

Royal Hotel Dundee, Scotland, 29th Jan. 1846

My dear friend Jackson:

I have been promising myself the pleasure of sending you a line from this side the sea, but have been compelled to deny myself in consequence of immediate and pressing engagements here. If you demand an apology for the liberty I am now about to take, I beg you to do what I feel confident you are seldom inclined to do—namely, look over the many acts of kindness you have performed toward myself and the people with whom I am identified. These acts justify me in thinking you will not object to having a line from me. From the first day I stepped out of obscurity on the anti-slavery platform at Nantucket to the day I stepped on the deck of the Cambria for these shores you stood by me to encourage, strengthen, and defend me from the assaults of my foes, and the foes of my race. I will not trouble you with any eulogy, for I know such would be disagreeable to your ears, but you must allow me to tell you that your acts are not forgotten. When I was a stranger, rough, unpolished, just from the bellows-handle in Richmond's brass foundry in New Bedford, when I was scarce able to write two sentences of the English language correctly, you took me into your drawing room, welcomed me to your table, put me in your best bed, and treated me in every way as an equal brother at a time when to do so was to expose yourself to the hot displeasure of nearly all your neighbours. These things I still remember, and it affords me great pleasure to speak of them. Pardon me for reminding you of these things now.

I am now as you will perceive by the date of this letter in Scotland, almost every hill, river, mountain and lake of which has been made classic by the heroic deeds of her noble sons. Scarcely a stream but has been poured into song, or a hill that is not associated with some fierce and bloody conflict between liberty and slavery. I had a view the other day of what are called the Grampion mountains that divide eastern Scotland from the west. I was told that here the ancient crowned heads used to meet, contend and struggle in deadly conflict for supremacy, causing those grand old hills to run blood-warming cold steel in the others heart. My soul sickens at the thought, yet I see in myself all those elements of character which were I to yield to their promptings might lead me to deeds as bloody as those at which my soul now sickens and from which I now turn with disgust and shame. Thank God liberty is no longer to be contended for and gained by instruments of death. A higher, a nobler, a mightier than carnal weapon is placed into our hands—one which hurls defiance at all the improvements of carnal warfare. It is the righteous appeal to the understanding and the heart—with this we can withstand the most fiery of all the darts of perdition itself. I see that America is boasting of her naval, and military power—let her boast—she may build her walls and her forts making them proof against ball and bomb. But while there is a single voice in her midst to charge home upon her the duty of emancipation, neither her army nor her navy can protect her from the gnawing of a guilty conscience.

I am travelling in company with my good friend James N. Buffum. Our meetings here have been of the most soul cheering character. The present position of the free Church in Scotland makes it important to expend as much labor here as possible. You know they sent delegates to the United States to raise money to build their churches and to pay their ministers. They succeeded in getting about four thousand pounds sterling. Well, our efforts are directed to making them disgorge their ill-gotten gain—return it to the Slaveholders. Our rallying cry is "No union with Slaveholders and send back the blood-stained money." Under these rallying cries, old Scotland boils like a pot. I half think if the free Church had for a moment supposed that her conduct would have been arraigned before the Scottish people by thorough Garrisonians as H. C. Wright, James N. Buffum and myself, she would never have taken the money. She thought to get the gold and nobody see her. It was a sad mistake. It would indeed be a grand anti-slavery triumph if we could get her to send back the money. It would break upon the confounded Slaveholders and their [allies] like a clap from the sky. We shall continue to deal our blows upon them—crying out disgorge—disgorge—disgorge your horrid plunder and to this cry the great mass of the people have cried Amen, Amen.

I have disposed of nearly all the first Edition of my Narrative and am publishing a second which will be out about the sixteenth of February. I realize enough from it to meet my expenses. I shall probably remain in Scotland till the middle of March. I shall then proceed to England, as I have not yet delivered a single lecture on Slavery in that country. It is quite an advantage to be a n——r here. I find I am hardly black enough for British taste, but by keeping my hair as woolly as possible I make out to pass for at least for half a Negro at any rate. My good friend Buffum finds the tables turned upon him here completely—the people lavish nearly all their attention on the Negro. I can easily understand that such a state of things would greatly embarrass a person with less sense than he, but he stems the current thus far nobly. I have received letters from America expressing fears that I may be spoiled by the attention which I am receiving—well 'tis possible—but if I thought it probable, the next steamer should bring me home to encounter again the kicks and cuffs of pro-slavery. Indeed I shall rejoice in the day that shall see me again by your side battling the enemy, and I should rejoice in it though I were to be subjected to all the regulations of color-phobia with which we used [to] encounter. I glory in the fight as well as in the victory. Make my love to all your family.

Gratefully yours,
Frederick Douglass

Anti-Slavery Collection, Boston Public Library

1. *Free Church Alliance with Manstealers, Glasgow, 1846*, p. 11; *Letter from the Executive Committee of the American and Foreign Anti-Slavery Society to the Commissioners of the Free Church of Scotland, April 2, 1844*, Edinburgh, 1844; Douglass to Richard D. Webb, Feb. 10, 1846; Anti-Slavery Letters to Garrison, Boston Public Library.

Pro-slavery journals in the United States went to ridiculous lengths in their demands that the British refuse Douglass a platform, even arguing that the Negro orator was embarrassing the three million Negro people held in slavery. "The slaves," said one journal, "would be very indignant at the conduct of their representative in England could they be made acquainted with his tantrums." There was scarcely a Negro "on a South Carolina rice plantation, or in a Louisiana sugar house, but what, amid all his degradation, would scorn the acts of Frederick Douglass. The man is lowering, in the eyes of English courtesy and intelligence, the character of our slave population."[1] To the charge that he was a menace to his native land because he was "running amuck in greedy-eared Britain against America, its people, its institutions, and even against its peace," Douglass had a ready answer. [I:69]

TO HORACE GREELEY

Glasgow (Scotland), April 15, 1846

My Dear Sir:

I never wrote nor attempted to write a letter for any other than a strictly anti-slavery press; but being greatly encouraged by your magnanimity, as shown in copying my letter written from Belfast, Ireland, to the *Liberator* at Boston, I venture to send you a few lines, direct from my pen.

I know not how to thank you for the deep and lively interest you have been pleased to take in the cause of my long neglected race, or in what language to express the gratification I feel in witnessing your unwillingness to lend your aid to "break a bruised reed," by adding your weight to the already insupportable burden to crush, the feeble though virtuous efforts of one who is laboring for the emancipation of a people, who, for two long centuries, have endured, with the utmost patience, a bondage, one hour of which, in the graphic language of the immortal Jefferson, is worse than ages of that which your fathers rose in rebellion to oppose.[2]

It is such indications on the part of the press—which, happily, are multiplying throughout all the land—that kindle up within me an ardent hope that the curse of slavery will not much longer be permitted to make its iron foot-prints in the lacerated hearts of my sable brethren, or to spread its foul mantle of moral blight, mildew and infamy, over the otherwise noble character of the American people.

I am very sorry to see that some of your immediate neighbors are very much displeased with you, for this act of kindness to myself, and the cause of which I am an humble advocate; and that an attempt has been made, on the part of some of them, by misrepresenting my sayings, motives and objects in this country, to stir up against me the already too bitter antipathy of the American people. I am called, by way of reproach, a runaway slave. As if it were a crime—an unpardonable crime—for a man to take his inalienable rights! If I had not run away, but settled down in the degrading arms of slavery, and made no effort to gain my freedom, it is quite probable that the learned gentlemen, who now brand me with being a miserable runaway slave, would have adduced the fact in proof of the Negro's adaptation to slavery, and his utter unfitness for freedom! *"There's no pleasing some people."* But why should Mr. James Brooks feel so much annoyed by the attention shown me in this country, and so anxious to excite against me the hatred and jealousy of the American people? I can very readily understand why a slaveholder—a trader in slaves—one who has all his property in human flesh, blinded by ignorance as to his own best interest, and under the dominion of violent passions engendered by the possession of discretionary and irresponsible power over the bodies and souls of his victims—accustomed to the inhuman sight of men and women sold at auction in company with horses, sheep and swine, and in every way treated more like brutes than human beings—should repine at my success, and, in his blindness, seek to throw every discouragement and obstacle in the way of the slave's emancipation. But why a New-York editor, born and reared in the State of Maine, far removed from the contaminated and pestilential atmosphere of slavery, should pursue such a course, is not so apparent. I will not, however, stop here to ascertain the cause, but deal with fact; and I cannot better do this than by giving your readers a simple and undisguised statement of the motives and objects of my visit to this country. I feel it but just to myself to do so, since I have been denounced by the New-York Express as a "glibtongued scoundrel," and gravely charged, in its own elegant and dignified language, with "running a muck in greedy-eared Britain against America, its people, its institutions, and even against its peace."

Of the low and vulgar epithets, coupled with the false and somewhat malicious charges, very little need be said. I am used to them. Their force is lost upon me, in the frequency of their application. I was reared where they were in the most common use. They form a large and very important portion of the vocabulary of characters known in the South as plantation "Negro drivers." A slaveholding gentleman would scorn to use them. He leaves them to find their way into the world of sound, through the polluted lips of his hired "Negro driver"— a being for whom the haughty slaveholder feels incomparably more contempt than he feels toward his slave. And for the best of all reasons—he knows the slave to be degraded, because he cannot help himself; but a white "Negro driver" is degraded, because of original, ingrained meanness. If I agree with the slaveholders in nothing else, I can say I agree with them in all their burning contempt for a "Negro driver," whether born North or South. Such epithets will have no prejudicial effect against me on the mind of the class of American people, whose good opinion I sincerely desire to cultivate and deserve. And it is to these I would address this brief word of explanation.

The object, then, of my visit to this country is simply to give such an exposition of the degrading influence of slavery upon the master and his abettors as well as upon the slave—to excite such an intelligent interest on the subject of

American slavery—as may react upon that country, and tend to shame her out of her adhesion to a system which all must confess to be at variance with justice, repugnant to Christianity, and at war with her own free institutions. "The head and front of my offending hath this extent, no more." I am one of those who think the best friend of a nation is he who most faithfully rebukes her for her sins—and he her worst enemy, who, under the specious and popular garb of patriotism, seeks to excuse, palliate, and defend them. America has much more to fear from such than all the rebukes of the abolitionists at home or abroad.

I am nevertheless aware, that the wisdom of exposing the sins of one nation in the ear of another, has been seriously questioned by good and clear-sighted people, both on this and on your side of the Atlantic. And the thought is not without its weight upon my own mind. I am satisfied that there are many evils which can be best removed by confining our efforts to the immediate locality where such evils exist. This, however, is by no means the case with the system of slavery. It is such a giant sin—such a monstrous aggregation of iniquity, so hardening to the human heart, so destructive to the moral sense, and so well calculated to beget a character in every one around it favorable to its own continuance, that I feel not only at liberty, but abundantly justified in appealing to the whole world to aid in its removal. Slavery exists in the United States because it is reputable, and it is reputable in the United States because it is not *dis*reputable out of the United States as it ought to be, and it is not so disreputable out of the United States as it ought to be because its character is not so well known as it ought to be. Believing this most firmly, and being a lover of Freedom, a hater of Slavery, one who has felt the bloody whip and worn the galling chain—sincerely and earnestly longing for the deliverance of my sable brethren from their awful bondage, I am bound to expose its character, whenever and wherever an opportunity is afforded me. I would attract to it the attention of the world. I would fix upon it the piercing eye of insulted Liberty. I would arraign it at the bar of Eternal Justice, and summon the Universe to witness against it. I would concentrate against it the moral and religious sentiment of Christian people of every "class, color and clime." I would have the guilty slaveholder see his condemnation written on every human face, and hear it proclaimed in every human voice, till, overwhelmed with shame and confusion, he resolved to cease his wicked course, undo the heavy burden, and let the oppressed go free.

The people in this country who take the deepest interest in the removal of Slavery from America, and the spread of Liberty throughout the world, are the same who oppose the bloody spirit of war, and are earnestly laboring to spread the blessings of peace all over the globe. I have ever found the abolitionists of this country the warmest friends of America and American institutions. I have frequently seen in their houses, and sometimes occupying the most conspicuous places in their parlors, the American Declaration of Independence.

An aged anti-slavery gentleman in Dublin, with whom I had the honor several times to dine during my stay in that city, has the Declaration of Independence and a number of the portraits of the distinguished founders of the American Republic. He bought them many years ago, in token of his admiration of the men and their principles. But, said he, after speaking of the sentiments of the Declaration—looking up as it hung in a costly frame—I am often tempted to turn its face to the wall, it is such a palpable contradiction of the spirit and practices of the American people at this time. This instrument was once the watchword of Freedom in this land, and the American people were regarded as the best friends and truest representatives of that sacred cause. But they are not so regarded now. They have allowed the crowned heads of Europe to outstrip them. While Great Britain has emancipated all her slaves, and is laboring to extend the blessings of Liberty wherever her power is felt, it seems, in the language of John Quincy Adams, that the preservation, propagation and perpetuation of slavery is the vital and animating spirit of the American Government. Even Haiti, the black Republic, is not to be spared; the spirit of Freedom, which a sanguinary and ambitious despot could not crush or extinguish, is to be exterminated by the free American Republic, because that spirit is dangerous to slavery. While the people of this country see such facts and indications, as well as the great fact that three millions of people are held in the most abject bondage, deprived of all their God-given rights—denied by law and public opinion to learn to read the sacred Scriptures, by a people professing the largest liberty and devotion to the religion of Jesus Christ—while they see this monstrous anomaly, they must look elsewhere for a paragon of civil and religious freedom. Sir, I am earnestly and anxiously laboring to wipe off this foul blot from the otherwise fair fame of the American people, that they may accomplish in behalf of human freedom that which their exalted position among the nations of the earth amply fits them to do. Would they but arise in their moral majesty and might—repent and purify themselves from this foul crime—break the galling fetters, and restore the long lost rights to the sable bondmen in their midst—they would encircle her name with a wreath of imperishable glory. Her light would indeed break forth as the morning—its brilliant beams would flash across the Atlantic, and illuminate the Eastern world.

I am, dear sir, very gratefully yours,
Frederick Douglass

The *Liberator,* June 26, 1846

1. *Oswego Daily Advertiser,* reprinted in *Anti-Slavery Standard,* Oct. 29, 1846.
2. In 1786, Thomas Jefferson wrote to M. de Meusnier: "What a stupendous, what an incomprehensible machine is man! Who can endure toil, famine, stripes, imprisonment, and death itself, in vindication of his own liberty, and, the next moment, be deaf to all those motives whose power supported him through his trial, and inflict on his fellow men a bondage, one hour of which is fraught with more misery, than ages of that which he rose in rebellion to oppose." (Philip S. Foner, ed., *Thomas Jefferson: Selections from his Writings,* New York, 1943, p. 67.)

While in Edinburgh, Douglass was invited by George Thompson, a leading English Abolitionist, to speak at a mammoth public meeting to be arranged in London under the auspices of the British and Foreign Anti-Slavery Society, which six years before had broken away from the Garrisonians. Well aware that his friends in America would look with disfavor upon his presence at the meeting, Douglass believed that it was his duty to "speak in any meeting where freedom of speech is allowed and where I may do any thing toward exposing the bloody system of slavery." Hence, he accepted the invitation, making it clear that his presence did not signify an endorsement of the doctrines of the organization.[1]

On his arrival in London, Douglass learned that a crowded schedule had been planned for him. "Frederick has crammed a year's sensations in the last five days," wrote George Thompson on May 23. "On Monday he poured forth at the Anti-Slavery Meeting. On Tuesday at the Peace Meeting. On Wednesday at the Complete Suffrage Meeting. On Thursday at the Temperance Meeting, and last night he had an audience of 2,500 to hear him for nearly three hours. . . ." At the final meeting held at Finsbury Chapel in his honor, "with the edifice crowded to suffocation," Douglass delivered a devastating attack on American slavery. . . .

At the conclusion of the address, Thompson arose and referred to a conversation in which Douglas spoke of how he missed his wife and children. Thompson proposed a subscription to bring Douglass' family to England. Fifty pounds were contributed while he was talking and thirty more at the end of his appeal. Thompson was certain that "an ample sum" would be raised "to bring them over and make them comfortable while they are among us."[2] [I:66–67]

AN APPEAL TO THE BRITISH PEOPLE, reception speech at Finsbury Chapel, Moorfields, England, May 12, 1846

I feel exceedingly glad of the opportunity now afforded me of presenting the claims of my brethren in bonds in the United States to so many in London and from various parts of Britain who have assembled here on the present occasion. I have nothing to commend me to your consideration in the way of learning, nothing in the way of education, to entitle me to your attention; and you are aware that slavery is a very bad school for rearing teachers of morality and religion. Twenty-one years of my life have been spent in slavery—personal slavery—surrounded by degrading influences, such as can exist nowhere beyond the pale of slavery; and it will not be strange, if under such circumstances, I should betray, in what I have to say to you, a deficiency of that refinement which is seldom or ever found, except among persons that have experienced superior advantages to those which I have enjoyed. But I will take it for granted that you know something about the degrading influences of slavery, and that you will not expect great things from me this evening, but simply such facts as I may be able to advance immediately in connection with my own experience of slavery.

Now, what is this system of slavery? This is the subject of my lecture this evening—what is the character of this institution? I am about to answer this inquiry, what is American slavery? I do this the more readily, since I have found persons in this country who have identified the term slavery with which I think it is not, and in some instances, I have feared, in so doing, have rather (unwittingly, I know) detracted much from the horror with which the term slavery is contemplated. It is common in this country to distinguish every bad thing by the name of slavery. Intemperance is slavery; to be deprived of the right to vote is slavery, says one; to have to work hard is slavery, says another; and I do not know but that if we should let them go on, they would say that to eat when we are hungry, to walk when we desire to have exercise, or to minister to our necessities, or have necessities at all, is slavery.

I do not wish for a moment to detract from the horror with which the evil of intemperance is contemplated—not at all; nor do I wish to throw the slightest obstruction in the way of any political freedom that any class of persons in this country may desire to obtain. But I am here to say that I think the term slavery is sometimes abused by identifying it with that which it is not. Slavery in the United States is the granting of that power by which one man exercises and enforces a right of property in the body and soul of another. The condition of a slave is simply that of the brute beast. He is a piece of property—a marketable commodity, in the language of the law, to be bought or sold at the will and caprice of the master who claims him to be his property; he is spoken of, thought of, and treated as property. His own good, his conscience, his intellect, his affections, are all set aside by the master. The will and the wishes of the master are the law of the slave. He is as much a piece of property as a horse. If he is fed, he is fed because he is property. If he is clothed, it is with a view to the increase of his value as property. Whatever of comfort is necessary to him for his body or soul that is inconsistent with his being property is carefully wrested from him, not only by public opinion, but by the law of the country. He is carefully deprived of everything that tends in the slightest degree to detract from his value as property. He is deprived of education. God has given him an intellect; the slaveholder declares it shall not be cultivated. If his moral perception leads him in a course contrary to his value as property, the slaveholder declares he shall not exercise it. The marriage institution cannot exist among slaves, and one-sixth of the population of democratic America is denied its privileges by the law of the land. What is to be thought of a nation boasting of its liberty, boasting of its humanity, boasting of its Christianity, boasting of its love of justice and purity, and yet having within its own borders three millions of persons denied by law the right of marriage?—what must be the condition of that people?

I need not lift up the veil by giving you any experience of my own. Every one that can put two ideas together must see the most fearful results from such a state of things as I have just mentioned. If any of these three millions find for themselves companions, and prove themselves honest, upright, virtuous persons to each other, yet in these cases—few as I am bound to confess they are—the virtuous live in constant apprehension of being torn asunder by the merciless menstealers that claim them as their property. This is American slavery; no marriage—no education—the light of the gospel shut out from the dark mind of the bondman—and he forbidden by the law to learn to read. If a mother shall teach her children to read, the law in Louisiana proclaims that she may be hanged by the neck. If the father attempt to give his son a knowledge of letters, he may be punished by the whip in one instance, and in another be killed, at the discretion of the court. Three millions of people shut out from the light of knowledge! It is easy for you to conceive the evil that must result from such a state of things.

I now come to the physical evils of slavery. I do not wish to dwell at length upon these, but it seems right to speak of them, not so much to influence your minds on this question, as to let the slaveholders of America know that the curtain which conceals their crimes is being lifted abroad; that we are opening the dark cell, and leading the people into the horrible recesses of what they are pleased to call their domestic institution. We want them to know that a knowledge of their whippings, their scourgings, their brandings, their chainings, is not confined to their plantations, but that some Negro of theirs has broken loose from his chains—has burst through the dark incrustation of slavery, and is now exposing their deeds of deep damnation to the gaze of the Christian people of England.

The slaveholders resort to all kinds of cruelty. If I were disposed, I have matter enough to interest you on this question for five or six evenings, but I will not dwell at length upon these cruelties. Suffice it to say, that all the peculiar modes of torture that were resorted to in the West India islands are resorted to, I believe, even more frequently in the United States of America. Starvation, the bloody whip, the chain, the gag, the thumb-screw, cathauling, the cat-o'-nine-tails, the dungeon, the blood-hound, are all in requisition to keep the slave in his condition as a slave in the United States. If any one has a doubt upon this point, I would ask him to read the chapter on slavery in [Charles] Dickens's Notes on America. If any man has a doubt upon it, I have here the "testimony of a thousand witnesses,"[3] which I can give at any length, all going to prove the truth of my statement. The blood-hound is regularly trained in the United States, and advertisements are to be found in the southern papers of the Union, from persons advertising themselves as blood-hound trainers, and offering to hunt down slaves at fifteen dollars a piece, recommending their hounds as the fleetest in the neighborhood, never known to fail. Advertisements are from time to time inserted, stating that slaves have escaped with iron collars about their necks, with bands of iron about their feet, marked with the lash, branded with red-hot irons, the initials of their master's name burned into their flesh; and their masters advertise the fact of their being thus branded with their own signature, thereby proving to the world that, however damning it may appear to non-slaveholders, such practices are not regarded discreditable among the slaveholders themselves. Why, I believe if a man should brand his horse in this country—burn the initials of his name into any of his cattle, and publish the ferocious deed here—that the united execrations of Christians in Britain would descend upon him. Yet, in the United States, human beings are thus branded. As Whittier says—

> . . . Our countrymen in chains,
>   The whip on woman's shrinking flesh,
> Our soil yet reddening with the stains
>   Caught from her scourgings warm and fresh.

The slave-dealer boldly publishes his infamous acts to the world. Of all things that have been said of slavery to which exception has been taken by slaveholders, this, the charge of cruelty, stands foremost, and yet there is no charge capable of clearer demonstration than that of the most barbarous inhumanity on the part of the slaveholders toward their slaves. And all this is necessary; it is necessary to resort to these cruelties, in order to make the slave a slave, and to keep him a slave. Why, my experience all goes to prove the truth of what you will call a marvelous proposition, that the better you treat a slave, the more you destroy his value as a slave, and enhance the probability of his eluding the grasp of the slaveholder; the more kindly you treat him, the more wretched you make him, while you keep him in the condition of a slave. My experience, I say, confirms the truth of this proposition. When I was treated exceedingly ill; when my back was being scourged daily; when I was whipped within an inch of my life—life was all I cared for. "Spare my life," was my continual prayer. When I was look-ing for the blow about to be inflicted upon my head, I was not thinking of my liberty; it was my life. But, as soon as the blow was not to be feared, then came the longing for liberty. If a slave has a bad master, his ambition is to get a bet-ter; when he gets a better, he aspires to have the best; and when he gets the best, he aspires to be his own master. But the slave must be brutalized to keep him as a slave. The slaveholder feels this necessity. I admit this necessity. If it be right to hold slaves at all, it is right to hold them in the only way in which they can be held; and this can be done only by shutting out the light of education from their minds, and brutalizing their persons.

The whip, the chain, the gag, the thumb-screw, the blood-hound, the stocks, and all the other bloody paraphernalia of the slave system are indispensably nec-essary to the relation of master and slave. The slave must be subjected to these, or he ceases to be a slave. Let him know that the whip is burned; that the fetters have been turned to some useful and profitable employment; that the chain is no longer for his limbs; that the blood-hound is no longer to be put upon his track; that his master's authority over him is no longer to be enforced by taking his life—and immediately he walks out from the house of bondage and asserts his freedom as a man. The slaveholder finds it necessary to have these implements to keep the slave in bondage; finds it necessary to be able to say, "Unless you do so and so; unless you do as I bid you—I will take away your life!"

Some of the most awful scenes of cruelty are constantly taking place in the middle states of the Union. We have in those states what are called the slave-breeding states. Allow me to speak plainly. Although it is harrowing to your feeling, it is necessary that the facts of the case should be stated. We have in the United States slave-breeding states. The very state from which the minister from our court to yours comes is one of these states—Maryland, where men, women, and children are reared for the market, just as horses, sheep, and swine are raised for the market. Slave-rearing is there looked upon as a legitimate trade; the law sanctions it, public opinion upholds it, the church does not condemn it. It goes on in all its bloody horrors, sustained by the auctioneer's block. If you would see the cruelties of this system, hear the following narrative. Not long since the following scene occurred. A slave-woman and a slave-man had united themselves as man and wife in the absence of any law to protect them as man and wife. They had lived together by the permission, not by right, of their mas-ter, and they had reared a family. The master found it expedient, and for his in-terest, to sell them. He did not ask them their wishes in regard to the matter at all; they were not consulted. The man and woman were brought to the auc-tioneer's block, under the sound of the hammer. The cry was raised, "Here goes;

who bids cash?" Think of it—a man and wife to be sold! The woman was placed on the auctioneer's block; her limbs, as is customary, were brutally exposed to the purchasers, who examined her with all the freedom with which they would examine a horse. There stood the husband, powerless; no right to his wife; the master's right preeminent. She was sold. He was next brought to the auctioneer's block. His eyes followed his wife in the distance; and he looked beseechingly, imploringly, to the man that had bought his wife to buy him also. But he was at length bid off to another person. He was about to be separated forever from her whom he loved. No word of his, no work of his, could save him from this separation. He asked permission of his new master to go and take the hand of his wife at parting. It was denied him. In the agony of his soul he rushed from the man who had just bought him, that he might take a farewell of his wife; but his way was obstructed, he was struck over the head with a loaded whip, and was held for a moment; but his agony was too great. When he was let go, he fell a corpse at the feet of his master. His heart was broken. Such scenes are the every-day fruits of American slavery.

Some two years since, the Hon. Seth M. Gates, an anti-slavery gentleman of the state of New York, a representative in the congress of the United States, told me he saw with his own eyes the following circumstance. In the national District of Columbia, over which the star-spangled emblem is constantly waving, where orators are ever holding forth on the subject of American liberty, American democracy, American republicanism, there are two slave prisons. When going across a bridge, leading to one of these prisons, he saw a young woman run out, bare-footed and bare-headed, and with very little clothing on. She was running with all speed to the bridge he was approaching. His eye was fixed upon her, and he stopped to see what was the matter. He had not paused long before he saw three men run out after her. He now knew what the nature of the case was: a slave escaping from her chains—a young woman, a sister—escaping from the bondage in which she had been held. She made her way to the bridge, but had not reached it, ere from the Virginia side there came two slaveholders. As soon as they saw them, her pursuers called out, "Stop her!" True to their Virginian instincts, they came to the rescue of their brother kidnappers across the bridge. The poor girl now saw that there was no chance for her. It was a trying time. She knew if she went back, she must be a slave forever—she must be dragged down to the scenes of pollution which the slaveholders continually provide for most of the poor, sinking, wretched young women whom they call their property. She formed her resolution; and just as those who were about to take her were going to put hands upon her, to drag her back, she leaped over the balustrades of the bridge, and down she went to rise no more. She chose death, rather than to go back into the hands of those Christian slaveholders from whom she had escaped.

Can it be possible that such things as these exist in the United States? Are not these the exceptions? Are any such scenes as this general? Are not such deeds condemned by the law and denounced by public opinion? Let me read you a few of the laws of the slaveholding states of America. I think no better exposure of slavery can be made than is made by the laws of the states in which slavery exists. I prefer reading the laws to making my statement in confirmation of what I have said myself; for the slaveholders cannot object to this testimony, since it is the calm, the cool, the deliberate enactment of their wisest heads, of their most clear-sighted, their own constituted representatives. "If more than seven slaves together are found in any road without a white person, twenty lashes a piece; for visiting a plantation without a written pass, ten lashes; for letting loose a boat from where it is made fast, thirty-nine lashes for the first offense; and for the second shall have cut off from his head one ear; for keeping or carrying a club, thirty-nine lashes; for having any article for sale, without a ticket from his master, ten lashes; for traveling in any other than the most usual and accustomed road, when going alone to any place, forty lashes; for traveling in the night without a pass, forty lashes."

I am afraid you do not understand the awful character of these lashes. You must bring it before your mind. A human being in a perfect state of nudity, tied hand and foot to a stake, and a strong man standing behind with a heavy whip, knotted at the end, each blow cutting into the flesh, and leaving the warm blood dripping to the feet; and for these trifles. For being found in another person's Negro-quarters, forty lashes; for hunting with dogs in the woods, thirty lashes; for being on horseback without the written permission of his master, twenty-five lashes; for riding or going abroad in the night, or riding horses in the day time, without leave, a slave may be whipped, cropped, or branded in the cheek with the letter R, or otherwise punished, such punishment not extending to life, or so as to render him unfit for labor. The laws referred to may be found by consulting Brevard's Digest; Haywood's Manual; Virginia Revised Code; Prince's Digest; Missouri Laws; Mississippi Revised Code. A man, for going to visit his brethren, without the permission of his master—and in many instances he may not have that permission; his master, from caprice or other reasons, may not be willing to allow it—may be caught on his way, dragged to a post, the branding-iron heated, and the name of his master or the letter R branded into his cheek or on his forehead.

They treat slaves thus, on the principle that they must punish for light offenses in order to prevent the commission of larger ones. I wish you to mark that in the single state of Virginia there are seventy-one crimes for which a colored man may be executed; while there are only three of these crimes which, when committed by a white man, will subject him to that punishment. There are many of these crimes which if the white man did not commit he would be regarded as a scoundrel and a coward. In the state of Maryland there is a law to this effect: that if a slave shall strike his master, he may be hanged, his head severed from his body, his body quartered, and his head and quarters set up in the most prominent places in the neighborhood. If a colored woman, in the defense of her own virtue, in defense of her own person, should shield herself from the brutal attacks of her tyrannical master, or make the slightest resistance, she may be killed on the spot. No law whatever will bring the guilty man to justice for the crime.

But you will ask me, can these things be possible in a land professing Christianity? Yes, they are so; and this is not the worst. No, a darker feature is yet to be presented than the mere existence of these facts. I have to inform you that the religion of the southern states, at this time, is the great supporter, the great sanctioner of the bloody atrocities to which I have referred. While America is printing tracts and Bibles; sending missionaries abroad to convert the heathen; expending her money in various ways for the promotion of the Gospel in foreign lands—the slave not only lies forgotten, uncared for, but is trampled under foot by the very churches of the land. What have we in America? Why, we have slavery made part of the religion of the land. Yes, the pulpit there stands up as the great defender of this cursed institution, as it is called. Ministers of religion come forward and torture the hallowed pages of inspired wisdom to sanction the bloody deed. They stand forth as the foremost, the strongest defenders of this "institution."

As a proof of this, I need not do more than state the general fact, that slavery has existed under the droppings of the sanctuary of the south for the last two hundred years, and there has not been any war between the religion and the slavery of the south. Whips, chains, gags, and thumb-screws have all lain under the droppings of the sanctuary, and instead of rusting from off the limbs of the bondman, those droppings have served to preserve them in all their strength. Instead of preaching the Gospel against this tyranny, rebuke, and wrong, ministers of religion have sought, by all and every means, to throw in the background whatever in the Bible could be construed into opposition to slavery, and to bring forward that which they could torture into its support.

This I conceive to be the darkest feature of slavery, and the most difficult to attack, because it is identified with religion, and exposes those who denounce it to the charge of infidelity. Yes, those with whom I have been laboring, namely, the old organization anti-slavery society of America, have been again and again stigmatized as infidels, and for what reason? Why, solely in consequence of the faithfulness of their attacks upon the slaveholding religion of the southern states, and the northern religion that sympathizes with it. I have found it difficult to speak on this matter without persons coming forward and saying, "Douglass, are you not afraid of injuring the cause of Christ? You do not desire to do so, we know; but are you not undermining religion?" This has been said to me again and again, even since I came to this country, but I cannot be induced to leave off these exposures. I love the religion of our blessed Savior. I love that religion that comes from above, in the "wisdom of God, which is first pure, then peaceable, gentle, and easy to be entreated, full of mercy and good fruits, without partiality and without hypocrisy." I love that religion that sends its votaries to bind up the wounds of him that has fallen among thieves. I love that religion that makes it the duty of its disciples to visit the fatherless and the widow in their affliction. I love that religion that is based upon the glorious principle, of love to God and love to man; which makes its followers do unto others as they themselves would be done by. If you demand liberty to yourself, it says, grant it to your neighbors. If you claim a right to think for yourself, it says, allow your neighbors the same right. If you claim to act for yourself, it says, allow your neighbors the same right. It is because I love this religion that I hate the slaveholding, the woman-whipping, the mind-darkening, the soul-destroying religion that exists in the southern states of America. It is because I regard the one as good, and pure, and holy, that I cannot but regard the other as bad, corrupt, and wicked. Loving the one I must hate the other; holding to the one I must reject the other.

I may be asked why I am so anxious to bring this subject before the British public—why I do not confine my efforts to the United States? My answer is, first, that slavery is the common enemy of mankind, and all mankind should be made acquainted with its abominable character. My next answer is, that the slave is a man, and, as such, is entitled to your sympathy as a brother. All the feelings, all the susceptibilities, all the capacities, which you have he has. He is a part of the human family. He has been the prey—the common prey—of christendom for the last three hundred years, and it is but right, it is but just, it is but proper, that his wrongs should be known throughout the world.

I have another reason for bringing this matter before the British public, and it is this: slavery is a system of wrong, so blinding to all around, so hardening to the heart, so corrupting to the morals, so deleterious to religion, so sapping to all the principles of justice in its immediate vicinity, that the community surrounding it lacks the moral stamina necessary to its removal. It is a system of such gigantic evil, so strong, so overwhelming in its power, that no one nation is equal to its removal. It requires the humanity of Christianity, the morality of the world to remove it. Hence, I call upon the people of Britain to look at this matter, and to exert the influence I am about to show they possess, for the removal of slavery from America. I can appeal to them, as strongly by their regard for the slaveholder as for the slave, to labor in this cause. I am here, because you have an influence on America that no other nation can have. You have been drawn together by the power of steam to a marvelous extent; the distance between London and Boston is now reduced to some twelve or fourteen days, so that the denunciations against slavery, uttered in London this week, may be heard in a fortnight in the streets of Boston, and reverberating amidst the hills of Massachusetts. There is nothing said here against slavery that will not be recorded in the United States.

I am here, also, because the slaveholders do not want me to be here; they would rather that I were not here. I have adopted a maxim laid down by Napoleon, never to occupy ground which the enemy would like me to occupy. The slaveholders would much rather have me, if I will denounce slavery, denounce it in the northern states, where their friends and supporters are, who will stand by and mob me for denouncing it. They feel something as the man felt, when he uttered his prayer, in which he made out a most horrible case for himself, and one of his neighbors touched him and said, "My friend, I always had the opinion of you that you have now expressed for yourself—that you are a very great sinner." Coming from himself, it was all very well, but coming from a stranger it was rather cutting.

The slaveholders felt that when slavery was denounced among themselves, it was not so bad; but let one of the slaves get loose, let him summon the people of Britain, and make known to them the conduct of the slaveholders toward their slaves, and it cuts them to the quick, and produces a sensation such as would be produced by nothing else. The power I exert now is something like the power that is exerted by the man at the end of the lever; my influence now is just in proportion to the distance that I am from the United States. My exposure of slavery abroad will tell more upon the hearts and consciences of slaveholders than if I was attacking them in America; for almost every paper that I now receive from the United States, comes teeming with statements about this fugitive Negro, calling him a "glib-tongued scoundrel," and saying that he is running out against the institutions and people of America.

I deny the charge that I am saying a word against the institutions of America, or the people, as such. What I have to say is against slavery and slaveholders. I feel at liberty to speak on this subject. I have on my back the marks of the lash; I have four sisters and one brother now under the galling chain. I feel it my duty to cry aloud and spare not. I am not averse to having the good opinion of my fellow-creatures. I am not averse to being kindly regarded by all men; but I am bound, even at the hazard of making a large class of religionists in this country hate me, oppose me, and malign me as they have done—I am bound by the prayers, and tears, and entreaties of three millions of kneeling bondsmen, to have no compromise with men who are in any shape or form connected with the slaveholders of America.

I expose slavery in this country, because to expose it is to kill it. Slavery is one of those monsters of darkness to whom the light of truth is death. Expose slavery, and it dies. Light is to slavery what the heat of the sun is to the root of a tree; it must die under it. All the slaveholder asks of me is silence. He does not ask me to go abroad and preach in favor of slavery; he does not ask any one to do that. He would not say that slavery is a good thing, but the best under the circumstances. The slaveholders want total darkness on the subject. They want the hatchway shut down, that the monster may crawl in his den of darkness, crushing human hopes, and happiness, destroying the bondman at will, and having no one to reprove or rebuke him. Slavery shrinks from the light; it hateth the light, neither cometh to the light, lest its deed should be reproved. To tear off the mask from this abominable system, to expose it to the light of heaven, aye, to the heat of the sun, that it may burn and wither it out of existence, is my object in coming to this country. I want the slaveholder surrounded, as by a wall of anti-slavery fire, so that he may see the condemnation of himself and his system glaring down in letters of light. I want him to feel that he has no sympathy in England, Scotland, or Ireland; that he has none in Canada, none in Mexico, none among the poor wild Indians; that the voice of the civilized, aye, and savage world, is against him. I would have condemnation blaze down upon him in every direction, till, stunned and overwhelmed with shame and confusion, he is compelled to let go the grasp he holds upon the persons of his victims, and restore them to their long-lost rights.

Report of a public meeting held at Finsbury Chapel, Moorfields, to receive Frederick Douglass, the American slave, on Friday, May 12, 1846. London, 1846

1. Douglass to Maria W. Chapman, Aug. 18, 1846, Anti-Slavery Letters to Garrison, Boston Public Library.

2. George Thompson to Henry C. Wright, May 23, 1846, Anti-Slavery Letters to Garrison, Boston Public Library.

Douglass told Thompson that he could not remain away from his family much longer and would be forced to return home in August unless he should decide to bring his family to England.

The conversation led to a fund for this purpose. "This result was entirely unexpected to me," wrote Douglass to Garrison on May 23, 1846. (*Liberator,* June 26, 1846.)

3. The reference is to *Slavery as it is: the testimony of a thousand witnesses,* prepared by Theodore D. Weld and published in 1839 by the American Anti-Slavery Society. From fugitive slaves in the North and from Southern newspapers Weld assembled facts on conditions of slaves in the South. In 1886, Douglass wrote that "His [Weld's] 'Testimony of a Thousand Witnesses' did as much for the cause of the Slave in the early times as 'Uncle Tom's Cabin' did for it in the later years." (Douglass to Garrison, May 1, 1886, Douglass *Mss.,* Frederick Douglass Memorial Home, Anacostia, D. C.)

In the summer of 1846 Douglass was happy to have William Lloyd Garrison with him in England. The Abolitionist leader had been invited by the Glasgow Emancipation Society in the belief that his influence would be decisive in the campaign to compel the Free Church to return the gift to the southern clergy. On July 31 Garrison arrived at Liverpool and a few days later he and Douglass began a journey from one part of England to the other—reorganizing the enemies of slavery in Britain and denouncing the slaveholders and their apologists in America. On August 4, they attended the opening session of the World Temperance Convention held at Covent Garden Theater in London. Neither was an official delegate, but they were "politely furnished . . . with a ticket" admitting them as members of the convention.

Before the convention adjourned, Douglass had stirred up a hornet's nest with a speech attacking the official American temperance movement. . . . The American delegates were furious. Reverend Kirk, a Boston clergyman, charged that Douglass had given a false picture of the temperance societies in the United States. Reverend Samuel Hanson Cox of Brooklyn, New York delivered a broadside against Douglass in a long, angry letter to the *New York Evangelist.*

Douglass' reply to Reverend Cox was extremely effective and resulted in making friends for himself and the Abolition cause in England and in his own country. . . . [The] conflict . . . revealed to a wide public on both sides of the Atlantic that in the North as well as the South there was an indifferent, if not pro-slavery, element among the clergy who did not want the evils of slavery exposed to the intelligence of the world. It also showed how deeply the pro-slavery forces feared the influence of the brilliant fugitive slave and how eagerly they sought to silence him.[1] [I:67-69]

TO SAMUEL HANSON COX, D.D.

Salisbury Road, Edinburgh, October 30, 1846

Sir:

I have two objects in addressing you at this time. The first is, to deny certain charges, and to reply to certain injurious statements, recently made by yourself, respecting my conduct at a meeting of the "World's Temperance Convention," held in Covent Garden Theatre, London, in the month of August last. My second object will be to review so much of your course as relates to the anti-slavery question, during your recent tour through Great Britain and a part of Ireland. There are times when it would evince a ridiculous sensibility to the good or evil opinions of men, and when it would be a wasteful expenditure of thought, time and strength, for one in my circumstances to reply to attacks made by those who hate me, more bitterly than the cause of which I am an humble advocate. While it is all quite true, it is equally true, that there are times when it is quite proper to make such replies; and especially so, when to defend one's self is to defend great and vital principles, the vindication of which is essential to the triumph of righteousness throughout the world.

Sir, I deem it neither arrogant nor presumptuous to assume to represent three millions of my brethren, who are, while I am penning these words, in chains and slavery on the American soil, the boasted land of liberty and light. I have been one with them in their sorrow and suffering—one with them in their ignorance and degradation—one with them under a burning sun and the slavedriver's bloody lash—and am at this moment freed from those horrible inflictions only because the laws of England are commensurate with freedom, and do not permit the American man-stealer, whose Christianity you endorse, to lay his foul clutch upon me, while upon British soil. Being thus so completely identified with the slaves, I may assume that an attack upon me is an attack upon them—and especially so, when the attack is obviously made, as in the present instance, with a view to injure me in the advocacy of their cause. I am resolved that their cause shall not suffer through any misrepresentations of my conduct, which evil-minded men, in high or low places, may resort to, while I have the ability to set myself right before the public. As much as I hate American slavery, and as much as I abominate the infernal spirit which in that land seems to pervade both Church and State, there are bright spots there which I love, and a large and greatly increasing population, whose good opinion I highly value, and which I am determined never to forfeit, while it can be maintained consistently with truth and justice.

Sir, in replying to you, and in singling out the conduct of one of your age, reputation and learning, for public animadversion, I should, in most cases, deem an apology necessary—I should approach such an one with great delicacy and guardedness of language. But, in this instance, I feel entirely relieved from all such necessity. The obligations of courtesy, which I should be otherwise forward to discharge to persons of your age and standing, I am absolved from by your obviously bitter and malignant attack. I come, therefore, without any further hesitancy to the subject.

In a letter from London to the *New-York Evangelist,* describing the great meeting at Covent Garden Theatre, you say:

> "They all advocated the same cause, showed a glorious unity of thought and feeling, and the effect was constantly raised—the moral scene was superb and glorious— when Frederick Douglass, the colored abolition agitator and ultraist, came to the platform, and so spoke *a la mode,* as to ruin the influence, almost, of all that preceded! He lugged in anti-slavery or abolition, no doubt prompted to it by some of the politic ones, who can use him to do what they would not themselves adventure to do in person. He is supposed to have been well paid for the abomination.
>
> "What a perversion, an abuse, an iniquity against the law of reciprocal righteousness, to call thousands together to get them, some certain ones, to seem conspicuous and devoted for one sole and grand object, and then, all at once, with obliquity, open an avalanche on them for some imputed evil or monstrosity, for which, whatever be the wound or injury inflicted, they were both too fatigued and

too hurried with surprise, and too straitened for time to be properly prepared. I say it is a trick of meanness! It is abominable!

"On this occasion Mr. Douglass allowed himself to denounce America and all its temperance societies together, and a grinding community of the enemies of his people; said evil, with no alloy of good, concerning the whole of us; was perfectly indiscriminate in his severities, talked of the American delegates, and to them, as if he had been our schoolmaster, and we his docile and devoted pupils; and launched his revengeful missiles at our country, without one palliative, and as if not a Christian or a true anti-slavery man lived in the whole of the United States. The fact is, the man has been petted, and flattered, and used, and paid by certain abolitionists not unknown to us, of the *ne plus ultra* stamp, till he forgets himself; and though he may gratify his own impulses and those of old Adam in others, yet sure I am that all this is just the way to ruin his influence, to defeat his object, and to do mischief, not good, to the very cause he professes to love. With the single exception of one cold-hearted parricide, whose character I abhor, and whom I will not name, and who has, I fear, no feeling of true patriotism or piety within him, all the delegates from our country were together wounded and indignant. No wonder at it! I write freely. It was not done in a corner. It was inspired, I believe, from beneath, and not from above. It was adapted to rekindle, on both sides of the Atlantic, the flames of national exasperation and war. And this is the game which Mr. Frederick Douglass and his silly patrons are playing in England and in Scotland, and wherever they can find 'some mischief still for idle hands to do'! I came here his sympathizing friend—I am so no more, as I more know him.

"My own opinion is increasingly that this abominable spirit must be exorcised out of England and America, before any substantial good can be effected for the cause of the slave. It is adapted only to make bad worse, and to inflame the passions of indignant millions to an incurable resentment. None but an ignoramus or a mad man could think that this way was that of the inspired apostles of the Son of God. It may gratify the feelings of a self-deceived and malignant few, but it will do no good in any direction—least of all to the poor slave! It is short-sighted, impulsive, partisan, reckless, and tending only to sanguinary ends. None of this, with men of sense and principle.

"We all wanted to reply, but it was too late; the whole theatre seemed taken with the spirit of the Ephesian uproar; they were furious and boisterous in the extreme; and Mr. Kirk could hardly obtain a moment, though many were desirous in his behalf, to say a few words, as he did, very calm and properly, that the cause of Temperance was not at all responsible for slavery, and had no connexion with it. There were some sly agencies behind the scenes—we know!"

Now, the motive for representing, in this connexion, "the effect constantly raised," the "moral scene sublime and glorious," is very apparent. It is obviously not so much to do justice to the scene, as to magnify my assumed offence. You have drawn an exceedingly beautiful picture, that you might represent me as marring and defacing its beauty, in the hope thereby to kindle against me the fury of its admirers.

"Frederick Douglass, the colored abolitionist and ultraist, came to the platform." Well, sir, what if I did come to the platform? How did I come to it? Did I come with, or without, the consent of the meeting? Had your love of truth equalled your desire to cover me with odium, you would have said that, after loud and repeated calls from the audience, and a very pressing invitation from the chairman, "Frederick Douglass came to the platform." But, sir, this would not have served your purpose—that being to make me out an intruder, one without the wedding garment, fit to be cast out among the unbidden and unprepared. This might do very well in America, where for a Negro to stand upon a temperance platform, on terms of perfect equality with white persons, it would be regarded as an insolent assumption, not to be borne with; but, sir, it is scarcely necessary to say, that it will not serve your purpose in England. It is now pretty well known throughout the world, that color is no crime in England, and it is becoming almost equally known, that color is treated as a crime in America. "*Frederick Douglass, the colored abolition agitator and ultraist, came to the platform!*" Shocking! How could democratic Americans sit calmly by, and behold such a flagrant violation of one of the most cherished American customs—this most unnatural amalgamation! Was it not an aggravating and intolerable insult, to allow a Negro to stand upon a platform, on terms of perfect equality with pure white American *gentlemen!* Monarchical England should be taught better manners; she should know that democratic America has the sole prerogative of deciding what shall be the social and civil position of the colored race. But, sarcasm aside, Sir, you claim to be a Christian, a philanthropist, and an abolitionist. Were you truly entitled to any one of these names, you would have been delighted at seeing one of Africa's despised children cordially received, and warmly welcomed to a world's temperance platform, and in every way treated as a man and a brother. But the truth probably is, that you felt both yourself and your country severely rebuked by my presence there; and, besides this, it was undoubtedly painful to you to be placed on the same platform, on a level with a Negro, a fugitive slave. I do not assert this positively—it may not be quite true. But if it be true, I sincerely pity your littleness of soul.

You sneeringly call me an "*abolition agitator and ultraist.*" Sir, I regard this as a compliment, though you intend it as a condemnation. My only fear is, that I am unworthy of those epithets. To be an abolition agitator is simply to be one who dares to think for himself—who goes beyond the mass of mankind in promoting the cause of righteousness—who honestly and earnestly speaks out his soul's conviction, regardless of the smiles or frowns of men—leaving the pure flame of truth to burn up whatever hay, wood and stubble it may find in its way. To be such an one is the deepest and sincerest wish of my heart. It is a part of my daily prayer to God, that He will raise up and send forth more to unmask a pro-slavery church, and to rebuke a man-stealing ministry—to rock the land with agitation, and give America no peace till she repent, and be thoroughly purged of this monstrous iniquity. While Heaven lends me health and strength, and intellectual ability, I shall devote myself to this agitation; and I believe that, by so acting, I shall secure the smiles of an approving God, and the grateful approbation of my down-trodden and long abused fellow-countrymen. With these on my side, of course I ought not to be disturbed by your displeasure; nor am I disturbed. I speak now in vindication of my cause, caring very little for your good or ill opinion.

You say I spoke "so as to ruin the influence of all that had preceded"! My speech, then, must have been very powerful; for I had been preceded by yourself, and some ten or twelve others, all powerful advocates of the Temperance cause, some of them the most so of any I ever heard. But I half fear my speech was not so powerful as you seem to imagine. It is barely possible that you have fallen into a mistake, quite common to persons of your turn of mind,—that of confounding your own pride with the cause which you may happen to plead. I think you will upon reflection confess, that I have now hit upon a happy solution of the difficulty. As I look back to that occasion, I remember certain facts, which seem to confirm me in this view of the case. You had eulogized in no measured or qualified terms, America and American Temperance Societies; and in this, your co-delegates were not a whit behind you. Is it not possible that the applause, following each brilliant climax of your fulsome panegyric, made you feel the moral effect raised, and the scene superb and glorious? I am not unaware of the effect of such demonstrations: it is very intoxicating, very inflating. Now, Sir, I should be very sorry, and would make any amends within my power, if I supposed I had really committed, the "*abomination*" of which you accuse me. The Temperance cause is dear to me. I love it for myself, and for the black man, as well as for the white man. I have labored, both in England and America, to promote the cause, and am ready still to labor; and I should grieve to think of any act of mine, which would inflict the slightest injury upon the cause. But I am satisfied that no such injury was inflicted. No, Sir, it was not the poor bloated drunkard, who was "*ruined*" by my speech, but your own bloated pride, as I shall presently show—as I mean to take up your letter in the order in which it is written, and reply to each part of it.

You say I lugged in anti-slavery, or abolition. Of course, you meant by this to produce the impression, that I introduced the subject illegitimately. If such were your intention, it is an impression utterly at variance with the truth. I said nothing, on the occasion referred to, which in fairness can be construed into an outrage upon propriety, or something foreign to the temperance platform—and especially a "world's Temperance platform." The meeting at Covent Garden was not a *white* temperance meeting, such as are held in the United States, but a "world's temperance meeting," embracing the black as well as the white part of the creation—practically carrying out the scriptural declaration, that "God has made of one blood, all nations of men, to dwell on all the face of the earth." It was a meeting for promoting temperance throughout the world. All nations had a right to be represented there; and each speaker had a right to make known to that body, the peculiar difficulties which lay in the way of the temperance reformation, in his own particular locality. In that Convention, and upon that platform, I was the recognized representative of the colored population of the United States; and to their cause I was bound to be faithful. It would have been quite easy for me to have made a speech upon the general question of temperance, carefully excluding all reference to my enslaved, neglected and persecuted brethren in America, and thereby secured your applause;—but to have pursued such a course, would have been selling my birthright for a mess of pottage,—would have been to play the part of Judas, a part which even you profess to loathe and detest. Sir, let me explain the motive which animated me, in speaking as I did at Covent Garden Theatre. As I stood upon that platform, and surveyed the deep depression of the colored people of America, and the treatment uniformly adopted, by white temperance societies, towards them— the impediments and absolute barriers thrown in the way of their moral and social improvement, by American slavery, and by an inveterate prejudice against them, on account of their color—and beheld them in rags and wretchedness, in fetters and chains, left to be devoured by intemperance and kindred vices—and slavery like a very demon, standing directly in the way of their reformation, as with a drawn sword, ready to smite down any who might approach for their deliverance—and found myself in a position where I could rebuke this evil spirit, where my words would be borne to the shores of America, upon the enthusiastic shouts of congregated thousands—I deemed it my duty to embrace the opportunity. In the language of John Knox, "I was in the place where I was demanded of conscience to speak the truth—and the truth I *did* speak—impugn it who so list." But, in so doing, I spoke perfectly in order, and in such a manner as no one, having a sincere interest in the cause of Temperance, could take offence at—as I shall show by reporting, in another part of this letter my speech as delivered on that occasion.

"He was, no doubt, prompted to do it by some of the politic ones, who can use him to do what they themselves would not adventure to do in person." The right or wrong of obeying the promptings of another depends upon the character of the thing to be done. If the thing be right, I should do it, no matter by whom prompted; if wrong, I should refrain from it, no matter by whom commanded. In the present instance, I was prompted by no one—I acted entirely upon my own responsibility. If, therefore, blame is to fall anywhere, it should fall upon me.

"He is supposed to have been well paid for the abomination." This, Sir, is a cowardly way of stating your own conjecture. I should be pleased to have you tell me, what harm there is in being well paid! Is not the laborer worthy of his hire? Do you preach without pay? Were you not paid by those who sent you to represent them in the World's Temperance Convention? There is not the slightest doubt that you were paid—and *well paid*. The only difference between us, in the matter of pay, is simply this—you were paid, and I was not. I can with a clear conscience affirm that, so far from having been well paid, as you supposed, I never received a single farthing for my attendance—or for any word which I uttered on the occasion referred to—while you were in all probability well supported, "well paid," for all you did during your attendance. My visit to London was at my own cost. I mention this, not because I blame you for taking pay, or because I regard as specially meritorious my attending the meeting without pay; for I should probably have taken pay as readily as you did, had it been offered; but it was not offered, and therefore I got none.

You stigmatize my speech as an "abomination"; but you take good care to suppress every word of the speech itself. There can be but one motive for this, and that motive obviously is, because there was nothing in the speech which, standing alone, would inspire others with the bitter malignity against me, which unhappily rankles in your own bosom.

Now, Sir, to show the public how much reliance ought to be placed on your statements, and what estimate they should form of your love of truth and Christian candor, I will give the substance of my speech at Covent Garden Theatre, and the circumstances attending and growing out of its delivery. As "the thing was not done in a corner," I can with safety appeal to the FIVE THOUSAND that heard the speech, for the substantial correctness of my report of it. It was as follows:—

Mr. Chairman—Ladies and Gentlemen—I am not a delegate to this Convention. Those who would have been most likely to elect me as a delegate, could not, because they are to-night held in the most abject slavery in the United States. Sir, I regret that I cannot fully unite with the American delegates, in their patriotic eulogies of America, and American Temperance Societies. I cannot do so, for this good reason—there are, at this moment, three millions of the American population, by slavery and prejudice, placed entirely beyond the pale of American Temperance Societies. The three million slaves are completely excluded by slavery—and four hundred thousand free colored people are almost as completely excluded by an inveterate prejudice against them, on account of their color. [Cries of shame! shame!]

I do not say these things to wound the feelings of the American delegates. I simply mention them in their presence, and before this audience, that, seeing how you regard this hatred and neglect of the colored people, they may be induced, on their return home, to enlarge the field of their Temperance operations, and embrace within the scope of their influence, my long neglected race—[great cheering and some confusion on the platform]. Sir, to give you some idea of the difficulties and obstacles in the way of the Temperance reformation of the colored population in the United States, allow me to state a few facts. About the year 1840, a few intelligent, sober and benevolent colored gentlemen in Philadelphia, being acquainted with the appalling ravages of intemperance among a numerous class of colored people in that city, and finding themselves neglected and excluded from white societies, organized societies among themselves—appointed committees—sent out agents—built temperance halls, and were earnestly and successfully rescuing many from the fangs of intemperance.

The cause went nobly on till the 1st of August, 1842, the day when England gave liberty to eight hundred thousand souls in the West Indies. The colored Temperance Societies selected this day to march in procession through the city, in the hope that such a demonstration would have the effect of bringing others into their ranks. They formed their procession, unfurled their teetotal banners, and proceeded to the accomplishment of their purpose. It was a delightful sight. But, Sir, they had not proceeded down two streets, before they were brutally assailed by a ruthless mob—their banner was torn down, and trampled in the dust—their ranks broken up, their persons beaten, and pelted with stones and brickbats. One of their churches was burned to the ground, and their best temperance hall was utterly demolished.[2] [Shame! shame! shame! from the audience—great confusion and cries of "sit down" from the American delegates on the platform.]

In the midst of this commotion, the chairman tapped me on the shoulder, and whispering, informed me that the fifteen minutes allotted to each speaker had expired; whereupon the vast audience simultaneously shouted, "Don't interrupt!—don't dictate! go on! go on! Douglass! Douglass!!" This continued several minutes; after which, I proceeded as follows:—

"Kind friends, I beg to assure you that the chairman has not, in the slightest degree, sought to alter any sentiment which I am anxious to express on the present occasion. He was simply reminding me, that the time allotted for me to speak had expired. I do not wish to occupy one moment more than is allotted to other speakers. Thanking you for your kind indulgence, I will take my seat."

Proceeding to do so, again there were loud cries of "go on! go on!" with which I complied, for a few moments, but without saying any thing more that particularly related to the colored people of America.

When I sat down, the Rev. Mr. Kirk, of Boston, rose, and said—"Frederick Douglass has unintentionally misrepresented the Temperance Societies of America. I am afraid that his remarks have produced the impression on the public mind, that the Temperance Societies support slavery—['No! no! no! no!!' shouted the audience.] If that be not the impression produced, I have nothing more to say."

Now, Dr. Cox, this is a fair unvarnished story of what took place at Covent Garden Theatre, on the 7th of August, 1846. For the truth of it, I appeal to all the Temperance papers in the land, and the "Journal of the American Union," published at New-York, Oct. 1, 1846. With this statement, I might safely submit the whole question to both the American and British public; but I wish not merely to correct your misrepresentations, and expose your falsehoods, but to show that you are animated by a fierce, bitter and untruthful spirit toward the whole anti-slavery movement.

And for this purpose, I shall now proceed to copy and comment upon extracts from your letter to the *New-York Evangelist*. In that letter, you exclaim, respecting the foregoing speech, delivered by me, every word of which you take pains to omit: "What a perversion, an abuse, an iniquity against the law of reciprocal righteousness, to call thousands together, and get them, some certain ones, to seem conspicuous and devoted for one sole and grand object, and then, all at once, with obliquity, open an avalanche on them for some imputed evil or monstrosity, for which, whatever be the wound or the injury inflicted, they were both too fatigued and too hurried with surprise, and too straitened for time, to be properly prepared. I say it is a trick of meanness! It is abominable!"

As to the "perversion," "abuse," "iniquity against the law of reciprocal righteousness," "obliquity," "a trick of meanness," "abominable,"—not one word is necessary to show their inappropriateness, as applied to myself, and the speech in question, or to make more glaringly apparent the green and poisonous venom with which your mouth, if not your heart, is filled. You represent me as opening "an avalanche upon you for some *imputed* evil or monstrosity." And is slavery only an *imputed evil*? Now, suppose I had lugged in Anti-Slavery, (which I deny,)—you profess to be an abolitionist. You, therefore, ought to have been the last man in the world to have found fault with me on that account. Your great love of liberty, and sympathy for the downtrodden slave, ought to have led you to "pardon something to the spirit of Liberty," especially in one who had the scars of the slave-drivers' whip on his back, and who, at this moment, has four sisters and a brother in slavery. But, Sir, you are not an abolitionist, and you only assumed to be one during your recent tour in this country, that you might sham your way through this land, and the more effectually stab and blast the character of the real friends of emancipation. Who ever heard of a true abolitionist speaking of slavery as an "imputed evil," or complaining of being "wounded and injured" by an allusion to it—and that, too, because that allusion was in opposition to the infernal system? You took no offence when the Rev. Mr. Kirk assumed the Christian name and character for the slaveholders in the World's Temperance Convention. You were not "wounded or injured,"—it was not a "perversion, an abuse, an iniquity against the law of reciprocal righteousness." You have no indignation to pour out upon him. Oh, no! But when a *fugitive slave* merely alluded to slavery as obstructing the moral and social improvement of my race, you were "wounded and injured," and rendered indignant! This, sir, tells the whole story of your abolitionism, and stamps your pretensions to abolition as brazen hypocrisy or self-deception.

You were "too fatigued, too hurried by surprise, too straitened for time." Why, Sir, you were in "an unhappy predicament." What would you have done, had you not been "too fatigued, too hurried by surprise, too straitened for time," and unprepared? Would you have denied a single statement in my address? I am persuaded you would not; and had you dared to do so, I could at once have given evidence in support of my statements, that would have put you to silence or to shame. My statements were in perfect accordance with historical facts—facts of so recent date that they are fresh in the memory of every intelligent American. You knew I spoke truly of the strength of American prejudice against the colored people. No man knows the truth on this subject better than yourself. I am, therefore, filled with amazement that you should seem to deny instead of confirming my statements.

Much more might be said on this point; but having already extended this letter to a much greater length than I had intended, I shall simply conclude by a reference to your remark respecting your professed sympathy and friendship for me previous to the meeting at Covent Garden. If your friendship and sympathy be of so mutable a character as must be inferred from your sudden abandonment of them I may expect that yet another change will return to me the lost treasure. At all events, I do not deem it of sufficient value to purchase it at so high a price as that of the abandonment of the cause of my colored brethren, which appears to be the condition you impose upon its continuance.

Very faithfully,
Frederick Douglass

The *Liberator*, November 27, 1846

1. W. P. Garrison and F. J. Garrison, *Life of William Lloyd Garrison*, vol. III, p. 157.

2. The riot began when a group of young hoodlums attacked a parade of colored men and boys organized to celebrate the progress of the temperance cause and the emancipation of the slaves in the British West Indies. The attack on the Negroes spread rapidly. In the next few days Negroes were stoned and beaten, a hall designed for the holding of their meetings was burned, and a Presbyterian Church set on fire. The cause of the riot was said to be a banner in the parade which carried the motto "Liberty or Death" over the figure of a Negro and showed St. Domingo in flames with white people massacred by the slaves. A reporter for the Philadelphia *Public Ledger* investigated this charge and found it to be completely false. "The banner," he wrote, "contains nothing more than the figure of an *emancipated slave,* pointing with one hand to the broken chains at his feet, and with the other to the word 'Liberty' in gold letters over his head. The burning town turns out to be a representation of the *rising sun,* and a *sinking ship,* emblematic of the dawn of freedom and the wreck of tyranny." (*Public Ledger,* Aug. 4, 1842.)

Late in 1846, [Douglass'] English friends, led by Ellen and Anna Richardson of Newcastle, . . . raised $710.96 to purchase his emancipation from Hugh Auld to whom his brother Thomas had transferred ownership. . . .[1] Douglass' joy was somewhat diminished by the storm of criticism the news of his freedom aroused among groups of Abolitionists in the United States. They charged that the purchase was a recognition of the "right to traffic in human beings." It was also "impolitic and inexpedient" because by the ransom Douglass had "lost much of that moral power which he possessed, as the representative of the three millions of his countrymen in chains, taking, as he did, his life in his hands, appearing, wherever he appeared, with all the liabilities which the law laid upon him to be returned to stripes, torture and death." Garrison, who had "gladly contributed" his "mite" to the purchase fund, was deluged with indignant letters accusing him of having violated a cardinal principle of the anti-slavery creed. Justifying the negotiation, he reminded his critics that although he had always contended that the demand of the slaveholder for compensation "was an unjust one," he had never maintained that it was wrong "to ransom one held in cruel bondage." "We deny," Garrison editorialized, "that purchasing the freedom of a slave is necessarily an implied acknowledgment of the master's right to property in human beings."[2] The heated controversy raged for more than three months in the columns of the *Liberator* and other anti-slavery journals. [I:72]

TO HENRY C. WRIGHT
                    22, St. Ann's Square, Manchester, December 22, 1846

Dear Friend:
   Your letter of the 12th December reached me at this place, yesterday. Please accept my heartfelt thanks for it. I am sorry that you deemed it necessary to assure me, that it would be the last letter of advice you would ever write me. It looked as if you were about to cast me off for ever! I do not, however, think you meant to convey any such meaning; and if you did, I am sure you will see cause to change your mind, and to receive me again into the fold of those, whom it should ever be your pleasure to advise and instruct.
   The subject of your letter is one of deep importance, and upon which, I have thought and felt much; and, being the party of all others most deeply concerned, it is natural to suppose I have an opinion, and ought to be able to give it on all fitting occasions. I deem this a fitting occasion, and shall act accordingly.
   You have given me your opinion: I am glad you have done so. You have given it to me direct, in your own emphatic way. You never speak insipidly, smoothly, or mincingly; you have strictly adhered to your custom, in the letter before me. I now take great pleasure in giving you my opinion, as plainly and unreservedly as you have given yours, and I trust with equal good feeling and purity of motive. I take it, that nearly all that can be said against my position is contained in your letter; for if any man in the wide world would be likely to find valid objections to such a transaction as the one under consideration, I regard you as that man. I must, however, tell you, that I have read your letter over, and over again, and have sought in vain to find anything like what I can regard a valid reason *against the purchase of my body, or against my receiving the manumission papers, if they are ever presented to me.*

Let me, in the first place, state the facts and circumstances of the transaction which you so strongly condemn. It is your right to do so, and God forbid that I should ever cherish the slightest desire to restrain you in the exercise of that right. I say to you at once, and in all the fulness of sincerity, speak out; speak freely; keep nothing back; let me know your whole mind. "Hew to the line, though the chips fly in my face." Tell me, and tell me plainly, when you think I am deviating from the strict line of duty and principle; and when I become unwilling to hear, I shall have attained a character which I now despise, and from which I would hope to be preserved. But to the facts.

I am in England, my family are in the United States. My sphere of usefulness is in the United States; my public and domestic duties are there; and there it seems my duty to go. But I am *legally* the property of Thomas Auld, and if I go to the United States, (no matter to what part, for there is no City of Refuge there, no spot sacred to freedom there,) Thomas Auld, *aided by the American Government,* can seize, bind and fetter, and drag me from my family, feed his cruel revenge upon me, and doom me to unending slavery. In view of this simple statement of facts, a few friends, desirous of seeing me released from the terrible liability, and to relieve my wife and children from the painful trepidation, consequent upon the liability, and to place me on an equal footing of safety with all other anti-slavery lecturers in the United States, and to enhance my usefulness by enlarging the field of my labors in the United States, have nobly and generously paid Hugh Auld, the agent of Thomas Auld, £150—in consideration of which, Hugh Auld (acting as his agent) and the Government of the United States agree, that I shall be free from all further liability.

These, dear friend, are the facts of the whole transaction. The principle here acted on by my friends, and that upon which I shall act in receiving the manumission papers, I deem quite defensible.

First, *as to those who acted as my friends, and their actions.* The actuating motive was, to secure me from a liability full of horrible forebodings to myself and family. With this object, I will do you the justice to say, I believe you fully unite, although some parts of your letters would seem to justify a different belief.

Then, as to the measure adopted to secure this result. Does it violate a fundamental principle, or does it not? This is the question, and to my mind the only question of importance, involved in the discussion. I believe that, on our part, no just or holy principle has been violated.

Before entering upon the argument in support of this view, I will take the liberty (and I know you will pardon it) to say, I think you should have pointed out some principle violated in the transaction, before you proceeded to exhort me to repentance. You have given me any amount of indignation against "Auld" and the United States, in all which I cordially unite, and felt refreshed by reading; but it has no bearing whatever upon the conduct of myself, or friends, in the matter under consideration. It does not prove that I have done wrong, nor does it demonstrate what is right, or the proper course to be pursued. Now that the matter has reached its present point, before entering upon the argument, let me say one other word; it is this—I do not think you have acted quite consistently with your character for promptness, in delaying your advice till the transaction was completed. You knew of the movement at its conception, and have known it through its progress, and have never, to my knowledge, uttered one syllable against it, in conversation or letter, till now that the deed is done. I regret this, not because I think your earlier advice would have altered the result, but because it would have left me more free than I can now be, since the thing is done. Of course, you will not think hard of my alluding to this circumstance. Now, then, to the main question.

The principle which you appear to regard as violated by the transaction in question, may be stated as follows:—*Every man has a natural and inalienable right to himself.* The inference from this is, "*that man cannot hold property in man*"—*and as man cannot hold property in man, neither can Hugh Auld nor the United States have any right of property in me—and having no right of property in me, they have no right to sell me—and, having no right to sell me, no one has a right to buy me.* I think I have now stated the principle, and the inference from the principle, distinctly and fairly. Now, the question upon which the whole controversy turns is, simply, this: does the transaction, which you condemn, really violate this principle? I own that, to a superficial observer, it would seem to do so. But I think I am prepared to show, that, so far from being a violation of that principle, it is truly a noble vindication of it. Before going further, let me state here, briefly, what sort of a purchase would have been a violation of this principle, which, in common with yourself, I reverence, and am anxious to preserve inviolate.

1st. It would have been a violation of that principle, had those who purchased me done so, *to make me a slave, instead of a free-man.* And,

2ndly. It would have been a violation of that principle, had those who purchased me done so with a view to compensate the slaveholder, for what he and they regarded as his rightful property.

In neither of these ways was my purchase effected. My liberation was, in their estimation, of more value than £150; the happiness and repose of my family were, in their judgment, more than paltry gold. The £150 was paid to the remorseless plunderer, not because he had any just claim to it, but to induce him to give up his legal claim to something which they deemed of more value than money. It was not to compensate the slaveholder, but to release me from his power; not to establish my *natural right* to freedom, but to release me from all legal liabilities to slavery. And all this, you and I, and the slaveholders, and all who know anything of the transaction, very well understand. The very letter to Hugh Auld, proposing terms of purchase, informed him that those who gave, *denied his right to it.* The error of those, who condemn this transaction, consists in their confounding the crime of buying men *into slavery,* with the meritorious act of buying men out of slavery, and the purchase of legal freedom with abstract right and natural freedom. They say, "If you buy, you recognize the right to sell. If you receive, you recognize the right of the giver to give." And this has a show of truth, as well as of logic. But a few plain cases will show its entire fallacy.

There is now, in this country, a heavy duty on corn. The government of this country has imposed it; and though I regard it a most unjust and wicked imposition, no man of common sense will charge me with endorsing or recognizing the right of this government to impose this duty, simply because, to prevent myself and family from starving, I buy and eat this corn.

Take another case:—I have had dealings with a man. I have owed him one hundred dollars, and have paid it; I have lost the receipt. He comes upon me the second time for the money. I know, and he knows, he has no right to it; but he is a villain, and has me in his power. The law is with him, and against me. I must pay or be dragged to jail. I choose to pay the bill a second time. To say I sanctioned his right to rob me, because I preferred to pay rather than go to jail, is to utter an absurdity, to which no sane man would give heed. And yet the principle of action, in each of these cases, is the same. The man might indeed say, the claim is unjust—and declare, I will rot in jail, before I will pay it. But this would not, certainly, be demanded by any principle of truth, justice, or humanity; and however much we might be disposed to respect his daring, but little deference could be paid to his wisdom. The fact is, we act upon this principle every day of our lives, and we have an undoubted right to do so. When I came to this country from the United States, I came in the *second* cabin. And why? Not because my natural right to come in the *first* cabin was not as good as that of any other man, but because a wicked and cruel prejudice decided, that the second cabin was the place for me. By coming over in the second, did I sanction or justify this wicked proscription? Not at all. It was the best I could do. I acted from necessity.

One other case, and I have done with this view of the subject. I think you will agree with me, that the case I am now about to put is pertinent, though you may not readily pardon me for making yourself the agent of my illustration. The case respects the passport system on the continent of Europe. That system you utterly condemn. You look upon it as an unjust and wicked interference, a bold and infamous violation of the *natural* and *sacred* right of locomotion. You hold, (and so do I,) that the image of our common God ought to be a passport all over the habitable world. But bloody and tyrannical governments have ordained otherwise; they usurp authority over you, and decide for you, on what conditions you shall travel. They say, you shall have a passport, or you shall be put in prison. Now, the question is, have they a right to prescribe any such terms? and do you, by complying with these terms, sanction their interference? I think you will answer, no; submission to injustice, and sanction of injustice, are different things; and he is a poor reasoner who confounds the two, and makes them one and the same thing. Now, then, for the parallel, and the application of the passport system to my own case.

I wish to go to the United States. I have a natural right to go there, and be free. My natural right is as good as that of Hugh Auld, or James K. Polk; but that plundering government says, I shall not return to the United States in safety—it says, I must allow Hugh Auld to rob me, or my friends, of £150, or be hurled into the infernal jaws of slavery. I must have a "bit of paper, signed and sealed," or my liberty must be taken from me, and I must be torn from my family and friends. The government of Austria said to you, "Dare to come upon my soil, without a passport, declaring you to be an American citizen, (which you say you are not,) you shall at once be arrested, and thrown into prison." What said you to that Government? Did you say that the threat was a villainous one, and an infamous invasion of your right of locomotion? Did you say, "I will come upon your soil; I will go where I please! I dare and defy your government!" Did you say, "I will spurn your passports; I would not stain my hand, and degrade myself, by touching your miserable parchment. You have no right to give it, and I have no right to take it. I trample your laws, and will put your constitutions under my feet! I will not recognize them!" Was this your course? No! dear friend, it was not. Your practice was wiser than your theory. You took the passport, submitted to be examined while travelling, and availed yourself of all the advantages of your "passport"—or, in other words, escaped all the evils which you ought to have done, without it, and would have done, but for the tyrannical usurpation in Europe.

I will not dwell longer upon this view of the subject; and I dismiss it, feeling quite satisfied of the entire correctness of the reasoning, and the principle attempted to be maintained. As to the expediency of the measures, different opinions may well prevail; but in regard to the principle, I feel it difficult to conceive of two opinions. I am free to say, that, had I possessed one hundred and fifty pounds, I would have seen Hugh Auld *kicking,* before I would have given it to him. I would have waited till the emergency came, and only given up the money when nothing else would do. But my friends thought it best to provide against the contingency; they acted on their own responsibility, and I am not disturbed about the result. But, having acted on a true principle, *I do not feel free to disavow their proceedings.*

In conclusion, let me say, I anticipate no such change in my position as you predict. I shall be Frederick Douglass still, and once a slave still. I shall neither be made to forget nor cease to feel the wrongs of my enslaved fellow-countrymen. My knowledge of slavery will be the same, and my hatred of it will be the same. By the way, I have never made my own person and suffering the theme of public discourse, but have always based my appeal upon the wrongs of the three millions now in chains; and these shall still be the burthen of my speeches. You intimate that I may reject the papers, and allow them to remain in the hands of those friends who have effected the purchase, and thus avail myself of the security afforded by them, without sharing any part of the responsibility of the transaction. My objection to this is one of honor. I do not think it would be very honorable on my part, to remain silent during the whole transaction, and giving it more than my silent approval; and then, when the thing is completed, and I am safe, attempt to play the *hero,* by throwing off all responsibility in the matter. It might be said, and said with great propriety, "Mr. Douglass, your indignation is very good, and has but one fault, and that is, *it comes too late!*" It would be a show of bravery when the danger is over. From every view I have been able to take of the subject, I am persuaded to receive the papers, if presented,—not, however, as a proof of my right to be free, for *that is self-evident,* but as a proof that my friends have been legally robbed of £150, in order to secure that which is the birth-right of every man. And I will hold up those papers before the world, in proof of the plundering character of the American government. It shall be the brand of infamy, stamping the nation, in whose name the deed was done, as a great aggregation of hypocrites, thieves and liars,—and their condemnation is just. They declare that all men are created equal, and have a natural and in-alienable right to liberty, while they rob me of £150, as a condition of my en-joying this natural and inalienable right. It will be their condemnation, in their own hand-writing, and may be held up to the world as a means of humbling that haughty republic into repentance.

I agree with you, that the contest which I have to wage is against the govern-ment of the United States. But the representative of that government is the slave-holder, *Thomas Auld*. He is commander-in-chief of the army and navy. The whole civil and naval force of the nation are at his disposal. He may command all these to his assistance, and bring them all to bear upon me, until I am made entirely subject to his will, or submit to be robbed myself, or allow my friends to be robbed, of seven hundred and fifty dollars. And rather than be subject to his will, I have submitted to be robbed, or allowed my friends to be robbed, of the seven hundred and fifty dollars.

Sincerely yours,
Frederick Douglass

The Liberator, January 29, 1847

1. The manumission document read: "To all whom it may concern: Be it known, that I, Hugh Auld, of the city of Baltimore, in Baltimore county, in the State of Maryland, for divers good causes and considerations, me thereunto moving, have released from slavery, liberated, manumitted, and set free, and by these presents do hereby release from slavery, manumit, and set free, *My Negro Man,* named *Frederick Bailey,* otherwise called *Douglass,* being of the age of twenty-eight years, or thereabouts, and able to work and gain a sufficient livelihood and maintenance; and him the said Negro man, named *Frederick Bailey,* otherwise called *Freder-ick Douglass,* I do declare to be henceforth free, manumitted and discharged from all manner of servitude to me, my executors, and administrators forever.

"In witness whereof, I the said Hugh Auld, have hereunto set my hand and seal, the fifth of December, in the year one thousand eight hundred and forty-six.

"*Hugh Auld.*"

To this document was annexed the bill of sale.

Douglass published these documents in *The North Star,* December 3, 1847. He added these words as a preface: "We give our readers the evidence of our right to be free in this democ-ratic and Christian country—not so much however to establish our right to ourself as to ex-pose the cold-blooded Methodist man-stealer, who claimed us as his property, and the hypo-critical nation that has sanctioned his infamous claim. We shall send him a copy of this paper."

2. Lucretia Mott to Richard D. Webb, Feb. 21, 1847, Anti-Slavery Letters to Garrison, Boston Public Library; Philadelphia Female Anti-Slavery Society in *Liberator,* Mar. 19, 1847; Increase S. Smith in *Ibid.,* Jan. 15, 1847; Garrison to Elizabeth Pease, Apr. 1, 1847, Garrison Mss., Boston Public Library; *Liberator,* Mar. 19, 1847.

Douglass' last months abroad were so crammed with lecture engagements that in one month, he spoke almost every night. By March the pace was beginning to tell, and some of his addresses lacked their usual forceful delivery. An observer at Warrington noted that he appeared "to be suffering from great debility owing to the large amount of fatigue he has lately endured." Nevertheless he continued to score success after success and to convert large audiences to the cause.

Late in March Douglass prepared for his departure. In London, on March 30, his friends tendered him a public farewell attended by 1,400 persons "of great respectability." Deeply moved, the honored guest spoke regretfully of leaving the country. . . .[1] [I:73]

FAREWELL SPEECH TO THE BRITISH PEOPLE, at London Tavern, London, England, March 30, 1847

Mr. Chairman, Ladies and Gentlemen:

I never appear before an audience like that which I now behold, without feeling my incompetency to do justice to the cause which I am here to advocate, or to meet the expectations which are generally created for me, by the friends who usually precede me in speaking. Certainly, if the eulogiums bestowed upon me this evening were correct, I should be able to chain the attention of this audience for hours by my eloquence. But, sir, I claim none of these qualities. While I feel grateful for the generosity of my friends in bestowing them upon me, I am conscious of possessing very little just right to them; for I am but a plain, blunt man—a poor slave, or, rather, one who has been a slave. [Cheers.] Never had I a day's schooling in my life; all that I have of education I have stolen. [Laughter.] I am desirous, therefore, at once to relieve you from any anticipation of a great speech, which, from what you have heard from our esteemed friend, the chairman, and the gentlemen who preceded me, you might have been led to expect. That I am deeply, earnestly, and devotedly engaged in advocating the cause of my oppressed brethren, is most true; and in that character, as their representative, I hail your kind expression of feeling towards me this evening, and receive it with the profoundest gratitude. I will make use of these demonstrations of your warm approbation hereafter; I will take them home in my memory; they shall be written upon my heart; and I will employ them in that land of boasted liberty and light, but, at the same time, of abject slavery, to which I am going, for the purpose of overthrowing that accursed system of bondage, and restoring the Negroes, throughout its wide domain, to their lost liberty and rights. Sir, the time for argument upon this question is over, so far as the right of the slave to himself is concerned; and hence I feel less freedom in speaking here this evening, than I should have done under other circumstances. Place me in the midst of a pro-slavery mob in the United States, where my rights as a man are cloven down—let me be in an assembly of ministers or politicians who call in question my claim to freedom—and then, indeed, I can stand up and open my mouth; then assert boldly and strongly the rights of my manhood. [Cheers.] But where all is admitted—where almost every man is waiting for the end of a sentence that he may respond to it with a cheer—listening for the last words of the most radical resolution that he may hold up his hand in favour of it—why, then, under such circumstances, I certainly have very little to do. You have done all for me. Still, sir, I may manage, out of the scraps of the cloth which you have left, to make a coat of many colours, not such an one as Joseph was clothed in, yet still bearing some resemblance to it. I do not, however, promise to make you a very connected speech. I have listened to the patriotic, or rather respectful, language applied to America and Americans this evening. I confess, that although I am going back to that country, though I have many dear friends there, though I expect to end my days upon its soil, I am, nevertheless, not here to make any profession whatever of respect for that country, of attachment to its politicians, or love for its churches or national institutions. The fact is, the whole system, the entire network of American society, is one great falsehood, from beginning to end. I might say, that the present generation of Americans have become dishonest men from the circumstances by which they are surrounded. Seventy years ago, they went to the battle-field in defence of liberty. Sixty years ago, they framed a constitution, over the very gateway of which they inscribed, "To secure the blessings of liberty to ourselves and posterity." In their celebrated Declaration of Independence, they made the loudest and clearest assertions of the rights of man; and yet at that very time the identical men who drew up that Declaration of Independence, and framed the American democratic constitution, were trafficking in the blood and souls of their fellow men. [Hear, hear.] From the period of the first adoption of the constitution of the United States downward, everything good and great in the heart of the American people—everything patriotic within their breasts—has been summoned to defend this great lie before the world. They have been driven from their very patriotism, to defend this great falsehood. How have they done it? Why, by wrapping it up in honeyed words. [Hear.] By disguising it, and calling it "our peculiar institution;" "our social system;" "our patriarchal institution;" "our domestic institution;" and so forth. They have spoken of it in every possible way, except the right way. In no less than three clauses of their constitution may be found a spirit of the most deadly hostility to the liberty of the black man in that country, and yet clothed in such language as no Englishman, to whom its meaning was unknown, could take offence at. For instance, the President of the United States is required, at all times and under any circumstances, to call out the army and navy to suppress "domestic insurrection." Of course, all Englishmen, upon a superficial reading of that clause of the constitution, would very readily assent to the justice of the proposition involved in it; they would agree at once in its perfect propriety. "The army and navy! what are they good for if not to suppress insurrections, and preserve the peace, tranquillity, and harmony of the state?" But what does this language really mean, sir ? What is its signification, as shadowed forth practically, in that constitution? What is the idea it conveys to the mind of the American? Why, that every man who casts a ball into the American ballot-box—every man who pledges himself to raise his hand in support of the American constitution—every individual who swears to support this instrument—at the same time swears that the slaves of that country shall either remain slaves or die. [Hear, hear.] This clause of the constitution, in fact, converts every white American into an enemy to the black man in that land of professed liberty. Every bayonet, sword, musket, and cannon has its deadly aim at the bosom of the Negro: 3,000,000 of the coloured race are lying there under the heels of 17,000,000 of their white fellow creatures.

There they stand, with all their education, with all their religion, with all their moral influence, with all their means of co-operation—there they stand, sworn before God and the universe, that the slave shall continue a slave or die. [Hear, hear, and cries of "Shame."] Then, take another clause of the American constitution. "No person held to service or labour, in any state within the limits thereof, escaping into another, shall in consequence of any law or regulation therein, be released from such service or labour, but shall be delivered up to be claimed by the party to whom such service or labour may be due." Upon the face of this clause there is nothing of injustice or inhumanity in it. It appears perfectly in accordance with justice, and in every respect humane. It is, indeed, just what it should be, according to your English notion of things and the general use of words. But what does it mean in the United States? I will tell you what it signifies there—that if any slave, in the darkness of midnight, looks down upon himself, feeling his limbs and thinking himself a man, and entitled to the rights of a man, shall steal away from his hovel or quarter, snap the chain that bound his leg, break the fetter that linked him to slavery, and seek refuge from the free institutions of a democracy, within the boundary of a monarchy, that that slave, in all his windings by night and by day, in his way from the land of slavery to the abode of freedom, shall be liable to be hunted down like a felon, and dragged back to the hopeless bondage from which he was endeavouring to escape. So that this clause of the constitution is one of the most effective safeguards of that slave system of which we have met here this evening to express our detestation. This clause of the American constitution makes the whole land one vast hunting-ground for men: it gives to the slaveholder the right at any moment to set his well-trained bloodhounds upon the track of the poor fugitive; hunt him down like a wild beast, and hurl him back to the jaws of slavery, from which he had, for a brief space of time, escaped. This clause of the constitution consecrates every rood of earth in that land over which the star-spangled banner waves as slave-hunting ground. Sir, there is no valley so deep, no mountain so high, no plain so expansive, no spot so sacred, throughout the length and breadth of America, as to enable a man, not having a skin coloured like your own, to enjoy the free and unrestrained right to his own hands. If he attempt to assert such a right he may be hunted down in a moment. Sir, in the Mosaic economy, to which reference has been made this evening by a preceding speaker, we have a command given, as it were, amid the thunders and lightnings from Sinai, "Thou *not* deliver unto his master the servant that is escaped unto thee: he shall dwell with thee in the place that liketh him best: thou shalt not oppress him!" America, religious America, has run into the very face of Jehovah, and said, "Thou *shalt* deliver him unto his master." [Hear, hear.] "Thou shalt deliver unto the tyrant, who usurps authority over his fellow man, the trembling bondman that escapes into your midst." Sir, this clause of the American constitution is one of the most deadly enactments against the natural rights of man: above and beyond all its other provisions, it serves to keep up that system of fraud, wrong, and inhumanity which is now crushing 3,000,000 of human beings identified with me in their complexion, and formerly in their chains. How is it? Why, the slave-holders of the South would be wholly unable to hold their slaves were it not for the existence of the protection afforded by this constitution; but for this the slaves would run away. No, no; they do not love their masters so well as the tyrants sometimes flatter themselves; they do frequently run away. You have an instance of their disposition to run away before you. [Loud cheers.]

Why, sir, the Northern States claim to be exempt from all responsibility in the matter of the slaveholding of America, because they do not actually hold slaves themselves upon their own soil. But this is a mere subterfuge. What is the actual position of those Northern States? If they are not actual slaveholders, they stand around the slave system and support it. They say to the slaveholder, "We have a sentiment against—we have a feeling opposed to—we have an abhorrence of—slavery. We would not hold slaves ourselves, and we are most sincerely opposed to slavery; but, still, if your Negroes run away from you to us, we will return them to you. And, while you can make the slaves believe that we will so return them, why, of course, they will not run away into our states: and, then, if they should attempt to gain their freedom by force, why, we will bring down upon them the whole civil, military, and naval power of the nation and crush them again into subjection. While we make them believe that we will do this, we give them the most complete evidence that we will, by our votes in congress and in the senate, by our religious assemblies, our synods, presbyteries and conferences, by our individual votes, by our deadly hate and deep prejudice against the coloured man, even when he is free, we will, by all these evidences, give you the means of convincing the slave, that, if he does attempt to gain his freedom, we will kill him. But still, notwithstanding all this, let it be clearly understood that we hate slavery." [Laughter and cheers.] This is the guilty position even of those who do not themselves hold slaves in America. And, under such circumstances, I really cannot be very patriotic when speaking of their national institutions and boasted constitution, and, therefore, I hope you will not expect any very eloquent outbursts of eulogy or praise of America from me upon the present occasion. [Loud cheers.] No, my friends; I am going back, determined to be honest with America. I am going to the United States in a few days, but I go there to do, as I have done here, to unmask her pretensions to republicanism, and expose her hypocritical professions of Christianity; to denounce her high claims to civilisation, and proclaim in her ears the wrongs of those who cry day and night to Heaven, "How long! how long! O Lord God of Sabaoth!" [Loud cheers.] I go to that land, not to foster her national pride, or utter fulsome words about her greatness. She is great in territory; great in numerical strength; great in intellectual sagacity; great in her enterprise and industry. She may boast of her broad lakes and mighty rivers; but, sir, while I remember, that with her broadest lakes and finest rivers, the tears and blood of my brethren are mingled and forgotten, I cannot speak well of her; I cannot be loud in her praise, or pour forth warm eulogiums upon her name or institutions. [Cheers.] No; she is unworthy of the name of great or free. She stands upon the quivering heartstrings of 3,000,000 of people. She punishes the black man for crimes, for which she allows the white man to escape. She declares in her statute-book, that the black man shall be seventy times more liable to the punishment of death than the white man. In the state of Virginia, there are seventy-one crimes for which a black man may be punished with death, only one of which crimes will bring upon the white man a like punishment. [Hear, hear.] She will not allow her black population to meet together and worship God according to the dictates of their own consciences. If they assemble together more than seven in number for the purpose of worshipping God, or improving their minds in any way, shape, or form, each one of them may legally be taken and whipped with thirty-nine lashes upon his bare back. If any one of them shall be found riding a horse, by day or by night, he may be taken and whipped forty lashes on his naked back, have his ears cropped, and his cheek branded with a red-hot iron. In all the slave states south, they make it a crime punishable with severe fines, and imprisonment in many cases, to teach or instruct a slave to read the pages of Inspired Wisdom. In the state of Mississippi, a man is liable to a heavy fine for teaching a slave to read. In the state of Alabama, for the third offence, it is death to teach a slave to read. In the state of Louisiana, for the second offence, it is death to teach a slave to read. In the state of South Carolina, for the third offence of teaching a slave to read, it is death by the law. To aid a slave in escaping from a brutal owner, no matter how inhuman the treatment he may have received at the hands of his tyrannical master, it is death by the law. For a woman, in defence of her own person and dignity, against the brutal and infernal designs of a determined master, to raise her hand in protection of her chastity, may legally subject her to be put to death upon the spot. [Loud cries of "Shame, shame."] Sir, I cannot speak of such a nation as this with any degree of complacency, [cheers], and more especially when that very nation is loud and long in its boasts of holy liberty and light; when, upon the wings of the press, she is hurling her denunciations at the despotisms of Europe, when she is embracing every opportunity to scorn and scoff at the English government, and taunt and denounce her people as a community of slaves, bowing under a haughty monarchy; when she has stamped upon her coin, from the cent to the dollar, from the dollar to the eagle, the sacred name of liberty; when upon every hill may be seen erected, a pole, bearing the cap of liberty, under which waves the star-spangled banner; when, upon every 4th of July, we hear declarations like this: "O God! we thank Thee that we live in a land of religious and civil liberty!" when from every platform, upon that day, we hear orators rise and say:—

> Ours is a glorious land;
>   Her broad-arms stretch from shore to shore,
> The broad Pacific chafes her strand,
>   She hears the dark Atlantic roar;
> Enamelled on her ample breast,
>   A many a goodly prospect stands.
> Ours is the land of the free and the home of the brave.

I say, when professions like these are put forth vauntingly before the world, and I remember the scenes I have witnessed in, and the facts I know, respecting that country, why, then, let others do as they will, I have no word of patriotic applause for America or her institutions. [Enthusiastic and protracted cheering.] America presents to the world an anomaly, such as no other nation ever did or can present before mankind. The people of the United States are the boldest in their pretensions to freedom, and the loudest in their profession of love of liberty; yet no nation upon the face of the globe can exhibit a statute-book so full of all that is cruel, malicious, and infernal, as the American code of laws. Every page is red with the blood of the American slave. O'Connell once said, speaking of Ireland—no matter for my illustration, how truly or falsely—that "her history may be traced, like the track of a wounded man through a crowd." If this description can be given of Ireland, how much more true is it when applied to the sons and daughters of Africa, in the United States? Their history is nothing but blood! blood!—blood in the morning, blood at noon, blood at night! They have had blood to drink; they have had their own blood shed. At this moment we may exclaim

> What, ho! our countrymen in chains!
> The whip on woman's shrinking flesh!
> Our soil still redd'ning with the stains
>   Caught from her scourging, warm and fresh!
> What! mothers from their children riven!
> What! God's own image bought and sold!
> Americans to market driven,
>   And barter'd, as the brutes, for gold!

And this, too, sir, in the midst of a people professing, not merely republicanism, not merely democratical institutions, but civilisation; nay, more—Christianity, in its highest, purest, and broadest sense [hear, hear]; claiming to be the heaven-appointed nation, in connexion with the British, to civilise, christianise, and evangelise the world. For this purpose, sir, we have our Tract, Bible, and Missionary Societies; our Sabbath-school and Education Societies; we have in array all these manifestations of religious life, and yet, in the midst of them all—amid the eloquence of the orators who swagger at all these meetings—may be heard the clanking of the fetter, the rattling of the chain, and the crack of the slave-driver's whip. The very man who ascends the platform, and is greeted with rounds of applause when he comes forward to speak on the subject of extending the victories of the cross of Christ, "from the rivers to the ends of the earth," has actually come to that missionary meeting with money red with the blood of the slave; with gold dripping with gore from the plantations. The very man who stands up there—Dr. Plummer, for instance, Dr. Marsh, Dr. Anderson, Dr. Cooper, or some other such doctor—comes to the missionary meeting for the purpose of promoting Christianity, Evangelical Christianity, with the price of blood in his possession. He stands up and preaches with it in his pocket, and gives it to aid the holy cause of sending missionaries to heathen lands. This is the spectacle we witness annually at New York and Philadelphia; and sometimes they have the temerity to come as far as Boston with their blood-stained money. We are a nation of inconsistencies; completely made up of inconsistencies. Mr. John C. Calhoun, the great Southern statesman of the United States, is regarded in that country as a real democrat, "dyed in the wool," "a right out-and-out democrat," "a back-bone democrat." By these and similar phrases they speak of him; and yet, sir, that very man stands upon the floor of the senate, and actually boasts that he is a robber! that he is an owner of slaves in the Southern states. He positively makes his boast of this disgraceful fact, and assigns it as a reason why he should be listened to as a man of consequence—a person of great importance. All his pretensions are founded upon the fact of his being a slaveowner. The audacity of these men is actually astounding; I scarcely know what to say in America, when I hear men deliberately get up and assert a right to property in my limbs—my very body and soul; that they have a right to *me!* that *I* am in their hands, "a chattel personal to all intents, purposes, and constructions whatsoever;" "a thing" to be bought and sold!—to be sure, having moral perceptions; certainly possessing intellect, and a sense of my own rights, and endowed with resolution to assert them whenever an opportunity occurred; and yet, notwithstanding, a slave! a marketable commodity! I do not know what to think of these men; I hardly know how to answer them when they speak in this manner. And, yet, this self-same John C. Calhoun, while he vehemently declaims for liberty, and asserts that any attempt to abridge the rights of the people should be met with the sternest resistance on all hands, deliberately stands forth at the head of the democracy of that country and talks of his right to property in me; and not only in my body, but in the bodies and souls of hundreds and thousands of others in the United States. As with this honorable gentleman, so is it with the doctors of divinity in America; for, after all, slavery finds no defenders there so formidable as them. They are more skilful, adroit, and persevering, and will descend even to greater meannesses, than any other class of opponents with whom the abolitionists have to contend in that country. The church in America is, beyond all question, the chief refuge of slavery. When we attack it in the state, it runs into the street, to the mob; when we attack it in the mob, it flies to the church; and, sir, it is a melancholy fact, that it finds a better, safer, and more secure protection from the shafts of abolitionism within the sacred enclosure of the Christian temple than from any other quarter whatever. [Hear, hear.] Slavery finds no champions so bold, brave, and uncompromising as the ministers of religion. These men come forth, clad in all the sanctity of the pastoral office, and enforce slavery with the Bible in their hands, and under the awful name of the Everlasting God. We there find them preaching sermon after sermon in support of the system of slavery as an institution consistent with the Gospel of Jesus Christ. We have commentary after commentary attempting to wrest the sacred pages of the Bible into a justification of the iniquitous system. And, sir, this may explain to you what might otherwise appear unaccountable in regard to the conduct and proceedings of American abolitionists. I am very desirous of saying a word or two on this point, upon which there has been much misrepresentation. I say, the fact that slavery takes refuge in the churches of the United States will explain to you another fact, which is, that the opponents of slavery in America are almost universally branded there—and, I am sorry to say, to some extent in this country also—as infidels. [Loud cries of "Shame, shame."] Why is this?

Simply because slavery is sheltered by the church. The warfare in favour of emancipation in America is a very different thing from the warfare which you had to wage on behalf of freedom in the West India Islands. On that occasion, thank God! religion was in its right position, and slavery in its proper place—in fierce antagonism to each other. Religion and slavery were then the enemies of each other. Slavery hated Religion with the utmost intensity; it pursued the missionary with the greatest malignity, burning down his chapel, mobbing his house, jeopardising his life, and rendering his property utterly insecure. There was an antipathy deep and lasting between slavery and the exponents of Christianity in the West India Islands. All honour to the names of Knibb and Burchell! [Loud cheers.] Those men were indeed found faithful to Him who commanded them to "Preach deliverance to the captive, and the opening of the prison to them that were bound." [Loud cheers.] But, sir, the natural consequence of such faithfulness was, that these men were hated with the most deadly hate by the slaveowners, who with their abettors, used every effort to crush that living voice of truth coming from the bosom of the Christian church, which was endeavouring to dash down the bloody altars of slavery, and scatter its guilty profits to the winds. Slavery was opposed by the church in the West Indies: not so in America; there, religion and slavery are linked and interlinked with each other—woven and interwoven together. In the United States we have slaveholders as class-leaders, ministers of the Gospel, elders, deacons, doctors of divinity, professors of theology, and even bishops. We have the slaveholder in all parts of the church. Wherever he is, he is an active, energetic, vigilant man. Slavery never sleeps or slumbers. The slaveholder who goes to his bed for the purpose of taking rest does not pass his night in tranquillity and peace; but, knowing his danger, he takes his pistol, bowie-knife, and dirk with him. He is uneasy; he is aware that he lies upon bleeding heartstrings, that he sleeps upon the wretchedness of men, that he rests himself upon the quivering flesh of his fellow creatures around him; he is conscious that there is intellect burning—a spark of divinity enkindled—within the bosoms of the men he oppresses, who are watching for, and will seize upon, the first opportunity to burst their bonds asunder, and mete out justice to the wretch who has doomed them to slavery. [Loud cheers.] The slaveowner, therefore, is compelled to be watchful; he cannot sleep; there is a morbid sensitiveness in his breast upon this subject: everything that looks like opposition to slavery is promptly met by him and put down. Whatever, either in the church or the state, may appear to have a tendency to undermine, sap, or destroy the foundation of slavery is instantly grappled with; and, by their religion, their energy, their perseverance, their unity of feeling, and identity of interest, the slaveholder and the church have ever had the power to command a majority to put down any efforts for the emancipation of the coloured race, and to sustain slavery in all its horrors. Thus has slavery been protected and sheltered by the church. Slavery has not only framed our civil and criminal code, it has not only nominated our presidents, judges, and diplomatic agents, but it has also given to us the most popular commentators on the Bible in America. [Hear, hear.] It has given to us our religion, shaped our morality, and fashioned it favourable to its own existence. Thus is it that slavery is ensconced at this moment; and, when the abolitionist sees slavery thus woven and interwoven with the very texture—with the whole network—of our social and religious organizations, why he resolves, at whatever hazard of reputation, ease, comfort, luxury, or even of life itself, to pursue, and, if possible, destroy it. [Loud cheers.] Sir, to illustrate our principle of action, I might say that we adopt the motto of Pat, upon entering a Tipperary row. Said he, "Wherever you see a head, hit it!" [Loud cheers and laughter.] Sir, the abolitionists have resolved, that wherever slavery manifests itself in the United States, they will hit it. [Renewed cheering.] They will deal out their heaviest blows upon it. Hence, having followed it from the state to the street, from the mob to the church, from the church to the pulpit, they are now hunting it down there. But slavery in the present day affects to be very pious; it is uncommonly devotional, all at once. It feels disposed to pray the very moment you touch it. The hideous fiend kneels down and pretends to engage in devotional exercises; and when we come to attack it, it howls piously—"Off! you are an infidel"; and straightway the press in America, and some portion of the press in this land also, take up the false cry. [Hear, hear.] Forthwith a clamour is got up here, not against the slaveholder, but against the man who is virtuously labouring for the overthrow of that which his assailants profess to hate—slavery. [Loud cheers.] A fierce outcry is raised, not in favour of the slave, but against him and against his best and only friends. Sir, when the history of the emancipation movement shall have been fairly written, it will be found that the abolitionists of the nineteenth century were the only men who dared to defend the Bible from the blasphemous charge of sanctioning and sanctifying Negro slavery. [Loud cheers.] It will be found that they were the only men who dared to stand up and demand, that the churches calling themselves by the name of Christ, should entirely, and for ever, purify themselves from all contact, connection, and fellowship with men who gain their fortunes by the blood of souls. It will be found that they were the men who "cried aloud and spared not;" who "lifted their voices like trumpets," against the giant iniquity by which they were surrounded. It will then be seen that they were the men who planted themselves on the immutable, eternal, and all-comprehensive principle of the sacred New Testament—"All things whatsoever ye would that men should do unto you, do ye even so unto them"—that, acting on this principle, and feeling that if the fetters were on their own limbs, the chain upon their own persons, the lash falling quick and hard upon their own quivering bodies, they would desire their fellow men about them to be faithful to their cause; and, therefore, carrying out this principle, they have dared to risk their lives, fortunes, nay, their all, for the purpose of rescuing from the tyrannous grasp of the slaveholder these 3,000,000 of trampled-down children of men. [Loud cheers.]

Sir, the foremost, strongest, and mightiest among those who have completely identified themselves with the Negroes in the United States, I will now name here; and I do so because his name has been most unjustly coupled with odium in this country. [Hear, hear.] I will name, if only as an expression of gratitude on my part, my beloved, esteemed, and almost venerated friend, William Lloyd Garrison. [Loud and prolonged cheering.] Sir, I have now been in this country for nineteen months; I have gone through its length and breadth; I have had sympathy here and sympathy there; co-operation here, and co-operation there; in fact, I have scarcely met a man who has withheld fellowship from me as an abolitionist, standing unconnected with William Lloyd Garrison. [Hear.] Had I stood disconnected from that great and good man, then numerous and influential parties would have held out to me the right hand of fellowship, sanctioned my proceedings in England, backed me up with money and praise, and have given me a great reputation, so far as they were capable; and they were men of influence. And why, sir, is William Lloyd Garrison hated and despised by certain parties in this country? What has he done to deserve such treatment at their hands? He has done that which all great reformers and pioneers in the cause of freedom or religion have ever been called upon to do—made himself unpopular for life in the maintenance of great principles. He has thrown himself, as it were, over the ditch as a bridge; his own body, his personal reputation, his individual property, his wide and giant-hearted intellect, all were sacrificed to form a bridge that others might pass over and enjoy a rich reward from the labours that he had bestowed, and the seed which he had sown. He has made himself disreputable. How? By his uncompromising hostility to slavery, by his bold, scathing denunciation of tyranny; his unwavering, inflexible adherence to principle; and by his frank, open, determined spirit of opposition to everything like cant and hypocrisy. [Loud cheers.] Such is the position in which he stands among the American people. And the same feeling exists in this country to a great extent. Because William Lloyd Garrison has upon both sides of the Atlantic fearlessly unmasked hypocrisy, and branded impiety in language in which impiety deserves to be characterized, he has thereby brought down upon himself the fierce execrations of a religious party in this land. But, sir, I do not like, upon the present occasion, even to allude to this subject; for the party who have acted in this manner is small and insignificant; so impotent for good, so well known for its recklessness of statement, so proverbial for harshness of spirit, that I will not dwell any longer on their conduct. I feel that I ought not to trespass upon your patience any further. [Loud cheers and cries of "Go on, go on."] Well, then, as you are so indulgent to me, I will refer to another matter. It would not be right and proper, from any consideration of regard and esteem which I feel for those who have honoured me by assembling here this evening to bid me farewell—especially to some who have honoured me and the cause I am identified with, honoured themselves and our common humanity, by being present to-night upon this platform—I say it would not be proper in me, out of deference to any such persons, on this occasion, to fail to advert to what I deem one of the greatest sins of omission ever committed by British Christians in this country. I allude to the recent meeting of the Ecumenical Evangelical Alliance. [Hear.] Sir, I must be permitted to say a word or two upon this matter. [Hear.] From my very love to British Christians—out of esteem for the very motives of those excellent men who composed the British part of that great convention—from all these considerations, I am bound to state here my firm belief, that they suffered themselves to be sadly hoodwinked upon this point. [Hear, hear.] They were misled and cajoled into a position on this question, which no subsequent action can completely obliterate or entirely atone for. They had it in their power to have given slavery a blow which would have sent it reeling to its grave, as if smitten by a voice or an arm from Heaven. They had moral power; they had more—they had religious power. They were in a position which no other body ever occupied, and in which no other association will ever stand, while slavery exists in the United States. [Hear.] They were raised up on a pinnacle of great eminence: they were "a city set on a hill." They were a body to whom the whole evangelical world was looking, during that memorable month of August. Pressed down deep among evangelical Christians, under the feet of some there, were 3,000,000 of slaves looking to the Evangelical Alliance, with uplifted hands, with imploring tones—or, rather, I should say in the absence of tones, for the slave is dead; he has no voice in such assemblies; he can send no delegates to Bible and Missionary Societies, Temperance Conventions, or Evangelican Alliances; he is not permitted to send representatives there to tell his wrongs. He has his pressing evils and deeply aggravated wrongs, to which he is constantly subject; but he is not allowed to depute any voice to plead his cause. Still, in the silence of annihilation—of mental and moral annihilation—in the very eloquence of extinction, he cried to the Evangelical Alliance to utter a word on behalf of his freedom. They "passed him by on the other side." [Loud cheers.] Sir, I am sorry for this, deeply sorry; sorry on their own account, for I know they are not satisfied with their position. I am sorry that they should, from a timidity on their part—a fear of offending those who were called "The American brethren"—have given themselves the pain and trouble to repent on this question. But still, I hope they will repent; and I believe that many of them have already repented [hear, hear]; I believe that those who were hoodwinked on that occasion, when they shall be brought to see that they were miserably deceived—misled by the jack o' lanterns from America, [laughter]—that they will add another element to their former opposition to slavery, and that is, the pain and sense of injustice done to themselves on the part of the American delegates. From the very feeling of having been betrayed into a wrong position, they will feel bound to deal a sharp, powerful, and pungent rebuke to those guilty men who dared to lead them astray. Sir, after all, I do not wonder at the manner in which the British delegates were deluded; when I reflect upon the subtlety of the Americans, their apparently open, free, frank, candid, and unsophisticated disposition—how they stood up and declared to the British brethren that they were honest, and looked so honestly, and smiled so blandly at the same time. No; I do not wonder at their success, when I think how old and skilful they are in the practice of misrepresentation—in the art of lying. [Hear.] Coarse as the expression I have here applied to them may be, Mr. Chairman, it is, nevertheless, true; the thing exists. If I am branded for coarseness on the present occasion, I must excuse myself by telling you I have a coarse thing and a foul business to lay before you. As with the president, so with these deputations from America; there is not a single inaugural speech, not an annual message, but teems with lies like this—that "in this land every man enjoys the protection of the law, the protection of his property, the protection of his person, the protection of his liberty." They iterate and reiterate these statements over and over again. Thus, these Americans, as I said before, are skilled in the art of falsehood. I do not wonder at their success, when I recollect that they brought religion to aid them in their fraud; for they not only told their falsehood with the blandness, oratory, and smiling looks of the politicians in their own country, but they combined with those seductive qualities a loud profession of piety; and in this way they have succeeded well in misleading the judgments of some of the most intrepid, bright, and illustrious of slavery's foes in the ranks of the ministers of religion of England. [Hear.] Among the arguments used at the meeting of the Evangelical Alliance, the following stood preeminent: "You, British ministers, should not interfere with slavery, or pass resolutions to exclude slaveholders from your fellowship, because," it was cooly said, "the slaveholders are placed in *difficult circumstances*." It was stated that the slaveholders could not get rid of their slaves if they wished; that they were anxiously desirous of emancipating their slaves, but that the laws of the states in which they lived were such as to compel them to hold them whether they would or not. It was alleged that their peculiar circumstances make it a matter of Christian duty in them to hold their slaves.

Sir, I know the stubborn and dogged manner in which these statements were made; and I am conscious how well calculated they were to excite sympathy for the slaveholders: but I am here to tell you, that there was not one word of truth in any of these plausible assertions. There was, indeed, a slight shadow of light; a glimmering might be detected by an argus eye, but not certainly by the eye of man. There was a faint semblance of truth in it; a slight shadow; but, after all, it was only a semblance. [Hear.] What are the facts of the case? Just these: that in three or four of the Southern states, when a man emancipates his slaves, he is obliged to give a bond that such slaves shall not become chargeable to the state as paupers. That is all the "impediment;" that is the whole of the "difficulty" as regards the law. But the fact is, that the free Negroes never become paupers. I do not know that I ever saw a black pauper. The free Negroes in Philadelphia, 25,000 in number, not only support their own poor, by their own benevolent societies, but actually pay 500 dollars per annum for the support of the white paupers in the state. [Loud cheers.] No, sir, the statement is false; we do not have black paupers in America; we leave pauperism to be fostered and taken care of by white people; not that I intend any disrespect to my audience in making this statement. [Hear.] I can assure you I am in nowise prejudiced against colour. [Laughter.] But the idea of a black pauper in the United States is most absurd. But, after all, what does the objection amount to? What if really they have to give a bond to the State that the slaves whom they emancipate should not become chargeable to the state? Why, sir, one would think this would be a very little matter of consideration to a just and Christian man; considering that all the wealth that this conscientious slave-holder possesses, he has wrung from the unrequited toil of the slave. It is not much, when it is recollected that he kept the poor Negro in ignorance, and worked him twenty-eight or thirty years of his life, and that he has had the fruit of his labour during the best part of his days. But yet, it is gravely stated, that the slave-owner looks on it as a great hardship, that if he emancipates his slave he is bound not to suffer him to become chargeable to the state. Why, the money which the slave should have earned in his youthful days, to support him in the season of age, has been wrung from him by his Christian master. But the slaveholder of America had no occasion ever to have had such a difficulty as this to contend with before he gets rid of his slave. I may mention a fact, which is not generally known here, that this law was adopted in the slave states—for what purpose? I will tell you why: because it was previously the custom of a large class of slaveholders to hold their slaves in bondage from infancy to old age, so long as they could toil and struggle and were worth a penny a day to their masters. While they could do this, they were kept; but, as soon as they became old and decrepit—the moment they were unable to toil—their masters, from very benevolence and humanity of course, gave them their freedom. [Hear, hear.] The inhabitants of the states, to prevent this burden upon their community, made the masters liable for their support under such circumstances. Dr. Cox did not tell you that in his famous speech in the Evangelical Alliance. [Hear,

hear.] I mean Dr. Cox of America. (Mr. Douglass here turned to Dr. Cox of Hackney, which caused much laughter.) I do rejoice that there is another Dr. Cox in the world, of a very different character from the one in America, to redeem the name of Cox from the infamy that must necessarily settle down upon the head of that Cox, who, with wiles and subtlety, led the Evangelical Alliance astray upon this question. [Cheers.] I am glad—I am delighted—I am grateful—profoundly grateful, in review of all the facts, that my friend—the slave's friend—Dr. Cox of Hackney, has been pleased to give us his presence to-night. [Renewed cheers.] But now, really if the slaveholder is watching for an opportunity to get rid of his slaves, what has he to do? Why, just nothing at all—he has only to *cease to do*. He has to undo what he has already done; nothing more. He has only to tell the slave, "I have no longer any claim upon you as a slave." That is all that is necessary; and then the work is done. The Negro, simple in his understanding as he was represented this evening—somewhat unjustly, by the by [referring to some remarks made in a former part of the evening by the vocalist, Mr. Henry Russell]—would take care of the rest of the matter. He would have no difficulty in finding some way to gain his freedom, if his master only gave him permission so to do. The truth is, that the whole of America is cursed with slavery. There is upon our Northern and Western borders a land uncursed by slavery—a territory ruled over by the British power. There—

> The lion at a virgin's feet
>   Crouches, and lays his mighty paw
> Upon her lap—an emblem meet
>   Of England's queen and England's law. [Cheers.]

From the slave plantations of America the slave could run, under the guidance of the North-star, to that same land, and in the mane of the British lion he might find himself secure from the talons and beak of the American eagle. The American slave-holder has only to say to his slave, "To-morrow, I shall no longer hold you in bondage," and the slave forthwith goes, and is permitted—not merely "permitted"—oh! no, he is *welcomed* and received with open arms, by the British authorities; he is welcomed, not as a slave, but as a man; not as a bondman, but as a freeman; not as a captive, but as a brother. [Cheers.] He is received with kindness, and regarded and treated with respect as a man. The Americans have only to say to their slaves, "Go and be free;" and they go and are free. No power within the states, or out of the states, attempts to disturb the master in the exercise of his right of transferring his Negro from one country to the other. "Oh! but then," Dr. Cox would say, "brethren, although all this which Douglass states may be very true, yet you must know that there are some very poor masters, who are so situated in regard to pecuniary matters"—for the doctor is a very indirect speaker—"so situated, in regard to pecuniary concerns, that they would not be able to remove their slaves. I know a brother in the South—a dear brother" (Mr. Douglass here imitated the tone and style of Dr. Cox, in a manner which caused great laughter) "to whom I spoke on this subject; and I told him what a great sin I thought it was for him to hold slaves; but he said to me, 'Brother, I feel it as much as you do, [loud laughter], but what can I do? Here are my slaves; take them; you may have them; you may take them out of the state if your please.' Said he, "I could not; and I left them. [Renewed laughter.] Now what would you do?" said the doctor to the brethren at Manchester and Liverpool—"what would you do, if placed in such difficult circumstances?" The fact is, there is no truth in the existence of these difficulties at all. Sir, let me tell you what has stood as a standing article in our anti-slavery journals for the last ten years. When this plea was first put forth in America, and those intrepid champions of the slave, Gerrit Smith, Arthur Tappan, and other noble-minded abolitionists heard of it, what did they do? They inserted their cards in all the most respectable papers in America, and stated that there were 10,000 dollars ready at the service of any poor slaveholders who might not have the means of removing the Negroes they were desirous of emancipating. [Cheers.] Now, sir, the slaveholders must have seen this advertisement, for whatever difficulties they have to encounter, they find none in seeing money. [Hear, and laughter.] But, sir, was there ever a demand for a single red copper of the whole of those 10,000 dollars? Never; never. Now what does this fact prove? Why that there were no slaveholders who stood in need of such assistance; not one who wanted it for the purpose for which it might have been easily obtained, to meet the "difficult circumstances" stated by Dr. Cox. How Dr. Cox could, knowing that fact, as he must have done—for he is not so blind that he cannot see a dollar—I say how he could set up this false and contemptible plea before the world, and attempt to mislead the public mind of England upon the subject—I will not use a harsh expression, but I will say—that I cannot see how he could reconcile its concealment with honesty at any rate. That is the strongest word I will use in regard to this portion of his conduct. [Hear, hear.] He certainly knew better; at least, I think he must have known better; he ought to have done so; for it is astonishing how quickly he sees things generally. Another brother, the Reverend Doctor Marsh, also went into this subject, and told the brethren of the difficult circumstances in which the slaveholders were placed, especially the "Christian slaveholders;" for, mark this, they never apologise for infidel slaveholders! [Hear.] You never heard one of the whole deputation apologise for that brutal man—the uneducated slavedriver. No; it is the refined, polite, highly civilised, genteel, Christian part of the slaveholders, for whom they stand up and plead. Yes; they apologise for what they call "Christian slaveholders"—*white blackbirds!* [Loud cheers and laughter.]

Dr. Marsh stated, that if any persons in the United States were to emancipate their slaves, they would instantly be put into the penitentiary. [Laughter, and cries of "Oh, oh."] I have sometimes been astonished at the credulity of their English auditory; but I do not wonder at it, for John Bull is pretty honest himself, and he thinks other people are so also. But, yet, I must say that I am surprised when I find sagacious, intelligent men really carried away by such assertions as these. Why, sir, if this statement were true, another tinge, deeper and darker than any previously exhibited, would have appeared in the character of the American people. What! men are not only *permitted* to enslave, not only allowed by the government to rob and plunder, but actually *compelled* by the first government upon earth to live by plunder! Why, these men, by such statements, stamp their country with an infamy deeper than I can cast upon it by anything I could say; that is, admitting their statements were true. But, sir, America, deeply fallen and lost as she is to moral principle, has not embodied in the form of law any such compulsion of slavery as that which these reverend gentlemen attempt to make out. No, sir; the slaveholder can free his slaves. Why, he has the same right to emancipate as he has to whip his Negro. He whips him; he has a right to do what he pleases with his own; he may give his slave away. I was given away [hear]; I was given away by my father, or the man who was called my father, to his own brother. My master was a methodist class-leader. [Hear.] When he found that I had made my escape, and was a good distance out of his reach, he felt a little spark of benevolence kindled up in his heart; and he cast his eyes upon a poor brother of his—a poor, wretched, out-at-elbows, hat-crown-knocked-in brother [laughter]—a reckless brother, who had not been so fortunate as to possess such a number of slaves as he had done. Well, looking over the pages of some British newspaper, he saw his son Frederick a fugitive slave in a foreign country, in a state of exile; and he determined now, for once in his life, that he would be a little generous to this brother out at the elbows, and he therefore said to him, "Brother, I have got a Negro; that is, I have not got him, but the English have [cheers]. When a slave, his name was Frederick—Fred. Bailey. We called him Fred" (for the Negroes never have but one name); "but he fancied that he was something better than a slave, and so he gave himself two names. Well, that same Fred. is now actually changed into Frederick Douglass, and is going through the length and breadth of Great Britain, telling the wrongs of the slaves. Now, as you are very poor, and certainly will not be made poorer by the gift I am about to bestow upon you, I transfer to you all legal right to property in the body and soul of the said Frederick Douglass." [Laughter.] Thus was I transferred by my father to my uncle. Well, really, after all, I feel a little sympathy for my uncle, Hugh Auld. I did not wish to be altogether a losing game for Hugh, although, certainly, I had no desire myself to pay him any money; but if any one else felt disposed to pay him money, of course they might do so. But at any rate I confess I had less reluctance at seeing £150 paid to poor Hugh Auld than I should have had to see the same amount of money paid to his brother, Thomas Auld, for I really think poor Hugh needed it, while Thomas did not. Hugh is a poor scamp. I hope he may read or hear of what I am now saying. I have no doubt he will, for I intend to send him a paper containing a report of this meeting.

By-the-by, though, I want to tell the audience one thing which I forgot, and that is, that I have as much right to sell Hugh Auld as Hugh Auld had to sell me. If any of you are disposed to make a purchase of him, just say the word. [Laughter.] However, whatever Hugh and Thomas Auld may have done, I will not traffic in human flesh at all; so let Hugh Auld pass, for I will not sell him. [Cheers.] As to the kind friends who have made the purchase of my freedom, I am deeply grateful to them. I would never have solicited them to have done so, or have asked them for money for such a purpose. I never could have suggested to them the propriety of such an act. It was done from the prompting or suggestion of their own hearts, entirely independent of myself. While I entertain the deepest gratitude to them for what they have done, I do not feel like shouldering the responsibility of the act. I do, however, believe that there has been no right or noble principle sacrificed in the transaction. Had I thought otherwise, I would have been willingly "a stranger and a foreigner, as all my fathers were," through my life, in a strange land, supported by those dear friends whom I love in this country. I would have contented myself to have lived here rather than have had my freedom purchased at the violation or expense of principle. But, as I said before, I do not believe that any good principle has been violated. If there is anything to which exception may be taken, it is in the expediency, and not the principle, involved in the transaction. I wish to say one word more respecting another body who have been alluded to this evening. You see that I keep harping on the church and its ministers, and I do so for the best of all reasons, that however low the ministry in a country may be (they may take this admission and make what they can of it: I know they will interpret it in their own favour, as it may be so interpreted)—that however corrupt the stream of politics and religion, nevertheless the fountain of the purity, as well as of the corruption, of the community may be found in the pulpit. (Hear.) It is in the pulpit and the press—in the publications especially of the religious press—that we are to look for our right moral sentiment. [Hear, hear.] I assert this as my deliberate opinion, I know, against the views of many of those with whom I co-operate. I do believe, however dark and corrupt they may be in any country, the ministers of religion are always higher—of necessity higher—than the community about them. I mean, of course, as a whole. There are exceptions. They cannot be enunciating those great abstract principles of right without their exerting, to some extent, a healthy influence upon their own conduct, although their own conduct is often in violation of those great principles. I go, therefore, to the churches, and I ask the churches of England for their sympathy and support in this contest. Sir, the growing contact and communication between this country and the United States, renders it a matter of the utmost importance that the subject of slavery in America should be kept before the British public. [Hear.] The reciprocity of religious deputations—the interchange of national addresses—the friendly addresses on peace and upon the subject of temperance—the ecclesiastical connections of the two countries—their vastly increasing commercial intercourse resulting from the recent relaxation of the restrictive laws upon the commerce of this country—the influx of British literature into the United States as well as of American literature into this country—the constant tourists—the frequent visits to America by literary and philanthropic men—the improvement in the facility for the transportation of letters through the post-office, in steam navigation, as well as other means of locomotion—the extraordinary power and rapidity with which intelligence is transmitted from one country to another—all conspire to make it a matter of the utmost importance that Great Britain should maintain a healthy moral sentiment on the subject of slavery. Why, sir, does slavery exist in the United States? Because it is reputable: that is the reason. Why is it thus reputable in America? Because it is not so disreputable out of America as it ought to be. Why, then, is it not so disreputable out of the United States as it should be? Because its real character has not been so fully known as it ought to have been. Hence, sir, the necessity of an Anti-slavery League [Hear, hear, and cheers]—of men leaguing themselves together for the purpose of enlightening, raising, and fixing the public attention upon this foulest of all blots upon our common humanity. Let us, then, agitate this question. [Hear.] But, sir, I am met by the objection, that to do so in this country, is to excite, irritate, and disturb the slaveholder. Sir, this is just what I want. I wish the slaveholder to be irritated. I want him jealous: I desire to see him alarmed and disturbed. Sir, by thus alarming him, you have the means of blistering his conscience, and it can have no life in it unless it is blistered. Sir, I want every Englishman to point to the star-spangled banner and say—

United States! Your banner wears
Two emblems, one of fame:
Alas! the other that it bears
Reminds us of your shame,
The white man's liberty in types
Stands blazoned on your stars;
But what's the meaning of your stripes?
They mean your Negroes' scars.

"Oh!" it is said, "but by so doing you would stir up war between the two countries." Said a learned gentleman to me, "You will only excite angry feelings, and bring on war, which is a far greater evil than slavery." Sir, you need not be afraid of war with America while they have slavery in the United States. We have 3,000,000 of peace-makers there. Yes, 3,000,000, sir—3,000,000 who have never signed the pledge of the noble Burrit,[2] but who are, nevertheless, as strong and as invincible peace-men as even our friend Elihu Burrit himself. Sir, the American slaveholders can appreciate these peace-makers: 3,000,000 of them stand there on the shores of America, and when our statesmen get warm, why these 3,000,000 keep cool. [Laughter]. When our legislators' tempers are excited, these peace-makers say, "Keep your tempers down, brethren!" The Congress talks about going to war, but these peace-makers suggest, "But what will you do at home?" When these slaveholders declaim about shouldering their muskets, buckling on their knapsacks, girding on their swords, and going to beat back and scourge the foreign invaders, they are told by these friendly monitors, "Remember, your wives and children are at home! Reflect that we are at home! We are on the plantations. You had better stay at home and look after us. True, we eat the bread of freemen; we take up the room of freemen; we consume the same commodities as freemen: but still we have no interest in the state, no attachment for the country: we are slaves! You cannot fight a battle in your own land, but, at the first tap of a foreign drum—the very moment the British standard shall be erected upon your soil, at the first trumpet-call to freedom—millions of slaves are ready to rise and to strike for their own liberty." [Loud cheers.] The slaveholders know this; they understand it well enough. No, no; you need not fear about war between Great Britain and America.[3] When Mr. Polk tells you that he will have the whole of Oregon, he only means to brag a little. When this boasting president tells you that he will have all that territory or go to war, he intends to retract his words the first favourable opportunity. When Mr. Webster says, fiercely, If you do not give back Madison Washington—the noble Madison Washington, who broke his fetters on the deck of the Creole,[4] achieved liberty for himself and one hundred and thirty-five others, and took refuge within your dominions—when this proud statesman tells you, that if you do not send this noble Negro back to chains and slavery, he will go to war with you, do not be alarmed; he does not mean any such thing. Leave him alone; he will find some way—some diplomatic stratagem almost inscrutable to the eyes of common men—by which to take back every syllable he has said. [Hear, hear.] You need not fear that you will have any war with America while slavery lasts, and while you as a people maintain your opposition to the accursed system. When you cease to feel any hostility to slavery, the slave-holders will then have no fear that the slaves will desert them for you, or will hate and fight against them in favour of you. So that, if only as a means of preserving peace, it were wise policy to advocate in England the cause of the emancipation of the American slaves. But, sir, England not only has power to do great good in this matter, but it is her duty to do so to the utmost of her ability. But I fear I am speaking too long. [Loud cheers, and cries of "No, no"; "Go on, go on."] Oh, my friends, you are very kind, but you are not very wise in saying so, allow me to tell you, with all due deference.

I must conclude, and that right early; for I have to speak again to-morrow night almost 200 miles from this place; and it becomes necessary, therefore, that I should bring my address to a close, if only from motives of self-preservation, which the Americans say is the first law of slavery. But before I sit down, let me say a few words at parting to my London friends, as well as those from the country, for I have reason to believe that there are friends present from all parts of the United Kingdom. I look around this audience, and I see those who greeted me when I first landed on your soil. I look before me here, and I see representatives from Scotland, where I have been warmly received and kindly treated. Manchester is represented on this occasion, as well as a number of other towns. Let me say one word to all these dear friends at parting; for this is probably the last time I shall ever have an opportunity of speaking to a British audience, at all events in London. I have now been in this country nineteen months, and I have travelled through the length and breadth of it. I came here a slave. I landed upon your shores a degraded being, lying under the load of odium heaped upon my race by the American press, pulpit, and people. I have gone through the wide extent of this country, and have steadily increased—you will pardon me for saying so, for I am loath to speak of myself—steadily increased the attention of the British public to this question. Wherever I have gone, I have been treated with the utmost kindness, with the greatest deference, the most assiduous attention; and I have every reason to love England. Sir, liberty in England is better than slavery in America. Liberty under a monarchy is better than despotism under a democracy. [Cheers.] Freedom under a monarchical government is better than slavery in support of the American capitol. Sir, I have known what it was for the first time in my life to enjoy freedom in this country. I say that I have here, within the last nineteen months, for the first time in my life, known what it was to enjoy liberty. I remember, just before leaving Boston for this country, that I was even refused permission to ride in an omnibus. Yes, on account of the colour of my skin, I was kicked from a public conveyance just a few days before I left that "cradle of liberty." Only three months before leaving that "home of freedom,"

I was driven from the lower floor of a church, because I tried to enter as other men, forgetting my complexion, remembering only that I was a man, thinking, moreover, that I had an interest in the gospel there proclaimed; for these reasons I went into the church, but was driven out on account of my colour. Not long before I left the shores of America I went on board several steamboats, but in every instance I was driven out of the cabin, and all the respectable parts of the ship, onto the forward deck, among horses and cattle, not being allowed to take my place with human beings as a man and a brother. Sir, I was not permitted even to go into a menagerie or to a theatre, if I wished to have gone there. The doors of every museum, lyceum and athenaeum were closed against me if I wanted to go into them. There was the gallery, if I desired to go. I was not granted any of these common and ordinary privileges of free men. All were shut against me. I was mobbed in Boston, driven forth like a malefactor, dragged about, insulted, and outraged in all directions. Every white man—no matter how black his heart—could insult me with impunity. I came to this land—how greatly changed! Sir, the moment I stepped on the soil of England—the instant I landed on the quay at Liverpool—I beheld people as white as any I ever saw in the United States; as noble in their exterior, and surrounded by as much to commend them to admiration, as any to be found in the wide extent of America. But, instead of meeting the curled lip of scorn, and seeing the fire of hatred kindled in the eyes of Englishmen, all was blandness and kindness. I looked around in vain for expressions of insult. Yes, I looked around with wonder! for I hardly believed my own eyes. I searched scrutinizingly to find if I could perceive in the countenance of an Englishman any disapprobation of me on account of my complexion. No; there was not one look of scorn or enmity. [Loud cheers.] I have travelled in all parts of the country: in England, Ireland, Scotland, and Wales. I have journeyed upon highways, byways, railways, and steamboats. I have myself gone, I might say, with almost electric speed; but at all events my trunk has been overtaken by electric speed. In none of these various conveyances, or in any class of society, have I found any curled lip of scorn, or an expression that I could torture into a word of disrespect of me on account of my complexion; not one. Sir, I came to this city accustomed to be excluded from athenaeums, literary institutions, scientific institutions, popular meetings, from the colosseum—if there were any such in the United States—and every place of public amusement or instruction. Being in London, I of course felt desirous of seizing upon every opportunity of testing the custom at all such places here, by going and presenting myself for admission as a man. From none of them was I ever ejected. I passed through them all; your colosseums, museums, galleries of painting, even into your House of Commons; and, still more, a nobleman—I do not know what to call his office, for I am not acquainted with anything of the kind in America, but I believe his name was the Marquis of Lansdowne—permitted me to go into the House of Lords, and hear what I never heard before, but what I had long wished to hear, but which I could never have heard anywhere else, the eloquence of Lord Brougham. In none of these places did I receive one word of opposition against my entrance. Sir, as my friend Buffum, who used to travel with me, would say, "I mean to tell these facts, when I go back to America." [Cheers.] I will even let them know, that wherever else I may be a stranger, that in England I am at home. [Renewed cheering.] That whatever estimate they may form of my character as a human being, England has no doubt with reference to my humanity and equality. That, however much the Americans despise and affect to scorn the Negroes, that Englishmen—the most intelligent, the noblest and best of Englishmen—do not hesitate to give the right hand of fellowship, of manly fellowship, to a Negro such as I am. I will tell them this, and endeavour to impress upon their minds these facts, and shame them into a sense of decency on this subject. Why, sir, the Americans do not know that I am a man. They talk of me as a box of goods; they speak of me in connexion with sheep, horses, and cattle. But here, how different! Why, sir, the very dogs of old England know that I am a man! [Cheers.] I was in Beckenham for a few days, and while at a meeting there, a dog actually came up to the platform, put his paws on the front of it, and gave me a smile of recognition as a man. [Laughter.] The Americans would do well to learn wisdom upon this subject from the very dogs of Old England; for these animals, by instinct, know that I am a man; but the Americans somehow or other do not seem to have attained to the same degree of knowledge. But I go back to the United States not as I landed here—I came a slave; I go back a free man. I came here a thing—I go back a human being. I came here despised and maligned—I go back with reputation and celebrity; for I am sure that if the Americans were to believe one tithe of all that has been said in this country respecting me, they would certainly admit me to be a little better than they had hitherto supposed I was. I return, but as a human being in better circumstances than when I came. Still I go back to toil. I do not go to America to sit still, remain quiet, and enjoy ease and comfort. Since I have been in this land I have had every inducement to stop here. The kindness of my friends in the north has been unbounded. They have offered me house, land, and every inducement to bring my family over to this country. They have even gone so far as to pay money, and give freely and liberally, that my wife and children might be brought to this land. I should have settled down here in a different position to what I should have been placed in the United States. But, sir, I prefer living a life of activity in the service of my brethren. I choose rather to go home; to return to America. I glory in the conflict, that I may hereafter exult in the victory. I know that victory is certain. [Cheers.] I go, turning my back upon the ease, comfort, and respectability which I might maintain even here, ignorant as I am. Still, I will go back, for the sake of my brethren. I go to suffer with them; to toil with them; to endure insult with them; to undergo outrage with them; to lift up my voice in their behalf; to speak and write in their vindication; and struggle in their ranks for that emancipation which shall yet be achieved by the power of truth and of principle for that oppressed people. [Cheers.] But, though I go back thus to encounter scorn and contumely, I return gladly. I go joyfully and speedily. I leave this country for the United States on the 4th of April, which is near at hand. I feel not only satisfied, but highly gratified, with my visit to this country. I will tell my colored brethren how Englishmen feel for their miseries. It will be grateful to their hearts to know that while they are toiling on in chains and degradation, there are in England hearts leaping with indignation at the wrongs inflicted upon them. I will endeavour to have daguerreotyped on my heart this sea of upturned faces, and portray the scene to my brethren when I reach America; I will describe to them the kind looks, the sympathetic desires, the determined hostility to everything like slavery sitting heavily or beautifully on the brow of every auditory I have addressed since I came to England. Yes, I will tell these facts to the Negroes, to encourage their hearts and strengthen them in their sufferings and toils; and I am sure that in this I shall have your sympathy as well as their blessing. Pardon me, my friends, for the disconnected manner in which I have addressed you; but I have spoken out of the fulness of my heart; the words that came up went out, and though not uttered altogether so delicately, refinedly, and systematically as they might have been, still, take them as they are—the free upgushings of a heart overborne with grateful emotions at the remembrance of the kindness I have received in this country from the day I landed until the present moment. With these remarks I beg to bid all my dear friends, present and at a distance—those who are here and those who have departed—farewell!

Farewell Speech of Mr. Frederick Douglass Previously to Embarking on Board The Cambria *Upon His Return to America, Delivered at the Valedictory Soiree Given to Him at the London Tavern on March 30, 1847*, London, 1847

1. *Liberator*, Apr. 30, 1847; *London Morning Advertiser*, reprinted in *Liberator*, Apr. 30, 1847.
2. In 1846 the League of Universal Brotherhood was founded by Elihu Burritt (1810–1879), to lead a movement against war. Its members, numbering in a few years 20,000 Americans and 20,000 Englishmen, took an iron-clad oath never to support any war for whatever purpose. During the Oregon crisis, when Burritt was also editing the *Advocate of Peace and Universal Brotherhood,* he co-operated with friends in Manchester, England, in an exchange of "Friendly Addresses" between British and American cities, merchants, ministers, and laborers.
3. The territory west of the Rocky Mountains, north of 42° and south of 54° 40′, was claimed by Spain, Great Britain, the United States, and Russia, but in 1818 by the terms of the Joint Occupation Treaty the territory was jointly occupied by Great Britain and the United States. On April 27, 1846, Congress authorized President James K. Polk to give notice of the termination of this treaty and claim the area for the United States. The situation seemed likely to lead to war, but on June 18, 1846, a compromise was agreed upon which settled the Oregon dispute by continuing the boundary east of the Rockies to the sea.
4. In October, 1841, the brig *Creole* sailed from Virginia for New Orleans, laden with over 100 slaves. During the voyage the slaves, led by Madison Washington, rose in revolt, killed one owner, overpowered the crew, and brought the vessel into the English port of Nassau. At the request of the American consul, the governor imprisoned nineteen involved in the mutiny, allowing the others to go free. Secretary of State Daniel Webster demanded the surrender of all the slaves, but the British refused. Finally, in 1853, an Anglo-American Commission awarded an idemnity of $110,330 to the United States.

At the meetings of the American Anti-Slavery Society in New York during the second week of May, Douglass was officially welcomed [home] by his leading co-workers. On this occasion he made his first important address since his return, and startled even the most avid Garrisonians with the fervor of his remarks. He out-Garrisoned the Garrisonians as he launched into a bitter attack upon his native land, . . . replying to Garrison who had referred to the Negro orator's "love and attachment" to America. . . .

The full text of the speech, as it appeared in the *New York Tribune,* was reprinted as a pamphlet by a group of Baltimore slaveholders who pointed to it as proof of the dangers inherent in the Abolitionist movement.[1] But most readers of the *Tribune* agreed with John Greenleaf Whittier that it was "a notable refutation of the charge of the natural inferiority urged against the colored man."[2] [I:75–76]

THE RIGHT TO CRITICIZE AMERICAN INSTITUTIONS, speech before the American Anti-Slavery Society, May 11, 1847

I am very glad to be here. I am very glad to be present at this Anniversary, glad again to mingle my voice with those with whom I have stood identified, with those with whom I have laboured, for the last seven years, for the purpose of undoing the burdens of my brethren, and hastening the day of their emancipation.

I do not doubt but that a large portion of this audience will be disappointed, both by the *manner* and the *matter* of what I shall this day set forth. The extraordinary and unmerited eulogies, which have been showered upon me, here and elsewhere, have done much to create expectations which, I am well aware, I can never hope to gratify. I am here, a simple man, knowing what I have experienced in Slavery, knowing it to be a bad system, and desiring, by all Christian means, to seek its overthrow. I am not here to please you with an eloquent speech, with a refined and logical address, but to speak to you the sober truths of a heart overborne with gratitude to God that we have in this land, cursed as it is with Slavery, so noble a band to second my efforts and the efforts of others, in the noble work of undoing the yoke of bondage, with which the majority of the States of this Union are now unfortunately cursed.

Since the last time I had the pleasure of mingling my voice with the voices of my friends on this platform, many interesting and even trying events have occurred to me. I have experienced, within the last eighteen or twenty months, many incidents, all of which it would be interesting to communicate to you, but many of these I shall be compelled to pass over at this time, and confine my remarks to giving a general outline of the manner and spirit with which I have been hailed abroad, and welcomed at the different places which I have visited during my absence of twenty months.

You are aware, doubtless, that my object in going from this country, was to get beyond the reach of the clutch of the man who claimed to own me as his property. I had written a book, giving a history of that portion of my life spent in the gall and bitterness and degradation of Slavery, and in which, I also identified my oppressors as the perpetrators of some of the most atrocious crimes. This had deeply incensed them against me, and stirred up within them the purpose of revenge, and, my whereabouts being known, I believed it necessary for me, if I would preserve my liberty, to leave the shores of America, and take up my abode in some other land, at least until the clamor had subsided. I went to England, monarchical England, to get rid of Democratic Slavery; and I must confess that at the very threshold I was satisfied that I had gone to the right place. Say what you will of England—of the degradation—of the poverty—and there is much of it there,—say what you will of the oppression and suffering going on in England at this time, there is Liberty there, not only for the white man, but for the black man also. The instant that I stepped upon the shore, and looked into the faces of the crowd around me, I saw in every man a recognition of my manhood, and an absence, a perfect absence, of everything like that disgusting hate with which we are pursued in this country. [Cheers.] I looked around in vain to see in any man's face a token of the slightest aversion to me on account of my complexion. Even the cabmen demeaned themselves to me as they did to other men, and the very dogs and pigs of old England treated me as a man! I cannot, however, my friends, dwell upon this anti-prejudice, or rather the many illustrations of the absence of prejudice against colour in England, but will proceed, at once, to defend the right and duty of invoking English aid and English sympathy for the overthrow of American Slavery, for the education of coloured Americans, and to forward, in every way, the interests of humanity; inasmuch as the right of appealing to England for aid in overthrowing Slavery in this country has been called in question, in public meetings and by the press, in this city.

I cannot agree with my friend Mr. Garrison, in relation to my love and attachment to this land. I have no love for America, as such; I have no patriotism. I have no country. What country have I? The institutions of this country do not know me, do not recognize me as a man. I am not thought of, spoken of, in any direction, out of the anti-slavery ranks, as a man. I am not thought of, or spoken of, except as a piece of property belonging to some *Christian* slaveholder, and all the religious and political institutions of this country, alike pronounce me a slave and a chattel. Now, in such a country as this, I cannot have patriotism. The only thing that links me to this land is my family, and the painful consciousness that here there are three millions of my fellow-creatures, groaning beneath the iron rod of the worst despotism that could be devised, even in Pandemonium; that here are men and brethren, who are identified with me by their complexion, identified with me by their hatred of Slavery, identified with me by their love and aspirations for liberty, identified with me by the stripes upon their backs, their inhuman wrongs and cruel sufferings. This, and this only, attaches me to this land, and brings me here to plead with you, and with this country at large, for the disenthralment of my oppressed countrymen, and to overthrow this system of Slavery which is crushing them to the earth. How can I love a country that dooms three millions of my brethren, some of them my own kindred, my own brothers, my own sisters, who are now clanking the chains of Slavery upon the plains of the South, whose warm blood is now making fat the soil of Maryland and of Alabama, and over whose crushed spirits rolls the dark shadow of oppression, shutting out and extinguishing forever, the cheering rays of that bright sun of Liberty lighted in the souls of all God's children by the Omnipotent hand of Deity itself? How can I, I say, love a country thus cursed, thus bedewed with the blood of my brethren? A country, the Church of which, and the Government of which, and the Constitution of which, is in favour of supporting and perpetuating this monstrous system of injustice and blood? I have not, I cannot have, any love for this country, as such, or for its Constitution. I desire to see its overthrow as speedily as possible, and its Constitution shivered in a thousand fragments, rather than this foul curse should continue to remain as now. [Hisses and Cheers.]

In all this, my friends, let me make myself understood. I do not hate America as against England, or against any other country, or land. I love humanity all over the globe. I am anxious to see righteousness prevail in all directions. I am anxious to see Slavery overthrown here; but, I never appealed to Englishmen in a manner calculated to awaken feelings of hatred or disgust, or to influence their prejudices towards America as a nation, or in a manner provocative of national jealousy or ill-will; but I always appealed to their conscience—to the higher and nobler feelings of the people of that country, to enlist them in this cause. I always appealed to their manhood, that which preceded their being Englishmen, (to quote an expression of my friend Phillips,) I appealed to them as men, and I had a right to do so. They are men, and the slave is a man, and we have a right to call upon all men to assist in breaking his bonds, let them be born when, and live where they may.

But it is asked, "What good will this do?" or "What good has it done?" "Have you not irritated, have you not annoyed your American friends, and the American people rather, than done them good?" I admit that we have irritated them. They deserve to be irritated. I am anxious to irritate the American people on this question. As it is in physics, so in morals, there are cases which demand irritation, and counter irritation. The conscience of the American public needs this irritation. And I would *blister it all over, from centre to circumference,* until it gives signs of a purer and a better life than it is now manifesting to the world.

But why expose the sins of one nation in the eyes of another? Why attempt to bring one people under the odium of another people? There is much force in this question. I admit that there are sins in almost every country which can be best removed by means confined exclusively to their immediate locality. But such evils and such sins pre-suppose the existence of a moral power in this immediate locality sufficient to accomplish the work of renovation. But where, pray, can we go to find moral power in this nation, sufficient to overthrow Slavery? To what institution, to what party shall we apply for aid? I say, we admit that there are evils which can be best removed by influences confined to their immediate locality. But in regard to American Slavery, it is not so. It is such a giant crime, so darkening to the soul, so blinding in its moral influence, so well calculated to blast and corrupt all the humane principles of our nature, so well adapted to infuse its own accursed spirit into all around it, that the people among whom it exists have not the moral power to abolish it. Shall we go to the Church for this influence? We have heard its character described. Shall we go to politicians or political parties? Have they the moral power necessary to accomplish this mighty task? They have not. What are they doing at this moment? Voting supplies for Slavery—voting supplies for the extension, the stability, the perpetuation of Slavery in this land. What is the Press doing? The same. The pulpit? Almost the same. I do not flatter myself that there is moral power in the land sufficient to overthrow Slavery, and I welcome the aid of England. And that aid will come. The growing intercourse between England and this country, by means of steam-navigation, the relaxation of the protective system in various countries in Europe, gives us an opportunity to bring in the aid, the moral and Christian aid of those living on the other side of the Atlantic. We welcome it, in the language of the resolution. We entreat our British friends to continue to send in their remonstrances across the deep, against Slavery in this land. And these remonstrances will have a powerful effect here. Sir, the Americans may tell of their ability, and I have no doubt they have it, to keep back the invader's hosts, to repulse the strongest force that its enemies may send against this country. It may boast, and it may *rightly* boast, of its capacity to build its ramparts so high that no foe can hope to scale them, to render them so impregnable as to defy the assault of the world. But, Sir, there is one thing it cannot resist, come from what quarter it may. It cannot resist TRUTH. You cannot build your forts so strong, nor your ramparts so high, nor arm yourself so powerfully, as to be able to withstand the overwhelming MORAL SENTIMENT against Slavery now flowing into this land. For example; prejudice against color is continually becoming weaker in this land (and more and more consider this) sentiment as unworthy a lodgment in the breast of an enlightened community. And the American abroad dare not now, even in a public conveyance, to lift his voice in defence of this disgusting prejudice.

I do not mean to say that there are no practices abroad which deserve to receive an influence favourable to their extermination, from America. I am most glad to know that Democratic freedom—not the bastard democracy, which, while loud in its protestations of regard for liberty and equality, builds up Slavery, and, in the name of Freedom, fights the battles of Despotism—is making great strides in Europe. We see abroad, in England especially, happy indications of the progress of American principles. A little while ago England was cursed by a Corn monopoly—by that giant monopoly, which snatched from the mouths of the famishing poor the bread which you sent them from this land. The community, the *people* of England, demanded its destruction, and they have triumphed! We have aided them, and they aid us, and the mission of the two nations, henceforth, is *to serve each other.*

Sir, it is said that, when abroad, I misrepresented my country on this question. I am not aware of any misrepresentation. I stated facts, and facts only. A gentleman of your own city, Rev. Dr. Cox, has taken particular pains to stigmatize me as having introduced the subject of Slavery illegitimately into the World's Temperance Convention. But what was the fact? I went to that Convention, not as a delegate. I went into it by the invitation of the Committee of the Convention. I suppose most of you know the circumstances, but I wish to say one word in relation to the spirit and the principle which animated me at the meeting. I went into it at the invitation of the Committee, and spoke not only at their urgent request, but by public announcement. I stood on the platform on the evening referred to, and heard some eight or ten Americans address the seven thousand people assembled in that vast Hall. I heard them speak of the temperance movement in this land. I heard them eulogize the temperance societies in the highest terms, calling on England to follow their example; (and England may follow them with advantage to herself;) but I heard no reference made to the 3,000,000 of people in this country who are denied the privileges, not only of temperance, but of all other societies. I heard not a word of the American slaves, who, if seven of them were found together at a temperance meeting, or any other place, would be scourged and beaten by their cruel tyrants. Yes, nine-and-thirty lashes is the penalty required to be inflicted by the law if any of the slaves get together in a number exceeding seven, for any purpose however peaceable or laudable. And while these American gentlemen were extending their hands to me, and saying, "How do you do, Mr. Douglass? I am most happy to meet you here," &c. &c. I knew that, in America, they would not have touched me with a pair of tongs. I felt, therefore, that that was the place and the time to call to remembrance the 3,000,000 of slaves, whom I aspired to represent on that occasion. I did so, not maliciously, but with a desire, only, to subserve the best interests of my race. I besought the American delegates, who had at first responded to my speech with shouts of applause, when they should arrive at home to extend the borders of their temperance societies so as to include the 500,000 coloured people in the Northern States of the Union. I also called to mind the facts in relation to the mob that occurred in the city of Philadelphia, in the year 1842. I stated these facts to show to the British public how difficult it is for a coloured man in this country to do anything to elevate himself or his race from the state of degradation in which they are plunged; how difficult it is for him to be virtuous or temperate, or anything but a menial, an outcast. You all remember the circumstances of the mob to which I have alluded. A number of intelligent, philanthropic, manly coloured men, desirous of snatching their coloured brethren from the fangs of intemperance, formed themselves into a procession, and walked through the streets of Philadelphia with appropriate banners and badges and mottoes. I stated the fact that that procession was not allowed to proceed far, in the city of Philadelphia—the American city of Brotherly Love, the city of all others loudest in its boasts of freedom and liberty—before these noble-minded men were assaulted by the citizens, their banners torn in shreds and themselves trampled in the dust, and inhumanly beaten, and all their bright and fond hopes and anticipations, in behalf of their friends and their race, blasted by the wanton cruelty of their white fellow-citizens. And all this was done for no other reason than that they had presumed to walk through the street with temperance banners and badges, like human beings.

The statement of this fact caused the whole Convention to break forth in one general expression of intense disgust at such atrocious and inhuman conduct. This disturbed the composure of some of our American representatives, who, in serious alarm, caught hold of the skirts of my coat, and attempted to make me desist from my exposition of the situation of the coloured race in this country. There was one Doctor of Divinity there, the ugliest man that I ever saw in my life, who almost tore the skirts of my coat off, so vehement was he in his *friendly* attempts to induce me to yield the floor. But fortunately the audience came to my rescue, and demanded that I should go on, and I did go on, and, I trust, discharged my duty to my brethren in bonds and the cause of human liberty, in a manner not altogether unworthy the occasion.

I have been accused of *dragging* the question of Slavery into the Convention. I had a right to do so: It was the *World's* convention—not the Convention of any sect, or number of sects—not the Convention of any particular nation—not a man's or a woman's Convention, not a black man's nor a white man's Convention, but the *World's* Convention, the Convention of ALL, *black* as well as *white*, *bond* as well as *free*. And I stood there, as I thought, a representative of the 3,000,000 of men whom I had left in rags and wretchedness, to be devoured by the accursed institution which stands by them, as with a drawn sword, ever ready to fall upon their devoted and defenceless heads. I felt, as I said to Dr. Cox, that it was demanded of me by conscience, to speak out boldly in behalf of those whom I had left behind. [Cheers.] And, Sir, (I think I may say this, without subjecting myself to the charge of egotism,) I deem it very fortunate for the friends of the slave, that Mr. Garrison and myself were there just at that time. Sir, the churches in this country have long repined at the position of the churches in England on the subject of Slavery. They have sought many opportunities to do away the prejudices of the English churches against American Slavery. Why, Sir, at this time there were not far from seventy ministers of the Gospel from Christian America, in England, pouring their leprous pro-slavery distilment into the ears of the people of that country, and by their prayers, their conversation, and their public speeches, seeking to darken the British mind on the subject of Slavery, and to create in the English public the same cruel and heartless apathy that prevails in this country in relation to the slave, his wrongs and his rights. I knew them by their continuous slandering of my race; and at this time, and under these circumstances, I deemed it a happy interposition of God, in behalf of my oppressed and misrepresented and slandered people, that one of their number should burst up through the dark incrustation of malice, and hate, and degradation, which had been thrown over them, and stand before the British public to open to them the secrets of the prison-house of bondage in America. [Cheers.] Sir, the slave sends no delegates to the Evangelical Alliance. [Cheers.] The slave sends no delegates to the World's Temperance Convention. Why? Because chains are upon his arms and fetters fast bind his limbs. He must be driven out to be sold at auction by some *Christian* slaveholder, and the money for which his soul is bartered must be appropriated to spread the Gospel among the heathen.

Sir, I feel that it is good to be here. There is always work to be done. Slavery is everywhere. Slavery goes everywhere. Slavery was in the Evangelical Alliance, looking saintly in the person of the Rev. Dr. Smythe; it was in the World's Temperance Convention, in the person of the Rev. Mr. Kirk. Dr. Marsh went about saying, in so many words, that the unfortunate slaveholders in America were so peculiarly situated, so environed by uncontrollable circumstances, that they could not liberate their slaves; that if they were to emancipate them they would be, in many instances, cast into prison. Sir, it did me good to go around on the heels of this gentleman. I was glad to follow him around for the sake of my country, for the country is not, after all, so bad as the Rev. Dr. Marsh represented it to be.

My fellow-countrymen, what think ye he said of you, on the other side of the Atlantic? He said you were not only pro-slavery, but that you actually aided the slaveholder in holding his slaves securely in his grasp; that, in fact, you compelled him to be a slaveholder. This I deny. You are not so bad as that. You do not compel the slaveholder to be a slaveholder.

And Rev. Dr. Cox, too, talked a great deal over there; and among other things he said, "that many slaveholders—dear Christian men!—were sincerely anxious to get rid of their slaves"; and to show how difficult it is for them to get rid of their human chattels, he put the following case: A man living in a State, the laws of which compel all persons emancipating their slaves to remove them beyond its limits, wishes to liberate his slaves, but he is too poor to transport them beyond the confines of the State in which he resides; therefore he cannot emancipate them—he is necessarily a slaveholder. But, Sir, there was one fact, which I happened, fortunately, to have on hand just at that time, which completely neutralized this very affecting statement of the Doctor's. It so happens that Messrs. Gerrit Smith and Arthur Tappan have advertised for the especial benefit of this afflicted class of slaveholders that they have set apart the sum of $10,000 to be appropriated in aiding them to remove their emancipated slaves beyond the jurisdiction of the State, and that the money would be forthcoming on application being made for it; but *no such application was ever made!* This shows that, however truthful the statements of these gentlemen may be concerning the things of the world to come, they are lamentably reckless in their statements concerning things appertaining to this world. I do not mean to say that they would designedly tell that which is false, but they did make the statements I have ascribed to them.

And Dr. Cox and others charge me with having stirred up warlike feelings while abroad. This charge, also, I deny. The whole of my arguments and the whole of my appeals, while I was abroad, were in favour of anything else than war. I embraced every opportunity to propagate the principles of peace while I was in Great Britain. I confess, honestly, that were I not a peace-man, were I a believer in fighting at all, I should have gone through England, saying to Englishmen, as Englishmen, there are 3,000,000 of men across the Atlantic who are whipped, scourged, robbed of themselves, denied every privilege, denied the right to read the Word of the God who made them, trampled under foot, denied all the rights of human-beings; go to their rescue; shoulder your muskets, buckle on your knapsacks, and in the invincible cause of Human Rights and Universal Liberty, go forth, and the laurels which you shall win will be as fadeless and as imperishable as the eternal aspirations of the human soul after that freedom which every being made after God's image instinctively feels is his birth-right. This would have been my course had I been a war man. That such was not my course, I appeal to my whole career while abroad to determine.

> *Weapons of war we have cast from the battle;*
> TRUTH *is our armour, our watch-word is* LOVE;
> *Hushed be the sword, and the musketry's rattle,*
> *All our equipments are drawn from above.*
> *Praise then the God of Truth,*
> *Hoary age and ruddy youth,*
> *Long may our rally be*
> *Love, Light and Liberty,*
> *Ever our banner the banner of Peace.*

National Anti-Slavery Standard, May 20, 1847

1. *Abolition Fanaticism in New York: Speech of a Runaway Slave from Baltimore at an Abolition meeting in New York Held May 11, 1847.*

The introduction to the pamphlet went: "The following report will show to Marylanders, how a runaway slave talks, when he reaches the Abolition regions of the country. This presumptive Negro was even present at the London World's Temperance Convention last year; and in spite of all the efforts of the American Delegates to prevent it, he palmed off his Abolition bombast upon an audience of 7000 persons! Of this high-handed measure he now makes his boast in New-York, one of the hot-beds of Abolitionism. The Report is given exactly as published in The New York Tribune. The reader will make his own comments."

2. *The National Era,* June 3, 1847.

TO THOMAS VAN RENSSELAER

Lynn, Massachusetts, May 18, '47

My dear Sir:

I am at home again; and, in compliance with your earnest request, avail myself of this, my first opportunity, to send you an article for your gallant little sheet. I have to thank you for the file you sent me on board the *"Hendrick Hudson."* I have given each number a hasty perusal, and have quite satisfied myself that you are on the right ground—of the right spirit—and that you possess the energy of head and of heart to make your paper a powerful instrument in defending, improving, and elevating our brethren in the (so called) free states, as well as hastening the downfall of the fierce and blood-thirsty *evangelical* tyrants in the slave States. Blow away on your "Ram's Horn"![1] Its wild, rough, uncultivated notes may grate harshly on the ear of refined and cultivated *chimers;* but sure I am that its voice will be pleasurable to the slave, and terrible to the slaveholder. Let us have a full, clear, shrill, unmistakable sound. "No compromise—no concealment"—no lagging for those who tarry—no *"slurs"* for popular favor—no lowering your tone for the sake of harmony. The harmony of this country is discord with the ALMIGHTY. To be in harmony with God is to be in open discord and conflict with the powers of Church and State in this country. Both are drunk on the warm blood of our brethren. "Blow on—blow on," and may the God of the oppressed give effect to your blowing.

Through the kindness of a friend, I have before me the *New York Sun* of 13th May. It contains a weak, puerile, and characteristic attack upon me, on account of my speech in the Tabernacle, before the American Anti-Slavery Society on the 11th instant. The article in question affords me a text from which I could preach you a long sermon; but I will neither trespass on your space, nor weary the patience of your readers, by treating the article in that way. I do not call attention to it, because I am anxious to defend myself from its malevolent contents, but to congratulate you upon the favorable change in the public mind which it indicates, and to enjoy a little (I trust innocent) sport at the expense of the editor.

We have been laughed at and ridiculed so much, that I am glad, once in a while, to be able to turn the tables on our white brethren. The editor informs his readers, that his object in writing the article is, to protest against "the unmitigated abuse heaped upon our country by the colored man Douglass." Now, who will doubt the patriotism of a man who will venture so much on behalf of his country? The *Sun* is truly a patriot. "The colored *man* Douglass." Well done! Not "*n——r*" Douglass—not *black*, but *colored*—not *monkey*, but *man*—the colored MAN Douglass. This, dear sir, is a decided improvement on the old mode of speaking of us. In the brilliant light of the *Sun*, I am no longer a *monkey*, but a MAN—and, henceforth, I may claim to be treated as a man by the *Sun*. In order to prepare the patient for the pill, and prove his title to be regarded an unmixed American, he gilds the most bloody and detestable tyranny all over with the most holy and beautiful sentiments of liberty. Hear him—"*Freedom of speech in this country should receive the greatest* LATITUDE." This sounds well; but is it not a strange text, from which to preach a sermon in favor of putting down freedom of speech by *mob violence?* "If men do not speak freely of our institutions, how are we to discover their errors or reform their abuses, should any exist?" A pertinent question, truly, and worthy of the thought and study of the profound and philosophical editor of the *Sun*. But now see a nobler illustration of the story of the "cow and the milk pail"—blowing hot and blowing cold, and blowing neither hot nor cold. The editor says—"*There is, however, a limit to this very freedom of speech. We cannot be permitted to go into a gentleman's house, accept his hospitality, yet* ABUSE *his fare, and we have no right to abuse a country under whose government, we are safely residing and securely protected.*"

Here we have it, all reasoned out as plain as logic can make it—the limit of freedom of speech accurately defined. But allow me to throw a little light upon the *Sun's* logic—if I can do so without entirely spoiling his *simile*. Poor thing, it would be a pity to hurt that. Does it not strike you as being first rate? To my mind, it is the best thing in the whole piece, and lacks only one thing—(but this probably makes no difference with the *Sun*—it may be its chief merit,) and that is, *likeness*—it lacks likeness. A gentleman's house and the government of this country are wholly dissimilar. Let me suggest to him—without meaning any disrespect to you, that a cook shop (a thing which I am surprised he should ever forget) bears a far greater resemblance to the government of this country, than that of a gentleman's house and hospitality. Let cook shop represent Country—"Bill of Fare"—"Bill of Rights;" and the "Chief Cook"—Commander-in-chief.—(I fancy I hear the editor say, this looks better.) Enters editor of the *Sun* with a keen appetite. He reads the bill of fare. It contains the names of many palatable dishes. He asks the cook for soup, he gets "dish water." For salmon, he gets a serpent; for beef, he gets bullfrogs; for ducks, he gets dogs; for salt, he gets sand; for pepper, he gets powder; and for vinegar, he gets gall; in fact, he gets for you the very opposite of everything for which you ask, and which from the bill of fare, and loudmouthed professions, you had a right to expect. This is just the treatment which the colored people receive in this country at the hand of this government. Its Bill of Rights is to practise towards us a bill of wrongs. Its self-evident truths are self-evident lies. Its majestic liberty, malignant tyranny. The foundation of this government—the great Constitution itself—is nothing more than a compromise with man-stealers, and a cunningly devised complication of falsehoods, calculated to deceive foreign Nations into a belief that this is a free country; at the same time that it pledges the whole Civil, Naval and Military power of the Nation to keep three millions of people in the most abject slavery. He says I abuse a country under whose government I am safely residing, and securely protected. I am neither safely residing, nor securely protected in this country. I am living under a government which authorized Hugh Auld to rob me of seven hundred and fifty dollars, and told me if I do not submit, if I resisted this robber, I should be put to death. This is the protection given to me, and every other colored man from the South, and no one knows this better than the Editor of the New York *Sun*. And this piece of robbery, the *Sun* calls the *rights* of the Master, and says that the English people recognized those rights by giving me money with which to purchase my freedom. The *Sun* complains that I defend the right of invoking England for the overthrow of American Slavery. Why not receive aid from England to overthrow American Slavery, as well as for Americans to send bread to England to feed the hungry? Answer me that! What would the *Sun* have said, if the British press had denounced this country for sending a shipload of grain into Ireland, and denied the right of American people to sympathize, and succor the afflicted and famine-stricken millions of that unhappy land?[2] What would it have said? Why, it and the whole American Press would have poured forth one flood of unmixed censure and scathing rebuke. England would have been denounced; the British public would have been branded as murderers. And if England had forbidden Captain Forbes to land his cargo, it might have been regarded just cause for war. And yet the interference in the one case is as justifiable as in the other. My Dear Sir, I have already extended this letter to a much greater length than I at first intended, and will now stop by wishing you every success in your noble enterprise.

Ever yours in our righteous cause,

Frederick Douglass

The *Liberator,* June 4, 1847

1. *The Ram's Horn,* a Negro paper, appeared in New York City on January 1, 1847, and lasted until June, 1848. Thomas Van Rensselaer and Willis Hodges were its editors, the latter raising money to put out the paper by working as a whitewasher. The paper had as many as 2,500 subscribers. Douglass assisted in editing the paper for a time.

2. Hundreds of thousands starved in Ireland during the potato famine of 1845–1847. Nearly 307,000 tenants in Ireland held less than five acres each, and when their crop failed, death and migration reduced the population 20 per cent. (For detailed descriptions of American aid during the famine, see *The Voyage of the Jamestown on her Errand of Mercy,* Boston, 1847, and *Report of the General Executive Committee for the relief of Ireland of the City and County of Philadelphia, Appointed by the Town Meeting of February 17, 1847, to provide means to relieve the sufferings in Ireland,* Philadelphia, 1847.)

BIBLES FOR THE SLAVES

The above is the watch-word of a recent but quite numerous class of persons, whose ostensible object seems to be to give Bibles to the American Slaves. They propose to induce the public to give, of their abundance, a large sum of money, to be placed in the hands of the American Bible Society, to be employed in purchasing Bibles and distributing them among the Slaves.

In this apparently benevolent and Christian movement they desire to unite all persons friendly to the long imbruted and long neglected Slave. The religious press has already spoken out in its favor. So full of promise and popularity is this movement that many of the leaders in Church and State are pressing into it. Churches, which have all along slumbered unmoved over the cruel wrongs and bitter woes of the Slave,—which have been as deaf as Death to every appeal of the fettered bondman for liberty,—are at last startled from their heartless stupor by this new cry of Bibles for the Slaves. Ministers of Religion, and learned Doctors of Divinity, who would not lift a finger to give the Slave to himself, are now engaged in the *professed* work of giving to the Slave the Bible. Into this enterprize have been drawn some who have been known as advocates for emancipation. One Anti-Slavery Editor has abandoned his position at the head of a widely circulating journal, and has gone forth to lecture and solicit donations in its behalf. Even the American Bible Society, which a few years ago peremptorily refused to entertain the offensive subject, and refused the offer of ten thousand dollars, has at last relented, if not repented, and now condescends to *receive money* for this object. To be sure we have had no public assurance of this from that society. It is, however, generously inferred by the friends of the movement, that they will *consent to receive money* for this purpose. Now what does all this mean? Are the men engaged in this movement sane? and if so, can they be honest? Do they seriously believe that the American Slave can receive the Bible? Do they believe that the American Bible Society cares one straw about giving Bibles to the Slaves? Do they suppose that Slaveholders, in open violation of their wicked laws, will allow their Slaves to have the Bible? How do they mean to get the Bible among the Slaves? It cannot go itself,—it must be carried. And who among them all has either the faith or the folly to undertake the distribution of Bibles among the Slaves?

Then, again, of what value is the Bible to one who may not read its contents? Do they intend to send teachers into the Slave States, with the Bibles, to teach the Slaves to read them? Do they believe that on giving the Bible, the unlettered Slave will all at once—by some miraculous transformation—become a man of letters, and be able to read the sacred Scriptures? Will they first obtain the Slaveholder's consent, or will they proceed without it? And if the former, by what means will they seek it? And if the latter, what success do they expect?

Upon these points, and many others, the public ought to be enlightened before they are called upon to give money and influence to such an enterprize. As a mere indication of the growing influence of Anti-Slavery sentiment this movement may be regarded by Abolitionists with some complacency; but as a means of abolishing the Slave system of America, it seems to me a sham, a delusion, and a snare, and cannot be too soon exposed before all the people. It is but another illustration of the folly of putting new cloth into an old garment, and new wine into old bottles. The Bible is peculiarly the companion of liberty. It belongs to a new order of things—Slavery is of the old—and will only be made worse by an attempt to mend it with the Bible. The Bible is only useful to those who can read and practise its contents. It was given to Freemen, and any attempt to give it to the Slave must result only in hollow mockery.

Give Bibles to the poor Slaves! It sounds well. It looks well. It wears a religious aspect. *It is a Protestant rebuke to the Pope,* and seems in harmony with the purely evangelical character of the great American people. It may also forestall some movement in England to give Bibles to our Slaves,—*and this is very desirable!* Now admitting (however difficult it may be to do so) the entire honesty of all engaged in this movement,—the immediate and only effect of their efforts must be to turn off attention from the main and only momentous question connected with the Slave, and absorb energies and money in giving to him the Bible that ought to be used in giving him to *himself.* The Slave is property. He cannot hold property. He cannot own a Bible. To give him a Bible is but to give his master a Bible. The Slave is a thing,—and it is the all commanding duty of the American people to make him a man. To demand this in the name of humanity, and of God, is the solemn duty of every living soul. To demand less than this, or anything else than this, is to deceive the fettered bondman, and to soothe the conscience of the Slaveholder on the very point where he should be most stung with remorse and shame.

Away with all tampering with such a question! Away with all trifling with the man in fetters! Give a hungry man a stone, and tell what beautiful houses are made of it,—give ice to a freezing man, and tell him of its good properties in hot weather,—throw a drowning man a dollar, as a mark of your good will,—but do not mock the bondman in his misery, by giving him a Bible when he cannot read it.

The Liberty Bell, June, 1847

PART TWO

From the Founding of *The North Star* to the Compromise of 1850

On Friday, December 3, 1847, a new era in Negro journalism in the United States was inaugurated. The first issue of *The North Star* came off the press, its masthead proclaiming the slogan: "Right is of no Sex—Truth is of no Color—God is the Father of us all, and we are all Brethren." The role of the paper was that of a "terror to evil doers," and while it would be "mainly Anti-Slavery," its columns would be "freely opened to the candid and decorous discussion of all measures and topics of a moral and humane character, which may serve to enlighten, improve and elevate mankind. . . ." A report of the National Convention of Colored People held at Troy early in October, and a long letter by Douglass to Henry Clay commenting on the Kentuckian's speech in behalf of colonization, were the main features of the first number. The first page stated that the subscription rates were two dollars a year, "*always in advance,*" and that advertisements not exceeding ten lines would be carried three times for one dollar.

The editors were Douglass and Martin R. Delany who had just resigned the editorship of the Pittsburgh *Mystery,* a Negro paper. William C. Nell, a self-taught Negro and a devoted Garrisonian, was listed as publisher. The printing office was located at 25 Buffalo Street, in the Talman Building, opposite Reynolds Arcade. It was a simple room. Douglass' desk was in one corner; cases of type and the printing press occupied the rest of the space. Two white apprentices, William A. Atkinson and William Oliver, and Douglass' children assisted in setting the type, locking the forms, folding, wrapping and mailing the paper. Although Douglass had his own press, the paper itself was printed in the shop of the *Rochester Democrat.*[1]

On the whole, reaction to the first issue was favorable. Samuel J. May spoke of his "delight" in reading the paper, Garrison praised it, and Edmund Quincy observed in the *Liberator* that its "literary and mechanical execution would do honor to any paper new or old, anti-slavery or pro-slavery, in the country." In England, *Howitt's Journal* augmented the chorus of approval with the remark: "*The North Star* may rank with any American paper, for ability and interest; it is full of buoyancy and variety. . . ."[2]

Not all joined in welcoming the new arrival. The *New York Herald* urged the people of Rochester to throw Douglass' printing press into the lake and exile the editor to Canada. The *Albany Dispatch* was a bit more subtle. It merely warned the citizens of Rochester that the presence of a paper published by "the n——r pet of the British Abolitionists" would be a "serious detriment" to the community, and suggested that they "buy him off." Undoubtedly there were those in Rochester who approved of these suggestions, but they were a distinct minority. The Rochester *Daily Advertiser* observed that the mechanical appearance of the first issue was "exceedingly neat," that the leading article indicated "a high order of talent," and that the editor was "a man of much more than ordinary share of intellect."[3] [I:84–85]

TO HENRY CLAY

Sir:

I have just received and read your Speech, delivered at the Mass Meeting in Lexington, Kentucky, 13th November 1847, and after a careful and candid perusal of it, I am impressed with the desire to say a few words to you on one or two subjects which form a considerable part of that speech. You will, I am sure, pardon the liberty I take in thus publicly addressing you, when you are acquainted with the fact, that I am one of those "unfortunate victims" whose case you seem to commiserate, and have experienced the cruel wrongs of Slavery in my own person. It is with no ill will, or bitterness of spirit that I address you. My position under this government, even in the State of N.Y., is that of a disfranchised man. I can have, therefore, no political ends to serve, nor party antipathy to gratify. My "intents" are not wicked but truly charitable. I approach you simply in the character of one of the unhappy millions enduring the evils of Slavery, in this otherwise highly favored and glorious land.

In the extraordinary speech before me, after dwelling at length upon the evils, disgrace, and dangers of the present unjust, mean, and iniquitous war waged by the United States upon Mexico, you disavow for yourself and the meeting, "in the most positive manner," any wish to acquire any foreign territory whatever for the purpose of introducing slavery into it. As one of the oppressed, I give you the full expression of sincere gratitude for this declaration, and the pledge which it implies, and earnestly hope that you may be able to keep your vow unsullied by compromises, (which, pardon me,) have too often marred and defaced the beauty and consistency of your humane declarations and pledges on former occasions. It is not, however, any part of my present intention to reproach you invidiously or severely for the past. Unfortunately for the race, you do not stand alone in respect to deviations from a strict line of rectitude. Poor, erring and depraved humanity, has surrounded you with a throng of guilty associates, it would not, therefore, be magnanimous in me to reproach you for the past, above all others.

Forgetting the things that are behind, I simply propose to speak to you of what you are at this time—of the errors and evils of your present, as I think, wicked position, and to point out to you the path of repentance, which if pursued, must lead you to the possession of peace and happiness, and make you a blessing to your country and the world.

In the speech under consideration, you say,

"My opinions on the subject of slavery are well known; they have the merit, if it be one, of consistency, uniformity and long duration."

The first sentence is probably true. Your opinions on slavery may be well known, but that they have the merit of consistency or of uniformity, I cannot so readily admit. If the speech before me be a fair declaration of your present opinions, I think I can convince you that even this speech abounds with inconsistencies such as materially to affect the consolation you seem to draw from this source. Indeed if you are uniform at all, you are only so in your inconsistencies.

You confess that

"Slavery is a great evil, and a wrong to its victims, and you would rejoice if not a single slave breathed the air within the limits of our country."

These are noble sentiments, and would seem to flow from a heart overborne with a sense of the flagrant injustice and enormous cruelty of slavery, and of one earnestly and anxiously longing for a remedy. Standing alone, it would seem that the author had long been in search of some means to redress the wrongs of the *"unfortunate victims"* of whom he speaks—that his righteous soul was deeply grieved, every hour, on account of the foul blot inflicted by this curse on his country's character.

But what are the facts? You are yourself a Slaveholder at this moment, and your words on this point had scarcely reached the outer circle of the vast multitude by which you were surrounded, before you poured forth one of the most helpless, illogical, and cowardly apologies for this same wrong, and *"great evil"* which I ever remember to have read. Is this consistency, and uniformity? if so, the oppressed may well pray the Most High that you may be soon delivered from it.

Speaking of "the unfortunate victims" of this "great evil," and "wrong," you hold this most singular and cowardly excuse for perpetuating the wrongs of my "unfortunate" race.

"But here they are to be dealt with as well as we can, with a due considera-tion of all circumstances affecting the security and happiness of both races."

What do you mean by the security, safety and happiness of both races? do you mean that the happiness of the slave is augmented by his being a slave, and if so, why call him an "unfortunate victim." Can it be that this is mere cant, by which to seduce the North into your support, on the ground of your sympathy for the slave. I cannot believe you capable of such infatuation. I do not wish to believe that you are capable of either the low cunning, or the vanity which your language on this subject would seem to imply, but will set it down to an uncontrollable conviction of the innate wickedness of slavery, which forces itself out, and defies even your vast powers of concealment.

But further, you assert,

"Every State has the supreme, uncontrolled and exclusive power to decide for itself whether slavery shall cease or continue within its limits, without any exte-rior intervention from any quarter."

Here I understand you to assert the most profligate and infernal doctrine, that any State in this Union has a right to plunder, scourge and enslave any part of the human family within its borders, just so long as it deems it for its interest so to do, and that no one or body of persons beyond the limits of said state has a right to interfere by word or deed against it. Is it possible that you hold this mon-strous and blood-chilling doctrine? If so, what confidence can any enlightened lover of liberty place in your pretended opposition to Slavery. I know your an-swer to all this, but it only plunges you into lower depths of infamy than the hor-rible doctrines avowed above. You go on to say:

"In States where the *Slaves outnumber the whites,* as is the case in several [which I believe are only two out of fifteen] the blacks could not be emancipated without *becoming the governing power in these states."*

This miserable bug-bear is quite a confession of the mental and physical equal-ity of the races. You pretend that you are a Republican. You loudly boast of your Democratic principles: why then do you object to the application of your prin-ciples in this case. Is the democratic principle good in one case, and bad in an-other? Would it be worse for a black majority to govern a white minority than it now is for the latter to govern the former? But you conjure up an array of frightful objections in answer to this.

"Collisions and conflicts between the two races would be inevitable, and af-ter shocking scenes of *rapine and carnage, the extinction or expulsion of the blacks would certainly take place."*

How do you know that any such results would be inevitable? Where, on the page of history, do you find anything to warrant even such a conjecture? You will probably point me to the Revolution in St. Domingo,[4] the old and thread-bare falsehood under which democratic tyrants have sought a refuge for the last forty years. But the facts in that direction are all against you. It has been clearly proven that that revolution was not the result of emancipation, but of a cruel attempt to re-enslave an already emancipated people. I am not aware that you have a single fact to support your truly terrible assertion, while on the other hand I have many all going to show what is equally taught by the voice of reason and of God, "that it is always safe to do right." The promise of God is, "that thy light shall break forth as the morning, and thy health shall spring forth speedily, and thy righteousness shall go before thee, the glory of the Lord shall be thy reward: then shalt thou call and the Lord shall answer; thou shalt cry and he will say, Here I am."

The history of the world is in conformity with the words of inspired wisdom. Look, for instance, at the history of Emancipation in the British West Indies. There the blacks were, and still are, an overwhelming majority. Have there been any "*shocking scenes of rapine and carnage, extinction or expulsion.*" You know there have not. Why then do you make use of this unfounded and irrational conjecture to frighten your fellow-countrymen from the righteous performance of a simple act of justice to millions now groaning in almost hopeless bondage.

I now give your argument in support of the morality of your position.

"It may be argued that, in admitting the injustice of slavery, I grant the necessity of an instantaneous separation of that injustice. Unfortunately, however, it is not always safe, practicable or possible in the great movements of States or public affairs of nations, to remedy or repair the infliction of previous injustice. In the inception of it, we may oppose and denounce it by our most strenuous exertions, but, after its consummation, there is often no other alternative left us but to deplore its perpetration, and to acquiesce as the only alternative, in its existence, as a less evil than the frightful consequences which might ensue from the vain endeavor to repair it. Slavery is one of these unfortunate instances."

The cases which you put in support of the foregoing propositions, are only wanting in one thing, and that is analogy. The plundering of the Indians of their territory, is a crime to which no honest man can look with any degree of satisfaction. It was a wrong to the Indians then living, and how muchsoever we might seek to repair that wrong, the victims are far beyond any benefit of it; but with reference to the slave, the wrong to be repaired is a present one, the slave holder is the every day robber of the slave, of his birthright to liberty, property, and the pursuit of happiness—his right to be free is unquestionable—the wrong to enslave him is self evident—the duty to emancipate him is imperative. Are you aware to what your argument on this point leads? do you not plainly see that the greatest crimes that ever cursed our common earth, may take shelter under your reasoning, and may claim perpetuity on the ground of their antiquity?

Sir, I must pass over your allusions to that almost defunct and infernal scheme which you term "unmixed benevolence" for expelling not the slave but the *free colored people* from these United States, as well as your charge against the Abolitionists.

"*It is a philanthropic and consoling reflection that the moral and physical condition of the African in the United States in a state of slavery is far better than it would have been had their ancestors not been brought from their native land.*"

I can scarce repress the flame of rising indignation, as I read this cold blooded and cruel sentence; there is so much of Satan dressed in the livery of Heaven, as well as taking consolation from crime, that I scarcely know how to reply to it. Let me ask you what has been the cause of the present unsettled condition of Africa? Why has she not reached forth her hand unto God? Why have not her fields been made Missionary grounds, as well as the Feejee Islands? Because of this very desolating traffic from which you seem to draw consolation. For three hundred years Christian nations, among whom we are foremost, have looked to Africa only as a place for the gratification of their lust and love of power, and every means have been adopted to stay the onward march of civilization in that unhappy land.

Your declaration on this point, places your consolation with that of the wolf in devouring the lamb. You next perpetrate what I conceive to be the most revolting blasphemy. You say:

"And if it should be the decree of the Great Ruler of the Universe, that their descendants shall be made instruments in his hands in the establishment of civilization and the Christian religion throughout Africa—our regrets on account of the original wrong will be greatly mitigated."

Here, Sir, you would charge home upon God the responsibility of your own crimes, and would seek a solace from the pangs of a guilty conscience by sacrilegiously assuming that in robbing Africa of her children, you acted in obedience to the great purposes, and were but fulfilling the decrees of the Most High God; but as if fearing that this refuge of lies might fail, you strive to shuffle off the responsibility of this "great evil" on Great Britain. May I not ask if you were fulfilling the great purposes of God in the share you took in this traffic, and can draw consolation from that alleged fact, is it honest to make England a sinner above yourselves, and deny her all the mitigating circumstances which you apply to yourselves?

You say that *"Great Britain inflicted the evil upon you."* If this be true, it is equally true that she inflicted the same evil upon herself; but she has had the justice and the magnanimity to repent and bring forth fruits meet for repentance. You copied her bad example, why not avail yourself of her good one also?

Now, Sir, I have done with your Speech, though much more might be said upon it. I have a few words to say to you personally.

I wish to remind you that you are not only in the "*autumn*," but in the very winter of life. Seventy-one years have passed over your stately brow. You must soon leave this world, and appear before God, to render up an account of your stewardship. For fifty years of your life you have been a slaveholder. You have robbed the laborer who has reaped down your fields, of his rightful reward. You are at this moment the robber of nearly fifty human beings, of their liberty, compelling them to live in ignorance. Let me ask if you think that God will hold you guiltless in the great day of account, if you die with the blood of these fifty slaves clinging to your garments. I know that you have made a profession of religion, and have been baptized, and am aware that you are in good and regular standing in the church, but I have the authority of God for saying that you will stand rejected at his bar, unless you "put away the evil of your doings from before his eyes—cease to do evil, and learn to do well—seek judgment, relieve the oppressed—and plead for the widow." You must "break every yoke, and let the oppressed go free," or take your place in the ranks of "evil doers," and expect to "reap the reward of corruption."

At this late day in your life, I think it would be unkind for me to charge you with any ambitious desires to become the President of the United States. I may be mistaken in this, but it seems that you cannot indulge either the wish or expectation. Bear with me, then, while I give you a few words of further counsel, as a private individual, and excuse the plainness of one who has felt the wrongs of Slavery, and fathomed the depths of its iniquity.

Emancipate your own slaves. Leave them not to be held or sold by others. Leave them free as the Father of his country left his,[5] and let your name go down to posterity, as his came down to us, a slaveholder, to be sure, but a repentant one. Make the noble resolve, that so far as you are personally concerned, "America shall be Free."

In asking you to do this, I ask nothing which in any degree conflicts with your argument against general emancipation. The dangers which you conjecture of the latter cannot be apprehended of the former. Your own slaves are too few in number to make them formidable or dangerous. In this matter you are without excuse. I leave you to your conscience, and your God,

And subscribe myself,

Faithfully, yours,

Frederick Douglass

The North Star, December 3, 1847

1. Douglass to Gerrit Smith, May 1, 1851, Gerrit Smith Papers, Syracuse University; Horace McGuire, "Two Episodes of Anti-Slavery Days," *Publications of the Rochester Historical Society,* Rochester, N.Y., vol. IV. 1925, p. 219. Douglass laid the blame for frequent errors and inaccuracies in *The North Star* on the fact that the paper was printed outside of his shop.

2. *The North Star,* Jan. 8, 1848; *Liberator,* Jan. 28, 1848; *Anti-Slavery Standard,* Jan. 27, 1848; Frederick G. Detweiler, *The Negro Press in the United States,* Chicago, 1922, p. 42; *Howitt's Journal,* vol. III, 1848, p. 288.

3. *Sunday Dispatch* reprinted in *The North Star,* Jan. 21, 1848; *Rochester Daily Advertiser,* Dec. 18, 1847.

4. In August, 1791, after two years of the French Revolution, the slaves in San Domingo revolted. The struggle lasted for twelve years during which time the slaves defeated in turn their local white rulers and the soldiers of the French monarchy, a Spanish invasion, a British expedition of some 60,000 men, and a French expedition of similar size under Napoleon Bonaparte's brother-in-law. The defeat of Bonaparte's expedition in 1803 led to the establishment of the Negro republic of Haiti which has lasted to this day.

5. In his will George Washington provided for the manumission of all his slaves after his wife's death. He likewise provided for the support of those thus freed who were either too old or too young to support themselves. In the case of the children he provided further that they were "to be taught to read and write and to be brought up to some useful occupation." (John C. Fitzpatrick, ed., *George Washington. Writings from the Original Manuscript Sources,* Washington, 1931–1940, vol. XXXI, pp. 279–80.)

WHAT OF THE NIGHT?

A crisis in the Anti-Slavery movement of this country, is evidently at hand. The moral and religious, no less than the political firmaments, North and South, at home and abroad, are studded with brilliant and most significant indications, pointing directly to a settlement of this all-commanding subject. Slavery is doomed to destruction; and of this slaveholders are rapidly becoming aware. Opposed or encouraged, the grand movement for its overthrow has, under God, attained a point of progress when its devoted advocates may press its claims in the full assurance that success will soon crown their righteous endeavors. We have labored long and hard. The prospect has at times been gloomy, if not hopeless. At present, we feel hopeful. In our humble judgment, there is no power within reach of the slaveholder, with all their arts, cunning and depravity, which can uphold a system at once so dark, foul and bloody as that of American slavery. The power which they have derived from the unconstitutional and perfidious annexation of Texas to the United States; the vast territories which they may acquire by our atrocious war with distracted and enfeebled Mexico; the sacrilegious support which they receive from a corrupt church and degenerate priesthood; the character and position they secure by a slaveholding President, are all transient, temporary and unavailing. They are powerful, but must give way to a mightier power.—Like huge trees in the bed of a mighty river, they only await the rising tide which, without effort, shall bear them away to the vortex of destruction. The Spirit of Liberty is sweeping in majesty over the whole European continent, encountering and shattering dynasties, overcoming and subverting monarchies, causing thrones to crumble, courts to dissolve, and royalty and despotism to vanish like shadows before the morning sun. This spirit cannot be bound by geographical boundaries or national restrictions. It hath neither flesh nor bones; there is no way to chain it; swords and guns, armies and ramparts, are as impotent to stay it as they would be if directed against the Asiatic cholera. We cannot but be affected. These stupendous overturnings throughout the world, proclaim in the ear of American slaveholders, with all the terrible energy of an earthquake, the downfall of slavery. They have heard the royal sound—witness their reluctance on the floor of Congress to pass resolutions congratulating the French on the downfall of royalty and the triumph of republicanism; witness the course of that prince of tyrants, John C. Calhoun; witness the mean and heartless response given by the misnamed Democrats of the country. These friends of the hell-born system of slavery are painfully aware that the cause of liberty and equality are one the world over; and that its triumph in any portion of the globe foreshadows and hastens the downfall of tyranny throughout the world.

Not among the least important and significant signs of the times, are the recent debates and occurrences in Washington. A combination of events has within a few days transpired there, which may well be regarded as a Providential interference in behalf of the enslaved and plundered of our land. The bold attempt of more than seventy slaves to escape their chains—their unfortunate and mortifying recapture—the wild clamor for the blood of the men who are willing to aid them in their escape—the mobocratic demonstrations against the Era office—the violent and assassin speeches made in both branches of Congress—their utter failure to intimidate the noble-hearted Giddings, Palfrey, and Hale—the sovereign and increasing contempt with which these gentlemen treat the bullying speeches of these bowie-knife legislators, are not only signs, but facts, fixing attention on slavery, and demonstrating a progress in public opinion, directly pointing to the speedy overthrow of slavery, or a dissolution of our unhallowed Union. Should the latter come, the former must come; slavery is doomed in either case. God speed the day! Never could there have been a better place, or more fitting opportunity for such facts, than at the place and time which they transpired. Slaves escaping from the Capital of the "model Republic"! What an idea!—running *from* the Temple of Liberty to be free! Then, too, our slaveholding Belshazzars were in the midst of feasting and rejoicing over the downfall of Louis Philippe, and the establishment of a republic in France! They were all pleasure and joyous delight; "but pleasures are like poppies spread." Their joy was soon turned into moaning, their laughter into fury.

The hand-writing on the wall to these joyous congratulationists, was the fact, that more than seventy thousand dollars' worth of their human cattle had made a peaceful attempt to gain their liberty by flight.[1] At once these thoughts of glorious liberty abroad gave way to the more urgent demands of slavery at home. These "worthless" Negroes are valuable. *These miserable creatures,* which we would gladly get rid of, must be brought back. And lo and behold! these very men who had been rejoicing over French liberty, are now armed kidnappers, and even on the Sabbath day have gone forth on the delectable business of man-hunting. Well, they have succeeded in overtaking and throttling their victims; they have brought them back before the musket's mouth, and doubtless most of them have been scourged for their temerity, and sold into Louisiana and Texas, where they will be worked to death in seven years; but as sure as there is a God, this will not be the last of it. Slavery in the District of Columbia will receive a shock from this simple event, which no earthly power can prevent or cure. The broad eye of the nation will be opened upon slavery in the District as it has never before; the North and West will feel keenly the damning disgrace of their Capital being a slave mart, and a deeper hatred of slavery will be engendered in the popular mind throughout the Union.

The North Star, May 5, 1848

1. In the spring of 1848 the schooner *Pearl,* with 77 fugitive slaves aboard, was captured at the mouth of the Potomac River and was brought back to Washington. The slaves and their white rescuers, Daniel Drayton, Capton Sayres, and Chester English, were imprisoned. The Negroes were turned over to slave-dealers to be sold in the lower South, and the white men were brought to trial. During the excitement of this event, a mob attempted to destroy the office of the *National Era* in Washington, and to force Dr. Bailey, its editor, to leave the district. Drayton and Sayres were found guilty of transporting slaves and were sentenced to life imprisonment. Exceptions were taken to the judge's rulings and a new trial was ordered, which took place in May, 1849. Once again the men were convicted and returned to the district jail, remaining there until 1852, when Charles Sumner, who had just been elected to the United States Senate, began a campaign for their release. Sumner submitted to the attorney-general an elab-

orate treatise on the injustice of the sentence, and President Fillmore granted the men an unconditional pardon. When it was learned that the governor of Virginia intended to arrest them at their release, Drayton and Sayres were taken by night to Baltimore, and then sent to Harrisburg and Philadelphia.

"PREJUDICE AGAINST COLOR"

Prejudice against color! Pray tell us *what* color? Black? brown? copper color? yellow? tawny? or olive? Native Americans of all these colors everywhere experience hourly indignities at the hands of persons claiming to be white. Now, is all this for *color's* sake? If so, which of these colors excites such commotion in those sallow-skinned Americans who call themselves white? Is it black? When did they begin to be so horrified at black? Was it before black stocks came into fashion? Black coats? black hats? black walking canes? black reticules? black umbrellas? black-walnut tables? black ebony picture frames and sculptural decorations? black eyes, hair and whiskers? bright black shoes, and glossy black horses? How this American colorphobia would have lashed itself into a foam at the sight of the celebrated *black* goddess Diana, of Ephesus! How it would have gnashed upon the old statue and hacked away at it out of sheer spite at its color! What exemplary havoc it would have made of the most celebrated statues of antiquity. Forsooth they were *black!* Their color would have been their doom. These half-white Americans owe the genius of sculpture a great grudge. She has so often crossed their path in the hated color, it would fare hard with her if she were to fall into their clutches. By the way, it would be well for Marshall and other European sculptors to keep a keen lookout upon all Americans visiting their collections. American colorphobia would be untrue to itself if it did not pitch battle with every black statue and bust that came in its way in going the rounds. A black Apollo, whatever the symmetry of his proportions, the majesty of his attitude, or the divinity of his air, would meet with great good fortune if it escaped mutilation at its hands, or at least defilement from its spittle. If all foreign artists, whose collections are visited by Americans, would fence off a corner of their galleries for a "Negro pew," and staightway colonize in thither every specimen of ancient and modern art that is chiselled or cast in *black,* it would be wise precaution. The only tolerable substitute for such colonization would be plenty of *whitewash,* which would avail little as a peace-offering to brother Jonathan unless *freshly* put on: in that case a thick coat of it might sufficiently placate his outraged sense of propriety to rescue the finest models of art from American Lynch-law: but it would not be best to presume too far, for colorphobia has no lucid intervals, *the fit is on all the time.* The anti-black feeling, being "a law of nature," must have vent; and unless it be provided, wherever it goes, with a sort of portable Liberia to scrape the offensive color into it twitches and jerks in convulsions directly. But stop—this anti-black passion is, we are told, "a law of nature," and not to be trifled with! "Prejudice against color" "a law of nature!" Forsooth! What a sinner against *nature* old Homer was! He goes off in ecstasies in his description, of the *black* Ethiopians, praises their beauty, calls them the favorites of the gods, and represents all the ancient divinities as selecting them from all the nations of the world as their intimate companions, the objects of their peculiar complacency. If Homer had only been indoctrinated into this "law of nature," he would have insulted his deities by representing them as making Negroes their chosen associates. What impious trifling with this sacred "law," was perpetrated by the old Greeks, who represented Minerva their favorite goddess of Wisdom as an *African* princess. Herodotus pronounces the Ethiopians the most majestic and beautiful of men. The great father of history was fated to live and die in the dark, as to this great "law of nature!" Why do so many Greek and Latin authors adorn with eulogy the beauty and graces of the black Memnon who served at the siege of Troy, styling him, in their eulogiums, the son of Aurora? Ignoramuses! They knew nothing of this great "law of nature." How little reverence for this sublime "law" had Solon, Pythagoras, Plato, and those other master spirits of ancient Greece, who, in their pilgrimage after knowledge, went to Ethiopia and Egypt, and sat at the feet of black philosophers, to drink in wisdom. Alas for the multitudes who flocked from all parts of the world to the instructions of that Negro, Euclid, who three hundred years before Christ, was at the head of the most celebrated mathematical school in the world. However learned in the mathematics, they were plainly numbskulls in the "law of nature!"

How little had Antiochus the Great the fear of this "law of nature" before his eyes, when he welcomed to his court, with the most signal honors, the black African Hannibal; and what an impious perverter of this same law was the great conqueror of Hannibal, since he made the *black* poet Terence one of his most intimate associates and confidants. What heathenish darkness brooded over the early ages of Christianity respecting this "law of nature." What a sin of ignorance! The most celebrated fathers of the church, Origen, Cyprian, Tertullian, Augustine, Clemens, Alexandrinus, and Cyril—why were not these black African bishops colonized into a "Negro pew," when attending the ecclesiastical councils of their day? Alas, though the sun of righteousness had risen on primitive Christians, this great "law of nature" had not! This leads us reverently to ask the age of this law. A law of nature, being a part of nature, must be as old as nature: but perhaps human nature was created by piecemeal, and this part was overlooked in the early editions, but supplied in a later revisal. Well, what is the date of the revised edition? We will save our readers the trouble of fumbling for it, by just saying that this "law of nature" was never heard of till long after the commencement of the African slave trade; and that the feeling called "prejudice against color," has never existed in Great Britain, France, Spain, Portugal, the Italian States, Prussia, Austria, Russia, or in any part of the world where colored persons have not been held as slaves. Indeed, in many countries, where multitudes of Africans and their descendants have been long held slaves, no prejudice against color has ever existed. This is the case in Turkey, Brazil, and Persia. In Brazil there are more than two millions of slaves. Yet some of the highest offices of state are filled by black men. Some of the most distinguished officers in the Brazilian army are blacks and mulattoes. Colored lawyers and physicians are found in all parts of the country. Besides this, hundreds of the Roman Catholic clergy are black and colored men, these minister to congregations made up indiscriminately of blacks and whites.

The North Star, May 5, 1848

_____

Next to Abolition and the battle for equal rights for the Negro people, the cause closest to Douglass' heart was woman's rights. In the anti-slavery agitation women took an active and significant part, and no one knew better than Douglass how deeply the Negro people were indebted to the tireless efforts of the women's anti-slavery societies. In reports from communities he was visiting, Douglass regularly devoted space in his paper to descriptions of the work of the anti-slavery women. . . .

While Douglass believed that the anti-slavery movement was doing much "for the elevation and improvement of women," he understood fully the need for an independent, organized movement to achieve equal rights for women. On July 14, 1848, *The North Star,* which featured the slogan, "Right is of no sex," carried an historic announcement:

"A Convention to discuss the Social, Civil and Religious Condition and Rights of Women, will be held in the Wesleyan Chapel at Seneca Falls, New York, on Wednesday and Thursday, the 19th and 20th of July instant.

"During the first day, the meetings will be exclusively for women, which all are earnestly invited to attend. The public generally are invited to be present on the second day, when Lucretia Mott, of Philadelphia, and others, both ladies and gentlemen, will address the Convention."

Thirty-five women and thirty-two men, courageous enough to run the risk of being branded "hermaphrodites" and "Aunt Nancy Men," responded to the call for the world's first organized gathering for woman's rights. Douglass was the only man to play a prominent part in the proceedings.

A "Declaration of Sentiments" adopted by the convention proclaimed: "The history of mankind is a history of repeated injuries and usurpations on the part of man and toward woman, having in direct object the establishment of an absolute tyranny over her." Sixteen facts were "submitted to a candid world" by way of proof, after which the Declaration demanded that women "have immediate admission to all the rights and privileges which belong to them as citizens of the United States." Eleven resolutions were then introduced which made such demands as the right of women to personal and religious freedom, the right to vote and to be elected to public office, to testify in courts, equality in marriage and the right to their own children, the right to own property and to claim their own wages; the right to education and equality in trades and professions.[1]

The only resolution that aroused controversy and was not unanimously adopted was the ninth, asserting that it was "the duty of the women of this country to secure to themselves their sacred right to the elective franchise." Many of the delegates, even Lucretia Mott, felt that the demand for the right to vote was too advanced for the times and would only heap ridicule on the entire movement. But Elizabeth Cady Stanton who had introduced the proposal and was determined to press the issue, and looked about the Convention for an ally. "I knew Frederick, from personal experience, was just the man for the work," she told an audience of suffragists years later. Hurrying to Douglass' side, Mrs. Stanton read the resolution and asked him to speak on the question. Douglass promptly arose, and addressed the delegates. He argued convincingly that political equality was essential for the complete liberation of women. The resolution was adopted by a small majority.[2] [II:15–17]

THE RIGHTS OF WOMEN

One of the most interesting events of the past week, was the holding of what is technically styled a Woman's Rights Convention at Seneca Falls. The speaking, addresses, and resolutions of this extraordinary meeting was almost wholly conducted by women; and although they evidently felt themselves in a novel position, it is but simple justice to say that their whole proceedings were characterized by marked ability and dignity. No one present, we think, however much he might be disposed to differ from the views advanced by the leading speakers on that occasion, will fail to give them credit for brilliant talents and excellent dispositions. In this meeting, as in other deliberative assemblies, there were frequent differences of opinion and animated discussion; but in no case was there the slightest absence of good feeling and decorum. Several interesting documents setting forth the rights as well as the grievances of women were read. Among these was a Declaration of Sentiments, to be regarded as the basis of a grand movement for attaining the civil, social, political, and religious rights of women. We should not do justice to our own convictions, or to the excellent persons connected with this infant movement, if we did not in this connection offer a few remarks on the general subject which the Convention met to consider and the objects they seek to attain. In doing so, we are not insensible that the bare mention of this truly important subject in any other than terms of contemptuous ridicule and scornful disfavor, is likely to excite against us the fury of bigotry and the folly of prejudice. A discussion of the rights of animals would be regarded with far more complacency by many of what are called the *wise* and the *good* of our land, than would a discussion of the rights of women. It is, in their estimation, to be guilty of evil thoughts, to think that woman is entitled to equal rights with man. Many who have at last made the discovery that the Negroes have some rights as well as other members of the human family, have yet to be convinced that women are entitled to any. Eight years ago a number of persons of this description actually abandoned the anti-slavery cause, lest by giving their influence in that direction they might possibly be giving countenance to the dangerous heresy that woman, in respect to rights, stands on an equal footing with man. In the judgment of such persons the American slave system, with all its concomitant horrors, is less to be deplored than this *wicked* idea. It is perhaps needless to say, that we cherish little sympathy for such sentiments or respect for such prejudices. Standing as we do upon the watch-tower of human freedom, we cannot be deterred from an expression of our approbation of any movement, however humble, to improve and elevate the character of any members of the human family. While it is impossible for us to go into this subject at length, and dispose of the various objections which are often urged against such a doctrine as that of female equality, we are free to say that in respect to political rights, we hold woman to be justly entitled to all we claim for man. We go farther, and express our conviction that all political rights which it is expedient for man to exercise, it is equally so for woman. All that distinguishes man as an intelligent and accountable being, is equally true of woman, and if that government only is just which governs by the free consent of the governed, there can be no reason in the world for denying to woman the exercise of the elective franchise, or a hand in making and administering the laws of the land. Our doctrine is that "right is of no sex." We therefore bid the women engaged in this movement our humble Godspeed.

The North Star, July 28, 1848

1. Elizabeth Cady Stanton, Susan B. Anthony, Mathilda Joslyn Gage, editors, *History of Woman Suffrage,* New York, 1881, vol. I, pp. 70–71.
2. *The Woman's Journal,* Apr. 14, 1888, p. 116; Stanton, Anthony, Gage, *op. cit.,* vol. I, p. 73. Years later a tablet was erected commemorating the occasion. It read:

> *On this spot stood the Wesleyan Chapel*
> *Where the first Woman's Rights Convention*
> *in the World's History was held*
> *July 19 and 20, 1848*
> *Elizabeth Cady Stanton*
> *moved this resolution*
> *which was seconded by Frederick Douglass*
> *That it was the duty of the women*
> *of this country to secure to themselves*
> *their sacred right*
> *to the elective franchise.*

THE REVOLUTION OF 1848, speech at West India Emancipation celebration, Rochester, New York, August 1, 1848

Mr. President and Friends:

We have met to commemorate no deed of sectional pride, or partial patriotism; to erect no monument to naval or military heroism; to applaud the character or commend the courage of no blood-stained warrior; to gloat over no fallen or vanquished foe; to revive no ancient or obsolete antipathy; to quicken and perpetuate the memory of no fierce and bloody struggle; to take from the ashes of oblivion no slumbering embers of fiery discord.

We attract your attention to no horrid strife; to no scenes of blood and carnage, where foul and unnatural murder carried its true designation, because regimentally attired. We brighten not the memories of brave men slain in the hostile array and the deadly encounter. The celebration of such men, and such deeds, may safely be left to others. We [can] thank Heaven, that [to us] is committed a more grateful and congenial task.

The day we have met to commemorate, is marked by no deeds of violence, associated with no scenes of slaughter, and excites no malignant feelings. Peace, joy and liberty shed a halo of unfading and untarnished glory around this annual festival. On this occasion, no lonely widow is reminded of a slaughtered husband; no helpless orphans are reminded of slaughtered fathers; no aged parents are reminded of slaughtered sons; no lovely sisters meet here to mourn over the memory of slaughtered brothers. Our gladness revives no sorrow; our joyous acclamation awakens no responsive mourning. The day, the deed, the event, which we have met to celebrate, is the Tenth Anniversary of West India Emancipation—a day, a deed, an event, all glorious in the annals of Philanthropy, and as pure as the stars of heaven! On this day, ten years ago, eight hundred thousand slaves became freemen. To congratulate our disenthralled brethren of the West Indies on their peaceful emancipation; to express our unfeigned gratitude to Almighty God, their merciful deliverer; to bless the memory of the noble men through whose free and faithful labors the grand result was finally brought about; to hold up their pure and generous examples to be admired and copied; and to make this day, to some extent, subservient to the sacred cause of human freedom in our own land, and throughout the world, is the grand object of our present assembling.

I rejoice to see before me white as well as colored persons; for though this is our day peculiarly, it is not so exclusively. The great fact we this day recognize—the great truth to which we have met to do honor, belongs to the whole human family. From this meeting, therefore, no member of the human family is excluded. We have this day a free platform, to which, without respect to class, color, or condition, all are invited. Let no man here feel that he is a mere spectator—that he has no share in the proceedings of this day, because his face is of a paler hue than mine. The occasion is not one of color, but of universal man—from the purest black to the clearest white, welcome, welcome! In the name of liberty and justice, I extend to each and to all, of every complexion, form and feature, a heartfelt welcome to a full participation in the joys of this anniversary.

The great act which distinguishes this day, and which you have this day heard read, is so recent, and its history perhaps so fresh in the memory of all, as to make a lengthy and minute detail of the nature and character of either superfluous. In the address which I had the honor to deliver twelve months since, on an occasion similar to this, at our neighboring town, Canandaigua, I entered quite largely into that investigation; and presuming that I now stand before thousands of the same great audience who warmly greeted me there, I shall be allowed to call your attention to a more extended view of the cause of human freedom than seemed possible at that time. The subject of human freedom, in all its grades, forms and aspects, is within the record of this day. Tyranny, in all its varied guises, may on this day be exposed—oppression and injustice denounced, and liberty held up to the admiration of all.

In appearing here to-day, and presuming to be the first to address you, frankness requires me to proclaim, at the outset, what otherwise might become evident in the end, my own inaptitude to the task which your Committee of Arrangements have in their kindness assigned me. Aside from other causes of my incompetency which I might name, and which I am sure all present would appreciate, I may, in justice to myself, state that my other numerous engagements and occupations have denied me the necessary time for suitable preparation. I would not, however, forget that there is an apparent fitness in your selection. I have stood on each side of Mason and Dixon's line; I have endured the frightful horrors of slavery, and have enjoyed the blessings of freedom. I can enter fully into the sorrows of the bondman and the blessings of freemen. I am one of your-selves, enduring daily the proscription and confronting the tide of malignant prejudice by which the free colored man of the North is continually and univer-sally opposed. There is, therefore, at least an apparent fitness in your selection. If my address should prove dull and uninteresting, I am cut off from the plea that the incidents and facts of our times are commonplace and uninteresting. In this respect, our meetings is most fortunate. We live in stirring times, and amid thrilling events. There is no telling what a day may bring forth. The human mind is everywhere filled with expectation. The moral sky is studded with signs and wonder. High upon the whirlwind, Liberty rides as on a chariot of fire. Our brave old earth rocks with might agitation. Whether we look at home or abroad, Lib-erty greets us with the same majestic air.

We live in times which have no parallel in the history of the world. The grand commotion is universal and all-pervading. Kingdoms, realms, empires, and re-publics, roll to and fro like ships upon a stormy sea. The long pent up energies of human rights and sympathies, are at last let loose upon the world. The grand conflict of the angel Liberty with the monster Slavery, has at last come. The globe shakes with the contest.—I thank God that I am permitted, with you, to live in these days, and to participate humbly in this struggle. We are, Mr. President, par-ties to what is going on around us. We are more than spectators of the scenes that pass before us. Our interests, sympathies and destiny compel us to be par-ties to what is passing around us. Whether the immediate struggle be baptized by the Eastern or Western wave of the waters between us, the water is one, and the cause one, and we are parties to it. Steam, skill, and lightning, have brought the ends of the earth together. Old prejudices are vanishing. The magic power of human sympathy is rapidly healing national divisions, and bringing mankind into the harmonious bonds of a common brotherhood. In some sense, we real-ize the sublime declaration of the Prophet of Patmos, "And there shall be no more sea." The oceans that divided us, have become bridges to connect us, and the wide "world has become a whispering gallery." The morning star of freedom is seen from every quarter of the globe.

> From spirit to spirit—from nation to nation,
> From city to hamlet, thy dawning is cast;
> And tyrants and slaves are like shadows of night,[1]

Standing in the far West, we may now hear the earnest debate of the Western world.—The means of intelligence is so perfect, as well as rapid, that we seem to be mingling with the thrilling scenes of the Eastern hemisphere.

In the month of February of the present year, we may date the commencement of the great movements now progressing throughout Europe. In France, at that time, we saw a king to all appearance firmly seated on his costly throne, guarded by two hundred thousand bayonets. In the pride of his heart, he armed himself for the destruction of liberty. A few short hours ended the struggle. A shout went up to heaven from countless thousands, echoing back to earth, "Liberty—Equal-ity—Fraternity." The troops heard the glorious sound, and fraternized with the people in the court yard of the Tuilleries.—Instantly the King was but a man. All that was kingly fled. The throne whereon he sat was demolished; his splendid palace sacked; his royal carriage was burnt with fire; and he who had arrayed himself against freedom, found himself, like the great Egyptian tyrant, completely overwhelmed. Out of the ruins of this grand rupture, there came up a Republican Provisional Government, and snatching the revolutionary motto of "Liberty—Equality—Fraternity," from the fiery thousands who had just rolled back the tide of tyranny, they commenced to construct a State in accordance with that noble motto. Among the first of its acts, while hard pressed from without and perplexed within, beset on every hand—to the everlasting honor of that Government, it decreed the complete, unconditional emancipation of every slave throughout the French colonies. This act of justice and consistency went into effect on the 23d of last June. Thus were three hundred thousand souls admitted to the joys of freedom.—That provisional government is now no more. The brave and brilliant men who formed it, have ceased to play a conspicuous part in the political affairs of the nation. For the present, some of the brightest lights are obscured. Over the glory of the great-hearted Lamartine, the dark shadow of suspicion is cast.—The most of the members of that government are now distrusted, suspected, and slighted.—But while there remains on the earth one man of sable hue, there will be one witness who will ever remember with unceasing gratitude this noble act of that provisional government.

Sir, this act of justice to our race, on the part of the French people, has had a widespread effect upon the question of human freedom in our own land. Seldom, indeed, has the slave power of the nation received what they regarded such bad news. It placed our slaveholding Republic in a dilemma which all the world could see. We desired to rejoice with her in her republicanism, but it was impossible to do so without seeming to rejoice over abolitionism. Here inconsistency, hypocrisy, covered even the brass face of our slaveholding Republic with confusion. Even that staunch Democrat and Christian, John C. Calhoun, found himself embarrassed as to how to vote on a resolution congratulating the French people on the triumph of Republicanism over Royalty.

But to return to Europe. France is not alone the scene of commotion. Her excitable and inflammable disposition makes her an appropriate medium for lighting more substantial fires. Austria has dispensed with Metternich, while all the German States are demanding freedom; and even iron-hearted Russia is alarmed and perplexed by what is going on around her. The French metropolis is in direct communication with all the great cities of Europe, and the influence of her example is everywhere powerful. The Revolution of the 24th February has stirred the dormant energies of the oppressed classes all over the continent. Revolutions, outbreaks, and provisional governments, followed that event in almost fearful succession. A general insecurity broods over the crowned heads of Europe. Ireland, too, the land of O'Connell, among the most powerful that ever advocated the cause of human freedom—Ireland, ever chafing under oppressive rule, famine-stricken, ragged and wretched, but warm-hearted, generous and unconquerable Ireland, caught up the inspiring peal as it swept across the bosom of St. George's Channel, and again renewed her oath, to be free or die. Her cause is already sanctified by the martyrdom of Mitchell, and millions stand ready to be sacrificed in the same manner. England, too—calm, dignified, brave old England—is not unmoved by what is going on through the sisterhood of European nations. Her toiling sons, from the buzz and din of the factory and workshop, to her endless coal mines deep down below the surface of the earth, have heard the joyful sound of "Liberty—Equality—Fraternity" and are lifting their heads and hearts in hope of better days.

These facts though unfortunately associated with great and crying evils—evils which you and I, and all of us must deeply deplore, are nevertheless interesting to the lovers of freedom and progress. They show that all sense of manhood and moral life, has not departed from the oppressed and plundered masses. They prove, that there yet remains an energy, when supported with the will that can roll back the combined and encroaching powers of tyranny and injustice. To teach this lesson, the movements abroad are important. Even in the recent fierce strife in Paris,[2] which has subjected the infant republic to a horrid baptism of blood, may be scanned a ray of goodness. The great mass of the *Blouses* behind the barricade of the Faubourgs, evidently felt themselves fighting in the righteous cause of equal rights. Wrong in head, but right in heart; brave men in a bad cause, possessing a noble zeal but not according to knowledge. Let us deplore their folly, but honor their courage; respect their aims, but eschew their means. Tyrants of the old world, and slaveholders of our own, will point in proud complacency to this awful outbreak, and say "Aha! aha! aha! *we told you so*—we told you so: this is but the result of undertaking to counteract the purposes of the Most High, who has ordained and annointed Kings and Slaveholders to rule over the people. So much for attempting to make that equal, which God made unequal!" These sentiments in other words, have already been expressed by at least one of the classes to which I have referred. To such, I say rejoice while you may, for your time is short. The day of freedom and order, is at hand. The beautiful infant may stagger and fall, but it will rise, walk and become a man. There may, and doubtless will be, many failures, mistakes and blunders attending the transition from slavery to liberty. But what then? shall the transition never be made? Who is so base, as to harbor the thought? In demolishing the old framework of the Bastille of civil tyranny, and erecting on its ruins the beautiful temple of freedom, some lives may indeed be lost; but who so craven, when beholding the noble structure—its grand proportions, its magnificent domes, its splendid towers and its elegant turrets, all pointing upward to heaven, as to say, That glorious temple ought never to have been built.

I look, Mr. President and friends, with the profoundest interest on all these movements, both in and out of France. Their influence upon our destiny here, is greater than may at first be perceived. Mainly, however, my confidence is reposing upon what is passing in England—brave and strong old England.—Among the first to do us wrong, and the first to do us justice. England the heart of the civilized world. The nation that gave us the deed—the glorious deed, which we, on this day humbly celebrate.

In these days of great movements, she is neither silent nor slumbering. It is true, the world is not startled by her thunder, or dazzled by her splendor. Her stillness, however, is of deeper signification, than the noise of many nations.—

Like her own fuel, she has less blaze—but more heat. Her passage to freedom is not through rivers of blood; she has discovered a more excellent way. What is bloody revolution in France, is peaceful reformation in England. The friends and enemies of freedom, meet not at the barricades thrown up in the streets of London; but on the broad platform of Exeter Hall. Their weapons are not pointed bayonets, but arguments. Friends of freedom rely not upon brute force but moral power. Their courage is not that of the tiger, but that of the Christian. Their ramparts are, right and reason, and can never be stormed! Their Hotel de Ville, is the House of Commons. Their fraternity, is the unanimous sympathy of the oppressed and hungry millions, whose war cry is not "Bread or death," but bread! bread! bread!—Give this day our daily bread! That cry cannot, must not be disregarded. The last mails, brought us accounts of a stirring debate in the House of Commons, on the extension of suffrage. The opponents of the measure appeared like pigmies in the hands of giants. Friends of freedom in the House, are strong men. Among them is a man, whose name when I mention it, will call forth from this vast audience, a round of grateful applause. I allude to one, who, when he was but yet a youth, full eighteen years ago, dedicated himself to the cause of the West Indian bondman, and pleaded that cause with an eloquence the most pathetic, thrilling, and powerful ever before known to British ears—and who, when he had stirred the British heart to the core, until justice to the West India bondman rung through the British Empire—and the freedom which we celebrate, was gloriously triumphant; with life in hand, he left his native shores, to plead the cause of the bondman—and went through our land taking his lot with the despised abolitionists, and nominally free colored man; amid floods of abuse and fiery trials, he hazarded his precious life in our cause, at last was finally induced to leave our shores by the strong persuasion of his friends lest the enemies of liberty should kill him, as they had sworn to do, and returned to his own country, and is now an honorable member of the British Parliament. That man, is George Thompson. In grateful remembrance of whose labors, I now propose three cheers.

If there be one living orator more than another to whom we are indebted, that man is George Thompson. Faithful to the monitions of conscience which led him to devote himself to the cause of the West Indian Slave, he has now consecrated his great talents to the cause of liberty in his own country. There are other noble men Champions of liberty in the House of Commons, deserving honorable mention; but none, so intimately connected with the great event which distinguishes this day, as that of George Thompson. His life has been mainly devoted to our cause—and his very name carries with it an advocacy of our freedom. It is a gratifying fact, that Mr. Thompson, the reviled, abused, and rejected of this country, at this moment occupies the proud position of a British Legislator. It shows, that even in England, reward waits on merit. That a man with great talents and devotion to truth, may rise to eminence even in a monarchical and aristocratical government.

I now turn from the contemplation of men and movements in Europe, to our own great country. Great we are, in many and very important respects. As a nation, we are great in numbers and geographical extent—great in wealth—great in internal resources—great in the proclamations of great truths—great in our professions of republicanism and religion—great in our inconsistencies—great in our hypocrisy—and great in our atrocious wickedness. While our boast is loud and long of justice, freedom, and humanity, the slavewhip rings to the mockery; while we are sympathising with the progress of freedom abroad, we are extending the foul curse of slavery at home; while we are rejoicing at the progress of freedom in France, Italy, Germany, and the whole European continent, we are propagating slavery in Oregon, New Mexico, California, and all our blood-bought possessions in the South and South-west.—While we are engaged in congratulating the people of the East on casting down tyrants, we are electing tyrants and men-stealers to rule over us. Truly we are a great nation! At this moment, three million slaves clank their galling fetters and drag their heavy chains on American soil. Three million from whom all rights are robbed. Three millions, a population equal to that of all Scotland, who in this land of liberty and light, are denied the right to learn to read the name of God.—They toil under a broiling sun and a driver's lash; they are sold like cattle in the market—and are shut out from human regards—thought of and spoken of as property—sanctioned as property by cruel laws, and sanctified as such by the Church and Clergy of the country.—While I am addressing you, four of my own dear sisters and one brother are enduring the frightful horrors of American slavery. In what part of the Union, they may be, I do not know; two of them, Sarah and Catharine, were sold from Maryland before I escaped from there. I am cut off from all communication with—I cannot hear from them, nor can they hear from me—we are sundered forever.

My case, is the case of thousands; and the case of my sisters, is the case of Millions. I have no doubt, that there are hundreds here to-day, that have parents, children, sisters and brothers, who are now in slavery. Oh! how deep is the damnation of America—under what a load of crime does she stagger from day to day! What a hell of wickedness is there coiled up in her bosom, and what awful judgment awaits her impenitence! My friends, words cannot express my feelings. My soul is sick of this picture of an awful reality.—The wails of bondmen are on my ear, and their heavy sorrows weigh down my heart.

I turn from these horrors—from these God-defying, man imbruting crimes, to those who in my judgment are responsible for them. And I trace them to the door of every American citizen. Slavery exists in this land because of the moral, constitutional, political and religious support which it receives from the people of this country, especially the people of the North. As I stand before many to whom this subject may be new, I may be allowed here to explain. The people of this country are held together by a Constitution. That Constitution contains certain compromises in favor of slavery, and which bind the citizens to uphold slavery. The language of every American citizen to the slave, so far as he can comprehend that language is, "You shall be a slave or die." The history and character of the American people confirms the slave in this belief. To march to the attainment of his liberty, is to march directly upon the bristling bayonets of the whole military power of the nation. About eighteen years ago, a man of noble courage, rose among his brethren in Virginia. "We have long been subjected to slavery. The hour for our deliverance has come. Let us rise and strike for liberty. In the name of a God of justice let us stay our oppressors."[3] What was the result? He fell amid showers of American bullets, fired by *United States* troops. The fact that the Constitution guarantees to the slaveholder the naval and military support of the nation; the fact that he may under that Constitution, recapture his flying bondman in any State or territory within or belonging to this Union; and the fact that slavery alone enjoys a representation in Congress, makes every man who in good faith swears to support that Constitution and to execute its provisions, responsible for all the outrages committed on the millions of our brethren now in bonds. I therefore this day, before this large audience, charge home upon the voters of this city, county and state, the awful responsibility of enslaving and imbruting my brothers and sisters in the Southern States of this Union. Carry it home with you from this great gathering in Washington Square, that you, my white fellow-countrymen, are the enslavers of men, women, and children, in the Southern States; that what are called the compromises of your glorious Constitution, are but bloody links in the chain of slavery; and that they make you parties to that chain. But for these compromises—but for your readiness to stand by them, "in the fullness of their letter and the completeness of their letter," the slave might instantly assert and maintain his rights. The contest now would be wonderfully unequal. Seventeen millions of armed, disciplined, and intelligent people, against three millions of unarmed and uninformed. Sir, we are often taunted with the inquiry from Northern white men—"Why do your people submit to slavery? and does not that submission prove them an inferior race? Why have they not shown a desire for freedom?" Such language is as disgraceful to the insolent men who use it, as it is tantalising and insulting to us.

It is mean and cowardly for any white man to use such language toward us. My language to all such, is, Give us fair play and if we do not gain our freedom, it will be time to taunt us thus.

Before taking my seat, I will call your attention to some charges and misrepresentations of the American press, respecting the result of the great measure which we this day commemorate. We continually find statements and sentiments like this, in the whirlpool of American newspapers—"The British Colonies are ruined," "The emancipated Negroes are lazy and won't work," "Emancipation has been a failure." Now, I wish to reply to these sentiments and statements—and to say something about laziness in general, as applied to the race to which I belong. By the way, I think I may claim a superior industry for the colored man over the white man, on the showing of the white men themselves. We are just now appropriating to ourselves, vast regions of country in the Southwest.—What is the language of white men, as to the best population to develop the great resources of those vast countries? Why, in good plain English this: that white industry is unequal to it, and that none but the sinewy arm of the sable race is capable of doing so. Now, for these lazy drones to be taunting us with laziness, is a little too bad. I will answer the statements respecting the ruined condition of the West India Islands, by a declaration recently made on this very subject by Lord John Russell, present Prime Minister of England, a man remarkable for coolness and accuracy of speech. In regard to the measure of emancipation, he says, and I read from the London Times of the 17th of June, 1848:—

"The main purpose of the act of 1834 was as I have stated, to give freedom to 800,000 persons, to place those then living in a condition of slavery in a state of independence, prosperity, and happiness. That object, I think, every one admits has been accomplished. [Cheers.] I believe a class of laborers more happy, more in possession of all the advantages and enjoyments of life than the Negro population of the West Indies, does not exist. [Cheers.]—That great object has been accomplished by the act of 1834."

"It appears by evidence that the Negroes of the West India colonies since the abolition of slavery had been in the best condition. They had the best food, and were in all respects better clothed and provided for than any peasantry in the world. There was a resolution passed by a committee in 1842 declaring that the measure of emancipation had completely succeeded so far as the welfare of the Negroes was concerned. I believe the noble lord the member for Lynn, moved a similar resolution on a subsequent occasion. We have it in evidence that the Negroes were able to indulge in the luxury of dress, which they carried to an almost ridiculous excess. Some were known to have dress worth 50*l.*"

Now, sir, I call upon the press of Rochester and of this country at large, to let these facts be known, that a long abused and injured race may at last have justice done them.

I must thank you now my friends, for your kind and patient attention: asking your pardon for having trespassed so long upon your hearing, I will take my seat.

The North Star, August 4, 1848

1. Last line of poem missing.
2. On May 15, 1848, the working class of Paris broke into the Assembly to protest the manipulations of the bourgeoisie in emasculating the socialist National Workshops program. A month later, on the morning of June 23, civil war broke out in Paris. After two days of fighting, the working class uprising was crushed with the loss of 3,000 workers' lives. Soon afterwards, the reaction set in in full force, ending on Dec. 10, 1848, with the election of Louis Napoleon as President of the Republic.
3. The reference is to Nat Turner (1800–1831), the leader of the great Negro slave insurrection in Southampton County, Virginia, in 1831.

TO THOMAS AULD

September 3d, 1848

Sir:

The long and intimate, though by no means friendly relation which unhappily subsisted between you and myself, leads me to hope that you will easily account for the great liberty which I now take in addressing you in this open and public manner. The same fact may possibly remove any disagreeable surprise which you may experience on again finding your name coupled with mine, in any other way than in an advertisement, accurately describing my person, and offering a large sum for my arrest. In thus dragging you again before the public, I am aware that I shall subject myself to no inconsiderable amount of censure. I shall probably be charged with an unwarrantable, if not a wanton and reckless disregard of the rights and proprieties of private life. There are those North as well as South who entertain a much higher respect for rights which are merely conventional, than they do for rights which are personal and essential. Not a few there are in our country, who, while they have no scruples against robbing the laborer of the hard earned results of his *patient industry,* will be shocked by the extremely indelicate manner of bringing your name before the public. Believing this to be the case, and wishing to meet every reasonable or plausible objection to my conduct, I will frankly state the ground upon which I justify myself in this instance, as well as on former occasions when I have thought proper to mention your name in public. All will agree that a man guilty of theft, robbery, or murder, has forfeited the right to concealment and private life; that the community have a right to subject such persons to the most complete exposure. However much they may desire retirement, and aim to conceal themselves and their movements from the popular gaze, the public have a right to ferret them out, and bring their conduct before the proper tribunals of the country for investigation. Sir, you will undoubtedly make the proper application of these generally admitted principles, and will easily see the light in which you are regarded by me. I will not therefore manifest ill temper, by calling you hard names. I know you to be a man of some intelligence, and can readily determine the precise estimate which I entertain of your character. I may therefore indulge in language which may seem to others indirect and ambiguous, and yet be quite well understood by yourself.

I have selected this day on which to address you, because it is the anniversary of my emancipation; and knowing of no better way, I am led to this as the best mode of celebrating that truly important event. Just ten years ago this beautiful September morning, yon bright sun beheld me a slave—a poor, degraded chattel—trembling at the sound of your voice, lamenting that I was a man, and wishing myself a brute. The hopes which I had treasured up for weeks of a safe and successful escape from your grasp, were powerfully confronted at this last hour by dark clouds of doubt and fear, making my person shake and my bosom to heave with the heavy contest between hope and fear. I have no words to describe to you the deep agony of soul which I experienced on that never to be forgotten morning—(for I left by daylight). I was making a leap in the dark. The probabilities, so far as I could by reason determine them, were stoutly against the undertaking. The preliminaries and precautions I had adopted previously, all worked badly. I was like one going to war without weapons—ten chances of defeat to one of victory. One in whom I had confided, and one who had promised me assistance, appalled by fear at the trial hour, deserted me, thus leaving the responsibility of success or failure solely with myself. You, sir, can never know my feelings. As I look back to them, I can scarcely realize that I have passed through a scene so trying. Trying however as they were, and gloomy as was the prospect, thanks be to the Most High, who is ever the God of the oppressed, at the moment which was to determine my whole earthly career. His grace was sufficient, my mind was made up. I embraced the golden opportunity, took the morning tide at the flood, and a free man, young, active and strong, is the result.

I have often thought I should like to explain to you the grounds upon which I have justified myself in running away from you. I am almost ashamed to do so now, for by this time you may have discovered them yourself. I will, however, glance at them. When yet but a child about six years old, I imbibed the determination to run away. The very first mental effort that I now remember on my part, was an attempt to solve the mystery, Why am I a slave? and with this question my youthful mind was troubled for many days, pressing upon me more heavily at times than others. When I saw the slave-driver whip a slave woman, cut the blood out of her neck, and heard her piteous cries, I went away into the corner of the fence, wept and pondered over the mystery. I had, through some medium, I know not what, got some idea of God, the Creator of all mankind, the black and the white, and that he had made the blacks to serve the whites as slaves. How he could do this and be *good,* I could not tell. I was not satisfied with this theory, which made God responsible for slavery, for it pained me greatly, and I have wept over it long and often. At one time, your first wife, Mrs. Lucretia, heard me singing and saw me shedding tears, and asked of me the matter, but I was afraid to tell her. I was puzzled with this question, till one night, while sitting in the kitchen, I heard some of the old slaves talking of their parents having been stolen from Africa by white men, and were sold here as slaves. The whole mystery was solved at once. Very soon after this my aunt Jinny and uncle Noah ran away, and the great noise made about it by your father-in-law, made me for the first time acquainted with the fact, that there were free States as well as slave States. From that time, I resolved that I would some day run away. The morality of the act, I dispose as follows: I am myself; you are yourself; we are two distinct persons, equal persons. What you are, I am. You are a man, and so am I. God created both, and made us separate beings. I am not by nature bound to you, or you to me. Nature does not make your existence depend upon me, or mine to depend upon yours. I cannot walk upon your legs, or you upon mine. I cannot breathe for you, or you for me; I must breathe for myself, and you for yourself. We are distinct persons, and are each equally provided with faculties necessary to our individual existence. In leaving you, I took nothing but what belonged to me, and in no way lessened your means for obtaining an *honest* living. Your faculties remained yours, and mine became useful to their rightful owner. I therefore see no wrong in any part of the transaction. It is true, I went off secretly, but that was more your fault than mine. Had I let you into the secret, you would have defeated the enterprise entirely; but for this, I should have been really glad to have made you acquainted with my intentions to leave.

You may perhaps want to know how I like my present condition. I am free to say, I greatly prefer it to that which I occupied in Maryland. I am, however, by no means prejudiced against the State as such. Its geography, climate, fertility and products, are such as to make it a very desirable abode for any man; and but for the existence of slavery there, it is not impossible that I might again take up my abode in that State. It is not that I love Maryland less, but freedom more. You will be surprised to learn that people at the North labor under the strange delusion that if the slaves were emancipated at the South, they would flock to the North. So far from this being the case, in that event, you would see many old and familiar faces back again to the South. The fact is, there are few here who would not return to the South in the event of emancipation. We want to live in the land of our birth, and to lay our bones by the side of our fathers'; and nothing short of an intense love of personal freedom keeps us from the South. For the sake of this, most of us would live on a crust of bread and a cup of cold water.

Since I left you, I have had a rich experience. I have occupied stations which I never dreamed of when a slave. Three out of the ten years since I left you, I spent as a common laborer on the wharves of New Bedford, Massachusetts. It was there I earned my first free dollar. It was mine. I could spend it as I pleased. I could buy hams or herring with it, without asking any odds of any body. That was a precious dollar to me. You remember when I used to make seven or eight, or even nine dollars a week in Baltimore, you would take every cent of it from me every Saturday night, saying that I belonged to you, and my earnings also. I never liked this conduct on your part—to say the best, I thought it a little mean. I would not have served you so. But let that pass. I was a little awkward about counting money in New England fashion when I first landed in New Bedford. I like to have betrayed myself several times. I caught myself saying phip, for fourpence; and at one time a man actually charged me with being a runaway, whereupon I was silly enough to become one by running away from him, for I was greatly afraid he might adopt measures to get me again into slavery, a condition I then dreaded more than death.

I soon, however, learned to count money, as well as to make it, and got on swimmingly. I married soon after leaving you: in fact, I was engaged to be married before I left you; and instead of finding my companion a burden, she was truly a helpmeet. She went to live at service, and I to work on the wharf, and though we toiled hard the first winter, we never lived more happily. After remaining in New Bedford for three years, I met with Wm. Lloyd Garrison, a person of whom you have *possibly* heard, as he is pretty generally known among slaveholders. He put it into my head that I might make myself serviceable to the cause of the slave by devoting a portion of my time to telling my own sorrows, and those of other slaves which had come under my observation. This was the commencement of a higher state of existence than any to which I had ever aspired. I was thrown into society the most pure, enlightened and benevolent that the country affords. Among these I have never forgotten you, but have invariably made you the topic of conversation—thus giving you all the notoriety I could do. I need not tell you that the opinion formed of you in these circles, is far from being favorable. They have little respect for your honesty, and less for your religion.

But I was going on to relate to you something of my interesting experience. I had not long enjoyed the excellent society to which I have referred, before the light of its excellence exerted a beneficial influence on my mind and heart. Much of my early dislike of white persons was removed, and their manners, habits and customs, so entirely unlike what I had been used to in the kitchen-quarters on the plantations of the South, fairly charmed me, and gave me a strong disrelish for the coarse and degrading customs of my former condition. I therefore made an effort so to improve my mind and deportment, as to be somewhat fitted to the station to which I seemed almost providentially called. The transition from degradation to respectability was indeed great, and to get from one to the other without carrying some marks of one's former condition, is truly a difficult matter. I would not have you think that I am now entirely clear of all plantation peculiarities, but my friends here, while they entertain the strongest dislike to them, regard me with that charity to which my past life somewhat entitles me, so that my condition in this respect is exceedingly pleasant. So far as my domestic affairs are concerned, I can boast of as comfortable a dwelling as your own. I have an industrious and neat companion, and four dear children—the oldest a girl of nine years, and three fine boys, the oldest eight, the next six, and the youngest four years old. The three oldest are now going regularly to school—two can read and write, and the other can spell with tolerable correctness words of two syllables: Dear fellows! they are all in comfortable beds, and are sound asleep, perfectly secure under my own roof. There are no slaveholders here to rend my heart by snatching them from my arms, or blast a mother's dearest hopes by tearing them from her bosom. These dear children are ours—not to work up into rice, sugar and tobacco, but to watch over, regard, and protect, and to rear them up in the nurture and admonition of the gospel—to train them up in the paths of wisdom and virtue, and, as far as we can to make them useful to the world and to themselves. Oh! sir, a slaveholder never appears to me so completely an agent of hell, as when I think of and look upon my dear children. It is then that my feelings rise above my control. I meant to have said more with respect to my own prosperity and happiness, but thoughts and feelings which this recital has quickened unfits me to proceed further in that direction. The grim horrors of slavery rise in all their ghastly terror before me, the wails of millions pierce my heart, and chill my blood. I remember the chain, the gag, the bloody whip, the death-like gloom overshadowing the broken spirit of the fettered bondman, the appalling liability of his being torn away from wife and children, and sold like a beast in the market. Say not that this is a picture of fancy. You well know that I wear stripes on my back inflicted by your direction; and that you, while we were brothers in the same church, caused this right hand, with which I am now penning this letter, to be closely tied to my left, and my person dragged at the pistol's mouth, fifteen miles, from the Bay side to Easton to be sold like a beast in the market, for the alleged crime of intending to escape from your possession. All this and more you remember, and know to be perfectly true, not only of yourself, but of nearly all of the slaveholders around you.

At this moment, you are probably the guilty holder of at least three of my own dear sisters, and my only brother in bondage. These you regard as your property. They are recorded on your ledger, or perhaps have been sold to human flesh mongers, with a view to filling your own ever-hungry purse. Sir, I desire to know how and where these dear sisters are. Have you sold them? or are they still in your possession? What has become of them? are they living or dead? And my dear old grandmother, whom you turned out like an old horse, to die in the woods—is she still alive? Write and let me know all about them. If my grandmother be still alive, she is of no service to you, for by this time she must be nearly eighty years old—too old to be cared for by one to whom she has ceased to be of service, send her to me at Rochester, or bring her to Philadelphia, and it shall be the crowning happiness of my life to take care of her in her old age. Oh! she was to me a mother, and a father, so far as hard toil for my comfort could make her such. Send me my grandmother! that I may watch over and take care of her in her old age. And my sisters, let me know all about them. I would write to them, and learn all I want to know of them, without disturbing you in any way, but that, through your unrighteous conduct, they have been entirely deprived of the power to read and write. You have kept them in utter ignorance, and have therefore robbed them of the sweet enjoyments of writing or receiving letters from absent friends and relatives. Your wickedness and cruelty committed in this respect on your fellow-creatures, are greater than all the stripes you have laid upon my back, or theirs. It is an outrage upon the soul—a war upon the immortal spirit, and one for which you must give account at the bar of our common Father and Creator.

The responsibility which you have assumed in this regard is truly awful—and how you could stagger under it these many years is marvellous. Your mind must have become darkened, your heart hardened, your conscience seared and petrified, or you would have long since thrown off the accursed load and sought relief at the hands of a sin-forgiving God. How, let me ask, would you look upon me, were I some dark night in company with a band of hardened villains, to enter the precincts of your elegant dwelling and seize the person of your own lovely daughter Amanda, and carry her off from your family, friends and all the loved ones of her youth—make her my slave—compel her to work, and I take her wages—place her name on my ledger as property—disregard her personal rights—fetter the powers of her immortal soul by denying her the right and privilege of learning to read and write—feed her coarsely—clothe her scantily, and whip her on the naked back occasionally; more and still more horrible, leave her unprotected—a degraded victim to the brutal lust of fiendish overseers, who would pollute, blight, and blast her fair soul—rob her of all dignity—destroy her virtue, and annihilate all in her person the graces that adorn the character of virtuous womanhood? I ask how would you regard me, if such were my conduct? Oh! the vocabulary of the damned would not afford a word sufficiently infernal, to express your idea of my God-provoking wickedness. Yet sir, your treatment of my beloved sisters is in all essential points, precisely like the case I have now supposed. Damning as would be such a deed on my part, it would be no more so than that which you have committed against me and my sisters.

I will now bring this letter to a close, you shall hear from me again unless you let me hear from you. I intend to make use of you as a weapon with which to assail the system of slavery—as a means of concentrating public attention on the system, and deepening their horror of trafficking in the souls and bodies of men. I shall make use of you as a means of exposing the character of the American church and clergy—and as a means of bringing this guilty nation with yourself to repentance. In doing this I entertain no malice towards you personally. There is no roof under which you would be more safe than mine, and there is nothing in my house which you might need for your comfort, which I would not readily grant. Indeed, I should esteem it a privilege, to set you an example as to how mankind ought to treat each other.

I am your fellow man, but not your slave,

Frederick Douglass

The *Liberator,* September 22, 1848

In September, 1848, between sixty and seventy delegates met in Cleveland and chose Douglass as president of the National Negro Convention. Douglass was delighted to discover in examining the delegates' credentials that they represented a cross-section of the free Negro people—printers, carpenters, blacksmiths, shoemakers, engineers, dentists, gunsmiths, editors, tailors, merchants, wheelwrights, painters, farmers, physicians, plasterers, masons, clergymen, barbers, hairdressers, coopers, livery stable keepers, bath-house keepers, and grocers.

Reversing the position adopted a year before on the national Negro press, the convention announced that *The North Star* answered the needs and purposes of such a press and urged its support by all Negro people. The delegates also endorsed the Free Soil Party, but declared that they were "determined to maintain the higher stand and more liberal views which heretofore characterized us as *abolitionists.*" This meeting recommended "a change in the conduct of colored barbers who refused to treat colored men on a basis of equality with the whites." Committees were appointed in different states to organize vigilante groups, "so as to enable them to measure arms with assailants without and invaders within."[1]

Douglass' voice was heard throughout the proceedings. He opposed the preamble to the seventeenth resolution "inasmuch as it intimated that slavery could not be abolished by moral means alone." He moved to amend the thirty-third resolution, declaring that the word "persons" used in the resolution designating delegates be understood "to include *women.*" The motion was seconded, and carried "with three cheers for woman's rights."[2]

Douglass' role at the Cleveland Convention won him nationwide attention. The proceedings were printed in the press, and special comments on the presiding officer appeared in the editorial columns. The pro-southern papers exhausted their vocabulary in slandering Douglass, but other journals were extravagant in their praise. Answering an attack by the *Plain Dealer* of its city, the Cleveland *Daily True Democrat* declared: "Frederick Douglass is a man, who if divided into fifty parts would make fifty better men than the editor of the *Plain Dealer.*" Gerrit Smith was so delighted with Douglass' conduct at the convention that he ventured the opinion that "he has the talents and dignity that would adorn the Presidency of the nation."[3] [II:25–26]

AN ADDRESS TO THE COLORED PEOPLE OF THE UNITED STATES

Fellow Countrymen:

Under a solemn sense of duty, inspired by our relation to you as fellow sufferers under the multiplied and grievous wrongs to which we as a people are universally subjected,—we, a portion of your brethren, assembled in National Convention, at Cleveland, Ohio, take the liberty to address you on the subject of our mutual improvement and social elevation.

The condition of our variety of the human family, has long been cheerless, if not hopeless, in this country. The doctrine perseveringly proclaimed in high places in church and state, that it is impossible for colored men to rise from ignorance and debasement, to intelligence and respectability in this country, has made a deep impression upon the public mind generally, and is not without its effect upon us. Under this gloomy doctrine, many of us have sunk under the pall of despondency, and are making no effort to relieve ourselves, and have no heart to assist others. It is from this despond that we would deliver you. It is from this slumber we would rouse you. The present, is a period of activity and hope. The heavens above us are bright, and much of the darkness that overshadowed us has passed away. We can deal in the language of brilliant encouragement, and speak of success with certainty. That our condition has been gradually improving, is evident to all, and that we shall yet stand on a common platform with our fellow countrymen, in respect to political and social rights, is certain. The spirit of the age—the voice of inspiration—the deep longings of the human soul—the conflict of right with wrong—the upward tendency of the oppressed throughout the world, abound with evidence complete and ample, of the final triumph of right over wrong, of freedom over slavery, and equality over caste. To doubt this, is to forget the past, and blind our eyes to the present, as well as to deny and oppose the great law of progress, written out by the hand of God on the human soul.

Great changes for the better have taken place and are still taking place. The last ten years have witnessed a mighty change in the estimate in which we as a people are regarded, both in this and other lands. England has given liberty to nearly one million, and France has emancipated three hundred thousand of our brethren, and our own country shakes with the agitation of our rights. Ten or twelve years ago, an educated colored man was regarded as a curiosity, and the thought of a colored man as an author, editor, lawyer or doctor, had scarce been conceived. Such, thank Heaven, is no longer the case. There are now those among us, whom we are not ashamed to regard as gentlemen and scholars, and who are acknowledged to be such, by many of the most learned and respectable in our land. Mountains of prejudice have been removed, and truth and light are dispelling the error and darkness of ages. The time was, when we trembled in the presence of a white man, and dared not assert, or even ask for our rights, but would be guided, directed, and governed, in any way we were demanded, without ever stopping to enquire whether we were right or wrong. We were not only slaves, but our ignorance made us willing slaves. Many of us uttered complaints against the faithful abolitionists, for the broad assertion of our rights; thought they went too far, and were only making our condition worse. This sentiment has nearly ceased to reign in the dark abodes of our hearts; we begin to see our wrongs as clearly, and comprehend our rights as fully, and as well as our white countrymen. This is a sign of progress; and evidence which cannot be gainsayed. It would be easy to present in this connection, a glowing comparison of our past with our present condition, showing that while the former was dark and dreary, the present is full of light and hope. It would be easy to draw a picture of our present achievements, and erect upon it a glorious future.

But, fellow countrymen, it is not so much our purpose to cheer you by the progress we have already made, as it is to stimulate you to still higher attainments. We have done much, but there is much more to be done.—While we have undoubtedly great cause to thank God, and take courage for the hopeful changes which have taken place in our condition, we are not without cause to mourn over the sad condition which we yet occupy. We are yet the most oppressed people in the world. In the Southern states of this Union, we are held as slaves. All over that wide region our paths are marked with blood. Our backs are yet scarred by the lash, and our souls are yet dark under the pall of slavery.—Our sisters are sold for purposes of pollution, and our brethren are sold in the market, with beasts of burden. Shut up in the prison-house of bondage—denied all rights, and deprived of all privileges, we are blotted from the page of human existence, and placed beyond the limits of human regard. Death, moral death, has palsied our souls in that quarter, and we are a murdered people.

In the Northern states, we are not slaves to individuals, not personal slaves, yet in many respects we are the slaves of the community. We are, however, far enough removed from the actual condition of the slave, to make us largely responsible for their continued enslavement, or their speedy deliverance from chains. For in the proportion which we shall rise in the scale of human improvement, in that proportion do we augment the probabilities of a speedy emancipation of our enslaved fellow-countrymen. It is more than a mere figure of speech to say, that we are as a people, chained together. We are one people— one in general complexion, one in a common degradation, one in popular estimation. As one rises, all must rise, and as one falls all must fall. Having now, our feet on the rock of freedom, we must drag our brethren from the slimy depths of slavery, ignorance, and ruin. Every one of us should be ashamed to consider himself free, while his brother is a slave.—The wrongs of our brethren, should be our constant theme. There should be no time too precious, no calling too holy, no place too sacred, to make room for this cause. We should not only feel it to be the cause of humanity, but the cause of christianity, and fit work for men and angels. We ask you to devote yourselves to this cause, as one of the first, and most successful means of self improvement. In the careful study of it, you will learn your own rights, and comprehend your own responsibilities, and, scan through the vista of coming time, your high, and God-appointed destiny. Many of the brightest and best of our number, have become such by their devotion to this cause, and the society of white abolitionists. The latter have been willing to make themselves of no reputation for our sake, and in return, let us show ourselves worthy of their zeal and devotion. Attend anti-slavery meetings, show that you are interested in the subject, that you hate slavery, and love those who are laboring for its overthrow.—Act with white Abolition societies wherever you can, and where you cannot, get up societies among yourselves, but without exclusiveness. It will be a long time before we gain all our rights; and although it may seem to conflict with our views of human brotherhood, we shall undoubtedly for many years be compelled to have institutions of a complexional character, in order to attain this very idea of human brotherhood. We would, however, advise our brethren to occupy memberships and stations among white persons, and in white institutions, just so fast as our rights are secured to us.

Never refuse to act with a white society or institution because it is white, or a black one, because it is black. But act with all men without distinction of color. By so acting, we shall find many opportunities for removing prejudices and establishing the rights of all men. We say avail yourselves of *white* institutions, not because they are white, but because they afford a more convenient means of improvement. But we pass from these suggestions, to others which may be deemed more important. In the Convention that now addresses you, there has been much said on the subject of labor, and especially those departments of it, with which we as a class have been long identified. You will see by the resolutions there adopted on that subject, that the Convention regarded those employments though right in themselves, as being nevertheless, degrading to us as a class, and therefore, counsel you to abandon them as speedily as possible, and to seek what are called the more respectable employments. While the Convention do not inculcate the doctrine that any kind of needful toil is in itself dishonorable, or that colored persons are to be exempt from what are called menial employments, they do mean to say that such employments have been so long and universally filled by colored men, as to become a badge of degradation, in that it has established the conviction that colored men are only fit for such employments. We therefore, advise you by all means, to cease from such employments, as far as practicable, by pressing into others. Try to get your sons into mechanical trades; press them into the blacksmith's shop, the machine shop, the joiner's shop, the wheelwright's shop, the cooper's shop, and the tailor's shop.

Every blow of the sledge hammer, wielded by a sable arm, is a powerful blow in support of our cause. Every colored mechanic, is by virtue of circumstances, an elevator of his race. Every house built by black men, is a strong tower against the allied hosts of prejudice. It is impossible for us to attach too much importance to this aspect of the subject. Trades are important. Wherever a man may be thrown by misfortune, if he has in his hands a useful trade, he is useful to his fellow man, and will be esteemed accordingly; and of all men in the world who need trades we are the most needy.

Understand this, that independence is an essential condition of respectability. To be dependent, is to be degraded. Men may indeed pity us, but they cannot respect us. We do not mean that we can become entirely independent of all men; that would be absurd and impossible, in the social state. But we mean that we must become equally independent with other members of the community. That other members of the community shall be as dependent upon us, as we upon them.—That such is not now the case, is too plain to need an argument. The houses we live in are built by white men—the clothes we wear are made by white tailors—the hats on our heads are made by white hatters, and the shoes on our feet are made by white shoe-makers, and the food that we eat, is raised and cultivated by white men. Now it is impossible that we should ever be respected as a people, while we are so universally and completely dependent upon white men for the necessaries of life. We must make white persons as dependent upon us, as we are upon them. This cannot be done while we are found only in two or three kinds of employments, and those employments have their foundation chiefly, if not entirely, in the pride and indolence of the white people. Sterner necessities, will bring higher respect.

The fact is, we must not merely make the white man dependent upon us to shave him but to feed him; not merely dependent upon us to black his boots, but to make them. A man is only in a small degree dependent on us when he only needs his boots blacked, or his carpet bag carried; as a little less pride, and a little more industry on his part, may enable him to dispense with our services entirely. As wise men it becomes us to look forward to a state of things, which appears inevitable. The time will come, when those menial employments will afford less means of living than they now do. What shall a large class of our fellow countrymen do, when white men find it economical to black their own boots, and shave themselves. What will they do when white men learn to wait on themselves? We warn you brethren, to seek other and more enduring vocations.

Let us entreat you to turn your attention to agriculture. Go to farming. Be tillers of the soil. On this point we could say much, but the time and space will not permit. Our cities are overrun with menial laborers, while the country is eloquently pleading for the hand of industry to till her soil, and reap the reward of honest labor. We beg and intreat you, to save your money—live economically—dispense with finery, and the gaities which have rendered us proverbial, and save your money. Not for the senseless purpose of being better off than your neighbor, but that you may be able to educate your children, and render your share to the common stock of prosperity and happiness around you. It is plain that the equality which we aim to accomplish, can only be achieved by us, when we can do for others, just what others can do for us. We should therefore, press into all the trades, professions and callings, into which honorable white men press.

We would in this connection, direct your attention to the means by which we have been oppressed and degraded. Chief among those means, we may mention the press. This engine has brought to the aid of prejudice, a thousand stings. Wit, ridicule, false philosophy, and an impure theology, with a flood of low blackguardism, come through this channel into the public mind; constantly feeding and keeping alive against us, the bitterest hate. The pulpit too, has been arrayed against us. Men with sanctimonious face, have talked of our being descendants of Ham—that we are under a curse, and to try to improve our condition, is virtually to counteract the purposes of God!

It is easy to see that the means which have been used to destroy us, must be used to save us. The press must be used in our behalf: aye! we must use it ourselves; we must take and read newspapers; we must read books, improve our minds, and put to silence and to shame, our opposers.

Dear Brethren, we have extended these remarks beyond the length which we had allotted to ourselves, and must now close, though we have but hinted at the subject. Trusting that our words may fall like good seed upon good ground; and hoping that we may all be found in the path of improvement and progress,

We are your friends and servants,
(Signed by the Committee, in behalf of the Convention)
Frederick Douglass,
H. Bibb,
W. L. Day,
D. H. Jenkins,
A. H. Francis.

The North Star, September 29, 1848

1. *The North Star,* Sept. 19, 1848; *Liberator,* Oct. 20, 1848.

2. *Report of Proceedings of Colored National Convention, Held at Cleveland, Ohio, on Wednesday, September 6, 1848,* Rochester, 1848, pp. 8, 12.

3. Cleveland *True Democrat,* Sept. 11, 1848; Gerrit Smith to Chas. B. Ray, Nov. 11, 1848, *Model Worker,* Dec. 29, 1848, reprinted in leaflet form, the Gerrit Smith Papers, Syracuse University.

On September 10, 1848, *The North Star* editorially recommended the Free Soil candidates, Van Buren and Adams. . . . Douglass understood that this was the beginning of a great movement which would finally split the Democrats, destroy the Whig Party, and create a new political anti-slavery movement with a mass following.[1] [He] was excited by the colorful campaign. . . .

Although Van Buren did not carry a single state, the Free Soil Party received 291,678 votes out of the 2,882,120 which were cast, and elected five men to Congress. . . . While Douglass was bitter over Taylor's election, he was encouraged by the vote cast for the Free Soil candidates. He was convinced that it was the duty of all anti-slavery men to promulgate their principles among the Free Soilers so that gradually "a true Free Soil Party" could be established. "We must go on and lead the Free Soilers," he told his audience at the Thirteenth Annual Meeting of the Rhode Island Anti-Slavery Society a month after the election.[2] [II:72–73]

THE BLOOD OF THE SLAVE ON THE SKIRTS OF THE NORTHERN PEOPLE

A victim of your power and oppression, humbly craves your attention to a few words, (in behalf of himself and three millions of his brethren, whom you hold in chains and slavery,) with respect to the election just completed. In doing so, I desire to be regarded as addressing you, individually and collectively. If I should seem severe, remember that the iron of slavery has pierced and rankled in my heart, and that I not only smart under the recollection of a long and cruel enslavement, but am even now passing my life in a country, and among a people, whose prejudices against myself and people subjects me to a thousand poisonous stings. If I speak harshly, my excuse is, that I speak in fetters of your own forging. Remember that oppression hath the power to make even a wise man mad.

In the selection of your national rulers just completed, you have made another broad mark on the page of your nation's history, and have given to the world and the coming generation a certain test by which to determine your present integrity as a people. That actions speak louder than words—that within the character of the representative may be seen that of the constituency—that no people are better than their laws or lawmakers—that a stream cannot rise higher than its source—that a sweet fountain cannot send forth bitter water, and that a tree is to be known by its fruits, are truisms; and in their light let us examine the character and pretensions of your boasted Republic.

As a people, you claim for yourselves a higher civilization—a purer morality—a deeper religious faith—a larger love of liberty, and a broader philanthropy, than any other nation on the globe. In a word, you claim yours to be a model Republic, and promise, by the force and excellence of your institutions, and the purity and brightness of your example, to overthrow the thrones and despotisms of the old world, and substitute your own in their stead. Your missionaries are found in the remotest parts of the globe, while our land swarms with churches and religious institutions. In words of Religion and Liberty, you are abundant and preeminent. You have long desired to get rid of the odium of being regarded as pro-slavery, and have even insisted that the charge of pro-slavery made against you was a slander and that those who made it were animated by wild and fanatical spirit. To make your innocence apparent, you have now had a fair opportunity. The issue for freedom or slavery has been clearly submitted to you, and you have deliberately chosen slavery.

General Taylor and General Cass were the chosen and admitted Southern and slavery candidates for the Presidency. Martin Van Buren, though far from being an abolitionist, yet in some sort represented the Anti-Slavery idea of the North, in a political form—him you have rejected, and elected a slaveholder to rule over you in his stead. When the question was whether New Mexico and California shall be Free or Slave States, you have rejected him who was solemnly pledged to maintain their freedom, and have chosen a man whom you knew to be pledged, by his position, to the maintenance of slavery. By your votes, you have said that slavery is better than freedom—that war is better than peace, and that cruelty is better than humanity. You have given your sanction to slave rule and slavery propagandism, and interposed whatever of moral character and standing you possess, to shield the reputation of slaveholders generally. You have said, that to be a man-stealer is no crime—to traffic in human flesh shall be a passport, rather than a barrier to your suffrages. To slaveholders you have said, Chain up your men and women, and before the bloody lash drive them to new fields of toil in California and New Mexico. To the slave in his chains you have said, Be content in your chains, and if you dare to gain your freedom by force, whether in New Mexico or California, in numbers indicated by our votes, our muskets shall find you out. In a word, you have again renewed your determination to support the Constitution of the United States, in its parts of freedom to the whites, and slavery to the blacks. If General Taylor's slaves run away, you have promised again to return them to bondage. While General Taylor is the well-known robber of three hundred human beings of all their hard earnings, and is coining their hard earnings into gold, you have conferred upon him an office worth twenty-five thousand dollars a year, and the highest honor within your power. By this act, you have endorsed his character and history. His murders in Mexico—his "bloodhound" cruelty in the Florida war—his awful profanity, together with the crimes attendant upon a slave plantation, such as theft, robbery, murder, and adultery, you have sanctioned as perfectly consistent with your morality, humanity, liberty, religion and civilization. You have said that the most available and suitable person in all this great nation, to preside over this model Republic, is a warrior, slaveholder, swearer, and bloodhound importer.—During the campaign just ended, your leaders have dubbed this man-stealer as an *honest man,* and many of you have shouted over the lie, as being a truth, thus destroying all moral distinctions. To talk of a veracious liar, a pious blasphemer, a righteous robber, a candid hypocrite, a sober drunkard, or a humane cannibal, would be quite as just and rational as to call an admitted man-stealer an honest man. Yet in the wildness of a wicked enthusiasm, you have given your countenance and support to this.

Now is it too much to say that you have made his crimes your own, and that the blood of the slave is on your garments? You have covered his theft with honesty, his blasphemy with piety, and, as far as in your power, you have rendered the blows intended to destroy slavery nugatory and innoxious. Before high heaven and the world, you are responsible for the blood of the slave. You may shut your eyes to the fact, sport over it, sleep over it, dance over it, and sing psalms over it, but so sure as there is a God of Justice and an unerring Providence, just so sure will the blood of the bondman be required at your hands.— An opportunity was presented to you by which you could have fixed an indelible mark of your utter detestation of slavery, and given a powerful blow to that bitter curse. This you have failed to do. When Christ and Barabbas were presented, you have cried out in your madness, Give us Barabbas the robber, in preference to Christ, the innocent. The perishing slave, with uplifted hands and bleeding hearts, implored you, in the name of the God you profess to serve, and the humanity you profess to cherish, not to add this mill-stone to the weight already crushing his heart and hopes. But he has appealed in vain. You have turned a deaf ear to his cries, hardened your hearts to his appeal, turned your back upon his sorrows, and united with the tyrant to perpetuate his enslavement. The efforts made in your presence to impress you with the awful sin of slavery, and to awaken you to a sense of your duty to the oppressed, have thus far been unavailing. You continue to fight against God, and declare that *injustice* exalteth a nation, and that sin is an *honor* to any people.

Do you really think to circumvent God?—Do you suppose that you can go on in your present career of injustice and political profligacy undisturbed? Has the law of righteous retribution been repealed from the statutes of the Almighty? Or what mean ye that ye bruise and bind my people? Will justice sleep forever? Oh, that you would lay these things to heart! Oh, that you would consider the enormity of your conduct, and seek forgiveness at the hands of a merciful Creator. Repent of this wickedess, and bring forth fruit meet for repentance, by delivering the despoiled out of the hands of the despoiler.

You may imagine that you have now silenced the annoying cry of abolition— that you have sealed the doom of the slave—that abolition is stabbed and dead; but you will find your mistake. You have stabbed, but the cause is not dead. Though down and bleeding at your feet, she shall rise again, and going before you, shall give you no rest till you break every yoke and let the oppressed go free. The Anti-Slavery Societies of the land will rise up and spring to action again, sending forth from the press and on the voice of the living speaker, words of burning truth, to alarm the guilty, to unmask the hypocrite, to expose the frauds of political parties, and rebuke the spirit of a corrupt and sin-sustaining church and clergy. Slavery will be attacked in its stronghold—the compromises of the

Constitution, and the cry of disunion shall be more fearlessly proclaimed, till slavery be abolished, the Union dissolved, or the sun of this guilty nation must go down in blood.—F. D.

The North Star, November 17, 1848

1. *The North Star,* Aug. 18, Nov. 10, 1848.
2. Charles H. Wesley, "The Participation of Negroes in Anti-Slavery Political Parties," *Journal of Negro History,* vol. XLII, 1945, p. 44.

Douglass' vigorous denunciation of colonization is an outstanding example of the contribution he made as an editor to clarifying problems confronting the Negro people. For some time after 1835, colonization agitation was unable to get much of a hearing in the North, as it came to be considered, to paraphrase Cornish and Garrison, merely an effort to strengthen the props of slave institutions. In the late 1840s, however, Henry Clay and the various compromise groups around him renewed the colonization program in the hope that it might lessen the tensions growing in the country over the slavery question. When Douglass founded *The North Star,* colonization agitation was again in full swing. Immediately he dedicated the journal to the battle against the colonizationists. . . .

In editorial after editorial Douglass hammered away at the theme that colonization was the "twin sister of slavery"; that the United States was the native land of the Negro; that "he, of any one has a right to the soil of this continent" having for more than two hundred years "toiled over the soil of America, under a burning sun and a driver's lash—ploughing, planting, reaping, that white men might loll in ease," and having "fought and bled for this country"; that "his attachment to the place of his birth is stronger than iron," and that those who advised the Negro to emigrate were "his worst and most deadly enemies."[1] . . .

The capstone of Douglass' argument and his most useful contribution to the discussion of colonization was his claim that Negroes and whites could live and work together as equals; that prejudice against color was not invincible; that it was already giving way "and must give way"; that it was an inevitable by-product of slavery and would be overcome as soon as the Negro people were given the same opportunities as their white brothers. The free Negroes, he declared, were making rapid advances in this direction, and were being retarded by the colonizationists who strengthened prejudice against the Negro people by declaring that it was inevitable and God-ordained because of "the natural inferiority of the colored race." It was the duty of the Negro people to defeat the vicious campaign which sought to prove that they were a blight upon American civilization, to "help free their brethren, rather than leave them in chains, to go and civilize Africa." We are Americans, cried Douglass, and we want to live in America on equal terms with all other Americans. "Brethren" he appealed, "stay where you are, so long as you can stay. Stay here and worthily discharge the duties of honest men, and of good citizens."[2] [I:97–99]

COLONIZATION

In order to divert the hounds from the pursuit of the fox, a *"red herring"* is sometimes drawn across the trail, and the hounds mistaking it for the real scent, the game is often lost. We look upon the recent debate in the Senate of the United States, over this wrinkled old "red herring" of colonization as a *ruse* to divert the attention of the people from that foul abomination which is sought to be forced upon the free soil of California and New Mexico, and which is now struggling for existence in Kentucky, Virginia and the District of Columbia. The slaveholders are evidently at a stand to know what trick they shall try next to turn the scorching rays of anti-slavery light and truth from the bloodshot eyes of the monster slavery. The discussion of it is most painful and agonizing; and if it continues, the very life of this foul, unnatural and adulterous beast will be put in imminent peril; so the slaveholding *charmers* have conjured up their old *familiar spirits* of colonization, making the old *essence* of abomination to flounder about in its grave clothes before the eyes of Northern men, to their utter confusion and bewilderment. A drowning man will catch at a straw. Slavery is sinking in public estimation. It is going down. It wants help, and asks through Mr. Underwood, of Kentucky, how much of the public money (made by the honest toil of Northern men) will be at its service in the event of emancipation, "as some are in favor of emancipation, provided that the Negroes can be sent to Liberia, or beyond the limits of the United States."

Here we have the old colonization spirit revived, and the impudent proposition entertained by the Senate of the United States of expelling the free colored people from the United States, their native land, to Liberia.

In view of this proposition, we would respectfully suggest to the assembled wisdom of the nation, that it might be well to ascertain the number of free colored people who will be likely to need the assistance of government to help them out of this country to Liberia, or elsewhere, beyond the limits of these United States—since this course might save any embarrassment which would result from an appropriation more than commensurate to the numbers who might be disposed to leave this, our own country, for one we know not of. We are of opinion that the *free* colored people generally mean to live in America, and not in Africa; and to appropriate a large sum for our removal, would merely be a waste of the public money. We do not mean to go to Liberia. Our minds are made up to live here if we can, or die here if we must; so every attempt to remove us, will be, as it ought to be, labor lost. Here we are, and here we shall remain. While our brethren are in bondage on these shores; it is idle to think of inducing any considerable number of the free colored people to quit this for a foreign land.

For two hundred and twenty-eight years has the colored man toiled over the soil of America, under a burning sun and a driver's lash—plowing, planting, reaping, that white men might roll in ease, their hands unhardened by labor, and their brows unmoistened by the waters of genial toil; and now that the moral sense of mankind is beginning to revolt at this system of foul treachery and cruel wrong, and is demanding its overthrow, the mean and cowardly oppressor is meditating plans to expel the colored man entirely from the country. Shame upon the guilty wretches that dare propose, and all that countenance such a proposition. We live here—have lived here—have a right to live here, and mean to live here.—F. D.

The North Star, January 26, 1849

1. *The North Star,* Mar. 23, 1849; *Frederick Douglass' Paper,* Feb. 26, 1852; *Douglass' Monthly,* Feb., 1859. *The African Repository* (vol. XXVI, Oct., 1850, pp. 289–94) contains

several excerpts from Douglass' editorials dealing with colonization as well as the answer of the emigrationists.

2. *The North Star,* Feb. 18, 1848; *Frederick Douglass' Paper,* Jan. 22, 1852. Douglass made it quite clear that he did not oppose missionary work in Africa. In a letter to Benjamin Coates he wrote: "My heart can never be indifferent to any legitimate movement for spreading the blessings of Christianity and civilization in that country. But the effort must not be to get the Negroes out of this country but to get Christianity into that." (Douglass to Benjamin Coates, April 17, 1856, William M. Coates Papers, Historical Society of Pennsylvania.)

During the first ten years of his work as an Abolitionist, Douglass had accepted all of the doctrines of the Garrisonian school. In his speeches, letters, and early editorials in *The North Star,* he reiterated his belief that the Constitution was wholly a pro-slavery document, called for the destruction of the American Union, reaffirmed his opposition to the use of the ballot against slavery and again asserted his conviction that moral suasion was the major instrumentality for ending slavery. "I am willing at all times to be known as a Garrisonian Abolitionist," he wrote on September 4, 1849.[1]

But as he moved outside the orbit of the Massachusetts Abolitionists and came into contact with anti-slavery men who differed with the Garrisonian school, Douglass began for the first time to examine his beliefs critically. After considerable study and extensive reading in law, political philosophy, and American government, he concluded that there were serious flaws in the Garrisonian doctrines. Gradually he formulated a new anti-slavery creed. . . .

As Douglass abandoned sole reliance on moral power for the overthrow of slavery, he was forced to re-examine his attitude toward political action. During 1841–1848 he had placed his hopes in the non-political activities of the anti-slavery societies. In a speech at the Higham Anti-Slavery Convention in November, 1841, he ridiculed political action, exclaiming that the slaveholders "care nothing about your political action, they don't dread the political movement; it is the *moral* movement, the appeal to men's sense of right, which makes them and all our opponents tremble."[2]

The belief in non-political action Douglass maintained consistently during the next few years. Like all Abolitionists under the influence of the Garrisonian wing of anti-slavery thought, he would have nothing to do with a government and a constitution framed and administered by men who "were and have been until now, little better than a band of pirates." Until the government and the Constitution were replaced by institutions which would "better answer the ends of justice," no true friend of liberty in the United States could vote or hold office.[3]

The key to Douglass' anti-political views was his interpretation of the Constitution "as a most foul and bloody conspiracy against the rights of three millions of enslaved and imbruted men." As a Negro, he knew at first hand the farce that history had made of the Declaration of Independence; his personal suffering made him only too ready to accept the Garrisonian doctrine that the Constitution was "a Covenant with death and an agreement with hell." If slaveholders appealed to the Constitution, he would appeal to a higher law, to divine morality. The founders of the American Union, he told an audience in England, while proclaiming liberty throughout the land, were themselves trafficking in their fellow men, and since then American government and society had been dedicated to defending the great lie of slavery. Slavery, he claimed, was not a southern but an American institution, a system that derived its support as much from the non-slaveholding states as from those where slavery was accepted. By swearing to uphold the American Constitution and the American Union, the people of the North had sworn before high heaven that the slave would be kept a slave. As long as they accepted the Constitution and its compromises in favor of the slaveholders, they were responsible for the existence of slavery in the United States and must share the guilt for that great crime.[4]

It required two years of study and discussion for Douglass to change his attitude toward the Constitution. The first indication he gives that he was beginning to re-examine his thinking is the [following] brief comment. . . . Six weeks later he wrote that if he could be convinced that the Constitution was essentially anti-slavery in its origins and purposes, he would be quick to use the ballot box against slavery, and to urge others to do likewise. He doubted, however, that he could be easily persuaded that such were the origins and purposes of the document. [II:49–52]

THE CONSTITUTION AND SLAVERY

Rochester, January 23, 1849

Frederick Douglass—Dear Sir:

I have called twice at the *Star* office, for the purpose of conferring with you about our discussion on American slavery, but did not find you. I am very anxious, in view of the good which I think may be done, to have the discussion immediately, and will cheerfully meet you at any time and place in this city, which you may propose, provided it shall be soon, as business will call me from the city in a few days. The resolution to be discussed, as you doubtless recollect, is the one which I presented at the Anti-Slavery Convention recently held in this city, at which time you challenged me to debate it, and I accepted the challenge.

"Resolved, That the Constitution of the United States, if strictly construed according to its reading, is anti-slavery in all of its provisions."

The word ALL was accepted from your suggestion. An immediate answer is especially requested.

Respectfully and truly yours,
C. H. Chase

My dear Sir:

I owe you an apology for not sooner publishing and replying to the above letter. On a close examination of the Constitution, I am satisfied that if strictly "construed according to its reading," it is not a pro-slavery instrument; and while I disagree with you as to the inference to be drawn from this admission, you will see that in the resolution, between us there is no question for debate.

I now hold, as I have ever done, that the original intent and meaning of the Constitution (the one given to it by the men who framed it, those who adopted, and the one given to it by the Supreme Court of the United States) makes it a pro-slavery instrument—such an one as I cannot bring myself to vote under, or swear to support.

Very respectfully,
Frederick Douglass

The North Star, February 9, 1849

1. Douglass to Oliver Johnson, *Anti-Slavery Bugle,* Oct. 6, 1849; *Liberator,* Nov. 26, 1841.
2. *Liberator,* Nov. 26, Dec. 3, 1841; *Anti-Slavery Standard,* Feb. 24, 1842.
3. *The North Star,* Mar. 30, 1849.
4. *Report of a Public Meeting at Finsbury Chapel, Moorefields, to Receive Frederick Douglass . . .* , 1846, p. 6.

THE CONSTITUTION AND SLAVERY

The assertion which we made five weeks ago, that "the Constitution, *if strictly construed according to its reading*," is not a pro-slavery instrument, has excited some interest amongst our Anti-Slavery brethren. Letters have reached us from different quarters on the subject. Some of these express agreement and pleasure with our views, and others, surprise and dissatisfaction. Each class of opinion and feeling is represented in the letters which we have placed in another part of this week's paper. The one from our friend Gerrit Smith, represents the view which the Liberty party take of this subject, and that of Mr. Robert Forten is consistent with the ground occupied by a majority of the American Anti-Slavery Society.

Whether we shall be able to set ourselves right in the minds of those on the one side of this question or the other, and at the same time vindicate the correctness of our former assertion, remains to be seen. Of one thing, however, we can assure our readers, and that is, that we bring to the consideration of this subject no partisan feelings, nor the slightest wish to make ourselves consistent with the creed of either Anti-Slavery party, and that our only aim is to know what is truth and what is duty in respect to the matter in dispute, holding ourselves perfectly free to change our opinion in any direction, and at any time which may be indicated by our immediate apprehension of truth, unbiased by the smiles or frowns of any class or party of abolitionists. The only truly consistent man is he who will, for the sake of being right today, contradict what he said wrong yesterday. "Sufficient unto the day is the evil thereof." True stability consists not in being of the same opinion now as formerly, but in a fixed principle of honesty, even urging us to the adoption or rejection of that which may seem to us true or false at the ever-present now.

Before entering upon a discussion of the main question, it may be proper to remove a misapprehension into which Gerrit Smith and Robert Forten seem to have fallen, in respect to what we mean by the term, "strictly construed according to its reading," as used by us in regard to the Constitution. Upon a second reading of these words, we can readily see how easily they can be made to mean more than we intended. What we meant then, and what we would be understood to mean now, is simply this—that the Constitution of the United States, standing alone, and construed *only* in the light of its letter, without reference to the opinions of the men who framed and adopted it, or to the uniform, universal and undeviating practice of the nation under it, from the time of its adoption until now, is not a pro-slavery instrument. Of this admission we are perfectly willing to give our esteemed friend Gerrit Smith, and all who think with him on this subject, the fullest benefit; accompanied, however, with this explanation, that it was made with no view to give the public to understand that we held this construction to be the proper one of that instrument, and that it was drawn out merely because we were unwilling to go before the public on so narrow an issue, and one about which there could be so little said on either side. How a document would appear under one construction, is one thing; but whether the construction be the right one, is quite another and a very different thing. Confounding these two things, has led Gerrit Smith to think too favorably of us, and Robert Forten too unfavorably. We may agree with the Roman Catholic, that the language of Christ, with respect to the sacrament, if construed according to reading, teaches the doctrine of transubstantiation. But the admission is not final, neither are we understood by so doing, to sanction that irrational though literal doctrine. Neither Roman Catholic nor Protestant could attach any importance to such an admission. It would neither afford pleasure to the Catholic, nor pain to the Protestant. Hoping that we have now made ourselves understood on this point, we proceed to the general question.

THE CONSTITUTIONALITY OF SLAVERY

The Constitution of the United States.—What is it? Who made it? For whom and for what was it made? Is it from heaven or from men? How, and in what light are we to understand it? If it be divine, divine light must be our means of understanding it; if human, humanity, with all its vices and crimes, as well as its virtues, must help us to a proper understanding of it. All attempts to explain it in the light of heaven must fail. It is human, and must be explained in the light of those maxims and principles which human beings have laid down as guides to the understanding of all written instruments, covenants, contracts and agreements, emanating from human beings, and to which human beings are parties, both on the first and the second part. It is in such a light that we propose to examine the Constitution; and in this light we hold it to be a most cunningly-devised and wicked compact, demanding the most constant and earnest efforts of the friends of righteous freedom for its complete overthrow. It was "conceived in sin, and shapen in iniquity." But this will be called mere declamation, and assertion—mere "heat without light"—sound and fury signify nothing.—Have it so. Let us then argue the question with all the coolness and clearness of which an unlearned fugitive slave, smarting under the wrongs inflicted by this unholy Union, is capable. We cannot talk "lawyer like" about law—about its emanating from the bosom of God!—about government, and of its seat in the great heart of the Almighty!—nor can we, in connection with such an ugly matter-of-fact looking thing as the United States Constitution, bring ourselves to split hairs about the alleged legal rule of interpretation, which declares that an "act of the Legislature may be set aside when it contravenes natural justice." We have to do with facts, rather than theory. The Constitution is not an abstraction. It is a living, breathing fact, exerting a mighty power over the nation of which it is the bond of Union.

Had the Constitution dropped down from the blue overhanging sky, upon a land uncursed by slavery, and without an interpreter, although some difficulty might have occurred in applying its manifold provisions, yet so cunningly is it framed, that no one would have imagined that it recognized or sanctioned slavery. But having a terrestrial, and not a celestial origin, we find no difficulty in ascertaining its meaning in all the parts which we allege to relate to slavery. Slavery existed before the Constitution, in the very States by whom it was made and adopted.—Slaveholders took a large share in making it. It was made in view of the existence of slavery, and in a manner well calculated to aid and strengthen that heaven-daring crime.

Take, for instance, article 1st, section 2d, to wit: "Representatives and direct taxes shall be apportioned among the several States which may be included within this Union, according to their respective numbers, which shall be determined by adding to the whole number of *free* persons, including those bound to service for a term of years, and including Indians not taxed, *three-fifths of all other persons.*"

A diversity of persons are here described—*persons* bound to service for a *term of years,* Indians not taxed, and three-fifths of *all other persons.* Now, we ask, in the name of common sense, can there be an honest doubt that, in States where there are slaves, that they are included in this basis of representation? To us, it is as plain as the sun in the heavens that this clause does, and was intended to mean, that the slave States should enjoy a representation of their human chattels under this Constitution. Beside, the term free, which is generally, though not always, used as the correlative of slave, "all other persons," settles the question forever that slaves are here included.

It is contended on this point by Lysander Spooner and others, that the words, "all other persons," used in this article of the Constitution, relates *only* to aliens. We deny that the words will bear any such construction. Are we to presume that the Constitution, which so carefully points out a class of persons for exclusion, such as "Indians not taxed," would be silent with respect to another class which it was meant equally to exclude? We have never studied logic, but it does seem to us that such a presumption would be very much like an absurdity. And the absurdity is all the more glaring, when it is remembered that the language used immediately after the words "excluding Indians not taxed," (having done with exclusions) it includes "*all other persons.*" It is as easy to suppose that the Constitution contemplates *including* Indians, (against its express declaration to the contrary,) as it is to suppose that it should be construed to mean the exclusion of slaves from the basis of representation, against the express language, "including all other persons." Where all are included, none remain to be excluded. The reasonings of those who take the opposite view of this clause, appears very much like quibbling, to use no harsher word. One thing is certain about this clause of the Constitution. It is this—that under it, the slave system has enjoyed a large and domineering representation in Congress, which has given laws to the whole Union in regard to slavery, ever since the formation of the government.

Satisfied that the view we have given of this clause of the Constitution is the only sound interpretation of it, we throw at once all those parts and particulars of the instrument which refer to slavery, and constitute what we conceive to be the slaveholding compromises of the Constitution, before the reader, and beg that he will look with candor upon the comments which we propose to make upon them.

"Art. 5th, Sec. 8th.—Congress shall have power to suppress insurrections."

"Art. 1st, Sec. 9th.—The migration or importation of any such persons as any of the States now existing shall think proper to admit, shall not be prohibited by

Congress prior to the year one thousand eight hundred and eight; but a tax or a duty may be imposed, not exceeding ten dollars for each person."

"Art. 4th, Sec. 2d.—No person held to service or labor in one State, escaping into another, shall in consequence of any law or regulation therein, be discharged from such service or labor, but shall be delivered up on claim of the party to whom such service or labor may be due."

"Art. 4th, Sec. 4th.—The United States shall guarantee to every State in this Union a Republican form of Government; and shall protect each of them against invasion; and on application of the Legislature, or of the Executive, (when the Legislature cannot be convened,) against domestic violence."[1]

The first article and ninth section is a full, complete and broad sanction of the slavetrade for twenty years. In this compromise of the Constitution, the parties to it pledged the national arm to protect that infernal trade for twenty years. While all other subjects of commerce were left under the control of Congress, this species of commerce alone was Constitutionally exempted. And why was this the case? Simply because South Carolina and Georgia declared, through their delegates that framed the Constitution, that they would not come into the Union if this traffic in human flesh should be prohibited. Mr. Rutledge, of South Carolina, (a distinguished member of the Convention that framed the Constitution,) said, "if the Convention thinks that North Carolina, South Carolina, and Georgia, will ever agree to the plan, *unless their right to import slaves be untouched,* the expectation is vain." Mr. Pinckney said, South Carolina could never receive the plan, "*if it prohibits the slavetrade.*" In consequence of the determination of these States to stand out of the Union in case the traffic in human flesh should be prohibited, and from one general desire to establish a Union, this ninth section of the first article was adopted, as *a compromise;* and shameful as it is, it is by no means more shameful than others which preceded and succeeded it. The slaveholding South, by that unyielding tenacity and consistency with which they usually contend for their measures, triumphed, and the doughface North was brought to the disgraceful terms in question, just as they have been ever since on all questions touching the subject of slavery.

As a compensation for their base treachery to human freedom and justice, the North were permitted to impose a tax of ten dollars for each person imported, with which to swell the coffers of the national treasury, thus baptising the infant Republic with blood-stained gold.

Art. 4, Sec. 2.—This article was adopted with a view to restoring fugitive slaves to their masters—ambiguous, to be sure, but sufficiently explicit to answer the end sought to be attained. Under it, and in accordance with it, the Congress enacted the atrocious "law of '93," making it penal in a high degree to harbor or shelter the flying fugitive. The whole nation that adopted it, consented to become kidnappers, and the whole land converted into slave-hunting ground.

Art. 4, Sec. 4—Pledges the national arm to protect the slaveholder from *domestic violence,* and is the safeguard of the Southern tyrant against the vengeance of the outraged and plundered slave. Under it, the nation is bound to do the bidding of the slaveholder, to bring out the whole naval and military power of the country, to crush the refractory slaves into obedience to their cruel masters. Thus has the North, under the Constitution, not only consented to form bulwarks around the system of slavery, with all its bloody enormities, to prevent the slave from escape, but has planted its uncounted feet and tremendous weight on the heaving hearts of American bondmen, to prevent them from rising to gain their freedom. Could Pandemonium devise a Union more inhuman, unjust, and affronting to God and man, than this? Yet such is the Union consummated under the Constitution of the United States. It is truly a compact demanding immediate disannulment, and one which, with our view of its wicked requirements, we can never enter.

We might just here drop the pen and the subject, and assume the Constitution to be what we have briefly attempted to prove it to be, radically and essentially pro-slavery, in fact as well as in its tendency; and regard our position to be correct beyond the possibility of an honest doubt, and treat those who differ from us as mere cavillers, bent upon making the worse appear the better reason; or we might anticipate the objections which are supposed to be valid against that position. We are, however, disposed to do neither.—We have too much respect for the men opposed to us to do the former, and have too strong a desire to have those objections put in their most favorable light, to do the latter.—We are prepared to hear all sides, and to give the arguments of our opponents a candid consideration. Where an honest expression of views is allowed, Truth has nothing to fear.

And now if our friend Gerrit Smith desires to be heard on the other side, the columns of the *North Star* are at his service. We can assure him that he cannot have a stronger wish to turn every rightful instrumentality against slavery, than we have; and if the Constitution can be so turned, and he can satisfy us of the fact, we shall readily, gladly and zealously turn our feeble energies in that direction. The case which our friend Gerrit Smith put to us in his letter is a good one, but fails in a most important particular, and that is, *analogy*. The only likeness which we can see in the supposed case of a bargain with Brown, to that of the bargain entered into by the North and the South, is that there is gross dishonesty in both. So far, there is a striking similarity, but no further. The parties that made the Constitution, aimed to cheat and defraud the slave, who was not himself a party to the compact or agreement. It was entered into understandingly on both sides. They both designed to purchase their freedom and safety at the expense of the imbruted slave. The North were willing to become the body guards of slavery—suppressing insurrection—returning fugitive slaves to bondage—importing slaves for twenty years, and as much longer as the Congress should see fit to leave it unprohibited, and virtually to give slaveholders three votes for every five slaves they could plunder from Africa, and all this to form a Union by which to repel invasion, and otherwise promote their interest. No, friend Smith, we are not asked to act the honorable part of *"Judge Douglass"* with respect to this "contract," but to become a guilty party to it, and in reply we say—No!—F. D.

The North Star, March 16, 1849

1. Clauses in Constitution, quoted as in Douglass' editorial.

An important phase of the anti-slavery activity in Rochester was the struggle for the abolition of segregated schools for Negro children. Douglass, the leader of the movement, felt a personal interest in the outcome. The Rochester Board of Education refused to allow his children to enter Public School 15 near his home, and insisted that they travel to the other side of the city to attend the school for Negro children.

Refusing to accept the system of segregated schools, Douglass, in August, 1848, arranged for his daughter, Rosetta, to attend Seward Seminary, a fashionable school for girls in Rochester. . . . [When] Rosetta was asked to leave the school, Douglass . . . did not permit the incident to pass over quietly. In [this] scathing letter . . . he promised that he would use all his powers to proclaim this "infamy" to the nation. Scores of papers reprinted the letter with its blistering conclusion. . . .[1]

Publicly announcing that "*in no emergency*" would he send any child of his to a segregated school, Douglass dispatched Rosetta to a private institution in Albany for two or three years; in 1851, he secured the services of a governess for her and the other children. Meanwhile, he worked unceasingly with Samuel D. Porter and other citizens of Rochester to abolish the separate school system which he called "the question of questions for the colored people of this place."[2]

For eight years Douglass pressed the issue of separate schools in Rochester. In 1857 the campaign bore fruit; the separate schools were abolished and Negro children were permitted to attend the public schools. [II:39–41]

TO H. G. WARNER, ESQ., (Editor of the *Rochester Courier*)

Sir:

My reasons—I will not say my apology, for addressing to you this letter, will become evident, by perusing the following brief statement of facts.

About the middle of August of the present year—deeply desiring to give my daughter, a child between nine and ten years old, the advantages of a good school—and learning that "Seward Seminary" of this city was an institution of that character—I applied to its principal, Miss Tracy, for the admission of my daughter into that Seminary. The principal—after making suitable enquiries into the child's mental qualifications, and informing me of the price of tuition per term, agreed to receive the child into the school at the commencement of the September term. Here we parted. I went home, rejoicing that my child was about to enjoy advantages for improving her mind, and fitting her for a useful and honorable life. I supposed that the principal would be as good as her word—and was more disposed to his belief, when I learned that she was an abolitionist—a woman of religious principles and integrity—and would be faithful in the performance of her promises, as she had been prompt in making them. In all this I have been grievously—if not shamefully disappointed.

While absent from home, on a visit to Cleveland, with a view to advance the cause of education and freedom among my despised fellow countrymen—with whom I am in all respects identified, the September term of the "Seward Seminary" commenced, and my daughter was promptly sent to that school.—But instead of receiving her into the school according to agreement—and as in honor the principal was bound to do, she was merely thrust into a room separate from all other scholars, and in this prison-like solitary confinement received the occasional visits of a teacher appointed to instruct her. On my return home, I found her still going to school, and not knowing the character of the treatment extended to her, I asked with a light heart, as I took her to my side, well, my daughter, how do you get on at the Seminary? She answered with tears in her eyes, "*I get along pretty well, but father, Miss Tracy does not allow me to go into the room with the other scholars because I am colored.*" Stung to the heart's core by this grievous statement, and suppressing my feelings as well as I could, I went immediately to the Seminary to remonstrate with the principal against the cruelty and injustice of treating my child as a criminal on account of her color—subjecting her to solitary confinement because guilty of a skin not colored like her own. In answer to all that I could say against such treatment, I was answered by the principal, that since she promised to receive the child into school, she had consulted with the trustees, (a body of persons I believe unknown to the public,) and that they were opposed to the child's admission to the school—that she thought at first of disregarding their opposition, but when she remembered how much they had done for her in sustaining the institution, she did not feel at liberty to do so; but she thought if I allowed her to remain and be taught separately for a term or more, that the prejudice might be overcome, and the child admitted into the school with the other young ladies and misses. At a loss to know what to do for the best interest of the child, I consulted with Mrs. Douglass and others, and the result of the consultation was, to take my child from the Seminary, as allowing her to remain there in such circumstances, could only serve to degrade her in her own eyes, and those of the other scholars attending the school. Before, however, carrying out my determination to withdraw the child from the Seminary, Miss Tracy, the principal, submitted the question of the child's reception to each scholar individually, and I am sorry to say, in a manner well calculated to rouse their prejudices against her. She told them if there was one objection to receiving her, she should be excluded; and said if any of them felt that she had a prejudice, and that that prejudice needed to be strengthened, that they might have time to whisper among themselves, in order to increase and strengthen that prejudice. To one young lady who voted to receive the child, she said, as if in astonishment; "did you mean to vote so? Are you *accustomed* to black persons?" The young lady stood silent; the question was so extraordinary, and withal so ambiguous, that she knew not what answer to make to it. Despite however, of the unwomanly conduct of the principal, (who, whatever may be her religious faith, has not yet learned the simplest principle of Christianity—do to others as ye would that others should do unto you)—thanks to the uncorruptible virtue of childhood and youth, in the fulness of their affectionate hearts, they welcomed my child among them, to share with them the blessings and privileges of the school; and when asked where she should sit if admitted, several young ladies shouted "By me, by me, by me." After this manifestation of sentiment on the part of the scholars, one would have supposed that all opposition on the part of the principal would have ceased; but this was not the case. The child's admission was subjected to a severer test. Each scholar was then told by the principal, that the question must be submitted to their parents, and that if one parent objected, the child would not be received into the school. The next morning my child went to school as usual, but returned with her books and other materials, saying that one person objected, and that she was therefore excluded from the Seminary.

Now, sir, these are the whole facts, with one important exception, and that fact is, that you are the person, the only person of all the parents sending young ladies and misses to that Seminary, who was hardened and mean enough to take the responsibility of excluding that child from school. I say, to you exclusively belongs the honor or infamy, of attempting to degrade an innocent child by excluding her from the benefit of attending a respectable school.

If this were a private affair, only affecting myself and family, I should possibly allow it to pass without attracting public attention to it; but such is not the case. It is a deliberate attempt to degrade and injure a large class of persons, whose rights and feelings have been the common sport of yourself, and such persons as yourself, for ages, and I think it unwise to allow you to do so with impunity.—Thank God, oppressed and plundered as we are, and have been, we are not without help. We have a press, open and free, and have ample means by which we are able to proclaim our wrongs as a people, and your own infamy, and that proclamation shall be as complete as the means in my power can make it. There is a sufficient amount of liberality in the public mind of Rochester to see that justice is done to all parties, and upon that liberality I rely. The young ladies of the school who saw the child, and had the best means of determining whether her presence in the schoolroom would be offensive or degrading to them, have decided in favor of admitting her, without a dissenting vote. Out of all the parents to whom the question of her admission was submitted, not one, except yourself, objected. You are in a minority of *one*. You may not remain so; there are perhaps others, whom you may corrupt, and make as much like yourself in the blindness of prejudice, as any ordinarily wicked person can be.

But you are still in a minority, and if I mistake not, you will be in a *despised minority*.—You have already done serious injury to Seward Seminary. Three young ladies left the school immediately after the exclusion of my daughter, and I have heard of three more, who had intended to go, but who have now declined going to that institution, because it has given its sanction to that anti-democratic, and ungodly caste. I am also glad to inform you that you have not succeeded as you hoped to do, in depriving my child of the means of a decent education, or the privilege of going to an excellent school. She had not been excluded from Seward Seminary five hours, before she was gladly welcomed into another quite as respectable, and *equally* christian to the one from which she was excluded. She now sits in a school among children as pure, and as white as you or yours, and no one is offended. Now I should like to know how much better are you than me, and how much better your children than mine? We are both worms of the dust, and our children are like us. We differ in color, it is true, (and not much in that respect,) but who is to decide which color is most pleasing to God, or most honorable among men? But I do not wish to waste words or argument on one whom I take to be as destitute of honorable feeling, as he has shown himself full of pride and prejudice.

Frederick Douglass

The North Star, March 30, 1849

1. "No one," observed the *Liberator* in reprinting the letter, "who begins to read the following admirable and manly letter of Mr. Douglass, will fail to finish it." (*Liberator*, Oct. 6, 1848)

2. *The North Star*, Nov. 9, 1849.

COMMENTS ON GERRIT SMITH'S ADDRESS

It will be remembered that Mr. Smith referred us in last week's paper to this address, for his views respecting the Constitutionality of slavery; and virtually said to us, Dispose of these, and if it shall then be necessary, you shall have more. To us, the address is quite unsatisfactory and unsound. About what a government ought to be so far as relates to a crime like slavery, there is no difference of opinion between us. That it is the duty of a government to protect the rights and liberties of its subjects, there is no question; and that that government which fails to do this is extremely guilty, there is equal agreement. What a government ought to do, is one thing; but not the thing germane to the question at issue between Mr. Smith and ourselves. That government ought to be just, merciful, holy, is granted. The question is not, however, what a government ought to be, or to do, but what the government of the United States is *authorized to be, and to do, by the Constitution of the United States.* The two questions should be kept separate, that the simplest may understand, as blending them only leads to confusion.

It is because we hold civil government to be solemnly bound to protect the weak against the strong, the oppressed against the oppressor, the few against the many, and to secure the humblest subject in the full possession of his rights of person and of property, that we utterly abhor and repudiate this government and the Constitution as a dark and damning conspiracy against all the purposes of government. Both its framers and administrators were, and have been until now, little better than a band of pirates.—We would make clean work of both the government and the Constitution, and not amend or force a new construction upon either, contradicted by the whole history of the nation; but would abolish both, and reconstruct a Constitution and a government which shall better answer the ends of justice. To think of good government in a Union with slaveholders, and under a Constitution framed by slaveholders, the practical operation of which for sixty years has been to strengthen, sustain and spread slavery, does seem to us delusive. We are not for mending old clothes with new cloth, or putting new wine into old bottles, but for starting afresh under a new and higher light than our piratical fathers saw, and form a Constitution and government which shall be so clear and explicit that no doubt can be entertained as to its minutest purposes.

That this cannot be truthfully affirmed of our present Constitution, we need not insist upon at this time. Even our friend Smith virtually admits that it would be dangerous to leave the question of the slave's redemption to be decided in the light of the Constitution. The "old tattered parchment" receives no great deference from him after all. Disdaining it altogether, he says, "*Whatever may be said of the lawfulness of slavery, government must abolish it. If it have a Constitution under which it cannot abolish slavery, then it must override the Constitution, and abolish slavery. But whether under or over the Constitution, it must abolish slavery.*" We like this for its whole-souled devotion to a glorious object. It is revolutionary, and looks as much like the fanaticism of Wendell Phillips and William Lloyd Garrison, as if it had been cast in their mould. In plain terms, Mr. Smith is for the abolition of slavery, whether in accordance with, or in violation of, the Constitution; and while the declaration is worthy of his noble heart, we cannot think such of his head. The doctrine laid down in this declaration, runs through the whole address, and gives it a vigor and warmth from beginning to end. We shall therefore express a few thoughts upon it.

It will be seen that the doctrine in question makes the government superior to, and independent of, the Constitution, which is the very charter of the government, and without which the government is nothing better than a lawless mob, acting without any other or higher authority than its own convictions or impulses as to what is right or wrong. If this doctrine be sound, it is a mere farce to have a written Constitution at all; for if the government can override and violate its Constitution in one point, it may do so in all.—There is no limit, or safety, or certainty. If it can abolish slavery in violation of the Constitution, because it conflicts with the moral sentiments of the majority, the same may be done in other cases for the same reason. All the safe-guards of that instrument, providing for its own interpretation and its own amendment, are worthless and needless, if this doctrine be true, and government will merely be the voice of an ever-shifting majority, be that good or evil.

Among the causes which have convulsed and revolutionized Europe during the past year, none has been more prominent or effective than the want and rational desire of the people for Constitutional government—not an unwritten, but a written Constitution, accurately defining the powers of government. But these revolutions and Constitutions would be a mere mockery, if government has a character independent of, and powers superior to the Constitution creating it. In the light of such doctrine, Constitutions are impotent and useless, and not worth the trouble of making them, to say nothing of the blood and treasure expended in their support. We hold this doctrine to be radically unsound, (and although brought forward to promote a noble object,) its tendency immoral. We say to our friend Smith, and to all others who sympathize with his views on this subject, If you profess to hold to the Constitution, maintain its provisions. If you cannot, in accordance with your conscience, perform its requirements, or submit to its limitations, then we say, it is your plain duty to come out from it, forsake it, repudiate it, abandon it, do anything rather than seem to be in harmony with an instrument which you would set aside and destroy. Do not, for the sake of honesty and truth, solemnly swear to protect and defend an instrument which it is your firm and settled purpose to disregard and violate in any one particular. Such a course would unsettle all confidence, invert all the principles of trust and reliance which bind society together, and leave mankind to all the horrors of anarchy, and all the confusion of Babel. We hold in respect to this, as the apostle held of old in respect to another Constitution—"They that be under the law, are bound to do the things contained in the law." We repudiate the law, and the things contained in it, while friend Smith holds to the law, but makes it subject to the understanding of right. But, says Mr. Smith—

> "Civil Government is to protect rights; and that it might as well, be openly repudiating its functions, and destroying its very existence, as to be giving countenance to searches after authorities for destroying rights. Laws, which interpret, define, secure rights, Government is to respect: and laws, which mistakingly, yet honestly, aim at this end, it is not to despise. But laws, which are enacted to destroy rights, it should trample under foot,—for, to say nothing worse of them, they are a gross insult upon it, inasmuch as they are a shameless attempt to turn it from good to evil, and from its just and Heaven-intended uses, to uses of a diametrically opposite character."

Here again, the argument goes to the extent of assuming, that civil government in this country has a separate existence from the Constitution, and, as if the Constitution were not the supreme law of the land, and that the government can consistently overthrow the Constitution whenever it shall think proper to do so. In answer to this statement, it is enough to say that the government of the United States is limited in its powers and action by the Constitution, and that beyond those limits it cannot go, by any pretext whatever; and that the Supreme Court, the appointed agent to decide the meaning of that instrument, has only to decide a law to be unconstitutional, and it is null and void.—It may indeed be said, that the Supreme Court of the United States has no right to legalize what is unjust and in derogation or against human freedom; but the answer is, that that is legal in this country which is Constitutional, and that the Supreme Court has no conscience above the Constitution of the United States, and certainly no power to set that instrument aside, either by declaring it to be null and void, or wrest it from its true intent and meaning, by a class of rules unknown and unsustained by a single precedent in this country.

As to what Mr. Smith says of determining the meaning of the Constitution by its letter alone, and disregarding as utterly worthless the intentions of the framers of that instrument, it may require consideration when he gives us some fixed and settled legal rules sustaining his views on this point. Such rules may exist, but we have not yet seen them; and until we do, we shall continue to understand the Constitution not only in the light of its letter, but in view of its history, the meaning attached to it by its framers, the men who adopted it, and the circumstances in which it was adopted. We have not read law very extensively, but so far as we have read, we have found many rules of interpretation favoring this mode of understanding the Constitution of the United States, and none against it, though there may be such.

It can scarcely be necessary, after what we have already said, to spend much time upon the following extraordinary declaration of Mr. Smith, respecting the Constitution, in which he declares that it "is drawn up with the intelligent and steadfast purpose of having it serve and be forever fully and gloriously identified with the cause of liberty, republicanism and equal rights, must of necessity be shut against the claims and pretensions of slavery." That it was drawn up with the purpose of serving the cause of the white man's liberty, is true; but that it was meant to serve the cause of the black man's liberty, is false. That a Constitution so drawn, must necessarily be shut against the claims of slavery, is an error. We are not deeply skilled in the science of human language, and use language in the sense in which it is generally used, rather than scientifically, and we do know that "Liberty, Republicanism, and Equal Rights," words constantly on the lips of this nation, are deemed to be no more hostile to Negro slavery, than the same words, when used by the Greeks, were supposed to be against the enslavement of the Helots. Ours is not the business of a lexicographer, but to receive the idea meant to be conveyed by the language of those who use it, and condemn or approve accordingly.

In the letter of Mr. Smith which we published last week, he assumes that the material thing for us to prove, in order to establish the wrongfulness of voting and acting under the United States Constitution, is, that the Federal Government has no right to abolish slavery under that instrument. With all deference, we must say, we see no such necessity laid upon us. We might, for argument's sake, grant all that Mr. Smith claims as to the power of the Federal Government to abolish slavery under the Constitution, and yet hold, as we certainly do hold, that it is wrong to vote and take office under the Constitution. It is not enough that a man can demonstrate that his plan will abolish slavery, to satisfy us that his plan is the right and best one to be adopted. Slavery might be abolished by the aid of a foreign arm; but shall we therefore invoke that aid? We might, to feed the hungry and clothe the naked, break into the house of Mr. Smith and steal the wherewithal to do these things, but the question of the rightfulness of such conduct would be still open. If there is one Christian principle more firmly fixed in our heart than another, it is this, that it is wrong to do evil that good may come; and if there is one heresy more to be guarded against than another, it is the doctrine that the end justifies the means. We say, therefore, that it is not incumbent upon us to show that, by a forced and latitudinarian construction of the Constitution, Congress may not abolish slavery in all the slaveholding States, in order to establish the doctrine which we lay down and justify the course which we feel bound to pursue in regard to voting under the Constitution of the United States. It is enough for us to know that the Constitution requires of those who are parties to it to return the fugitive slave to the house of bondage, and to shoot down the slave if he rises to gain his freedom, to justify us in repudiating and forever casting from us, as a covenant with death, the American Constitution.

Of course those who regard the Constitution in the light that Mr. Smith does, are bound by their convictions of duty to pursue an opposite course; and we candidly confess that, could we see the Constitution as they do, we should not be slow in using the ballot-box against the system of slavery, or urging others to do so. But we have learned enough of the elements of moral power, to know that a man is lame, impotent, and worse than weak, when he ceases to regard the clear convictions of his understanding, to accomplish anything, no matter how desirable that thing may be. We shall therefore continue to denounce the Constitution and government of the United States as a most foul and bloody conspiracy against the rights of three millions of enslaved and imbruted men; for such is the conviction of our conscience in respect to both the Constitution and the government. Down with both, for it is not fit that either should exist!—F. D.

The North Star, March 30, 1849

It was Douglass' firm conviction that a Negro leader should take issue with every case encountered of prejudice against color. The readers of his paper knew that the editor applied this principle, for they regularly came upon lengthy accounts describing Douglass' battles against segregation. . . . The frequent appearance of such reports . . . gave courage to large sections of the Negro population in the North and made them more determined to combat segregation wherever they met it. [I:96–97]

COLORPHOBIA IN NEW YORK!

The fifth of May will long be remembered as the most trying day ever experienced by the unfortunate victims of colorphobia in the city of New York. The disease was never more malignant or general than on that day. The streets were literally crowded with persons of all classes afflicted with this terrible malady. Whole omnibus loads were attacked at the same moment, and their hideous and unearthly howls were truly distressing, excruciating. It will be impossible to describe, or give the reader any correct idea either of the extent of the disease or the agony it seemed to occasion. Like most epidemics, its chief havoc was among the baser sort. The suffering here was fearful and intense. If the genteel suffered from the plague, they managed to suppress and control their feelings better than what are called the "lower orders." But, even here, there could be no successful concealment. The strange plague defied all concealment, and would show itself in spite of veils, white pocket handkerchiefs, parasols, hats, bonnets and umbrellas. In the refined the presence of the plague might be seen by a distortion of the countenance, a red and furious look about the cheek, a singular turn up of the nose, and a *"lower me!"* expression of the eyes.

Among the low and vulgar the symptoms were different;—the hand clinched, head shaking, teeth grating, hysteric yells and horrid imprecation, marked the presence of the disease and the agony of the miserable creatures who were its unfortunate victims. Persons who, at a distance of thirty or forty yards, appeared the very pictures of health, were found, on a nearer approach, most horribly cut and marred.

But the effect upon the outward man was not half so strange and dreadful as that upon the mind. Here all was utter ruin. Gough's description of "delirium tremens" would not be much out of place in describing one haunted and afflicted with colorphobia. Monsters, goblins, demons, snakes, lizards and scorpions—all that was foul, strange and loathsome—seized upon their bewildered imaginations. Pointing with outstretched arm towards us, its victims would exclaim, as if startled by some terrible sight—"Look! look!" "Where?" "Ah, what?" "Why?" "Why, don't you see?" "See what?" "Why, that BLACK! black! *black!*" Then, with eyes turned up in horror, they would exclaim in the most unearthly manner, and start off in a furious gallop—running all around us, and gazing at us, as if they would read our very hearts. The whole scene was deeply afflicting and terrible.

But to the cause of this wide-spread plague, or rather the manifestation of it. We think it can all be made plain to the dullest comprehension. There had arrived in New York, a few days previous, two *English* Ladies, from London—friends of Frederick Douglass—and had taken apartments at the Franklin House, Broadway; and were not only called upon at that Hotel by Mr. Douglass, but really allowed themselves to take his arm, and to walk many times up and down Broadway, in broad-day light, when that great thoroughfare was crowded with pure American ladies and gentlemen. Such an open, glaring outrage upon *pure American* tastes had never before been perpetrated. Two ladies, elegantly attired, educated, and of the most approved manners, faultless in appearance and position, actually walking, and leaning upon the arm of a person, with a skin not colored like their own! Oh! monstrous! Was it not enough to cause the very stones to leap up with indignation from the pavement! and to "stir them up to mutiny and rage"? More and worse still, these ladies appeared wholly indifferent to, and oblivious of, all the indignation and fury going on about them; but walked, talked and acted as though nothing unusual was passing. In a word, they seemed to forget that they were in the greatest Commercial Emporium of this, the mightiest Nation in the world, and to act as though they had been in the paltry city of London!! instead of New York. What could they have been thinking about? How strange that they had not made themselves acquainted with the institutions and customs of the great Nation, upon whose sacred soil they were *allowed* to land? How singular that their friends had not warned them against such a monstrous outrage upon the established customs of this, the "*freest*" country in the world? They certainly must have been deceived. It is impossible "that nature so could err." "Charms, conjuration—mighty magic," must have bewildered and misled them. They would have been kindly received and hospitably entertained by some of the most respectable and refined families in the city of New York; but, with a strange hallucination, they preferred to identify themselves with the most despised and injured portion of all the people of America—and thus to make themselves of no reputation, and cut themselves off from all sympathy and attention of the highly favored and accomplished sons and daughters of America. Before quitting this subject, we wish to call attention to certain singular inconsistencies connected with the development of the feeling, called (erroneously) prejudice against color. The first is this. The poor creatures who seemed most disturbed by the fact that these ladies walked through the streets of New York in company with a colored man, felt in no wise shocked at seeing ladies seated in their gilded carriages, with colored persons seated near them, driving their horses and otherwise assisting such ladies. All this was perfectly right. They were in the capacity of servants. Hence New York toadyism is rather pleased than disgusted. It is not with colored servants that New York loafers are displeased; but with colored *gentlemen*. It is with the colored man as a gentleman that they feel the most intense displeasure. They cannot bear it, and they must pour out their pent-up wrath, whenever an opportunity is afforded for doing so.

In this same Franklin Hotel, in which we could not be allowed to dine on account of our color, we saw a large number of colored waiters in the nearest proximity to white gentlemen and ladies, without offence.

We, however, tire of this subject. This prejudice is so unjust, unnatural and irrational, that ridicule and indignation seem to be the only weapons with which to assail it.

Our friends informed us that when they landed, they were assured that they had reached the shores of a free country, and were congratulated upon that fact. But they had scarcely reached the hotel, when they were informed that a friend of theirs, who was not deemed unfit to be associated with in London, and who would have been kindly received at the best hotels in that city, and in Paris, would not be allowed to take dinner with them at the Franklin Hotel, in the city of New York. In this free country one is not permitted to choose and enjoy the society of his friends, without being subjected to innumerable insults and annoyances.

We shall not, however, despair on this point. A marked improvement has already taken place in the manner of treating colored travelers, and the change is going on still. Nothing, however, facilitates this more than such examples of fidelity to principle, and indifference to a corrupt and brutal public opinion, as is presented in the conduct of these two English ladies, and others. This prejudice must be removed; and the way for abolitionists and colored persons to remove it, is to act as though it did not exist, and to associate with their fellow creatures irrespective of all complexional differences. We have marked out this path for ourselves, and we mean to pursue it at all hazards.—F. D.

The North Star, May 25, 1849

TO CAPT. THOMAS AULD, FORMERLY MY MASTER
No. 4 Alexander St., Rochester, September 3d, 1849

Dear Sir:

I propose to celebrate this, the 11th anniversary of my escape from your dominion, by addressing to you a friendly epistle on the subject of slavery.

I do this partly with a view to the fulfilment of a promise I made you on this day one year ago, and partly to neutralize certain charges which I then brought against you.

Ungrateful and unjust as you, perhaps, deem me, I should despise myself if I could wilfully malign the character even of a slaveholder; and if, at any time, I have appeared to you guilty of such conduct, you have greatly misapprehended me. I can say, with a clear conscience, in all that I have ever written or spoken respecting yourself, I have tried to remember that, though I am beyond your power and control, I am still accountable to our common Father and Judge, in the sight of whom I believe that I stand acquitted of all intentional misrepresentation against you. Of course, I said many hard things respecting yourself; but all has been based upon what I knew of you at the time I was a slave in your family. Of the past, therefore, I have nothing to take back; but information concerning you and your household, lately received, makes it unjust and unkind for me to continue the style of remark, in regard to your character, which I primarily adopted.

I have been told by a person intimately acquainted with your affairs, and upon whose word I can rely, that you have ceased to be a slaveholder, and have emancipated all your slaves, except my poor old grandmother, who is now too old to sustain herself in freedom; and that you have taken her from the desolate hut in which she formerly lived, into your own kitchen, and are providing for her in a manner becoming a man and a Christian.

This, sir, is good news; it is all the more gratifying to me, since it deprives the pro-slavery public of the North of what they deem a powerful argument against me, and the abolitionists generally. It proves that the agitation of the subject of slavery does not hinder, if it does not help, the emancipation of slaves at the South. I have been frequently told that my course would have an unfavorable influence upon the condition of my friends and relatives in your possession; and the common argument against abolitionists may be stated as follows: Let slaveholders alone, and they will emancipate their slaves; and that agitation only retards the progress of the slave's liberation. It is alleged that the slaveholder is induced to clutch more firmly what is attempted to be wrested from him. To this argument, your case is a plain contradiction. If the effect of anti-slavery were such as is thus alleged, you would have been among the first to have experienced it; for few slaveholders in this land have had a larger share of public exposure and denunciation than yourself; and this, too, from a quarter most calculated to annoy, and to provoke resentment. All this, however, has not prevented you from nobly discharging the high duty you owed alike to God and to the slaves in your possession. I congratulate you warmly, and I rejoice most sincerely, that you have been able, against all the suggestions of self-interest, of pride, and of love of power, to perform this act of pure justice and humanity. It has greatly increased my faith in man, and in the *latent virtue* even of slaveholders. I say *latent virtue,* not because I think slaveholders are worse than all other men, but because, such are the power and influence of education and habit upon even the best constituted minds, that they paralyze and disorder, if not destroy their moral energy; and of all persons in the world, slaveholders are in the most unfavorable position for retaining their power. It would be easy for me to give you the reason of this, but you may be presumed to know it already.

Born and brought up in the presence and under the influence of a system which at once strikes at the very foundation of morals, by denying—if not the existence of God—the equal brotherhood of mankind, by degrading one part of the human family to the condition of brutes, and by reversing all right ideas of justice and of brotherly kindness, it is almost impossible that one so environed can greatly grow in virtuous rectitude.

You, however, sir, have risen superior to these unhallowed influences, and have added another striking proof to those already existing, that the heart of the slaveholder is still within the reach of the truth, and that to him the duty of letting "the oppressed go free," is not in vain.

I shall no longer regard you as an enemy to freedom, nor to myself—but shall hail you as a friend to both.—Before doing so, however, I have one reasonable request to make of you, with which you will, I hope, comply. It is thus: That you make your conversion to anti-slavery known to the world, by precept as well as example. A publication of the facts relating to the emancipation of the slaves, with the reasons that have led you to this humane act, would doubtless prove highly beneficial to the cause of freedom generally—at the same time that it would place yourself in that high estimation of the public mind to which your generous conduct justly entitles you. I think you have no right to put your candle under a bushel. Your case is different in many respects from that of most repentant slaveholders. You have been publicly and peculiarly exposed before the world for being a slaveholder; and, since you have ceased to be such, a just regard for your own standing among men, as well as a desire to promote the happiness of a deeply injured people, requires you to make known your sentiments on this important subject. It would be truly an interesting and a glorious spectacle to see *master* and *slave*, hand in hand, laboring together for the overthrow of American slavery. I am sure that such an example would tell with thrilling effect upon the public mind of this section. We have already had the example of slaves and slaveholders side by side battling for freedom; but we yet lack a master working by the side of his former slave on the anti-slavery platform. You have it in your power to supply this deficiency; and if you can bring yourself to do so, you will attain a larger degree of happiness for yourself, and will confer a greater blessing on the cause of freedom, than you have already done by the generous act of emancipating your own slaves. With the example before me, I shall not despair of yet having the pleasure of giving you the right hand of fellowship on the anti-slavery platform.

Before closing the present letter, I wish to set you right about a matter which is, perhaps, of small importance to yourself, but is of considerable consequence to me.

In your letter, written three years ago, to Mr. A. C. C. Thompson, of Wilmington, respecting the validity of my narrative, you complained that I failed to mention your intention to emancipate me at the age of 25. The reason of this failure is as follows: You will remember that your promise to emancipate me preceded my first attempt to escape; and that you then told me that you would have emancipated me, had I not made the attempt in question. If you ask me why I distrusted your promise in the first instance, I could give you many reasons; but the one that weighed most with me was the passage of a law in Maryland, throwing obstructions in the way of emancipation; and I had heard you refer to that law as an excuse for continuing your slaves in bondage; and, supposing the obstructions alluded to might prove insuperable barriers to my freedom, I resolved upon flight as the only alternative left me short of a life of slavery. I hope this explanation will be satisfactory. I do not regret what I have done, but rather rejoice in it, as well for your sake as mine. Nevertheless, I wish to be fairly understood, and have, therefore, made the explanation.

I shall here conclude this letter, by again expressing my sincere gratitude at the magnanimous deed with which your name is now associated—and by repeating the ardent hope that you will publicly identify yourself with the holy cause of freedom, to which, since I left your service, I have been most unremittingly devoting myself.

I am, Dear Sir, very respectfully yours,

Frederick Douglass

The *Liberator*, September 14, 1849

GOVERNMENT AND ITS SUBJECTS

It has long been regarded as the dictate of wisdom, by sagacious legislators, that a government should conciliate, as far as possible, every class of its subjects. It is always deemed unpardonable folly, and flagrant wickedness, for any government needlessly to afflict and insult a portion of its people. Governments are, either exceedingly strong, or exceedingly weak; and that government is strongest which has the fewest foes. This is peculiarly true of our own; it, of all others, should make friends with its subjects, and with every class of its subjects, for the day may come when it will need them all. It is not to be disguised that, in the matter of slave-holding, our nation stands before the world, preeminent in infamy; that the existence of slavery, in this country, is looked upon by other nations, as the peculiar weakness, as well as the crime, of the American people; and it is quite easy to perceive that, in the event of a conflict between this and any European power, this vulnerable point would be the first to be attacked. The colored people of this country would be counted as the natural allies of any power which should inscribe on its banners, *Liberty for the black, as well as for the white man.*

But with these truths so obvious to common sense before them, our legislators appear to take the utmost pleasure in wantonly displaying their contempt for the rights and feelings of the growing colored population of the United States. It would be impossible for a government to devise a policy better calculated to make itself the object of hatred than that adopted by our government toward its free colored people; to make us detest the land of our birth— to abhor the government under which we live—and to welcome the approach of an invading enemy as our only salvation, would seem to be the animating spirit and purpose of all the legislative enactments of the country with respect to us. With all its boasted wisdom and dignity, it does not hesitate to use every opportunity of persecuting, insulting and assailing the weakest, and most defenceless part of its subjects or citizens. It acts towards us as though the highest crime we could commit is that of patriotism; and all manner of insult, neglect and contempt, are necessary to prevent the commission of this crime on our part. Our thoughts have been turned in this direction by the contemptible meanness of our present Secretary of State, in refusing to grant to William W. Brown the usual passport granted to citizens about to travel in foreign countries. Mr. Brown remarks (in a recent letter to Mr. Garrison,) that one of his fellow passengers to Europe, was accompanied by a colored servant, and that this servant had with him a regular passport, signed by the Secretary of State, Mr. Buchanan.

This fact presents the American government in its true light. It has no objection whatever to extend its protection to colored servants, but it is resolved, on no occasion, to grant protection to colored gentlemen. A colored man who travels for the benefit of a white man, will have thrown over him the shield and panoply of the United States; but, if he travels for his own profit or pleasure, he forfeits all the immunities of an American citizen. The government in this particular, fairly reflects the lights and shades of the whole American mind; as appendages to white men we are universally esteemed; as independent and responsible men we are universally despised.

In keeping with this spirit, and in pursuance of this policy, the colored man is not permitted to carry a United States' mail bag across the street, nor hand it from a stage driver to a post-master. In the navy, no matter how great may be his talents, skill and acquirements—no matter how daring, heroic, and patriotic he may be, he is forbidden, by the government, to rise above the office of a cook, or a steward, under the flag of the United States.

The colored man, if a slave, may travel in company with his master, into any state or territory in the Union; but if he be a free man, he may not even visit the capitol of the nation (which he helps to support by his taxes), without the liability of being cast into prison, kept there for months together, and then taken out, and sold like a beast of burden, under the auctioneer's hammer, for his jail fees. Besides the gross frauds and ruinous wrongs, heaped, with scandalous profusion, on the heads of the colored people, by the government, the white population at large, (saints and sinners,) are constantly exerting their skill and ingenuity in devising schemes which serve to embitter our lot, and to destroy our happiness.

From places of instruction and amusement, open to all other nations under the sun, we are *excluded;* from the cabins of steamboats, and the tables of Hotels (which are free to English, Irish, Dutch, Scotch and also to the most rude Hoosier of the West) we are *excluded;* from the ecclesiastical convention, and the political caucus, we are generally *excluded;* from the bar and the jury-box of our country we are *excluded;* from respectable trades and employments, and from nearly all the avenues to wealth and power, we are *excluded;* from the Lyceum Hall and the common school, the sources of light and education, we are as a people *excluded.* Meanwhile societies are organized under the guise of philanthropy and religion, whose chief business it is to propagate the most malignant slanders against us, and to keep up in the public mind a violent animosity between us and our white fellow-citizens. Upon this the government smiles with approbation, and exerts its utmost powers to execute the behests of this unnatural and cruel prejudice. What is this but the most discreditable disregard of sound political wisdom, to say nothing of the dictates of justice and magnanimity? Can the colored man be expected to entertain for such a government any feelings but those of intense hatred? Or can he be expected to do other than to seize the first moment which shall promise him success to gratify his vengeance? To apprehend that he would not do so would evince the most deplorable ignorance of the elements of human nature.

We warn the American people, and the American Government to be wise in their day and generation. The time may come that those whom they now despise and hate, may be needed. Those compelled foes may, by and by be wanted as friends. America cannot always sit, as a queen, in peace and repose. Prouder and stronger governments than hers have been shattered by the bolts of the wrath of a *just God*. We beseech her to have a care how she goads the *sable oppressed* in the land. We warn her in the name of retribution, to look to her ways, for in an evil hour those hands that have been engaged in beautifying and adorning the fair fields of our country, may yet become the instruments of spreading desolation, devastation, and death throughout our borders.—F. D.

The North Star, November 9, 1849

THE DESTINY OF COLORED AMERICANS

It is impossible to settle, by the light of the present, and by the experience of the past, any thing, definitely and absolutely, as to the future condition of the colored people of this country; but, so far as present indications determine, it is clear that this land must continue to be the home of the colored man so long as it remains the abode of civilization and religion. For more than two hundred years we have been identified with its soil, its products, and its institutions; under the sternest and bitterest circumstances of slavery and oppression—under the lash of Slavery at the South—under the sting of prejudice and malice at the North—and under hardships the most unfavorable to existence and population, we have lived, and continue to live and increase. The persecuted red man of the forest, the original owner of the soil, has, step by step, retreated from the Atlantic lakes and rivers; escaping, as it were, before the footsteps of the white man, and gradually disappearing from the face of the country. He looks upon the steamboats, the railroads, and canals, cutting and crossing his former hunting grounds; and upon the ploughshare, throwing up the bones of his venerable ancestors, and beholds his glory departing—and his heart sickens at the desolation. He spurns the civilization—he hates the race which has despoiled him, and unable to measure arms with his superior foe, he dies.

Not so with the black man. More unlike the European in form, feature and color—called to endure greater hardships, injuries and insults than those to which the Indians have been subjected, he yet lives and prospers under every disadvantage. Long have his enemies sought to expatriate him, and to teach his children that this is not their home, but in spite of all their cunning schemes, and subtle contrivances, his footprints yet mark the soil of his birth, and he gives every indication that America will, for ever, remain the home of his posterity. We deem it a settled point that the destiny of the colored man is bound up with that of the white people of this country; be the destiny of the latter what it may.

It is idle—worse than idle, ever to think of our expatriation, or removal. The history of the colonization society must extinguish all such speculations. We are rapidly filling up the number of four millions; and all the gold of California combined, would be insufficient to defray the expenses attending our colonization. We are, as laborers, too essential to the interests of our white fellow-countrymen, to make a very grand effort to drive us from this country among probable events.

While labor is needed, the laborer cannot fail to be valued; and although passion and prejudice may sometimes vociferate against us, and demand our expulsion, such efforts will only be spasmodic, and can never prevail against the sober second thought of self-interest. *We are here,* and here we are likely to be. To imagine that we shall ever be eradicated is absurd and ridiculous. We can be remodified, changed, and assimilated, but never extinguished. We repeat, therefore, that *we are here;* and that this is *our* country; and the question for the philosophers and statesmen of the land ought to be, What principles should dictate the policy of the action towards us? We shall neither die out, nor be driven out; but shall go with this people, either as a testimony against them, or as an evidence in their favor throughout their generations. We are clearly on their hands, and must remain there for ever. All this we say for the benefit of those who hate the Negro more than they love their country. In an article, under the caption of "Government and its Subjects," (published in our last week's paper,) we called attention to the unwise, as well as the unjust policy usually adopted, by our Government, towards its colored citizens. We would continue to direct attention to that policy, and in our humble way, we would remonstrate against it, as fraught with evil to the white man, as well as to his victim.

The white man's happiness cannot be purchased by the black man's misery. Virtue cannot prevail among the white people, by its destruction among the black people, who form a part of the whole community. It is evident that white and black "must fall or flourish together." In the light of this great truth, laws ought to be enacted, and institutions established—all distinctions, founded on complexion, ought to be repealed, repudiated, and for ever abolished—and every right, privilege, and immunity, now enjoyed by the white man, ought to be as freely granted to the man of color.

Where "knowledge is power," that nation is the most powerful which has the largest population of intelligent men; for a nation to cramp, and circumscribe the mental faculties of a class of its inhabitants, is as unwise as it is cruel, since it, in the same proportion, sacrifices its power and happiness. The American people, in the light of this reasoning, are, at this moment, in obedience to their pride and folly, (we say nothing of the wickedness of the act,) wasting one sixth part of the energies of the entire nation by transforming three millions of its men into beasts of burden.—What a loss to industry, skill, invention, (to say nothing of its foul and corrupting influence,) is *Slavery!* How it ties the hand, cramps the mind, darkens the understanding, and paralyses the whole man! Nothing is more evident to a man who reasons at all, than that America is acting an irrational part in continuing the slave system at the South, and in oppressing its free colored citizens at the North. Regarding the nation as an individual, the act of enslaving and oppressing thus, is as wild and senseless as it would be for Nicholas to order the amputation of the right arm of every Russian soldier before engaging in a war with France. We again repeat that Slavery is the peculiar weakness of America, as well as its peculiar crime; and the day may yet come when this visionary and oft repeated declaration will be found to contain a great truth.—F. D.

The North Star, November 16, 1849

PART THREE

From the Compromise of 1850 to
the Kansas-Nebraska Act of 1854

Long and assiduously have the derided and contemned advocates of emancipation labored in the work of disseminating their principles and opinions at the North; and anxiously have they looked forward to the period when these opinions and principles should be brought before the entire nation. That time has now arrived. Notwithstanding that the slaveholders of the South, with equal assiduity have been active in originating schemes, with a view to stay the progress of these opinions and principles, and in fortifying the system of slavery against attack, by trampling upon the right of petition, by suppressing free discussion, by fettering the American press, by gagging the American pulpit, and by enlarging their borders,—the judgment-day of slavery is dawning—the devices of the oppressor, thanks to the God of the oppressed, have most signally failed—the "wisdom of the crafty" has been confounded, and the "counsels of the ungodly have been brought to nought;" the great movement for freedom has rolled onward with a speed accelerated in proportion to the amount of opposition arrayed against it. This should be a time of rejoicing with the humble laborers in the cause. We speak advisedly, and in no canting spirit, when we term this cause holy; for if to have triumphed over foes mighty and multitudinous—to have removed mountains of difficulty,—if to have, with one, "chased a thousand," and with two, to have "put ten thousand to flight," be any evidence of the guardianship of Heaven, we can say, with one of old, "Truly the Lord is with us." This dreaded agitation, so feeble in its commencement, now rocks the land, from end to end. The vexed question of slavery has forced itself into the councils of the nation; and, like the rod of the Hebrew deliverer, it has swallowed up all other topics. Scarcely a day has passed since the meeting of the present Congress, but that the hated subject has been the theme of fiery discourse. Our entire exchange comes to us laden with leaders and speeches on this once obscure and strictly avoided topic. The public mind has reached a point of interest and excitement unprecedented. The South demands the extension of slavery into the new territories; while the North sternly insists upon its exclusion; but words pass on both sides, and the waves of agitation rise higher and higher. It is at this juncture that the crafty Clay, with his characteristic temper and skill, has thrown himself on the turbid waters of debate. He comes, as he is wont to do, with that soft and gentle diction, and in that spirit of conciliation and compromise, for which he has been so long and so highly distinguished. He wishes, as usual, to revive the expiring embers of patriotism—to soothe all asperities—to allay all sectional jealousies, and to knit the nation into a firmer bond of union. He has presented a string of resolutions to the Senate, for the purpose, (to use his own language,) of making *"an amicable arrangement of all questions in controversy between the free and the slave States, growing out of the subject of slavery."*[1] This object, it must be admitted, is a comprehensive one; and it displays no small ambition that any one man should essay to accomplish it. But let this pass. Will he succeed? is the question. We think not. The plan which Mr. Clay proposes, like all Southern compromises, gives everything to Liberty, *in words,* and secures everything to Slavery, *in deeds.* He is most generous in giving away that which he does not possess; but is never betrayed into the weakness of bestowing that which he has the power to retain. The first Resolution of his compromise goes the enormous length of proposing the admission of California into the Union, without forcing her to open her golden domain to the foul and corrupting system of slavery. What a magnificent concession is here! Ought not every Northern man to bow, with grateful emotion, to the magnanimous man by whom it is proffered? This liberal and generous concession, to be fully appreciated, must be viewed in the light of certain notorious facts. The first fact is, that California has already, with singular unanimity, adopted a constitution which excludes for ever the foul system of bondage from her borders. The next fact is, that she has already received, from the present Administration of the United States government, especial marks of its approbation. Another fact is, with the growing population of California, her vast extent and boundless wealth, she is, of herself sufficiently strong to command respect, without asking the favor of any; and the last and most important fact of all is, that the North has the disposition and power to admit her into the Union, with or without the generous compromise, so nobly and complacently presented by that father of compromises, Henry Clay. Mr. Clay's proffered liberality is about as noble as that of a highwayman, who, when in the power of a traveller, and on his way to prison, proposes a consultation, and offers to settle the unhappy difficulty which has occurred between himself and the latter, by accepting the half of the contents of his purse, assuring him, at the same time, that IF his pistol had NOT missed fire, he might have possessed himself of the whole. This assuming to concede, as a mark of liberality, the right of a State to enter this Union, without being compelled to have the foul curse of slavery fastened upon her, would be about as ridiculous as it is disgraceful; but that the slightest token of concession, on the part of the South to the North, is hailed by so many doughfaces with marks of humble gratitude! The impudence of slaveholders exceeds everything! They talk about *the rights* (!!) of slavery, just as if it were possible for slavery to have rights. The *right* to introduce it into the new territories! the constitutional right, &c. Shame on such insolent pretensions! Slavery has NO RIGHTS. It is a foul and damning outrage upon all rights, and has no right to exist anywhere, in or out of the territories. "The earth is the Lord's," and "righteousness" should "cover it;" and he who concedes any part of it to the introduction of slavery, is an enemy to God, an invader of his dominion, and a rebel against his government.

The next resolution of Mr. Clay adopts practically, the non-intervention doctrine so universally held up to ridicule by the Whig press of the North, as the offspring of that prince of sycophants, Gen. Cass. They are as follows:

> "Resolved, that the western boundary of the State of Texas, ought to be fixed on the Rio del Norte, commencing one marine league from its mouth, and running up that river to the Southern line of New Mexico; thence with that line eastwardly, and so continuing in the same direction, to the line established between the United States and Spain, excluding any portion of New Mexico, whether lying on the east or west of that river.
>
> "Resolved, That it be proposed to the State of Texas, that the United States will provide for the payment of all that portion of the legitimate and *bona fide* public debt of that State, contracted prior to its annexation to the United States, and for which the

duties on foreign imports were pledged by the said State to its creditors, not exceeding the sum of $———, in consideration of the said duties so pledged having been no longer applicable to that object, after the said annexation, but having thenceforward become payable to the United States; and upon the condition, also, that the State of Texas shall, by some solemn and authentic act of her Legislature, or of a Convention, relinquish to the United States any claim which it has to any part of New Mexico."

No comments on the foregoing resolutions, are needed from us. We put them on record merely as links in the chain of this compromise. It will be seen that Mr. Clay does not concede the justice of the claims which Texas has recently set up, for a large portion of New Mexico. So far so good.

The fifth and sixth resolutions are as follows:

"Resolved, That it is inexpedient to abolish Slavery in the District of Columbia, while that institution continues to exist in the State of Maryland, without the consent of that State, without the consent of the people of the District, and without just compensation to the owners of slaves within the District.

"But, Resolved, That it is expedient to prohibit within the District the slave-trade, in slaves brought into it from States or places beyond the limits of the District, either to be sold therein as merchandize, or to be transported to other markets without the District of Columbia."

If the abolition of slavery is to depend upon the assent of the slaveholders of Maryland, and the other contingencies specified, it is easy to see that slavery in the District of Columbia cannot be reached until the last vestige of slavery has disappeared from the State of Maryland. When that event takes place, there will be no necessity for compromise. And so far as these resolution have any bearing at all, their effect will be to clog the wheels of emancipation.

What is said about abolishing the slave-trade in the District of Columbia, is a mere *ruse:* since the slavetraders of Maryland can easily reside in Washington, and sell their slaves out of that city, under the very management which pretends to obstruct the trade. While slavery remains in the District, and the right to buy and sell is retained by the slaveholders, it will be impossible to suppress the slave-trade there.

The seventh resolution in the series is as follows:

"Resolved, That more effectual provision ought to be made by law, according to the requirement of the Constitution, for the restitution and delivery of persons bound to service or labor in any State who may escape into any other State or territory in the Union."

Hardened as we have had reason to believe Mr. Clay to be, and inconsistent as he always is, we scarcely expected such a resolution from him as the foregoing, at this time, and in such a connection. When the sympathy of the nation has, by his eloquence and that of others, just been wrought up to the greatest intensity for the Hungarian fugitives from oppression, that he should propose *such* a resolution, at *such* a time, for hunting down fugitives *in our own land,* who are fleeing from a bondage and tyranny far more terrible than that of Austria, is almost as shocking to our sense of consistency and propriety, as it is revolting to our moral perceptions of right and wrong.

But we give Mr. Clay's eighth and last resolution, that the reader may judge for himself as to the benefit which freedom will derive from this mis-named compromise. To us, the whole seems like the handle of a jug—all on one side.

> "Resolved, That Congress has no power to prohibit or obstruct the trade in slaves between the slaveholding States; but that the admission or exclusion of slaves brought from one into another of them, depends exclusively upon their own particular laws."

This resolution declares what is not true.—If there be any meaning in words, the Constitution of the U.S. does confer upon Congress full powers to abolish the slave trade between the States. Having already extended this article beyond the limits we had prescribed, we bring it at once to a close.—F. D.

The North Star, February 8, 1850

1. On January 29, 1850, Henry Clay introduced a series of resolutions which he believed would provide the basis for the settlement of "all questions of controversy . . . arising out of the institution of slavery, upon a fair, equitable, and just basis." His "comprehensive scheme of adjustment" proposed that California be admitted as a state with her free-state Constitution; that Congress provide territorial governments for New Mexico and Utah, without restriction as to slavery, but without authorizing slaveholders to take their slaves there; that taxes be granted a sum of money for the payment of her public debt; that slavery should not be abolished in the District of Columbia without the consent of Maryland, and but that the slave trade in the District should be prohibited; that a more effective fugitive slave law should be enacted, and that Congress had no power to prohibit or obstruct the trade in slaves between the slaveholding states.

These resolutions were referred to a select committee of thirteen of which Clay was made chairman, and its report was basically the proposals advanced by its chairman.

AT HOME AGAIN

Having been, during the past few weeks, the special object of attack, marked out by a corrupt and fiendish Press, for assassination, the victim of a continuous train of almost unprecedented abuse—harassed and dogged from day to day by the furious blood-hounds of American Slavery,—I should be something more than a Stoic, if I did not feel and acknowledge a sense of profound gratitude to the God of the oppressed, that I am again permitted safely to occupy my editorial chair. Never since the day I entered the field of public effort in the cause of my enslaved brethren, have I been called to endure persecution more bitter, insults more brutal, violence more fierce, scorn and contempt more malicious and demoniacal, than that heaped upon me in the city of New York, during the past three weeks. I have been made to feel keenly that I am in an enemy's land—surrounded on all sides by hardships, difficulties and dangers—that on the side of the oppressor there is power, and that there are few to take up the cause of my deeply injured and down-trodden people. These things grieve, but do not appal me. Not an inch will I retreat—not one jot of zeal will I abate—not one word will I retract; and, in the strength of God, while the red current of life flows through my veins, I will continue to labor for the downfall of slavery and the freedom of my race. I am denounced as an offender. I am not ignorant of my offences. I plead guilty to the worst of those laid to my charge. Amplified as they have been, enormous as they are alleged to be, I do not shrink from looking them full in the face, and glorying in having committed them. My *crime* is, that I have assumed to be a man, entitled to all the rights, privileges and dignity, which belong to human nature—that color is no crime, and that all men are brothers. I have acted on this presumption. The very "head and front of my offending hath this extent—no more." I have not merely talked of human brotherhood and human equality, but have reduced that talk to practice. This I have done in broad open day, scorning concealment. I have walked through the streets of New York, in company with white persons, not as a menial, but as an equal. This was done with no purpose to inflame the public mind; not to provoke popular violence; not to make a display of my contempt for public opinion; but simply as a matter of course, and because it was right so to do. The right to associate with my fellow worms of the dust, on terms of equality, without regard to color, is a right which I will yield only with my latest breath.

My readers will have observed, in the *North Star* of last week, an account of a most cowardly assault made upon me in the Battery at New York. Like most other statements which emanate from the American press, this one (though partly true) is false in several particulars. It is not true that I walked down Broadway with two white females resting on my arm, in the case alluded to, although I *insist* upon the right to do so. It is not true that the ladies in company with me placed themselves under the care of the gentleman (ruffian?) who assaulted me, nor any of the villainous party, nor of anybody else. It is not true that I sneered or spoke to the loafing assailants. The facts briefly are these. Myself and friends were going to Philadelphia, and supposing that the "John Porter" departed from New York at twelve o'clock, we rode down a quarter before twelve but found on our arrival, that we had been mistaken; the time of starting being half-past one o'clock. The interval, therefore, we passed in the Battery. When about to leave for the Steamer, five or six men surrounded us, assailing us with all sorts of coarse and filthy language, and two of them finally struck the ladies on the head, while another attacked me. I warded off the blows with my umbrella, and the cowardly creatures left without doing any personal harm. Thinking that we should not be disturbed by them again we walked slowly toward the Steamer, one of the mob observing that I was off my guard, ran up behind me and before I could put myself in a position to ward off the assassin's blow, I was struck in the face. These are the whole facts in the case. I never was more calm or self-possessed than when under his beastly assault. I felt no indignation towards the poor miserable wretches who committed the outrage. They were but executing upon me the behests of the proslavery church and the clergy of the land; doing the dirty work of the men who despise them, and who have no more respect for them in reality than they have for me.

F.D.

The North Star, May 30, 1850

On August 21, 1850, four weeks before the Fugitive Slave bill became law, Douglass presided at a convention at Cazenovia, New York, known as the "Fugitive Slave Convention." Over 2,000 people attended the meeting among whom were thirty fugitives. [The following letter] was drawn up urging the slaves to escape to freedom. The convention pledged itself to raise funds for the defense of William Chaplin, who had been imprisoned in Maryland for assisting in the escape of the slaves of Robert Toombs and Alexander H. Stephens. A week later at an "Anti-Fugitive Slave Bill Meeting" at Syracuse, Douglass and J. C. Hathaway raised three hundred and fifty dollars for Chaplin's defense.[1] [II:43]

A LETTER TO THE AMERICAN SLAVES FROM THOSE WHO HAVE FLED FROM AMERICAN SLAVERY

Afflicted and Beloved Brothers:

The meeting which sends you this letter, is a meeting of runaway slaves. We thought it well, that they, who had once suffered, as you still suffer, that they, who had once drunk of that bitterest of all bitter cups, which you are still compelled to drink of, should come together for the purpose of making a communication to you.

The chief object of this meeting is, to tell you what circumstances we find ourselves in—that, so you may be able to judge for yourselves, whether the prize we have obtained is worth the peril of the attempt to obtain it.

The heartless pirates, who compelled us to call them "master," sought to persuade us, as such pirates seek to persuade you, that the condition of those, who escape from their clutches, is thereby made worse, instead of better. We confess, that we had our fears, that this might be so. Indeed, so great was our ignorance, that we could not be sure that the abolitionists were not the friends, which our masters represented them to be. When they told us, that the abolitionists, could they lay hands upon us would buy and sell us, we could not certainly know, that they spoke falsely; and when they told us, that abolitionists are in the habit of skinning the black man for leather, and of regaling their cannibalism on his flesh, even such enormities seemed to us to be possible. But owing to the happy change in our circumstances, we are not as ignorant and credulous now, as we once were; and if we did not know it before, we know it now, that slaveholders are as great liars, as they are great tyrants.

The abolitionists act the part of friends and brothers to us; and our only complaint against them is, that there are so few of them. The abolitionists, on whom it is safe to rely, are, almost all of them, members of the American Anti-Slavery Society, or of the Liberty Party. There are other abolitionists: but most of them are grossly inconsistent; and, hence, not entirely trustworthy abolitionists. So inconsistent are they, as to vote for anti-abolitionists for civil rulers, and to acknowledge the obligation of laws, which they themselves interpret to be pro-slavery.

We get wages for our labor. We have schools for our children. We have opportunities to hear and to learn to read the Bible—that blessed book, which is all for freedom, notwithstanding the lying slaveholders who say it is all for slavery. Some of us take part in the election of civil rulers. Indeed, but for the priests and politicians, the influence of most of whom is against us, our condition would be every way eligible. The priests and churches of the North, are, with comparatively few exceptions, in league with the priests and churches of the South; and this, of itself, is sufficient to account for the fact, that a caste-religion and a Negro-pew are found at the North, as well as at the South. The politicians and political parties of the North are connected with the politicians and political parties of the South; and hence, the political arrangements and interests of the North, as well as the ecclesiastical arrangements and interests, are adverse to the colored population. But, we rejoice to know, that all this political and ecclesiastical power is on the wane. The callousness of American religion and American democracy has become glaring: and, every year, multitudes, once deluded by them, come to repudiate them. The credit of this repudiation is due, in a great measure, to the American Anti-Slavery Society, to the Liberty Party, and to antisectarian meetings, and conventions. The purest sect on earth is the rival of, instead of one with, Christianity. It deserves not to be trusted with a deep and honest and earnest reform. The temptations which beset the pathway of such a reform, are too mighty for it to resist. Instead of going forward for God, it will slant off for itself. Heaven grant, that, soon, not a shred of sectarianism, not a shred of the current religion, not a shred of the current politics of this land, may remain. Then will follow, aye, that will itself be, the triumph of Christianity: and, then, white men will love black men and gladly acknowledge that all men have equal rights. Come, blessed day—come quickly.

Including our children, we number in Canada, at least, twenty thousand. The total of our population in the free States far exceeds this. Nevertheless, we are poor, we can do little more to promote your deliverance than pray for it to the God of the oppressed. We will do what we can to supply you with pocket compasses. In dark nights, when his good guiding star is hidden from the flying slave, a pocket compass greatly facilitates his exodus. Candor requires the admission, that some of us would not furnish them, if we could; for some of us have become nonresistants, and have discarded the use of these weapons: and would say to you: "love your enemies; do good to them, which hate you; bless them that curse you; and pray for them, which despitefully use you." Such of us would be glad to be able to say, that all the colored men of the North are nonresistants. But, in point of fact, it is only a handful of them, who are. When the insurrection of the Southern slaves shall take place, as take place it will unless speedily prevented by voluntary emancipation, the great majority of the colored men of the North, however much to the grief of any of us, will be found by your side, with deep-stored and long-accumulated revenge in their hearts, and with death-dealing weapons in their hands. It is not to be disguised, that a colored man is as much disposed, as a white man, to resist, even unto death, those who oppress him. The colored American, for the sake of relieving his colored brethren, would no more hesitate to shoot an American slaveholder, than would a white American, for the sake of delivering his white brother, hesitate to shoot an Algerine slaveholder. The State motto of Virginia: "Death to Tyrants;" is as well the black man's, as the white man's motto. We tell you these things not to encourage, or justify, your resort to physical force; but, simply, that you may know, be it to your joy or sorrow to know it, what your Northern colored brethren are, in these important respects. This truth you are entitled to know, however the knowledge of it may affect you, and however you may act, in view of it.

We have said, that some of us are non-resistants. But, while such would dissuade you from all violence toward the slaveholder, let it not be supposed, that they regard it as guiltier than those strifes, which even good men are wont to justify. If the American revolutionists had excuse for shedding but one drop of blood, then have the American slaves excuse for making blood to flow "even unto the horse-bridles."

Numerous as are the escapes from slavery, they would be far more so, were you not embarrassed by your misinterpretations of the rights of property. You hesitate to take even the dullest of your master's horses—whereas it is your duty to take the fleetest. Your consciences suggest doubts, whether in quitting your bondage, you are at liberty to put in your packs what you need of food and clothing. But were you better informed, you would not scruple to break your master's locks, and take all their money. You are taught to respect the rights of property. But, no such right belongs to the slaveholder. His right to property is but the robber-right. In every slaveholding community, the rights of property all center in them, whose coerced and unrequited toil has created the wealth in which their oppressors riot. Moreover, if your oppressors have rights of property, you, at least, are exempt from all obligations to respect them. For you are prisoners of war, in an enemy's country—of a war, too, that is unrivalled for its injustice, cruelty, meanness—and therefore, by all the rules of war, you have the fullest liberty to plunder, burn, and kill, as you may have occasion to do to promote your escape.

We regret to be obliged to say to you, that it is not everyone of the Free States, which offers you an asylum. Even within the last year, fugitive slaves have been arrested in some of the Free States, and replunged into slavery. But, make your way to New York or New England, and you will be safe. It is true, that even in New York and New England, there are individuals, who would rejoice to see the poor flying slave cast back into the horrors of slavery. But, even these are restrained by public sentiment. It is questionable whether even Daniel Webster, or Moses Stuart, would give chase to a fugitive slave; and if they would not, who would?—for the one is chief-politician and the other chief-priest.

We do not forget the industrious efforts, which are now in making to get new facilities at the hands of Congress for re-enslaving those, who have escaped from slavery. But we can assure you, that as to the State of New York and the New England States, such efforts must prove fruitless. Against all such devilism—against all kidnappers—the colored people of these States will "stand for their life," and, what is more, the white people of these States will not stand against them. A regenerated public sentiment has, forever, removed these States beyond the limits of the slaveholders' hunting ground. Defeat—disgrace—and, it may be, death—will be their only reward for pursuing their prey into this *abolitionized* portion of our country.

A special reason why you should not stop in that part of the Nation which comes within the bounds of John McLean's judicial district, is, that he is a great man in one of the religious sects, and an aspirant for the Presidency. Fugitive slaves and their friends fare hard in the hands of this judge. He not only puts a pro-slavery construction on the Federal Constitution, and holds, that law can make property of man—a marketable commodity of the image of God, but, in various other ways, he shows that his sympathies are with the oppressor. Shun Judge McLean, then, even as you would the Reverend Moses Stuart.[2] The law of the one is as deadly an enemy to you, as is the religion of the other.

There are three points in your conduct, when you shall have become inhabitants of the North, on which we cannot refrain from admonishing you.

1st. If you will join a sectarian church, let it not be one which approves of the Negro-pew, and which refuses to treat slaveholding as a high crime against God and man. It were better, that you sacrifice your lives than that by going into the Negro-pew, you invade your self-respect—debase your souls—play the traitor to your race—and crucify afresh Him who died for the one brotherhood of man.

2d. Join no political party, which refuses to commit itself fully, openly, and heartfully, in its newspapers, meetings, and nominations, to the doctrine, that slavery is the grossest of all absurdities, as well as the guiltiest of all abominations, and that there can no more be a law for the enslavement of man, made in the image of God, than for the enslavement of God himself. Vote for no man for civil office, who makes your complexion a bar to political, ecclesiastic or social equality. Better die than insult yourself and insult our social equality. Better die than insult yourself and insult every person of African blood, and insult your Maker, by contributing to elevate to civil office he who refuses to eat with you, to sit by your side in the House of Worship, or to let his children sit in the school by the side of your children.

3d. Send not your children to the school which the malignant and murderous prejudice of white people has gotten up exclusively for colored people. Valuable as learning is, it is too costly, if it is acquired at the expense of such self-degradation.

The self-sacrificing, and heroic, and martyr-spirit, which would impel the colored men of the North to turn their backs on pro-slavery churches and pro-slavery politics, and pro-slavery schools, would exert a far mightier influence against slavery, than could all their learning, however great, if purchased by concessions of their manhood, and surrenders of their rights, and coupled, as it then would be, by characteristic meanness and servility.

And now, brethren, we close this letter with assuring you, that we do not, cannot, forget you. You are ever in our minds, our hearts, our prayers. Perhaps, you are fearing, that the free colored people of the United States will suffer themselves to be carried away from you by the American Colonization Society. Fear it not. In vain is it, that this greatest and most malignant enemy of the African race is now busy in devising new plans, and in seeking the aid of Government, to perpetuate your enslavement. It wants us away from your side, that you may be kept in ignorance. But we will remain by your side to enlighten you. It wants us away from your side, that you may be contented. But we will remain by your side, to keep you, and make you more, discontented. It wants us away from your side to the end, that your unsuccored and conscious helplessness may make you the easier and surer prey of your oppressors. But we will remain by your side to sympathize with you, and cheer you, and give you the help of our rapidly swelling members. The land of our enslaved brethren is our land, and death alone shall part us.

We cannot forget you, brethren, for we know your sufferings and we know your sufferings because we know from experience, what it is to be an American slave. So galling was our bondage, that, to escape from it, we suffered the loss of all things, and braved every peril, and endured every hardship. Some of us left parents, some wives, some children. Some of us were wounded with guns and dogs, as we fled. Some of us, to make good our escape, suffered ourselves to be nailed up in boxes, and to pass for merchandise. Some of us secreted ourselves in the suffocating holds of ships. Nothing was so dreadful to us, as slavery; and hence, it is almost literally true, that we dreaded nothing, which could befall us, in our attempt to get clear of it. Our condition could be made no worse, for we were already in the lowest depths of earthly woe. Even should we be overtaken, and resubjected to slavery, this would be but to return to our old sufferings and sorrows and should death itself prove to be the price of our endeavor after freedom, what would that be but a welcome release to men, who had, all their lifetime, been killed every day, and "killed all the day long."

We have referred to our perils and hardships in escaping from slavery. We are happy to be able to say, that every year is multiplying the facilities for leaving the Southern prison house. The Liberty Party, the Vigilance Committee of New York,[3] individuals, and companies of individuals in various parts of the country, are doing all they can, and it is much to afford you a safe and a cheap passage from slavery to liberty. They do this however, not only at great expense of property, but at great peril of liberty and life. Thousands of you have heard, ere this, that, within the last fortnight, the precious name of William L. Chaplin has been added to the list of those, who, in helping you gain your liberty, have lost their own.[4] Here is a man, whose wisdom, cultivation, moral worth, bring him into the highest and best class of men—and, yet, he becomes a willing martyr for the poor, despised, forgotten slave's sake. Your remembrance of one such fact is enough to shed light and hope upon your darkest and most disponding moments.

Brethren, our last word to you is to bid you be of good cheer, and not to despair of your deliverance. Do not abandon yourselves, as have many thousands of American slaves, to the crime of suicide. Live! live to escape from slavery, live to serve God! Live till He shall Himself call you into eternity! Be prayerful—be brave—be hopeful. "Lift up your heads, for your redemption draweth nigh."

The North Star, September 5th, 1850

1. *New York Tribune,* Aug. 23, 1830; *Anti-Slavery Standard,* Aug. 29, Sept. 5, 1850; *Syracuse Daily Standard,* Aug. 29, 1850.

2. Judge John McLean of Boston handed down several decisions upholding the Fugitive Slave Law of 1850 and ordering the return fugitives to slavery.

Moses Stuart (1780–1852), a leading clergyman and biblical scholar in New England, upheld the constitutionality of the Fugitive Slave Law.

The Fugitive Slave Law of 1850 provided for the appointment of special federal commissioners to facilitate the reclaiming of runaways. These commissioners could appoint marshals to arrest fugitives, and these marshals could, in turn, "call to their aid" any bystanders at the scene of an arrest, who were "commanded" to "assist in the prompt and efficient execution of the law. . . . " Slave owners could "pursue and reclaim" fugitives with or without a warrant; the commissioner would judge the case without a jury. In addition, "In no trial or hearing under this act shall the testimony of such alleged fugitive be admitted in evidence." "Satisfactory" written or oral "proof" being offered that the person arrested was the sought-for fugitive, the commissioner would issue a certificate. The slave owner was authorized to use all "reasonable force" necessary to take a fugitive back to the place of his or her escape. If the slave owner feared "that such fugitive will be rescued by force" it was the duty of the officer involved to employ any number of persons necessary "to overcome such force," and deliver the fugitive back to the fugitive's owner. Any marshal who failed to properly execute the fugitive law was to be fined $100; the marshal was also liable for the full value of any fugitive escaping from his custody. Finally, an officer was "entitled to a fee of five dollars each" for every person he arrested; a commissioner was "entitled to a fee of ten dollars" if he delivered a fugitive to a slave owner, but only five dollars if he freed the black claimed.

The new Fugitive Slave Law was approved by Congress on September 18, 1850.

3. The New York City Committee of Vigilance was established to guard blacks from kidnappers who would return them to Southern bondage. Its secretary was the militant David Ruggles (1810–1849) who was jailed several times because of his frank criticism of the police who collaborated with slave hunters. See Dorothy Porter, "David M. Ruggles, An Apostle of Human Rights," *Journal of Negro History,* volume XVIII, Jan. 1943, pp. 23–50.

4. In August 1850, William L. Chaplin and others were arrested by Washington police on Maryland soil, for taking part in the escape of two slaves, the property of Robert Toombs and Alexander H. Stephens. Chaplin was kept in jail at Rockville, Maryland, until December; was subsequently indicted in the District of Columbia on a charge of assault with intent to kill, and in Maryland he was indicted on seven counts: three for assault with intent to murder, two for assisting slaves to escape, and two for larceny of slaves. Bail was fixed at $6,000 in the District and $19,000 in Maryland.

(In an appeal to the Liberty Party, the fugitive slaves, meeting in Cazenovia, New York, recommended that it nominate Chaplin for President of the United States. "He is emphatically a scholar, a statesman, a philanthropist, a gentleman, and a Christian Job, who was the supreme magistrate in the community, in which he dwelt, numbers among his own qualifications for office, 'I WAS A FATHER TO THE POOR.'—Beautiful, precious, indispensable qualification is this! and who had it more abundantly than William L. Chaplin." The fact that Chaplin was imprisoned for a worthy cause was another reason that merited his nomination. "It is true, that we would not, for this reason, ask for his nomination, were it not also, that he is fit for it. But, being fit for it, we find in the fact of his imprisonment, good cause why he, among all, who have such fitness, should be singled out for the nomination." *The North Star,* September 5, 1850.)

With the aid of Gerrit Smith, Lewis Tappan, William H. Seward and others, Chaplin's bail was secured and he was released from jail. Smith served as treasurer of the Chaplin fund, and contributed $10,000 to the movement to free Chaplin.

Under the sponsorship of the Rochester anti-slavery group, Douglass spoke frequently in Corinthian Hall, the city's most popular auditorium. Here, during the winter of 1850–51, he taught a course on slavery. The aim of the course, which consisted of seven lectures, was to counteract the influence of the local press and the pulpit in creating among the people of Rochester "an indifference and coldness" toward the enslavement of their fellowmen "which might be looked for only in men hardened by the most atrocious and villainous crimes." The lectures were well attended and they contributed to the growth of anti-slavery sentiment in the community; several were reported in full in the local press and reprinted in pamphlet form. [II:39]

LECTURE ON SLAVERY, NO. 1, delivered in Corinthian Hall, Rochester, N.Y., on Sunday evening, December 1, 1850

I come before you this evening to deliver the first lecture of a course which I purpose to give in this city, during the present winter, on the subject of American Slavery.[1]

I make this announcement with no feelings of self-sufficiency. If I do not mistake my own emotions, they are such as result from a profound sense of my incompetency to do justice to the task which I have just announced, and have now entered upon.

If any, then, demand of me why I speak, I plead as my apology, the fact that abler and more eloquent men have failed to speak, or what, perhaps, is more true, and therefore more strong, such men have spoken only on the wrong side of the question, and have thus thrown their influence against the cause of liberty, humanity and benevolence.

There are times in the experience of almost every community, when even the humblest member thereof may properly presume to teach—when the wise and great ones, the appointed leaders of the people, exert their powers of mind to complicate, mystify, entangle and obscure the simple truth—when they exert the noblest gifts which heaven has vouchsafed to man to mislead the popular mind, and to corrupt the public heart,—*then* the humblest may stand forth and be excused for opposing even his weakness to the torrent of evil.

That such a state of things exists in this community, I have abundant evidence. I learn it from the Rochester press, from the Rochester pulpit, and in my intercourse with the people of Rochester. Not a day passes over me that I do not meet with apparently good men, who utter sentiments in respect to this subject which would do discredit to savages. They speak of the enslavement of their fellow-men with an indifference and coldness which might be looked for only in men hardened by the most atrocious and villainous crimes.

The fact is, we are in the midst of a great struggle. The public mind is widely and deeply agitated; and bubbling up from its perturbed waters, are many and great impurities, whose poisonous miasma demands a constant antidote.

Whether the contemplated lectures will in any degree contribute towards answering this demand, time will determine.

Of one thing, however, I can assure my hearers—that I come up to this work at the call of duty, and with an honest desire to promote the happiness and well-being of every member of this community, as well as to advance the emancipation of every slave.

The audience will pardon me if I say one word more by way of introduction. It is my purpose to give this subject a calm, candid and faithful discussion. I shall not aim to shock nor to startle my hearers; but to convince their judgment and to secure their sympathies for the enslaved. I shall aim to be as stringent as truth, and as severe as justice; and if at any time I shall fail of this, and do injustice in any respect, I shall be most happy to be set right by any gentleman who shall hear me, subject, of course, to order and decorum. I shall deal, during these lectures, alike with individuals and institutions—men shall no more escape me than things. I shall have occasion, at times, to be even personal, and to rebuke sin in high places. I shall not hesitate to arraign either priests or politicians, church or state, and to measure all by the standard of justice, and in the light of truth. I shall not forget to deal with the unrighteous spirit of *caste* which prevails in this community; and I shall give particular attention to the recently enacted fugitive slave bill. I shall keep my eye upon the Congress which is to commence to-morrow, and fully inform myself as to its proceedings. In a word, the whole subject of slavery, in all its bearings, shall have a full and impartial discussion.

A very slight acquaintance with the history of American slavery is sufficient to show that it is an evil of which it will be difficult to rid this country. It is not the creature of a moment, which to-day is, and to-morrow is not; it is not a pigmy, which a slight blow may demolish; it is no youthful upstart, whose impertinent pratings may be silenced by a dignified contempt. No: it is an evil of gigantic proportions, and of long standing.

Its origin in this country dates back to the landing of the pilgrims on Plymouth rock.—It was here more than two centuries ago. The first spot poisoned by its leprous presence, was a small plantation in Virginia. The slaves, at that time, numbered only twenty. They have now increased to the frightful number of three millions; and from that narrow plantation, they are now spread over by far the largest half of the American Union. Indeed, slavery forms an important part of the entire history of the American people. Its presence may be seen in all American affairs. It has become interwoven with all American institutions, and has anchored itself in the very soil of the American Constitution. It has thrown its paralysing arm over freedom of speech, and the liberty of the press; and has created for itself morals and manners favorable to its own continuance. It has seduced the church, corrupted the pulpit, and brought the powers of both into degrading bondage; and now, in the pride of its power, it even threatens to bring down that grand political edifice, the American Union, unless every member of this republic shall so far disregard his conscience and his God as to yield to its infernal behests.

That must be a powerful influence which can truly be said to govern a nation; and that slavery governs the American people, is indisputably true. If there were any doubt on this point, a few plain questions (it seems to me) could not fail to remove it. *What* power has given this nation its Presidents for more than fifty years? *Slavery.* What power is that to which the present aspirants to presidential honors are bowing? *Slavery.* We may call it "Union," "Constitution," "Harmony," or "American institutions," that to which such men as Cass, Dickinson, Webster, Clay and other distinguished men of this country, are devoting their energies, is nothing more nor less than American slavery. It is for this that they are writing letters, making speeches, and promoting the holding of great mass meetings, professedly in favor of "*the Union.*" These men know the service most pleasing to their master, and that which is most likely to be richly rewarded. Men may "serve God for nought," as did Job; but he who serves the devil has an eye to his reward. "Patriotism," "obedience to the law," "prosperity to the country," have come to mean, in the mouths of these distinguished statesmen, a mean and servile acquiescence in the most flagitious and profligate legislation in favor of slavery. I might enlarge here on this picture of the slave power, and tell of its influence upon the press in the free States, and upon the condition and rights of the free colored people of the North; but I forbear for the present.—Enough has been said, I trust, to convince all that the abolition of this evil will require time, energy, zeal, perseverance and patience; that it will require fidelity, a martyr-like spirit of self-sacrifice, and a firm reliance on Him who has declared Himself to be *"the God of the oppressed."* Having said thus much upon the power and prevalence of slavery, allow me to speak of the nature of slavery itself; and here I can speak, in part, from experience—I can speak with the authority of positive knowledge.

More than twenty years of my life were consumed in a state of slavery. My childhood was environed by the baneful peculiarities of the slave system. I grew up to manhood in the presence of this hydra-headed monster—not as a master— not as an idle spectator—not as the guest of the slaveholder; but as A SLAVE eating the bread and drinking the cup of slavery with the most degraded of my brother bondmen, and sharing with them all the painful conditions of their wretched lot. In consideration of these facts, I feel that I have a right to speak, and to speak *strongly.* Yet my friends, I feel bound to speak truly.

Goading as have been the cruelties to which I have been subjected—bitter as have been the trials through which I have passed—exasperating as have been (*and still are*) the indignities offered to my manhood, I find in them no excuse for the slightest departure from truth in dealing with any branch of this subject.

First of all, I will state, as well as I can, the legal and social relation of master and slave. A master is one (to speak in the vocabulary of the Southern States) who claims and exercises a right of property in the person of a fellow man. This he does with the force of the law and the sanction of Southern religion. The law gives the master absolute power over the slave. He may work him, flog him, hire him out, sell him, and, in certain contingencies, *kill* him, with perfect impunity. The slave is a human being, divested of all rights—reduced to the level of a brute—a mere "chattel" in the eye of the law—placed beyond the circle of human brotherhood—cut off from his kind—his name, which the "recording angel" may have enrolled in heaven, among the blest, is impiously inserted in a *master's ledger,* with horses, sheep and swine. In law, the slave has no wife, no children, no country, and no home. He can own nothing, possess nothing, acquire nothing, but what must belong to another. To eat the fruit of his own toil, to clothe his person with the work of his own hands, is considered stealing. He toils that another may reap the fruit; he is industrious that another may live in idleness; he eats unbolted meal, that another may eat the bread of fine flour; he labors in chains at home, under a burning sun and a biting lash, that another may ride in ease and splendor abroad; he lives in ignorance, that another may be educated; he is abused, that another may be exalted; he rests his toil-worn limbs on the cold, damp ground, that another may repose on the softest pillow; he is clad in coarse and tattered raiment, that another may be arrayed in purple and fine linen; he is sheltered only by the wretched hovel, that a master may dwell in a magnificent mansion; and to this condition he is bound down as by an arm of iron.

From this monstrous relation, there springs an unceasing stream of most revolting cruelties. The very accompaniments of the slave system, stamp it as the offspring of hell itself. To ensure good behavior, the slaveholder relies on *the whip;* to induce proper humility, he relies on *the whip;* to rebuke what he is pleased to term insolence, he relies on *the whip,* to supply the place of wages, as an incentive to toil, he relies on *the whip;* to bind down the spirit of the slave, to imbrute and to destroy his manhood, he relies on *the whip,* the chain, the gag, the thumb-screw, the pillory, the bowie-knife, the pistol, and the blood-hound. These are the necessary and unvarying accompanyments of the system. Wherever slavery is found, these horrid instruments are also found. Whether on the coast of Africa, among the savage tribes, or in South Carolina, among the refined and civilized, slavery is the same, and its accompanyments one and the same. It makes no difference whether the slaveholder worships the God of the Christians or is a follower of Mahomet, he is the minister of the same cruelty, and the author of the same misery. *Slavery* is always *slavery*—always the same foul, haggard, and damning scourge, whether found in the Eastern or in the Western Hemisphere.

There is a still deeper shade to be given to this picture. The physical cruelties are indeed sufficiently harassing and revolting; but they are but as a few grains of sand on the sea shore, or a few drops of water in the great ocean, compared with the stupendous wrongs which it inflicts upon the mental, moral and religious nature of its hapless victims. It is only when we contemplate the slave as a moral and intellectual being, that we can adequately comprehend the unparalleled enormity of slavery, and the intense criminality of the slaveholder. I have said that the slave is a man. "What a piece of work is man! How noble in reason! How infinite in faculties! In form and moving how express and admirable! In action how like an angel! In apprehension how like a God! The beauty of the world! the paragon of animals!"

The slave is a man, "the image of God," but " a little lower than the angels;" possessing a soul, eternal and indestructible; capable of endless happiness, or immeasurable woe; a creature of hopes and fears, of affections and passions, of joys and sorrows; and he is endowed with those mysterious powers by which man soars above the things of time and sense, and grasps with undying tenacity, the elevating and sublimely glorious idea of a God. It is *such* a being that is smitten and blasted. The first work of slavery is to mar and deface those characteristics of its victims which distinguish *men* from *things,* and *persons* from *property*. Its first aim is to destroy all sense of high moral and religious responsibility. It reduces man to a mere machine. It cuts him off from his maker, it hides from him the laws of God, and leaves him to grope his way from time to eternity in the dark, under the arbitrary and despotic control of a frail, depraved and sinful fellow-man.

As the serpent-charmer of India is compelled to extract the deadly teeth of his venomous prey before he is able to handle him with impunity, so the slaveholder must strike down the conscience of the slave, before he can obtain the entire mastery over his victim.

It is, then, the first business of the enslaver of men to blunt, deaden and destroy the central principle of human responsibility. Conscience is to the individual soul and to society, what the law of gravitation is to the universe. It holds society together; it is the basis of all trust and confidence; it is the pillar of all moral rectitude. Without it, suspicion would take the place of trust; vice would be more than a match for virtue; men would prey upon each other, like the wild beasts of the desert; and earth would become a *hell*.

Nor is slavery more adverse to the conscience than it is to the mind.

This is shown by the fact that in every State of the American Union, where slavery exists, except the State of Kentucky, there are laws, *absolutely* prohibitory of education among the slaves. The crime of teaching a slave to read is punishable with severe fines and imprisonment, and, in some instances, with *death itself*.

Nor are the laws respecting this matter, a dead letter. Cases may occur in which they are disregarded, and a few instances may be found where slaves may have learned to read; but such are isolated cases, and only prove the rule. The great mass of slaveholders look upon education among the slaves as utterly subversive of the slave system. I *well* remember when my mistress first announced to my master that she had discovered that I could read. His face colored at once, with surprise and chagrin. He said that "I was ruined, and my value as a slave destroyed; that a slave should know nothing but to obey his master; that to give a Negro an inch would lead him to take an ell; that having learned how to read, I would soon want to know how to write; and that, bye and bye, I would be running away." I think my audience will bear witness to the correctness of this philosophy, and to the literal fulfilment of this prophecy.

It is perfectly well understood at the South that to educate a slave is to make him discontented with slavery, and to invest him with a power which shall open to him the treasures of freedom; and since the object of the slaveholder is to maintain complete authority over his slave, his constant vigilance is exercised to prevent everything which militates against, or endangers the stability of his authority. Education being among the menacing influences, and, perhaps, the most dangerous, is, therefore, the most cautiously guarded against.

It is true that we do not often hear of the enforcement of the law, punishing as crime the teaching of slaves to read, but this is not because of a want of disposition to enforce it. The true reason, or explanation of the matter is this, there is the greatest unanimity of opinion among the white population of the South, in favor of the policy of keeping the slave in ignorance. There is, perhaps, another reason why the law against education is so seldom violated. The slave is *too* poor to be able to offer a temptation sufficiently strong to induce a white man to violate it; and it is not to be supposed that in a community where the moral and religious sentiment is in favor of slavery, many martyrs will be found sacrificing their liberty and lives by violating those prohibitory enactments.

As a general rule, then, darkness reigns over the abodes of the enslaved, and "how great is that darkness!"

We are sometimes told of the contentment of the slaves, and are entertained with vivid pictures of their happiness. We are told that they often dance and sing; that their masters frequently give them wherewith to make merry; in fine, that that they have little of which to complain. I admit that the slave *does* sometimes sing, dance, and appear to be merry. But what does this prove? It only proves to my mind, that though slavery is armed with a thousand stings, it is not able entirely to kill the elastic spirit of the bondman. That spirit will rise and walk abroad, despite of whips and chains, and extract from the cup of nature, occasional drops of joy and gladness. No thanks to the slaveholder, nor to slavery, that the vivacious captive may sometimes dance in his chains, his very mirth in such circumstances, stands before God, as an accusing angel against his enslaver.

But *who* tells us of the extraordinary contentment and happiness of the slave? What traveller has explored the balmy regions of our Southern country and brought back "these glad tidings of joy"? Bring him on the platform, and bid him answer a few plain questions, we shall then be able to determine the weight and importance that attach to his testimony. Is he a minister? Yes. Were you ever in a slave State, sir? Yes. May I inquire the object of your mission South? To preach the gospel, sir. Of what denomination are you? A Presbyterian, sir. To whom were you introduced? To the Rev. Dr. Plummer. Is he a slaveholder, sir? Yes, sir. Has slaves about his house? Yes, sir. Were you then the guest of Dr. Plummer? Yes, sir. Waited on by slaves while there? Yes, sir. Did you preach for Dr. Plummer? Yes, sir. Did you spend your nights at the great house, or at the quarter among the slaves? At the great house. You had, then, no social intercourse with the slaves? No, sir. You fraternized, then, wholly with the *white* portion of the population while there? Yes, sir. This is sufficient, sir; you can leave the platform.

Nothing is more natural than that those who go into slave States, and enjoy the hospitality of slaveholders, should bring back favorable reports of the condition of the slave. If that ultra republican, the Hon. Lewis Cass could not return from the Court of France, without paying a compliment to royalty simply because King Louis Phillippe patted him on the shoulder, called him "friend," and invited him to dinner, it is not to be expected that those hungry shadows of men in the shape of ministers, that go South, can escape a contamination even more beguiling and insidious. Alas! for the weakness of poor human nature! "Pleased with a rattle, tickled with a straw!"

Why is it that all the reports of contentment and happiness among the slaves at the South come to us upon the authority of slaveholders, or (what is equally significant,) of slaveholder's friends? *Why* is it that we do not hear from the slaves direct? The answer to this question furnishes the darkest features in the American slave system.

It is often said, by the opponents of the anti-slavery cause, that the condition of the people of Ireland is more deplorable than that of the American slaves. *Far* be it from me to underrate the sufferings of the Irish people. They have been long oppressed; and the same heart that prompts me to plead the cause of the American bondman, makes it impossible for me *not* to sympathize with the oppressed of all lands. Yet I must say that there is no analogy between the two cases. The Irishman is poor, but he is *not* a slave. He *may* be in rags, but he is *not* a slave. He is still the master of his own body, and can say with the poet, "The hand of Douglass is his own." "The world is all before him, where to choose," and poor as may be my opinion of the British Parliament, I cannot believe that it will ever sink to such a depth of infamy as to pass a law for the recapture of Fugitive Irishmen! The shame and scandal of kidnapping will long remain wholly monopolized by the American Congress! The Irishman has not only the liberty to emigrate from his country, but he has liberty at home. He can write, and speak, and co-operate for the attainment of his rights and the redress of his wrongs.

The multitude can assemble upon all the green hills, and fertile plains of the Emerald Isle—they can pour out their grievances, and proclaim their wants without molestation; and the press, that "swift-winged messenger," can bear the tidings of their doings to the extreme bounds of the civilized world. They have their "Conciliation Hall" on the banks of the Liffey, their reform Clubs, and their newspapers; they pass resolutions, send forth addresses, and enjoy the right of petition. But how is it with the American slave? *Where* may he assemble? *Where* is his Conciliation Hall? Where are his newspapers? Where is his right of petition? Where is his freedom of speech? his liberty of the press? and his right of locomotion? He is said to be happy; happy men can speak. But ask the slave—*what* is his condition?—*what* his state of mind?—*what* he thinks of his enslavement? and you had as well address your inquiries to the *silent dead*. There comes no *voice* from the enslaved, we are left to gather his feelings by imagining what ours would be, were our souls in his soul's stead.

If there were no other fact descriptive of slavery, than that the slave is dumb, this alone would be sufficient to mark the slave system as a grand aggregation of human horrors.

Most who are present will have observed that leading men, in this country, have been puting forth their skill to secure quiet to the nation. A system of measures to promote this object was adopted a few months ago in Congress.[2]

The result of those measures is known. Instead of quiet, they have produced alarm; instead of peace, they have brought us war, and so must ever be.

While this nation is guilty of the enslavement of three millions of innocent men and women, it is as idle to think of having a sound and lasting peace, as it is to think there is no God, to take cognizance of the affairs of men. There can be no peace to the wicked while slavery continues in the land, it will be condemned, and while it is condemned there will be agitation; Nature must cease to be nature; Men must become monsters; Humanity must be transformed; Christianity must be exterminated; all ideas of justice, and the laws of eternal goodness must be utterly blotted out from the human soul, ere a system so foul and infernal can escape condemnation, or this guilty Republic can have a sound and enduring Peace.

The North Star, December 5, 1850

1. Douglass gave seven lectures during the course.
2. Douglass is referring to the Compromise of 1850.

Operating in central New York among men who adhered to an anti-slavery constitutional interpretation, Douglass was constantly being called upon to justify his view that the Constitution was a pro-slavery instrument. The more he discussed this question with Gerrit Smith and William Goodell and the more he studied their writings the more difficult it became for him to uphold his theory. Through these discussions and readings, Douglass became convinced that the preamble to the Constitution—that the national government had been formed to establish a more perfect union, promote the general welfare and secure the blessings of liberty—governed the meaning of the document in all its parts and details. The Constitution was thus, by its avowed purpose, anti-slavery, Slavery was not, nor could it become legalized, and it was the duty of the federal government to eradicate it. Political action to secure that end was both warranted and necessary.

As Douglass saw it, national necessity compelled him to accept an interpretation of the Constitution which might not be evident in the document itself. Realizing the importance of having the Constitution fight for him, he interpreted it in a way most convenient for the anti-slavery crusade. The Garrisonians, by their insistence on an interpretation which the slaveholders shared, no matter how apparently correct that interpretation might be, not only played directly into the hands of their enemies, but created enmity for themselves. Whatever the average Northerner felt about slavery, he did not believe that his country was built upon falsehood and iniquities. While the Garrisonians announced their determination to destroy the Constitution and the Union to end slavery, Douglass decided to use both in the struggle against "a system of lawless violence; that never was lawful and never can be made so."[1] [II:52–53]

TO GERRIT SMITH, ESQR.

Rochester, Jan. 21st, 1851

My Dear Friend:

I thank you sincerely for your donation, and feel much pleased that amid the multitudinous demands made upon your purse, you yet find the means of encouraging me in my humble labors in the cause of human redemption.

I have thought much since my personal acquaintance with you and since hearing your reasons for regarding the Constitution of the United States an Anti-Slavery instrument, and although I can not yet see that instrument in the same light in which you view it, I am so much impressed by your reasoning that I have about decided to let Slaveholders and their Northern abettors have the Laboring *oar* in putting a proslavery interpretation upon the Constitution. I am sick and tired of arguing on the slaveholders' side of this question, although they are doubtless right so far as the intentions of the framers of the Constitution are concerned. But these intentions you fling to the winds. Your legal rules of interpretation override all speculations as to the opinions of the Constitution makers and these *rules* may be sound and I confess I know not how to meet or refute them on *legal* grounds. You will now say I have conceded all that you require, and it may be so. But there is a consideration which is of much importance between us. It is this: may we avail ourselves of legal rules which enable us to defeat even the wicked intentions of our Constitution makers? It is this question which puzzles me more than all others involved in the subject. Is it good morality to take advantage of a legal flaw and put a meaning upon a legal instrument the very opposite of what we have good reason to believe was the intention of the men who framed it? Just here is the question of difficulty with me. I know well enough that slavery is an outrage, contrary to all ideas of justice, and therefore cannot be law according to Blackstone. But may it not be law according to American legal authority?

You will observe by reading the resolutions adopted at the Annual meeting of the Western N.Y. Anti-Slavery Society, that I have already ceased to affirm the pro-slavery character of the Constitution. In drawing up the resolutions for that meeting, I purposely avoided all affirmation of the pro-slavery "Compromises," as they are termed.

My good friend, Julia Griffith, forwarded to your address one copy of my two first lectures in Rochester this morning. I hope it will reach you. I am greatly pleased by your good opinion of these lectures. I sometimes fear that being delivered by a fugitive slave who has never had a day's school constitutes the only merit they possess. Yet I am so much encouraged by my friends here, and elsewhere, that I am seriously intending, if I can command the money, to publish them in Book form.[1] Your generous offer of 25 dollars for that purpose, was timely and very thankfully received. I shall give four or five more lectures to complete the course. The fact that Negroes are turning Book makers may possibly serve to remove the popular impression that they are fit only for Bootblacking, and although they may not *shine* in the former profession as they have long done in the latter, I am not without hope that they will do themselves good by making the effort. I have often felt that what the colored people want most in this country is character. They want manly aspirations and a firm though modest self-reliance, and this we must have, or be like all other worthless things swept away before the march of events.

I see now that a strong effort is being made to get us out of this country. The speech of Mr. Clay in the Senate the other day, an article in the New York *Tribune* now before me on the subject, the starting up of a new Colonization paper in New York,[2] are facts which all point the way, and that is "Out with the Negroes," and I really fear that some whose presence in this country is necessary to the elevation of the colored people will leave us, while the degraded and worthless will remain to help bind us to our present debasement.

But I have already trespassed upon your time long enough. I know how closely your time is occupied. Miss Griffiths[3] unites with me in kind regards to yourself and Mrs. Smith.

Very gratefully yours,
Frederick Douglass

I would say excuse my writing, but that your own *writing* suggests that consideration so often that I do not wish to weary you by such a reminder. I am however rapidly getting over the difficulty of reading letters from your pen and am always glad to get one at any rate.

Gerrit Smith Papers, Syracuse University

1. For a detailed analysis of Douglass' position on the Constitution and the Union, see his speeches, *The Constitution of the United States: Is it Pro-Slavery or Anti-Slavery?* Halifax, 1860, and *The Anti-Slavery Movement,* Rochester, 1855.

2. For Henry Clay's speech in the Senate in behalf of measures to transport free Negroes to Liberia, see Carl Schurz, *Life of Henry Clay,* Boston and New York, 1899, vol. II, p. 378.

An editorial entitled "The African Race" appeared in the New York *Tribune* of Jan. 17,

1851, which asserted that the Negro "cannot flourish surrounded by and mixed up with whites. His only sure resource against debasement is separation." It concluded with the hope that Negroes "will come to realize that colonization is the means whereby oppressed Races and communities renew their youth and strength."

3. Julia Griffiths, the daughter of a close friend of William Wilbeforce, came to the United States with her sister from England, moved into Douglass' home and helped him with his business problems and running *The North Star*. (She also assisted Douglass in perfecting his writing as editor.) When *The North Star* and the *Liberty Party Paper* merged, Miss Griffiths became business manager of the new paper.

———

The change in Douglass' anti-slavery creed had been developing for a number of years but it did not become public until 1851.[1] At the eighteenth annual meeting of the American Anti-Slavery Society held in Syracuse in May, 1851, a resolution was submitted by Edmund Quincy proposing that the *Anti-Slavery Standard,* the *Pennsylvania Freeman,* the *Anti-Slavery Bugle,* and *The North Star* receive the recommendation of the society. When Samuel J. May suggested that the *Liberty Party Paper* be added to the list, Garrison opposed this motion on the ground that this journal did not stand for the dissolution of the Union and believed that the Constitution was an anti-slavery document. This in turn led to a resolution that no paper should be endorsed which did not assume the Constitution to be a pro-slavery document. Douglass thereupon announced that he could not consider his paper eligible for endorsement since he had "arrived at the firm conviction that the Constitution, construed in the light of well-established rules of legal interpretation, might be made consistent in its details with the noble purposes in its preamble," and that in the future he would insist that the Constitution "be wielded in behalf of emancipation." . . . His opinions had "recently changed materially in relation to political action," and he now believed that it was "the first duty of every American citizen, whose conscience permits him so to do, to use his political as well as his moral power for its [slavery's] overthrow."

These words created a stir. Enraged, Garrison cried out: "There is roguery somewhere." He moved that *The North Star* be stricken from the list and this was promptly voted by the convention.

Douglass never forgot Garrison's "insulting remark," though in his paper he wrote that he could "easily forgive" the man for whom he still cherished "a veneration only inferior in degree to that we owe to our conscience and to our God." [II:53–54]

CHANGE OF OPINION ANNOUNCED

The debate on the resolution relative to anti-slavery newspapers [at the annual meeting of the American Anti-Slavery Society] assumed such a character as to make it our duty to define the position of the *North Star* in respect to the Constitution of the United States. The ground having been distinctly taken, that no paper ought to receive the recommendation of the American Anti-Slavery Society that did not assume the Constitution to be a pro-slavery document, we felt in honor bound to announce at once to our old anti-slavery companions that we no longer possessed the requisite qualification for their official approval and commendation; and to assure them that we had arrived at the firm conviction that the Constitution, construed in the light of well established rules of legal interpretation, might be made consistent in its details with the noble purposes avowed in its preamble; and that hereafter we should insist upon the application of such rules to that instrument, and demand that it be wielded in behalf of emancipation. The change in our opinion on this subject has not been hastily arrived at. A careful study of the writings of Lysander Spooner, of Gerrit Smith, and of William Goodell, has brought us to our present conclusion. We found, in our former position, that, when debating the question, we were compelled to go behind the letter of the Constitution, and to seek its meaning in the history and practice of the nation under it—a process always attended with disadvantages; and certainly we feel little inclination to shoulder disadvantages of any kind, in order to give slavery the slightest protection. In short, we hold it to be a system of lawless violence; that it *never was lawful, and never can be made so;* and that it is the first duty of every American citizen, whose conscience permits so to do, to use his *political* as well as his *moral* power for its overthrow. Of course, this avowal did not pass without animadversion, and it would have been strange if it had passed without some crimination; for it is hard for any combination or party to attribute good motives to any one who differs from them in what they deem a vital point. Brother Garrison at once exclaimed, "There is roguery somewhere!" but we can easily forgive this hastily expressed imputation, falling, as it did, from the lips of one to whom we shall never cease to be grateful, and for whom we have cherished (and do now cherish) a veneration only inferior in degree to that which we owe to our conscience and to our God.

The North Star, May 15, 1851, reprinted in the *Liberator,* May 23, 1851

1. Douglass privately informed Stephen S. Foster and Samuel J. May of his new beliefs early in the spring of 1851. In his letter to the *Liberator* of May 16, 1851, May wrote that Douglass' announcement of his changed sentiments was "not unexpected."

———————————

[Douglass'] former associates greeted the union of *The North Star* and the *Liberty Party Paper* in June, 1851, with the cry that he had sold out his principles to gain financial support from Gerrit Smith and other political Abolitionists. Douglass hotly denied that this change had been sudden and unheralded or that he had been primarily influenced by his financial dependence upon Smith. He offered proof that he had gradually altered his attitude toward political action and had reached the conclusion that the Constitution was an anti-slavery document long before the question of uniting his paper with the *Liberty Party Paper* was broached. But neither his protests nor his evidence convinced his former associates. Samuel J. May voiced the sentiments of the Garrisonians when he wrote: "It would be a strange thing, indeed, if a mind so acute as that of Mr. D. could not find plausible reasons for the change he has made."[1] [II:54]

TO GERRIT SMITH, ESQR.

Rochester, May 21st, 1851

My Dear Sir:
    It needs no ghost to assure me, that I am to be made for a time, an object of special attack. I am not afraid of it and am not pained in view of it. I know too

well the temper of very old companions to hope to escape the penalty which all others have paid who have ventured to differ from them. The leaders in the American Anti-slavery Society are strong men, noble champions in the cause of human freedom, and yet they are not after all the most charitable in construing the motives of those who see matters in a different light from themselves. Insinuations have already been thrown out and will be again.

There are two ways of treating assaults from that quarter and that character. They can be replied to or be allowed to spend their force unanswered. Judgment is needed here. A word of advice from you will at any time be most welcome. You will do me the kindness and the cause of truth and freedom the service, of giving a little attention to any controversy which may arise between my old friends and me, in regard to my present position on the *Constitutional* question. That my ground is correct I am satisfied, and can easily, I think, defend it against the strongest. But I am persuaded that the war will be waged, not against opinions but *motives,* especially if the union of papers which we contemplate shall go into effect.[2] If in this, time shall prove me correct, I shall need a word from you which I am sure you will generously give. You can prove that even in the *North Star* more than two years ago, I gave up the ground that the Constitution, when strictly construed, is a pro-slavery document, and that the only points which prevented me from declaring at that time in favor of voting and against the disunion ground related to the intentions of the framers of the Constitution. I had not made up my mind then, as I have now, that I am only in reason and in conscience bound to learn the intentions of those who framed the Constitution *in the Constitution itself.*

You yourself do know that before I could have had the slightest hope of affecting the union of papers which we now contemplate, that I distinctly assured you of the change in my opinion which I have now publicly avowed. For months I have made no secret of my present opinion. I talked the matter over with S. S. Foster. I told him soon after leaving your house this spring that I no longer hewed to the no voting theory. I assured S. J. May of the same thing. The only reason which I had in not publicly avowing before the change in my mind, was a desire to do so in open court. I espoused the doctrine among my old companions. I wished to reject it in their presence. I write from the office or I am sure that my wife would unite with Miss Griffiths (who is industriously wielding her pen at another desk) in sending love to yourself and Dear Lady.

Yours most truly,

Frederick Douglass

Gerrit Smith Papers, Syracuse University

1. *Liberator,* July 4, 1851.
2. The union of papers was the amalgamation of *The North Star* with the *Liberty Party Paper,* a weekly journal edited and published by John Thomas in Syracuse. This paper had fewer than seven hundred subscribers and was in great financial distress. The merger resulted from a suggestion by Gerrit Smith, the financial backer of Thomas's paper. Douglass was to become the editor of the new publication, Thomas the assistant editor. A new printing office and a good

press would result in a "good looking paper . . . free from all typographical, grammatical, or-thographical, and rhetorical errors and blunders." Smith advanced two hundred dollars for the purchase of the press and type and promised to provide a monthly donation toward the paper's upkeep.

After considerable bickering with John Thomas over the salary of the assistant editor and the location of the paper, the merger became an accomplished fact. On June 30, 1851, the first issue of the new weekly, now named *Frederick Douglass' Paper,* appeared.

[As Douglass] began "wielding the Federal Constitution for the abolition of American Slav-ery," and decided to use both moral and political power, he . . . allied himself with the Lib-erty Party, associating himself with the Gerrit Smith wing of the organization. On May 15, 1851, he wrote that he knew "of no one principle of that party that I should oppose." The following autumn he attended the convention of the Liberty Party in Buffalo and was ap-pointed to the National Committee and to the Committee on Nominations. And in the fall elections he assured anti-slavery voters that there was "no way in which the cause of the slave can be better promoted than by voting the Liberty Party ticket."[1] [II:74]

THE FREE NEGRO'S PLACE IS IN AMERICA, Speech delivered at National Convention of Liberty Party, Buffalo, New York, September 18, 1851

. . . It is my purpose to occupy but a few moments of the meeting on this subject, as I know you are anxious to hear our other friend (Mr. Scoble) from England.[2] In listening to the remarks of our friend from Jamaica,[3] I was struck with the similarity of the reasons given by him for the emigration of colored persons from his country, to those which are given, but with very different motives, by the agents of the American Colonization Society—a society which ever has and, I hope, ever will receive the utter detestation of every colored man in the land. I know that our friend (Mr. A.) will find it difficult to appreciate the reasons which induce the free colored people of these states to insist upon remaining here. He sees us, a suffering people, hemmed in on every side by the malignant and bitter prejudice which excludes us from nearly every profitable employment in this country, and which, as he has well said, has had several of the states to legislate for our expulsion. In the extremity of our need, he comes to us in the spirit of benevolence, I believe, and holds out to us the prospect of a better country, the prospect of a home, where none shall molest or make us afraid. And he will think it strange that we do not accept of his benevolent proffer, and welcome him in his mission of mercy and good will towards us. And yet we must say that such a welcome cannot be given by the colored people of this country without stabbing their own cause to the vitals, without conceding a point which every black man should feel that he must die for rather than yield, and that is, that the prejudice and the mal-administration toward us in this country are invincible to truth, in-vincible to combined and virtuous effort for their overthrow. We must make no such concession. Sir, the slaveholders have long been anxious to get rid of the free colored persons of this country. They know that where we are left free, blacks though we are, thick skulled as they call us, we shall become intelligent, and, moreover, that as we become intelligent, in just that proportion shall we become an annoyance to them in their slaveholding. They are anxious therefore to get us out of the country.—They know that a hundred thousand intelligent, upright, industrious and persevering black men in the northern states must command respect and sympathy, must encircle themselves with the regard of a large class of the virtue-loving, industry-loving people of the North, and that whatever sympathy, whatever respect they are able to command must have a reflex influence upon slavery. And, therefore, they say *"out with them,"* let us get rid of them! For my part, I am not disposed to leave, and, I think, our friend must have been struck with the singular kind of applause at certain sayings of his, during the address—an applause that seemed to come from the galleries, from the door, and from that part of the house that does not wish to be mixed up with the platform. Straws show which way the wind blows,. I fancied, too, that when our friend was portraying the blessings that would result from our removal from this land to Jamaica, that delightful visions were floating before the minds of those gentlemen in the distance. Now, sir, I want to say on behalf of any Negroes I have the honor to represent, that we *have been* with, and still *are* with you, and mean to be with you *to the end.* It may seem ungrateful, but there are some of us who are resolved that you shall not get rid of your colored relations.—Why should we not stay with you? Have we not a right here? I know the cry is raised that we are out of our native land, that this land is the land of the white man; that Africa is the home of the Negro, and not America.

But how stands the matter? I believe that simultaneously with the landing of the Pilgrims, there landed slaves on the shores of this continent, and that for two hundred and thirty years and more we have had a foothold on this continent. We have grown up with you; we have watered your soil with our tears; nourished it with our blood, tilled it with our hard hands. Why should we not stay here? We came when it was a wilderness, and were the pioneers of civilization on this continent. *We* levelled your forests; *our hands* removed the stumps from your fields, and raised the first crops and brought the first produce to your tables. We have been with you, are still with you, have been with you in adversity, and by the help of God will be with you in prosperity.

There was a time when certain learned men of this country undertook to argue us out of existence. Professor *Grant* of New York reckoned us of a race belonging to a by-gone age, which, in the progress of the human family, would become perfectly extinct. Yet we do not die. It does seem that there is a Providence in this matter.—Chain us, lash us, hunt us with bloodhounds, surround us with utter insecurity, render our lives never so hard to be borne, and yet we do live on—smile under it all and are able to smile. Amid all our afflictions there is an invincible determination to stay right here, because a large portion of the American people desire to get rid of us. In proportion to the strength of their desire to have us go, in just that proportion is the strength of our determination to stay, and in staying we ask nothing but justice. We have fought for this country, and we only ask to be treated as well as those who fought against it. We are American citizens, and we only ask to be treated as well as you treat aliens. And you will treat us so yet. Most men assume that we cannot make progress here.

It is untrue, sir. That we can make progress in the future is proved by the progress we have already made. Our condition is rapidly improving. Sir, but a few years ago, if I attempted to ride on the railroad cars in New England, and presumed to take my seat in the cars with white persons, I was dragged out like a beast. I have often been beaten until my hands were blue with the blows in order to make me disengage those hands from the bench on which I was seated.— On every railroad in New England this was the case. How is it now? Why, a Negro may ride just where he pleases and there is not the slightest objection raised, and I have very frequently rode over those same roads since, and never received the slightest indignity on account of my complexion. Indeed the white people are becoming more and more disposed to associate with the blacks. I am constantly annoyed by these pressing attentions. I used to enjoy the privilege of an entire seat, and riding a great deal at night, it was quite an advantage to me, but sometime ago, riding up from Geneva, I had curled myself up, and by the time I had got into a good snooze, along came a man and lifted up my blanket. I looked up and said, "pray do not disturb me, I am a black man." "I don't care who the devil you are, only give me a seat," was the reply. I told you the white people about here are beginning "to don't care who the devil you are." If you can put a dollar in their way, or a seat under them, they don't care "who the devil you are." But I will not detain you longer. I know you are anxious to hear our friend from England.

Frederick Douglass' Paper, October 2, 1851

1. Douglass to Gerrit Smith, May 15, 1851, Gerrit Smith Papers, Syracuse University.

2. In his speech, John Scoble defended the abolition of slavery in the British West Indies from criticism that it had resulted in the degradation of the free black population. He described a visit to the West Indies since emancipation, and told how in general, the conditions of the black population had improved. As for economic depression resulting from emancipation, Scoble insisted that "whatever of depression may exist in our West India Colonies, is not to be traced to emancipation, but to other causes, plain to the man of reflection and knowledge."

3. W. W. Anderson of Jamaica was the speaker referred to. Anderson spoke highly of conditions in Jamaica and recommended emigration of free blacks from the United States to the island.

In September, 1851, Douglass came to the assistance of three fugitive Negroes who had fought back against the slave-catchers. The leader of the group, William Parker, a free Negro in Sadsbury, Pennsylvania, had sheltered a fugitive slave. The slaveowner, one Gorsuch, together with United States marshals, arrived in Sadsbury to claim the fugitive. Warned by the Philadelphia Vigilance Committee the people of Sadsbury were prepared.

When Gorsuch demanded the fugitive, he was refused. His home attacked, Parker sounded a horn and up sprang a large body of Negroes armed with clubs, axes, and guns. A battle ensued, the slave catchers were routed, several were wounded, and Gorsuch himself was killed.

Parker and two fugitives fled, and, after an exciting journey on the Underground, arrived in Rochester. Douglass, aware that the authorities were hot on their trail, took them into his home and gave them shelter.[1] While the men remained in hiding, Julia Griffiths

drove to the boat landing on the Genesee River and made arrangements for their ship-
ment to Canada. When the fugitives boarded the boat, Parker handed Douglass the gun
with which he had killed Gorsuch.[2]

"I could not look upon them as murderers," Douglass wrote years later, "to me they
were heroic defenders of the just rights of men against men-stealers and murderers."[3]
[II:44–45]

FREEDOM'S BATTLE AT CHRISTIANA

The fight at Christiana between the slavecatchers and the alleged fugitive slaves,
continues to excite general discussion. The sensation produced by the death of
the kidnappers is not surpassed by that which occurred throughout the country
on hearing of the fate of the Cuban invaders.[4] The failure of these two patriotic
expeditions, undertaken so nobly by our *law-abiding* citizens, must long be regarded as among the most memorable events of this eventful year.

Everybody seems astonished, that in this land of gospel light and liberty, after
all the sermons of the *Lords, Lathrops, Spencers, Coxes, Springs, Deweys,
Sharpes, Tyngs,*[5] and a host of other Doctors of Divinity, there should be found
men so firmly attached to liberty and so bitterly averse to slavery, as to be willing
to peril even life itself to gain the one and to avoid the other. Pro-slavery men especially are in a state of amazement at the strange affair. That the hunted men
should fight with the biped bloodhounds that had tracked them, even when the animals had a *"paper"* authorizing them to hunt, is to them inexplicable audacity.
"This not that the Negroes fought the kidnappers (no, let no one misrepresent) that
we are astonished, but that they should fight them and kill them when they knew
they had *'papers'.*" That they should kill the men-hunters is, perhaps, natural, and
may be explained in the light of the generally admitted principle "that self-preservation is the first law of nature," but, the rascals! they killed their pursuers, when
they knew they had *"papers!"* Just here is the point of difficulty. What could have
got into these men of sable coating? Didn't they know that slavery, not freedom,
is their natural condition? Didn't they know that their legs, arms, eyes, hands and
heads, were the rightful property of the white men who claimed them?

Can we in charity suppose these Negroes to have been ignorant of the fact that
our *"own dear Fillmore"* (than whom there is none higher—not according to
northern Whiggery, not even in the heavens above nor in the earth beneath) did,
on the eighteenth day of September, in the year one thousand eight hundred and
fifty of the Christian era and in the seventy-fifth year of the freedom and independence of the American people *from the bondage of a foreign yoke,* approve
and send forth a decree, (with all the solemn authority of his great name.) or-
daining that thereafter *Men Should Cease to be Men!*[6]—Oh! ye most naughty
and rebellious fellows! Why stand ye up like men, after this mighty decree? Why
have not your hands become paws, and your arms, legs? Why are you not down
among four-footed beasts with the fox, the wolf and the bear, sharing with them
the chances of the chase, but constituting the most choice game—the peculiar
game of this free and Christian country? We say again that here is the point of
difficulty which demands explanation. For you see, friends and brethren, if the
story gets afloat that these Negroes of Christiana did really hear the words of the

mighty *Fillmore* commanding them to be brutes instead of men, and they did not change as ordered, why, the dangerous doctrine will also get afloat presently that there is a law higher than the law of *Fillmore*. If his voice cannot change the nature of things, it is certain that there is a power above him, and that that frightful heresy, (which has been so justly condemned by the most learned clergy,) called the "Higher Law,"[7] will be received, the evil consequences of which, even the great Daniel cannot portray.

We have said that the pro-slavery people of this country don't know what to make of this demonstration on the part of the alleged fugitive slaves of Christiana. This, however, is possibly a mistake. There is in that translation a lesson which the most obtuse may understand, namely, that all Negroes are not such fools and dastards as to cling to *life* when it is coupled with chains and slavery.

This lesson, though most dearly bought is quite worth the price paid. It was needed. The lamb-like submission with which men of color have allowed themselves to be dragged away from liberty, from family and all that is dear to the hearts of man, had well nigh established the impression that they were conscious of their own fitness for slavery. The frequency of arrests and the ease with which they were made quickened the rapacity, and invited these aggressions of slave-catchers. The Christiana conflict was therefore needed to check these aggressions and to bring the hunters of men to the sober second thought. But was it right for the colored men to resist their enslavers? We answer, Yes, or the whole structure of the world's theory of right and wrong is a lie.—If it be right for any man to resist those who would enslave them, it was right for the men of color at Christiana to resist. If an appeal to arms may ever be innocently made, the appeal in this instance was innocently made; and if it were wrong in them to fight, it can never be right in any case to fight.—For never were there, never can there be more sacred rights to defend than were menaced on this occasion. Life and liberty are the most sacred of all man's rights. If these may be invaded with impunity, all others may be for they comprehend all others. But we take still higher ground. It was right in the light of absolute justice, which says to the aggressor, he that leadeth into captivity shall go into captivity, and he that taketh the sword shall perish by the sword. The man who rushes out of the orbit of his own rights, to strike down the rights of another, does, by that act, divest himself of the right to live; if he be shot down, his punishment is just.

Now what are the facts in the case, for these have been most scandalously misrepresented by the newspapers? The slaveholder's side of the story has been told, but the other side has been dumb, for colored men cannot write. Could they speak for themselves, we dare be sworn that they would testify substantially as follows: Early in the evening of September tenth, a colored man, a fugitive slave, went to the house of Wm. Parker, a sober, well-behaved, and religious man of color,[8] and said to him, William, there is a warrant out for the arrest of some of us, and it is said the kidnappers will be up to-night from Philadelphia. What had we better do? The answer to this was worthy of the man. Come to my house said Parker. Accordingly, five men of color, all told, spent the night at William's house. They sat up late in the apprehension of an attack, but finally went to bed, but sleep—they could not. About two hours before day-light, one of the colored men went into the yard, and on raising his eyes, saw, at that unseasonable hour, fifteen men, coming stealthily along the lane. He ran into the house, and told the inmates that the slave-catchers had come, and the truth of his story was soon confirmed, for a minute elapsed before the whole fifteen were in Parker's yard. The man who went into the yard, did not fasten the door securely, and it was therefore easily forced. The slaveholders rushed into the lower part of the house, and called upon the occupants to give themselves up. Here commenced the conflict. The kidnappers undertook to force their way upstairs, but were met, and compelled to retreat. A parley ensued. Gorsuch was spokesman for himself and his kidnapping comrades, and Parker for himself and guests. Gorsuch said, you have got my property in your house. I have not, said Parker; there is no property here but what belongs to me. I own every trunk, and chair and article of furniture about this house, and none but robbers and murderers would make any attack upon me at this hour of the night. You have got my men in your house, said Gorsuch, and I will have them, or go to hell in the attempt to get them. Parker said I have got none of your men, I never owned a man in my life. I believe it to be a sin to own men; I am no slave-owner. Gorsuch here interrupted Parker, saying, I don't want to hear your abolition lecture. After a long parley, during which Parker repeatedly advised the slave-catchers to go away, stating that he did not wish to hurt them, although they had fired into his house fifteen times, shooting once through his hat crown, the five colored men came downstairs, and walked in front of the slave-catchers, and both parties were now arrayed face to face. Parker then rook the old man, Gorsuch, by the arm, and said to him, old man, we don't want to harm you. You profess to be a Christian; you are a Methodist class-leader, and you ought to be ashamed to be in such business. At this point, young Gorsuch, "father, do you allow a 'n——r' to talk so to you? why don't you shoot him, father?" Parker than answered: "Young man, I would say to you, just what I have said to your father, you had better go about *your* business." Young Gorsuch then fired at Parker, but missed him, and he, Gorsuch, was instantly shot down.—There was now general shooting, and striking with clubs, during which the elder Gorsuch was killed, his son shot through the lungs, and his nephew dangerously wounded. We must not omit to state that the first man to take the advice of the colored preacher, (as Parker is called,) was the Marshal from Philadelphia. *He topped his boom* before the heat of the battle came on, undoubtedly feeling that he had barked up the wrong tree, and that it was best for him to make tracks! The time occupied in parleying between the two parties, was full two hours.

The colored men who are alleged to have taken part in the conflict at Christiana, are to be tried, we are informed, for high treason. This is to cap the climax of American absurdity, to say nothing of American infamy. Our government has virtually made every colored man in the land an outlaw, one who may be hunted by any villain who may think proper to do so, and if the hunted man, finding himself stript of all legal protection, shall lift his arm in his own defense, why, forsooth, he is arrested, arraigned, and tried for high treason, and if found guilty, he must suffer death!

The basis of allegiance is protection. We owe allegiance to the government that protects us, but to the government that destroys us, we owe no allegiance.

The only law which the alleged slave has a right to know anything about, is the law of nature. This is his only law. The enactments of this government do not recognize him as a citizen, but as a thing. In the light of the law, a slave can no more commit treason than a horse or an ox can commit treason. A horse kicks out the brains of his master. Do you try the horse for treason? Then why the slave who does the same thing? You answer, because the slave is a man, and he is therefore responsible for his acts. The answer is sound. The slave is a man and ought not to be treated like a horse, but like a man, and his manhood is his justification for shooting down any creature who shall attempt to reduce him to the condition of a brute.

But there is one consolation after all about this arraignment for treason. It admits our manhood. Sir Walter Scott says that treason is the crime of a gentleman. We shall watch this trial in Philadelphia, and shall report the result when it transpires. Meanwhile, we think that fugitives may sleep more soundly than formerly.

Frederick Douglass' Paper, September 25, 1851

1. About 30 Negroes and two white men were arrested and charged with treason and with levying war against the government of the United States. The defense was conducted so brilliantly by John M. Read and Thaddeus Stevens that all the defendants were acquitted. (*The History of the Trial of Castner Hanway for Treason, by a Member of the Philadelphia Bar,* Philadelphia, 1852.)

2. The following hastily scribbled note sent by Douglass to Samuel D. Porter in September, 1851, probably refers to the three fugitives who had been involved in the Sadsbury affair: "There are three men now at my house who are in great peril. I am unwell, I need your advice. Please come at once." The note was signed "D.F." (Samuel D. Porter Papers, University of Rochester.)

3. Amy Hamner Croughton, "Anti-Slavery Days in Rochester," *Publications of the Rochester Historical Society,* Rochester, N.Y., vol. XV, 1936, pp. 133–34.

4. The reference is to the capture by the Spanish of filibusters, led by Narciso López, who sought to end Spanish rule over Cuba and unite the island with the United States. (López was executed.) For Douglass' criticism of the filibusters, see his editorial, "Cuba and the United States," *Frederick Douglass' Paper,* September 4, 1851. For a discussion of the López filibustering expedition, see Philip S. Foner, *A History of Cuba and its Relations with the United States,* New York, 1963, vol. II, pp. 41–65.

5. Daniel Sharp (1783–1853), Baptist; Gardiner Spring (1785–1873), Presbyterian; Jesse Ames Spencer (1816–1898), Episcopalian; Nathan Lord (1792–1870) and Orville Dewey (1794–1882), Unitarians—all defended the Fugitive Slave Act in their sermons and urged obedience to the law.

6. Millard Fillmore (1800–1874), thirteenth president of the United States, signed the Fugitive Slave Act of 1850.

7. Popularized by William H. Seward in his Senate speech opposing the Compromise of 1850, the "Higher Law" doctrine held that there was a "Higher Law" than the Constitution, and the argument was advanced to justify resistance to the Fugitive Slave Act of 1850.

8. For William Parker, see William Parker, "The Freedman's Story," *Atlantic Monthly,* vol. XVII, February and March, 1866, and Jonathan Katz, *Resistance at Christiana: The Fugitive Slave Rebellion, Christiana, Pennsylvania, September 11, 1851: A Documentary Account,* New York, 1974.

At the Whig Convention in Rochester in October, 1851, the Free Soil delegates proposed Douglass as representative for the Second Assembly District in the State Legislature and secured twenty-two votes on the first ballot for their candidate. The convention finally nominated another candidate, but the press generally admitted that if the "Free Soilers had been in a majority," Douglass would have secured the nomination.[1] Douglass, however, rebuffed all overtures from the Free Soilers. [II:74]

ON BEING CONSIDERED FOR THE LEGISLATURE

To F. Gorton, B. E. Hecock, N. H. Gardner, James Abrams, of American office, Joseph Putnam, S. F. Witherspoon, William Breck, United States Deputy Collector, G. S. Jennings, James H. Delly, John C. Stevens, L. R. Jerome, United States Deputy and of American office, Sulivan Gray, Edward French, William Thorn, Justin Day, Jr., E. R. Warren, John Cornwall, Rev. Charles G. Lee, formerly preacher in Syracuse, M. H. Jennings, Jared Coleman, United States Deputy Collector.

Gentlemen: I have learned with some surprise, that in the Whig Convention held in this city on Saturday last, you signified, by your votes, a desire to make me your representative in the Legislature of this State. Never having, at any time that I can recollect, thought, spoken, or acted, in any way, to commit myself to either the principles or the policy of the Whig party, but on the contrary, having always held, and publicly expressed opinions diametrically opposed to those held by that part of the Whig party which you are supposed to represent, your voting for me, I am bound in courtesy to suppose, is founded in a misapprehension of my political sentiments.

Lest you should, at any other time, commit a similar blunder, I beg to state, once for all, that I do not believe that the slavery question is settled, and settled forever. I do not believe that slave-catching is either a Christian duty, or an innocent amusement. I do not believe that he who breaks the arm of the kidnapper, or wrests the trembling captive from his grasp is a "traitor." I do not believe that human enactments are to be obeyed when they are point blank against the laws of the living God. And believing most fully, (as I do,) the reverse of all this, you will easily believe me to be a person wholly unfit to receive the suffrages of gentlemen holding the opinion and favoring the policy of that wing of the Whig party, denominated "the *Silver Grays.*"

With all the respect which your derision permits me to entertain for you,

I am gentlemen,

Your faithful fellow-citizen,

Frederick Douglass

Frederick Douglass' Paper, October 30, 1851; reprinted in the *New York Times,* November 6, 1851

1. Buffalo *Commercial Advertiser,* reprinted in *Frederick Douglass' Paper,* Oct. 30, 1851. In an appeal to the workingmen of the United States from the working classes of Glasgow there appeared the remark: "As a matter of self-interest, we conceive that any community within the Union who are unable to discern the representative powers of Frederick Douglass,

are wholly at fault. In all earnestness our opinion of him is, that he would do honor to the most gifted legislative assembly in the world, and from such statement you may possibly draw your own conclusions as to what interests we would confide to his care, were it in our power to honor such an one with our suffrages either in matters municipal or parliamentary." (*The North Star*, Jan. 16, 1851.)

EXTRACT FROM A SPEECH at Providence, Nov. 6. Phonographic Report by
    J. L. Crosby.

God, the foundation and source of all goodness, must be loved in order that we may love our fellow-man. In order to produce and cultivare this love, abolitionists should pray, abolitionists should meditate, abolitionists should make it a matter of thought, of deep thought; they should make it so when they come before the people, and that God who seeth in secret will reward them openly. This may seem rather ministerial, than after the fashion of an anti-slavery speech; but I am not sure that we have not, in our utter detestation of the subserviency of the ministry and of the church, cast aside something which we might justly highly prize. I know I have. I know that a few years ago, when engaged more especially in exposing the pro-slavery character of the American Church and clergy (and, as I now believe, justly) still, in coupling together all manner of churches and ministers, I have no doubt that I destroyed in myself that very reverence for God and for religion which is necessary to give vital power to my anti-slavery efforts; and hence I am led to make confession of having erred—greatly erred. I believe that others will make the same confession before long—that they have to some extent undermined that principle in the human mind which is essential for carrying forward a great and holy cause, namely reverence.

Now I believe, it is good for us to meditate on this question, and to take the slave with us in our meditations, to take the slave with us everywhere, to take the slave into our thoughts when we go before God; and if we do this, we shall not be wanting in words to say on this subject.

We believe that there never was a time when we had more strong and powerful reasons for being active in the cause than now. The time was when abolitionists could gather themselves together, when they spoke and prayed, and sang and had a good meeting, and returned to their homes with none to molest them or make them afraid; but at this time we are all prostrate under the arm of the Slave Power to an extent which we never were before and this consideration if no other, should induce greater activity on our part, greater earnestness, greater determination to wage war upon this inhuman *slave* system, of which the Fugitive Slave Law is but a branch, a shoot, a leaf. This, I say, should prompt us to more energetic exertion in behalf of the slave.

I have been, for the past year under a cloud. I have never been so hopeful of the American people on this subject as many of my friends. I never believed, for instance, that slavery would be limited by any action of the last Congress. I never believed that the Fugitive Slave Law would not be enacted and if enacted that it would not be enforced. I believed that the Slave Power would be extended. I believed that the Fugitive Slave Law would be enacted, and, if enacted the nation would be ready to execute it. It has been enacted and it has been executed.

Scarcely a week passes, but some poor fugitive is hunted down in the streets of some of our large cities. In Philadelphia, week after week, instances of this kind are occurring; men and women hunted down in the streets of brotherly love! Men and women hunted down, chained and fettered under the very steeples, and in the shadow of the very churches of our land or dragged through the streets with none to pity, none to succor them, none to help them, Man after man is dragged and chained and fettered into hopeless bondage—hopeless, unending bondage, so far as bondage in this life can be unending. Facts like these are occurring over our land and if there are souls within us, we cannot be indifferent at such a time as this.

Frederick Douglass' Paper, December 11, 1851

HON. HORACE GREELEY AND THE PEOPLE OF COLOR

There is not, perhaps, a single public man in all the United States, unconnected with the Anti-Slavery movement, who has, at any time, evinced a more generous and manly spirit towards the Free People of color, nor indicated the entertainment of a more genuine desire for their welfare and happiness than Horace Greeley of the *New York Tribune*. He has often defended our people from the brutal attacks of the press, *far* more effectively than ever our technical friends could do; for while they speak to tens, Greeley speaks to thousands. Regarding us in the light of a misunderstood, under-estimated, and oppressed people, struggling against immense odds, to be men and citizens, he has, at times extended to us a helping hand, almost fraternal. Did a colored man rise up among his brethren, and by industry, perseverance and talents, make himself master of a position among men of high moral and intellectual worth, Mr. Greeley was among the first of all American Editors to recognize and to proclaim the fact with apparent satisfaction. There is not a colored public man in the United States who has signalized himself, either by his devotion to liberty, or by his ability, who is not, to some extent, indebted to Mr. Greeley for a friendly word of encouragement. Even within the last two years, he has poured such a torrent of denunciation upon the slave system; attacked with such boldness the slave power; portrayed with such faithfulness, the disgraceful and shocking slave hunts; despised with such hearty good will, the demagoguism of Webster and Fillmore; as displayed in their pretended alarm for the safety of the Union; battled so earnestly against the new doctrine of treason as almost to win for himself the unpopular yet enviable title of being the Negro's friend. What black man did not feel grateful to the *Tribune*, a few months ago, for the gallant manner in which it exposed the frauds and falsehoods practiced upon this nation in respect to the true character of Haiti? *Who* among us did not feel a thrill of gratitude when he read, in September last, the defense of the heroic colored men at Christiana? Why, every one of us. But while we do not forget all this, we must nevertheless, recognize Mr. Greeley as being among the most effective and dangerous of our foes. We say this more in sadness than in bitterness of spirit. We may misapprehend his motives: they are between himself and the Searcher of all hearts; yet we repeat, that by his present position he is, practically, among our deadliest enemies. He is the advocate of Colonization, which, to us, means *ultimate extermination;* and in this advocacy, Henry Clay himself, whose olfactory nerves are disturbed by the most distant allusion to "*Free* people of color," does not assume a more haughty, imperious, and overbearing spirit towards us than this same Horace Greeley. In urging our departure from our native land to Africa, this gentleman appeals more to our fears than to our hopes. He paints our ignorance, degradation and wretchedness in the darkest colors and warns us that *worse,* not better, days await us in this country. He points us to the inhuman, barbarous, and unconstitutional legislation of Indiana,[1] and without pouring forth a true man's abhorrence of such legislation, he complacently asks us what such legislation means; and intimates that this is but the beginning of the "Reign of Terror." He does not call upon the people of Indiana to wipe out its disgraceful Statute; but he calls upon the free people of color to *take the hint from such legislation,* and *clear out to Africa.* He has even become so averse to our remaining here of late, as to frown upon all efforts of ours to obtain our civil and political rights. He held up the Committee who signed the call for the "Colored State Convention," to the ridicule of his readers last week, for proposing such a convention, and stated that he had always advised Negroes to refrain from agitating for the right of suffrage. If his advice were taken, he would probably point to our inertness as an evidence of our unfitness for the exercise of that right. A queer and incomprehensible man is Mr. Greeley. For the poverty and misery of the poor white man in this country, his mind is fruitful of remedies. "Working men's union," "Co-operative associations" have his hearty concurrence and advocacy. At their conventions and congresses, he is prophet, priest, and philosopher—soothing their poverty by his sympathy, increasing their courage by his counsel, and stimulating them to exertion by the fruits of his own example. But for the poor black man, he has neither sympathy, prophecy, nor plan. His advice to us may be stated in two words, and is such as is commonly addressed to dogs—"*Be gone.*"

Mr. Greeley is called a benevolent man; and, as such, we ask him, how he reconciles his course towards the Free Colored People with the spirit of benevolence? Does he not know that the certain effect of urging them to depart, and alarming them with the idea that it is impossible for them to remain here, is to damp their aspirations, to fill them with doubt, and to paralyze their energies for improvement and elevation? To us, this circumstance constitutes one of the strongest objections to the Colonization discussion.—Slaveholders will not emigrate with their slaves to New Mexico, while there are doubt and uncertainity of their ability to hold them when they get there; and colored people will not exert themselves to acquire property, and settle down as good citizens of the State, while they are alarmed and terrified by the prospect of being (ultimately) driven out of the country. This truth is *well* known by our oppressors; and it is, doubtless, one motive for the constant agitation of the Colonization scheme.

Frederick Douglass' Paper, January 29, 1852

1. Soon after Indiana became a state, laws were passed discouraging immigration of free Negroes, forbidding their entrance into and residence in the state, unless heavy bonds for good behavior and support were forthcoming; denying all Negroes the right of testimony against a white person; cutting them off from any share in the public school fund, and excluding them entirely from the public schools. Most of these laws became a dead letter, but in remodeling the State Constitution in 1851, the pro-slavery element in the state pushed for the adoption of these laws as part of the State Constitution. They were incorporated as the "Thirteenth Article," and provided generally for banishing "Negroes" and "mulattoes" from the state, fining heavily any who might employ them, and instructing the legislature to pass the necessary laws for their colonization beyond the state.

HORACE GREELEY AND COLONIZATION

Frederick Douglass' Paper is requested to take notice that the *Tribune* is quite as willing that the blacks should colonize in this country as out of it. Our opinion is that the work of civilizing and Christianizing Africa is one which especially commends itself to the civilized and Christianized blacks of this country; but we would like to see them buy out a township in Southern Jersey, or a county in Nebraska for a beginning, and see what work they would make of colonizing that. What we mean to make them do, even at the expense of incurring their deadliest hatred, is to stop currying horses, blacking boots and opening oysters for a living and go to plowing, hoeing and harvesting their own fields, where the world can see what they do and who does it. Hitherto the great mass of them have acted as if their race were made for servitude and unfit for anything else.— We don't believe that, but they act as if they did, and we mean to make them act differently if we can.—*Tribune.*

We are glad to know that the *Tribune* is *"willing"* that the blacks should colonize in this country; for, however indifferent such *willingness* may seem, when viewed from the stand-point of right and justice, it is magnified into a shining virtue, when compared with the cruel and bitter spirit which would drive every freeman of color off this continent. But we differ from the *Tribune,* even in its more innocent notion of colonization. We say to every colored man, *be a man where you are*; neither a "township in Southern Jersey," nor a "county in Nebraska," can serve you. You must be a man here, and force your way to intelligence, wealth and respectability. If you can't do that here, you can't do it there. By changing your place, you don't change your character. We believe that contact with the white race, even under the many unjust and painful restrictions to which we are subjected, does more toward our elevation and improvement, than the mere circumstance of being separated from them could do. The truth is sometimes acknowledged by Colonizationists themselves. They argue (for a diabolical purpose it is true) that the condition of our race has been improved by their situation as slaves, since it has brought them into contact with a superior people, and afforded them facilities for acquiring knowledge. This position is sound, though the hearts that gave it birth, are rotten. We hold, that while there is personal liberty in the Northern States for the colored people, while they have the privilege to educate their children, to speak and write out their sentiments, to petition, and in some instances, and with some qualifications, to exercise the right of suffrage, the time has not come for them to emigrate from these States to any other country, and last of all, to the wilds of Africa. The *Tribune* need not, we think, apprehend the "deadliest hatred" of the colored people, by urging them to "stop currying horses, blacking boots, and opening oysters for a living." Numbers of them are taking this advice, and urging it upon others. Be patient, Mr. Greeley, a nation may not be born in a day, without a miracle.

Frederick Douglass' Paper, February 26, 1852

It was in [Rochester's] Corinthian Hall . . . that Douglass delivered [this] famous address . . . commemorating the anniversary of the signing of the Declaration of Independence. In bitter, eloquent prose, he told his audience that had he the ability and could he reach the nation's ear he would "pour out a fiery stream of biting ridicule, blasting reproach, withering sarcasm, and stern rebuke"; for it was not light that was needed but fire. He asked his listeners if they had meant to mock him when they invited him to speak on such an occasion; to him the fourth of July was not a day for rejoicing, but for mourning. Then followed what is probably the most moving passage in all of Douglass' speeches: [that which begins,] "What, to the American slave, is your 4th of July?" [II:39]

THE MEANING OF JULY FOURTH FOR THE NEGRO, speech at Rochester, New York, July 5, 1852

Mr. President, Friends and Fellow Citizens:

He who could address this audience without a quailing sensation, has stronger nerves than I have. I do not remember ever to have appeared as a speaker before any assembly more shrinkingly, nor with greater distrust of my ability, than I do this day. A feeling has crept over me quite unfavorable to the exercise of my limited powers of speech. The task before me is one which requires much previous thought and study for its proper performance. I know that apologies of this sort are generally considered flat and unmeaning. I trust, however, that mine will not be so considered. Should I seem at ease, my appearance would much misrepresent me. The little experience I have had in addressing public meetings, in country school houses, avails me nothing on the present occasion.

The papers and placards say that I am to deliver a Fourth of July Oration. This certainly sounds large, and out of the common way, for me. It is true that I have often had the privilege to speak in this beautiful Hall, and to address many who now honor me with their presence. But neither their familiar faces, nor the perfect gage I think I have of Corinthian Hall seems to free me from embarrassment.

The fact is, ladies and gentlemen, the distance between this platform and the slave plantation, from which I escaped, is considerable—and the difficulties to be overcome in getting from the latter to the former are by no means slight. That I am here to-day is, to me, a matter of astonishment as well as of gratitude. You will not, therefore, be surprised, if in what I have to say I evince no elaborate preparation, nor grace my speech with any high sounding exordium. With little experience and with less learning, I have been able to throw my thoughts hastily and imperfectly together; and trusting to your patient and generous indulgence, I will proceed to lay them before you.

This, for the purpose of this celebration, is the Fourth of July. It is the birthday of your National Independence, and of your political freedom. This, to you, is what the Passover was to the emancipated people of God. It carries your minds back to the day, and to the act of your great deliverance; and to the signs, and to the wonders, associated with that act, and that day. This celebration also marks the beginning of another year of your national life; and reminds you that the Republic of America is now 76 years old. I am glad, fellow-citizens, that your nation is so young. Seventy-six years, though a good old age for a man, is but a mere speck in the life of a nation. Three score years and ten is the allotted time for individual men; but nations number their years by thousands. According to this fact, you are, even now, only in the beginning of your national career, still lingering in the period of childhood. I repeat, I am glad this is so. There is hope in the thought, and hope is much needed, under the dark clouds which lower above the horizon. The eye of the reformer is met with angry flashes, portending disastrous times; but his heart may well beat lighter at the thought that America is young, and that she is still in the impressible stage of her existence. May he not hope that high lessons of wisdom, of justice and of truth, will yet give direction to her destiny? Were the nation older, the patriot's heart might be sadder, and the reformer's brow heavier. Its future might be shrouded in gloom, and the hope of its prophets go out in sorrow. There is consolation in the thought that America is young.—Great streams are not easily turned from channels, worn deep in the course of ages. They may sometimes rise in quiet and stately majesty, and inundate the land, refreshing and fertilizing the earth with their mysterious properties. They may also rise in wrath and fury, and bear away, on their angry waves, the accumulated wealth of years of toil and hardship. They, however, gradually flow back to the same old channel, and flow on as serenely as ever. But, while the river may not be turned aside, it may dry up, and leave nothing behind but the withered branch, and the unsightly rock, to howl in the abyss-sweeping wind, the sad tale of departed glory. As with rivers so with nations.

Fellow-citizens, I shall not presume to dwell at length on the associations that cluster about this day. The simple story of it is, that, 76 years ago, the people of this country were British subjects. The style and title of your "sovereign people" (in which you now glory) was not then born. You were under the British Crown. Your fathers esteemed the English Government as the home government; and England as the fatherland. This home government, you know, although a

considerable distance from your home, did, in the exercise of its parental prerogatives, impose upon its colonial children, such restraints, burdens and limitations, as, in its mature judgment, it deemed wise, right and proper.

But your fathers, who had not adopted the fashionable idea of this day, of the
infallibility of government, and the absolute character of its acts, presumed to
differ from the home government in respect to the wisdom and the justice of
some of those burdens and restraints. They went so far in their excitement as to
pronounce the measures of government unjust, unreasonable, and oppressive,
and altogether such as ought not to be quietly submitted to. I scarcely need say,
fellow-citizens, that my opinion of those measures fully accords with that of your
fathers. Such a declaration of agreement on my part would not be worth much
to anybody. It would certainly prove nothing as to what part I might have taken
had I lived during the great controversy of 1776. To say now that America was
right, and England wrong, is exceedingly easy. Everybody can say it; the dastard,
not less than the noble brave, can flippantly discant on the tyranny of England
towards the American Colonies. It is fashionable to do so; but there was a time
when, to pronounce against England, and in favor of the cause of the colonies,
tried men's souls. They who did so were accounted in their day plotters of mischief, agitators and rebels, dangerous men. To side with the right against the
wrong, with the weak against the strong, and with the oppressed against the oppressor! here lies the merit, and the one which, of all others, seems unfashionable in our day. The cause of liberty may be stabbed by the men who glory in the
deeds of your fathers. But, to proceed.

Feeling themselves harshly and unjustly treated, by the home government,
your fathers, like men of honesty, and men of spirit, earnestly sought redress.
They petitioned and remonstrated; they did so in a decorous, respectful, and
loyal manner. Their conduct was wholly unexceptionable. This, however, did
not answer the purpose. They saw themselves treated with sovereign indifference, coldness and scorn. Yet they persevered. They were not the men to look
back.

As the sheet anchor takes a firmer hold, when the ship is tossed by the storm,
so did the cause of your fathers grow stronger as it breasted the chilling blasts of
kingly displeasure. The greatest and best of British statesmen admitted its justice,
and the loftiest eloquence of the British Senate came to its support. But, with that
blindness which seems to be the unvarying characteristic of tyrants, since
Pharaoh and his hosts were drowned in the Red Sea, the British Government persisted in the exactions complained of.

The madness of this course, we believe, is admitted now, even by England; but
we fear the lesson is wholly lost on our present rulers.

Oppression makes a wise man mad. Your fathers were wise men, and if they
did not go mad, they became restive under this treatment. They felt themselves
the victims of grievous wrongs, wholly incurable in their colonial capacity. With
brave men there is always a remedy for oppression. Just here, the idea of a total
separation of the colonies from the crown was born! It was a startling idea, much
more so than we, at this distance of time, regard it. The timid and the prudent
(as has been intimated) of that day were, of course, shocked and alarmed by it.

Such people lived then, had lived before, and will, probably, ever have a place on this planet; and their course, in respect to any great change (no matter how great the good to be attained, or the wrong to be redressed by it), may be calculated with as much precision as can be the course of the stars. They hate all changes, but silver, gold and copper change! Of this sort of change they are always strongly in favor.

These people were called Tories in the days of your fathers; and the appellation, probably, conveyed the same idea that is meant by a more modern, though a somewhat less euphonious term, which we often find in our papers, applied to some of our old politicians.

Their opposition to the then dangerous thought was earnest and powerful; but, amid all their terror and affrighted vociferations against it, the alarming and revolutionary idea moved on, and the country with it.

On the 2d of July, 1776, the old Continental Congress, to the dismay of the lovers of ease, and the worshipers of property, clothed that dreadful idea with all the authority of national sanction. They did so in the form of a resolution; and as we seldom hit upon resolutions, drawn up in our day, whose transparency is at all equal to this, it may refresh your minds and help my story if I read it.

> "Resolved, That these united colonies are, and of right, ought to be free and Independent States; that they are absolved from all allegiance to the British Crown; and that all political connection between them and the State of Great Britain is, and ought to be, dissolved."

Citizens, your fathers made good that resolution. They succeeded; and to-day you reap the fruits of their success. The freedom gained is yours; and you, therefore, may properly celebrate this anniversary. The 4th of July is the first great fact in your nation's history—the very ringbolt in the chain of your yet undeveloped destiny.

Pride and patriotism, not less than gratitude, prompt you to celebrate and to hold it in perpetual remembrance. I have said that the Declaration of Independence is the ringbolt to the chain of your nation's destiny; so, indeed, I regard it. The principles contained in that instrument are saving principles. Stand by those principles, be true to them on all occasions, in all places, against all foes, and at whatever cost.

From the round top of your ship of state, dark and threatening clouds may be seen. Heavy billows, like mountains in the distance, disclose to the leeward huge forms of flinty rocks! That bolt drawn, that chain broken, and all is lost. Cling to this day—cling to it, and to its principles, with the grasp of a storm-tossed mariner to a spar at midnight.

The coming into being of a nation, in any circumstances, is an interesting event. But, besides general considerations, there were peculiar circumstances which make the advent of this republic an event of special attractiveness.

The whole scene, as I look back to it, was simple, dignified and sublime. The population of the country, at the time, stood at the insignificant number of three millions. The country was poor in the munitions of war. The population was weak and scattered, and the country a wilderness unsubdued. There were then no means of concert and combination, such as exist now. Neither steam nor lightning had then been reduced to order and discipline. From the Potomac to the Delaware was a journey of many days. Under these, and innumerable other disadvantages, your fathers declared for liberty and independence and triumphed.

Fellow Citizens, I am not wanting in respect for the fathers of this republic. The signers of the Declaration of Independence were brave men. They were great men, too—great enough to give frame to a great age. It does not often happen to a nation to raise, at one time, such a number of truly great men. The point from which I am compelled to view them is not, certainly, the most favorable; and yet I cannot contemplate their great deeds with less than admiration. They were statesmen, patriots and heroes, and for the good they did, and the principles they contended for, I will unite with you to honor their memory.

They loved their country better than their own private interests; and, though this is not the highest form of human excellence, all will concede that it is a rare virtue, and that when it is exhibited it ought to command respect. He who will, intelligently, lay down his life for his country is a man whom it is not in human nature to despise. Your fathers staked their lives, their fortunes, and their sacred honor, on the cause of their country. In their admiration of liberty, they lost sight of all other interests.

They were peace men; but they preferred revolution to peaceful submission to bondage. They were quiet men; but they did not shrink from agitating against oppression. They showed forbearance; but that they knew its limits. They believed in order; but not in the order of tyranny. With them, nothing was "settled" that was not right. With them, justice, liberty and humanity were "final"; not slavery and oppression. You may well cherish the memory of such men. They were great in their day and generation. Their solid manhood stands out the more as we contrast it with these degenerate times.

How circumspect, exact and proportionate were all their movements! How unlike the politicians of an hour! Their statesmanship looked beyond the passing moment, and stretched away in strength into the distant future. They seized upon eternal principles, and set a glorious example in their defence. Mark them!

Fully appreciating the hardships to be encountered, firmly believing in the right of their cause, honorably inviting the scrutiny of an on-looking world, reverently appealing to heaven to attest their sincerity, soundly comprehending the solemn responsibility they were about to assume, wisely measuring the terrible odds against them, your fathers, the fathers of this republic, did, most deliberately, under the inspiration of a glorious patriotism, and with a sublime faith in the great principles of justice and freedom, lay deep, the corner-stone of the national super-structure, which has risen and still rises in grandeur around you.

Of this fundamental work, this day is the anniversary. Our eyes are met with demonstrations of joyous enthusiasm. Banners and pennants wave exultingly on the breeze. The din of business, too, is hushed. Even mammon seems to have quitted his grasp on this day. The ear-piercing fife and the stirring drum unite their accents with the ascending peal of a thousand church bells. Prayers are made, hymns are sung, and sermons are preached in honor of this day; while the quick martial tramp of a great and multitudinous nation, echoed back by all the hills, valleys and mountains of a vast continent, bespeak the occasion one of thrilling and universal interest—a nation's jubilee.

Friends and citizens, I need not enter further into the causes which led to this anniversary. Many of you understand them better than I do. You could instruct me in regard to them. That is a branch of knowledge in which you feel, perhaps, a much deeper interest than your speaker. The causes which led to the separation of the colonies from the British crown have never lacked for a tongue. They have all been taught in your common schools, narrated at your firesides, unfolded from your pulpits, and thundered from your legislative halls, and are as familiar to you as household words. They form the staple of your national poetry and eloquence.

I remember, also, that, as a people, Americans are remarkably familiar with all facts which make in their own favor. This is esteemed by some as a national trait—perhaps a national weakness. It is a fact, that whatever makes for the wealth or for the reputation of Americans and can be had cheap! will be found by Americans. I shall not be charged with slandering Americans if I say I think the American side of any question may be safely left in American hands.

I leave, therefore, the great deeds of your fathers to other gentlemen whose claim to have been regularly descended will be less likely to be disputed than mine!

My business, if I have any here to-day, is with the present. The accepted time with God and His cause is the ever-living now.

> Trust no future, however pleasant,
> Let the dead past bury its dead;
> Act, act in the living present,
> Heart within, and God overhead.

We have to do with the past only as we can make it useful to the present and to the future. To all inspiring motives, to noble deeds which can be gained from the past, we are welcome. But now is the time, the important time. Your fathers have lived, died, and have done their work, and have done much of it well. You live and must die, and you must do your work. You have no right to enjoy a child's share in the labor of your fathers, unless your children are to be blest by your labors. You have no right to wear out and waste the hard-earned fame of your fathers to cover your indolence. Sydney Smith tells us that men seldom eulogize the wisdom and virtues of their fathers, but to excuse some folly or wickedness of their own. This truth is not a doubtful one. There are illustrations of it near and remote, ancient and modern. It was fashionable, hundreds of years ago, for the children of Jacob to boast, we have "Abraham to our father," when they had long lost Abraham's faith and spirit. That people contented themselves under the shadow of Abraham's great name, while they repudiated the deeds which made his name great. Need I remind you that a similar thing is being done all over this country to-day? Need I tell you that the Jews are not the only people who built the tombs of the prophets, and garnished the sepulchers of the righteous? Washington could not die till he had broken the chains of his slaves. Yet his monument is built up by the price of human blood, and the traders in the bodies and souls of men shout—"We have Washington to *our father.*"—Alas! that it should be so; yet so it is.

> *The evil that men do, lives after them,*
> *The good is oft interred with their bones.*

Fellow-citizens, pardon me, allow me to ask, why am I called upon to speak here to-day? What have I, or those I represent, to do with your national independence? Are the great principles of political freedom and of natural justice, embodied in that Declaration of Independence, extended to us? and am I, therefore, called upon to bring our humble offering to the national altar, and to confess the benefits and express devout gratitude for the blessings resulting from your independence to us?

Would to God, both for your sakes and ours, that an affirmative answer could be truthfully returned to these questions! Then would my task be light, and my burden easy and delightful. For *who* is there so cold, that a nation's sympathy could not warm him? Who so obdurate and dead to the claims of gratitude, that would not thankfully acknowl edge such priceless benefits? Who so stolid and selfish, that would not give his voice to swell the hallelujahs of a nation's jubilee, when the chains of servitude had been torn from his limbs? I am not that man. In a case like that, the dumb might eloquently speak, and the "lame man leap as an hart."

But such is not the state of the case. I say it with a sad sense of the disparity between us. I am not included within the pale of this glorious anniversary! Your high independence only reveals the immeasurable distance between us. The blessings in which you, this day, rejoice, are not enjoyed in common.—The rich inheritance of justice, liberty, prosperity and independence, bequeathed by your fathers, is shared by you, not by me. The sunlight that brought light and healing to you, has brought stripes and death to me. This Fourth July is *yours,* not *mine.* *You* may rejoice, *I* must mourn. To drag a man in fetters into the grand illuminated temple of liberty, and call upon him to join you in joyous anthems, were inhuman mockery and sacrilegious irony. Do you mean, citizens, to mock me, by asking me to speak to-day? If so, there is a parallel to your conduct. And let me warn you that it is dangerous to copy the example of a nation whose crimes, towering up to heaven, were thrown down by the breath of the Almighty, burying that nation in irrevocable ruin! I can to-day take up the plaintive lament of a peeled and woe-smitten people!

"By the rivers of Babylon, there we sat down. Yea! we wept when we remembered Zion. We hanged our harps upon the willows in the midst thereof. For there, they that carried us away captive, required of us a song; and they who wasted us required of us mirth, saying, Sing us one of the songs of Zion. How can we sing the Lord's song in a strange land? If I forget thee, O Jerusalem, let my right hand forget her cunning. If I do not remember thee, let my tongue cleave to the roof of my mouth."

Fellow-citizens, above your national, tumultuous joy, I hear the mournful wail of millions! whose chains, heavy and grievous yesterday, are, to-day, rendered more intolerable by the jubilee shouts that reach them. If I do forget, if I do not faithfully remember those bleeding children of sorrow this day, "may my right hand forget her cunning, and may my tongue cleave to the roof of my mouth!" To forget them, to pass lightly over their wrongs, and to chime in with the popular theme, would be treason most scandalous and shocking, and would make me a reproach before God and the world. My subject, then, fellow-citizens, is American slavery. I shall see this day and its popular characteristics from the slave's point of view. Standing there identified with the American bondman, making his wrongs mine, I do not hesitate to declare, with all my soul, that the character and conduct of this nation never looked blacker to me than on this 4th of July! Whether we turn to the declarations of the past, or to the professions of the present, the conduct of the nation seems equally hideous and revolting. America is false to the past, false to the present, and solemnly binds herself to be false to the future. Standing with God and the crushed and bleeding slave on this occasion, I will, in the name of humanity which is outraged, in the name of liberty which is fettered, in the name of the constitution and the Bible which are disregarded and trampled upon, dare to call in question and to denounce, with all the emphasis I can command, everything that serves to perpetuate slavery— the great sin and shame of America! "I will not equivocate; I will not excuse";[1] I will use the severest language I can command; and yet not one word shall escape me that any man, whose judgment is not blinded by prejudice, or who is not at heart a slaveholder, shall not confess to be right and just.

But I fancy I hear some one of my audience say, "It is just in this circumstance that you and your brother abolitionists fail to make a favorable impression on the public mind. Would you argue more, and denounce less; would you persuade more, and rebuke less; your cause would be much more likely to succeed." But, I submit, where all is plain there is nothing to be argued. What point in the anti-slavery creed would you have me argue? On what branch of the subject do the people of this country need light? Must I undertake to prove that the slave is a man? That point is conceded already. Nobody doubts it. The slaveholders themselves acknowledge it in the enactment of laws for their government. They acknowledge it when they punish disobedience on the part of the slave. There are seventy-two crimes in the State of Virginia which, if committed by a black man (no matter how ignorant he be), subject him to the punishment of death; while only two of the same crimes will subject a white man to the like punishment. What is this but the acknowledgment that the slave is a moral, intellectual, and responsible being? The manhood of the slave is conceded. It is admitted in the fact that Southern statute books are covered with enactments forbidding, under severe fines and penalties, the teaching of the slave to read or to write. When you can point to any such laws in reference to the beasts of the field, then I may consent to argue the manhood of the slave. When the dogs in your streets, when the fowls of the air, when the cattle on your hills, when the fish of the sea, and the reptiles that crawl, shall be unable to distinguish the slave from a brute, *then* will I argue with you that the slave is a man!

For the present, it is enough to affirm the equal manhood of the Negro race. Is it not astonishing that, while we are ploughing, planting, and reaping, using all kinds of mechanical tools, erecting houses, constructing bridges, building ships, working in metals of brass, iron, copper, silver and gold; that, while we are reading, writing and ciphering, acting as clerks, merchants and secretaries, having among us lawyers, doctors, ministers, poets, authors, editors, orators and teachers; that, while we are engaged in all manner of enterprises common to other men, digging gold in California, capturing the whale in the Pacific, feeding sheep and cattle on the hill-side, living, moving, acting, thinking, planning, living in families as husbands, wives and children, and, above all, confessing and worshipping the Christian's God, and looking hopefully for life and immortality beyond the grave, we are called upon to prove that we are men!

Would you have me argue that man is entitled to liberty? that he is the rightful owner of his own body? You have already declared it. Must I argue the wrongfulness of slavery? Is that a question for Republicans? Is it to be settled by the rules of logic and argumentation, as a matter beset with great difficulty, involving a doubtful application of the principle of justice, hard to be understood? How should I look to-day, in the presence of Americans, dividing, and subdividing a discourse, to show that men have a natural right to freedom? speaking of it relatively and positively, negatively and affirmatively. To do so, would be to make myself ridiculous, and to offer an insult to your understanding.—There is not a man beneath the canopy of heaven that does not know that slavery is wrong *for him*.

What, am I to argue that it is wrong to make men brutes, to rob them of their liberty, to work them without wages, to keep them ignorant of their relations to their fellow men, to beat them with sticks, to flay their flesh with the lash, to load their limbs with irons, to hunt them with dogs, to sell them at auction, to sunder their families, to knock out their teeth, to burn their flesh, to starve them into obedience and submission to their masters? Must I argue that a system thus marked with blood, and stained with pollution, is *wrong?* No! I will not. I have better employment for my time and strength than such arguments would imply.

What, then, remains to be argued? Is it that slavery is not divine; that God did not establish it; that our doctors of divinity are mistaken? There is blasphemy in the thought. That which is inhuman, cannot be divine! *Who* can reason on such a proposition? They that can, may; I cannot. The time for such argument is passed.

At a time like this, scorching irony, not convincing argument, is needed. O! had I the ability, and could reach the nation's ear, I would, to-day, pour out a fiery stream of biting ridicule, blasting reproach, withering sarcasm, and stern rebuke. For it is not light that is needed, but fire; it is not the gentle shower, but thunder. We need the storm, the whirlwind, and the earthquake. The feeling of the nation must be quickened; the conscience of the nation must be roused; the propriety of the nation must be startled; the hypocrisy of the nation must be exposed; and its crimes against God and man must be proclaimed and denounced.

What, to the American slave, is your 4th of July? I answer; a day that reveals to him, more than all other days in the year, the gross injustice and cruelty to which he is the constant victim. To him, your celebration is a sham; your boasted liberty, an unholy license; your national greatness, swelling vanity; your sounds of rejoicing are empty and heartless; your denunciation of tyrants, brass fronted impudence; your shouts of liberty and equality, hollow mockery; your prayers and hymns, your sermons and thanksgivings, with all your religious parade and solemnity, are, to Him, mere bombast, fraud, deception, impiety, and hypocrisy—a thin veil to cover up crimes which would disgrace a nation of savages. There is not a nation on the earth guilty of practices more shocking and bloody than are the people of the United States, at this very hour.

Go where you may, search where you will, roam through all the monarchies and despotisms of the Old World, travel through South America, search out every abuse, and when you have found the last, lay your facts by the side of the everyday practices of this nation, and you will say with me, that, for revolting barbarity and shameless hypocrisy, America reigns without a rival.

Take the American slave-trade, which we are told by the papers, is especially prosperous just now. Ex-Senator Benton tells us that the price of men was never higher than now. He mentions the fact to show that slavery is in no danger. This trade is one of the peculiarities of American institutions. It is carried on in all the large towns and cities in one-half of this confederacy; and millions are pocketed every year by dealers in this horrid traffic. In several states this trade is a chief source of wealth. It is called (in contradistinction to the foreign slave-trade) *"the internal slave-trade."* It is, probably, called so, too, in order to divert from it the horror with which the foreign slave-trade is contemplated. That trade has long since been denounced by this government as piracy. It has been denounced with burning words from the high places of the nation as an execrable traffic. To arrest it, to put an end to it, this nation keeps a squadron, at immense cost, on the coast of Africa. Everywhere, in this country, it is safe to speak of this foreign slave-trade as a most inhuman traffic, opposed alike to the laws of God and of man. The duty to extirpate and destroy it, is admitted even by our doctors of divinity. In order to put an end to it, some of these last have consented that their colored brethren (nominally free) should leave this country, and establish themselves on the western coast of Africa! It is, however, a notable fact that, while so much execration is poured out by Americans upon all those engaged in the foreign slave-trade, the men engaged in the slave-trade between the states pass without condemnation, and their business is deemed honorable.

Behold the practical operation of this internal slave-trade, the American slave-trade, sustained by American politics and American religion. Here you will see men and women reared like swine for the market. You know what is a swine-drover? I will show you a man-drover. They inhabit all our Southern States. They perambulate the country, and crowd the highways of the nation, with droves of human stock. You will see one of these human flesh jobbers, armed with pistol, whip, and bowie-knife, driving a company of a hundred men, women, and children, from the Potomac to the slave market at New Orleans. These wretched people are to be sold singly, or in lots, to suit purchasers. They are food for the cotton-field and the deadly sugar-mill. Mark the sad procession, as it moves wearily along, and the inhuman wretch who drives them. Hear his savage yells and his blood-curdling oaths, as he hurries on his affrighted captives! There, see the old man with locks thinned and gray. Cast one glance, if you please, upon that young mother, whose shoulders are bare to the scorching sun, her briny tears falling on the brow of the babe in her arms. See, too, that girl of thirteen, weeping, *yes!* weeping, as she thinks of the mother from whom she has been torn! The drove moves tardily. Heat and sorrow have nearly consumed their strength; suddenly you hear a quick snap, like the discharge of a rifle; the fetters clank, and the chain rattles simultaneously; your ears are saluted with a scream, that seems to have torn its way to the centre of your soul! The crack you heard was the sound of the slave-whip; the scream you heard was from the woman you saw with the babe. Her speed had faltered under the weight of her child and her chains! that gash on her shoulder tells her to move on. Follow this drove to New Orleans. Attend the auction; see men examined like horses; see the forms of women rudely and brutally exposed to the shocking gaze of American slave-buyers. See this drove sold and separated forever; and never forget the deep, sad sobs that arose from that scattered multitude. Tell me, citizens, where, under the sun, you can witness a spectacle more fiendish and shocking. Yet this is but a glance at the American slave-trade, as it exists, at this moment, in the ruling part of the United States.

I was born amid such sights and scenes. To me the American slave-trade is a terrible reality. When a child, my soul was often pierced with a sense of its horrors. I lived on Philpot Street, Fell's Point, Baltimore, and have watched from the wharves the slave ships in the Basin, anchored from the shore, with their cargoes of human flesh, waiting for favorable winds to waft them down the Chesapeake. There was, at that time, a grand slave mart kept at the head of Pratt Street, by Austin Woldfolk. His agents were sent into every town and county in Maryland, announcing their arrival, through the papers, and on flaming *"hand-bills,"* headed cash for Negroes. These men were generally well dressed men, and very captivating in their manners; ever ready to drink, to treat, and to gamble. The fate of many a slave has depended upon the turn of a single card; and many a child has been snatched from the arms of its mother by bargains arranged in a state of brutal drunkenness.

The flesh-mongers gather up their victims by dozens, and drive them, chained, to the general depot at Baltimore. When a sufficient number has been collected here, a ship is chartered for the purpose of conveying the forlorn crew to Mobile, or to New Orleans. From the slave prison to the ship, they are usually driven in the darkness of night; for since the antislavery agitation, a certain caution is observed.

In the deep, still darkness of midnight, I have been often aroused by the dead, heavy footsteps, and the piteous cries of the chained gangs that passed our door. The anguish of my boyish heart was intense; and I was often consoled, when speaking to my mistress in the morning, to hear her say that the custom was very wicked; that she hated to hear the rattle of the chains and the heart-rending cries. I was glad to find one who sympathized with me in my horror.

Fellow-citizens, this murderous traffic is, to-day, in active operation in this boasted republic. In the solitude of my spirit I see clouds of dust raised on the highways of the South; I see the bleeding footsteps; I hear the doleful wail of fettered humanity on the way to the slave-markets, where the victims are to be sold like *horses, sheep,* and *swine,* knocked off to the highest bidder. There I see the tenderest ties ruthlessly broken, to gratify the lust, caprice and rapacity of the buyers and sellers of men. My soul sickens at the sight.

> *Is this the land your Fathers loved,*
> *The freedom which they toiled to win?*
> *Is this the earth whereon they moved?*
> *Are these the graves they slumber in?*

But a still more inhuman, disgraceful, and scandalous state of things remains to be presented. By an act of the American Congress, not yet two years old, slavery has been nationalized in its most horrible and revolting form. By that act, Mason and Dixon's line has been obliterated; New York has become as Virginia; and the power to hold, hunt, and sell men, women and children, as slaves, remains no longer a mere state institution, but is now an institution of the whole United States. The power is co-extensive with the star-spangled banner, and American Christianity. Where these go, may also go the merciless slave-hunter. Where these are, man is not sacred. He is a bird for the sportsman's gun. By that most foul and fiendish of all human decrees, the liberty and person of every man are put in peril. Your broad republican domain is hunting ground for *men*. Not for thieves and robbers, enemies of society, merely, but for men guilty of no crime. Your law-makers have commanded all good citizens to engage in this hellish sport. Your President, your Secretary of State, your *lords, nobles,* and ecclesiastics enforce, as a duty you owe to your free and glorious country, and to your God, that you do this accursed thing. Not fewer than forty Americans have, within the past two years, been hunted down and, without a moment's warning, hurried away in chains, and consigned to slavery and excruciating torture. Some of these have had wives and children, dependent on them for bread; but of this, no account was made. The right of the hunter to his prey stands superior to the right of marriage, and to *all* rights in this republic, the rights of God included! For black men there is neither law nor justice, humanity nor religion. The Fugitive Slave *Law* makes mercy to them a crime; and bribes the judge who tries them. An American judge gets ten dollars for every victim he consigns to slavery, and five, when he fails to do so. The oath of any two villains is sufficient, under this hell-black enactment, to send the most pious and exemplary black man into the remorseless jaws of slavery! His own testimony is nothing. He can bring no witnesses for himself. The minister of American justice is bound by the law to hear but *one* side; and *that* side is the side of the oppressor. Let this damning fact be perpetually told. Let it be thundered around the world that in tyrant-killing, king-hating, people-loving, democratic, Christian America the seats of justice are filled with judges who hold their offices under an open and palpable *bribe,* and are bound, in deciding the case of a man's liberty, *to hear only his accusers!*

In glaring violation of justice, in shameless disregard of the forms of administering law, in cunning arrangement to entrap the defenceless, and in diabolical intent this Fugitive Slave Law stands alone in the annals of tyrannical legislation. I doubt if there be another nation on the globe having the brass and the baseness to put such a law on the statute-book. If any man in this assembly thinks differently from me in this matter, and feels able to disprove my statements, I will gladly confront him at any suitable time and place he may select.

I take this law to be one of the grossest infringements of Christian Liberty, and, if the churches and ministers of our country were not stupidly blind, or most wickedly indifferent, they, too, would so regard it.

At the very moment that they are thanking God for the enjoyment of civil and religious liberty, and for the right to worship God according to the dictates of their own consciences, they are utterly silent in respect to a law which robs religion of its chief significance and makes it utterly worthless to a world lying in wickedness. Did this law concern the *"mint, anise, and cummin"*—abridge the right to sing psalms, to partake of the sacrament, or to engage in any of the ceremonies of religion, it would be smitten by the thunder of a thousand pulpits. A general shout would go up from the church demanding *repeal, repeal, instant repeal!*—And it would go hard with that politician who presumed to solicit the votes of the people without inscribing this motto on his banner. Further, if this demand were not complied with, another Scotland would be added to the history of religious liberty, and the stern old covenanters would be thrown into the shade. A John Knox would be seen at every church door and heard from every pulpit, and Fillmore would have no more quarter than was shown by Knox to the beautiful, but treacherous, Queen Mary of Scotland. The fact that the church of our country (with fractional exceptions) does not esteem "the Fugitive Slave Law" as a declaration of war against religious liberty, implies that that church regards religion simply as a form of worship, an empty ceremony, and *not* a vital principle, requiring active benevolence, justice, love, and good will towards man. It esteems sacrifice above mercy; psalm-singing above right doing; solemn meetings above practical righteousness. A worship that can be conducted by persons who refuse to give shelter to the houseless, to give bread to the hungry, clothing to the naked, and who enjoin obedience to a law forbidding these acts of mercy is a curse, not a blessing to mankind. The Bible addresses all such persons as "scribes, pharisees, hypocrites, who pay tithe of *mint, anise,* and *cummin,* and have omitted the weightier matters of the law, judgment, mercy, and faith."

But the church of this country is not only indifferent to the wrongs of the slave, it actually takes sides with the oppressors. It has made itself the bulwark of American slavery, and the shield of American slave-hunters. Many of its most eloquent Divines, who stand as the very lights of the church, have shamelessly given the sanction of religion and the Bible to the whole slave system. They have taught that man may, properly, be a slave; that the relation of master and slave is ordained of God; that to send back an escaped bondman to his master is clearly the duty of all the followers of the Lord Jesus Christ; and this horrible blasphemy is palmed off upon the world for Christianity.

For my part, I would say, welcome infidelity! welcome atheism! welcome anything! in preference to the gospel, *as preached by those Divines!* They convert the very name of religion into an engine of tyranny and barbarous cruelty, and serve to confirm more infidels, in this age, than all the infidel writings of Thomas Paine, Voltaire, and Bolingbroke put together have done! These ministers make religion a cold and flinty-hearted thing, having neither principles of right action nor bowels of compassion. They strip the love of God of its beauty and leave the throne of religion a huge, horrible, repulsive form. It is a religion for oppressors, tyrants, man-stealers, and *thugs*. It is not that *"pure and unde-filed religion"* which is from above, and which is *"first pure, then peaceable, easy to be entreated,* full of mercy and good fruits, *without partiality, and with-out hypocrisy."* But a religion which favors the rich against the poor; which ex-alts the proud above the humble; which divides mankind into two classes, tyrants and slaves; which says to the man in chains, *stay there;* and to the op-pressor, *oppress on;* it is a religion which may be professed and enjoyed by all the robbers and enslavers of mankind; it makes God a respecter of persons, de-nies his fatherhood of the race, and tramples in the dust the great truth of the brotherhood of man. All this we affirm to be true of the popular church, and the popular worship of our land and nation—a religion, a church, and a wor-ship which, on the authority of inspired wisdom, we pronounce to be an abom-ination in the sight of God. In the language of Isaiah, the American church might be well addressed, "Bring no more vain oblations; incense is an abomination unto me: the new moons and Sabbaths, the calling of assemblies, I cannot away with; it is iniquity, even the solemn meeting. Your new moons, and your ap-pointed feasts my soul hateth. They are a trouble to me; I am weary to bear them; and when ye spread forth your hands I will hide mine eyes from you. Yea! when ye make many prayers, I will not hear. Your hands are full of blood; cease to do evil, learn to do well; seek judgment; relieve the oppressed; judge for the fatherless; plead for the widow."

The American church is guilty, when viewed in connection with what it is do-ing to uphold slavery; but it is superlatively guilty when viewed in its connection with its ability to abolish slavery.

The sin of which it is guilty is one of omission as well as of commission. Al-bert Barnes but uttered what the common sense of every man at all observant of the actual state of the case will receive as truth, when he declared that "There is no power out of the church that could sustain slavery an hour, if it were not sus-tained in it."

Let the religious press, the pulpit, the Sunday School, the conference meeting, the great ecclesiastical, missionary, Bible and tract associations of the land array their immense powers against slavery, and slave-holding; and the whole system of crime and blood would be scattered to the winds, and that they do not do this involves them in the most awful responsibility of which the mind can conceive.

In prosecuting the anti-slavery enterprise, we have been asked to spare the church, to spare the ministry; but *how,* we ask, could such a thing be done? We are met on the threshold of our efforts for the redemption of the slave, by the church and ministry of the country, in battle arrayed against us; and we are com-pelled to fight or flee. From *what* quarter, I beg to know, has proceeded a fire so deadly upon our ranks, during the last two years, as from the Northern pulpit? As the champions of oppressors, the chosen men of American theology have ap-peared—men honored for their so-called piety, and their real learning. The Lords of Buffalo, the Springs of New York, the Lathrops of Auburn, the Coxes and Spencers of Brooklyn, the Gannets and Sharps of Boston, the Deweys of Wash-ington, and other great religious lights of the land have, in utter denial of the au-thority of *Him* by whom they professed to be called to the ministry, deliberately taught us, against the example of the Hebrews, and against the remonstrance of the Apostles, *that we ought to obey man's law before the law of God.*[2]

My spirit wearies of such blasphemy; and how such men can be supported, as the "standing types and representatives of Jesus Christ," is a mystery which I leave others to penetrate. In speaking of the American church, however, let it be distinctly understood that I mean the *great mass* of the religious organizations of our land. There are exceptions, and I thank God that there are. Noble men may be found, scattered all over these Northern States, of whom Henry Ward Beecher, of Brooklyn; Samuel J. May, of Syracuse; and my esteemed friend (Rev. R. R. Raymond) on the platform, are shining examples; and let me say further, that, upon these men lies the duty to inspire our ranks with high religious faith and zeal, and to cheer us on in the great mission of the slave's redemption from his chains.

One is struck with the difference between the attitude of the American church towards the anti-slavery movement, and that occupied by the churches in England towards a similar movement in that country. There, the church, true to its mission of ameliorating, elevating and improving the condition of mankind, came forward promptly, bound up the wounds of the West Indian slave, and restored him to his liberty. There, the question of emancipation was a high religious question. It was demanded in the name of humanity, and according to the law of the living God. The Sharps, the Clarksons, the Wilberforces, the Buxtons, the Burchells, and the Knibbs were alike famous for their piety and for their philanthropy. The anti-slavery movement *there* was not an anti-church movement, for the reason that the church took its full share in prosecuting that movement: and the anti-slavery movement in this country will cease to be an anti-church movement, when the church of this country shall assume a favorable instead of a hostile position towards that movement.

Americans! your republican politics, not less than your republican religion, are flagrantly inconsistent. You boast of your love of liberty, your superior civilization, and your pure Christianity, while the whole political power of the nation (as embodied in the two great political parties) is solemnly pledged to support and perpetuate the enslavement of three millions of your countrymen. You hurl your anathemas at the crowned headed tyrants of Russia and Austria and pride yourselves on your Democratic institutions, while you yourselves consent to be the mere *tools* and *body-guards* of the tyrants of Virginia and Carolina. You invite to your shores fugitives of oppression from abroad, honor them with banquets, greet them with ovations, cheer them, toast them, salute them, protect them, and pour out your money to them like water; but the fugitives from your own land you advertise, hunt, arrest, shoot, and kill. You glory in your refinement and your universal education; yet you maintain a system as barbarous and dreadful as ever stained the character of a nation—a system begun in avarice, supported in pride, and perpetuated in cruelty. You shed tears over fallen Hungary, and make the sad story of her wrongs the theme of your poets, statesmen, and orators, till your gallant sons are ready to fly to arms to vindicate her cause against the oppressor; but, in regard to the ten thousand wrongs of the American slave, you would enforce the strictest silence, and would hail him as an enemy of the nation who dares to make those wrongs the subject of public discourse! You are all on fire at the mention of liberty for France or for Ireland; but are as cold as an iceberg at the thought of liberty for the enslaved of America. You discourse eloquently on the dignity of labor; yet, you sustain a system which, in its very essence, casts a stigma upon labor. You can bare your bosom to the storm of British artillery to throw off a three-penny tax on tea; and yet wring the last hard earned farthing from the grasp of the black laborers of your country. You profess to believe "that, of one blood, God made all nations of men to dwell on the face of all the earth," and hath commanded all men, everywhere, to love one another; yet you notoriously hate (and glory in your hatred) all men whose skins are not colored like your own. You declare before the world, and are understood by the world to declare that you "*hold these truths to be self-evident, that all men are created equal; and are endowed by their Creator with certain inalienable rights; and that among these are, life, liberty, and the pursuit of happiness;* and yet, you hold securely, in a bondage which, according to your own Thomas Jefferson, "*is worse than ages of that which your fathers rose in rebellion to oppose,*" a seventh part of the inhabitants of your country.

Fellow-citizens, I will not enlarge further on your national inconsistencies. The existence of slavery in this country brands your republicanism as a sham, your humanity as a base pretense, and your Christianity as a lie. It destroys your moral power abroad: it corrupts your politicians at home. It saps the foundation of religion; it makes your name a hissing and a bye-word to a mocking earth. It is the antagonistic force in your government, the only thing that seriously disturbs and endangers your *Union*. It fetters your progress; it is the enemy of improvement; the deadly foe of education; it fosters pride; it breeds insolence; it promotes vice; it shelters crime; it is a curse to the earth that supports it; and yet you cling to it as if it were the sheet anchor of all your hopes. Oh! be warned! be warned! a horrible reptile is coiled up in your nation's bosom; the venomous creature is nursing at the tender breast of your youthful republic; *for the love of God, tear away,* and fling from you the hideous monster, and *let the weight of twenty millions crush and destroy it forever!*

But it is answered in reply to all this, that precisely what I have now denounced is, in fact, guaranteed and sanctioned by the Constitution of the United States; that, the right to hold, and to hunt slaves is a part of that Constitution framed by the illustrious Fathers of this Republic.

Then, I dare to affirm, notwithstanding all I have said before, your fathers stooped, basely stooped

> To palter with us in a double sense:
> And keep the word of promise to the ear,
> But break it to the heart.

And instead of being the honest men I have before declared them to be, they were the veriest impostors that ever practised on mankind. This is the inevitable conclusion, and from it there is no escape; but I differ from those who charge this baseness on the framers of the Constitution of the United States. It is a slander upon their memory, at least, so I believe. There is not time now to argue the constitutional question at length; nor have I the ability to discuss it as it ought to be discussed. The subject has been handled with masterly power by Lysander Spooner, Esq., by William Goodell, by Samuel E. Sewall, Esq., and last, though not least, by Gerrit Smith, Esq. These gentlemen have, as I think, fully and clearly vindicated the Constitution from any design to support slavery for an hour.

Fellow-citizens! there is no matter in respect to which the people of the North have allowed themselves to be so ruinously imposed upon as that of the pro-slavery character of the Constitution. In that instrument I hold there is neither warrant, license, nor sanction of the hateful thing; but interpreted, as it ought to be interpreted, the Constitution is a glorious liberty document. Read its preamble, consider its purposes. Is slavery among them? Is it at the gateway? or is it in the temple? it is neither. While I do not intend to argue this question on the present occasion, let me ask, if it be not somewhat singular that, if the Constitution were intended to be, by its framers and adopters, a slaveholding instrument, why neither slavery, slaveholding, nor slave can anywhere be found in it. What would be thought of an instrument, drawn up, legally drawn up, for the purpose of entitling the city of Rochester to a tract of land, in which no mention of land was made? Now, there are certain rules of interpretation for the proper understanding of all legal instruments. These rules are well established. They are plain, commonsense rules, such as you and I, and all of us, can understand and apply, without having passed years in the study of law. I scout the idea that the question of the constitutionality, or unconstitutionality of slavery, is not a question for the people. I hold that every American citizen has a right to form an opinion of the constitution, and to propagate that opinion, and to use all honorable means to make his opinion the prevailing one. Without this right, the liberty of an American citizen would be as insecure as that of a Frenchman. Ex-Vice-President Dallas tells us that the constitution is an object to which no American mind can be too attentive, and no American heart too devoted. He further says, the Constitution, in its words, is plain and intelligible, and is meant for the home-bred, unsophisticated understandings of our fellow-citizens. Senator Berrien tells us that the Constitution is the fundamental law, that which controls all others. The charter of our liberties, which every citizen has a personal interest in understanding thoroughly. The testimony of Senator Breese, Lewis Cass, and many others that might be named, who are everywhere esteemed as sound lawyers, so regard the constitution. I take it, therefore, that it is not presumption in a private citizen to form an opinion of that instrument.

Now, take the Constitution according to its plain reading, and I defy the presentation of a single pro-slavery clause in it. On the other hand, it will be found to contain principles and purposes, entirely hostile to the existence of slavery.

I have detained my audience entirely too long already. At some future period I will gladly avail myself of an opportunity to give this subject a full and fair discussion.

Allow me to say, in conclusion, notwithstanding the dark picture I have this day presented, of the state of the nation, I do not despair of this country. There are forces in operation which must inevitably work the downfall of slavery.

"The arm of the Lord is not shortened," and the doom of slavery is certain. I, therefore, leave off where I began, with hope. While drawing encouragement from "the Declaration of Independence," the great principles it contains, and the genius of American Institutions, my spirit is also cheered by the obvious tendencies of the age. Nations do not now stand in the same relation to each other that they did ages ago. No nation can now shut itself up from the surrounding world and trot round in the same old path of its fathers without interference. The time was when such could be done. Long established customs of hurtful character could formerly fence themselves in, and do their evil work with social impunity. Knowledge was then confined and enjoyed by the privileged few, and the multitude walked on in mental darkness. But a change has now come over the affairs of mankind. Walled cities and empires have become unfashionable. The arm of commerce has borne away the gates of the strong city. Intelligence is penetrating the darkest corners of the globe. It makes its pathway over and under the sea, as well as on the earth. Wind, steam, and lightning are its chartered agents. Oceans no longer divide, but link nations together. From Boston to London is now a holiday excursion. Space is comparatively annihilated.—Thoughts expressed on one side of the Atlantic are distinctly heard on the other.

The far off and almost fabulous Pacific rolls in grandeur at our feet. The Celestial Empire, the mystery of ages, is being solved. The fiat of the Almighty, "Let there be Light," has not yet spent its force. No abuse, no outrage whether in taste, sport or avarice, can now hide itself from the all-pervading light. The iron shoe, and crippled foot of China must be seen in contrast with nature. Africa must rise and put on her yet unwoven garment. "Ethiopia shall stretch out her hand unto God." In the fervent aspirations of William Lloyd Garrison, I say, and let every heart join in saying it:

> God speed the year of jubilee
>   The wide world o'er!
> When from their galling chains set free,
> Th' oppress'd shall vilely bend the knee,
>
> And wear the yoke of tyranny
>   Like brutes no more.
> That year will come, and freedom's reign,
> To man his plundered rights again
>   Restore.
>
> God speed the day when human blood
>   Shall cease to flow!
> In every clime be understood,
> The claims of human brotherhood,
> And each return for evil, good,
>   Not blow for blow;
>
> That day will come all feuds to end,
> And change into a faithful friend
>   Each foe.

> *God speed the hour, the glorious hour,*
> *When none on earth*
> *Shall exercise a lordly power,*
> *Nor in a tyrant's presence cower;*
> *But to all manhood's stature tower,*
> *By equal birth!*
> *That hour will come, to each, to all,*
> *And from his prison-house, to thrall*
> *Go forth.*
>
> *Until that year, day, hour, arrive,*
> *With head, and heart, and hand I'll strive,*
> *To break the rod, and rend the gyve,*
> *The spoiler of his prey deprive—*
> *So witness Heaven!*
> *And never from my chosen post,*
> *Whate'er the peril or the cost,*
> *Be driven.*

Oration delivered in Corinthian Hall, Rochester, by Frederick Douglass, July 5, 1852, Rochester, 1852

1. These words were used by William Lloyd Garrison in the first issue of the *Liberator*.

2. At the request of the Union Safety Committee of New York City, formed by conservative merchants, the clergymen of New York agreed to set aside December 12, 1850, as a day on which sermons would be delivered upholding the Compromise of 1850, especially the Fugitive Slave Act. Practically all the sermons advised acquiescence on the part of the people to the law and denounced the "higher law" doctrine. The sermons were published and distributed by the Union Safety Committee. (See the pamphlets, *The Law-Abiding Conscience and the Higher Law Conscience, with Remarks on the Fugitive Slave Question*, New York, 1850; John C. Lord, *The Higher Law in Its Application to the Fugitive Slave Bill*, New York, 1851; and Philip S. Foner, *Business and Slavery*, pp. 56–58.)

As [Douglass] marked the busy preparations of the Free Soilers for the national campaign and noted the enthusiasm evoked by this growing mass movement, he realized the futility of the isolationist policy he had been advocating. Recalling his original position that it was the duty of the Abolitionists to lead the Free Soilers, he wrote to Smith on July 15, 1852, that it was their political responsibility to attend the approaching Pittsburgh convention of the Free Soil Party. The gathering could be "made to occupy such a position as the 'Liberty Party' may properly vote for its candidates." The masses who would be present in Pittsburgh were far ahead of their leaders, and were quite prepared to support a program in advance of "mere *Free Soil*." It remained for men like Smith to bring up the issues around which the delegates would rally.[1]

On August 11, 1852, two thousand persons crowded into the Masonic Hall in Pittsburgh to attend the second national convention of the Free Soil Party. Douglass and Smith sat in the New York section. Soon after convening, Douglass was nominated as a secretary of the convention by Lewis Tappan, was elected by acclamation, and took his seat "amid loud applause." Barely had the next speaker started to address the delegates, when loud calls for Douglass drowned out his voice. Amid cheers Douglass moved to the platform. Taken by surprise, he had no prepared address. But he launched immediately into what reporters described as "an aggressive speech."[2] . . .

The audience applauded Douglass throughout and cheered as he concluded with the advice that "numbers should not be looked to as much as right." As the afternoon session drew to a close, the delegates again called on Douglass to speak, but he declined with the brief statement that his throat was sore from his previous exertion.

The reception of Douglass at the Free Soil Convention aroused comment in Europe as well as in this country. In London *The Anti-Slavery Reporter* viewed it as one of the brightest signs of the time. "The appointment of Frederick Douglass as one of the secretaries of the convention," it observed, "is a cheering indication of the advance of anti-slavery sentiment in the United States. That a colored man should be called upon to act as an officer in a large political meeting is a sign of progress in that country, where to belong to the enslaved race has been to be proscribed and neglected."[3]

Douglass informed his readers that he had been favorably impressed by the "spirit" displayed at the Free Soil Convention "no less than with its principles" and candidates. John P. Hale of New Hampshire was "a large-hearted philanthropist . . . a dreaded foe to slavery," and George W. Julian of Indiana was "one of the truest and most disinterested friends of freedom whom we have ever met." He urged the Liberty Party convention about to assemble at Canastota, New York, to endorse the Free Soil nominations. [II:75–76]

THE FUGITIVE SLAVE LAW, speech to the National Free Soil Convention at Pittsburgh, August 11, 1852

Gentlemen, I take it that you are in earnest, and mean all you say by this call, and therefore I will address you. I am taken by surprise, but I never withhold a word on such an occasion as this. The object of this Convention is to organize a party, not merely for the present, but a party identified with eternal principles and therefore permanent. I have come here, not so much of a free soiler as others have come. I am, of course, for circumscribing and damaging slavery in every way I can. But my motto is extermination—not only in New Mexico, but in New Orleans—not only in California but in South Carolina. No where has God ordained that this beautiful land shall be cursed with bondage by enslaving men. Slavery has no rightful existence anywhere. The slaveholders not only forfeit their right to liberty, but to life itself.—[Applause.] The earth is God's, and it ought to be covered with righteousness, and not slavery. We expect this great National Convention to lay down some such principle as this. What we want is not a temporary organization, for a temporary want, but a firm, fixed, immovable, liberty party. Had the old liberty party continued true to its principles, we never should have seen such a hell born enactment as the Fugitive Slave Law.

In making your Platform, nothing is to be gained by a timid policy. The more closely we adhere to principle, the more certainly will we command respect. Both National Conventions acted in open contempt of the antislavery sentiment of the North, by incorporating, as the corner stone of their two platforms, the infamous law to which I have alluded—a law which, I think, will never be repealed—it is too bad to be repealed—a law fit only to trampled under foot, (suiting the action to the word). The only way to make the Fugitive Slave Law a dead letter is to make half a dozen or more dead kidnappers. [Laughter and applause.] A half dozen more dead kidnappers carried down South would cool the ardor of Southern gentlemen, and keep their rapacity in check. That is perfectly right as long as the colored man has no protection. The colored men's rights are less than those of a jackass. No man can take away a jackass without submitting the matter to twelve men in any part of this country. A black man may be carried away without any reference to a jury. It is only necessary to claim him, and that some villain should swear to his identity. There is more protection there for a horse, for a donkey, or anything, rather than a colored man—who is, therefore, justified in the eye of God, in maintaining his right with his arm.

A Voice.—Some of us do not believe that doctrine.

Douglass.—The man who takes the office of a bloodhound ought to be treated as a bloodhound; and I believe that the lines of eternal justice are sometimes so obliterated by a course of long continued oppression that it is necessary to revive them by deepening their traces with the blood of a tyrant. [Much applause.] This Fugitive Slave Law had the support of the Lords, and the Coxes, the Tyngs, the Sharps and the flats. [Laughter.] It is nevertheless a degradation and a scandalous outrage on religious liberty; and if the American people were not sunk into degradation too deep for one possessing so little eloquence as I do to describe, they would feel it, too. This vile, infernal law does not interfere with singing of psalms, or anything of that kind, but with the weightier matters of the law, judgment, mercy, and faith. It makes it criminal for you, sir, to carry out the principles of Christianity. It forbids you the right to do right—forbids you to show mercy—forbids you to follow the example of the good Samaritan.

Had this law forbidden any of the rites of religion, it would have been a very different thing. Had it been a law to strike at baptism, for instance, it would have been denounced from a 1000 pulpits, and woe to the politician who did not come to the rescue.—But, I am spending my strength for nought; what care we for religious liberty? what are we—an unprincipled set of knaves. [Laughter.] You feel it to be so. Not a man of you that looks a fellow Democrat or Whig in the face, but knows it. But it has been said that this law is constitutional—if it were, it would be equally the legitimate sphere of government to repeal it. I am proud to be one of the disciples of Gerrit Smith, and this is his doctrine; and he only utters what all law writers have said who have risen to any eminence. Human government is for the protection of rights; and when human government destroys human rights, it ceases to be a government, and becomes a foul and blasting conspiracy; and is entitled to no respect whatever.

It has been said that our fathers entered into a covenant for this slavecatching. Who were your daddies? [Laughter.] I take it they were men, and so are you. You are the sons of your fathers; and if you find your fathers exercising any rights that you don't find among your rights, you may be sure that they have transcended their limits. If they have made a covenant that you should do that which they have no right to do themselves, they transcended their own authority, and surely it is not binding on you. If you look over the list of your rights, you do not find among them any right to make a slave of your brother. [Many cries of "no, no, no—and so say we, all of us."]

Well, you have just as good a right to do so as your fathers had. It is a fundamental truth that every man is the rightful owner of his own body. If you have no right to the possession of another man's body your fathers had no such right. But suppose that they have written in a constitution that they have a right, you and I have no right to conform to it. Suppose you and I had made a deed to give away two or three acres of blue sky; would the sky fall—and would anybody be able to plough it? You will say that this is an absurdity, and so it is. The binding quality of law, is its reasonableness. I am safe, therefore, in saying, that slavery cannot be legalized at all. I hope, therefore, that you will take the ground that this slavery is a system, not only of wrong, but is of a lawless character, and cannot be christianized nor legalized. [Applause.]

Can you hear me in that end of the hall now? [Laughter and applause.] I trust that this Convention will be the means of laying before the country the principles of the Liberty Party which I have the honor to represent, to some extent, on this floor. Slavery is such a piracy that it is known neither to law nor gospel—it is neither human nor divine—a monstrosity that cannot be legalized. If they took this ground it would be the handwriting on the wall to the Belshazzars of the South. It would strip the crime of its legality, and all the forms of law would shrink back with horror from it. As I have always an object when speaking on such subjects as this, I wish you to supply yourselves with Gerrit Smith's pamphlet on civil government, which I now hold in my hand. I thought you doubted the impossibility of legalizing slavery. [Cries of no.]

Could a law be made to pass away any of your individual rights? No. And so neither can a law be made to pass away the right of the black man. This is more important than most of you seem to think. You are about to have a party, but I hope not such a party as will gather up the votes, here and there, to be swallowed up at a meal by the great parties. I think I know what some leading men are now thinking. We hear a great deal of the independent, free democracy—at one time independent and another time dependent—but I want always to be independent, and not hurried to and fro into the ranks of Whigs or Democrats. It has been said that we ought to take the position to gain the greatest number of voters, but that is wrong.

We have had enough of that folly. It was said in 1848 that Martin Van Buren would carry a strong vote in New York; he did so but he almost ruined us. He merely looked at us as into the pigpen to see how the animal grew; but the table was the final prospect in view; he regarded the Free Soil party as a fatling to be devoured. [Great laughter.] Numbers should not be looked to so much as right. The man who is right is a majority. He who has God and conscience on his side, has a majority against the universe. Though he does not represent the present state, he represents the future state. If he does not represent what we are, he represents what we ought to be. In conclusion, this party ought to extend a hand to the noble, self-sacrificing patriot—glorious Kossuth. But I am a voting delegate, and must now go to the convention. You will excuse me for breaking off so abruptly.

Frederick Douglass' Paper, August, 1852

1. Gerrit Smith Papers, Syracuse University.
2. *Frederick Douglass' Paper,* Aug. 20, 1852; Frederic May Holland, *Frederick Douglass,* pp. 210–12.
3. *The Anti-Slavery Reporter,* Aug. 20, Sept. 10, 1852.

[Douglass'] main concern in the autumn of 1852 was in the campaign for representative from the twenty-second Congressional district of New York. His friend and mentor, Gerrit Smith, had been nominated for the office by the Liberty or Free Democrat's Party. Douglass campaigned through the state even though he doubted that Smith, being "too far in advance of the people and of the age," could possibly be elected. He could not believe his ears when people said they were "going to vote for Gerrit Smith" and expressed confidence in Smith's election. "This however, I deem unreasonable," he wrote to Smith from Chittenango Falls on October 21. "How could such a thing be? Oh! if it could only be so, the cup of my joy would be full. It is too good to be true. Yet *I* am the only man whom I have heard speak disparagingly in private about the matter."[1]

The Free Soil vote of 1852 was about one-half of what it had been in 1848, but Douglass' disappointment was speedily forgotten with the announcement of the election of Gerrit Smith to Congress by an overwhelming majority. The "grand event," which even Garrison admitted was "among the most extraordinary political events of this most extraordinary age," completely filled his "cup of joy." "The election of *Gerrit Smith*—what an era!" he exulted. . . . As his excitement mounted, he predicted that "with men and money," the Liberty Party could carry New York state "for freedom" in 1856.[2]

Douglass placed great hope in Smith's congressional career. On August 18, 1853, four months before the session convened, he wrote to his co-reformer advising him to master the parliamentary rules of Congress so as "to defy all the mantraps which they will surely set for your feet." Unfortunately Smith did not remain in Washington long enough to put this sound advice to much use. After joining in the attack on the Kansas-Nebraska Bill, introduced into Congress early in 1854, and leading the movement to strike out the word "white" from the bill granting land to actual settlers in New Mexico, he decided he had had enough of life in the nation's capital and returned to Peterboro. On August 7, 1854, Smith resigned his seat in Congress. The only explanation he gave was the "pressure of my far too extensive business."[3] [II:77]

TO GERRIT SMITH, ESQR.

Rochester, Nov. 6th, 1852

My dear Sir:

The cup of my joy is full. If my humble labors have in any measure contributed (as you kindly say they have) to your election, I am most amply rewarded. You are now, thank heaven, within sight and hearing of this guilty nation. For the rest, I fear nothing. You will do the work of an apostle of Liberty. May God give you strength. Your election forms an era in the great Anti-Slavery struggle. For the first time, a man will appear in the American Congress completely imbued with the spirit of freedom. Heretofore, virtue has had to ask pardon of men. Our friends who have nobly spoken great truths in Congress, on the subject of Slavery, have all of them found themselves in straits where they have been compelled to disavow or qualify their abolitionism so as to seriously damage the beauty and force of their testimony. Not so will it be with you. Should your life and health be spared (which blessings are devoutly prayed for), you will go into Congress with the "Jerry Level" in your hand, regarding Slavery as "naked piracy." You go to Congress, not by the grace of a party caucus, bestowed as a reward for party services; not by concealment, bargain or compromise, but by the unbought suffrages of your fellow citizens acting independently of, and in defiance of party! The odds against you were not insignificant. The *Dixes,* the *Woodburys,* the *Stantons,* the *Seymours,* and the *Conklings,* the very flower of your opponents were pitted against you. You are elected and they are defeated. "Nough said." You go to Congress, not for quiet nor seclusion, shut out from the eye of the world, where your thoughts and feelings had to be imagined, but you go from the very whirlwind of agitation, from "rescue trials," from womans' rights conventions and from "Jerry celebrations," where your lightest words were caught up and perverted to your hurt. You go to Congress a *free man.* I will not weary you with congratulations. My friend Julia, is even more ecstatic than myself about your election.

    Please remind, favourably, Mrs. Smith, of your faithful friend,

Frederick Douglass

Gerrit Smith Papers, Syracuse University

    1. Douglass to Gerrit Smith, Oct. 21, 1852, Gerrit Smith Papers, Syracuse University.

    Actually the candidates of the Liberty Party were William Goodell and S. M. Bell of Virginia. A committee of Liberty Party men had been appointed to ask Hale and Julian certain questions with the understanding that the party's support hinged on their answers. They asked whether a political party should regard itself as organized for the purpose of securing equal rights to all, and "whether you believe that slavery, so far as capable of legislation is a naked piracy, around which there can be no legal covering." Hale and Julian ignored the questions, so the Liberty Party met again in Syracuse on September 30 and made the nominations referred to above. Douglass was one of the vice-presidents of the convention, but he did not remove the names of Hale and Julian from the masthead of his paper.

    2. *Liberator,* reprinted in *Frederick Douglass' Paper,* Nov. 19, 1852; Douglass to Samuel J. May [?], Nov. 10, 1852, Frederick Douglass *Mss.,* New York Historical Society.

    3. Douglass to Gerrit Smith, Aug. 18, 1853, Gerrit Smith Papers, Syracuse University; *New York Tribune,* Aug. 19, 1854.

A CALL TO WORK

The mission of the political abolitionists of this country is to abolish slavery. The means to accomplish this great end is, first, to disseminate antislavery sentiment; and, secondly, to combine that sentiment and render it a political force which shall, for a time, operate as a check on violent measures for supporting slavery; and, finally, overthrow the great evil of slavery itself.—The end sought is sanctioned by God and all his holy angels, by every principle of justice, by every pulsation of humanity, and by all the hopes of this republic. A better cause never summoned men to its support, nor invoked the blessings of heaven for success. Its opponents (whether they know it or not) are fighting against all that is noble in man—all that is best in society; and if their principles shall prove uneradicable, and their measures successful, then, just so sure as there is a God in the universe, the hope of this republic will go out in blood. Men may laugh— they may scoff—they may wrap themselves in heedless indifference; but every fact of history, every sentiment of religion, every indication of Providence proclaims, trumpet-tongued, that a day of reckoning will come. If this guilty country be saved—if it be made a blessing to mankind, that result will be accomplished, under God, by the faithful and self-sacrificing labors of the abolitionists. The work is great—very great. There has been a great deal done; but there is much more to do. There never was a time when we should advance to that work with a lighter heart or a firmer tread. The anti-slavery sentiment of the country has just made its mark on the public records in a manner not to be despised, and well calculated to inspire confidence in final success. The means are at hand to carry that mark higher still. Whoever lives to see the year 1856, will see anti-slavery in the field, with a broader front and loftier mien than it ever wore before.

Causes are in operation greatly calculated to concentrate the anti-slavery sentiment, and to bring it to bear directly against slavery. One of these causes is the complete overthrow of the Whig party,[1] and the necessity which it imposes upon its Northern anti-slavery members to assume an attitude more in harmony with their convictions than they could do on the Baltimore platform. The Southern wing of this party (never very reliable) will naturally become fused into the Democratic party, with which it is now more in sympathy than it can be with Northern Whigs. It is evident, that the Whigs of the North must stand alone or stand with us. It is equally evident that they cannot, and do not, desire to array themselves against the only living sentiment of the North, since they would, by such a course, only commit political suicide and make themselves of no political consequence. The danger now to be apprehended is, not that our numbers will not increase, and increase rapidly and largely, but that we shall be tempted to modify our platform of principles and abate the stringency of our testimonies, so as to accommodate the wishes of those who have not hitherto distinctly acted with us, and who now wish to do so.

Now the way to swell our vote for freedom and to prevent the evil, thus briefly hinted at, is, to spread anti-slavery light, and to educate the people on the whole subject of slavery—circulate the documents—let the anti-slavery speaker, more than ever, go abroad—let every town be visited, and let truth find its way into every house in the land. The people want to do what is best. They must be shown that to do right is best. The great work to be done is to educate the people, and to this work the abolitionist should address himself with full purpose of heart.—This is no time for rest; but a time for every one to be up and doing. The battle, though not just begun, is far from being completed. The friends of freedom, in their various towns and counties, should, without waiting for some central organization to move in the matter, take up the work themselves—collect funds—form committees—send for documents— call in lecturers, and bring the great question of the day distinctly and fully before their fellow-citizens. We would not give the snap of our finger for one who begins and ends his anti-slavery labors on election day. Anti-slavery papers are to be upheld—lecturers are to be sustained—correspondence is to be kept up— acquaintances are to be formed with those who sympathize with us, and a fraternal and brotherly feeling is to be increased, strengthened and kept up. Here, then, is work—work for every one to do—work which must be done if ever the great cause in which we have embarked is brought to a happy consummation. Let every one make this cause his own. Let him remember the deeply injured and imbruted slave as bound with him. Let him not forget that he is but a steward, and that he is bound to make a righteous use of his Lord's money. Let him make his anti-slavery a part of his very being, and God will bless him and increase him an hundred fold. Now is the time for a real anti-slavery revival. The efforts to silence discussion should be rebuked. We *ought* not, we must not be "hushed and mum" at the bidding of slave power conventions, or any other power on earth.

Frederick Douglass' Paper, November 19, 1852

1. Winfield Scott, the Whig candidate, was overwhelmingly defeated by Franklin Pierce in the electoral college. Pierce carried every state but four, but his popular majority was small, less than 50,000 out of 3,100,000 votes.

In March, 1853, Douglass visited Harriet Beecher Stowe at her home in Andover, Ohio, to consult with the author of *Uncle Tom's Cabin* "as to some method which should contribute successfully, and permanently, to the improvement and elevation of the free colored people in the United States. . . ." Mrs. Stowe asked Douglas to propose the best plan to achieve the goal.[1]

Anxious to secure approval of his plan, Douglass read his reply to Mrs. Stowe to the Rochester National Negro Convention. A number of delegates, Charles L. Remond and George T. Downing among them, were hostile to the proposal. They argued that the college would be too costly; that the Negro people would not be interested in the institution. The old contention that a Negro college was a capitulation to prejudice against color was also raised.

Douglass, Dr. James McCune Smith, and James W. C. Pennington led the battle for the industrial college. They pointed out that there were few Negro apprentices since there were not many Negro craftsmen and most white craftsmen were opposed to taking a Negro into service. An industrial college would produce skilled workers, and the presence of an "industrious, enterprising, upright, thrifty, and intelligent free black population would be a killing refutation of slavery." Since the college would be open to all students regardless of color, it could hardly be considered a segregated institution.

The majority of the delegates concurred with the arguments in favor of the industrial college, and voted to sponsor the institution.[2] [II:32]

TO HARRIET BEECHER STOWE

Rochester, March 8th, 1853

My Dear Mrs. Stowe:

You kindly informed me, when at your house, a fortnight ago, that you designed to do something which should permanently contribute to the improvement and elevation of the free colored people in the United States. You especially expressed an interest in such of this class as had become free by their own exertions, and desired most of all to be of service to them. In what manner, and by what means, you can assist this class most successfully, is the subject upon which you have done me the honor to ask my opinion.

Begging you to excuse the unavoidable delay, I will now most gladly comply with your request, but before doing so, I desire to express, dear Madam, my deep sense of the value of the services which you have already rendered my afflicted and persecuted people, by the publication of your inimitable book on the subject of slavery. That contribution to our bleeding cause, alone, involves us in a debt of gratitude which cannot be measured; and your resolution to make other exertions on our behalf excites in me emotions and sentiments, which I scarcely need try to give forth in words. Suffice it to say, that I believe you to have the blessings of your enslaved countrymen and countrywomen; and the still higher reward which comes to the soul in the smiles of our merciful Heavenly father, whose ear is ever open to the cries of the oppressed.

With such sentiments, dear Madam, I will at once proceed to lay before you, in as few words as the nature of the case will allow, my humble views in the premises. First of all, let me briefly state the nature of the disease, before I undertake to prescribe the remedy. Three things are notoriously true of us as a people. These are POVERTY, IGNORANCE AND DEGRADATION. Of course there are exceptions to this general statement; but these are so few as only to prove its essential truthfulness. I shall not stop here to inquire minutely into the causes which have produced our present condition; nor to denounce those whom I believe to be responsible for these causes. It is enough that we shall agree upon the character of the evil, whose existence we deplore, and upon some plan for its removal.

I assert then, that *poverty, ignorance* and *degradation* are the combined evil or, in other words, these constitute the social disease of the Free Colored people in the United States.

To deliver them from this triple malady, is to improve and elevate them, by which I mean simply to put them on an equal footing with their white fellow-countrymen in the sacred right to "*Life, Liberty* and the pursuit of happiness." I am for no fancied or artificial elevation, but only ask fair play. How shall this be obtained? I answer, first, not by establishing for our use high schools and colleges. Such institutions are, in my judgment, beyond our immediate occasions, and are not adapted to our present most pressing wants. High schools and colleges are excellent institutions, and will, in due season, be greatly subservient to our progress; but they are the result, as well as they are the demand of a point of progress, which we, as a people, have not yet attained. Accustomed, as we have been, to the rougher and harder modes of living, and of gaining a livelihood, we cannot, and we ought not to hope that, in a single leap from our low condition, we can reach that of *Ministers, Lawyers, Doctors, Editors, Merchants, &c.* These will, doubtless, be attained by us; but this will only be, when we have patiently and laboriously, and I may add successfully, mastered and passed through the intermediate gradations of agriculture and the mechanic arts. Besides, there are (and perhaps this is a better reason for my view of the case) numerous institutions of learning in this country, already thrown open to colored youth. To my thinking, there are quite as many facilities now afforded to the colored people, as they can spare the time, from the sterner duties of life, to avail themselves of. In their present condition of poverty, they cannot spare their sons and daughters two or three years at boarding schools or colleges, to say nothing of finding the means to sustain them while at such institutions. I take it, therefore, that we are well provided for in this respect; and that it may be fairly inferred from the past that the facilities for our education, so far as schools and colleges in the Free States are concerned, will increase quite in proportion with our future wants. Colleges have been open to colored youth in this country during the last dozen years. Yet few, comparatively, have acquired a classical education; and even this few have found themselves educated far above a living condition, there being no methods by which they could turn their learning to account. Several of this latter class have entered the ministry; but you need not be told that an educated people is needed to sustain an educated ministry. There must be a certain amount of cultivation among the people to sustain such a ministry. At present, we have not that cultivation amongst us; and therefore, we value, in the preacher, strong lungs, rather than high learning. I do not say that educated ministers are not needed amongst us.—Far from it! I wish there were more of them; but to increase their number is *not* the largest benefit you can bestow upon us.

You, dear Madam, can help the masses. You can do something for the thousands; and by lifting these from the depths of poverty and ignorance, you can make an educated ministry and an educated class possible. In the present circumstances, prejudice is a bar to the educated black minister among the whites; and ignorance is a bar to him among the blacks.

We have now two or three colored lawyers in this country; and I rejoice in the fact; for it affords very gratifying evidence of our progress. Yet it must be confessed that, in point of success, our lawyers are as great failures as are our ministers. White people will not employ them to the obvious embarrassment of their causes, and the blacks, taking their *cue* from the whites, have not sufficient confidence in their abilities to employ them. Hence, educated colored men, among the colored people, are at a very great discount. It would seem that education and emigration go together with us; for as soon as a man rises amongst us, capable, by his genius and learning, to do us great service, just so soon he finds that he can serve himself better by going elsewhere. In proof of this, I might instance the Russwurms—the Garnetts—the Wards—the Crummells and others—all men of superior ability and attainments, and capable of removing mountains of prejudice against their race, by their simple presence in the country; but these gentlemen, finding themselves embarrassed here by the peculiar disadvantages to which I have referred—disadvantages in part growing out of their education—being repelled by ignorance on the one hand, and prejudice on the other, and having no taste to continue a contest against such odds, they have sought more congenial climes, where they can live more peaceable and quiet lives. I regret their election—but I cannot blame them; for, with an equal amount of education, and the hard lot which was theirs, I might follow their example.

But, again, it has been said that the colored people must become farmers—that they must go on the land, in order to their elevation. Hence, many benevolent people are contributing the necessary funds to purchase land in Canada, and elsewhere, for them. That prince of good men, Gerrit Smith, has given away thousands of acres to colored men in this State, thinking, doubtless, that in so doing he was conferring a blessing upon them.[3] Now, while I do not undervalue the efforts which have been made, and are still being made in this direction, yet I must say that I have far less confidence in such efforts, than I have in the benevolence which prompts them. Agricultural pursuits are not, as I think, suited to our condition. The reason of this is not to be found so much in the occupation, (for it is a noble and ennobling one,) as in the people themselves. That is only a remedy, which can be applied to the case; and the difficulty in agricultural pursuits, as a remedy for the evils of poverty and ignorance amongst us, is that it cannot, for various reasons, be applied.

We cannot apply it, because it is almost impossible to get colored men to go on the land. From some cause or other, (perhaps the adage that misery loves company will explain,) colored people will congregate in the large towns and cities; and they will endure any amount of hardship and privation, rather than separate, and go into the country. Again, very few have the means to set up for themselves, or to get where they could do so.

Another consideration against expending energy in this direction is our want of self-reliance. Slavery more than all things else, robs its victims of self-reliance. To go into the western wilderness, and there to lay the foundation of future society, requires more of that important quality than a life of slavery has left us. This may sound strange to you, coming as it does from a colored man; but I am dealing with facts, and these never accommodate themselves to the feelings or wishes of any. They don't *ask*, but *take leave to be*. It is a fact then, and not less so because I wish it were otherwise, that the colored people are wanting in self-reliance—too fond of society—too eager for immediate results—and too little skilled in mechanics or husbandry to attempt to overcome the wilderness; at least, until they have overcome obstacles less formidable. Therefore, I look to other means than agricultural pursuits for the elevation and improvement of colored people. Of course, I allege this of the many. There are exceptions. Individuals among us, with commendable zeal, industry, perseverance and self-reliance, have found, and are finding, in agricultural pursuits, the means of supporting, improving and educating their families.

The plan which I contemplate will, (if carried into effect,) greatly increase the number of this class—since it will prepare others to meet the rugged duties which a pioneer agricultural condition must impose upon all who take it upon them. What I propose is intended simply to prepare men for the work of getting an honest living—not out of dishonest men—but out of an honest earth.

Again, there is little reason to hope that any considerable number of the free colored people will ever be induced to leave this country, even if such a thing were desirable. This black man—*un*like the Indian—loves civilization. He does not make very great progress in civilization himself but he likes to be in the midst of it, and prefers to share its most galling evils, to encountering barbarism. Then the love of the country, the dread of isolation, the lack of adventurous spirit, and the thought of seeming to desert their "brethren in bonds," are a powerful check upon all schemes of colonization which look to the removal of the colored people, without the slaves. The truth is, dear madam, we are *here,* and here we are likely to remain. Individuals emigrate—nations never. We have grown up with this republic, and I see nothing in her character, or even in the character of the American people as yet, which compels the belief that we must leave the United States. If then, we are to remain here, the question for the wise and good is precisely that you have submitted to me—namely: What can be done to improve the condition of the free people of color in the United States? The plan which I humbly submit in answer to this inquiry—and in the hope that it may find favor with you, and with many friends of humanity who honor, love and co-operate with you—is the establishment in Rochester, N.Y., or in some other part of the United States equally favorable to such an enterprise, of an INDUSTRIAL COLLEGE in which shall be taught several important branches of the mechanical arts. This college is to be opened to colored youth. I will pass over, for the present, the details of such an institution as I propose. It is not worth while that I should dwell upon these at all. Once convinced that something of the sort is needed, and the organizing power will be forthcoming. It is the peculiarity of your favored race that they can always do what they think necessary to be done. I can safely trust all details to yourself, and the wise and good people whom you represent in the interest you take in my oppressed fellow-countrymen.

Never having had a day's schooling in all my life I may not be expected to map out the details of a plan so comprehensive as that involved in the idea of a college. I repeat, then, I leave the organization and administration to the superior wisdom of yourself and the friends who second your noble efforts. The argument in favor of an Industrial College—a college to be conducted by the best men—and the best workmen which the mechanical arts can afford; a college where colored youth can be instructed to use their hands, as well as their heads; where they can be put into possession of the means of getting a living whether their lot in after life may be cast among civilized or uncivilized men; whether they choose to stay here, or prefer to return to the land of their fathers—is briefly this: Prejudice against the free colored people in the United States has shown itself nowhere so invincible as among mechanics. The farmer and the professional man cherish no feeling so bitter as that cherished by these. The latter would starve us out of the country entirely. At this moment I can more easily get my son into a lawyer's office to learn law than I can into a blacksmith's shop to blow the bellows and to wield the sledge-hammer. Denied the means of learning useful trades we are pressed into the narrowest limits to obtain a livelihood. In times past we have been the hewers of wood and the drawers of water for American society, and we once enjoyed a monopoly in the menial enjoyments, but this is so no longer. Even these enjoyments are rapidly passing away out of our hands. The fact is—every day begins with the lesson, and ends with the lesson—the colored men must learn trades; and must find new employment; new modes of usefulness to society, or that they must decay under the pressing wants to which their condition is rapidly bringing them.

We must become mechanics; we must build as well as live in houses; we must make as well as use furniture; we must construct bridges as well as pass over them, before we can properly live or be respected by our fellow men. We need mechanics as well as ministers. We need workers in iron, clay, and leather. We have orators, authors, and other professional men, but these reach only a certain class, and get respect for our race in certain select circles. To live here as we ought we must fasten ourselves to our countrymen through their every day cardinal wants. We must not only be able to *black* boots, but to *make* them. At present we are unknown in the Northern States as mechanics. We give no proof of genius or skill at the county, State, or national fairs. We are unknown at any of the great exhibitions of the industry of our fellow-citizens, and being unknown we are unconsidered.

The fact that we make no show of our ability is held conclusive of our inability to make any, hence all the indifference and contempt with which incapacity is regarded, fall upon us, and that too, when we have had no means of disproving the infamous opinion of our natural inferiority. I have during the last dozen years denied before the Americans that we are an inferior race; but this has been done by arguments based upon admitted principles rather than by the presentation of facts. Now, firmly believing, as I do, that there are skill, invention, power, industry, and real mechanical genius, among the colored people, which will bear favorable testimony for them, and which only need the means to develop them, I am decidedly in favor of the establishment of such a college as I have mentioned. The benefits of such an institution would not be confined to the Northern States, nor to the free colored people. They would extend over the whole Union. The slave not less than the freeman would be benefited by such an institution. It must be confessed that the most powerful argument now used by the Southern slaveholder, and the one most soothing to his conscience, is that derived from the low condition of the free colored people of the North. I have long felt that too little attention has been given by our truest friends in this country to removing this stumbling block out of the way of the slave's liberation.

The most telling, the most killing refutation of slavery, is the presentation of an industrious, enterprising, thrifty, and intelligent free black population. Such a population I believe would rise in the Northern States under the fostering care of such a college as that supposed.

To show that we are capable of becoming mechanics I might adduce any amount of testimony; dear madam, I need not ring the changes on such a proposition. There is no question in the mind of any unprejudiced person that the Negro is capable of making a good mechanic. Indeed, even those who cherish the bitterest feelings towards us have admitted that the apprehension that Negroes might be employed in their stead, dictated the policy of excluding them from trades altogether. But I will not dwell upon this point as I fear I have already trespassed too long upon your precious time, and written more than I ought to expect you to read. Allow me to say in conclusion, that I believe every intelligent colored man in America will approve and rejoice at the establishment of some such institution as that now suggested. There are many respectable colored men, fathers of large families, having boys nearly grown up, whose minds are tossed by day and by night with the anxious enquiry, "what shall I do with my boys?" Such an institution would meet the wants of such persons. Then, too, the establishment of such an institution would be in character with the eminently practical philanthropy of your trans-Atlantic friends. America could scarce object to it as an attempt to agitate the public mind on the subject of slavery, or to *dissolve the Union.* It could not be tortured into a cause for hard words by the American people, but the noble and good of all classes, would see in the effort an excellent motive, a benevolent object, temperately, wisely, and practically manifested.

Wishing, you, dear madam, renewed health, a pleasant passage, and safe return to your native land.

I am most truly, your grateful friend,

Frederick Douglass

Proceedings of the Colored National Convention Held in Rochester, July 6th, 7th and 8th, 1853, Rochester, 1853, pp. 33–38

1. In July, 1851, after she had published five installments of *Uncle Tom's Cabin* in the *National Era,* Harriet Beecher Stowe wrote to Douglass asking him to assist her in gathering information about life on a cotton plantation which he could use in her novel. The main part of her letter was devoted to a long defense of the church against the charge of many abolitionists, Douglass among them, that it was pro-slavery. We do not know if Douglass answered the letter. (See Charles Edwards Stowe, *The Life of Harriet Beecher Stowe,* Boston and New York, 1890, pp. 149–53.)

2. *Proceedings of the Colored National Convention Held in Rochester, July 6th, 7th and 8th, 1853,* Rochester, 1853, pp. 17–22.

3. On August 1, 1846, Gerrit Smith wrote to Rev. Theodore S. Wright, Rev. Charles B. Ray, and Dr. J. McCune Smith asking them to prepare a list of the colored men in certain counties eligible to receive a deed of land from him. The following conditions were attached to the offer: no person younger than twenty-one or older than sixty should be included, nor any person well-off and already an owner of land, and no drinker of intoxicating liquor. One hundred and twenty thousand acres of land were distributed by Smith to three thousand Negroes in New York. (See *An Address to the Three Thousand Colored Citizens of New York who are the Owners of One Hundred and Twenty Thousand Acres of Land, in the State of New York, Given to them by Gerrit Smith, Esq. of Peterboro,* New York, 1846.)

With the assistance of the Rochester Ladies' Anti-Slavery Society, of which she was secretary, [Julia] Griffiths in 1853 published a gift-book, *Autographs for Freedom,* to aid Douglass' paper. Several hundred gift-books had been issued in this country before the Civil War, and the anti-slavery cause alone had produced five before *Autographs for Freedom* made its appearance. The new feature of Miss Griffiths' volume was the autographs which followed the author's essays, letters, and speeches. Like the other anti-slavery gift-books, it was designed to be sold at Abolitionist fairs and bazaars, though Douglass also offered the volume to subscribers as a means of extending the circulation of his journal.[1]

Commenting on the English edition of *Autographs for Freedom,* the *British Banner* observed: "The book is deeply interesting, and as presenting the aggregate of liberal sentiments from cultivated and enlightened minds, possesses a peculiar value." Among the "cultivated and enlightened" contributors were Negro leaders such as J. McCune Smith, George B. Vashon, William G. Allen, Charles L. Reason, James M. Whitfield, William Wells Brown, J. M. Langston and Douglass himself; public figures such as William H. Seward, Horace Greeley, Gerrit Smith, Horace Mann, and Joshua R. Giddings; preachers and philosophers such as Theodore Parker, Ralph Waldo Emerson, and Henry Ward Beecher; and women reformers such as Harriet Beecher Stowe, Antoinette Brown, Caroline M. Kirkland, Catherine M. Sedgwick, and Jane Swisshelm. Most of the contributions were brief—frequently a page in length—and few were outstanding for their literary merit. But the volumes did contain some previously unpublished work by prominent writers, and some of the contributions by the Negro authors rank high in the literature of the anti-slavery movement.[2] The 1853 issue featured a little-known work of fiction by Frederick Douglass entitled *The Heroic Slave*, a short story about Madison Washington, who led the famous uprising in 1841 on the Creole, a ship engaged in the domestic slave trade. [I:89–90]

THE HEROIC SLAVE

PART I.

Oh! child of grief, why weepest thou?
Why droops thy sad and mournful brow?
Why is thy look so like despair?
What deep, sad sorrow lingers there?

The State of Virginia is famous in American annals for the multitudinous array of her statesmen and heroes. She has been dignified by some the mother of statesmen. History has not been sparing in recording their names, or in blazoning their dead. Her high position in this respect, has given her an enviable distinction among her sister States. With Virginia for his birthplace, even a man of ordinary parts, on account of the general partiality for her sons, easily rises to eminent stations. Men, not great enough to attract special attention in their native States, have, like a certain distinguished citizen in the State of New York, sighed and repined that they were not born in Virginia. Yet not all the great ones of the Old Dominion have, by the fact of their birth-place, escaped undeserved obscurity. By some strange neglect, one of the truest, manliest, and bravest of her children,—one who, in after years, will, I think, command the pen of genius to set his merits forth, holds now no higher place in the records of that grand old Commonwealth than is held by a horse or an ox. Let those account for it who can, but there stands the fact, that a man who loved liberty as well as did Patrick Henry—who deserved it as much as Thomas Jefferson,—and who fought for it with a valor as high, and arms as strong, and against odds as great, as he who led all the armies of the American colonies through the great war for freedom and independence, lives now only in the chattel records of his native State.

Glimpses of this great character are all that can now be presented. He is brought to view only by a few transient incidents, and these afford but partial satisfaction. Like a guiding star on a stormy night, he is seen through the parted clouds and the howling tempests; or, like the gray peak of a menacing rock on a perilous coast, he is seen by the quivering flash of angry lightning, and he again disappears covered with mystery.

Curiously, earnestly, anxiously we peer into the dark, and wish even for the blinding flash, or the light of northern skies to reveal him. But alas! he is still enveloped in darkness, and we return from the pursuit like a wearied and disheartened mother, (after a tedious and unsuccessful search for a lost child,) who returns weighed down with disappointment and sorrow. Speaking of marks, traces, possibles, and probabilities, we come before our readers.

In the spring of 1835, on a Sabbath morning, within hearing of the solemn peals of the church bells at a distant village, a Northern traveller through the State of Virginia drew up his horse to drink at a sparkling brook, near the edge of a dark pine forest. While his weary and thirsty steed drew in the grateful water, the rider caught the sound of a human voice, apparently engaged in earnest conversation.

Following the direction of the sound, he descried, among the tall pines, the man whose voice had arrested his attention. "To whom can he be speaking?" thought the traveller. "He seems to be alone." The circumstance interested him much, and he became intensely curious to know what thoughts and feelings, or, it might be, high aspirations, guided those rich and mellow accents. Tieing his horse at a short distance from the brook, he stealthily drew near the solitary speaker; and, concealing himself by the side of a huge fallen tree, he distinctly heard the following soliloquy:—

"What, then, is life to me? It is aimless and worthless, and worse than worthless. Those birds, perched on you swinging boughs, in friendly conclave, sounding forth their merry notes in seeming worship of the rising sun, though liable to the sportsman's fowling-piece, are still my superiors. They *live free,* though they may die slaves. They fly where they list by day, and retire in freedom at night. But what is freedom to me, or I to it? I am a slave,—born a slave, an abject slave,—even before I made part of this breathing world, the scourge was plaited for my back; the fetters were forged for my limbs. How mean a thing am I. That accursed and crawling snake, that miserable reptile, that has just glided into its slimy home, is freer and better off than I. He escaped my blow, and is safe. But here am I, a man,—yes, a man!—with thoughts and wishes, with powers and faculties as far as angel's flight above that hated reptile,—yet he is my superior, and scorns to own me as his master, or to stop to take my blows. When he saw my uplifted arm, he darted beyond my reach, and turned to give me battle. I dare not do as much as that. I neither run nor fight, but do meanly stand, answering each heavy blow of a cruel master with doleful wails and piteous cries. I am galled with irons; but even these are more tolerable than the consciousness, the galling consciousness of cowardice and indecision. Can it be that I dare not run away? Perish the thought, I dare do anything which may be done by another. When that young man struggled with the waves, for life, and others stood back appalled in helpless horror, did I not plunge in, forgetful of life, to save his? The raging bull from whom all others fled, pale with fright, did I not keep at bay with a single pitch-fork? Could a coward do that? No,—no,—I wrong myself,—I am no coward. Liberty I will have, or die in the attempt to gain it. This working that others may live in idleness! This cringing submission to insolence and curses! This living under the constant dread and apprehensions of being sold and transferred, like a mere brute, is too much for me. I will stand it no longer. What others have done, I will do. These trusty legs, or these sinewy arms shall place me among the free. Tom escaped; so can I. The North Star will not be less kind to me than to him. I will follow it. I will at least make the trial. I have nothing to lose. If I am caught, I shall only be a slave. If I am shot, I shall only lose a life which is a burden and a curse. If I get clear, (as something tells me I shall,) liberty, the inalienable birth-right of every man, precious and priceless, will be mine. My resolution is fixed. *I shall be free.*"

At these words the traveller raised his head cautiously and noiselessly, and caught, from his hiding-place, a full view of the unsuspecting speaker. Madison (for that was the name of our hero) was standing erect, a smile of satisfaction rippled upon his expressive countenance, like that which plays upon the face of one who has but just solved a difficult problem, or vanquished a malignant foe; for at that moment he was free, at least in spirit. The future gleamed brightly before him, and his fetters lay broken at his feet. His air was triumphant.

Madison was of manly form. Tall, symmetrical, round, and strong. In his movements he seemed to combine, with the strength of the lion, a lion's elasticity. His torn sleeves disclosed arms like polished iron. His face was "black, but comely." His eye, lit with emotion, kept guard under a brow as dark and as glossy as the raven's wing. His whole appearance betokened Herculean strength; yet there was nothing savage or forbidding in his aspect. A child might play in his arms, or dance on his shoulders. A giant's strength, but not a giant's heart was in him. His broad mouth and nose spoke only of good nature and kindness. But his voice, that unfailing index of the soul, though full and melodious, had that in it which could terrify as well as charm. He was just the man you would choose when hardships were to be endured, or danger to be encountered,—intelligent and brave. He had the head to conceive, and the hand to execute. In a word, he was one to be sought as a friend, but to be dreaded as an enemy.

As our traveller gazed upon him, he almost trembled at the thought of his dangerous intrusion. Still he could not quit the place. He had long desired to sound the mysterious depths of the thoughts and feelings of a slave. He was not, therefore, disposed to allow so providential an opportunity to pass unimproved. He resolved to hear more; so he listened again for those mellow and mournful assents which, he says, made such an impression upon him as can never be erased. He did not have to wait long. There came another gush from the same full fountain; now bitter, and now sweet. Scathing denunciations of the cruelty and unjustice of slavery; heart-touching narrations of his own personal suffering, intermingled with prayers to the God of the oppressed for help and deliverance, were followed by presentations of the dangers and difficulties of escape, and formed the burden of his eloquent utterances; but his high resolution clung to him,—for he ended each speech by an emphatic declaration of his purpose to be free. It seemed that the very repetition of this imparted a glow to his countenance. The hope of freedom seemed to sweeten, for a season, the bitter cup of slavery, and to make it, for a time, tolerable; for when in the very whirlwind of anguish,—when the heart's cord seemed screwed up to snapping tension, hope sprung up and soothed his troubled spirit. Fitfully he would exclaim, "How can I leave her? Poor thing! what can she do when I am gone? Oh! oh! 'tis impossible that I can leave poor Susan!"

A brief pause intervened. Our traveller raised his head, and saw again the sorrow-smitten slave. His eye was fixed upon the ground. The strong man stag-

gered under a heavy load. Recovering himself, he argued, thus aloud: "All is uncertain here. To-morrow's sun may not rise before I am sold, and separated from
her I love. What, then, could I do for her? I should be in more hopeless slavery,
and she no nearer to liberty,—whereas if I were free,—my arms my own,—I
might devise the means to rescue her."

This said, Madison cast around a searching glance, as if the thought of being
overheard had flashed across his mind. He said no more, but, with measured
steps, walked away, and was lost to the eye of our traveller amidst the wildering
woods.

Long after Madison had left the ground, Mr. Listwell (our traveller) remained
in motionless silence, meditating on the extraordinary revelations to which he
had listened. He seemed fastened to the spot, and stood half hoping, half fearing
the return of the sable preacher to his solitary temple. The speech of Madison
rung through the chambers of his soul, and vibrated through his entire frame.
"Here is indeed a man," thought he, "of rare endowments,—a child of God,—
guilty of no crime but the color of his skin,—hiding away from the face of humanity, and pouring out his thoughts and feelings, his hopes and resolutions to
the lonely woods; to him those distant church bells have no grateful music. He
shuns the church, the altar, and the great congregation of Christian worshippers,
and wanders away to the gloomy forest, to utter in the vacant air complaints and
griefs, which the religion of his times and his country can neither console nor relieve. Goaded almost to madness by the sense of the injustice done him, he resorts hither to give vent to his pent up feelings, and to debate with himself the
feasibility of plans of his own invention, for his own deliverance. From this hour
I am an abolitionist. I have seen enough and heard enough, and I shall go to my
home in Ohio resolved to atone for my past indifference to this ill-starred race,
by making such exertions as I shall be able to do, for the speedy emancipation
of every slave in the land.

PART II.

The gaudy, babbling and remorseful day
Is crept into the bosom of the sea;
And now loud-howling wolves arouse the jades
That drag the tragic melancholy night;
Who with their drowsy, slow, and flagging wings
Clip dead men's graves, and from their misty jaws
Breathe foul contagions, darkness in the air.
                                    Shakespeare

Five years after the foregoing singular occurrence, in the winter of 1840, Mr.
and Mrs. Listwell sat together by the fireside of their own happy home, in the
State of Ohio. The children were all gone to bed. A single lamp burnt brightly
on the center table. All was still and comfortable within; but the night was cold
and dark; a heavy wind sighed and moaned sorrowfully around the house and
barn, occasionally bringing against the chattering windows a stray leaf from the
large oak trees that embowered their dwelling. It was a night for strange noises
and for strange fancies. A whole wilderness of thought might pass through one's

mind during such an evening. The smouldering embers, partaking of the sprit of the restless night, became fruitful of varied and fantastic pictures, and revived many bygone scenes and old impressions. The happy pair seemed to sit in silent fascination, gazing on the fire. Suddenly this reverie was interrupted by a heavy growl. Ordinarily such an occurrence would have scarcely provoked a single word, or excited the least apprehension. But there are certain seasons when the slightest sound sends a jar through all the subtle chambers of the mind; and such a season was this. The happy pair started up, as if some sudden danger had come upon them. The growl was from their trusty watch-dog.

"What can it mean? Certainly no one can be out on such a night as this," said Mrs. Listwell.

"The wind has deceived the dog, my dear; he has mistaken the noise of falling branches, brought down by the wind, for that of the footsteps of persons coming to the house. I have several times to-night thought that I heard the sound of footsteps. I am sure, however, that it was but the wind. Friends would not be likely to come out at such an hour, or such a night; and thieves are too lazy and self-indulgent to expose themselves to this biting frost; but should there be any one about, our brave old Monte, who is on the look-out, will not be slow in sounding the alarm."

Saying this they quietly left the window, whither they had gone to learn the cause of the menacing growl, and re-seated themselves by the fire, as if reluctant to leave the slowly expiring embers, although the hour was late. A few minutes only intervened after resuming their seats, when again their sober meditations were disturbed. Their faithful dog now growled and barked furiously, as if assailed by an advancing foe. Simultaneously the good couple arose, and stood in mute expectation. The contest without seemed fierce and violent. It was, however, soon over,—the barking ceased, for, with true canine instinct, Monte quickly discovered that a friend, not an enemy of the family, was coming to the house, and instead of rushing to repel the supposed intruder, he was now at the door, whimpering and dancing for the admission of himself and his newly made friend.

Mr. Listwell knew by this movement that all was well; he advanced and opened the door, and saw by the light that streamed out into the darkness, a tall man advancing slowly towards the house, with a stick in one hand, and a small bundle in the other. "It is a traveller," thought he, "who has missed his way, and is coming to inquire the road. I am glad we did not go to bed earlier,—I have felt all the evening as if somebody would be here to-night."

The man had now halted a short distance from the door, and looked prepared alike for flight or battle. "Come in, sir, don't be alarmed, you have probably lost your way."

Slightly hesitating, the traveller walked in; not, however, without regarding his host with a scrutinizing glance. "No, sir," said he "I have come to ask you a greater favor."

Instantly Mr. Listwell exclaimed, (as the recollection of the Virginia forest scene flashed upon him,) "Oh, sir, I know not your name, but I have seen your face, and heard your voice before. I am glad to see you. I know all. You are flying for your liberty,—be seated,—be seated,—banish all fear. You are safe under my roof."

This recognition, so unexpected, rather disconcerted and disquieted the noble fugitive. The timidity and suspicion of persons escaping from slavery are easily awakened, and often what is intended to dispel the one, and to allay the other, has precisely the opposite effect. It was so in this case. Quickly observing the unhappy impression made by his words and action, Mr. Listwell assumed a more quiet and inquiring aspect, and finally succeeded in removing the apprehensions which his very natural and generous salutation had aroused.

Thus assured, the stranger said, "Sir, you have rightly guessed, I am, indeed, a fugitive from slavery. My name is Madison,—Madison Washington my mother used to call me. I am on my way to Canada, where I learn that persons of my color are protected in all the rights of men; and my object in calling upon you was, to beg the privilege of resting my weary limbs for the night in your barn. It was my purpose to have continued my journey till morning; but the piercing cold, and the frowning darkness compelled me to seek shelter; and, seeing a light through the lattice of your window, I was encouraged to come here to beg the privilege named. You will do me a great favor by affording me shelter for the night."

"A resting-place, indeed, sir, you shall have; not, however, in my barn, but in the best room of my house. Consider yourself, if you please, under the roof of a friend; for such I am to you, and to all your deeply injured race."

While this introductory conversation was going on, the kind lady had revived the fire, and was diligently preparing supper; for she, not less than her husband, felt for the sorrows of the oppressed and hunted ones of earth, and was always glad of an opportunity to do them a service. A bountiful repast was quickly prepared, and the hungry and toil-worn bondman was cordially invited to partake thereof. Gratefully he acknowledged the favor of his benevolent benefactress; but appeared scarcely to understand what such hospitality could mean. It was the first time in his life that he had met so humane and friendly a greeting at the hands of persons whose color was unlike his own; yet it was impossible for him to doubt the charitableness of his new friends, or the genuiness of the welcome so freely given; and he therefore, with many thanks, took his seat at the table with Mr. and Mrs. Listwell, who, desirous to make him feel at home, took a cup of tea themselves, while urging upon Madison the best that the house could afford.

Supper over, all doubts and apprehensions banished, the three drew around the blazing fire, and a conversation commenced which lasted till long after midnight.

"Now," said Madison to Mr. Listwell, "I was a little surprised and alarmed when I came in, by what you said; do tell me, sir, why you thought you had seen my face before, and by what you knew me to be a fugitive from slavery; for I am sure that I never was before in this neighborhood, and I certainly sought to conceal what I supposed to be the manner of a fugitive slave."

Mr. Listwell at once frankly disclosed the secret; describing the place where he first saw him; rehearsing the language which he (Madison) had used; referring to the effect which his manner and speech had made upon him; declaring the resolution he there formed to be an abolitionist; telling how often he had spoken of the circumstance, and the deep concern he had ever since felt to know what had become of him; and whether he had carried out the purpose to make his escape, as in the woods he declared he would do.

"Ever since that morning," said Mr. Listwell, "you have seldom been absent from my mind, and though now I did not dare to hope that I should ever see you again, I have often wished that such might be my fortune; for, from that hour, your face seemed to be daguerreotyped on my memory." Madison looked quite astonished, and felt amazed at the narration to which he had listened. After recovering himself he said, "I well remember that morning, and the bitter anguish that wrung my heart; I will state the occasion of it. I had, on the previous Saturday, suffered a cruel lashing; had been tied up to the limb of a tree, with my feet chained together, and a heavy iron bar placed between my ankles. Thus suspended, I received on my naked back, forty stripes, and was kept in this distressing position three or four hours, and was then let down, only to have my torture increased; for my bleeding back, gashed by the cow-skin, was washed by the overseer with old brine, partly to augment my suffering, and partly, as he said, to prevent inflammation. My crime was that I had stayed longer at the mill, the day previous, than it was thought I ought to have done, which, I assured my master and the overseer, was no fault of mine; but no excuses were allowed. 'Hold your tongue, you impudent rascal,' met my every explanation. Slave-holders are so imperious when their passions are excited, as to construe every word of the slave into insolence. I could do nothing but submit to the agonizing infliction. Smarting still from the wounds, as well as from the consciousness of being whipt for no cause, I took advantage of the absence of my master, who had gone to church, to spend the time in the woods, and brood over my wretched lot. Oh, sir, I remember it well,—and can never forget it."

"But this was five years ago; where have you been since?"

"I will try to tell you," said Madison. "Just four weeks after that Sabbath morning, I gathered up the few rags of clothing I had and started, as I, supposed, for the North and for freedom. I must not stop to describe my feelings on taking this step. It seemed like taking a leap into the dark. The thought of leaving my poor wife and two little children caused me indescribable anguish; but consoling myself with the reflection that once free, I could, possibly, devise ways and means to gain their freedom also, I nerved myself up to make the attempt. I started, but ill-luck attended me; for after being out a whole week, strange to say, I still found myself on my master's grounds; the third night after being out, a season of clouds and rain set in, wholly preventing me from seeing the North Star, which I had trusted as my guide, not dreaming that clouds might intervene between us.

"This circumstance was fatal to my project, for in losing my star, I lost my way; so when I supposed I was far towards the North, and had almost gained my freedom, I discovered myself at the very point from which I had started. It was a severe trial, for I arrived at home in great destitution; my feet were sore, and in travelling in the dark, I had dashed my foot against a stump, and started a nail, and lamed myself. I was wet and cold; one week had exhausted all my stores; and when I landed on my master's plantation, with all my work to do over again,—hungry, tired, lame, and bewildered,—I almost cursed the day that I was born. In this extremity I approached the quarters. I did so stealthily, although in my desperation I hardly cared whether I was discovered or not. Peeping through the rents of the quarters, I saw my fellow slaves seated by a warm fire, merrily passing away the time, as though their hearts knew no sorrow. Although I envied their seeming contentment, all wretched as I was, I despised the cowardly acquiescence in their own degradation which it implied, and felt a kind of pride and glory in my own desperate lot. I dared not enter the quarters,—for where there is seeming contentment with slavery, there is certain treachery to freedom. I proceeded towards the great house, in the hope of catching a glimpse of my poor wife, whom I knew might be trusted with my secrets even on the scaffold. Just as I reached the fence which divided the field from the garden, I saw a woman in the yard, who in the darkness I took to be my wife; but a nearer approach told me it was not she. I was about to speak; had I done so, I would not have been here this night; for an alarm would have been sounded, and the hunters been put on my track. Here were hunger, cold, thirst, disappointment, and chagrin, confronted only by the dim hope of liberty. I tremble to think of that dreadful hour. To face the deadly cannon's mouth in warm blood unterrified, is, I think, a small achievement, compared with a conflict like this with gaunt starvation. The gnawings of hunger conquers by degrees, till all that a man has he would give in exchange for a single crust of bread. Thank God, I was not quite reduced to this extremity.

"Happily for me, before the fatal moment of utter despair, my good wife made her appearance in the yard. It was she; I knew her step. All was well now. I was, however, afraid to speak, lest I should frighten her. Yet speak I did; and, to my great joy, my voice was known. Our meeting can be more easily imagined than described. For a time hunger, thirst, weariness, and lameness were forgotten. But it was soon necessary for her to return to the house. She being a house-servant, her absence from the kitchen, if discovered, might have excited suspicion. Our parting was like tearing the flesh from my bones; yet it was the part of wisdom for her to go. She left me with the purpose of meeting me at midnight in the very forest where you last saw me. She knew the place well, as one of my melancholy resorts, and could easily find it, though the night was dark.

"I hastened away, therefore, and concealed myself, to await the arrival of my good angel. As I lay there among the leaves, I was strongly tempted to return again to the house of my master and give myself up; but remembering my solemn pledge on that memorable Sunday morning, I was able to linger out the two long hours between ten and midnight. I may well call them long hours. I have endured much hardship; I have encountered many perils, but the anxiety of those two hours, was the bitterest, I ever experienced. True to her word, my wife came laden with provisions, and we sat down on the side of a log, at that dark and lonesome hour of the night. I cannot say we talked; our feelings were too great for that; yet we came to an understanding that I should make the woods my home, for if I gave myself up, I should be whipped and sold away; and if I started for the North, I should leave a wife doubly dear to me. We mutually determined, therefore, that I should remain in the vicinity. In the dismal swamps I lived, sir, five long years,—a cave for my home during the day. I wandered about at night with the wolf and the bear,—sustained by the promise that my good Susan would meet me in the pine woods at least once a week. This promise was redeemed I assure you, to the letter, greatly to my relief. I had partly become contented with my mode of life, and had made up my mind to spend my days there; but the wilderness that sheltered me thus long took fire, and refused longer to be my hiding-place.

"I will not harrow up your feelings by portraying the terrific scene of this awful conflagration. There is nothing to which I can liken it. It was horribly and indescribably grand. The whole world seemed on fire, and it appeared to me that the day of judgment had come; that the burning bowels of the earth had burst forth, and that the end of all things was at hand. Bears and wolves scorched from their mysterious hiding-places in the earth, and all the wild inhabitants of the untrodden forest, filled with a common dismay, ran forth, yelling, howling, bewildered amidst the smoke and flame. The very heavens seemed to rain down fire through the towering trees; it was by the merest chance that I escaped the devouring element. Running before it, and stopping occasionally to take breath, I looked back to behold its frightful ravages, and to drink in its savage magnificence. It was awful, thrilling, solemn, beyond compare. When aided by the fitful wind, the merciless tempest of fire swept on, sparkling, creaking, cracking, curling, roaring, out-doing in its dreadful splendor a thousand thunderstorms at once. From tree to tree it leaped, swallowing them up in its lurid, baleful glare; and leaving them leafless, limbless, charred, and lifeless behind. The scene was overwhelming, stunning,—nothing was spared,—cattle, tame and wild, herds of swine and of deer, wild beasts of every name and kind,—huge night-birds, bats, and owls, that had retired to their homes in lofty tree-tops to rest, perished in that fiery storm. The long-winged buzzard and croaking raven mingled their dismal cries with those of the countless myriads of small birds that rose up to the skies, and were lost to the sight in clouds of smoke and flame. Oh, I shudder when I think of it! Many a poor wandering fugitive, who, like myself, had sought among wild beasts the mercy denied by our fellow men, saw, in helpless consternation, his dwelling-place and city of refuge reduced to ashes forever. It was this grand conflagration that drove me hither; I ran alike from fire and from slavery."

After a slight pause, (for both speaker and hearers were deeply moved by the above recital,) Mr. Listwell, addressing Madison, said, "If it does not weary you too much, do tell us something of your journeyings since this disastrous burning,—we are deeply interested in everything which can throw light on the hardships of persons escaping from slavery; we could hear you talk all night; are there no incidents that you could relate of your travels hither? Or are they such that you do not like to mention them?"

"For the most part, sir, my course has been uninterrupted; and, considering the circumstances, at times even pleasant. I have suffered little for want of food; but I need not tell you how I got it. Your moral code may differ from mine, as your customs and usages are different. The fact is sir, during my flight, I felt myself robbed by society of all my just rights; that I was in an enemy's land, who sought both my life and my liberty. They had transformed me into a brute; made merchandise of my body, and, for all the purposes of my flight, turned day into night,—and guided by my own necessities, and in contempt of their conventionality, I did not scruple to take bread where I could get it."

"And just there you were right," said Mr. Listwell; "I once had doubts on this point myself, but a conversation with Gerrit Smith, (a man, by the way, that

I wish you could see, for he is a devoted friend of your race, and I know he would receive you gladly,) put an end to all my doubts on this point. But do not let me interrupt you."

"I had but one narrow escape during my whole journey," said Madison.

"Do let us hear of it," said Mr. Listwell.

"Two weeks ago," continued Madison, "after travelling all night, I was over-taken by daybreak, in what seemed to me an almost interminable wood. I deemed it unsafe to go farther, and, as usual, I looked around for a suitable tree in which to spend the day. I liked one with a bushy top, and found one just to my mind. Up I climbed, and hiding myself as well as I could, I, with this strap, (pulling one out of his old coat-pocket,) lashed myself to a bough, and flattered myself that I should get a good night's sleep that day; but in this I was soon disappointed. I had scarcely got fastened to my natural hammock, when I heard the voices of a number of persons, apparently approaching the part of the woods where I was. Upon my word, sir, I dreaded more these human voices than I should have done those of wild beasts. I was at a loss to know what to do. If I descended, I should probably be discovered by the men; and if they had dogs I should, doubtless, be 'treed.' It was an anxious moment, but hardships and dangers have been the accompaniments of my life; and have, perhaps, imparted to me a certain hardness of character, which, to some extent, adapts me to them. In my present predicament, I decided to hold my place in the tree-top, and abide the consequences. But here I must disappoint you; for the men, who were all colored, halted at least a hundred yards from me, and began with their axes, in right good earnest, to attack the trees. The sound of their laughing axes was like the report of as many well-charged pistols. By and by there came down at least a dozen trees with a terrible crash. They leaped upon the fallen trees with an air of victory. I could see no dog with them, and felt myself comparatively safe, though I could not forget the possibility that some freak or fancy might bring the axe a little nearer my dwelling than comported with my safety.

"There was no sleep for me that day, and I wished for night. You may imagine that the thought of having the tree attacked under me was far from agreeable, and that it very easily kept me on the look-out. The day was not without diversion. The men at work seemed to be a gay set; and they would often make the woods resound with that uncontrolled laughter for which we, as a race, are remarkable. I held my place in the tree till sunset,—saw the men put on their jackets to be off. I observed that all left the ground except one, whom I saw sitting on the side of a stump, with his head bowed, and his eyes apparently fixed on the ground. I became interested in him. After sitting in the position to which I have alluded ten or fifteen minutes, he left the stump, walked directly towards the tree in which I was secreted, and halted almost under the same. He stood for a moment and looked around, deliberately and reverently took off his hat, by which I saw that he was a man in the evening of life, slightly bald and quite gray. After laying down his hat carefully, he knelt and prayed aloud, and such a prayer, the most fervent, earnest, and solemn, to which I think I ever listened. After reverently addressing the Almighty, as the all-wise, all-good, and the common Father of all mankind, he besought God for grace, for strength, to bear up and under, and to endure, as a good soldier, all the hardships and trials which beset the journey of life, and to enable him to live in a manner which accorded with the gospel of Christ. His soul now broke out in humble supplication for deliverance from bondage. 'O thou,' said he, 'that hearest the raven's cry, take pity on poor me! O deliver me! O deliver me! in mercy, O God, deliver me from the chains and manifold hardships of slavery! With thee, O Father, all things are possible. Thou canst stand and measure the earth. Thou hast beheld and drove asunder the nations,— all power is in thy hand,—thous didst say of old, 'I seen the affliction of my people, and am come to deliver them',—Oh look down upon our afflictions, and have mercy upon us.' But I cannot repeat his prayer, nor can I give you an idea of its deep pathos. I had given but little attention to religion. and had but little faith in it; yet, as the old man prayed, I felt almost like coming down and kneeling by his side, and mingling my broken complaint with his.

"He had already gained my confidence; as how could it be otherwise? I knew enough of religion to know that the man who prays in secret is far more likely to be sincere than he who loves to pray standing in the street, or in the great congregation. When he arose from his knees, like another Zacheus, I came down from the tree. He seemed a little alarmed at first, but I told him my story, and the good man embraced me in his arms, and assured me of his sympathy.

"I was now about out of provisions, and thought I might safely ask him to help me replenish my store. He said he had no money; but if he had, he would freely give it me. I told him I had one dollar; it was all the money I had in the world. I gave it to him, and asked him to purchase some crackers and cheese, and to kindly bring me the balance; that I would remain in or near that place, and would come to him on his return, if he would whistle. He was gone only about an hour. Meanwhile, from some cause or other, I know not what, (but as you shall see very wisely,) I changed my place. On his return I started to meet him; but it seemed as if the shadow of approaching danger fell upon my spirit, and checked my progress. In a very few minutes, closely on the heels of the old man, I distinctly saw fourteen men, with something like guns in their hands."

"Oh! the old wretch!" exclaimed Mrs. Listwell "he had betrayed you, had he?"

"I think not," said Madison, "I cannot believe that the old man was to blame. He probably went into a store, asked for the articles for which I sent, and presented the bill I gave him; and it is so unusual for slaves in the country to have money, that fact, doubtless, excited suspicion, and gave rise to inquiry. I can easily believe that the truthfulness of the old man's character compelled him to disclose the facts; and thus were these blood-thirsty men put on my track. Of course I did not present myself; but hugged my hiding-place securely. If discovered and attacked, I resolved to sell my life as dearly as possible.

"After searching about the woods silently for a time, the whole company gathered around the old man; one charged him with lying, and called him an old villain; said he was a thief; charged him with stealing money; said if he did not instantly tell where he got it, they would take the shirt from his old back, and give him thirty-nine lashes.

" 'I did not steal the money,' said the old man, it was given me, as I told you at the store; and if the man who gave it to me is not here, it is not my fault.'

" 'Hush! you lying old rascal; we'll make you smart for it. You shall not leave this spot until you have told where you got the money.'

"They now took hold of him, and began to strip him; while others went to get sticks with which to beat him. I felt, at the moment, like rushing out in the midst of them; but considering that the old man would be whipped the more for having aided a fugitive slave, and that, perhaps, in the melée he might be killed outright, I disobeyed this impulse. They tied him to a tree, and began to whip him. My own flesh crept at every blow, and I seem to hear the old man's piteous cries even now. They laid thirty-nine lashes on his bare back, and were going to repeat that number, when one of the company besought his comrades to desist. 'You'll kill the d——d old scoundrel! You've already whipt a dollar's worth out of him, even if he stole it!' 'O yes,' said another, 'let him down. He'll never tell us another lie, I'll warrant ye!' With this, one of the company untied the old man, and bid him go about his business.

The old man left, but the company remained as much as an hour, scouring the woods. Round and round they went, turning up the underbrush, and peering about like so many bloodhounds. Two or three times they came within six feet of where I lay. I tell you I held my stick with a firmer grasp than I did in coming up to your house to-night. I expected to level one of them at least. Fortunately, however, I eluded their pursuit, and they left me alone in the woods.

"My last dollar was now gone, and you may well suppose I felt the loss of it; but the thought of being again free to pursue my journey, prevented that depression which a sense of destitution causes; so swinging my little bundle on my back, I caught a glimpse of the Great Bear (which ever points the way to my beloved star,) and I started again on my journey. What I lost in money I made up at a hen-roost that same night, upon which I fortunately came."

"But you didn't eat your food raw? How did you cook it?" said Mrs. Listwell.

"O no, Madam," said Madison, turning to his little bundle;—"I had the means of cooking." Here he took out of his bundle an old fashioned tinderbox, and taking up a piece of a file, which he brought with him, he struck it with a heavy flint, and brought out at least a dozen sparks at once. "I have had this old box," said he, "more than five years. It is the only property saved from the fire in the dismal swamp. It had done me good service. It has given me the means of broiling many a chicken!"

It seemed quite a relief to Mrs. Listwell to know that Madison had, at least, lived upon cooked food. Women have a perfect horror of eating uncooked food.

By this time thoughts of what was best to be done about getting Madison to Canada, began to trouble Mr. Listwell; for the laws of Ohio were very stringent against any one who should aid, or who were found aiding a slave to escape through that State. A citizen, for the simple act of taking a fugitive slave in his carriage, had just been stripped of all his property, and thrown penniless upon the world. Notwithstanding this, Mr. Listwell was determined to see Madison safely on his way to Canada. "Give yourself no uneasiness," said he to Madison, "for if it cost my farm, I shall see you safely out of the States, and on your way to the land of liberty. Thank God that there is such a land so near us! You will spend to-morrow with us, and to-morrow night I will take you in my carriage to the Lake. Once upon that, and you are safe."

"Thank you! thank you," said the fugitive; "I will commit myself to your care."

For the first time during five years, Madison enjoyed the luxury of resting his limbs on a comfortable bed, and inside a human habitation. Looking at the white sheets he said to Mr. Listwell, "What, sir! you don't mean that I shall sleep in that bed?"

"Oh yes, oh yes."

After Mr. Listwell left the room, Madison said he really hesitated whether or not he should lie on the floor; for that was far more comfortable and inviting than any bed to which he had been used.

We pass over the thoughts and feelings, the hopes and fears, the plans and purposes, that revolved in the mind of Madison during the day that he was secreted at the house of Mr. Listwell. The readers will be content to know that nothing occurred to endanger his liberty, or to excite alarm. Many were the little attentions bestowed upon him in his quiet retreat and hiding-place. In the evening, Mr. Listwell, after treating Madison to a new suit of winter clothes, and replenishing his exhausted purse with five dollars, all in silver, brought out his two-horse wagon, well provided with buffaloes, and silently started off with him to Cleveland. They arrived there without interruption, a few minutes before sunrise the next morning. Fortunately the steamer Admiral lay at the wharf, and was to start for Canada at nine o'clock. Here the last anticipated danger was surmounted. It was feared that just at this point the hunters of men might be on the look-out, and, possibly pounce upon their victim. Mr. Listwell saw the captain of the boat; cautiously sounded him on the matter of carrying liberty-loving passengers, before he introduced his precious charge. This done, Madison was conducted on board. With usual generosity this true subject of the emancipating queen welcomed Madison, and assured him that he should be safely landed in Canada, free of charge. Madison now felt himself no more a piece of merchandise, but a passenger, and, like any other passenger, going about his business, carrying with him what belonged to him, and nothing which rightfully belonged to anybody else.

Wrapped in his new winter suit, snug and comfortable, a pocket full of silver, safe from his pursuers, embarked for a free country, Madison gave every sign of sincere gratitude, and bade his kind benefactor farewell, with such a grip of the hand as bespoke a heart full of honest manliness, and a soul that knew how to appreciate kindness. It need scarcely be said that Mr. Listwell was deeply moved by the gratitude and friendship he had excited in a nature so noble as that of the fugitive. He went to his home that day with a joy and gratification which knew no bounds. He had done something "to deliver the spoiled out of the hands of the spoiler," he had given bread to the hungry, and clothes to the naked; he had befriended a man to whom the laws of his country forbade all friendship,—and in proportion to the odds against his righteous deed, was the delightful satisfaction that gladdened his heart. On reaching home, he exclaimed, "He is safe,—he is safe,—he is safe,"—and the cup of his joy was shared by his excellent lady. The following letter was received from Madison a few days after.

Windsor, Canada West, Dec. 16, 1840.

My dear Friend,—for such you truly are:—

Madison is out to the woods at last; I nestle in the mane of the British lion, protected by the mighty paw from the talons and the beak of the American eagle. I AM FREE, and breathe an atmosphere too pure for slaves, slave-hunters, or slave-holders. My heart is full. As many thanks to you, sir, and to your kind lady, as there are pebbles on the shores of Lake Erie; and may the blessing of God rest upon you both. You will never be forgotten by your profoundly grateful friend.

Madison Washington.

PART III.

——— *His head was with his heart,*
And that was far away!
Childe Harold.

Just upon the edge of the great road from Petersburg, Virginia, to Richmond, and only about fifteen miles from the latter place, there stands a somewhat ancient and famous public tavern, quite notorious in its better days, as being the grand resort for most of the leading gamblers, horse-racers, cock-fighters, and slave-traders from all the country round about. This old rookery, the nucleus of all sorts of birds, mostly those of ill omen, has, like everything else peculiar to Virginia, lost much of its ancient consequence and splendor; yet it keeps up some appearance of gaiety and high life, and is still frequented, even by respectable travellers, who are unacquainted with its past history and present condition. Its fine old portico looks well at a distance, and gives the building an air of grandeur. A nearer view, however, does little to sustain this pretension. The house is large, and its style imposing, but time and dissipation, unfailing in their results, have made ineffaceable marks upon it, and it must, in the common course of events, soon be numbered with the things that were. The gloomy mantle of ruin is, already, outspread to envelop it, and its remains, even but now remind one of a human skull, after the flesh has mingled with the earth. Old hats and rags fill the places in the upper windows once occupied by large panes of glass, and the molding boards along the roofing have dropped off from their places, leaving holes and crevices in the rented wall for hats and swallows to build their nests in. The platform of the portico, which fronts the highway is a rickety affair, its planks are loose, and in some places entirely gone, leaving effective mantraps in their stead for nocturnal ramblers. The wooden pillars, which once supported it, but which now hang as encumbrances, are all rotten, and tremble with the touch. A part of the stable, a fine old structure in its day, which has given comfortable shelter to hundreds of the noblest steeds of "the Old Dominion" at once, was blown down many years ago, and never has been, and probably never will be rebuilt. The doors of the barn are in wretched condition; they will shut with a little human strength to help their worn out hinges, but not otherwise. The side of the great building seen from the road is much discolored in sundry places by slops poured from the upper windows, rendering it unsightly and offensive in other respects. Three or four great dogs, looking as dull and gloomy as the mansion itself, lie stretched out along the door-sills under the portico; and double the number of loafers, some of them completely rum-ripe, and others ripening, dispose themselves like so many sentinels about the front of the house. These latter understand the science of scraping acquaintance to perfection. They know every-body, and almost every-body knows them. Of course, as their title implies, they have no regular employment. They are (to use an expressive phrase) hangers-on, or still better, they are what sailors would denominate holder-on to the slack, in every-body's mess, and in nobody's watch. They are, however, as good as the newspaper for the events of the day, and they sell their knowledge almost as cheap. Money they seldom have; yet they always have capital the most reliable. They make their way with a succeeding traveller by intelligence gained from a preceding one. All the great names of Virginia they know by heart, and have seen their owners often. The history of the house is folded in their lips, and they rattle off stories in connection with it, equal to the guides at Dryburgh Abbey. He must be a shrewd man, and well skilled in the art of evasion, who gets out of the hands of these fellows without being at the expense of a treat.

It was at this old tavern, while on a second visit to the State of Virginia in 1841, that Mr. Listwell, unacquainted with the fame of the place, turned aside, about sunset, to pass the night. Riding up to the house, he had scarcely dismounted, when one of the half dozen bar-room fraternity met and addressed him in a manner exceedingly bland and accommodating.

"Fine evening, sir."

"Very fine," said Mr. Listwell. "This is a tavern, I believe?"

"O yes, sir, yes; although you may think it looks a little the worse for wear, it was once as good a house as any in Virginy. I make no doubt if ye spend the night here, you'll think it a good house yet; for there aint a more accommodating man in the country than you'll find the landlord."

Listwell. "The most I want is a good bed for myself, and a full manger for my horse. If I get these, I shall be quite satisfied."

Loafer. "Well, I alloys like to hear a gentleman talk for his horse; and just because the horse can't talk for itself. A man that don't care about his beast, and don't look after it when he's travelling, aint much in my eye nay how. Now, sir, I likes a horse, and I'll guarantee your horse will be taken good care on here. That old stable, for all you see it looks so shabby now, once sheltered the great Eclipse, when he run here again Batchelor and Jumping Jenny. Them was fast horses, but he beat 'em both."

Listwell. "Indeed."

Loafer. "Well I rather reckon you've travelled a right smart distance to-day, from the look of your horse?"

Listwell. "Forty miles only."

Loafer. "Well! I'll be darned if that aint a pretty good only. Mister, that beast of yours is a singed cat, I warrant you. I never see'd a creature like that that wasn't good on the road. You've come about forty miles, then?"

Listwell. "Yes, yes, and a pretty good pace at that."

Loafer. "You're somewhat in a hurry, then, I make no doubt? I reckon I could guess if I would, what you're going to Richmond for? It wouldn't be much of a guess either; for it's rumored hereabouts, that there's to be the greatest sale of N——s at Richmond to-morrow that has taken place there in a long time; and I'll be bound you're a going there to have a hand in it."

Listwell. "Why, you must think, then, that there's money to be made at that business?"

Loafer. "Well, 'pon my honor, sir, I never made any that way myself; but it stands to reason that it's a money making business; for almost all other business in Virginia is dropped to engage in this. One thing is sartain, I never see'd a n——r-buyer yet that hadn't a plenty of money, and he wasn't as free with it as water. I has known one on'em to treat as high as twenty times in a night; and, generally speaking, they's men of edication, and knows all about the government. The fact is, sir, I alloys like to hear 'em talk, becase I alloys can learn something from them."

Listwell. "What may I call your name, sir?"

Loafer. "Well, now, they calls me Wilkes. I'm known all around all the gentlemen that comes here. They all knows old Wilkes."

Listwell. "Well, Wilkes, you seem to be accquainted here, and I see you have a strong liking for a horse. Be so good as to speak a kind word for mine to the hostler to-night, and you'll not lose anything by it."

Loafer. "Well, sir, I see you don't say much, but you've got an insight into things. It's alloys wise to get the good will of them that's acquainted about a tavern; for a man don't know when he goes into a house what may happen, or how much he may need a friend." Here the loafer gave Mr. Listwell a significant grin, which expressed a sort of triumphant pleasure at having, as he supposed, by his tact succeeded in placing so fine appearing a gentleman under obligations to him.

The pleasure, however, was mutual; for there was something so insinuating in the glance of this loquacious customer, that Mr. Listwell was very glad to get quit of him, and to do so more successfully, he ordered his supper to be brought to him in his private room, private to the eye, but not to the ear. This room was directly over the bar, and the plastering being off, nothing but pine boards and naked laths separated him from the disagreeable company below,—he could easily hear what was said in the bar-room, and was rather glad of the advantage it afforded, for, as you shall see, it furnished him important hints as to the manner and deportment he should assume during his stay at that tavern.

Mr. Listwell says he had got into his room but a few moments, when he heard the officious Wilkes below, in a tone of disappointment, exclaim, "Whar's that gentleman?" Wilkes was evidently expecting to meet with his friend at the barroom, on his return, and had no doubt of his doing the handsome thing. "He has gone to his room," answered the landlord, "and has ordered his supper to be brought to him."

Here some one shouted out, "Who is he, Wilkes? Where's he going?"

"Well, now, I'll be hanged if I know; but I'm willing to make any man a bet of this old hat against a five dollar bill, that that gent is as full of money as a dog is of fleas. He's going down to Richmond to buy n——s, I make no doubt. He's no fool, I warrant ye."

"Well, he acts d—d strange," said another, "anyhow. I likes to see a man, when he comes up to a tavern, to come straight into the bar-room, and show that he's a man among men. Nobody was going to bite him."

"Now, I don't blame him a bit for not coming in here. That man knows his business, and means to take care on his money," answered Wilkes.

"Wilkes, you're a fool. You only say that, because you hope to get a few coppers out of him."

"You only measure my corn by your half-bushel, I won't say that you're only mad because I got the chance of speaking to him first."

"O Wilkes! you're known here. You'll praise up anybody that will give you a copper; besides, 'tis my opinion that that fellow who took his long slab-sides up stairs, for all the world just like a half-scared woman, afraid to look honest men in the face, is a Northerner, and as mean as dish-water."

"Now what will you bet of that," said Wilkes. The speaker said, "I make no bets with you, 'case you can get that fellow upstairs there to say anything."

"Well," said Wilkes, "I am willing to bet any man in the company that that gentleman is a n——r-buyer. He didn't tell me so right down, but I reckon I knows enough about men to give a pretty clean guess as to what they are arter."

The dispute as to who Mr. Listwell was, what his business, where he was going, etc., was kept up with much animation for some time, and more than once threatened a serious disturbance of the peace. Wilkes had his friends as well as his opponents. After this sharp debate, the company amused themselves by drinking whiskey, and telling stories. The latter consisting of quarrels, fights, rencontres, and duels, in which distinguished persons of that neighborhood, and frequenters of that house, had been actors. Some of these stories were frightful enough, and were told, too, with a relish which bespoke the pleasure of the parties with the horrid scenes they portrayed. It would not be proper here to give the reader any idea of the vulgarity and dark profanity which rolled, as "a sweet morsel," under these corrupt tongues. A more brutal set of creatures, perhaps, never congregated.

Disgusted, and a little alarmed withal, Mr. Listwell, who was not accustomed to such entertainment, at length retired, but not to sleep. He was too much wrought upon by what he had heard to rest quietly, and what snatches of sleep he got, were interrupted by dreams which were anything than pleasant. At eleven o'clock, there seemed to be several hundreds of persons crowding into the house. A loud and confused clamor, cursing and cracking of whips, and the noise of chains startled him from his bed; for a moment he would have given the half of his farm in Ohio to have been at home. This uproar was kept up with undulating course, till near morning. There was loud laughing—loud singing—loud cursing—and yet there seemed to be weeping and mourning in the midst of all. Mr. Listwell said had heard enough during the forepart of the night to convince him that a buyer of men and women stood the best chance of being respected. And he, therefore, thought it best to say nothing which might undo the favorable opinion that had been formed of him in the bar-room by at least one of the fraternity that swarmed about it. While he would not avow himself a purchaser of slaves, he deemed it not prudent to disavow it. He felt that he might, properly, refuse to cast such a pearl before parties which, to him, were worse than swine. To reveal himself, and to impart a knowledge of his real character and sentiments would, to say the least, be imparting intelligence with the certainty of seeing it and himself both abused. Mr. Listwell confesses, that this reasoning did not altogether satisfy his conscience, for, hating slavery as he did, and regarding it to be the immediate duty of every man to cry out against it, "without compromise and without concealment," it was hard for him to admit to himself the possibility of circumstances wherein a man might, properly, hold his tongue on the subject. Having as little of the spirit of a martyr as Erasmus, he concluded, like the latter, that it was wiser to trust to the mercy of God for his soul, than the humanity of the slave-trader for his body. Bodily fear, not conscientious scruples, prevailed.

In this spirit he rose early in the morning, manifesting no surprise at what he had heard during the night. His quondam friend was soon at his elbow, boring him with all sorts of questions. All, however, directed to find out his character, business, residence, purposes, and destination. With the most perfect appearance of good nature and carelessness, Mr. Listwell evaded these meddlesome inquiries, and turned conversation to general topics, leaving himself and all that specially pertained to him, out of discussion. Disengaging himself from their troublesome companionship, he made his way towards an old bowling-alley, which was connected with the house, and which, like all the rest, was in very bad repair.

On reaching the alley Mr. Listwell saw for the first time in his life, a slave-gang on their way to market. A sad sight truly. Here were one hundred and thirty human beings,—children of a common Creator—guilty of no crime—men and women, with hearts, minds, and deathless spirits, chained and fettered, and bound for the market, in a Christian country,—in a country boasting of its liberty, independence, and high civilization! Humanity converted into merchandise, and linked in iron bands, with no regard to decency or humanity! All sizes, ages, and sexes, mothers, fathers, daughters, brothers, sisters,—all huddled together, on their way to market to be sold and separated from home, and from each other forever. And all to fill the pockets of men too lazy to work for an honest living, and who gain their fortune by plundering the helpless, and trafficking in the souls and sinews of men. As he gazed upon this revolting and heart-rending scene, our informant said he almost doubted the existence of a God of justice! And he stood wondering that the earth did not open and swallow up such wickedness.

In the midst of these reflections, and while running his eye up and down the fettered ranks, he met the glance of one whose face he thought he had seen before. To be resolved, he moved towards the spot. It was MADISON WASHINGTON! Here was a scene for the pencil! Had Mr. Listwell been confronted by one risen from the dead, he could not have been more appalled. He was completely stunned. A thunderbolt could not have struck him more dumb. He stood, for a few moments as motionless as one petrified; collecting himself, he at length exclaimed, "Madison! is that you?"

The noble fugitive, but little less astonished than himself, answered cheerily, "O yes, sir, they've got me again."

Thoughtless of consequences for the moment, Mr. Listwell ran up to his old friend, placing his hands upon his shoulders, and looked him in the face! Speechless they stood gazing at each other as if to be doubly resolved that there was no mistake about the matter, till Madison motioned his friend away, intimating a fear lest the keepers should find him there, and suspect him of tampering with the slaves.

"They will soon be out to look after us. You can come when they go to breakfast, and I will tell you all."

Pleased with this arrangement, Mr. Listwell passed out of the alley; but only just in time to save himself, for, while near the door, he observed three men making their way to the alley. The thought occurred to him to await their arrival, as the best means of diverting the ever ready suspicions of the guilty.

While the scene between Mr. Listwell and his friend Madison was going on, the other slaves stood as mute spectators,—at a loss to know what all this could mean. As he left, he heard the man chained to Madison ask, "Who is that gentleman?"

"He is a friend of mine. I cannot tell you now. Suffice it to say he is a friend. You shall hear more of him before long, but mark me! whatever shall pass between that gentleman and me, in your hearing, I pray you will say nothing about it. We are chained here together,—ours is a common lot; and that gentleman is not less your friend than mine." At these words, all mysterious as they were, the unhappy company gave signs of satisfaction and hope. It seems that variable accompaniment of genius, had already won the confidence of the gang and was sort of general-in-chief among them.

By this time the keepers arrived. A horrid trio, well fitted for their demoniacal work. Their uncombed hair came down over foreheads "villainously low," and with eyes, mouths, and noses to match. "Hello! hallo!" they growled out as they entered, "Are you all there!"

"All there," said Madison.

"Well, well, that's right! your journey will soon be over. You'll be in Richmond by eleven to-day, and then you'll have an easy time on it."

"I say, gal, what in the devil are you crying about?" said one of them. I'll give you something to cry about, if you don't mind." This was said to a girl, apparently not more than twelve years old, who had been weeping bitterly. She had, probably, left behind her loving mother, affectionate sisters, brothers, and friends, and her tears were but the natural expression of her sorrow, and the only solace. But the dealers in human flesh have no respect for such sorrow. They look upon it as a protest against their cruel injustice, and they are prompt to punish it.

This is a puzzle not easily solved. How came he here? what can I do for him? may I not even now be in some way compromised in this affair? were thoughts that troubled Mr. Listwell, and made him eager for the promised opportunity of speaking to Madison.

The bell now sounded for breakfast, and keepers and drivers, with pistols and bowie-knives gleaming from their belts, hurried in, as if to get the best places.

Taking the chance now afforded, Mr. Listwell hastened back to the bowling-alley. Reaching Madison, he said, "Now do tell me all about the matter. Do you know me?"

"Oh, yes," said Madison, "I know you well, and shall never forget you nor that cold and dreary night you gave me shelter. I must be short," he continued, "for they'll soon be out again. This, then, is the story in brief. On reaching Canada, and getting over the excitement of making my escape; sir, my thoughts turned to my poor wife, who had well deserved my love by her virtuous fidelity and undying affection for me. I could not bear the thought of leaving her in the cruel jaws of slavery, without making an effort to rescue her. First, I tried to get money to her; but oh! the process was too slow. I despaired of accomplishing it. She was in all my thoughts by day, and my dreams by night. At times I could almost hear her voice, saying, 'O Madison! Madison! will you then leave me here? can you leave me here to die? No! no! you will come! you will come!' I was wretched. I lost my appetite. I could neither work, eat, nor sleep, till I resolved to hazard my own liberty, to gain that of my wife! But I must be short. Six weeks ago I reached my old master's place. I laid about the neighborhood nearly a week, watching my chance, and, finally, I ventured upon the desperate attempt to reach the window, but the noise in raising it frightened my wife, and she screamed and fainted. I took her in my arms, and was descending the ladder, when the dog began to bark furiously, and before I could get to the woods the white folks were roused. The cool night air soon restored my wife, and she readily recognized me. We made the best of our way to the woods, but it was now too late,—the dogs were after us as though they would have torn us to pieces. It was all over with me now! My old master and his two sons ran out with loaded rifles, and before we were out of gunshot, our ears were assailed with 'Stop! stop! or be shot down.' Nevertheless we ran on. Seeing that we gave no heed to their call, they fired, and my poor wife fell by my side dead, while I received but a slight flesh wound. I now became desperate, and stood my ground, and awaited their attack over her dead body. They rushed upon me, with their rifles in hand. I parried their blows, and fought them till I was knocked down and overpowered."

"Oh! it was madness to have returned," said Mr. Listwell.

"Sir, I could not be free with the galling thought that my poor wife was still a slave. With her in slavery, my body, not my spirit, was free. I was taken to the house,—chained to a ring-bolt,—my wounds dressed. I was kept there three days. All slaves, for miles around, were brought to see me. Many slave-holders came with their slaves, using me as proof of the completeness of their power, and of the impossibility of slaves getting away. I was taunted, jeered at, and berated by them, in a manner that pierced me to the soul. Thank God, I was able to smother my rage, and to bear it all with seeming composure. After my wounds were nearly healed, I was taken to a tree and stripped, and I received sixty lashes on my naked back. A few days after, I was sold to a slave-trader, and placed in this gang for the New Orleans market."

"Do you think your master would sell you to me?"

"O no, sir! I was sold on condition of my being taken South. Their motive is revenge."

"Then, then," said Mr. Listwell, "I fear I can do nothing for you. Put your trust in God, and bear your sad lot with the manly fortitude which becomes a man. I shall see you at Richmond, but don't recognize me." Saying this, Mr. Listwell handed Madison ten dollars; said a few words to the other slaves; received their hearty "God bless you," and made his way to the house.

Fearful of exciting suspicion by too long delay, our friend went to the breakfast table, with the aid of one who half reproved the greediness of those who rushed in at the sound of the bell. A cup of coffee was all that he could manage. His feelings were too bitter and excited, and his heart was too full with the fate of poor Madison (whom he loved as well as admired) to relish his breakfast; and although he sat long after the company had left the table, he really did little more than change the position of his knife and fork. The strangeness of meeting again one whom he had met on two several occasions before, under extraordinary circumstances, was well calculated to suggest the idea that a supernatural power, a wakeful providence, or an inexorable fate, had linked their destiny together; and that no efforts of his could disentangle him from the mysterious web of circumstances which enfolded him.

On leaving the table, Mr. Listwell nerved himself up and walked firmly into the bar-room. He was at once greeted again by that talkative chatter-box, Mr. Wilkes.

"Them's a likely set of n——s in the alley there," said Wilkes.

"Yes, they're fine looking fellows, one of them I should like to purchase, and for him I would be willing to give a handsome sum."

Turning to one of his comrades, and with a grin of victory, Wilkes said, "Aha, Bill, did you hear that? I told you I know'd that gentleman wanted to buy n——s, and would bid as high as any purchaser in the market."

"Come, come," said Listwell, "don't be too loud in your praise, you are old enough to know that prices rise when purchasers are plenty."

"That's a fact," said Wilkes, "I see you knows the ropes—and there's not a man in old Virginy whom I'd rather help to make a good bargain than you, sir."

"Mr. Listwell here threw a dollar at Wilkes, (which the latter caught with a dexterous hand,) saying, "Take that for your kind good will." Wilkes held up the dollar to his right eye, with a grin of victory, and turned to the morose grumbler in the corner who had questioned the liberality of a man of whom he knew nothing.

Mr. Listwell now stood as well with the company as any other occupant of the bar-room.

We pass over the hurry and bustle, the brutal vociferations of the slave-drivers in getting their unhappy gang in motion for Richmond; and we need not narrate every application of the lash to those who faltered in the journey. Mr. Listwell followed the train at a long distance, with a sad heart; and on reaching Richmond, left his horse at a hotel, and made his way to the wharf in the direction of which he saw the slave-coffle driven. He was just in time to see the whole company embark for New Orleans. The thought struck him that, while mixing with the multitude, he might do his friend Madison one last service, and he stept into a hardware store and purchased three strong files. These he took with him, standing near the small boat, which lay in waiting to bear the company by parcels to the side of the brig that lay in the stream, he managed, as Madison passed him, to slip the files into his pocket, and at once darted back among the crowd.

All the company now on board, the imperious voice of the captain sounded, and instantly a dozen hardy seamen were in the rigging, hurrying aloft to unfurl the broad canvas of our Baltimore-built American Slaver. The sailors hung about the ropes, like so many black cats, now in the round-tops, now in the cross-trees, now on the yard-arms; all was bluster and activity. Soon the broad fore topsail, the royal and top gallant sail were spread to the breeze. Round went the heavy windlass, clank, clank went the fall-bit,—the anchors weighed,—jibs, mainsails, and topsails hauled it to the wind, and the long, low, black slaver, with her cargo of human flesh, careened and moved forward to the sea.[3]

Mr. Listwell stood on the shore, and watched the slaver till the last speck of her upper sails faded from sight, and announced the limit of human vision. "Farewell! farewell! brave and true man! God grant that brighter skies may smile upon your future than have yet looked down upon your thorny pathway."

Saying this to himself, our friend lost no time in completing his business, and in making his way homewards, gladly shaking off from his feet the dust of Old Virginia.

PART IV.

> *Oh, where's the slave so lowly*
> *Condemn'd to chains unholy,*
> *Who could he burst*
> *His bonds at first*
> *Would pine beneath them slowly?*
> *—Moore*

> ——*Know ye not*
> *Who would be free, themselves must strike the blow.*
> *—Childe Harold*

What a world of inconsistency, as well as of wickedness, is suggested by the smooth and gliding phrase, *American Slave Trade;* and how strange and perverse is that moral sentiment which loathes, execrates, and brands as piracy and as deserving of death the carrying away into captivity men, women, and children from the African coast; but which is neither shocked nor disturbed by a similar traffic, carried on with the same motives and purposes, and characterized by even more odious peculiarities on the coast of our MODEL REPUBLIC. We execrate and hang the wretch guilty of this crime on the coast of Guinea, while we respect and applaud the guilty participators in this murderous business on the enlightened shores of the Chesapeake. The inconsistency is so flagrant and glaring, that it would seem to cast a doubt on the doctrine of the innate moral sense of mankind.

Just two months after the sailing of the Virginia slave brig, which the reader has seen move off to sea so proudly with her human cargo for the New Orleans market, there chanced to meet, in the Marine Coffee-house at Richmond, a company of ocean birds, when the following conversation, which throws some light on the subsequent history, not only of Madison Washington, but of the hundred and thirty human beings with whom we last saw him chained.

"I say, shipmate, you had rather rough weather on your late passage to Orleans?" said Jack Williams, a regular old salt, tauntingly, to a trim, compact, manly looking person, who proved to be the first mate of the slave brig in question.

"Foul play, as well as foul weather," replied the firmly knit personage, evidently but little inclined to enter upon a subject which terminated so ingloriously to the captain and officers of the American slaver.

"Well, betwixt you and me," said Williams, "that whole affair on board of the *Creole* was miserably and disgracefully managed. Those black rascals got the upper hand of ye altogether; and, in my opinion, the whole disaster was the result of ignorance of the real character of darkies in general. With half a dozen resolute white men, (I say it not boastingly,) I could have had the rascals in irons in ten minutes, not because I'm so strong, but I know how to manage 'em. With my back against the caboose, I could, myself, have flogged a dozen of them; and had I been on board, by every monster of the deep, every black devil of 'em all would have had his neck stretched from the yard-arm. Ye made a mistake in yer manner of fiting 'em. All that is needed in dealing with a set of rebellious darkies, is to show that ye're not afraid of 'em. For my own part, I would not honor a dozen n——s, by pointing a gun at one on 'em,—a good stout whip, or a stiff rope's end, is better than all the guns at Old Point to quell a n——r insurrection. Why, sir, to take a gun to a n——r is the best way you can select to tell him you are afraid of him, and the best way of inviting his attack."

This speech made made quite a sensation among the company, and a part of them indicated solicitude for the answer which might be made to it. Our first mate replied, "Mr. Williams, all that you've now said sounds very well here on shore, where, perhaps, you have studied Negro character. I do not profess to understand the subject as well as yourself; but it strikes me, you apply the same rule in dissimilar cases. It is quite easy to talk of flogging n——s here on land, where you have the sympathy of the community, and the whole physical force of the government, State and national, at your command, and where, if a Negro shall lift his hand against a white man, the whole community, with one accord, are ready to unite in shooting him down. I say, in such circumstances, it's easy to talk of flogging Negroes and of Negro cowardice; but, sir, I deny that the Negro is, naturally, a coward, or that your theory of managing slaves will stand the test of salt water. It may do very well for an overseer, a contemptible hireling, to take advantage of fears already in existence, and which his presence has no power to inspire; to swagger about whip in hand, and discourse on the timidity and cowardice of Negroes; for they have a smooth sea and fair wind. It is one thing to manage a company of slaves on a Virginia plantation, and quite another thing to quell an insurrection on the lonely billows of the Atlantic, where every breeze speaks of courage and liberty. For the Negro to act cowardly on shore, may be to act wisely; and I've some doubts whether you, Mr. Williams, would find it very convenient were you a slave in Algiers, to raise your hand against the bayonets of a whole government."

"By George, shipmates," said Williams, "you're coming rather too near. Either I've fallen very low in your estimation, or your notions of Negro courage have got up a button-hole too high. Now I more than ever wish I'd been on board of that luckless craft. I'd have given ye practical evidence of the truth of my theory. I don't doubt there's some difference in being at sea. But a n———r's a n———r, on sea or land, and is a coward, find him where you will; a drop of blood from one on 'em will skeer a hundred. A knock on the nose, or a kick on the shin, will tame the wildest 'darkey' you can fetch me. I say again, and will stand by it, I could, with half a dozen men, put the whole nineteen on 'em in irons, and have carried them safe to New Orleans too. Mind, I don't blame you, but I do say, and every gentleman here will bear me out in it, that the fault was somewhere, or them n———s would never have got off as they have done. For my part I feel ashamed to have the idea go abroad, that a ship load of slaves can't be safely taken from Richmond to New Orleans. I should like, merely to redeem the character of Virginia sailors, to take charge of a ship load on 'em to-morrow."

Williams went on in this strain, occasionally casting an imploring glance at the company for applause for his wit, and sympathy for his contempt of Negro courage. He had, evidently, however, waked up the wrong passenger; for besides being in the right, his opponent carried that in his eye which marked him a man not to be trifled with.

"Well, sir," said the sturdy mate, "You can select your own method for distinguishing yourself;—the path of ambition in this direction is quite open to you in Virginia, and I've no doubt that you will be highly appreciated and compensated for all your valiant achievements in that line; but for myself, while I do not profess to be a giant, I have resolved never to set my foot on the deck of a slave ship, either as officer, or common sailor again; I have got enough of it."

"Indeed! indeed!" exclaimed Williams, derisively.

"Yes, indeed," echoed the mate, "but don't misunderstand me. It is not the high value that I set upon my life that makes me say what I have said; yet I'm resolved never to endanger my life again in a cause which my conscience does not approve. I dare say here what many men feel, but dare not speak, that this whole slave-trading business is a disgrace and scandal to Old Virginia."

"Hold! hold on! shipmate," said Williams, "I hardly thought you'd have shown your colors so soon,—I'll be hanged if you're not as good an abolitionist as Garrison himself."

The mate now rose from his chair, manifesting some excitement. "What do you mean, sir," said he, in a commanding tone. "That man does not live who shall offer me an insult with impunity."

The effect of these words was marked; and the company clustered around. Williams, in an apologetic tone, said, "Shipmate! keep you temper. I meant no insult. We all know that Tom Grant is no coward, and what I said about you being an abolitionist was simply this: you might have put down them black mutineers and murderers, but your conscience held you back."

"In that, too," said Grant, "you were mistaken. I did all that any man with equal strength and presence of mind could have done. The fact is, Mr. Williams, you underrate the courage as well as the skill of these Negroes, and further, you do not seem to have been correctly informed about the case in hand at all."

"All I know about it is," said Williams, "that on the ninth day after you left Richmond, a dozen or two of the n——s ye had on board, came on deck and took the ship from you;—had her steered into a British port, where, by the by, every woolly head of them went ashore and was free. Now I take this to be a discreditable piece of business, and one demanding explanation."

"There are a great many discreditable things in the world," said Grant. "For a ship to go down under a calm sky is, upon the first flush of it, disgraceful either to sailors or caulkers. But when we learn, that by some mysterious disturbance in nature, the waters parted beneath, and swallowed the ship up, we lose our indignation and disgust in lamentation of the disaster, and in awe of the Power which controls the elements."

"Very true, very true," said Williams, "I should be very glad to have an explanation which would relieve the affair of its present discreditable features. I have desired to see you ever since you got home, and to learn from you a full statement of the facts in the case. To me the whole thing seems unaccountable. I cannot see how a dozen or two of ignorant Negroes, not one of whom had ever been to sea before, and all of them were closely ironed between decks should be able to get their fetters off, rush out of the hatchway in open daylight, kill two white men, the one the captain and the other their master, and then carry the ship into a British port, where every 'darkey' of them was set free. There must have been great carelessness, or cowardice somewhere!"

The company which had listened in silence during most of this discussion, now became much excited. One said, I agree with Williams; and several said the thing looks black enough. After the temporary tumultous exclamations had subsided,—

"I see," said Grant, "how you regard this case, and how difficult it will be for me to render our ship's company blameless in your eyes. Nevertheless, I will state the facts precisely as they came under my own observation. Mr. Williams speaks of 'ignorant Negroes,' and, as a general rule, they are ignorant; but had he been on board the *Creole* as I was, he would have seen cause to admit that there are exceptions to this general rule. The leader of the mutiny in question was just as shrewd a fellow as ever I met in my life, and was as well fitted to lead in a dangerous enterprise as any one white man in ten thousand. The name of this man, strange to say, (ominous of greatness,) was MADISON WASHINGTON. In the short time he had been on board, he had secured the confidence of every officer. The Negroes fairly worshipped him. His manner and bearing were such, that no one could suspect him of a murderous purpose. The only feeling with which we regarded him was, that he was a powerful, good-disposed Negro. He seldom spoke to anyone, and when he did speak, it was with the utmost propriety. His words were well chosen, and his pronunciation equal to that of any schoolmaster. It was a mystery to us where he got his knowledge of language; but as little was said to him, none of us knew the extent of his intelligence and ability till it was too late. It seems he brought three files with him on board, and must have gone to work upon his fetters the first night out; and he must have worked well at that; for on the day of the rising, he got the irons off eighteen besides himself.

"The attack began just about twilight in the evening. Apprehending a squall, I had commanded the second mate to order all hands on deck to take in sail. A few minutes before this I had seen Madison's head above the hatchway, looking out upon the white-capped waves at the leeward. I think I never saw him look more good-natured. I stood just about midship, on the larboard side. The captain was pacing the quarterdeck on the starboard side, in company with Mr. Jameson, the owner of most of the slaves on board. Both were armed. I had just told the men to lay aloft, and was looking to see my orders obeyed, when I heard the discharge of a pistol on the starboard side; and turning suddenly around, the very deck seemed covered with fiends from the pit. The nineteen Negroes were all on deck,[4] with their broken fetters in their hands, rushing in all directions. I put my hand quickly in my pocket to draw out my jack-knife; but before I could draw it, I was knocked senseless to the deck. When I came to myself, (which I did in a few minutes, I suppose, for it was yet quite light), there was not a white man on deck. The sailors were all aloft in the rigging, and dared not come down. Captain Clarke and Mr. Jameson lay stretched on the quarter-deck,—both dying,[5]—while Madison himself stood at the helm unhurt.

"I was completely weakened by the loss of blood, and had not recovered from the stunning blow which felled me to the deck; but it was a little too much for me, even in my prostrate condition, to see our good brig commanded by a black murderer. So I called out to the men to come down and take the ship, or die in the attempt. Suiting the action to the word, I started aft. 'You murderous villain,' said I, to the imp at the helm, and rushed upon him to deal him a blow, when he pushed me back with his strong, black arm, as though I had been a boy of twelve. I looked around for the men. They were still in the rigging. Not one had come down. I started towards Madison again. The rascal now told me to stand back. 'Sir,' said he, 'your life is in my hands. I could have killed you a dozen times over during this last half hour, and could kill you now. You call me a black murderer. I am not a murderer. God is my witness that LIBERTY, not malice, is the motive for this night's work. I have done no more to those dead men yonder, than they would have done to me in like circumstances. We have struck for our freedom, and if a true man's heart be in you, you will honor us for the deed. We have done that which you applaud your fathers for doing, and if we are murderers, so were they.'

"I felt little disposition to reply to this impudent speech. By heaven, it disarmed me. The fellow loomed up before me. I forgot his blackness in the dignity of his manner, and the eloquence of his speech. It seemed as if the souls of both the great dead (whose names he bore) had entered him. To the sailors in the rigging he said: 'Men! the battle is over,—your captain is dead. I have complete command of this vessel. All resistance to my authority will be in vain. My men have won their liberty, with no other weapons but their own *Broken Fetters*. We are nineteen in number. We do not thirst for your blood, we demand only our rightful freedom. Do not flatter yourselves that I am ignorant of chart or compass. I know both. We are now only about sixty miles from Nassau. Come down, and do your duty. Land us in Nassau, and not a hair of your heads shall be hurt.'

"I shouted, 'Stay where you are, men,—when a sturdy black fellow ran at me with a handspike, and would have split my head open, but for the interference of Madison, who darted between me and the blow. 'I know what you are up to,' said the latter to me. 'You want to navigate this brig into a slave port, where you would have us all hanged; but you'll miss it; before this brig shall touch a slave-cursed shore while I am on board, I will myself put a match to the magazine, and blow her, and be blown with her, into a thousand fragments. Now I have saved your life twice within these last twenty minutes,—for, when you lay helpless on deck, my men were about to kill you. I held them in check. And if you now (seeing I am your friend and not your enemy) persist in your resistance to my authority, I give you fair warning, you *Shall Die.*'

"Saying this to me, he cast a glance into the rigging where the terror-stricken sailors were slinging, like so many frightened monkeys, and commanded them to come down, in a tone from which there was no appeal; for four men stood by with muskets in hand, ready at the word of command to shoot them down.

"I now became satisfied that resistance was out of the question; that my best policy was to put the brig into Nassau, and secure the assistance of the American consul at the port. I felt sure that the authorities would enable us to secure the murderers, and bring them to trial.

"By this time the apprehended squall had burst upon us. The wind howled furiously,—the ocean was white with foam, which, on account of the darkness, we could see only by the quick flashes of lightning that darted occasionally from the angry sky. All was alarm and confusion. Hideous cries came up from the slave women. Above the roaring billows a succession of heavy thunder rolled along, swelling the terrific din. Owing to the great darkness, and a sudden shift of the wind, we found ourselves in the trough of the sea. When shipping a heavy sea over the starboard bow, the bodies of the captain and Mr. Jameson were washed overboard. For awhile we had dearer interests to look after than slave property. A more savage thunder-gust never swept the ocean. Our brig rolled and creaked as if every bolt would be started, and every thread of oakum would be pressed out of the seams. 'To the pumps! to the pumps!' I cried, but not a sailor would quit his grasp. Fortunately this squall soon passed over, or we must have been food for sharks.

"During all the storm, Madison stood firmly at the helm,—his keen eye fixed upon the binnacle. He was not indifferent to the dreadful hurricane; yet he met it with the equanimity of an old sailor. He was silent but not agitated. The first words he uttered after the storm had slightly subsided were characteristic of the man. 'Mr. mate, you cannot write the bloody laws of slavery on those restless billows. The ocean, if not the land, is free.' I confess, gentlemen, I felt myself in the presence of a superior man; one who, had he been a white man, I would have followed willingly and gladly in any honorable enterprise. Our difference of color was the only ground for difference of action. It was not that his principles were wrong in the abstract; for they are the principles of 1776. But I could not bring myself to recognize their application to one whom I deemed my inferior.

"But to my story. What happened now is soon told. Two hours after the frightful tempest had spent itself, we were plump at the wharf in Nassau. I sent two of our men immediately to our consul with a statement of facts, requesting his interference in our behalf. What he did, or whether he did anything, I don't know; but, by order of the authorities, a company of *black* soldiers came on board, for the purpose, as they said, of protecting the property. These impudent rascals, when I called on them to assist me in keeping the slaves on board, sheltered themselves adroitly under the instructions only to protect property,—and said they did not recognize persons as *property*. I told them that by the law of Virginia and the laws of the United States, the slaves on board were as much property as the barrels of flour in the hold. At this the stupid blockheads showed their *ivory*, rolled up their white eyes in horror, as if the idea of putting men on footing with merchandise was revolting to their humanity. When these instructions were understood among the Negroes, it was impossible for us to keep them on board. They deliberately gathered up their baggage before our eyes, and against our remonstrances, poured through the gangway,—formed themselves into a procession on the wharf,—bid farewell to all on board, and, uttering the wildest shouts of exultation, they marched, amidst the deafening cheers of a multitude of sympathizing spectators, under the triumphant leadership of their heroic chief and deliverer, *Madison Washington.*"[6]

Frederick Douglass

Autographs for Freedom, edited by Julia W. Griffiths, 1853, pp. 174–238[7]

1. *Frederick Douglass' Paper,* Feb. 24, 1854.

2. *British Banner,* reprinted in *Frederick Douglass' Paper,* April 8, 1853; *Autographs for Freedom,* Rochester, 1854, pp. 44–60, 70–76.

3. The *Creole* sailed from Hampton Roads, Virginia, for New Orleans in October 1841 with eight crew members, five sailors, a cargo of tobacco, 135 slaves, and six white passengers (three white men in charge of the slaves, together with the captain's wife, child, and niece). See *Senate Documents,* 27 Congress, 2nd Session, vol. II, No. 51, pp. 1–46. This is a fairly complete documentary collection on the *Creole* affair.

4. Only nineteen slaves, led by Madison Washington, participated in the slave uprising, but they quickly took control of the brig.

5. Only one white man died, John Hewell, owner of thirty-nine of the slaves. Two of the blacks in the revolt were seriously wounded, one of them later dying.

6. Douglass' account here is basically correct, but he omits the fact that the slaves aboard the *Creole* were actually released by the black islanders who surrounded the brig in boats, an action which led the authorities to release the slaves of the *Creole.* British officials in Nassau warned Americans of the *Creole* that resistance to the slaves' liberation would incite the blacks on the island and cause bloodshed.

In 1855 an Anglo-American Claims Commission awarded $110,330 to owners of the liberated slaves. The British government was required to compensate owners of the *Creole*'s slaves on the ground that the brig had been on a lawful voyage, and had had the right to expect shelter from a friendly power when "unavoidable necessity" drove it into Nassau. See Howard Jones, "The Peculiar Institution and National Honor: The Case of the *Creole* Slave Revolt," *Civil War History,* March 1975, pp. 45–47.

7. Sections of the short story also appeared in *Frederick Douglass' Paper,* March 11, 1853.

THE BLACK SWAN, ALIAS MISS ELIZABETH GREENFIELD

How mean, bitter, and malignant is *prejudice against color!* It is the most brainless, brutal, and inconsistent thing of which we know anything. It can dine heartily on dishes prepared by colored hands? It can drink heartily from the glass filled by colored hands? It can ride languishingly behind horses driven by colored hands? It can snooze soundly under a razor guided by colored hands! Finally, it can go to Metropolitan Hall, and listen with delight to the enchanting strains of a black woman! if in all those relations there be conditions acknowledging the inferiority of black people to white. This brainless and contemptible creature, neither man nor beast, caused the following particular notice to be placed on the placard, announcing the Concert of "The Black Swan" in Metropolitan Hall, New York:

> "PARTICULAR NOTICE.—No colored person can be admitted, as there is no part of the house appropriated for them."

We marvel that Miss Greenfield can allow herself to be treated with such palpable *disrespect;* for the insult is *to her,* not less than to her race.

She must have felt *deep humiliation* and depression while attempting to sing in the presence of an audience and under arrangements which had thus degraded and dishonored the people to which she belongs.—Oh! that she could be a *woman* as well as a songstress—brave and dauntless—resolved to fall or flourish with her outraged race—to scorn the mean propositions of the oppressor, and to refuse sternly to acquiesce in her own degradation. She is *quite mistaken* if she supposes that her success, as an artist depends upon her entire abandonment of self-respect. There are *generous hearts* enough in this country who, if she but lead the way, would extend to her the meed of praise and patronage commensurate with her merits. We warn her also, that this yielding, on her part, to the cowardly and contemptible exactions of the Negro haters of this country may meet her in a distant land in a manner which she little imagines.

Frederick Douglass' Paper, April 8, 1853

THE KEY TO UNCLE TOM'S CABIN[1]

American Slavery, like every other form of wickedness, has a strong desire just to be let alone; and slaveholders, above all other preachers, to whom we ever listened, insist most strongly on the duty of every man's minding his own business. They are sure that to drag slavery out of its natural darkness, will only rivet the fetters more firmly on their slaves; still, they have very strong reasons against coming to the light. "Let us declare," said a Carolina journal, some years ago, "that the subject of slavery *is* not and *shall* not be open to discussion within our borders—that the moment any preacher or private citizen shall attempt to enlighten us on that subject, his tongue shall be cut out and cast upon a dung hill!" Unlike Ajax, the cry is, give us but darkness, and slavery asks no more. "Mind your own business," said the late Mr. Clay to Mr. Mendenhall. "*Look at home,*" said the amiable *Mrs. Julia Gardner Ex-President John Tyler,* of Virginia, to the Duchess of Sutherland.

Well, there is a good deal in the idea of one's minding his own business; and we are not sure that, if that idea were fully carried out, it would not abolish slavery.— Suppose every slaveholder should some day resolve to mind his own business, take care of his own concerns, be at the pains and industry of providing for his own wants with his own hands, or with the money obtained by his own energies—and suppose he should say to his slaves, "follow my example, mind your own business, don't look after mine, but look after your own business in your own way"—why, just here would be the end of slavery. Slaveholders preach to others this doctrine while they are themselves most grossly and scandalously intermeddling with the business of others to the utter neglect of their own.

It is noticeable, too, that the complaint of interference is never preferred against any of our sainted priesthood who bulwark the system with the gospel. These holy Doctors are held to be very properly employed. It is only your hot-headed men who think a "n——r" has rights as well as a white man—that a slave is as good as his master—who are supposed to need counsel to mind their own business.

But to return. Slavery dreads exposure. The light, which strengthens other systems, weakens slavery; and slaveholders know this very well. The wonder is, that, knowing it so well, they do not more skilfully manage their affairs. It is surprising that they allow such fiendish advertisements to find their way into their public journals—permit such bloody enactments to stain their statute books— and, publicly, commit such shocking atrocities as fill the pages of the "Thousand Witnesses," and swell the volume of the "Key" to "Uncle Tom's Cabin." Some one should call attention to this unguarded point. How would it do, instead of advertising in the everywhere circulating newspaper for "blood-hounds to hunt slaves," "cash for Negroes," &c., to use small hand-bills for the purpose? These would not come North, telling their tales of misery on the one hand, and of deep wickedness on the other. Then, too, would it not be well to repeal most of the laws regulating the whipping, branding, ironing, shooting, stabbing, hanging and quartering, of slaves? Could not all these ends be attained without their being provided for in the statute book? Could not "the spirit" be retained without "the letter?" for it is "the letter" which, in this instance, is deadly—while "the spirit" of these laws is the life of the system of slavery. We should not be surprised if some such suggestions prevailed at the South; for slavery cannot bear to be looked at. The slaveholder must become a madman, and forget the eyes of just men and of a just God, when he burns his name into the flesh of a woman.

Bold and incorrigible as slaveholders, generally, are, they are, nevertheless, far from being indifferent to the good opinions of their fellow-men. They are seldom found willing to acknowledge themselves cruel, or wanting at all in the sentiments of humanity. On the contrary, none are more anxious than they to be regarded as kind and humane. Hence, they are ever anticipating objections to the slave system, by asserting the mildness of the treatment of their slaves, the excellency of their condition and the quiet of their minds. The best of them, however, would find the presence, for any considerable time, of a Northern man of anti-slavery principles on their plantations, watching the intercourse between themselves and their contented and happy, unpaid laborers, very inconvenient and irksome! No. Masters should be seen apart from their slaves.

They find it easier to commend slavery in its absence, than when confronted by its ugly features.

Willingly enough are these slaveholding gentlemen and ladies to be seen at Saratoga Springs, at Niagara, where they are arrayed in purple and fine linen, and are covered with silks, satins and broadcloth—their hands shining with gold, and their bosoms sparkling with diamonds. Their manner is so genteel—their conversation so winning—their smiles are full of kindness, that they easily make their way, win friends, and conceal their abominations. But bring them out from their hiding place—tear off the gold with which their sin is plated, and they stand out, by all the deductions of reason, morality, and religion, naked pirates before God and man, guilty of cruelty which might make a devil blush. Concealment, then, is the constant care of slaveholders. To see a slave speaking to a Northern man throws them into agony. So anxious are they to retain the secrets of the slave prison, that they denounce death against any in their midst who undertakes to reveal them.

But all efforts to conceal the enormity of slavery fail. The most unwise thing which, perhaps, was ever done by slaveholders, in order to hide the ugly features of slavery, was the calling in question, and denying the truthfulness of "*Uncle Tom's Cabin.*" They had better have owned the "soft impeachment" therein contained—for the "Key" not only proves the correctness of every essential part of "Uncle Tom's Cabin," but proves more and worse things against the murderous system than are alleged in that great book. Since the publication of that repository of human horrors—"*The Testimony of a Thousand Witnesses*"—there has not been an exposure of slavery so terrible as the *Key* to "*Uncle Tom's Cabin.*" Let it be circulated far and wide, at home and abroad; let young and old read it, think of it, and learn from it to hate slavery with unappeasable intensity. The book, then, will be not only a *Key* to "Uncle Tom's Cabin," but a key to unlock the prison-house for the deliverance of millions who are now pining in chains, crying, "How long! How long! O Lord God of Sabaoth! How long shall these things be?"

Frederick Douglass' Paper, April 29, 1853

1. Harriet Beecher Stowe wrote the volume entitled *The Key to Uncle Tom's Cabin* to defend the veracity of her great novel, *Uncle Tom's Cabin.* It consisted of a mass of supporting data, court decisions, newspaper clippings, church proceedings, etc. It did not, however, consist of materials she had used when she wrote *Uncle Tom's Cabin.*

THE PRESENT CONDITION AND FUTURE PROSPECTS OF THE NEGRO PEOPLE, speech at annual meeting of the American and Foreign Anti-Slavery Society, New York City, May 11, 1853

Mr. President, Ladies and Gentlemen:

The resolution upon which I propose to make a few remarks, respects the present condition and future prospects of the whole colored people of the United States. The subject is a great one, and opens ample scope for thought and feeling. I feel a diffidence in undertaking the consideration for two causes: first, my own incompetence to do it justice; and the second is, the peculiar relation subsisting between me and the audience I am to address. Sir, I am a colored man, and this is a white audience. No colored man, with any nervous sensibility, can stand before an American audience without an intense and painful sense of the disadvantages imposed by his color. He feels little borne up by that brotherly sympathy and generous enthusiasm, which give wings to the eloquence, and strength to the hearts of other men, who advocate other and more popular causes. The ground which a colored man occupies in this country is, every inch of it, sternly disputed. Sir, were I a white man, speaking for the rights of white men, I should in this country have a smooth sea and a fair wind. It is, perhaps, creditable to the American people (and I am not the man to detract from their credit) that they listen eagerly to the report of wrongs endured by distant nations. The Hungarian, the Italian, the Irishman, the Jew and the Gentile, all find in this goodly land a home; and when any of them, or all of them, desire to speak, they find willing ears, warm hearts, and open hands. For these people, the Americans have principles of justice, maxims of mercy, sentiments of religion, and feelings of brotherhood in abundance. But for *my* poor people (alas, how poor!), enslaved, scourged, blasted, overwhelmed, and ruined, it would appear that America had neither justice, mercy, nor religion. She has no scales in which to weigh our wrongs, and no standard by which to measure our rights. Just here lies the grand difficulty of the colored man's cause. It is found in the fact, that we may not avail ourselves of the just force of admitted American principles. If I do not misinterpret the feelings and philosophy of my white fellow-countrymen generally, they wish us to understand distinctly and fully that they have no other use for us whatever, than to coin dollars out of our blood.

Our position here is anomalous, unequal, and extraordinary. It is a position to which the most courageous of our race can look without deep concern. Sir, we are a hopeful people, and in this we are fortunate: but for this trait of our character, we should have, long before this seemingly unpropitious hour, sunk down under a sense of utter despair.

Look at it, sir. Here, upon the soil of our birth, in a country which has known us for two centuries, among a people who did not wait for us to seek them, but who sought us, found us, and brought us to their own chosen land, a people for whom we have performed the humblest services, and whose greatest comforts and luxuries have been won from the soil by our sable and sinewy arms—I say, sir, among such a people, and with such obvious recommendations to favor, we are far less esteemed than the veriest stranger and sojourner.

Aliens are we in our native land. The fundamental principles of the republic, to which the humblest white man, whether born here or elsewhere, may appeal with confidence in the hope of awakening a favorable response are held to be inapplicable to us. The glorious doctrines of your revolutionary fathers, and the more glorious teachings of the Son of God, are construed and applied against us. We are literally scourged beyond the beneficent range of both authorities, human and divine. We plead for our rights, in the name of the immortal Declaration of Independence, and of the written constitution of government, and we are answered with imprecations and curses. In the sacred name of Jesus we beg for mercy, and the slave-whip, red with blood, cracks over us in mockery. We invoke the aid of the ministers of Him who came "to preach deliverance to the captive," and to set at liberty them that are bound, and from the loftiest summits of this ministry comes the inhuman and blasphemous response, saying: if one prayer would move the Almighty arm in mercy to break your galling chains, that prayer would be withheld. We cry for help to humanity—a common humanity, and here too we are repulsed. American humanity hates us, scorns us, disowns and denies, in a thousand ways, our very personality. The outspread wing of American Christianity, apparently broad enough to give shelter to a perishing world, refuses to cover us. To us, its bones are brass, and its feathers iron. In running thither for shelter and succor, we have only fled from the hungry bloodhound to the devouring wolf, from a corrupt and selfish world to a hollow and hypocritical Church; and may I not add, from the agonies of earth to the flames of hell! Sir, this is strong language. For the sake of my people, I would to God it were extravagantly strong. But, Sir, I fear our fault here to-day will not be that we have pleaded the cause of the slave too vehemently, but too tamely; that we have not contemplated his wrongs with too much excitement, but with unnatural calmness and composure. For my part, I cannot speak as I feel on this subject. My language, though never so bitter, is less bitter than my experience. At best, my poor speech is, to the facts in the case, but as the shadow to the substance. Sir, it is known to you, and to many who hear me, that I am alike familiar with the whip and chain of slavery, and the lash and sting of public neglect and scorn; that my back is marked with the one, and my soul is fretted with the other. My neck is galled by both yokes—that imposed by one master, and that imposed by many masters. More than twenty years of my life were passed in slavery, and nearly fifteen years have been passed in nominal freedom. Mine has been the experience of the colored people of America, both slave and free. I was born a slave. Even before I made part of this breathing world, the scourge was plaited for my back, and the fetters were forged for my limbs. My earliest recollections are associated with the appalling thought that I was a slave—a slave for life. How that crushing thought wrung my young heart I shall never be able fully to tell. But of some things I can tell—some things which are incident to the free and to the slave people of this country. Give me leave, then, in my own language to speak freely all that can be uttered of the thoughts of my heart in regard to the wrongs of the people with whom I thus stand associated in the two conditions to which I have thus alluded; for when I have said all, "the half will not then have been told." Sir, it was once said by that greatest of modern Irish orators, Daniel O'Connell, (a man whose patriotism was equalled only by his love of universal freedom,) that the history of the Irish people might be traced like a wounded man through a crowd, by the blood. That is a most startling saying. I read it with a shudder soon after it was said, and felt, if this were true in relation to the Irish people, it was still more true in relation to the colored people of the United States. Our wrongs and outrages are as old as our country. They date back to its earliest settlement, and extend through two hundred and thirty years, and they are as numerous and as oft-repeated as the days of all those years. Even now, while I speak and you listen, the work of blood and sorrow goes on. Methinks I hear the noise of chains and the clang of the whip. There is not a day, not an hour in any day, not a minute in any hour of the day, that the blood of my people does not gush forth at the call of the scourge; that the tenderest ties of humanity are not sundered; that parents are not torn from children, and husbands from their wives, for the convenience of those who gain fortunes by the blood of their souls. But I do not propose to confine your attention to the details of slavery. They are harrowing to think of, and too shocking to fix the mind upon for any length of time. I rather wish to speak of the condition of the colored people of the United States generally. This people, free and slave, are rapidly filling up the number of four millions. They are becoming a nation, in the midst of a nation which disowns them, and for weal or for woe this nation is united. The distinction between the slave and the free is not great, and their destiny seems one and the same. The black man is linked to his brother by indissoluble ties. The one cannot be truly free while the other is a slave. The free colored man is reminded by the ten thousand petty annoyances with which he meets of his identity with an enslaved people, and that with them he is destined to fall or flourish. We are one nation, then. If not one in immediate condition, at least one in prospects. I will not argue that we are men of like passions with the rest of mankind: that is unnecessary. All know at any rate that we are capable at least of love and hate, friendship and enmity. But whatever character or capacity you ascribe to us, I am not ashamed to be numbered with this race. I am not ashamed to speak here as a Negro. Sir, I utterly abhor and spurn with all the contempt possible that cowardly meanness (I will not call it pride) which leads any colored man to repudiate his connection with his race. I cannot say, therefore, as was said recently by a distinguished colored man at a Convention in Cincinnati, that "he did not speak as a colored man," for, Sir, as a colored man I do speak; as a colored man I was invited here to speak; and as a colored man there are peculiar reasons for my speaking. The man struck is the man to cry out. I would place myself—nay, I am placed among the victims of American oppression. I view this subject from their stand-point, and scan the moral and political horizon of the country with their hopes, their fears, and their intense solicitude. Standing here, then, and judging from the events and indications of the past few years, the black man must see that a crisis has arrived in his relations with the American people. He is reminded that trials and hardships await him; that the times are portentous of storms which will try the strength of his bark. Sir, it is evident that there is in this country a purely slavery party; a party which exists for no other earthly purpose but to promote the interests of slavery. The presence of this party is felt everywhere in the republic. It is known by no particular name, and has assumed no definite shape, but its branches reach far and wide in the Church and in the State. This shapeless and nameless party is not intangible in other and more important respects. That party, Sir, has determined upon a fixed, definite, and comprehensive policy towards the whole colored population of the United States. What that policy is, it becomes us as Abolitionists, and especially does it become the colored people themselves to consider and understand fully. We ought to know who our enemies are, where they are, and what are their objects and measures. Well, Sir, here is my version of it; not original with me, but mine because I hold it to be true. I understand this policy to comprehend five cardinal objects. They are these: 1st.

The complete suppression of all anti-slavery discussion; 2d. The expatriation of the entire free people of color from the United States; 3d. The unending perpetuation of slavery in this republic; 4th. The nationalization of slavery to the extent of making slavery respected in every State of the Union; 5th. The extension of slavery over Mexico and the entire South American States. Sir, these objects are forcibly presented to us in the stern logic of passing events—in the facts which are and have been passing around us during the last three years. The country has been and is now dividing on these grand issues. In their magnitude these issues cast all others into the shade, depriving them of all life and vitality. Old party lines are broken. Like is finding its like on either side of these great issues, and the great battle is at hand. For the present, the best representative of the slavery party in politics is the Democratic party. Its great head for the present is President Pierce, whose boast it is that his whole life has been consistent with the interests of slavery; that he is above reproach on that score. In his inaugural address he reassures the South on this point. The head of the slave power being in power, it is natural that the pro-slavery elements should cluster around the Administration, and this is rapidly being done. A fraternization is going on. The stringent Protectionists and the Free Traders strike hands. The supporters of Fillmore are becoming the supporters of Pierce. The Silver Gray Whig shakes hands with the Hunker Democrat, the former only differing from the latter in name.[1] They are of one heart, one mind, and the union is natural, and perhaps inevitable. Both hate Negroes, both hate progress, both hate the "Higher Law," both hate Wm. H. Seward, both hate the Free Democratic party, and upon these hateful bases they are forming a union of hatred. "Pilate and Herod are thus made friends." Even the central organ of the Whig party is extending its beggar-hand for a morsel from the table of Slavery Democracy; and when spurned from the feast by the more deserving, it pockets the insult; when kicked on one side, it turns the other, and perseveres in its importunities. The fact is, that paper comprehends the demands of the times. It understands the age and its issues. It wisely sees that slavery and freedom are the great antagonistic forces in the country, and it goes to its own side. Silver Grays and Hunkers all understand this. They are, therefore, rapidly sinking all other questions to nothing, compared with the increasing demands of slavery. They are collecting, arranging, and consolidating their forces for the accomplishment of their appointed work. The keystone to the arch of this grand union of the slavery party of the United States is the Compromise of 1850. In that Compromise we have all the objects of our slaveholding policy specified. It is, Sir, favorable to this view of the designs of the slave power that both the Whig and the Democratic party bent lower, sunk deeper, and strained harder in their conventions, preparatory to the late presidential election, to meet the demands of the slavery party than at any previous time in their history. Never did parties come before the Northern people with propositions of such undisguised contempt for the moral sentiment and the religious ideas of that people. They virtually asked them to unite in a war upon free speech, upon conscience, and to drive the Almighty Presence from the councils of the nation. Resting their platforms upon the Fugitive Slave Bill, they boldly asked the people for political power to execute the horrible and hell-black provisions of that bill. The history of that election reveals with great clearness the extent to which slavery has shot its leprous distilment through the life-blood of the nation. The party most thoroughly opposed to the cause of justice and humanity triumphed, while the party suspected of a leaning towards liberty was overwhelmingly defeated—some say, annihilated. But here is a still more important fact, illustrating the designs of the slave power. It is a fact full of meaning, that no sooner did this Democratic leading party come into power than a system of legislation was presented to the Legislatures of the Northern States designed to put the States in harmony with the Fugitive Slave Law, and the malignant bearing of the National Government towards the colored inhabitants of the country. This whole movement on the part of the States bears the evidence of having one origin, emanating from one head, and urged forward by one power. It was simultaneous, uniform, and general, and looked to one end. It was intended to put thorns under feet already bleeding, to crush a people already bowed down, to enslave a people already but half free. In a word, it was intended to discourage, dishearten, and drive the free colored people out of the country. In looking at the recent Black Law of Illinois, one is struck with its enormity.[2] It would seem that the men who enacted that law had not only banished from their minds all sense of justice, but all sense of shame. It coolly proposes to sell the bodies and souls of the blacks to increase the intelligence and refinement of the whites; to rob every black stranger who ventures among them to increase their literary fund. While this is going on in the States, a pro-slavery Political Board of Health is established at Washington. Senators Hale, Chase and Sumner are robbed of a part of their senatorial dignity and consequence, as representing sovereign States, because they have refused to be inoculated with the slavery virus.[3] Among the services which a Senator is expected by his State to perform are many that can only be done efficiently by Committees; and in saying to these honorable Senators, You shall not serve on the Committees of this body, the slavery party took the responsibility of robbing and insulting the States that sent them. It is an attempt at Washington to decide for the States who shall be sent to the Senate. Sir, it strikes me that this aggression on the part of the slave power did not meet at the hands of the proscribed Senators the rebuke which we had a right to expect would be administered. It seems to me that an opportunity was lost; that the great principles of senatorial equality were left undefended at a time when its vindication was sternly demanded. But it is not to the purpose of my present statement to criticise the conduct of our friends. I am persuaded that much ought to be left to the discretion of anti-slavery men in Congress, and charges of recreancy should never be made but on the most sufficient grounds. For, of all the places in the world where an anti-slavery man needs the confidence and encouragement of friends, I take Washington to be that place. Let me now call attention to the social influences which are operating and coöperating with the slavery party of the country, designed to contribute to one or all of the grand objects aimed at by that party. We see here the black man attacked in his vital interests. Prejudice and hate are excited against him. Enmity is stirred up between him and other laborers. The Irish people, warm-hearted, generous, and sympathizing with the oppressed everywhere when they stand on their own green island, are instantly taught on arriving in this Christian country to hate and despise the colored people. They are taught to believe that we eat the bread which of right belongs to them. The cruel lie is told the Irish that our adversity is essential to their prosperity. Sir, the Irish American will find out his mistake one day. He will find that in assuming our avocation he also has assumed our degradation. But for the present we are the sufferers. The old employments by which we have heretofore gained our livelihood are gradually, and it may be inevitably, passing into other hands. Every hour sees us elbowed out of some employment, to make room perhaps for some newly arrived immigrants, whose hunger and color are thought to give them a title to especial favor. White men are becoming house-servants, cooks and stewards, common laborers and flunkeys to our gentry, and for aught that I see, they adjust themselves to their stations with a becoming obsequiousness. This fact proves that if we cannot rise to the whites, the whites can fall to us. Now, Sir, look once more. While the colored people are thus elbowed out of employment; while the enmity of immigrants is being excited against us; while State after State enacts laws against us; while we are hunted down like wild game, and oppressed with a general feeling of insecurity, the American Colonization Society—that old offender against the best interests, and slanderer of the colored people—awakens to new life, and vigorously presses its scheme upon the consideration of the people and the Government. New papers are started; some for the North and some for the South, and each in its tone adapting itself to its latitude. Government, State and National, is called upon for appropriations to enable the Society to send us out of the country by steam. They want steamers to carry letters and Negroes to Africa. Evidently this Society looks upon our "extremity as its opportunity," and we may expect that it will use the occasion well. It does not deplore, but glories in our misfortunes. But, Sir, I must hasten. I have thus briefly given my view of one aspect of the present condition and future prospects of the colored people of the United States. And what I have said is far from encouraging to my afflicted people. I have seen the cloud gather upon the sable brows of some who hear me. I confess the case looks black enough. Sir, I am not a hopeful man. I think I am apt even to undercalculate the benefits of the future. Yet, Sir, in this seemingly desperate case, I do not despair for my people. There is a bright side to almost every picture of this kind, and ours is no exception to the general rule. If the influences against us are strong, those for us are also strong. To the inquiry, Will our enemies prevail in the execution of their designs? in my God and in my soul I believe they *will not*. Let us look at the first object sought for by the slavery party of the country, viz., the suppression of anti-slavery discussion. They desire to suppress discussion on this subject, with a view to the peace of the slaveholder and the security of slavery. Now, Sir, neither the principal nor the subordinate objects here declared can be all gained by the slave power, and for this reason: It involves the proposition to padlock the lips of the whites, in order to secure the fetters on the limbs of the blacks. The right of speech, precious and priceless, *cannot, will not* be surrendered to slavery. Its suppression is asked for, as I have said, to give peace and security to slaveholders. Sir, that thing cannot be done. God has interposed an insuperable obstacle to any such result. "There can be *no peace,* saith my God, to the wicked." Suppose it were possible to put down this discussion, what would it avail the guilty slave-holder, pillowed as he is upon the heaving bosoms of ruined souls? He could not have a peaceful spirit. If every anti-slavery tongue in the nation were silent; every anti-slavery organization dissolved; every antislavery press demolished; every anti-slavery periodical, paper, book, tract, pamphlet or what not were searched out, gathered together, deliberately burnt to ashes, and their ashes given to the four winds of heaven, still, still the slaveholder could have "*no peace.*" In every pulsation of his heart, in every throb of his life, in every glance of his eye, in the breeze that soothes and in the thunder that startles, would be waked up an accuser whose language is, "Thou art verily guilty concerning thy brother." Oh! Sir, I can say with the poet Cowper—and I speak from observation—

I would not have a slave to till my ground.

Again: The prospect, Sir, of putting down this discussion is anything but flattering at the present moment. I am unable to detect any signs of the suppression of this discussion. I certainly do not see it in this crowded assembly, nor upon this platform, nor do I see it in any direction. Why, Sir, look all over the North; look South, look at home, look abroad! Look at the whole civilized world! And what are all this vast multitude doing at this moment? Why, Sir, they are reading *Uncle Tom's Cabin,* and when they have read that, they will probably read *The Key to Uncle Tom's Cabin*—a key not only to the cabin, but I believe to the slave's darkest dungeon. A nation's hand, with that "Key," will unlock the slave-prison to millions. Then look at the authoress of *Uncle Tom's Cabin.* There is nothing in her reception abroad which indicates a declension of interest in the great subject which she has done so much to unfold and illustrate. The sending of a princess on the shores of England would not have produced the same sensation. I take it, then, that the slavery party will find this item of their programme the most difficult of execution, since it is the voice of all experience that opposition to agitation is the most successful method of promoting it. Men will write. Men will read. Men will think. Men will feel. And the result of all this is, men will speak. And it were as well to chain the lightning as to repress the moral convictions and humane prompting of enlightened human nature. Herein, Sir, is our hope. Slavery cannot bear discussion. It is a matter of darkness; and as Junius said of the character of Lord Granby, "it can only pass without censure, as it passes without observation." The second cardinal object of this party, viz.: the expatriation of the free colored people of the United States, is a very desirable one to our enemies; and we read, in the vigorous efforts making to accomplish it, an acknowledgment of our manhood, and the danger to slavery arising out of our presence. Despite the tremendous pressure brought to bear against us, the colored people are gradually increasing in wealth, in intelligence, and in respectability. Here is the secret of the Colonization scheme. It is easily seen that just in proportion to the intelligence and respectability of the free colored race at the North is their power to endanger the stability of slavery. Hence the desire to get rid of us. But, Sir, the desire is not merely to get us out of this country, but to get us at a convenient and harmless distance from slavery. And here, Sir, I think I can speak as if by authority for the free colored people of the United States. The people of this republic may commit the audacious and high-handed atrocity of driving us out of the limits of their borders. They may virtually confiscate our property; they may invade our civil and personal liberty, and render our lives intolerable burdens, so that we may be induced to leave the United States; but to compel us to go to Africa is quite another thing. Thank God, the alternative is not quite so desperate as that we must be slaves here, or go to the pestilential shores of Africa. Other and more desirable lands are open to us. We can plant ourselves at the very portals of slavery. We can hover about the Gulf of Mexico. Nearly all the isles of the Caribbean Seas bid us welcome; while the broad and fertile valleys of British Guiana, under the sway of the emancipating Queen, invite us to their treasures, and to nationality. With the Gulf of Mexico on the South, and Canada on the North, we may still keep within hearing of the wails of our enslaved people in the United States. From the isles of the sea and from the mountain-tops of South America we can watch the meandering destiny of those we have left behind. Americans should remember that there are already on this continent, and in the adjacent islands, all of 12,370,000 Negroes, who only wait for the lifegiving and organizing power of intelligence to mould them into one body, and into a powerful nation. The following estimate of our numbers and localities is taken from one of the able reports of the British and Foreign Anti-slavery Society, carefully drawn up by its former Secretary, John Scoble, Esq.:

United States,	3,650,000	Dutch Colonies	50,000
Brazil,	4,050,000	Danish Colonies,	45,000
Spanish Colonies,	1,470,000	Mexico,	70,000
S. American Republics,	1,130,000	Canada,	35,000
British Colonies,	750,000		
Haiti,	850,000	Total,	12,370,000
French Colonies,	270,000		

Now, Sir, it seems to me that the slavery party will gain little by driving us out of this country, unless it drives us off this continent and the adjacent islands. It seems to me that it would be after all of little advantage to slavery to have the intelligence and energy of the free colored people all concentrated in the Gulf of Mexico. Sir, I am not for going any where. I am for staying precisely where I am, in the land of my birth. But, Sir, if I must go from this country; if it is impossible to stay here, I am then for doing the next best, and that will be to go wherever I can hope to be of most service to the colored people of the United States. Americans, there is a meaning in those figures I have read. God does not permit twelve millions of his creatures to live without the notice of his eye. That this vast people are tending to one point on this continent is not without significance. All things are possible with God. Let not the colored man despair, then. Let him remember that a home, a country, a nationality, are all attainable this side of Liberia. But for the present the colored people should stay just where they are, unless they are compelled to leave. I have faith left yet in the wisdom and justice of the country, and it may be that there are enough left of these to save the nation. But there is a third object sought by the slavery party, namely, to render slavery a permanent system in this republic, and to make the relation of master and slave respected in every State in the Union. Neither part of this object can be accomplished. Slavery has no means within itself of perpetuation or permanence. It is a huge lie. It is of the Devil, and will go to its place. It is against nature, against progress, against improvement, and against the government of God. It cannot stand. It has an enemy in every bar of railroad iron, in every electric wire, in every improvement in navigation, in the growing intercourse of nations, in cheap postage, in the relaxation of tariffs, in common schools, in the progress of education, the spread of knowledge, in the steam engine, and in the World's Fair, now about to assemble in New York, and in everything that will be exhibited there. About making slavery respectable in the North, laws have been made to accomplish just that thing; the law of '50 and the law of '93. And those laws, instead of getting respect for slavery, have begot distrust and abhorrence. Congress might pass slave-laws every day in the year for all time, if each one should be followed by such publications as *Uncle Tom* and the *Key*. It is not in the power of human law to make men entirely forget that the slave is a man. The freemen of the North can never be brought to look with the same feelings upon a man escaping from his claimants as upon a horse running from his owner. The slave is a man, and no slave. Now, Sir, I had more to say on the encouraging aspects of the times, but the time fails me. I will only say, in conclusion, greater is He that is for us than they that are against us; and though labor and peril beset the Anti-slavery movements, so sure as that a God of mercy and justice is enthroned above all created things, so sure will that cause gloriously triumph. [Great applause.]

Annual Report of the American and Foreign Anti-Slavery Society for 1853

1. The Hunkers was the conservative faction of New York's Democratic Party in the 1840s who opposed the Abolitionists and deprecated anti-slavery agitation. By 1853–1855 the distinction between Hunkers and Barnburners, the more progressive wing of the Democratic Party in New York, was replaced by the terms "Hards" and "Softs." Most of the Hunkers became "Hards."

The Silver Grays was the name given to the conservative minority of the Whig Party in New York who, approving of the conciliatory policies of President Fillmore, bolted the Whig State Convention of 1850 in New York when the delegates endorsed the anti-slavery views of William H. Seward. They were so called because of the color of the hair of Francis Granger, leader of the bolters. After this incident the conservative anti-Abolitionist Whigs were known as Silver Grays or Cotton Whigs.

2. The reference is to an act passed by the Illinois legislature in 1853 which provided that anyone aiding a Negro, bond or free, to secure settlement in Illinois was to be fined not less than $100 or more than $500 and was to be imprisoned in the county jail not longer than a year. The Negro was to be fined $50 if he stayed in the state for ten days with the purpose of continuing his residence. Upon failure to pay his fine he would be arrested and be advertised for ten days by the sheriff and then sold to the person who would pay the fine and costs for the shortest term of service. During this period the temporary owner was to work the Negro at his own pleasure. The prosecuting witness was to receive half the fine imposed. The law was called by its opponents "An Act to establish slavery in this State." (See Mason McCloud Fishback, "Illinois Legislation on Slavery and Free Negroes, 1818–1865," *Transactions of the Illinois State Historical Society for the year 1904*, p. 428.)

3. In January, 1853, in the arrangement of the Senate Committees, Hale of New Hampshire, Sumner of Massachusetts, and Chase of Ohio, were excluded from the committee list upon the express ground that they were "outside of any healthy political organization in this country." A resolution protesting this action was defeated in the Massachusetts legislature.

For five years after the Cleveland convention, the National Convention movement lay dormant. Following the passage of the Fugitive Slave Act in 1850, many Negroes were too terrified to attend public gatherings. Any Negro who was unable to produce proof of his freedom satisfactory to a southern deputy was in danger of being returned to slavery. Hundreds of Negro families from Ohio, Pennsylvania, and New York fled to Canada, abandoning their homes and work. Professor Fred Landon estimates that approximately twenty thousand Negroes, the greater percentage of whom were probably former slaves, fled to Canada during the decade 1850–1860.[1]

The very intensity of the drive against the Negro population in the North compelled the revival of the National Convention. In July, 1853, a hundred and forty delegates from nine states gathered in Rochester, New York, in what was the most important of all conventions. The call for the gathering indicated some of the major problems which made the reconvening of the National Convention necessary: "The Fugitive Slave Act, . . . the proscriptive legislation of several States with a view to drive our people from their borders—the exclusion of our children from schools supported by our money—the prohibition of the exercise of the franchise—the exclusion of colored citizens from the jury box—the social barriers erected against our learning trades—the wiley and vigorous efforts of the American Colonization Society to employ the arm of the government to expel us from our native land—and withal the propitious awakening to the fact of our condition at home and abroad, which has followed the publication of 'Uncle Tom's Cabin'—calls trumpet-tongued for our union, co-operation, and action. . . ." Reverend J. W. C. Pennington was elected president of the Rochester Convention and the vice-presidents included Douglass, William C. Nell, and John B. Vashon.

Douglass was also chairman of the committee on Declaration of Sentiments and drew up the "Address of the Colored Convention to the People of the United States." This remarkable "Address" set forth the basic demands of the Negro people for justice and equality. Today . . . it may still be read, not only for the clarity and grace of its prose but also for its significance. . . .

Realizing that [his] claim of citizenship was denied by the national government, Douglass presented a masterly historical analysis to buttress his argument, quoting extensively from state Constitutional Conventions, from congressional debates, and from Andrew Jackson's proclamation to the free colored inhabitants of Louisiana during the Battle of New Orleans. . . .

"No nobler paper was ever put forth by any body of men," commented the reporter for the *New York Tribune*.[2]

THE CLAIMS OF OUR COMMON CAUSE, address of the Colored Convention held in Rochester, July 6–8, 1853, to the People of the United States

Fellow citizens:

Met in convention as delegates, representing the Free Colored people of the United States; charged with the responsibility of inquiring into the general condition of our people, and of devising measures which may, with the blessing of God, tend to our mutual improvement and elevation; conscious of entertaining no motives, ideas, or aspirations, but such as are in accordance with truth and justice, and are compatible with the highest good of our country and the world, with a cause as vital and worthy as that for which (nearly eighty years ago) your fathers and our fathers bravely contended, and in which they gloriously triumphed—we deem it proper, on this occasion, as one method of promoting the honorable ends for which we have met, and of discharging our duty to those in whose name we speak, to present the claims of our common cause to your candid, earnest, and favorable consideration.

As an apology for addressing you, fellow-citizens! we cannot announce the discovery of any new principle adapted to ameliorate the condition of mankind. The great truths of moral and political science, upon which we rely, and which we press upon your consideration, have been evolved and enunciated by you. We point to your principles, your wisdom, and to your great example as the full justification of our course this day. That "all men are created equal": that "life, liberty, and the pursuit of happiness" are the right of all; that "taxation and representation" should go together; that governments are to protect, not to destroy, the rights of mankind; that the Constitution of the United States was formed to establish justice, promote the general welfare, and secure the blessing of liberty to all the people of this country; that resistance to tyrants is obedience to God—are American principles and maxims, and together they form and constitute the constructive elements of the American government. From this elevated platform, provided by the Republic for us, and for all the children of men, we address you. In doing so, we would have our spirit properly discerned. On this point we would gladly free ourselves and our cause from all misconception. We shall affect no especial timidity, nor can we pretend to any great boldness. We know our poverty and weakness, and your wealth and greatness. Yet we will not attempt to repress the spirit of liberty within us, or to conceal, in any wise, our sense of the justice and the dignity of our cause.

We are Americans, and as Americans, we would speak to Americans. We address you not as aliens nor as exiles, humbly asking to be permitted to dwell among you in peace; but we address you as American citizens asserting their rights on their own native soil. Neither do we address you as enemies, (although the recipients of innumerable wrongs); but in the spirit of patriotic good will. In assembling together as we have done, our object is not to excite pity for ourselves, but to command respect for our cause, and to obtain justice for our people. We are not malefactors imploring mercy; but we trust we are honest men, honestly appealing for righteous judgment, and ready to stand or fall by that judgment. We do not solicit unusual favor, but will be content with roughhanded "fair play." We are neither lame or blind, that we should seek to throw off the responsibility of our own existence, or to cast ourselves upon public charity for support. We would not lay our burdens upon other men's shoulders; but we do ask, in the name of all that is just and magnanimous among men, to be freed from all the unnatural burdens and impediments with which American customs and American legislation have hindered our progress and improvement. We ask to be disencumbered of the load of popular reproach heaped upon us—for no better cause than that we wear the complexion given us by our God and our Creator.

We ask that in our native land, we shall not be treated as strangers, and worse than strangers.

We ask that, being friends of America, we should not be treated as enemies of America.

We ask that, speaking the same language and being of the same religion, worshipping the same God, owing our redemption to the same Savior, and learning our duties from the same Bible, we shall not be treated as barbarians.

We ask that, having the same physical, moral, mental, and spiritual wants, common to other members of the human family, we shall also have the same means which are granted and secured to others, to supply those wants.

We ask that the doors of the school-house, the workshop, the church, the college, shall be thrown open as freely to our children as to the children of other members of the community.

We ask that the American government shall be so administered as that beneath the broad shield of the Constitution, the colored American seaman, shall be secure in his life, liberty and property, in every State in the Union.

We ask that as justice knows no rich, no poor, no black, no white, but, like the government of God, renders alike to every man reward or punishment, according as his works shall be—the white and black man may stand upon an equal footing before the laws of the land.

We ask that (since the right of trial by jury is a safeguard to liberty, against the encroachments of power, only as it is a trial by impartial men, drawn indiscriminately from the country) colored men shall not, in every instance, be tried by white persons; and that colored men shall not be either by custom or enactment excluded from the jury-box.

We ask that (inasmuch as we are, in common with other American citizens, supporters of the State, subject to its laws, interested in its welfare liable to be called upon to defend it in time of war, contributors to its wealth in time of peace) the complete and unrestricted right of suffrage, which is essential to the dignity even of the white man, be extended to the Free Colored man also.

Whereas the colored people of the United States have too long been retarded and impeded in the development and improvement of their natural faculties and powers, even to become dangerous rivals to white men, in the honorable pursuits of life, liberty and happiness; and whereas, the proud Anglo-Saxon can need no arbitrary protection from open and equal competition with any variety of the human family; and whereas, laws have been enacted limiting the aspirations of colored men, as against white men—we respectfully submit that such laws are flagrantly unjust to the man of color, and plainly discreditable to white men; and for these and other reasons, such laws ought to be repealed.

We especially urge that all laws and usages which preclude the enrollment of colored men in the militia, and prohibit their bearing arms in the navy, disallow their rising, agreeable to their merits and attainments—are unconstitutional—the constitution knowing no color—are anti-Democratic, since Democracy respects men as equals—are unmagnanimous, since such laws are made by the many, against the few, and by the strong against the weak.

We ask that all those cruel and oppressive laws, whether enacted at the South or the North, which aim at the expatriation of the free people of color, shall be stamped with national reprobation, denounced as contrary to the humanity of the American people, and as an outrage upon the Christianity and civilization of the nineteenth century.

We ask that the right of pre-emption, enjoyed by all white settlers upon the public lands, shall also be enjoyed by colored settlers; and that the word "*white*" be struck from the pre-emption act. We ask that no appropriations whatever, state or national, shall be granted to the colonization scheme; and we would have our right to leave or to remain in the United States placed above legislative interference.

We ask that the Fugitive Slave Law of 1850, that legislative monster of modern times, by whose atrocious provisions the writ of "*habeas corpus*," the "right of trial by jury," have been virtually abolished, shall be repealed.

We ask, that the law of 1793 be so construed as to apply only to apprentices, and others really owing service or labor; and not to slaves, who can *owe* nothing. Finally, we ask that slavery in the United States shall be immediately, unconditionally, and forever abolished.

To accomplish these just and reasonable ends, we solemnly pledge ourselves to God, to each other, to our country, and to the world, to use all and every means consistent with the just rights of our fellow men, and with the precepts of Christianity.

We shall speak, write and publish, organize and combine to accomplish them.

We shall invoke the aid of the pulpit and the press to gain them.

We shall appeal to the church and to the government to gain them.

We shall vote, and expend our money to gain them.

We shall send eloquent men of our own condition to plead our cause before the people.

We shall invite the co-operation of good men in this country and throughout the world—and above all, we shall look to God, the Father and Creator of all men, for wisdom to direct us and strength to support us in the holy cause to which we this day solemnly pledge ourselves.

Such, fellow-citizens are our aims, ends, aspirations and determinations. We place them before you, with the earnest hope, that upon further investigation, they will meet your cordial and active approval.

And yet, again, we would free ourselves from the charge of unreasonableness and self-sufficiency.

In numbers we are few and feeble; but in the goodness of our cause, in the rectitude of our motives, and in the abundance of argument on our side, we are many and strong.

We count our friends in the heavens above, in the earth beneath, among good men and holy angels. The subtle and mysterious cords of human sympathy have connected us with philanthropic hearts throughout the civilized world. The number in our own land who already recognize the justice of our cause, and are laboring to promote it, is great and increasing.

It is also a source of encouragement, that the genuine American, brave and independent himself, will respect bravery and independence in others. He spurns servility and meanness, whether they be manifested by nations or by individuals. We submit, therefore, that there is neither necessity for, nor disposition on our part to assume a tone of excessive humility. While we would be respectful, we must address you as men, as citizens, as brothers, as dwellers in a common country, equally interested with you for its welfare, its honor and for its prosperity.

To be still more explicit: We would, first of all, be understood to range ourselves no lower among our fellow-countrymen than is implied in the high appellation of "*citizen.*"

Notwithstanding the impositions and deprivations which have fettered us—notwithstanding the disabilities and liabilities, pending and impending—notwithstanding the cunning, cruel, and scandalous efforts to blot out that right, we declare that we are, and of right we ought to be *American citizens.* We claim this right, and we claim all the rights and privileges, and duties which, properly, attach to it.

It may, and it will, probably, be disputed that we are citizens. We may, and, probably, shall be denounced for this declaration, as making an inconsiderate, impertinent and absurd claim to citizenship; but a very little reflection will vindicate the position we have assumed, from so unfavorable a judgment. Justice is never inconsiderate; truth is never impertinent; right is never absurd. If the claim we set up be just, true and right, it will not be deemed improper or ridiculous in us so to declare it. Nor is it disrespectful to our fellow-citizens, who repudiate the aristocratic notions of the old world that we range ourselves with them in respect to all the rights and prerogatives belonging to American citizens. Indeed, we believe, when you have duly considered this subject, you will commend us for the mildness and modesty with which we have taken our ground.

By birth, we are American citizens; by the principles of the Declaration of Independence, we are American citizens; within the meaning of the United States Constitution, we are American citizens; by the facts of history, and the admissions of American statesmen, we are American citizens; by the hardships and trials endured; by the courage and fidelity displayed by our ancestors in defending the liberties and in achieving the independence of our land, we are American citizens. In proof of the justice of this primary claim, we might cite numerous authorities, facts and testimonies,—a few only must suffice.

In the Convention of New York, held for amending the Constitution of that State, in the year 1821, an interesting discussion took place, upon a proposition to prefix the word "*white*" to male citizens. Nathan Sandford, then late Chancellor of the State, said:

> "Here there is but one estate—*the people*—and to me the only qualification seems to be their virtue and morality. If they may be safely trusted to vote for one class of rulers, why not for all? The principle of the scheme is, that those who bear the burdens of the State, shall choose those that rule it."

Dr. Robert Clark, in the same debate, said:

> "I am unwilling to retain the word '*white,*' because it is repugnant to all the principles and notions of liberty, to which we have heretofore professed to adhere, and to our 'Declaration of Independence,' which is a concise and just expose of those principles." He said "it had been appropriately observed by the Hon. gentleman from Westchester, (Mr. Jay,) that by retaining this word, you violate the Constitution of the United States."

Chancellor Kent supported the motion of Mr. Jay to strike out the word "*white.*"

"He did not come to this Convention," said he, "to disfranchise any portion of the community."

Peter A. Jay, on the same occasion, said, "It is insisted that this Convention, clothed with all the powers of the sovereign people of the State, have a right to construct the government in a manner they think most conducive to the general good. If Sir, right and power be equivalent terms, then I am far from disputing the rights of this assembly. We have power, Sir, I acknowledge, not only to disfranchise every black family, but as many white families also, as we may think expedient. We may place the whole government in the hands of a few and thus construct an aristocracy. * * * * * * But, Sir, right and power are not convertible terms. No man, no body of men, however powerful, have a right to do wrong."

In the same Convention, Martin Van Buren said:

"There were two words which have come into common use with our revolutionary struggle—words which contained an abridgement of our political rights—words which, at that day, had a talismanic effect—which led our fathers from the bosom of their families to the tented field—which for seven long years of toil and suffering, had kept them to their arms, and which finally conducted them to a glorious triumph. They were 'Taxation and Representation.' Nor did they lose their influence with the close of the struggle. They were never heard in our halls of legislation without bringing to our recollection the consecrated feelings of those who won our liberties, or, reminding us of everything that was sacred in principle."

Ogden Edwards without, said, "he considered it no better than robbery to demand the contributions of colored people towards defraying the public expenses, and at the same time to disfranchise them."

But we must close our quotations from these debates. Much more could be cited, to show that colored men are not only citizens, but that they have a right to the exercise of the elective franchise in the State of New York. If the right of citizenship is established in the State of New York, it is in consequence of the same facts which exist at least in every free State of the Union. We turn from the debates in the State of New York to the nation; and here we find testimony abundant and incontestible, that Free Colored people are esteemed as citizens, by the highest authorities in the United States.

The Constitution of the United States declares "that the citizens of each State shall be entitled to all the privileges and immunities of citizens in the United States."

There is in this clause of the Constitution, nothing whatever, of that watchful malignity which has manifested itself lately in the insertion of the word "*white*," before the term "*citizen*." The *word* "*white*" was unknown to the framers of the Constitution of the United States in such connections—unknown to the signers of the Declaration of Independence—unknown to the brave men at *Bunker Hill*, *Ticonderoga* and at *Red Bank*. It is a modern word, brought into use by modern legislators, despised in revolutionary times. The question of our citizenship came up as a national question, and was settled during the pendency of the Missouri question, in 1820.

It will be remembered that that State presented herself for admission into the Union, with a clause in her Constitution prohibiting the settlement of colored citizens within her borders. Resistance was made to her admission into the Union, upon that very ground; and it was not until that State receded from her unconstitutional position, that President Monroe declared the admission of Missouri into the Union to be complete.

According to *Niles' Register*, August 18th, vol. 20, page 338–339, the refusal to admit Missouri into the Union was not withdrawn until the General Assembly of that State, in conformity to a fundamental condition imposed by Congress, had, by an act passed for that purpose, solemnly enacted and declared:

> "That this State [Missouri] has assented, and does assent, that the fourth clause of the 26th section of the third article of their Constitution should never be construed to authorize the passage of any law, and that no law shall be passed in conformity thereto, by which any citizen of either of the United States shall be excluded from the enjoyment of any of the privileges and immunities to which such citizens are entitled, under the Constitution of the United States."

Upon this action by the State of Missouri, President Monroe proclaimed the admission of Missouri into the Union.

Here, fellow-citizens, we have a recognition of our citizenship by the highest authority of the United States; and here we might rest our claim to citizenship. But there have been services performed, hardships endured, courage displayed by our fathers, which modern American historians forget to record—a knowledge of which is essential to an intelligent judgment of the merits of our people. Thirty years ago, slavery was less powerful than it is now; American statesmen were more independent then, than now; and as a consequence, the black man's patriotism and bravery were more readily recognized. The age of slave-hunting had not then come on. In the memorable debate on the Missouri question, the meritorious deeds of our fathers obtained respectful mention. The Hon. Wm. Eustis, who had himself been a soldier of the revolution, and Governor of the State of Massachusetts, made a speech in the Congress of the United States, 12th December, and said:

> "The question to be determined is, whether the article in the Constitution of Missouri, requiring the legislature to provide by law, 'that free negroes and mulattoes shall not be admitted into that State,' is, or is not repugnant to that clause of the Constitution of the United States which declares 'that the citizens of each State shall be entitled to all the privileges and immunities of citizens in the several States?' This is the question. Those who contend that the article is not repugnant to the Constitution of the United States, take the position that free blacks and mulattoes are not citizens. *Now I invite the gentlemen who maintain this to go with me and examine this question to its root.* At the early part of the revolutionary war, there were found in the middle and northern States, many blacks and other people of color, capable of bearing arms, a part of them free, and a greater part of them slaves. The freemen entered our ranks with the whites. The time of those who were slaves were purchased by the State, and they were induced to enter the service in consequence of a law, by which, on condition of their serving in the ranks during the war, they were made freemen. In Rhode Island, where their numbers were more considerable, they were formed under the same considerations into a regiment, commanded by white officers; and it is required in justice to them, to add that they discharged their duty with zeal

and fidelity. The gallant defence of Red Bank, in which the black regiment bore a part, is among the proofs of their valor.

"Not only the rights but the character of those men do not seem to be understood; nor is it to me at all extraordinary that gentlemen from other States in which the condition, character, the moral facilities, and the rights of men of color differ so widely, should entertain opinions so variant from ours. In Massachusetts, Sir, there are among them who possess all the virtues which are deemed estimable in civil and social life. They have their public teachers of religion and morality—their schools and other institutions. On anniversaries which they consider interesting to them, they have their public processions, in all of which they conduct themselves with order and decorum. Now, we ask only, that in a disposition to accommodate others, their avowed rights and privileges be not taken from them. If their number be small, and they are feebly represented, we, to whom they are known, are proportionately bound to protect them. But their defence is not founded on their numbers; it rests on the immutable principles of justice. If there be only one family, or a solitary individual who has rights guaranteed to him by the Constitution, whatever may be his color or complexion, it is not in the power, nor can it be the inclination of Congress to deprive him of them. And I trust, Sir, that the decision on this occasion will show that we will extend good faith even to the blacks."—*National Intelligencer,* January 2, 1821.

The following is an extract from a speech of the Hon. Mr. Morrill, of New Hampshire, delivered in the United States Senate in the same month, and reported in the *National Intelligencer,* Jan. 11th, 1821:

"Sir, you excluded, not only the citizens from their constitutional privileges and immunities, but also your soldiers of color, to whom you have given patents of land. You had a company of this description. They have fought your battles. They have defended your country. They have preserved your privileges; but have lost their own. What did you say to them on their enlistment? 'We will give you a monthly compensation, and, at the end of the war, 160 acres of good land, on which you may settle, and by cultivating the soil, spend your declining years in peace and in the enjoyment of those immunities for which you have fought and bled.' Now, Sir, you restrict them, and will not allow them to enjoy the fruit of their labor. Where is the public faith in this case? Did they suppose, with a patent in their hand, declaring their title to land in Missouri, with the seal of the nation, and the President's signature affixed thereto, it would be said unto them by any authority, you shall not possess the premises? This could never have been anticipated; and yet this must follow, if colored men are not citizens."

Mr. Strong, of New York, said, in the same great debate, "The federal constitution knows but two descriptions of freemen: these are citizens and aliens. Now Congress can naturalize only aliens—i.e., persons who owe allegiance to a foreign government. But a slave has no country, and owes no allegiance except to his master. How, then, is he an alien? If restored to his liberty, and made a freeman, what is his national character? It must be determined by the federal constitution, and without reference to policy; for it respects liberty. Is it that of a citizen, or alien? But it has been shown that he is not an alien. May we not, therefore, conclude—nay, are we not bound to conclude that he is a citizen of the United States?"

Charles Pinckney, of South Carolina, speaking of the colored people, in Congress, and with reference to the same question, bore this testimony:

"They then were (during the Revolution) as they still are, as valuable a part of our population to the Union, as any other equal number of inhabitants. They were, in numerous instances, the pioneers; and in all the labors of your armies, to their hands were owing the erection of the greatest part of the fortifications raised for the protection of our country. Fort Moultrie gave at an early period the experience and untired valor of our citizens' immortality to American arms; and in the Northern States, numerous bodies of them were enrolled, and fought, side by side, with the whites, the battles of the Revolution."

General Jackson, in his celebrated proclamations to the free colored inhabitants of Louisiana, uses these expressions: "*Your* white fellow-citizens;" and again: "*Our* brave *citizens are united,* and *all* contention has ceased *among them.*"

FIRST PROCLAMATION (*Extracts*)

HEADQUARTERS, 7th Military Dis't.,
Mobile, Sept. 21st, 1814

To the Free Colored Inhabitants of Louisiana:
Through a mistaken policy you have heretofore been deprived of a participation in the glorious struggle for national rights, in which your country is engaged.
This no longer shall exist.
As sons of freedom, you are now called on to defend our most inestimable blessings. As *Americans,* your country looks with confidence to her adopted children for a valorous support. As fathers, husbands, and brothers, you are summoned to rally round the standard of the Eagle, to defend all which is dear to existence.
Your country, although calling for your exertions, does not wish you to engage in her cause without remunerating you for the services rendered.
In the sincerity of a soldier, and in the language of truth, I address you.—To every noble-hearted free man of color, volunteering to serve during the present contest with Great Britain, and no longer, there will be paid the same bounty in money and land now received by the white soldiers of the United States, viz: $124 in money, and 160 acres of land. The non-commissioned officers and privates will also be entitled to *the same* monthly pay and daily rations, and clothes, furnished *to any American soldier.*
The Major General commanding will select officers for your government from your white fellow-citizens. Your non-commissioned officers will be selected from yourselves. Due regard will be paid to the feelings of freemen and soldiers. As a distinct, independent battalion or regiment, pursuing the path of glory, you will, undivided, receive the applause and gratitude of *your* countrymen.

Andrew Jackson,
Major Gen. Commanding.

Niles' Register, Dec. 3, 1814, vol. 7, p. 205

SECOND PROCLAMATION

To the Free People of Color:
Soldiers! when on the banks of the Mobile I called you to take up arms, inviting you to partake the perils and glory of your *white* fellow-citizens, I expected much from you; for I was not ignorant that you possessed qualities most formidable to an invading enemy. I knew with what fortitude you could endure hunger and thirst, and all the fatigues of a campaign.
I knew well how you loved your native country, and that you, as well as ourselves, had to defend what *man* holds most dear—his parents, wife, children, and property.

You have done more than I expected. In addition to the previous qualities I before knew you to possess, I found among you a noble enthusiasm which leads to the performance of great things.

Soldiers! the President of the United States shall hear how praiseworthy was your conduct in the hour of danger, and the representatives of the American people will give you the praise your exploits entitle you to. Your General anticipates them in applauding your noble ardor.

The enemy approaches—his vessels cover our lakes—*our brave citizens are united,* and all contention has ceased among them. Their only dispute is, who shall win the prize of valor, or who the most glory, its noblest reward.—By order,

Thomas Butler, Aide-de-Camp.

Such, fellow-citizens, is but a sample of a mass of testimony, upon which we found our claim to be American citizens. There is, we think, no flaw in the evidence. The case is made out. We and you stand upon the same broad national basis. Whether at home or abroad, we and you owe equal allegiance to the same government—have a right to look for protection on the same ground. We have been born and reared on the same soil; we have been animated by, and have displayed the same patriotic impulses; we have acknowledged and performed the same duty; we have fought and bled in the same battles; we have gained and gloried in the same victories; and we are equally entitled to the blessings resulting therefrom.

In view of this array of evidence of services bravely rendered, how base and monstrous would be the ingratitude, should the republic disown us and drive us into exile!—how faithless and selfish, should the nation persist in degrading us! But we will not remind you of obligations—we will not appeal to your generous feelings—a naked statement of the case is our best appeal. Having, now, upon the testimony of your own great and venerated names completely vindicated our right to be regarded and treated as American citizens, we hope you will now permit us to address you in the plainness of speech becoming the dignity of American citizens.

Fellow-citizens, we have had, and still have, great wrongs of which to complain. A heavy and cruel hand has been laid upon us.

As a people, we feel ourselves to be not only deeply injured, but grossly misunderstood. Our white fellow-countrymen do not know us. They are strangers to our character, ignorant of our capacity, oblivious of our history and progress, and are misinformed as to the principles and ideas that control and guide us as a people. The great mass of American citizens estimate us as being a characterless and purposeless people; and hence we hold up our heads, if at all, against the withering influence of a nation's scorn and contempt.

It will not be surprising that we are so misunderstood and misused when the motives for misrepresenting us and for degrading us are duly considered. Indeed, it will seem strange, upon such consideration, (and in view of the ten thousand channels through which malign feelings find utterance and influence,) that we have not even fallen lower in public estimation than we have done. For, with the single exception of the Jews, under the whole heavens, there is not to be found a people pursued with a more relentless prejudice and persecution, than are the Free Colored people of the United States.

Without pretending to have exerted ourselves as we ought, in view of an intelligent understanding of our interest, to avert from us the unfavorable opinions and unfriendly action of the American people, we feel that the imputations cast upon us, for our want of intelligence, morality and exalted character, may be mainly accounted for by the injustice we have received at your hands. What stone has been left unturned to degrade us? What hand has refused to fan the flame of popular prejudice against us? What American artist has not caricatured us? What wit has not laughed at us in our wretchedness? What songster has not made merry over our depressed spirits? What press has not ridiculed and condemned us? What pulpit has withheld from our devoted heads its angry lightning, or its sanctimonious hate? Few, few, very few; and that we have borne up with it all—that we have tried to be wise, though denounced by all to be fools—that we have tried to be upright, when all around us have esteemed us as knaves—that we have striven to be gentlemen, although all around us have been teaching us its impossibility—that we have remained here, when all our neighbors have advised us to leave, proves that we possess qualities of head and heart, such as cannot but be commended by impartial men. It is believed that no other nation on the globe could have made more progress in the midst of such an universal and stringent disparagement. It would humble the proudest, crush the energies of the strongest, and retard the progress of the swiftest. In view of our circumstances, we can, without boasting, thank God, and take courage, having placed ourselves where we may fairly challenge comparison with more highly favored men.

Among the colored people, we can point, with pride and hope, to men of education and refinement, who have become such, despite of the most unfavorable influences; we can point to mechanics, farmers, merchants, teachers, ministers, doctors, lawyers, editors, and authors against whose progress the concentrated energies of American prejudice have proved quite unavailing.—Now, what is the motive for ignoring and discouraging our improvement in this country? The answer is ready. The intelligent and upright free man of color is an unanswerable argument in favor of liberty, and a killing condemnation of American slavery. It is easily seen that, in proportion to the progress of the free man of color, in knowledge, temperance, industry, and righteousness, in just that proportion will he endanger the stability of slavery; hence, all the powers of slavery are exerted to prevent the elevation of the free people of color.

The force of fifteen hundred million dollars is arrayed against us; hence, the *press,* the pulpit, and the platform, against all the natural promptings of uncontaminated manhood, point their deadly missiles of ridicule, scorn and contempt at us; and bid us, on pain of being pierced through and through, to remain in our degradation.

Let the same amount of money be employed against the interest of any other class of persons, however favored by nature they may be, the result could scarcely be different from that seen in our own case. Such a people would be regarded with aversion; the money-ruled multitude would heap contumely upon them, and money-ruled institutions would proscribe them. Besides this money consideration, fellow-citizens, an explanation of the erroneous opinions prevalent concerning us is furnished in the fact, less creditable to human nature, that men are apt to hate most those whom they have injured most.—Having despised us, it is not strange that Americans should seek to render us despicable; having enslaved us, it is natural that they should strive to prove us unfit for freedom; having denounced us as indolent, it is not strange that they should cripple our enterprise; having assumed our inferiority, it would be extraordinary if they sought to surround us with circumstances which would serve to make us direct contradictions to their assumption.

In conclusion, fellow-citizens, while conscious of the immense disadvantages which beset our pathway, and fully appreciating our own weakness, we are encouraged to persevere in efforts adapted to our improvement, by a firm reliance upon God, and a settled conviction, as immovable as the everlasting hills, that all the truths in the whole universe of God are allied to our cause.

Frederick Douglass,
J. M. Whitfield,
H. O. Wagoner,
Rev. A. N. Freeman,
George B. Vashon.

Proceedings of the Colored National Convention Held in Rochester, July 6th, 7th and 8th, 1853, Rochester, 1853.

1. Fred Landon, "The Negro Migration to Canada after 1850," *Journal of Negro History,* vol. V, Jan., 1920, p. 22.
2. *New York Tribune,* July 9, 1853.

A TERROR TO KIDNAPPERS

Such is the title of a huge and highly finished cane, recently presented to Frederick Douglass by John Jones and J.D. Bonner, members of the National Council for Illinois. This was a happy thought, this *stick*—present not altogether inappropriate, for it is believed in these parts that a good stick is sometimes as much needed as a good speech and often more effective. Where you have a dog deal with, stick will perform wonders where speech would be powerless!—There are among the children of men, and I have gained the fact from personal observation, to be found representatives of all the animal world, from the most savage and ferocious, to the most gentle and docile. Everything must be dealt with according to its kind. What will do for the Lamb will not do for the Tiger. A man would look foolish if he attempted to bail out a leaking boat with the Bible, or to extinguish a raging fire by throwing in a Prayer Book. Equally foolish would he look if he attempted to soften a slave-catcher's heart without first softening his head. This is a capital stick, and I thank my friends for it. I hope never to meet with a creature requiring its use; but should I meet with such an one, I shall use it with stout arm and humane motive.

Frederick Douglass' Paper, November 25, 1853

PART FOUR

From the Kansas-Nebraska Act
to the Election of Abraham Lincoln

THE WORD "WHITE."

The *Homestead Bill,*[1] which has just passed the House of Representatives, and is now likely to pass the Senate, contains a provision limiting the advantages which it is designed to secure, solely to that part of God's children, who happen to live in a skin which passes for white. Blacks, browns, mulattoes, and quadroons, &c., are to have no part or lot in the rights it secures, to the settlers on the wild lands of the Republic. In the political eyes of our legislators, these latter have no right to live. The great Legislator above, according to our magnanimous republicans, legislated unwisely, and in a manner which independent Americans can never sanction, in giving life to blacks, browns, mulattoes, and quadroons, equally with his dear white children! and this, Congress is determined to make evident before Heaven and Earth and Hell! Alas! poor, robbed and murdered people! for what were we born? Why was life given us? We may not live in the old states; we may not emigrate to the new, and are told not to settle with any security on the wild lands! Were we made to sport?—given life to have it starved out of us?—provided with blood simply that it may gush forth at the call of the scourge? and thus to gratify the white man's love of torture. Some deeds there are, so wantonly cruel, so entirely infernal, as to stun the feeling, and confound all the powers of reason.—And such an one is this. What kind of men are those who voted for the Homestead Bill with such an amendment! Do they eat bread afforded by our common mother earth? and do they ever pray that God, the common father of mankind, will preserve them from famine? Men that act as they have now acted, do not appear to believe either in the existence of, or in the justice of God. It is impossible for us to argue against such mean, cowardly and wanton cruelty. Americans by birth—attached to the country by every association that can give a right to share in the benefits of its institutions, the first successful tillers of the soil—and yet foreigners, aliens, Irish, Dutch, English and French, are to be made welcome to a quarter section of American land, while we are to be kept off from it by the flaming sword, of the Republic. Shame on the outrage!

Frederick Douglass' Paper, March 17, 1854

1. The amendment barring blacks from participating in homestead benefits passed both the House and Senate.

THE END OF ALL COMPROMISES WITH SLAVERY—NOW AND FOREVER

Against the indignant voice of the Northern people—against the commonest honesty—against the most solemn warnings from statesmen and patriots—against the most explicit and public pledges of both the great parties—against the declared purpose of Pres't Pierce on assuming the reins of government—against every obligation of honor, and the faith of mankind—against the stern resistance of a brave minority of our representatives—against the plainest dictates of the Christian religion, and the voice of its ministers, the hell-black scheme for extending slavery over Nebraska, where thirty-four years ago it was solemnly protected from slavery forever, has triumphed. The audacious villainy of the slave power, and the contemptible pusillanimity of the North, have begotten this monster, and sent him forth to blast and devour whatsoever remains of liberty, humanity and justice in the land. The North is again whipt—driven to the wall. The brick is knocked down at the end of the row, by which the remainder are laid prostrate. The Republic swings clear from all her ancient moorings, and moves off upon a tempestuous and perilous sea. Woe! woe! woe to slavery! Her mightiest shield is broken. A bolt that bound the North and South together has been surged asunder, and a mighty barricade, which has intervened between the forces of slavery and freedom, has been madly demolished by the slave power itself; and for one, we now say, in the name of God, let the battle come. Is this the language of excitement? It may be; but it is also the language of truth. The man who is unmoved now, misconceives the crisis; or he is intensely selfish, caring nothing about the affairs of his country and kind. Washington, long the abode of political profligacy and corruption, is now the scene of the revelry of triumphant wickedness, laughing to scorn the moral sense of the nation, and grinding the iron heel of bondage into the bleeding heart of living millions. Great God in mercy, overrule this great wrath to thy praise!

But what is to be done? Why, let this be done: let the whole North awake, arise; let the people assemble in every free State of the Union; and let a great party of freedom be organized, on whose broad banner let it be inscribed, All compromises with slavery ended—The abolition of slavery essential to the preservation of liberty. Let the old parties go to destruction, whither they have nearly sunk the nation. Let their names be blotted out, and their memory rot; and henceforth let there be only a free party, and a slave party. The banner of God and liberty, and the bloody flag of slavery and chains shall then swing out from our respective battlements, and rally under them our respective armies, and let the inquiry go forth now, as of old, Who is on the Lord's side? Let the ministers of religion, all over the country, whose remonstrances have been treated with contempt—whose calling has been despised—whose names have been made a byword—whose rights as citizens have been insolently denied—and whose God has been blasphemed by the plotters of this great wickedness, now buckle on the armor of their master, and heartily strive with their immense power, to arrest the nation in its downward progress, and save it from the deep damnation to which it is sinking.

> If ye have whispered truth, whisper no longer,
> Speak as the tempest does, sterner and stronger.

The time for action has come. While a grand political party is forming, let companies of emigrants from the free States be collected together—funds provided—and with every solemnity which the name and power of God can inspire. Let them be sent out to possess the goodly land, to which, by a law of Heaven and a law of man, they are justly entitled.

Frederick Douglass' Paper, May 26, 1854

IS IT RIGHT AND WISE TO KILL A KIDNAPPER?

A kidnapper has been shot dead, while attempting to execute the fugitive slave bill in Boston.[1] The streets of Boston in sight of Bunker Hill Monument, have been stained with the warm blood of a man in the act of perpetrating the most atrocious robbery which one man can possibly commit upon another—even the wresting from him his very person and natural powers. The deed of blood, as of course must have been expected, is making a tremendous sensation in all parts of the country, and calling forth all sorts of comments. Many are branding the deed as "murder," and would visit upon the perpetrator the terrible penalty attached to that dreadful crime. The occurrence naturally brings up the question of the reasonableness, and the rightfulness of killing a man who is in the act of forcibly reducing a brother man who is guilty of no crime, to the horrible condition of a slave. The question bids fair to be one of important and solemn interest, since it is evident that the practice of slave-hunting and slave-catching, with all their attendant enormities, will either be pursued, indefinitely, or abandoned immediately according to the decision arrived at by the community.

Cherishing a very high respect for the opinions of such of our readers and friends as hold to the inviolability of the human life, and differing from them on this vital question, we avail ourselves of the present excitement in the public mind, calmly to state our views and opinions, in reference to the case in hand, asking for them an attentive and candid perusal.

Our moral philosophy on this point is our own—never having read what others may have said in favor of the views which we entertain.

The shedding of human blood at first sight, and without explanation is, and must ever be, regarded with horror; and he who takes pleasure in human slaughter is very properly looked upon as a moral monster. Even the killing of animals produces a shudder in sensitive minds, uncalloused by crime; and men are only reconciled to it by being shown, not only its reasonableness, but its necessity. These tender feelings so susceptible to pain, are most wisely designed by the Creator, for the preservation of life. They are, especially, the affirmation of God, speaking through nature, and asserting man's right to live. Contemplated in the light of warmth of these feelings, it is in all cases, a crime to deprive a human being of life: but God has not left us solely to the guidance of our feelings, having endowed us with reason, as well as with feeling, and it is in the light of reason that this question ought to be decided.

All will agree that human life is valuable or worthless, as to the innocent or criminal use that is made of it. Most evidently, also, the possession of life was permitted and ordained for beneficent ends, and not to defeat those ends, or to render their attainment impossible. Comprehensively stated, the end of man's creation is his own good, and the honor of his Creator. Life, therefore, is but a means to an end, and must be held in reason to be not superior to the purposes for which it was designed by the All-wise Creator. In this view there is no such thing as an absolute right to live; that is to say, the right to live, like any other human right, may be forfeited, and if forfeited, may be taken away. If the right to *life* stands on the same ground as the right to *liberty,* it is subject to all the exceptions that apply to the right to liberty. All admit that the right to enjoy *liberty* largely depends upon the use made of that liberty; hence Society has erected jails and prisons, with a view to deprive men of their liberty when they are so wicked as to abuse it by invading the liberties of their fellows. We have a right to arrest the locomotion of a man who insists upon walking and trampling on his brother man, instead of upon the highway. This right of society is essential to its preservations; without it a single individual would have it in his power to destroy the peace and the happiness of ten thousand otherwise right minded people. Precisely on the same ground, we hold that a man may, properly, wisely and even mercifully be deprived of life. Of course life being the most precious is the most sacred of all rights, and cannot be taken away, but under the direst necessity; and not until all reasonable modes had been adopted to prevent this necessity, and to spare the aggressor.

It is no answer to this view, to say that society is selfish in sacrificing the life of an individual, or of many individuals, to save the mass of mankind, or society at large. It is in accordance with nature, and the examples of the Almighty, in the execution of his will and beneficent laws. When a man flings himself from the top of some lofty monument, against a granite pavement, in that act he forfeits his *right* to live. He dies according to law, and however shocking may be the spectacle he presents, it is no argument against the beneficence of the law of gravitation, the suspension of whose operation must work ruin to the well-being of mankind. The observance of this law was necessary to his preservation; and his wickedness or folly, in violating it, could not be excused without imperilling those who are living in obedience to it. The atheist sees no benevolence in the law referred to; but to such minds we address not this article. It is enough for us that the All-Wise has established the law, and determined its character, and the penalty of its violation; and however we may deplore the mangled forms of the foolish and the wicked who transgress it, the beneficence of the law itself is fully vindicated by the security it gives to all who obey it.

We hold, then, in view of this great principle, or rule, in the physical world, we may properly infer that other law or principle of justice is the moral and social world, and vindicate its practical application to the preservation of the rights and liberties of the race, as against such exceptions furnished in the monsters who deliberately violate it by taking pleasure in enslaving, imbruting and murdering their fellow-men. As human life is not superior to the laws for the preservation of the physical universe, so, too, it is not superior to the eternal law of justice, which is essential to the preservation of the rights, and the security, and happiness of the race.

The argument thus far is to the point, that society has the right to preserve itself even at the expense of the life of the aggressor; and it may be said that, while what we allege may be right enough, as regards society, it is false as vested in an individual, such as the poor, powerless, and almost friendless wretch, now in the clutches of this proud and powerful republican government. But we take it to be a sound principle, that when government fails to protect the just rights of any individual man, either he or his friends may be held in the sight of God and man, innocent, in exercising any right for his preservation which society may exercise for its preservation. Such an individual is flung, by his untoward circumstances, upon his original right of self defence. We hold, therefore, that when James Batchelder, the truckman of Boston, abandoned his useful employment, as a common laborer, and took upon himself the revolting business of a kidnapper, and undertook to play the bloodhound on the track of his crimeless brother Burns, he labelled himself the common enemy of mankind, and his slaughter was as innocent, in the sight of God, as would be the slaughter of a ravenous wolf in the act of throttling an infant. We hold that he had forfeited his right to live, and that his death was necessary, as a warning to others liable to pursue a like course.

It may be said, that though the right to kill in defence of one's liberty be admitted, it is still unwise for the fugitive slave or his friends to avail themselves of this right; and that submission, in the circumstances, is far wiser than resistance. To this it is a sufficient answer to show that submission is valuable only so long as it has some chance of being recognized as a virtue. While it has this chance, it is well enough to practice it, as it may then have some moral effect in restraining crime and shaming aggression, but no longer. That submission on the part of the slave, has ceased to be a virtue, is very evident. While fugitives quietly cross their hands to be tied, adjust their ankles to be chained, and march off unresistingly to the hell of slavery, there will ever be fiends enough to hunt them and carry them back. Nor is this all nor the worst. Such submission, instead of being set to the credit of the poor sable ones, only creates contempt for them in the public mind, and becomes an argument in the mouths of the community, that Negroes are, by nature, only fit for slavery; that slavery is their normal condition. Their patient and unresisting disposition, their unwillingness to peril their own lives, by shooting down their pursuers, is already quoted against them, as marking them as an inferior race. This reproach must be wiped out, and nothing short of resistance on the part of colored men, can wipe it out. Every slave-hunter who meets a bloody death in his infernal business, is an argument in favor of the manhood of our race. Resistance is, therefore, wise as well as just.

At this point of our writing, we meet with the following plea, set up for the atrocious wretch, "gone to his own place," by the Rochester *Daily American*, a Silver Grey paper.

> "An important inquiry arises,—Who are the murderers of Batchelder? There are several. First, and most guilty, are Wendell Phillips, Theodore Parker, and their Fanueil Hall coadjutors. All just minds will regard their conduct as more atrocious than even that of the ruffians who shot and mangled the unfortunate officer. Cold, remorseless, and bloody as the cruel axe, they deliberately worked up the crowd to a murderous frenzy, and pointed out the path which led to murder. The guilt which rests upon the infuriated assassins is light compared with that which blackens the cowardly orators of Fanueil Hall.
>
> "What had Batchelder done, that Phillips, Parker and their minions should steep their souls in his blood? Why did these men make his wife a widow,—his children fatherless, and send his unwarned spirit to the presence of God?"

This is very pathetic. The *widow* and the *fatherless* of this brutal truckman—a truckman who, it seems, was one of the swell-head bullies of Boston, selected for the office of Marshal or Deputy Marshal, solely because of his brutal nature and ferocious disposition.

We would ask Mr. Mann whether if such a wretch should lay his horney paws upon his own dignified shoulders, with a view to reduce him to bondage, he would hold, as a murderer, any friend of his, who, to save him from such a fate, shot down the brute?—There is not a citizen of Rochester worthy of the name, who would not shoot down any man in defence of his own liberty—or who, if set upon, by a number of robbers, would not thank any friend who interposed, even to the shedding of blood, for his release.—*The widow and orphans* are far better off with such a wretch in the grave, than on the earth. Then again, the law which he undertook to execute, has *no tears* for the *widows and orphans* of poor innocent fugitives, who make their homes at the North. With a hand as relentless as that of death, it snatches the husband from the wife, and the father from his children, and this for no crime.—Oh! that man's ideas of justice and of right depended *less* upon the circumstance of color, and *more* upon the indestructible nature of things. For a *white* man to defend his friend unto blood is praiseworthy, but for a *black* man to do precisely the same thing is crime. It was glorious for Patrick Henry to say, "*Give me liberty or give me death!*" It was glorious for Americans to drench the soil, and crimson the sea with blood, *to escape the payment of three-penny tax upon tea;* but it is crime to shoot down a monster in defence of the liberty of a black man and to save him from a bondage "one hour of which (in the language of Jefferson) is worse than ages of that which our fathers rose in rebellion to oppose." Until Mr. Mann is willing to be a slave—until he is ready to admit that human legislation can rightfully reduce him to slavery, by a simple vote—until he abandons the right of self defence—until he ceases to glory in the deeds of Hancock, Adams, and Warren—and ceases to look with pride and patriotic admiration upon the sombre pile at Bunker Hill, where the blood of the oppressor was poured out in torrents making thousands of *widows and orphans,* it does not look graceful in him to brand as *murderers* those that killed the atrocious *Truckman* who attempted to play the blood-hound on the track of the poor, defenceless Burns.

Frederick Douglass' Paper, June 2, 1854

1. The reference is to the slaying in Boston of James Batchelder, a truckman, during the attack of a crowd seeking to release Anthony Burns, a fugitive slave held in the Court House. Burns had escaped from Richmond in February, 1854, and was hiding in Boston. He was arrested on May 24, 1854. The next morning he was about to be delivered to his master, when Richard H. Dana, Jr., who happened to be in the court-room, secured an adjournment of the hearing for two days.

Many conventions were being held in Boston at this time, and when the story reached the ears of the Abolitionists, they determined to prevent Burns' return to slavery. During an attack on the Court House to free Burns, James Batchelder, a truckman serving as the United States Marshal, was killed.

President Pierce ordered out federal troops to force Burns' return to his master, and an army carried him down State Street and flung him, manacled, into the hold of a vessel bound for Virginia.

ANTHONY BURNS RETURNED TO SLAVERY

Now are our brows bound with victorious wreaths;
Our bruised arms hung up for monuments;
Our stern alarums chang'd to merry meetings,
Our dreadful marches to delightful measures.

Now let all true patriotic Christian Republicans rejoice and be glad! Let a grand Festal day be at once proclaimed from the august seat of government. Let the joyous thunders of ten thousand cannon jar the earth and shake the sky with notes of gratitude, in fitting acknowledgement of this mighty victory! Let the churches be flung open and the pulpit resound with thanksgiving, that our beloved country has been saved, and that Republican Liberty is still secure, and the example of the model republic still shines refulgently, to the confusion of tyrants and oppressors in Europe. After a mighty struggle continued through a great many bitter, dreadful, stormy and anxious days and nights the arms of the Republic have gloriously succeeded in capturing Anthony Burns—the clothes cleaner—in Brattle Street, Boston! Under the Star Spangled Banner, on the deck of our gallant warship Morris, the said Burns, whose liberation would have perhaps rent asunder our Model Republic, has been safely conveyed to slavery and chains, in sight of our nation's proud Capitol!

How sweet to the ear and heart of every true American, are the shrieks of Anthony Burns, as the American eagle sends his remorseless beak and bloody talons into him!! How grateful to the taste and pleasant to the eye, is the warm blood of the sable fugitive. He is now getting his desert. How dare he walk on the legs given him by the Almighty? He thought to take possession of his own body! to go at large among men, but he forgot that this is a civilized and Christian nation, and that no such unnatural and monstrous conduct could be allowed.—Had our churches been dens, and Christians been but tigers, he might have escaped. But he knows by this time that Christian bayonets are more terrible than the claws of the tiger or the fangs of the wolf! He perpetrated the folly of calling upon our churches and ministers to pray for him. He might as well have prayed to the devil to keep him out of hell! Did he not know that our churches are built up, and our religion is supported by the blood and tears of such as he? Was not the Fugitive Slave Bill defended by the very lights of Christianity? Had he forgotten that Rev. Doctor Stewart, of Andover, Doctor Spring, of New York, Doctor Cox, of Brooklyn, and Doctor Lord, of Buffalo, all mighty in doctrine, read in all the languages of the sacred books, enforced his capture as a Christian duty? How foolish was it, then, of him to look to the church for sympathy and to the pulpit for prayers. Was he not the property of brother Suttle, bought with his money, and would it not have been a piece of naked robbery to have deprived dear Brother Suttle of his rightful property?—A few madcaps— dangerous ones—whose infatuation would almost surpass belief, but for their reckless deeds, sought to rescue him; they said he was a man; that he was a brother; that God and nature proclaimed him free; and that it was a sin to enslave him; that it was monstrous and inhuman to enslave him; but we sent these mischievous and infidel persons to prison, and told them to read the Bible. Oh! how our brave troops did trample them down; and how our cannon would have swept them into eternity, had they lifted a finger for the release of our prey!

Hail Columbia! happy land.

Frederick Douglass' Paper, June 9, 1854

———————

Douglass' paper . . . combated the doctrines of white chauvinism which provided the slaveowners with ideological weapons "proving" the "inherent supremacy" of white people, and therefore their right to be masters, and the "inherent inferiority" of Negro people, and therefore their duty to be slaves. Especially did Douglass lash out against the so-called ethnologists, anthropologists, sociologists, and historians who offered alleged proof of the "natural inferiority" of the Negro and the necessity of his filling the God-ordained role of slave to the white man. He pointed out that the ideology of "white supremacy" was as necessary to the system of chattel slavery as the slave trader, the lash, and the bloodhound, and demonstrated that the fostering of a belief in the innate inferiority of the Negro people was part of slavocracy's complex system of control. Douglass called on every Abolitionist to develop the sharpest struggle to expose the propaganda from colleges, pulpits, politicians, and press which constantly drummed out the concept of the inferiority of an entire people.[1]

Douglass himself contributed considerably to the exposure of these pseudo-scientific theories. On August 4, 1854, his paper carried the entire text of his speech at Western Reserve College. . . . Douglass' address demolished the theories of a number of ethnologists and anthropologists who had prostituted their science in the interests of slavery by proclaiming that the Negro was not a man. . . . Douglass demonstrated that the Negro was a man and that he had a common origin with all other men. This he proved by arguments in which, as the *Ohio Observer* remarked, "he exhibited considerable knowledge and research."

So wide was the interest aroused by the publication of this address in *Frederick Douglass' Paper* that it became necessary to reprint it as a pamphlet. Distributed throughout the North and West and even in Europe, it became a powerful weapon to combat the presumed "sub-humanity of Negroes" dictum of the pro-slavery ethnologists and anthropologists. "It is one of the marvels of the age," commented the *National Era* when the address first appeared in Douglass' paper, "that a fugitive from slavery, reared to manhood under all the weight of its depressing influences, should be the author of this able and learned Address. This fact alone is the best refutation of the atheistical fanatics, who would exclude the Negro from the pale of manhood." [I:99–100]

THE CLAIMS OF THE NEGRO ETHNOLOGICALLY CONSIDERED, address delivered at Western Reserve College, July 12, 1854

Gentlemen, in selecting the Claims of the Negro as the subject of my remarks to-day, I am animated by a desire to bring before you a matter of living importance—a matter upon which action, as well as thought is required. The relation subsisting between the white and black people of this country is the vital question of the age. In the solution of this question, the scholars of America will have to take an important and controlling part. This is the moral battle field to which their country and their God now call them. In the eye of both, the neutral scholar is an ignoble man. Here, a man must be hot, or be accounted cold, or, perchance, something worse than hot or cold. The lukewarm and the cowardly, will be rejected by earnest men on either side of the controversy. The cunning man who avoids it, to gain the favor of both parties, will be rewarded with scorn; and the timid man who shrinks from it, for fear of offending either party, will be despised. To the lawyer, the preacher, the politician, and to the man of letters, there is no neutral ground. He that is not for us, is against us. Gentlemen, I assume at the start, that wherever else I may be required to speak with bated breath, here, at least, I may speak with freedom the thought nearest my heart. This liberty is implied, by the call I have received to be here; and yet I hope to present the subject so that no man can reasonably say, that an outrage has been committed, or that I have abused the privilege with which you have honored me. I shall aim to discuss the claims of the Negro, general and special, in a manner, though not scientific, still sufficiently clear and definite to enable my hearers to form an intelligent judgment respecting them.

The first general claim which may here be set up, respects the manhood of the Negro. This is an elementary claim, simple enough, but not without question. It is fiercely opposed. A respectable public journal, published in Richmond, Va., bases its whole defence of the slave system upon a denial of the Negro's manhood.

> "The white peasant is free, and if he is a man of will and intellect, can rise in the scale of society; or at least his offspring may. He is not deprived by law of those 'inalienable rights,' 'liberty and the pursuit of happiness,' by the use of it. But here is the essence of slavery—that we do declare the Negro destitute of these powers. We bind him by law to the condition of the laboring peasant for ever, without his consent, and we bind his posterity after him. Now, the true question is, have we a right to do this? If we have not, all discussions about his comfortable situation, and the actual condition of free laborers elsewhere, are quite beside the point. If the Negro has the same right to his liberty and the pursuit of his own happiness that the white man has, then we commit the greatest wrong and robbery to hold him a slave—an act at which the sentiment of justice must revolt in every heart and Negro slavery is an institution which that sentiment must sooner or later blot from the face of the earth."—*Richmond Examiner*.

After stating the question thus, the *Examiner* boldy asserts that the Negro has no such right—BECAUSE HE IS NOT A MAN!

There are three ways to answer this denial. One is by ridicule; a second is by denunciation; and a third is by argument. I hardly know under which of these modes my answer to-day will fall. I feel myself somewhat on trial; and that this is just the point where there is hesitation, if not serious doubt. I cannot, however, argue; I must assert. To know whether a Negro is a man, it must first be known what constitutes a man. Here, as well as elsewhere, I take it, that the "coat must be cut according to the cloth." [It is not necessary, in order to establish the manhood of any one making the claim, to prove that such an one equals Clay in eloquence, or Webster and Calhoun in logical force and directness; for, tried by such standards of mental power as these, it is apprehended that very few could claim the high designation of *man*. Yet something like this folly is seen in the arguments directed against the humanity of the Negro. His faculties and powers, uneducated and unimproved, have been contrasted with those of the highest cultivation; and the world has then been called upon to behold the immense and amazing difference between the man admitted, and the man disputed. The fact that these intellects, so powerful and so controlling, are almost, if not quite as exceptional to the general rule of humanity, in one direction, as the specimen Negroes are in the other, is quite overlooked.]

Man is distinguished from all other animals, by the possession of certain definite faculties and powers, as well as by physical organization and proportions. He is the only two-handed animal on the earth—the only one that laughs, and nearly the only one that weeps. Men instinctively distinguish between men and brutes. Common sense itself is scarcely needed to detect the absence of manhood in a monkey, or to recognize its presence in a Negro. His speech, his reason, his power to acquire and to retain knowledge, his heaven-erected face, his habitudes, his hopes, his fears, his aspirations, his prophecies, plant between him and the brute creation, a distinction as eternal as it is palpable. Away, therefore, with all the scientific moonshine that would connect men with monkeys; that would have the world believe that humanity, instead of resting on its own characteristic pedestal—gloriously independent—is a sort of sliding scale, making one extreme brother to the ourangoutang, and the other to angels, and all the rest intermediates! Tried by all the usual, and all the *un*usual tests, whether mental, moral, physical, or psychological, the Negro is a MAN—considering him as possessing knowledge, or needing knowledge, his elevation or his degradation, his virtues, or his vices—whichever road you take, you reach the same conclusion, the Negro is a MAN. His good and his bad, his innocence and his guilt, his joys and his sorrows, proclaim his manhood in speech that all mankind practically and readily understand.

A very recondite author says, that "man is distinguished from all other animals, in that he resists as well as adapts himself to his circumstances." He does not take things as he finds them, but goes to work to improve them. Tried by this test, too, the Negro is a man. You may see him yoke the oxen, harness the horse, and hold the plow. He can swim the river; but he prefers to fling over it a bridge. The horse bears him on his back—admits his mastery and dominion. The barnyard fowl know his step, and flock around to receive their morning meal from his sable hand. The dog dances when he comes home, and whines piteously when he is absent. All these know that the Negro is a MAN. Now, presuming that what is evident to beast and to bird, cannot need elaborate argument to be made plain to men, I assume, with this brief statement, that the Negro is a man.

The first claim conceded and settled, let us attend to the second, which is beset with some difficulties, giving rise to many opinions, different from my own, and which opinions I propose to combat.

There was a time when, if you established the point that a particular being is a man, it was considered that such a being, of course, had a common ancestry with the rest of mankind. But it is not so now. This is, you know, an age of science, and science is favorable to division. It must explore and analyze, until all doubt is set at rest. There is, therefore, another proposition to be stated and maintained, separately, which, in other days, (the days before the Notts, the

Gliddens, the Agassiz, and Mortons, made their profound discoveries in ethnological science,) might have been included in the first.

It is somewhat remarkable, that, at a time when knowledge is so generally diffused, when the geography of the world is so well understood—when time and space, in the intercourse of nations, are almost annihilated—when oceans have become bridges—the earth a magnificent hall—the hollow sky a dome—under which a common humanity can meet in friendly conclave—when nationalities are being swallowed up and the ends of the earth brought together—I say it is remarkable—nay, it is strange that there should arise a phalanx of learned men—speaking in the name of *science*—to forbid the magnificent reunion of mankind in one brotherhood. A mortifying proof is here given, that the moral growth of a nation, or an age, does not always keep pace with the increase of knowledge, and suggests the necessity of means to increase human love with human learning.

The proposition to which I allude, and which I mean next to assert, is this, that what are technically called the Negro race, are a part of the human family, and are descended from a common ancestry, with the rest of mankind. The discussion of this point opens a comprehensive field of inquiry. It involves the question of the unity of the human race. Much has and can be said on both sides of that question.

Looking out upon the surface of the Globe, with its varieties of climate, soil, and formations, its elevations and depressions, its rivers, lakes, oceans, islands, continents, and the vast and striking differences which mark and diversify its multitudinous inhabitants, the question has been raised, and pressed with increasing ardor and pertinacity, (especially in modern times,) can all these various tribes, nations, tongues, kindreds, so widely separated, and so strangely dissimilar, have descended from a common ancestry? That is the question, and it has been answered variously by men of learning. Different modes of reasoning have been adopted, but the conclusions reached may be divided into two the one YES, and the other NO. *Which* of these answers is most in accordance with facts, with reason, with the welfare of the world, and reflects most glory upon the wisdom, power, and goodness of the Author of all existence, is the question for consideration with us? On which side is the weight of the argument, rather than which side is absolutely proved?

It must be admitted at the beginning, that, viewed apart from the authority of the Bible, neither the unity, nor diversity of origin of the human family, can be demonstrated. To use the terse expression of the Rev. Dr. Anderson, who speaking on this point, says; "It is impossible to get far enough back for that." This much, however, can be done. The evidence on both sides, can be accurately weighed, and the truth arrived at with almost absolute certainty.

It would be interesting, did time permit, to give here, some of the most striking features of the various theories, which have, of late, gained attention and respect in many quarters of our country—touching the origin of mankind—but I must pass this by. The argument to-day, is to the unity, as against that theory, which affirms the diversity of human origin.

THE BEARINGS OF THE QUESTION

A moment's reflection must impress all, that few questions have more important and solemn bearings, than the one now under consideration. It is connected with eternal as well as with terrestrial interests. It covers the earth and reaches heaven. The unity of the human race—the brotherhood of man—the reciprocal duties of all to each, and of each to all, are too plainly taught in the Bible to admit of cavil.—The credit of the Bible is at stake—and if it be too much to say, that it must stand or fall, by the decision of this question, *it is* proper to say, that the value of that sacred Book—as a record of the early history of mankind—must be materially affected, by the decision of the question.

For myself I can say, my reason (not less than my feeling, and my faith) welcomes with joy, the declaration of the Inspired Apostle, "that God has made of one blood all nations of men for to dwell upon all the face of the earth." But this grand affirmation of the unity of the human race, and many others like unto it, together with the whole account of the creation, given in the early scriptures, must all get a new interpretation or be overthrown altogether, if a diversity of human origin can be maintained.—Most evidently, this aspect of the question makes it important to those, who rely upon the Bible, as the sheet anchor of their hopes—and the frame work of all religious truth. The young minister must look into this subject and settle it for himself, before he ascends the pulpit, to preach redemption to a fallen race.

The bearing of the question upon Revelation, is not more marked and decided than its relation to the situation of things in our country, at this moment. *One seventh* part of the population of this country is of Negro descent. The land is peopled by what may be called the most dissimilar races on the globe. The black and the white—the Negro and the European—these constitute the American people—and, in all the likelihoods of the case, they will ever remain the principal inhabitants of the United States, in some form or other. The European population are greatly in the ascendant in numbers, wealth and power. They are the rulers of the country—the masters—the Africans, are the slaves—the proscribed portion of the people—and precisely in proportion as the truth of human brotherhood gets recognition, will be the freedom and elevation, in this country, of persons of African descent. In truth, this question is at the bottom of the whole controversy, now going on between the slaveholders on the *one* hand, and the abolitionists on the other. It is the same old question which has divided the selfish, from the philanthropic part of mankind in all ages. It is the question whether the rights, privileges, and immunities enjoyed by some ought not to be shared and enjoyed by all.

It is not quite two hundred years ago, when such was the simplicity (I will not now say the pride and depravity) of the Anglo-Saxon inhabitants of the British West Indies, that the learned and pious Godwin, a missionary to the West Indies, deemed it necessary to write a book, to remove what he conceived to be the injurious belief that it was sinful in the sight of God to baptize Negroes and Indians. The West Indies have made progress since that time.—God's emancipating angel has broken the fetters of slavery in those islands, and the praises of the Almighty are now sung by the sable lips of eight hundred thousand freemen, before deemed only fit for slaves, and to whom even baptismal and burial rights were denied.

The unassuming work of *Godwin* may have had some agency in producing this glorious result. One other remark before entering upon the argument. It may be said, that views and opinions, favoring the unity of the human family, coming from one of lowly condition, are open to the suspicion, that *"the wish is father to the thought,"* and so, indeed, it may be.—But let it be also remembered, that this deduction from the—weight of the argument on the one side, is more than counterbalanced by the pride of race and position arrayed on the other. Indeed, ninety-nine out of every hundred of the advocates of a diverse origin of the human family in this country, are among those who hold it to be the privilege of the *Anglo-Saxon* to enslave and oppress the African—and slaveholders, not a few, like the Richmond Examiner to which I have referred, have admitted, that the whole argument in defence of slavery, becomes utterly worthless the moment the African is proved to be equally a man with the Anglo-Saxon. The temptation therefore, to read the Negro out of the human family is exceedingly strong, and may account somewhat for the repeated attempts on the part of Southern pretenders to science, to cast a doubt over the Scriptural account of the origin of mankind. If the origin and motives of most works, opposing the doctrine of the unity of the human race, could be ascertained, it may be doubted whether *one* such work could boast an honest parentage. Pride and selfishness, combined with mental power, never want for a theory to justify them—and when men oppress their fellow-men, the oppressor ever finds, in the character of the oppressed, a full justification for his oppression. Ignorance and depravity, and the inability to rise from degradation to civilization and respectability, are the most usual allegations against the oppressed. The evils most fostered by slavery and oppression, are precisely those which slaveholders and oppressors would transfer from their system to the inherent character of their victims. Thus the very crimes of slavery become slavery's best defence. By making the enslaved a character fit only for slavery, they excuse themselves for refusing to make the slave a freeman. A wholesale method of accomplishing this result, is to overthrow the instinctive consciousness of the common brotherhood of man. For, let it be once granted that the human race are of multitudinous origin, naturally different in their moral, physical, and intellectual capacities, and at once you make plausible a demand for classes, grades and conditions, for different methods of culture, different moral, political, and religious institutions, and a chance is left for slavery, as a necessary institution. The debates in Congress on the Nebraska Bill during the past winter, will show how slaveholders have availed themselves of this doctrine in support of slaveholding. There is no doubt that Messrs. Nott, Glidden, Morton, Smith and Agassiz were duly consulted by our slavery propagating statesmen.

ETHNOLOGICAL UNFAIRNESS TOWARDS THE NEGRO

The lawyers tell us that the credit of a witness is always in order. Ignorance, malice or prejudice, may disqualify a witness, and why not an author? Now, the disposition everywhere evident, among the class of writers alluded to, to separate the Negro race from every intelligent nation and tribe in Africa, may fairly be regarded as one proof, that they have staked out the ground beforehand, and that they have aimed to construct a theory in support of a foregone conclusion. The desirableness of isolating the Negro race, and especially of separating them from the various peoples of Northern Africa, is too plain to need a remark. Such isolation would remove stupendous difficulties in the way of getting the Negro in a favourable attitude for the blows of scientific christendom.

Dr. Samuel George Morton may be referred to as a fair sample of American Ethnologists. His very able work "*Crania Americana,*" published in Philadelphia in 1839, is widely read in this country.—In this great work his contempt for Negroes, is ever conspicuous. I take him as an illustration of what had been alleged as true of his class.

The fact that Egypt was one of the earliest abodes of learning and civilization, is as firmly established as are the everlasting hills, defying, with a calm front the boasted mechanical and architectural skill of the nineteenth century—smiling serenely on the assaults and the mutations of time, there she stands in overshadowing grandeur, riveting the eye and the mind of the modern world—upon her, in silent and dreamy wonder—Greece and Rome—and through them Europe and America have received their civilization from the ancient Egyptians. This fact is not denied by anybody. But Egypt is in Africa. Pity that it had not been in Europe, or in Asia, or better still in America! Another unhappy circumstance is, that the ancient Egyptians were not white people; but were, undoubtedly, just about as dark in complexion as many in this country who are considered genuine Negroes; and that is not all, their hair was far from being of that graceful lankness which adorns the fair Anglo-Saxon head. But the next best thing, after these defects, is a positive unlikeness to the Negro. Accordingly, our learned author enters into an elaborate argument to prove that the ancient Egyptians were totally distinct from the Negroes, and to deny all relationship between. Speaking of the "Copts and Fellahs," whom everybody knows are descendants of the Egyptians, he says, "*The Copts, though now remarkably distinct from the people that surround them, derive from their remote ancestors some mixture of Greek, Arabian, and perhaps even Negro blood.*" Now, mark the description given of the Egyptians in this same work: "*Complexion brown. The nose is straight, excepting the end, where it is rounded and wide; the lips are rather thick, and the hair black and curly.*" This description would certainly seem to make it safe to suppose the presence of "*even* Negro blood." A man, in our day, with brown complexion, "nose rounded and wide, lips thick, hair black and curly," would, I think, have no difficulty in getting himself recognized as a Negro!!

The same authority tells us that the "Copts are supposed by *Niebuhr, Denon* and others, to be the descendants of the ancient Egyptians"; and Dr. Morton adds, that it has often been observed that a strong resemblance may be traced between the Coptic visage and that presented in the ancient mummies and statues. Again, he says, the "*Copts can be, at most, but the degenerate remains, both physically and intellectually, of that mighty people who have claimed the admiration of all ages.*" Speaking of the Nubians, Dr. Morton says, (page 26,)——

"The hair of the Nubian is thick and black—often curled, either by nature or art, and sometimes *partially frizzled,* but *never woolly."*

Again:——

"Although the Nubians occasionally present their national characters unmixed, they generally show traces of their social intercourse with the Arabs, and *even* with the Negroes."

* * *

The repetition of the adverb here, *"even,"* is important, as showing the spirit in which our great American Ethnologist pursues his work, and what deductions may be justly made from the value of his researches on that account. In everything touching the Negro, Dr. Morton, in his "Crania Americana," betrays the same spirit. He thinks that the *Sphinx* was not the representative of an Egyptian Deity, but was a shrine, worshiped at by the degraded *Negroes* of Egypt; and this fact he alleges as the secret of the mistake made by Volney, in supposing that the Egyptians were real Negroes. The absurdity of this assertion will be very apparent, in view of the fact that the great Sphinx in question was the chief of a series, full two miles in length. Our author again repels the supposition that the Egyptians were related to Negroes, by saying there is no mention made of *color* by the historian, in relating the marriage of Solomon with Pharaoh's daughter; and with genuine American feeling, he says, such a circumstance as the marrying of an European monarch with the daughter of a Negro would not have been passed over in silence in our day. This is a sample of the reasoning of men who reason from *prejudice* rather than from *facts.* It assumes that a *black skin* in the *East* excites the same prejudice which we see here in the West. Having denied all relationship of the Negro to the ancient Egyptians, with characteristic American assumption, he says, "It is easy to prove, that whatever may have been the hue of their skin, they belong to the same race with ourselves."

Of course, I do not find fault with Dr. Morton, or any other American, for claiming affinity with Egyptians. All that goes in that direction belongs to my side of the question, and is really right.

The leaning here indicated is natural enough, and may be explained by the fact, that an educated man in Ireland ceases to be an Irishman; and an intelligent black man is always supposed to have derived his intelligence from his connection with the white race. To be intelligent is to have one's Negro blood ignored.

There is, however, a very important physiological fact, contradicting this last assumption; and that fact is, that intellect is uniformly derived from the maternal side. Mulattoes, in this country, may almost wholly boast of Anglo-Saxon male ancestry.

It is the province of prejudice to blind; and scientific writers, not less than others, write to please, as well as to instruct, and even unconsciously to themselves, (sometimes,) sacrifice what is true to what is popular. Fashion is not confined to dress; but extends to philosophy as well—and it is fashionable now, in our land, to exaggerate the differences between the Negro and the European. If, for instance, a phrenologist, or naturalist undertakes to represent in portraits, the differences between the two races—the Negro and the European—he will invariably present the *highest* type of the European, and the *lowest* type of the Negro.

The European face is drawn in harmony with the highest ideas of beauty, dignity and intellect. Features regular and brow after the Websterian mold. The Negro, on the other hand, appears with features distorted, lips exaggerated, forehead depressed—and the whole expression of the countenance made to harmonize with the popular idea of Negro imbecility and degradation. I have seen many pictures of Negroes and Europeans, in phrenological and ethnological works; and all, or nearly all, excepting the work of Dr. Prichard, and that other great work, Combs' Constitution of Man, have been more or less open to this objection. I think I have never seen a single picture in an American work, designed to give an idea of the mental endowments of the Negro, which did any thing like justice to the subject; nay, that was not infamously distorted. The heads of *A. Crummel, Henry H. Garnet, Sam'l R. Ward, Chas. Lenox Remond, W. J. Wilson, J. W. Penington, J. I. Gaines, M. R. Delany, J. W. Loguen, J. M. Whitfield, J. C. Holly,* and hundreds of others I could mention, are all better formed, and indicate the presence of intellect more than any pictures I have seen in such works; and while it must be admitted that there are Negroes answering the description given by the American ethnologists and others, of the Negro race, I contend that there is every description of head among them, ranging from the highest Indoo Caucasian downward. If the very best type of the European is always presented, I insist that *justice*, in all such works, demands that the very best type of the Negro should also be taken. The importance of this criticism may not be apparent to all;—to the *black* man it is very apparent. He sees the injustice, and writhes under its sting. But to return to Dr. Morton, or rather to the question of the affinity of the Negroes to the Egyptians.

It seems to me that a man might as well deny the affinity of the American to the Englishman, as to deny such affinity between the Negro and the Egyptian. He might make out as many points of difference, in the case of the one as in that of the other. Especially could this be done, if, like ethnologists, in given cases, only typical specimens were resorted to. The lean, slender American, pale and swarthy, if exposed to the sun, wears a very different appearance to the full, round Englishman, of clear, *blonde* complexion. One may trace the progress of this difference in the common portraits of the American Presidents. Just study those faces, beginning with *Washington;* and as you come thro' the *Jeffersons,* the *Adamses,* and the *Madisons,* you will find an increasing bony and wiry appearance about those portraits, & a greater remove from that serene amplitude which characterises the countenances of the earlier Presidents. I may be mistaken, but I think this is a correct index of the change going on in the nation at large—converting Englishmen, Germans, Irishmen, and Frenchmen, into Americans, and causing them to lose, in a common American character, all traces of their former distinctive national peculiarities.

AUTHORITIES AS TO THE RESEMBLANCE OF THE EGYPTIANS TO NEGROES

Now, let us see what the best authorities say, as to the personal appearance of the Egyptians. I think it will be at once admitted, that while they differ very strongly from the Negro, debased and enslaved, that difference is not greater than may be observed in other quarters of the globe, among people notoriously belonging to the same variety, the same original stock; in a word, to the same family. If it shall be found that the people of Africa have an African character, as general, as well defined, and as distinct, as have the people of Europe, or the people of Asia, the exceptional differences among them afford no ground for supposing a difference of race; but, on the contrary, it will be inferred that the people of Africa constitute one great branch of the human family, whose origin may be as properly referred to the families of Noah, as can be any other branch of the human family, from whom they differ. Denon, in his 'Travels in Egypt,' describes the Egyptians, as of full, but "delicate and voluptuous forms, countenances sedate and placid, round and soft features, with eyes long and almond shaped, half shut and languishing and turned up at the outer angles, as if habitually fatigued by the light and heat of the sun; cheeks round; thick lips, full and prominent; mouth large, but cheerful and smiling; complexion dark, ruddy and coppery, and the whole aspect displaying—as one of the most graphic delineators among modem travelers has observed—the genuine African character, of which the *Negro* is the exaggerated and extreme representation." Again, Prichard says, (page 152,)—

> "Herodotus traveled in Egypt, and was, therefore, well acquainted with the people from personal observation. He does not say anything directly, as to the descriptions of their persons, which were too well known to the Greeks to need such an account, but his indirect testimony is very strongly expressed. After mentioning a tradition, that the people of Colchis were a colony from Egypt, Herodotus says, that 'there was one fact strongly in favor of this opinion—the Colchians were *black* in complexion and woolly haired.'"

These are the words by which the complexion and hair of Negroes are described. In another passage, he says that

> "The pigeon, said to have fled to Dodona, and to have founded the Oracle, was declared to be *black*, and that the meaning of the story was this: The Oracle was, in reality, founded by a female captive from the Thebaid; she was *black*, being an Egyptian."

"Other Greek writers," says Pritchard, "have expressed themselves in similar terms."

Those who have mentioned the Egyptians as a *swarthy* people, according to Prichard, might as well have applied the term *black* to them, since they were doubtless of a chocolate color. The same author brings together the testimony of Eschylus and others as to the color of the ancient Egyptians, all corresponding, more or less, with the foregoing. Among the most direct testimony educed by Prichard, is, first that of Volney, who, speaking of the modern Copts, says:

> "They have a puffed visage, swollen eyes, flat nose, and thick lips, and bear much resemblance to mulattoes."

Baron Larrey says, in regard to the same people:

> "They have projecting check bones, dilating nostrils, thick lips, and hair and beard black and *crisp*."

Mr. Ledyard, (whose testimony, says our learned authority, is of the more value, as he had no theory to support,) says:

> "I suspect the *Copts* to have been the *origin* of the *Negro* race; the nose and lips correspond with those of the Negro; the hair, wherever I can see it among the people here, is curled, *not* like that of the Negroes, but like the mulattoes."

Here I leave our learned authorities, as to the resemblance of the Egyptians to Negroes.

It is not in my power, in a discourse of this sort, to adduce more than a very small part of the testimony in support of a near relationship between the present enslaved and degraded Negroes, and the ancient highly civilized and wonderfully endowed Egyptians. Sufficient has already been adduced, to show a marked similarity in regard to features, hair, color, and I doubt not that the philologist can find equal similarity in the structures of their languages. In view of the foregoing, while it may not be claimed that the ancient Egyptians were Negroes,—viz:—answering, in all respects, to the nations and tribes ranged under the general appellation, Negro; still, it may safely be affirmed, that a strong affinity and a direct relationship may be claimed by the Negro race, to *that grandest of all the nations of antiquity, the builders of the pyramids.*

But there are other evidences of this relationship, more decisive than those alledged in a general similarity of personal appearance. Language is held to be very important, by the best ethnologists, in tracing out the remotest affinities of nations, tribes, classes and families. The color of the skin has sometimes been less enduring than the speech of a people. I speak by authority, and follow in the footsteps of some of the most learned writers on the natural and ethnological history of man, when I affirm that one of the most direct and conclusive proofs of the general affinity of Northern African nations, with those of West, East and South Africa, is found in the general similarity of their language. The philologist easily discovers, and is able to point out something like the original source of the multiplied tongues now in use in that yet mysterious quarter of the globe. *Dr. R. G. Latham,* F. R. S., corresponding member of the Ethnological Society, New York—in his admirable work, entitled "Man and his Migrations"—says:

> "In the languages of Abyssinia, the Gheez and Tigre, admitted, as long as they have been known at all, to be *Semitic,* graduate through the Amharic, the Talasha, the Harargi, the Gafat and other languages, which may be well studied in Dr. Beke's valuable comparative tables, into the Agow tongue, unequivocally indigenous to Abyssinia, and through this into the true Negro classes. But, unequivocal as may be the Semitic elements of the Berber, Coptic and Galla, their affinities with the tongues of Western and Southern Africa are more so. I weigh my words when I say, not *equally,* but *more;* changing the expression, for every foot in advance which can be made towards the Semitic tongues in one direction, the African philologist can go a yard towards the Negro ones in the other."

In a note, just below this remarkable statement, Dr. Latham says:

> "A short table of the Berber and Coptic, as compared with the other African tongues, may be seen in the Classical Museum of the British Association, for 1846. In the Transactions of the Philological Society is a grammatical sketch of the Tumali language, by

Dr. S. Tutshek of Munich. The Tumali is a truly Negro language, of Kordufan; whilst, in respect to the extent to which its inflections are formed, by internal changes of vowels and accents, it is fully equal to the Semitic tongues of Palestine and Arabia."

This testimony may not serve prejudice, but to me it seems quite sufficient.

SUPERFICIAL OBJECTIONS

Let us now glance again at the opposition. A volume, on the Natural History of the Human Species, by Charles Hamilton Smith, quite false in many of its facts, and as mischievous as false, has been published recently in this country, and will, doubtless, be widely circulated, especially by those to whom the thought of human brotherhood is abhorrent. This writer says, after mentioning sundry facts touching the dense and spherical structure of the Negro head:

> "This very structure may influence the erect gait, which occasions the practice common also to the Ethiopian, or mixed nations, of carrying burdens and light weights, even to a tumbler full of water, upon the head."

No doubt this seemed a very sage remark to Mr. Smith, and quite important in fixing a character to the Negro skull, although different to that of Europeans. But if the learned Mr. Smith had stood, previous to writing it, at our door (a few days in succession), he might have seen hundreds of Germans and of Irish people, not bearing burdens of "*light* weight," but of *heavy* weight, upon the same vertical extremity. The carrying of burdens upon the head is as old as Oriental Society; and the man writes himself a blockhead, who attempts to find in the custom a proof of original difference. On page 227, the same writer says:

> "The voice of the Negroes is feeble and hoarse in the male sex."

The explanation of this mistake in our author, is found in the fact, that an oppressed people, in addressing their superiors—perhaps I ought to say, their oppressors—usually assume a minor tone, as less likely to provoke the charge of intrusiveness. But it is ridiculous to pronounce the voice of the Negro feeble; and the learned ethnologist must be hard pushed, to establish differences, when he refers to this as one. Mr. Smith further declares, that

> "The typical woolly haired races have never discovered an alphabet, framed a grammatical language, nor made the least step in science or art."

Now, the man is still living (or was but a few years since), among the Mandingoes of the Western coast of Africa, who has framed an alphabet; and while Mr. Smith may be pardoned for his ignorance of that fact, as an ethnologist, he is inexcusable for not knowing that the Mpongwe language, spoken on both sides of the Gaboon River, at Cape Lopez, Cape St. Catharine, and in the interior, to the distance of two or three hundred miles, is as truly a grammatically framed language as any extant. I am indebted, for this fact, to Rev. Dr. *M. B. Anderson*, President of the Rochester University; and by his leave, here is the Grammar—[holding up the Grammar.] Perhaps, of all the attempts ever made to disprove the unity of the human family, and to brand the Negro with natural inferiority, the most compendious and barefaced is the book, entitled "*Types of Mankind*," by Nott and Glidden. One would be well employed, in a series of Lectures, directed to an exposure of the unsoundness, if not the wickedness of this work.

THE AFRICAN RACE BUT ONE PEOPLE

But I must hasten. Having shown that the people of Africa are, probably, one people; that each tribe bears an intimate relation to other tribes and nations in that quarter of the globe, and that the Egyptians may have flung off the different tribes seen there at different times, as implied by the evident relations of their language, and by other similarities; it can hardly be deemed unreasonable to suppose, that the African branch of the human species—from the once highly civilized Egyptian to the barbarians on the banks of the Niger—may claim brotherhood with the great family of Noah, spreading over the more Northern and Eastern parts of the globe. I will now proceed to consider those physical peculiarities of form, features, hair and color, which are supposed by some men to mark the African, not only as an inferior race, but as a distinct species, naturally and originally different from the rest of mankind, and as really to place him nearer to the brute than to man.

THE EFFECT OF CIRCUMSTANCES UPON THE PHYSICAL MAN

I may remark, just here, that it is impossible, even were it desirable, in a discourse like this, to attend to the anatomical and physiological argument connected with this part of the subject. I am not equal to that, and if I were, the occasion does not require it. The form of the *Negro*—[I use the term *Negro,* precisely in the sense that you use the term Anglo Saxon; and I believe, too, that the former will one day be as illustrious as the latter]—has often been the subject of remark. His flat feet, long arms, high cheek bones and retreating forehead, are especially dwelt upon, to his disparagement, and just as if there were no white people with precisely the same peculiarities. I think it will ever be found, that the *well* or *ill* condition of any part of mankind, will leave its mark on the physical as well as on the intellectual part of man. A hundred instances might be cited, of whole families who have degenerated, and others who have improved in personal appearance, by a change of circumstances. A man is worked upon by what *he* works on. He may carve out his circumstances, but his circumstances will carve him out as well. I told a boot maker, in New Castle upon Tyne, that I had been a plantation slave. He said I must pardon him; but he could not believe it; no plantation laborer ever had a high instep. He said he had noticed, that the coal heavers and work people in low condition, had, for the most part, flat feet, and that he could tell, by the shape of the feet, whether a man's parents were in high or low condition. The thing was worth a thought, and I have thought of it, and have looked around me for facts. There is some truth in it; though there are exceptions, in individual cases.

[The day I landed in Ireland, nine years ago, I addressed] (in company with Father *Spratt,* and that good man who has been recently made the subject of bitter attack; I allude to the philanthropic *James Haughton, of Dublin*) [a large meeting of the common people of Ireland, on temperance. Never did human faces tell a sadder tale. More than five thousand were assembled; and I say, with no wish to wound the feelings of any Irishman, that these people lacked only a black skin and woolly hair, to complete their likeness to the plantation Negro. The open, uneducated mouth—the long, gaunt arm—the badly formed foot and ankle—the shuffling gait—the retreating forehead and vacant expression—and, their petty quarrels and fights—all reminded me of the plantation, and my own cruelly abused people.] Yet, *that* is the land of *Grattan,* of *Curran,* of *O'Connell,* and of *Sheridan.* [Now, while what I have said is true of the common people, the fact is, there are no more really handsome people in the world, than the educated Irish people. The Irishman educated, is a model gentleman; the Irishman ignorant and degraded, compares in form and feature, with the Negro!]

I am stating facts. If you go into Southern Indiana, you will see what climate and habit can do, even in one generation. The man may have come from New England, but his hard features, sallow complexion, have left little of New England on his brow. The right arm of the blacksmith is said to be larger and stronger than his left. The ship carpenter is at forty round shouldered. The shoemaker carries the marks of his trade. One locality becomes famous for one thing, another for another. Manchester and Lowell, in America, Manchester and Sheffield, in England, attest this. But what does it all prove? Why, nothing positively, as to the main point; still it raises the inquiry—May not the condition of men explain their various appearances? Need we go behind the vicissitudes of barbarism for an explanation of the gaunt, wiry, apelike appearance of some of the genuine Negroes? Need we look higher than a vertical sun, or lower than the damp, black soil of the Niger, the Gambia, the Senegal, with their heavy and enervating miasma, rising ever from the rank growing and decaying vegetation, for an explanation of the Negro's color? If a cause, full and adequate, can be found here, *why seek further?*

The Eminent Dr. *Latham,* already quoted, says that nine tenths of the white population of the globe are found between 30 and 65 degrees North latitude. Only about one fifth of all the inhabitants of the globe are white; and they are as far from the Adamic complexion as is the Negro. The remainder are—*what?* Ranging all the way from the brunette to jet black. There are the red, the reddish copper color, the yellowish, the dark brown, the chocolate color, and so on, to the jet black. On the mountains on the North of Africa, where water freezes in winter at times, branches of the same people who are *black* in the valley are *white* on the mountains. The Nubian, with his beautiful curly hair, finds it becoming frizzled, crisped, and even woolly, as he approaches the great Sahara. The Portuguese, white in Europe, is brown in Asia. The Jews, who are to be found in all countries, never intermarrying, are white in Europe, brown in Asia, and black in Africa. Again, what does it all prove? Nothing, absolutely; nothing which places the question beyond dispute; but it *does* justify the conjecture before referred to, that outward circumstances *may* have something to do with modifying the various phases of humanity; and that color itself is at the control of the world's climate and its various concomitants. It is the sun that paints the peach—and may it not be, that he paints the *man* as well? My reading, on this point, however, as well as my own observation, have convinced me, that from the beginning the Almighty, within certain limits, endowed mankind with organizations capable of countless variations in form, feature and color, without having it necessary to begin a new creation for every new variety.

A powerful argument in the favor of the oneness of the human family, is afforded in the fact that nations, however dissimilar, may be united in one social state, not only without detriment to each other, but, most clearly, to the advancement of human welfare, happiness and perfection. While it is clearly proved, on the other hand, that those nations freest from foreign elements, present the most evident marks of deterioration. Dr. JAMES MCCUNE SMITH, himself a colored man, a gentleman and scholar, alleges—and not without excellent reason—that this, our own great nation, so distinguished for industry and enterprise, is largely indebted to its composite character. [We all know, at any rate, that now, what constitutes the very heart of the civilized world—(I allude to England)—has only risen from barbarism to its present lofty eminence, through successive invasions and alliances with her people.] The Medes and Persians constituted one of the mightiest empires that ever rocked the globe. The most terrible nation which now threatens the peace of the world, to make its will the law of Europe, is a grand piece of Mosaic work, in which almost every nation has its characteristic feature, from the wild Tartar to the refined Pole.

But, gentlemen, the time fails me, and I must bring these remarks to a close. My argument has swelled beyond its appointed measure. What I intended to make special, has become, in its progress, somewhat general. I meant to speak here to-day, for the lonely and the despised ones, with whom I was cradled, and with whom I have suffered; and now, gentlemen, in conclusion, what if all this reasoning be unsound? What if the Negro may not be able to prove his relationship to Nubians, Abyssinians and Egyptians? What if ingenious men are able to find plausible objections to all arguments maintaining the oneness of the human race? What, after all, if they are able to show very good reasons for believing the Negro to have been created precisely as we find him on the Gold Coast along the Senegal and the Niger—I say, what of all this?—"*A man's a man for a' that.*" I sincerely believe, that the weight of the argument is in favor of the unity of origin of the human race, or species—that the arguments on the other side are partial, superficial, utterly subversive of the happiness of man, and insulting to the wisdom of God. Yet, what if we grant they are not so? What, if we grant that the case, on our part, is not made out? Does it follow, that the Negro should be held in contempt? Does it follow, that to enslave and imbrute him is either just or wise? I think not. Human rights stand upon a common basis; and by all the reason that they are supported, maintained and defended, for one variety of the human family, they are supported, maintained and defended for *all* the human family; because all mankind have the same wants, arising out of a common nature. A diverse origin does not disprove a common nature, nor does it disprove a united destiny. The essential characteristics of humanity are everywhere the same. In the language of the eloquent *Curran*, "No matter what complexion, whether an Indian or an African sun has burnt upon him," his title deed to freedom, his claim to life and to liberty, to knowledge and to civilization, to society and to Christianity, are just and perfect. It is registered in the Courts of Heaven, and is enforced by the eloquence of the God of all the earth.

I have said that the Negro and white man are likely ever to remain the principal inhabitants of this country. I repeat the statement now, to submit the reasons that support it. The blacks can disappear from the face of the country by three ways. They may be colonized,—they may be exterminated,—or, they may die out.

Colonization is out of the question; for I know not what hardships the laws of the land can impose, which can induce the colored citizen to leave his native soil. He was here in its infancy; he is here in its age. Two hundred years have passed over him, his tears and blood have been mixed with the soil, and his attachment to the place of his birth is stronger than iron. It is not probable that he will be exterminated; two considerations must prevent a crime so stupendous as that—the influence of Christianity on the one hand, and the power of self interest on the other; and, in regard to their dying out, the statistics of the country afford no encouragement for such a conjecture. The history of the Negro race proves them to be wonderfully adapted to all countries, all climates, and all conditions. Their tenacity of life, their powers of endurance, their malleable toughness, would almost imply especial interposition on their behalf. The ten thousand horrors of slavery, striking hard upon the sensitive soul, have bruised, and battered, and stung, but have not killed. The poor bondman lifts a smiling face above the surface of a sea of agonies, *hoping on, hoping ever.* His tawny brother, the Indian, dies, under the flashing glance of the Anglo Saxon. *Not* so the Negro; civilization cannot kill him. He accepts it—becomes a part of it. In the Church, he is an Uncle Tom, in the State, he is the most abused and least offensive. All the facts in his history mark out for him a destiny, united to America and Americans. Now, whether this population shall, by *Freedom, Industry, Virtue and Intelligence,* be made a blessing to the country and the world, or whether their multiplied wrongs shall kindle the vengeance of an offended God, will depend upon the conduct of no class of men so much as upon the Scholars of the country. The future public opinion of the land, whether anti-slavery or pro-slavery, whether just or unjust, whether magnanimous or mean, must redound to the honor of the Scholars of the country or cover them with shame. There is but one safe road for nations or for individuals. The fate of a wicked man and of a wicked nation is the same. The flaming sword of offended justice falls as certainly upon the nation as upon the man. God has no children whose rights may be safely trampled upon. The sparrow may not fall to the ground without the notice of His eye, and men are more than sparrows.

Now, gentlemen, I have done. The subject is before you. I shall not undertake to make the application. I speak as unto wise men. I stand in the presence of Scholars. We have met here to-day from vastly different points in the world's condition. I have reached here—if you win pardon the egotism—by little short of a miracle; at any rate, by dint of some application and perseverance. Born, as I was, in obscurity, a stranger to the halls of learning, environed by ignorance, degradation, and their concomitants, from birth to manhood, I do not feel at liberty to mark out, with any degree of confidence, or dogmatism, what is the precise vocation of the Scholar. Yet, this I *can* say, as a denizen of the world, and as a citizen of a country rolling in the sin and shame of Slavery, the most flagrant and scandalous that ever saw the sun, "Whatsoever things are true, whatsoever things are honest, whatsoever things are just, whatsoever things are pure, whatsoever things are lovely, whatsoever things are of good report, if there be any virtue, and if there be any praise, think on these things."

Pamphlet, Rochester, 1854

1. *Frederick Douglass' Paper,* Jan. 12, 1855.

THE KANSAS-NEBRASKA BILL, speech at Chicago, October 30, 1854

Friends and Fellow Citizens:

A great national question, a question of transcendent importance—one upon which the public mind is deeply moved, and not my humble name—has assembled this multitude of eager listeners in Metropolitan Hall this evening. You have come up here in obedience to a humane and patriotic impulse, to consider of the requirements of patriotism and humanity, at an important crisis in the affairs of this nation.

In this patriotic and holy purpose, I hail your presence here with grateful, sincere, and heart-felt pleasure. I am anxious to address you on the great subject which has called you together—and will do so—but circumstances will justify me in saying a few words first of a personal nature.

I have the misfortune of being deemed an intruder by some of your fellow citizens.—My visit among you is thought to be untimely, and to savor of impudence, and the like. Upon this matter I have a word to say in my own defence. A man that will not defend himself is not fit to defend a good cause.

And first, ladies and gentlemen, I am not sure that a visit on my part to Chicago would at any time afford those who are now complaining of me any special pleasure. But, gentlemen, I am not ashamed of being called an intruder. I have met it a thousand times in a thousand different places, and I am quite prepared to meet it now—and here, as I have met it, at other times and in other places.

Every inch of ground occupied by the colored man in this country is sternly disputed. At the ballot box and at the altar—in the church and in the State—he is deemed an intruder. He is, in fact, seldom a welcome visitor anywhere. Marvel not, therefore, if I seem somewhat used to the charge of intrusiveness, and am not more embarrassed in meeting it. Men have been known to get used to conditions and objects which, at the first, seemed utterly repulsive and insufferable. And so may I.

One reason why I am not ashamed to be here is this: I have a right to be here and a duty to perform here. That right is a constitutional right, as well as a natural right. It belongs to every citizen of the United States. It belongs not less to the humblest than to the most exalted citizens. The genius of American institutions knows no privileged class or classes. The plebian and the (would be) patrician stand here upon a common level of equality, and the last man in the world who should complain of this is the earnest advocate of popular sovereignty.

I have a right to come into this State to prosecute any lawful business in a lawful manner. This is a natural right, and is a part of the supreme law of the land. By that law the citizens of each state are the citizens of the United States, with rights alike and equal in all the States. The only question of right connected with my case here respects my citizenship. If I am a citizen, I am clothed all over with the star spangled banner and defended by the American Constitution, in every State of the American Union. That constitution knows no man by the color of his skin. The men who made it were too noble for any such limitation of humanity and human rights. The word white is a modern term in the legislation of this country. It was never used in the better days of the Republic, but has sprung up within the period of our national degeneracy.

I claim to be an American citizen. The constitution knows but two classes: Firstly, citizens, and secondly, aliens. I am not an alien; and I am, therefore, a citizen. I am moreover a free citizen. Free, thank God, not only by the law of the State in which I was born and brought up but free by the laws of nature.

In the State of New York where I live, I am a citizen and a legal voter, and may therefore be presumed to be a citizen of the United States. I am here simply as an American citizen, having a stake in the weal or woe of the nation, in common with other citizens. I am not even here as an agent of any sect or party. Parties are too politic and sects are too sectarian, to select one of my odious class, and of my radical opinions, at this important time and place, to represent them. Nevertheless, I do not stand alone here. There are noble minded men in Illinois who are neither ashamed of their cause nor their company. Some of them are here tonight, and I expect to meet with them in every part of the State where I may travel. But, I pray, hold no man or party responsible for my words, for I am no man's agent; and I am no parties' agent; and I beg that my respected friends— the reporters—will be good enough to make a note of that. I have a very good reason for making this request—a reason which I may some day give to the world, but which I need not give now.

One other remark; and it shall be in regard to a matter about which you wish to hear at once. It touches the matter involved on my mission here. I wish not only to stand within my rights as a man, but to stand approved at the bar of propriety as a gentleman, when, as in this case, I can do so without the sacrifice of principle. It has been given out, I believe, by some friends and also by some of the enemies of the principles I am' here to sustain that I have come into this State to confront in public debate, my distinguished namesake, the Hon. Stephen A. Douglas.

Fellow citizens, I wish to disclaim so much of this report as can possibly imply the slightest disrespect for the talents of your honorable Senator. His fame as an orator, and as a man of energy and perseverance, has not risen higher anywhere than in my own judgment. He is a man of the people. He came up from among them, and that by the native energy of his character and his manly industry. I am ever pleased to see a man rise from among the people. Every such man is prophetic of the good time coming. I have watched him during the past winter, when apparently overwhelmed with learning and eloquence, rise again, and with more than the tact and skill of a veteran, drive all before him. There is perhaps something in a name, and that may possibly explain the peculiar interest with which I have watched and contemplated the fortune of Mr. S. A. Douglas.

This feeling, I think, you will admit, is quite natural. No man likes to read in a newspaper of the hanging of a man bearing his own name.[1]

On the other hand, no man bearing the name of Douglas, would think less of his name, if this great nation should, in the abundance of goodness be pleased to place that name in the scroll of its Presidents; and this, notwithstanding the trite saying, that a rose by any other name would smell as sweet.

But the times, the times bid us to have done with names. Names have lost their significance, in more ways than one—deeds, not words, are the order of the day; names are valued so long as they are associated with honor, justice and liberty; and become execrable when associated with falsehood, treachery and tyranny?

It is alleged that I am come to this State to insult Senator Douglas. Among gentlemen, that is only an insult which is intended to be such, and I disavow all such intention. I am not even here with the desire to meet in public debate, that gentleman. I am here precisely as I was in this State one year ago—with no other change in my relations to you, or to the great question of human freedom, than time and circumstances have brought about. I shall deal with the subject in the same spirit now as then; approving such men and such measures as I look to the security of liberty in the land and with my whole heart condemning all men and measures as serve to subvert or endanger it.

If Hon. S. A. Douglas, your beloved and highly gifted Senator, has designedly, or through mistaken notions of public policy ranged himself, on the side of oppressors and the deadliest enemies of liberty, I know of no reason, either in this world or any other world, which should prevent me, or prevent any one else, from thinking so, or from saying so.

The people in whose cause I come here to-night, are not among those whose right to regulate their own domestic concerns, is so feelingly and eloquently contended for in certain quarters. They have no Stephen Arnold Douglas—no Gen. Cass, to contend at North Market Hall for their Popular Sovereignty. They have no national purse—no offices, no reputation, with which to corrupt Congress, or to tempt men, mighty in eloquence and influence into their service. Oh, no! They have nothing to commend them but their unadorned humanity. They are human—that's all—only human. Nature owns them as human—God owns them as human; but men own them as property!—Every right of human nature, as such, is denied them—they are dumb in their chains! To utter one groan, or scream, for freedom in the presence of the Southern advocate of Popular Sovereignty, is to bring down the frightful lash upon their quivering flesh. I knew this suffering people; I am acquainted with their sorrows; I am one with them in experience; I have felt the lash of the slave driver, and stand up here with all the bitter recollections of its horrors vividly upon me.

There are special reasons, therefore, why I should speak and speak freely. The right of speech is a very precious one, especially to the oppressed.

I understand that Mr. Douglas regards himself as the most abused man in the United States and that the greatest outrage ever committed upon him, was in the case in which your indignation raised your voices so high that his could not be heard. No personal violence, as I understand, was offered him. It seems to have been a trial of vocal powers between the individual and the multitude; as might have been expected, the voice of one man was not equal in volume to the voice of five hundred.

I do not mention this circumstance to approve it; I do not approve it; I am for free speech as well as for freemen and free soil; but how ineffably insignificant is this wrong done in a single instance, and to a single individual, compared with the stupendous iniquity perpetrated against more than three millions of the American people, who are struck dumb by the very men in whose cause Mr. Senator Douglas was here to plead. While I would not approve the silencing of Mr. Douglas, may we not hope that this slight abridgment of his rights may lead him to respect in some degree the rights of other men, as good in the eyes of Heaven, as himself.

Let us now consider the great question of the age; the only great national question which seriously agitates the public mind at this hour. It is called the vexed question; and excites alarm in every quarter of the country.

Efforts have been made to set it at rest.—Statesmen, and political parties, and churches have exerted themselves to settle it forever. They sought to bind it with cords; to resist it with revolutions, and bury it under platforms; but all to no purpose. The waves of the ocean still roll, and the earthquakes still shake the earth, and men's hearts still fail them for fear of those judgments which threaten to come upon the land.

Fellow Citizens: some things are settled, and settled forever—not by the laws of man, but by the laws of God; by the constitution of mankind; by the relations of things and by the facts of human experience.

It is, I think, pretty well settled, that liberty and slavery cannot dwell in the United States in peaceful relations; the history of the last five and twenty years settles that.

It is pretty well settled, too, that one or the other of these must go to the wall. The South must either give up slavery, or the North must give up liberty. The two interests are hostile, and are irreconcilable.—The just demands of liberty are inconsistent with the overgrown exactions of the slave power.

There is not a single tendency of slavery but is adverse to freedom. The one is adapted to progress, to industry, and to dignify industry. Slavery is anti-progressive—sets a premium on idleness, and degrades both labor and laborers. The fetters on the limbs of the slave, to be secure, must be accompanied with fetters on society as well. A free press and a free gospel, are as hostile as fire and gunpowder—separation or explosion, are the only alternatives.

No people in this country better understand this peculiarity than the slaveholders themselves. Hence the repeated violations of your Post Office laws in Southern towns and cities; hence the expurgations of Northern literature, and the barbarous outrages committed upon the persons of Northern travellers in the Southern States. Light and love, justice and mercy, must be guarded against in a community where the cruel lash is the law, and human lust is religion.

For a long time, it has been seen that the ideas and institutions of liberty, if allowed their natural course, would finally overthrow slavery. That slaveholders themselves would after a while come to loathe it.

Selfishness combined with this knowledge has at length ultimated into the formation of a party, ranged under the very taking appellation of National—the greatest business of which is to hold at bay, and restrain, and if possible to extinguish in the heart of this great nation every sentiment supposed to be at variance with the safety of slavery.

This party has arisen out of the teachings of that great man of perverted faculties, the late John C. Calhoun. No man of the nation has left a broader or a blacker mark on the politics of the nation, than he. In the eye of Mr. Calhoun every right guaranteed by the American constitution, must be held in subordination to slavery. It was he who first boldly declared the self-evident truths of the declaration of independence, self-evident falsehoods.[2] He has been followed in this by Mr. Benton's D.D. from Indiana.

The very spirit of Mr. Calhoun animates the slavery party of to-day. His principles are its principles, and his philosophy its philosophy. He looked upon slavery as the great American interest. The slavery party of to-day so esteem it. To preserve it, shield it, and support it, is its constant duty, and the object and aim of all its exertions. With this party the right of free men, free labor, and a free north are nothing. Daniel Webster never said a truer word than at Marshfield, in '48—"Why the North? There is no North!" But there is a South and ever has been a South controlling both parties, at every period of their existence.

The grand inauguration of this slavery party took place in the Summer of 1852.—That party was represented in both the great parties; and demanded as a condition of their very existence, that they should give their solemn endorsement, as a finality to the compromise measures of 1850. Abhorrent as were its demands, and arrogant and repulsive as was its manner of pressing them—that party was obeyed. Both conventions took upon them the mark of the beast; and called upon the whole North to do the same.—The Democratic party consented to be branded thus:

"That Congress has no power, under the constitution, to interfere with, or control the domestic institutions of the several States; and that such States are the sole and proper judges of everything appertaining to their own affairs, not prohibited by the constitution—that all efforts of the Abolitionists or others to induce Congress to interfere with the question of slavery, or to take incipient steps in relation thereto, are calculated to lead to the most alarming and dangerous consequences; and that all such efforts have an inevitable tendency to diminish the happiness of the people, and endanger the stability and permanency of the Union; and ought not to be countenanced by any friend of our political institution.

"*Resolved,* That the foregoing proposition covers and was intended to embrace the whole subject of the slavery agitation in Congress; and, therefore, the Democratic party of this Union, standing on this National platform, will abide by, and adhere to a faithful execution of the acts known as the compromise measures, settled by the last Congress—the act for reclaiming fugitives from service or labor included, which act being decided to carry out an express provision of the constitution, cannot, with fidelity, be repealed or be changed as to destroy or impair its efficacy.

"*Resolved,* That the Democratic party will resist all attempts at renewing, in Congress or out of it, the agitation of the slavery question, under whatever shape or color the attempt may be made."

Gentlemen: Such was the Democratic *mark,* and such was the Democratic *pledge.* It was taken in sight of all the nation, and in the sight of God, only two years ago. Has it kept that pledge? Does it stand acquitted to-day at the bar of public honor? or does it stand forth black with perfidy towards the North, while it wallows in the mire of deeper servility to the South? Has the Democratic party a single claim on your confidence, more than any notorious liar would have upon your credulity? Can you believe in a party that keeps its word, only as it has no temptation to break it? Is there a single man that can pretend to say that the Democrats—the Baltimore platform Democrats, have been true to their solemn declarations? Have they not renewed, and, in a manner to peril the cause of liberty—the agitation of slavery, which they solemnly promised to resist? Do you say they have not? Then there is no longer an intelligible proposition in the English language—nor is it possible to frame one.

But let me read to you the resolution imposed on the Whig National Convention, as the vital condition of its existence; and which was given to the world as the faith of that great organization, touching the matter of slavery. Here it is:

"That the series of acts, of the 31st Congress, known as the compromise, including the fugitive slave act, are received and acquiesced in by the Whig party of the United States, as a final settlement, in principle and substance, of the dangerous and exciting subjects which they embrace; and so far as the fugitive slave law is concerned, we will maintain the same, and insist upon its strict enforcement, until time and experience shall demonstrate the necessity of further legislation to guard against the evasion of the laws on the one hand, and the abuse of their powers on the other—not impairing their present efficacy—and deprecate all further agitation of the questions thus settled, as dangerous to our peace; and we will discountenance a continuance or renewal of such agitation, whenever, wherever, or however, the attempt may be made; and we will maintain this system as essential to the nationality of the Whig party, and the integrity of the Union."

Now, fellow-citizens: In those platforms, and in the events which have since transpired, it is easy to read the designs of the slave power. Something is gained when the plans and purposes of an enemy are discovered.

I understand the first purpose of the slave power to be the suppression of all anti-slavery discussion. Next, the extension of slavery over all the territories. Next, the nationalizing of slavery, and to make slavery respected in every State in the Union.

First, the right of speech is assailed, and both parties pledge themselves to put it down. When parties make platforms, they are presumed to put nothing into them, which, if need be, they may not organize into law. These parties on this presumption, are pledged to put down free discussion by law—to make it an offence against the law to speak, write, and publish against slavery, here in the free States, just as it now is an offence against the law to do so in the slave States. One end of the slave's chain must be fastened to a padlock in the lips of Northern freemen, else the slave will himself become free.

Now, gentlemen, are you ready for this?—Are you ready to give up the right of speech, and suppress every human and Christ-inspired sentiment, lest the conscience of the guilty be disturbed?

Our parties have attempted to give peace to slaveholders. They have attempted to do what God has made impossible to be done; and that is to give peace to slaveholders.—"There is no peace to the wicked, saith my God." In the breast of every slaveholder, God has placed, or stationed an anti-slavery lecturer, whose cry is *guilty*, guilty, guilty; "thou art verily guilty concerning thy brother."

But now let me come to the points of this great question which touch us most nearly to-night.

I take the case to be this: The citizens of this State are now appealed to, to give their sanction to the repeal of the law, by which slavery has been, during a period of thirty four years, restricted to the south Of 36 deg. 30 min. of north latitude, in the territory acquired by the purchase of Louisiana.

This is but a simple and truthful statement of the real question.

The question is not, whether "popular sovereignty" is the true doctrine for the territories—it is not whether the chief agents in the repeal of that line, acted from good or bad motives; nor is it whether they are able or feeble men.

These are points of very little consequence in determining the path of duty in this case.

When principles are at stake, persons are of small account; and the safety of a Republic is found in a rigid adherence to principles. Once give up these, and you are a ship in a storm, without anchor or rudder.

Fellow-Citizens: The proposition to repeal the Missouri Compromise, was a stunning one. It fell upon the nation like a bolt from a cloudless sky. The thing was too startling for belief. You believed in the South, and you believed in the North; and you knew that the repeal of the Missouri Compromise was a breach of honor; and, therefore, you said the thing could not be done. Besides, both parties had pledged themselves directly, positively and solemnly against re-opening in Congress the agitation on the subject of slavery; and the President himself had declared his intention to maintain the national quiet. Upon those assurances you rested, and rested fatally.

But you should have learned long ago that "men do not gather grapes of thorns, nor figs of thistles." It is folly to put faith in men who have broken faith with God. When a man has brought himself to enslave a child of God, to put fetters on his brother, he has qualified himself to to disregard the most sacred of compacts—beneath the sky there is nothing more sacred than man, and nothing can be properly respected when manhood is despised and trampled upon. Now let us attend to the defence made before the people by the advocates of the Kansas-Nebraska bill.

They tell us that the bill does not open the Territories to slavery, and complain that they are misrepresented and slandered by those charging them with flinging open the Territories to slavery. I wish to slander no man. I wish to misrepresent no man. They point us to the bill itself as proof that no such opening of the Territories to slavery is contemplated, or intended by it. I will read to you from the bill itself, to see what is relied upon at this point:

"It being the true intent and meaning of this act not to legislate slavery into any Territory or State; *nor to exclude it therefrom,* but to leave the people thereof perfectly free to form and regulate their domestic institutions in their own way; subject only to the constitution of the United States."

One part of this declaration is true and carries the evidence of its truth on its face. It is true that it is no part of the true intent and meaning of the act to exclude slavery from any Territory or State. If its true intent and meaning had been otherwise, it would not have repealed the law, the only law, which had excluded slavery from those territories, and from those States which may be formed out of them. I repeat, this part of the bill needs no explanation. It is plain enough already. There is not a slaveholder in the land, however ardent an advocate of slavery extension he may be, who has ever complained that the true intent and meaning of the Kansas-Nebraska bill was to exclude slavery from the territories in question, or from any States which might be formed out of them. Slaveholders do not so understand the bill. Had they so understood it, they would never have gone in a *body* to sustain the bill. It is very significant that on this part of this "stump speech" in the declaration, the country is agreed, everybody understanding it alike, while on the other hand, the words in the bill, directly preceding it, are the subject of controversy. Why is this so? You are told that it is owing to the perversity of man's understanding. But this is not the answer. I will tell you why it is. The people, like the old rat, do not deny that the white dust they see here is meal—real and genuine meal—but under the meal they detect the treacherous form of the cat. Under that smooth exterior there are the sharp teeth and destructive claws, and hence they avoid, shun and detest it.

But again: it is claimed that the Nebraska bill does not open the territories to Slavery for another reason. It is said that Slavery is the creature of positive law, and that it can only exist where it is sustained by positive law—that neither in Kansas nor in Nebraska is there any law establishing Slavery, and that, therefore, the moment a slaveholder carries his slaves into those Territories they are free, and restored to the rights of human nature. This is the ground taken by General Cass. He contended for it in the North Market Hall, with much eloquence and skill. I thought, while I was hearing him on this point, that slaveholders would not be likely to thank him for the argument. Theoretically the argument is good, practically the argument is bad. It is not true that slavery cannot exist without being established by positive law. On the contrary, the instance cannot be shown where a law was ever made establishing slavery, where the relation of master and slave did not previously exist. The law is always an aftercoming consideration. Wicked men first overpower, and subdue their fellow-men to slavery, and then call in the law to sanction the deed.

Even in the slave States of America, slavery has never been established by positive law. It was not so established under the colonial charters of the original States, nor the constitution of the States. It is now, and always has been, a system of lawless violence.

On this proposition, I hold myself ready and willing to meet any defender of the Nebraska bill. I would not even hesitate to meet the author of that bill himself. I insist upon it that the very basis upon which this bill is defended, is utterly and entirely false as applied to the practice of slavery in this country. The South itself scouts the theory of Messrs. Douglas and Cass at this point, and esteem it simply as a gull-trap in which to catch the simple. They look upon it simply as a piece of plausible stump oratory, and censure it as such. But that slavery is not the tame creature of law, as alleged, I will not rely solely on my own declaration.

Senator Mason, of Virginia, the author of the Fugitive Slave bill, and one of the most influential members of the American Senate, during the debate on the Fugitive Slave bill in 1850, scouted such a basis for slavery, and confessed that no such existed. He said, and I quote his own words:

"Then again, it is proposed (by one of the opponents of the bill) as a part of the proof to be adduced at the hearing after the fugitive has been recaptured, that evidence shall be brought by the claimant to show that slavery is established in the State from whence the fugitive has absconded. Now, this very thing, in a recent case in the city of New York, was required by one of the judges of that State, which case attracted the attention of the authorities of Maryland, and against which they protested, because of the indignities heaped upon their citizens, and the losses which they sustained in that city. In that case, the Judge of the State Court required proof that slavery was established in Maryland, and went so far as to say that the only mode of proving it was by reference to the statute book. Such proof is required in the Senator's amendment; and if he means by this that proof shall be brought that slavery is established by existing laws, it is impossible to comply with the requisition, for no such proof can be produced, I apprehend, in any of the slave States. *I am not aware that there is a single State in which the institution is established by positive law.* On a former occasion, and on a different topic, it was my duty to endeavor to show to the Senate that no such law was necessary for its establishment; certainly none could be found, and none was required in any of the States of the Union."

There you have it. It cannot be shown that slavery is established by law even in the slaveholding States. But slavery exists there—and so may it exist in Nebraska and in Kansas—and I had almost said that this is well known to the very men who are now trying to persuade the people of the north that it cannot.

But there is another defence set up for the repeal of the Missouri restriction. It is said to be a patriotic defence, supported by patriotic reasons. It is the defence which Senator Douglas uses with much effect wherever he goes.

He says he wants no broad black line across this continent. Such a line is odious and begets unkind feelings between the citizens of a common country.

Now, fellow-citizens, why is the line of thirty-six degrees thirty minutes, a broad black line? What is it that entitles it to be called a *black line?* It is the fashion to call whatever is odious in this country, black.—You call the Devil black— and he may be, but what is there in the line of thirty-six degrees thirty minutes, which makes it blacker than the line which separates Illinois from Missouri, or Michigan from Indiana? I can see nothing in the line itself which should make it black or odious. It is a line, that's all.

If it is black, black and odious, it must be so not because it is a line, but because of the things it separates.

If it keeps asunder what God has joined together—or separates what God intended should be fused—then it may be called an odious line, a black line; but if on the other hand, it marks only a distinction—natural and eternal—a distinction, fixed in the nature of things by the Eternal God, then I say, withered be the arm and blasted be the hand that would blot it out.

But we are told that the people of the North were originally opposed to that line, that they burnt in effigy the men from the North who voted for it, and that it comes with a bad grace from the North now to oppose its repeal.

Fellow-citizens, this may do in the Barroom. It may answer somewhere outside of where the moon rises, but it won't do among men of intelligence.

Why did the North condemn the Missouri line? This it was: they believed that it gave slavery an advantage to which slavery had no right. By establishing the Missouri Compromise line, slavery got all south of it. By repealing that line it may get all north of it. Now are any so blind as not to see that the same reasons for opposing the original line, are good against repeal.

Allow me to illustrate. Thirty-four years ago, a man succeeds in getting a decision unjustly, by which he comes in possession of one half of your farm. You protest against that decision, and say it is corrupt. But the man does not heed your protests. He builds his house upon it, and fences in his lands and warns you to keep off his premises. You cannot help yourself. You live by his side thirty-four years. You have lost the means of regaining your lost property. But just at this time there comes a new judge, a Daniel, a very Daniel, and he reverses so much of the judgment by which you lost the first half of your farm, and makes another decision by which you may lose the other half.

You meekly protest against this new swindle. When the judge in question, with great affectation of impartiality, denounces you as very difficult to please, and as flagrantly inconsistent.

Such, gentlemen, is the plain and simple truth in the matter.

By the Missouri Compromise, slavery—an alien to the Republic, and enemy to every principle of free Institutions, and having no right to exist anywhere— got one half of a territory rightfully belonging to Freedom.—You complained of that. Now a law is repealed whereby you may lose the other half also, and you are forbidden to complain.

But hear again:

It is said with much adroitness by the advocates of the Nebraska bill, that we are unnecessarily solicitous for the rights of Negroes, that if the people of the territories can be trusted to make laws for white men, they may be safely left to make laws for black men.

Now, gentlemen, this is a favorite point of the author of the Nebraska bill. Under its fair seeming front, is an appeal to all that is mean, cowardly, and vindictive in the breast of the white public. It implies that the opponents of the Nebraska bill feel a deeper concern for the Negroes as such, than for white men, that we are unnaturally sensitive to rights of the blacks, and unnaturally indifferent to the rights of the whites.

With such an unworthy implication on its face, I brand it as a mean, wicked and bitter appeal to Popular Prejudice, against a people wholly defenceless, and at the mercy of the public.

The argument of Senator Douglas at this point, assumes the absurd position that a slaveholding people will be as careful of the rights of their black slaves as they are of their own. They might as well say that wolves may be trusted to legislate for themselves, and why not for lambs, as to say that slaveholders may do so for themselves, and why not for their slaves?

Shame on the miserable sophistry, and shame on the spirit that prompted its utterance! There is nothing manly or honorable in either. Take another specimen of senatorial logic; a piece of the same roll to which I have just referred.

Senator Douglas tells you, that the people may be as safely left to make laws respecting slavery, as to regulate theft, robbery, or murder. Very well—so they may. There is no doubt about that; but as usual, the Hon. Senator fails to bring out the whole truth.—To bring out the whole truth here, is to cover him with shame.

To put the matter in its true light, let us suppose that in the Southern States of this Union, the people are so benighted as to practice and support "theft," "robbery," and "murder," but that in the other States that practice is loathed and abhorred.

Suppose, also, that up to a certain line in a territory belonging alike and equally to all the States, these wicked practices were prohibited by law; and then, suppose a grave Senator from a State where theft, robbery and murder are looked upon with horror, rising in his place in the national legislature and moving to repeal the line excluding "theft," "robbery" and "murder," and demanding that "theft," "robbery" and "murder," be placed upon the same footing with honesty, uprightness and innocence.—I say, suppose this, and you have a parallel to the conduct of Senator Douglas, in repealing the line of 36 deg. 30 min.

But the grand argument, and the one which seems to be relied upon as unanswerable and overwhelming, is this: The people of the territories are American citizens, and carry with them the right of self-government; that this Nebraska bill is based upon this great American principle of Popular Sovereignty, and that to oppose this principle, is to act as did King George towards the American colonies.

Let me answer this argument. It may not need an answer here in Chicago, for it has been answered here, and answered well.—Nevertheless, let me answer it again, and prove by the bill itself, that it is a stupendous shame with every motive to deceive without the power.

What is meant by Popular Sovereignty?—It is the right of the people to establish a government for themselves, as against all others. Such was its meaning in the days of the revolution. It is the independent right of a people to make their own laws, without dictation or interference from any quarter. A sovereign subject is a contradiction in terms, and is an absurdity. When sovereignty becomes subject, it ceases to be sovereignty. When what was future becomes the present, it ceases to be the future and so with sovereignty and subjection, they cannot exist at the same time in the same place, any more than an event can be future and present at the same time. This much is clear.

Now the question is, does the Kansas-Nebraska bill give to the people of these territories the sovereign right to govern themselves? Is there a man here who will say that it does?

The author of the bill, in his stump speeches in the country, says that it does; and some men think the statement correct. But what say you, who have read the bill?

Nothing could be further from the truth, than to say that Popular Sovereignty is accorded to the people who may settle the territories of Kansas and Nebraska.

The three great cardinal powers of government are the Executive, Legislative and Judicial. Are these powers secured to the people of Kansas and Nebraska?

That bill places the people of that territory as completely under the powers of the federal government as Canada is under the British crown. By this Kansas-Nebraska bill the federal government has the substance of all governing power, while the people have the shadow. The judicial power of the territories is not from the people of the territories, who are so bathed in the sunlight of popular sovereignty by stump eloquence, but from the federal government.—The executive power of the territories derives its existence not from the overflowing fountain of popular sovereignty, but from the federal government. The Secretaries of the territories are not appointed by the sovereign people of the territories, but are appointed independently of popular sovereignty.

But is there nothing in this bill which justifies the supposition that it contains the principle of popular sovereignty? No, not one word. Even the territorial councils, elected, not by the people who may settle in the territories, but by only certain descriptions of people are subject to a double veto power, vested first in a governor, which they did not elect, and second in the President of the United States. The only shadow of popular sovereignty is the power given to the people of the territories by this bill to have, hold, buy and sell human beings. The sovereign right to make slaves of their fellowmen if they choose is the only sovereignty that the bill secures.

In all else, popular sovereignty means only what the boy meant when he said he was going to live with his uncle Robert. He said he was going there, and that he meant while there, to do just as he pleased, if his uncle Robert would let him!

I repeat, that the only seeming concession to the idea of popular sovereignty in this bill is authority to enslave men, and to concede that right or authority is a hell black denial of popular sovereignty itself.

Whence does popular sovereignty take rise? What and where is its basis? I should really like to hear from the author of the Nebraska bill, a philosophical theory, of the nature and origin of popular sovereignty. I wonder where he would begin, how he would proceed and where he would end.

The only intelligible principle on which popular sovereignty is founded, is found in the Declaration of American Independence, there and in these words: We hold these truths to be self-evident, that all men are created equal and are endowed by their Creator with the right of life, liberty and the pursuit of happiness.

The right of each man to life, liberty and the pursuit of happiness, is the basis of all social and political right, and, therefore, how brass-fronted and shameless is that impudence, which while it aims to rob men of their liberty, and to deprive them of the right to the pursuit of happiness—screams itself hoarse to the words of popular sovereignty.

But again: This bill, this Nebraska bill, gives to the people of the territories the right to hold slaves. Where did this bill get this right, which it so generously gives away? Did it get it from Hon. Stephen A. Douglas? Then I demand where he got that right?—Who gave it to him? Was he born with it? Or has he acquired it by some noble action? I repeat, how came he by it, or with it, or to have it?

Did the people of this State, from whom he derived his political and legislative life, give him this right, the right to make slaves of men? Had he any such right?

The answer is, he had not. He is in the condition of a man who has given away that which is not his own.

But it may be said that Congress has the right to allow the people of the territories to hold slaves.

The answer is, that Congress is made up of men, and possesses only the rights of men, and unless it can be shown, that some men have a right to hold their fellow-men as property, Congress has no such right.

There is not a man within the sound of my voice, who has not as good a right to enslave a brother man, as Congress has. This will not be denied even by slaveholders.

Then I put the question to you, each of you, all of you, have you any such right?

To admit such a right is to charge God with folly, to substitute anarchy for order, and to turn earth into a hell. And you know it.

Now, friends and fellow-citizens, I am uttering no new sentiments at this point, and am making no new argument. In this respect there is nothing new under the sun.

Error may be new or it may be old, since it is founded in a misapprehension of what truth is. It has its beginnings and has its endings. But not so with truth. Truth is eternal. Like the great God from whose throne it emanates, it is from everlasting unto everlasting, and can never pass away.

Such a truth is man's right to freedom.—He was born with it. It was his before he comprehended it. The title deed to it is written by the Almighty on his heart, and the record of it is in the bosom of the eternal—and never can Stephen A. Douglas efface it unless he can tear from the great heart of God this truth. And this mighty government of ours will never be at peace with God until it shall, practically and universally, embrace this great truth as the foundation of all its institutions, and the rule of its entire administration.

Now, gentlemen, I have done. I have no fear for the ultimate triumph of free principles in this country. The signs of the times are propitious. Victories have been won by slavery, but they have never been won against the onward march of anti-slavery principles. The progress of these principles has been constant, steady, strong and certain. Every victory won by slavery has had the effect to fling our principles more widely and favorably among the people.—The annexation of Texas—the Florida war—the war with Mexico—the compromise measures and the repeal of the Missouri Compromise, have all signally vindicated the wisdom of that great God, who has promised to overrule the wickedness of men for His own glory—to confound the wisdom of the crafty and bring to naught the counsels of the ungodly.

Frederick Douglass' Paper, November 24, 1854

1. The allusion is to the hanging of Stephen A. Douglas in effigy in Chicago and many other communities, from Iowa to Maine, during the debates in Congress on the Nebraska Bill.

2. On January 12, 1838, Calhoun declared in the Senate: "Many in the South once believed it [slavery] was a moral and political evil. That folly and delusion are gone. We see it now in its true light and regard it as the most safe and stable basis for free institutions in the world." (R. K. Cralle, ed., *The Works of John C. Calhoun,* New York, 1854–1856, vol. III, p. 180.)

THE ANTI-SLAVERY MOVEMENT, lecture delivered before the Rochester Ladies' Anti-Slavery Society, March 19, 1855

Ladies and Gentlemen:

Had I consulted my own health, or the advice of my physician, I should have been elsewhere, and otherwise employed this evening. I am not well, and have not been so for several weeks. I have usually come to this platform to lecture on slavery—that darkest and hugest of all wrongs—the vilest (in the language of John Wesley) that ever saw the sun. But it has pleased the Rochester Ladies' Anti-Slavery Society to have presented here, during the winter, almost every phase of that terrible wrong; and I have, therefore, selected my topic in view of that fact. It will, probably, amount to the same thing in the end.

Some one has, happily, said, that it matters very little which path the traveller may take; he has but to go forward to go round the world. In like manner it may be said, that it matters little which path of inquiry a man may pursue, or which great moral or spiritual fact he may investigate; he has but to honestly persevere to find himself, at last, at the portals of the whole universe of truth, and speedily walking amidst its golden glories.

The subject of my lecture this evening is, the nature, character, and history of the anti-slavery movement. I own that, were I here on any ordinary occasion, to deliver a lecture on the question of slavery, I should select topics of a more popular and stirring character than those I propose to touch this evening. When I speak of the anti-slavery movement, I mean to refer to that combination of moral, religious and political forces which has long been, and is now, operating and cooperating for the abolition of slavery in this country, and throughout the world. I wish to speak of that movement, to-night, more as the calm observer, than as the ardent and personally interested advocate. For, while I am willing to have it known, that every fibre of my soul is enlisted in the cause of emancipation, I would not have it thought that I am less capable than others, of calmly and rationally contemplating the movement designed to accomplish that important and much desired end. In making this statement, I am quite aware of the common impression concerning the mental abilities of my race. It has been said, that the variety of the human family, to which I belong, excels less in the intellectual, than in the emotional characteristics of men; and the great leader of the anti-slavery movement in our country allowed himself to say, in the columns of his paper, not long ago, that "the anti-slavery movement, both religiously and politically, has transcended the ability of the sufferers from American slavery and prejudice, as a class, to keep pace with it, or to perceive what are its demands, or to understand the philosophy of its operations."[1] Notwithstanding such discouraging considerations, I presume to speak to you, to-night, on the subject selected. In doing so, I have one consolation, and that is, as I apprehend it, the anti-slavery movement is, after all, no cold abstraction, requiring a sharp and flinty intellect to analyze it. While it is a subject of surpassing dignity, and one upon which the wisest and best minds may be employed, it is, nevertheless, a subject upon which the humblest may venture to think and speak, without justly being exposed to the reproach of treading upon ground which should be trodden only by men of the "superior race."

One other word for my subject. A grand movement on the part of mankind, in any direction, or for any purpose, moral or political, is an interesting fact, fit and proper to be studied. It is such, not only for those who eagerly participate in it, but also for those who stand aloof from it—even for those by whom it is opposed. I take the anti-slavery movement to be such an one, and a movement as sublime and glorious, in its character, as it is holy and beneficent in the ends it aims to accomplish. At this moment, I deem it safe to say, it is properly engrossing more minds in this country than any other subject now before the American people. The late John C. Calhoun—one of the mightiest men that ever stood up in the American Senate—did not deem it beneath him; and he probably studied it as deeply, though not as honestly, as Gerrit Smith, or William Lloyd Garrison. He evinced the greatest familiarity with the subject; and the greatest efforts of his last years in the Senate had direct reference to this movement. His eagle eye watched every new development connected with it; and he was ever prompt to inform the South of every important step in its progress. He never allowed himself to make light of it; but always spoke of it and treated it as a matter of grave import; and, in this, he showed himself a master of the mental, moral, and religious constitution of human society. Daniel Webster, too, in the better days of his life, before he gave his assent to the Fugitive Slave Bill, and trampled upon all his earlier and better convictions—when his eye was yet single—he clearly comprehended the nature of the elements involved in this movement; and in his own majestic eloquence, warned the South, and the country, to have a care how they attempted to put it down. He is an illustration that it is easier to give, than to take good advice. To these two men—the greatest men to whom the nation has yet given birth—may be, traced the two great facts of the present—the South triumphant, and the North humbled. Their names may stand thus: Calhoun and domination—Webster and degradation. Yet again. If to the enemies of liberty this subject is one of engrossing interest, vastly more so should it be such to freedom's friends. The latter, it leads to the gates of all valuable knowledge, philanthropic, ethical and religious; for it brings them to the study of man, wonderfully and fearfully made—the proper study of man through all time—the open book, in which are the records of time and eternity!

Of the existence and power of the anti-slavery movement, as a fact, you need no evidence. The nation has seen its face, and felt the controlling pressure of its hand. You have seen it moving in all directions, and in all weathers, and in all places, appearing most where desired least, and pressing hardest where most resisted. No place is exempt. The quiet prayer meeting, and the stormy halls of national debate, share its presence alike. It is a common intruder, and, of course, has got the name of being ungentlemanly. Brethren who had long sung, in the most affectionate fervor, and with the greatest sense of security,

Together let us sweetly live—together let us die,

have been suddenly and violently separated by it, and ranged in hostile attitude towards each other. One of the most powerful religious organizations (I allude to the Methodists) of this country, has been rent asunder, and its strongest bolts of denominational brotherhood started at a single surge. It has changed the tone of the Northern pulpit, and modified that of the press. A celebrated Divine, who, four years ago, was for flinging his own mother, or brother, into the remorseless jaws of the monster Slavery, lest he should swallow up the Union, now recognizes anti-slavery as a characteristic of future civilization. Signs and wonders follow this movement; and the fact just stated is one of them. Party ties are loosened by it; and men are compelled to take sides for or against it, whether they will or not. Come from where he may, or come for what he may, he is compelled to show his hand. What is this mighty force? What is its history? and what is its destiny? Is it ancient or modern, transient or permanent? Has it turned aside, like a stranger and a sojourner, to tarry for a night? or has it come to rest with us forever? Excellent chances are here for speculation; and some of them are quite profound. We might, for instance, proceed to inquire not only into the philosophy of the anti-slavery movement, but into the philosophy of the law, in obedience to which that movement started into existence. We might demand to know what is that law or power which, at different times, disposes the minds of men to this or that particular object—now for peace, and now for war—now for freedom, and now for slavery; but this profound question I leave to the Abolitionists of the superior class to answer. The speculations which must precede such answer, would afford, perhaps, about the same satisfaction as the learned theories which have rained down upon the world, from time to time, as to the origin of evil. I shall, therefore, avoid water in which I cannot swim, and deal with anti-slavery as a fact, like any other fact in the history of mankind, capable of being described and understood, both as to its internal forces, and its external phases and relations.

First, then, let us consider its history. About this there is much error, and little truth in many minds. Some who write and speak on the subject, seem to regard the anti-slavery movement as a recent discovery, brought out for the first time less than a quarter of a century ago. I cannot consent to view it thus. This movement is older and weightier than that. I would deprive William Lloyd Garrison of no honor justly his. All credit must forever redound to him as the man to whose earnest eloquence—more than to that of any other living man—we owe the revival of the antislavery movement in this country; but it is due to truth to say, he neither discovered its principles, originated its ideas, nor framed its arguments. These are all older than the preacher. It is an error to speak of this venerable movement as a new thing under the sun. The causes producing it, and the particles composing it, like the great forces of the physical world, fire, steam, and lightning, have slumbered in the bosom of nature since the world began. There are coal and iron, and lead, and copper, and silver, and gold, and precious gems in the hillsides, whereon the shepherd-boy sings, unconsciously, his evening song. They are all there, though he knows it not, awaiting the thoughtful discoverer, and the skillful workman to bring them forth in the varied and multitudinous forms of beauty, power, and glory, of which they are capable. And so it is with the elements of this history. They are prior to the present anti-slavery movement. Whence are these elements? I trace them to nature and to nature's God. From heaven come the rain, the snow, and the crystalizing blast, which pile up the glaciers; and from the same source come also those melting beams and softening breezes, which send down the thundering avalanche, to awe and astonish the hearts of man. What, though one passed by at the moment! shall he ascribe to his tiny tread the solemn crash, and the stunning reverberation? Rather let him stand, awe-struck, ascribing to God all the glory and honor for his wondrous works. It is a thought no less true, than consoling, that, in fitting out this globe for its mighty and mysterious voyage in time and space, the Great Mind who loosed it from its moorings, foresaw all its perils, and comprehended all its vicissitudes—and better still, bountifully provided for the moral, as well as for the physical safety of its passengers. In the very heart of humanity are garnered up, as from everlasting to everlasting, all those elementary principles, whose vital action constitutes what we now term the "anti-slavery movement." They are the treasures of our common store-house. The humblest may approach, enter, and be supplied with arms, to meet the ills that flesh is heir to. A thousand moral battles have been fought with them, and they are as good as ever. Ages of oppression, and iron-hearted selfishness, have rolled over them, and covered them with their blinding dust; but these have had no power to extinguish, or to destroy them. Occasional glimpses of these important principles have gladdened the eyes of good men, at different stages of the world's progress, who have wisely written down, to be read by after coming generations, their apprehensions of them. Noble testimonies of this sort may be found all along the way trodden by the race. They are the common inheritance of all men, without money and without price. In reading these ancient testimonies, some of them reaching back to the grand exodus of Israel, and some to the earliest days of our country, more than a century ago, one is filled with veneration for the vast accumulation, the mighty bulwark of judgment, of solemn conviction, of holy protest, reared for the defence of the rights of man.

The anti-slavery movement has little to entitle it to being called a new thing under the sun, in view of any just historical test. I know nothing original about it. Its ideas and arguments were already to the hand of the present workmen; the oldest abolitionist of to-day is but the preacher of a faith framed and practised long before he was born. The patriots of the American Revolution clearly saw, and with all their inconsistency, they had the grace to confess the abhorrent character of slavery, and to hopefully predict its overthrow and complete extirpation. Washington, and Jefferson, Patrick Henry, and Luther Martin, Franklin, and Adams, Madison, and Monroe, and a host of the earlier statesmen, jurists, scholars, and divines of the country, were among those who looked forward to this happy consummation. But, now, let us come to the sober record, and it will be seen that the anti-slavery movement in this country, is older than the Republic. In the records of the churches, especially, we find most important data, showing that the anti-slavery sentiment was national at the very beginning of the Republic, and that this sentiment got its fullest and most earnest expression through the churches at that time. The Methodist, Baptist, and Presbyterian churches of the country, stood upon radical anti-slavery ground. It will not be easy to find anywhere, in the records of any modern anti-slavery society, testimony more vital and stringent than is found in the proceedings of the Methodist church against slavery, nearly a hundred years ago; and the same is true of the Baptist churches of the South. The Methodist church vaulted up to the highest position occupied by the most ultra Abolitionists of to-day. It denied slavery all sanction, human and divine, against the laws of God, and against the laws of man. In 1780, that denomination said: "The Conference acknowledges that slavery is contrary to the laws of God, man and nature, and hurtful to society—contrary to the dictates of conscience, and true religion, and doing to others that we would not they should do unto us." In 1784, the same church declared, "that those who buy, sell, or give slaves away, except for the purpose to free them, shall be expelled immediately." In 1785, the Conference spoke even more stringently on the subject. It then said: "We hold in the deepest abhorrence the practice of slavery, and shall not cease to seek its destruction by all wise and proper means."

Still later, in 1801:—

> "We declare that we are more than ever convinced of the great evil of African slavery, which still exists in these United States, and every member of the Society who sells a slave shall immediately, on full proof, be excluded from the Society. The Conferences are directed to draw up addresses, for the gradual emancipation of the slaves, to the Legislatures. Proper committees shall be appointed, out of the most respectable of our friends, for the conducting of the business. And the presiding elders, deacons, and travelling preachers, shall do all in their power to further the blessed undertaking. Let this be continued from year to year, till the desired end be accomplished."

So reads the record of the Methodist Episcopal Church of America, more than half a century ago. Here was an anti-slavery movement springing out of the very bosom of the church. In what did this movement differ from the present one? In this, and in this only, *as to time.* The first looked for the gradual abolition of slavery; and the other looks for immediate emancipation. Under the operation of the one doctrine, nearly sixty thousand slaves have been emancipated in Maryland, and as many in Virginia, and many more in the several Southern States, besides universal emancipation in the Northern States. The only new idea brought to the anti-slavery movement, by Mr. Garrison, is the doctrine of immediatism, as against gradualism, and thus far, it must be confessed, that fewer slaves have been emancipated under the influence of this doctrine, in this country, than under the old doctrine of gradual emancipation. So much as this is due to facts. Nevertheless, I would not give up a just principle because it has been slower of adoption than a principle less just. The doctrine of immediatism was not, however, original with Mr. Garrison. Dr. Hopkins, of Newport, R.I., had urged that doctrine upon the consideration of his slaveholding congregation before Mr. Garrison was born. That brave, old philanthropist met the slave-holder face to face with the stern demand of emancipation, "*without delay.*" Dr. Hopkins was a strong reasoner, and an earnest reformer. The Abolitionist of to-day will lose nothing by perusing the anti-slavery works of their noble predecessor. The Methodist Episcopal Church, whose course on the slavery question I have been unfolding, was not singular in its position respecting slavery fifty years ago. Elizabeth Herrick, too, of England, as early as 1824, published a pamphlet in favor of immediate and unconditional emancipation. The Presbyterian Church, and the Methodist, stood on the same ground. In 1794, the General Assembly of that body, pronounced the following judgment on the character of slavery, and that of slave-holders:—

> "1st Timothy, 1st chapter, 10th v.—'The law is made for manstealers.' 'This crime among the Jews exposed the perpetrators of it to capital punishment.'—Exodus xxi. 15. And the apostle here classes them with sinners of the first rank. The word he uses in its original import, comprehends all who are concerned in bringing any of the human race into slavery, or in retaining them in it. Stealers of men are all those who bring off slaves or freemen, and keep, sell, or buy them. 'To steal a freeman,' says Grotius, 'is the highest kind of theft.' In other instances we only steal human property, but when we steal or retain men in slavery, we seize those who, in common with ourselves, are constituted, by the original grant, lords of the earth."

A good deal has been said and written about harsh language, but I think it would be difficult to find, in the writings of any modern Abolitionist, language more severe than this held by a religious assembly. Slaveholders are declared to be sinners of the first rank, man-stealers, worthy of capital punishment, guilty of the highest kind of theft. Prior to this action of the Presbyterian General Assembly, the Baptist Church in Virginia had declared itself opposed to slavery, and was actively at work in the cause of emancipation in that State. My assertion can be verified by referring to Semple's History of the rise and progress of the Baptists of Virginia:—

> "In the year 1783, a General Committee, composed of delegates from local associations, was instituted in Virginia, charged with 'considering matters that might be for the good of the whole Society.' It was especially the duty of this committee to be the medium through which the Baptists should address themselves to the Legislature, for redress of grievances, &c. At a meeting of this General Committee, March 7, 1788, delegates from four associations being present, among 'the religious political subjects' taken up was this:
>
> "'3d. Whether a petition should be offered to the General Assembly, praying that the yoke of slavery may be made more tolerable. Referred to the next session.'"

I do not discover that in the next session anything was done; but at the meeting of August 8, 1789, delegates from seven associations being present, the subject was considered, and the account is thus given by Semple, in his History of the Rise and Progress of the Baptists of Virginia, p. 79. He says:

> "'The propriety of hereditary slavery was also taken up at this session, and after some time employed in the consideration of the subject, the following resolution was offered by Mr. Seland and adopted:
>
> "'Resolved, That slavery is a violent deprivation of the rights of nature, and inconsistent with a republican government, and, therefore (we) recommend it to our brethren, to make use of every legal measure to extirpate this horrid evil from the

land; and pray Almighty God that our honorable Legislature may have it in their power to proclaim the great jubilee, consistent with the principles of good policy.' "

A fact like this could not be an isolated one; and there are incidental circumstances scattered in the history of those times which have come down to us, showing that the anti-slavery sentiment was widespread and effective.

To it I presume is to be attributed the rise of the powerful anti-slavery party, which for some time existed among the Baptists of Kentucky, known as Emancipators. For accounts of this party, I must refer you to Benedict's History of the Baptists, (edition of 1813,) vol. 2; pages 231, 235, 245, 250. This edition of Benedict's contains other allusions to the subject of slavery, which are interesting. You will find some account of the Emancipators of Kentucky, in the first volume of the Baptist Memorial, edited by Dr. Babcock, under the head 'Kentucky Baptists.' The Rev. Dr. Peck, of Illinois, has lately furnished, for the *New York Recorder,* articles on the Emancipators, which I will send you, if we have spare copies.

In the minutes of the Philadelphia Baptist Association, for the year 1789—the year of the passage of the above named resolution by the General Committee of Virginia—I find the following:—(See edition of the American Baptist Publication Society, edited by Rev. A. D. Gillette, p. 247.)

> " 'Agreeably to a recommendation in the letter from the Church at Baltimore, this Association declare their high approbation of the several Societies formed in the United States and Europe, for the gradual abolition of the slavery of the Africans, and for guarding against their being detained or sent off as slaves, after having obtained their liberty; and do hereby recommend to the churches as represent, to form similar Societies, to become members thereof, and exert themselves to obtain this important object.' "

I have the above from a distinguished Baptist, who, has fully investigated the subject; and I must express my deep gratitude for the assistance that gentleman has rendered me in the collection of these valuable facts, which, though well known to the Baptists of the country, are yet quite unknown to the public generally. Not having at my command the books to which he refers, I have preferred to incorporate his letter to me as it stands.

It is hardly necessary, in this connection, to refer to the Society of Friends, in these early times. All who know anything of them, know that they were emancipationists. That venerable Society had made Abolitionism a fundamental religious duty, long before the oldest Abolitionist, now living, was on the stage. Wherever that Society obtained a footing in this country, the work of amelioration went on. Slaves were emancipated, and the condition of the free people of color was improved. The broad brim, and the plain dress, were a terror to slaveholders, and a praise to the slave. When running from slavery, only seventeen years ago, I had not transferred my confidence from the Quakers to the Abolitionists. I believed in them for what they had done, years ago, for my race; and when the Abolitionists, of modern times, have done as much for freedom as the early Friends, they will not have to complain that the confidence of the colored people has been withdrawn from them. I now deny, in view of the facts of this history, that any man, now living, has any business to lay claim to the anti-slavery movement, as a thing of his invention, or of his discovery. We, who now work, have inherited, derived, received this movement from the churches of earlier times. Good men, who wrought before us, laid the foundation upon which we are building. All along the pages of the holy Bible, from Moses to John, may be found the constructive principles upon which this movement is based; and the organizers of the present anti-slavery societies, found here an inexhaustible mine of material, ready to be fused into that solid bolt, with which they now shake the land. It was here that Godwin, and Sharpe, and Clarkson, and Wilberforce, and Fox, and Benezet, and Wesley, and Woolman, forged the magnificent, moral armory, with which they began the mighty struggle, and with which Lundy, Walker, Garrison, and Leavitt, and Elizur Wright, and William Goodell, and Beriah Green, and the Tappans, and Gerrit Smith, and Judge Jay, have nobly continued until now. Honor to the memory of the departed, and honor to those who remain.

But what was the condition of the anti-slavery movement twenty years ago, and how came it in that condition? It is much easier to answer the first, than to answer the last question. There were witnesses for freedom in the church, but the church had become comparatively dead on the subject. The friends continued to work, though with flagging zeal. The other churches had become complicated with slavery, and the slave was forgotten by those who were once his friends. Lundy was at work for an anti-slavery revival, when Mr. Garrison joined him, and raised the note of immediate emancipation. Alas! for human frailty! and alas! for the poor slave. Present efforts may promise much, but we cannot but remember that one anti-slavery generation nearly died out without leaving men to take their places, and so may the present. The country which had been deploring the existence of slavery, and deeply desiring its abolition, had become like the world. The price of human flesh had risen, and man stealers had become gentlemen. This brings me to notice the revival of the anti-slavery movement twenty-five years ago. The country was soon in a blaze, as all know; yet, nothing strange happened to the early advocates of a cause, new to be sure, but only new by the new zeal and fresh eloquence brought to its service. The plainer the truth, and the more obvious the justice of the demand made, the more stern and bitter is the opposition; and for this reason, the plainer the truth, the brighter the prospect of its realization. The enunciation, and persistent proclamation of anti-slavery principles twenty-five years ago, demonstrate this. Never was there a cause more just—never one more peaceful and harmless in its character—never truths more self-evident. Immediate and unconditional emancipation was proclaimed, as the right of the slave, and as the duty of the slave-holder. This demand was enforced in the name, and according to the law of the living God. No sword, no bayonet, the simple truth uttered in the love of it. That is all.

> "Weapons of war we have cast from the battle
> Truth is our armor, our watchword is love;
> Hushed be the sword and the musketry's rattle,
> All our equipments are drawn from above."

The slave-holder was not, then, an object of hate and of execration. Had he gone into an abolition meeting, he would have been heard with patience and courtesy in his own defence. Yet, at this point, how was this cause met? How was it met by the American people, and how was it met by the church, to which latter, indeed, the movement owes its origin in this country, as well as in England?

The facts of this history are too recent, too notorious, and too fresh in the minds of all to need minute narration; and even if this were not so, it would scarcely be necessary to dwell long upon this aspect of the subject. Find out what happened on the presentation of any new truth, or any truth, which an age had lost sight of or discarded, and you are masters of the facts which attended the anti-slavery revival. As with the mission of the Savior of mankind, so with the anti-slavery movement. The latter could say, "had ye believed Moses, ye would have believed me." The new gospel of liberty was tried as by fire. The old folly was attempted, of crucifying the body to quench the spirit—of killing men to kill their principles. There was much trial in those early days. Lovejoy, a noble martyr, in defence of a free press and a free gospel, weltered in his warm blood at Alton. A brother of his, as true an Abolitionist, is now a member of the Legislature of the State, which received this bloody baptism. Crandal perished in prison at Washington, for having, and carrying a few anti-slavery papers in his portmanteau.[2] The *National Era* is now published there, and has the largest circulation of any paper at the seat of Government. Mr. Garrison was dragged through the streets of Boston by a mob, and took refuge in the common jail;[3] and is now, comparatively, a popular man in that city, surrounded by friends, rich, and powerful.

But to drop the present, and to refer exclusively to the past. The country was like a savage drunkard, roused from his slumbers. Speaking and writing on the subject of slavery became dangerous. Mob violence menaced the persons and property of the Abolitionists, and their very homes became unsafe for themselves and their families. Boston, New York, and Philadelphia, Cincinnati, and Utica, were under mob law. Pennsylvania Hall was burned with fire, because it had given shelter to the hunted spirit of liberty for a few brief hours. As to the free colored people, a more than demoniacal hate was roused against them—assault and insult came down upon them without measure, and without mixture, and a wild and clamorous cry of blood! blood! came howling over all the broad savannahs of the South.

> Then to side with truth is noble, when we share her wretched crust,
> Ere her cause bring fame and profit, and 'tis prosperous to be just;
> Then it is the brave man chooses, while the coward stands aside,
> Doubting in his abject spirit, till his Lord is crucified;
> And the multitude make virtue of the faith they had denied.

Someone has called the period to which I have been referring, "the martyr age of anti-slavery;" and not having been an actor in those scenes, I may properly admire—as who could do other than admire—the manly heroism displayed by the Abolitionists at this trying point of their experience.

Like true apostles, as they were, their faith in their principles knew no wavering. The heathen raged, and the people imagined a vain thing. Conventions were broken up, only to be held again; presses were demolished, to be erected again. The anti-slavery lecturer was pelted from one town, only to flee into another; and the new faith of the prophets waxed stronger and stronger. For every advocate struck down, ten new ones stood up. With them, obstacles were converted into facilities—hindrances into helps—curtailments into increase—and curses into blessings. If you will turn to the letters and speeches of that period, you will find that they burn with love to the *slave,* as a wronged, and bitterly abused fellow-man. His sorrows and sufferings were the burden of early anti-slavery eloquence. It was remembering the bondman as bound with him; and the thought that their suffering as freemen, was as nothing compared to that of their enslaved brother, which enabled the early Abolitionists of this country to preserve, and to make a deep impression on the hearts of men. Mr. Garrison had been so true to the slave, that when in England he was supposed to be, till seen, a veritable *Negro.* He was proud of it then, and spoke of it in proof of his faithfulness. I shall be pardoned if I say, he would scarcely consider this mission complimentary to him now. I have now glanced at the reception which the anti-slavery revival met at the hands of the world. Now, let us see how it was received by the Church. Besides the early anti-slavery position of the Church, to which I have already directed attention, there were special reasons for anticipating a better reception at the hands of the Church, than it had received at the hands of the cold and selfish world. The American Churches stood already committed to causes, analogous in their spirit and purpose to the anti-slavery cause. The heathen in Asia, Africa, and in the isles of the sea, were not only remembered by the Church, but were objects of special, earnest, and energetic exertion. Prayers, and contribution boxes, were abundant for these, to save them from the bondage of sin and superstition. Our Church sent bibles and missionaries "from the rivers to the ends of the earth." Under its outspread wings, were warmly sheltered the Missionary Society, the Tract Society, the Sabbath School Society, and innumerable sewing societies, composed of honorable women connected with the Church. These were all, apparently, animated by an honest desire to improve the condition of the human race, in other and distant lands. I say, therefore, it was both reasonable and natural to expect a better reception for the anti-slavery cause from the church than from the world.

And, yet again, there was something in the condition of the enslaved millions at our own doors, which appealed directly to the Church, supposing the heart of the Church to beat in unison with the heart of the Son of God. At the very outset of his mission among the children of men, he was careful to range himself on the side of the poor, the enslaved, and heart-broken victims of oppression.

"The spirit of the Lord is upon me," said the great one, who spake as never man spake, "because he hath anointed me to preach the Gospel to the poor. He hath sent me to bind up the broken-hearted—to preach deliverance to the captive, and recovery of sight to the blind; to set at liberty them that are bruised."

The Abolitionist could point to this sublime declaration of the Son of God, and then point to the millions of enslaved, captured, bruised, maimed, and heart-broken people, whose cries of anguish ascend to God continually—and this they did. They carried those bleeding and heart-broken millions—poor, helpless and forlorn—to the very altar of the Church; and cried, "men of Israel, help!" They described their physical suffering—their mental, moral debasement, and destitution; and said to the Church: "In the name of mercy open unto us." An angel of mercy, with benignant aspect, and streaming eyes, stood at the door of the Church, veiled in deep sorrow, imploring, entreating, in the name of God, and down-trodden man, for entrance; but those who held the key, repulsed her with iron bolts. The cry for mercy disturbed the worship and it drove the angel away, and went on praying. But this is not all. In imitation, perhaps, of the example set by the world, the Church not only rejected, but became an active persecutor of the anti-slavery movement. She sent forth some of her ablest champions to battle against it. The Holy Bible, which had furnished arguments against slave-holding seventy years ago, was found to contain now the best arguments for slavery.

So recently as the year 1850, she rained down millions of sermons, to prove it right to hunt slaves, and consign them to life-long bondage. The Methodist Church which, in its infancy and purity held so high a position, forgot her ancient testimonies; and led off, in a grand crusade, to put down the anti-slavery movement. It undertook to censure and silence such of its members as believed with John Wesley; that slavery is the sum of all villainies. In what striking, strange and painful contrast are the resolutions adopted at Cincinnati by the General Conference, in 1836, with those adopted by the same Conference in 1801. Here they are, preamble and all:—

> "*Whereas* great excitement has prevailed in this country on the subject of modern abolitionism, which is reported to have been increased in this city, by the unjustifiable conduct of two members of the General Conference, in lecturing upon, and in favor of that agitating topic; and whereas such a course on the part of any of its members is calculated to bring upon this body the suspicion and distrust of the community, and to misrepresent its sentiments in regard to the point at issue; and whereas, in this aspect of the case, a due regard for its character, as well as just concern for the interests of the Church confided to its care, demand a full, decided, and unequivocal expression of the views of the General Conference in the premises; therefore,
>
> "*Resolved,* 1st. By the delegates of the Annual Conference, in General Conference assembled, that they disapprove in the most unqualified sense of the conduct of the two members of the General Conference, who are reported to have lectured in this city recently, upon and in favor of that agitating topic.
>
> "*Resolved,* 2d. By the delegates of the Annual Conference, in General Conference assembled, that they are decidedly opposed to Modem Abolitionism; and wholly disclaim any right, wish or intention to interfere in the civil and political relation between master and slave, as it exists in the States of this Union."

Here, then, was an entire change in the attitude of the Methodist Episcopal Church, on the subject of slavery. The traffickers in the bodies and souls of men were set at ease in her Zion; and the victims of the bloody lash were literally driven from her gates.

As went the Methodist Episcopal Church, so went the Baptist and Presbyterian Churches. They receded from their anti-slavery ground; despised the claims of the movement, which their earlier and holier precepts and example had called into being. The Churches which began their career in love for the oppressed, had now become the friends of the oppressor, and the bulwark of slavery.

Here arose that crisis in the anti-slavery movement, from the evil effects of which it has not yet recovered. It will never be forgotten. The conflict was terrible to all concerned, flinging the Church against man, and some of the advocates of emancipation against God. The Church stepped between the slave's chains, and the uplifted blow aimed to break them. The alternative presented was to oppose the Church, or abandon the slave! Here were religion and slavery on the one hand, and freedom and humanity on the other. The Church raised the cry of infidelity, and her opponents laughed at her forms and ceremonies, and poured contempt upon her prayers. The Church cherished her forms all the more for being assailed, and the advocates of emancipation clung the more to anti-slavery, because it was assailed by the Church, and thus unbelief and irreligion are seen thickest where this battle has raged hottest. The Church, by her professions, should have been the right arm and shield of this beneficent movement; but alas! she proved false to her trust, abandoned her right mission of striking down slavery, and attempted to strike down liberty. The slave, under the uplifted lash of the taskmaster, quivering with fear, and imploring mercy, could no longer look to the Church for succor. The buyers and sellers of men were welcomed to her bosom, and the slave, in his chains, was driven away.

Is it strange, then, that those who once loved, began now to loathe the Church? Is it strange, that their faith, in her regard for the souls of men, should wane when they saw her shameless contempt for the bodies of men? Could they believe that she loved God truly, who hated the image of God so intensely? Had the Church of this country welcomed this movement, as a long lost child, which had stayed away from its home, in the church—had she given to it the endorsement of her name, adopted it as her own, lent to it the aid of her coöperation, the influence of her example—had she given it the facilities of her widespread organization, the support of her press, and the might of her eloquence, the great battle of liberty would, long ere this, have been decided. The slave's chains would have been broken into a thousand fragments, and millions, now pining in bondage, would have been rejoicing in their liberty. Not only was here lost a splendid opportunity for blessing the world, but a golden opportunity was lost for bringing honor to the name of the Church, and reverence to her ministry. A new occasion, a new harvest, was given unto her, which she might have gathered and garnered up for the days of drought and moral famine, which have since rolled over her. An invincible army of sable soldiers, with ample means to scourge and drive back the allied host of infidelity and atheism now marching against her, were foolishly and wickedly left in chains. Three millions of joyful hearts, clapping their glad hands in freedom, ascribing their great deliverance from thraldom to the beneficent interposition of the Church of God, would have thundered into silence the clamor of scoffers, and made her name glorious throughout the world.

But she flung away the golden chance, and is now exposed not only to the assaults of sin, but on her hands, is a more solemn controversy. The attacks of unbelief are not so galling as the fire from the ramparts of justice and humanity. Not only has the slave been converted into an enemy of the Church, and taught to look elsewhere for succor and deliverance, but the sober thinking philanthropist has been led to raise the dangerous enquiry—Of what use to this sin-cursed world is a church, whose religion and gospel are the dread of the oppressed and the delight of the oppressor? This aspect of this history is of the profoundest significance and deserves to be pondered on. The usefulness, and the very existence of the Church, as an organization, are involved in the use made of this subject. Let the Church look to it. Organizations are strong, but there is something in the world much stronger than any human organization. The eternal spirit is mightier than all the external world; religion is greater than the form created to express it. Forms and organizations are but the "*mint,*" "*annis*" and "*cummin.*" The weightier matters of the law are judgment, mercy and faith; and the latter are with the oppressed and enslaved everywhere. Forms and ceremonies may pass current for a time; but there is too much love among mankind for what is real, true and genuine, to endure always what is empty, hollow and hypocritical. It won't do for the Church to weep over the heathen abroad, and laugh over the heathen at home. It will not do to send Bibles and missionaries to India, with money wrung from the blood and sweat of the heathen of South Carolina and Georgia, to whom we prohibit, under pains and penalties, the privilege of learning to read the name of Almighty God! It will not do to save souls abroad, and enslave souls at home. Let the Church, then, look to it, for here is the source of her weakness, attracting, as well from the sky of truth, as from the clouds of error, the exterminating bolt and the devouring fire. Her new moons, appointed feasts, Sabbath days, solemn assemblies, are no atonement for refusing to do justice. She is under the law to cease to do evil, and learn to do well. She must seek justice and relieve the oppressed. In a word, she must abolish slavery, or be abolished by slavery. The voice of one crying in the wilderness, has the same lesson to-day as in the days of Jesus. The axe is laid at the root of the tree. Usefulness is the price of existence. Do or die, wear out or rust out, bring forth fruit or be cut down, is the law now and always. Men may go often, but they will not go always to an exhausted fountain; they will not long search for substance where they are only rewarded with shadows. If they do not find God and his eternal attributes among the solemn splendors of the Church, they will turn away from its altars and aisles, and go forth into the temple of God's creation, and strive to interpret for themselves the heavenly inscriptions of divine love.

Many who once stood with delight in the Church, apart from the world, go not up with the great congregation to worship now; and they tell us the Church must make peace with the slave before it can make peace with God. She must bring back the child of her early love, from the wandering exile into which she has driven it. She must return to her early testimonies, and teach the oppressor now, as at the beginning, to "break every yoke, and let the oppressed go free," and gather around her the affections of those who esteem mercy more than sacrifice.

Let us now turn away from the Church, and examine the anti-slavery movement in its branches, for divisions are here, as well as elsewhere. I will not enter into an examination of their causes. God forbid! that I should open here those bitter fountains. I may say, however, that the first grand division took place fourteen years ago, and on the very minor question—Shall a woman be a member of a committee in company with men? The majority said she should be; and the minority seceded. Thus was a grand philanthropic movement rent asunder by a side issue, having nothing, whatever, to do with the great object which the American

Anti-Slavery Society was organized to carry forward. Before I would have stood in such an attitude, and taken the responsibility of dividing the ranks of freedom's army, I would have suffered my right arm to be taken off. How beautiful would it have been for that woman, how nobly would her name have come down to us in this history, had she said: "All things are lawful for me, but all things are not expedient! While I see no objection to my occupying a place on your committee, I can for the slave's sake forego that privilege. The battle of Woman's Rights should be fought on its own ground; as it is, the slave's cause, already too heavy laden, had to bear up under this new addition; but I will not go further on that subject, except to characterize it as a sad mistake."

But I propose to speak of the different anti-slavery sects and parties, and to give my view of them very briefly. There are four principal divisions.

1st. The Garrisonians, or the American Anti-Slavery Society.

2d. The Anti-Garrisonians, or the American and Foreign Anti-Slavery Society.

3d. The Free Soil Party, or Political Abolitionists.

4th. The Liberty Party, or Gerrit Smith School of Abolitionists.

There are others, and among them those conscientious men and women, principally of the Society of Friends, who may be called *"free labor people"*—since their remedy for slavery is an abstinence from slave produce. This Society formerly published in Philadelphia a periodical, called "The Non-Slaveholder," and kept open a store for the sale of free labor goods; and besides this, it promoted the growth of free cotton in several of the more Southern States. This Society is still in existence, and is quietly doing its work.[4]

I shall consider, first, the Garrisonian Anti-Slavery Society. I call this the Garrisonian Society, because Mr. Garrison is, confessedly, its leader. This Society is the oldest of modern Anti-Slavery Societies. It has, strictly speaking, two weekly papers, or organs—employs five or six lecturers—and holds numerous public meetings for the dissemination of its views. Its peculiar and distinctive feature is, its doctrine of *"no union with slaveholders."* This doctrine has, of late, become its bond of union, and the condition of good fellowship among its members. Of this Society, I have to say, its logical result is but negatively, anti-slavery. Its doctrine, of "no union with slaveholders," carried out, dissolves the Union, and leaves the slaves and their masters to fight their own battles, in their own way. This I hold to be an abandonment of the great idea with which that Society started. It started to free the slave. It ends by leaving the slave to free himself. It started with the purpose to imbue the heart of the nation with sentiments favorable to the abolition of slavery, and ends by seeking to free the North from all responsibility of slavery, other than if slavery were in Great Britain, or under some other nationality. This, I say, is the practical abandonment of the idea, with which that Society started. It has given up the faith, that the slave can be freed short of the overthrow of the Government; and then, as I understand that Society, it leaves the slaves, as it must needs leave them, just where it leaves the slaves of Cuba, or those of Brazil. The nation, as such, is given up as beyond the power of salvation by the foolishness of preaching; and hence, the aim is now to save the North; so that the American Anti-Slavery Society, which was inaugurated to convert the nation, after ten years' struggle, parts with its faith, and aims now to save the North. One of the most eloquent of all the members of that Society, and the man who is only second to Mr. Garrison himself, defines the Garrisonian doctrine thus:

> "All the slave asks of us, is to stand out of his way, withdraw our pledge to keep the peace on the plantation; withdraw our pledge to return him; withdraw that representation which the Constitution gives in proportion to the number of slaves, and without any agitation here, without any individual virtue, which the times have eaten out of us, God will vindicate the oppressed, by the laws of justice which he has founded. Trample under foot your own unjust pledges, break to pieces your compact with hell by which you become the abettors of oppression. Stand alone, and let no cement of the Union bind the slave, and he will right himself."

That is it. "Stand alone;" the slave is to "right himself." I dissent entirely from this reasoning. It assumes to be true what is plainly absurd, and that is, that a population of slaves, without arms, without means of concert, and without leisure, is more than a match for double its number, educated, accustomed to rule, and in every way prepared for warfare, offensive or defensive. This Society, therefore, consents to leave the slave's freedom to a most uncertain and improbable, if not an impossible, contingency.

But, "*no union with slaveholders.*"

As a mere expression of abhorrence of slavery, the sentiment is a good one; but it expresses no intelligible principle of action, and throws no light on the pathway of duty. Defined, as its authors define it, it leads to false doctrines, and mischievous results. It condemns Gerrit Smith for sitting in Congress, and our Savior for eating with publicans and sinners. Dr. Spring uttered a shocking sentiment, when he said, if one prayer of his would emancipate every slave, he would not offer that prayer. No less shocking is the sentiment of the leader of the disunion forces, when he says, that if one vote of his would emancipate every slave in this country, he would not cast that vote. Here, on a bare theory, and for a theory which, if consistently adhered to, would drive a man out of the world— a theory which can never be made intelligible to common sense—the freedom of the whole slave population would be sacrificed.

But again: "no union with slaveholders." I dislike the morality of this sentiment, in its application to the point at issue. For instance: A. unites with B. in stealing my property, and carrying it away to California, or to Australia, and, while there, Mr. A. becomes convinced that he did wrong in stealing my property, and says to Mr. B., "no union with property stealers," and abandons him, leaving the property in his hands. Now, I put it to this audience, has Mr. A., in this transaction, met the requirements of stringent morality? He, certainly, has not. It is not only his duty to separate from the thief, but to restore the stolen property to its rightful owner. And I hold that in the Union, this very thing of restoring to the slave his long-lost rights, can better be accomplished than it can possibly be accomplished outside of the Union. This, then, is my answer to the motto, "No union with slaveholders."

But this is not the worst fault of this Society. Its chief energies are expended in confirming the opinion, that the United States Constitution is, and was, intended to be a slave-holding instrument—thus piling up, between the slave and his freedom, the huge work of the abolition of the Government, as an indispensable condition to emancipation. My point here is, first, the Constitution is, according to its reading, an anti-slavery document; and, secondly, to dissolve the Union, as a means to abolish slavery, is about as wise as it would be to burn up this city, in order to get the thieves out of it. But again, we hear the motto, "no union with slaveholders;" and I answer it, as that noble champion of liberty, N. P. Rogers, answered it with a more sensible motto, namely—"No union with slaveholding." I would unite with anybody to do right; and with nobody to do wrong. And as the Union, under the Constitution, requires me to do nothing which is wrong, and gives me many facilities for doing good, I cannot go with the American Anti-Slavery Society in its doctrine of disunion.

But to the second branch of the anti-slavery movement. The American and Foreign Anti-Slavery Society has not yet departed from the original ground, but stands where the American Anti-Slavery Society stood at the beginning. The energies of this association are mainly directed to the revival of anti-slavery in the Church. It is active in the collection, and in the circulation of facts, exposing the character of slavery, and in noting the evidences of progress in the Church on the subject. It does not aim to abolish the Union, but aims to avail itself of the means afforded by the Union to abolish slavery. The Annual Report of this Society affords the amplest and truest account of the anti-slavery movement, from year to year. Nevertheless, I am somewhat against this Society, as well as against the American Anti-Slavery Society. It has almost dropped the main and most potent weapon with which slavery is to be assailed and overthrown, and that is speech. At this moment, when every nerve should be strained to prevent a reaction, that Society has not a single lecturing agent in the field.

The next recognized anti-slavery body is the Free Soil party, alias—the Free Democratic party, alias—the Republican party. It aims to limit and denationalize slavery, and to relieve the Federal Government from all responsibility for slavery. Its motto is, "*Slavery Local—Liberty National.*" The objection to this movement is the same as that against the American Anti-Slavery Society. It leaves the slaves in his fetters—in the undisturbed possession of his master, and does not grapple with the question of emancipation in the States.

The fourth division of the anti-slavery movement is, the "*Liberty Party*"—a small body of citizens, chiefly in the State of New York, but having sympathizers all over the North. It is the radical, and to my thinking, the *only* abolition organization in the country, except a few local associations. It makes a clean sweep of slavery everywhere. It denies that slavery is, or *can* be legalized. It denies that the Constitution of the United States is a pro-slavery instrument, and asserts the power and duty of the Federal Government to abolish slavery in every State of the Union. Strictly speaking, I say this is the only party in the country which is an abolition party. The mission of the Garrisonians ends with the dissolution of the Union—that of the Free Soil party ends with the relief of the Federal Government from all responsibility for slavery; but the Liberty Party, by its position and doctrines, and by its antecedents, is pledged to continue the struggle while a bondman in his chains remains to weep. Upon its platform must the great battle of freedom be fought out—if upon any short of the bloody field. It must be under no partial cry of "no union with slaveholders;" nor selfish cry of "no more slavery extension;" but it must be, "no slavery for man under the whole heavens." The slave as a man and a brother, must be the vital and animating thought and impulse of any movement, which is to effect the abolition of slavery in this country. Our anti-slavery organizations must be brought back to this doctrine, or they will be scattered and left to wander, and to die in the wilderness, like God's ancient people, till another generation shall come up, more worthy to go up and possess the land.

One anti-slavery movement nearly died out fifty years ago, and I am not prepared to deny the possibility of a like fate for this one. The elements of discord and deterioration are already in it, and working their legitimate results. And yet I am not gloomy. Present organizations may perish, but the cause will go on. That cause has a life, distinct and independent of the organizations patched up from time to time to carry it forward. Looked at apart from the bones and sinews, and body, it is a thing immortal. It is the very essence of justice, liberty and love. The moral life of human society—it cannot die, while conscience, honor and humanity remain. If but one be filled with it, the cause lives. Its incarnation in any one individual man, leaves the whole world a priesthood, occupying the highest moral eminence—even that of disinterested benevolence. Whoso has ascended this height, and has the grace to stand there, has the world at his feet, and is the world's teacher, as of divine right. He may sit in judgment on the age, upon the civilization of the age, and upon the religion of the age; for he has a test, a sure and certain test, by which to try all institutions, and to measure all men. I say, he may do this, but this is not the chief business for which he is qualified. The great work to which he is called is not that of judgment. Like the Prince of Peace, he may say, if I judge, I judge righteous judgment; still mainly, like him, he may say, this is not his work. The man who has thoroughly embraced the principles of justice, love, and liberty, like the true preacher of Christianity, is less anxious to reproach the world of its sins, than to win it to repentance. His great work on earth is to exemplify, and to illustrate, and to engraft those principles upon the living and practical understandings of all men within the reach of his influence. This is his work; long or short his years, many or few his adherents, powerful or weak his instrumentalities, through good report, or through bad report, this is his work. It is to snatch from the bosom of nature the latent facts of each individual man's experience, and with steady hand to hold them up fresh and glowing, enforcing, with all his power, their acknowledgment and practical adoption. If there be but *one* such man in the land, no matter what becomes of abolition societies and parties, there will be an anti-slavery cause, and an anti-slavery movement. Fortunately for that cause, and fortunately for him by whom it is espoused, it requires no extraordinary amount of talent to preach it or to receive it when preached. The grand secret of its power is, that each of its principles is easily rendered appreciable to the faculty of reason in man, and that the most unenlightened conscience has no difficulty in deciding on which side to register its testimony. It can call its preachers from among the fishermen, and raise them to power. In every human breast, it has an advocate which can be silent only when the heart is dead. It comes home to every man's understanding, and appeals directly to every man's conscience. A man that does not recognize and approve for himself the rights and privileges contended for, in behalf of the American slave, has not yet been found. In whatever else men may differ, they are alike in the apprehension of their natural and personal rights. The difference between abolitionists, and those by whom they are opposed, is not as to principles. All are agreed in respect to these. The manner of applying them is the point of difference.

The slave-holder himself, the daily robber of his equal brother, discourses eloquently as to the excellency of justice, and the man who employs a brutal driver to flay the flesh of his Negroes, is not offended when kindness and humanity are commended. Every time the abolitionist speaks of justice, the anti-abolitionist assents—says, yes, I wish the world were filled with the disposition to render to every man what is rightfully due him. I should then get what is due me. That's right; let us have justice. By all means, let us have justice. Every time the abolitionist speaks in honor of human liberty, he touches a chord in the heart of the anti-abolitionist, which responds in harmonious vibrations. Liberty—yes, that is very evidently my right, and let him beware who attempts to invade or abridge that right. Every time he speaks of love, of human brotherhood, and the reciprocal duties of man and man, the anti-abolitionist assents—says, yes, all right— all true—we cannot have such ideas too often, or too fully expressed. So he says, and so he feels, and only shows thereby that he is a man as well as an anti-abolitionist. You have only to keep out of sight the manner of applying your principles, to get them endorsed every time. Contemplating himself he sees truth with absolute clearness and distinctness. He only blunders when asked to lose sight of himself. In his own cause he can beat a Boston lawyer, but he is dumb when asked to plead the cause of others. He knows very well, whatsoever he would have done unto himself, but is quite in doubt as to having the same things done unto others. It is just here that lions spring up in the path of duty, and the battle once fought in heaven is refought on the earth. So, it is, so hath it ever been, and so must it ever be, when the claims of justice and mercy make their demand at the door of human selfishness. Nevertheless, there is that within which ever pleads for the right and the just.

In conclusion, I have taken a sober view of the present anti-slavery movement. I am sober, but not hopeless. There is no denying, for it is everywhere admitted, that the anti-slavery question is the great moral and social question now before the American people. A state of things has gradually been developed, by which that question has become the first thing in order. It has got to be met. Herein is my hope. The great idea of impartial liberty is now fairly before the American people. Anti-slavery is no longer a thing to be prevented. The time for prevention is past. This is great gain. When the movement was younger and weaker— when it wrought in a Boston garret to human apprehension, it might have been silently put out of the way. Things are different now. It has grown too abundant—its ramifications too extended—its power too omnipotent, to be snuffed out by the contingencies of infancy. A thousand strong men might be struck down and its ranks still be invincible. One flash from the heart-supplied intellect of Harriet Beecher Stowe could light a million camp fires in front of the embattled hosts of slavery, which, not all the waters of the Mississippi, mingled as they are, with blood, could extinguish. The present will be looked to by after coming generations, as the age of anti-slavery literature—when supply on the gallop could not keep pace with the ever growing demand—when a picture of a Negro on the cover a help to the sale of a book—when conservative lyceums and other American literary associations began first to select their orators for distinguished occasions, from the ranks of the previously despised Abolitionists. If the anti-slavery movement shall fail now, it will not be from outward opposition, but from inward decay. Its auxiliaries are everywhere. Scholars, authors, orators, poets, and statesmen, give it their aid. The most brilliant of American poets volunteer in its service. Whittier speaks in burning verse, to more than thirty thousand, in the *National Era*. Your own Longfellow whispers, in every hour of trial and disappointment, "labor and wait." James Russell Lowell is reminding us, that "men are more than institutions." Pierpont cheers the heart of the pilgrim in search of liberty, by singing the praises of "the north star." Bryant, too, is with us; and though chained to the car of party, and dragged on amidst a whirl of political excitement, he snatches a moment for letting drop a smiling verse of sympathy for the man in chains. The poets are with us. It would seem almost absurd to say it, considering the use that has been made of them, that we have allies in the Ethiopian songs; those songs that constitute our national music, and without which we have no national music. They are heart songs, and the finest feelings of human nature are expressed in them. "Lucy Neal," "Old Kentucky Home," and "Uncle Ned," can make the heart sad as well as merry, and can call forth a tear as well as a smile. They awaken the sympathies for the slave, in which anti-slavery principles take root, grow and flourish. In addition to authors, poets, and scholars at home, the moral sense of the civilized world is with us. England, France, and Germany, the three great lights of modern civilization, are with us, and every American traveller learns to regret the existence of slavery in his country. The growth of intelligence, the influence of commerce, steam, wind, and lightning, are our allies. It would be easy to amplify this summary, and to swell the vast conglomeration of our material forces; but there is a deeper and truer method of measuring the power of our cause, and of comprehending its vitality. This is to be found in its accordance with the best elements of human nature. It is beyond the power of slavery to annihilate affinities recognized and established by the Almighty. The slave is bound to mankind, by the powerful and inextricable net-work of human brotherhood. His voice is the voice of a man, and his cry is the cry of a man in distress, and man must cease to be man before he can become insensible to that cry. It is the righteousness of the cause—the humanity of the cause—which constitutes its potency. As one genuine bank bill is worth more than a thousand counterfeits, so is one man, with right on his side, worth more than a thousand in the wrong. "One may chase a thousand, and put ten thousand to flight." It is, therefore, upon the goodness of our cause, more than upon all other auxiliaries, that we depend for its final triumph.

Another source of congratulation is the fact that, amid all the efforts made by the Church, the Government, and the people at large, to stay the onward progress of this movement, its course has been onward, steady, straight, unshaken, and unchecked from the beginning. Slavery has gained victories, large and numerous; but never, as against this movement—against a temporizing policy, and against Northern timidity, the slave power has been victorious; but against the spread and prevalence in the country, of a spirit of resistance to its aggression, and of sentiments favorable to its entire overthrow, it has yet accomplished nothing. Every measure, yet devised and executed, having for its object the suppression of anti-slavery, has been as idle and fruitless as pouring oil to extinguish fire. A general rejoicing took place, on the passage of "the Compromise Measures" of 1850. Those measures were called peace measures, and were afterwards termed by both the great parties of the country, as well as by leading statesmen, a final settlement of the whole question of slavery; but experience has laughed to scorn the wisdom of pro-slavery statesmen; and their final settlement of agitation seems to be the final revival, on a broader and grander scale than ever before, of the question which they vainly attempted to suppress forever. The Fugitive Slave Bill has especially been of positive service to the anti-slavery movement. It has illustrated before all the people the horrible character of slavery toward the slave, in hunting him down in a free State, and tearing him away from wife and children, thus setting its claims higher than marriage or parental claims. It has revealed the arrogant and over-bearing spirit of the slave States towards the free States; despising their principles—shocking their feelings of humanity, not only by bringing before them the abominations of slavery, but by attempting to make them parties to the crime. It has called into exercise among the colored people, the hunted ones, a spirit of manly resistance well calculated to surround them with a bulwark of sympathy and respect hitherto unknown. For men are always disposed to respect and defend rights, when the victims of oppression stand up manfully for themselves.

There is another element of power added to the anti-slavery movement of great importance; it is the conviction, becoming every day more general and universal, that slavery must be abolished in the South, or it will demoralize and destroy liberty in the North. It is the nature of slavery to beget a state of things all around it, favorable to its own continuance. This fact connected with the system of bondage, is beginning to be more fully realized. The slave-holder is not satisfied to associate with men in the Church or in the State, unless he can thereby stain them with the blood of his slaves. To be a slave-holder, is to be a propagandist from necessity; for slavery can only live by keeping down the undergrowth morality which nature supplies. Every new-born white babe comes armed from the Eternal presence, to make war on slavery. The heart of pity, which would melt in due time over the brutal chastisements it sees inflicted on the helpless, must be hardened. And this work goes on every day in the year, and every hour in the day.

What is done at home, is being done also abroad here in the North. And even now the question may be asked, have we at this moment a single free State in the Union? The alarm at this point will become more general. The slave power must go on in its career of exactions. Give, give, will be its cry, till the timidity which concedes shall give place to courage, which shall resist. Such is the voice of experience, such has been the past, such is the present, and such will be that future, which, so sure as man is man, will come. Here I leave the subject; and I leave off where I began, consoling myself and congratulating the friends of freedom upon the fact that the anti-slavery cause is not a new thing under the sun; not some moral delusion which a few years' experience may dispel. It has appeared among men in all ages, and summoned its advocates from all ranks. Its foundations are laid in the deepest and holiest convictions, and from whatever soul the demon, selfishness, is expelled, there will this cause take up its abode. Old as the ever-lasting hills; immovable as the throne of God; and certain as the purposes of eternal power against all hindrances, and against all delays, and despite all the mutations of human instrumentalities, it is the faith of my soul that this Anti-Slavery cause will triumph.

Ladies and gentlemen, I am not superstitious, but I recognize an arm stronger than any human arm, and an intelligence higher than any human intelligence, guarding and guiding this Anti-Slavery cause, through all the dangers and perils that beset it, and making even auxiliaries of enemies, and confounding all worldly wisdom for its advancement. Let us trust that arm—let us confide in that intelligence—in conducting this movement; and whether it shall be ours to witness the fulfilment of our hopes, the end of American slavery or not, we shall have the tranquil satisfaction of having faithfully adhered to eternal principles of rectitude, and may lay down life in the triumphant faith, that those principles will, ultimately, prevail.

The Anti-Slavery Movement. A lecture by Frederick Douglass, before the Rochester Ladies' Anti-Slavery Society, Rochester, 1855

1. William Lloyd Garrison made this statement in December, 1853, in the course of his controversy with Douglass. (See *Liberator,* Dec. 16, 1853; *National Anti-Slavery Standard,* Dec. 24, 1853.)

2. Dr. Reuben Crandall went to Washington in 1835 to lecture on the natural sciences. While engaged in this work, he received some packages, wrapped in newspapers, among which were a few copies of the *Emancipator* and of the *Anti-Slavery Reporter.* These papers were circulated unwittingly by someone who obtained them from Dr. Crandall, and lead to the latter's arrest. Dr. Crandall was forced to remain in jail for nearly eight months before he was brought to trial and acquitted.

3. In 1835 the English Abolitionist George Thompson came to the United States on a lecture tour. On October 21, the Boston Female Anti-Slavery Society held a meeting, at which a mob of several thousand persons assembled, expecting to tar-and-feather Thompson. The latter, however, had been warned, and the crowd, searching for a victim, seized Garrison, dragged him with a rope around his neck through the street, and would probably have lynched him if Mayor Theodore Lyman had not intervened. Garrison spent the night in the Leverett Street jail and in the morning left the city for several weeks.

4. The Free Produce Movement was the attempt to strike at the slaveholding system by a boycott upon the products of slave labor. Since free produce societies had a membership of only about fifteen hundred, most of whom were Quakers, and probably not more than five or six thousand people tried to purchase free labor goods, it is obvious that the movement could not be very successful. Douglass, however, strongly endorsed the free produce cause, considering it as rendering an important moral impetus to the struggle against slavery. (See Ruth Ketring Neuerinburger, "The Free Produce Movement: A Quaker Protest Against Slavery," *Historical Papers of the Trinity College Historical Society,* Series XXV, Duke University Press, 1942.)

TO HON. CHAS. SUMNER

Rochester, April 24, 1855

My dear Sir:

There were two points in your address,[1] which grated a little on my ear at the moment, and which I would have called to your attention immediately after its delivery in Rochester had opportunity permitted. The first claimed that Mr. Garrison originated the present Anti-Slavery movement—a claim which I do not regard as well grounded, and I think I have succeeded in showing this in a lecture recently delivered in Rochester and in several other places during the past winter. Mr. Garrison found the Anti-Slavery movement already in existence when he stepped to the side of Benjamin Lundy in Baltimore. The second point was your very guarded disclaimer touching the social elevation of the colored race. It seemed to me that considering the obstinate and persecuting character of American prejudice against color, and the readiness with which those who entertain it avail themselves of every implication in its favor, your remark on that point was unfortunate.

I may be a little sensitive on the subject of our social position. I think I have become more so of late, because I have detected, in some of my old comrades, something like a falling away from their first love, touching the recognition of the entire manhood and social equality of the colored people. I do not mean by this, that every colored man, without regard to his character or attainments, shall be recognized as socially equal to white people who are in these respects superior to him; but I do mean to say that the simple fact of *color* should not be the criterion by which to ascertain or to fix the social station of any. Let every man, without regard to color, go wherever his character and abilities naturally carry him. And further, let there be no public opinion already to repel any who are in these respects fit for high social position.

For my own individual part as a colored man, I have little of which to complain. I have found myself *socially* higher than I am placed politically. The most debased white man in New York is my superior at the ballot box, but not so in a social point of view. In the one case color is the standard of fitness or unfitness; in the other, character.

I thank you heartily, my dear Sir, for honoring me with the opportunity of dropping these suggestions for your perusal.

With the spirit and manner of your noble address, I was not only pleased but profoundly gratified, and I thank God that talents and acquirements so high as yours, are devoted to the service of my crushed and bleeding race.

Believe me, my dear Sir,
Your faithful and grateful friend,
Frederick Douglass

Charles Sumner Papers, Harvard University

1. For the text of the lecture entitled, "The Necessity, the Practicability and the Dignity of the Anti-Slavery Enterprise," see *The Works of Charles Sumner*, vol. IV, pp. 1–51. See also Douglass' editorial on Sumner's speech in *Frederick Douglass' Paper*, June 1, 1855.

THE TRUE GROUND UPON WHICH TO MEET SLAVERY

If one half of the time, talent and money, which has been spent in attempts to fix upon the Constitution of the United States, a pro-slavery interpretation, had been devoted to showing its anti-slavery character, and in pointing out the duty of the citizen and statesman to abolish slavery under the Constitution, the anti-slavery cause would be in a far more hopeful condition than it now is. Never, in our judgment, will the North be roused to intelligent and efficient action against slavery, until it shall become the settled conviction of the people, that slavery is anarchical, unconstitutional, and wholly incapable of legalization. While men admit that slavery can be lawful anywhere, they concede that it may be made lawful everywhere; the morality which concedes the legality of slavery in Missouri, is impotent as against slavery in Kansas or anywhere else.—Slavery cannot be legal and illegal at the same time. It cannot be constitutional and unconstitutional at the same time. Grant that the constitution recognizes the right of slaveholders to their slaves in any State of this Union; and all the laws of comity, good neighborhood, and good faith, require that the parties to the constitution should respect the slaveholder's right of property everywhere in the Union.—Free Soilism is lame, halt and blind, while it battles against the spread of slavery, and admits its right to exist anywhere. If it has the right to exist, it has a right to grow and spread. The slaveholder has the best of the argument the very moment the legality and constitutionality of slavery is conceded. There is much reason in the logic of the late John C. Calhoun. If slaves are property in the eye of the constitution of the United States, they are subject to the same condition of all other property contemplated in that instrument, and their owners are entitled to all the advantages of this property equally with other citizens in their property.—We repeat, slaves are property, or they are not property. They are persons, or they are beasts of burden. The constitution must recognize them as one or the other. It cannot regard them as men and regard them as things at the same time. If it regards them as things, legitimate objects of property, then the laws that govern the rights and privileges of property must prevail in respect to them. But if it regards them as persons, then all the thunders of the constitution may be launched at the head of him who dares to treat them contrary to the rights sacred to persons in the constitution.

Now, the question is, does the constitution, in any of its provisions, know any man as a slave? Does it know anything under the name and character of slavery? Is there a single word in the constitution about slaves, slaveholders or slavery? We utterly deny that there is one such word, sentence or syllable to be found in that instrument, and will thank any reader of our paper to point out any such, as he may even think, by any necessary implication, and contradict our assertion. But there is no such reference to recognition of slavery in the constitution.

The concession that the constitution recognizes and allows slavery in the slave States, is a most false, injurious, and hurtful concession.—The doctrine resulting from it, drives conscientious abolitionists from the ballot-box, reduces the masses—who would be practical abolitionists into mere *"Free Soilers,"* and arms the slaveholder with almost the only available power this side of *revolution* to defeat the anti-slavery movement. Out of this needless concession has arisen the partial and impatient watchwords of Northern anti-slavery men. Instead of the immediate, unconditional, and universal abolition of slavery in this country, we have liberty national, and slavery sectional—"no more slave States"—"no slavery outside the slave States." Instead of walking straight up to the giant wrong and demanding its utter overthrow, we are talking of limiting it, circumscribing it, surrounding it with free States, and leaving it to die of inward decay. A theory more fanciful and false, for getting rid of slavery, it would be difficult to conceive of. There was far more plausibility in the old notion that the abolition of the foreign slave trade would be the abolition of slavery. Cut off the stream and the pond will dry up, thought our fathers and the history of slavery demonstrates their folly, by showing that slavery has become more and more powerful every hour after the abolition of the slave trade. Before that trade was abolished, the antislavery sentiment of the country was active and energetic, and withal, bearing most precious fruits in gradual emancipation. But the slave trade at an end, the conscience of the people began to be at rest, and slavery took a new and more vigorous growth, and has been growing ever since. By surrounding the slave States with free States, it is contended that the influence of the latter upon the former, will naturally undermine and eventually overthrow slavery in the slave States. Now, when will men reason in accordance with facts? When will they learn wisdom from the past, and reduce that wisdom to practice? The lesson taught by the facts of history, and the facts of the present, is, that the free States on the borders of slave States, are far more likely to be corrupted by slavery than to abolish slavery.—The influence of Maryland on Pennsylvania has resulted in the conversion of the latter into a slave State, in a very important sense, making her mob and burn the property of the abolitionists, and converting her very halls of justice into slave prisons.

The only way to put an end to the aggressions of slavery, is to put an end to slavery itself. While the system of slavery exists, it must, from its very nature, be aggressive. The safety of liberty requires the complete extinction of its opposite; and since the U.S. Constitution was established to secure the blessing of liberty, there is, therefore, a high constitutional, as well as moral obligation, resting upon the American people to abolish slavery. Liberty can never be national while slavery is sectional, for the reason that a thing cannot exist and non-exist at the same time. Down with slavery everywhere, and proclaim the law of liberty everywhere is the truest, wisest and best course, and the manifest duty of abolitionists now and always.

Frederick Douglass' Paper, August 24, 1855

Late in October Douglass traveled to Boston to attend the convention of the Radical Abolitionists. [Gerrit] Smith, Beriah Green, and Abram Pyne, a Negro editor, were also present. A terrific downpour and the simultaneous opening of the National Agricultural Fair accounted for the small attendance. Under these circumstances the body decided to take no definite action. Still Douglass was not discouraged. He was as confident as ever in "the ultimate triumph" of the views of this handful of Liberty Party men and Radical Abolitionists. Sooner or later those interested in the struggle against slavery would come to see that these views were correct.[1] [II:81]

THE FINAL STRUGGLE

Among the varied and multitudinous array of opposition to the anti-slavery movement, no Abolitionist should abate his zeal, or relax his energy, but rather redouble his diligence, and resolve, if need be, to die upon the battle field, struggling for the victory. There is some consolation in the reflection, that the conflict will not, cannot, last forever. The hour which shall witness *the final struggle,* is on the wing. Already we hear the *booming* of the bell which shall yet toll the death knell of human slavery.

Liberty and Slavery cannot dwell together forever in the same country. There is not one iota of affinity existing between them. They hate each other, with a hatred which is unto Death. They ever have been, and they ever must remain, in a state of irreconcilable hostility. Before a union can be effected between them, the laws which govern the moral universe must be repealed. It is absurd in any one to expect to witness the spirit of Liberty being led, by the demon of Slavery, to the hymeneal altar.—As well expect the pains and sorrows of hell, to mingle, in happy unison, with the pleasures and the joys of heaven; the spirits of just men made perfect, with the spirits of the lost.

It is useless, then, to attempt to effect a union between them. No compromise can effect it. No legislation can change the inflexible law of adaptation, the eternal fitness of things. No compact can make that Right, which is wrong from its first principles to its crowning assumptions.

It is, then, perfectly apparent to every reflecting mind, that a crisis more critical than any which has preceded it, is pending. This crisis cannot much longer be delayed. It must come to pass as the legitimate result of the past and the present struggle for the mastery in which we behold these deadly enemies engaged. We may attempt to bind up the wounds of the respective hostile parties, with mollifying ointment, but this will not avert the impending hour. It must come, as sure as the laws of God cannot be trampled upon with impunity.

Then, as a nation, if we are wise, we will prepare for the last conflict, for that final struggle in which the enemy of Freedom must capitulate. Instead of indulging in delusive dreams of safety, the Slave Power should prepare for the era of its disastrous doom; it will be wise and consider its latter end.

The motto to be inscribed upon the banner of Freedom, in the last conflict is not, "No more Slave States," nor "No Slavery outside of the Slave States;" but no Slavery where it does exist; no Slavery in the Republic. We shall not be burdened or annoyed by unhallowed compromises, we shall make no contracts with the perfidious enemy. Not one word of concession or compromise, shall escape our lips, not one syllable of apology. Truth and Error, Liberty and Slavery, in a hand-to-hand conflict. This is what we want; this is what we will have. The utter extinction of Slavery, everywhere in our national domain; the subversion of the Black Power, wherever, in all our widespread territory, it dare lift its defiant head toward Heaven.

Again; in the final struggle, in order to be successful, there must exist a thorough organization of freemen, with the single issue presented, Liberty everywhere, Slavery nowhere; there must be unity of effort; every man who loves freedom, must array himself in her defence, whatever may have been his past political predilections. The magnet of Human Freedom, must be held high above the din of party tumult, and every man who is willing to peril his life, his fortune, and his sacred honor, in its defence, will ultimately be attracted to the magnet, whether Whig, or Democrat, or Freesoiler, or Abolitionist. This will form the great Abolition Party of the land. In fact, there must be, and there will be, but two Parties in the country; these will be known not as Whigs, nor as Democrats, nor as Republicans, so far as party names are concerned, but simply as the Anti-Slavery and Pro-Slavery parties of the country. All who are desirous of maintaining a sort of assumed neutrality on the question, as well as the most inveterate haters of the Abolition movement, will constitute the Pro-Slavery Party. Neither of these parties, in the last conflict, will be *wheedled* from the arena, by the presentation of incidental issues. Each party, forming a unit, and rallying under its own banner, will fight for the triumph of its respective Principles.

We do not fear the result of such a struggle. The sooner the last battle shall be fought, the sooner victory will perch upon the standard of the free. The Principles which form the basis of the Abolition movement, are as unchanging and as undying as their Eternal Author. They must triumph *for Heaven has nowhere promised to delegate his power to another.* Let us then prepare for the battle, and for victory. Already are the masses moving. The disintegration of the once powerful political Parties, is a cheering and significant sign of the times. The throne of the despot is trembling to its deep foundations. There is a good time coming. We yet shall make the welkin ring with the mighty hallelujahs of the free.

Frederick Douglass' Paper, November 16, 1855

1. *Radical Abolitionist*, Dec., 1855 (copy in library of Cornell University).
Gerrit Smith was the chief sponsor of the Radical Abolitionist Party as he was of the Liberty Party. He financed its organs, *The American Jubilee*, which was published in March and April, 1855, and *The Radical Abolitionist*, which replaced it and appeared from August, 1855, to December, 1859.

———————

In the summer of 1851, *The North Star* [had] amalgamated with the *Liberty Party Paper*, a weekly journal edited and published by John Thomas in Syracuse. . . . With Gerrit Smith contributing to its support, [*Frederick Douglass' Paper*] was able for two years to meet its expenses. But after 1853 it . . . ran into difficulties. "Money! Money!!

Money!!" Douglass appealed to delinquent subscribers on April 8, 1853. " . . . We greatly need your assistance, just now. The expense of publishing a paper like ours is very great—and depending, as it does, almost wholly upon its *subscription* list, it can only be sustained and its Editor left unembarrassed by *prompt payment* on the part of *subscribers.*" The situation grew worse. By June, 1855, when Douglass instituted the policy of advanced subscription payments, the journal was fifteen hundred dollars in debt, and almost double that amount was due from delinquent subscribers. [I:88–89]

TO GERRIT SMITH

Rochester, May 23, 1856

My Dear Sir:

I hope you are the better of your cold. If all be well I shall certainly meet you at Syracuse. I am released from my earlier appointments in Ohio.

Now I want your counsel. Your unceasing interest in me and in my paper, and in the cause to which it is devoted, makes it right that I should seek your counsel.

I am almost convinced that my paper cannot be sustained. I am now full fifteen hundred dollars in debt for it, and have on hand only six hundred dollars from my friend Julia Griffiths to pay my creditors. My paper is deep in its ninth year. I have done my part toward putting it on a permanent footing. I have failed, at least for the present. My credit is good and I might go on. But is it right and best? I am almost persuaded that it is not. The prospect is dark. My paper is dying of the disease which carried the *Model Worker* to its grave. It is opposed to the Republicans of fifty six as it was opposed to Free Soilers in forty eight. My paper is not Republican and therefore Republicans look coldly on it. It is not Garrisonian and therefore Garrisonians hate and spare no pains to destroy it. Meanwhile, the colored people do very little to support it. Now what shall be done? Shall the paper go down and be a total wreck—or shall it be saved—by being merged into the *Radical Abolitionist?* Cannot the *Radical Abolitionist* be made a weekly journal and some way be devised by which my subscription list be transferred to that of the *Abolitionist?* I am sick at the thought of the failure of my paper and humbled by the thought that no Negro has yet succeeded in establishing a press in the United States—but when a man cannot stand up he must fall down. I have struggled about nine years to establish such a press—and although I had when I began five or six thousand dollars, I should not have now half that sum but for the success attending my lectures last winter and the sale of my Book. The nine years have almost gone. My children are growing up and increasing their demands upon me, and it becomes me to submit to the humiliation of failure rather than blindly go on till all is lost. I ask nothing for myself in this business. I do not even ask for a place in the paper but simply ask that you will help me to save my paper from positive failure by merging it into the *Radical Abolitionist.* I suggest this to your own private eye. While I do not ask any place in the *Radical Abolitionist* as an editor or assistant in case my paper is merged, yet it might be an element of strength to the concern to have me in some way connected with it.

I am, my dear friend, very truly yours,

Frederick Douglass

I lectured last night to the largest audience in Corinthian Hall which has assembled here during the past winter.

I hope you will not consider the foregoing an appeal to your pockets, for it honestly is not.

Personally I am quite "well off" in the world having health, and heart, a good house and lot, a little money, and a wide field of usefulness as a lecturer in the cause of freedom. *My Bondage and My Freedom* will sell, as long as I can lecture—so that I regard myself well provided for for the present.

Love to dear Mrs. Smith,

Again yours F. D.

Gerrit Smith Papers, Syracuse University

On August 15, Douglass . . . informed his readers of his purpose "to support, with whatever influence we possess, little or much, John C. Fremont, and William L. Dayton, the candidates of the Republican Party for the presidency and vice-presidency of the United States, in the present political canvass." Coming after his continuous denunciations of the Republican Party and especially after his characterization of it in June as "a heterogenous mass of political antagonism, gathered from defunct Whiggery, disaffected Democracy, and demented, defeated and disappointed Native Americanism," Douglass knew that his political somersault would arouse consternation among his readers. So he accompanied his announcement with a careful explanation of this new course which apparently seemed to inconsistent with the policies he had hitherto advocated.[1]

In subsequent editorials Douglass enlarged on reasons for his action and in cogent, well-defined arguments set down the correct role for any vanguard reform group. Instead of isolating itself from a mass movement which was not ready to accept a more advanced program, the duty of the vanguard was to work inside the movement, gradually bringing to its membership the understanding that would result in the adoption of an advanced position. [II:83–84]

FREMONT AND DAYTON

The readers of our journal will observe that the honored names which, for some time, stood at the head of our columns, as its candidates for the president and vice-president of the United States, have been withdrawn and although no other names have been or shall be placed at the head of our columns, we deem it proper frankly to announce our purpose to support, with whatever influence we possess, little or much, John C. Fremont and William L. Dayton, the candidates of the Republican Party for the presidency and vice-presidency of the United States, in the present political canvass.

To a part of our readers, this announcement, considering our previous position, will be an unwelcome surprise. We have, hitherto, advocated to the best of our ability, a course of political action inconsistent with our Present course. It is,

therefore, eminently fit that we should accompany the foregoing announcement
with something like a statement of reasons for our newly adopted policy.

1. A step so important as to lead to a separation in action, at least, between
ourselves and of loved, honored, and tried friends, should not be hastily or in-
considerately taken. In full view of this truth, we have with much care examined
and re-examined the subject of our political relations and duties regarding Slavery and the colored people of the United States. Our position, as well as the suggestion of wisdom just referred to, very naturally cause hesitation. The name of
Gerrit Smith has long been synonymous with us as genuine, unadulterated Abolitionism. Of all men beneath the sky, we would rather see this just man made
President. Our heart and judgment cling and twine around this man and his
counsels as the ivy to the oak. To differ from him, and the beloved friends who
may still intend to vote for him at the approaching election, is the result only of
stern and irresistible conviction, the voice of which we cannot feel ourselves at
liberty to disregard.

2. The time has passed for an honest man to attempt any defence of a right to
change his opinion as to political methods of opposing Slavery. Anti-Slavery consistency itself, in our view, requires of the Anti-Slavery voter that disposition of
his vote and his influence, which, in all the circumstances and likelihoods of the
case tend most to the triumph of Free Principles in the Councils and Government
of the nation. It is not to be consistent to pursue a course politically this year,
merely because that course seemed the best last year, or at any previous time.
Right Anti-Slavery action is that which deals the severest deadliest blow upon
Slavery that can be given at that particular time. Such action is always consistent, however different may be the forms through which it expresses itself.

3. Again, in supporting Fremont and Dayton, we are in no wise required to
abandon a single Anti-Slavery Truth or Principle which we have hitherto cherished, and publicly advocated. The difference between our paper this week and
last week is a difference of Policy, not of Principle. Hereafter, as hitherto, we
shall contend for every principle, and maintain [mutilated] the platform of the
Radical Abolitionists. The unconstitutionality of Slavery, the illegality of Slavery, the Right of the Federal Government to abolish Slavery in every part of the
Republic, whether in States or Territories, will be as firmly held, and as sternly
insisted upon, as hitherto. Nor do we wish, by supporting the Republican Candidate in the approaching election, to be understood as merging our individuality, body and soul, into that Party, nor as separating ourselves from our Radical
Abolition friends in their present endeavors to enforce the great Principles of Justice and Liberty, upon which the Radical Abolition movement is based. Fur-
thermore, we here concede, that upon Radical Abolition grounds, the final battle against Slavery in this country must be fought out—Slavery must be seen and
felt to be a huge crime, a system of lawless violence, before it can be abolished.
In our Paper, upon the Platform, at home and abroad, we shall endeavor to bring
Slavery before the People in this hateful light; and by so doing, shall really be upholding the Radical Abolition Platform in the very ranks of the Republican Party.

4. Beyond all controversy, the commanding and vital issue with Slavery at the
approaching Presidential election, is the extension or the limitation of Slavery.

The malign purpose of extending, strengthening, and perpetuating Slavery, is the conclusion of the great mass of the slaveholders. The execution of this purpose upon Kansas, is plainly enough the business set down for the present by the friends of Slavery, North and South. And it cannot be denied that the election either of Buchanan or Fillmore would be the success of this malign purpose of the Slave Power. Other elements enter into the issue, such, for instance, as Northern or Southern ascendency of the Slave power in the Councils of the Nation, the continued humiliation of the Northern People, the reign of Terror at Washington, the crippling of the Anti-Slavery movement, and the security and preservation of Slavery from inward decay or outside destroying influences. The fact that Slaveholders had taken a united stand in favor of this measure, is, at least, an argument why Anti-Slavery men should take a stand to defeat them. The greatest triumphs of Slavery have been secured by the division of its enemies, one party insisting on attacking one point, and another class equally in earnest bending their energies in another direction. Were it in our power, the order of battle between Liberty and Slavery would be arranged differently. Anti-Slavery in our hands, at the ballot box, should be the aggressor; but it is not within our power, or within that of any other man, to control the order of events, or the circumstances which shape our course, and determine our conduct at particular times. All men will agree, that, generally speaking, the point attacked, is the point to be defended. The South has tendered to us the issue of Slavery Extension; and to meet the Slave Power here, is to rouse its most devilish animosity. It is to strike hardest, where the Slaveholders feel most keenly. The most powerful blow that could be given at that point would in our judgment, be the election to the Presidency and Vice Presidency of the Republic the Candidates of the Republican Party.

5. Briefly, then, we shall support Fremont and Dayton in the present crisis of the Anti-Slavery movement, because they are, by position, and from the very nature of the organization which supports them, the admitted and recognized antagonists of the Slave Power, of gag-law, and of all the hellish designs of the Slave Power to extend and fortify the accursed slave system. We shall support them because they are the most numerous Anti-Slavery Party, and, therefore, the most powerful to inflict a blow upon, and the most likely to achieve a valuable victory over, the Slave Oligarchy. There is not a trafficker in the bodies and souls of men, from Baltimore to New Orleans, that would not crack his bloody slave whip with fiendish delight over the defeat of Fremont and Dayton. Whereas, on the other hand, the moral effect of the Radical Abolition vote, separated as it must be from the great Anti-Slavery body of the North, must, from the nature of the case, be very limited for good, and only powerful for mischief, where its effect would be to weaken the Republican Party. We shall support Fremont and Dayton, because there is no chance whatever in the present contest of electing better men than they. And we are the more reconciled to accepting them, by the fact that they are surrounded by a Party of progressive men. Take them, therefore, not merely for what they are, but for what we have good reason to believe they will become when they have lived for a time in the element of Anti-Slavery discussion. We shall support them by pen, by speech, by vote, because it is by no means certain that they can succeed in this State against the powerful combinations opposed to

them without the support of the full and complete Abolition vote. Bitter indeed, would be the reproach, and deep and pointed would be the regret, if, through the Radical Abolitionists, victory should perch on the bloody standard of Slave Rule, as would be the case if Fremont and Dayton were defeated, and Buchanan and Breckenridge elected. For one, we are not disposed to incur this reproach, nor to experience this regret, and shall, therefore, vote for Fremont and Dayton. In supporting them, we neither dishonor our Principles nor lessen our means of securing their adoption and active application. We can reach the ears and heart of as great a number within the ranks of the Republican Party as we could possibly do by remaining outside of those ranks. We know of no law applicable to the progress and promulgation of Radical Abolition Principles which would act less favorably towards our Principles inside the Party, than outside of it.

6. Another reason for supporting the Republican Party at the ballot-box and thus supporting the Anti-Slavery vote as a unit, is, that such action conforms exactly to the facts of our existing relations as citizens. There is now, evidently, but one great question of widespread and of all-commanding national interest; and that question is Freedom or Slavery. In reality, there can be but two Parties to this question; and for ourselves, we wish it to be with the natural division for Freedom, in form, as well as in fact.

7. It seems to us both the dictate of good morals and true wisdom, that if we cannot abolish Slavery in all the States by our votes at the approaching election, we ought, if we can, keep Slavery out of Kansas by our vote. To pursue any other policy is to abandon at present, practical advantage to Freedom in an assertion of more comprehensive claims, right enough in themselves, but which reason and fact assure us can only be attained by votes in the future, when the public mind shall have been educated up to those claims. We are quite well aware that to the foregoing, objections of apparent weight may be urged by those for whose conscientious convictions we cherish the profoundest respect. And although we do not propose to anticipate objections, but intend to meet them as they shall be presented in the progress of the canvass, we will mention and reply to one. Most plainly the greatest difficulty to be met with by a Radical Abolitionist in supporting Fremont and Dayton, is the fact that these Candidates have not declared and do not declare any purpose to abolish Slavery by legislation, in the States. They neither entertain nor declare any such purpose, and in this they are far from occupying the high Anti-Slavery position of the Radical Abolition Society. But let us not be unreasonable or impatient with the Republican Party. In considering this defect in the Anti-Slavery character and creed of the Republican Candidates, it should be borne in mind that they stand now in respect to this doctrine precisely where the Liberty Party stood ten years ago. The Right and duty of the Federal Government to abolish Slavery everywhere in the United States, is entirely true and deeply important; and yet, it must be confessed that this doctrine has been made appreciable but to a few minds, the dwellers in the mountain peaks of the moral world, who catch the first beams of morning, long before the slumberers in the valleys awake from their dreams. This new doctrine, we think, may very properly be left to take its turn in the arena of discussion. Time and argument will do more for its progress, and its final adoption by the people, than

can be done for it in the present crisis, by the few votes of the isolated Radical Abolitionists. In further extenuation or apology, it may be very properly urged, that while the Republican Party has not at this point adopted the Abolition creed, it has laid down principles and promulgated doctrines, which in their application, directly tend to the Abolition of Slavery in the States. But the conclusive answer to all who object upon this ground is the indisputable Truth, that neither in Religion nor Morals, can a man be justified in refusing to assist his fellow-men to accomplish a possible good thing, simply because his fellows refuse to accomplish some other good things which they deem impossible. Most assuredly, that theory cannot be a sound one which would prevent us from voting with men for the Abolition of Slavery in Maryland simply because our companions refuse to include Virginia. In such a case, the path of duty is plainly this; go with your fellow-citizens for the Abolition of Slavery in Maryland when they are ready to go for that measure, and do all you can, meanwhile, to bring them to whatever work of righteousness may remain and which has become manifest to your clearer vision. Such, then, is the conclusion forced upon us by the philosophy of the facts of our condition as a nation. A great crime against Freedom and Civilization is about to be perpetrated. The Slave Power is resolved to plant the deadly Upas, Slavery, in the virgin soil of Kansas. This great evil may be averted, and all the likelihoods of the case, the election of John C. Fremont and William L. Dayton, will be instrumental in averting it. Their election will prevent the establishment of Slavery in Kansas, overthrow Slave Rule in the Republic, protect Liberty of Speech and of the Press, give ascendency to Northern civilization over the bludgeon and blood-hound civilization of the South, and the mark of national condemnation on Slavery, scourge doughfaces from place and from power, and inaugurate a higher and purer standard of Politics and Government. Therefore, we go for Fremont and Dayton.

Frederick Douglass' Paper, August 15, 1856

1. *Frederick Douglass' Paper*, June 20, 1856, reprinted in *Liberator*, Sept. 5, 1856.

THE DO-NOTHING POLICY

When will colored men learn to discard the do-nothing tactics, the "masterly inactivity," for which their course in the past has been distinguished? When the American People were almost to a man arrayed against us, when to present a petition from the colored citizens of a State would provoke a storm of violence upon the head of the individual who had the hardihood to present it, then the cry was we are powerless, we are bound hand and foot, and delivered to the spoiler. Now, when there is a more hopeful state of public sentiment; when the friends of impartial liberty may be counted by thousands; the cry is we must be quiet, we must not make ourselves be heard or felt in this contest, lest we injure the cause for which we pray. And we fold our hands and indolently gaze at the tremendous struggle going on in the nation, by which our rights will be determined.

This is a false position. Who of all the people in this country have the deepest stake in the contest for supremacy between slavery and freedom? The colored people. Who ought then to be the most active, the most vigilant and self sacrificing? The colored people. It is vain for us to expect to realize any degree of liberty and respect in our country, unless we are willing to bear our share in the struggle. What deprivation of right have the whites met with in Kansas, which is greater than the disabilities inflicted on colored men in nearly every state; yet we submit quietly, scarcely mustering enough of energy to make an annual and spasmodic protest against our wrongs, while they, forsaking the comforts and refinements of their homes, taking their lives in their hands, are contending bravely for their rights, and many of them are lying stark and stiff, under the soil of Kansas. We may learn a lesson of them; the man deprived of rights is the man to contend for them. The revolutionary worthies of our early history pledged their lives, their fortunes and their sacred honors, for the success of their cause and nobly have they redeemed their pledge. Are we prepared to make the same pledge, and having made it to redeem it as they did? If so the day of our emancipation is near at hand, even at the door.

No race on earth have greater incentives to exertion than we. Not only our equality as a race is denied, but we are even denied our rank as men; we are enslaved, oppressed, and even those most favorably disposed towards us, are so from motives more of pity than respect. For the first time since the dawn of history, is there a chance afforded us to prove our equal manhood. What a noble work is here before us then, to redeem an entire race from the obloquy and scorn of the world, and place it upon the same level with the rest of mankind. Generations unborn will envy us the felicity of having been born at a time when such noble work could be accomplished, when the foundations can be laid deep and strong for the future liberation of the race. The American people, with all their lack of justice, and cruel oppression of our people, are yet of that stock which admires and respects a sturdy contender for his own rights. Happily the strife we are called upon to enter is not, in the northern States, a war-like one. The republicans of France and of Italy, can achieve their freedom only by bloodshed, by the overthrow of their governments, and the slaughter of their enemies. With us the only hardship is, the industry and persistence with which our efforts must be made. The right of petition, the right of the press, and free speech, are left to us, and the use of these is all that is required for the acquisition of our rights in the northern States. Will we use them? Now while the masses of the people are loud in their professions of love for freedom—now while the slave power is measuring to their whites of the North, the same degree of oppression and violence to which we have so long been subjected—now while the waters of the political Siloam are stirred, have we enough of energy to step into its healing waters and be cured?

There are two States of the North in which we believe equal political rights are within the reach of their colored citizens, only needing a determined and united move on their part. New York is one of those States, Ohio, the other. The colored citizens of New York meet next month at Syracuse to confer together on the subject. If they are united, if they are resolved to use with unwavering energy the press, the orator, and the petition, they will gain all they desire. To meet and pass resolutions will do no good; but appoint reliable, energetic men to conduct the canvass, raise money to support them, and unite with them afterward in perfecting and executing the plans proposed, and all will be well. On the other hand, to float quietly with the current, allowing others to win and bestow the freedom which we lazily propose to enjoy, will go far to prove the charges of our enemies true, and sink us lower in the estimation of our white countrymen. The open sesame for the colored man is action! action!! action!!

Frederick Douglass' Paper, September 12, 1856

PEACEFUL ANNIHILATION OF SLAVERY IS HOPELESS

While we feel bound to use all our powers of persuasion and argument; to welcome every instrumentality that promises to peacefully destroy that perpetual contemner of God's laws, and disturber of a nation's peace—Slavery; we yet feel that its peaceful annihilation is almost hopeless, and hence stand by the doctrines enunciated in those resolutions, and contend that the slave's right to revolt is perfect, and only wants the occurrence of favourable circumstances to become a duty. . . . We cannot but shudder as we call to mind the horrors that have ever marked servile insurrections—we would avert them if we could; but shall the millions forever submit to robbery, to murder, to ignorance, and every unnamed evil which an irresponsible tyranny can devise, because the overthrow of that tyranny would be productive of horrors? We say not. The recoil, when it comes, will be in exact proportion to the wrongs inflicted; terrible as it will be, we accept and hope for it. The slaveholder has been tried and sentenced, his execution only waits the finish to the training of his executioners. He is training his own executioners.

William Chambers, *American Slavery and Colour*, New York, 1857, p. 174

THE DRED SCOTT DECISION, speech delivered before American Anti-Slavery Society, New York, May 14, 1857[1]

Mr. Chairman, Friends, and Fellow Citizens:
    While four millions of our fellow countrymen are in chains—while men, women, and children are bought and sold on the auction-block with horses, sheep, and swine—while the remorseless slave-whip draws the warm blood of our common humanity—it is meet that we assemble as we have done to-day, and

lift up our hearts and voices in earnest denunciation of the vile and shocking abomination. It is not for us to be governed by our hopes or our fears in this great work; yet it is natural on occasions like this, to survey the position of the great struggle which is going on between slavery and freedom, and to dwell upon such signs of encouragement as may have been lately developed, and the state of feeling these signs or events have occasioned in us and among the people generally. It is a fitting time to take an observation to ascertain where we are, and what our prospects are.

To many, the prospects of the struggle against slavery seem far from cheering. Eminent men, North and South, in Church and State, tell us that the omens are all against us. Emancipation, they tell us, is a wild, delusive idea; the price of human flesh was never higher than now; slavery was never more closely entwined about the hearts and affections of the southern people than now; that whatever of conscientious scruple, religious conviction, or public policy, which opposed the system of slavery forty or fifty years ago, has subsided; and that slavery never reposed upon a firmer basis than now. Completing this picture of the happy and prosperous condition of this system of wickedness, they tell us that this state of things is to be set to our account. Abolition agitation has done it all. How deep is the misfortune of my poor, bleeding people, if this be so! How lost their condition, if even the efforts of their friends but sink them deeper in ruin!

Without assenting to this strong representation of the increasing strength and stability of slavery, without denouncing what of untruth pervades it, I own myself not insensible to the many difficulties and discouragements that beset us on every hand. They fling their broad and gloomy shadows across the pathway of every thoughtful colored man in this country. For one, I see them clearly, and feel them sadly. With an earnest, aching heart, I have long looked for the realization of the hope of my people. Standing, as it were, barefoot, and treading upon the sharp and flinty rocks of the present, and looking out upon the boundless sea of the future, I have sought, in my humble way, to penetrate the intervening mists and clouds, and, perchance, to descry, in the dim and shadowy distance, the white flag of freedom, the precise speck of time at which the cruel bondage of my people should end, and the long entombed millions rise from the foul grave of slavery and death. But of that time I can know nothing, and you can know nothing. All is uncertain at that point. One thing, however, is certain; slaveholders are in earnest, and mean to cling to their slaves as long as they can, and to the bitter end. They show no sign of a wish to quit their iron grasp upon the sable throats of their victims. Their motto is, "a firmer hold and a tighter grip" for every new effort that is made to break their cruel power. The case is one of life or death with them, and they will give up only when they must do that or do worse.

In one view the slaveholders have a decided advantage over all opposition. It is well to notice this advantage—the advantage of complete organization. They are organized; and yet were not at the pains of creating their organizations. The State governments, where the system of slavery exists, are complete slavery organizations. The church organizations in those States are equally at the service of slavery; while the Federal Government, with its army and navy, from the chief magistracy in Washington, to the Supreme Court, and thence to the chief marshalship at New York, is pledged to support, defend, and propagate the crying curse of human bondage. The pen, the purse, and the sword, are united against the simple truth, preached by humble men in obscure places.

This is one view. It is, thank God, only one view; there is another, and a brighter view. David, you know, looked small and insignificant when going to meet Goliath, but looked larger when he had stain his foe. The Malakoff was, to the eye of the world, impregnable, till the hour it fell before the shot and shell of the allied army. Thus hath it ever been. Oppression, organized as ours is, will appear invincible up to the very hour of its fall. Sir, let us look at the other side, and see if there are not some things to cheer our heart and nerve us up anew in the good work of emancipation.

Take this fact—for it is a fact—the anti-slavery movement has, from first to last, suffered no abatement. It has gone forth in all directions, and is now felt in the remotest extremities of the Republic.

It started small, and was without capital either in men or money. The odds were all against it. It literally had nothing to lose, and everything to gain. There was ignorance to be enlightened, error to be combatted, conscience to be awakened, prejudice to be overcome, apathy to be aroused, the right of speech to be secured, mob violence to be subdued, and a deep, radical change to be inwrought in the mind and heart of the whole nation. This great work, under God, has gone on, and gone on gloriously.

Amid all changes, fluctuations, assaults, and adverses of every kind, it has remained firm in its purpose, steady in its aim, onward and upward, defying all opposition, and never losing a single battle. Our strength is in the growth of anti-slavery conviction, and this has never halted.

There is a significant vitality about this abolition movement. It has taken a deeper, broader, and more lasting hold upon the national heart than ordinary reform movements. Other subjects of much interest come and go, expand and contract, blaze and vanish, but the huge question of American Slavery, comprehending, as it does, not merely the weal or the woe of four millions, and their countless posterity, but the weal or the woe of this entire nation, must increase in magnitude and in majesty with every hour of its history. From a cloud not bigger than a man's hand, it has overspread the heavens. It has risen from a grain not bigger than a mustard seed. Yet see the fowls of the air, how they crowd its branches.

Politicians who cursed it, now defend it; ministers, once dumb, now speak in its praise; and presses, which once flamed with hot denunciations against it, now surround the sacred cause as by a wall of living fire. Politicians go with it as a pillar of cloud by day, and the press as a pillar of fire by night. With these ancient tokens of success, I, for one, will not despair of our cause.

Those who have undertaken to suppress and crush out this agitation for Liberty and humanity, have been most woefully disappointed. Many who have engaged to put it down, have found themselves put down. The agitation has pursued them in all their meanderings, broken in upon their seclusion, and, at the very moment of fancied security, it has settled down upon them like a mantle of unquenchable fire. Clay, Calhoun, and Webster each tried his hand at suppressing the agitation; and they went to their graves disappointed and defeated.

Loud and exultingly have we been told that the slavery question is settled, and settled forever. You remember it was settled thirty-seven years ago, when Missouri was admitted into the Union with a slaveholding constitution, and slavery prohibited in all territory north of thirty-six degrees of north latitude. Just fifteen years afterwards, it was settled again by voting down the right of petition, and gagging down free discussion in Congress. Ten years after this it was settled again by the annexation of Texas, and with it the war with Mexico. In 1850 it was again settled. This was called a final settlement. By it slavery was virtually declared to be the equal of Liberty, and should come into the Union on the same terms. By it the right and the power to hunt down men, women, and children, in every part of this country, was conceded to our southern brethren, in order to keep them in the Union. Four years after this settlement, the whole question was once more settled, and settled by a settlement which unsettled all the former settlements.

The fact is, the more the question has been settled, the more it has needed settling. The space between the different settlements has been strikingly on the decrease. The first stood longer than any of its successors.

There is a lesson in these decreasing spaces. The first stood fifteen years—the second, ten years—the third, five years—the fourth stood four years—and the fifth has stood the brief space of two years.

This last settlement must be called the Taney settlement. We are now told, in tones of lofty exultation, that the day is lost—all lost—and that we might as well give up the struggle. The highest authority has spoken. The voice of the Supreme Court has gone out over the troubled waves of the National Conscience, saying peace, be still.

This infamous decision of the Slaveholding wing of the Supreme Court maintains that slaves are within the contemplation of the Constitution of the United States, property; that slaves are property in the same sense that horses, sheep, and swine are property; that the old doctrine that slavery is a creature of local law is false; that the right of the slaveholder to his slave does not depend upon the local law, but is secured wherever the Constitution of the United States extends; that Congress has no right to prohibit slavery anywhere; that slavery may go in safety anywhere under the star-spangled banner; that colored persons of African descent have no rights that white men are bound to respect; that colored men of African descent are not and cannot be citizens of the United States.

You will readily ask me how I am affected by this devilish decision—this judicial incarnation of wolfishness? My answer is, and no thanks to the slaveholding wing of the Supreme Court, my hopes were never brighter than now.

I have no fear that the National Conscience will be put to sleep by such an open, glaring, and scandalous tissue of lies as that decision is, and has been, over and over, shown to be.

The Supreme Court of the United States is not the only power in this world. It is very great, but the Supreme Court of the Almighty is greater. Judge Taney can do many things, but he cannot perform impossibilities. He cannot bale out the ocean, annihilate the firm old earth, or pluck the silvery star of liberty from our Northern sky. He may decide, and decide again; but he cannot reverse the decision of the Most High. He cannot change the essential nature of things— making evil good, and good evil.

Happily for the whole human family, their rights have been defined, declared, and decided in a court higher than the Supreme Court. "There is a law," says Brougham, "above all the enactments of human codes, and by that law, unchangeable and eternal, man cannot hold property in man."

Your fathers have said that man's right to liberty is self-evident. There is no need of argument to make it clear. The voices of nature, of conscience, of reason, and of revelation, proclaim it as the right of all rights, the foundation of all trust, and of all responsibility. Man was born with it. It was his before he comprehended it. The *deed* conveying it to him is written in the center of his soul, and is recorded in Heaven. The sun in the sky is not more palpable to the sight than man's right to liberty is to the moral vision. To decide against this right in the person of Dred Scott, or the humblest and most whip-scarred bondman in the land, is to decide against God. It is an open rebellion against God's government. It is an attempt to undo what God has done, to blot out the broad distinction instituted by the *All-wise* between men and things, and to change the image and superscription of the everliving God into a speechless piece of merchandise.

Such a decision cannot stand. God will be true though every man be a liar. We can appeal from this hell-black judgment of the Supreme Court, to the court of common sense and common humanity. We can appeal from man to God. If there is no justice on earth, there is yet justice in. heaven. You may close your Supreme Court against the black man's cry for justice, but you cannot, thank God, close against him the ear of a sympathising world, nor shut up the Court of Heaven. All that is merciful and just, on earth and in Heaven, will execrate and despise this edict of Taney.

If it were at all likely that the people of these free States would tamely submit to this demoniacal judgment, I might feel gloomy and sad over it, and possibly it might be necessary for my people to look for a home in some other country. But as the case stands, we have nothing to fear.

In one point of view, we, the abolitionists and colored people, should meet this decision, unlocked for and monstrous as it appears, in a cheerful spirit. This very attempt to blot out forever the hopes of an enslaved people may be one necessary link in the chain of events preparatory to the downfall and complete overthrow of the whole slave system.

The whole history of the anti-slavery movement is studded with proof that all measures devised and executed with a view to ally and diminish the anti-slavery agitation, have only served to increase, intensify, and embolden that agitation. This wisdom of the crafty has been confounded, and the counsels of the ungodly brought to nought. It was so with the Fugitive Slave Bill. It was so with the Kansas-Nebraska Bill; and it will be so with this last and most shocking of all pro-slavery devices, this Taney decision.

When great transactions are involved, where the fate of millions is concerned, where a long enslaved and suffering people are to be delivered, I am superstitious enough to believe that the finger of the Almighty may be seen bringing good out of evil, and making the wrath of man redound to his honor, hastening the triumph of righteousness.

The American people have been called upon, in a most striking manner, to abolish and put away forever the system of slavery. The subject has been pressed upon their attention in all earnestness and sincerity. The cries of the slave have gone forth to the world, and up to the throne of God. This decision, in my view, is a means of keeping the nation awake on the subject. It is another proof that God does not mean that we shall go to sleep, and forget that we are a slave-holding nation.

Step by step we have seen the slave power advancing; poisoning, corrupting, and perverting the institutions of the country; growing more and more haughty, imperious, and exacting. The white man's liberty has been marked out for the same grave with the black man's.

The ballot box is desecrated, God's law set at nought, armed legislators stalk the halls of Congress, freedom of speech is beaten down in the Senate. The rivers and highways are infested by border ruffians, and white men are made to feel the iron heel of slavery. This ought to arouse us to kill off the hateful thing. They are solemn warnings to which the white people, as well as the black people, should take heed.

If these shall fail, judgment, more fierce or terrible, may come. The lightning, whirlwind, and earthquake may come. Jefferson said that he trembled for his country when he reflected that God is just, and his justice cannot sleep forever. The time may come when even the crushed worm may turn under the tyrant's feet. Goaded by cruelty, stung by a burning sense of wrong, in an awful moment of depression and desperation, the bondman and bondwoman at the south may rush to one wild and deadly struggle for freedom. Already slaveholders go to bed with bowie knives, and apprehend death at their dinners. Those who enslave, rob, and torment their cooks, may well expect to find death in their dinner-pots.

The world is full of violence and fraud, and it would be strange if the slave, the constant victim of both fraud and violence, should escape the contagion. He, too, may learn to fight the devil with fire, and for one, I am in no frame of mind to pray that this may be long deferred.

Two remarkable occurrences have followed the presidential election; one was the unaccountable sickness traced to the National Hotel at Washington, and the other was the discovery of a plan among the slaves, in different localities, to slay their oppressors.[2] Twenty or thirty of the suspected were put to death. Some were shot, some hanged, some burned, and some died under the lash. One brave man owned himself well acquainted with the conspiracy, but said he would rather die than disclose the facts. He received seven hundred and fifty lashes, and his noble spirit went away to the God who gave it. The name of this hero has been by the meanness of tyrants suppressed. Such a man redeems his race. He is worthy to be mentioned with the Hoffers and Tells, the noblest heroes of history. These insurrectionary movements have been put down, but they may break out at any time, under the guidance of higher intelligence, and with a more invincible spirit.

> The fire thus kindled, may be revived again;
> The flames are extinguished, but the embers remain;
> One terrible blast may produce an ignition,
> Which shall wrap the whole South in wild conflagration.
>
> The pathway of tyrants lies over volcanoes
> The very air they breathe is heavy with sorrows;
> Agonizing heart-throbs convulse them while sleeping,
> And the wind whispers Death as over them sweeping.

By all the laws of nature, civilization, and of progress, slavery is a doomed system. Not all the skill of politicians, North and South, not all the sophistries of Judges, not all the fulminations of a corrupt press, not all the hypocritical prayers, or the hypocritical refusals to pray of a hollow-hearted priesthood, not all the devices of sin and Satan, can save the vile thing from extermination.

Already a gleam of hope breaks upon us from the southwest. One Southern city has grieved and astonished the whole South by a preference for freedom. The wedge has entered. Dred Scott, of Missouri, goes into slavery, but St. Louis declares for freedom. The judgment of Taney is not the judgment of St. Louis.

It may be said that this demonstration in St. Louis is not to be taken as an evidence of sympathy with the slave; that it is purely a white man's victory. I admit it. Yet I am glad that white men, bad as they generally are, should gain a victory over slavery. I am willing to accept a judgment against slavery, whether supported by white or black reasons—though I would much rather have it supported by both. He that is not against us, is on our part.

Come what will, I hold it to be morally certain that, sooner or later, by fair means or foul means, in quiet or in tumult, in peace or in blood, in judgment or in mercy, slavery is doomed to cease out of this otherwise goodly land, and liberty is destined to become the settled law of this Republic.

I base my sense of the certain overthrow of slavery, in part, upon the nature of the American Government, the Constitution, the tendencies of the age, and the character of the American people; and this, notwithstanding the important decision of Judge Taney.

I know of no soil better adapted to the growth of reform than American soil. I know of no country where the conditions for affecting great changes in the settled order of things, for the development of right ideas of liberty and humanity, are more favorable than here in these United States.

The very groundwork of this government is a good repository of Christian civilization. The Constitution, as well as the Declaration of Independence, and the sentiments of the founders of the Republic, give us a platform broad enough, and strong enough, to support the most comprehensive plans for the freedom and elevation of all the people of this country, without regard to color, class, or clime.

There is nothing in the present aspect of the anti-slavery question which should drive us into the extravagance and nonsense of advocating a dissolution of the American Union as a means of overthrowing slavery, or freeing the North from the malign influence of slavery upon the morals of the Northern people. While the press is at liberty, and speech is free, and the ballot-box is open to the people of the sixteen free States; while the slaveholders are but four hundred thousand in number, and we are fourteen millions; while the mental and moral power of the nation is with us; while we are really the strong and they are the weak, it would look worse than cowardly to retreat from the Union.

If the people of the North have not the power to cope with these four hundred thousand slaveholders inside the Union, I see not how they could get out of the Union. The strength necessary to move the Union must ever be less than is required to break it up. If we have got to conquer the slave power to get out of the Union, I for one would much rather conquer, and stay in the Union. The latter, it strikes me, is the far more rational mode of action.

I make these remarks in no servile spirit, nor in any superstitious reverence for a mere human arrangement. If I felt the Union to be a curse, I should not be far behind the very chiefest of the disunion Abolitionists in denouncing it. But the evil to be met and abolished is not in the Union. The power arrayed against us is not a parchment.

It is not in changing the dead form of the Union, that slavery is to be abolished in this country. We have to do not with the dead, but the living; not with the past, but the living present.

Those who seek slavery in the Union, and who are everlastingly dealing blows upon the Union, in the belief that they are killing slavery, are most woefully mistaken. They are fighting a dead form instead of a living and powerful reality. It is clearly not because of the peculiar character of our Constitution that we have slavery, but the wicked pride, love of power, and selfish perverseness of the American people. Slavery lives in this country not because of any paper Constitution, but in the moral blindness of the American people, who persuade themselves that they are safe, though the rights of others may be struck down.

Besides, I think it would be difficult to hit upon any plan less likely to abolish slavery than the dissolution of the Union. The most devoted advocates of slavery, those who make the interests of slavery their constant study, seek a dissolution of the Union as their final plan for preserving slavery from Abolition, and their ground is well taken. Slavery lives and flourishes best in the absence of civilization; a dissolution of the Union would shut up the system in its own congenial barbarism.

The dissolution of the Union would not give the North one single additional advantage over slavery to the people of the North, but would manifestly take from them many which they now certainly possess.

Within the Union we have a firm basis of anti-slavery operation. National welfare, national prosperity, national reputation and honor, and national scrutiny; common rights, common duties, and common country, are so many bridges over which we can march to the destruction of slavery. To fling away these advantages because James Buchanan is President, or Judge Taney gives a lying decision in favor of slavery, does not enter into my notion of common sense.

Mr. Garrison and his friends have been telling us that, while in the Union, we are responsible for slavery; and in so telling us, he and they have told us the truth. But in telling us that we shall cease to be responsible for slavery by dissolving the Union, he and they have not told us the truth.

There now, clearly, is no freedom from responsibility for slavery, but in the Abolition of slavery. We have gone too far in this business now to sum up our whole duty in the cant phrase of "no Union with slaveholders."

To desert the family hearth may place the recreant husband out of the sight of his hungry children, but it cannot free him from responsibility. Though he should roll the waters of three oceans between him and them, he could not roll from his soul the burden of his responsibility to them; and, as with the private family, so in this instance with the national family. To leave the slave in his chains, in the hands of cruel masters who are too strong for him, is not to free ourselves from responsibility. Again: If I were on board of a pirate ship, with a company of men and women whose lives and liberties I had put in jeopardy, I would not clear my soul of their blood by jumping in the long boat, and singing out no union with pirates. My business would be to remain on board, and while I never would perform a single act of piracy again, I should exhaust every means given me by my position, to save the lives and liberties of those against whom I had committed piracy. In like manner, I hold it is our duty to remain inside this Union, and use all the power to restore to enslaved millions their precious and God-given rights. The more we have done by our voice and our votes, in times past, to rivet their galling fetters, the more clearly and solemnly comes the sense of duty to remain, to undo what we have done. Where, I ask, could the slave look for release from slavery if the Union were dissolved? I have an abiding conviction founded upon long and careful study of the certain effects of slavery upon the moral sense of slaveholding communities, that if the slaves are ever delivered from bondage, the power will emanate from the free States. All hope that the slaveholders will be self-moved to this great act of justice, is groundless and delusive. Now, as of old, the Redeemer must come from above, not from beneath. To dissolve the Union would be to withdraw the emancipating power from the field.

But I am told this is the argument of expediency. I admit it, and am prepared to show that what is expedient in this instance is right. "Do justice, though the heavens fall." Yes, that is a good motto, but I deny that it would be doing justice to the slave to dissolve the Union and leave the slave in his chains to get out by the clemency of his master, or the strength of his arms. Justice to the slave is to break his chains, and going out of the union is to leave him in his chains, and without any probable chance of getting out of them.

But I come now to the great question as to the constitutionality of slavery. The recent slaveholding decision, as well as the teachings of anti-slavery men, make this a fit time to discuss the constitutional pretensions of slavery.

The people of the North are a law abiding people. They love order and respect the means to that end. This sentiment has sometimes led them to the folly and wickedness of trampling upon the very life of law, to uphold its dead form. This was so in the execution of that thrice accursed Fugitive Slave Bill. Burns and Simms were sent back to the hell of slavery after they had looked upon Bunker Hill, and heard liberty thunder in Faneuil Hall. The people permitted this outrage in obedience to the popular sentiment of reverence for law. While men thus respect law, it becomes a serious matter so to interpret the law as to make it operate against liberty. I have a quarrel with those who fling the Supreme Law of this land between the slave and freedom. It is a serious matter to fling the weight of the Constitution against the cause of human liberty, and those who do it, take upon them a heavy responsibility. Nothing but absolute necessity, shall, or ought to drive me to such a concession to slavery.

When I admit that slavery is constitutional, I must see slavery recognized in the Constitution. I must see that it is there plainly stated that one man of a certain description has a right of property in the body and soul of another man of a certain description. There must be no room for a doubt. In a matter so important as the loss of liberty, everything must be proved beyond all reasonable doubt.

The well known rules of legal interpretation bear me out in this stubborn refusal to see slavery where slavery is not, and only to see slavery where it is.

The Supreme Court has, in its day, done something better than make slaveholding decisions. It has laid down rules of interpretation which are in harmony with the true idea and object of law and liberty.

It has told us that the intention of legal instruments must prevail; and that this must be collected from its words. It has told us that language must be construed strictly in favor of liberty and justice.

It has told us where rights are infringed, where fundamental principles are overthrown, where the general system of the law is departed from, the Legislative intention must be expressed with irresistible clearness, to induce a court of justice to suppose a design to effect such objects.

These rules are as old as law. They rise out of the very elements of law. It is to protect human rights, and promote human welfare. Law is in its nature opposed to wrong, and must everywhere be presumed to be in favor of the right. The pound of flesh, but not one drop of blood, is a sound rule of legal interpretation.

Besides there is another rule of law as well of common sense, which requires us to look to the ends for which a law is made, and to construe its details in harmony with the ends sought.

Now let us approach the Constitution from the standpoint thus indicated, and instead of finding in it a warrant for the stupendous system of robbery, comprehended in the term slavery, we shall find it strongly against that system.

"We, the people of the United States, in order to form a more perfect Union, establish justice, insure domestic tranquility, provide for the common defence, promote the general welfare, and secure the blessings of liberty to ourselves and our posterity, do ordain and establish this constitution for the United States of America."

Such are the objects announced by the instrument itself, and they are in harmony with the Declaration of Independence, and the principles of human wellbeing.

Six objects are here declared, "Union," "defence," "welfare," "tranquility," and "justice," and "liberty."

Neither in the preamble nor in the body of the Constitution is there a single mention of the term *slave* or *slave holder, slave master* or *slave state,* neither is there any reference to the color, or the physical peculiarities of any part of the people of the United States. Neither is there anything in the Constitution standing alone, which would imply the existence of slavery in this country.

"We, the people"—not we, the white people—not we, the citizens, or the legal voters—not we, the privileged class, and excluding all other classes but we, the people; not we, the horses and cattle, but we the people—the men and women, the human inhabitants of the United States, do ordain and establish this Constitution, &c.

I ask, then, any man to read the Constitution, and tell me where, if he can, in what particular that instrument affords the slightest sanction of slavery?

Where will he find a guarantee for slavery? Will he find it in the declaration that no person shall be deprived of life, liberty, or property, without due process of law? Will he find it in the declaration that the Constitution was established to secure the blessing of liberty? Will he find it in the right of the people to be secure in their persons and papers, and houses, and effects? Will he find it in the clause prohibiting the enactment by any State of a bill of attainder?

These all strike at the root of slavery, and any one of them, but faithfully carried out, would put an end to slavery in every State in the American Union.

Take, for example, the prohibition of a bill of attainder. That is a law entailing on the child the misfortunes of the parent. This principle would destroy slavery in every State of the Union.

The law of slavery is a law of attainder. The child is property because its parent was property, and suffers as a slave because its parent suffered as a slave.

Thus the very essence of the whole slave code is in open violation of a fundamental provision of the Constitution, and is in open and flagrant violation of all the objects set forth in the Constitution.

While this and much more can be said, and has been said, and much better said, by Lysander Spooner, William Goodell, Beriah Green, and Gerrit Smith, in favor of the entire unconstitutionality of slavery, what have we on the other side?

How is the constitutionality of slavery made out, or attempted to be made out?

First, by discrediting and casting away as worthless the most beneficent rules of legal interpretation; by disregarding the plain and common sense reading of the instrument itself; by showing that the Constitution does not mean what it says, and says what it does not mean, by assuming that the written Constitution is to be interpreted in the light of a secret and unwritten understanding of its framers, which understanding is declared to be in favor of slavery. It is in this mean, contemptible, underhand method that the Constitution is pressed into the service of slavery.

They do not point us to the Constitution itself, for the reason that there is nothing sufficiently explicit for their purpose; but they delight in supposed intentions—intentions nowhere expressed in the Constitution, and everywhere contradicted in the Constitution.

Judge Taney lays down this system of interpreting in this wise:

"The general words above quoted would seem to embrace the whole human family, and, if they were used in a similar instrument at this day, would be so understood. But it is too clear for dispute that the enslaved African race were not intended to be included, and formed no part of the people who framed and adopted this declaration; for if the language, as understood in that day, would embrace them, the conduct of the distinguished men who framed the Declaration of Independence would have been utterly and flagrantly inconsistent with the principles they asserted; and instead of the sympathy of mankind, to which they appealed, they would have deserved and received universal rebuke and reprobation.

"It is difficult, at this day, to realize the state of public opinion respecting that unfortunate class with the civilized and enlightened portion of the world at the time of the Declaration of Independence and the adoption of the Constitution; but history shows they had, for more than a century, been regarded as beings of an inferior order, and unfit associates for the white race, either socially or politically, and had no rights which white men are bound to respect; and the black man might be reduced to slavery, bought and sold, and treated as an ordinary article of merchandise. This opinion, at that time, was fixed and universal with the civilized portion of the white race. It was regarded as an axiom of morals, which no one thought of disputing, and everyone habitually acted upon it, without doubting, for a moment, the correctness of the opinion. And in no nation was this opinion more fixed, and generally acted upon, than in England; the subjects of which government not only seized them on the coast of Africa, but took them, as ordinary merchandise, to where they could make a profit on them. The opinion, thus entertained, was universally maintained on the colonies this side of the Atlantic; accordingly, Negroes of the African race were regarded by them as property, and held and bought and sold as such in every one of the thirteen colonies, which united in the Declaration of Independence, and afterwards formed the Constitution."

The argument here is, that the Constitution comes down to us from a slaveholding period and a slaveholding people; and that, therefore, we are bound to suppose that the Constitution recognizes colored persons of African descent, the victims of slavery at that time, as debarred forever from all participation in the benefit of the Constitution and the Declaration of Independence, although the plain reading of both includes them in their beneficent range.

As a man, an American, a citizen, a colored man of both Anglo-Saxon and African descent, I denounce this representation as a most scandalous and devilish perversion of the Constitution, and a brazen misstatement of the facts of history.

But I will not content myself with mere denunciation; I invite attention to the facts.

It is a fact, a great historic fact, that at the time of the adoption of the Constitution, the leading religious denominations in this land were anti-slavery, and were laboring for the emancipation of the colored people of African descent.

The church of a country is often a better index of the state of opinion and feeling than is even the government itself.

The Methodists, Baptists, Presbyterians, and the denomination of Friends, were actively opposing slavery, denouncing the system of bondage, with language as burning and sweeping as we employ at this day.

Take the Methodists. In 1780, that denomination said: "The Conference acknowledges that slavery is contrary to the laws of God, man, and nature, and hurtful to society—contrary to the dictates of conscience and true religion, and doing to others that we would not do unto us." In 1784, the same church declared, "that those who buy, sell, or give slaves away, except for the purpose to free them, shall be expelled immediately." In 1785, it spoke even more stringently on the subject. It then said: "We hold in the deepest abhorrence the practice of slavery, and shall not cease to seek its destruction by all wise and proper means."

So much for the position of the Methodist Church in the early history of the Republic, in those days of darkness to which Judge Taney refers.

Let us now see how slavery was regarded by the Presbyterian Church at that early date.

In 1794, the General Assembly of that body pronounced the following judgment in respect to slavery, slaveholders, and slaveholding.

"1st Timothy, 1st chapter, 10th verse: 'The law was made for mansteaders.' 'This crime among the Jews exposed the perpetrators of it to capital punishment.' Exodus, xxi, 15.—And the apostle here classes them with sinners of the first rank. The word he uses in its original import, comprehends all who are concerned in bringing any of the human race into slavery, or in retaining them in it. Stealers of men are all those who bring off slaves or freemen, and keep, sell, or buy them. 'To steal a freeman,' says Grotius, 'is the highest kind of theft.' In other instances, we only steal human property, but when we steal or retain men in slavery, we seize those who, in common with ourselves, are constituted, by the original grant, lords of the earth."

I might quote, at length, from the sayings of the Baptist Church and the sayings of eminent divines at this early period, showing that Judge Taney has grossly falsified history, but will not detain you with these quotations.

The testimony of the church, and the testimony of the founders of this Republic, from the declaration downward, prove Judge Taney false; as false to history as he is to law.

Washington and Jefferson, and Adams, and Jay, and Franklin, and Rush, and Hamilton, and a host of others, held no such degrading views on the subject of slavery as are imputed by Judge Taney to the Fathers of the Republic.

All, at that time, looked for the gradual but certain abolition of slavery, and shaped the constitution with a view to this grand result.

George Washington can never be claimed as a fanatic, or as the representative of fanatics. The slaveholders impudently use his name for the base purpose of giving respectability to slavery. Yet, in a letter to Robert Morris, Washington uses this language—language which, at this day, would make him a terror of the slaveholders, and the natural representative of the Republican party.

"There is not a man living, who wishes more sincerely than I do, to see some plan adopted for the abolition of slavery; but there is only one proper and effectual mode by which it can be accomplished, and that is by Legislative authority; and this, as far as my suffrage will go, shall not be wanting."

Washington only spoke the sentiment of his times. There were, at that time, Abolition societies in the slave States—Abolition societies in Virginia, in North Carolina, in Maryland, in Pennsylvania, and in Georgia—all slaveholding States. Slavery was so weak, and liberty so strong, that free speech could attack the monster to its teeth. Men were not mobbed and driven out of the presence of slavery, merely because they condemned the slave system. The system was then on its knees imploring to be spared, until it could get itself decently out of the world.

In the light of these facts, the Constitution was framed, and framed in conformity to it.

It may, however, be asked, if the Constitution were so framed that the rights of all the people were naturally protected by it, how happens it that a large part of the people have been held in slavery ever since its adoption? Have the people mistaken the requirements of their own Constitution?

The answer is ready. The Constitution is one thing, its administration is another, and, in this instance, a very different and opposite thing. I am here to vindicate the law, not the administration of the law. It is the written Constitution, not the unwritten Constitution, that is now before us. If, in the whole range of the Constitution, you can find no warrant for slavery, then we may properly claim it for liberty.

Good and wholesome laws are often found dead on the statute book. We may condemn the practice under them and against them, but never the law itself. To condemn the good law with the wicked practice, is to weaken, not to strengthen our testimony.

It is no evidence that the Bible is a bad book, because those who profess to believe the Bible are bad. The slaveholders of the South, and many of their wicked allies at the North, claim the Bible for slavery; shall we, therefore, fling the Bible away as a pro-slavery book? It would be as reasonable to do so as it would be to fling away the Constitution.

We are not the only people who have illustrated the truth, that a people may have excellent law, and detestable practices. Our Savior denounces the Jews, because they made void the law by their traditions. We have been guilty of the same sin.

The American people have made void our Constitution by just such traditions as Judge Taney and Mr. Garrison have been giving to the world of late, as the true light in which to view the Constitution of the United States. I shall follow neither. It is not what Moses allowed for the hardness of heart, but what God requires, ought to be the rule.

It may be said that it is quite true that the Constitution was designed to secure the blessings of liberty and justice to the people who made it, and to the posterity of the people who made it, but was never designed to do any such thing for the colored people of African descent.

This is Judge Taney's argument, and it is Mr. Garrison's argument, but it is not the argument of the Constitution. The Constitution imposes no such mean and satanic limitations upon its own beneficent operation. And, if the Constitution makes none, I beg to know what right has anybody, outside of the Constitution, for the special accommodation of slaveholding villainy, to impose such a construction upon the Constitution?

The Constitution knows all the human inhabitants of this country as "the people." It makes, as I have said before, no discrimination in favor of, or against, any class of the people, but is fitted to protect and preserve the rights of all, without reference to color, size, or any physical peculiarities. Besides, it has been shown by William Goodell and others, that in eleven out of the old thirteen States, colored men were legal voters at the time of the adoption of the Constitution.

In conclusion, let me say, all I ask of the American people is, that they live up to the Constitution, adopt its principles, imbibe its spirit, and enforce its provisions.

When this is done, the wounds of my bleeding people will be healed, the chain will no longer rust on their ankles, their backs will no longer be torn by the bloody lash, and liberty, the glorious birthright of our common humanity, will become the inheritance of all the inhabitants of this highly favored country.

Two speeches by Frederick Douglass; one on West India emancipation, delivered at Canandaigua, Aug. 4th, and the other on the Dred Scott decision, delivered in New York, on the occasion of the anniversary of the American Abolition Society, May, 1857, Rochester, 1857

1. Dred Scott, a slave, was brought by his master, Dr. Emerson, into the Louisiana Territory above the line where slavery was legally prohibited. Here Scott lived a number of years, married, and raised a family. Eventually Dred Scott and his family were brought back to the slave state of Missouri. After Dr. Emerson's death, they were sold to a New Yorker, Sanford, whom they eventually sued for their freedom.

The case was decided by the Supreme Court on March 6, 1857. Chief Justice Taney, writing the majority decision, held that the Missouri Circuit Court had no jurisdiction over the case since the Scotts were not and could never be citizens within the meaning of the Constitution, and therefore had no right to sue in a federal court. Taney argued that when the Constitution was adopted, Negroes were regarded as persons of an inferior order, and not as "citizens," and they were not intended to be included by the constitutional provision giving to citizens of different states the right to sue in federal courts.

Instead of resting the matter here, the Chief Justice went on to express an opinion not vital to the case. In this opinion, Taney upheld the right of slave owners to take their slaves to any territory of the United States and to hold them there in bondage no matter what Congress or the territorial legislature said to the contrary. Dred Scott, he declared, had not become free by residence in the territory covered by the Missouri Compromise, since Congress had no constitutional power to enact the Missouri Compromise.

In a powerful dissenting opinion, Justice Curtis of Massachusetts attacked the majority decision of the Court.

2. On November 7, 1856, "an extensive scheme of Negro insurrection" was discovered in Lavoca, De Witt, and Victoria counties in the southeastern part of Texas. A week later a plot was disclosed in St. Mary Parish, Louisiana. Conspiracies were also discovered in Obion, Tennessee; Fulton, Kentucky; New Madrid, and Scott counties, Missouri. In December conspiracies were discovered in nearly all of the southern states. (See Herbert Aptheker, *American Negro Slave Revolts*, New York, 1943, pp. 345–50; Harvey Wish, "The Slave Insurrection Panic of 1856," Journal of Southern History, vol. V, pp. 208–14; *Annual Report of the American Anti-Slavery Society*, New York, 1856, pp. 76–79.)

WEST INDIA EMANCIPATION, speech delivered at Canandaigua, New York, August 3, 1857

. . . Friends and fellow-citizens: We have met here to-day to celebrate with all fitting demonstrations of joy and gladness, this the twenty-third anniversary of the inauguration of freedom as the ruling law of the British West Indies. The day and the deed are both greatly distinguished. They are as a city set upon a hill. All civilized men at least, have looked with wonder and admiration upon the great deed of justice and humanity which has made the first of August illustrious among all the days of the year. But to no people on the globe, leaving out the emancipated men and women of the West Indies themselves, does this day address itself with so much force and significance, as to the people of the United States. It has made the name of England known and loved in every Slave Cabin, from the Potomac to the Rio Grande, and has spread alarm, hatred, and dread in all the accursed slave markets of our boasted Republic from Baltimore to New Orleans.

Slavery in America, and slavery everywhere, never received a more stunning and killing condemnation.

The event we celebrate is the finding and the restoration to the broken ranks of human brotherhood, eight hundred thousand lost members of the human family. It is the resurrection of a mighty multitude, from the grave of moral, mental, social, and spiritual death, where ages of slavery and oppression, and lust and pride and cruelty, had bound them. Here they were instantly clothed with all the rights, responsibilities, powers, and duties, of free men and women.

Up to the morning of the first of August, 1834, these people were slaves, numbered with the beasts of the field, marked, branded, priced, valued, and ranged as articles of property. The gates of human brotherhood were bolted and barred against them. They were outside of both law and gospel. The love taught in the Bible, and the justice recorded in the Statute Book, did not embrace them: they were outside. Their fellow men had written their names with horses, sheep, and swine, and with horned cattle. They were not governed by the law, but the lash, they were not paid for their work, but whipped on to toil as the American slave now is. Their degradation was complete. They were slaves; and when I have said that, I have said all. The essence of wickedness, the intensified sum of all iniquity, the realization of the idea of a burning hell upon the earth, in which every passion is an unchained devil, let loose to deal out ten thousand pains, and horrors start up to view at the very mention of slavery!—It comprehends all that is foul, shocking, and dreadful. Human nature shudders, and turns pale at its presence, and flies from it as from a den of lions, a nest of scorpions, or an army of rattlesnakes. The very soul sickens, and the mind revolts at the thought of slavery, and the true man welcomes instant death in preference to being reduced to its degradation and ruin.

Yet such was the condition of our brothers and sisters in the British West Indies, up to the morning of the first of August, 1834. The wicked love of dominion by man over man, had made strong their fetters and multiplied their chains. But on the memorable morning which we are met to celebrate, one bolt from the moral sky of Britain left these bloodstained irons all scattered and broken throughout the West Indies, and the limbs they had bruised, out-stretched in praise and thanksgiving to God for deliverance. No man of any sensibility can read the account of that great transaction without emotions too great for utterance. There was something Godlike in this decree of the British nation. It was the spirit of the Son of God commanding the devil of slavery to go out of the British West Indies.

It said tyrant slave-driver, fling away your blood-stained whip, and bury out of sight your broken fetters and chains. Your accursed occupation is gone. It said to the slave, with wounds, bruises, and scars yet fresh upon him, you are emancipated—set free—enfranchised—no longer slaves, but British subjects, and henceforth equal before the British law!

Such, my friends, was the change—the revolution—the wondrous transformation which took place in the condition of the colored people in the British West Indies, twenty-three years ago. With the history of the causes, which led to this great consummation, you are perhaps already sufficiently acquainted. I do not intend in my present remarks to enter into the tedious details of this history, although it might prove quite instructive to some in this assembly. It might prove especially interesting to point out various steps in the progress of the British Anti-Slavery movement, and to dwell upon some of the more striking analogies between that and our movement in this country. The materials at this point are ample, did the limits of the hour permit me to bring them forward.

One remark in this connection I will make. The abolition movement in America, like many other institutions of this country, was largely derived from England. The defenders of American slavery often excuse their villainy on the ground that they inherited the system from England. Abolitionism may be traced to the same source, yet I don't see that it is any more popular on that account. Mr. Garrison applied British abolitionism to American slavery. He did that and nothing more. He found its principles here plainly stated and defined; its truths glowingly enunciated, and the whole subject illustrated, and elaborated in a masterly manner. The sin—the crime—the curse of slavery, were all demonstrated in the light of reason, religion, and morality, and by a startling array of facts. We owe Mr. Garrison our grateful homage in that he was among the first of his countrymen who zealously applied the British argument for abolition, against American slavery. Even the doctrine of immediate emancipation as against gradualism, is of English, not American origin. It was expounded and enforced by Elizabeth Herrick, and adopted by all the earnest abolitionists in England. It came upon the British nation like Uncle Tom's Cabin upon our land after the passing of the fugitive slave law, and it is remarkable that the highest services rendered the anti-slavery cause in both countries, were rendered by women. Elizabeth Herrick, who wrote only a pamphlet, will be remembered as long as the West India Emancipation is remembered, and the name of Harriet Beecher Stowe can never die while the love of freedom lives in the world.

But, my friends, it is not with these analogies and minute references that I mean in my present talk, to deal.

I wish you to look at West India Emancipation as one complete transaction of vast and sublime significance, surpassing all power of exaggeration. We hear and read much of the achievements of this nineteenth century, and much can be said, and truthfully said of them. The world has literally shot forward with the speed of steam and lightning. It has probably made more progress during the last fifty years, than in any five hundred years to which we can refer in the history of the race. Knowledge has been greatly increased, and its blessing widely diffused.

Locomotion has been marvelously improved, so that the very ends of the earth are being rapidly brought together. Time to the traveler has been annihilated.

Deep down beneath the stormy surface of the wide, wide waste of waters, a pathway has been formed for human thought. Machinery of almost every conceivable description, and for almost every conceivable purpose, has been invented and applied; ten thousand discoveries and combinations have been made during these last fifty years, till the world has ceased to ask in astonishment "what next?" for there seems scarcely any margin left for a next. We have made hands of iron and brass, and copper and wood, and though we have not been able to endow them with life and soul, yet we have found the means of endowing them with intelligent motion, and of making them do our work, and to do it more easily, quickly and more abundantly than the hands in their palmiest days were able to perform it. I am not here to disparage or underrate this physical and intellectual progress of the race. I thank my God for every advance which is made in this direction.

I fully appreciate the beautiful sentiment which you farmers, now before me, so highly regard, "that he who makes two blades of grass grow where only one grew before," is a benefactor. I recognize and honor, as you do, all such benefactors. There is not the slightest danger that those who contribute directly to the world's wealth and ease will ever be forgotten by the world. The world loves its own. A hungry man will not forget the hand that feeds him, though he may forget that Providence which caused the bread to grow. Arkwright, Watt, Fulton, Franklin, Morse, and Daguerre, are names which will not fade from the memories of men. They are grand civilizers, but civilizers after their kind—and great as are their achievements, they sink to nothingness when compared with that great achievement which has given us the first day of August as a sacred day. "What shall it profit a man if he gain the whole world and lose his own soul?" We are to view this grand event in the light of this sublime enquiry.

"Men do not live by bread alone," said the great Redeemer. What is true of individual men, is also true of societies, and nations of men. Nations are not held in their spheres, and perpetuated in health by cunning machinery. Railroads, steamships, electric wires, tons of gold and silver, and precious stones cannot save them. A nation may perish in the midst of them all, or in the absence of them all. The true life principle is not in them.

Egypt died in the sight of all her imposing wealth and her everlasting Pyramids. The polished stone is there, but Egypt is gone. Greece has vanished, her life disappeared as it were, in a trance of artistic beauty and architectural splendor. Great Babylon, the mother of harlots and the abominations of the earth, fell in the midst of barbaric wealth and glory. The lesson taught by the history of nations is that the preservation or destruction of communities does not depend upon external prosperity. Men do not live by bread alone, so with nations. They are not saved by art, but by honesty. Not by the gilded splendors of wealth, but by the hidden treasure of manly virtue. Not by the multitudinous gratification of the flesh, but by the celestial guidance of the spirit.

It is in this view that West India Emancipation becomes the most interesting and sublime event of the nineteenth century. It was the triumph of a great moral principle, a decisive victory, after a severe and protracted struggle, of freedom over slavery; of justice and mercy against a grim and bloody system of devilish brutality. It was an acknowledgment by a great nation of the sacredness of humanity, as against the claims of power and cupidity. . . .

Now, my friends, how has this great act of freedom and benevolence been received in the United States. How has our American Christian Church and our American Democratic Government received this glorious new birth of National Righteousness.

From our professions as a nation, it might have been expected that a shout of joy and gladness would have shook the hollow sky, that loud hallelujahs would have rolled up to heaven from all our borders, saying, "Glory to God, in the highest, on earth peace and good will toward man. Let the earth be glad." "The Lord God omnipotent reigneth."

Alas, no such responsive note of rejoicing has reached my ear, except from a part of the colored people and their few white friends. As a nation, we are deaf, dumb, and blind to the moral beauty and transcendent sublimity of West India Emancipation. We have passed it by with averted eyes, regarding it rather as a reflection to be resented than as an example to be imitated. First, we looked for means of impeaching England's motives for abolishing Slavery, and not being able to find any such, we have made ourselves hoarse in denouncing emancipation as a failure.

We have not viewed the great fact in the light of a liberal philosophy, but have applied to it rules of judgment which were not intended to reveal its true character and make known its actual worth. We have taken a microscope to view the stars, and a fish line to measure the ocean's depths.

We have approached it as though it were a railroad, a canal, a steamship, or a newly invented mowing machine, and out of the fullness of our dollar-loving hearts, we have asked with owl-like wisdom, Will it pay? Will it increase the growth of sugar? Will it cheapen tobacco? Will it increase the imports and exports of the Islands? Will it enrich or ruin the planters? How will it effect Jamaica spirits? Can the West Indies be successfully cultivated by free labor? These and sundry other questions, springing out of the gross materialism of our age and nation, have been characteristically put respecting West India Emancipation. All our tests of the grand measure have been such as we might look for from slaveholders themselves. They all proceed from the slave-holders' side, and never from the side, of the emancipated slaves.

The effect of freedom upon the emancipated people of the West Indies passes for nothing. It is nothing that the plundered slave is now a freeman; it is nothing with our sagacious, economical philosophers, that the family now takes the place of concubinage; it is nothing that marriage is now respected where before it was a mockery; it is nothing that moral purity has now a chance to spring up, where before pollution was only possible; it is nothing that education is now spreading among the emancipated men and women, bearing its precious fruits, where only ignorance, darkness, superstition and idolatry prevailed before; it is nothing that the whipping post has given way to the schoolhouse; it is nothing that the church stands now where the slave prison stood before; all these are nothing, I say, in the eyes of our slavery-cursed country.

But the first and last question, and the only question which we Americans have to press in the premises, is the great American question (viz.) *will it pay?*

Sir, if such a people as ours had heard the beloved disciple of the Lord, exclaiming in the rapture of the apocalyptic vision, "And I saw another angel fly in the midst of heaven, having the everlasting gospel to preach to them that dwell on the earth, and to every nation, kindred, tongue, and people;" they, instead of answering, Amen Glory to God in the Highest, would have responded,—But brother John, *will it pay?* Can money be made out of it? Will it make the rich richer, and the strong stronger? How will it affect property? In the eyes of such people, there is no God but wealth; no right and wrong but profit and loss.

Sir, our national morality and religion have reached a depth of baseness than which there is no lower deep. They both allow that if men can make money by stealing men and women, and by working them up into sugar, rice, and tobacco, they may innocently continue the practice, and that he who condemns it is an unworthy citizen, and a disturber of the church. Money is the measure of morality, and the success or failure of slavery, as a money-making system, determines with many whether the thing is virtuous, or villainous, and whether it should be maintained or abolished. They are for Slavery where climate and soil are said to be for it, and are really not opposed to it anywhere, though as a nation we have made a show of opposition to it where the system does not exist. With our geographical ethics, and climatic religion, we have naturally sided with the slaveholders and women-whippers of the West Indies, in denouncing the abolition of slavery in the West Indies a failure.

Sir: As to what has been the effect of West India freedom upon the material condition of the people of those Islands, I am happy that there is one on this platform, who can speak with the authority of positive knowledge. Henry Highland Garnet has lived and labored among those emancipated people. He has enjoyed ample opportunity for forming an intelligent judgment in respect to all that pertains to the subject. I therefore most willingly leave this branch of the subject to him.

One remark, however, I will venture to make—and that is this: I take it that both the friends and the enemies of the emancipated have been too impatient for results. They seem to forget that although a nation can be born in a day, it can mature only in centuries—that though the fetters on the limbs can be broken in an instant, the fetters on the soul can wear off only in the ages.

Degradation, mental, moral, and physical, ground into the very bones of a people by ages of unremitting bondage, will not depart from that people in the course even of many generations.

West India freedom, though more than twenty-one years old, is yet but an infant. And to predicate its future on its present weakness, awkwardness, and improvidence now, is about as wise as to apply the same rule to your little toothless children. It has taken at least a thousand years to bring some of the leading nations of the earth from the point where the Negroes of the West Indies started twenty-three years ago, to their present position. Let considerations like these be duly weighed, and black man though I am, I do not fear the world's judgment.

Now, sir, I like these annual celebrations. I like them because they call us to the contemplation of great interests, and afford an opportunity of presenting salutary truths before the American people. They bring our people together, and enable us to see and commune with each other to mutual profit. If these occasions are conducted wisely, decorously, and orderly, they increase our respectability in the eyes of the world, and silence the slanders of prejudice. If they are otherwise conducted they cover us with shame and confusion. But, sir, these celebrations have been objected to by our slaveholding democracy; they do not think it in good taste. Slaveholders are models of taste. With them, propriety is everything; honesty, nothing. For a long time they have taught our Congress, and Senate, and Pulpits, what subjects should be discussed, and what objects should command our attention. Senator Sumner fails to observe the proscribed rules and he falls upon the Senate floor, stunned and bleeding beneath the ruffian blows of one of our southern models of propriety.[1] By such as these, and by their timid followers, this is called a *British* celebration.

From the inmost core of my soul I pity the mean spirits, who can see in these celebrations nothing but British feeling. The man who limits his admiration of good actions to the country in which he happens to be born, (if he ever was born,) or to the nation or community of which he forms a small part, is a most pitiable object. With him to be one of a nation is more than to be one of the human family. He don't live in the world, but he lives in the United States. Into his little soul the thought of God as our common Father, and of man our common Brother has never entered. To such a soul as that, this celebration cannot but be exceedingly distasteful.

But sarcasm aside, I hold it to be eminently fit that we keep up those celebrations from year to year, at least until we shall have an American celebration to take its place. That the event we thus commemorate transpired in another country, and was wrought out by the labors and sacrifices of the people of another nation, forms no valid objection to its grateful, warm, hearty, and enthusiastic celebration by us. In a very high sense, we may claim that great deed as our own. It belongs not exclusively to England and the English people, but to the lovers of Liberty and of mankind the world over. It is one of those glorious emanations of Christianity, which, like the sun in the Heavens, takes no cognizance of national lines or geographical boundaries, but pours its golden floods of living light upon all. In the great Drama of Emancipation, England was the theatre, but universal and everywhere applying principles of Righteousness, Liberty, and Justice were the actors. The great Ruler of the Universe, the God and Father of all men, to whom be honor, glory, and praise for evermore, roused the British conscience by his truth, moved the British heart, and West India Emancipation was the result. But if only Englishmen may properly celebrate this great concession to justice and liberty, then, sir, we may claim to be Englishmen, Englishmen in the love of Justice and Liberty, Englishmen in magnanimous efforts to protect the weak against the strong, and the slave against the slaveholder. Surely in this sense, it ought to be no disgrace to be an Englishman, even on the soil of the freest people on the globe.

But, Mr. Chairman, we celebrate this day on the broad platform of Philanthropy—whose country is the world, and whose countrymen are all mankind. On this platform we are neither Jews nor Greeks, strangers nor foreigners, but fellow citizens of the household of faith. We are the brothers and friends of Clarkson, Wilberforce, Granville, Sharpe, Richard Baxter, John Wesley, Thomas Day, Bishop Portius, and George Fox, and the glorious company of those who first wrought to turn the moral sense of mankind in active opposition to slavery. They labored for freedom not as Englishmen, but as men, and as brothers to men—the world over—and it is meet and right to commemorate and imitate their noble example. So much for the Anti-British objection.

I will now notice a special objection. It is said that we, the colored people, should do something ourselves worthy of celebration, and not be everlastingly celebrating the deeds of a race by which we are despised.

This objection, strange as it may seem, comes from no enemy of our people, but from a friend. He is himself a colored man, a high spirited and patriotic man, eminent for learning and ability, and to my mind, he has few equals, and no superior among us. I thank Dr. J. M'Cune Smith for this objection, since in the answer I may make to it, I shall be able to give a few of my thoughts on the relation subsisting between the white and colored people of this country, a subject which it well becomes us to consider whenever and wherever we congregate.

In so far as this objection to our celebrating the first of August has a tendency to awaken in us a higher ambition than has hitherto distinguished us, and to raise our aims and activities above the dull level of our present physical wants, and so far as it shall tend to stimulate us to the execution of great deeds of heroism worthy to be held in admiration and perpetual remembrance, for one, sir, I say amen to the whole of it. I am free to say, that nothing is more humiliating than the insignificant part we, the colored people, are taking in the great contest now going on with the powers of oppression in this land. I can stand the insults, assaults, misrepresentations, and slanders of the known haters of my race, and brave them all. I look for such opposition. It is a natural incident of the war, and I trust I am to a certain degree prepared for it; but the stolid contentment, the listless indifference, the moral death which reigns over many of our people, we who should be all on fire, beats down my little flame of enthusiasm and leaves me to labor, half robbed of my natural force. This indifference, in us, is outrageous. It is giving aid and comfort to the men who are warring against our very manhood. The highest satisfaction of our oppressors, is to see the Negro degraded, divested of public spirit, insensible to patriotism, and to all concern for the freedom, elevation, and respectability of the race.

Senator Toombs with a show of truth, lyingly said in Boston a year or two ago in defence of the slavery of the black race, they are mentally and morally inferior, and that if the whole colored population were swept from this country, there would be nothing in twenty years to tell that such a people had ever existed. He exulted over our assumed ignorance and over our destitution of valuable achievements. Of course the slaveholder uttered a falsehood, but to many it seemed to be a truth, and vast numbers of the American people receive it as a truth to-day, and shape their action accordingly.

The general sentiment of mankind is, that a man who will not fight for himself, when he has the means of doing so, is not worth being fought for by others, and this sentiment is just. For a man who does not value freedom for himself will never value it for others, nor put himself to any inconvenience to gain it for others. Such a man, the world says, may lie down until he has sense enough to stand up. It is useless and cruel to put a man on his legs, if the next moment his head is to be brought against a curb-stone.

A man of that type will never lay the world under any obligation to him, but will be a moral pauper, a drag on the wheels of society, and if he, too, be identified with a peculiar variety of the race he will entail disgrace upon his race as well as upon himself. The world in which we live is very accommodating to all sorts of people. It will co-operate with them in any measure which they propose; it will help those who earnestly help themselves, and will hinder those who hinder themselves. It is very polite, and never offers its services unasked.—Its favors to individuals are measured by an unerring principle in this: viz—respect those who respect themselves, and despise those who despise themselves. It is not within the power of unaided human nature to persevere in pitying a people who are insensible to their own wrongs, and indifferent to the attainment of their own rights. The poet was as true to common sense as to poetry when he said,

"Who would be free, themselves must strike the blow."

When O'Connell, with all Ireland at his back, was supposed to be contending for the just rights and liberties of Ireland, the sympathies of mankind were with him, and even his enemies were compelled to respect his patriotism. Kossuth, fighting for Hungary with his pen long after she had fallen by the sword, commanded the sympathy and support of the liberal world till his own hopes died out. The Turks, while they fought bravely for themselves and scourged and drove back the invading legions of Russia, shared the admiration of mankind. They were standing up for their own rights against an arrogant and powerful enemy; but as soon as they let out their fighting to the Allies, admiration gave way to contempt. These are not the maxims and teachings of a cold-hearted world. Christianity itself teaches that a man shall provide for his own house. This covers the whole ground of nations as well as individuals. Nations no more than individuals can innocently be improvident. They should provide for all wants, mental, moral, and religious, and against all evils to which they are liable as nations. In the great struggle now progressing for the freedom and elevation of our people, we should be found at work with all our might, resolved that no man or set of men shall be more abundant in labors, according to the measure of our ability, than ourselves.

I know, my friends, that in some quarters the efforts of colored people meet with very little encouragement. We may fight, but we must fight like the Sepoys of India, under white officers. This class of Abolitionists don't like colored celebrations, they don't like colored conventions, they don't like colored Anti-Slavery fairs for the support of colored newspapers. They don't like any demonstrations whatever in which colored men take a leading part. They talk of the proud Anglo-Saxon blood, as flippantly as those who profess to believe in the natural inferiority of races. Your humble speaker has been branded as an ingrate, because he has ventured to stand up on his own right, and to plead our common cause as a colored man, rather than as a Garrisonian. I hold it to be no part of gratitude to allow our white friends to do all the work, while we merely hold their coats. Opposition of the sort now referred to, is partisan opposition, and we need not mind it. The white people at large will not largely be influenced by it. They will see and appreciate all honest efforts on our part to improve our condition as a people.

Let me give you a word of the philosophy of reform. The whole history of the progress of human liberty shows that all concessions yet made to her august claims, have been born of earnest struggle. The conflict has been exciting, agitating, all-absorbing, and for the time being, putting all other tumults to silence. It must do this or it does nothing. If there is no struggle there is no progress. Those who profess to favor freedom and yet deprecate agitation, are men who want crops without plowing up the ground, they want rain without thunder and lightning. They want the ocean without the awful roar of its many waters.

This struggle may be a moral one, or it may be a physical one, and it may be both moral and physical, but it must be a struggle. Power concedes nothing without a demand. It never did and it never will. Find out just what any people will quietly submit to and you have found out the exact measure of injustice and wrong which will be imposed upon them, and these will continue till they are resisted with either words or blows, or with both. The limits of tyrants are prescribed by the endurance of those whom they oppress. In the light of these ideas, Negroes will be hunted at the North, and held and flogged at the South so long as they submit to those devilish outrages, and make no resistance, either moral or physical. Men may not get all they pay for in this world, but they must certainly pay for all they get. If we ever get free from the oppressions and wrongs heaped upon us, we must pay for their removal. We must do this by labor, by suffering, by sacrifice, and if needs be, by our lives and the lives of others.

Hence, my friends, every mother who, like Margaret Garner, plunges a knife into the bosom of her infant to save it from the hell of our Christian Slavery,[2] should be held and honored as a benefactress. Every fugitive from slavery who like the noble William Thomas at Wilkesbarre, prefers to perish in a river made red by his own blood, to submission to the hell hounds who were hunting and shooting him, should be esteemed as a glorious martyr, worthy to be held in grateful memory by our people. The fugitive Horace, at Mechanicsburgh, Ohio, the other day, who taught the slave catchers from Kentucky that it was safer to arrest white men than to arrest him, did a most excellent service to our cause. Parker and his noble band of fifteen at Christiana, who defended themselves from the kidnappers with prayers and pistols, are entitled to the honor of making the first successful resistance to the Fugitive Slave Bill. But for that resistance, and the rescue of Jerry, and Shadrack,[3] the man-hunters would have hunted our hills and valleys here with the same freedom with which they now hunt their own dismal swamps.

There was an important lesson in the conduct of that noble Krooman in New York, the other day, who, supposing that the American Christians were about to enslave him, betook himself to the mast head, and with knife in hand, said he would cut his throat before he would be made a slave. Joseph Cinque on the deck of the Amistad, did that which should make his name dear to us. He bore nature's burning protest against slavery. Madison Washington who struck down his oppressor on the deck of the Creole, is more worthy to be remembered than the colored man who shot Pitcairn at Bunker Hill.

My friends, you will observe that I have taken a wide range, and you think it is about time that I should answer the special objection to this celebration. I think so too. This, then, is the truth concerning the inauguration of freedom in the British West Indies. Abolition was the act of the British Government. The motive which led the Government to act, no doubt was mainly a philanthropic one, entitled to our highest admiration and gratitude. The National Religion, the justice, and humanity, cried out in thunderous indignation against the foul abomination, and the government yielded to the storm. Nevertheless a share of the credit of the result falls justly to the slaves themselves. "Though slaves, they were rebellious slaves." They bore themselves well. They did not hug their chains, but according to their opportunities, swelled the general protest against oppression. What Wilberforce was endeavoring to win from the British Senate by his magic eloquence, the Slaves themselves were endeavoring to gain by outbreaks and violence. The combined action of one and the other wrought out the final result. While one showed that slavery was wrong, the other showed that it was dangerous as well as wrong. Mr. Wilberforce, peace man though he was, and a model of piety, availed himself of this element to strengthen his case before the British Parliament, and warned the British government of the danger of continuing slavery in the West Indies. There is no doubt that the fear of the consequences, acting with a sense of the moral evil of slavery, led to its abolition. The spirit of freedom was abroad in the Islands. Insurrection for freedom kept the planters in a constant state of alarm and trepidation. A standing army was necessary to keep the slaves in their chains. This state of facts could not be without weight in deciding the question of freedom in these countries.

I am aware that the rebellious disposition of the slaves was said to arise out of the discussions which the abolitionists were carrying on at home, and it is not necessary to refute this alleged explanation. All that I contend for is this: that the slaves of the West Indies did fight for their freedom, and that the fact of their discontent was known in England, and that it assisted in bringing about that state of public opinion which finally resulted in their emancipation. And if this be true, the objection is answered.

Again, I am aware that the insurrectionary movements of the slaves were held by many to be prejudicial to their cause. This is said now of such movements at the South. The answer is that abolition followed close on the heels of insurrection in the West Indies, and Virginia was never nearer emancipation than when General Turner kindled the fires of insurrection at Southampton.

Sir, I have now more than filled up the measure of my time. I thank you for the patient attention given to what I have had to say. I have aimed, as I said at the beginning, to express a few thoughts having some relation to the great interests of freedom both in this country and in the British West Indies, and I have said all that I meant to say, and the time will not permit me to say more.

Two speeches by Frederick Douglass; one on West India emancipation, delivered at Canandaigua, Aug. 4th, and the other on the Dred Scott decision, delivered in New York, on the occasion of the anniversary of the American Abolition Society, May, 1857, Rochester, 1857

1. On May 22, 1856, two days after Senator Sumner delivered his speech, "The Crime against Kansas," he was accosted at his desk by Representative Preston S. Brooks (1819–1857) of South Carolina who denounced him for having uttered "a libel on South Carolina, and Mr. Butler, who is a relative of mine." Brooks then struck Sumner a blow on the head with his heavy walking stick. Pinioned by his desk, Sumner could not rise till he had wrenched the desk from its fastenings. In this condition, he was beaten until he fell bleeding and unconscious to the floor. Three and a half years passed before Sumner was sufficiently recovered to return to the Senate. Meanwhile he had been re-elected by the almost unanimous vote of the Massachusetts legislature.

A special investigating committee of the House reported in favor of the expulsion of Brooks, but the report on a strictly party vote failed to receive the necessary two-thirds majority. Brooks, however, resigned after a speech in his own justification and was unanimously re-elected by his constituents. In the North he was fiercely denounced for his cowardly attack, but in the South he was hailed as a hero, and was presented with a number of gold-headed canes and a gold-handled cowhide.

2. In January, 1856, the Garner family, slaves of Archibald K. Gaines of Kentucky, escaped and found refuge in Cincinnati. They were pursued and attacked. Before the group was captured, Margaret Garner killed one of her children, and severely wounded two others "to save them all from Slavery by death." She was tried on a murder charge in Cincinnati and found guilty, but due to jurisdictional difficulties was returned to slavery in Kentucky. (For a detailed account of this story, see *Annual Report of the American Anti-Slavery Society,* New York, 1856, pp. 44–47.)

3. In February, 1851, Shadrach, a Negro waiter in Boston, was arrested on the complaint of John de Bree of Norfolk, Virginia, and was charged with having escaped from the South in May, 1850. Before the case was decided, a body of Negroes, led by Lewis Hayden, broke into the prison, seized Shadrach, and dispatched him to Canada.

Douglass' paper featured many calls for the abolition of capital punishment, and offered prayers that the day would come when "throughout the Union and throughout the world, this barbarity will be forever cancelled."[1] But Douglass did not confine himself to pious utterances in behalf of the cause. In the fall of 1858 he took part in a pioneer effort in which he suffered bitter discrimination but showed his moral courage. That year he joined Susan B. Anthony, Isaac and Amy Post, Samuel D. Porter, and others in an effort to prevent the execution of one, Ira Stout, who was about to be hanged for murder. Douglass drew up a call for a mass meeting which Susan B. Anthony circulated. "The undersigned, citizens of Rochester, and others, believing Capital Punishment to be unfriendly to the progress of civilization, hostile to a true religion, repulsive to the best instincts of humanity, and deprecating the effects of executions on the public mind, do respectively invite a general attendance of the public at a meeting to be held at City Hall, Thursday Evening, October 7th, at 7 o'clock, with a view of securing, in the case of Ira Stout, condemned to be hung for the crime of murder, commutation of the sentence of death to imprisonment for life."

A counter handbill was immediately distributed by the more conservative citizens of Rochester calling upon the public to assemble in the City Hall and "rescue the meeting from the hands of the fanatics and save the city from the disgrace of being supposed in favor of the abolition of the gallows." Fully aware that trouble was brewing, the adherents of the abolition of capital punishment went ahead with their plans, and Douglass prepared a set of resolutions to be read to the meeting for approval.[2]

When the person designated to serve as chairman failed to make an appearance at the meeting, Douglass was chosen to replace him. "We all felt that a man of *power* must be obtained for chairman," explained one of the sponsors of the gathering, "or the meeting was lost. Such a man is Frederick Douglass; he yielded his own feelings to serve, in this most trying hour, the cause of humanity." A storm of hisses greeted Douglass when he mounted the platform. The mob yelled: "Put in a white man!" "Down with the n——r!" "Whitewash him!" Douglass lashed into the crowd. "Seldom," wrote an observer, "have we heard such earnest eloquence as fell from the lips of Mr. Douglass, as he stood before the maddening crowd, and defended the right of Free Speech. Insulted almost beyond parallel, and . . . beyond endurance, not once did he forget the dignity of his position or the responsibility of the office with which he was invested. Much of his speech, so happily did he use his rich and powerful voice, was distinctly heard above the terrible noise of the mob."

Douglass read his resolutions denouncing capital punishment and asking Governor King to commute Ira Stout's punishment to imprisonment for life. But it was impossible to act on them. Yells, groans, hisses, stamping of feet, whistling, and vile epithets greeted the reading. When some of the rowdies attempted to attack Douglass, the mayor came to the platform and asked the chairman to adjourn the meeting. Douglass, with his daughter upon his arm and his sons by his side, left the hall, "surrounded by a gang of ruffians, heaping all measure of sayings upon him, for the simple and only reason that 'he wore a skin not colored like their own.' "[3] [II:14-15]

RESOLUTIONS PROPOSED FOR ANTI-CAPITAL PUNISHMENT MEETING, ROCHESTER, NEW YORK, OCTOBER 7, 1858

Resolved, That life is the great primary and most precious and comprehensive of all human rights—that whether it be coupled with virtue, honor, or happiness, or with sin, disgrace and misery, the continued possession of it is rightfully not a matter of volition; that it is neither deliberately nor voluntarily assumed, nor to be deliberately or voluntarily destroyed, either by individuals separately, or combined in what is called Government; that it is a right derived solely and directly from God—the source of all goodness and the center of all authority—and is most manifestly designed by Him to be held, esteemed, and reverenced among men as the most sacred, solemn and inviolable of all his gifts to man.

Resolved, That the love of man as manifested in his actions to his fellows, whether in his public or private relations, has ever been the surest test of the presence of God in the soul; that the degree in which the sacredness of human life has been exemplified in all ages of the world, has been the truest index of the measure of human progress; that in proportion as the tide of barbarism has receded, a higher regard has been manifested for the God-given right to life, its inviolability has been strengthened in proportion to the development of the intellect and moral sentiments, and that conscience, reason and revelation unite their testimony against the continuance of a custom, barbarous in its origin, anti-christian in its continuance, vindictive in its character, and demoralizing in its tendencies.

Resolved, That any settled custom, precept, example or law, the observance of which necessarily tends to cheapen human life, or in any measure serves to diminish and weaken man's respect for it, is a custom, precept, example and law utterly inconsistent with the law of eternal goodness written on the constitution of man by his Maker, and is diametrically opposed to the safety, welfare and happiness of mankind; and that however ancient and honorable such laws and customs may be in the eyes of prejudice, superstition and bigotry, they ought to be discountenanced, abolished, and supplanted by a higher civilization and a holier and more merciful Christianity.

Resolved, That in the opinion of this meeting, when a criminal is firmly secured in the iron grasp of the government, and on that account can no longer endanger the peace and safety of society; that when he is wasted and emaciated by heavy chains and horrid thoughts, and long confinement in a gloomy cell—when, as is often the case, he is completely transformed, both in temper and spirit—the execution of the death penalty on such an one is an act of cold blooded and barbarous enormity, and is as cowardly as it is cruel, and that instead of repressing and preventing the horrid crime of murder, it really serves by shocking and blunting the finer and better feelings of human nature, to undermine respect for human life, and leads directly to the perpetration of the crime which it would extinguish.

Resolved, That the time to advance opinions and principles is when those opinions and principles are upon trial, and threatened with outrage; and that while we have respectfully remained silent till the ends of justice have been served in fixing the guilt of the criminal, we now come in the sacred office of humanity and benevolence, to appeal for mercy at the hands of his Excellency, Governor King, on behalf of young Ira Stout, and to ask that his punishment shall be commuted from being capitally executed to imprisonment for life.

Resolved, That punishment as such, is a form of revenge, wreaking upon the criminal the pain he has inflicted on another, wrong in principle and pernicious in practice; arises out of the lowest propensities of human nature, and is opposed to the highest civilization; that it has no sanction in the spirit and teachings of Christ, which everywhere abound in loving kindness and forgiveness.

Resolved, That rather than visit the crime upon the head of the criminal, thus descending to his level, we ought to place him in a position to develop his higher nature; and instead of descending to a spirit of revenge, and degrading ourselves on the one hand, and the criminal on the other, we should urge a thorough reform in our criminal laws—basing them on the truly Christian principle of love and good will towards man, and to reject forever the cold blooded and barbarous principle of retaliation.

Resolved, That a copy of the foregoing resolutions, and the proceedings of this meeting, be transmitted to his Excellency, Governor King, as an expression of the sense of this meeting, and that the same be subscribed by the Chairman and Secretary thereof.

Frederick Douglass, Chairman.
J. Bower, Secretary.

The *Liberator*, October 22, 1858

1. *The North Star*, Mar. 9, 1848.
2. *Liberator*, Oct. 22, 1858; Rochester *Daily American*, Oct. 5–6, 1858.
3. Lucy N. Colman in *Liberator*, Oct. 22, 1858.

Douglass' relations with John Brown . . . began more than ten years before the raid on Harpers Ferry. It was at Brown's home in Springfield that Douglass first learned of the former's plan to aid the slaves, a project which embraced the setting up of an armed force which would function in the very heart of the South. . . . Despite his original skepticism, Douglass came to think favorable of Brown's plan. The more he examined the project, the more convinced he became that it might contribute to undermining slavery, for "men do not like to buy runaway horses, nor to invest their money in a species of property likely to take legs and walk off with itself."[1] At the very least, the plan would reawaken the slumbering conscience of the nation. His sympathy for Brown's project grew as his confidence in the efficacy of moral suasion waned.

Douglass and Brown discussed the project many times after their first meeting in 1847. On several occasions Brown stopped at Douglass' home in Rochester,[2] and spent the night outlining the project for a chain of hide-outs in the Maryland and Virginia mountains from which men could go down to the plantations and encourage the slaves to escape. . . .

On February 1, 1858, Brown arrived at Douglass' home. He would not stay long, he assured his host, and insisted upon paying for his accommodations. He remained several weeks, spending most of the time in his own room writing to numerous friends for financial assistance for his venture, the nature of which he did not reveal. At other times Brown would talk at length of his plan for mountain strongholds, even explaining them to Douglass' children and illustrating "each detail with a set of blocks."[3] Before he left Rochester he had secured a recruit in the person of Shields Green, a runaway slave who was staying at Douglass' home. . . .

In the early summer of 1859, Brown fixed upon Harpers Ferry as the base of his operations in Virginia and rented a farm about five miles from there to collect his arms and his band of followers. By mid-summer he had recruited a little army of twenty-one men, including several Negroes, and was almost ready to strike. In August, Brown decided to reveal the full details of his plan to Douglass in the hope of enlisting him as a member of the company preparing to attack Harpers Ferry. Douglass received a letter from Brown asking him to be present at Chambersburg, Pennsylvania, and to bring Shields Green along. The meeting took place on the night of August 20, in a stone quarry near Chambersburg. Brown, his lieutenant Kagi, Douglass and Green were present. It was in the old quarry that Douglass for the first time learned of Brown's plan to seize Harpers Ferry, capture the leading citizens and hold them as hostages while his band rounded up the slaves in the surrounding areas.[4] Brown was dismayed by the emphatic disapproval registered in Douglass' reaction to his plan. Douglass assured Brown that he was still prepared to join with him in carrying out the original plan of running slaves through the Alleghenies, but the raid on Harpers Ferry was an attack on the national government and was doomed to failure. But no amount of argument could dissuade Brown. The seizure would dramatize the evils of slavery, he argued, capture the attention of the nation and arouse the people to action.[5]

Brown's eloquence and his burning enthusiasm for the cause moved Douglass tremendously, but he remained adamant to all entreaties to participate in the enterprise. As he was preparing to leave, Brown made a final appeal: "Come with me, Douglass! I will defend you with my life, I want you for a special purpose. When I strike, the bees will begin to swarm and I shall want you to help me hive them." Douglass shook his head sadly, and turning to Shields Green he asked him if he had made up his mind. The former slave indicated his decision with the now famous reply that he would go with the "old man."[6] . . .

The Chambersburg meeting between Douglass and Brown marked the last time these good friends were to see one another. On the night of October 16, Brown gave the order to march on Harpers Ferry. When the morning dawned, Brown and his men were in possession of the United States armory and the bridges leading to the Ferry. A few slaves had been persuaded to join them. The following night a company of United States marines, under the command of Colonel Robert E. Lee, arrived; at dawn the building was taken by assault. Brown fought with amazing coolness and courage, but was finally overpowered. Amid popular excitement, he was tried for treason and found guilty. On December 2, 1859, Brown was hanged at Charlestown.

Douglass received the startling news of Brown's capture while lecturing in the National Hall at Philadelphia. He was informed that letters had been found in Brown's possession implicating him, among others, of knowledge of the plot.[7] He knew at once that with the mounting hysteria his life was in extreme danger. At the advice of his friends he left Philadelphia and hastened to New York City, pausing at Hoboken to wire to B. F. Blackball, telegraph operator in Rochester: "Tell Lewis to secure all the important papers in my high desk."[8] Later Douglass learned how fortunate he had been in following the advice of friends in Philadelphia. John W. Hurn, a telegraph operator, and an admirer of Douglass, suppressed for three hours the delivery of a message to the sheriff of Philadelphia ordering him to arrest Frederick Douglass.[9]

Douglass' alarm increased as he read the New York papers. The *New York Herald* headlined a report of Brown's alleged confession to Governor Wise of Virginia: "*Gerrit Smith, Joshua Giddings, Fred Douglass and Other Abolitionists and Republicans Implicated.*" "Enough it seems has been ascertained to justify a requisition from Governor Wise of Virginia, upon Governor Morgan, of New York, for the delivery over to the hands of justice of Gerrit Smith and Fred. Douglass, as parties implicated in the crime of murder and as accessories before the fact." From Richmond came an announcement that one hundred Southerners were offering rewards for the heads of "Traitors" among whom Douglass' name was prominently featured.

On his arrival in Rochester, several friends warned Douglass that the New York Governor would probably surrender him to the Virginia authorities upon request. As most citizens of Rochester would resist the attempt to return Douglass to the South and bloodshed and rioting would follow, he was advised both for his own safety and for the peace of the community, to cross over the border to Canada.[10] Aware that President Buchanan would employ the full power of the federal government to achieve his arrest, Douglass took the advice of his friends and fled to Canada.

Douglass barely evaded his pursuers. He had already been charged in Virginia with "murder, robbery and inciting to servile insurrection in the State of Virginia." Moreover, Governor Wise had asked President Buchanan and the Post-Master General of the United States to grant two agents from Virginia authority to serve as detectives for the post-office department for the purpose of delivering Douglass to the Virginia courts.[11] On October 25, 1859, the Rochester *Union and Advertiser* reported: "It is understood that United States Attorney Ould of Washington, and other federal officers, were here yesterday. It is supposed they came hither for the purpose of arresting Frederick Douglass for his alleged participation in the organized scheme against the slaveholding states, of which the Harper's Ferry insurrection was one of the appointed results."[12]

Had Douglas been arrested by federal authorities at that time the chances are that in the prevailing tense atmosphere he would have followed Brown to the gallows. Despite its facetious tone, the *New York Herald* knew whereof it spoke when it commented: "The black Douglass having some experience in his early life of the pleasures of Southern society had no desire to trust himself again even on the borders of the Potomac."[13] No evidence would have been required to sentence a Negro Abolitionist to death in Virginia during the weeks following the attack on Harpers Ferry. . . .

Two weeks after Harpers Ferry, Douglass wrote an editorial on John Brown which cut through the hysterical outpourings of the press and predicted the course the nation would soon follow. [II:86–93]

CAPT. JOHN BROWN NOT INSANE

One of the most painful incidents connected with the name of this old hero, is the attempt to prove him insane.[14] Many journals have contributed to this effort from a friendly desire to shield the prisoner from Virginia's cowardly vengeance. This is a mistaken friendship, which seeks to rob him of his true character and dim the glory of his deeds, in order to save his life. Was there the faintest hope of securing his release by this means, we would choke down our indignation and be silent. But a Virginia court would hang a crazy man without a moment's hesitation, if his insanity took the form of hatred of oppression; and this plea only blasts the reputation of this glorious martyr of liberty, without the faintest hope of improving his chance of escape.

It is an appalling fact in the history of the American people, that they have so far forgotten their own heroic age, as readily to accept the charge of insanity against a man who has imitated the heroes of Lexington, Concord, and Bunker Hill.

It is an effeminate and cowardly age, which calls a man a lunatic because he rises to such self-forgetful heroism, as to count his own life as worth nothing in comparison with the freedom of millions of his fellows. Such an age would have sent Gideon to a mad-house, and put Leonidas in a strait-jacket. Such a people would have treated the defenders of Thermopylae as demented, and shut up Caius Marcus in bedlam. Such a marrowless population as ours has become under the debaucheries of Slavery, would have struck the patriot's crown from the brow of Wallace, and recommended blisters and bleeding to the heroic Tell. Wallace was often and again as desperately forgetful of his own life in defense of Scotland's freedom, as was Brown in striking for the American slave; and Tell's defiance of the Austrian tyrant, was as far above the appreciation of cowardly selfishness as was Brown's defiance of the Virginia pirates. Was Arnold Winkelried insane when he rushed to his death upon an army of spears, crying "make way for Liberty!" Are heroism and insanity synonyms in our American dictionary? Heaven help us! when our loftiest types of patriotism, our sublimest historic ideals of philanthropy, come to be treated as evidence of moon-struck madness. Posterity will owe everlasting thanks to John Brown for lifting up once more to the gaze of a nation grown fat and flabby on the garbage of lust and oppression, a true standard of heroic philanthropy, and each coming generation will pay its installment of the debt. No wonder that the aiders and abettors of the huge, overshadowing and many-armed tyranny, which he grappled with in its own infernal den, should call him a mad man; but for those who profess a regard for him, and for human freedom, to join in the cruel slander, "is the unkindest cut of all."

Nor is it necessary to attribute Brown's deeds to the spirit of vengeance, invoked by the murder of his brave boys. That the barbarous cruelty from which he has suffered had its effect in intensifying his hatred of slavery, is doubtless true. But his own statement, that he had been contemplating a bold strike for the freedom of the slaves for ten years, proves that he had resolved upon his present course long before he, or his sons, ever set foot in Kansas. His entire procedure in this matter disproves the charge that he was prompted by an impulse of mad revenge, and shows that he was moved by the highest principles of philanthropy. His carefulness of the lives of unarmed persons—his humane and courteous treatment of his prisoners—his cool self-possession all through his trial—and especially his calm, dignified speech on receiving his sentence, all conspire to show that he was neither insane or actuated by vengeful passion; and we hope that the country has heard the last of John Brown's madness. The explanation of his conduct is perfectly natural and simple on its face. He believes the Declaration of Independence to be true, and the Bible to be a guide to human conduct, and acting upon the doctrines of both, he threw himself against the serried ranks of American oppression, and translated into heroic deeds the love of liberty and hatred of tyrants, with which he was inspired from both these forces acting upon his philanthropic and heroic soul. This age is too gross and sensual to appreciate his deeds, and so calls him mad; but the future will write his epitaph upon the hearts of a people freed from slavery, because he struck the first effectual blow.

Not only is it true that Brown's whole movement proves him perfectly sane and free from merely revengeful passion, but he has struck the bottom line of the philosophy which underlies the abolition movement. He has attacked slavery with the weapons precisely adapted to bring it to the death. Moral considerations have long since been exhausted upon slaveholders. It is in vain to reason with them. One might as well hunt bears with ethics and political economy for weapons, as to seek to "pluck the spoiled out of the hand of the oppressor" by the mere force of moral law. Slavery is a system of brute force. It shields itself behind *might,* rather than right. It must be met with its own weapons. Capt. Brown has initiated a new mode of carrying on the crusade of freedom, and his blow has sent dread and terror throughout the entire ranks of the piratical army of slavery. His daring deeds may cost him his life, but priceless as is the value of that life, the blow he has struck, will, in the end, prove to be worth its mighty cost. Like Samson, he has laid his hands upon the pillars of this great national temple of cruelty and blood, and when he falls, that temple will speedily crumble to its final doom, burying its denizens in its ruins.

Douglass' Monthly, November, 1859

1. *Life and Times of Frederick Douglass,* pp. 339–41.

2. On November 15, 1856, Elizabeth Cady Stanton wrote that in December she expected to see Brown at Rochester where he would be "on a visit to Frederick Douglass." (T. Stanton and H. S. Blatch, *Elizabeth Cady Stanton,* New York, 1901, vol. II, p. 69.)

3. J. M. Parker, "Reminiscences of Frederick Douglass," *Outlook,* vol. LI, Apr. 6, 1895, p. 553; F. B. Sanborn, *The Life and Letters of John Brown,* Boston, 1885, p. 434. Brown probably stayed a little more than two weeks at Douglass' home. There are, however, conflicting reports on this question. Richard J. Hinton says he was at Douglass' home "for three weeks," and Douglass says he "remained for about a month." (Richard J. Hinton, *John Brown and His Men,* New York, 1899, p. 165; *Life and Times of Frederick Douglass,* p. 385.)

4. On August 9, 1867, Douglass wrote to Gerrit Smith: "I wish to say distinctly that John Brown never declared nor intimated to me that he was about to embark in a grand or unqualified insurrection; that the only insurrection he proposed was the escaping of slaves and their

376 Frederick Douglass: Selected Speeches and Writings

standing for their lives against any who should pursue them. For years before, Captain Brown's long entertained plan was to go to the mountains in the Slave States and invite the Slaves to flee there. . . . Three or four weeks previous to his invasion of Harpers Ferry Captain Brown requested me to have an interview with him at Chambersburg, Pennsylvania. I did it and in this interview he had determined upon that invasion instead of carrying out his old plan of going into the mountains. . . . I do not suppose that any of his friends at the North knew of it." (Frederick Douglass Mss., Frederick Douglass Memorial Home, Anacostia, D.C.) The last sentence would seem to indicate that Douglass was the first person outside of his band to whom Brown told his plan for attacking Harpers Ferry.

5. Sanborn, *Life and Letters of John Brown,* pp. 536–38; *Life and Times of Frederick Douglass,* p. 387. Douglass brought with him a letter to Brown containing twenty-five dollars from Mrs. J. N. Gloucester, a prosperous Negro woman in Brooklyn.

6. *Life and Times of Frederick Douglass,* p. 390. Douglass' meeting with Brown lasted for three days. (Douglass to F. B. Sanborn, Apr. 15, 1885, Sanborn, *Life and Letters of John Brown,* p. 538.)

7. Sanborn, *Recollections of Seventy Years,* p. 153. Only a brief, unimportant letter to Douglass was found by Brown's captors. No other material involving Douglass was discovered among his papers at the farm.

8. Amy Hamner-Croughton, "Anti-Slavery Days in Rochester," *Publications of the Rochester Historical Society,* Rochester, N. Y., vol. XV, 1936, p. 143. Letters from Brown and a copy of the "Provisional Constitution" Brown had drawn up while at Douglass' home were in the desk. After the message was received they were removed.

9. Washington *Evening Star,* Feb. 21, 1895.

10. *New York Herald,* Oct. 20, 1859; *Liberator,* Dec. 23, 1859; Hamner-Croughton, *op. cit.,* p. 144.

11. *Life and Times of Frederick Douglass,* p. 379; *New York Herald,* Oct. 22, 1859.

12. See also Rochester *Democrat,* Oct. 26, 1859, and Rochester *Union,* Oct. 25, 1859, reprinted in *New York Herald,* Oct. 28, 1859.

13. *New York Herald,* Nov. 4, 1859.

14. Brown's counsel attempted to raise the plea of his alleged insanity as a reason why the Governor of Virginia should show him clemency, but John Brown absolutely refused "to avail himself of this possible means of escape from the hangman. Not even to save his life would he consent to have the sacrifices already made minimized, and his entire twenty years' war upon slavery written down as the mere mania of a lunatic." (Oswald Garrison Villard, *John Brown,* New York, 1943, pp. 506–07.) In December, 1859, Brown was hanged at Charlestown.

Douglass [was] severely criticized for his refusal to join Brown's expedition and for having fled to Canada after the raid.[1] John E. Cook, one of the men captured with Brown, even blamed Douglass for the failure of the expedition, charging that the latter had been assigned to bring a large body of men to reinforce Brown. In [this] letter,. . . a brilliant document,. . . Douglass denied the charge. [II:92]

TO THE ROCHESTER *DEMOCRAT AND AMERICAN*

Canada West, Oct. 31, 1859.

Mr. Editor:

I notice that the telegraph makes Mr. Cook (one of the unfortunate insurgents at Harper's Ferry, and now in the hands of the thing calling itself the Government of Virginia, but which in fact is but an organized conspiracy by one party of the people against the other and weaker,) denounce me as a coward—and to assert that I promised to be present at the Harper's Ferry insurrection. This is certainly a very grave impeachment, whether viewed in its bearings upon friends or upon foes, and you will not think it strange that I should take a somewhat serious notice of it. Having no acquaintance whatever with Mr. Cook, and never having exchanged a word with him about the Harper's Ferry insurrection, I am induced to doubt that he could have used the language concerning me which the wires attribute to him. The lightning, when speaking for itself, is among the most direct, reliable and truthful of things; but when speaking for the terror-stricken slaveholders at Harper's Ferry, it has been made the swiftest of liars. Under their nimble and trembling fingers, it magnified seventeen men into seven hundred—and has since filled the columns of the New York *Herald* for days with interminable contradictions. But, assuming that it has told only the simple truth, as to the sayings of Mr. Cook in this instance, I have this answer to make to my accuser: Mr. Cook may be perfectly right in denouncing me as a coward. I have not one word to say in defence or vindication of my character for courage. I have always been more distinguished for running than fighting—and, tried by the Harper's Ferry insurrection test, I am most miserably deficient in courage—even more so than Cook, when he deserted his old brave captain, and fled to the mountains. To this extent Mr. Cook is entirely right, and will meet no contradiction from me or from anybody else. But wholly, grievously, and most unaccountably wrong is Mr. Cook, when he asserts that I promised to be present in person at the Harper's Ferry insurrection. Of whatever other imprudence and indiscretion I may have been guilty, I have never made a promise so rash and wild as this. The taking of Harper's Ferry was a measure never encouraged by my word or by my vote, at any time or place; my wisdom or my cowardice has not only kept me from Harper's Ferry, but has equally kept me from making any promise to go there. I desire to be quite emphatic here—for of all guilty men, he is the guiltiest who lures his fellowmen to an undertaking of this sort, under promise of assistance, which he afterwards fails to render. I therefore declare that there is no man living, and no man dead, who if living, could truthfully say that I ever promised him or anybody else, either conditionally or otherwise, that I would be present in person at the Harper's Ferry insurrection. My field of labor for the abolition of slavery has not extended to an attack upon the United States arsenal. In the teeth of the documents already published, and of those which hereafter may be published, I affirm no man connected with that insurrection, from its noble and heroic leader down, can connect my name with a single broken promise of any sort whatever. So much I deem it proper to say negatively.

The time for a full statement of what I know, and of *all* I know, of this desperate but sublimely disinterested effort to emancipate the slaves of Maryland and Virginia, from their cruel taskmasters, has not yet come, and may never come. In the denial which I have now made, my motive is more a respectful consideration for the opinions of the slave's friends, than from my fear of being made an accomplice in the general *conspiracy* against Slavery. I am ever ready to write, speak, publish, organize, combine, and even to conspire against Slavery, when there is a reasonable hope for success. Men who live by robbing their fellow-men of their labor and liberty, have forfeited their right to know anything of the thoughts, feelings, or purposes of those whom they rob and plunder. They have by the single act of slaveholding voluntarily placed themselves beyond the laws of justice and honor, and have become only fitted for companionship with thieves and pirates—the common enemies of God and of all mankind. While it shall be considered right to protect oneself against thieves, burglars, robbers and assassins, and to slay a wild beast in the act of devouring his human prey, it can never be wrong for the imbruted and whip-scarred slaves, or their friends, to hunt, harass and even strike down the traffickers in human flesh. If anybody is disposed to think less of me on account of this sentiment; or because I may have had a knowledge of what was about to occur, and did not assume the base and detestable character of an informer, he is a man whose good or bad opinion of me may be equally repugnant and despicable. Entertaining this sentiment, I may be asked, why I did not join John Brown—the noble old hero whose one right hand has shaken the foundation of the American Union, and whose ghost will haunt the bed-chambers of all the born and unborn slaveholders of Virginia through all their generations, filling them with alarm and consternation! My answer to this has already been given, at least, impliedly given: "The tools to those that can use them." Let every man work for the abolition of Slavery in his own way. I would help all, and hinder none. My position in regard to the Harper's Ferry insurrection may be easily inferred from these remarks, and I shall be glad if those papers which have spoken of me in connection with it would find room for this brief statement.

I have no apology for keeping out of the way of those gentlemanly United States Marshals, who are said to have paid Rochester a somewhat protracted visit lately, with a view to an interview with me. A government recognizing the validity of the *Dred Scott* decision, at such a time as this, is not likely to have any very charitable feelings towards me; and if I am to meet its representatives, I prefer to do so, at least, upon equal terms. If I have committed any offence against Society, I have done so on the soil of the State of New York, and I should be perfectly willing *there* to be arraigned before an impartial jury; but I have quite insuperable objections to being caught by the hands of Mr. Buchanan, and "*bagged*" by Gov. Wise. For this appears to be the arrangement. Buchanan does the fighting and hunting, and Wise "*bags*" the game.

Some reflections may be made upon my leaving on a tour to England, just at this time. I have only to say, that my going to that country has been rather delayed than hastened by the insurrection at Harper's Ferry. All knew that I had intended to leave here in the first week of November.

Frederick Douglass

Reprinted in New York *Herald,* November 4, 1859

1. As late as 1919 several of the surviving members of Brown's family, Henry Thompson, Salmon Brown, Annie Brown Adams, and Sarah Brown, told Oswald Garrison Villard that they had always believed that Douglass had failed "to live up to his obligations." (Oswald Garrison Villard, *John Brown,* New York, 1943, pp. 323, 627.)

TO HELEN BOUCASTER, SECR., SHEFFIELD A.S.A.

North Parade, Halifax, Dec. 7, 1859

My dear Friend:

Having, for the moment, very much upon my hands, I cannot go fully into the question of the right of an enslaved people to gain their freedom by a resort to force. Nor indeed is it necessary that I should. I can, however, at once, give you the assurance that my advocacy of the cause of the slave in England has no reference whatever to any plan or purpose involving a resort to arms, for the liberation of my Brothers & Sisters in slavery. My mission is wholly peaceful. On that point you may feel wholly at rest. On the subject of Harper's Ferry, I can be equally explicit. I neither took part in that transaction nor counselled the taking it, but opposed the measure as fraught only with disaster and ruin to the main object of the enterprise, which was to run off slaves into the mountains, and into Canada where they could protect and defend themselves. I do hope that a difference of opinion on any one point will not defeat our co-operating against slavery at other points where we agree; but of that you must judge. The liberties of England are bulwarked about by ten thousand cannon. The slave is a victim of a constant *insurrection,* by which his blood is drawn out drop by drop! It may not be altogether impartial to lay down the rule of submission to him, too sternly, especially since he has submitted already two hundred years. First pure, then peaceable.

Very truly & gratefully your friend,

Frederick Douglass

Ms., The John Rylands University Library of Manchester, Deansgate, Manchester, England

---

The news that Frederick Douglass was on the high seas bound for England aroused considerable excitement in British anti-slavery circles. Here was the one man who could revive the drooping spirits of anti-slavery forces and inspire the English people into vigorous activity for the cause of abolition. His talents and reputation were enough, but the report of his implication in the Harpers Ferry affair and his narrow escape from imprisonment were additional guarantee that he would address capacity audiences. The British *Anti-Slavery Reporter* was confident that Douglass' visit would do much "to stimulate the energy and increase the efficiency of the existing Societies, and to lead to the formation of many new ones."[1]

As in his previous visit thirteen years before, Douglass did much to strengthen the British anti-slavery movement. His lectures, dealing mainly with the significance of John Brown's raid and the anti-slavery interpretation of the Constitution, were not only well-attended but were widely distributed in pamphlet form. "His *powerful* and eloquent appeals," wrote James Walker, secretary of the Leeds Young Men's Anti-Slavery Society, "deepen our detestation of slavery, and have imparted to us a stronger impulse for, and led us more actively and devotedly into anti-slavery work than ever."[2] The impetus Douglass gave the British anti-slavery forces during his five months' visit in 1859–1860 became evident during the Civil War and was in some measure responsible for the tremendous support of the English masses for the Union cause. [II:94–95]

THE CONSTITUTION OF THE UNITED STATES: IS IT PRO-SLAVERY OR ANTISLAVERY? speech delivered in Glasgow, Scotland, March 26, 1860

... I proceed to the discussion. And first a word about the question. Much will be gained at the outset if we fully and clearly understand the real question under discussion. Indeed, nothing is or can be understood till this is understood. Things are often confounded and treated as the same, for no better reason than that they resemble each other, even while they are in their nature and character totally distinct and even directly opposed to each other. This jumbling up things is a sort of dust-throwing which is often indulged in by small men who argue for victory rather than for truth. Thus, for instance, the American Government and the American Constitution are spoken of in a manner which would naturally lead the hearer to believe that the one is identical with the other; when the truth is, they are as distinct in character as is a ship and a compass. The one may point right and the other steer wrong. A chart is one thing, the course of the vessel is another. The Constitution may be right, the Government wrong. If the Government has been governed by mean, sordid, and wicked passions, it does not follow that the Constitution is mean, sordid, and wicked. What, then, is the question? I will state it. But first let me state what is not the question. It is not whether slavery existed in the United States at the time of the adoption of the Constitution; it is not whether slaveholders took part in framing the Constitution; it is not whether those slaveholders, in their hearts, intended to secure certain advantages in that instrument for slavery; it is not whether the American Government has been wielded during seventy-two years in favour of the propagation and permanence of slavery; it is not whether a pro-slavery interpretation has been put upon the Constitution by the American Courts—all these points may be true or they may be false, they may be accepted or they may be rejected, without in any wise affecting the real question in debate. The real and exact question between myself and the class of persons represented by the speech at the City Hall[3] may be fairly stated thus:—1st, Does the United States Constitution guarantee to any class or description of people in that country the right to enslave, or hold as property, any other class or description of people in that country? 2nd, Is the dissolution of the union between the slave and free States required by fidelity to the slaves, or by the just demands of conscience? Or, in other words, is the refusal to exercise the elective franchise, and to hold office in America, the surest, wisest, and best way to abolish slavery in America?

To these questions the Garrisonians say Yes. They hold the Constitution to be a slaveholding instrument, and will not cast a vote or hold office, and denounce all who vote or hold office, no matter how faithfully such persons labour to promote the abolition of slavery. I, on the other hand, deny that the Constitution guarantees the right to hold property in man, and believe that the way to abolish slavery in America is to vote such men into power as will use their powers for the abolition of slavery. This is the issue plainly stated, and you shall judge between us. Before we examine into the disposition, tendency, and character of the Constitution, I think we had better ascertain what the Constitution itself is. Before looking for what it means, let us see what it is. Here, too, there is much dust to be cleared away. What, then, is the Constitution? I will tell you. It is no vague, indefinite, floating, unsubstantial, ideal something, coloured according to any man's fancy, now a weasel, now a whale, and now nothing. On the contrary, it is a plainly written document, not in Hebrew or Greek, but in English, beginning with a preamble, filled out with articles, sections, provisions, and clauses, defining the rights, powers, and duties to be secured, claimed, and exercised under its authority. It is not even like the British Constitution, which is made up of enactments of Parliament, decisions of Courts, and the established usages of the Government. The American Constitution is a written instrument full and complete in itself. No Court in America, no Congress, no President, can add a single word thereto, or take a single word therefrom. It is a great national enactment done by the people, and can only be altered, amended, or added to by the people. I am careful to make this statement here; in America it would not be necessary. It would not be necessary here if my assailant had showed the same desire to set before you the simple truth, which he manifested to make out a good case for himself and friends. Again, it should be borne in mind that the mere text, and only the text, and not any commentaries or creeds written by those who wished to give the text a meaning apart from its plain reading, was adopted as the Constitution of the United States. It should also be borne in mind that the intentions of those who framed the Constitution, be they good or bad, for slavery or against slavery, are to be respected so far, and so far only, as we find those intentions plainly stated in the Constitution. It would be the wildest of absurdities, and lead to endless confusion and mischiefs, if, instead of looking to the written paper itself, for its meaning, it were attempted to make us search it out, in the secret motives, and dishonest intentions, of some of the men who took part in writing it. It was what they said that was adopted by the people, not what they were ashamed or afraid to say, and really omitted to say. Bear in mind, also, and the fact is an important one, that the framers of the Constitution sat with closed doors, and that this was done purposely, that nothing but the result of their labours should be seen, and that that result should be judged of by the people free from any of the bias shown in the debates. It should also be borne in mind, and the fact is still more important, that the debates in the convention that framed the Constitution, and by means of which a pro-slavery interpretation is now attempted to be forced upon that instrument, were not published till more than a quarter of a century after the presentation and the adoption of the Constitution.

These debates were purposely kept out of view, in order that the people should adopt, not the secret motives or unexpressed intentions of any body, but the simple text of the paper itself. Those debates form no part of the original agreement. I repeat, the paper itself, and only the paper itself, with its own plainly-written purposes, is the Constitution. It must stand or fall, flourish or fade, on its own individual and self-declared character and objects. Again, where would be the advantage of a written Constitution, if, instead of seeking its meaning in its words, we had to seek them in the secret intentions of individuals who may have had something to do with writing the paper? What will the people of America a hundred years hence care about the intentions of the scriveners who wrote the Constitution? These men are already gone from us, and in the course of nature were expected to go from us. They were for a generation, but the Constitution is for ages. Whatever we may owe to them, we certainly owe it to ourselves, and to mankind, and to God, to maintain the truth of our own language, and to allow no villainy, not even the villainy of holding men as slaves—which Wesley says is the sum of all villainies—to shelter itself under a fair-seeming and virtuous language. We owe it to ourselves to compel the devil to wear his own garments, and to make wicked laws speak out their wicked intentions. Common sense, and common justice, and sound rules of interpretation all drive us to the words of the law for the meaning of the law. The practice of the Government is dwelt upon with much fervour and eloquence as conclusive as to the slaveholding character of the Constitution. This is really the strong point, and the only strong point, made in the speech in the City Hall. But good as this argument is, it is not conclusive. A wise man has said that few people have been found better than their laws, but many have been found worse. To this last rule America is no exception. Her laws are one thing, her practice is another thing. We read that the Jews made void the law by their tradition, that Moses permitted men to put away their wives because of the hardness of their hearts, but that this was not so at the beginning. While good laws will always be found where good practice prevails, the reverse does not always hold true. Far from it. The very opposite is often the case. What then? Shall we condemn the righteous law because wicked men twist it to the support of wickedness? Is that the way to deal with good and evil? Shall we blot out all distinction between them, and hand over to slavery all that slavery may claim on the score of long practice? Such is the course commended to us in the City Hall speech. After all, the fact that men go out of the Constitution to prove it pro-slavery, whether that going out is to the practice of the Government, or to the secret intentions of the writers of the paper, the fact that they do go out is very significant. It is a powerful argument on my side. It is an admission that the thing for which they are looking is not to be found where only it ought to be found, and that is in the Constitution itself. If it is not there, it is nothing to the purpose, be it wheresoever else it may be. But I shall have more to say on this point hereafter.

The very eloquent lecturer at the City Hall doubtless felt some embarrassment from the fact that he had literally to *give* the Constitution a pro-slavery interpretation; because upon its face it of itself conveys no such meaning, but a very opposite meaning. He thus sums up what he calls the slaveholding provisions of the Constitution. I quote his own words:—"Article I, section 9, provides for the continuance of the African slave trade for 20 years, after the adoption of the Constitution. Art. 4, section 9, provides for the recovery from other States of fugitive slaves. Art. I, section 2, gives the slave States a representation of three-fifths of all the slave population; and Art. I, section 8, requires the President to use the military, naval, ordnance, and militia resources of the entire country for the suppression of slave insurrection, in the same manner as he would employ them to repel invasion." Now any man reading this statement, or hearing it made with such a show of exactness, would unquestionably suppose that the speaker or writer had given the plain written text of the Constitution itself. I can hardly believe that he intended to make any such impression. It would be a scandalous imputation to say he did. And yet what are we to make of it? How can we regard it? How can he be screened from the charge of having perpetrated a deliberate and point-blank misrepresentation? That individual has seen fit to place himself before the public as my opponent, and yet I would gladly find some excuse for him. I do not wish to think as badly of him as this trick of his would naturally lead me to think. Why did he not read the Constitution? Why did he read that which was not the Constitution? He pretended to be giving chapter and verse, section and clause, paragraph and provision. The words of the Constitution were before him. Why then did he not give you the plain words of the Constitution? Oh, sir, I fear that that gentleman knows too well why he did not. It so happens that no such words as "African slave trade," no such words as "slave representation," no such words as "fugitive slaves," no such words as "slave insurrections," are anywhere used in that instrument. These are the words of that orator, and not the words of the Constitution of the United States. Now you shall see a slight difference between my manner of treating this subject and that which my opponent has seen fit, for reasons satisfactory to himself, to pursue. What he withheld, that I will spread before you: what he suppressed, I will bring to light: and what he passed over in silence, I will proclaim: that you may have the whole case before you, and not be left to depend upon either his, or upon my inferences or testimony. Here then are the several provisions of the Constitution to which reference has been made. I read them word for word just as they stand in the paper, called the United States Constitution, Art. I, sec. 2. "Representatives and direct taxes shall be apportioned among the several States which may be included in this Union, according to their respective numbers, which shall be determined by adding to the whole number of free persons, including those bound to service for a term of years, and excluding Indians not taxed, three-fifths of all other persons; Art. I, sec. 9. The migration or importation of such persons as any of the States now existing shall think fit to admit, shall not be prohibited by the Congress prior to the year one thousand eight hundred and eight, but a tax or duty may be imposed on such importation, not exceeding ten dollars for each person; Art. 4, sec. 2. No person held to service or labour in one State, under the laws thereof, escaping into another shall, in consequence of any law or regulation therein, be discharged from such service or labour; but shall be delivered up on claim of the party to whom such service or labour may be due; Art. I, sec. 8. To provide for calling for the militia to execute the laws of the Union, suppress insurrections, and repel invasions." Here, then, are those provisions of the Constitution, which the most extravagant defenders of slavery can claim to guarantee a right of property in man. These are the provisions which have been pressed into the service of the human fleshmongers of America. Let us look at them just as they stand, one by one. Let us grant, for sake of the argument, that the first of these provisions, referring to the basis of representation and taxation, does refer to slaves. We are not compelled to make that admission, for it might fairly apply to aliens—persons living in the country, but not naturalized. But giving the provisions the very worst construction, what does it amount to? I answer—It is a downright disability laid upon the slaveholding States; one which deprives those States of two-fifths of their natural basis of representation. A black man in a free State is worth just two-fifths more than a black man in a slave State, as a basis of political power under the Constitution. Therefore, instead of encouraging slavery, the Constitution encourages freedom by giving an increase of "two-fifths" of political power to free over slave States. So much for the three-fifths clause; taking it at its worst, it still leans to freedom, not to slavery; for, be it remembered that the Constitution nowhere forbids a coloured man to vote. I come to the next, that which it is said guaranteed the continuance of the African slave trade for twenty years. I will also take that for just what my opponent alleges it to have been, although the Constitution does not warrant any such conclusion. But, to be liberal, let us suppose it did, and what follows? why, this—that this part of the Constitution, so far as the slave trade is concerned, became a dead letter more than 50 years ago, and now binds no man's conscience for the continuance of any slave trade whatever. Mr. Thompson is just 52 years too late in dissolving the Union on account of this clause. He might as well dissolve the British Government, because Queen Elizabeth granted to Sir John Hawkins to import Africans into the West Indies 300 years ago! But there is still more to be said about this abolition of the slave trade. Men, at that time, both in England and in America, looked upon the slave trade as the life of slavery. The abolition of the slave trade was supposed to be the certain death of slavery. Cut off the stream, and the pond will dry up, was the common notion at that time.

Wilberforce and Clarkson, clear-sighted as they were, took this view; and the American statesmen, in providing for the abolition of the slave trade, thought they were providing for the abolition of slavery. This view is quite consistent with the history of the times. All regarded slavery as an expiring and doomed system, destined to speedily disappear from the country. But, again, it should be remembered that this very provision, if made to refer to the African slave trade at all, makes the Constitution anti-slavery rather than for slavery, for it says to the slave States, the price you will have to pay for coming into the American Union is, that the slave trade, which you would carry on indefinitely out of the Union, shall be put an end to in twenty years if you come into the Union. Secondly, if it does apply, it expired by its own limitation more than fifty years ago. Thirdly, it is anti-slavery, because it looked to the abolition of slavery rather than to its perpetuity. Fourthly, it showed that the intentions of the framers of the Constitution were good, not bad. I think this is quite enough for this point. I go to the "slave insurrection" clause, though, in truth, there is no such clause. The one which is called so has nothing whatever to do with slaves or slaveholders any more than your laws for the suppression of popular outbreaks has to do with making slaves of you and your children. It is only a law for suppression of riots or insurrections. But I will be generous here, as well as elsewhere, and grant that it applies to slave insurrections. Let us suppose that an anti-slavery man is President of the United States (and the day that shall see this the case is not distant) and this very power of suppressing slave insurrection would put an end to slavery. The right to put down an insurrection carries with it the right to determine the means by which it shall be put down. If it should turn out that slavery is a source of insurrection, that there is no security from insurrection while slavery lasts, why, the Constitution would be best obeyed by putting an end to slavery, and an anti-slavery Congress would do that very thing. Thus, you see, the so-called slave-holding provisions of the American Constitution, which a little while ago looked so formidable, are, after all, no defence or guarantee for slavery whatever. But there is one other provision. This is called the "Fugitive Slave Provision." It is called so by those who wish to make it subserve the interest of slavery in America, and the same by those who wish to uphold the views of a party in this country. It is put thus in the speech at the City Hall:—"Let us go back to 1787, and enter Liberty Hall, Philadelphia, where sat in convention the illustrious men who framed the Constitution—with George Washington in the chair. On the 27th of September, Mr. Butler and Mr. Pinckney, two delegates from the State of South Carolina, moved that the Constitution should require that fugitive slaves and servants should be delivered up like criminals, and after a discussion on the subject, the clause, as it stands in the Constitution, was adopted. After this, in the conventions held in the several States to ratify the Constitution, the same meaning was attached to the words. For example, Mr. Madison (afterwards President), when recommending the Constitution to his constituents, told them that the clause would secure them their property in slaves." I must ask you to look well to this statement. Upon its face, it would seem a full and fair statement of the history of the transaction it professes to describe and yet I declare unto you, knowing as I do the facts in the case, my utter amazement at the downright untruth conveyed under the fair seeming words now quoted. The man who could make such a statement may have all the craftiness of a lawyer, but who can accord to him the candour of an honest debater? What could more completely destroy all confidence in his statements? Mark you, the orator had not allowed his audience to hear read the provision of the Constitution to which he referred. He merely characterized it as one to "deliver up fugitive slaves and servants like criminals," and tells you that that provision was adopted as it stands in the Constitution. He tells you that this was done "after discussion." But he took good care not to tell you what was the nature of that discussion. He would have spoiled the whole effect of his statement had he told you the whole truth. Now, what are the facts connected with this provision of the Constitution? You shall have them. It seems to take two men to tell the truth. It is quite true that Mr. Butler and Mr. Pinckney introduced a provision expressly with a view to the recapture of fugitive slaves: it is quite true also that there was some discussion on the subject—and just here the truth shall come out. These illustrious kidnappers were told promptly in that discussion that no such idea as property in man should be admitted into the Constitution. The speaker in question might have told you, and he would have told you but the simple truth, if he had told you that the proposition of Mr. Butler and Mr. Pinckney—which he leads you to infer was adopted by the convention that framed the Constitution—was, in fact, promptly and indignantly rejected by that convention. He might have told you, had it suited his purpose to do so, that the words employed in the first draft of the fugitive clause were such as applied to the condition of slaves, and expressly declared that persons held to "servitude" should be given up; but that the word "servitude" was struck from the provision, for the very reason that it applied to slaves. He might have told you that that same Mr. Madison declared that that word was struck out because the convention would not consent that the idea of property in men should be admitted into the Constitution. The fact that Mr. Madison can be cited on both sides of this question is another evidence of the folly and absurdity of making the secret intentions of the framers the criterion by which the Constitution is to be construed. But it may be asked—if this clause does not apply to slaves, to whom does it apply?

I answer, that when adopted, it applies to a very large class of persons— namely, redemptioners—persons who had come to America from Holland, from Ireland, and other quarters of the globe—like the Coolies to the West Indies— and had, for a consideration duly paid, become bound to "serve and labour" for the parties to whom their service and labour was due. It applies to indentured apprentices and others who had become bound for a consideration, under contract duly made, to serve and labour. To such persons this provision applies, and only to such persons. The plain reading of this provision shows that it applies, and that it can only properly and legally apply, to persons "bound to service." Its object plainly is, to secure the fulfilment of contracts for "service and labour." It applies to indentured apprentices, and any other persons from whom service and labour may be due. The legal condition of the slave puts him beyond the operation of this provision. He is not described in it. He is a simple article of property. He does not owe and cannot owe service. He cannot even make a contract. It is impossible for him to do so. He can no more make such a contract than a horse or an ox can make one. This provision, then, only respects persons who owe service, and they only can owe service who can receive an equivalent and make a bargain. The slave cannot do that, and is therefore exempted from the operation of this fugitive provision. In all matters where laws are taught to be made the means of oppression, cruelty, and wickedness, I am for strict construction. I will concede nothing. It must be shown that it is so nominated in the bond. The pound of flesh, but not one drop of blood. The very nature of law is opposed to all such wickedness, and makes it difficult to accomplish such objects under the forms of law. Law is not merely an arbitrary enactment with regard to justice, reason, or humanity. Blackstone defines it to be a rule prescribed by the supreme power of the State commanding what is right and forbidding what is wrong. The speaker at the City Hall laid down some rules of legal interpretation. These rules send us to the history of the law for its meaning. I have no objection to such a course in ordinary cases of doubt. But where human liberty and justice are at stake, the case falls under an entirely different class of rules. There must be something more than history—something more than tradition. The Supreme Court of the United States lays down this rule, and it meets the case exactly—"Where rights are infringed—where the fundamental principles of the law are overthrown—where the general system of the law is departed from, the legislative intention must be expressed with irresistible clearness." The same court says that the language of the law must be construed strictly in favour of justice and liberty. Again, there is another rule of law. It is—Where a law is susceptible of two meanings, the one making it accomplish an innocent purpose, and the other making it accomplish a wicked purpose, we must in all cases adopt that which makes it accomplish an innocent purpose. Again, the details of a law are to be interpreted in the light of the declared objects sought by the law. I set these rules down against those employed at the City Hall. To me they seem just and rational. I only ask you to look at the American Constitution in the light of them, and you will see with me that no man is guaranteed a right of property in man, under the provisions of that instrument. If there are two ideas more distinct in their character and essence than another, those ideas are "persons" and "property," "men" and "things." Now, when it is proposed to transform persons into "property" and men into beasts of burden, I demand that the law that contemplates such a purpose shall be expressed with irresistible clearness. The thing must not be left to inference, but must be done in plain English. I know how this view of the subject is treated by the class represented at the City Hall. They are in the habit of treating the Negro as an exception to general rules. When their own liberty is in question they will avail themselves of all rules of law which protect and defend their freedom; but when the black man's rights are in question they concede everything, admit everything for slavery, and put liberty to the proof. They reverse the common law usage, and presume the Negro a slave unless he can prove himself free. I, on the other hand, presume him free unless he is proved to be otherwise. Let us look at the objects for which the Constitution was framed and adopted, and see if slavery is one of them. Here are its own objects as set forth by itself:—"We, the people of these United States, in order to form a more perfect union, establish justice, ensure domestic tranquillity, provide for the common defence, promote the general welfare, and secure the blessings of liberty to ourselves and our posterity, do ordain and establish this Constitution for the United States of America." The objects here set forth are six in number: union, defence, welfare, tranquillity, justice, and liberty. These are all good objects, and slavery, so far from being among them, is a foe of them all. But it has been said that Negroes are not included within the benefits sought under this declaration. This is said by the slaveholders in America—it is said by the City Hall orator—but it is not said by the Constitution itself. Its language is "we the people;" not we the white people, not even we the citizens, not we the privileged class, not we the high, not we the low, but we the people; not we the horses, sheep, and swine, and wheel-barrows, but we the people, we the human inhabitants; and, if Negroes are people, they are included in the benefits for which the Constitution of America was ordained and established. But how dare any man who pretends to be a friend to the Negro thus gratuitously concede away what the Negro has a right to claim under the Constitution? Why should such friends invent new arguments to increase the hopelessness of his bondage? This, I undertake to say, as the conclusion of the whole matter, that the constitutionality of slavery can be made out only by disregarding the plain and common-sense reading of the Constitution itself; by discrediting and casting away as worthless the most beneficent rules of legal interpretation; by ruling the Negro outside of these beneficent rules; by claiming everything for slavery; by denying everything for freedom; by assuming that the Constitution does not mean what it says, and that it says what it does not mean; by disregarding the written Constitution, and interpreting it in the light of a secret understanding. It is in this mean, contemptible, and underhand method that the American Constitution is pressed into the service of slavery. They go everywhere else for proof that the Constitution is pro-slavery but to the Constitution itself. The Constitution declares that no person shall be deprived of life, liberty, or property without due process of law; it secures to every man the right of trial by jury, the privilege of the writ of habeas corpus—that great writ that put an end to slavery and slave-hunting in England—it secures to every State a republican form of government. Any one of these provisions, in the hands of abolition statesmen, and backed up by a right moral sentiment, would put an end to slavery in America. The Constitution forbids the passing of a bill of attainder: that is, a law entailing upon the child the disabilities and hardships imposed upon the parent. Every slave law in America might be repealed on this very ground. The slave is made a slave because his mother is a slave. But to all this it is said that the practice of the American people is against my view. I admit it. They have given the Constitution a slaveholding interpretation. I admit it. They have committed innumerable wrongs against the Negro in the name of the Constitution. Yes, I admit it all; and I go with him who goes farthest in denouncing these wrongs. But it does not follow that the Constitution is in favour of these wrongs because the slaveholders have given it that interpretation. To be consistent in his logic, the City Hall speaker must follow the example of some of his brothers in America—he must not only fling away the Constitution, but the Bible. The Bible must follow the Constitution, for that, too, has been interpreted for slavery by American divines. Nay, more, he must not stop with the Constitution of America, but make war upon the British Constitution, for, if I mistake not, that gentleman is opposed to the union of Church and State. In America he called himself a Republican. Yet he does not go for breaking down the British Constitution, although you have a Queen on the throne, and bishops in the House of Lords.

My argument against the dissolution of the American Union is this: It would place the slave system more exclusively under the control of the slaveholding States, and withdraw it from the power in the Northern States which is opposed to slavery. Slavery is essentially barbarous in its character. It, above all things else, dreads the presence of an advanced civilisation. It flourishes best where it meets no reproving frowns, and hears no condemning voices. While in the Union it will meet with both. Its hope of life, in the last resort, is to get out of the Union. I am, therefore, for drawing the bond of the Union more closely, and bringing the Slave States more completely under the power of the Free States. What they most dread, that I most desire. I have much confidence in the instincts of the slaveholders. They see that the Constitution will afford slavery no protection when it shall cease to be administered by slaveholders. They see, moreover, that if there is once a will in the people of America to abolish slavery, there is no word, no syllable in the Constitution to forbid that result. They see that the Constitution has not saved slavery in Rhode Island, in Connecticut, in New York, or Pennsylvania; that the Free States have increased from one up to eighteen in number, while the Slave States have only added three to their original number. There were twelve Slave States at the beginning of the Government: there are fifteen now. There was one Free State at the beginning of the Government: there are eighteen now. The dissolution of the Union would not give the North a single advantage over slavery, but would take from it many. Within the Union we have a firm basis of opposition to slavery. It is opposed to all the great objects of the Constitution. The dissolution of the Union is not only an unwise but a cowardly measure—15 millions running away from three hundred and fifty thousand slaveholders. Mr. Garrison and his friends tell us that while in the Union we are responsible for slavery. He and they sing out "No Union with slaveholders," and refuse to vote. I admit our responsibility for slavery while in the Union, but I deny that going out of the Union would free us from that responsibility. There now clearly is no freedom from responsibility for slavery to any American citizen short of the abolition of slavery. The American people have gone quite too far in this slaveholding business now to sum up their whole business of slavery by singing out the cant phrase, "No union with slaveholders." To desert the family hearth may place the recreant husband out of the presence of his starving children, but this does not free him from responsibility. If a man were on board of a pirate ship, and in company with others had robbed and plundered, his whole duty would not be performed simply by taking the longboat and singing out "No union with pirates." His duty would be to restore the stolen property. The American people in the Northern States have helped to enslave the black people. Their duty will not have been done till they give them back their plundered rights. Reference was made at the City Hall to my having once held other opinions, and very different opinions to those I have now expressed. An old speech of mine delivered fourteen years ago was read to show—I know not what. Perhaps it was to show that I am not infallible. If so, I have to say in defence, that I never pretended to be. Although I cannot accuse myself of being remarkably unstable, I do not pretend that I have never altered my opinion both in respect to men and things. Indeed, I have been very much modified both in feeling and opinion within the last fourteen years. When I escaped from slavery, and was introduced to the Garrisonians, I adopted very many of their opinions, and defended them just as long as I deemed them true. I was young, had read but little, and naturally took some things on trust. Subsequent experience and reading have led me to examine for myself. This has brought me to other conclusions. When I was a child, I thought and spoke as a child. But the question is not as to what were my opinions fourteen years ago, but what they are now. If I am right now, it really does not matter what I was fourteen years ago. My position now is one of reform, not of revolution. I would act for the abolition of slavery through the Government—not over its ruins. If slaveholders have ruled the American Government for the last fifty years, let the anti-slavery men rule the nation for the next fifty years. If the South has made the Constitution bend to the purposes of slavery, let the North now make that instrument bend to the cause of freedom and justice. If 350,000 slaveholders have, by devoting their energies to that single end, been able to make slavery the vital and animating spirit of the American Confederacy for the last 72 years, now let the freemen of the North, who have the power in their own hands, and who can make the American Government just what they think fit, resolve to blot out for ever the foul and haggard crime, which is the blight and mildew, the curse and the disgrace of the whole United States.

Pamphlet, Howard University Library

1. *The Anti-Slavery Reporter*, Dec. 1, 1859, p. 276.
2. *The Anti-Slavery Advocate*, vol. II, No. 42, June 1, 1860, pp. 393–94.
3. The speech referred to was delivered by George Thompson in the City Hall, Glasgow, on February 27, 1860. It was a fairly bitter attack on Douglass' interpretation of the Constitution. (See *Lecture on the Constitution of the United States by Mr. Thompson Delivered in the City Hall, Glasgow, February 27th, 1860*. London Emancipation Committees Tracts, No. 5, London, 1860 and *The Anti-Slavery Advocate*, London, Apr. 2, 1860, vol. II, no. 40, pp. 317–21. Copies of both are in the Boston Public Library.)

––––––––––

Douglass' tour of England was cut short by the tragic news of the death of his youngest daughter, Annie, "the light and life of my house." Very devoted to her father, the ten-year-old child had grieved since his abrupt departure for Canada. She had been a constant companion of John Brown during the weeks he had spent in Rochester. . . .

Although he was urged to continue his tour into Ireland and the south of England, Douglass decided "to fly to my sorrow-stricken family." He promised to resume his tour in the fall but this was not to be. He did not return to England until long after the Civil War. [II:95]

TO MY BRITISH ANTI-SLAVERY FRIENDS

Dear Friends:—You will have learned ere this the cause of my sudden departure from Great Britain to the United States, and will be glad to know that up to this date no harm has befallen me, or is likely to befall me, on account of the troubles in this country during the Autumn of last year. I am in Rochester, N.Y., at my office daily, walking the streets openly, known to be in the country by our slaveholding Government officials; yet, either because they are too busy in electioneering for a new President, or because they have no definite proof of my complicity in the Harper's Ferry insurrection, or because they dread the difficulty of taking me from Rochester, they allow me for the present to go unmolested, and do not even call me to Washington to give evidence before the Committee of the American Senate to trace out the ramifications of the John Brown plot.[1]—The Committee has thus far proved an entire failure. It has elicited nothing on the subject beyond the statements and disclosures of noble old John Brown himself. Nothing has really been added to the honest declaration of motives, plans and purposes, made by the brave old man to the alarmed and vindictive slaveholders, after he was overpowered and completely in their cruel hands. He spoke to them from the open gate of death in which he stood, and his words were solemn, searching and truthful. Of all the witnesses thus far summoned, none have given any other coloring to the Harper's Ferry affair than was given by the man who originated and attempted to carry out that uprising against slavery. One reason, perhaps, why I have not been compelled to appear before the Committee, is the doubt which has arisen as to the constitutional power of a purely legislative body, like the American Senate, to exercise a function so entirely judicial in its character as that of enforcing the attendance of witnesses, and compelling them to testify. In this respect our Senate differs from your House of Lords, of which it is in some respects a copy. It is not judicial. Nevertheless, I am yet liable to be called upon at any moment to go before this body, for while there is evidently no written constitutional grant of power of this sort to the Senate, the long exercise of the power unquestioned, makes it in some degree authoritative and conclusive. While I have no desire to go to Washington to testify before the Committee, the danger of violence toward me there would be light compared with what it would have been when the country was deeply and fiercely excited by the trials of the insurgents, and the reign of terror everywhere prevailing at the South. Yet, if summoned, I should hesitate before placing myself on slaveholding soil. Not even a white man with anti-slavery opinions is safe in the slave States. I am an offender both by color and conduct. I have done too much to give slaveholding a bad name, to be readily forgiven, or allowed to escape unharmed. I shall therefore see to it that I am not drawn into a slave State if I can help it, and my present conviction is that I can help it.

Very many of you, my kind, good friends, could not assent to the wisdom of my returning to this country, and regretted my determination to do so; but all of you sympathized with me in the sentiment which led me so suddenly to break off my anti-slavery work among you, and in the face of perils by sea and land, to fly to my sorrow-stricken family. My presence nowhere else, after the long months of anxiety, sickness, sorrow and death which have intervened, could be so sacredly beneficial as *at home*. My wife, my children, and the condition of my business affairs, all needed me; and although I ran some risk and suffered much during the voyage from a severe fall, caused by a sudden and unexpected motion of the ship, I do not regret having returned. For all your kindness, hospitality, sympathy, aid and co-operation while a stranger and sojourner among you, my heart overflows with the warmest gratitude. Especially do I remember the many touching marks of sympathy with me in the loss of my dearly beloved daughter, whose death was all the more painful because resulting, no doubt, from overanxiety for the safety of her father, and deep sorrow for the death of dear old John Brown, upon whose knee she had often sat only a few months before.

I am still intending to resume my tour in the Fall. All Ireland and the south of England remain to be visited, and I hope to enter upon my duties as early as the month of October.

On looking into the accounts of my weekly anti-slavery paper, and finding that its receipts had fallen much below its current expenses, I at first decided to discontinue its publication until after my return from Europe, for I then thought of leaving home for England about the first of this month. I have now, however, determined to continue its publication, and employ the interval between the present month and the time of my leaving the U.S., in enlarging its circulation, collecting outstanding subscriptions, and otherwise securing its permanence and increasing its usefulness.—The paper is as much needed as ever. Even in the event of the election of a Republican President, which I still hopefully anticipate, the real work of abolitionizing the public mind will still remain, and every pen, press and voice now employed will then, as now, be needed to carry forward that great work. The Republican party is, as I have often said in conversation with you, only negatively anti-slavery. It is opposed to the *political power* of slavery, rather than to slavery itself, and would arrest the spread of the slave system, humble the slave power, and defeat all plans for giving slavery any further guarantee of permanence. This is very desirable, but it leaves the great work of abolishing slavery, and giving freedom to the four millions now groaning in the chains and under the lash of slavery, still to be accomplished. The triumph of the Republican party will only open the way for this great work. While life, and health, and strength endure, I hope under God to be found faithfully and earnestly devoting whatever of power and skill I possess to this object—an object which I am glad to know is deeply dear to your hearts, and to the promotion of which you gladly extend your aid and sympathy.

I have nothing to add on the present aspect of anti-slavery affairs here to what will be found in the other columns of the *Monthly,* except to say, that I have never known the slaves to be escaping from slavery more rapidly than during the several weeks I have been at home. Ten have found food, shelter, counsel and comfort under my roof since I came home, and have been duly forwarded where they are beyond the reach of the slave-hunter. God speed the year of Jubilee the wide world o'er!

Yours, truly,   F.D.
Rochester, May 26, 1860.

Douglass' Monthly, June, 1860

1. The Thirty-Sixth Congress assembled three days after the execution of John Brown. A resolution was immediately offered by Senator John M. Mason for the appointment of a committee to investigate every aspect of the affair at Harpers Ferry. The resolution was unanimously adopted, and a Senate Committee was appointed.

When Douglass returned to this country, he found that the Presidential campaign was already under way. At their national convention at Charleston in April, the Democrats had split into two separate factions with Stephen A. Douglas heading one and John C. Breckenridge the other. Early the following month, the Constitutional Union Party had selected James A. Bell and Edward Everett as their candidates for President and Vice-President. In mid-May, the Republicans, in high glee over the dissension in the Democracy, assembled at Chicago and nominated Abraham Lincoln to head their national ticket.

The readers of *Douglass' Monthly* for June, 1860, were treated to a masterly analysis of the significance of Lincoln's nomination. Douglass did not share the prevailing opinion among eastern journalists that "the Rail-Splitter candidate" for President was an absolute nonentity whose nomination was the result of pure accident plus vote-swapping, logrolling and wirepulling. [Instead he wrote that] Lincoln merited the support of the more radical elements among the Republicans. [II:95–96]

THE CHICAGO NOMINATIONS

The nomination of Mr. Lincoln has taken the people of this part of the Country by surprise. The popular feeling in favor of Mr. Seward was nowhere stronger, or more earnest, than in this part of the State. The people felt that he had a stronger claim upon his party than any other man, having done more to give that party shape, and to systematise the elements composing it, and to furnish it with ideas, than any other man in the nation.

The Republican party is justly proud of Mr. Seward, proud of his history, proud of his talents, and proud of his attainments as a statesman, and it is not without strong feeling that it sees him shoved aside to make room for a man whose abilities are untried, and whose political history is too meagre to form a basis on which to judge of his future.

Still there does not appear to be the slightest disposition, on the part of Mr. Seward's friends to be factional under their disappointment, but they acquiesce in the decision of the Convention, with a grace which speaks much in praise of the party discipline in the Republican ranks.

There are a few of the more radical men, who regard Mr. Seward's defeat as a sort of political "judgment" upon him for his late speech in the Senate.[1] To them, that speech was so full of concession to the slave power, so clear a bid for the nomination at Chicago, and so nearly sunk the progressive statesman in the political trimmer, that they are well content with his defeat.

The road to the Presidency does not lead through the swamps of compromise and concession any longer, and Mr. Seward ought to have made that discovery, before John Brown frightened him into making his last great speech. In that speech he stooped quite too low for his future fame, and lost the prize that tempted the stoop after all. He had far better have lost it while standing erect.

Mr. Lincoln is a man of unblemished private character; a lawyer, standing near the front rank at the bar of his own State, has a cool, well balanced head; great firmness of will; is perseveringly industrious; and one of the most frank, honest men in political life. He cannot lay claim to any literary culture beyond the circle of his practical duties, or to any of the graces found at courts, or in diplomatic circles, but must rely upon his "good hard sense" and honesty of purpose, as capital for the campaign, and the qualities to give character to his administration. His friends cannot as yet claim for him a place in the front rank of statesmanship, whatever may be their faith in his latent capacities. His political life is thus far to his credit, but it is a political life of fair promise rather than one of rich fruitage.

It was, perhaps, this fact that obtained for him the nomination. Our political history has often illustrated the truth that a man may be too great a statesman to become President. The failure of Webster, Clay and Silas Wright in the Presidential race, is in point here, and the success of Harrison, Polk, Taylor and Pierce, tends to prove the same proposition.

If, therefore, Mr. Lincoln possesses great capacities, and is yet to be proved a great statesman, it is lucky for him that a political exigency moved his party to take him on trust and before his greatness was ripe, or he would have lost the chance. But when once elected it will be no longer dangerous for him to develop great qualities, and we hope that in taking him on a "profession of his faith," rather than on the recommendations of his political life, his party will witness his continual "growth in grace," and his administration will redound to the glory of his country, and his own fame.

As to his principles, there is no reason why the friends of Mr. Seward should not heartily support him. He is a radical Republican, and is fully committed to the doctrine of the "irrepressible conflict."[2] In his debates with Douglas, he came fully up to the highest mark of Republicanism, and he is a man of will and nerve, and will not back down from his own assertions. He is not a compromise candidate by any means. Mr. Bates was to have played that part, with Horace Greeley for prompter. But the Chicago Convention did not fall into the melting mood. Greeley "piped unto them but they would not dance;" he mourned unto them, but they did not "lament," and his "betweenity" candidate fell flat between the two stools of Somewhere and Nowhere. Mr. Greeley has the greatest passion for making political nominations from the ranks of his enemies of any man in America. His candidates are like the frogs bred along the Nile; the head begins to croak and show signs of life while the body is yet plain mud. So Mr. Greeley is forever digging up some man for a candidate, whose head just begins to appear, while his whole body is yet enveloped in pro-slavery mud, and we are glad he was defeated.

The Presidential contest, this fall, is likely to be rather sharply defined. If Mr. Douglas is put on the course, the old personal rivalry between him and Mr. Lincoln will render the campaign especially spicy.

Illinois will form a sort of pivot, around which the waves of the political sea will sweep and dash with great force.

The nomination of Bell and Everett[3] will tend to divert strength from the Democracy, and give advantage to Lincoln, but will have no great influence on the general result. Slavery propagandism, whether led by the vigorous and impulsive "little giant," or by the more staid and conservative Bell, will be the great enemy which the Republican party must meet.

For ourselves, we are sorry that the hosts of freedom could not have been led forth upon a higher platform, and have had inscribed upon their banners, "Death to Slavery," instead of "No more Slave States." But the people will not have it so, and we are compelled to work and wait for a brighter day, when the masses shall be educated up to a higher standard of human rights and political morality.

But as between the hosts of Slavery propagandism and the Republican party— incomplete as is its platform of principles—our preferences cannot hesitate.

While we should be glad to co-operate with a party fully committed to the doctrine of "All rights to all men," in the absence of all hope of rearing up the standard of such a party for the coming campaign, we can but desire the success of the Republican candidates.

It will be a great work accomplished when this Government is divorced from the active support of the inhuman slave system. To pluck executive patronage out of the hands of the pliant tools of the whip and the chain; to turn the tide of the National Administration against the man-stealers of this country and in favor of even a partial application of the principles of justice, is a glorious achievement, and we hope for its success.

To save a prospective empire, yet to be planted in the Great West, from the desecrating foot prints of inhuman oppression, and open these mountain slopes and river bottoms, to a hardy, industrious, and enlightened population of freemen, who are sure to follow the "Star of Empire" toward the Pacific, marching to the inspiring songs of "Free labor and free men," is a consummation devoutly to be wished—a vision of prospective good, inspiring to the patriot.

It is a sad fact that the people of this country are, as yet, on a plane of morality and philanthropy far below what the exigencies of the cause of human progress demands. It is to be regretted that they will not come up to the glorious work of striking the shackles from four million slaves at a single blow—but even though they persist in approaching the blood-cemented Bastille of oppression, by the slow processes of a cautious siege, rather than by the more brave and inspiring march of a storming party, we are compelled to submit for the present, and take with gratitude the little good thus proffered.

Douglass' Monthly, June, 1860

1. In an effort to placate the conservatives and assure his nomination as the Republican candidate for President, Seward, early in 1860, tried to live down his reputation of radicalism. He had originally endorsed Hinton Rowan Helper's *The Impending Crisis,* but in the edition printed in January, 1860, his endorsement was deleted. And in late February, 1860, in a speech in the Senate upon a bill for the admission of Kansas, Seward scrupulously avoided the "higher law" and "irrepressible conflict" doctrines. Nor did he demand, as formerly, that the Supreme Court rescind the Dred Scott decision. "Differences of opinion," he said, "even on the subject of slavery, are with us political, not social or personal differences. There is not one disunionist or disloyalist among us all. We are altogether unconscious of any process of dissolution going on among us or around us. We have never been more patient, and never loved the representatives of other sections more than now." (*Congressional Globe,* 36th Cong., 1st Sess., p. 913.)

2. In a speech in Rochester in the fall of 1858, Seward said: "Our country exhibits, in full operation, two radically different political systems; the one resting on the basis of servile or slave labor, the other on the basis of voluntary labor of freemen. . . . Hitherto, the two systems have existed in different States, but side by side, within the American Union. These antagonist systems are continually coming into closer contact, and collision results. Shall I tell you what this collision means? They who think it is accidental, unnecessary, the work of interested, or fanatical agitators, and therefore ephemeral, mistake the case altogether. It is an irrepressible conflict between opposing and enduring forces; and it means that the United States must and will, sooner or later, become either entirely a slave-holding nation, or entirely a free-labor nation." (Frederick W. Seward, *Seward at Washington, 1846–1861,* New York, 1891, p. 351.)

3. The Constitutional Union Party met in convention at Baltimore on May 9, 1860, and nominated John Bell for President and Edward Everett for Vice President. They ran on a platform that no political principles be recognized other than "the Constitution of the country, the Union of the States, and the enforcement of the laws."

On his return to Rochester in May 1860, Douglass found that sentiment around John Brown and those associated with him had changed. In December, 1859, a Senate Committee, headed by James M. Mason of Virginia, had been appointed to investigate the attack on Harpers Ferry. On June 14, 1860, the committee submitted an innocuous report which stated that while Brown had planned "to commence a servile insurrection" which he hoped to extend "throughout the entire South," he did not appear to have intrusted even his immediate followers with his plans. After much consideration, the committee announced that it was "not prepared to suggest any legislation."[1]

[The following is] a letter to a group of Abolitionists assembling at North Elba, in the Adirondacks, . . . to do honor to the memory of John Brown. [II:94]

TO JAMES REDPATH, ESQ.

Rochester, June 29, 1860

My Dear Sir:

Your kind note, inviting me to meet with yourself and other friends on the 4th of July, at North Elba, came into my hands only yesterday. Had it reached me only a day or two earlier, I certainly should have complied with it. Very gladly would I assemble with you and the others on that revolutionary day, to do honor to the memory of one whom I regard as THE man of the nineteenth century. Little, indeed, can you and I do to add lustre to his deathless fame.—The principles of John Brown, attested by a life of spotless integrity and sealed by his blood, are self-vindicated. His name is covered with a glory so bright and enduring, as to require nothing at our hands to increase or perpetuate it. Only for our own sake, and that of enslaved and imbruted humanity must we assemble. To have been acquainted with John Brown, shared his counsels, enjoyed his confidence, and sympathized with the great objects of his life and death, I esteem as among the highest privileges of my life. We do but honor to ourselves in doing honor to him, for it implies the possession of qualities akin to his.

I have little hope of the freedom of the slave by peaceful means. A long course of peaceful slaveholding has placed the slaveholders beyond the reach of moral and humane considerations. They have neither ears nor hearts for the appeals of justice and humanity. While the slave will tamely submit his neck to the yoke, his back to the lash, and his ankle to the fetter and chain, the Bible will be quoted, and learning invoked to justify slavery. The only penetrable point of a tyrant is the *fear of death*. The outcry that they make, as to the danger of having their *throats cut* is because they deserve to have them *cut*. The efforts of John Brown and his brave associates, though apparently unavailing, have done more to upset the logic and shake the security of slavery, than all other efforts in that direction for twenty years.

The sleeping dust, over which yourself and friends proposed to meet on the 4th, cannot be revived; but the noble principles and disinterested devotion which led John Brown to step serenely to the gallows and lay down his life will never die. They are all the more potent for his death.

Not anxiously are the eyes and hearts of the American slaves and their friends turned to the lofty peaks of the Alleghanies. The innumerable glens, caves, ravines and rocks of those mountains, will yet be the hiding-places of hunted liberty. The eight-and-forty hours of John Brown's school in Virginia taught the slaves more than they could have otherwise learned in a half-century. Even the mistake of remaining in the arsenal after the first blow was struck, may prove the key to future successes. The tender regard which the dear old man evinced for the life of the tyrants—and which should have secured him his life—will not be imitated by future insurgents. Slaveholders are as insensible to magnanimity as to justice, and the measure they meter must be meted to them again. My heart is with you.

Very truly,
Fred'k Douglass

The *Liberator,* July 27, 1860

1. Henry Wilson, *History of the Rise and Fall of the Slave Power in America,* vol. II, p. 606.

———

The secrecy of the Underground Railroad makes it impossible to determine the number of slaves Douglass aided. But it was a figure which easily ran into the hundreds.[1] "Fugitives are constantly passing through here," William C. Nell wrote from Rochester in 1852, "giving no rest to their feet nor slumber to their eyelids, until the protecting aegis of Queen Victoria makes them welcome freemen on Canada's shore. A party of fifteen thus rid themselves of republican slavery on Thanksgiving day!!!"[2] In 1854 Douglass stated that in two weeks, he had aided over thirty fugitives on their way to Canada. In June, 1857, he informed his subscribers that four fugitives "passed through our hands to the Queen's dominions." On January 8, 1858, he wrote to the Ladies' Irish Anti-Slavery Association: ". . . you will be glad to know that the number escaping from Slavery has latterly been unusually large. We have passed over our section of the underground railroad about forty within the last sixty days." The *Rochester Express* of October 25, 1859, reported that in one day "not less than fifteen thousand dollars worth of 'property' passed through this city, on the 'underground,'" in the shape of "a dozen smart, intelligent, young and middle-aged men and women." In May, 1860, ten fugitives found "food and shelter, counsel and comfort," under Douglass' roof, and during the following month he sped ten more on the road to Canada and freedom.[3] [II:46]

TO WILLIAM STILL

Rochester, July 2d, 1860

. . . You hold up before me the glorious promises contained in the sacred Scriptures. These are needed by none more than by those who have presumed to put themselves to the work of accomplishing the abolition of Slavery in this country. There is scarcely one single interest, social, moral, religious, or physical, which is not in some way connected with this stupendous evil. On the side of the oppressor there is power, now as in the earlier days of the world. I find much comfort in the thought that I am but a passenger on board of this ship of life. I have not the management committed to me. I am to obey orders, and leave the rest to the great Captain whose wisdom is able to direct. I have only to go on in His fear and in His spirit, uttering with pen and tongue the whole truth against Slavery, leaving to Him the honor and the glory of destroying this mighty work of the devil. I long for the end of my people's bondage, and would give all I possess to witness the great jubilee; but God can wait, and surely I may. If He, whose pure eyes cannot look upon sin with allowance, can permit the day of freedom to be deferred, I certainly can work and wait. The times are just now a little brighter; but I will walk by faith, not by right, for all grounds of hope founded on external appearance, have thus far signally failed and broken down under me. Twenty years ago, Slavery did really *seem* to be rapidly hastening I to its fall, but ten years ago, the Fugitive Slave Bill, and the efforts to enforce it, changed the whole appearance of the struggle. Anti-slavery in an abolition sense has been ever since battling against heavy odds, both in Church and State. Nevertheless, God reigns, and we need not despair, and I for one do not. I know, at any rate, no better work for me during the brief period I am to stay on the earth, than is found in pleading the cause of the down-trodden and the dumb.

Since I reached home, I have had the satisfaction of passing nearly a score [of fugitive slaves] on to Canada, only two women among them all. The constant meeting with these whip-scarred brothers will not allow me to become forgetful of the four millions still in bonds.

William Still, *The Underground Railroad,* Philadelphia, 1872, p. 598

1. Benjamin Quarles estimates that in ten years "Douglass personally helped approximately four hundred fugitives gain their freedom." ("The Public Life of Frederick Douglass," unpublished Ph.D. thesis, University of Wisconsin, 1938, p. 118.)

2. William C. Nell to Garrison, Feb. 19, 1852, *Liberator,* Mar. 5, 1852.

3. *Frederick Douglass' Paper,* May 19, 1854, June 19, 1857; *The Anti-Slavery Reporter,* July 1, 1858, p. 168; *Annual Report of the American Anti-Slavery Society for the Year Ending May 1, 1860,* New York, 1861, p. 49; *Douglass' Monthly,* June, 1860; Douglass to Anna H. Richardson, July 2, 1860.

THE PROSPECT IN THE FUTURE

The future of the anti-slavery cause is shrouded in doubt and gloom. The labors of a quarter of a century, instead of culminating in success, seem to have reached a point of weary hopelessness, so far as Radical Abolitionists are concerned. The great work of enlightening the people as to the wicked enormities of slavery, is well-nigh accomplished, but the practical results of this work have disappointed our hopes. The grim and bloody tragedies of outrage and cruelty are rehearsed day by day to the ears of the people, but they look on as coolly indifferent as spectators in a theatre. The dangers to our common country produce as little emotion as the revelation of the wrongs of our common humanity. They assent to all the horrid truths which reveal the inhuman secrets of the gloomy prison house, but are not moved to action. They commend the iron-linked logic and soul-born eloquence of Abolitionists, but never practice the principles laid bare by the one, or act upon the emotions called up by the other. An able advocate of human rights gratifies their intellectual tastes, pleases their imaginations, titillates their sensibilities into a momentary sensation, but does not move them from the downy seat of inaction. They are familiar with every note in the scale of abstract rights, from the Declaration of Independence to the orations of Charles Sumner, but seem to regard the whole as a grand operatic performance, of which they are mere spectators. You cannot relate a new fact, or frame an unfamiliar argument on this subject.—Reason and morality have emptied their casket of richest jewels into the lap of this cause, in vain. Religion has exhausted her volleyed thunders of denunciation upon the head of this gigantic crime, but it stands unmoved and defiant. She has poured out floods of the tears of love and sympathy before this people, but their hearts have never been so melted as to produce an appropriate response to her divine ardor. Art, literature and poetry have all expended their treasures to arouse the callous hearts of the American people to the duty of letting the oppressed go free, and yet four millions struggle out their lives in blood-rusted chains. Europe is rocking and heaving with the struggle for liberty, while America is comparatively indifferent under a system of bondage more terrible than Europe has known for centuries. Garibaldi lands on the coast of Sicily with a few hundred men, as the forlorn hope of Italian freedom, and a brave and generous and appreciating people flock to his standard, and drive the tyrant of Naples from his bloody throne. John Brown takes up arms against a system of tyranny more cruel and barbarous than that of the murderer of Palermo, and is hung on a Virginia gallows, while thirty millions of people, whose civil catechism is the Declaration of Independence, look on unmoved to interference.

What is the explanation of this terrible paradox of passing history? Are the people of this country of an inferior race? Are they lacking in physical courage? Do they fail to appreciate the value of liberty? Our history, if we shall confine its revelations to the descendants of the Anglo-Saxon, the Teutonic, or the Celtic races, answers all these questions in the negative. This conglomerate people, made up from the crossing of all these races, have shown great courage and patriotism in defending *their own freedom,* but have utterly failed in the magnanimity and philanthropy necessary to prompt respect for the rights of another and a weaker race than those mentioned above. It is not because we fail to appreciate or lack the courage to defend our own rights that we permit the existence of slavery among us, but it is because our patriotism is intensely selfish, our courage lacks generosity, and our love of liberty is circumscribed by our narrow and wicked selfhood, that we quietly permit a few tyrants to crush a weak people in our midst. Whoever levies a tax upon our Bohea or Young Hyson, will find the whole land blazing with patriotism and bristling with bayonets the next morning. Let the mightiest maritime nation on the globe but impress a few Yankee sailors, and our merchant ships will be punctured with port holes, and manned with sailors who fight like heroes. Let any power on earth claim sovereignty over a single rood of the scraggy pine woods of Maine, or a foot of the drifted sand of some island on our western border, and Congress will burst forth with such a flood of pyrotechnic oratory as to stir our warlike blood to the tune of battle. But millions of a foreign race may be stolen from their homes, and reduced to hopeless and inhuman bondage among us, and we either approve the deed, or protest as gently as "sucking doves." Our courage, our love of liberty, our statesmanship, our literature, our ethics, and our religion, are all most intensely and wickedly selfish. Our national character fails to present a single fulcrum for the lever of justice or humanity. We only ask to be permitted to enjoy our own heritage, and on this condition are content to see others crushed in our midst. Ours is the philosophy of Cain. When God and humanity cry out against the oppression of the African, we coolly ask what of it? "Am I my brother's keeper?" If his blood cry to us for redress, we say, "let it cry; it is not our blood." If his children are stolen and enslaved, we look on and say "they are not our children; don't you see their noses are flat and their hair curls." If his daughters are debauched, our blood remains cool, for they are neither our daughters nor sisters. If his wife is stolen, we have nothing to do so long as our wives are protected by law. If the way to heaven is open to the white man, and we have a chance to "land our souls in glory," we are sublimely indifferent to the fact that the Bible and the Gospel are withheld from the Negro, and go on shouting our amens, and singing our anthems so loud that nobody but God can hear his wail of agony above the din of our voiceful, but heartless piety. Heaven help the poor slave, whose only hope of freedom is in the selfish hearts of such a people!—Nor can heaven help him, except by moving him to help himself. The motive power which shall liberate the slave must be looked for in slavery itself—must be generated in the bosom of the bondman. Outside philanthropy never disenthralled any people. It required a Spartacus, himself a Roman slave and gladiator, to arouse the servile population of Italy, and defeat some of the most powerful armies of Rome, at the head of an army of slaves; and the slaves of America await the advent of an African Spartacus.

There is one element of American character which has as yet never been fairly appealed to in behalf of the slave. Our philanthropy melts itself away into maudlin tears at the story of his wrongs. Our sense of justice kicks the beam when his master's cotton bales are in the adverse scale. Our religion whines and snivels over his sufferings, but cannot leave its formal devotions long enough to bind up its wounds. Our politics bellow in his behalf on the stump, but only employ his cause as a stalking horse for party effect, and to carry self-seekers into power. But there is a latent clement in our national character which, if fairly called into action, will sweep anything down in its course. The American people admire courage displayed in defense of liberty, and will catch the flame of sympathy from the sparks of its heroic fire.— The strength of this trait of character has been long manifest in the reception of the patriots who have been cast upon our shores from the wrecks of European revolutions; and when some African Eunus or Salvius shall call the servile population of the South to arms, and inspire them to fight a few desperate battles for freedom, the mere animal instincts and sympathies of this people will do more for them than has been accomplished by a quarter of a century of oratorical philanthropy. We can

never cease to regret that an appeal to the higher and better elements of human nature is, in this case, so barren of fitting response. But so it is, and until this people
have passed through several generations of humanitarian culture, so it will be.—In
the meantime the slave must continue to suffer or rebel, and did they know their
strength they would not wait the tardy growth of our American sense of justice.

To the Negro-hating conservative this language sounds harsh and vengeful,
no doubt. But that same law-and-order conservative reads of the glorious deeds
of Garibaldi and the Sicilian insurrectionists, with a shout of responsive enthusiasm springing to his lips, and rejoices at the downfall of the tyrants of Naples.
The cruelties inflicted by the brutal police of Francis II, are reproduced every
week on hundreds of plantations in America, and a people far outnumbering the
Sicilians are crushed under the heel of a democracy which is far heavier than that
of any crowned and booted Bourbon. Why should we shout when a tyrant is driven from his throne by Garibaldi's bayonets,[1] and shudder and cry peace at the
thought that the American slave may one day learn the use of bayonets also?

Douglass' Monthly, August, 1860

1. Giuseppe Garibaldi (1807–1882) led his victorious expedition to Sicily and Naples in
1860 and with his thousand "red shirts" overthrew the Bourbon monarchy and made possible
the accession of these states to a United Italy. The movement culminated in the establishment
of the Kingdom of Italy under the Piedmontese dynasty.

THE PRESIDENTIAL CAMPAIGN OF 1860, speech at celebration of West India Emancipation, August 1, 1860

Mr. President:—I thank you very sincerely for the kind and cordial welcome you
have been pleased, on behalf of this vast audience, to extend to me, and also for
the words of sympathy with me in the experiences through which I have passed
since our last meeting in this place. I esteem it a high privilege, especially in view
of the many vicissitudes and exciting incidents of the past twelve months, to join
you again in appropriate recognition of this anniversary of freedom. It is now
twenty-six years since the justice and humanity of England represented in the
British Parliament and throne, abolished and put an end to slavery in the British
West Indies forever. No greater demonstration of philanthropy has occurred
during the present century. It astonished the world by its grandeur. Men could
hardly believe that humanity could so succeed against the selfishness of property.—The transition for the slaves emancipated was a most wonderful experience. In all our emancipations in the United States, we have had nothing so sudden and so startling as this. The slaves were eight hundred thousand chattels
yesterday; they were eight hundred thousand free men and women the next day.
It was a trying event. It tested the mettle of slaves as well as masters, and the
behavior of the former proved them worthy of their newly gained freedom.

Emancipation had been looked for and prayed for by the scarred and mutilated bondman; but even *they* must have found it hard to believe that they were now forever free. Yet, in the doubt, and in the assurance, and in the great joy of the occasion, their behavior was equally orderly and beautiful.

Many of the old slave-drivers anticipated the event with the gloomiest forebodings. Knowing how well they had deserved vengeance, they shuddered at the thought of its possible approach. Guilty men! they read human nature wrong. They who study mankind with a whip in their hands, will always go wrong. They see but one side of everything about them, and that is the worst side. They only *see without,* the qualities they feel within themselves. Pride, self-love, cruelty, brutality and revenge had been cultivated with all the approved instruments of torture on the plantation. These qualities they knew and well understood; but they did not see the higher elements of human nature. According to their dismal fears and predictions, the Islands were to be desolated. The white inhabitants were to be slaughtered. Fire and sword were to be let loose, and neither age nor sex were to be spared.

It is one of the glories of the occasion and the event, that every such prediction and objection was refuted by the grand result. Not even the most unscrupulous and eager slanderers of the Negro race have been able to sustain a charge of violence against the emancipated bondmen. Peace, joy and gratitude combined to sanctify and hallow the glorious advent of liberty.

We meet here to-day, as we met here last year, to honor this high and brilliant example of British justice towards a people everywhere spoken against. The event is worthy the attention of all men, but to the American people it addresses itself with tenfold power and force as an example fit to be honored and imitated. The First of August is, and of right ought to be, the great abolition day for all the friends of freedom. In regard to England, a very significant and gratifying fact may be stated. Notwithstanding all the years of clamor against the results of emancipation, England has steadily persisted in its abolition policy.

The abolition of slavery in the West Indies is now, as at the beginning, esteemed by every true-hearted Britain as the chief glory of his country. And well it may be.—It was the result of the very best elements of cultivated human nature. The labor, the zeal, the earnestness, and the perseverance employed in bringing the British people to see slavery in its true character, and to bring them to act for its abolition, were never excelled by those of any other great reformatory movement. The people there talk to this day of the mighty enthusiasm that rocked the land, and every man is proud to say that he had a hand in the great work. The British public, though weighed down and staggering under a heavy weight of taxation, bore, without a murmur, the additional burden of twenty millions sterling. If there was any complaint at all, it was that the masters got it instead of the slaves. How striking and humiliating is the contrast in respect to slavery, between England and America, the mother and the daughter! If the merits of republican institutions, as against those of a monarchy, were made to depend upon the character and history of the American Republic, monarchical institutions would most certainly bear off the palm. The British monarchy, self-moved and self-sustained, emancipated, set free, and clothed with the dignity of citizenship, nearly a million slaves at a single stroke of the pen, and then began to exert, and continues to exert her great moral influence to make her noble example felt throughout the world.

It is really amazing how far into the regions of darkness and sorrow this knowledge of British feeling has penetrated. The most ignorant slave on the banks of the Red River has by some means or other come to learn that the English are the friends of the African race. Her ships are on the gold coast; they are in the Gulf of Mexico, and along the coast of the Brazils in search of slave pirates, only secure from arrest when they hoist the American flag. While the British monarchy thus employs its powers, how is it with our so-called Christian Protestant Republic? The story is soon told. Four millions clank their fetters at the very doors of our churches and our Government. The slave trade, long ago abolished by the humanity of your revolutionary fathers, is now openly defended, and is secretly carried on, with the evident connivance of the Government in various ports of the South. The policy of limiting slavery, which comes down to us from the founders of the government, has been set aside by the Dred Scott decision. Free colored men, who, in the better days of the Republic, were regarded and treated as American citizens, have been made aliens and enemies in the land of their birth. Slavehunting, which had died out under the quiet influence of a partial civilization, has now, in the middle of the nineteenth century, been thoroughly revived. Thus, while the British Government, with far less pretension to liberty than we, is wielding the mighty power and influence which her position and greatness give her, for the promotion of liberty and humanity throughout the world—the American Government is worse than winking at the slave trade, and slavers are fitted out in sight of our business men's prayer meetings. It is evidently the design of the Slave Power of this Republic to fasten the terrible curse of human bondage upon every quarter of this continent.

But England is not the only nation whose conduct stands in marked and striking contrast with our own. There stands Russia, grim and terrible, half way between barbarism and civilization—a conglomeration of many races, darkened by ages of wide-spread cruelty and blood—governed by a despotism, cold and hard as granite—supremely indifferent to the good or ill opinion of mankind—with no freedom of tongue, no freedom of press—yet even she proves herself more just and wise in her day and generation than we. She knows enough, and is wise enough to make friends of her own household. The car of emancipation is advancing gloriously in that country; the shouts of millions, headed by the Emperor Alexander himself, go up in joy over the freedom of the Russian serf.

But with us how different is the spectacle! Slavery is everywhere the pet monster of the American people. All our political parties, and most of our churches, kneel with humility at its accursed shrine of tears and blood! Each party vies with the other in its zealous self-abasement and servile devotion. In our politics, as well as in our religion, he who refuses to join in the worship of whips, and in acknowledgment of the charity of chains, is stigmatized as a blasphemer, and an enemy to the State. We read, the Chaldean monarch set up an image of gold for his subjects to worship. That was bad enough, and one may rejoice that there was virtue enough in the three Hebrews to refuse to kneel. But bad as the image was as an object of worship, the thing itself was not undesirable. But our object of worship is in itself revolting. A vulture feeding on a living and quivering human heart, tearing it to pieces with his remorseless talons and bloody beak, would be an appropriate symbol of the object of our national devotion. For where under the whole heavens can there be found any system of wrong and cruelty to compare with our slavery? Who has measured its vast extent, found its limits, or sounded the depths of its wickedness? Language fails to describe it, and the human mind, though winged with a fancy outflying the lightning, fails to overtake and comprehend this huge and many-headed abomination. I know slavery as well as most men. I was born in it, as most of you know; but though I have been a victim to what has broken the spirit and cowed into servility many a better man than myself, I have not yet been able to convey even *my* limited sense of the ten thousand wrongs of slavery. I have spoken and written much on the subject during the last twenty years, and have been at times accused of exaggeration; and yet I can say, with truth, that I have fallen far short in describing the pains and woes, and in painting the unbroken stream of sorrow and sighing mercilessly poured down upon the sable millions doomed to life-long bondage in this boasted free country. Slavery has been denounced as the sum of an villainies. The language is well chosen. But who can grapple with a thing so huge as the sum of all villainies? The idea is too large and dreadful for the imagination. The warp and woof of slavery is yet to be unravelled.—Each bloody thread must yet be disentangled and drawn forth, before men will thoroughly understand and duly hate the enormity, or properly abhor its upholders and work its abolition. This is the work still to be done. After all the books, pamphlets and periodicals—after all the labors of the Abolitionists at home and abroad—we have still to make the American people acquainted with the sin and crime of our slave system.

In this good work, let me acknowledge the sentiment of gratitude which you and I feel on this occasion to Hon. Charles Sumner, of Massachusetts. It is more than empty praise to say that we recognize him as the Wilberforce of America. He has brought to the right side of the discussion a quenchless zeal, and an irresistible earnestness. His large culture and eminent talents have been industriously applied to the work of placing before the world the monstrous crime and withering barbarism of our country. For this great service, I embrace this occasion to thank him, in my own name, and in the name of our whole people. Many other noble men have spoken and have spoken well. We thank them all—we appreciate them all; but among them all, none has uttered the feelings of the black man so well; none have hurled at slavery such a succession of moral thunder-bolts as he. Were Mr. Sumner only a non-extensionist, we might not mention his name for special honor on this memorable day. But the brave Senator from Massachusetts takes rank with a higher order of men, and is engaged in a sublimer work. The principles which he enunciates, the doctrines which he maintains, with an eloquence unmatched in the American Senate, and unsurpassed out of it, compel us to rank him with the Sharpes, the Clarksons, the Buxtons, and the Broughams of England—the great men whose mighty efforts have given us and our people the event we have met this day to celebrate. Like them, Charles Sumner is an Abolitionist. Owing to a difference in the civilization of the two countries, Mr. Sumner has suffered as they did not, for the faithful utterance of his opinions. His sacred blood has stained the Senate floor. Assassin blows have fallen upon him; and yet we have him still with us, in all the strength, fertility and grandeur of his well-stored intellect. Four years of painful anxiety have been dispelled by the sight of his rising, as he has risen, with redoubled zeal, and with powers of action and utterance augmented, quickened and intensified. His assailants and would-be murderers were not spared, as I almost wish they had been, to experience the mortification of seeing the noble Senator rise, as if from the very grave to which they had aimed to consign him. They have both ceased from the earth, and Mr. Sumner looks in vain around the Senate hall to find any to imitate the example of his dead assassins. A mighty change has been going on in Washington during these last four years. The Massachusetts Senator could well indulge in what he calls the easy victory of charity towards his fallen foes.

But there is a charity which falls upon the head of the wrong-doers like coals of living fire. Such charity was deserved, and such was meted out to the haughty slave-masters of the Senate. I would have given a great deal to have looked upon them during the execration. A man more politic than Mr. Sumner might have broken the ominous silence of four years in a tone better suited to the taste of those who are just now desiring the success of the Republican party with principles or without principles. But Mr. Sumner is better than his company. He not only talks of the irrepressible conflict, but nobly flings himself into it with all the ardor of his great soul, and becomes himself a part of it. I hail him with a full heart, as a man of the right metal. Let us thank God and take courage, that such a man in this hour of pro-slavery truckling, backed up by the Legislature of such a State, bravely stands up in the highest council of the nation the champion of liberty and equal rights to all men of whatever class, clime, condition or color.

Friends, I shall not detain you to-day with any history of West India Emancipation.—Elsewhere, and on other occasions, I have done this at length. Nor shall I stop to justify emancipation by an appeal to its material results. The chief objection that we have ever heard against it, is, that when free, and left to decide the question for himself, the black man will not work. This objection comes from those who have as little taste for work under a tropical sun as the Negroes. A kind and humane lady in England, who took an earnest interest in emancipation, when told that the Negroes of Jamaica were lazy and would not work, answered the objection by saying she was glad that after working so long and hard under cruel task masters, the poor people could now take a little time to rest.—This charge of special indolence I have met on other occasions, and shall not repeat my refutation of it here. My work is nearer home. This is a free day—a day for free speech—and all things touching the cause of human freedom are in order here to-day.—Subjects of discourse are abundant, and invite us on every side. Our Democratic Republic is just now undergoing one of its periodical political convulsions. It is engaged in the quadrennial business of electing its King. We are a strange people. We flatter ourselves that the people govern, and that the government is directly and immediately responsible to the people. And so, indeed, it seems in theory; but the matter is quite different in practice. In this respect we are even in the rear of old England and our neighbors across the lakes. We have a less responsible Government than either. It should be distinguished from all other Governments as *the irresponsible Government.*

By the Constitution of the United States our King reigns over us for the term of four years. It seems a short term; but experience shows that it is quite long enough for the perpetration of almost innumerable mischiefs, and to thwart and defeat the most beneficent measures. Our King is armed with mighty powers, the veto power among them. He is Commander-in-Chief of the army and navy.— During his reign he can exercise his power as rigorously as any of the crowned heads of Europe, and do so with greater impunity. I assert fearlessly, that while Americans are ever boasting of the sovereignty of the people, there is no Government on the earth which can be administered in more open violation of the principles of freedom, or in more flagrant contempt for the rights and wishes of the people, than the American Government during a Presidential term. Commanding the purse, the sword and the patronage of the Government, and being safely installed in the Presidential chair, with a Cabinet of his own selection about him, the President is thereafter beyond the reach of the people. You cannot get at him. He is above inquiry, and therefore above impeachment and below assassination. The limits set to his term of office protect him. Any hardened old sinner, such as now reigns over us, once in office, may luxuriate in corruption and tyranny to his heart's content, (if such men have hearts and can feel content). Mr. Buchanan has been reveling in rascality from the very commencement of his reign. He began with the Dred Scott decision, advanced to the Lecompton Constitution, and has improved like a young bear from bad to worse ever since. We boast of our self-government. What superlative nonsense! It has no existence except one day in four years. The first Minister in England, who is in fact the ruler of the country, may be outvoted and compelled to resign his office any day in the year. The House of Commons, or any member of it, may call him to account upon the first appearance of misconduct in the direction of public affairs. All is different here. Once well mounted with the reins of Government in his fists, the Presidential rider may force in his spurs, lay on the whip, draw the blood at every blow, and defy the national animal to throw him off. We have been kicking and tossing about very wildly since we felt Mr. Buchanan in the saddle; but there the old fellow sits as calm as a summer morning. The rulers over yonder, who have crowns annexed to them, must look out for their heads. Conspiracies, revolutions and assassinations are more than possible to them, as Louis Napoleon himself can tell you. But here we have a political safety valve. Freedom to choose a new ruler one day in four years, compensates for all the tyranny, injustice and corruption, inaugurated and submitted to during the Presidential term.—Schemes of villainy may be set in motion during such a term, which may cling to the country and curse it for ages. You have no remedy. You must bear it for four years, and then possibly take another a little more dishonest and tyrannical than his predecessor. What better was Fillmore and the Fugitive Slave Bill, than Tyler and Texas? What better is Buchanan with Lecompton and bribery, than Pierce with his shameless and violent measures for making Kansas a slave State? From bad to worse all the time.—The lesson which each gives his successor, is, steal all you can during your term, enrich yourself and your friends, for

behave well or ill, you are sure to go out of office with as many curses as coppers. One scripture at least is followed by these Christian gentlemen. Make to
yourselves friends of the mammon of unrighteousness. After each election one
host of incompetent kin folks takes the place of another; and hence the offices of
Government are constantly kept in green and incompetent hands. Such is the machine, and such are its workings. It looks well on paper. It sounds well on the
stump, but its works testify trumpet tongued against it.

Well, we are about to try our hand again. A new political crisis is upon the
country. The Presidential track is crowded with aspirants. A frightful number of
patriots are modestly consenting to assume the burden of Presidential honors.
Instead of the five loaves and two fishes—the usual number of political principles—we have five parties and no principles in the present canvass. And yet, since
the organization of Government, there has been no election so exciting and interesting as this. The elements are everywhere deeply stirred, and nowhere are
they more deeply stirred than at the South. Our political philosophers call the
present contest a sectional strife: as if there could be conscious antagonism between two pieces of land not even separated by a stream of fresh water; as if the
stately oaks and elms of New York had all at once become offended with the noble pines of North Carolina; as if the wheat, rye and oats of the North had all at
once conceived a deadly hatred towards the rice, cotton and tobacco of the sunny
South; or as if the bleak and cold granite hills of New Hampshire had declared
open war against the hot and feverish rice swamps of Georgia, or the sugar plantations of Louisiana.

The irrepressible conflict has no such explanation. The present strife is one of
sentiments, ideas and systems. It respects not so much the rights of labor, the
rights of capital, as the rights of man. Under all the deceptive phrases of the political speech of the times, the real meaning of the contest forces itself into view,
and defies all arts of concealment. Slavery is the real issue—the single bone of
contention between all parties and sections. It is the one disturbing force, and explains the confused and irregular motion of our political machine. All other issues died ten years ago. This is the only living one. Every thoughtful man who
goes to the ballot box this fall will go there either to help or to hinder slavery, or
with the idea of neither helping nor hindering slavery. In any case, slavery is the
object. Taking broad abolition ground, as I hope many of us do, we have much
to regret, as well as much to congratulate ourselves upon in the present state of
the abolition question, and in the relations and prospects of the political parties
in reference to that question.

It is sad to think that after a struggle so long and perilous, marked by the blood
and tears of martyrs, we are still confronted by the slave system, unconquered, unsubdued, fierce, greedy, turbulent, and more rampant than ever. But such is the fact.
Twenty years ago, slaveholders and their advocates and abettors contented themselves with asking to be let alone. The people of the North were told to mind their
own business, that slavery was purely a local system, one with which the North had
nothing to do. If it were a curse, it was the curse of the South, and the South would
bear it alone. If it were a blessing, it belonged alone to the South.—Very different
is the tone of the Slave Power to-day. Now, slavery seems to be the only *national*

interest, and the whole power of the Federal Government is invoked to fortify and perpetuate the system on pain of a dissolution of the Union and civil war.

How has this altered state of the question been brought about? Through what blunder on the part of the Abolitionists themselves has this advantage been given to the enemies of justice and freedom? Without question, one great and deplorable mistake has been committed by the opponents of slavery, and that mistake explains to some extent the present proud and arrogant behavior of the defenders of the huge abomination.—We have allowed them to prepare and make the issues of all our late elections, and to decide the character of the controversy before the people. Instead of basing ourselves firmly and immovably on the principle of immediate, unconditional emancipation, as the right of the slave, and as the duty of the masters, and being the aggressors, we have been defending outposts and allowing them to be the aggressors. We have permitted them the advantage of selecting the ground and stipulating the conditions. The result has been that we have been constantly battling against slavery where it does not exist, and conceding rights and privileges where it does exist.—Carefully guarding the slave system within its present limits, the slaveholders have now impudently demanded the right to extend the evil over all the land.

In attestation of what I have now affirmed, let me give a few pages in our national history. You are familiar with the facts, and still it is well to revive them and keep them before the public mind. I wish to impress upon your minds how the anti-slavery sentiment of the country has been abused and deadened—how the anti-slavery cause has been subverted—how the whole abolition movement, or *train,* (to use a railroad phrase,) has been switched off the abolition track to that of non-extension. The deep game by which this was accomplished was brought to light sixteen years ago.

In the year 1844, while all that was honest and upright in the country was sighing over the atrocious scourge and the deep disgrace and scandal of America; while we were sedulously teaching the infant lips of the Republic to denounce the existence of slavery as a curse; to abolish the hateful thing forever—the slaveholders, with an audacity half sublime, openly flung into the Presidential canvass an imperative demand for the annexation of Texas, a country as large as the French empire.—There was no concealment of the motives for this measure. The slaveholders told the country and the world just what they wanted with Texas. Mr. John C. Calhoun, then Secretary of State under John Tyler, was, as all know, the leading spirit in this bold enterprise and the part he took in it showed his satanic sagacity. His policy still lives, and his spectre now leads the infernal hosts of slavery and the slave trade. Texas was in debt, like most other slave countries. She wanted money and wanted credit. Two ways were open to her by which she could get both. England was willing to assist her, on condition that she would abolish her slavery; and America would assist her, provided she would make her slavery perpetual.

Again you have the Monarchy for freedom and the model Republic for slavery and chains. Mr. Calhoun at Washington, and Mr. Everett at London, both pressed the claims of this barbarism against the humanity and civilization of Europe. Mr. Calhoun told the British Government, in the name of the whole American people, that Texas was desired as a means of propping up slavery, and that America could not permit Texas to come under the anti-slavery policy of England. This bold and skillful maneuver of the slaveholders worked admirably. It sent Mr. Van Buren in silence to Kinderhood, Henry Clay to the shades of Ashland, and James K. Polk, a man unknown to fame, to the Presidential chair. Mr. Van Buren was moderately opposed to annexation; Mr. Clay was against it at the North, and for it at the South; and Mr. Polk for it North and South alike. This decided the conflict. Mr. Polk was triumphantly elected, and you all know what followed. The war with Mexico, with all its waste of blood and treasure, was the bitter fruit of annexation; for, as all know, Texas was a revolted province of Mexico.—She had revolted in part because of the humane laws of Mexico for the abolition of slavery. In taking her we took her debts, her quarrels, her slavery, and all the disgrace and scandal attaching to her name. Hers was the bad reputation of criminals, slaveholders and cut throats.

The people of the North are and have ever been a strangely hopeful and confiding people. They have always presumed upon the good disposition and good intentions of their Southern brethren. I remember well, when a man would have been laughed at as a simpleton or frowned at as a fanatic if he ventured to whisper a danger of the annexation of Texas. Up to the very year in which the perfidious deed was consummated, scarcely anyone at the North believed that Texas could be annexed. Even after it was done, we went on hoping. Some went on so far as to tell the people that as Texas had been voted in, she could be voted out. Boston took the lead in denouncing the perfidy of forcing the old members of the Confederacy into this fellowship, without their consent or consultation. Others of the hopeful class said the South had got Texas, but the victory would be rendered barren by making the largest part of it into free States. Deluded and infatuated men!—They did not know the rapacious spirit and fatal skill at work against them. Disappointed and defeated, they nevertheless maintained the same hopeful and confiding tone in regard to the Territories acquired from Mexico after the war.

The Abolitionists who refused to vote for Mr. Clay—the man who was either for or against, or neither for nor against the annexation of Texas—were, during the interval between 1844 and 1848, placed in a trying position before the people of the North. They were kept under a galling fire of all the Whig guns of the country. They were charged with defeating Mr. Clay, by voting for James G. Birney, electing Mr. Polk, and annexing Texas. The thing was, to be sure, only a *lie;* but having the advantage of being well stuck to, it produced a visible effect upon the abolition party. Voting directly for the abolition of slavery declined. The leaders of the party began to look for available candidates outside of the abolition ranks. Abolition lecturers were supplanted by merely Free Soil lecturers. Abolition newspapers, one after another, faded from view, and Free Soil papers took their places. The Buffalo Convention of 1848, being the first confluence of the abolition sentiment with the old corrupt political elements of the country, was higher toned in its anti-slavery than any Convention since held. The abolition element has by no means kept pace with the growth of the non-extension party. The National Conventions, held successively in Pittsburgh, Philadelphia and

Chicago, have formed a regular gradation of descent from the better utterances of '48 at Buffalo, till at last good readers have been puzzled to find *even a fibre*, to saying nothing of a plank of abolition in the platform adopted at Chicago. We have constantly been acquiescing in present attainments of slavery, and only battle against its future acquisitions. We hear nothing now of no more slave States. We hear nothing of the abolition of slavery in the District of Columbia. We hear nothing of the repeal of the Fugitive Slave Law; and even the Declaration of Independence, declaring all men free and equal, came near being voted down in the Chicago Convention, and was admitted at last only on the strength of the eloquence of Geo. W. Curtis, who warned the Convention against rejecting it.[1]

This declaration is one of the disheartening features of the times. The facts wear anything but a cheering aspect to those of us who looked hopefully to the speedy abolition of slavery by moral and political action; and yet our cause is not lost, nor is it powerless. The abolition idea is still abroad, and may yet be made effective. It has no powerful party committed distinctly to its realization, but has a party distinctly committed to a policy which the people generally think will do certain preliminary work essential to the overthrow of slavery. While I see with others, and our noble friends Gerrit Smith and William Goodell among them, that the Republican party is far from an abolition party, I cannot fail to see also that the Republican party carries with it the anti-slavery sentiment of the North, and that a victory gained by it in the present canvass will be a victory gained by that sentiment over the wickedly aggressive pro-slavery sentiment of the country. I would gladly have a party openly combined to put down slavery at the South. In the absence of such a party, I am glad to see a party in the field against which all that is slaveholding, malignant and Negro-hating, both at the North and the South, is combined. I know of no class of men whose instincts as to men and measures touching slavery are more to be depended upon than those of the slaveholders. There are gradations in all things, and reforms among them. A man need not to be a William Lloyd Garrison or a William H. Seward in order to get himself recognized as an enemy to slavery. The slaveholders know that the day of their power is over when a Republican President is elected. The mobs gotten up to put down the Republican Conventions at Baltimore, Alexandria and Wheeling, the threats of violence offered to Cassius M. Clay and his Republican associates in Kentucky, and the threats of a dissolution of the Union in case of the election of Lincoln, are tolerable endorsements of the anti-slavery tendencies of the Republican party; and for one, Abolitionist though I am, and resolved to cast my vote for an Abolitionist, I sincerely hope for the triumph of that party over all the odds and ends of slavery combined against it. I do not accord with those who prefer the defeat of the Republican party from a fear that it will serve slavery as faithfully as the Democratic party, or either branch of it. To do anything of the kind would be to cut its own thread of existence.

If the Republican party shall arrest the spread of slavery; if it shall exclude from office all such in the slave States who know only slavery as master and lawgiver, who burn every newspaper and letter supposed to contain anti-slavery matter, who refuse to hand a black man a letter from the Post Office because he is of the hated color, and will put men into office who will administer them justly and impartially; if it will send ministers and other agents to foreign courts who will represent other interests than slavery, and will give a colored citizen of a free State a passport as any other citizen—place the honor of the nation on the side of freedom, encourage freedom of speech and of the press, protect Republican principles and organizations in the slave States—that party, though it may not abolish slavery, will not have existed in vain. But if, on the other hand, it shall seek first of all to make itself acceptable to slaveholders—do what it can to efface all traces of its anti-slavery origin—fall to slave-catching—swear by the Dred Scott decision, and perpetuate slavery in the District of Columbia—it will disappoint the hopes of all its heart friends, and will be deserted, shunned and abhorred as the other parties now are and its place will be taken by another and better party, organized on higher ground and animated by a nobler spirit. Bad as the moral condition of this country is, and powerful as may be the influence of prejudice, the sun of science and civilization has risen too high in the heavens for any party to stand long on the mean, narrow and selfish idea of a "white man's party." This is an age of universal ideas. Men are men, and governments cannot afford much longer to make discriminations between men in regard to personal liberty.—Surely the Republican party will not fall into the mistake or the crime of competing with the old parties in the old wornout business of feeding popular malignity, by acts of discrimination against the free colored people of the United States. I certainly look to that party for a nobler policy than that avowed by some connected with the Republican organization.

How stands the case with the two wings of the so-called Democratic party? What is the difference between Douglas and Breckinridge? I will tell you: Breckinridge believes that the Supreme Court has decided that the slaveholder has a right to carry his slaves into any Territory belonging to the U.S., and that while Congress is bound to protect the slaveholders in this right, there is no power either in Congress, or in any such Territory, to prohibit the relation of master and slave. Mr. Douglas does not believe that the Supreme Court has so decided, but avows himself ready to abide by the decision as soon as the Court shall so decide. The difference between the two, is the difference between two obedient servants of the same master.—One thinks himself already sent, and the other holds himself ready upon the moment of receiving orders. Mr. Douglas, addressing the slaveholders, says:—I am your humble, obedient servant. I stand by the Dred Scott decision; and if that, or any other decision of the Supreme Court establishes slavery in the Territories, I am for it also. I am ready, upon a knowledge of this fact, to send all the moonshine I now hold, about the right of the people to govern themselves, to the winds.—The difference between Douglas and Breckinridge is, therefore, simply the difference between *now* and *then*—a difference which seems wide before the election, but which will vanish immediately after the election, let who will attain the Presidency—for there can be no doubt as to how the Supreme Court, with a majority of slaveholders, will decide the question, if it has not already decided.

In view of this state of the case, it is scarcely worth while to do more than denounce the humbug with which Mr. Douglas is just now seeking to win your votes. By a peculiar use of words, he confounds *power* with *right* in such a manner as to make the *power* to do wrong the *right* to do wrong. By his notion of human rights, everything depends upon the majority. It is not a bit more absurd and monstrous to say that the first settlers in a Territory have the right to protect murder, than that they have the right to protect slavery. The right to do the one is just as good as the right to do the other. The right of the slaveholder is precisely the right of the highway robber. The one says your money or your life, and the other says your liberty or your life, and both depend upon superior force for their existence.

I say nothing here and now about the Bell and Everett party. A party without any opinion need have no opinion expressed of it. If a party is of a mind to be blind and dumb, it cannot be surprised at being considered deaf as well. There is doubt now that there is any such party in existence, since the leaders of it have been endeavoring to sell the party out. It is a question who holds the bill of sale in this State—Mr. Brooks or Mr. Douglas. But could such a party as the Bell and Everett party, made up of the old effete Know Nothing elements, succeed in gaining power, there is nothing in its character to inspire a single ray of hope for the slave or humanity, but in addition to Negro hate, we should have an equally abominable hate toward foreigners.

Of the Houston and Stockton party, (the South Americans,) we may say just what has been said of the Bell and Everett party, and that is *as much as nothing*. It is impossible to distinguish between the two factions. On the great question of slavery they stand together, and may be relied upon in any emergency for slavery.

I alluded at the beginning to the exciting vicissitudes and incidents of the past year.—Three months after our last anniversary, there appeared upon the theatre of American life a man whose character and deeds dazzled, astonished and bewildered the whole nation.—A knowledge of him flashed across the oceans and continents like a splendid meteor. For a time, the whole civilized world stood amazed and gazing. There was that peculiarity in him, which in all the ages had awakened the reverence of men, the sage not less than the simple—a human soul illuminated with divine qualities in such high degree as to raise the question, was he our brother?—a man of like passions with ourselves. His behavior was so unusual that men did not know what to make of him. It was thought that the race of such men had become extinct. Men had read of them, as beings belonging to another age. They could not believe that any such man could now be on the earth, and not until they were startled by the reality could they admit the possibility. We have not yet recovered from the wonder with which this man's deeds filled us. His character is yet the study of great minds. Poets, statesmen and philosophers study him as the astronomers the heavenly bodies. He was as a comet, whose brightness overspread half the sky, and men, timid men, thought that a second visit might fire the earth. I need not tell you who this strange man was. You have anticipated me.

You know that I allude to the hero of Harper's Ferry. The ablest and best men of the land have spoken of John Brown, and have confessed their inability to do him justice.—The *Tribune* never said a truer thing than when it said the time had not come to pronounce judgment upon the character and deeds of John Brown. Our land is too fat with the lost sweat and warm blood of slaves driven to toil and death; our civilization is yet too selfish and barbarous; our statesmen are yet too narrow, base and mobocratic; our press is yet too venal and truckling; our religion is too commercial, too much after the pattern of the pride and prejudices of our times, to understand and appreciate the great character who sacrificed himself for the hated Negroes of this country. With the statesmanship, civilization and Christianity of America, the Negro is simply a piece of property, having no rights which white men are required to respect; but with John Brown and his noble associates, *the Negro is a man,* entitled to all the rights claimed by the whitest man on the earth. Brave and glorious old man! Yours was the life of a true friend of humanity, and the triumphant death of a hero.—The friends of freedom shall be nerved to the glorious struggle with slavery by your example; the hopes of the slave shall not die while your name shall live, and after ages shall rejoice to do justice to your great history.

Douglass' Monthly, September, 1860

1. At the Republican convention in Chicago, J. R. Giddings proposed an amendment to a series of resolutions reported by Judge William Jessup, reaffirming the principles of the Declaration of Independence. When this was voted down, Giddings retired from the convention. But George W. Curtis took up the issue, and asked the delegates if they were prepared to appear before the country as a party which had voted down the Declaration of Independence, and which refused to reassert its basic principle "that all men are created equal" and were "endowed by their creator with certain inalienable rights; among these are Life, Liberty and the Pursuit of Happiness." His amendment was adopted amid shouts of approval.

THE LATE ELECTION

Our last monthly paper announced the probable election of Abraham Lincoln and Hannibal Hamlin, the Republican candidates for President and Vice President of the U.S. What was then only speculation and probability, is now an accomplished fact. Pennsylvania, in her State election of October, it is true, had made this result, to a degree, certain; but there were efforts and appliances resorted to by the enemies of the Republican party, which could not fail to cause doubt and anxiety in the minds of the most sanguine.—The deed is, however, now done, and a new order of events connected with the great question of slavery, is now fairly opening upon the country, the end whereof the most sagacious and far-sighted are unable to see and declare. No preceding election resembles this in its issues and parties, and none resembles it in the effects it has already produced, and is still likely to produce. It was a contest between sections, North and South, as to what shall be the principles and policy of the national Government in respect to the slave system of the fifteen Southern States. The broadest assertion of a right of property in man, holding such property equally innocent, sacred and legal under the Constitution, as property in houses, lands, horses, sheep, and horned cattle, and like the latter entitled to Congressional protection in all the Territories, and by parity of reasoning, in all the States of the American Union. The Southern candidate for the Presidency, Mr. Breckinridge, fully represented this broad assertion of what Lord Mansfield well declared to be so opposed to nature, that nothing short of positive law could support it, and Brougham denounced as the "wild and guilty fantasy" of property in man. Mr. Lincoln, the Northern Republican candidate, while admitting the right to hold men as slaves in the States already existing, regards such property as peculiar, exceptional, local, generally an evil, and not to be extended beyond the limits of the States where it is established by what is called positive law. We thus simply state the issue, more for the benefit of our trans-Atlantic friends and readers, than for those at home, who have heard and read little else during the last three or four months. The clamor now raised by the slaveholders about "Northern aggression," "sectional warfare," as a pretext of dissolving the Union, has this basis only: The Northern people have elected, against the opposition of the slaveholding South, a man for President who declared his opposition to the further extension of slavery over the soil belonging to the United States. Such is the head and front, and the full extent of the offense, for which "minute men" are forming, drums are beating, flags are flying, people are arming, "banks are closing," "stocks are falling," and the South generally taking on dreadfully.

By referring to another part of our present monthly, our respected readers will find a few samples of the spirit of the Southern press on the subject. They are full of intrigue, smell of brimstone, and betoken a terrific explosion. Unquestionably, "secession," "disunion," "Southern Confederacy," and the like phrases, are the most popular political watch words of the cotton-growing States of the Union. Nor is this sentiment to be entirely despised. If Mr. Lincoln were really an Abolition President, which he is not; if he were a friend to the Abolition movement, instead of being, as he is, its most powerful enemy, the dissolution of the Union might be the only effective mode of perpetuating slavery in the Southern States—since if it could succeed, it would place slavery beyond the power of the President and his Government. But the South has now no such cause for disunion. The present alarm and perturbation will cease; the Southern fire-eaters will be appeased and will retrace their steps.—There is no sufficient cause for the dissolution of the Union. Whoever lives through the next four years will see Mr. Lincoln and his Administration attacked more bitterly for their pro-slavery truckling, than for doing any anti-slavery work. He and his party will become the best protectors of slavery where it now is, and just such protectors as slaveholders will most need. In order to defeat him, the slaveholders took advantage of the ignorance and stupidity of the masses, and assured them that Lincoln is an Abolitionist. This, Mr. Lincoln and his party will lose no time in scattering to the winds as false and groundless. With the single exception of the question of slavery extension, Mr. Lincoln proposes no measure which can bring him into antagonistic collision with the traffickers in human flesh, either in the States or in the District of Columbia. The Union will, therefore, be saved simply because there is no cause in the election of Mr. Lincoln for its dissolution. Slavery will be as safe, and safer, in the Union under such a President, than it can be under any President of a Southern Confederacy. This is our impression, and we deeply regret the facts from which it is derived.

With an Abolition President we should consider a successful separation of the slave from the free States a calamity, greatly damaging to the prospects of our long enslaved, bruised and mutilated people; but under what may be expected of the Republican party, with its pledges to put down the slaves should they attempt to rise, and to hunt them should they run away, a dissolution of the Union would be highly beneficial to the cause of liberty.—The South would then be a Sicily, and the North a Sardinia. Mr. Lincoln would then be entirely absolved from his slave-hunting, slave-catching and slave-killing pledges, and the South would have to defend slavery with her own guns, and hunt her Negroes with her own dogs. In truth, we really wish those brave, fire-eating, cotton-growing States would just now go at once outside the Union and set up for themselves, where they could be got at without disturbing other people, and got away from without encountering other people. Such a consummation was "one devoutly to be wished." But no, cunning dogs, they will smother their rage, and after all the dust they can raise, they will retire within the Union and claim its advantages.

What, then, has been gained to the anti-slavery cause by the election of Mr. Lincoln? Not much, in itself considered, but very much when viewed in the light of its relations and bearings. For fifty years the country has taken the law from the lips of an exacting, haughty and imperious slave oligarchy. The masters of slaves have been masters of the Republic. Their authority was almost undisputed, and their power irresistible. They were the President makers of the Republic, and no aspirant dared to hope for success against their frown. Lincoln's election has vitiated their authority, and broken their power. It has taught the North its strength, and shown the South its weakness. More important still, it has demonstrated the possibility of electing, if not an Abolitionist, at least an *anti-slavery reputation* to the Presidency of the United States. The years are few since it was thought possible that the Northern people could be wrought up to the exercise of such startling courage. Hitherto the threat of disunion has been as potent over the politicians of the North, as the cat-o'-nine-tails is over the backs of the slaves. Mr. Lincoln's election breaks this enchantment, dispels this terrible nightmare, and awakes the nation to the consciousness of new powers, and the possibility of a higher destiny than the perpetual bondage to an ignoble fear.

Another probable effect will be to extinguish the reviving fires of the accursed foreign slave trade, which for a year or two have been kindled all along the Southern coast of the Union. The Republican party is under no necessity to pass laws on this subject. It has only to enforce and execute the laws already on the statute book. The moral influence of such prompt, complete and unflinching execution of the laws, will be great, not only in arresting the specific evil, but in arresting the tide of popular demoralization with which the successful prosecution of the horrid trade in naked men and women was overspreading the country. To this duty the Republican party will be prompted, not only by the conscience of the North, but by what perhaps will be more controlling party interests.

It may also be conceded that the election of Lincoln and Hamlin, notwithstanding the admission of the former that the South is entitled to an efficient Fugitive Slave Law, will render the practice of recapturing and returning to slavery persons who have heroically succeeded, or may hereafter succeed in reaching the free States, more unpopular and odious than it would have been had either Douglas, Bell or Breckinridge been elected. Slaves may yet be hunted, caught and carried back to slavery, but the number will be greatly diminished, because of the popular disinclination to execute the cruel and merciless Fugitive Slave Law. Had Lincoln been defeated, the fact would have been construed by slaveholders, and their guilty minions of the country, as strong evidence of the soundness of the North in respect to the alleged duty of hounding down and handing over the panting fugitive to the vengeance of his infuriated master. No argument is needed to prove this gain to the side of freedom.

But chief among the benefits of the election, has been the canvass itself. Notwithstanding the many cowardly disclaimers, and miserable concessions to popular prejudice against the colored people, which Republican orators have felt themselves required, by an intense and greedy desire of success, to make, they have been compelled also to recur to first principles of human liberty, expose the baseless claim of property in man, exhibit the hideous features of slavery, and to unveil, for popular execration, the brutal manners and morals of the guilty slavemasters.—The canvass has sent all over the North most learned and eloquent men to utter the great truths which Abolitionists have for twenty years been earnestly, but unsuccessfully endeavoring to get before the public mind and conscience. We may rejoice in the dissemination of the truth by whomsoever proclaimed, for the truth will bear its own weight, and bring forth its own fruit.

Nevertheless, this very victory threatens and may be the death of the modern Abolition movement, and finally bring back the country to the same, or a worse state, than Benj. Lundy and Wm. Lloyd Garrison found it thirty years ago. The Republican party does not propose to abolish slavery anywhere, and is decidedly opposed to Abolition agitation. It is not even, by the confession of its President elect, in favor of the repeal of that thrice-accursed and flagrantly unconstitutional Fugitive Slave Bill of 1850. It is plain to see, that once in power, the policy of the party will be only to seem a little less yielding to the demands of slavery than the Democratic or Fusion party,[1] and thus render ineffective and pointless the whole Abolition movement of the North. The safety of our movement will be found only by a return to all the agencies and appliances, such as writing, publishing, organizing, lecturing, holding meetings, with the earnest aim not to prevent the extension of slavery, but to abolish the system altogether. Congress should be at once memorialized for the abolition of slavery in the District of Columbia, and the slave trade between the States. The same zeal, activity, energy and earnestness should be displayed in circulating petitions, as in the earlier stages of the movement. We have the pen, voice and influence of only one man, and that man of the most limited class; but with few or many, in whatever vicissitudes which may surround the cause, now or hereafter, we shall join in no cry, and unite in no demand less than the complete and universal *abolition* of the whole slave system. Slavery shall be destroyed.

Douglass' Monthly, December, 1860

1. On September 23, 1860, a committe of fifteen, appointed at a Grand Mass Meeting in New York City, announced that it had drawn up a fusion ticket consisting of eighteen Douglas,

ten Bell, and seven Breckenridge electors. Thus the separate anti-Republican parties were united into a single Union electoral ticket for New York State. (For a discussion of the fusion movement, see Philip S. Foner, *Business and Slavery*, pp. 172–80.)

It was no simple task . . . to revive the old spirit of the anti-slavery movement in the weeks following Lincoln's election. As threats of secession of the southern states mounted, northern conservatives tried to convince the slaveholders that they had nothing to fear from remaining in the Union. Personal liberty laws to prevent the return of fugitive slaves were repealed, resolutions condemning the Abolitionists were adopted by Union-Saving gatherings, and paid hoodlums were hired to disrupt anti-slavery meetings. Northern newspapers fanned the flames of hysteria, calling for demonstrations wherever Abolitionists gathered.[1]

Douglass was once again the special target for attack. At a meeting in Boston on December 3, 1860, to commemorate the anniversary of John Brown's execution, ruffians, hired by merchants engaged in the southern trade, invaded the hall, disrupted the proceedings, and singled out Douglass for attack. Fighting "like a trained pugilist," the Negro Abolitionist was thrown "down the staircase to the floor of the hall."[2]

The meeting was adjourned to a church on Joy Street. As the audience poured into the street, Negroes were seized, knocked down, trampled upon, and a number seriously injured. "The mob was howling with rage," Douglass recalled years later. "Boston wanted a victim to appease the wrath of the south already bent upon the destruction of the Union."[3] (II: 99–100)

SPEECH ON JOHN BROWN, delivered in Tremont Temple, Boston, December 3, 1860

Mr. President, Ladies and Gentlemen:—I occupied considerable attention this morning, and I do not feel called upon to take up much of the time this evening. There are other gentlemen here from whom I desire to hear, and to whom, I doubt not, you wish to listen.

This is a meeting to discuss the best method of abolishing slavery, and each speaker is expected to present what he regards as the best way of prosecuting the anti-slavery movement. From my heart of hearts I endorse the sentiment expressed by Mr. Phillips, of approval of all methods of proceeding against slavery, politics, religion, peace, war, Bible, Constitution, disunion, Union—[laughter]—every possible way known in opposition to slavery is my way. But the moral and social means of opposing slavery have had a greater prominence, during the last twenty-five years, than the way indicated by the celebration of this day—I mean the John Brown way. That is a recent way of opposing slavery; and I think, since it is in consequence of this peculiar mode of advocating the abolition of slavery that we have had a mob in Boston today, it may be well for me to occupy the few moments I have in advocating John Brown's way of accomplishing our object. [Applause]

Sir, we have seen the number of slaves increase from half a million to four millions.—We have seen, for the last sixty years, more or less of resistance to slavery in the U.S. As early as the beginning of the U.S. Government, there were abolition societies in the land. There were abolition societies in Virginia, abolition societies in Maryland, abolition societies in South Carolina, abolition societies in Pennsylvania. These societies appealed to the sense of justice, appealed to humanity, in behalf of the slave. They appealed to the magnanimity of the slaveholders and the nation; they appealed to the Christianity of the South and of the nation, in behalf of the slave. Pictures of slavery were presented.—The ten thousand enormities daily occurring in the Southern States were held up—men sold on the auction-block—women scourged with a heavy lash—men tied to the stake and deliberately burned, the blood gushing from their nose and eyes, asking rather to be shot than to be murdered by such slow torture. The facts of these charges have been flung before the public by ten thousand eloquent lips, and by more than ten thousand eloquent pens.—The humanity, the common human nature of the country has been again and again appealed to. Four millions have bowed before this nation, and with uplifted hands to Heaven and to you, have asked, in the name of God, and in the name of humanity, to break our chains! To this hour, however, the nation is dumb and indifferent to these cries for deliverance, coming up from the South; and instead of the slaveholders becoming softened, becoming more disposed to listen to the claims of justice and humanity—instead of being more and more disposed to listen to the suggestions of reason, they have become madder and madder, and with every attempt to rescue the bondman from the clutch of his enslaver, his grip has become tighter and tighter, his conscience more and more callous. He has become harder and harder, with every appeal made to his sense of justice, with every appeal made to his humanity, until at length he has come even to confront the world with the pretension that to rob a man of his liberty, to pocket his wages, or to pocket the fruits of his labor without giving him compensation for his work, is not only right according to the law of nature and the laws of the land, but that it is right and just in sight of the living God. Doctors of Divinity—the Stuarts and the Lords, the Springs, the Blagdens, the Adamses, and ten thousand others all over the country—have come out in open defense of the slave system. Not only is this the case, but the very submission of the slave to his chains is held as an evidence of his fitness to be a slave; it is regarded as one of the strongest proofs of the divinity of slavery, that the Negro tamely submits to his fetters. His very non-resistance—what would be here regarded a Christian virtue—is quoted in proof of his cowardice, and his unwillingness to suffer and to sacrifice for his liberty.

Now what remains? What remains? Sir, it is possible for men to trample on justice and liberty so long as to become entirely oblivious of the principles of justice and liberty. It is possible for men so far to transgress the laws of justice as to cease to have any sense of justice. What is to be done in that case?—You meet a man on the sidewalk, in the morning, and you give him the way. He thanks you for it. You meet him again, and you give him the way, and he may thank you for it, but with a little less emphasis than at first. Meet him again, and give him the way, and he almost forgets to thank you for it. Meet him again, and give him the way, and he comes to think that you are conscious either of your inferiority or of his superiority; and he begins to claim the inside of the walk as his right.—This is human nature; this is the nature of the slaveholders. Now, something must be done to make these slaveholders feel the injustice of their course. We must, as John Brown, Jr.—thank God that he lives and is with us to-night! [applause]—we must, as John Brown, Jr., has taught us this evening, reach the slaveholder's conscience through his fear of personal danger. We must make him feel that there is death in the air about him, that there is death in the pot before him, that there is death all around him. We must do this in some way. It can be done. When you have a good horse, a kind and gentle horse, a horse that your wife can drive, you are disposed to keep him—you wouldn't take any money for that horse. But when you have one that at the first pull of the reins takes the bit in his teeth, kicks up behind, and knocks off the dasher-board, you generally want to get rid of that horse. [Laughter.]—The Negroes of the South must do this; they must make these slaveholders feel that there is something uncomfortable about slavery—must make them feel that it is not so pleasant, after all, to go to bed with bowie-knives, and revolvers, and pistols, as they must. This can be done, and will be done—[cheers]—yes, I say, *will* be done. Let not, however, these suggestions of mine be construed into the slightest disparagement of the various other efforts, political and moral.

I believe in agitation; and it was largely this belief which brought me five hundred miles from my home to attend this meeting. I am sorry—not for the part I humbly took in the meeting this morning—but I am sorry that Mr. Phillips was not there to look that Fay in the face. ["Hear!"] I believe that he, and a few Abolitionists like him in the city of Boston, well-known, honorable men, esteemed among their fellow-citizens—had they been there to help us take the initiatory steps in the organization of that meeting, we might, perhaps, have been broken up, but it would have been a greater struggle, certainly, than that which it cost to break up the meeting this morning. [Applause.]

I say, sir, that I want the slaveholders to be made uncomfortable. Every slave that escapes helps to add to their discomfort. I rejoice in every uprising at the South. Although the men may be shot down, they may be butchered upon the spot, the blow tells, notwithstanding, and cannot but tell. Slaveholders sleep more uneasily than they used to. They are more careful to know that the doors are locked than they formerly were. They are more careful to know that their bowie-knives are sharp; they are more careful to know that their pistols are loaded. This element will play its part in the abolition of slavery. I know that all hope of a general insurrection is vain. We do not need a general insurrection to bring about this result. We only need the fact to be known in the Southern States generally, that there is liberty in yonder mountains, planted by John Brown. [Cheers.]—The slaveholders have but to know, and they do now know, but will be made to know it even more certainly before long—that from the Alleghanies, from the State of Pennsylvania, there is a vast broken country extending clear down into the very heart of Alabama—mountains flung there by the hand and the providence of God for the protection of liberty—[cheers]—mountains where there are rocks, and ravines, and fastnesses, dens and caves, ten thousand Sebastopols piled up by the hand of the living God, where one man for defense will be as good as a hundred for attack. There let them learn that there are men hid in those fastnesses, who will sally out upon them and conduct their slaves from the chains and fetters in which they are now bound, to breathe the free air of liberty upon those mountains. Let, I say, only a thousand men be scattered in those hills, and slavery is dead. It cannot live in the presence of such a danger. Such a state of things would put an end to planting cotton; it would put an end not only to planting cotton, but to planting anything in that region.

Something is said about the dissolution of the Union under Mr. Lincoln or under Mr. Buchanan. I am for a dissolution of the Union—decidedly for a dissolution of the Union! Under an abolition President, who would wield the army and the navy of the Government for the abolition of slavery, I should be for the union of these States. If this Union is dissolved, I see many ways in which slavery may be attacked by force, but very few in which it could be attacked by moral means. I see that the moment you dissolve the union between the South and the North, the slave part going by itself and doing so peaceably—as the cry is from the *Tribune* and the Albany *Evening Journal,* and other such papers, that it shall do[4]—establishing an independent government—that very moment the feeling of responsibility for slavery in the North is at an end. But men will tell us to mind our own business. We shall care no more for slavery in the Carolinas or in Georgia than we care for kingcraft or priestcraft in Canada, or slavery in the Brazils or in Cuba. My opinion is that if we only had an anti-slavery President, if we only had an abolition President to hold these men in the Union, and execute the declared provisions of the Constitution, execute that part of the Constitution which is in favor of liberty, as well as put upon those passages which have been construed in favor of slavery, a construction different from that and more in harmony with the principles of eternal justice that lie at the foundation of the government—if we could have such a government, a government that would force the South to behave herself, under those circumstances I should be for the continuance of the Union. If, on the contrary—no *if* about it—we have what we have, I shall be glad of the news, come when it will, that the slave States are an independent government, and that you are no longer called upon to deliver fugitive slaves to their masters, and that you are no longer called upon to shoulder your arms and guard with your swords those States—no longer called to go into them to put down John Brown, or anybody else who may strike for liberty there.—[Applause.] In case of such a dissolution, I believe that men could be found at least as brave as Walker, and more skillful than any other filibusterer, who would venture into those States and raise the standard of liberty there, and have ten thousand and more hearts at the North beating in sympathy with them. I believe a Garibaldi would arise who would march into those States with a thousand men, and summon to his standard sixty thousand, if necessary, to accomplish the freedom of the slave. [Cheers.]

We need not only to appeal to the moral sense of these slaveholders; we have need, and a right, to appeal to their fears. Sir, moral means are good, but we need something else. Moral means were very little to poor John Thomas on the banks of the Wilkesbarre river, in Pennsylvania, when the slave-catchers called upon him to provide them with a breakfast at the hotel, that while in the act of serving them with their beef-steak they might fall upon him and return him to slavery.—They did fall upon him; they struck him down; but, recovering himself, he ran and plunged into the Wilkesbarre. There he stood, up to his shoulders, and the slave-catchers gathered on the banks—and the moral suasion people of that vicinity gathered also on the banks—they looked indignantly on the slave-catchers. But the slave-catchers did not heed the cries of indignation and shame; they fired their revolvers until the river about that man was red with his blood, and no hand was lifted to strike down those assassins.—They went off, indeed, without their victim, but they supposed he was dead. Sir, what was wanted at that time was just what John Brown, Jr., has told us to-night—a few resolute men, determined to be free, and to free others, resolved, when men were being shot, to shoot again. Had a few balls there whistled, as at Christiana, about the heads of the slave-catchers, it would have been the end of this slave-catching business there. There is no necessity of permitting it. The only way to make the Fugitive Slave Law a dead letter is to make a few dead slave-catchers. [Laughter and applause.] There is no need to kill them either—shoot them in the legs, and send them to the South living epistles of the free gospel preached here at the North. [Renewed laughter.]

But, Sir, I am occupying too much time.—["Go on!" Go on!"] I see a friend on my right, whose voice to-night I have not heard for many years. These troublous times in which we live, and have been living for a few years past, make that voice doubly dear to me on this occasion; and I seize this occasion, as the first that has happened to me in at least six to eight years, to say that I rejoice, most heartily rejoice, in the privilege—for a privilege I esteem it—not only of hearing Mr. Phillips's voice, but of standing on a platform with him in vindication of free speech. [Applause.] But I hope to speak in Boston on Friday. I, therefore, will not prolong my remarks further. I thank you for this hearing. [Applause.]

Douglass' Monthly, January, 1861

1. For an analysis of conditions following Lincoln's election, see Philip S. Foner, *Business and Slavery*, pp. 224–84.

2. *Boston Evening Transcript*, Dec. 3, 1860; *New York Tribune*, Dec. 6, 1860; *Liberator*, Dec. 7, 1860. "The mob," wrote James Redpath, "was incited, and chiefly composed of merchants, traders with the South—nearly all of whom have uncollected debts there, and many of them mortgages on slaves."

3. *Douglass' Monthly*, Jan. 1861; Douglass to Mrs. Livermore, April 19, 1886, Douglass Mss., Frederick Douglass Memorial Home, Anacostia, D.C.

4. Three days after Lincoln's election, Horace Greeley published an editorial in his New York *Tribune* in which he wrote: "If the cotton States shall decide that they can do better out of the Union than in it, we insist on letting them go in peace . . . whenever a considerable section of our Union shall resolve to go out, we shall resist all coercive measures designed to keep it in. We hope never to live in a republic whereof one section is pinned to the residue by bayonets." (See also New York *Tribune*, Nov. 16, 19, 24, 1860.) "The *Tribune* policy," writes Ralph Ray Fahrney, "not only encouraged the further alienation of Southern loyalty, but it discouraged the formation of public sentiment in the North favorable to the maintenance of the Union." (*Horace Greeley and the Tribune in the Civil War*, Cedar Rapids, Iowa, 1936, p. 49.)

During this same period, Thurlow Weed proposed in the albany *Evening Journal* that concessions be granted to the South to keep the southern states in the Union. He also advocated peaceful secession and denounced any plan to keep the seceded states in the Union by force. (See Howard Cecil Perkins, ed., *Northern Editorials on Secession*, New York, 1942, pp. 107, 199, 300; Glyndon G. Van Deusen, *Thurlow Weed*, New York, 1947, pp. 267–70.)

PART FIVE

From Secession to the Emancipation Proclamation

DISSOLUTION OF THE AMERICAN UNION

The event so long and so loudly threatened by the State of South Carolina, and dreaded by the other States, has at last happened, and is a matter of history.[1] She has seceded, separated, repealed, quitted, dissolved the Union, declared her independence, set up for herself, assumed a place among the sisterhood of nations, pulled down the star spangled banner of the great American Confederacy, and upon innumerable pine poles has unfurled the Palmetto flag, preferring to be a large piece of nothing, to being any longer a small piece of something. Her ordinance of secession passed unanimously. Her people (except those of them held in slavery, which are more than half her population) have hailed the event as another and far more glorious Fourth of July, and are celebrating it with plenty of gunpowder, bad brandy, but as yet no balls, except those where perfumed ladies and gentlemen move their feet to the inspiring notes of the fiddle. Other balls may yet come; and unless South Carolina shall retreat, or the Federal Government shall abdicate its functions, they must come. But for the present all is remarkably pleasant and agreeable. Secession seems a newly invented game, and the people are much delighted with it. They play it over and over again—never tire of it. They play till midnight, and sing "We'll not go home till morning." For once the Palmetto State seems happy. Once in a while there is a word of apprehension, a murmur, that all is not well from a thoughtful source; but this is soon hushed in the general hilarity of her people, on account of their transition from Federal bondage to national independence and freedom. South Carolina is very happy indeed. She sends word to the world on the wings of the lightning, that she has met with a change, and is attesting her great joy by bonfires, pyrotechnics, cannons, illuminations, music and dancing. And yet, as we have said, there is an undercurrent of doubt, uncertainty, distrust and foreboding. The fact is, the new Republic has cleared, taken her papers, but has not yet weighed anchor, drawn a hawser, or set a single thread on canvas.—There is much noise, much pulling and hauling, and a lively stir generally; but the ship is still anchored in the safe harbor of the Union, and those having her in charge seem, after all, rather reluctant about venturing out upon the untried billows of the dissolution sea. We think, however, she will not hesitate much longer, but will soon fire a parting salute, and bid the Union defiance, instead of an affectionate farewell.

To speak plainly, South Carolina is out of the Union, just as the nonvoting Abolitionists are out of the Union—the former to preserve slavery, and the latter to abolish slavery. She is out of the Union, on paper, in speeches, letter, resolutions and telegrams. The head and front of her independence hath this extent, no more. The postal arrangements of the United States are still extended over her; the revenue laws of the United States are still enforced in her ports, and no hand, thus far, has been lifted against the one or the other. The United States flag yet waves over Fort Moultrie, and a United States revenue cutter is lying in Charleston harbor. The South Carolinians have accomplished what they call peaceful secession—a thing quite as easily done as the leaving of a society of Odd Fellows, or bidding good night to a spiritual circle.

But, unfortunately, human governments are neither held together, nor broken up by such mild and gentle persuasives as are implied in the soft phrase—peaceful secession. Theirs is a voice of command, not of persuasion. They rest not upon paper, but upon power. They do not solicit obedience as a favor, but compel it as a duty. The work is not done yet. Though boasting of her sovereignty, her independence, and her freedom, instead of being out of the Union, South Carolina has really accomplished little more than to make known to the world the wish of certain politicians to take her out, and their design, either to take her out, or to *scare* the Northern people and the Republican party into such guarantees for slavery, as even an Algerine pirate, on the score of humanity, might hesitate to grant. Nothing short of irrepealable and eternal bondage will satisfy South Carolina. She can only be satisfied when Cotton is declared king, and South Carolina admitted to be the kingdom of Cotton. Evidently, however, if she really means to go out of the Union, she has yet an immensely difficult and dangerous work before her. The moorings that bind these States together can only be broken by opinion, backed up by force.

She must exclude the mail service, put an end to United States Post Offices, drive United States Custom House officers from her ports, capture public property, take the forts and arsenals, and drive out every officer from her borders who holds and exercises any authority whatsoever under the Government of the U.S. This may be an easy task, and may also be, under Mr. Buchanan, (who is clearly in the plot,) speedily done; but even when this is done, South Carolina is still in the Union.—The incoming President is elected to preside over the *United* States; and if any of them have been permitted, by the treachery and weakness of his predecessor, to break away from the Government, his business will be to bring them back, and see that the laws of the United States are duly extended over them, and faithfully executed. The coolest and wisest statesmen of the Republic deny the right of peaceful secession. They admit the right of revolution; but revolution in this country is rebellion, and rebellion is treason, and treason is levying war against the United States, with something more substantial than paper resolutions and windy declamations.—There must be swords, guns, powder, balls, and men behind them to use them.

Now, when matters reach that point, South Carolina must conquer the United States, or the United States must conquer South Carolina. The right of South Carolina to secede, therefore, depends upon her ability to do so, and to stay so. If she can whip the Federal Government and scourge and keep it beyond her borders, and compel the United States to regard her as other than a revolt province, she can get out of the Union. But until she does all this, Abraham Lincoln is bound by his oath of office to regard her as one of the United States, and subject to the "Union, the Constitution and the laws."

Such every body knows to be the true legal view of secession; but the question comes—is there virtue enough in the Federal Government to enforce the law? When a poor slave escapes to Boston, and hides in the cellars and garrets of humane men, the U.S. Government is strong. It can line the streets with soldiers, surround the granite Court House with chains, and convert the temple of justice into a prison to catch, hold and hurl the fugitive back into the house of bondage; but has that Government virtue enough to enforce the laws against the slaveholding women-whipping rebels of Charleston? We do not ask, has Mr.

Buchanan the virtue to do this? The fact is, that old man is in a fair way to win for himself the infamy of another Benedict Arnold. Only under his fostering care could the state of disorder and alarm have reached its present magnitude. His message was a virtual invitation to the Slave States to secede from the Union, assuring them that no force would be employed against them.[2] Of all old sinners, there is less hope of him who paints his crimes with prayers, who prays for light when he means to walk in darkness, who repents only of righteousness and clings to wrong, turns his back on justice, and flings around slavery the mantle of religion. Of such a man there is no hope. Even should he resist, it would be a sham resistance, more to show the enemies of the Government in a favorable light, than to punish and to subdue them to law and order. Of him nothing can be expected but weakness, cunning, treachery and gross hypocrisy; and we believe naught else is expected of him. Like Louis XI., he can pray and poison, count beads and cut throats. In the crafty wording of his proclamation of fast, you might suppose that Mr. Buchanan had slavery in his eye as one of the sins of the nation; but we have only to read his message to know what he regards as our great sin. It is *opposition* to slavery, to making merchandise of men, to trading in human flesh, to sell women at auction, to driving them to toil, and giving them naught for their work. It is anti-slavery, according to this old saint, not slavery, that has brought the frown of Heaven upon our land! Oh! what a stench arises from the rottenness of such piety; and yet such is the current religion of the Bell-Everett and Squatter Sovereignty religion of the national fusion parties of the country. Nothing will so rapidly and effectually bring religion into utter contempt, as this making it the mantle to hide the monstrous and shocking enormities, the blood-chilling and unutterable cruelty and wickedness of slavery. Mr. Buchanan threw around his character the very poetry of villainy, when he called upon the nation to join him in prayer and fasting.

But to the dissolution of the Union, and its chances of success. Conquering a Federal army, and driving out all Federal officers, is not the only difficulty to be overcome. The slave population of South Carolina may at last prove the most serious check upon disunion. They are more than equal to the whites in number, and cannot have failed to learn something from passing events. All the precautions of their tyrant masters have not hid from them the fact that *they*, in some sort, have a direct interest in the controversy between the State and the Federal Government. It is more than probable that they have given Mr. Lincoln credit for having intentions towards them far more benevolent and just than any he is known to cherish.—His pledges to protect and uphold slavery in the States have not reached them; while certain dim, undefined, but large and exaggerated notions of his emancipating purposes have taken firm hold of them, and have grown larger and firmer with every look, nod and undertone of their oppressors. They were taught to look for freedom by the election of John C. Fremont.[3] He failed; but he so nearly succeeded, that hope was entertained that another trial would bring certain victory. That victory they have been taught to believe has now been achieved; that a friend of theirs is now about to take the reins of Government; that he is a *"Black Republican,"* that his mission is to free the slaves. Let them learn that there is enmity between the State and the Federal Government, and that South Carolina has broken away from the Union to defeat their liberation from bondage; that Abraham Lincoln, the President, is on their side, and against their masters; that he has only been defeated in giving them their liberty by taking the State out of the Union, and it is easy to see that such impressions and ideas might burst forth and spread havoc and death among slaveholders to an extent never surpassed even in the annals of St. Domingo. South Carolina, in such an event, would be more likely to fight her way back into the Union, than to fight her way out of it. Her salvation as a slave State might be made to depend upon Federal arms.

But will not the cotton States join South Carolina? They probably will; but the elements of weakness would be the same. South Carolina would only be presented on a larger scale: with her, those cotton States have to extinguish the life of the Federal Government within their limits, and keep that extinguished. This can only be done *by force, by treachery, or by negotiation;* and to neither will Abraham Lincoln succumb. To do so would be to put the razor to the throat of his party, write himself down a coward, make political platforms worse than a mockery, and to become the pliant tool of the very barbarism which he was elected to restrain, and "place it where the public mind would rest in the belief in its ultimate extinction."—He is pledged to the maintenance of the Union; and if he has the *will,* he will not lack the power to maintain it against all foes. But if the Union can only be maintained by new concessions to the slaveholders; if it can only be stuck together and held together by a new drain on the Negro's blood; if the North is to forswear the exercise of all rights incompatible with the safety and perpetuity of slavery; that slavery shall be the only right, the only system superior to investigation, and superior to progress—we say, if this (and it is all demanded) be the price of the Union, then will every right minded man and woman in the land say, let the Union perish, and perish forever. As against compromises and national demoralization, welcome, ten thousand times over, the hardships consequent upon a dissolution of the Union.

Douglass' Monthly, January, 1861

1. As soon as the election of Lincoln was certain, the South Carolina legislature summoned a state convention. On December 20, 1860, the convention of 169 delegates met at Charleston in secret session, and unanimously resolved "that the Union now susbsisting between South Carolina and other states under the name of 'The United States of America' is hereby dissolved."

2. In his message to Congress, December 3, 1860, President Buchanan asserted that a state had no right to secede from the Union if it felt aggrieved. At the same time, he denied that the Federal government had the power to preserve the Union by force, and urged upon Congress the remedy of "conciliation." He proposed an explanatory amendment to the Constitution which would contain a recognition of the right of property in slaves in the States, of the duty of protecting slavery in all the common territories, and of the right of the master to have his escaping slave restored to him.

3. "The slaves," writes Herbert Aptheker, "were certain that the Republican Party stood for their liberation, and some felt that Colonel Frémont would aid them forcibly, in their efforts for freedom." (*Essays in the History of the American Negro,* New York, 1945, p. 58.)

THE UNION AND HOW TO SAVE IT

In viewing the alleged causes of the present perilous and dilapidated condition of the Federal Union, and the various plans by which it is proposed to set that Union in safety, all manly sensibility is shocked, and all human patience breaks down in disgust and indignation at the spectacle. The attitude of the Northern people in this crisis will crimson the cheeks of their children's children with shame. As between the North and the South, history will record the fact, that the latter, though engaged in a villainous and wicked cause, acted bravely, and displayed a manly spirit, while the former, with the best of causes, and pledged to it in open daylight before millions of their countrymen, acted the part of miserable cowards, insensible alike to the requirements of self-respect or duty. Was ever a people so terribly frightened as are we of the North at this moment? We have been singing and shouting *free speech! free speech!* on every Northern stump during the last ten years, and yet one rebellious frown of South Carolina has muzzled the mouths of all our large cities, and filled the air with whines for compromise. Boston gets up a mob; Philadelphia shuts her halls; Rochester follows in the humiliating train. The South in thus scaring us, and succeeding in possessing herself of the palpable evidence of our fright, has attained one essential condition to complete mastery. We are now as pliant and obedient to our Southern masters, as are the subdued *"Cruisers,"* and other fractious horses under the strap of the matchless Mr. Rarey. We used to hear and read of the aggressions of slavery, of the insolent demands of the Slave Power, and cries of down with the slave-holding oligarchy.

> *"But all is now so hushed and mum;*
> *You'd think your Atherton had come."*

What is this but a premium to insolence, a petition for increased contempt, and humble solicitation to be kicked again? Faith, the human flesh-mongers see at every step the effect of their medicine, and every day they "down with another dose." First they talk of the slow process of "co-operation" as a condition to breaking up the Union; then they talk of the right of individual States to secede; and finding both Government and people appalled with fear, they fall to seizing forts, arsenals, arms and ammunition, capturing Custom Houses, Post Offices, tearing down the national flag, and firing upon an unarmed Government vessel, with the national flag flying at her mast-head. After all this, they send their Commissioners to Washington to denounce coercion in the very teeth of the Government which they have robbed, plundered, insulted, spit upon and defied. Any other Government on the earth would have hanged every traitor Commissioner venturing into its presence. They build forts day and night and man them with a thousand men, and yet demand the removal from among them the keepers of the only fort they have not stolen, to save the effusion of blood! Aftercoming generations will hardly believe the story of the present hour. The arrogance and impudence of the traitors are only exceeded by the sneaking cowardice and pitiful imbecility of the Government, and of the Northern people, who, by mobbing down freedom of speech, crying "no coercion," and whining for compromise, prove themselves of a piece with the Government. The position of the North in this crisis is really too selfish, mean and craven for the slaveholder, and they despise and scorn all overtures from this quarter. Well might Mr. Slaveholder Iverson ask what are concessions worth, wrung from the fears of the North? The doughface who concedes, from fear, can be made to *recede* under the same mean impulse. Iverson has flogged too many slaves to put much confidence in promises of obedience made under the lash. The children of this generation are wiser than the children of light.

Look at our statesmen in and out of Congress. In assuming to deal with this subject, they neither appear to apprehend the causes of the trouble, nor the remedy. Their speeches and letters would make the impression that right and wrong, good and evil, justice and injustice, humanity and cruelty, honesty and perfidy, progression and retrogression, can have their natures, characters and results all changed by some cunning legislative device; that there is some process for circumventing the natural operation of the eternal laws of the universe by which they may do evil and obtain good, sow the wind and escape the whirlwind, touch pitch and not be defiled, gather grapes of thorns, and figs of thistles, and all other like impossible things in all sorts of impossible ways. Shame upon this cowardly, guilty and fantastical method of dealing with the stupendous crime and curse, which our statesmen are either too blind to see, or too dishonest to confess to be the real cause of our national troubles. They beat the bush, but dare not enter; they talk of "passion," "sectional feeling," "misrepresentation of object," the "South deceived," as the causes of the treason and rebellion which, thirsting for blood, are about to plunge the nation into all the horrors of civil war, and all the dark and dreadful possibilities of anarchy.

Now, what disturbs, divides and threatens to bring on civil war, and to break up and ruin this country, but slavery. Who but one morally blind can fail to see it; and who but a moral coward can hesitate to declare it.—Fifteen States are bent upon the ascendency, and endless perpetuation of this system of immeasurable wickedness and numberless crimes, and are determined either to make it the law of the whole country, or destroy the Government. Against this inhuman and monstrous purpose are arraigned the enlightenment of the age, checking and overthrowing tyranny, liberating the bondman from his chains in all quarters of the globe, and extending constitutional liberty to long oppressed nationalities; against it are the instinctive sentiments of humanity, shuddering at the thought of chattelized humanity; against it are the eternal laws of liberty, goodness, justice and progress, dispelling the darkness of barbarism, exposing the hollowness of a corrupt priesthood, under the sanction of whose dark mummeries all the hell-black crimes of human bondage have found, in this country, their greatest security; against it are the ever-increasing triumphs in the arts of civilization, reducing the importance of mere brute force to nothing in comparison with intellectual power; against it are all the promptings, aspirations, convictions and sympathies of unperverted human nature, and the God in history everywhere pronouncing the doom of those nations which frame mischief by law, and revel in selfishness and blood. It is the concussion of these natural elements against slavery which now rock the land, and sends us staggering about as if shaken by an earthquake. Here is the cause of the trouble. It is slavery, the sum of all villainies, on the one hand, and all the silent but mighty forces of nature on the other. Here is and must ever remain the irrepressible conflict, until slavery is abolished or human nature, with all its divine attributes, is changed and made to reflect the image of hell instead of heaven.

Slavery is the disease, and its abolition in every part of the land is essential to the future quiet and security of the country. Any union which can possibly be patched up while slavery exists, must either completely demoralize the whole nation, or remain a heartless form, disguising, under the smiles of friendship, a vital, active and ever-increasing hate, sure to explode in violence. It is a matter of life and death. Slavery must be all in the Union, or it can be nothing. This is fully understood by the slaveholders of the cotton States and hence they can accept no compromise, no concession, no settlement that does not exalt slavery above every other interest in the country. While there is a press unfettered, or a human tongue left free, the land will be filled with alarm and agitation. Any compromise which shall leave men free in any corner of the Republic to feel, think, and utter their thoughts, will contain the seeds of its own destruction, and leave to the future what ought to be done to-day. Instead of looking around for means of reconciling freedom and slavery, how immeasurably better would it be if, in our national councils, some Wilberforce or a Buxton could arise, and, looking at the subject from the highest point of a wise statesmanship, which is ever in harmony with immutable laws of progress and development, scorning all the petty tricks of the mere politician, propose a plan for the complete abolition of slavery. Is America more selfish and less humane than Russia?—Is she less honest and benevolent than England? Is she more stolid and insensible to the claims of humanity than the Dutch?—What should hinder her from following the human example, and adopting the enlightened policy of those nations? Whether this is done or not, herein, and herein alone is the basis of solid peace, and the country must remain a spectacle of anarchy, and be a byword and a hissing to a mocking earth, till this basis of eternal justice and liberty shall be the foundation of our Union.

All compromises now are but as new wine to old bottles, new cloth to old garments. To attempt them as a means of peace between freedom and slavery, is as to attempt to reverse irreversible law. The "irrepressible conflict" still proceeds, and must continue till the merciful spirit of Christianity and civilization shall be extinguished and cease to have a single heart and voice to plead her cause, or slavery dies. If there is not wisdom and virtue enough in the land to rid the country of slavery, then the next best thing is to let the South go to her own place, and be made to drink the wine cup of wrath and fire, which her long career of cruelty, barbarism and blood shall call down upon her guilty head.

Douglass' Monthly, February, 1861

As the secession movement progressed, Douglass saw only one ray of hope for the cause—Lincoln's inauguration. His admiration of Lincoln had increased in the weeks following the election. He observed with satisfaction the President-elect's determination not to capitulate to the demands for a compromise policy that would appease secessionists and "his refusal to have concessions extorted from him under the terror instituted by thievish conspirators and traitors. . . ." The Negro leader shared Lincoln's attitude toward the pro-compromise advocates, pointing out: "All compromises are now but as new wine to old bottles, new cloth to old garments. To attempt them as a means of peace between freedom and slavery, is as to attempt to reverse irreversible law."[1]

Together with the entire nation Douglass looked forward to Lincoln's inaugural address. Late in February, 1861, a convention of slave owners had set up a provisional government at Montgomery, Alabama, with Jefferson Davis as President of the Confederate States of America. How would Lincoln meet this unprecedented crisis?

Douglass was bitterly disappointed by the inaugural address. Lincoln had pledged himself not to interfere directly or indirectly with slavery in the states where it then existed; promised to support the enforcement of the fugitive slave law; and declared he would maintain the Union. Douglass saw little in this message to gladden the hearts of the Negro people. (II:100–101)

THE INAUGURAL ADDRESS

Elsewhere in the columns of our present monthly, our readers will find the Inaugural Address of Mr. Abraham Lincoln, delivered on the occasion of his induction to the office of President of the United States. The circumstances under which the Address was delivered, were the most extraordinary and portentous that ever attended any similar occasion in the history of the country. Threats of riot, rebellion, violence and assassination had been freely, though darkly circulated, as among the probable events to occur on that memorable day. The life of Mr. Lincoln was believed, even by his least timid friends, to be in most imminent danger.[2] No mean courage was required to face the probabilities of the hour. He stood up before the pistol or dagger of the sworn assassin, to meet death from an unknown hand, while upon the very threshold of the office to which the suffrages of the nation had elected him. The outgoing Administration, either by its treachery or weakness, or both, had allowed the Government to float to the very verge of destruction. A fear, amounting to agony in some minds, existed that the great American Republic would expire in the arms of its newly elected guardian upon the very moment of his inauguration. For weeks and months previously to the 4th of March, under the wise direction and management of General Scott, elaborate military preparations were made with a view to prevent the much apprehended outbreak of violence and bloodshed, and secure the peaceful inauguration of the President elect. How much the nation is indebted to General Scott for its present existence, it is impossible to tell. No doubt exists that to him, rather than to any forbearance of the rebels, Washington owes its salvation from bloody streets on the fourth of March. The manner in which Mr. Lincoln entered the Capital was in keeping with the menacing and troubled state of the times. He reached the Capital as the poor, hunted fugitive slave reaches the North, in disguise, seeking concealment, evading pursuers, by the underground railroad, between two days, not during the sunlight, but crawling and dodging under the sable wing of night. He changed his programme, took another route, started at another hour, travelled in other company, and arrived at another time in Washington. We have no censure for the President at this point. He only did what braver men have done. It was, doubtless, galling to his very soul to be compelled to avail himself of the methods of a fugitive slave, with a nation howling on his track. The great party that elected him fairly wilted under it. The act, in some sense, was an indication of the policy of the new Government—more cunning than bold, evading rather than facing danger, outwitting rather than bravely conquering and putting down the enemy. The whole thing looked bad, but it was not adopted without reason. Circumstances gave to an act which, upon its face, was cowardly and mean, the merit of wisdom, forethought and discretion.

Once in Washington, Mr. Lincoln found himself in the thick atmosphere of treason on the one hand, and a cowardly, sentimental and deceitful profession of peace on the other. With such surroundings, he went to work upon his Inaugural Address, and the influence of those surroundings may be traced in the whole character of his performance. Making all allowance for circumstances, we must declare the address to be but little better than our worst fears, and vastly below what we had fondly hoped it might be. It is a double-tongued document, capable of two constructions, and conceals rather than declares a definite policy. No man reading it could say whether Mr. Lincoln was for peace or war, whether he abandons or maintains the principles of the Chicago Convention upon which he was elected. The occasion required the utmost frankness and decision. Overlooking the whole field of disturbing elements, he should have boldly rebuked them. He saw seven States in open rebellion, the Constitution set at naught, the national flag insulted, and his own life murderously sought by slave-holding assassins. Does he expose and rebuke the enemies of his country, the men who are bent upon ruling or ruining the country? Not a bit of it. But at the very start he seeks to court their favor, to explain himself where nobody misunderstands him, and to deny intentions of which nobody had accused him. He turns away from his armed enemy and deals his blows on the head of an innocent bystander. He knew, full well, that the grand objection to him and his party respected the one great question of slavery extension. The South want to extend slavery, and the North want to confine it where it is, "where the public mind shall rest in the belief of its ultimate extinction." This was the question which carried the North and defeated the South in the election which made Mr. Abraham Lincoln President. Mr. Lincoln knew this, and the South has known it all along; and yet this subject only gets the faintest allusion, while others, never seriously in dispute, are dwelt upon at length.

Mr. Lincoln opens his address by announcing his complete loyalty to slavery in the slave States, and quotes from the Chicago platform a resolution affirming the rights of property in slaves, in the slave States. He is not content with declaring that he has no lawful power to interfere with slavery in the States, but he also denies having the least *"inclination"* to interfere with slavery in the States. This denial of all feeling against slavery, at such a time and in such circumstances, is wholly discreditable to the head and heart of Mr. Lincoln. Aside from the inhuman coldness of the sentiment, it was a weak and inappropriate utterance to such an audience, since it could neither appease nor check the wild fury of the rebel Slave Power. Any but a blind man can see that the disunion sentiment of the South does not arise from any misapprehension of the disposition of the party represented by Mr. Lincoln. The very opposite is the fact. The difficulty is, the slaveholders understand the position of the Republican party too well. Whatever may be the honied phrases employed by Mr. Lincoln when confronted by actual disunion; however silvery and beautiful may be the subtle rhetoric of his long-headed Secretary of State, when wishing to hold the Government together until its management should fall into other hands; all know that the masses at the North (the power behind the throne) had determined to take and keep this Government out of the hands of the slave-holding oligarchy, and administer it here-after to the advantage of free labor as against slave labor. The slaveholders knew full well that they were hereafter to change the condition of rulers to that of be-ing ruled; they knew that the mighty North is outstripping the South in numbers, and in all the elements of power, and that from being superior, they were to be doomed to hopeless inferiority. This is what galled them. They are not afraid that Lincoln will send out a proclamation over the slave States declaring all the slaves free, nor that Congress will pass a law to that effect. They are no such fools as to believe any such thing; but they do think, and not without reason, that the power of slavery is broken, and that its prestige is gone whenever the people have made up their minds that Liberty is safer in the hands of freemen than in those of slaveholders. To those sagacious and crafty men, schooled into mastery over bondmen on the plantation, and thus the better able to assume the airs of supe-riority over Northern doughfaces, Mr. Lincoln's disclaimer of any power, right or inclination to interfere with slavery in the States, does not amount to more than a broken shoe-string! They knew it all before, and while they do not accept it as a satisfaction, they do look upon such declarations as the evidence of cow-ardly baseness, upon which they may safely presume.

The slaveholders, the parties especially addressed, may well inquire if you, Mr. Lincoln, and the great party that elected you, honestly entertain this very high respect for the rights of slave property in the States, how happens it that you treat the same rights of property with scorn and contempt when they are set up in the Territories of the United States?—If slaves are property, and our rights of property in them are to be so sacredly guarded in the States, by what rule of law, justice or reason does that property part with the attributes of property, upon entering into a Territory owned in part by that same State? The fact is, the slave-holders have the argument all their own way, the moment that the right of prop-erty in their slaves is conceded under the Constitution. It was, therefore, weak, uncalled for and useless for Mr. Lincoln to begin his Inaugural Address by thus at the outset prostrating himself before the foul and withering curse of slavery. The time and the occasion called for a very different attitude. Weakness, timid-ity and conciliation towards the tyrants and traitors had emboldened them to a pitch of insolence which demanded an instant check. Mr. Lincoln was in a posi-tion that enabled him to wither at a single blast their high blown pride. The oc-casion was one for honest rebuke, not for palliations and apologies. The slave-holders should have been told that their barbarous system of robbery is contrary to the spirit of the age, and to the principles of Liberty in which the Federal Government was founded, and that they should be ashamed to be everlastingly pressing that scandalous crime into notice. Some thought we had in Mr. Lincoln the nerve and decision of an Oliver Cromwell; but the result shows that we merely have a continuation of the Pierces and Buchanans, and that the Republican President bends the knee to slavery as readily as any of his infamous predecessors. Not content with the broadest recognition of the right of property in the souls and bodies of men in the slave States, Mr. Lincoln next proceeds, with nerves of steel, to tell the slaveholders what an excellent slave hound he is, and how he regards the right to recapture fugitive slaves a constitutional duty; and lest the poor bondman should escape being returned to the hell of slavery by the application of certain well known rules of legal interpretation, which any and every white man may claim in his own case, Mr. Lincoln proceeds to cut off the poor, trembling Negro who had escaped from bondage from all advantages from such rules. He will have the pound of flesh, blood or no blood, be it more or less, a just pound or not. The Shylocks of the South, had they been after such game, might have exclaimed, in joy, an Abraham come to judgment! But they were not to be caught with such fodder. The hunting down a few slaves, the sending back of a few Lucy Bagleys, young and beautiful though they be, to the lust and brutality of the slavebreeders of the Border States, is to the rapacity of the rebels only as a drop of water upon a house in flames. The value of the thing was wholly in its quality. "Mr. Lincoln, you will catch and return our slaves if they run away from us, and will help us hold them where they are;" what cause, then, since you have descended to this depth of wickedness, withholds you from coming down to us entirely? Indeed, in what respect are you better than ourselves, or our overseers and drivers who hunt and flog our Negroes into obedience?—Again, the slaveholders have a decided advantage over Mr. Lincoln, and over his party. He stands upon the same moral level with them, and is in no respect better than they. If we held the Constitution, as held by Mr. Lincoln, no earthly power could induce us to swear to support it. The fact is, (following the lead of the Dred Scott decision, and all the Southern slaveholding politicians, with all the doughfaces of the North who have been engaged in making a Constitution, for years, outside of the Constitution of 1789,) Mr. Lincoln has taken everything at this point in favor of slavery for granted. He is like the great mass of his countrymen, indebted to the South for both law and gospel.

But the Inaugural does not admit of entire and indiscriminate condemnation. It has at least one or two features which evince the presence or something like a heart as well as a head. Horrible as is Mr. Lincoln's admission of the constitutional duty of surrendering persons claimed as slaves, and heartily as he seems determined that that revolting work shall be performed, he has sent along with his revolting declaration a timid suggestion which, tame and spiritless as it is, must prove as unpalatable as gall to the taste of slaveholders. He says: "In any law on this subject, ought not all the safeguards of liberty known in humane and civilized jurisprudence be introduced, so that a free man be not in any case surrendered as a slave." For so much, little as it is, let the friends of freedom thank Mr. Lincoln. This saves his Address from the gulf of infamy into which the Dred

Scott decision sunk the Supreme Court of the United States. Two ideas are embraced in this suggestion: First, a black man's rights should be guarded by all the safeguards known to liberty and to humane jurisprudence; secondly, that slavery is an inhuman condition from which a free man ought by all lawful means to be saved. When we remember the prevailing contempt for the rights of all persons of African descent, who are mostly exposed to the operation of these slave-catching laws, and the strenuous efforts of the American Church and clergy to make slavery a divine relation, and especially blissful to our much hated variety of the human family, we are disposed to magnify and rejoice over even this slight recognition of rights, and this implied acknowledgment of the hatefulness of slavery. One of the safeguards of liberty is trial in open court. Another is the right of bringing evidence in one's own favor, and of confronting and questioning opposing witnesses. Another is the trial by a jury of our peers. Another is that juries are judges both of the law and the evidence in the case. There are other safeguards of liberty which we might specify, any one of which, faithfully applied, would not only make it difficult to surrender a free man as a slave, but would make it almost impossible to surrender any man as such. Thanking Mr. Lincoln for even so much, we yet hold him to be the most dangerous advocate of slave-hunting and slave-catching in the land.

He has laid down a general rule of legal interpretation which, like most, if not all general rules, may be stretched to cover almost every conceivable villainy. "*The intention of the law-giver is the law,*" says Mr. Lincoln. But we say that this depends upon whether the *intention* itself is lawful. If law were merely an arbitrary rule, destitute of all idea of right and wrong, the intention of the law-giver might indeed be taken as the law, provided that intention were certainly known. But the very idea of law carries with it ideas of right, justice and humanity. Law, according to Blackstone, commands that which is right and forbids that which is wrong. A law authorizing murder is now law, because it is an outrage upon all the elements out of which laws originate. Any man called to administer and execute such a law is bound to treat such an edict as a nullity, having no binding authority over his action or over his conscience. He would have a right to say, upon the authority of the Supreme Court, that "laws against fundamental morality are void"; that a law for murder is an absurdity, and not only from the purpose of all law and government, but wholly at war with every principle of law. It would be no avail in such a case to say that the "intention of lawmakers is the law." To prove such an intention is only to destroy the validity of the law.

But the case is not murder, but simply the surrendering of a person to slavery who has made his or her escape from slavery into a free State. But what better is an act of this kind than murder? Would not Mr. Lincoln himself prefer to see a dagger plunged to the hilt into the heart of his own daughter, than to see that daughter given up to the lust and brutality of the slaveholders of Virginia, as was poor, trembling Lucy Bagley given up a few weeks ago by the Republicans of Cleveland?[3] What is slavery but a slow process of soul murder? What but murder is its chief reliance? How do slaveholders hold their slaves except by asserting their right and power to murder their slaves if they do not submit to slavery?

Does not the whole slave system rest upon a basis of murder? Your money or your life, says the pirate; your liberty or your life, says the slaveholder. And where is the difference between the pirate and the slaveholder?

But the "intention of the law is the law." Well, suppose we grant it in the present case, that the intention of the law-maker is the law, and two very important questions arise—first, as to who were the makers, and, secondly, by what means are we required to learn their intentions? Who made the Constitution? The preamble to the Constitution answers that question. "We, the people, do ordain and establish this Constitution." The people, then, made the law. How stood their intention as to the surrender of fugitive slaves? Were they all agreed in this intention to send slaves to bondage who might escape from it? Or were only a part? and if a part, how many? Surely, if a minority only were of the intention, that intention could not be the law, especially as the law itself expresses no such intention. The fact is, there is no evidence whatever that any considerable part of the people who made and adopted the American Constitution intended to make that instrument a slave-hunting or a slaveholding instrument, while there is much evidence to prove the very reverse. Daniel Webster, even in his famous 7th of March speech, was sufficiently true to the letter of the Constitution, and to the history of the times in which the Constitution was framed and adopted, to deny that the Constitution required slaves to be given up, and quoted Mr. James Madison in corroboration of his statement. This is Mr. Webster's language: "It may not be important here to allude to that—I had almost said celebrated—opinion of Mr. Madison. You observe, sir, that the term slavery is not used in the Constitution. The Constitution does not require that fugitive slaves shall be delivered up; it requires that persons bound to service in one States escaping into another, shall be delivered up. Mr. Madison opposed the introduction of the term slave, or slavery, into the Constitution; for he said he did not wish to see it recognized by the Constitution of the United States of America, that there could be property in men."

How sadly have the times changed, not only since the days of Madison—the days of the Constitution—but since the days even of Daniel Webster. Cold and dead as that great bad man was to the claims of humanity, he was not sufficiently removed from the better days of the Republic to claim, as Mr. Lincoln does, that the surrender of fugitive slaves is a plain requirement of the Constitution.

But there comes along a slight gleam of relief. Mr. Lincoln tremblingly ventures to *inquire* (for he is too inoffensive to the slaveholders to assert and declare, except when the rights of the black men are asserted and declared away) if it "might not be well to provide by law for the enforcement of that clause in the Constitution which guarantees that the citizens of each State shall be entitled to all the privileges and immunities of citizens in the several States."

Again we thank Mr. Lincoln. He has, however, ventured upon a hazardous suggestion. The man has not quite learned his lesson. He had not been long enough in Washington to learn that Northern citizens, like persons of African descent, have no rights, privileges or immunities that slaveholders are bound to respect. To break open a man's trunk, to read the letters from his wife and daughters, to tar and feather him, to ride him on a rail and give him the alternative of being hanged or of leaving town the same hour, simply because he resides in a free State, is a privilege and immunity which our Southern brethren will not give up, though the requirement were made in every line of the Constitution. Yet, we say, we are thankful. It is something even to have a sickly intimation that other American citizens, not belonging to the privileged slaveholding class, have rights which it "*might be well*" to secure by law, and that the mere fact of living in a free State ought not to subject the unfortunate traveler either to being whipped, hanged or shot. Yes, this is something to be thankful for and is more than any other American President has ever ventured to say, either in his Inaugural Speech or Annual Message. It is, perhaps, this latter fact that gives Mr. Lincoln's casual remark its chief importance.—Hitherto our Presidents had pictured the South as the innocent lamb, and the greedy North as the hungry wolf, ever ready to tear and devour.

From slave-catching, Mr. Lincoln proceeds to give a very lucid exposition of the nature of the Federal Union, and shows very conclusively that this Government from its own nature and the nature of all Governments, was intended to be perpetual, and that it is revolutionary, insurrectionary and treasonable to break it up. His argument is excellent; but the difficulty is that the argument comes too late. When men deliberately arm themselves with the avowed intention of breaking up the Government; when they openly insult its flag, capture its forts, seize its munitions of war, and organize a hostile Government, and boastfully declare that they will fight before they will submit, it would seem of little use to argue with them. If the argument was merely for the loyal citizen, it was unnecessary. If it was for those already in rebellion, it was casting pearls before swine. No class of men in the country understood better than the rebels themselves the nature of the business on which they are engaged.—They tell us this in the thousands of pounds of powder they have been buying, and the millions of money and arms they have been stealing. They know that unless the Government is a miserable and contemptible failure, destitute of every attribute of a Government except the name, that that Government must meet them on the field and put them down, or be itself put down. To parley with traitors is but to increase their insolence and audacity.

It remains to be seen whether the Federal Government is really able to do more than hand over some John Brown to be hanged, suppress a slave insurrection, or catch a runaway slave—whether it is powerless for liberty, and only powerful for slavery. Mr. Lincoln says, "I shall take care that the laws of the Union shall be faithfully executed in all the States"—that is, he will do so as "*as far as practicable,*" and *unless* the American people, his masters, shall, in some authoritative manner direct the contrary. To us, both these provisions had better have been omitted. They imply a want of confidence in the ability of the Government to execute its own laws, and open its doors to all that border tribe who have nothing but smiles for the rebels and peace lectures for the Government. The American people have placed the Government in the hands of Abraham Lincoln for the next four years, and his instructions are in the Constitution. He had no right to suppose that they will reverse those instructions in a manner to give immunity to traitors; and it was a mistake to admit such a possibility, especially in the presence of the very traitors themselves. But we are dwelling longer upon Mr. Lincoln's speech than we had intended, and longer than we are warranted either by the patience of our readers, or the extent of our space. The perusal of it has left no very hopeful impression upon our mind for the cause of our down-trodden and heart-broken countrymen. Mr. Lincoln has avowed himself ready to catch them if they run away, to shoot them down if they rise against their oppressors, and to prohibit the Federal Government *irrevocably* from interfering for their deliverance. With such declarations before them, coming from our first modern anti-slavery President, the Abolitionists must know what to expect during the next four years, (should Mr. Lincoln not be, as he is likely to be, driven out of Washington by his rival, Mr. Jeff. Davis, who has already given out that should Mr. Lincoln attempt to do, what he has sworn to do—namely, execute the laws, fifty thousand soldiers will march directly upon Washington!) This might be taken as an empty threat on the part of the President of the Confederated States, if we did not see with what steadiness, promptness and certainty the rebels have from the first executed all their designs and fulfilled all their promises. A thousand things are less probable than that Mr. Lincoln and his Cabinet will be driven out of Washington, and made to go out, as they came in, by the Underground Railroad. The game is completely in the hands of Mr. Jefferson Davis, and no doubt he will avail himself of every advantage.

Douglass' Monthly, April, 1861

1. *Douglass' Monthly,* Feb., Mar., 1861.

2. On February 21, 1861, information was conveyed by Allan Pinkerton to President-Elect Lincoln, en route to the nation's capital, that a band of conspirators in Baltimore were planning to assassinate him. At the same time Lincoln was told by Frederick Seward that detectives in Baltimore had also discovered a plot there to assassinate him.

3. Sarah Lucy Bagby fled from her owner in Virginia in October, 1860, and went to Cleveland. On January 19, 1861, she was arrested and committed to the county jail. Despite a vigorous effort on the part of the colored people of Cleveland to rescue her, she was returned to her owner in Wheeling, Virginia.

A TRIP TO HAITI

A dream, fondly indulged, a desire, long cherished, and a purpose, long meditated, are now quite likely to be realized. At this writing, we are on the eve of starting for a visit of a few weeks to Haiti; and before the announcement can reach all our readers and friends, especially those in Great Britain, we shall probably be well on our ocean-way to the shores of *la Republic de l'Haiti.*

For this piece of good fortune (for such we esteem it, and hope it will prove to be) we are indebted for all, save the disposition to go the voyage, to the considerate kindness of the Haitian Government. That Government has removed an important obstacle out of the way, which might have delayed, though it could not have prevented our long-desired visit. Too late to apprize our readers in our April number of the fact, we were informed that a steamer was being chartered by the Haitian Bureau at Boston to carry emigrants and passengers to Haiti from the United States. The intimation was accompanied with a generous offer of a free passage to ourself and daughter to and from Haiti, by Mr. Redpath, the Haitian Consulate at Philadelphia. We are not more thankful for this generous offer from the quarter whence it comes, than sensible of the kind consideration which it implies. We gratefully appreciate both, and shall promptly avail ourselves of the double favors.

The steamer secured for the voyage is to sail from New Haven, Connecticut, about the 25th of April, and will, if all be well, reach *Port-au-Prince* by the first of May.

In making this announcement, we do not wish in any wise to conceal the fact that we are much elated by the prospect of standing once upon the soil of San Domingo, the theatre of many stirring events and heroic achievements, the work of a people, bone of our bone, and flesh of our flesh.

We began life too late to accomplish much. More than twenty-one years of it were lost for all proper educational advantage. Slavery stole from us those years when study and travel should do most for a man; but the world is still new and beautiful to us, and we still rejoice in any opportunity to increase our knowledge of its works and ways. We have seen much of it, but mostly its sterner features. Clouds and storms, ice and snow, moral as well as physical, have been our familiar elements. We have felt the keenly cutting, frosty air, from off the desolate coast of Labrador, amid the snows of winter; but we have never felt the beams of a tropical sun, seen the luminous stars of the tropical sky, heard the sweet warblings of tropical birds, inhaled the fragrance of tropical breezes, nor beheld the endless wealth of a tropical soil. We are going to a land where nature is in full dress, and unfolds her charms in all their loveliness. But we go to Haiti not to enjoy its delightful and soothing climate, to rest in the shadow of its stately palms, nor to luxuriate in its delicious fruits, and its glorious flowers. While not insensible to those delightful attractions, we are drawn towards the sunny region at this time by other considerations than those of pleasure—considerations connected with the sacred cause to which we have gladly given twenty years of unremitting toil.

A visit to Haiti at any time would be a high privilege to us. Our whole experience makes such a visit desirable. Born a slave as we were, in this boasted land of liberty, tinged with a hated color, despised by the rulers of the State, accustomed from childhood to hear the colored race disparaged and denounced, their mental and moral qualities held in contempt, treated as an inferior race, incapable of self government, and of maintaining, when left to themselves, a state of civilization, set apart by the laws of our being to a condition of slavery—we, naturally enough, desire to see, as we doubtless shall see, in the free, orderly and Independent Republic of Haiti, a refutation of the slanders and disparagements of our race. We want to experience the feeling of being under a Government which has been administered by a race denounced as mentally and morally incapable of self-government.

While, however, we shall go to Haiti with strong prepossessions in its favor, we hope to go with the eyes of a truthful observer, able to see things as they really are, to consider the circumstances, and report the philosophy as well as the facts of the situation. Truth can hurt nobody, and we have no fear to tell even that which may seem to make against our cause, if truth shall require it. One thing we know in advance, of Haiti, and that is, her people are *"naught but men and women"*; and that men and women under a vertical sun, where nature responds at the merest touch of industry to every physical want, will not tax themselves to make the same exertion as when in a colder climate and upon a sterner soil.—Another thing we know in advance, which is this: that against all disparagements from the United States against the crafty machinations of two continents to crush her, Haiti has during more than sixty years maintained a free and independent system of government and that no hostile power has been able to bend the proud necks of her people to a foreign yoke. She stands forth among the nations of the earth richly deserving respect and admiration.

Both the press and the platform of the United States have long made Haiti the bugbear and scare-crow of the cause of freedom. Ignorant of her real character in some instances; willfully blind to her obvious virtues in others, we have done her people the most marked injustice. The fact is, white Americans find it hard to tell the truth about colored people. They see us with a dollar in their eyes. Twenty hundred millions of dollars invested in the bodies and souls of the Negro race in this Republic—a mountain of gold—constitutes a standing bribe, a perpetual temptation to do injustices to the colored race. Haiti has thus constantly been the victim of something like a downright conspiracy to rob her of the natural sympathy of the civilized world, and to shut her out of the fraternity of nations. No people have been compelled to meet and live down a prejudice so stubborn and so hatefully unjust. For a time it was fashionable to call them even in our Congress a nation of murderers and cut-throats, and for no better reason than that they won their freedom by their arms. It is quite time that this interesting people should be better understood. Though a city set on an hill, she has been hid; and though a light of glorious promise, she has been compelled to shine only under a bushel. A few names of her great men have been known to the world; but her real character as a whole, we are persuaded, has been grossly misunderstood and perversely misrepresented. One object of our mission, therefore, will be to do justice to Haiti, to paint her as she is, and to add the testimony of an honest witness to honest worth.

But besides these general motives, there are special ones growing out of the state of things at present existing in this country.—During the last few years the minds of free colored people in all the States have been deeply exercised in relation to what may be their future in the United States. To many it has seemed that the portents of the moral sky were all against us. At the South they have been taught to believe that they must soon be forced to choose between slavery or expulsion. At the North there are, alas! too many proofs that the margin of life and liberty is becoming more narrow every year. There are many instances where the black man's places are taken by the white man, but few where, in the free States, the places of the white man are taken by the man of sable hue. The apprehension is general, that proscription, persecution and hardships are to wax more and more rigorous and more grievous with every year; and for this reason they are now, as never before, looking out into the world for a place of retreat, an asylum from the apprehended storm which is about to beat pitilessly upon them.

Without attempting to dispel this apprehension by appeals to facts, which have failed to satisfy, and to general principles of development and progress, which most of our people have deemed too abstract and transcendental for practical life, we propose to act in view of the settled fact that many of them are already resolved to look for homes beyond the boundaries of the United States, and that most of their minds are turned towards Haiti. Though never formally solicited by any organized body of our people to acquire information which may be useful to those who are looking to that country for a home, we have been repeatedly urged to do so by individuals of the highest character and respectability. Without at all discrediting the statements of others, we have desired to see for ourselves. For the next six or eight weeks, therefore, we know of no better use to which we can put ourselves, than in a tour of observation in this modern land of Canaan, where so many of our people are journeying from the rigorous bondage and oppression of our modern Egypt.

—Since this article upon Haiti was put in type, we find ourselves in circumstances which induce us to forego our much desired trip to Haiti, for the present. The last ten days have made a tremendous revolution in all things pertaining to the possible future of the colored people of the United States. We shall stay here and watch the current of events, and serve the cause of freedom and humanity in any way that shall be open to us during the struggle now going on between the slave power and the government. When the Northern people have been made to experience a little more of the savage barbarism of slavery, they may be willing to make war upon it, and in that case we stand ready to lend a hand in any way we can be of service. At any rate, this is no time for us to leave the country.

Douglass' Monthly, May, 1861

With the outbreak of the Civil War, Frederick Douglass entered upon a new phase of his career as an Abolitionist. Up to this time he had fought the slaveholders as an individual or together with the many thousands of men and women who abhorred slavery and gave freely of their time and money in the struggle against it. Now the full might of an aroused North was to be thrown against the slavocracy. And the forces of circumstance would compel the country to listen attentively to what the Abolitionists had to say. Before the war was many months old, Douglass was to find himself no longer the despised agitator, but the distinguished anti-slavery advocate who had warned that the nation must abolish slavery or be abolished by it. Many Americans, remembering that for years Douglass had insisted that slavery would be drowned in a sea of blood since its "peaceful annihilation" was "almost hopeless," now weighed carefully his observations on the nature and conduct of the war.

These observations related mainly to one aspect of the conflict. Douglass had little time to discuss the problems relating to the tariff, internal improvements, and a national banking system. One issue alone consumed his thoughts night and day—the Negro slave. He viewed the conduct of the war "more as a bondman than as a freeman." His mission in the war, he announced early in the conflict, was "to stand up for the downtrodden, to open my mouth for the dumb, to remember those in bonds as bound with them."[1]

When the news flashed over the North on April 12, 1861, that "Fort Sumter has surrendered," Douglass cried out: "God be praised!" The tension was broken; the war had begun. In that moment the current of popular feeling changed. Gone were the months of appeasement when politicians and business men had vied with each other "to purchase peace and prosperity for the North by granting the most demoralizing concessions to the Slave Power." The cannons booming over Charleston had compelled everyone "to elect between patriotic fidelity and pro-slavery treason." The flag had been fired on, and from the North and West came countless expressions of patriotism and loyalty. "Since they will have it so," declared Governor Andrew of Massachusetts, "in the name of God—amen." To this Douglass added: "Again, we say out of a full heart, and on behalf of our enslaved and bleeding brothers, thank God."[2]

There were different views as to the causes and purposes of the war. Some Abolitionists and politically advanced German-American Communists entered the struggle with a consciousness of the need to abolish Negro slavery as well as to save the Union. But the vast majority of the northern people who took to arms the moment Fort Sumter was attacked joined the Union forces with the sole aim of saving the Union. They shared with Lincoln the belief that the only issue at stake in the war was "whether in a free government the minority have the right to break it up whenever they choose."[3] Some argued that the war was simply a conflict between states' rights and nationalism. Others saw in the war merely a struggle between low and high tariffs.

From the very beginning, Douglass perceived clearly that the war was a struggle to complete the historic task left uncompleted by the first American Revolution which had failed to root out the cancer of slavery from the body of America, that it would mean the emancipation of the Negro people and the liberation of the North from slaveholding domination.

The fact that in the popular uprising pledging full support to the federal government there were few references to slavery was of little importance to him. Slavery was involved in the war whether or not the people or their government knew it.... With amazing power of acute observation, Douglass pointed out directly after the bombardment of Fort Sumter: "It is not merely a war for slavery, but it is a war for slavery dominion." [III:11–12]

THE FALL OF SUMTER

As a friend of freedom, earnestly laboring for the abolition of slavery, we have no tears to shed, no lamentations to make over the fall of Fort Sumter. By that event, one danger which threatened the cause of the American slave has been greatly diminished. Through many long and weary months, the American people have been on the mountain with the wily tempter, and have been liable at any moment of weakness to grant a new lease of life to slavery. The whole power of the Northern pro-slavery press, combined with the commercial and manufacturing interests of the country, has been earnestly endeavoring to purchase peace and prosperity for the North by granting the most demoralizing concessions to the insatiate Slave Power. This has been our greatest danger. The attack upon Fort Sumter bids fair to put an end to this cowardly, base and unprincipled truckling. To our thinking, the damage done to Fort Sumter is nothing in comparison with that done to the secession cause. The hail and fire of its terrible batteries has killed its friends and spared its enemies. Anderson lives,[4] but where are the champions of concession at the North? Their traitor lips are pale and silent.

While secession confined its war operation to braggart threats, pompous declarations, exciting telegrams, stealing arms, planting liberty poles, wearing cockades, and displaying palmetto and rattlesnake flags, it exercised a potent influence over the public mind, and held the arm of the Government paralyzed. It commanded the artillery of a thousand cannon. But the secessionists themselves have now "smashed" up these magnificent machines, and have spiked their own most efficient guns. They have completely shot off the legs of all trimmers and compromisers, and compelled everybody to elect between patriotic fidelity and pro-slavery treason.

For this consummation we have watched and wished with fear and trembling. God be praised! that it has come at last. We should have been glad if the North, of its own proper virtue, had given this *quietus* to doubt and vacillation. She did not do it, and perhaps it is best that she did not. What her negative wisdom withheld has now come to us through the vengeance and rashness of slaveholders. Another instance of the wrath of man working out the purposes and praise of eternal goodness!

Had Mr. Jefferson Davis continued to allow Major Anderson, with his harmless garrison, to receive his daily bread from the markets of Charleston, or even permitted the Government at Washington to feed his men, the arm of the nation might have slept on, and the South might have got the most extravagant concessions to its pet monster, slavery. Every Personal Liberty Bill might have been swept from the statute books of the North, and every trembling fugitive hunted by Northern bloodhounds from his hiding place to save the Union. Already the hateful reaction had begun. Chicago and Cleveland, headquarters of Republicanism, had both betrayed innocent blood, while "down with Abolition" was fast becoming the cry of the mob on the one hand, and clergy on the other. The color of the Negro, always hated, was fast becoming more hated, and the few rights and liberties enjoyed by the free colored citizen were threatened. But now, thanks to the reckless impetuosity of the dealers in the bodies and souls of men, their attack upon Sumter has done much to arrest this retrograde and cowardly movement, and has raised the question as to the wisdom of thus pampering treason. Our rulers were ready enough to sacrifice the Negro to the Union so long as there was any hope of saving the Union by that means. The attack upon Sumter, and other movements on the part of the cotton lords of the lash, have about convinced them that the insatiate slaveholders not only mean peace and safety of slavery, but to make themselves masters of the Republic. It is not merely a war for slavery, but it is a war for slavery dominion. There are points in which different nations excel.—England is mighty on the land, but mightier on the water. The slaveholders have always surpassed the North in the matter of party politics. In the arts of persuasion, the management of men, in tact and address, they have ever been remarkably successful. Accustomed to rule over slaves, and to assume the airs of vaunted superiority, they easily intimidate the timid, overawe the servile, while they artfully cultivate the respect and regard of the brave and fearless.

It remains to be seen whether they have acted wisely in transferring the controversy with the North from the halls of diplomacy, to the field of battle. They were not forced to the measure. The Government at Washington stood waiting to be gracious. It treated treason in its embryo form, merely as an *"eccentricity,"* which a few months would probably cure. They had no purpose to resort to the straight jacket. To some of us there was far too little importance attached to the slaveholding movement by the Government at Washington. But all is changed now. The Government is active, and the people aroused. Again, we say, out of a full heart, and on behalf of our enslaved and bleeding brothers and sisters, thank God!—The slaveholders themselves have saved our cause from ruin! They have exposed the throat of slavery to the keen knife of liberty, and have given a chance to all the righteous forces of the nation to deal a death-blow to the monster evil of the nineteenth century.—*Friends of freedom! be up and doing;—now is your time.* The tyrant's extremity is your opportunity! Let the long crushed bondman arise! and in this auspicious moment, snatch back the liberty of which he has been so long robbed and despoiled. Now is the day, and now is the hour!

Is it said that we exult in rebellion? We repel the allegation as a slander. Every pulsation of our heart is with the legitimate American Government, in its determination to suppress and put down this slaveholding rebellion. The *Stars and Stripes* are now the symbols of liberty. The Eagle that we left last month something like as good as dead, has revived again, and screams terror in the ears of the slaveholding rebels. None but the worst of traitors can now desire victory for any flag but that of the old Confederacy. He who faithfully works to put down a rebellion undertaken and carried on for the extension and perpetuity of slavery, performs an anti-slavery work. Even disunion Abolitionists, who have believed that the dissolution of the Union would be the dissolution of slavery, will, we have no doubt, rejoice in the success of the Government at Washington, in suppressing and putting down this slaveholding rebellion.

Douglass' Monthly, May, 1861

1. *Douglass' Monthly,* Mar., 1862.
2. Ibid., May, 1861; Henry G. Pearson, *The Life of John A. Andrew,* Boston, 1904, vol. I, p. 176.
3. Carl Sandburg, *Storm over the Land: A Profile of the Civil War,* New York, 1942, p. 43.
4. Major Robert Anderson commanded the Fort Sumter garrison in Charleston Harbor. After thirty-three hours of bombardment which began at dawn on April 12, Anderson gave up the fort. On Sunday, April 14, he marched his garrison out, and they boarded a relief ship and headed north for New York harbor. They had lost one man, killed in the accidental explosion of one of their own cannon.

SUDDEN REVOLUTION IN NORTHERN SENTIMENT

During the first three weeks after the inauguration of Mr. Lincoln's Administration, there was a general sentiment all over the North looking to a peaceful solution of the revolutionary crisis now upon the country.—The Government at Washington seemed to be paralyzed, the Border States were active in their efforts to avert civil war, partly by securing new and stronger guarantees for slavery, and partly by threats of disunion if the Government should attempt to defend itself by force against the rebel force of the so-called Confederate States. Fort Sumter was to be abandoned; other Southern forts were to follow in the same path, and the Secession States were to be acknowledged and to have an easy time generally. Southern Commissioners remained at Washington, and kept up the hopes of the Cotton States by sending encouraging telegrams over the country that things were working well and favorably to all their plans and purposes. Democrats were doing what they could all over the North to cripple and fetter the Republicans, and Republicans themselves were divided as between a policy of peace and a policy of war, each wing of the latter party claiming to represent the spirit and purposes of the Administration. In this general disjointed condition of facts, the Northern people stood apparently powerless.

But what a change now greets us! The Government is aroused, the dead North is alive, and its divided people united. Never was a change so sudden, so universal, and so portentous. The whole North, East and West is in arms. Drums are beating, men are enlisting, companies forming, regiments marching, banners are flying, and money is pouring into the national treasury to put an end to the slave-holding rebellion.

The rebels have all along based the probabilities of success to their unhallowed scheme of battering down the present Government at Washington upon treacherous divisions among the people of the North. An united North was not among their calculations, and there was much in the history of Northern subserviency to the Slave Power to encourage their reckoning. But now all is changed—quite changed. People, press and pulpit, with exceptions too insignificant to mention, are knitted together like the iron links of a coat of mail. "Southern brethren," "forbearance," "concession," "compromise," "peace," and "reconstruction," have everywhere been exchanged for sterner watch-words. The cry now is for war, vigorous war, war to the bitter end, and war till the traitors are effectually and permanently put down. The moral tone of the North has risen, the manly spirit of the North is quickened, and its activity, enterprize and energy are all ranged on the side of the National Government.

If, however, the change in the popular feeling has been quick and sudden, the causes leading thereto have been long maturing.—The Government has been patient, forbearing and long suffering beyond all example. It had seen inflammatory appeals and heard rebellious threats six months ago, and for the last four months it has seen treason actively organizing itself in Conventions for Secession, into all sorts of military bodies for resisting and defying the power of the United States; it has seen seven States formally secede from the Union, and set up a Government for themselves; it has seen the armed traitors robbing and plundering its property, and seizing its own means of self-preservation; it has seen its own flag insulted and hauled down over its own forts and arsenals; it has seen frowning forts and batteries erected for the very purpose of disputing its authority and securing its overthrow; and still it hoped and waited for the return of reason and good feeling, without lifting an arm or firing a ball; but when it saw an attempt to starve out Major Anderson and his men from Fort Sumter, and open all their rebel batteries for the destruction of that fortress, both Government and people were compelled to awake from all dreams of peace.

Whatever else may take place, one thing at least is certain, the slaveholding rebellion will be crushed out, and its leaders covered with execrations and curses in the very sections where they have been most popular. They have blinded and befooled the people into the belief that great masses of men at the North and in the Middle States would stand by them in their unprovoked and fratricidal war upon the Government. They have boasted their ability to send more men into the field because of their slavery. They have spoken of themselves as giants and heroes, and of Northern men as pigmies and cowards. They have laughed at the President's proclamation, and contrasted the strength and sagacity of Montgomery with the weakness and imbecility of Washington. What a revulsion in popular feeling will come over the South when it finds it has been deceived, misled and ruined, for ruined it will be. Let the ports of the South be blockaded; let business there be arrested; let provisions, arms and ammunition be no longer sent there; let the grim visage of a Northern army confront them from one direction, a furious slave insurrection meet them at another, and starvation threaten them from still another, and they will begin to murmur a discontent which will surely break out at last in bitter execration and curses upon the guilty authors of their triple woes. The confederate slaveholding traitors are now only on the outer wave of the whirlpool of treason; every circle they now make will bring them nearer the centre that is certain to swallow them up, and hurl them to the bottom of its howling waters.

Douglass' Monthly, May, 1861

Two ideas . . . took possession of Douglass from the moment the war started: free the slaves as a war measure and recruit Negroes into the Union Army. He urged this policy without compromise. In editorials, speeches, letters, and interviews, he stressed again and again the theme—"The Negro is the key of the situation—the pivot upon which the whole rebellion turns." A proclamation of freedom to the slaves would "smite rebellion in the very seat of its life," depriving it of the labor which kept the rebel army supplied with food, clothing, and the sinews of war. It would also unmask the rebels' cry that they were fighting for the right to govern themselves. Abolition of the slaves would immediately unite the world in favor of the government of the United States. "From the first," Douglass wrote later in his autobiography, "I reproached the North that they fought the rebels with only one hand, when they might strike effectively with two—that they fought with their soft white hand, while they kept their black iron hand chained and helpless behind them—that they fought the effect, while they protected the cause, and that the Union Cause would never prosper till the war assumed an anti-slavery attitude, and the Negro was enlisted on the loyal side."[1]

Negroes rushed to offer their services to the Union, but they were rejected. Moved by Douglass' call, Philadelphia Negroes offered to go South to organize slave revolts. Everywhere in the North Negroes asked to be received into the Union Army. At a meeting of Boston Negroes late in April, a resolution was passed urging the government to enlist them: "Our feelings urge us to say to our countrymen that we are ready to stand by and defend our Government as the equals of its white defenders; to do so with 'our lives, our fortunes, and our sacred honor,' for the sake of freedom, and as good citizens; and we ask you to modify your laws, that we may enlist,—that full scope may be given to the patriotic feelings burning in the colored man's breast."[2]

These appeals fell on deaf ears. Determined to mollify the border slave states—Delaware, Maryland, Kentucky, and Missouri—and keep them in the Union, Lincoln was deaf to pleas that the war be turned into a war against slavery and that Negroes be recruited into the Union Army. [III:13–14]

HOW TO END THE WAR

To our mind, there is but one easy, short and effectual way to suppress and put down the desolating war which the slaveholders and their rebel minions are now waging against the American Government and its loyal citizens. Fire must be met with water, darkness with light, and war for the destruction of liberty must be met with war for the destruction of slavery. *The simple way, then, to put an end to the savage and desolating war now waged by the slaveholders, is to strike down slavery itself,* the primal cause of that war.

Freedom to the slave should now be proclaimed from the Capitol, and should be seen above the smoke and fire of every battle field, waving from every loyal flag! The time for mild measures is past. They are pearls cast before swine, and only increase and aggravate the crime which they would conciliate and repress. The weak point must be found, and when found should be struck with the utmost vigor. Any war is a calamity; but a peace that can only breed war is a far greater calamity. A long and tame war, waged without aim or spirit, paralyzes business, arrests the wheels of civilization, benumbs the national feeling, corrodes the national heart, and diffuses its baleful influence universally. Sharp, quick, wise, strong and sudden, are the elements for the occasion. The sooner this rebellion is put out of its misery, the better for all concerned. A lenient war is a lengthy war, and therefore the worst kind of war. Let us stop it, and stop it effectually—stop it before its evils are diffused throughout the Northern States—stop it on the soil upon which it originated, and among the traitors and rebels who originated the war. This can be done at once, by "*carrying the war into Africa.*" *Let the slaves and free colored people be called into service, and formed into a liberating army,* to march into the South and raise the banner of Emancipation among the slaves. The South having brought revolution and war upon the country, and having elected and consented to play at that fearful game, she has no right to complain if some good as well as calamity shall result from her own act and deed.

The slaveholders have not hesitated to employ the sable arms of the Negroes at the South in erecting the fortifications which silenced the guns of Fort Sumter, and brought the star-spangled banner to the dust. They often boast, and not without cause, that their Negroes will fight for them against the North. They have no scruples against employing the Negroes to exterminate freedom, and in overturning the Government. They work with spade and barrow with them, and they will stand with them on the field of battle, shoulder to shoulder, with guns in their hands, to shoot down the troops of the U.S. Government.—They have neither pride, prejudice nor *pity* to restrain them from employing Negroes *against white men, where slavery is to be protected and made secure*. Oh! that this Government would only now be as true to liberty as the rebels, who are attempting to batter it down, are true to slavery. We have no hesitation in saying that ten thousand black soldiers might be raised in the next thirty days to march upon the South. One black regiment alone would be, in such a war, the full equal of two white ones. The very fact of color in this case would be more terrible than powder and balls. The slaves would learn more as to the nature of the conflict from the presence of one such regiment, than from a thousand preachers. Every consideration of justice, humanity and sound policy confirms the wisdom of calling upon black men just now to take up arms in behalf of their country.

We are often asked by persons in the street as well as by letter, what our people will do in the present solemn crisis in the affairs of the country. Our answer is, would to God you would let us do something! We lack nothing but your consent. We are ready and would go, counting ourselves happy in being permitted to serve and suffer for the cause of freedom and free institutions. But you won't let us go. Read the heart-rending account we publish elsewhere of the treatment received by the brave fellows, who broke away from their chains and went through marvelous suffering to defend Fort Pickens against the rebels.—They were instantly seized and put in irons and returned to their guilty masters to be whipped to death! Witness Gen. Butler's offer to put down the slave insurrection in the State of Maryland. The colored citizens of Boston have offered their services to the Government, and were refused.[3] There is, even now, while the slaveholders are marshaling armed Negroes against the Government, covering the ocean with pirates, destroying innocent lives, to sweep down the commerce of the country, tearing up railways, burning bridges to prevent the march of Government troops to the defence of its capital, exciting mobs to stone the Yankee soldiers; there is still, we say, weak and contemptible tenderness towards the blood thirsty, slaveholding traitors, by the Government and people of the country. Until the nation shall repent of this weakness and folly, until they shall make the cause of their country the cause of freedom, until they shall strike down slavery, the source and center of this gigantic rebellion, they don't deserve the support of a single sable arm, nor will it succeed in crushing the cause of our present troubles.

Douglass' Monthly, May, 1861

1. *Douglass' Monthly*, Sept., 1861; *Life and Times of Frederick Douglass*, p. 421.

2. *Boston Courier*, Apr. 24, 1861.

3. A report in the *Boston Daily Courier*, April 24, 1861, declared that "a meeting of the colored citizens of this city was held last evening in Rev. Mr. Grimes' church . . . [at which] a series of resolutions . . . were adopted, asking for a modification of the militia laws, so that colored persons may enlist." Five days later, April 29, 1861, Secretary of War Simon Cameron announced that "this Department has no intention at present to call into the service of the government any colored soldiers." (*War of the Rebellion: A Compilation of the Official Records of the Union and Confederate Armies*. Washington, 1880–1901, Series 3, vol. I, pp. 106, 133.)

NEMESIS

At last our proud Republic is overtaken. Our National Sin has found us out. The National Head is bowed down, and our face is mantled with shame and confusion. No foreign arm is made bare for our chastisement. No distant monarch, offended at our freedom and prosperity, has plotted our destruction; no envious tyrant has prepared for our necks his oppressive yoke. Slavery has done it all. Our enemies are those of our own household. It is civil war, the worst of all wars, that has unveiled its savage and wrinkled front amongst us. During the last twenty years and more, we have as a nation been forging a bolt for our own national destruction, collecting and augmenting the fuel that now threatens to wrap the nation in its malignant and furious flames. We have sown the wind, only to reap the whirlwind. Against argument, against all manner of appeal and remonstrances coming up from the warm and merciful heart of humanity, we have gone on like the oppressors of Egypt, hardening our hearts and increasing the burdens of the American slave, and strengthening the arm of his guilty master, till now, in the pride of his giant power, that master is emboldened to lift rebellious arms against the very majesty of the law, and defy the power of the Government itself. In vain have we plunged our souls into new and unfathomed depths of sin, to conciliate the favor and secure the loyalty of the slaveholding class. We have hated and persecuted the Negro; we have scourged him out of the temple of justice by the Dred Scott decision; we have shot and hanged his friends at Harper's Ferry; we have enacted laws for his further degredation, and even to expel him from the borders of some of our States; we have joined in the infernal chase to hunt him down like a beast, and fling him into the hell of slavery; we have repealed and trampled upon laws designed to prevent the spread of slavery, and in a thousand ways given our strength, our moral and political influence to increase the power and ascendency of slavery over all departments of Government; and now, as our reward, this slaveholding power comes with sword, gun and cannon to take the life of the nation and overthrow the great American Government. Verily, they have their reward. The power given to crush the Negro now overwhelms the white man. The Republic has put one end of the chain upon the ankle of the bondman, and the other end about its own neck. They have been planting tyrants, and are now getting a harvest of civil war and anarchy. The land is now to weep and howl, amid ten thousand desolations brought upon it by the sins of two centuries against millions on both sides of eternity. Could we write as with lightning, and speak as with the voice of thunder, we should write and cry to the nation, *Repent, Break Every Yoke, let the Oppressed Go Free for Herein alone is deliverance and safety!* It is not too late. The moment is propitious, and we may even yet escape the complete vengeance of the threatened wrath and fury, whose balls of fire are already dropping to consume us. Now is the time to put an end to the source of all our present national calamities. Now is the time to change the cry of vengeance long sent up from the tasked and toiling bondman, into a grateful prayer for the peace and safety of the Government. Slaveholders have in their madness invited armed abolition to march to the deliverance of the slave. They have furnished the occasion, and bound up the fate of the Republic and that of the slave in the same bundle, and the one and the other must survive or perish together. Any attempt now to separate the freedom of the slave from the victory of the Government over slaveholding rebels and traitors; any attempt to secure peace to the whites while leaving the blacks in chains; any attempt to heal the wounds of the Republic, while the deadly virus of slavery is left to poison the blood, will be labor lost. The American people and the Government at Washington may refuse to recognize it for a time; but the "inexorable logic of events" will force it upon them in the end; that the war now being waged in this land is a war for and against slavery; and that it can never be effectually put down till one or the other of these vital forces is completely destroyed. The irrepressible conflict, long confined to words and votes, is now to be carried by bayonets and bullets, and may God defend the right!

Douglass' Monthly, May, 1861

THE PAST AND THE PRESENT

Whoever will calmly and impartially contemplate the present aspect of the slavery question, cannot fail to read in the stern logic of passing events, the resolute determination on the part of the South to subjugate every other section of the country, and bring it wholly within the sphere of its unlimited control. This is no hyperbole, but the language of that stubborn reality which is shadowed forth in every act of the Black Power. Emboldened by its past achievements, and encouraged by the suicidal admissions of the majority of professed anti-slavery men in the free States, slavery has grown more imperious and exacting, boldly threatening in the person of its Toombs, to call the roll of its slaves on Bunker Hill, then, through Douglas in the Senate, lifting up its haggard brow, and to the representatives of anti-slavery sentiment declaring in defiant tone, "*we will subdue you*"; or, through its chivalrous champion, Brooks, attempting, on the floor of Congress, to murder in cold blood the noble and gifted Sumner, because he spoke forth the words of truth and soberness. Thus has it gone on, until now it has reached the climax of its defiant iniquity. Men and women, because of their complexion, are driven in their old age from their hard-earned homes, or allowed to remain where they were born only on condition of their becoming slaves.

Nor is the poor black man alone the victim of the barbaric cruelties and indignities upon which our would-be masters feast and fatten. In violation of the Constitution, in violation of the comity of States, in violation of the rudimental principles of our Government, men and women, of the *orthodox* and *constitutional* complexion, accused of no crime save a lack of sympathy with slavery, are treated with every indignity which satanic malice could invent, or brutal frenzy inflict; their property confiscated, their houses burned over their heads, their lives hanging upon the caprice of a mob, hunted like wild beasts, driven from their homes, in some instances, without a moment's warning. No more flagrant outrages against unoffending citizens are recorded in the annals of persecution.— In no other community of the civilized world, could such flagrant usurpations of tyranny be perpetrated with impunity.

These heart-rending developments were a part of the *modus operandi* by which the promised subjugation of freedom was to be effected. The threatened victory was not primarily expected to be achieved by the dissolution of the Union, or by the arbitrament of the sword. The South did not expect to bring the North to terms by effecting a complete change in the growing anti-slavery sentiment of the free States. This, Jefferson Davis declares, is wholly impossible. How, then, did she expect to accomplish her purpose? Her prospects of success were summed up in two words: *Continued Aggressions.* The South contemplated persistence in her wholesale aggressions upon the free States, her burglary upon the rights of human nature, until every right dear to a freeman's heart should be wrested from him, and freedom becomes so emasculated and dispirited, as to render abortive all attempts to rally our scattered, peeled, and *worried* forces; and thus we were to be subdued. For years has she made known her intentions, leaving her place of ambush, and recklessly rushing into the highway. She has exhibited the plan of operations with an audacity commensurate with her stupendous iniquity.

We are not disposed to deny that the usually cautious South, in thus reasoning from premise to conclusion, had a right to expect much from the spaniel-like servility which has been a prominent and disgraceful characteristic of the North. It would seem, after all, that the North has something more than "a local habitation and a name," and that Southern insolence and bravado have counted altogether too largely upon our constitutional proclivity to crush out liberty to "save the Union." Our new President and his Cabinet, as ardently as they desire Peace, are not content to accept as its condition, the proffered ultimatum of the rebels. The compromises manufactured to order by Weed, Corwin & Co., look not only to a repeal of our Personal Liberty Bills, &c., but they contemplate an abrogation of the fundamental principles of all legitimate civil government, the first, prime, sole law of social organization, the primal law of human relations. Mr. Lincoln knows very well, that for him to adopt a policy which involves such abrogation, is to disband the Republican party, and cover himself with merited and imperishable infamy.—It is to make the extension and perpetration of slavery a fixed fact, and fling a solemn pall over the sanguine hopes of the eighteen hundred thousand men who placed him in power, firmly believing that he was the man for the hour.

We sincerely trust that the hopes which have been engendered by the disposition and determination of the new Administration to act firmly with the traitors and rebels of the seceded States, will not be blasted by any renewed attempts to "compromise," and "concede," and "conciliate." There is, in fact, but one alternative—either to recognize the secession movement as a successful revolution, to be treated as such, or, as a causeless rebellion, to be promptly suppressed. Successful compromise is wholly out of the question. Indeed, the traitors with that impertinent coolness and diabolic candor peculiar to them, have repeatedly declared that they will listen to no compromises which acknowledge the right of the people of the free States to regard slavery as a moral and political evil, and thus to denounce it.

We cannot tell what a day or an hour may bring forth; but at the present moment, a peaceful settlement is scarcely within the range of human probability. *The Decisive Blow Must Be Struck.* The question must be decided very shortly in one way or another. Our opinion is, that it is only necessary, in order to humble the haughty and defiant South, for Mr. Lincoln to develop that inflexible Jacksonian firmness[1] for which he has obtained credit; to show the South that he is in earnest, if need be, in *terrible* earnest; and that he will, at all hazards, enforce the laws. Let the South understand that *he* is President of the American Republic, and come weal, or come woe, he will, as such, exercise his authority. Then, and not till then, will there be an end to their pugnacious, developments. But let him, Buchanan-like, tamper with the rapacious rebels, or show them any quarter, and he will eventually be driven by them from Washington, his inglorious Cabinet bearing him "faithful company."

We earnestly desire to see the South humbled. The "high looks" of the lordly Assyrians must be "brought low." The North has all things to hope for, and nothing to fear from such humility. We know something by experience of the character of slaveholders. To use a trite maxim, "give them an inch and they will take an ell." Refuse the ell, and they will rant, and bluster, and swear, in order to obtain it. So long as they can frighten an opponent, they act very frightfully. But let them understand that "no one's afraid," and they'll soon be in a *status quo!* For example: the "Confederate" authorities have hitherto declared that Anderson should not be supplied with provisions carried to Fort Sumter in the vessels of the United States. They had reason to believe that the attempt would not be made. They thus interpreted the Delphic utterances of the distinguished Premier. But now, when Jeff. Davis, the President of the new Confederacy, ascertains that the Administration is determined to re-enforce the forts, then, presto! change! he telegraphs, in eager haste to Charleston, "not to fire on vessels carrying supplies to Fort Sumter." This must have been humiliating, and from this letting down, Mr. Lincoln should learn a lesson, if he has not done so already, and inflict upon the enemy such a chastisement as will give all to understand that there *is* a Government, and that we have at last a President who belongs to "*a healthy organization.*"*

The policy which Messrs. Davis and Stephens propose to execute, can be consummated, if at all, only by the assistance which it could derive from the want of unanimity of sentiment and action by which the North has been characterized. From the numerical strength of the South we have nothing to fear. Their very strength is weakness. But one thousand united and determined men can at any time defeat five thousand who are distracted and vacillating. The South has triumphed hitherto, not because of its inherent vitality or its recuperative energy; much less has it been successful because of the justice of its policy; but because it has been one and indivisible. When the institution of slavery has been assailed from any quarter, whatever diversity of opinion may have previously existed upon other questions, each and all of its supporters have flung their banner to the breeze, with the motto thereon blazing, "*Negroes and Slavery—one and Inseparable—Now*

---

*We must own that the rebels have been as good as their word, after all.

and Forever!" Pilate and Herod friends! singing the same song, indulging in the same hopes and fears, living the same life, and dying the same death!

Let the Administration, then, in its well directed efforts to *humble the South,* receive the cordial sympathy and co-operation of every well-wisher of his country, and of the world at large. The crisis has come, and it must be met manfully.

One word more. However timid men at this juncture may alternate between hope and fear, one thing is certain—slavery is a doomed institution. The traitors themselves have accelerated its rapid decline, and precipitated its disastrous doom. Perhaps, they now remember that the gallows erected for Mordecai was the identical instrument upon which Haman himself swung into eternity. A like fate attends them. The land may yet be drenched in human blood. The now slumbering and paralyzed arm of our sable millions may yet awake, instinct with superhuman energy.—Their smothered aspirations may yet burst through the startling gloom; and, driven to desperation, they may settle with the weight of doom upon their hard hearted oppressors. Heaven prevent the dire catastrophe, unless there can be no other way opened for the redemption of the now crushed millions! If this be the alternative demanded by the exigency of their condition, then let the worst be upon us, and that right speedily. Meanwhile, let us lift our hearts and voices far above the noise and strife of battle; far above where the storm-cloud crashes the tall pines upon the mountain cliffs; and look unto Him who is "mighty to save, and strong to deliver;" remembering that "He who is for us, is more than all that are against us." Let us act well our part; for

> *"Oppression shall not always reign,*
> *There comes a brighter day."*

Douglass' Monthly, May, 1861

1. In July, 1832, President Jackson signed a tariff bill which aroused widespread dissatisfaction in South Carolina. A movement, led by John C. Calhoun, called for nullification and secession, a special session of the South Carolina legislature was held and the calling of a convention ordered. This body adopted an ordinance nullifying the tariff acts of 1828 and 1832, and openly proclaimed the right of a state to secede if an attempt was made to coerce it. The ordinance was to go into effect in February, 1833.

President Jackson moved swiftly to crush the nullificationists and secessionists. After announcing his intention to enforce all federal laws in South Carolina, he dispatched troops and ships to Charleston. With none of the other southern states prepared to follow her, South Carolina soon acquiesced.

NOTES ON THE WAR

Though the destruction of life and property has been frightful and appalling, we are yet at the beginning of the horrors of our civil war. The slaveholders, though less hopeful of the result, are not less determined to fight, and fight to the last. They rely for success not more upon their arms in the field, than upon the faithful industry of their slaves to keep their rebel army supplied with food, and clothing, and the sinews of war. They boast that the slave population is a grand element of strength, and that it enables them to send and sustain a stronger body of rebels to overthrow the Government than they could otherwise do if the whites were required to perform the labors of cultivation;[1] and in this they are unquestionably in the right, provided the National Government refuses to turn this mighty element of strength into one of weakness. While the rebels are tearing up railways, cutting telegraph wires, burning bridges, building forts, guarding fords, fighting behind batteries, marching and countermarching, and doing all they can to destroy the lives and property of loyal citizens, one species of their own property, in the shape of men and women, are busily at work with spade, shovel, plow and hoe, to feed and clothe the destroyers. Why? Oh! why, in the name of all that is national, does our Government allow its enemies this powerful advantage? The war has made little progress, physical or moral. We are stupidly applying maxims of peace to a condition of war—maxims of loyalty to a condition of treason and rebellion—obligations of friendship towards implacable enemies.—The lives of loyal men are being sacrificed by scores, and will, bye and bye, be sacrificed by thousands. Rebels and pirates sweep peaceful commerce from the sea, and the country is full of desolation and ruin; and yet the vital, necessary and animating cause of all our national calamities is spared the slightest shock, and the Government at Washington utterly refuses to call that cause in question. The passion of selfishness, murder and rebellion are fired by slavery; the physical strength of rebellion is found less in the attenuated arm of the slaveholder, than in the sinewy arm of steel, which wields, without wages, the hoe and spade on the plantation. All this is plain. The very stomach of this rebellion is the Negro in the condition of a slave. Arrest that hoe in the hands of the Negro, and you smite rebellion in the very seat of its life.— Change the status of the slave from bondage to freedom, and you change the rebels into loyal citizens. The Negro is the key of the situation—the pivot upon which the whole rebellion turns.

The rulers at Washington, and those who direct public opinion at the North, seem to be utterly in the fog on this point. They have made some progress, but they are still far behind the plain requirements of the hour. Even the New York *Tribune* protests against making this a war for the destruction of slavery, and insists that such a war would alienate a large body of the Northern people at present who adhere to the Government in the prosecution of the war.[2] When the *Tribune* has watched the progress of the war a little longer, it will see that what it calls a diversion from the objects of the war, is the only effective and certain way to accomplish those objects. The clear-sighted and earnest men of the North are forever checked in carrying forward measures of justice and principle, from the fear of giving offence to some conservatives whose influence and co-operation it is desirable to have. In nine cases out of ten, these very conservatives would be secured rather than repelled by bold and vigorous measures. Men who a little while ago denounced coercion, are now in the foremost ranks of the Government to suppress rebellion. The men who applauded Gen. Butler for offering his army to put down a slave insurrection, applauded him more when he refused to return slaves to their masters, although his duty under the Constitution is as plain to do this latter as the former. But we believe that the *Tribune* and other papers have over-estimated the tenderness of the commercial classes towards slavery. They are under a cloud, in a perfect haze, concerning the rights of slave property; but let the Government once lift itself up to the dignity of a sound principle, and it will draw the whole people up to it. The Government must lead the people. The people will follow in any just and necessary path, and do so joyfully.

We know that rebellion cannot be talked down, written down, or coaxed down. It has got to be beaten down, and the heaviest blow that can be given is the right blow to be given. There is no whipping the traitors without hurting them. War was made to hurt, and those who provoke it ought to be hurt; and the only conceivable good which can come out of war, comes because it hurts.

What our rulers at Washington most of all stand in need of, in order to a speedy suppression of this slaveholding rebellion, and to place the nation on a firm foundation of peace and prosperity, is neither men nor money, but a living and all-controlling faith in the principles of freedom avowed in the Declaration of Independence, and which are the foundation of the Government; they need faith in the Bible truth, that righteousness exalteth a nation, and that sin is a reproach to any people; they want faith in justice and humanity, and in the fullest application of them. They have men, money and arms in abundance. A call is made for a thousand men, and lo! ten thousand start up as from the ground to answer that call. They ask for thirty millions of treasure, and at once sixty millions, like a golden flood, is rolled into the National treasury. The world has never seen a government so suddenly thus made opulent in all the munitions of war. But alas! while strong in men, rich in money and in the munitions of war, we are neither rich nor strong in what is far more important in moral consistency.—To fight against slaveholders, without fighting against slavery, is but a half-hearted business, and paralyzes the hands engaged in it. Our army presents the appearance, while thus fettered, of seeming to be trying how not to put down a rebellion and treason among the slaveholders. It would knock them down, but it would see that they fall upon feathers, and not upon forks or flints. It is still clinging to the delusion—for it is nothing else—that they can win the slaveholders to loyalty by showing friendship to slavery, and by admitting, within certain limits, that slavery has constitutional rights—the wildest possible mistake.

They know that slavery is the crime, the curse and the scandal of the American name; that to it they owe all their present National troubles; and that while slavery lasts, there can be no lasting peace. They know that there is, and must ever remain an "irrepressible conflict" between slavery and freedom, and that one or the other must be eventually and totally extinguished; but still they hesitate to adopt the only mode of warfare which can secure the permanent triumph of freedom, and the lasting peace of the country.—What is this mode of warfare which we recommend, and which is required by the exigency now upon the land? This it is: Accept the aid of the slaves wherever the National army is required to march to suppress rebellion, and proclaim freedom and protection to men of all colors who will rally to the support of the established Government.—Teach the rebels and traitors that the price they are to pay for the attempt to abolish this Government must be the abolition of slavery in every State and Territory where the National arm is required to march in vindication of the National flag. Send no more slaves back to their rebel master; offer to put down no more slave insurrections *"with an iron hand;"* reject no more black troops; release no more slaveholding rebels on their word of honor; hang or imprison for life all pirates; and henceforth let the war cry be down with treason, and down with slavery, the cause of treason.

There are objections to this programme; but they are by no means so strong as those which can be urged against the policy at present pursued. It is urged, for instance, that upon any declaration of the emancipation of the slaves on the part of the Federal army, the slaveholders would at once proceed to a work of indiscriminate slaughter of the male portion of their slaves; and this threat has been already made in a letter from the South to Ex-President Fillmore. Horrible purpose! but quite worthy of the guilty wretches from whom it proceeds. The thought of it chills the blood and stuns the mind; but horrible as would be such wholesale murder the work once begun would soon cure itself and out of it would come in the end peace to the country and freedom to the slave. Anything but unending slavery, and if the abolition of slavery must and can only end in blood at any time, no time can be better than now for that bloody end. There are good reasons for believing, however, that with all the known savage ferocity of slaveholders, that even they, within sight of the American people and the world, would proceed only to a very limited extent in the sanguinary slaughter which they now so shamelessly threaten. But whatever might be the consequences, nothing worse can happen than victory to the slaveholding rebels, either for the country or for the slaves.

Douglass' Monthly, July, 1861

1. Even before the war started, the *Savannah Republican* observed: "They [the northern people] forget the peculiar character of our institutions, the permanency of our industrial system, the fact that the labor of the South is not as elsewhere, the fighting element of the State. When wars occur in Europe or at the North, they take the laboring man from the plow, the workshop and factory to fight for them. Production, to the extent of the force required, must accordingly cease. In the Southern, and especially in the cotton-growing states, the case is entirely different. A wholly different system of labor prevails. Our cotton-fields are tilled by slaves, and Georgia alone might send 20,000 troops to the field without diminishing the production of her staple to the amount of a hundred bales." (*Savannah Republican* reprinted in *Boston Daily Courier,* Feb. 21, 1861.)

2. On May 14, 1861, the *New York Tribune* rejected the program calling for the emancipation of the slaves, fearing it would alienate many Democrats pledged to the maintenance of the Union. It warned, however, that if the South prolonged the war, patriots would have to respond to the call, "The Republic must live, even though Slavery should have to die!"

THE DECISION OF THE HOUR, substance of a lecture delivered at Zion
   Church, Sunday, June 16, 1861

I am not surprised, my respected hearers, though I am most deeply gratified by
the continued interest which you have manifested in these now somewhat protracted anti-slavery lectures. The subject of slavery is a most fruitful one, and it
seems impossible to exhaust it. I seldom retire from this place without thinking
of something left unsaid, which might have been said to profit.

More than thirty years of earnest discussion has augmented rather than diminished the interest which surrounds the subject. Tongues the most eloquent,
and pens the most persuasive, the highest talent and genius of the country have
been arduously employed in the attempt to unfold the matchless and measureless abominations comprehended in that one little word—slavery. Yet those who
have succeeded best, own that they have fallen far short of the terrible reality.
You, yourselves, have read much, thought much, and have felt much respecting
the slave system, and yet you come up here and crowd this church every Sunday
to hear the subject further discussed.

Vain as I may be, I have not the vanity to suppose that you come here because
of any eloquence of mine, or any curiosity to hear a colored man speak—for I
have been speaking among you more or less frequently nearly a score of years;
and I recognize among my hearers to-day some of those kind friends who greeted
me the first time I attempted to plead the cause of the slave in this city. No—the
explanation of this continued, and I may say increasing interest, is not to be
found in your humble speaker; nor can it be ascribed altogether to the temper of
the times, and the mighty events now transpiring in the country. We shall find it
in the deep significance, the solemn importance and unfathomable fullness of the
subject itself. It sweeps the whole horizon of human rights, powers, duties and
responsibilities. The grand primal principles which form the basis of human society, are here.

Those who love peace more than justice; those who prefer grim and hoary oppression to agitation and liberty, condemn the discussion of slavery because it is
an exciting subject. They cry, away with it; we have had enough of it; it excites
the people, excites the Church, excites the Congress, excites the North, excites
the South, and excites everybody. It is, in a word, an exciting subject. I admit it
all. The subject is, indeed, an exciting one. Herein is one proof of its importance.
Small pots boil quick; empty barrels make the most noise when rolled; but that
which has the power to stir a nation's heart, and shake the foundations of
Church and State, is something more than empty clamor. Individual men of excitable temperament may be moved by trifles; they may give to an inch the importance of a mile—elevate a mote to the grandeur of a mountain—but the
masses of men are not of this description.—Only mighty forces, resting deep
down among the foundations of nature and life, can lash the deep and tranquil
sea of humanity into a storm, like that which the world is now witnessing.

The human mind is so constructed as that, when left free from the blinding
and hardening power of selfishness, it bows reverently to the mandates of truth
and justice. It becomes loyal and devoted to an idea. Good men, once fully pos-

sessed of this loyalty, this devotion, have bravely sacrificed fortune, reputation, and life itself. All the progress towards perfection ever made by mankind, and all the blessings which are now enjoyed, are ascribable to some brave and good man, who, catching the illumination of a heaven-born truth, has counted it a joy, precious and unspeakable, to toil, suffer, and often to die for the glorious realization of that heaven-born truth. Hence the excitement. Cold water added to cold water, makes no disturbance. Error added to error causes no jar. Selfishness and selfishness walk together in peace, because they are agreed; but when fire is brought in direct contact with water, when flaming truth grapples with some loathsome error, when the clear and sweet current of benevolence sets against the foul and bitter stream of selfishness, when mercy and humanity confront iron-hearted cruelty, and ignorant brutality, there cannot fail to be agitation and excitement.

Men have their choice in this world. They can be angels, or they may be demons. In the apocalyptic vision, John describes a war in heaven. You have only to strip that vision of its gorgeous Oriental drapery, divest it of its shining and celestial ornaments, clothe it in the simple and familiar language of common sense, and you will have before you the eternal conflict between right and wrong, good and evil, liberty and slavery, truth and falsehood, the glorious light of love, and the appalling darkness of human selfishness and sin. The human heart is a seat of constant war. Michael and his angels are still contending against the infernal host of bad passions, and excitement will last while the fight continues, and the fight will continue till one or the other is subdued. Just what takes place in individual human hearts, often takes place between nations, and between individuals of the same nation. Such is the struggle now going on in the United States. The slaveholders had rather reign in hell than serve in heaven.

What a whirlwind, what a tempest of malignant passion greets us from that quarter! Behold how they storm with rage, and yet grow pale with terror! Their demonstrations of offended pride are only equaled by their consummate impudence and desperate lying. Let me read you a paragraph from a recent speech of Mr. Henry A. Wise, as a specimen of the lies with which the leaders of this slaveholding rebellion inflame the base passions of their ignorant followers. He lyingly says of the Northern people:

> "Your political powers and rights, which were enthroned in the Capitol when you were united with them under the old constitutional bond of the Confederacy, have been annihilated. They have undertaken to annul laws within their own limits that would render your property unsafe within those limits. They have abolitionized your border, as the disgraced North-West will show. They have invaded your moral strongholds, and the rights of your religion, and have undertaken to teach you what should be the moral duties of men. They have invaded the sanctity of your homes and firesides, and endeavored to play master, father and husband for you in your households."

Such lies answer themselves at the North, but do their work at the South. The strong and enduring power which anti-slavery truth naturally exercises upon the minds of men, when earnestly presented, is explained, as I have already intimated, not by the cunning arts of rhetoric, for often the simplest and most broken utterances of the uneducated fugitive slave, will be far more touching and powerful than the finest flights of oratory. The explanation of the power of anti-slavery is to be found in the inner and spontaneous consciousness, which every man feels of the comprehensive and stupendous criminality of slavery. There are many wrongs and abuses in the world that shock and wound the sensibilities of men. They are felt to be narrow in their scope, and temporary in their duration, and to require little effort for their removal. But not so can men regard slavery. It compels us to recognize it, as an ever active, ever increasing, all comprehensive crime against human nature. It is not an earthquake swallowing up a town or city, and then leaving the solid earth undisturbed for centuries. It is not a Vesuvius which, belching forth its fire and lava at intervals, causes ruin in a limited territory; but slavery is felt to be a moral volcano, a burning lake, a hell on the earth, the smoke and stench of whose torments ascend upward forever. Every breeze that sweeps over it comes to us tainted with its foul miasma, and weighed down with the sighs and groans of its victims. It is a compendium of all the wrongs which one man can inflict upon a helpless brother. It does not cut off a right hand, nor pluck out a right eye, but strikes down at a single blow the God-like form of man. It does not merely restrict the right, or lay heavy burdens upon its victims, grievous to be borne; but makes deliberate and constant war upon human nature itself, robs the slave of personality, cuts him off from the human family, and sinks him below even the brute. It leaves nothing standing to tell the world that here was a man and a brother.

In the eye of the law of slavery, the slave is only property. He cannot be a father, a husband, a brother, or a citizen, in any just sense of these words. To be a father, a husband, a brother, and a citizen, implies the personal possession of rights, powers, duties and responsibilities, all of which are denied the slave. Slavery being the utter and entire destruction of all human relations, in opposing it, we are naturally enough bound to the consideration of a wide range of topics, involving questions of the greatest importance to all men. But for the universal character of the anti-slavery question, it would have been impossible to have held the public mind suspended upon this discussion during the space of thirty years. The best informed men have candidly confessed that anti-slavery meetings have been the very best schools of the nation during the last quarter of a century.— The nation has been taught here, as nowhere else, law, morals and Christianity. Untrammelled by prescription, unrestrained by popular usage, unfettered by mouldly creeds, despising all the scorn of vulgar prejudice, our anti-slavery speakers and writers have dared to call in question every doctrine and device of man, which could strengthen the hands of tyrants, and bind down the bodies and souls of men. The manhood of the slave has been the test of all our laws, customs, morals, civilization, governments, and our religions.—With a single eye here, the whole anti-slavery body has been full of light. With the golden rule, they have measured American Christianity, and found it hollow—its votaries doing precisely unto others that which they would shoot, stab, burn and devour others for doing unto themselves. To all who press the Bible into the service of slavery, we have said, if you would not be the slave, you cannot be the master.

The fact is, slavery is at the bottom of all mischief amongst us, and will be until we shall put an end to it. We have seen three attempts within less than thirty years to break up the American Government in this the first century of its existence, and slavery has been the moving cause in each instance. The attempt was made in 1832, again in 1850, again in 1860. Some of us were surprised and astonished that the slaveholders should rebel against the American Government, simply because they could not rule the Government to the full extent of their wishes.—Little cause had we for such surprise and astonishment. We ought to have known slaveholders better.

What is a slaveholder but a rebel and a traitor? That is, and must be in the nature of his vocation, his true character. Treason and rebellion are the warp and woof of the relation of master and slave. A man cannot be a slaveholder without being a traitor to humanity and a rebel against the law and government of the ever-living God. He is a usurper, a spoiler. His patriotism means plunder, and his principles are those of the highway robber. Out of such miserable stuff you can make nothing but conspirators and rebels.

So far as the American Government is entitled to the loyal support and obedience of American citizens, so far that Government is, in the main, in harmony with the highest good and the just convictions of the people. Justice, goodness, conscience are divine. Conformity to these, on the part of human governments, make them binding and authoritative. These attributes, wherever exhibited, whether in the government of States, in the government of families, or wherever else exhibited, command the reverence and loyal regard of honest men and women. But slaveholders, by the very act of slaveholding, have thrown off all the trammels of conscience and right. They are open, brazen, self-declared rebels and traitors to all that makes loyalty a virtue, and fidelity a duty. The greater includes the lesser crime. In the one high-handed act of rebellion against truth, justice and humanity, comprehended in making one man the slave of another, we have the ascertained sum of treason and rebellion which now rages and desolates the whole slaveholding territory in the United States.

This is no new idea in these lectures. I have presented it before, and shall probably repeat it again. I wish at any rate to underscore it now, for I deem it important that we should thoroughly understand the foe with which we have to deal. Let it, then, be written down in every man's mind, as no longer a matter of dispute, that a thief and a robber cannot be safely trusted; that a slaveholder cannot be a good citizen of a free republic; and that the relation of master and slave is in the nature of it treason and rebellion. It has long been obvious to common sense— it is now known to common experience—that a slaveholder who is a slaveholder at heart is a natural born traitor and rebel. He is a rebel against manhood, womanhood and brotherhood. The essence of his crime is nothing less than the complete destruction of all that dignifies and ennobles human character.

I don't know how it seems to you, in reading the authoritative utterances of our Government, and the officers of our army, respecting slavery; but it really seems to me that they are woefully mistaken if they think this country can ever have peace while slavery is allowed to live. Every little while you learn that slaves have been sent back to their loyal masters. We hear that while other property is freely confiscated, this peculiar property is only held to the end of the war, and the inference seems to be that these slaves, by and by, are to enter into the basis of negotiations between the Government and the slave-holding rebels. I am anxious to look charitably upon everything looking to the suppression of rebellion and treason. I want to see the monster destroyed; but I think that while our Government uses its soldiers to catch and hold slaves, and offers to put down slave insurrections, and subject them to the control and authority of their rebel masters, it will make precious little headway in putting down the rebels, or in establishing the peace of the country hereafter.

There is still an effort to conciliate the Border States. Our Government does not know slavery. Our rulers do not yet know slaveholders. We are likely to find them out after a while. We are just now in a pretty good school. The revolution through which we are passing is an excellent instructor. We are likely to find out what is meant by Southern chivalry and Southern honor.—When you have watched a while longer the course of Southern men, whether in the cotton States or in the slavebreeding States, you will have become convinced that they are all of the same species, and that the Border States are as bad as any. John Bell, the Union man, is as much a traitor as Frank Pickens of South Carolina. We shall learn by and by that such men as Letcher of Virginia, Jackson of Missouri, Magoffin of Kentucky, were traitors and rebels in the egg, only waiting to be hatched by the heat of surrounding treason. The ties that bind slaveholders together are stronger than all other ties, and in every State where they hold the reins of government, they will take sides openly or secretly with the slaveholding rebels.—Conciliation is out of the question. They know no law, and will respect no law but the law of force. The safety of the Government can be attained only in one way, and that is, by rendering the slaveholders powerless.

Slavery, like all other gross and powerful forms of wrong which appeal directly to human pride and selfishness, when once admitted into the frame work of society, has the ability and tendency to beget a character in the whole network of society surrounding it, favorable to its continuance. The very law of its existence is growth and dominion. Natural and harmonious relations easily repose in their own rectitude, while all such as are false and unnatural are conscious of their own weakness, and must seek strength from without. Hence the explanation of the uneasy, restless, eager anxiety of slaveholders.—Our history shows that from the formation of this Government, until the attempt now making to break it up, this class of men have been constantly pushing schemes for the safety and supremacy of the slave system. They have had marvelous success. They have completely destroyed freedom in the slave States, and were doing their best to accomplish the same in the free States. He is a very imperfect reasoner who attributes the steady rise and ascendency of slavery to anything else than the nature of slavery itself. Truth may be careless and forgetful, but a lie cannot afford to be either. Truth may repose upon its inherent strength, but a falsehood rests for support upon external props. Slavery is the most stupendous of all lies, and depends for existence upon a favorable adjustment of all its surroundings. Freedom of speech, of the press, of education, of labor, of locomotion, and indeed all kinds of freedom, are felt to be a standing menace to slavery. Hence, the friends of slavery are bound by the necessity of their system to do just what the history of the country shows they have done—that is, to seek to subvert all liberty, and to pervert all the safeguards of human rights. They could not do otherwise. It was the controlling law of their situation.

Now, if these views be sound, and are borne out by the whole history of American slavery, then for the statesman of this hour to permit any settlement of the present war between slavery and freedom, which will leave untouched and undestroyed the relation of master and slave, would not only be a great crime, but a great mistake, the bitter fruits of which would poison the life blood of unborn generations. No grander opportunity was ever given to any nation to signalize, either its justice and humanity, or its intelligence and statesmanship, than is now given to the loyal American people. We are brought to a point in our National career where two roads meet and diverge. It is the critical moment for us. The destiny of the mightiest Republic in the modern world hangs upon the decision of that hour. If our Government shall have the wisdom to see, and the nerve to act, we are safe. If it fails, we perish, and go to our own place with those nations of antiquity long blotted from the maps of the world. I have only one voice, and that is neither loud nor strong. I speak to but few, and have little influence; but whatever I am or may be, I may, at such a time as this, in the name of justice, liberty and humanity, and in that of the permanent security and welfare of the whole nation, urge all men, and especially the Government, to the abolition of slavery. Not a slave should be left a slave in the returning footprints of the American army gone to put down this slaveholding rebellion. Sound policy, not less than humanity, demands the instant liberation of every slave in the rebel States.

Douglass' Monthly, July, 1861

THE WAR AND SLAVERY

We have no change to report of the moral position of the Federal Government in respect to slavery. As the beginning of July left us, so the beginning of August finds us. We are still treading the unsteady billows of events, and walking amid the flitting shadows of doubt and uncertainty. Aside from the mere compelling obedience to the laws, no high and inflexible principle of public policy has been announced by the Government.—From present appearances, nothing is contemplated but the restoration of the country to the same condition in which rebellion and bloodshed found it, leaving the elements of mischief to repeat, under more favorable circumstances, the atrocities and crimes by which the country is now afflicted. Thus far we are contenting ourselves with trimming off the leaves and branches, and leaving the trunk and roots of rebellion firmly fixed in the soil, ready to gather new sap, and to sprout forth again with renewed vigor. The great army of the North has moved into Eastern Virginia, and the Federal arms have been victorious in Western Virginia; but no moral progress yet marks the career of the Federal Government. The political horizon is scanned with breathless suspense. Those amongst us who believe that freedom is always right and best, and that slavery is always wrong and worst, watch and wait with longing hearts to see the Government stumble upon the only true and sound policy suggested and required by the crisis.—That policy is nothing more nor less than the complete and unalterable abolition of slavery, the known cause of our present national troubles. But thus far we have watched and waited in vain. When Congress voted upon the resolution of Mr. Lovejoy, declaring the recapture of runaway slaves no part of the present business of our army,[1] we seemed on the verge of the right path; but when the Government decided that no more slaves should be allowed within the lines of our army, and that none should follow our soldiers, the loss was greater than the gain. This decision evades, ignores the real issue. The Government, in taking it, has settled nothing, but its own moral cowardice and insufficiency. In this, however, the Government but reflects the mind of the people.

Self-deception is a chronic disease of the American mind and character. The crooked way is ever preferred to the straight in all our mental processes, and in all our studied actions. We are masters in the art of substituting a pleasant falsehood for an ugly and disagreeable truth, and of clinging to a fascinating delusion while rejecting a palpable reality. Every reflecting man knows, and knows full well, that the real source and centre of the treason, rebellion and bloodshed under which the country is now staggering as if to its fall, is slavery. Every one knows that this is a slaveholder's rebellion, and nothing else. Every one knows that here is the source of its power, the fountain of its motives, and the explanation of its purposes; that the measureless enormity of rebellion and treason can be traced to no other parentage than that of the American slave system.—Neither merchants, manufacturers, lawyers, mechanics or laborers, whatever might have been their hardships, would have turned from the peaceful methods of the ballot box, to the deadly one of the cartridge box, to redress their wrongs, real or fancied. Neither of these classes have possessed the ability, the temptation or the disposition to perpetuate such a crime. The peril and misfortune of the country has been the existence among us of a privileged class of irresponsible despots, authorized tyrants and blood-suckers, who fasten upon the Negro's flesh, and draw political power and consequence from their legalized crimes, rather than from their virtues.—Such a body are the slaveholders. Proud, grasping, ambitious, nursed in lies and cruelty, these men are fitted for their present infernal work. Feeble at the beginning, tolerated as a necessity rather than as a right, regarded as a transient evil by the fathers of the Government, destined soon to pass away, something entirely extraneous to, and inconsistent with the constructive elements of American institutions—slavery, through various phases, but by regular processes of development, of repeated disturbances, and of multiplied compromises, has naturally reached the point at which we now see it, full of wrath and fury, covering the land with a mantle of fire and blood. We all see it and feel it. Nobody doubts it, and every body believes it; and yet the Government and people, owing to their chronic self-deception, their cowardly spirit and want of fixed principle, are practically rejecting what they know to be true, and accepting what they know to be false.

In the late Message of our honest President, which purports to give an honest history of our present difficulties, no mention is, at all, made of slavery.[2] Any one reading that document, with no previous knowledge of the United States, would never dream from anything there written that we have a slaveholding war waged upon the Government, determined to overthrow it, or so to reconstruct it as to make it the instrument of extending the slave system and enlarging its powers; while all here know that *that* is the vital and animating motive of the rebellion. The proclamation goes forth at the head of all our armies, assuring the slaveholding rebels that slavery shall receive no detriment from our arms.—While fugitive slaves are not sent back just now to known rebels, the inducement is held out to all loyal slaveholders that they shall have their slaves sent back to them. While the slaveholders do not scruple to employ their slaves in the work of rebellion against the Government, our rulers at Washington steadily refuse to accept the aid of free colored citizens in defense of the Government.—Thus do we belie and reject the issue presented to us in this contest. Thus do we refuse to see even what it is impossible to hide from ourselves, that slavery is the cause of the war, and that its abolition is the true and only remedy for the war, and that all other remedies are but patch work, putting new wine into old bottles, and new cloth in old garments, and thus making the rent worse than before. Up to this time, slavery has lost nothing in point of doctrine, or principle, by the war, and no principle has been laid down by the Government which can necessarily give the soul-drivers of the South the least possible alarm for the safety of slavery. The impression which our Government seeks to make upon the slaveholders seems to be that slavery is safer in, than out of the Union.

The only circumstance which has thus far transpired, indicating an anti-slavery tendency on the part of the Government, was the approval of the action of Gen. Butler in treating slaves as contraband of war.[3] But even this was but a temporary arrangement, and was carefully left open to the most sudden reversal. The final disposition of those already within the lines of the Federal army is even yet a matter of painful uncertainty.—They may even yet be handed over to the tender mercies of the cruel taskmasters from whom they escaped, or in some way be made an element in a trumped up paper settlement of the contest between the Government and the rebels.

From every view we have been able to get of the conflict through all the debates in Congress, the proclamations of Generals, and over all the smoke and fire of the battle field, we see the dark shadow of Compromise—the outlines of a new bargain—by which the slaveholders, though whipt, shall not be humbled, and though criminals of the deepest die, shall yet hold up their heads as free citizens and as honest men. We are doing now all that we can to whip them without offending their tastes or injuring their interests. History will, we think, set this down as the most amiable and forbearing Government ever assaulted by the sword of treason and rebellion. We will not consent to the employment of negroes or Indians in our army. That would offend the prejudices of our Southern traitors, and exalt these proscribed races to the dignity of citizenship, and might possibly embarrass the Government in its efforts to accomplish a speedy settlement. The fact is we are living in troublous times, on a mighty stream afloat, without pilot, rudder or chart, and no man knows just where the winds and the waves of events may yet carry us.

—Since the above was written, the Federal army has met that of the rebels, under Beauregard and Jeff. Davis, at Bull's Run, near Manassas Junction, Va.[4] The battle was hot and bloody, and was decided in favor of the rebels, they having repulsed the Federal army, causing it to retreat to Washington, with great losses in killed and wounded and in provisions and munitions of war. Among the rebels were black troops,[5] no doubt pressed into the service by their tyrant masters. This disastrous and deeply melancholy event, which has brought sorrow and mourning to thousands of Northern hearts and homes, and covered the friends of the Government with the deepest sadness, has much changed the tone of Northern sentiment as to the proper mode of prosecuting the war, in reference to slavery, the cause of the war. Men now call not only for vengeance and righteous retribution, but for the destruction of the cause of their great national disaster. A cry has gone forth for the abolition of slavery. It is not merely a cry of passion, but of sound policy, the speediest method of terminating the war, and setting the Government in permanent safety from future disturbance. The strength of the rebels, the vigor with which they prosecute the war, the deadly hate towards the North which they cherish, the strong bond of Union which a common interest in slavery affords, the employment of slaves to do the drudgery of the rebel army, and to shoot down the Government troops—the fact that this is a slaveholder's rebellion and nothing else, all point out slavery as the thing to be struck down, as the best means of the successful and permanent establishment of the peace and prosperity of the nation. If the defeat at Bull's Run shall have the effect to teach the Government this high wisdom, and to distinguish between its friends and its foes at the South, that defeat, terrible as it is, will not have been entirely disastrous. It would, indeed, greatly mitigate the sorrow and suffering which it has occasioned, if out of it shall come a policy of liberty and justice, extending its blessings impartially to all, and effectively putting down the whole class of pestiferous slaveholders, so that the nation shall know them no more, except in history, to be execrated and loathed, with all other robbers and tyrants which have cursed and ruined human society, and made the earth red with innocent blood. Why should the people of this great nation longer hesitate? Does not every man know the cause of all our national troubles? Why should they spare that which is not only the crime and the shame of America, but the rot and ruin of the Republic? How long must rebellion rage?—How long must red-handed slaughter, fear and alarm stalk through the land, to convince the Government at Washington, and the people of the country, that their true and only method of escape from both present and future trouble, is by battering down the prison of the bondman.

We are happy to believe—indeed, *we have very good evidence of the fact*— that the Administration at Washington, notwithstanding appearances, stand ready to inaugurate and carry out a policy towards slavery which will most certainly eventuate in breaking down slavery in all the rebel States, just so soon as the people shall require it. By the simple process of calling upon the blacks of the South to rally under the Star Spangled Banner, and to work and fight for freedom under it—precisely as they are now working and fighting for slavery under the hateful flag of rebellion—we could in a few months emancipate the great body of slaves, and thus break the back bone of the rebellion. Now is the time to press this idea upon public notice. The Government should be addressed through the press, by petitions, by letters, by personal representations, and in every way, in a manner to convince it that the people of this great Republic are ready to receive and support every measure consistent with the general welfare and the common defense, to have an end put to slavery in every State requiring Federal arms to repress and put down rebellion.

Nor are the people quite as far from this requirement of wisdom, justice and humanity, as at first sight it might seem. Though it is generally true that governments only move as they are moved upon by the people, they do sometimes find themselves moved by events which they cannot control, and when so moved in a just cause, they never move alone, but infallibly draw the people with them. Let but the Administration firmly occupy the ground pointed out by John Quincy Adams twenty years ago, that the war power of the Government gives power to abolish slavery,[6] and asserts the necessity of acting upon it, and tardy and blind as the people have seemed, they will go for it with startling unanimity and enthusiasm. Half the North but a few months ago denounced coercion, i.e. the armed enforcement of the laws and the Constitution against slaveholding traitors and rebels. They would probably have yet been divided, had the Government remained undecided and in doubt. The moment the Government was resolved, the people were also resolved, and have so remained through good report and through evil report. The people at heart are against slavery. None other than a wolf's heart can be otherwise. All they want is a leader, with power and authority, and they are ready to follow where he leads. They are yet checked by supposed constitutional objections, and by practical difficulties. President Lincoln, Secretaries Seward, Chase, Cameron and Blair have only to devise the mode of avoiding those difficulties of law and practice, and they will have the joyous support of the great heart of America, and the blessings of those ready to perish.

Douglass' Monthly, August, 1861

1. On July 9, 1861, the House passed Owen Lovejoy's resolution which asserted that "it is no part of the duty of the soldiers of the United States to capture and return fugitive slaves." (*Congressional Globe*, 37 Cong., 1st sess., p. 32.)

2. Congress convened in special session on July 4, 1861. Lincoln's message on this occasion did not mention slavery, and stressed only the national obligation to maintain the Union. (See John G. Nicolay and John Hay, eds., *Complete Works of Abraham Lincoln*, New York, 1905, vol. VII, pp. 77–78.)

3. After General Butler refused to return escaped slaves to their masters, Negroes from the South flocked into his camp in such numbers that he decided to report the case to Washington and ask for instructions. Secretary of War Cameron approved his action.

4. The First Battle of Bull Run took place on Sunday, July 21, 1861. It ended in a smashing Confederate victory. The Union staff men reported 16 officers and 444 men killed, 78 officers and 1,046 men wounded, 50 officers and 1,262 men missing. Confederate losses were officially reported at 378 killed, 1,489 wounded, and 30 missing.

5. A fugitive Negro from a Confederate corps in Nansemond County, Virginia, spoke in Boston on February 5, 1862, and stated "that there was one regiment of 700 black men from Georgia, 1,000 from South Carolina, and about 1,000, including his own, in Virginia, destined for Manassas, when he ran away." (*Boston Daily Journal*, Feb. 6, 1862.)

6. In December, 1838, the House of Representatives adopted a resolution, by a vote of 194 to 6, declaring that Congress had no power over slavery in the states. John Quincy Adams opposed the resolution, arguing that in case of war the government would have power to abolish slavery, in order that the nation might be saved.

THE REBELS, THE GOVERNMENT, AND THE DIFFERENCE BETWEEN THEM

Thus far our Government has made very little progress in suppressing the slave-holding rebellion. Aside from the movements of Gen. Lyon in Missouri, and of Gen. McClellan in Western Virginia, where the forces have been mainly from the slave States, the rebels have had a decided advantage, and are probably stronger than at the beginning of the war. The defeat of the Government forces at Bull's Run on Sunday, July 21st, has inspired the rebels with new confidence, and confirmed their high hopes of ultimate success. At Great Bethel, at Vienna, at Acquia Creek, and wherever there has been fighting aside from Western Virginia and Missouri, the rebels have been on the winning side, and to-day they send up shouts of exultation and defiance. The Government has men, money, and munitions of war in abundance, and the complete freedom of the sea. The rebels are poor in men, money, munitions of war, and are suffering all the hardships of a rigorous blockade. Yet with all these, and the disadvantages of an atrociously wicked cause, they are to this hour masters of the field. Who shall explain to us why this is so? Why does wrong so prosper against right? Many answers come to us. One alleges that it is the incompetency of our Generals; another, that it is the strong positions occupied by the rebels; and a third tells us, that it is all owing to the treachery of the late Administration. These, and a thousand other explanations, come to us; but the real difficulty of the case remains untouched.

Our solution of the whole matter is this: The South is *in earnest,* and the North is not. The South is whole, and the North is half. The South has one animus, the North another. The contest is unequal in the spirit and purpose of the fight. The feeling of the North towards the South is destitute of every element of malice. It seeks to conquer as much by conciliation as by the sword. It would commend itself more by the gentleness of its temper, than by the irresistibleness of its power. The South fights from choice—the North from necessity. The one is positive, and the other is merely negative. The one strikes with all the exterminating vigor of a settled and deadly hate—the other with the hesitating reluctance of a compassionating parent, careful not to wound too deeply the offending child. So to our mind stands the matter. The South hates the North, and the North even yet loves the South, and would rather win her back to loyalty by kind words than by hard blows.

All this is made very manifest in the conduct of both belligerents. Witness the scenes of Bull's Run the other day, when the rebels amused themselves in sticking bayonets in the dead, and setting the wounded up against stumps, and shooting at them as targets.—Witness the deceptions, the cheats, the unscrupulous lying, and the firing upon and killing their prisoners of war, to which they have resorted. Witness their throwing shot and shell at every point where they had reason to know that they were killing only the sick and wounded. Witness their shooting down our men when they could have taken them as prisoners, and in these things learn that the South is to its finger ends filled with the fiercest and deadliest hate.[1]

How marked and striking is the contrast between the two peoples, and the two armies. Where the one tortures and sometimes kills its prisoners, the other treats them kindly, and often releases them upon taking the oath of allegiance. Where the one slays only in battle, the other shoots down our unarmed men in cold blood. While the South does not hesitate to employ their slaves against the Government, the Government refuses to accept the services of any colored citizen in suppressing the rebellion, lest they should lead to the freedom of the slaves, and thus inflict too heavy a blow upon the slaveholding rebels. The one is very careful about the rights of property, while the other fills the sea with pirates, and plunders the Government of every thing it can get its hand upon. The slaveholders have no scruples; they wage this war with unrelenting and desperate earnestness, sustained and fed by immeasurable malice, unmixed, and as deadly as the poison from the fang of a rattlesnake. Herein is the secret of their success. It is not their numbers, not their wealth, not the goodness of their cause, not their skill, but the quenchless fire of a deadly hate, which spurns all restraints of law and humanity, and walks to its purpose with a single eye and a determined hand. The battle at Bull's Run has done something to open Northern eyes to the real character of their Southern brethren; but it may require other lessons of the same sort to lead them to strike the South only where it can do so effectually, and that is the abolition of slavery.

Douglass' Monthly, August, 1861

1. See the document, "Barbarities of the Enemy," Frank Moore, ed., *The Rebellion Record,* vol. II, 1862, section "Rumors and Incidents," p. 25.

TO REV. SAMUEL J. MAY

Rochester, August 30, 1861

My Dear Sir:

I do not [know] Mr. Copeland nor his plan, and I should like to know something of the latter before offering myself or procuring any other man to act as his body servant.

It now seems to me that our Government has resolved that no good shall come to the Negro from this war, and that it means by every means in its power to convince the slaveholders that slavery is safer in than out of the union—that the slaveholding rebel is an object of higher regard than is his humble slave. The hope that the war would finally become an abolition war has been dissipated and men are now preparing for another attempt to preserve the liberty of the white man at the expense of that of the black. I have tried to be hopeful and do still try to be so—but I confess that it seems much like hoping against hope. What I feared would result from sudden success has come from defeat. The Government defeated seems as little disposed to carry the war to the abolition point as before. Who would have supposed that General Banks would have signalized the first week of his campaign on the Potomac by capturing slaves and returning them to their masters? He has done less to punish the rebels than to punish their victims. Only think too, of Fremont with Edward M. Davis for quartermaster, cooping up two fugitive slaves in the arsenal of St. Louis and when the poor fellows succeeded in getting away from these their federal and abolition friends, their Loyal owners were assured that they might expect to be duly paid for their runaway chattels with your money and mine. Looking at the government in the light of these and similar examples, and the fact that the government consents only that Negroes shall smell powder in the character of cooks and body servants in the army, my anti-slavery confidence is blown to the winds. I wait and work relying more upon the stern logic of events than upon any disposition of the Federal army towards slavery.

When I join any movement such as I suppose contemplated, I must have a country or the hope of a country under me—a government around me—and some flag of a Northern or Southern nation floating over me. The Negro can do much, but he can not hope to whip two nations at once. Not even the allowance that the Government at Washington would wink at a John Brown movement could induce me to join it. Nothing short of an open recognition of the Negro's manhood, his rights as such to have a country, to bear arms, and to defend that country equally with others would induce me to join the army in any capacity. I am sick of seeing mere isolated, extemporaneous insurrections the only result of which is the shooting and hanging of the few brave men who take part in them—and not being willing to take the chances of such an insurrection myself I could not advise any one else to take part in them. Whenever the government is ready to make the war, a war for freedom and progress and will receive the services of black men on the same terms upon which it receives that of other men I pledge myself to do one man's work in supplying the Government. I honor Mr. Copeland for his supposed good intentions—but he will not succeed in getting the Government to do justice by persuasion. Nothing short of dire necessity will bring it to act wisely.

Yours very truly,
Fred'k Douglass

Frederick Douglass Mss., Arthur H. Spingarn Collection

WHAT SHALL BE DONE WITH THE SLAVES IF EMANCIPATED?

It is curious to observe, at this juncture, when the existence of slavery is threatened by an aroused nation, when national necessity is combining with an en-

lightened sense of justice to put away the huge abomination forever, that the enemies of human liberty are resorting to all the old and ten thousand times refuted
objections to emancipation with which they confronted the abolition movement
twenty-five years ago. Like the one stated above, these pro-slavery objections
have their power mainly in the slavery-engendered prejudice, which every where
pervades the country. Like all other great transgressions of the law of eternal rectitude, slavery thus produces an element in the popular and depraved moral sentiment favorable to its own existence. These objections are often urged with a
show of sincere solicitude for the welfare of the slaves themselves. It is said, what
will you do with them? they can't take care of themselves; they would all come
to the North; they would not work; they would become a burden upon the State,
and a blot upon society; they'd cut their masters' throats; they would cheapen
labor, and crowd out the poor white laborer from employment; their former
masters would not employ them, and they would necessarily become vagrants,
paupers and criminals, overrunning all our alms houses, jails and prisons. The
laboring classes among the whites would come in bitter conflict with them in all
the avenues of labor, and regarding them as occupying places and filling positions which should be occupied and filled by white men; a fierce war of races
would be the inevitable consequence, and the black race would, of course, (being the weaker,) be exterminated. In view of this frightful, though happily somewhat contradictory picture, the question is asked, and pressed with a great show
of earnestness at this momentous crisis of our nation's history, What shall be
done with the four million slaves if they are emancipated?

This question has been answered, and can be answered in many ways. Primarily, it is a question less for man than for God—less for human intellect than for the
laws of nature to solve. It assumes that nature has erred; that the law of liberty is
a mistake; that freedom, though a natural want of the human soul, can only be enjoyed at the expense of human welfare, and that men are better off in slavery than
they would or could be in freedom; that slavery is the natural order of human relations, and that liberty is an experiment. What shall be done with them?

Our answer is, do nothing with them; mind your business, and let them mind
theirs. Your *doing* with them is their greatest misfortune. They have been undone by your doings, and all they now ask, and really have need of at your hands,
is just to let them alone. They suffer by every interference, and succeed best by
being let alone. The Negro should have been let alone in Africa—let alone when
the pirates and robbers offered him for sale in our Christian slave markets—
(more cruel and inhuman than the Mohammedan slave markets)—let alone by
courts, judges, politicians, legislators and slave-drivers—let alone altogether, and
assured that they were thus to be let alone forever, and that they must now make
their own way in the world, just the same as any and every other variety of the
human family. As colored men, we only ask to be allowed to *do* with ourselves,
subject only to the same great laws for the welfare of human society which apply to other men, Jews, Gentiles, Barbarian, Sythian. Let us stand upon our own
legs, work with our own hands, and eat bread in the sweat of our own brows.
When you, our white fellow-countrymen, have attempted to do anything for us,
it has generally been to deprive us of some right, power or privilege which you

yourself would die before you would submit to have taken from you. When the planters of the West Indies used to attempt to puzzle the pure-minded Wilberforce with the question, How shall we get rid of slavery? his simple answer was, "quit stealing." In like manner, we answer those who are perpetually puzzling their brains with questions as to what shall be done with the Negro, "let him alone and mind your own business." If you see him plowing in the open field, leveling the forest, at work with a spade, a rake, a hoe, a pick-axe, or a bill—let him alone; he has a right to work. If you see him on his way to school, with spelling book, geography and arithmetic in his hands—let him alone. Don't shut the door in his face, nor bolt your gates against him; he has a right to learn—let him alone. Don't pass laws to degrade him. If he has a ballot in his hand, and is on his way to the ballot-box to deposit his vote for the man whom he thinks will most justly and wisely administer the Government which has the power of life and death over him, as well as others—let him *alone;* his right of choice as much deserves respect and protection as your own. If you see him on his way to the church, exercising religious liberty in accordance with this or that religious persuasion—let him alone.—Don't meddle with him, nor trouble yourselves with any questions as to what shall be done with him.

The great majority of human duties are of this negative character. If men were born in need of crutches, instead of having legs, the fact would be otherwise. We should then be in need of help, and would require outside aid; but according to the wiser and better arrangement of nature, our duty is done better by not hindering than by helping our fellow-men; or, in other words, the best way to help them is just to let them help themselves.

We would not for one moment check the outgrowth of any benevolent concern for the future welfare of the colored race in America or elsewhere; but in the name of reason and religion, we earnestly plead for justice before all else. Benevolence with justice is harmonious and beautiful; but benevolence without justice is a mockery. Let the American people, who have thus far only kept the colored race staggering between partial philanthropy and cruel force, be induced to try what virtue there is in justice. First pure, then peaceable—first just, then generous.—The sum of the black man's misfortunes and calamities are just here: He is everywhere treated as an exception to all the general rules which should operate in the relations of other men. He is literally scourged beyond the beneficent range of truth and justice.—With all the purifying and liberalizing power of the Christian religion, teaching, as it does, meekness, gentleness, brotherly kindness, those who profess it have not yet even approached the position of treating the black man as an equal man and a brother. The few who have thus far risen to this requirement, both of reason and religion, are stigmatized as fanatics and enthusiasts.

What shall be done with the Negro if emancipated? Deal justly with him. He is a human being, capable of judging between good and evil, right and wrong, liberty and slavery, and is as much a subject of law as any other man; therefore, deal justly with him. He is, like other men, sensible of the motives of reward and punishment. Give him wages for his work, and let hunger pinch him if he don't work. He knows the difference between fullness and famine, plenty and scarcity.

"But will he work?" Why should he not? He is used to it. His hands are already hardened by toil, and he has no dreams of ever getting a living by any other means than by hard work. But would you turn them all loose? Certainly! We are no better than our Creator. He has turned them loose, and why should not we?

But would you let them all stay here?—Why not? What better is *here* than *there*? Will they occupy more room as freemen than as slaves? Is the presence of a black freeman less agreeable than that of a black slave? Is an object of our injustice and cruelty a more ungrateful sight than one of your justice and benevolence? You have borne the one more than two hundred years—can't you bear the other long enough to try the experiment? "But would it be safe?" No good reason can be given why it would not be. There is much more reason for apprehension from slavery than from freedom. Slavery provokes and justifies incendiarism, murder, robbery, assassination, and all manner of violence.— But why not let them go off by themselves? That is a matter we would leave exclusively to themselves. Besides, when you, the American people, shall once do justice to the enslaved colored people, you will not want to get rid of them. Take away the motive which slavery supplies for getting rid of the free black people of the South, and there is not a single State, from Maryland to Texas, which would desire to be rid of its black people. Even with the obvious disadvantage to slavery, which such contact is, there is scarcely a slave State which could be carried for the unqualified expulsion of the free colored people. Efforts at such expulsion have been made in Maryland, Virginia and South Carolina, and all have failed, just because the black man as a freeman is a useful member of society. To drive him away, and thus deprive the South of his labor, would be as absurd and monstrous as for a man to cut off his right arm, the better to enable himself to work.

There is one cheering aspect of this revival of the old and threadbare objections to emancipation—it implies at least the presence of danger to the slave system. When slavery was assailed twenty-five years ago, the whole land took the alarm, and every species of argument and subterfuge was resorted to by the defenders of slavery. The mental activity was amazing; all sorts of excuses, political, economical, social, theological and ethnological, were coined into barricades against the advancing march of anti-slavery sentiment. The same activity now shows itself, but has added nothing new to the argument for slavery or against emancipation.—When the accursed slave system shall once be abolished, and the Negro, long cast out from the human family, and governed like a beast of burden, shall be gathered under the divine government of justice, liberty and humanity, men will be ashamed to remember that they were ever deluded by the flimsy nonsense which they have allowed themselves to urge against the freedom of the long enslaved millions of our land. That day is not far off.

"O hasten it in mercy, gracious Heaven!"

Douglass' Monthly, January, 1862

In November, 1861, the Emancipation League was organized in Boston by Wendell Phillips, William Lloyd Garrison, George S. Boutwell, Samuel Gridley Howe, and others with the object "of urging upon the people and the Government emancipation of the Slaves, as a measure of justice, and military necessity." By means of public lectures the League hoped to arouse the nation for the annihilation of slavery.[1] Douglass was selected to deliver the fourth lecture in its course.

He accepted the invitation with joy. Now he could join with his former colleagues in the vital work of educating the people, delighted that they had revived their organizations and activity after the unfortunate lull in the early months of war. . . . Douglass directed a stinging attack at the "vacillation, doubt, uncertainty and hesitation" which characterized the administration "in regard to the true methods of dealing with the vital cause of the rebellion." The crowded auditorium agreed as he declared that "our policy seems to be, to have no policy." . . .

Six days later at Cooper Institute in New York, Douglass repeated the Emancipation League address. Again there was the insistent prodding, again the demands for action, for a summary destruction of the slave system. And again his remarks were greeted with "most hearty and enthusiastic applause." The *Anti-Slavery Standard* reported that "more than one judge expressed the opinion that no more effective discourse had been delivered in the city."[2]

To Douglass the most significant thing about both addresses was the response of the audience. There were no catcalls, no hissing, no disorder as he excoriated the administration. He was well aware that it was national safety and not burning hatred of the slave system which was responsible for the enthusiasm to his call for immediate emancipation. Nevertheless, he rejoiced in the change in public sentiment, for now he was less concerned with the motives which would lead the nation to abolish slavery than in achieving this goal. He directed all of his attention to winning recruits for the abolition of slavery.[3]
[III:20–21]

THE FUTURE OF THE NEGRO PEOPLE OF THE SLAVE STATES, speech delivered before the Emancipation League in Tremont Temple, Boston, February 5, 1862

Ladies and Gentlemen:

The progress of the present tremendous war has developed great qualities of mind and heart among the loyal people, and none more conspicuously than patience. We have seen our sons, brothers, and fathers led to the battle field by untried and unskillful generals, and have held our breath; we have seen them repeatedly marched in thousands upon concealed batteries of the enemy, to be swept down by storms of iron and fire, and have scarcely murmured: we have seen the wealth of the land poured out at the frightful rate of a million a day without complaint; we have seen our Capital surrounded, hemmed in, blockaded in the presence of a fettered but chafing loyal army of a quarter of a million on the Potomac during seven long months, and still we have cried patience and forbearance. We have seen able and earnest men displaced from high and important positions to make room for men who have yet to win our confidence, and still have believed in the Government. This is all right, all proper. Our Government however defective is still our Government. It is all we have to shield us from the fury and vengeance of treason, rebellion, and anarchy.

If I were asked to describe the most painful and mortifying feature presented in the prosecution and management of the present war on the part of the United States Government, against the slaveholding rebels now marshalled against it, I should not point to Ball's Bluff, Big Bethel, Bull Run, or any of the many blunders and disaster on flood or field; but I should point to the vacillation, doubt, uncertainty and hesitation, which have thus far distinguished our government in regard to the true method of dealing with the vital cause of the rebellion. We are without any declared and settled policy—and our policy seems to be, to have no policy.

The winds and currents are ever changing, and after beating about for almost a whole year on the perilous coast of a wildering ocean unable to find our bearings, we at last discover that we are in the same latitude as when we set sail, as far from the desired port as ever and with much less heart, health, and provisions for pursuing the voyage than on the morning we weighed anchor.

If it be true that he that doubteth is condemned already, there is certainly but little chance for this Republic.

At the opening session of the present Congress there was a marked, decided, and emphatic expression against slavery as the great motive power of the present slaveholding war. Many petitions, numerously and influentially signed, were duly sent in and presented to that body, praying, first, for the entire abolition of slavery in all the slaveholding States; secondly, that a just award be made by Congress to loyal slaveholders; and thirdly, that the slaves of rebels be wholly confiscated. The vigor, earnestness, and power with which these objects were advocated, as war measures, by Messrs. Stevens, Bingham, Elliott, Gurley, Lovejoy and others, inspired the loyal friends of Freedom all over the North with renewed confidence and hope, both for the country and for the slave. The conviction was general that at last the country was to have a policy, and that that policy would bring freedom and safety to the Republic.

Thus far, however, this hope, this confidence, this conviction has not been justified. The country is without a known policy. The enemies of the Abolition cause, taking alarm from these early efforts, have earnestly set themselves to the work of producing a reaction in favor of slavery, and have succeeded beyond what they themselves must have expected at the first.

Among other old, and threadbare, and worn out objections which they have raised against the Emancipation policy, is the question as to what shall be done with the four million slaves of the South, if they are emancipated? or in other words, what shall be the future of the four million slaves?

I am sensible, deeply sensible, of the importance of this subject, and of the many difficulties which are supposed to surround it.

If there is any one great, pressing, and all-commanding problem for this nation to solve, and to solve without delay, that problem is slavery. Its claims are urgent, palpable, and powerful. The issue involves the whole question of life and death to the nation.

Some who speak on this subject are already sure as to how this question will finally be decided. I am not, but one thing I know:—If we are a wise, liberty-loving, a just and courageous nation—knowing what is right and daring to do it—we shall solve this problem, and solve it speedily, in accordance with national safety, national unity, national prosperity, national glory, and shall win for our-selves the admiration of an onlooking world and the grateful applause of after-coming generations. If on the other hand, we are a cunning, cowardly, and self-ish nation given over—as other nations have been before us—to hardness of heart and blindness of mind, it needs no prophet to foretell our doom.

Before proceeding to discuss the future of the colored people of the slave States, you will allow me to make a few remarks, personal and general, respect-ing the tremendous crisis through which we are passing. In the first place I have not the vanity to suppose—and I say it without affectation—that I can add any thing to the powerful arguments of the able men who have preceded me in this course of lectures. I take the stand tonight more as an humble witness than as an advocate. I have studied slavery and studied freedom on both sides of Mason and Dixon's line. Nearly twenty-two years of my life were spent in Slavery, and more than twenty-three have been spent in freedom. I am of age in both conditions, and there seems an eminent fitness in allowing me to speak for myself and my race. If I take my stand to-night as I shall do, with the downtrodden and enslaved, and view the facts of the hour more as a bondman than as a freeman, it is not because I feel no interest in the general welfare of the country. Far from it.

I am an American citizen. In birth, in sentiment, in ideas, in hopes, in aspira-tions, and responsibilities, I am an American citizen. According to Judge Kent there are but two classes of people in America: they are citizens and aliens, na-tives and foreigners.—Natives are citizens—foreigners are aliens until naturalized.

But I am not only a citizen by birth and lineage, I am such by choice.

I once had a very tempting offer of citizenship in another country; but declined it because I preferred the hardships and duties of my mission here. I have never regretted that decision, although my pathway has been anything than a smooth one; and to-night, I allow no man to exceed me in the desire for the safety and welfare of this country. And just here do allow me to boast a little. There is noth-ing in the circumstances of the present hour, nothing in the behavior of the col-ored people, either North or South, which requires apology at my hands. Though everywhere spoken against, the most malignant and unscrupulous of all our slan-derers have not, in this dark and terrible hour of the nation's trial dared to ac-cuse us of a want of patriotism or loyalty. Though ignored by our friends and re-pelled by our enemies, the colored people, both north and south, have evinced the most ardent desire to serve the cause of the country, as against the rebels and traitors who are endeavoring to break it down and destroy it. That they are not largely represented in the loyal army, is the fault of the Government, and a very grievous fault it is. Mark here our nation's degeneracy. Colored men were good enough to fight under Washington. They are not good enough to fight under Mc-Clellan.—They were good enough to fight under Andrew Jackson. They are not good enough to fight under Gen. Halleck. They were good enough to help win American independence but they are not good enough to help preserve that in-dependence against treason and rebellion. They were good enough to defend New Orleans but not good enough to defend our poor beleaguered Capital. I am not arguing against, not condemning those in power, but simply stating facts in vindication of my people; and as these facts stand, I do say that I am proud to be recognized here as an humble representative of that rejected race. Whether in peace or in war, whether in safety or in peril, whether in evil report or good report, at home or abroad, my mission is to stand up for the downtrodden, to open my mouth for the dumb, to remember those in bonds as bound with them.

Happily, however, in standing up in their cause I do, and you do, but stand in defense of the cause of the whole country. The circumstances of this eventful hour make the cause of the slaves and the cause of the country identical. They must fall or flourish together. A blow struck for the freedom of the slave, is equally a blow struck for the safety and welfare of the country. As Liberty and Union have become identical, so slavery and treason have become one and inseparable. I shall not argue this point. It has already been most ably argued. All eyes see it, all hearts begin to feel it; and all that is needed is the wisdom and the manhood to perform the solemn duty pointed out by the stern logic of our situation. It is now or never with us.

The field is ripe for the harvest. God forbid that when the smoke and thunder of this slaveholding war shall have rolled from the troubled face of our country it shall be said that the harvest is past, the summer is ended and we are not saved.

There are two classes of men who are endeavoring to put down this strange and most unnatural rebellion. About patriotism and loyalty, they talk alike; but the difference between them is heaven wide—and if we fail to suppress the rebels and restore the country to a condition of permanent safety it will be chargeable less to the skill and power of the rebels themselves, than to this division and conflict among ourselves. Never could it be said more truly and sadly than now, that our enemies are those of our own household.—The traitors of the South are open, bold, decided. We know just where to find them.—They are on the battle field, with arms in their hands and bullets in their pockets. It is easy to deal with them, but it is not so easy to deal with the so-called Union men in Maryland, Western Virginia, and Kentucky, and those who sympathize with them in the Northern States.

One class is for putting down the rebellion if that can be done by force and force alone, and without abolishing slavery, and the other is for putting down the rebellion by putting down slavery upon every rod of earth which shall be made sacred by the footprints of a single loyal soldier. One class would strike down the effect, the other would strike at the cause. Can any man doubt for a moment that the latter is the wisest and best course? Is it not as plain as the sun in the heavens, that slavery is the life, the soul, the inspiration, and power of the rebellion? Is it not equally plain that any peace which may be secured which shall leave slavery still existing at the South, will prove a hollow and worthless peace, a mere suspension of hostilities, to be renewed again at the first favorable opportunity?—Does any man think that the slaveholders would relinquish all hope of Southern independence in the future because defeated in the present contest? Would they not come out of the war with a deadlier hate and a firmer purpose to renew the struggle hereafter, with larger knowledge and better means of success? He who thinks or flatters himself that they would not, has read history and studied human nature to little purpose.

But why, O why should we not abolish slavery now? All admit that it must be abolished at some time. What better time than now can be assigned for that great work?—Why should it longer live? What good thing has it done that it should be given further lease of life? What evil thing has it left undone? Behold its dreadful history! Saying nothing of the rivers of tears and streams of blood poured out by its 4,000,000 victims—saying nothing of the leprous poison it has diffused through the life blood of our morals and our religion—saying nothing of the many humiliating concessions already made to it—saying nothing of the deep and scandalous reproach it has brought upon our national good name—saying nothing of all this, and more the simple fact that this monster Slavery has eaten up and devoured the patriotism of the whole South, kindled the lurid flames of a bloody rebellion in our midst, invited the armies of hostile nations to desolate our soil, and break down our Government, is good and all-sufficient cause of smiting it as with a bolt from heaven. If it is possible for any system of barbarism to sing its own death warrant, Slavery, by its own natural working, is that system. All the arguments of conscience, sound expediency, national honor and safety unite in the fiat—let it die the death of its own election.

One feature of the passing hour is notable in showing how narrow and limited may be the channel through which a great reformatory movement can run for long and weary years, without once overflowing its banks and enriching the surrounding country through which it passes.

Notwithstanding all our books, pamphlets, newspapers, our great conventions, addresses, and resolutions, tens of thousands of the American people are now taking their *first* lessons as to the character and influence of slavery and slaveholders. Tongues that used to bless Slavery now curse it, and men who formerly found paragons of the race only among slave mongers and their abettors, are but now having the scales torn from their eyes by slaveholding treason and rebellion. They are just coming to believe what we have all along been trying to tell them, that is: that he who breaks faith with God may not be expected to keep faith with man. I gladly welcome this great change in the public sentiment of the country. And yet I do not rely very confidently upon it. I am not deceived either in regard to its origin or its quality.—I know that national self-preservation, national safety, rather than any regard to the bondman as a man and a brother, is at the bottom of much that now meets us in the shape of opposition to slavery. The little finger of him who denounced slavery from a high moral conviction of its enormity is more than the loins of him that merely denounces it for the peril into which it has brought the country. Nevertheless, I rejoice in this change, the result will be nearly the same to the slave, if from motives of necessity or any other motives the nation shall be led to the extinction of slavery. Every consideration of expediency and justice may be consistently brought to bear against that sum of all villanies.

A WORD AS TO THE COURSE OF THE ABOLITIONISTS

Upon the first outburst of the now raging rebellion, awakening the nation as from a sleep of death, the Abolitionists of the country very generally dropped their distinctive character, and were fused with the mass of their fellow-citizens. Patriotism for the moment took the place of philanthropy, and those who had for long years given their best energies to save the slave, were not behind any other class of citizens in their efforts to save the country. They suspended their agencies, postponed their meetings, and poured out their best eloquence with pen and tongue to fire the Northern heart to the great contest to which it was summoned in the name of an imperiled country. In this, however, we may have been more patriotic than wise. Every day bears witness that Slavery is not only the cause of the rebellion, but that it is and has been from the beginning, the only real obstacle to crushing out the rebellion; and that all efforts to save the country are utterly vain, unless guided by the principles which the Abolitionists know best how to teach.

I rejoice therefore in the formation of the Emancipation league. May its work be quick, certain and complete. I perceive that it has not entered upon its career unobserved. The guardians of slavery in Boston, for there are such guardians, have honored it by very lengthened and very bitter denunciations.—No better reception could have been expected, even if deserved, than that given it by the *Boston Courier.*[4] A like denunciation came from the Tory press of England when the anti-corn law League was formed. Nevertheless that grand League put down the Corn monopoly in seven years, gave bread to the starving millions, broke down the tory party beyond the hope of regaining power, changed the policy of the British nation, transferred the power of the landed aristocracy to the people and gave us the Brights, the Cobdens, the Wilsons, and the Thompsons, and the William Edward Forsters, the men who represent the middle classes of England and who are now in our days of trouble as in our days of peace and prosperity, America's best and truest friends. Humanity is proud of the triumphs of that League. It will not be otherwise of this League.

But I come now to the more immediate subject of my lecture, namely: What shall be done with the four millions of slaves if they are emancipated? This singular question comes from the same two very different and very opposite classes of the American people, who are endeavoring to put down the rebels. The first have no moral, religious, or political objection to Slavery, and, so far as they are concerned, Slavery might live and flourish to the end of time. They are the men who have an abiding affection for rebels, and at the beginning marched to the tune of "No Coercion—No subjugation." They have now dropped these unpopular "Noes," and have taken up another set, equally treacherous. Their tune now is, No Emancipation. No Confiscation of slave property, No Arming of the Negroes. They were driven from the first set of "Noes" by the gleaming of a half million bayonets, and I predict that they will be driven from the last set, though I cannot promise that they will not find another set.

The second class of persons are those who may be called young converts, newly awakened persons, who are convinced of the great evil and danger of Slavery, and would be glad to see some wise and unobjectionable plan of emancipation devised and adopted by the Government. They hate Slavery and love Freedom, but they are yet too much trammeled by the popular habit of thought respecting the Negro to trust the operation of their own principles. Like the man in the Scriptures, they see men only as trees walking. They differ from the first class only in motive and purpose, and not in premise and argument, and hence the answer to Pro-Slavery objections will answer those raised by our new anti-Slavery men. When some of the most potent, grave and reverend defenders of Slavery in England urged Wilberforce for a statement of his plan of Emancipation, his simple response was quit stealing.

My answer to the question, What shall be done with the four million slaves if emancipated? shall be alike short and simple: Do nothing with them, but leave them like you have left other men, to do with and for themselves. We would be entirely respectful to those who raise the inquiry, and yet it is hard not to say to them just what they would say to us, if we manifested a like concern for them, and that is; please to mind your business, and leave us to mind ours. If we cannot stand up, then let us fall down.—We ask nothing at the hands of the American people but simple justice, and an equal chance to live; and if we cannot live and flourish on such terms, our case should be referred to the Author of our existence. Injustice, oppression, and Slavery with their manifold concomitants have been tried with us during a period of more than two hundred years. Under the whole heavens you will find no parallel to the wrongs we have endured. We have worked without wages; we have lived without hope, wept without sympathy, and bled without mercy. Now, in the name of common humanity, and according to the laws of the Living God, we simply ask the right to bear the responsibility of our own existence.

Let us alone. Do nothing with us, for us, or by us as a particular class. What you have done with us thus far has only worked to our disadvantage. We now simply ask to be allowed to do for ourselves. I submit that there is nothing unreasonable or unnatural in all this request. The black man is said to be unfortunate. He is so. But I affirm that the broadest and bitterest of the black man's misfortunes is the fact that he is everywhere regarded and treated as an exception to the principles and maxims which apply to other men, and that nothing short of the extension of those principles to him can satisfy any honest advocate of his claims.

Even those who are sincerely desirous to serve us and to help us out of our difficulties, stand in doubt of us and fear that we could not stand the application of the rules which they freely apply to all other people.

Now, whence comes this doubt and fear? I will tell you. There is no difficulty whatever in giving ample and satisfactory explanation of the source of this estimate of the black man's capacity.

What have been his condition and circumstances for more than two centuries? These will explain all.

Take any race you please, French, English, Irish, or Scotch, subject them to slavery for ages—regard and treat them everywhere, every way, as property, as having no rights which other men are required to respect.—Let them be loaded with chains, scarred with the whip, branded with hot irons, sold in the market, kept in ignorance, by force of law and by common usage, and I venture to say that the same doubt would spring up concerning either of them, which now confronts the Negro. The common talk of the streets on this subject shows great ignorance. It assumes that no other race has ever been enslaved or could be held in slavery, and the fact that the black man submits to that condition is often cited as a proof of original and permanent inferiority, and of the fitness of the black man only for that condition. Just this is the argument of the Confederate States; the argument of Stephens in defense of S. C. But what are the facts? I believe it will not be denied that the Anglo-Saxons are a fine race of men, and have done something for the civilization of mankind, yet who does not know that this now grand and leading race was in bondage and abject slavery for ages upon their own native soil. They were not stolen away from their own country in small numbers, where they could make no resistance to their enslavers, but were enslaved in their own country.

Turn to the pages of the history of the Norman Conquest, by Monsieur Thierry, and you will find this statement fully attested.—He says: Foreigners visiting England, even so late as the sixteenth century, were astonished at the great number of serfs they beheld, and the excessive harshness of their servitude. The word bondage, in the Norman tongue, expressed at the time all that was most wretched in the condition of humanity. He again says: About the year 1381, all who were called bonds in English or in Anglo-Norman—that is, all the cultivators of land—were serfs in body and goods, abliged to pay heavy aids for the small portions of land which served them to feed their families, and were not at liberty to give up that portion of land without the consent of the Lords for whom they were obliged to do gratuitously their tillage, their gardening, and their carriage of all kinds. The Lords could sell them, together with their horses, their oxen, and their implements of husbandry—their children and their posterity—which in the English deeds was expressed in the following manner: Know that I have sold ——, my knave, and all his offspring, born or to be born.

Sir Walter Scott, after describing very minutely the dress of a Saxon serf, says: One part of the dress only remains, but it is too remarkable to be suppressed. It was a brass ring resembling a dog's collar, but without any opening, and soldered fast around the neck, so loose as to form no impediment to breathing, and yet so tight as to be incapable of being removed excepting by the use of the file. On this singular gorget was engraved, in Saxon letters, an inscription of the following purport; Gurth, the son of Beowulph, is the born thrall of Cedric Rotherwood.

As an evidence of the contempt and degradation in which the Saxons were held, Monsieur Thierry says that after the conquest the Bishop of Lincoln reckoned only two languages in England—Latin for men of letters and French for the ignorant, in which language he himself wrote pious books for the use of the French, making no account of the English language and those who spoke it.

The poets of the same period, even those of English birth, composed all their verses in French when they wished to derive from them either profit or honor. Such is a brief view of the social condition occupied for ages by a people now the mightiest on the globe. The Saxon was of no account then; the Negro is of no account now. May not history one day carry the analogy a step further? In the case of the Saxon, we have a people held in abject slavery, upon their own native soil by strangers and foreigners. Their very language made no account of, and themselves wearing brass collars on their necks like dogs, bearing the names of their masters. They were bought and sold like the beast of the field, and their offspring born and to be born doomed to the same wretched condition. No doubt that the people of this now proud and grand race in their then abject condition were compelled to listen to disparagement and insults from their Norman oppressors, as galling as those which meet the black man here. No doubt that these disparagements hung about their necks like a mountain weight to keep them down, and no doubt there were men of shallow brain and selfish hearts to tell them that Slavery was their normal condition.

The misfortunes of my own race in this respect are not singular. They have happened to all nations, when under the heel of oppression. Whenever and wherever any particular variety of the human family has been enslaved by another, their slavers and oppressors, in every such instance, have found their best apology for their own base conduct in the bad character of their victims. The cunning, the deceit, the indolence, and the manifold vices and crimes, which naturally grow out of the condition of Slavery, are generally charged as inherent characteristics of the oppressed and enslaved race. The Jews, the Indians, the Saxons and the ancient Britons, have all had a taste of this bitter experience.

When the United States coveted a part of Mexico, and sought to wrest from that sister Republic her coveted domain, some of you remember how our press teemed from day to day with charges of Mexican inferiority—How they were assailed as a worn-out race; how they were denounced as a weak, worthless, indolent, and turbulent nation, given up to the sway of animal passions, totally incapable of self-government, and how excellent a thing we were told it would be for civilization if the strong beneficent arms of the Anglo-Saxon could be extended over them; and how, with our usual blending of piety with plunder, we justified our avarice by appeals to the hand-writing of Divine Providence. All this, I say, you remember, for the facts are but little more than a dozen years old.

As between us and unfortunate Mexico, so it was with Russia and the Ottoman Empire. In the eyes of Nicholas, the Turk was the sick man of Europe—just as the Negro is now the sick man of America.

So, too, in former years, it was with England and Ireland. When any new burden was sought to be imposed upon that ill-fated country, or when any improvement in the condition of its people was suggested, and pressed by philanthropic and liberal statesmen, the occasion never failed to call forth the most angry and disparaging arguments and assaults upon the Irish race.

Necessity is said to be the plea of tyrants. The alleged inferiority of the oppressed is also the plea of tyrants. The effect upon these against whom it is directed is to smite them as with the hand of death. Under its paralyzing touch all manly aspirations and self-reliance die out and the smitten race comes almost to assent to the justice of their own degradation.

No wonder, therefore, that the colored people in America appear stupid, helpless and degraded. The wonder is rather that they evince so much spirit and manhood as they do. What have they not suffered and endured? They have been weighed, measured, marked and prized—in detail and in the aggregate. Their estimated value a little while ago was twenty hundred millions. Those twenty hundred millions of dollars have all the effect of twenty hundred millions of arguments against the Negro as a man and a brother. Here we have a mountain of gold, depending upon the continuance of our enslavement and degradation. No wonder that it has been able to bribe the press against us.—No wonder that it has been able to employ learning and eloquence against us. No wonder that it has bought up the American pulpit and obtained the sanction of religion against us. No wonder that it has turned every department of the Government into engines of oppression and tyranny toward us.—No nation, however gifted by nature, could hope to bear up under such oppressive weights.

But to return. What shall be done with the four million slaves, if emancipated. I answer, deal justly with them; pay them honest wages for honest work; dispense with the biting lash, and pay them the ready cash; awaken a new class of motives in them; remove those old motives of shriveling fear of punishment which benumb and degrade the soul, and supplant them by the higher and better motives of hope, of self-respect, of honor, and of personal responsibility. Reverse the whole current of feeling in regard to them. They have been compelled hitherto to regard the white man as a cruel, selfish, and remorseless tyrant, thirsting for wealth, greedy of gain, and caring nothing as to the means by which he obtains it. Now, let him see that the white man has a nobler and better side to his character, and he will love, honor, esteem the white man.

But it is said that the black man is naturally indolent, and that he will not work without a master. I know that this is a part of his bad reputation; but I also know that he is indebted for this bad reputation to the most indolent and lazy of all the American people, the slaveholders—men who live in absolute idleness, and eat their daily bread in the briny sweat of other men's faces. That the black man in Slavery shirks labor—aims to do as little as he can, and to do that little in the most slovenly manner—only proves that he is a man. Thackery says that all men are about as lazy as they can afford to be—and I do not claim that the Negro is an exception to this rule. He loves ease and abundance just as other people love ease and abundance. If this is a crime, then all men are criminals, and the Negro no more than the rest.

Again, it is affirmed that the Negro, if emancipated, could not take care of himself. My answer to this is, let him have a fair chance to try it. For 200 years he has taken care of himself and his master in the bargain. I see no reason to believe that he could not take care, and very excellent care, of himself when having only himself to support. The case of the freed slaves in the British West Indies has already been dwelt upon in the course of these lectures, and facts, arguments, and statistics have been presented demonstrating beyond all controversy that the black man not only has the ability and the disposition to work, but knows well how to take care of his earnings. The country over which he has toiled as a slave is rapidly becoming his property—that freedom has made him both a better producer and a better consumer.

LIBERTY AN EXPERIMENT

It is one of the strangest and most humiliating triumphs of human selfishness and prejudice over human reason, that it leads men to look upon emancipation as an experiment, instead of being, as it is, the natural order of human relations. Slavery, and not Freedom, is the experiment; and to witness its horrible failure we have to open our eyes, not merely upon the blasted soil of Virginia and other Slave States, but upon a whole land brought to the verge of ruin.

We are asked if we would turn the slaves all loose. I answer, Yes. Why not? They are not wolves nor tigers, but men. They are endowed with reason—can decide upon questions of right and wrong, good and evil, benefits and injuries—and are therefore subjects of government precisely as other men are.

But would you have them stay here? Why should they not? What better is here than there? What class of people can show a better title to the land on which they live than the colored people of the South? They have watered the soil with their tears and enriched it with their blood, and tilled it with their hard hands during two centuries; they have leveled its forests, raked out the obstructions to the plow and hoe, reclaimed the swamps, and produced whatever has made it a goodly land to dwell in, and it would be a shame and a crime little inferior in enormity to Slavery itself if these natural owners of the Southern and Gulf States should be driven away from their country to make room for others—even if others could be obtained to fill their places.

But unjust and revolting to every right-minded and humane man as is this talk of the expatriation of the slaves, the offense is not more shocking than it is unwise. For a nation to drive away its laboring population is to commit political suicide. It is like cutting off one's right hand in order to work the better and to produce the more. To say that Negroes shall not live in the Southern States is like saying that the lands of the South shall be no longer cultivated. The cry has all along been, We must have Negroes to work in the South, for white men cannot stand the hot sun and the fell diseases of the rice swamp and the sugar plantation. Even the leaders of the rebellion made it one of their grievances that they could not get more Negroes, though from motives of policy they have now dropped this plank from their platform.[5] No one doubts that the Gulf States mean to have more slaves from Africa just so soon as they shall get well settled in their independence. Again, why not allow the colored people of the South remain where they are? Will they occupy more room in freedom than slavery? If you could bear them as objects of your injustice, can they be more offensive as objects of your justice and your humanity? Why send them away? Who wants to take their places in the cotton field, in the rice swamp, and sugar fields, which they have tilled for ages? The whole scheme of colonization would be too absurd for discussion, but that the madness of the moment has drowned the voice of common sense as well as common justice.

There is a measure now before Congress duly reported from one of its Committees proposing, first, to make the Negroes leave the land of their birth, and secondly to pay the expense of their enforced removal.[6] If such a measure can become a law, the nation is more deeply wicked than any Abolitionist has hitherto ventured to believe. It is a most mischievous and scandalous proposition, unworthy of any man not dead to the claims of every sentiment of honor and humanity. I predict that if it passes it will become like the Fugitive Slave law—it will lie dead upon the statute book—having no other effect than to alarm the freed men of the South and disgrace the Congress by which it is passed.

Once free the slaves, and at once the motives which now require their expatriation will become too weak to breathe. In the single little State of Maryland, with climate and soil which invite the white laborer to its borders, there are at this moment nearly one hundred thousand free colored people. Now, notwithstanding that Maryland is a Slave State, and thus possesses a strong motive for getting rid of their free colored people, the better to hold her slaves—and notwithstanding the circumstances of climate and soil—that Slave States only a year or two ago voted down by a large majority of their people the inhuman and barbarous proposition concerning her free colored population.

The number of colored people now on this continent and in the adjacent islands cannot fall far below twenty millions. An attempt to remove them would be as vain as to bail out the ocean. The whole naval power of the United States could not remove the natural increase of our part of this population. Every fact in our circumstances here marks us as a permanent element of the American people. Mark the readiness with which we adapt ourselves to your civilization. You can take no step in any direction where the black man is not at your back or side.—Go to California and dig gold: the black man is there. Go to war with Mexico, and let your armies penetrate the very heart of the country, and the black man is there. Go down into the coast of North and South Carolina, and the black man is there, and there as your friend, to give you more important and more trustworthy information than you can find among all the loyal poor white trash you can scare up in that region. The Negro is sometimes compared with the Indian, and it is predicted that, like the Indian, he will die out before the onward progress of the Anglo-Saxon race. I have not the least apprehension at this point. In features and complexion, the Negro is more unlike the European than is his Mongolian brother. But the interior resemblance is greater than the exterior difference. The Indian wraps himself in gloom, and proudly glories in isolation—he retreats before the onward march of civilization. The humming of the honey bee warns him away from his hunting grounds. He sees the plowshare of civilization tossing up the bones of his venerated fathers, and he dies of a broken heart. Not so with the Negro. There is a vitality about him that seems alike invincible to hardship and cruelty. Work him, whip him, sell him, torment him, and he still lives, and clings to American civilization—an Uncle Tom in the Church, and an Uncle Ben on the Southern coast, to guide our Burnside expeditions.

My friends, the destiny of the colored American, however this mighty war shall terminate, is the destiny of America. We shall never leave you. The allotments of Providence seem to make the black man of America the open book out of which the American people are to learn lessons of wisdom, power, and goodness—more sublime and glorious than any yet attained by the nations of the old or the new world. Over the bleeding back of the American bondman we shall learn mercy. In the very extreme difference of color and features of the Negro and the Anglo-Saxon, shall be learned the highest ideas of the sacredness of man and the fullness and perfection of human brotherhood.

> *Throughout the delivery of his address, Mr. Douglass was interrupted with most hearty and enthusiastic applause.*

Douglass' Monthly, March, 1862

1. *Boston Courier,* Dec. 11, 16, 17, 1861.

2. *Douglass' Monthly,* Mar., 1862; *Anti-Slavery Reporter,* Feb. 22, 1862.

3. *Douglass' Monthly,* Mar., 1862.

4. The *Boston Courier,* long known for its anti-abolitionist and pro-southern viewpoint, attacked the Emancipation League viciously, charging that "the 'League' is a conspiracy against the Constitution and the Government" and that "all who join such a 'League' are outright opposers of the Constitution and the Government, and mean to destroy the Union, if they can." (*Boston Courier,* Dec. 2, 18, 1861.)

5. The reference is to the clause in the constitution of the Confederate States which declared: "The importation of Negroes of the African race from any foreign country other than the slaveholding States or Territories of the United States of America, is hereby forbidden; and Congress is required to pass such laws as shall effectually prevent the same. . . ." The clause was adopted as part of the Confederate campaign to gain recognition in Europe.

6. Many proposals were made in Congress providing for the colonization of Negroes outside of the United States, and in April, 1862, a hundred thousand dollars was appropriated to colonize slaves emancipated in the District of Columbia. The funds were placed at Lincoln's disposal, and the President, who favored this policy, sought in vain to carry the program into effect. Efforts were made to establish a colony on Cow Island in the Caribbean Sea, but they failed. (See Charles H. Wesley, "Lincoln's Plan for Colonizing the Emancipated Negroes," *Journal of Negro History,* vol. IV, January, 1919, pp. 7–21.)

THE WAR AND HOW TO END IT, speech delivered at Corinthian Hall, Rochester, New York, March 25, 1862

I stand here to-night to advocate in my humble way, the unrestricted and complete Emancipation of every slave in the United States, whether claimed by loyal or disloyal masters. This is the lesson of the hour.

Through the certain operation of the *changeless laws of the universe,* Emancipation, which has long been a great and solemn national duty, pressing heavily on the national conscience has at last become a great and all commanding national necessity.

I choose not to insist upon these comprehensive propositions as a colored man to-night nor as one having special reasons for hating slavery, although, upon these grounds I might well base a claim to be heard, but my ground is taken as an American citizen, feeling with all others a deep and living interest in the welfare of the whole country.

In the tremendous conflict through which we are passing, all events steadily conspire, to make the cause of the slave and the cause of the country identical. He who to-day fights for Emancipation, fights for his country and free Institutions, and he who fights for slavery, fights against his country and in favor of a slaveholding oligarchy.

This was always so, though only abolitionists perceived the fact. The difference between them and others is this: They got an earlier glimpse at the black heart of slavery—than others did. They saw in times of seeming peace, for the peace we have had, was only seeming—what we can only see in times of open war. They saw that a nation like ours, containing two such opposite forces as liberty and slavery, could not enjoy permanent peace, and they said so and got mobbed for saying so. But let that pass.

Before I proceed to discuss the subject announced for my lecture this evening, allow me to make a few remarks on the mighty events which have marked and are marking the progress of the war. It requires a large share of wisdom and coolness, to properly weigh and measure the great facts which have already passed into history; but it requires a much larger share of these qualities, to enable man to discriminate between, and to determine the proper relations and bearings of the great living facts, transpiring before our eyes.

The obvious reason is this: important events often succeed each other so rapidly, and take the place of each other so quickly, that it becomes almost impossible to give to any one of them, that measure of reflection, which is necessary to form an intelligent judgement.

We are an intelligent people, apt scholars, but I think that few of us fully appreciate the solemn events that are now passing before our eyes.

It is known that we are at war, at war among ourselves, civil war the worst of all wars, but the real scope and significance of this war is but imperfectly understood by millions of the American people.

The very air is filled with conflicting statements in respect to the cause of this war, and naturally enough, it is also filled with contradictory theories as to the manner of restoring the country to peace.

I shall not stay here to discuss the long train of events, and the certain action of social forces which have finally culminated in this rebellion. The limits of the occasion will not permit any such lengthy discussion. The most that I can do, is to point out a few of the leading features of the contest, and enforce the lesson which I think they plainly teach and the path of duty they mark out for our feet.

The first enquiry which concerned the loyal north upon the sudden outburst of this stupendous rebellion, naturally related to the strength of the rebels, and the amount of force and skill required for their speedy suppression. Even at this vital point we blundered. We misconceived the real state of the case, and misread the facts then passing before us. We were quite incredulous of the tremendous strength and vigor of the foe against whom we were called upon to battle.

We are a charitable people, and in excess of charity were disposed to put the very best construction upon the strange behavior of our southern brethren. We admitted that South Carolina might secede. It was like her to do so. She had talked extravagantly about going out of the union, and she must do something extravagant and startling to save a show of consistency. Georgia too, we thought might possibly go out, but we were quite sure that these twin rebel States, would stand alone in their infamy, and that they would soon tire of their isolation, repent of their folly, and come back to the union. Traitors fled the Cabinet, the House and the Senate, and hastened away to fan the flames of treason at home. Still we doubted that any thing very serious would come of it. We treated it as a bubble on the wave, a nine day's wonder. Calm and thoughtful men ourselves, we relied on the sober second thought of others. Even a shot at one of our ships, an insult offered to our flag, caused only a momentary feeling of indignation and resentment, such as a mother might feel toward a naughty child who had thrown away his bread and stamped defiance at her authority. It was not until Beauregard opened his slave built batteries upon the starving garrison in Charleston harbor, that the confiding North, like a sleeping lion, was roused from his lair, and shook his thundering mane in wrath. We were slow to wake, but we did awake. Still we were scarcely conscious of the skill, power and resources of the enemy. We still hoped that wiser and better counsels would ultimately prevail. We could not believe but that a powerful union sentiment still existed at the South, and that a strong reaction would yet take place there in favor of the union. To the very last we continued to believe in the border States. We could not believe that those States would plunge madly into the bloody vortex of rebellion. It required the assaults of a blood thirsty mob spilling the blood of loyal soldiers to convince us of Baltimore treason.

I need not tell you, how in all this study of passing events, we have been grossly mistaken. Every hope based upon the sanity, loyalty, and good disposition of the South has been woefully disappointed. While armies were forming, and the most formidable preparations were making, we continued to dream of peace, and even after the war was fairly begun, we thought to put down the rebellion by a show of force rather than by an exercise of force. We showed our teeth but did not wish to use them. We preferred to fight with dollars rather than daggers. The fewer battles the better was the motto, popular at Washington, and peace in sixty days trembled along the wires. We now see what we could not at first comprehend. We are astonished at the strength and vigor of the foe. Treason had shot its poisonous roots deeper, and has spread them farther than our calculations had allowed for. Now I have a reason for calling attention to this unwillingness on our part to know the worst. It has already caused much trouble, and I have reason to apprehend that it will cause us much more. We need warnings a thousand times repeated. A hint to the wise is enough for the wise, and although we are wise and can take a hint, the trouble is we don't heed it unless it comes in the shape of a rifled cannon ball battering against the walls of our forts, or an iron clad ram, sinking our navy and threatening our whole Atlantic Coast. Let me under score this point of weakness and as I think blindness on our part for it still lingers with us.

Even now, you need not go far to find newspapers clinging still to the delusion that there is a strong union sentiment at the South. While the rebels are waging a barbarous war, of unparalleled ferocity, marshalling the savage Indian to the slaughter of your sons, and poisoning the wells in their retreats, we are still speaking of them as our erring brothers, to be won back to the union by fondling, rather than fighting. This has been our great error. We failed to comprehend the vital force of the rebellion. First, because we were dazzled and bewildered by the wild rapidity of the strange events, which burst upon us, and secondly because of our habitual leniency to the South and to slaveholders grimly confronting us at the outset.

I have said that the first question was how to whip the rebels. That was the bitter problem. We were sadly unprepared to fight. Treason had become the warp and woof of the army and navy. Floyd had stolen all the arms, and Cobb had stolen all the money. The nation was at the mercy of the merciless. How to procure arms, and brave men to use them, was naturally first in order. Like the rod of Moses it swallowed all others. It even hushed the voice of abolitionists and wheeled them into line with its imperative demands.

It was the great physical question. Men of muscle understood it as well as men of mind. But now there is another and a mightier question destined to try men's souls more severely than the first.

For not that which is spiritual is first, but that which is natural; after that, that which is spiritual. The physical part of this tremendous conflict is at last in a hopeful way. The great armies of the North are in motion. Baltimore is at the mercy of McHenry, Western Virginia clings to the union, Kentucky is no longer neutral, Missouri has gone to Arkansas. North Carolina is invaded, Florida has followed the fortunes of Bragg, and Tennessee is under Foote.

Brave hearts and strong hands, have met and disposed of the first question. I knew they would from the first. The slaveholding rebels have fought, and have fought well, and will do so again. They are proud, brave and desperate, but proud, brave and desperate as they are, I tell no secret when I say, they can run as well as fight.

General McClellan in his recent address to his army—takes pains to compliment these traitors. He is "sad" at the thought of striking them. The traitors themselves show no such weakness. The language of their Generals is altogether of another character. There is no epithet too vile for them, by which to characterize our army. But McClellan, is careful to tell us that the Southern army is composed of foemen worthy of our steel. I do not like this. It looks bad. Instead of being foemen worthy of our steel, they are rebels and traitors worthy of our hemp.

I do not wonder that all the haters of Impartial Liberty at the North are especially devoted to this "sad" reluctant General, who instead of portraying the baseness of the traitors takes pains to compliment them. It is seriously doubted if he will ever try his steel upon them. Thus far he has entirely failed to do any thing of the sort. But, whether McClellan ever overtakes the rebels or not, the army of the Potomac has moved, and brave men sweep both the Eastern and Western border of the rebellion. So that I look upon the first question, the question as to how to break down the military power of the rebels as in good hands and the public mind is happily relieved at that point.

But now a higher and more important problem presses for consideration. It is a problem for statesmen rather than Generals. Soldiers can capture a State, but statesmen must govern a State. It is sometimes hard to pull down a house but it is always harder to build one up.

This is the question now to be decided, having broken down the rebel power in the seceded States, how shall we extend the Constitution and the Union over them? We know how to make war, we know how to conquer, but the question is do we know how to make peace? We can whip the South, but can we make the South loyal? Baltimore is in our hands, but her parlors and drawing rooms are full of Traitors. The army is at Nashville but the people have fled. General Sherman writes loving epistles to erring rebels, but no one will carry them to the rebels, nor will the rebels touch them. The fact is the South hates the north. It hates the Union. The feeling is genuine and all-pervading. Whence comes this hate? This is an imperative inquiry for statesmen, who would place the peace of this government on an immovable foundation. You are of the same race, the same language, the same sacred historic memories. Why do they hate you? Certainly not because you have been in any manner ungenerous or unjust to them. Why do they hate you? Is it because they are naturally worse than other men? Not at all. I hold that the slaveholder is just as good as his slave system will allow him to be. If I were a slaveholder, and was determined to remain such, I would equal the worst, both in cruelty to the slave and in hatred to the north. I should hate the declaration of Independence, hate the Constitution, hate the Golden rule, hate free schools, free speech, free press, and every other form of freedom. Because in them all, I should see an enemy to my claim of property in man. I should see that the whole North is a point blank and killing condemnation of all my pretensions. The real root of bitterness, that which has generated this intense Southern hate toward the North, is Slavery. Here is the stone of stumbling and the rock of offence. Once I felt it necessary to argue this point. The time for such argument has past. Slavery stands confessed as the grand cause of the war. It has drilled every rebel soldier, loaded, primed, aimed and fired every rebel cannon since the war began. No other interest, commercial, manufacturing or political, could have wrought such a social earthquake amongst us. It has within itself that which begets a character in all around it favorable to its own continuance. It makes slaves of the negroes, vassals of the poor whites and tyrants of the masters. Pride, injustice, ingratitude, lust of dominion, cruelty, scorn, and contempt are the qualities of this rebellion, and slavery breeds them all. The tyrant wants no law above his own will, no associates but men of his own stamp of baseness. He is willing to administer the laws when he can bend them to his will, but he will break them when he can no longer bend them. Where labor is performed under the lash, justice will be administered under the bowie knife. The south is in this respect just what slavery has made her. She has been breeding thieves, rebels and traitors, and this stupendous conflict is the result. She could not do otherwise and cherish slavery in the midst of her.

Now the great question is what shall be the conditions of peace? What shall be done with slavery? We have gradually drifted to this vital question. Slavery is the pivot on which turns all the machinery of this tremendous war, and upon it will depend the character of the future of our peace or want of it.

It is really wonderful how we have been led along towards this grand issue, and how all efforts to evade, postpone, and prevent its coming, have been mocked and defied by the stupendous sweep of events.

It was oracularly given out from Washington many months ago, that whether this rebellion should succeed or fail, the status of no man in the country would be changed by the result. You know what that meant. Europe knew what that meant. It was an assurance given to the world in general, and the slaveholding states in particular, that no harm should come to slavery in the prosecution of the war for the Union. It was a last bid for a compromise with the rebels. But despite of diplomatic disclaimers, despite border State influence, despite the earlier proclamation of the President himself, the grand question of Emancipation now compels attention and the most thoughtful consideration of men in high places of the nation.

By the events of this war, Washington has become to the nation what Syracuse was to the State of New York after the rescue of Jerry, the grand centre for abolition meetings. A new Congress has assembled there.

Dr. Cheever, Ralph Waldo Emerson, Gerrit Smith, Wendell Phillips, William Goodell and William Lloyd Garrison may now utter in safety their opinions on slavery in the national capital. Meanwhile Congress has a bill before it for the abolition of slavery in the District of Columbia. Kill slavery at the heart of the nation, and it will certainly die at the extremities. Down with it there, and it is the brick knocked down at the end of the row by which the whole line is prostrate.

More and better, the infernal business of slave catching by our army in Missouri and on the Potomac, is at last peremptorily forbidden under penalty of dismissal from the service. This looks small, but is not so. It is a giant stride toward the grand result.

I thank all the powers of earth and sky, that I am permitted to be a witness to this day's events. That slavery could always live and flourish in this country I have always known to be a foul and guilty heresy. That the vile system must eventually go down I have never doubted, even in the darkest days of my life in slavery. But that I should live to see the President of the United States deliberately advocating Emancipation was more than I ever ventured to hope.

It is true that the President lays down his propositions with many qualifications some of which to my thinking, are unnecessary, unjust and wholly unwise. There are spots on the Sun. A blind man can see where the President's heart is. I read the spaces as well as the lines of that message, I see in them a brave man trying against great odds, to do right. An honest patriot endeavoring to save his country in its day of peril. It is the first utterance, and first utterances are not according to Carlyle the most articulate and perfect. Time and practice will improve the President as they improve other men. He is tall and strong but he is not done growing, he grows as the nation grows. He has managed to say one good word, and to say it so distinctly that all the world may hear. He has dared to say that the highest interest of the country will be promoted by the abolition of slavery. And this, bear in mind, is not said in the bitterness of defeat, but when every morning brought news of glorious victories over the slaveholding rebels. The message comes at the call of no desperation. The time selected for sending it to Congress and the nation must be read with the document itself in order to appreciate its true significance.

Right upon the heels of the message comes the appointment of John C. Frémont, a man whose name thrills the young heart of America with every sentiment of honor, patriotism, and bravery. John C. Frémont carries his department in his name. He goes to free the mountains of rebels and traitors and the good wishes of all but traitors will go with him. Here is a new chapter of the war:

Frémont's proclamation, was revised and modified by the President; Frémont was removed from his post when in the act of striking the foe. Calumny did its worst upon Frémont. But he was brave and calm, with Jessie by his side he could not well be otherwise, and though strong himself without that pride of American women to support him, he must have fallen. I saw them as they passed eastward, after the chief had fallen. One glance at the young General and his noble wife told me that Frémont would rise again. He has risen. The rebels will hear it. His war horse is already pawing on all their mountains! But what shall be the conditions of peace? How shall the Union be reconstructed? To my mind complete Emancipation is the only basis of permanent peace. Any other basis will place us just at the point from which we started. To leave slavery standing in the rebel States, is to leave the eggs of treason in the nest from whence we shall have to meet a larger brood of traitors, and rebels at another time; it is to transmit to posterity the question that ought to be settled to-day. Leave slavery where it is, and you leave the same generator of hate towards the north which has already cost us rivers of blood and millions of treasure. Leave slavery in the south and it will be as dangerous for a Northern man to travel in the south, as for a man to enter a powder magazine with fire. Despots are suspicious, and every slaveholder is an unmitigated despot, a natural foe to every form of freedom. Leave slavery in the south, and you will fill the north with a full fledged breed of servile panderers to slavery, baser than all their predecessors.

Leave slavery where it is and you will hereafter, as heretofore, see in politics a divided, fettered, north, and an united south. You will see the statesmen of the country facing both ways, speaking two languages, assenting to the principles of freedom in the north, and bowing to the malign spirit and practices of slavery at the South. You will see all the pro-slavery elements of the country attracted to the south, giving that section ascendancy again in the counsels of the nation and making them masters of the destinies of the Republic. Restore slavery to its old status in the Union and the same elements of demoralization which have plunged this country into this tremendous war will begin again to dig the grave of free Institutions.

It is the boast of the South that her Institutions are peculiar and homogeneous, and so they are. Her statesmen have had the wit to see that contact with the free North must either make the North like herself, or that she herself must become like the North. They are right. The South must put off the yoke of slavery or the North must prepare her neck for that yoke, provided the union is restored. There is a middle path—We have pursued that middle path. It is *compromise* and by it we have reached the point of civil war with all its horrid consequences. The question is shall we start anew in the same old path?

Who wants a repetition of the same event thro' which we are passing? Who wants to see the nation taxed to keep a standing army in the South to maintain respect for the Federal Government and protect the rights of citizens of the United States? To such a man I say, leave slavery still dominant at the South and you shall have all your wants supplied.

On the other hand abolish slavery and the now disjointed nation like kindred drops would speedily mingle into one. Abolish slavery and the last hinderance to a solid nationality is abolished. Abolish slavery and you give conscience a chance to grow, and you will win the respect and admiration of mankind. Abolish slavery and you put an end to all sectional politics founded upon conflicting sectional interests, and imparting strife and bitterness to all our general elections, and to the debates on the floor of Congress. Abolish slavery and the citizens of each state will be regarded and treated as equal citizens of the United States, and may travel unchallenged and unmolested in all the states of the Union. Abolish slavery and you put an end to sectional religion and morals, and establish free speech and liberty of conscience throughout your common country. Abolish slavery and rational, law abiding Liberty will fill the whole land with peace, joy, and permanent safety now and forever.

Douglass' Monthly, April, 1862

[In early 1862,] Congress was debating a bill calling for the abolition of slavery in the District of Columbia, with compensation to slaveholders. The measure encountered bitter opposition from slaveholders and their sympathizers. "Senators," cried Senator Saulsbury of Delaware, "abandon now, at once and forever, your schemes of wild philanthropy and universal emancipation; proclaim to the people of this whole country everywhere that you mean to preserve the Union as established by the fathers of the Republic, and the rights of the people as secured by the Constitution they helped to frame, and your Union can never be destroyed; but go on with your wild schemes of emancipation, throw doubt and suspicion upon every man simply because he fails to look at your questions of wild philanthropy as you do, and the God of heaven only knows, after wading through scenes before which those of the French revolution 'pale their ineffectual fires,' what ultimately may be the result."[1]

But popular pressure for abolition of slavery in the nation's capital was too strong to be diverted by predictions of a reign of terror. On March 30, 1862, Senator Sumner, who with Henry Wilson, the junior Senator from Massachusetts, was most active in pushing the measure, delivered a notable address urging its speedy adoption. "It is the first instalment," he declared, "of the great debt which we will owe to an enslaved race, and will be recognized as one of the victories of humanity." The effect, he predicted, would soon be felt throughout the South. "What God and nature decree, rebellion cannot arrest," he concluded.[2]

Douglass hastened to send [this] letter of thanks to Sumner for his magnificent address. . . .

On April 3, 1862, the bill passed the Senate. Eight days later it received final approval in the House. On the sixteenth day of April, the President signed the bill outlawing slavery in the nation's capital.

For the first time since the outbreak of the war, Douglass' joy was unbounded. The measure, he informed his readers, was "the first great step towards that righteousness which exalts a nation." He called for hosannahs: "Let high swelling anthems (such as tuned the voice and thrilled the heart of ancient Israel, when they shouted to heaven the glad tidings of their deliverance from Egyptian bondage) now roll along the earth and sky. . . ."[3] [III:21–22]

TO HON. CHARLES SUMNER

Rochester, April 8th, 1862.

My Dear Sir:

I want only a moment of your time to give you my thanks for your speech in the Senate on the Bill for the abolition of Slavery in the District of Columbia. I trust I am not dreaming but the events taking place seem like a dream. If Slavery is really dead in the District of Columbia, and merely waiting for the ceremony of "Dust to dust," by the president, to you, more than to any other American statesman, belongs the honor of this great triumph of Justice, Liberty and Sound Policy. I rejoice for my freed brothers, and Sir, I rejoice for you. You have lived to strike down in Washington, the power which lifted the bludgeon against your own free voice. I take nothing from the good and brave men who have cooperated with you. There is, or ought to be, a head to every body, and whether you will or not, the Slaveholder and the Slave look to you as the best embodiment of the Anti-Slavery idea now in the counsels of the Nation. May God sustain you. This is my prayer for you and all the good men who surround you. I am Dear Sir, Truly and gratefully yours,

Frederick Douglass

Charles Sumner Papers, Harvard University

1. Henry Wilson, *History of the Rise and Fall of the Slave Power in America,* Boston and New York, 1877, vol. III, p. 276.
2. Ibid., p. 274.
3. *Douglass' Monthly,* May, 1862.

When on May 9, 1862, General David Hunter, commanding the Department of the South, issued an order proclaiming: "Slavery and martial law in a free country being altogether incompatible, the slaves in Georgia, Florida, and South Carolina are therefore declared free," Lincoln hesitated once more. He learned of Hunter's order through the newspapers a week after the proclamation. Secretary Chase urged him to let the order stand. "No commanding general shall do such a thing upon my responsibility without consulting me," the President replied. On May 19, even before receiving official notice, he issued a message declaring Hunter's order unauthorized and null and void.[1]

In a bitter mood Douglass assailed the administration at a Fourth of July meeting at Himrods Corner, New York. Bluntly and fearlessly he told the audience of two thousand that the President, the Cabinet and "our rebel worshipping Generals in the field" were guilty of treason. . . . Douglass picked up the theme he had been stressing since the first day of the war. Rebellion and slavery were "twin monsters," and "all attempts at upholding one while pulling down the other" would end in disaster for the nation. . . . He was certain that if only it had the will, the government could speedily abolish slavery. All that was necessary was a proclamation by the President announcing the freedom of the slaves. . . .

Unknown to Douglass, Lincoln was being forced to the same conclusion. The forces that Douglass had predicted would compel the government to pursue a revolutionary course of action were now in full operation. Lincoln was beginning to realize the impossibility of his own program. His pleas to the slave-owners to accept compensated emancipation had fallen on deaf ears. The slaveholders continued to use the labor of their slaves to wage their war, while the Union government continued to deprive itself of the valuable services of the slaves, the natural enemies of the slaveholders. Also, the failure of the Lincoln administration to make the war clearly one for the abolition of slavery was aiding the Confederate agents in Europe who were confusing the common people as to the nature of the war. Only when the war became clearly defined as an issue of slavery—for and against—would the danger of European recognition of the Confederacy end. [III:22–23]

THE SLAVEHOLDERS' REBELLION. A speech delivered on the 4th day of July, 1862, at Himrods Corners, Yates Co., N.Y.

Fellow Citizens:

Eighty-six years ago the fourth of July was consecrated and distinguished among all the days of the year as the birthday of American liberty and Independence. The fathers of the Republic recommended that this day be celebrated with joy and gladness by the whole American people, to their latest posterity. Probably not one of those fathers ever dreamed that this hallowed day could possibly be made to witness the strange and portentous Events now transpiring before our eyes, and which even now cast a cloud of more than midnight blackness over the face of the whole country. We are the observers of strange and fearful transactions.

Never was this national anniversary celebrated in circumstances more trying, more momentous, more solemn and perilous, than those by which this nation is now so strongly environed. We present to the world at this moment, the painful spectacle of a great nation, undergoing all the bitter pangs of a gigantic and bloody revolution. We are torn and rent asunder, we are desolated by large and powerful armies of our own kith and kin, converted into desperate and infuriated rebels and traitors, more savage, more fierce and brutal in their modes of warfare, than any recognized barbarians making no pretentions to civilization.

In the presence of this troubled and terrible state of the country, in the appalling jar and rumbling of this social Earthquake, when sorrow and sighing are heard throughout our widely extended borders, when the wise and brave men of the land are everywhere deeply and sadly contemplating this solemn crisis as one which may permanently decide the fate of the nation, I should greatly transgress the law of fitness, and violate my own feelings and yours, if I should on this occasion attempt to entertain you by delivering anything of the usual type of our 4th of July orations.

The hour is one for sobriety, thoughtfulness and stern truthfulness. When the house is on fire, when destruction is spreading its baleful wings everywhere, when helpless women and children are to be rescued from devouring flames, a true man can neither have ear nor heart for anything but the thrilling and heart-rending cry for help. Our country is now on fire. No man can now tell what the future will bring forth. The question now is whether this great Republic before it has reached a century from its birth, is to fall in the wake of unhappy Mexico, and become the constant theatre of civil war, or whether it shall become like old Spain, the mother of Mexico, and by folly and cruelty part with its renown among the nations of the earth, and spend the next seventy years in vainly attempting to regain what it has lost in the space of this one slaveholding rebellion.

Looking thus at the state of the country, I know of no better use to which I can put this sacred day, I know of no higher duty resting upon me, than to enforce my views and convictions, and especially to hold out to reprobation, the short sighted and ill judged, and inefficient modes adopted to suppress the rebels. The past may be dismissed with a single word. The claims of our fathers upon our memory, admiration and gratitude, are founded in the fact that they wisely, and bravely, and successfully met the crisis of their day. And if the men of this generation would deserve well of posterity they must like their fathers, discharge the duties and responsibilities of their age.

Men have strange notions nowadays as to the manner of showing their respect for the heroes of the past. They every where prefer the form to the substance, the seeming to the real.—One of our Generals, and some of our editors, seem to think that the fathers are honored by guarding a well, from which those fathers may have taken water, or the house in which they may have passed a single night, while our sick soldiers need pure water, and are dying in the open fields for water and shelter. This is not honoring, but dishonoring your noble dead. Nevertheless, I would not even in words do violence to the grand events, and thrilling associations, that gloriously cluster around the birth of our national independence. There is no need of any such violence. The thought of to-day and the work of to-day, are alike linked, and interlinked with the thought and work of the past. The conflict between liberty and slavery, between civilization and barbarism, between enlightened progress, and stolid indifference and inactivity is the same in all countries, in all ages, and among all peoples. Your fathers drew the sword for free and independent Government, Republican in its form, Democratic in its spirit; to be administered by officers duly elected by the free and unbought suffrages of the people, and the war of to-day on the part of the loyal north, the east and the west, is waged for the same grand and all commanding objects. We are only continuing the tremendous struggle, which your fathers and my fathers began eighty-six years ago. Thus identifying the present with the past, I propose to consider the great present question, uppermost and all absorbing in all minds and hearts throughout the land.

I shall speak to you of the origin, the nature, the objects of this war, the manner of conducting, and its possible and probable results.

ORIGIN OF THE WAR

It is hardly necessary at this very late day of this war, and in view of all the discussion through the press and on the platform which has transpired concerning it, to enter now upon any elaborate enquiry or explanation as to whence came this foul and guilty attempt to break up and destroy the national Government. All but the willfully blind or the malignantly traitorous, know and confess that this whole movement which now so largely distracts the country, and threatens ruin to the nation, has its root and its sap, its trunk and its branches, and the bloody fruit it bears only from the one source of all abounding abomination, and that is slavery. It has sprung out of a malign selfishness and a haughty and imperious pride which only the practice of the most hateful oppression and cruelty could generate and develop. No ordinary love of gain, no ordinary love of power, could have stirred up this terrible revolt.—The legitimate objects of property, such as houses, land, fruits of the earth, the products of art, science and invention, powerful as they are, could never have stirred and kindled this malignant flame, and set on fire this rebellious fury. The monster was brought to its birth by pride, lust and cruelty which could not brook the sober restraints of law, order and justice. The monster publishes its own parentage. Grim and hideous as this rebellion is, its shocking practices, digging up the bones of our dead soldiers slain in battle, making drinking vessels out of their skulls, drumsticks out of their arm bones, slaying our wounded soldiers on the field of carnage, when their gaping wounds appealed piteously for mercy, poisoning wells, firing upon unarmed men, stamp it with all the horrid characteristics of the bloody and barbarous system and society from which it derived its life.

Of course you know, and I know that there have been and still are, in certain out of the way places here at the north, where rebels, in the smooth disguise of loyal men, do meet and promulgate a very opposite explanation of the origin of this war, and that grave attempts have been made to refute their absurd theories. I once heard Hon. Edward Everett entertain a large audience by a lengthy and altogether unnecessary argument to prove that the south did not revolt on account of the fishing bounty paid to northern fishermen, nor because of any inequalities or discrimination in the revenue laws. It was the Irishman's gun aimed at nothing and hitting it every time. Yet the audience seemed pleased with the learning and skill of the orator, and I among the number, though I hope to avoid his bad example in the use of time.

There is however one false theory of the origin of the war to which a moment's reply may be properly given here. It is this. The abolitionists by their insane and unconstitutional attempt to abolish slavery have brought on the war. All that class of men who opposed what they were pleased to call coercion at the first, and a vigorous prosecution of the war at the present, charge the war directly to the abolitionists. In answer to this charge, I lay down this rule as a basis to which all candid men will assent. Whatever is said or done by any class of citizens, strictly in accordance with rights guaranteed by the Constitution, cannot be fairly charged as against the Union, or as inciting to a dissolution of the Union.

Now the slaveholders came into the Union with their eyes wide open, subject to a Constitution wherein the right to be abolitionists was sacredly guaranteed to all the people. They knew that slavery was to take its chance with all other evils against the power of free speech and national enlightenment. They came on board the national ship subject to these conditions, they signed the articles after having duly read them, and the fact that those rights, plainly written, have been exercised is no apology whatever for the slaveholder's mutiny and their attempt to lay piratical hands on the ship and its officers. When therefore I hear a man denouncing abolitionists on account of the war, I know that I am listening to a man who either does not know what he is talking about, or to one who is a traitor in disguise.

THE NATURE OF THE REBELLION

There is something quite distinct and quite individual in the nature and character of this rebellion. In its motives and objects it stands entirely alone, in the annals of great social disturbances. Rebellion is no new thing under the sun. The best governments in the world are liable to these terrible social disorders. All countries have experienced them. Generally however, rebellions are quite respectable in the eyes of the world, and very properly so. They naturally command the sympathy of mankind, for generally they are on the side of progress. They would overthrow and remove some old and festering abuse not to be otherwise disposed of, and introduce a higher civilization, and a larger measure of liberty among men. But this rebellion is in no wise analogous to such.—The pronounced and damning peculiarity of the present rebellion, is found in the fact, that it was conceived, undertaken, planned, and persevered in, for the guilty purpose of handing down to the latest generations the accursed system of human bondage. Its leaders have plainly told us by words as well as by deeds, that they are fighting for slavery. They have been stirred to this perfidious revolt, by a certain deep and deadly hate, which they warmly cherish toward every possible contradiction of slavery whether found in theory or in practice. For this cause they hate free society, free schools, free states, free speech,[2] the freedom asserted in the Declaration of Independence, and guaranteed in the Constitution.—Herein is the whole secret of the rebellion.—The plan is and was to withdraw the slave system from the hated light of liberty, and from the natural operations of free principles. While the slaveholders could hold the reins of government they could and did pervert the free principles of the Constitution to slavery, and could afford to continue in the union, but when they saw that they could no longer control the union as they had done for sixty years before, they appealed to the sword and struck for a government which should forever shut out all light from the southern conscience, and all hope of Emancipation from the southern slave. This rebellion therefore, has no point of comparison with that which has brought liberty to America, or with those of Europe, which have been undertaken from time to time, to throw off the galling yoke of despotism. It stands alone in its infamy.

Our slaveholding rebels with an impudence only belonging to themselves, have sometimes compared themselves to Washington, Jefferson, and the long list of worthies who led in the revolution of 1776, when in fact they would hang either of these men if they were now living, as traitors to slavery, because they each and all considered the system an evil.

THE CONFLICT UNAVOIDABLE

I hold that this conflict is the logical and inevitable result of a long and persistent course of national transgression. Once in a while you will meet with men who will tell you that this war ought to have been avoided. In telling you this, they only make the truth serve the place and perform the office of a lie. I too say that this war ought never to have taken place. The combustible material which has produced this terrible explosion ought long ago to have been destroyed.—For thirty years the abolitionists have earnestly sought to remove this guilty cause of our troubles. There was a time when this might have been done, and the nation set in permanent safety. Opportunities have not been wanting. They have passed by unimproved. They have sometimes been of a character to suggest the very work which might have saved us from all the dreadful calamities, the horrors and bloodshed, of this war. Events, powerful operators, have eloquently pleaded with the American people to put away the hateful slave system. For doing this great work we have had opportunities innumerable. One of these was presented upon the close of the war for Independence, the moral sentiment of the country was purified by that great struggle for national life. At that time slavery was young and small, the nation might have easily abolished it, and thus relieved itself forever of this alien element, the only disturbing and destructive force in our republican system of Government. Again there was another opportunity for putting away this evil in 1789, when we assembled to form the Constitution of the United States. At that time the anti-slavery sentiment was strong both in church and state, and many believed that by giving slavery no positive recognition in the Constitution and providing for the abolition of the slave trade, they had given slavery its death blow already. They made the great mistake of supposing that the existence of the slave trade was necessary to the existence of slavery, and having provided that the slave trade should cease, they flattered themselves that slavery itself must also speedily cease. They did not comprehend the radical character of the evil. Then again in 1819 the Missouri question gave us another opportunity to seal the doom of the slave system, by simply adhering to the early policy of the fathers and sternly refusing the admission of another State into the Union with a Constitution tolerating slavery.[3] Had this been done in the case of Missouri, we should not now be cursed with this terrible rebellion. Slavery would have fallen into gradual decay. The moral sentiment of the country, instead of being vitiated as it is, would have been healthy and strong against the slave system. Political parties and politicians would not, as they have done since, courted the slave power for votes and thus increased the importance of slavery.

THE FIRST PALPABLE DEPARTURE FROM RIGHT POLICY

The date of the Missouri Compromise forms the beginning of that political current which has swept us on to this rebellion, and made the conflict unavoidable. From this dark date in our nation's history, there started forth a new political and social power. Until now slavery had been on its knees, only asking time to die in peace. But the Missouri Compromise gave it a new lease of life. It became at once a tremendous power. The line of thirty-six degrees, thirty minutes, at once stamped itself upon our national politics, our morals, manners, character and religion.—From this time there was a south side to everything American, and the country was at once subjected to the slave power, a power as restless and vigilant as the eye of an escaping murderer. We became under its sway an illogical nation. Pure and simple truth lost its attraction for us. We became a nation of Compromisers.

It is curious to remark the similarity of national to individual demoralization. A man sets out in life with honest principles and with high purposes inspired at the family hearthstone, and for a time steadily and scrupulously keeps them in view. But at last under the influence of some powerful temptation he is induced to violate his principles and push aside his sense of right. The water for the first moment is smooth about him, but soon he finds himself in the rapids. He has lost his footing. The broad flood, resistless as the power of fate, sweeps him onward, from bad to worse, he becomes more hardened, blind and shameless in his crimes till he is overtaken by dire calamity, and at last sinks to ruin. Precisely this has been the case with the American people. No people ever entered upon the pathway of nations, with higher and grander ideas of justice, liberty and humanity than ourselves. There are principles in the Declaration of Independence which would release every slave in the world and prepare the earth for a millenium of righteousness and peace.—But alas! we have seen that declaration intended to be viewed like some colossal statue at the loftiest altitude, by the broad eye of the whole world, meanly subjected to a microscopic examination and its glorious universal truths craftily perverted into seeming falsehoods. Instead of treating it, as it was intended to be treated, as a full and comprehensive declaration of the equal and sacred rights of mankind, our contemptible Negro-hating and slaveholding critics have endeavored to turn it into absurdity by treating it as a declaration of the equality of man in his physical proportions and mental endowments. This gross and scandalous perversion of the true intents and meaning of the declaration did not long stand alone. It was soon followed by the heartless dogma, that the rights declared in that instrument did not apply to any but white men. The slave power at last succeeded, in getting this doctrine proclaimed from the bench of the Supreme Court of the United States. It was there decided that "all men" only means some men, and those white men. And all this in face of the fact, that white people only form one fifth of the whole human family—and that some who pass for white are nearly as black as your humble speaker. While all this was going on, lawyers, priests and politicians were at work upon national prejudice against the colored man.—They raised the cry and put it into the mouth of the ignorant, and vulgar and narrow minded, that "this is the white man's country," and other cries which readily catch the ear of the crowd. This popular method of dealing with an oppressed people has, while crushing the blacks, corrupted and demoralized the whites. It has cheered on the slave power, increased its pride and pretension, till ripe for the foulest treason against the life of the nation. Slavery, that was before the Missouri Compromise couchant, on its knees, asking meekly to be let alone within its own limits to die, became in a few years after rampant, throttling free speech, fighting friendly Indians, annexing Texas, warring with Mexico, kindling with malicious hand the fires of war and bloodshed on the virgin soil of Kansas, and finally threatening to pull down the pillars of the Republic, if you Northern men should dare vote in accordance with your constitutional and political convictions. You know the history; I will not dwell upon it. What I have said, will suffice to indicate the point at which began the downward career of the Republic. It will be seen that it began by bartering away an eternal principle of right for present peace. We undertook to make slavery the full equal of Liberty, and to place it on the same footing of political right with Liberty. It was by permitting the dishonor of the Declaration of Independence, denying the rights of human nature to the man of color, and by yielding to the extravagant pretensions set up by the slaveholder under the plausible color of State rights. In a word it was by reversing the wise and early policy of the nation, which was to confine slavery to its original limits, and thus leave the system to die out under the gradual oper-

ation of the principles of the Constitution and the spirit of the age. Ten years had
not elapsed, after this compromise, when the demon disunion lifted its ugly front,
in the shape of nullification. The plotters of this treason undertook the work of
disunion at that time as an experiment. They took the tariff as the basis of action.
The tariff was selected, not that it was the real object,[4] but on the wisdom of the
barber, who trains his green hands on wooden heads before allowing them to handle the razor on the faces of living men.

You know the rest. The experiment did not succeed. Those who attempted it
were thirty years before their time. There was no Buchanan in the Presidential
chair, and no Cobbs and Floyds in the Cabinet. Calhoun and his treasonable associates were promptly assured, on the highest authority, that their exit out of
the Union was possible only by one way and that by way of the Gallows.—They
were defeated, but not permanently.—They dropped the tariff and openly
adopted slavery as the ostensible, as well as the real ground of disunion. After
thirty years of persistent preparatory effort, they have been able under the fostering care of a traitorous Democratic President, to inaugurate at last this enormous rebellion. I will not stop here to pour out loyal indignation on that arch
traitor, who while he could find power in the Constitution to hunt down innocent men all over the North for violating the thrice accursed fugitive slave Bill,
could find no power in the Constitution to punish slaveholding traitors and
rebels, bent upon the destruction of the Government. That bad old man is already receiving a taste of the punishment due to his crimes. To live amid all the
horrors resulting from his treachery is of itself a terrible punishment. He lives
without his country's respect. He lives a despised old man. He is no doubt still a
traitor, but a traitor without power, a serpent without fangs, and in the agony
of his torture and helplessness will probably welcome the moment which shall
remove him from the fiery vision of a betrayed and half ruined country.

THE CONDUCT OF THE WAR

To-day we have to deal not with dead traitors, such as James Buchanan, How-
ell Cobb, Floyd, Thompson and others, but with a class of men incomparably
more dangerous to the country. They are our weak, paltering and incompetent
rulers in the Cabinet at Washington and our rebel worshipping Generals in the
field, the men who sacrifice the brave loyal soldiers of the North by thousands,
while refusing to employ the black man's arm in suppressing the rebels, for fear
of exasperating these rebels: men who never interfere with the orders of Generals, unless those orders strike at slavery, the heart of the Rebellion. These are the
men to whom we have a duty to discharge to-day, when the country is bleeding
at every pore, and when disasters thick and terrible convert this national festal
day, into a day of alarm and mourning. I do not underrate the power of the
rebels, nor the vastness of the work required for suppressing them. Jefferson
Davis is a powerful man, but Jefferson Davis has no such power to blast the hope
and break down the strong heart of this nation, as that possessed and exercised
by Abraham Lincoln. With twenty millions of men behind him, with wealth and
resources at his Command such as might pride the heart of the mightiest

monarch of Europe, and with a cause which kindles in every true heart the fires of valor and patriotism, we have a right to hold Abraham Lincoln sternly responsible for any disaster or failure attending the suppression of this rebellion. I hold that the rebels can do us no serious harm, unless it is done through the culpable weakness, imbecility or unfaithfulness of those who are charged with the high duty of seeing that the Supreme Law of the land is everywhere enforced and obeyed. Common sense will confess that five millions ought not to be a match for twenty millions. I know of nothing in the mettle of the slaveholder which should make him superior in any of the elements of a warrior to an honest Northern man. One slaveholder ought not longer to be allowed to maintain the boast that he is equal to three Northern men; and yet that boast will not be entirely empty, if we allow those five millions much longer to thwart all our efforts to put them down. It will be most mortifyingly shown that after all our appliances, our inventive genius, our superior mechanical skill, our great industry, our muscular energy, our fertility in strategy, our vast powers of endurance, our overwhelming numbers, and admitted bravery, that the eight or ten rebel slave States, sparsely populated, and shut out from the world by our possession of the sea, are invincible to the arms of the densely populated and every way powerful twenty free States. I repeat, these rebels can do nothing against us, cannot harm a single hair of the national head, if the men at Washington, the President and Cabinet, and the commanding Generals in the field will but earnestly do their most obvious duty.—I repeat Jeff. Davis and his malignant slaveholding Republic, can do this union no harm except by the permission of the reigning powers at Washington.

I am quite aware that some who hear me will question the wisdom of any criticisms upon the conduct of this war at this time and will censure me for making them. I do not dread those censures. I have on many occasions, since the war began, held my breath when even the stones of the street would seem to cry out. I can do so no longer. I believe in the absence of martial law, a citizen may properly express an opinion as to the manner in which our Government has conducted, and is still conducting this war. I hold that it becomes this country, the men who have to shed their blood and pour out their wealth to sustain the Government at this crisis, to look very sharply into the movements of the men who have our destiny in their hands.

Theoretically this is a responsible Government. Practically it can be made the very reverse. Experience demonstrates that our safety as a nation depends upon holding every officer of the nation strictly responsible to the people for the faithful performance of duty. This war has developed among other bad tendencies, a tendency to shut our eyes to the mistakes and blunders of those in power. When the President has avowed a policy, sanctioned a measure, or commended a general, we have been told that his action must be treated as final. I scout this assumption. A doctrine more slavish and abject than this does not obtain under the walls of St. Peter. Even in the Rebel States, the Confederate Government is sharply critical, and Jefferson Davis is held to a rigid responsibility.—There is no reason of right or of sound policy for a different course towards the Federal Government. Our rulers are the agents of the people. They are fallible men. They need instruction from the people, and it is no evidence of a factious disposition that any man presumes to condemn a public measure if in his judgment that measure is opposed to the public good.

This is already an old war. The statesmanship at Washington with all its admitted wisdom and sagacity, utterly failed for a long time to comprehend the nature and extent of this rebellion. Mr. Lincoln and his Cabinet will have by and by to confess with many bitter regrets, that they have been equally blind and mistaken as to the true method of dealing with the rebels.—They have fought the rebels with the Olive branch. The people must teach them to fight them with the sword. They have sought to conciliate obedience. The people must teach them to compel obedience.

There are many men connected with the stupendous work of suppressing this slaveholding rebellion, and it is the right of the American people to keep a friendly and vigilant eye upon them all, but there are three men in the nation, from whose conduct the attention of the people should never be withdrawn: The first is President Lincoln, the Commander-in-chief of the army and navy. The single word of this man can set a million of armed men in motion: He can make and unmake generals, can lift up or cast down at will. The other two men are McClellan and Halleck. Between these two men nearly a half a million of your brave and loyal sons are divided, the one on the Potomac and the other on the Mississippi. They are the two extended arms of the nation, stretched out to save the Union.

Are those two men loyal? are they in earnest? are they competent? We have a right, and it is our duty to make these inquiries, and report and act in reference to them according to the truth.

Whatever may be said of the loyalty or competency of McClellan, I am fully persuaded by his whole course that he is not in earnest against the rebels, that he is to-day, as heretofore, in war as in peace a real pro-slavery Democrat. His whole course proves that his sympathies are with the rebels, and that his ideas of the crisis make him unfit for the place he holds. He kept the army of the Potomac standing still on that river, marching and countermarching, giving show parades during six months. He checked and prevented every movement which was during that time proposed against the rebels East and West.

Bear in mind the fact that this is a slave-holding rebellion, bear in mind that slavery is the very soul and life of all the vigor which the rebels have thus far been able to throw into their daring attempt to overthrow and ruin this country. Bear in mind that in time of war, it is the right and duty of each belligerent to adopt that course which will strengthen himself and weaken his enemy.

Bear in mind also that nothing could more directly and powerfully tend to break down the rebels, and put an end to the struggle than the Insurrection or the running away of a large body of their slaves, and then, read General McClellan's proclamation, declaring that any attempt at a rising of the slaves against their rebel masters would be put down, and put down with an iron hand.[5] Let it be observed too, that it has required the intervention of Congress, by repeated resolutions to prevent this General from converting the army of the Potomac from acting as the slave dogs of the rebels, and that even now while our army are compelled to drink water from the muddy swamps, and from the Pamunky river, forbidden by George B. McClellan to take pure water from the Rebel General Lee's well. Let it be understood that Northern loyal soldiers have been compelled by the orders of this same General, to keep guard over the property of a leading rebel, because of a previous understanding between the loyal, and the traitor General. Bear in mind the fact that this General has in deference to the slave-holding rebels forbidden the singing of anti-slavery songs in his camp, and you will learn that this General's ideas of the demands of the hour are most miserably below the mark, and unfit him for the place he fills. Take another fact into account, General McClellan is at this moment the favorite General of the Richardsons, the Ben Woods, the Vallandighams, and the whole school of pro-slavery Buchanan politicians of the North, and that he is reported in the Richmond Dispatch to have said that he hated to war upon Virginia, and that he would far rather war against Massachusetts. This statement of the Richmond Dispatch in itself is not worth much, but if we find as I think we do find, in General McClellan's every movement an apparent reluctance to strike at Virginia rebels, we may well fear that his words have been no better than his deeds. Again, take the battles fought by him and under his order, and in every instance the rebels have been able to claim a victory, and to show as many prisoners and spoils taken as we. At Ball's Bluff, McClellan's first battle of the Potomac, it is now settled, that our troops were marched up only to be slaughtered. Nine hundred and thirty of our brave northern soldiers were deliberately murdered, as much so as if they had each been stabbed, bayonnetted, shot, or otherwise killed when asleep by some midnight assassin, for they were so ordered and handled, that they were perfectly harmless to their deadly foes, and helpless in their own defense. Then the battle of Seven Pines, where General Casey's Division was pushed out like an extended finger four miles beyond the lines of our army, towards the rebels, as if for no other purpose than to be cut to pieces or captured by the rebels, and then the haste with which this same Division was censured by Gen. McClellan, are facts looking all the same way. This is only one class of facts. They are not the only facts, nor the chief ones that shake my faith in the General of the Army of the Potomac.

Unquestionably time is the mightiest ally that the rebels can rely on. Every month they can hold out against the Government gives them power at home, and prestige abroad, and increases the probabilities of final success.—Time favors foreign intervention, time favors heavy taxation upon the loyal people, time favors reaction, and a clamor for peace. Time favors fevers, and pestilence, wasting and destroying our army. Therefore *time, time* is the great ally of the rebels.

Now I undertake to say that General McClellan has from the beginning so handled the army of the Potomac as to give the rebels the grand advantage of time. From the time he took command of the Potomac army in August 1861 until now, he has been the constant cause of delay, and probably would not have moved when he did, but that he was compelled to move or be removed. Then behold his movement. He moved upon Manassas when the enemy had been gone from there seven long days. When he gets there he is within sixty miles of Richmond. Does he go on? Oh! no, but he just says hush, to the press and the people, I am going to do something transcendentally brilliant in strategy. Three weeks pass away, and knowing ones wink and smile as much as to say you will see something wonderful soon. And so indeed we do, at the end of three weeks we find that General McClellan has actually marched back from Manassas to the Potomac, gotten together an endless number of vessels at a cost of untold millions, to transport his troops to Yorktown, where he is just as near to Richmond and not a bit nearer than he was just three weeks before, and where he is opposed by an army every way as strongly posted as any he could have met with by marching straight to Richmond from Manassas. Here we have two hundred and thirty thousand men moved to attack empty fortifications, and moved back again.

Now what is the state of facts concerning the nearly four months of campaign between the James and the York Rivers? The first is that Richmond is not taken, and in all the battles yet fought, the rebels have claimed them as victories, we have lost between thirty and forty thousand men, and the general impression is that there is an equal chance that our army will be again repulsed before Richmond and driven away.

You may not go the length that I do, in regard to Gen. McClellan, at this time, but I feel quite sure that this country will yet come to the conclusion that Geo. B. McClellan is either a cold blooded Traitor, or that he is an unmitigated military Impostor. He has shown no heart in his conduct, except when doing something directly in favor of the rebels, such as guarding their persons and property and offering his services to suppress with an iron hand any attempt on the part of the slaves against their rebel masters.

THE POLICY OF THE ADMINISTRATION

I come now to the policy of President Lincoln in reference to slavery. An administration without a policy is confessedly an administration without brains, since while a thing is to be done, it implies a known way to do it and he who professes his ability to do it, but cannot show how it is to be done, confesses his own imbecility. I do not undertake to say that the present administration has no policy, but if it has, the people have a right to know what it is, and to approve or disapprove of it as they shall deem it wise or unwise.

Now the policy of an administration can be learned in two ways. The first by what it says, and the second by what it does, and the last is far more certain and reliable than the first. It is by what President Lincoln has done in reference to slavery, since he assumed the reins of government, that we are to know what he is likely to do, and deems best to do in the premises. We all know how he came into power. He was elected and inaugurated as the representative of the anti-slavery policy of the Republican party. He had laid down and maintained the doctrine that Liberty and Slavery were the great antagonistic political elements in this country. That Union of these States could not long continue half free and half slave, that they must in the end be all free or all slave.

In the conflict between these two elements he arrayed himself on the side of freedom, and was elected with a view to the ascendancy of free principles. Now what has been the tendency of his acts since he became Commander in chief of the army and navy? I do not hesitate to say, that whatever may have been his intentions, the action of President Lincoln has been calculated in a marked and decided way to shield and protect slavery from the very blows which its horrible crimes have loudly and persistently invited. He has scornfully rejected the policy of arming the slaves, a policy naturally suggested and enforced by the nature and necessities of the war. He has steadily refused to proclaim, as he had the constitutional and moral right to proclaim, complete emancipation to all the slaves of rebels who should make their way into the lines of our army. He has repeatedly interfered with and arrested the anti-slavery policy of some of his most earnest and reliable generals. He has assigned to the most important positions, generals who are notoriously pro-slavery, and hostile to the party and principles which raised him to power.—He has permitted rebels to recapture their runaway slaves in sight of the capital. He has allowed General Halleck to openly violate the spirit of a solemn resolution by Congress forbidding the army of the United States to return the fugitive slaves to their cruel masters,[6] and has evidently from the first submitted himself to the guidance of the half loyal slave States, rather than to the wise and loyal suggestions of those States upon which must fall, and have fallen, the chief expense and danger involved in the prosecution of the war. It is from such action as this, that we must infer the policy of the Administration. To my mind that policy is simply and solely to reconstruct the union on the old and corrupting basis of compromise, by which slavery shall retain all the power that it ever had, with the full assurance of gaining more, according to its future necessities.

The question now arises, "Is such a reconstruction possible or desirable?" To this I answer from the depth of my soul, no. Mr. Lincoln is powerful, Mr. Lincoln can do many things, but Mr. Lincoln will never see the day when he can bring back or charm back, the scattered fragments of the Union into the shape and form they stood when they were shattered by this slaveholding rebellion.

What does this policy of bringing back the union imply? It implies first of all, that the slave States will promptly and cordially, and without the presence of compulsory and extraneous force, co-operate with the free States under the very constitution which they have openly repudiated, and attempted to destroy. It implies that they will allow and protect the collection of the revenue in all their ports.—It implies the security and safety of our postal arrangements within their border. It implies the regular election of the members of the Senate and the House of Representatives and the prompt and complete execution of all the Federal laws within their limits. It implies that the rebel States will repudiate the rebel leaders, and that they shall be punished with perpetual political degradation. So much it implies on the part of the rebel States.—And the bare statement, with what we know of the men engaged in the war, is sufficient to prove the impossibility of their fulfilment while slavery remains.

What is implied by a reconstruction of the union on the old basis so far as concerns the northern and loyal States? It implies that after all we have lost and suffered by this war to protect and preserve slavery, the crime and scandal of the nation, that we will as formerly act the disgusting part of the watch dogs of the slave plantation, that we will hunt down the slaves at the North, and submit to all the arrogance, bluster, and pretension of the very men who have imperilled our liberties and baptized our soil with the blood of our best and bravest citizens. Now I hold that both parties will reject these terms with scorn and indignation. Having thus condemned as impossible and undesirable the policy which seems to be that of the administration you will naturally want to know what I consider to be the true policy to be pursued by the Government and people in relation to slavery and the war. I will tell you: Recognise the fact, for it is the great fact, and never more palpable than at the present moment, that the only choice left to this nation, is abolition or destruction. You must abolish slavery or abandon the union. It is plain that there can never be any union between the north and the south, while the south values slavery more than nationality. A union of interest is essential to a union of ideas, and without this union of ideas, the outward form of the union will be but as a rope of sand. Now it is quite clear that while slavery lasts at the south, it will remain hereafter as heretofore, the great dominating interest, overtopping all others, and shaping the sentiments and opinions of the people in accordance with itself. We are not to flatter ourselves that because slavery has brought great troubles upon the South by this war, that therefore the people of the South will be stirred up against it. If we can bear with slavery after the calamities it has brought upon us, we may expect that the South will be no less patient. Indeed we may rationally expect that the South will be more devoted to slavery than ever. The blood and treasure poured out in its defense will tend to increase its sacredness in the eyes of southern people, and if slavery comes out of this struggle, and is retaken under the forms of old compromises, the country will witness a greater amount of insolence and bluster in favor of the slave system, than was ever shown before in or out of Congress.— But it is asked how will you abolish slavery. You have no power over the system before the rebellion is suppressed, and you will have no right or power when it is suppressed. I will answer this argument when I have stated how the thing may be done. The fact is there would be no trouble about the way, if the government only possessed the will. But several ways have been suggested. One is a stringent Confiscation Bill by Congress. Another is by a proclamation by the President at the head of the nation. Another is by the commanders of each division of the army. Slavery can be abolished in any or all these ways. There is plausiblity in the argument that we cannot reach slavery until we have suppressed the rebellion. Yet it is far more true to say that we cannot reach the rebellion until we have suppressed slavery. For slavery is the life of the rebellion. Let the loyal army but inscribe upon its banner, Emancipation and protection to all who will rally under it, and no power could prevent a stampede from slavery, such as the world has not witnessed since the Hebrews crossed the Red Sea. I am convinced that this rebellion and slavery are twin monsters, and that they must fall or flourish together, and that all attempts at upholding one while putting down the other, will be followed by continued trains of darkening calamities, such as make this anniversary of our national Independence, a day of mourning instead of a day of transcendant joy and gladness.

But a proclamation of Emancipation, says one, would only be a paper order. I answer, so is any order emanating from our Government. The President's proclamation calling his countrymen to arms, was a paper order. The proposition to retake the property of the Federal Government in the southern States, was a paper order. Laws fixing the punishment of traitors are paper orders. All laws, all written rules for the Government of the army and navy and people, are "paper orders," and would remain only such were they not backed up by force, still we do not object to them as useless, but admit their wisdom and necessity. Then these paper orders carry with them a certain moral force which makes them in a large measure self-executing. I know of none which would possess this self-executing power in larger measure than a proclamation of Emancipation. It would act on the rebel masters, and even more powerfully upon their slaves. It would lead the slaves to run away, and the masters to emancipate, and thus put an end to slavery. The conclusion of the whole matter is this: The end of slavery and only the end of slavery, is the end of the war, the end of secession, the end of disunion, and the return of peace, prosperity and unity to the nation. Whether Emancipation comes from the North or from the South, from Jeff Davis or from Abraham Lincoln, it will come alike for the healing of the nation, for slavery is the only mountain interposed to make enemies of the North and South.

Fellow Citizens: let me say in conclusion. This slavery begotten and slavery sustained, and slavery animated war, has now cost this nation more than a hundred thousand lives, and more than five hundred millions of treasure. It has weighed down the national heart with sorrow and heaviness, such as no speech can portray. It has cast a doubt upon the possibility of liberty and self Government which it will require a century to remove.—The question is, shall this stupendous and most outrageous war be finally and forever ended? Or shall it be merely suspended for a time, and again revived with increased and aggravated fury in the future? Can you afford a repetition of this costly luxury? Do you wish to transmit to your children the calamities and sorrows of to-day? The way to either class of these results is open to you. By urging upon the nation the necessity and duty of putting an end to slavery, you put an end to the war, and put an end to the cause of the war, and make any repetition of it impossible. But just take back the pet monster again into the bosom of the nation, proclaim an amnesty to the slaveholders, let them have their slaves, and command your services in helping to catch and hold them, and so sure as like causes will ever produce like effects, you will hand down to your children here, and hereafter, born and to be born all the horrors through which you are now passing. I have told you of great national opportunities in the past, a greater than any in the past is the opportunity of the present. If now we omit the duty it imposes, steel our hearts against its teachings, or shrink in cowardice from the work of to-day, your fathers will have fought and bled in vain to establish free Institutions, and American Republicanism will become a hissing and a byword to a mocking earth.

Douglass' Monthly, August, 1862

1. Wilson, *op. cit.*, vol. III, p. 383.

2. On February 22, 1856, the *Richmond Enquirer* editorialized: "We have got to hating everything with the prefix 'free'—from the free Negroes down and up through the whole catalogue of abominations, demagogueries, lusts, philosophers, fanaticism, and follies, free farms, free labor, free n———rs, free society, free will, free thinking, free love, free wives, free children, free schools."

3. In 1820, the South discovered to its dismay that the control of the House of Representatives had definitely passed into the hands of the free North. As a result, the South could stop the enactment of measures hostile to its "peculiar institution" only if it dominated the Senate. But its control in that body depended upon the entrance of Missouri as a slave state. To prevent the South from having a majority of one state in the upper house, the North demanded the admission of Maine. After prolonged and bitter debate, both states were admitted, an "equilibrium of forces" in the Senate being thus maintained. In addition, the Missouri Compromise provided for the prohibition of slavery in the Louisiana territory north of the 30° 36' line.

4. Jackson himself had emphasized this very point at the conclusion of the nullification controversy. "The tariff was only the pretext," he wrote, "and disunion and a southern confederacy the real object. The next pretext will be the negro, or slavery question." (Andrew Jackson to Rev. Andrew J. Crawford, May 1, 1833, J. S. Bassett, and J. F. Jameson, eds., *Correspondence of Andrew Jackson,* Washington, 1931, vol. V, p. 72.)

5. In his proclamation to the people of western Virginia, General George B. McClellan said his army did not come to interfere in any way with their slaves. "We will, on the contrary," he assured them, "with an iron hand, crush any attempt at insurrection on their part." (*Official Records of the Union and Confederate Armies,* Series 1, vol. II, p. 662.)

6. On November 20, 1861, General Henry W. Halleck published an order directing that all fugitive slaves within his lines be ejected, and that none be admitted in the future. He justified this decree on the ground that the Confederates were employing the fugitives as spies. It was widely believed in Radical Republican circles that Lincoln was responsible for this order. (See *New York Tribune,* Nov. 23, 1861.)

TO GERRIT SMITH

Rochester, Sept. 8th, 1862

My Dear Friend:

Let me sincerely thank you for your kind note and for twenty dollars to help me in the further publication of my monthly. I had not known of your poor health until your note came. May you soon recover your wonted vigor and live yet many years to cheer the heart of the lowly and suffering. I had attributed your silence of late, to what I supposed must be your ineffable disgust at the wretched management of the war. Your gloomiest predictions have been even now more than realized, and I shudder at what the future may still have in store for us. I think the nation was never more completely in the hands of the Slave power. This government is now in the hands of the Army, and the Army is in the hands of the very worst type of American Democracy, the chief representative of which[1] is now doing his utmost to destroy the country. I think, in such hands, we shall do well if we at last succeed in buying a peace from our Southern masters, without fully indemnifying them for the entire expense to which they have been put in humbling us. My good friend Julia seems to have been greatly delighted with her meeting with your dear household in London. I feel sure that a quiet visit to England would do wonders for your health.

Your friend,
Frederick Douglass

Gerrit Smith Papers, Syracuse University

1. The reference is to General George B. McClellan who was a member of the Democratic Party. Don Carlos Buell and Henry W. Halleck were other examples of members of the Democratic Party appointed to positions of power and influence in the Union army.

Lincoln read a draft of an emancipation proclamation to his Cabinet on July 21, 1862. Rebels were to be warned of the penalties of the Confiscation Act, reminded that they could still emancipate their slaves and receive compensation, and on January 1, 1863, all slaves in the possession of rebels were to be declared free. For two days the Cabinet debated the draft of the proclamation. Despite the opposition of most of the Cabinet members, Lincoln decided to go ahead with his plan to issue it. He agreed, however, with Seward that it was not wise to issue the proclamation until the military situation became more favorable.

But all this was known to only a few people. Lincoln's public utterances provided little encouragement for the friends of the slave; on one occasion he told a delegation that the Constitution did not allow the freeing of the slaves, because it could not be enforced in the rebel states. Douglass was filled with deeper despair when he saw how the President was riding the colonization hobby. [On] August [14], 1862, Lincoln called a group of prominent free Negroes to the White House and urged them to support colonization. "Your race suffer greatly, many of them, by living among us," he told them, "while ours suffer from your presence. In a word we suffer on each side. If this is admitted, it affords a reason why we should be separated." If not for the institution of slavery, he declared, "and the colored race as a basis, the war could not have an existence." The white people were not willing for the Negroes to remain in the country. New Granada in Central America had indicated that it was prepared to receive them. Lincoln urged the delegation to help him in a colonization plan to send Negroes to that country.[1]

Douglass' anger increased as he read the account of the interview. Overlooking the fact that this was the first time a President of the United States had addressed a Negro audience, he accused Lincoln of revealing "his pride of race and blood, his contempt for Negroes and his canting hypocrisy." . . . He cut to shreds Lincoln's argument that the presence of the Negro in the country was the basic cause of the war. [III:24]

THE PRESIDENT AND HIS SPEECHES

The President of the United States seems to possess an ever increasing passion for making himself appear silly and ridiculous, if nothing worse. Since the publication of our last number he has been unusually garrulous, characteristically foggy, remarkably illogical and untimely in his utterances, often saying that which nobody wanted to hear, and studiously leaving unsaid about the only things which the country and the times imperatively demand of him. Our garrulous and joking President has favored the country and the world with two speeches, which if delivered by any other than the President of the United States, would attract no more attention than the funny little speeches made in front of the arcade by our friend John Smith, inviting customers to buy his razor strops.—One of the speeches of the President was made at a war meeting in Washington in vindication of Mr. Stanton, and in justification of himself against the charge that he had failed to send reinforcements to Gen. McClellan.[2] Very little need be said of this first speech. In comparison with some speeches made on that occasion, the President's is short, but in comparison to the amount of matter it contains, it is tediously long, full of repetitions, and so remarkably careless in style that it reminds one strongly of the gossiping manner in which a loquacious old woman discusses her neighbors and her own domestic affairs, and explaining herself so lucidly that her audience, after listening with all due patience, are in the end as well informed about the subject in question as before the exposition. In short, the speech does not prove anything except that the Secretary of War is not responsible, but that the President is responsible for the failure to send re-enforcements to General McClellan. We may at once have done with this speech, especially since the information it contains was explicitly given to the country full three weeks before its utterance at the War meeting in Washington.

The other and more important communication of the President it appears was delivered in the White House before a committee of colored men assembled by his invitation. In this address Mr. Lincoln assumes the language and arguments of an itinerant Colonization lecturer, showing all his inconsistencies, his pride of race and blood, his contempt for Negroes and his canting hypocrisy. How an honest man could creep into such a character as that implied by this address we are not required to show. The argument of Mr. Lincoln is that the difference between the white and black races renders it impossible for them to live together in the same country without detriment to both. Colonization, therefore, he holds to be the duty and the interest of the colored people. Mr. Lincoln takes care in urging his colonization scheme to furnish a weapon to all the ignorant and base, who need only the countenance of men in authority to commit all kinds of violence and outrage upon the colored people of the country. Taking advantage of his position and of the prevailing prejudice against them he affirms that their presence in the country is the real first cause of the war, and logically enough, if the premises were sound, assumes the necessity of their removal.

It does not require any great amount of skill to point out the fallacy and expose the unfairness of the assumption, for by this time every man who has an ounce of brain in his head, no matter to which party he may belong, and even Mr. Lincoln himself, must know quite well that the mere presence of the colored race never could have provoked this horrid and desolating rebellion. Mr. Lincoln knows that in Mexico, Central America and South America, many distinct races live peaceably together in the enjoyment of equal rights, and that the civil wars which occasionally disturb the peace of those regions never originated in the difference of the races inhabiting them. A horse thief pleading that the existence of the horse is the apology for his theft or a highway man contending that the money in the traveler's pocket is the sole first cause of his robbery are about as much entitled to respect as is the President's reasoning at this point. No, Mr. President, it is not the innocent horse that makes the horse thief, not the traveler's purse that makes the highway robber, and it is not the presence of the Negro that causes this foul and unnatural war, but the cruel and brutal cupidity of those who wish to possess horses, money and Negroes by means of theft, robbery, and rebellion. Mr. Lincoln further knows or ought to know at least that

Negro hatred and prejudice of color are neither original nor invincible vices, but merely the offshoots of that root of all crimes and evils—slavery. If the colored people instead of having been stolen and forcibly brought to the United States had come as free immigrants, like the German and the Irish, never thought of as suitable objects of property, they never would have become the objects of aversion and bitter persecution, nor would there ever have been divulged and propagated the arrogant and malignant nonsense about natural repellancy and the incompatibility of races.

Illogical and unfair as Mr. Lincoln's statements are, they are nevertheless quite in keeping with his whole course from the beginning of his administration up to this day, and confirm the painful conviction that though elected as an anti-slavery man by Republican and Abolition voters, Mr. Lincoln is quite a genuine representative of American prejudice and Negro hatred and far more concerned for the preservation of slavery, and the favor of the Border Slave States, than for any sentiment of magnanimity or principle of justice and humanity. This address of his leaves us less ground to hope for anti-slavery action at his hands than any of his previous utterances. Notwithstanding his repeated declarations that he considers slavery an evil, every step of his Presidential career relating to slavery proves him active, decided, and brave for its support, and passive, cowardly, and treacherous to the very cause of liberty to which he owes his election. This speech of the President delivered to a committee of free colored men in the capital explains the animus of his interference with the memorable proclamation of General Fremont. A man who can charge this war to the presence of colored men in this country might be expected to take advantage of any legal technicalities for arresting the cause of Emancipation, and the vigorous prosecution of the war against slaveholding rebels. To these colored people, without power and without influence, the President is direct, undisguised, and unhesitating. He says to the colored people: I don't like you, you must clear out of the country. So too in dealing with anti-slavery Generals the President is direct and firm. He is always brave and resolute in his interferences in favor of slavery, remarkably unconcerned about the wishes and opinions of the people of the north; apparently wholly indifferent to the moral sentiment of civilized Europe; but bold and self-reliant as he is in the ignominious service of slavery, he is as timid as a sheep when required to live up to a single one of his anti-slavery testimonies. He is scrupulous to the very letter of the law in favor of slavery, and a perfect latitudinarian as to the discharge of his duties under a law favoring freedom. When Congress passed the Confiscation Bill,[3] made the Emancipation of the slaves of rebels the law of the land, authorized the President to arm the slaves which should come within the lines of the Federal army, and thus removed all technical objections, everybody who attached any importance to the President's declarations of scrupulous regard for law, looked at once for a proclamation emancipating the slaves and calling the blacks to arms. But Mr. Lincoln, formerly so strict and zealous in the observance of the most atrocious laws which ever disgraced a country, has not been able yet to muster courage and honesty enough to obey and execute that grand decision of the people. He evaded his obvious duty, and instead of calling the blacks to arms and to liberty he merely authorized the military commanders to use them as laborers, without even promising them their freedom at the end of their term of service to the government, and thus destroyed virtually the very object of the measure. Further when General Halleck issued his odious order No. 3, excluding fugitive slaves from our lines, an order than which none could be more serviceable to the slaveholding rebels, since it was a guarantee against the escape of their slaves, Mr. Lincoln was deaf to the outcry and indignation which resounded through the north and west, and saw no occasion for interference, though that order violated a twice adopted resolution of Congress. When General McClellan employed our men guarding rebel property and even when Gen. Butler committed the outrage paralled only by the atrocities of the rebels—delivering back into bondage thousands of slaves—Mr. Lincoln again was mute and did not feel induced to interfere in behalf of outraged humanity.

The tone of frankness and benevolence which he assumes in his speech to the colored committee is too thin a mask not to be seen through. The genuine spark of humanity is missing in it, no sincere wish to improve the condition of the oppressed has dictated it. It expresses merely the desire to get rid of them, and reminds one of the politeness with which a man might try to bow out of his house some troublesome creditor or the witness of some old guilt. We might also criticize the style adopted, so exceedingly plain and coarse threaded as to make the impression that Mr. L. had such a low estimate of the intelligence of his audience, as to think any but the simplest phrases and constructions would be above their power of comprehension. As Mr. Lincoln however in all his writings has manifested a decided awkwardness in the management of the English language, we do not think there is any intention in this respect, but only the incapacity to do better.

Douglass' Monthly, September, 1862

1. Philip Van Doren Stern, ed., *The Life and Writings of Abraham Lincoln*, New York, 1940, pp. 715–23.

In September, Lincoln submitted to his cabinet "the question of the propriety of seeking to make treaties with Latin America or European countries with colonies of tropics" for the purpose of providing a "refuge for colored people." Seward addressed a circular letter to the governments of England, France, Holland and Denmark, informing them of Lincoln's colonization plans and asking their cooperation. (See Edward Bates' diary, Sept. 25, 1862, Howard K. Beale, ed., *Diary of Edward Bates*, Washington, 1933, p. 262.) The arrangement with New Granada fell through, mainly because Negroes themselves did not want to emigrate.

2. Lincoln's address, delivered August 6, 1862, sought to put an end to discussions as to who was responsible for the failure of the Peninsular campaign. He declared: "General McClellan is not to blame for asking for what he wanted and needed, and the Secretary of War is not to blame for not giving when he had none to give." "I have no accusation against him," he said of Secretary of War Stanton.

3. On July 20, 1861, a bill to confiscate property used for insurrectionary purposes was reported to the Senate by the Committee on the Judiciary. It provided that all property used to aid or promote an insurrection against the government of the United States was to be regarded to be lawful subject to prize and capture wherever found. In addition, individuals engaging in this insurrection were to forfeit the right to the service or labor of any person used in resisting the laws of the United States. The bill was slightly amended during the debate on the measure in Congress, was adopted by both houses, and received the approval of President Lincoln on August 6, 1861.

PART SIX

From the Emancipation Proclamation to the Eve of Appomattox

[On] September 17, [1862,] the cannons roared for fourteen hours at Antietam and thousands went down to death. By the end of the week the Confederate Army was in retreat. On Monday, September 22, Lincoln issued the preliminary Emancipation Proclamation. He mentioned again the possibility of compensated emancipation and said that he would continue to encourage the voluntary colonization of Negroes "upon this continent or elsewhere." But the time had come for direct action. Hence he proclaimed:

"That on the First day of January, in the year of our Lord one thousand, eighteen hundred and sixty-three, all persons held as slaves within any State or any designated part of a state, the people whereof shall then be in rebellion against the United States, shall be then, henceforward, and forever free."[1]

"Forever free"—Douglass could scarcely believe his eyes as he read these words. He rushed into print to give vent to his happiness. . . . His pen was jubilant. . . .

There were distinct limitations to the Proclamation. It did not cover all the slaveholding territory. Then, what if the war should end and there were no states in rebellion on the first of January, 1863? Some Abolitionists viewed the Proclamation as an empty gesture. Douglass rejected this outlook. This was the most important document ever signed by a President of the United States. [III:25–26]

EMANCIPATION PROCLAIMED

Common sense, the necessities of the war, to say nothing of the dictation of justice and humanity have at last prevailed. We shout for joy that we live to record this righteous decree. *Abraham Lincoln,* President of the United States, Commander-in-Chief of the army and navy, in his own peculiar, cautious, forbearing and hesitating way, slow, but we hope sure, has, while the loyal heart was near breaking with despair, proclaimed and declared: "*That on the First of January, in the Year of Our Lord One Thousand, Eight Hundred and Sixty-three, All Persons Held as Slaves Within Any State or Any Designated Part of a State, The People Whereof Shall Then be in Rebellion Against the United States, Shall be Thenceforward and Forever Free.*" "Free forever" oh! long enslaved millions, whose cries have so vexed the air and sky, suffer on a few more days in sorrow, the hour of your deliverance draws nigh! Oh! Ye millions of free and loyal men who have earnestly sought to free your bleeding country from the dreadful ravages of revolution and anarchy, lift up now your voices with joy and thanksgiving for with freedom to the slave will come peace and safety to your country. President Lincoln has embraced in this proclamation the law of Congress passed more than six months ago, prohibiting the employment of any part of the army and naval forces of the United States, to return fugitive slaves to their masters, commanded all officers of the army and navy to respect and obey its provisions. He has still further declared his intention to urge upon the Legislature of all the slave States not in rebellion the immediate or gradual abolishment of slavery. But read the proclamation for it is the most important of any to which the President of the United States has ever signed his name.

Opinions will widely differ as to the practical effect of this measure upon the war. All that class at the North who have not lost their affection for slavery will regard the measure as the very worst that could be devised, and as likely to lead to endless mischief. All their plans for the future have been projected with a view to a reconstruction of the American Government upon the basis of compromise between slaveholding and non-slaveholding States. The thought of a country unified in sentiments, objects and ideas, has not entered into their political calculations, and hence this newly declared policy of the Government, which contemplates one glorious homogeneous people, doing away at a blow with the whole class of compromisers and corrupters, will meet their stern opposition. Will that opposition prevail? Will it lead the President to reconsider and retract? Not a word of it. Abraham Lincoln may be slow, Abraham Lincoln may desire peace even at the price of leaving our terrible national sore untouched, to fester on for generations, but Abraham Lincoln is not the man to reconsider, retract and contradict words and purposes solemnly proclaimed over his official signature.

The careful, and we think, the slothful deliberation which he has observed in reaching this obvious policy, is a guarantee against retraction. But even if the temper and spirit of the President himself were other than what they are, events greater than the President, events which have slowly wrung this proclamation from him may be relied on to carry him forward in the same direction.[2] To look back now would only load him with heavier evils, while diminishing his ability, for overcoming those with which he now has to contend. To recall his proclamation would only increase rebel pride, rebel sense of power and would be hailed as a direct admission of weakness on the part of the Federal Government, while it would cause heaviness of heart and depression of national enthusiasm all over the loyal North and West. No, Abraham Lincoln will take no step backward. His word has gone out over the country and the world, giving joy and gladness to the friends of freedom and progress wherever those words are read, and he will stand by them, and carry them out to the letter. If he has taught us to confide in nothing else, he has taught us to confide in his word. The want of Constitutional power, the want of military power, the tendency of the measure to intensify Southern hate, and to exasperate the rebels, the tendency to drive from him all that class of Democrats at the North, whose loyalty has been conditioned on his restoring the union as it was, slavery and all, have all been considered, and he has taken his ground notwithstanding. The President doubtless saw, as we see, that it is not more absurd to talk about restoring the union, without hurting slavery, than restoring the union without hurting the rebels. As to exasperating the South, there can be no more in the cup than the cup will hold, and that was full already. The whole situation having been carefully scanned, before Mr. Lincoln could be made to budge an inch, he will now stand his ground. Border State influence, and the influence of half-loyal men, have been exerted and have done their worst. The end of these two influences is implied in this proclamation. Hereafter, the inspiration as well as the men and the money for carrying on the war will come from the North, and not from half-loyal border States.

The effect of this paper upon the disposition of Europe will be great and increasing. It changes the character of the war in European eyes and gives it an important principle as an object, instead of national pride and interest. It recognizes and declares the real nature of the contest, and places the North on the side of justice and civilization, and the rebels on the side of robbery and barbarism. It will disarm all purpose on the part of European Government to intervene in favor of the rebels and thus cast off at a blow one source of rebel power. All through the war thus far, the rebel ambassadors in foreign countries have been able to silence all expression of sympathy with the North as to slavery. With much more than a show of truth, they said that the Federal Government, no more than the Confederate Government, contemplated the abolition of slavery.

But will not this measure be frowned upon by our officers and men in the field? We have heard of many thousands who have resolved that they will throw up their commissions and lay down their arms, just so soon as they are required to carry on a war against slavery. Making all allowances for exaggeration there are doubtless far too many of this sort in the loyal army. Putting this kind of loyalty and patriotism to the test, will be one of the best collateral effects of the measure. Any man who leaves the field on such a ground will be an argument in favor of the proclamation, and will prove that his heart has been more with slavery than with his country. Let the army be cleansed from all such pro-slavery vermin, and its health and strength will be greatly improved. But there can be no reason to fear the loss of many officers or men by resignation or desertion. We have no doubt that the measure was brought to the attention of most of our leading Generals, and blind as some of them have seemed to be in the earlier part of the war, most of them have seen enough to convince them that there can be no end to this war that does not end slavery. At any rate, we may hope that for every pro-slavery man[3] that shall start from the ranks of our loyal army, there will be two anti-slavery men to fill up the vacancy, and in this war one truly devoted to the cause of Emancipation is worth two of the opposite sort.

Whether slavery will be abolished in the manner now proposed by President Lincoln, depends of course upon two conditions, the first specified and the second implied. The first is that the slave States shall be in rebellion on and after the first day of January 1863 and the second is we must have the ability to put down that rebellion. About the first there can be very little doubt. The South is thoroughly in earnest and confident. It has staked everything upon the rebellion. Its experience thus far in the field has rather increased its hopes of final success than diminished them. Its armies now hold us at bay at all points, and the war is confined to the border States slave and free. If Richmond were in our hands and Virginia at our mercy, the vast regions beyond would still remain to be subdued. But the rebels confront us on the Potomac, the Ohio, and the Mississippi. Kentucky, Maryland, Missouri, and Virginia are in debate on the battlefields and their people are divided by the line which separates treason from loyalty. In short we are yet, after eighteen months of war, confined to the outer margin of the rebellion. We have scarcely more than touched the surface of the terrible evil. It has been raising large quantities of food during the past summer. While the masters have been fighting abroad, the slaves have been busy working at home to supply them with the means of continuing the struggle. They will not down at the bidding of this Proclamation, but may be safely relied upon till January and long after January. A month or two will put an end to general fighting for the winter. When the leaves fall we shall hear again of bad roads, winter quarters and spring campaigns. The South which has thus far withstood our arms will not fall at once before our pens. All fears for the abolition of slavery arising from this apprehension may be dismissed. Whoever, therefore, lives to see the first day of next January, should Abraham Lincoln be then alive and President of the United States, may confidently look in the morning papers for the final proclamation, granting freedom, and freedom forever, to all slaves within the rebel States. On the next point nothing need be said. We have full power to put down the rebellion. Unless one man is more than a match for four, unless the South breeds braver and better men than the North, unless slavery is more precious than liberty, unless a just cause kindles a feebler enthusiasm than a wicked and villainous one, the men of the loyal States will put down this rebellion and slavery, and all the sooner will they put down that rebellion by coupling slavery with that object. Tenderness towards slavery has been the loyal weakness during the war. Fighting the slaveholders with one hand and holding the slaves with the other, has been fairly tried and has failed. We have now inaugurated a wiser and better policy, a policy which is better for the loyal cause than an hundred thousand armed men. The Star Spangled Banner is now the harbinger of Liberty and the millions in bondage, inured to hardships, accustomed to toil, ready to suffer, ready to fight, to dare and to die, will rally under that banner wherever they see it gloriously unfolded to the breeze. Now let the Government go forward in its mission of Liberty as the only condition of peace and union, by weeding out the army and navy of all such officers as the late Col. Miles, whose sympathies are now known to have been with the rebels. Let only the men who assent heartily to the wisdom and the justice of the anti-slavery policy of the Government be lifted into command; let the black man have an arm as well as a heart in this war, and the tide of battle which has thus far only waved backward and forward, will steadily set in our favor. The rebellion suppressed, slavery abolished, and America will, higher than ever, sit as a queen among the nations of the earth.

Now for the work. During the interval between now and next January, let every friend of the long enslaved bondman do his utmost in swelling the tide of anti-slavery sentiment, by writing, speaking, money and example. Let our aim be to make the North a unit in favor of the President's policy, and see to it that our voices and votes, shall forever extinguish that latent and malignant sentiment at the North, which has from the first cheered on the rebels in their atrocious crimes against the union, and has systematically sought to paralyze the national arm in striking down the slaveholding rebellion. We are ready for this service or any other, in this, we trust the last struggle with the monster slavery.

Douglass' Monthly, October 1862

1. Philip Van Doren Stern, ed., *The Life and Writings of Abraham Lincoln,* New York, 1940, pp. 718–19.

2. Lincoln himself observed in 1864: "I claim not to have controlled events, but confess plainly that events have controlled me." (Philip S. Foner, ed., *Abraham Lincoln: Selections from His Writings,* p. 22.)

3. General McClellan, however, denounced the Proclamation, warned Lincoln that the Administration must under no circumstances abandon its conservative policies, and issued a counter-proclamation to the army denouncing any and all proposals to free the slaves. (See George B. McClellan, *McClellan's Own Story,* New York, 1887, pp. 487–88.)

At no time before the issuance of the Emancipation Proclamation had Douglass been under the illusion that legal emancipation alone would provide freedom for the Negro slaves.
He had continually reminded the Abolitionists that their work would really begin with
the abolition of slavery and the defeat of the rebel states. A new class of men in the South
would have to be trained to take the place of the leaders of the rebellion. They would have
to be educated to understand that slavery had ever been "their direct calamity and curse,"
that labor was honorable, not degrading, and that "the liberty of a part is never to be secured by the enslavement or oppression of any." The whole South would become missionary ground. Family relations which had no real existence under slavery would have
to be established, schools set up for ex-slaves, and all the benefits of republican institutions introduced. In short, the work that would confront the Abolitionists was "nothing
less than radical revolution in all the modes of thought which have flourished under the
blighting slave system."

And what of the ex-slave himself? Law and the sword could abolish slavery, but it was
too much to expect that those who had "a mountain of gold of twenty hundred millions
of dollars" invested in slavery would let such profits slip from their hands. They would
squirm and twist in every conceivable way to reinstate some form of slavery in the South.
The slaves might be emancipated in form but remain slaves in fact. [III:40]

THE WORK OF THE FUTURE

Already it seems well to look forward to the future to which we are hastening.
No nation was ever called to the contemplation of a destiny more important and
solemn than ours. Great duties and responsibilities are devolved upon us. Liberty, order, and civilization are staked against a slaveholding despotism, and social anarchy. To-day we have to put down a stupendous rebellion. To-morrow
we shall have to reconstruct the whole fabric of Southern society, and bring order out of anarchy. It is a tremendous undertaking. When the armies of the rebellion are entirely demoralized, broken and scattered beyond the possibility of
organized opposition to the National Government, when the flag of the Union
shall wave from the battlements of every fortress in the South, when slavery the
grim and guilty motive for this horrid war shall have been abolished, when the
poor whites of the South shall have been delivered from the rule and sway of the
slaveholding class, when sullen, silent, and gloomy but subdued hate shall settle
upon the Southern mind, then will come the time for the exercise of the highest
of all human faculties. A profounder wisdom, a holier zeal, than belongs to the
prosecution of war, will be required. Courage and patriotism are chiefly needed
now, a holy philanthropy and a deep insight into human nature will be needed
then. The sea of thought and feeling lashed into rage and fury by the war will remain to be calmed into the steady motions of peace and safety. The war will leave
Southern Society like a ship driven by the storm, without rudder or compass.
State and National constitutions, holding but feeble sway and exciting but feeble reverence. The people left to themselves, will each be disposed to do after his
own mind, and the discomfited rebels may among themselves, fulfill the prediction of Mr. Stephens of Georgia, who said he expected yet to see the rebels cutting each other's throats. The structure of the American Constitution and Government imply the existence among the whole people of a fraternal good will, an
earnest spirit of co-operation for the common good, a mutual dependence of all

upon each and of each upon all. The Government is not enthroned above the people but is of, by and through the people. A despotic form of Government with its standing armies, holds its existence in large measure independently of the people and in some sort against the people, looking at them very much as a slaveholder regards his slaves, to be worked and fed when obedient, and to be flogged and otherwise punished when they disobey. When such people raise an insurrection and are put down, the path before them is plain and simple: *It is submission.* To obey is the fulfillment of the whole law of despotism.—But our form of Government contemplates in such a case something more than mere cold obedience. It not only requires this, but a cordial co-operation. Its whole machinery is deranged when one of its parts fail to perform its functions. The rebellion has paralyzed the Federal Government in all the rebel States, but putting down the rebels in arms does not necessarily cure this paralysis. The benumbed or dead state must be called into life, and for this the highest wisdom must be employed. The State Senate, the State Legislature, the State Courts, the State Governors, and officers generally have to be gathered in under the fold of the Constitution and Union, and brought to co-operate in good faith with the National Government. How all this shall be done, is one of the great questions of the future. Foreseeing this state of things, Mr. Sumner of the Senate, with the comprehensible grasp of a true statesmanship, proposed that the States in rebellion shall be governed as Territories.[1] Though denounced and repudiated at the time, this theory of conducting the rebel States back to their former position will in the end be adopted.

It would be absurd and ridiculous to expect that the conquered traitors will at once cordially cooperate with the Federal Government. They must be set aside for a new class of men, men who have hitherto exercised but little influence in the State. For this, we shall have to educate the people. The arduous task of the future will be to make the Southern people see and appreciate Republican Government, as a blessing of inestimable value, and to be maintained at any and every cost. They have got to be taught that slavery which they have valued as a blessing has ever been their direct calamity and curse.—The work before us is nothing less than a radical revolution in all the modes of thought which have flourished under the blighting slave system. The idea that labor is an evil, that work is degrading and that idleness is respectable, must be dispelled and the idea that work is honorable made to take its place.—Above all they must be taught that the liberty of a part is never to be secured by the enslavement or oppression of any. Neither the slave or the slaveholder can instantly throw off the sentiments inspired and ground into them by long years of tyranny on the one hand and of abject and cringing submission on the other. The master will carry into the new relation of liberty much of the insolence, caprice and pretention exercised by him while the admitted lord of the lash. The slave in his turn will be bound in the invisible chains of slavery long after his iron chains are broken and forever buried out of sight. There is no such thing as immediate Emancipation either for the master or for the slave. Time, experience and culture must gradually bring society back to the normal condition from which long years of slavery have carried all under its iron sway.

Then for the freed men: What shall be their status in the new condition of things? Shall they exchange the relation of slavery to individuals, only to become the slaves of the community at large, having no rights which anybody is required to respect, subject to a code of black laws, denying them school privileges, denying them the right of suffrage, denying them the right to sit as jurors, denying them the right to testify in courts of Law, denying them the right to keep and bear arms, denying them the right of speech, and the right of petition? Or shall they have secured to them equal rights before the law. Oh! that the heart of this unbelieving nation could be at once brought to a faith in the Eternal Laws of justice, justice for all men, justice now and always, justice without reservation or qualification except those suggested by mercy and love.

It is not likely however, that at the outset, the Southern people will consent to an absolutely just and humane policy towards the newly emancipated black people so long enslaved and degraded. One, therefore, of the labors and duties which will require the exertions of those who have heretofore remembered those in bonds as bound with them, will be to ameliorate the condition of the partially emancipated. The whole South, as it never was before the abolition of slavery will become missionary ground. The family relation which has had no real existence under the region of slavery, will remain to be established, schools for the education of dusky millions will be required, and all the elevating and civilizing institutions of the country must be extended to these people. Men full of faith in the race, and of the sacred fire of love, must walk among these slavery-smitten columns of humanity and lift their forms towards Heaven. Verily, the work does not end with the abolition of slavery but only begins. Slavery has been the great hindrance. It has stood athwart the pathway of knowledge and progress, dreading nothing so much as the enlightenment of its slaves. This old and grim obstacle removed, and jets of heavenly light will speedily illumine the land long covered with darkness, cruelty and crime.

Douglass' Monthly, November, 1862

1. On February 11, 1862, Senator Sumner introduced his plan of Reconstruction known as the "State Suicide" theory. This plan declared that a state which had seceded from the Union had abdicated all its rights under the Constitution, and forfeited all functions and powers as a state, "so that from that time forward the territory falls under the exclusive jurisdiction of Congress as other territory, and the state being according to the language of the law, *felo-de-se*, ceases to exist." (For the full text of the plan, see Walter P. Fleming, ed., *Documentary History of Reconstruction*, Cleveland, 1906, vol. I, pp. 144-45.)

A DAY FOR POETRY AND SONG, remarks at Zion Church, December 28, 1862

My Friends:

This is scarcely a day for prose. It is a day for poetry and song, a new song. These cloudless skies, this balmy air, this brilliant sunshine, (making December as pleasant as May), are in harmony with the glorious morning of liberty about to dawn upon us. Out of a full heart and with sacred emotion, I congratulate you my friends and fellow citizens, on the high and hopeful condition of the cause of human freedom and the cause of our common country, for these two causes are now one and inseparable and must stand or fall together. We stand today in the presence of a glorious prospect.—This sacred Sunday in all the likelihoods of the case, is the last which will witness the existence of legal slavery in all the Rebel slaveholding States of America. Henceforth and forever, slavery in those States is to be recognized, by all the departments of the American Government, under its appropriate character, as an unmitigated robber and pirate, branded as the sum of all villainy, an outlaw having no rights which any man white or colored is bound to respect. It is difficult for us who have toiled so long and hard, to believe that this event, so stupendous, so far reaching and glorious is even now at the door. It surpasses our most enthusiastic hopes that we live at such a time and are likely to witness the downfall, at least the legal downfall of slavery in America. It is a moment for joy, thanksgiving and praise.

Among the first questions that tried the strength of my childhood mind—was first why are colored people slaves, and the next was will their slavery last forever. From that day onward, the cry that has reached the most silent chambers of my soul, by day and by night has been How long! How long oh! Eternal Power of the Universe, how long shall these things be.

This inquiry is to be answered on the first of January 1863.

That this war is to abolish slavery I have no manner of doubt. The process may be long and tedious but that that result must at last be reached is among the undoubted certainties of the future! Slavery once abolished in the Rebel States, will give the death wound to slavery in the border States. When Arkansas is a free State Missouri cannot be a slave State.

Nevertheless, this is no time for the friends of freedom to fold their hands and consider their work at an end. The price of Liberty is eternal vigilance. Even after slavery has been legally abolished, and the rebellion substantially suppressed, even when there shall come representatives to Congress from the States now in rebellion, and they shall have repudiated the miserable and disastrous error of disunion, or secession, and the country shall have reached a condition of comparative peace, there will still remain an urgent necessity for the benevolent activity of the men and the women who have from the first opposed slavery from high moral conviction.

Slavery has existed in this country too long and has stamped its character too deeply and indelibly, to be blotted out in a day or a year, or even in a generation. The slave will yet remain in some sense a slave, long after the chains are taken from his limbs; and the master will retain much of the pride, the arrogance, imperiousness and conscious superiority and love of power, acquired by his former relation of master. Time, necessity, education, will be required to bring all classes into harmonious and natural relations.

But the South will not be the only part of the country demanding vigilance and exertion on the part of the true friends of the colored people. Our chief difficulty will be hereafter, as it has been heretofore with pro-slavery doughfaces, at the North. A dog will continue to scratch his neck even after the collar is removed. The sailor a night or two after reaching land feels his bed swimming from side to side, as if tossed by the sea. Daniel Webster received a large vote in Massachusetts after he was dead. It will not be strange if many Northern men whose politics, habits of thought, and accustomed submission to the slave power, leads them to continue to go through the forms of their ancient servility long after their old master slavery is in his grave.

Law and the sword can and will in the end abolish slavery. But law and the sword cannot abolish the malignant slaveholding sentiment which has kept the slave system alive in this country during two centuries. Pride of race, prejudice against color, will raise their hateful clamor for oppression of the Negro as heretofore. The slave having ceased to be the abject slave of a single master, his enemies will endeavor to make him the slave of society at large.

For a time at least, we may expect that this malign purpose and principle of wrong will get itself more or less expressed in party presses and platforms. Pro-Slavery political writers and speakers will not fail to inflame the ancient prejudice against the Negro, by exaggerating his faults and concealing or disparaging his virtues. A crime committed by one of the hated race,[1] while any excellence found in one black man will grudgingly be set to his individual credit. Hence we say that the friends of freedom, the men and women of the land who regard slavery as a crime and the slave as a man will still be needed even after slavery is abolished.

Douglass' Monthly, January, 1863

1. A part of the sentence was omitted in the *Monthly.*

As the need for manpower increased, Washington countenanced the policy of local recruiting of Southern Negro troops. But up to December, 1862, a national call for Negro volunteers had not been issued. The final Emancipation Proclamation, however, announced that freed slaves would be received into the armed forces of the United States "to garrison forts, positions, stations, and other places, and to man vessels of all sorts in said service." Early in 1863, a bill was passed in the House of Representatives authorizing the President "to enroll, arm, equip and receive into the land and naval service of the United States such number of volunteers as he may deem useful to suppress the present rebellion." The Senate returned the bill to the House, deeming it unnecessary legislation since the President had such power under previous acts of Congress.[1]

Acting on this interpretation, Governor John A. Andrew of Massachusetts requested permission to raise two regiments of Negro troops to serve for three years. On January 20, 1863, the War Department issued a general order to the Massachusetts executive which contained the clause: "Such volunteers to be enlisted for three years, unless sooner discharged, and may include persons of African descent, organized into separate corps." Immediately upon receipt of the order, Governor Andrew announced the formation of the 54th Massachusetts regiment, the first Negro regiment to be recruited in the North.

But Massachusetts with a comparatively small Negro population could sign up only a hundred volunteers in the first six weeks. Governor Andrew turned to his friend George L. Stearns, a leading New England Republican and formerly a close associate of John Brown, and persuaded him to take full charge of recruiting. An able organizer, Stearns

promptly collected five thousand dollars, advertised widely for enlistments, and set up recruiting posts from Boston to St. Louis. To speed up the work, Stearns called on Negro
leaders to act as recruiting agents. On February 23, he left for Rochester to enroll Douglass as an agent.[2]

Douglass needed little prodding. He had been urging the recruiting of Negroes into the
Union army from the first month of the war. Within three days after Stearn's visit, he issued [this] famous call. . . . Originally appearing in Douglass' journal, the stirring message was republished by the leading papers of the North. Printed in pamphlet form, the
call was widely circulated and became the most important agent for recruiting Negro soldiers. [III:30–31]

"MEN OF COLOR, TO ARMS!"

When first the rebel cannon shattered the walls of Sumter and drove away its
starving garrison, I predicted that the war then and there inaugurated would not
be fought out entirely by white men. Every month's experience during these
dreary years has confirmed that opinion. A war undertaken and brazenly carried on for the perpetual enslavement of colored men, calls logically and loudly
for colored men to help suppress it. Only a moderate share of sagacity was
needed to see that the arm of the slave was the best defense against the arm of
the slaveholder. Hence with every reverse to the national arms, with every ex-
ulting shout of victory raised by the slaveholding rebels, I have implored the imperiled nation to unchain against her foes, her powerful black hand. Slowly and
reluctantly that appeal is beginning to be heeded. Stop not now to complain that
it was not heeded sooner. It may or it may not have been best that it should not.
This is not the time to discuss that question. Leave it to the future. When the
war is over, the country is saved, peace is established, and the black man's rights
are secured, as they will be, history with an impartial hand will dispose of that
and sundry other questions. Action! Action! not criticism, is the plain duty of
this hour. Words are now useful only as they stimulate to blows. The office of
speech now is only to point out when, where, and how to strike to the best advantage. There is no time to delay. The tide is at its flood that leads on to fortune. From East to West, from North to South, the sky is written all over, "Now
or never." Liberty won by white men would lose half its luster. "Who would be
free themselves must strike the blow." "Better even die free, than to live slaves."
This is the sentiment of every brave colored man amongst us. There are weak
and cowardly men in all nations. We have them amongst us. They tell you this
is the "white man's war"; that you will be "no better off after than before the
war"; that the getting of you into the army is to "sacrifice you on the first opportunity." Believe them not; cowards themselves, they do not wish to have
their cowardice shamed by your brave example. Leave them to their timidity,
or to whatever motive may hold them back. I have not thought lightly of the
words I am now addressing you. The counsel I give comes of close observation
of the great struggle now in progress, and of the deep conviction that this is your
hour and mine. In good earnest then, and after the best deliberation, I now for
the first time during this war feel at liberty to call and counsel you to arms. By
every consideration which binds you to your enslaved fellow-countrymen, and

the peace and welfare of your country; by every aspiration which you cherish for the freedom and equality of yourselves and your children; by all the ties of blood and identity which make us one with the brave black men now fighting our battles in Louisiana and in South Carolina, I urge you to fly to arms, and smite with death the power that would bury the government and your liberty in the same hopeless grave. I wish I could tell you that the State of New York calls you to this high honor. For the moment her constituted authorities are silent on the subject. They will speak by and by, and doubtless on the right side; but we are not compelled to wait for her. We can get at the throat of treason and slavery through the State of Massachusetts. She was first in the War of Independence; first to break the chains of her slaves; first to make the black man equal before the law; first to admit colored children to her common schools, and she was first to answer with her blood the alarm cry of the nation, when its capital was menaced by rebels. You know her patriotic governor, and you know Charles Sumner. I need not add more.

Massachusetts now welcomes you to arms as soldiers. She has but a small colored population from which to recruit. She has full leave of the general government to send one regiment to the war, and she has undertaken to do it. Go quickly and help fill up the first colored regiment from the North. I am authorized to assure you that you will receive the same wages, the same rations, the same equipments, the same protection, the same treatment, and the same bounty, secured to the white soldiers. You will be led by able and skillful officers, men who will take especial pride in your efficiency and success. They will be quick to accord to you all the honor you shall merit by your valor, and see that your rights and feelings are respected by other soldiers. I have assured myself on these points, and can speak with authority. More than twenty years of unswerving devotion to our common cause may give me some humble claim to be trusted at this momentous crisis. I will not argue. To do so implies hesitation and doubt, and you do not hesitate. You do not doubt. The day dawns; the morning star is bright upon the horizon! The iron gate of our prison stands half open. One gallant rush from the North will fling it wide open, while four millions of our brothers and sisters shall march out into liberty. The chance is now given you to end in a day the bondage of centuries, and to rise in one bound from social degradation to the plane of common equality with all other varieties of men. Remember Denmark Vesey of Charleston; remember Nathaniel Turner of Southampton;[3] remember Shields Green and Copeland, who followed noble John Brown, and fell as glorious martyrs for the cause of the slave. Remember that in a contest with oppression, the Almighty has no attribute which can take sides with oppressors. The case is before you. This is our golden opportunity. Let us accept it, and forever wipe out the dark reproaches unsparingly hurled against us by our enemies. Let us win for ourselves the gratitude of our country, and the best blessings of our posterity through all time. The nucleus of this first regiment is now in camp at Readville, a short distance from Boston. I will under take to forward to Boston all persons adjudged fit to be mustered into the regiment, who shall apply to me at any time within the next two weeks.

Broadside, Rochester, March 21, 1863

1. F. A. Shannon, "The Federal Government and the Negro Soldier, 1861–1865," *Journal of Negro History*, vol. XI, Oct., 1926, p. 572.

2. Luis F. Emilio, *History of the Fifty-Fourth Regiment of Massachusetts of the Massachusetts Volunteer Infantry, 1863–1865*, Boston, 1894, pp. 11–12.

3. Denmark Vesey, a free Negro, was the leader of the great slave conspiracy in and around Charleston, South Carolina, in 1822. The plot was revealed by some of the participants, and Vesey, together with thirty-four other Negroes, was hanged.

Nathaniel Turner was the leader of the great slave uprising in Southampton County, Virginia, in 1831. Turner evaded arrest for more than six weeks, but was finally captured and tried, and on Nov. 11, 1831, he was executed.

In March, Douglass covered numerous towns in western New York to recruit a company of one hundred men for the regiment being organized in Massachusetts. His son Charles was the first to enlist; soon afterward his other son, Lewis, signed up. In Buffalo, Douglass obtained seven recruits. Rochester furnished thirteen. By April 1 he had sent twenty-three Negroes to Boston.[1]

His recruiting tour convinced Douglass that many Negroes did not fully understand why they should join the Union army. To meet this problem, he wrote an article in his journal listing and discussing nine reasons why the Negro should enlist. [III:31–32]

WHY SHOULD A COLORED MAN ENLIST?

This question has been repeatedly put to us while raising men for the 54th Massachusetts regiment during the past five weeks, and perhaps we cannot at present do a better service to the cause of our people or to the cause of the country than by giving a few of the many reasons why a colored man should enlist.

First. You are a man, although a colored man. If you were only a horse or an ox, incapable of deciding whether the rebels are right or wrong, you would have no responsibility, and might like the horse or the ox go on eating your corn or grass, in total indifference, as to which side is victorious or vanquished in this conflict. You are however no horse, and no ox, but a man, and whatever concerns man should interest you. He who looks upon a conflict between right and wrong, and does not help the right against the wrong, despises and insults his own nature, and invites the contempt of mankind. As between the North and South, the North is clearly in the right and the South is flagrantly in the wrong. You should therefore, simply as a matter of right and wrong, give your utmost aid to the North. In presence of such a contest there is no neutrality for any man. You are either for the Government or against the Government. Manhood requires you to take sides, and you are mean or noble according to how you choose between action and inaction.—If you are sound in body and mind, there is nothing in your *color* to excuse you from enlisting in the service of the republic against its enemies. If *color* should not be a criterion of rights, neither should it be a standard of duty. The whole duty of a man, belongs alike to white and black.

"A man's a man for a' that."

Second. You are however, not only a man, but an American citizen, so declared by the highest legal adviser of the Government, and you have hitherto expressed in various ways, not only your willingness but your earnest desire to fulfil any and every obligation which the relation of citizenship imposes. Indeed, you have hitherto felt wronged and slighted, because while white men of all other nations have been freely enrolled to serve the country, you a native born citizen have been coldly denied the honor of aiding in defense of the land of your birth. The injustice thus done you is now repented of by the Government and you are welcomed to a place in the army of the nation. Should you refuse to enlist *now,* you will justify the past contempt of the Government towards you and lead it to regret having honored you with a call to take up arms in its defense. You cannot but see that here is a good reason why you should promptly enlist.

Third. A third reason why a colored man should enlist is found in the fact that every Negro-hater and slavery-lover in the land regards the arming of Negroes as a calamity and is doing his best to prevent it. Even now all the weapons of malice, in the shape of slander and ridicule, are used to defeat the filling up of the 54th Massachusetts (colored) regiment. In nine cases out of ten, you will find it safe to do just what your enemy would gladly have you leave undone. What helps you hurts him. Find out what he does not want and give him a plenty of it.

Fourth. You should enlist to learn the use of arms, to become familiar with the means of securing, protecting and defending your own liberty. A day may come when men shall learn war no more, when justice shall be so clearly apprehended, so universally practiced, and humanity shall be so profoundly loved and respected, that war and bloodshed shall be confined only to beasts of prey. Manifestly however, that time has not yet come, and while all men should labor to hasten its coming, by the cultivation of all the elements conducive to peace, it is plain that for the present no race of men can depend wholly upon moral means for the maintenance of their rights. Men must either be governed by love or by fear. They must love to do right or fear to do wrong. The only way open to any race to make their rights respected is to learn how to defend them. When it is seen that black men no more than white men can be enslaved with impunity, men will be less inclined to enslave and oppress them. Enlist therefore, that you may learn the art and assert the ability to defend yourself and your race.

Fifth. You are a member of a long enslaved and despised race. Men have set down your submission to Slavery and insult, to a lack of manly courage. They point to this fact as demonstrating your fitness only to be a servile class. You should enlist and disprove the slander, and wipe out the reproach. When you shall be seen nobly defending the liberties of your own country against rebels and traitors— brass itself will blush to use such arguments imputing cowardice against you.

Sixth. Whether you are or are not, entitled to all the rights of citizenship in this country has long been a matter of dispute to your prejudice. By enlisting in the service of your country at this trial hour, and upholding the National Flag, you stop the mouths of traducers and win applause even from the iron lips of ingratitude. Enlist and you make this your country in common with all other men born in the country or out of it.

Seventh. Enlist for your own sake. Decried and derided as you have been and still are, you need an act of this kind by which to recover your own self-respect. You have to some extent rated your value by the estimate of your enemies and hence have counted yourself less than you are. You owe it to yourself and your race to rise from your social debasement and take your place among the soldiers of your country, a man among men. Depend upon it, the subjective effect of this one act of enlisting will be immense and highly beneficial. You will stand more erect, walk more assured, feel more at ease, and be less liable to insult than you ever were before. He who fights the battles of America may claim America as his country—and have that claim respected. Thus in defending your country now against rebels and traitors you are defending your own liberty, honor, manhood and self-respect.

Eighth. You should enlist because your doing so will be one of the most certain means of preventing the country from drifting back into the whirlpool of Pro-Slavery Compromise at the end of the war, which is now our greatest danger. He who shall witness another Compromise with Slavery in this country will see the free colored man of the North more than ever a victim of the pride, lust, scorn and violence of all classes of white men. The whole North will be but another Detroit, where every white fiend may with impunity revel in unrestrained beastliness towards people of color; they may burn their houses, insult their wives and daughters, and kill indiscriminately. If you mean to live in this country now is the time for you to do your full share in making it a country where you and your children after you can live in comparative safety. Prevent a compromise with the traitors, compel them to come back to the Union whipped and humbled into obedience and all will be well. But let them come back as masters and all their hate and hellish ingenuity will be exerted to stir up the ignorant masses of the North to hate, hinder and persecute the free colored people of the North. That most inhuman of all modern enactments, with its bribed judges, and summary process, the Fugitive Slave Law, with all its infernal train of canting divines, preaching the gospel of kidnapping, as twelve years ago, will be revived against the free colored people of the North. One or two black brigades will do much to prevent all this.

Ninth. You should enlist because the war for the Union, whether men so call it or not, is a war for Emancipation. The salvation of the country, by the inexorable relation of cause and effect, can be secured only by the complete abolition of Slavery. The President has already proclaimed emancipation to the Slaves in the rebel States which is tantamount to declaring Emancipation in all the States, for Slavery must exist everywhere in the South in order to exist anywhere in the South. Can you ask for a more inviting, ennobling and soul enlarging work, than that of making one of the glorious Band who shall carry Liberty to your enslaved people? Remember that identified with the Slave in color, you will have a power that white soldiers have not, to attract them to your lines and induce them to take up arms in a common cause. One black Brigade will, for this work, be worth more than two white ones. Enlist, therefore, enlist without delay, enlist now, and forever put an end to the human barter and butchery which have stained the whole South with the warm blood of your people, and loaded its air with their groans. Enlist, and deserve not only well of your country, and win for yourselves, a name and a place among men, but secure to yourself what is infinitely more precious, the fast dropping tears of gratitude of your kith and kin marked out for destruction, and who are but now ready to perish.

When time's ample curtain shall fall upon our national tragedy, and our hillsides

and valleys shall neither redden with the blood nor whiten with the bones of kinsmen and countrymen who have fallen in the sanguinary and wicked strife; when
grim visaged war has smoothed his wrinkled front and our country shall have regained its normal condition as a leader of nations in the occupation and blessings
of peace—and history shall record the names of heroes and martyrs— who bravely
answered the call of patriotism and Liberty—against traitors, thieves and assassins—let it not be said that in the long list of glory, composed of men of all nations—there appears the name of no colored man.

Douglass' Monthly, April, 1863

1. Emilio, *op. cit.,* p. 13; Douglass to Gerrit Smith, Mar. 6, 1863, Gerrit Smith Papers, Syracuse University.

———————

ANOTHER WORD TO COLORED MEN

Let me sound once more the trump of war. We should have blast on blast from
that trumpet, till thrilled with its notes every brave black men of the North, capable of bearing arms, shall come forth, clad in complete steel, ready to make the
twin monsters, slavery and rebellion, crumble together in the dust. The white
man's soul was tried in 1776. The black man's soul is tried in 1863. The first stood
the test, and is received as genuine—so may the last. The broad eye of the nation
is fixed upon the black man. They are half in doubt as to whether his conduct in
this crisis will refute or confirm their allegations against the colored race. They
stand ready to applaud, or to hurl the bolt of condemnation.—Which shall it be,
my brave and strong hearted brothers? The decision of our destiny is now, as never
before, in our hands. We may lie here low in the dust, despised and spit upon by
every passer-by; or we may, like brave men, rise and unlock to ourselves the golden
gates of a glorious future. Depend upon it, we have no time to lose. To hold back
is to invite infamy upon ourselves, and upon our children. All the Negro hating
vermin of the land may crawl over us, if our courage quails at this hour. He is
whipped oftenest who is whipped easiest. As with individuals so with nations and
classes. It has been the fashion in this country—even in some of our Northern
cities—to assault and mob colored citizens, for no other reason than the ease with
which it could be done. We have it in our power to do something towards changing this cowardly fashion. When it is once found that black men can give blows as
well as take them, men will find more congenial employment than pounding them.
The black man, in arms to fight for the freedom of his race, and the safety and security of the country, will give his countrymen a higher and better revelation of his
character. The case stands thus: We have asked the nation for a chance to fight the
Rebels—to fight against slavery, and to fight for freedom. Well, the chance is now
given us. We must improve it, or sink deeper than ever in the pit of social and political degradation, from which we have been struggling for years to extricate our-

selves. When the nationality of the United States is set in safety, in part of your hands, the whole world would cry shame upon any attempt to denationalize you.

To fight for the Government in this tremendous war is, then, to fight for nationality and for a place with all other classes of our fellow-citizens. I know that Congress has been pleased to say in deference to prevailing prejudice that colored men shall not rise higher than company officers. They might as well have passed a law that black men shall not be brave; that they shall not learn to read; that they shall not shoot straight; and that they shall not grow taller than five feet nine inches and a half. The law is even more absurd than mean. Enter the army and deserve promotion, and you will be sure to get it in the end. To say you will not go into the army until you can be a Colonel or a General, is about as wise as to say you won't go into the water until you shall learn how to swim.—When the priest told Patrick that he had prayed his father's head and shoulders out of purgatory, and a little more money was wanted to complete the work, Paddy declined to give it, on the ground that if his father had been so fortunate as to get his head out, he would risk his getting his whole body out.—Pat's wisdom will be good in our case. Once let colored men be made Captains of companies, and demonstrate their capacity for such captaincy, and I'll risk their upward progress. The great thing to be done first of all is, to get an eagle on your button and a musket on your shoulder. "It is the first step that costs." Take it, and all will come right after that first step is well and firmly taken.

Some say wait till New York shall call us as a part of her quota. My answer to this objection is, that New York will be far more likely to call us if she finds us responding to the call of Massachusetts. If the call of Massachusetts shall prove a success, other States will follow her example. If she fails, visibly fails, no State will be foolish enough to follow in her footsteps. If you are in earnest, and really wish to get at the foe, you will go by way of Massachusetts, since that is the only way now open. Our first business is to make the Bay State regiment a success.

To fail there is to fail everywhere and to succeed there is to succeed everywhere.

Do not flatter yourselves that the colored troops at the South can do our work. They cannot do it, no matter how brave and enduring they may prove themselves to be. The fact that they make better soldiers than we will be quoted against us. Their good behavior will be set to the credit of slavery, and we shall be told that while slavery elevates the character of the colored man to the level of the soldier, freedom debases him to the level of a spiritless coward. There is no mistake about it, colored men of the North; we shall either go up, or we shall go down, precisely as we ourselves shall determine in view of the demands of this hour. The day that sees the fifty fourth regiment of Massachusetts march down Broadway, composed of well drilled, well-uniformed, well-armed, well-appointed colored soldiers, under the ample folds of the Star Spangled Banner—lifting their high and orderly footsteps to the inspiring notes of "Old John Brown," singing those words with a spirit and meaning with which they were never sung before, will be the proudest and happiest day for the colored race ever witnessed in the United States. After that spectacle, colored men and women in New York will walk among their country men and women without asking pardon for having been born—and with a higher consciousness of the dignity of human nature.

But enough of this. I have undertaken to raise at least one company for the fifty fourth Massachusetts regiment. I am anxious to have the work done speedily. This may be hastened by the co-operation of friends in different parts of the State. Let them get together and talk the matter over and send me the names of such of their number as are willing to go when called upon. During the past week I have twice visited Buffalo, and at one meeting obtained the names of seven good looking young men—every one of whom can read and write. In Rochester I have thirteen names, my son heading the list. A letter from Oswego assures me that eight or nine men are ready to go from there. This week I shall visit Auburn, Syracuse, Troy and Albany. If I were recruiting with advantages held out to white soldiers for this State I could raise a regiment more easily than I can raise a company under present circumstances.

Frederick Douglass

Douglass' Monthly, April, 1863

———

The unjust treatment of Negro soldiers made [Douglass' recruitment] work difficult. Audiences pointed out that wages of Negro soldiers did not equal those of the white soldiers. After July, 1862, the latter received rations, $13 a month, and a $3.50 allowance for clothing. The Negro was paid as a laborer, not as a soldier, receiving rations, $7 a month, and a $3 allowance for clothing.[1]

The Negro soldiers objected vigorously to this discrimination, and many Negroes refused to enlist because of the differential in pay. Recruiting agents found it more and more difficult to secure signatures.

No one understood more clearly than Douglass the strategic importance of the active participation of Negro troops in helping determine the successful outcome of the war. Hence nothing should interfere with participation of the Negro in the Union army. Discrimination against Negro soldiers must be consistently fought, but it must not serve as a barrier to the full participation of the Negro in the war. The major issue was to win the war against slavery, and just as necessity and organized protests had forced the administration to emancipate the slaves, they would compel it to place Negro soldiers on an equality with the white soldiers. "Colored men going into the army and navy," Douglass wrote as early as February, 1863, "must expect annoyance. They will be severely criticized and even insulted—but let no man hold back on this account. We shall be fighting a double battle, against slavery in the South and against prejudice and proscription in the North—and the case presents the very best assurances of success."[2]

But many Negroes were not convinced. On June 17, Philadelphia received permission to raise a Negro division. Encountering difficulty in securing enlistments, Stearns, now in charge of recruiting Negro regiments for the Federal government, arranged a mass meeting at National Hall on July 6 with Douglass as the main speaker.

In his speech to the Negro youth of Philadelphia Douglass offered a brilliant analysis of the two forces that were struggling for mastery in the War: the concept that the Negro people were an inferior people and should be enslaved forever as against the principle that all men are naturally fundamentally equal. [III:33–34]

ADDRESS FOR THE PROMOTION OF COLORED ENLISTMENTS, delivered at a mass meeting in Philadelphia, July 6, 1863

Mr. President and Fellow Citizens:

I shall not attempt to follow Judge Kelley and Miss Dickinson in their eloquent and thrilling appeals to colored men to enlist in the service of the United States. They have left nothing to be desired on that point. I propose to look at the subject in a plain and practical common-sense light. There are obviously two views to be taken of such enlistments—a broad view and a narrow view. I am willing to take both, and consider both. The narrow view of this subject is that which respects the matter of dollars and cents. There are those among us who say they are in favor of taking a hand in this tremendous war, but add they wish to do so on terms of equality with white men. They say if they enter the service, endure all the hardships, perils and suffering—if they make bare their breasts, and with strong arms and courageous hearts confront rebel cannons, and wring victory from the jaws of death, they should have the same pay, the same rations, the same bounty, and the same favorable conditions every way afforded to other men.

I shall not oppose this view. There is something deep down in the soul of every man present which assents to the justice of the claim thus made, and honors the manhood and self respect which insists upon it. I say at once, in peace and in war, I am content with nothing for the black man short of equal and exact justice. The only question I have, and the point at which I differ from those who refuse to enlist, is whether the colored man is more likely to obtain justice and equality while refusing to assist in putting down this tremendous rebellion than he would be if he should promptly, generously and earnestly give his hand and heart to the salvation of the country in this its day of calamity and peril. Nothing can be more plain, nothing more certain than that the speediest and best possible way open to us to manhood, equal rights and elevation, is that we enter this service. For my own part, I hold that if the Government of the United States offered nothing more, as an inducement to colored men to enlist, than bare subsistence and arms, considering the moral effect of compliance upon ourselves, it would be the wisest and best thing for us to enlist. There is something ennobling in the possession of arms, and we of all other people in the world stand in need of their ennobling influence.

The case presented in the present war, and the light in which every colored man is bound to view it, may be stated thus. There are two governments struggling now for the possession of and endeavoring to bear rule over the United States— one has its capital in Richmond, and is represented by Mr. Jefferson Davis, and the other has its capital at Washington, and is represented by "Honest Old Abe." These two governments are today face to face, confronting each other with vast armies, and grappling each other upon many a bloody field, north and south, on the banks of the Mississippi, and under the shadows of the Alleghanies. Now, the question for every colored man is, or ought to be, what attitude is assumed by these respective governments and armies towards the rights and liberties of the colored race in this country; which is for us, and which against us!

Now, I think there can be no doubt as to the attitude of the Richmond or Confederate Government. Wherever else there has been concealment, here all is frank, open, and diabolically straightforward. Jefferson Davis and his government make no secret as to the cause of this war, and they do not conceal the purpose of the war. That purpose is nothing more nor less than to make the slavery of the African race universal and perpetual on this continent. It is not only evident from the history and logic of events, but the declared purpose of the atrocious war now being waged against the country. Some, indeed, have denied that slavery has anything to do with the war, but the very same men who do this affirm it in the same breath in which they deny it, for they tell you that the abolitionists are the cause of the war. Now, if the abolitionists are the cause of the war, they are the cause of it only because they have sought the abolition of slavery. View it in any way you please, therefore, the rebels are fighting for the existence of slavery—they are fighting for the privilege, the horrid privilege, of sundering the dearest ties of human nature—of trafficking in slaves and the souls of men—for the ghastly privilege of scourging women and selling innocent children.

I say this is not the concealed object of the war, but the openly confessed and shamelessly proclaimed object of the war. Vice-President Stephens has stated, with the utmost clearness and precision, the difference between the fundamental ideas of the Confederate Government and those of the Federal Government.[3] One is based upon the idea that colored men are an inferior race, who may be enslaved and plundered forever and to the hearts' content of any men of a different complexion, while the Federal Government recognizes the natural and fundamental equality of all men.

I say, again, we all know that this Jefferson Davis government holds out to us nothing but fetters, chains, auction blocks, bludgeons, branding-irons, and eternal slavery and degradation. If it triumphs in this contest, woe, woe, ten thousands woes, to the black man! Such of us as are free, in all the likelihoods of the case, would be given over to the most excruciating tortures, while the last hope of the long crushed bondman would be extinguished forever.

Now, what is the attitude of the Washington Government towards the colored race? What reasons have we to desire its triumph in the present contest? Mind, I do not ask what was its attitude towards us before this bloody rebellion broke out. I do not ask what was its disposition when it was controlled by the very men who are now fighting to destroy it when they could no longer control it. I do not even ask what it was two years ago, when McClellan shamelessly gave out that in a war between loyal slaves and disloyal masters, he would take the side of the masters, against the slaves—when he openly proclaimed his purpose to put down slave insurrections with an iron hand—when glorious Ben. Butler, now stunned into a conversion to anti-slavery principles, (which I have every reason to believe sincere,) proffered his services to the Governor of Maryland, to suppress a slave insurrection, while treason ran riot in that State, and the warm, red blood of Massachusetts soldiers still stained the pavements of Baltimore.

I do not ask what was the attitude of this Government when many of the officers and men who had undertaken to defend it, openly threatened to throw down their arms and leave the service if men of color should step forward to defend it, and be invested with the dignity of soldiers. Moreover, I do not ask what was the position of this Government when our loyal camps were made slave hunting grounds, and United States officers performed the disgusting duty of slave dogs to hunt down slaves for rebel masters. These were all dark and terrible days for the republic. I do not ask you about the dead past. I bring you to the living present. Events more mighty than men, eternal Providence, all-wise and all-controlling, have placed us in new relations to the Government and the Government to us. What that Government is to us today, and what it will be tomorrow, is made evident by a very few facts. Look at them, colored men. Slavery in the District of Columbia is abolished forever; slavery in all the territories of the United States is abolished forever; the foreign slave trade, with its ten thousand revolting abominations, is rendered impossible; slavery in ten States of the Union is abolished forever; slavery in the five remaining States is as certain to follow the same fate as the night is to follow the day. The independence of Haiti is recognized;[4] her Minister sits beside our Prime Minister, Mr. Seward, and dines at his table in Washington, while colored men are excluded from the cars in Philadelphia; showing that a black man's complexion in Washington, in the presence of the Federal Government, is less offensive than in the city of brotherly love. Citizenship is no longer denied us under this government.

Under the interpretation of our rights by Attorney General Bates, we are American citizens. We can import goods, own and sail ships, and travel in foreign countries with American passports in our pockets; and now, so far from there being any opposition, so far from excluding us from the army as soldiers, the President at Washington, the Cabinet and the Congress, the generals commanding and the whole army of the nation unite in giving us one thunderous welcome to share with them in the honor and glory of suppressing treason and upholding the star-spangled banner. The revolution is tremendous, and it becomes us as wise men to recognize the change, and to shape our action accordingly.

I hold that the Federal Government was never, in its essence, anything but an anti-slavery government. Abolish slavery tomorrow, and not a sentence or syllable of the Constitution need be altered. It was purposely so framed as to give no claim, no sanction to the claim, of property in man. If in its origin slavery had any relation to the government, it was only as the scaffolding to the magnificent structure, to be removed as soon as the building was completed. There is in the Constitution no East, no West, no North, no South, no black, no white, no slave, no slaveholder, but all are citizens who are of American birth.

Such is the government, fellow-citizens, you are now called upon to uphold with your arms. Such is the government that you are called upon to co-operate with in burying rebellion and slavery in a common grave. Never since the world began was a better chance offered to a long enslaved and oppressed people. The opportunity is given us to be men. With one courageous resolution we may blot out the hand-writing of the ages against us. Once let the black man get upon his person the brass letters U.S.; let him get an eagle on his button, and a musket on his shoulder, and bullets in his pocket, and there is no power on the earth or under the earth which can deny that he has earned the right of citizenship in the United States. I say again, this is our chance, and woe betide us if we fail to embrace it. The immortal bard hath told us:

> "There is a tide in the affairs of men,
> Which, taken at the flood, leads on to fortune.
> Omitted, all the voyage of their life

Is bound in shallows and in miseries.
We must take the current when it serves,
Or lose our ventures."

Do not flatter yourselves, my friends, that you are more important to the government than the government is to you. You stand but as the plank to the ship. This rebellion can be put down without your help. Slavery can be abolished by white men; but liberty so won for the black man, while it may leave him an object of pity, can never make him an object of respect.

Depend upon it, this is no time for hesitation. Do you say you want the same pay that white men get? I believe that the justice and magnanimity of your country will speedily grant it. But will you be overnice about this matter? Do you get as good wages now as white men get by staying out of the service? Don't you work for less every day than white men get? You know you do. Do I hear you say you want black officers? Very well, and I have not the slightest doubt that in the progress of this war, we shall see black officers, black colonels, and generals even. But is it not ridiculous in us in all at once refusing to be commanded by white men in time of war, when we are everywhere commanded by white men in time of peace? Do I hear you say still that you are a son, and want your mother provided for in your absence?—a husband and want your wife cared for?—a brother, and want your sister secured against want? I honor you for your solicitude. Your mothers, your wives, and your sisters ought to be cared for, and an association of gentlemen, composed of responsible white and colored men, is now being organized in this city for this very purpose.

Do I hear you say you offered your services to Pennsylvania and were refused? I know it. But what of that? The State is not more than the nation. The greater includes the lesser. Because the State refuses, you should all the more readily turn to the United States. When the children fall out, they should refer the quarrel to the parent. "You came unto your own, and your own received you not." But the broad gates of the United States stand open night and day. Citizenship in the United States will, in the end, secure your citizenship in the State.

Young men of Philadelphia, you are without excuse. The hour has arrived, and your place is in the Union army. Remember that the musket—the United States musket with its bayonet of steel—is better than all mere parchment guarantees of liberty. In your hands that musket means liberty; and should your constitutional right at the close of this war be denied, which, in the nature of things, it cannot be, your brethren are safe while you have a Constitution which proclaims your right to keep and bear arms.

Douglass' Monthly, August, 1863

1. Herbert Aptheker, *Essays in the History of the American Negro,* New York, 1945, p. 195.
2. *Douglass' Monthly,* Feb., 1863.
3. In March, 1861, Alexander H. Stephens, Vice President of the Southern Confederacy, delivered a speech upon the causes of secession, during which he said: "The prevailing ideas entertained by him [Jefferson] and most of the leading statesmen at the time of formation of the old Constitution were that the enslavement of the African was in violation of the laws of nature; that it was wrong in principle, socially, morally, and politically. . . .

"Our new government is founded upon exactly the opposite ideas; the foundations are laid, its cornerstone rests upon the great truth that the Negro is not equal to the white man; that slavery—subordination to the superior race—is his natural and moral condition. . . . It is upon this . . . our social fabric is firmly planted; and I cannot permit myself to doubt the ultimate success of a full recognition of this principle throughout the civilized and enlightened world. . . ." (See Horace Greeley, *The American Conflict*, New York, 1867, vol. I, p. 417.)

4. In his first annual message to Congress, President Lincoln observed: "If any good reason exists why we should persevere longer in withholding our recognition of the independence and sovereignty of Hayti and Liberia, I am unable to discover it." He urged Congress to approve the proposal by an appropriation "for maintaining a *charge d'affaires* near each of those new states."

On February 4, 1862, Senator Sumner reported a bill from the Committee on Foreign Relations, authorizing the President to appoint diplomatic representatives to the republics of Haiti and Liberia. After considerable debate, the bill was passed by a vote of eighty-six to thirty-seven, and approved by the President on June 5, 1862.

Suffering from poor arms and equipment, inferior training, and incompetent officers, Negro soldiers were often hurried into battle without adequate preparation. Although they fought bravely in every engagement, earning the praise of Union officers, under such circumstances the slaughter was fearful. For example, in mid-July, 1863, the 54th Massachusetts, sick and exhausted from days of fighting and forced marches, was ordered to storm Fort Wagner. A weary regiment led the ill-starred assault and suffered about 42 percent casualties. Colonel Shaw and many of his soldiers were killed.

The treatment of Negro soldiers who fell into the hands of the enemy was particularly cruel. In December, 1862, Jefferson Davis announced that any Negro soldier who was taken prisoner would be turned over to state authorities and dealt with as an insurrectionist according to the slave codes of the South. As these codes stipulated death sentence for "subversive" activities, many free Negro soldiers died convicted of "conspiring to murder or maim a white person." Under the regulation no exchange of prisoners could be effected where Negroes were concerned. In most cases Negroes captured in battle were brutally murdered by the Confederates. Even the wounded were not spared.[1]

From the South came reports detailing grievances and complaints of Negro soldiers at the very time that Douglass was engaged in securing volunteers for Negro regiments. Infuriated, he published an open letter in which he lashed out at Lincoln for failing to redress the grievances of Negro soldiers. . . . Having set forth [his] demands, Douglass called a halt to his recruiting work until the government's policies for Negro soldiers were changed. His duty, he felt, was to provide decent conditions for Negroes in the armed forces before asking any more to enlist. [III:34–35]

TO MAJOR G. L. STEARNS

Rochester, August 1st, 1863

My Dear Sir:

Having declined to attend the meeting to promote enlistments, appointed for me at Pittsburgh, in present circumstances, I owe you a word of explanation. I have hitherto deemed it a duty, as it certainly has been a pleasure, to cooperate with you in the work of raising colored troops in the free states, to fight the battles of the Republic against the slaveholding rebels and traitors. Upon the first call you gave me to this work, I responded with alacrity. I saw, or thought I saw a ray of light, brightening the future of my whole race as well as that of our war troubled country, in arousing colored men to fight for the nation's life, I continue to believe in the black man's arm, and still have some hope in the integrity of our rulers. Nevertheless, I must for the present leave to others the work of persuading colored men to join the Union Army. I owe it to my long abused people, and especially of them already in the army, to expose their wrongs and plead their cause. I cannot do that in connection with recruiting. When I plead for recruits I want to do it with all my heart, without qualification. I cannot do that now. The impression settles upon me that colored men have much overrated the enlightenment, justice and generosity of our rulers at Washington. In my humble way I have contributed somewhat to that false estimate. You know, that when the idea of raising colored troops was first suggested, the special duty to be assigned them, was the garrisoning of forts and arsenals in certain warm, unhealthy and miasmatic localities in the South. They were thought to be better adapted to that service than white troops. White troops, trained to war, brave and daring, were to take fortifications, and the blacks were to hold them and keep them from falling again into the hands of the rebels.—Three advantages were to arise out of this wise division of labor. 1st. The spirit and pride of white troops was not to waste itself in dull and monotonous inactivity in fort-life. Their arms were to be kept bright by constant use. 2dly. The health of the white troops was to be preserved. 3dly. Black troops were to have the advantage of sound military training, and be otherwise useful at the same time that they should be tolerably secure from capture by the rebels, who early avowed their determination to enslave and slaughter them in defiance of the laws of war. Two out of the three advantages, were to accrue to the white troops. Thus far however, I believe that no such duty as holding fortifications has been committed to colored troops. They have done far other and more important work than holding fortifications. I have no special complaint to make at this point, and I simply mention it to strengthen the statement that from the beginning of this business it was the confident belief among both the colored and white friends of colored enlistments that President Lincoln as Commander-in-Chief of the army and navy would certainly see to it, that his colored troops should be so handled and disposed of as to be but little exposed to capture by the rebels, and that—if so exposed—as they have repeatedly been from the first, the President possessed both the disposition and the means for compelling the rebels to respect the rights of such as might fall in their hands. The piratical proclamation of President Davis announcing Slavery and assassination to colored prisoners was before the country and the world. But men had faith in Mr. Lincoln and his advisers. He was silent, to be sure, but charity suggested that being a man of action rather than words, he only waited for a case in which he should be required to act. This faith in the man enabled us to speak with warmth and effect in urging enlistments among colored men. That faith, my dear Sir, is now nearly gone. Various occasions have arisen during the last six months for the exercise of his power in behalf of the colored men in his service. But no word comes from Mr. Lincoln or from the War Department, sternly assuring the Rebel Chief that inquisitions shall yet be made for innocent blood. No word of retaliation when a black man is slain by a rebel in cold blood. No word was said when free men from Massachusetts were caught and sold into slavery in Texas. No word is said when brave black men who according to the testimony of both friend and foe, fought like heroes to plant the star spangled banner on the blazing parapets of Fort Wagner, and in doing so were captured, some multilated and killed, and others sold into slavery. The same crushing silence reigns over this scandalous outrage as over that of the slaughtered teamsters at Murfreesboro.—The same as over that at Millikens Bend and Vicksburg. I am free to say, my dear Sir, that the case looks as if the confiding colored soldiers had been betrayed into bloody hands by the very Government in whose defense they were heroically fighting. I know what you will say to this; you will say; "wait a little longer, and after all, the best way to have justice done to your people is to get them into the army as fast as possible." You may be right in this; my argument has been the same, but have we not already waited, and have we not already shown the highest qualities of soldiers and on this account deserve the protection of the Government for which we are fighting? Can any case stronger than that before Charleston ever arise? If the President is ever to demand justice and humanity for black soldiers, is not this the time for him to do it? How many 54ths must be cut to pieces, its mutilated prisoners killed and its living sold into Slavery, to be tortured to death by inches before Mr. Lincoln shall say: "Hold, enough!"

You know the 54th. To you, more than any one man belongs the credit of raising that Regiment. Think of its noble and brave officers literally hacked to pieces while many of its rank and file have been sold into a slavery worse than death, and pardon me if I hesitate about assisting in raising a fourth Regiment until the President shall give the same protection to them as to white soldiers. With warm and sincere regards,

Frederick Douglass

Since writing the foregoing letter, which we have now put upon record, we have received assurance from Major Stearns, that the Government of the United States is already taking measures which will secure for the captured colored soldiers, at Charleston and elsewhere, the same protection against slavery and cruelty, extended to white soldiers. What ought to have been done at the beginning, comes late, but it comes. The poor colored soldiers have purchased this interference dearly. It really seems that nothing of justice, liberty, or humanity can come to us except through tears and blood.

Douglass' Monthly, August, 1863

1. Herbert Aptheker, *To Be Free: Studies in American Negro History*, New York, 1948, pp. 83–92, 94–98; Brainerd Dyer, "The Treatment of Colored Union Troops by the Confederates," *Journal of Negro History*, vol. XX, July, 1935, pp. 273–86.

THE COMMANDER-IN-CHIEF AND HIS BLACK SOLDIERS

Whatever else may be said of President Lincoln, the most malignant Copperhead in the country cannot reproach him with any undue solicitude for the lives and liberties of the brave black men, who are now giving their arms and hearts to the support of his Government. When a boy, on a slave plantation the saying was common: "Half a cent to kill a Negro and half a cent to bury him."—The luxury of killing and burying could be enjoyed by the poorest members of Southern society, and no strong temptation was required to induce white men thus to kill and bury the black victims of their lust and cruelty.—With a Bible and pulpit affirming that the Negro is accursed of God, it is not strange that men should curse him, and that all over the South there should be manifested for the life and liberty of this description of man, the utterest indifference and contempt. Unhappily the same indifference and contempt for the lives of colored men is found wherever slavery has an advocate or treason an apologist. In the late terrible mobs in New York and elsewhere, the grim features of this malice towards colored men was everywhere present. Beat, shoot, hang, stab, kill, burn and destroy the Negro, was the cry of the crowd. Religion has cursed him and the law has enslaved him, and why may not the mob kill him?—Such has been our national education on this subject, and that it still has power over Mr. Lincoln seems evident from the fact, that no measures have been openly taken by him to cause the laws of civilized warfare to be observed towards his colored soldiers. The slaughter of blacks taken as captives, seems to affect him as little as the slaughter of beeves for the use of his army. More than six months ago Mr. Jefferson Davis told Mr. Lincoln and the world that he meant to treat blacks not as soldiers but as felons.[1] The threat was openly made, and has been faithfully executed by the rebel chief. At Murfreesboro twenty colored teamsters in the Federal service, were taken by the rebels, and though not soldiers, and only servants, they were in cold blood—every man of them—shot down. At Milliken's Bend, the same black flag with its death's head and cross-bones was raised. When Banks entered Port Hudson be found white federal prisoners, but no black ones. Those of the latter taken, were no doubt, in cold blood put to the sword. Today, news from Charleston tells us that Negro soldiers taken as prisoners will not be exchanged, but sold into slavery—that some twenty of such prisoners are now in their hands. Thousands of Negroes are now being enrolled in the service of the Federal Government. The Government calls them, and they come. They freely and joyously rally around the flag of the Union, and take all the risks, ordinary and extraordinary, involved in this war. They do it not for office, for thus far, they get none; they do it not for money, for thus far, their pay is less than that of white men. They go into this war to affirm their manhood, to strike for liberty and country.—If any class of men in this war can claim the honor of fighting for principle, and not from passion, for ideas, not from brutal malice, the colored soldier can make that claim preeminently. He strikes for manhood and freedom, under the forms of law and the usages of civilized warfare. He does not go forth as a savage with tomahawk and scalping knife, but in strict accordance with the rules of honorable warfare. Yet he is now openly threatened with slavery and assassination by the rebel Government—and the threat has been savagely executed.

What has Mr. Lincoln to say about this slavery and murder? What has he said?—Not one word. In the hearing of the nation he is as silent as an oyster on the whole subject. If two white men are threatened with assassination, the

Richmond Rebels are promptly informed that the Federal Government will retaliate sternly and severely. But when colored soldiers are so threatened, no word comes from the Capitol. What does this silence mean? Is there any explanation short of base and scandalous contempt for the just rights of colored soldiers?

For a time we tried to think that there might be solid reasons of state against answering the threats of Jefferson Davis—but the Government has knocked this favorable judgment from under us, by its prompt threat of retaliation in the case of the two white officers at Richmond who are under sentence of death. Men will ask, the world will ask, why interference should be made for those young white officers thus selected for murder, and not for the brave black soldiers who may be flung by the fortunes of war into the hands of the rebels? Is the right to "life, liberty and the pursuit of happiness" less sacred in the case of the one than the other?

It may be said that the black soldiers have enlisted with the threat of Jefferson Davis before them, and they have assumed their position intelligently, with a full knowledge of the consequences incurred. If they have, they have by that act shown themselves all the more worthy of protection. It is noble in the Negro to brave unusual danger for the life of the Republic, but it is mean and base in the Republic if it rewards such generous and unselfish devotion by assassination, when a word would suffice to make the laws of war respected, and to prevent the crime. Shocking enough are the ordinary horrors of war, but the war of the rebels toward the colored men is marked by deeds which well might "shame extremest hell." And until Mr. Lincoln shall interpose his power to prevent these atrocious assassinations of Negro soldiers, the civilized world will hold him equally with Jefferson Davis responsible for them. The question is already being asked: Why is it that colored soldiers which were first enlisted with a view to "garrison forts and arsenals, on the Southern coast"—where white men suffer from climate, should never be heard of in any such forts and arsenals? Was that a trick? Why is it that they who were enlisted to fight the fevers of the South, while white soldiers fight the rebels are now only heard of in "forlorn hopes," in desperate charges always in the van, as at Port Hudson, Milliken's Bend, James Island and Fort Wagner?[2] Green colored recruits are called upon to assume the position of veterans. They have performed their part gallantly and gloriously, but by all the proofs they have given of their patriotism and bravery we protest against the meanness, ingratitude and cruelty of the Government, in whose behalf they fight, if that Government remains longer a silent witness of their enslavement and assassination. Having had patience and forbearance with the silence of Mr. Lincoln a few months ago, we could at least imagine some excuses for his silence as to the fate of colored troops falling by the fortunes of war into the hands of the rebels, but the time for this is past. It is now for every man who has any sense of right and decency, to say nothing of gratitude, to speak out trumpet-tongued in the ears of Mr. Lincoln and his Government and demand from him a declaration of purpose, to hold the rebels to a strict account for every black federal soldier taken as a prisoner. For every black prisoner slain in cold blood, Mr. Jefferson Davis should be made to understand that one rebel officer shall suffer death, and for every colored soldier sold into slavery, a rebel shall be held as a hostage. For our Government to do less than this, is to deserve the indignation and the execration of mankind.

Douglass' Monthly, August, 1863

1. Jefferson Davis' proclamation, issued on December 23, 1862, declared: "That all negro slaves captured in arms be at once delivered over to the executive authorities of the respective States to which they belong, to be dealt with according to the laws of said states."

2. The attack on Fort Wagner, July 18, 1863, was led by the 54th Massachusetts, the first colored regiment from the North. Sergeant William H. Carney planted the colors of the regiment on top of the fort. Several of the commanders were killed, including Colonel Robert Gould Shaw; many were wounded, and the brigade was compelled to retire.

In the battle of Port Hudson, May 27, 1863, two colored regiments, the First and Third Louisiana Native Guards, distinguished themselves for bravery and received special commendation from General Banks.

At the battle of Milliken's Bend, June 7, 1863, the Negroes were extremely important, and in bitter hand-to-hand fighting were victorious. Negro soldiers who were wounded were killed in this and in other battles, the common slogan of the Confederates being that "no quarter" should be shown them.

[In July,] Douglass went to the war office where Secretary Stanton granted him an interview. When Douglass expressed a willingness to accept a military commission, Stanton promised him the rank of assistant adjutant on the staff of General Lorenzo Thomas. The latter had been sent to the Mississippi Valley in the spring of 1863 to put machinery into operation for recruiting Negro soldiers in the South.[1]

Douglass was delighted. In great glee he hastened to Rochester to bring out the last issue of his monthly journal. Any day now the commission would arrive from Secretary Stanton.

Douglass' decision to cease publication [of his *Monthly*] was not sudden. In the fall of 1862, he had informed his old friend, Julia Griffiths, that on January 1, 1863, when the President issued the Emancipation Proclamation, he would give up his editorial duties and retire to a farm. Julia's keen counsel evidently caused him to postpone his decision. She wrote from England on December 5, 1862: "Now a word, my dear friend, about your personal matters & *give attention* to what I say. Even if all goes as you wish it on the 1st January 63 *you must not give up your paper.* This is the *15th* year of its existence in some shape, & tho' the name has varied, the Editor has always been *one* & the *same* man, Now more known than ever. The paper was started from this side the water and the ground of obtaining material aid for your branch of the cause is the paper. Surely, the more free colored people are in the North, the more they will need a paper—to assist in elevating them & educating them. No, my dear friend, do not be led astray, or make a mistake by giving up the paper. You know nothing about farming yourself and would be like a fish out of water without mental *labors* & public work! I wish I could fly over the water & have a consultation with you. I have felt quite uneasy in my mind since this farm business was first mentioned."[2] . . .

The final, . . . touching . . . sentence of Douglass' "Valedictory" mark[ed] the end of sixteen years of continuous publication of his journal. [III:37–38]

VALEDICTORY

Rochester, N.Y., Aug 16th, 1863

My Respected Readers:

I beg to state that my relation to you as the Editor and publisher of a Journal devoted to the cause of Emancipation is, for the present, ended. That journal which has continued, under one form and designation or another, during nearly sixteen years, covering a period remarkable for the intensity and fierceness of the moral struggle between slavery and freedom, will be discontinued from the date of this publication.

In making this simple announcement emotions are excited for which I shall not attempt to find words to give suitable expression.—Although the result has been reached naturally, logically and necessarily, it is nevertheless accepted reluctantly and sadly. My relation to my readers has been in a high degree friendly, and in taking this formal leave of those readers, at home and abroad, I feel that I am taking leave of my true and tried friends. Great principles of justice and the most enduring sympathies known to the heart of man have united us in the cause of the American slave and swept us along the tide of these eventful sixteen years together. I know well enough, and knew from the first that my hold upon you, was not the result of shining talents or high mental attainments. I came to you fresh from the house of American bondage, with only such learning as I had stolen or picked up in the darkness of twenty-two years of slavery, and in a few years of liberty and toil. Yet you were pleased to receive me, and were not ashamed to cheer me on in my mission of deliverance to my enslaved people. Out of a full heart, my dear respected friends, I thank you at this parting, for your long continued and ever faithful cooperation. I shall never cease to regard these years of editorial toil on my part and of sympathy and support on your part, as among the most cheerful and happy of my life.

But you will ask me, Why do you cease the publication of your paper? "Why not continue to speak and write as formerly—Slavery is not yet abolished." The inquiry is pertinent and I will give it my answer: and to answer it more perfectly I will first answer it negatively. First then, I wish it distinctly understood, that I do not discontinue the publication of my paper because it can no longer be supported. In this respect my paper has been highly favored from the first. The kind friends, who in England, seventeen years ago gave me the means of purchasing a printing press, have stood by me through all the years of my journal and generously helped me in every time of need. The same friends would doubtless help me hereafter as heretofore, if the journal were continued, and needed their help for its continuance.

Again, I cannot allow that my course is dictated by a love of change or adventure. My stability is quite equal to that of most men. My paper ends its existence in the same room on the same street where it began. It has been during these sixteen years, immovable in its principles as it has been permanent in its local habitation. Often called elsewhere as more desirable localities for being heard and felt over the country, I have still remained in Rochester, and shown no taste for experimenting anywhere. Many times I could have sold my establishment, and formed alliances with other papers, but remembering that those who put me in possession of the press desired me to conduct it, I have refused all proposals for either sale or alliance. Neither do I discontinue the paper because I think that speaking and writing against slavery and its twin monster prejudice against the colored race are no longer needful. Such writing and speaking will be necessary so long as slavery and proscription shall remain in this country and in the world. Happily, however, I can write now through channels which were not opened fully to these subjects, when my journal was established. It will be grateful to my friends, especially to those over the sea, to know that the New York *Independent* and the New York *Tribune*, both powerful periodicals, counting their readers by the hundred thousand, welcome to their ample columns the best utterances in behalf of my race of which I am capable. These journals with many others, in my own town and elsewhere, are now quite ready to listen to what the colored man has to say for himself and for his much questioned and doubted people. Besides these, there is now, as there was not, at the beginning, a paper published in the city of New York by colored men entitled *"The Anglo-African,"* to whose columns all colored writers may gain access. I, at least have never been refused a place in its columns.—Indeed, I may say with gratitude and without boasting, that humble as I am in origin and despised as is the race to which I belong, I have lived to see the leading presses of the country, willing and ready to publish any argument or appeal in behalf of my race, I am able to make. So that while speaking and writing are still needful, the necessity for a special organ for my views and opinions on slavery no longer exists. To this extent at least, my paper has accomplished the object of its existence. It has done something towards battering down that dark and frowning wall of partition between the working minds of two races, hitherto thought impregnable. It found me an illiterate fugitive from slavery, and by the mental exercise in reflection and reading its publication imposed, and made indispensable, it has educated myself, and other colored men up to the average power of thought and expression of our times.

Let it also be understood that I do not abandon my paper, because I shall cease to think and write upon vital social questions concerning colored men and women. I shall think, write and speak as I have opportunity, while the slave needs a pen to plead his cause, or a voice to expose his wrongs before the people.

So much dear readers, negatively, and to prevent misapprehension. I will now tell affirmatively and directly why I lay down my pen and paper. The United States are now in the bitterest pangs of civil war. Slavery is the cause of this terrible war, and its abolition is decreed by one of the parties to the war. I am with the abolition party in war as in peace. I discontinue my paper, because I can better serve my poor bleeding country-men whose great opportunity has now come, by going South and summoning them to assert their just liberty, than I can do by staying here. I am going South to assist Adjutant General Thomas, in the organization of colored troops, who shall win for the millions in bondage the inestimable blessings of liberty and country.

Slavery has chosen to submit her claims to the decision of the God of battles. She has deliberately taken the sword and it is meet that she should perish by the sword. Let the oppressor fall by the hand of the oppressed, and the guilty slaveholder, whom the voice of truth and reason could not reach, let him fall by the hand of his slave. It is in accordance with the All-wise orderings of Providence that it should be so. Eternal justice can thunder forth no higher vindication of her majesty nor proclaim a warning more salutary to a world steeped in cruelty and wickedness, than in such a termination of our system of slavery. Reason, argument, appeal,—all moral influences have been applied in vain. The oppressor has hardened his heart, blinded his mind and deliberately rushed upon merited destruction. Let his blood be upon his own head. That I should take some humble part in the physical as well as the moral struggle against slavery and urge my long enslaved people to vindicate their manhood by bravely striking for their liberty and country is natural and consistent. I have indicated my course. You may not approve it, but I am sure you will appreciate the convictions of duty which impel me to it. With a heart full and warm with gratitude to you for all you have done in furtherance of the cause of these to whom I have devoted my life, I bid you an affectionate farewell.

Frederick Douglass

Douglass' Monthly, August, 1863

1. *Life and Times of Frederick Douglass*, pp. 372–74.
2. Julia G. Crofts to Douglass, Leeds, Dec. 5, 1862, Douglass Papers, Frederick Douglass Memorial Home, Anacostia, D.C.

Late in July, 1863, Douglass paid his first visit to Washington. "No man who had not worn the yoke of bondage and been scourged and driven beyond the beneficent range of the brotherhood of man by popular prejudice," he told an audience a quarter of a century later, "can understand the tumult of feeling with which I entered the White House."[1] . . .

After [some] introductory remarks, Douglass came directly to the point. As a recruiting agent he wished to present the case of the Negro soldier. If the War Department wished to recruit Negro men, it had to reverse its policies; give the Negro soldiers the same pay white soldiers received; compel the Confederacy to treat Negro soldiers, when taken prisoners, as prisoners of war; promote Negro soldiers who distinguished themselves for bravery in the field just as white men were promoted for similar service, and retaliate in kind when any Negro soldiers were murdered in cold blood.

Lincoln listened attentively and sympathetically to these proposals. The time was not yet ripe, he replied, to give Negro soldiers the same pay as a white man, for opposition to recruiting Negroes in the Union army was still too strong. "I assure you, Mr. Douglass," he continued, "that in the end they shall have the same pay as white soldiers." He admitted the justice of Douglass' request for the promotion of Negroes in the army, and promised "to sign any commission to colored soldiers" which the Secretary of War recommended. He agreed that Negro soldiers should be treated as prisoners of war when captured. But he balked at Douglass' suggestion for retaliation. "Once begun," he declared, "I do not know where such a measure would stop."[2]

Douglass left the White House with . . . impressions . . . which later interviews with Lincoln were to confirm. One was the President's "entire freedom from popular prejudice against the colored people. He was the first great man that I talked with in the United States freely, who in no single instance reminded me of the difference between himself and myself, of the difference of color. . . ." Throughout the interview with this great man, "as great as the greatest," Douglass had felt "as though I could go and put my hand on his shoulder. . . ."

These impressions were decisive in Douglass' decision to continue his recruiting work. He was not entirely satisfied with Lincoln's reactions to his requests, but he "was so well satisfied with the man and with the educating tendency of the conflict" that he was convinced the government's treatment of the Negro soldiers would soon radically change for the better.[3] [III:35–37]

OUR WORK IS NOT DONE, speech delivered at the annual meeting of the American Anti-Slavery Society held at Philadelphia, December 3–4, 1863

Ladies and Gentlemen:

I confess, at the outset, to have felt a very profound desire to utter a word at some period during the present meeting. As it has been repeatedly said here, it has been a meeting of reminiscences. I shall not attempt to treat you to any of my own in what I have now to say, though I have some in connection with the labors of this Society, and in connection with my experience as an American slave, that I might not inappropriately bring before you on this occasion. I desire to be remembered among those having a word to say at this meeting, because I began my existence as a free man in this country with this association, and because I have some hopes or apprehensions, whichever you please to call them, that we shall never, as a Society, hold another decade meeting.

I well remember the first time I ever listened to the voice of the honored President of this association, and I have some recollection of the feelings of hope inspired by his utterances at that time. Under the inspiration of those hopes, I looked forward to the abolition of slavery as a certain event in the course of a very few years. So clear were his utterances, so simple and truthful, and so adapted, I conceived, to the human heart were the principles and doctrines propounded by him, that I thought five years, at any rate, would be all that would be required for the abolition of slavery. I thought it was only necessary for the slaves, or their friends, to lift up the hatchway of slavery's infernal hold, to uncover the bloody scenes of American thraldom, and give the nation a peep into its horrors, its deeds of deep damnation, to arouse them to almost phrensied opposition to this foul curse. But I was mistaken. I had not been five years pelted by the mob, insulted by the crowds, shunned by the Church, denounced by the ministry, ridiculed by the press, spit upon by the loafers, before I became convinced that I might perhaps live, struggle, and die, and go down to my grave, and the slaves of the South yet remain in their chains.

We live to see a better hope to-night. I participate in the profound thanksgiving expressed by all, that we do live to see this better day. I am one of those who believe that it is the mission of this war to free every slave in the United States. I am one of those who believe that we should consent to no peace which shall not be an Abolition peace. I am, moreover, one of those who believe that the work of the American Anti-Slavery Society will not have been completed until the black men of the South, and the black men of the North, shall have been admitted, fully and completely, into the body politic of America. I look upon slavery as going the way of all the earth. It is the mission of the war to put it down. But a mightier work than the abolition of slavery now looms up before the Abolitionist. This Society was organized, if I remember rightly, for two distinct objects; one was the emancipation of the slave, and the other the elevation of the colored people. When we have taken the chains off the slave, as I believe we shall do, we shall find a harder resistance to the second purpose of this great association than we have found even upon slavery itself.

I am hopeful; but while I am hopeful, I am thoughtful withal. If I lean to either side of the controversy to which we have listened today, I lean to that side which implies caution, which implies apprehension, which implies a consciousness that our work is not done. Protest, affirm, hope, glorify as we may, it cannot be denied that Abolitionism is still unpopular in the United States. It cannot be denied that this war is at present denounced by its opponents as an Abolition war; and it is equally clear that it would not be denounced as an Abolition war, if Abolitionism was not odious. It is equally clear that our friends, Republicans, Unionists, Loyalists, would not spin out elaborate explanations and denials that this is the character of the war, if Abolition were popular. Men accept the term Abolitionist with qualifications. They do not come out square and openhanded, and affirm themselves to be Abolitionists. As a general rule, we are attempting to explain away the charge that this is an Abolition war. I hold that it is an Abolition war, because slavery has proved itself stronger than the Constitution; it has proved itself stronger than the Union; and has forced upon us the necessity of putting down slavery in order to save the Union, and in order to save the Constitution. [Applause.]

I look at this as an Abolition war instead of being a Union war, because I see that the lesser is included in the greater, and that you cannot have the lesser until you have the greater. You cannot have the Union, the Constitution, and Republican institutions, until you have stricken down that damning curse, and put it beyond the pale of the Republic. For, while it is in this country, it will make your Union impossible; it will make your Constitution impossible. I therefore call this just what the Democrats have charged it with being, an Abolition war. Let us emblazon it on our banners, and declare before the world that this is an Abolition war, [applause,] that it will prosper precisely in proportion as it takes upon itself this character. [Renewed applause.]

My respected friend, Mr. Purvis, called attention to the existence of prejudice against color in this country. This gives me great cause for apprehension, if not for alarm. I am afraid of this powerful element of prejudice against color. While it exists, I want the voice of the American Anti-Slavery Society to be continually protesting, continually exposing it. While it can be said that in this most antislavery city in the Northern States of our Union, in the city of Philadelphia, the city of Brotherly Love, the city of churches, the city of piety, the most genteel and respectable colored lady or gentleman may be kicked out of your commonest street car, we are in danger of a compromise. While it can be said that black men, fighting bravely for this country, are asked to take seven dollars per month, while the Government lays down as a rule or criterion of pay a complexional one, we are in danger of a compromise. While to be radical is to be unpopular, we are in danger of a compromise. While we have a large minority called Democratic, in every State of the North, we have a powerful nucleus for a most infernal reaction in favor of slavery. I know it is that we have recently achieved vast political victories. I am glad of it. I value these victories, however, more for what they have prevented than for what they have actually accomplished. I should have been doubly sad at seeing any of these States wheel into line with the Peace Democracy. But, however it may be in the State of Pennsylvania, I know that you may look for abolition in the creed of any party in New York with a microscope, and you will not find a single line of anti-slavery there. The victories were Union victories, victories to save the Union in such ways as the country may devise to save it. But whatever may have been the meaning of these majorities in regard to the Union, we know one thing, that the minorities, at least, mean slavery. They mean submission. They mean the degradation of the colored man. They mean everything but open rebellion against the Federal Government in the North. But the mob, the rioters in the city of New York, convert that city into a hell, and its lower orders into demons, and dash out the brains of little children against the curbstones; and they mean anything and everything that the Devil exacts at their hands. While we had in this State a majority of but 15,000 over this pro-slavery Democratic party, they have a mighty minority, a dangerous minority. Keep in mind when these minorities were gotten. Powerful as they are, they were gotten when slavery, with bloody hands, was stabbing at the very heart of the nation itself. With all that disadvantage, they have piled up these powerful minorities.

We have work to do, friends and fellow-citizens, to look after these minorities. The day that shall see Jeff. Davis fling down his Montgomery Constitution, and call home his Generals, will be the most trying day to the virtue of this people that this country has ever seen. When the slaveholders shall give up the contest, and ask for readmission into the Union, then, as Mr. Wilson has told us, we shall see the trying time in this country. Your Democracy will clamor for peace, and for restoring the old order of things, because that old order of things was the life of the Democratic party. "You do take away mine house, when you take away the prop that sustains my house," and the support of the Democratic party we all know to be slavery. The Democratic party is for war for slavery; it is for peace for slavery; it is for the *habeas corpus* for slavery; it is against the *habeas corpus* for slavery; it was for the Florida war for slavery; it was for the Mexican war for slavery; it is for jury trial for traitors, for slavery; it is against jury trial for men claimed as fugitive slaves, for slavery. It has but one principle, one master; and it is guided, governed, and directed by it. I say that, with this party among us, flaunting its banners in our faces, with the New York *World* scattered broadcast over the North, with the New York *Express,* with the mother and father and devil of them all, the New York *Herald,* [applause,] with those papers flooding our land, and coupling the term Abolitionist with all manner of course epithets, in all our hotels, at all our crossings, our highways and byways and railways all over the country, there is work to be done—a good deal of work to be done.

I have said that our Work will not be done until the colored man is admitted a full member in good and regular standing in the American body politic. Men have very nice ideas about the body politic where I have travelled; and they don't like the idea of having the Negro in the body politic. He may remain in this country, for he will be useful as a laborer—valuable, perhaps, in time of trouble, as a helper; but to make him a full and complete citizen, a legal voter, that would be contaminating the body politic. I was a little curious, some years ago, to find out what sort of a thing this body politic was; and I was very anxious to know especially about what amount of baseness, brutality, coarseness, ignorance, and bestiality could find its way into the body politic; and I was not long in finding it out. I took my stand near the little hole through which the body politic put its votes. [Laughter.] And first among the mob I saw Ignorance, unable to read its vote, asking *me* to read it, by the way, [great laughter,] depositing its vote in the body politic. Next I saw a man stepping up to the body politic, casting in his vote, having a black eye, and another one ready to be blacked, having been engaged in a street fight. I saw, again, Pat, fresh from the Emerald Isle, with the delightful brogue peculiar to him, stepping up—not walking, but leaning upon the arms of two of his friends, unable to stand, passing into the body politic! I came to the conclusion that this body politic was, after all, not quite so pure a body as the representations of its friends would lead us to believe.

I know it will be said that I ask you to make the black man a voter in the South. Yet you are for having brutality and ignorance introduced into the ballot-box. It is said that the colored man is ignorant, and therefore he shall not vote. In saying this, you lay down a rule for the black man that you apply to no other class of your citizens. I will hear nothing of degradation or of ignorance against the black man. If he knows enough to be hanged, he knows enough to vote. If he knows an honest man from a thief, he knows much more than some of our white voters. If he knows as much when sober as an Irishman knows when drunk, he knows enough to vote. If he knows enough to take up arms in defence of this Government, and bare his breast to the storm of rebel artillery, he knows enough to vote. [Great applause.]

Away with this talk of the want of knowledge on the part of the Negro! I am about as big a Negro as you will find anywhere about town; and any man that does not believe I know enough to vote, let him try it. I think I can convince him that I do. Let him run for office in my district, and solicit my vote, and I will show him.

All I ask, however, in regard to the blacks, is that whatever rule you adopt, whether of intelligence or wealth, as the condition of voting, you shall apply it equally to the black man. Do that, and I am satisfied, and eternal justice is satisfied; liberty, fraternity, equality, are satisfied; and the country will move on harmoniously.

Mr. President, I have a patriotic argument in favor of insisting upon the immediate enfranchisement of the slaves of the South; and it is this. When this rebellion shall have been put down, when the arms shall have fallen from the guilty hands of traitors, you will need the friendship of the slaves of the South, of those millions there. Four or five million men are not of inconsiderable importance at any time; but they will be doubly important when you come to reorganize and reestablish republican institutions in the South. Will you mock those bondmen by breaking their chains with one hand, and with the other giving their rebel masters the elective franchise, and robbing them of theirs? I tell you the Negro is your friend. You will make him your friend by emancipating him. But you will make him not only your friend in sentiment and heart by enfranchising him, but you will make him your best defender, your best protector against the traitors and the descendants of those traitors, who will inherit the hate, the bitter revenge which will crystallize all over the South, and seek to circumvent the Government that they could not throw off. You will need the black man there, as a watchman and patrol; and you may need him as a soldier. You may need him to uphold in peace, as he is now upholding in war, the star-spangled banner. [Applause.] I wish our excellent friend, Senator Wilson, would bend his energies to this point as well as the other—to let the Negro have a vote. It will be helping him from the jaws of the wolf. We are surrounded by those that, like the wolf, will use their jaws, if you give the elective franchise to the descendants of the traitors, and keep it from the black man. We ought to be the voters there. We ought to be members of Congress. [Applause.] You may as well make up your minds that you have got to see something dark down that way. There is no way to get rid of it. I am a candidate already! [Laughter and applause.]

For twenty-five years, Mr. President, you know that when I got as far South as Philadelphia, I felt that I was rubbing against my prison wall, and could not go any further. I dared not go over yonder into Delaware. Twenty years ago, when I attended the first decade meeting of this Society, as I came along the vales and hills of Gettysburg, my good friends, the anti-slavery people along there warned me to remain in the house during the day-time, and travel in the night, lest I should be kidnapped, and carried over into Maryland. My good friend, Dr. Fussell, was one of the number who did not think it safe for me to attend an anti-slavery meeting along the borders of this State. I can go down there now. I have been down there to see the President; and as you were not there, perhaps you may like to know how the President of the United States received a black man at the White House. I will tell you how he received me—just as you have seen one gentleman receive another [great applause]; with a hand and a voice well-balanced between a kind cordiality and a respectful reserve. I tell you I felt big there! [Laughter.] Let me tell you how I got to him; because everybody can't get to him. He has to be a little guarded in admitting spectators. The manner of getting to him gave me an idea that the cause was rolling on. The stairway was crowded with applicants. Some of them looked eager; and I have no doubt some of them had a purpose in being there, and wanted to see the President for the good of the country! They were white; and as I was the only dark spot among them, I expected to have to wait at least half a day; I had heard of men waiting a week; but in two minutes after I sent in my card, the messenger came out, and respectfully invited "Mr. Douglass" in. I could hear, in the eager multitude outside, as they saw me pressing and elbowing my way through, the remark, "Yes, damn it, I knew they would let the n—r through," in a kind of despairing voice—a Peace Democrat, I suppose. [Laughter.] When I went in, the President was sitting in his usual position, I was told, with his feet in different parts of the room, taking it easy. [Laughter.] Don't put this down, Mr. Reporter, I pray you; for I am going down there again to-morrow! [Laughter.] As I came in and approached him, the President began to rise, [laughter,] and he continued rising until he stood over me [laughter]; and, reaching out his hand, he said, "Mr. Douglass, I know you; I have read about you, and Mr. Seward has told me about you"; putting me quite at ease at once.

Now, you will want to know how I was impressed by him. I will tell you that, too. He impressed me as being just what every one of you have been in the habit of calling him—an honest man. [Applause.] I never met with a man, who, on the first blush, impressed me more entirely with his sincerity, with his devotion to his country, and with his determination to save it at all hazards. [Applause.] He told me (I think he did me more honor than I deserve) that I had made a little speech, somewhere in New York, and it had got into the papers, and among the things I had said was this: That if I were called upon to state what I regarded as the most sad and most disheartening feature in our present political and military situation, it would not be the various disasters experienced by our armies and our navies, on flood and field, but it would be the tardy, hesitating, vacillating policy of the President of the United States; and the President said to me, "Mr. Douglass, I have been charged with being tardy, and the like"; and he went on, and partly admitted that he might seem slow; but he said, "I am charged with vacillating; but, Mr. Douglass, I do not think that charge can be sustained; I think it cannot be shown that when I have once taken a position, I have ever retreated from it." [Applause.] That I regarded as the most significant point in what he said during our interview. I told him that he had been somewhat slow in proclaiming equal protection to our colored soldiers and prisoners; and he said that the country needed talking up to that point. He hesitated in regard to it, when he felt that the country was not ready for it. He knew that the colored man throughout this country was a despised man, a hated man, and that if he at first came out with such a proclamation, all the hatred which is poured on the head of the Negro race would be visited on his administration. He said that there was preparatory work needed, and that that preparatory work had now been done. And he said, "Remember this, Mr. Douglass; remember that Milliken's Bend, Port Hudson and Fort Wagner are recent events; and that these were necessary to prepare the way for this very proclamation of mine." I thought it was reasonable, but came to the conclusion that while Abraham Lincoln will not go down to posterity as Abraham the Great, or as Abraham the Wise, or as Abraham the Eloquent, although he is all three, wise, great and eloquent, he will go down to posterity, if the country is saved, as Honest Abraham [applause]; and going down thus, his name may be written anywhere in this wide world of ours side by side with that of Washington, without disparaging the latter. [Renewed applause.]

But we are not to be saved by the captain, at this time, but by the crew. We are not to be saved by Abraham Lincoln, but by that power behind the throne, greater than the throne itself. You and I and all of us have this matter in hand. Men talk about saving the Union, and restoring the Union as it was. They delude themselves with the miserable idea that that old Union can be brought to life again. That old Union, whose canonized bones we so quietly inurned under the shattered walls of Sumter, can never come to life again. It is dead, and you cannot put life in it. The first ball shot at Sumter caused it to fall as dead as the body of Julius Caesar, when stabbed by Brutus. We do not want it. We have outlived the old Union. We had outlived it long before the rebellion came to tell us—I mean the Union, under the old pro-slavery interpretation of it—and had become ashamed of it. The South hated it with our anti-slavery interpretation, and the North hated it with the Southern interpretation of its requirements. We had already come to think with horror of the idea of being called upon, here in our churches and literary societies, to take up arms, and go down South and pour the leaden death into the breasts of the slaves, in case they should rise for liberty; and the better part of the people did not mean to do it. They shuddered at the idea of so sacrilegious a crime. They had already become utterly disgusted with the idea of playing the part of bloodhounds for the slave-masters, watch-dogs for the plantations. They had come to detest the principle upon which the Slave States had a larger representation in Congress than the Free States. They had already come to think that the little finger of dear old John Brown was worth more to the world than all the slaveholders in Virginia put together. [Applause.] What business, then, have we to fight for the old Union? We are not fighting for it. We are fighting for something incomparably better than the old Union. We are fighting for unity; unity of idea, unity of sentiment, unity of object, unity of institutions, in which there shall be no North, no South, no East, no West, no black, no white, but a solidarity of the nation, making every slave free, and every free man a voter. [Great applause.]

Proceedings of the American Anti-Slavery Society at its Third Decade, Held in the City of Philadelphia, December 3, 4, 1863, New York, 1864, pp. 110–118

1. *Washington Post,* Feb. 13, 1888.
   It is difficult to determine the exact date of the interview, but very likely it took place between July 18 when the Fort Wagner disaster occurred and July 30 when Lincoln issued an order decreeing retaliation for every soldier enslaved or killed in violation of the laws of war.
   2. Allen Thordike Rice, ed., *Reminiscences of Abraham Lincoln by Distinguished Men of His Time,* New York, 1866, pp. 185–88.
   Lincoln's prediction that discrimination in pay would be abolished was to come true a year after his interview with Douglass. On July 14, 1864, Congress passed a bill granting Negro soldiers the same pay as white soldiers, retroactive to January 1, 1864.
   3. *Liberator,* Jan. 29, 1864; Rice, *op. cit.,* pp. 185–88.

[Douglass'] commission never materialized. Douglass did not doubt Stanton's sincerity, but concluded that, in thinking it over, the Secretary of War had decided that "the time had not come for a step so radical and aggressive."[1] The "radical" step involved conferring the rank of assistant adjutant on the outstanding Negro leader in the nation, on a man who, more than anyone else, had been responsible for recruiting Negro regiments in the

North. Yet the Lincoln administration feared to take this step. By offering Douglass the post in the first place, Secretary Stanton showed that he was fully aware of what it would mean to the Negro people in the South to have their outstanding protagonist by their side; how it would strengthen the entire campaign to recruit Negro soldiers and thus make an invaluable contribution to the war effort. But expediency, fear of criticism by the Copperhead elements, and anti-Negro prejudice in the administration itself pushed the nation's welfare into the background.

The failure to receive a military commission naturally made Douglass bitter, but there was no time for moroseness. There were too many issues confronting the nation that required clarification. Chief among them, as Douglass saw it, was the pressing problem of the Negro's status as a free man. In the fall of 1863, after a three weeks' vigil at the sick bed of his son Lewis, Douglass returned to the lecture platform. In his speech, "The Mission of the War," which he repeated week after week in different communities, he warned Abolitionists that "there never was a time when Anti-Slavery work was more needed than now," and impressed upon the nation the necessity of securing full freedom for the Negro people. On February 17, 1864, he wrote: "I am, this winter, doing more with my voice than with my pen. I am heard with more than usual attention and hope I am doing some good in my day and generation."[2] [III:39–40]

THE MISSION OF THE WAR, address sponsored by Women's Loyal League and delivered in Cooper Institute, New York City, January 13, 1864

Ladies and Gentlemen:

By the mission of the war I mean nothing occult, arbitrary or difficult to be understood, but simply those great moral changes in the fundamental condition of the people, demanded by the situation of the country, plainly involved in the nature of the war, and which if the war is conducted in accordance with its true character, it is naturally and logically fitted to accomplish.

Speaking in the name of Providence, some men tell me that Slavery is already dead, that it expired with the first shot at Sumter. This may be so, but I do not share the confidence with which it is asserted. In a grand Crisis like this, we should all prefer to look facts sternly in the face, and to accept their verdict whether it bless or blast us. I look for no miraculous destruction of Slavery. The war looms before me simply as a great national opportunity, which may be improved to national salvation, or neglected to national ruin. I hope much from the bravery of our soldiers, but in vain is the might of armies if our rulers fail to profit by experience, and refuse to listen to the suggestions of wisdom and justice. The most hopeful fact of the hour is that we are now in a salutary school—the school of affliction. If sharp and signal retribution, long protracted, widesweeping and overwhelming, can teach a great nation respect for the long-despised claims of justice, surely we shall be taught now and for all time to come. But if, on the other hand, this potent teacher, whose lessons are written in characters of blood, and thundered to us from a hundred battle-fields shall fail, we shall go down as we shall deserve to go down, as a warning to all other nations which shall come after us. It is not pleasant to contemplate the hour as one of doubt and danger. We naturally prefer the bright side, but when there is a dark side it is folly to shut our eyes to it or deny its existence.

I know that the acorn involves the oak, but I know also that the commonest accident may destroy its potential character and defeat its natural destiny. One wave brings its treasure from the briny deep, but another oftens sweeps it back to its primal depths. The saying that revolutions never go backward must be taken with limitations. The revolution of 1848 was one of the grandest that ever dazzled a gazing world. It overturned the French throne, sent Louis Philippe into exile, shook every throne in Europe, and inaugurated a glorious Republic. Looking from a distance, the friends of democratic liberty saw in the convulsion the death of kingcraft in Europe and throughout the world. Great was their disappointment. Almost in the twinkling of an eye, the latent forces of despotism rallied. The Republic disappeared. Her noblest defenders were sent into exile, and the hopes of democratic liberty were blasted in the moment of their bloom. Politics and perfidy proved too strong for the principles of liberty and justice in that contest. I wish I could say that no such liabilities darken the horizon around us. But the same elements are plainly involved here as there. Though the portents are that we shall flourish it is too much to say that we cannot fail and fall. Our destiny is to be taken out of our own hands. It is cowardly to shuffle our responsibilities upon the shoulders of Providence. I do not intend to argue but to state facts.

We are now wading into the third year of conflict with a fierce and sanguinary rebellion, one which at the beginning of it, we were hopefully assured by one of our most sagacious and trusted political prophets would be ended in less than ninety days: a rebellion which, in its worst features, stands alone among rebellions a solitary and ghastly horror, without a parallel in the history of any nation, ancient or modern: a rebellion inspired by no love of liberty and by no hatred of oppression, as most other rebellions have been, and therefore utterly indefensible upon any moral or social grounds: a rebellion which openly and shamelessly sets at defiance the world's judgment of right and wrong, appeals from light to darkness, from intelligence to ignorance, from the ever-increasing prospects and blessings of a high and glorious civilization to the cold and withering blasts of a naked barbarism: a rebellion which even at this unfinished stage of it, counts the number of its slain not by thousands nor tens of thousands, but by hundreds of thousands. A rebellion which in the destruction of human life and property has rivaled the earthquake, the whirlwind and the pestilence that walketh in darkness, and wasteth at noonday. It has planted agony at a million hearthstones, thronged our streets with the weeds of mourning, filled our land with mere stumps of men, ridged our soil with 200,000 rudely-formed graves, and mantled it all over with the shadow of death. A rebellion which, while it has arrested the wheels of peaceful industry and checked the flow of commerce, has piled up a debt, heavier than a mountain of gold to weigh down the necks of our children's children. There is no end to the mischief wrought. It has brought ruin at home, contempt abroad, cooled our friends, heated our enemies, and endangered our existence as a nation.

Now, for what is all this desolation, ruin, shame, suffering, and sorrow? Can anybody want the answer? Can anybody be ignorant of the answer? It has been given a thousand times from this and other platforms. We all know it is Slavery. Less than a half a million of Southern slaveholders—holding in bondage four million slaves—finding themselves outvoted in the effort to get possession of the

United States Government, in order to serve the interests of Slavery, have madly resorted to the sword—have undertaken to accomplish by bullets what they failed to accomplish by ballots. That is the answer.

It is worthy of remark that Secession was an afterthought with the Rebels. Their aim was higher; Secession was only their second choice. Who was going to fight for Slavery in the Union? It was not separation, but subversion. It was not Richmond, but Washington. It was not the Confederate rag, but the glorious Star Spangled Banner.

Whence came the guilty ambition equal to this atrocious crime. A peculiar education was necessary to this bold wickedness. Here all is plain again. Slavery— the peculiar institution—is aptly fitted to produce just such patriots, who first plunder, and then seek to destroy their country. A system which rewards labor with stripes and chains!—which robs the slave of his manhood, and the master of all just consideration for the rights of his fellow-man—has prepared the characters—male and female—that figure in this Rebellion—and for all its cold-blooded and hellish atrocities. In all the most horrid details of torture, starvation and murder in the treatment of our prisoners, I behold the features of the monster in whose presence I was born, and that is Slavery. From no sources less foul and wicked could such a Rebellion come. I need not dwell here. The country knows the story by heart. But I am one of those who think this Rebellion—inaugurated and carried on for a cause so unspeakably guilty and distinguished by barbarities which would extort a cry of shame from the painted savage—is quite enough for the whole lifetime of any one nation—though the lifetime should cover the space of a thousand years. We ought not to want a repetition of it. Looking at the matter from no higher ground than patriotism—setting aside the high considerations of justice, liberty, progress, and civilization—the American people should resolve that this shall be the last slaveholding Rebellion that shall ever curse this continent. Let the War cost more or cost little—let it be long or short—the work now begun should suffer no pause, no abatement, until it is done and done forever.

I know that many are appalled and disappointed by the apparently interminable character of this war. I am neither appalled nor disappointed without pretending to any higher wisdom than other men. I knew well enough and often said it—once let the North and South confront each other on the battle-field, and Slavery and Freedom be the inspiring motives of the respective sections, the contest will be fierce, long and sanguinary. Gov. Seymour charges us with prolonging the war, and I say the longer the better if it must be so—in order to put an end to the hell black cause out of which the Rebellion has risen.

Say not that I am indifferent to the horrors and hardships of the war. I am not indifferent. In common with the American people generally, I feel the prolongation of the war a heavy calamity—private as well public. There are vacant spaces at my hearthstone which I shall rejoice to see filled again by the boys who once occupied them—but which cannot be thus filled while the war lasts—for they have enlisted—"during the war."

But even from the length of this struggle, we who mourn over it may well enough draw some consolation when we reflect upon the vastness and grandeur of its mission. The world has witnessed many wars—and history records and perpetuates their memory, but the world has not seen a nobler and grander war than that which the loyal people of this country are now waging against the slaveholding Rebels. The blow we strike is not merely to free a country or continent—but the whole world from Slavery—for when Slavery fails here—it will fall everywhere. We have no business to mourn over our mission. We are writing the statutes of eternal justice and liberty in the blood of the worst of tyrants as a warning to all after-comers. We should rejoice that there was normal life and health enough in us to stand in our appointed place, and do this great service for mankind.

It is true that the war seems long. But this very slow progress is an essential element of its effectiveness. Like the slow convalescence of some patients the fault is less chargeable to the medicine than to the deep-seated character of the disease. We were in a very low condition before the remedy was applied. The whole head was sick and the whole heart faint. Dr. Buchanan and his Democratic friends had given us up, and were preparing to celebrate the nation's funeral. We had been drugged nearly to death by Pro-Slavery compromises. A radical change was needed in our whole system. Nothing is better calculated to effect the desired change than the slow, steady and certain progress of the war.

I know that this view of the case is not very consoling to the peace Democracy. I was not sent and am not come to console this breach of our political church. They regard this grand moral revolution in the mind and heart of the nation as the most distressing attribute of the war, and howl over it like certain characters of whom we read—who thought themselves tormented before their time.

Upon the whole, I like their mode of characterizing the war. They charge that it is no longer conducted upon constitutional principles. The same was said by Breckinridge and Vallandigham. They charge that it is not waged to establish the Union as it was. The same idea has occurred to Jefferson Davis. They charge that this is a war for the subjugation of the South. In a word, that it is an Abolition war.

For one, I am not careful to deny this charge. But it is instructive to observe how this charge is brought and how it is met. Both warn us of danger. Why is this war fiercely denounced as an Abolition war? I answer, because the nation has long and bitterly hated Abolition and the enemies of the war confidently rely upon this hatred to serve the ends of treason. Why do the loyal people deny the charge? I answer, because they know that Abolition, though now a vast power, is still odious. Both the charge and the denial tell how the people hate and despise the only measure that can save the country.

An Abolition war! Well, let us thank the Democracy for teaching us this word. The charge in a comprehensive sense is most true, and it is a pity that it is true, but it would be a vast pity if it were not true. Would that it were more true than it is. When our Government and people shall bravely avow this to be an Abolition war, then the country will be safe. Then our work will be fairly mapped out. Then the uplifted arm of the nation will swing unfettered to its work, and the spirit and power of the Rebellion will be broken. Had Slavery been abolished in the Border States at the very beginning of the war, as it ought to have been—had it been abolished in Missouri, as it would have been but for Presidential interference—there would now be no Rebellion in the Southern States—for instead of having to watch these Border States, as they have done, our armies would have marched in overpowering numbers directly upon the Rebels and overwhelmed them. I now hold that a sacred regard for truth, as well as sound policy, makes it our duty to own and avow before Heaven and earth that this war is, and of right ought to be, an Abolition war.

The Abolition of Slavery is the comprehensive and logical object of the war, for it includes everything else which the struggle involves. It is a war for the Union, a war for the Constitution, I admit; but it is logically such a war only in the sense that the greater includes the lesser. Slavery has proved itself the strong man of our national house. In every Rebel State it proved itself stronger than the Union, stronger than the Constitution, and stronger than the Republican Institutions. It overrode majorities, made no account of the ballot-box, and had everything its own way. It is plain that this strong man must be bound and cast out of our house before Union, Constitution and Republican institutions can become possible. An Abolition war, therefore, includes Union, Constitution, Republican Institutions, and all else that goes to make up the greatness and glory of our common country. On the other hand, exclude Abolition, and you exclude all else for which you are fighting.

The position of the Democratic party in relation to the war ought to surprise nobody. It is consistent with the history of the party for thirty years. Slavery, and only slavery, has been its recognized master during all that time. It early won for itself the title of being the natural ally of the South and of Slavery. It has always been for peace or against peace, for war and against war, precisely as dictated by Slavery. Ask why it was for the Florida War, and it answers, Slavery. Ask why it was for the Mexican War, and it answers, Slavery. Ask why it was for the annexation of Texas, and it answers, Slavery. Ask why it was opposed to the habeas corpus when a Negro was the applicant, and it answers, Slavery. Ask why it is now in favor of the habeas corpus, when Rebels and traitors are the applicants for its benefits, and it answers, Slavery. Ask why it was for mobbing down freedom of speech a few years ago, when that freedom was claimed by the Abolitionists, and it answers, Slavery. Ask why it now asserts freedom of speech, when sympathizers with traitors claim that freedom, and again Slavery is the answer. Ask why it denied the right of a State to protect itself against possible abuses of the Fugitive-Slave bill, and you have the same old answer. Ask why it now asserts the sovereignty of the States separately as against the States united, and again Slavery is the answer. Ask why it was opposed to giving persons claimed as fugitive slaves a jury trial before returning them to slavery; ask why it is now in favor of giving jury trial to traitors before sending them to the forts for safe keeping; ask why it was for war at the beginning of the Rebellion; ask why it has attempted to embarrass and hinder the loyal Government at every step of its progress, and you have but one answer, Slavery.

The fact is, the party in question, I say nothing of individual men who were once members of it, has had but one vital and animating principle for thirty years, and that has been the same old horrible and hell-born principle of Negro Slavery.

It has now assumed a saintly character. Its members would receive the benediction due to peace-makers. At one time they would slop bloodshed at the South by inaugurating bloody revolution at the North. The livery of peace is a beautiful livery, but in this case it is a stolen livery and sits badly on the wearer. These new apostles of peace call themselves Peace Democrats, and boast that they belong to the only party which can restore the country to peace. I neither dispute their title nor the pretensions founded upon it. The best that can be said of the peace-making ability of this class of men is their bitterest condemnation. It consists in their known treachery to the loyal Government. They have but to cross the Rebel lines to be hailed by the traitors as countrymen, clansmen, kinsmen, and brothers beloved in a common conspiracy. But, fellow-citizens, I have far less solicitude about the position and the influence of this party than I have about that of the great loyal party of the country. We have much less to fear from the bold and shameless wickedness of the one than from the timid and short-sighted policy of the other.

I know we have recently gained a great political victory; but it remains to be seen whether we shall wisely avail ourselves of its manifest advantages. There is danger that, like some of our Generals in the field, who, after soundly whipping the foe, generously allow him time to retreat in order, reorganize his forces, and intrench himself in a new and stronger position, where it will require more power and skill to dislodge him than was required to vanquish him in the first instance. The game is now in our hands. We can put an end to this disloyal party by putting an end to Slavery. While the Democratic party is in existence as an organization, we are in danger of a slaveholding peace, and of Rebel rule. There is but one way to avert this calamity, and that is destroy Slavery and enfranchise the black man while we have the power. While there is a vestige of Slavery remaining, it will unite the South with itself, and carry with it the Democracy of the North. The South united and the North divided, we shall be hereafter as heretofore, firmly held under the heels of Slavery.

Here is a part of the platform of principles upon which it seems to me every loyal man should take his stand at this hour:

First: That this war, which we are compelled to wage against slaveholding Rebels and traitors, at untold cost of blood and treasure, shall be, and of right ought to be, an Abolition War.

Secondly: That we, the loyal people of the North and of the whole country, while determined to make this a short and final war, will offer no peace, accept no peace, consent to no peace, which shall not be to all intents and purposes an Abolition peace.

Thirdly: That we regard the whole colored population of the country, in the loyal as well as in the disloyal States, as our countrymen—valuable in peace as laborers, valuable in war as soldiers—entitled to all the rights, protection, and opportunities for achieving distinction enjoyed by any other class of our countrymen.

Fourthly: Believing that the white race has nothing to fear from fair competition with the black race, and that the freedom and elevation of one race are not to be purchased or in any manner rightfully subserved by the disfranchisement of another, we shall favor immediate and unconditional emancipation in all the

States, invest the black man everywhere with the right to vote and to be voted for, and remove all discriminations against his rights on account of his color, whether as a citizen or as a soldier.

Ladies and gentlemen, there was a time when I hoped that events unaided by discussions would couple this Rebellion and Slavery in a common grave. But as I have before intimated, the facts do still fall short of our hopes. The question as to what shall be done with Slavery—and especially what shall be done with the Negro—threaten to remain open questions for some time yet.

It is true we have the Proclamation of January, 1863. It was a vast and glorious step in the right direction. But unhappily, excellent as that paper is—and much as it has accomplished temporarily—it settles nothing. It is still open to decision by courts, canons, and Congresses. I have applauded that paper and do now applaud it, as a wise measure—while I detest the motive and principle upon which it is based. By it the holding and flogging of Negroes is the exclusive luxury of loyal men.

Our chief danger lies in the absence of all moral feeling in the utterances of our rulers. In his letter to Mr. Greeley the President told the country virtually that the abolition or non-abolition of Slavery was a matter of indifference to him.[3] He would save the Union with Slavery or without Slavery. In his last Message he shows the same moral indifference, by saying as he does say that he had hoped that the Rebellion could be put down without the abolition of Slavery.[4]

When the late Stephen A. Douglas uttered the sentiment that he did not care whether Slavery were voted up or voted down in the Territories, we thought him lost to all genuine feeling on the subject, and no man more than Mr. Lincoln denounced that sentiment as unworthy of the lips of any American statesman. But today, after nearly three years of a Slaveholding Rebellion, we find Mr. Lincoln uttering substantially the same heartless sentiments. Douglas wanted Popular Sovereignty; Mr. Lincoln wants the Union. Now did a warm heart and a high moral feeling control the utterance of the President, he would welcome, with joy unspeakable and full of glory, the opportunity afforded by the Rebellion to free the country from the matchless crime and infamy. But policy, policy, everlasting policy, has robbed our statesmanship of all soul-moving utterances.

The great misfortune is and has been during all the progress of this war, that the Government and loyal people have not understood and accepted its true mission. Hence we have been floundering in the depths of dead issues. Endeavoring to impose old and worn-out conditions upon new relations—putting new wines into old bottles, new cloth into old garments, and thus making the rent worse than before.

Had we been wise we should have recognized the war at the outset as at once the signal and the necessity for a new order of social and political relations among the whole people. We could, like the ancients, discern the face of the sky, but not the signs of the times. Hence we have been talking of the importance of carrying on the war within the limits of a Constitution broken down by the very people in whose behalf the Constitution is pleaded! Hence we have from the first been deluding ourselves with the miserable dream that the old Union can be revived in the States where it has been abolished.

Now, we of the North have seen many strange things, and may see many more; but that old Union, whose canonized bones we saw hearsed in death and inurned under the frowning battlements of Sumter, we shall never see again while the world standeth. The issue before us is a living issue. We are not fighting for the dead past, but for the living present and the glorious future. We are not fighting for the old Union, nor for anything like it, but for that which is ten thousand times more important; and that thing, crisply rendered, is National unity. Both sections have tried Union. It has failed.

The lesson for the statesmen at this hour is to discover and apply some principle of Government which shall produce unity of sentiment, unity of idea, unity of object. Union without unity is, as we have seen, body without soul, marriage without love, a barrel without hoops, which falls at the first touch.

The statesmen of the South understood this matter earlier and better than the statesmen of the North. The dissolution of the Union on the old bases of compromise, was plainly foreseen and predicted 30 years ago. Mr. Calhoun and not Mr. Seward, is the original author of the doctrine of the irrepressible conflict. The South is logical and consistent. Under the teachings of their great leader they admit into their form of Government no disturbing force. They have based their Confederacy squarely on their corner-stone. Their two great and all commanding ideas are, first, that Slavery is right; and second, that the slaveholders are a superior order or class. Around these two ideas their manners, morals, politics, religion, and laws revolve. Slavery being right, all that is inconsistent with its entire security is necessarily wrong, and of course ought to be put down. There is no flaw in their logic.

They first endeavored to make the Federal Government stand upon their accursed corner-stone; and we but barely escaped, as you well know, that calamity. Fugitive Slave laws, Slavery Extension laws, and Dred Scott decisions were among the steps to get the nation squarely upon the corner-stone now chosen by the Confederate States. The loyal North is less definite in regard to the necessity of principles of National Unity. Yet, unconsciously to ourselves, and against our own protestations, we are in reality, like the South, fighting for national unity— a unity of which the great principles of liberty and equality, and not Slavery and class superiority, are the corner-stone.

Long before this rude and terrible war came to tell us of a broken Constitution and a dead Union, the better portion of the loyal people had outlived and outgrown what they had been taught to believe were the requirements of the old Union. We had come to detest the principle by which Slavery had a strong representation in Congress. We had come to abhor the idea of being called upon to suppress slave insurrections. We had come to be ashamed of slave-hunting, and being made the watch-dogs of slaveholders, who were too proud to scent out and hunt down their slaves for themselves. We had so far outlived the old Union four years ago that we thought the little finger of the hero of Harper's Ferry of more value to the world struggling for liberty than all the first families of old Virginia put together.

What business, then, have we to be pouring out our treasure and shedding our best blood like water for that old worn-out, dead and buried Union, which had already become a calamity and a curse? The fact is, we are not fighting for any such thing, and we ought to come out under our own true colors, and let the South and the whole world know that we don't want and will not have anything analogous to the old Union.

What we now want is a country—a free country—a country not saddened by the footprints of a single slave—and nowhere cursed by the presence of a slaveholder. We want a country which shall not brand the Declaration of Independence as a lie. We want a country whose fundamental institutions we can proudly defend before the highest intelligence and civilization of the age. Hitherto we have opposed European scorn of our Slavery with a blush of shame as our best defence. We now want a country in which the obligations of patriotism shall not conflict with fidelity to justice and Liberty. We want a country, and are fighting for a country, which shall be free from sectional political parties—free from sectional religious denominations—free from sectional benevolent associations—free from every kind and description of sect, party, and combination of a sectional character. We want a country where men may assemble from any part of it, without prejudice to their interests or peril to their persons. We are in fact, and from absolute necessity, transplanting the whole South with the higher civilization of the North. The New England schoolhouse is bound to take the place of the Southern whipping-post. Not because we love the Negro, but the nation; not because we prefer to do this, because we must or give up the contest, and give up the country. We want a country, and are fighting for a country, where social intercourse and commercial relations shall neither be embarrassed nor embittered by the imperious exactions of an insolent slaveholding Oligarchy, which required Northern merchants to sell their souls as a condition precedent to selling their goods.[5] We want a country, and are fighting for a country, through the length and breadth of which the literature and learning of any section of it may float to its extremities unimpaired, and thus become the common property of all the people—a country in which no man shall be fined for reading a book, or imprisoned for selling a book—a country where no man may be imprisoned or flogged or sold for learning to read, or teaching a fellow mortal how to read. We want a country, and are fighting for a country, in any part of which to be called an American citizen, shall mean as much as it did to be called a Roman citizen in the palmiest days of the Roman Empire.

We have heard much in other days of manifest destiny. I don't go all the lengths to which such theories are pressed, but I do believe that it is the manifest destiny of this war to unify and reorganize the institutions of the country—and that herein is the secret of the strength, the fortitude, the persistent energy, in a word the sacred significance of this war. Strike out the high ends and aims thus indicated, and the war would appear to the impartial eye of an on-looking world little better than a gigantic enterprise for shedding human blood.

A most interesting and gratifying confirmation of this theory of its mission is furnished in the varying fortunes of the struggle itself. Just in proportion to the progress made in taking upon itself the character I have ascribed to it has the war prospered and the Rebellion lost ground.

Justice and humanity are often overpowered—but they are persistent and eternal forces—and fearful to contend against. Let but our rulers place the Government fully within these trade winds of Omnipotence, and the hand of death is upon the Confederate Rebels. A war waged as ours seemed to be at first, merely for power and empire, repels sympathy though supported by legitimacy. If Ireland should strike for independence to-morrow, the sympathy of this country would be with her, and I doubt if American statesmen would be more discreet in the expression of their opinions of the merits of the contest, than British statesmen have been concerning the merits of ours. When we were merely fighting for the old Union the world looked coldly upon our Government. But now the world begins to see something more than legitimacy—something more than national pride. It sees national wisdom aiming at national unity; and national justice breaking the chains of a long enslaved people. It is this new complexion of our cause which warms our hearts and strengthens our hands at home, disarms our enemies and increases our friends abroad. It is this more than all else which has carried consternation into the blood-stained halls of the South. It has sealed the fiery and scornful lips of the Roebucks and Lindsays of England, and caused even the eloquent Mr. Gladstone to restrain the expression of this admiration for Jeff. Davis and his Rebel nation. It has placed the broad arrow of British suspicion on the prows of the Rebel rams in the Mersey, and performed a like service in France. It has driven Mason, the shameless man-hunter, from London, where he never should have been allowed to stay for an hour, except as a bloodhound is tolerated in Regent Park for exhibition.

We have had from the first warm friends in England. We owe a debt of respect and gratitude to William Edward Forster, John Bright, Richard Cobden, and other British statesmen, in that they outran us in comprehending the high character of our struggle. They saw that this must be a war for human nature, and walked by faith to its defense while all was darkness about us—while we were yet conducting it in profound reverence for Slavery.

I know we are not to be praised for this changed character of the war. We did our very best to prevent it. We had but one object at the beginning, and that was, as I have said, the restoration of the old Union; and for the first two years the war was kept to that object strictly, and you know full well and bitterly with what results. I will not stop here to blame and denounce the past; but I will say that the most of the blunders and disasters of the earlier part of the war might have been avoided had our armies and Generals not repelled the only true friends the Union cause had in the rebel States. The Army of the Potomac took up an anti-Negro position from the first, and has not entirely renounced it yet. The colored people told me a few days ago in Washington that they were the victims of the most brutal treatment by these Northern soldiers when they first came there. But let that pass. Few men, however great their wisdom, are permitted to see the end from the beginning. Events are mightier than our rulers, and these Divine forces, with overpowering logic, have fixed upon this war, against the wishes of our Government, the comprehensive character and mission I have ascribed to it. The collecting of revenue in the Rebel ports, the repossession of a few forts and arsenals and other public property stolen by the Rebels, have almost disappeared from the recollection of the people. The war has been a growing war in every sense of the word. It began weak, and has risen strong. It began low, and has risen high. It began narrow, and has become broad. It began with few, and now, behold, the country is full of armed men, ready, with courage and fortitude; to make the wisest and best idea of American statesmanship the law of the land.

Let, then, the war proceed in its strong, high, and broad course till the Rebellion is put down, and our country is saved beyond the necessity of being saved again!

I have already hinted at our danger. Let me be a little more direct and pronounced.

The Democratic party, though defeated in the elections last Fall, is still a power. It is the ready organized nucleus of a powerful Pro-Slavery and Pro-Rebel reaction. Though it has lost in members, it retains all the elements of its former power and malevolence.

That party has five very strong points in its favor, and its public men and journals know well how to take advantage of them.

First: There is the absence of any deep moral feeling among the loyal people against Slavery itself—their feeling against it being on account of its rebellion against the Government, and not because it is a stupendous crime against human nature.

Secondly: The vast expense of the war and the heavy taxes in money as well as men which the war requires for its prosecution. Loyalty has a strong back, but taxation has often broken it.

Thirdly: The earnest desire for peace which is shared by all classes except Government contractors who are making money out of the war; a feeling which may be kindled to a flame by any serious reverses to our arms. It is silent in victory but vehement and dangerous in defeat.

Fourthly: And superior to all others, is the national prejudice and hatred toward all colored people of the country, a feeling which has done more to encourage the hopes of the Rebels than all other powers beside.,

Fifthly: An Abolitionist is an object of popular dislike. The guilty Rebel who with broad blades and bloody hands seeks the life of the nation, is at this hour more acceptable to the northern Democracy than an Abolitionist guilty of no crime. Whatever may be a man's abilities, virtue, or service, the fact that he is an Abolitionist makes him an object of popular hate.

Upon these five strings the Democracy still have hopes of playing themselves into power, and not without reason. While our Government has the meanness to ask Northern colored men to give up the comfort of home, endure untold hardships, peril health, limbs and life itself, in its defense, and then degrades them in the eyes of other soldiers, by offering them the paltry sum of $7.00 per month, and refuses to reward their valor with even the hope of promotion—the Democratic party may well enough presume upon the strength of popular prejudice for support.

While our Republican Government at Washington makes color and not character the criterion of promotion in the army and degrades colored commissioned officers at New Orleans below the rank to which even the Rebel Government had elevated them, I think we are in danger of a compromise with Slavery.

Our hopeful Republican friends tell me this is impossible—that the day of compromise with Slavery is past. This may do for some men, but will not do for me.

The Northern people have always been remarkably confident of their own virtue. They are hopeful to the last. Twenty years ago we hoped that Texas could not be annexed; but if that could not be prevented we hoped that she would come in a Free State. Thirteen years ago we were quite sure that no such abomination as the Fugitive Slave Bill could get itself on our National statute book; but when it got there we were equally sure that it never could be enforced. Four years ago we were sure that the Slave States would not rebel, but if they did we were sure it would be a very short rebellion. I know that times have changed very rapidly, and that we have changed with them. Nevertheless, I know also we are the same old American people, and that what we have done once we may possibly do again. The leaven of compromise is among us—I repeat, while we have a Democratic party at the North trimming its sails to catch the Southern breeze in the next Presidential election, we are in danger of compromise. Tell me not of amnesties and oaths of allegiance. They are valueless in the presence of twenty hundred millions invested in human flesh. Let but the little finger of Slavery get back into this Union, and in one year you shall see its whole body again upon our backs.

While a respectable colored man or woman can be kicked out of the commonest street car in New York where any white ruffian may ride unquestioned—we are in danger of a compromise with Slavery. While the North is full of such papers as the The New York *World, Express,* and *Herald,* firing the nation's heart with hatred to Negroes and Abolitionists, we are in danger of a slaveholding peace. While the major part of anti-slavery profession is based upon devotion to the Union rather than hostility to Slavery, there is danger of a slaveholding peace. Until we shall see the election of November next, and that it has resulted in the election of a sound Anti-Slavery man as President, we shall be in danger of a slaveholding compromise. Indeed, as long as Slavery has any life in it, anywhere in the country, we are in danger of such a compromise.

Then there is the danger arising from the impatience of the people on account of the prolongation of the war. I know the American people. They are an impulsive people, impatient of delay, clamorous for change—and often look for results out of all proportion to the means employed in attaining them.

You and I know that the mission of this war is National regeneration. We know and consider that a nation is not born in a day. We know that large bodies move slowly—and often seem to move thus—when, could we perceive their actual velocity, we should be astonished at its greatness. A great battle lost or won is easily described, understood and appreciated, but the moral growth of a great nation requires reflection, as well as observation, to appreciate it. There are vast numbers of voters, who make no account of the moral growth of a great nation and who only look at the war as a calamity to be endured only so long as they have no power to arrest it. Now, this is just the sort of people whose votes may turn the scale against us in the last event.

Thoughts of this kind tell me that there never was a time when Anti-Slavery work was more needed than now. The day that shall see the Rebels at our feet, their weapons flung away, will be the day of trial. We have need to prepare for that trial. We have long been saved a Pro-Slavery peace by the stubborn, unbending persistence of the Rebels. Let them bend as they will bend—there will come the test of our sternest virtues.

I have now given, very briefly, some of the grounds of danger. A word as to the ground of hope. The best that can be offered is that we have made progress—vast and striking progress—within the last two years.

President Lincoln introduced his administration to the country as one which would faithfully catch, hold, and return runaway slaves to their masters. He avowed his determination to protect and defend the slaveholder's right to plunder the black laborer of his hard earnings. Europe was assured by Mr. Seward that no slave should gain his freedom by this war. Both the President and the Secretary of State have made progress since then.

Our Generals, at the beginning of the war, were horribly Pro-Slavery. They took to slave-catching and slave-killing like ducks to water. They are now very generally and very earnestly in favor of putting an end to Slavery. Some of them, like Hunter and Butler, because they hate Slavery on its own account, and others, because Slavery is in arms against the Government.

The Rebellion has been a rapid educator. Congress was the first to respond to the instinctive judgment of the people, and fixed the broad brand of its reprobation upon slave-hunting in shoulder-straps. Then came very temperate talk about confiscation, which soon came to be pretty radical talk. Then came propositions for Border-State, gradual, compensated, colonized Emancipation. Then came the threat of a proclamation, and then came the proclamation. Meanwhile the Negro had passed along from a loyal spade and pickax to a Springfield rifle.

Haiti and Liberia are recognized. Slavery is humbled in Maryland, threatened in Tennessee, stunned nearly to death in Western Virginia, doomed in Missouri, trembling in Kentucky, and gradually melting away before our arms in the rebellious States.

The hour is one of hope as well as danger. But whatever may come to pass, one thing is clear: The principles involved in the contest, the necessities of both sections of the country, the obvious requirements of the age, and every suggestion of enlightened policy demand the utter extirpation of Slavery from every foot of American soil, and the enfranchisement of the entire colored population of the country. Elsewhere we may find peace, but it will be a hollow and deceitful peace. Elsewhere we may find prosperity, but it will be a transient prosperity. Elsewhere we may find greatness and renown, but if these are based upon anything less substantial than justice they will vanish, for righteousness alone can permanently exalt a nation.

I end where I began—no war but an Abolition war; no peace but an Abolition peace; liberty for all, chains for none; the black man a soldier in war, a laborer in peace; a voter at the South as well as at the North; America his permanent home, and all Americans his fellow-countrymen. Such, fellow-citizens, is my idea of the mission of the war. If accomplished, our glory as a nation will be complete, our peace will flow like a river, and our foundations will be the everlasting rocks.

New York Tribune, January 14, 1864

1. *Life and Times of Frederick Douglass,* p. 380.

2. Douglass to Anonymous, Feb. 17, 1864, Henry P. Slaughter Collection. See also Douglass to Gerrit Smith, Oct. 10, 1863, Gerrit Smith Papers, Syracuse University; Charles R. Douglass to Frederick Douglass, Sept. 8, 1863, Douglass Papers, Frederick Douglass Memorial Home, Anacostia, D.C.

3. On August 19, 1862, Horace Greeley published in the *New York Tribune* an appeal to Lincoln entitled "The Prayer of Twenty Millions." Greeley demanded that Lincoln make emancipation one of the aims of the war. Although Lincoln had already determined to issue an emancipation proclamation, he did not reveal it in his public letter to Greeley. He wrote: "My paramount object in the struggle is to save the Union, and is not either to save or destroy slavery. If I could save the Union without freeing any slave, I would do it; and if I could save it by freeing all the slaves, I would do it; and if I could save it by freeing some and leaving others alone, I would also do that." (John G. Nicolay and John Hay, eds. *Complete Works of Abraham Lincoln,* New York, 1905, vol. VII, pp. 270–74.)

4. Douglass is referring to the following sentence in Lincoln's annual message to Congress, December 8, 1863: "According to our political system, as a matter of civil administration, the General Government had no lawful power to effect emancipation in any State, and for a long time it had been hoped that the rebellion could be suppressed without resorting to it as a military measure." (For the full text of the message, see Nicolay and Hay, *op. cit.,* vol. IX, pp. 224–52.)

5. During the decade 1850–1860, names of northern merchants suspected of being friendly to the anti-slavery movement or who were not deemed sufficiently active in denouncing the Abolitionists were published in southern newspapers, and southern merchants were called upon to boycott them. (See Philip S. Foner, *Business and Slavery,* pp. 43–44, 160–61.)

During the winter and spring of 1864 Douglass became increasingly distrustful of Lincoln's program for the freedmen. He was disturbed by the President's proposal to establish state governments in those southern states with a population loyal to the Union sufficient to cast a vote equal to one-tenth of that cast at the presidential election in 1860. Lincoln was obviously ready to reconstruct the southern states without Negro suffrage. Nor was the President doing anything to remove the disabilities against Negro soldiers. Negro troops had already demonstrated their competence and courage at Port Hudson, Milliken's Bend, and Fort Wagner, and were distinguishing themselves every day on the battlefield. Yet they still received less pay than white soldiers, were unable to secure commissions, and were slaughtered by the Confederate soldiers when captured in battle.[1] . . .

The summer of 1864 was a period of intense gloom throughout the North. The Union reverses, the sluggish character of the war, the open clamor of the Copperheads and even Republicans like Horace Greeley for peace at any price, the dissension in the President's cabinet, the conflict between Congress and the chief executive, all weakened the support of the administration. "Mr. Lincoln is already beaten," cried Greeley. "He cannot be elected." Senator Sherman predicted that if the Democrats should select a candidate who had "any particle of patriotism or sense," they would sweep the Republicans out of office like an avalanche."[2]

Until late in August, Douglass was unsparing in his criticism of Lincoln. Not only did he join Wendell Phillips in denouncing the President's policies, but he called upon his friends in England to expose "*the swindle* by which our Government claims the respect of mankind for abolishing slavery. . . ." [III:42–44]

TO AN ENGLISH CORRESPONDENT

[June, 1864]

[Dear Sir:]

... The more you can say of *the swindle* by which our Government claims the respect of mankind for abolishing slavery—at the same time that it is practically re-establishing that hateful system in Louisiana, under General Banks—*the better*. I have not readily consented to the claims set up in the name of anti-slavery for our Government, but I have tried to believe all for the best. My patience and faith are not very strong now. The treatment of our poor black soldiers—the refusal to pay them anything like equal compensation, though it was promised them when they enlisted; the refusal to insist upon the exchange of colored prisoners when colored prisoners have been slaughtered in cold blood, although the President has repeatedly promised thus to protect the lives of his colored soldiers—have worn my patience threadbare. The President has virtually laid down this as the rule of his statesmen: *Do evil by choice, right from necessity.* You will see that he does not sign the bill adopted by Congress, restricting the organization of State Governments only to those States where there is a loyal majority. His plan is to organize such Governments wherever there is one-tenth of the people loyal!—an entire contradiction of the constitutional idea of the Republican Government. I see no purpose on the part of Lincoln and his friends to extend the elective franchise to the colored people of the South, but the contrary. This is extremely dishonorable. *No rebuke of it can be too strong from your side of the water.* The Negro is deemed good enough to fight for the Government, but not good enough to enjoy the right to vote for the Government. We invest with the elective franchise those who with bloody blades and bloody hands have sought the life of the nation, but sternly refuse to invest those who have done what they could to save the nation's life. This discrimination becomes more dishonorable when the circumstances are duly considered. Our Government asks the Negro to espouse its cause; it asks him to turn against his master, and thus fires his master's hate against him. Well, when it has attained peace, what does it propose? Why this, to hand the Negro back to the political power of his master, without a single element of strength to shield himself from the vindictive spirit sure to be roused against the whole colored race.

[Frederick Douglass]

The *Liberator,* September 16, 1864

1. Wendell Phillips was the outstanding Abolitionist critic of Lincoln's policies during the winter and spring of 1864. Garrison, however, regarded support of Lincoln as a moral obligation upon Abolitionists. A split between these two close friends occurred at a meeting of the Massachusetts Anti-Slavery Society early in 1864. When Phillips proposed a resolution declaring "that the government is ready to sacrifice the honor and interest of the North to secure a sham peace and have the freedmen under the control of the late slaveholders," Garrison took exception and offered the amendment that "the government was only in danger of doing so." (*Liberator,* Feb. 5, 1864.) Phillips' resolution was upheld by a small majority.

2. Ruhly J. Bartlett, *John C. Frémont and the Republican Party,* Columbus, Ohio, 1930, p. 118.

TO WILLIAM LLOYD GARRISON, ESQ.

Rochester, N.Y., Sept. 17, 1864

Dear Sir:

You were pleased to remark in the last number of *The Liberator* (heading it with "Frederick Douglass on President Lincoln") that the secessionist newspapers in Great Britain are publishing with exultation a letter recently addressed by Mr. Douglass to an English correspondent, and you further favor your readers with an extract from the same letter, which criticizes in plain terms the policy of the present administration towards the colored people of the country. I am sure you will allow me space in the columns of the *Liberator* (not to qualify, not to take back any charge, statement, or argument contained in that letter, not even to find fault with its publication, here or elsewhere, though it was flung off in haste, and was not written for publication, but for the eyes of the esteemed friend to whom it was addressed) to remove an inference respecting my present political course, which may possibly and will probably be drawn from the extract in question. In the first place, it is proper to state that that letter was not written recently, as you mistakenly allege, but three months ago, and was in no wise intended to be used against the present administration in the canvass and issues as now made up between the great parties and especially by the disloyal and slavery perpetuating nominations placed before the country by the Chicago convention.[1] Since the date of those nominations, we are met by a new state of facts, and new considerations have arisen to guide and control the political action of all those who are animated by a sincere desire to see justice, liberty and peace permanently established in this rebellion and slavery cursed land. While there was, or seemed to be, the slightest possibility of securing the nomination and election of a man to the Presidency of more decided anti-slavery convictions and a firmer faith in the immediate necessity and practicability of justice and equality for all men, than have been exhibited in the policy of the present administration, I, like many other radical men, freely criticized, in private and in public, the actions and utterances of Mr. Lincoln, and withheld from him my support. That possibility is now no longer conceivable; it is now plain that this country is to be governed or misgoverned during the next four years, either by the Republican Party represented in the person of Abraham Lincoln, or by the (miscalled) Democratic Party, represented by George B. McClellan. With this alternative clearly before us, all hesitation ought to cease, and every man who wishes well to the slave and to the country should at once rally with all the warmth and earnestness of his nature to the support of Abraham Lincoln and Andrew Johnson, and to the utter defeat and political annihilation of McClellan and Pendleton; for the election of the latter, with their well known antecedents, declared sentiments, and the policy avowed in the Chicago platform, would be the heaviest calamity of these years of war and blood, since it would upon the instant sacrifice and wantonly cast away everything valuable, purchased so dearly by the precious blood of our brave sons and brothers on the battlefield for the perfect liberty and permanent peace of a common country. Let me say one other word. I would never give unintentionally the slightest joy to the enemies of human liberty. My rule is to do that *least* that they like *most*, and that *most* that they like *least*. But nothing strange has happened to me in the said exultation over my words by the secessionist newspapers in Great Britain or elsewhere. The common example of those who do not go at all, playing off those who go farthest against those who go, but do not go fast and far enough, is but repeated in this exultation; and if I mistake not, in other days, there were often utterances of *The Liberator* itself, both on the eve and in the middle of the Presidential campaigns, which caused even greater exultation among the known enemies of liberty against timid, shortsighted and trimming anti-slavery men in the high places of the country, than anything I ever wrote concerning Mr. Lincoln and his administration could produce.

Yours for freedom and the equal rights of all men,

Frederick Douglass

The *Liberator*, September 23, 1864

1. On August 30, 1864, the Democratic National Convention met in Chicago. Gov. Horatio Seymour was its permanent chairman, but Clement L. Vallandigham was the dominant figure at the sessions. George B. McClellan was nominated for President and George H. Pendleton for Vice President. The party platform was drawn up by the Copperhead element in the party, and included a plank, written by Vallandigham, which called for a negotiated peace.

About August 25, Douglass met Lincoln for the second time. He found the President in an "alarmed condition," frightened by the repercussions of Lincoln's "To Whom It May Concern" letter, in which he had guaranteed a careful hearing and safe conduct to anyone who brought an authoritative proposition "which embraces the restoration of peace, the integrity of the whole Union, and the abandonment of slavery. . . ."[1] The letter had been written on July 18, 1864, at the request of Horace Greeley, the distinguished editor of the *New York Tribune,* who was about to hold an interview with two Rebel emissaries at Niagara Falls. Greeley had asked Lincoln to grant a safe-conduct to these emissaries, in order that they might come to Washington and discuss terms of peace. In reply, the President sent the "To Whom It May Concern" letter by a special messenger, Colonel John Hay, one of his private secretaries.

Although nothing came of the peace negotiations, since it was soon apparent that the Rebel emissaries had no authority whatever to treat for peace, a howl had arisen from Copperheads and moderate Republicans on the publication of the letter. Lincoln was denounced for having said in so many words that even if the war were ended and the Union saved by a negotiated peace the conflict would go on until slavery was abolished. Pressure was being exerted upon Lincoln by Republicans to force him to modify his conditions for peace.

Lincoln had framed a letter to answer the charges. When Douglass entered, the President read the contents to him, and asked him if he should release it. . . .

Whether or not Douglass' advice was considered, the fact remains that Lincoln did not release the letter. Undoubtedly Douglass felt highly honored that the President had sought his advice on so vital a matter of national policy. He was equally impressed by the fact that at no time during the discussion did Lincoln assert, as he had in the past, that his aim was to save the Union with or without slavery. "What he said on this day," Douglass wrote later, "showed a deeper moral conviction against slavery than I have ever seen before in anything spoken or written by him."[2] . . .

Despite his criticism of the Republican Party, Douglass was anxious to take the stump for Lincoln. But Republican committees were cool to the offer. A campaign pamphlet issued by the Democrats, entitled *Miscegenation Indorsed by Republican Party*, quoted from Douglass' speech at the meeting of the American Anti-Slavery Society in December, 1863, describing his first visit to Lincoln. The Democrats pointed gleefully to Douglass' statement that "the President of the United States received a black man at the White House just as one gentleman received another." Republican politicians, frightened by the label attached to their candidate, felt that Douglass' campaign speeches would only provide further ammunition to the Democrats and rejected his offers to assist in the campaign.[3] Already the reactionary wing of the Republican Party was foreshadowing its later betrayal of the Negro people. [III:45–46, 51]

TO THEODORE TILTON

Rochester, October 15, 1864

My Dear Mr. Tilton:

I am obliged by your favor containing a copy of your recent speech in Latimer hall. I had read that speech in the *Tribune* several days ago,[4] and in my heart thanked you for daring thus to break the spell of enchantment with which slavery, though wounded, dying and despised, is still able to bind the tongues of our republican orators. It was a timely word wisely and well spoken, the best and most luminous spark struck from the flint and steel of this canvass. To all appearance we have been more ashamed of the Negro during this canvass than those of 56 and 60. The President's "To whom it may concern" frightened his party and his party in return frightened the President. I found him in this alarmed condition when I called upon him six weeks ago, and it is well to note the time. The country was struck with one of those bewilderments which dethrone reason for the moment. Everybody was thinking and dreaming of peace, and the impression had gone abroad that the President's anti-slavery policy was about the only thing which prevented a peaceful settlement with the Rebels. McClellan was nominated, and at that time his prospects were bright as Mr. Lincoln's were gloomy. You must therefore, judge the President's words in the light of the circumstances in which he spoke. Atlanta had not fallen;[5] Sheridan had not swept the Shenandoah, and men were ready for peace almost at any price. The President was pressed on every hand to modify his letter, "*To whom it may concern.*" How to meet this pressure he did me the honor to ask my opinion. He showed me a letter written with a view to meet the peace clamor raised against him. The first point made in it was the important fact that no man or set of men authorized to speak for the Confederate Government had ever submitted a proposition for peace to him. Hence the charge that he had in some way stood in the way of peace fell to the ground. He had always stood ready to listen to any such propositions. The next point referred to was the charge that he had in his Niagara letter committed himself and the country to an abolition war rather than a war for the union, so that even if the latter could be attained by negotiation, the war would go on for Abolition.

The president did not propose to take back what he had said in his Niagara letter, but wished to relieve the fears of his peace friends, by making it appear that the thing which they feared could not happen, and was wholly beyond his power. Even if I would, I could not carry on the war for the abolition of slavery. The country would not sustain such a war, and I could do nothing without the support of Congress. I could not make the abolition of slavery an absolute prior condition to the reestablishment of the Union. All that the President said on this point was to make manifest his want of power to do the thing which his enemies and pretended friends professed to be afraid he would do. Now the question he put to me was—Shall I send forth this letter—To which I answered—Certainly not. It would be given a broader meaning than you intend to convey; it would be taken as a complete surrender of your anti-slavery policy, and do you serious damage. In answer to your Copperhead accusers, your friends can make the argument of your want of power, but you cannot wisely say a word on that point.

I have looked and feared that Mr. Lincoln would say something of the sort, but he has been perfectly silent on that point, and I think will remain so. But the thing which alarmed me most was this: The President said he wanted some plan devised by which he could get more of the Slaves within our lines. He thought now was their time—*and that such only of them as succeeded in getting within our line would be free after the war was over.* This shows that the President only has faith in this proclamation of freedom, during the war, and that he believes the operation will cease with the war. We were long together and there was much said, but this is enough. . . .

I am not doing much in this Presidential canvass for the reason that Republican committees do not wish to expose themselves to the charge of being the "N—r" party. The Negro is the deformed child, which is put out of the room when company comes. I hope to speak some after the election—though not much before—and I am inclined to think I shall be able to speak all the more usefully because I have had so little to say during the present canvass. I now look upon the election of Mr. Lincoln as settled. When there was any shadow of a hope that a man of a more decided anti-slavery conviction and policy could be elected, I was not for Mr. Lincoln. But as soon as the Chicago convention, my mind was made up, and it is made still. All dates changed with the nomination of Mr. McClellan.

I hope that in listening to Mr. Stanton's version of my visit to the President that you kept in mind something of Mr. Stanton's own state of mind concerning public affairs. I found him in a very gloomy state of mind—much less hopeful than myself—and yet more cheerful than I expected to find him. I judge from your note that he must have imparted somewhat of the hue of his own mind to my statements. He thinks far less of the President's honesty than I do, and far less of his anti-slavery than I do. I have not yet come to think that honesty and politics are incompatible. Well, here I am, my dear Sir, writing you a long letter, needlessly taking up your precious time, and with no better excuse for the impertinence than a brief note from you and a knowledge of your good temper and disposition toward me. . . .

Truly yours always,
Frederick Douglass

Frederick Douglass MSS, Buffalo Public Library

1. Nicolay and Hay, *op. cit.,* vol. X, p. 161.

2. *Life and Times of Frederick Douglass,* p. 427.

3. *Liberator,* Jan. 29, 1864.

4. Theodore Tilton spoke at Latimer Hall, Brooklyn, on October 7, 1864. (For the text of his speech, see *New York Tribune,* Oct. 8, 1864, and *National Anti-Slavery Standard,* Oct. 15, 1864.)

5. The Confederate troops abandoned Atlanta on the night of September 1, 1864. On September 3, the newspapers announced, "General Sherman has taken Atlanta." Two days later Sherman's famous words flashed through the nation: "Atlanta is ours and fairly won." President Lincoln, on September 3, issued a proclamation asking the people to give thanks for Admiral Farragut's victory in Mobile and the capture of Atlanta when they assembled in church the next Sunday.

PART SEVEN

Reconstruction, 1865–1876

Two years before Appomattox Douglass had made it clear that Reconstruction meant not only the return of the rebellious states to the Union; it meant the most profound alteration in the entire manner of the South. The historical tasks of Reconstruction consisted in crushing forever the slave power and creating the conditions for a democratic South. The slavocracy had been routed on the battlefield, but its strangle-hold upon southern life had to be broke before the democratic forces could count the victory complete.

But many Abolitionists were ready to call it a day. With the end of the war Garrison held that the work of abolition was ended, and that the American Anti-Slavery Society could now be disbanded. At the annual meeting in May, 1865, he declared: "We organized expressly for the abolition of slavery; we called our Society an *Anti-Slavery Society*. The other work [Negro suffrage] was incidental. Now, I believe, slavery is abolished in this country, abolished constitutionally, abolished by a decree of this nation, never, never to be reversed, and, therefore, that it is ludicrous for us, a mere handful of people with little means, with no agents in the field, no longer separate, and swallowed up in the great ocean of popular feeling against slavery, to assume that we are of special importance, and that we ought not to dissolve."

Garrison was sure that the North in reconstructing the southern states would insist on "guarantees for the protection of the freedmen," would give them the vote, and protect them by force of arms. Douglass did not share his faith. . . . The majority agreed with Douglass that discontinuance of the American Anti-Slavery Society meant abandoning the Negro and the cause of freedom. Garrison's resolution to disband was rejected by a vote of 118 to 48. A new executive committee, with Wendell Phillips as president, was chosen.[1] [IV:15–16]

THE NEED FOR CONTINUING ANTI-SLAVERY WORK, speech at Thirty-Second Annual Meeting of the American Anti-Slavery Society, May 10, 1865

Several gentlemen have been so kind as to refer to me in the course of this discussion, and my friend, Mr. May, referred to me as being opposed to the disbandment of this Society at any time during the present year. Having been thus referred to, I wish to put myself properly before the meeting.

Almost the first work the American Anti-Slavery Society asked me to do, after employing me as an agent more than twenty years ago, was to accompany Stephen S. Foster and Abby Kelley (now Mrs. Foster) into the State of Rhode Island, to wage a most unrelenting war against what was called the "Dorr Constitution," because that Constitution contained the odious word "white" in it. That was regarded as legitimate and anti-slavery work at that time; and that work was most effectively performed, amid mobs and all sorts of violence. We succeeded in defeating that Dorr Constitution, and secured the adoption of a Constitution in which the word "white" did not appear. We thought it was a grand *anti-slavery* triumph, and it was; it was a good *anti-slavery* work. When I came North and went to Massachusetts, I found that the leading work of the Abolitionists was to put the State of Massachusetts in harmony with the platform of the American Anti-Slavery Society. They said charity began at home. They looked over their statute-book, and whenever they found the word "white," there they recognized slavery, and they made war upon it. The anti-slavery ladies made themselves of no reputation by going about with petitions, asking the Legislature to blot out that hated word "white" from the marriage law. That was good anti-slavery work twenty years ago; I do not see why it is not good anti-slavery work now. It was a part of anti-slavery work then; it is a part now, I think.

I do not wish to appear here in any fault-finding spirit, or as an impugner of the motives of those who believe that the time has come for this Society to disband. I am conscious of no suspicion of the purity and excellence of the motives that animate the President of this Society, and other gentlemen who are in favor its disbandment. I take this ground; whether this Constitutional Amendment is law or not, whether it has been ratified by a sufficient number of States to make it law or not, I hold that the work of Abolitionists is not done. Even if every State in the Union had ratified that Amendment, while the black man is confronted in the legislation of the South by the word "white," our work as Abolitionists, as I conceive it, is not done. I took the ground, last night, that the South, by unfriendly legislation, could make our liberty, under that provision, a delusion, a mockery, and a snare, and I hold that ground now. What advantage is a provision like this Amendment to the black man, if the Legislature of any State can to-morrow declare that no black man's testimony shall be received in a court of law? Where are we then? Any wretch may enter the house of a black man, and commit any violence he pleases; if he happens to do it only in the presence of black persons, he goes unwhipt of justice ["Hear, hear"]. And don't tell me that those people down there have become so just and honest all at once that they will not pass laws denying to black men the right to testify against white men in the courts of law. Why, our Northern States have done it. Illinois, Indiana and Ohio have done it. Here, in the midst of institutions that have gone forth from old Plymouth Rock, the black man has been excluded from testifying in the courts of law; and if the Legislature of every Southern State to-morrow pass a law, declaring that no Negro shall testify in any courts of law, they will not violate that provision of the Constitution. Such laws exist now at the South.[2] The next day, the Legislatures may pass a law that any black man who shall lift his arm in self-defence, even, against a white man, shall have that arm severed from his body, and may be hanged and quartered, and his head and quarters set up in the most public parts of the district where the crime shall have been committed. Such laws now exist at the South, and they might exist under this provision of the Constitution, that there shall be neither slavery nor involuntary servitude in any State of the Union.

Then another point. I have thought, for the last fifteen years, that we had an anti-slavery Constitution—a Constitution intended "to secure the blessings of liberty to ourselves and our posterity." But we have had slavery all along. We had a Constitution that declared that the citizen of old Massachusetts should enjoy all the rights and immunities of citizens in South Carolina—but what of it? Let Mr. Hoar go down, to South Carolina, and point to that provision in the Constitution, and they would kick him out of the State. There is something down in South Carolina higher than Constitutional provisions.

Slavery is not abolished until the black man has the ballot. While the Legislature of the South retain the right to pass laws making any discrimination between black and white, slavery still lives there. [Applause.] As Edmund Quincy once said, "While the word 'white' is on the statute-book of Massachusetts, Massachusetts is a slave State. While a black man can be turned out of a car in Massachusetts, Massachusetts is a slave State. While a slave can be taken from old Massachusetts, Massachusetts is a slave State." That is what I heard Edmund Quincy say twenty-three or twenty-four years ago. I never forget such a thing. Now, while the black man can be denied a vote, while the Legislatures of the South can take from him the right to keep and bear arms, as they can—they would not allow a Negro to walk with a cane where I came from, they would not allow five of them to assemble together—the work of the Abolitionists is not finished. Notwithstanding the provision in the Constitution of the United States, that the right to keep and bear arms shall not be abridged, the black man has never had the right either to keep or bear arms; and the Legislatures of the States will still have the power to forbid it, under this Amendment. They can carry on a system of unfriendly legislation, and will they not do it? Have they not got the prejudice there to do it with? Think you, that because they are for the moment in the talons and beak of our glorious eagle, instead of the slave being there, as formerly, that they are converted? I hear of the loyalty at Wilmington, the loyalty at South Carolina—what is it worth?

Mr. May—Not a straw.

Mr. Douglass—Not a straw. I thank my friend for admitting it. They are loyal while they see 200,000 sable soldiers, with glistening bayonets, walking in their midst. [Applause.] But let the civil power of the States be restored, and the old prejudices and hostility to the Negro will revive. Aye, the very fact that the Negro has been used to defeat this rebellion and strike down the standards of the Confederacy will be a stimulus to all their hatreds, to all their malice, and lead them to legislate with greater stringency towards this class than ever before. [Applause.] The American people are bound—bound by their sense of honor (I hope by their sense of honor, at least, by a just sense of honor), to extend the franchise to the Negro; and I was going to say, that the Abolitionists of the American Anti-Slavery Society were bound to "stand still, and see the salvation of God," until that work is done. [Applause.] Where shall the black man look for support, my friends, if the American Anti-Slavery Society fails him? ["Hear, hear."] From whence shall we expect a certain sound from the trumpet of freedom, when the old pioneer, when this Society that has survived mobs, and martyrdom, and the combined efforts of priest-craft and state-craft to suppress it, shall all at once subside, on the mere intimation that the Constitution has been amended, so that neither slavery nor involuntary servitude shall hereafter be allowed in this land? What did the slaveholders of Richmond say to those who objected to arming the Negro, on the ground that it would make him a freeman? Why, they said, "The argument is absurd. We may make these Negroes fight for us; but while we retain the political power of the South, we can keep them in their subordinate positions." That was the argument; and they were right. They might have employed the Negro to fight for them, and while they retained in their hands the power to exclude him from political rights, they could have reduced him to a condition similar to slavery. They would not call it slavery, but some other name. Slavery has been fruitful in giving itself names. It has been called "the peculiar institution," "the social system," and the "impediment," as it was called by the General Conference of the Methodist Episcopal Church. It has been called by a great many names, and it will call itself by yet another name; and you and I and all of us had better wait and see what new form this old monster will assume, in what new skin this old snake will come forth next.

e *Liberator,* May 26, 1865

1. *Liberator,* May 26, 1865. At a meeting of the colored people of New York City early in May, a resolution was adopted urging the American Anti-Slavery Society not to dissolve. The Society, it declared, had not accomplished its full objects, particularly that of "removing public prejudice," and "could not, in good faith, without a violation of assumed honorable trust, at present dissolve." (*New York Times,* May 3, 1865.)

2. In 1865–1866 Southern states enacted statutes known as the "Black Codes" which reduced the freedmen to a condition very close to slavery. Under these codes a Negro who was not at work was arrested and imprisoned. In order to pay off the prison charges and fines he was hired out. If the Negro quit work before his contract expired, he was arrested and imprisoned for a breach of contract and the reward to the person performing the arrest was deducted from his wages. Some of the codes also provided that if a Negro laborer left his employer he would "forfeit all wages to the time of abandonment." Negro children whose parents were considered too poor to support them were bound out as apprentices, girls until eighteen years of age and boys until twenty-one.

THE DOUGLASS INSTITUTE, lecture at Inauguration of Douglass Institute, Baltimore, September 29, 1865[1]

I have, during my public career, had the honor to address many assemblies, both at home and abroad, and in furtherance of various objects; but I do not remember ever to have appeared anywhere under a deeper sense of the importance of the occasion than I feel tonight. I know it is common to call all occasions, upon which we assemble in large numbers, great and important, and in some sense the characterization is just and proper; for the movement of large bodies of men in this or that direction, for any purpose, good or ill, is always important, and worthy of note. But the present occasion is one of no ordinary character. We come here to dedicate an institution which, in my opinion, is destined to play an important part in promoting the freedom and elevation of the colored people of this city and State, and I may say of the whole Union.

Let me at the outset put myself at ease by expressing to the founders of this Institution my sincere and heartfelt thanks for assigning to me the high place I occupy on this occasion, and above all, for associating my name with the Institute here established. It is an honor. I look upon this proceeding on your part not merely as a compliment to me personally, but as an open avowal of the great principles of progress, liberty, justice and equality, which I have for years endeavored to advocate. When I left Maryland, twenty-seven years ago, I did so with the firm resolve never to forget my brothers and sisters in bondage, and to do whatever might be in my power to accomplish their emancipation; and I have to say to-night, that in whatever else I may have failed, in this at least I have not failed. No man can truthfully say I ever deserted the post of duty.

The establishment of an Institute bearing my name by the colored people in the city of my boyhood, so soon after the act of emancipation in this State, looms before me as a *first* grand indication of progress. I say it is a *first,* and first indications, whether observed in the silent, mysterious phemomena of physical nature, or in the moral or intellectual developments of human society, are always interesting to thoughtful men. Every age has its prophet or its Messiah. We are ever waiting and watching like good old Simeon for our babe of Bethlehem. John Brown used to say he had looked over our people as over a dark sea, in the hope of seeing a head rise up with a mind to plan and a hand to deliver. Any movement of the water arrested his attention. In all directions, we desire to catch the first sign. The first sign of clear weather on the ocean after a season of darkness and storm; the first sign of returning health after long and weary months of wasting fever; the first sign of rain after a famine, threatening drouth; the first indication of spring, silently releasing the knotty and congealed earth from the frosty fetters of winter; the first sign of peace after the ten thousand calamities, horrors, desolations and alarms of war, evermore bring joy and gladness to the human heart.

The mind of man has a special attraction towards first objects. It delights in the dim and shadowy outlines of the coming fact. There is a calm and quiet satisfaction in the contemplation of present attainments; but the great future, and the yet unattained, awaken in the soul the deepest springs of poetry and enthusiasm.

The occasion that brings us here this evening may be properly viewed in the spirit of these brief reflections. It is an indication of the rise of a people long oppressed, enslaved and bound in the chains of ignorance, to a freer and higher plane of life, manhood, usefulness and civilization.

Peace, says the noble Sumner, has its trumphs no less than war. I avail myself of the aphorism, and claim the dedication of the Douglass Institute in this, the city of Baltimore, in the State of Maryland, dedicated as it will be to knowledge, virtue and liberty, as one such triumph. I think it quite difficult to over-estimate the importance and significance of the first effort of the kind in the city of Baltimore. I confess that the establishment of such an Institution here and now was a source of apprehension as well as joy; joy in the thought of its success, apprehension lest the effort should fail. It seemed too much to expect.

A people hitherto pronounced by American learning as incapable of any thing higher than the dull round of merely animal life—held to be originally and permanently inferior—fit only for the coarser and heavier labors of human society—shut out for ages from the arts, from science, and from all the more elevating forms of industry—deprived of the social incentives to excellence which everywhere act upon other men, dare here and now to establish an Institute, devoted to all the higher wants and aspirations of the human soul. It is a great fact.

Your very enemies, looking upon this event, will admit that it speaks well for the colored people of Baltimore. It is in itself a powerful appeal from the popular judgment under which the colored people of this city and of this State, and of the whole country, have staggered during more than two hundred years. I would bestow no extravagant and indiscriminate praise upon the founders of the Douglass Institute. You are sensible men, and would not thank me if I did. The colored people of this country have as much reason to deprecate flattery as they have disparagement. What they want is the simple truth, and this renders honor where honor is due. I say to you, gentlemen, what you all know, that this institution, viewed in comparison with those established by our white fellow-citizens for similar objects, stands but as a dwarf to a giant; but regarded in the light of our history, in view of our numbers and opportunities, the Douglass Institute is the equal of any in credit, and far more significant than most of them. It is a beginning, and though like all beginnings it is small, it is, nevertheless, a prophecy of larger and better things. It represents something, and important as it is for itself, it is ten-fold more important for what it represents in the character of its founders. It implies something. It implies that the colored people of Baltimore not only have the higher qualities attributed to the white race, but that they are awakening to a healthy consciousness of those qualities in themselves, and that they are beginning to see, as the dark cloud of slavery rolls away, the necessity of bringing those qualities into vigorous exercise. It implies an increased knowledge of the requirements of a high civilization, and a determination to comply with them. This Institute, in character and design, in some measure represents the abilities and possibilities of our race.

My friends, the present is a critical moment for the colored people of this country; our fate for weal or for woe, it may be yet for many generations, trembles now in the balance. No man can tell which way the scale will turn. There is not a breeze that sweeps to us from the South, but comes laden with the wail of our suffering people. Heaven only knows what will be in store for our people in the South. But dismal as is the hour, troubled and convulsed as are the times, we may congratulate ourselves upon the establishment of this institution. It comes as a timely argument on the right side of the momentous questions which now agitate the nation. It comes at a time when the American people are once more being urged to do from necessity what they should have done from a sense of right, and of sound statemanship. It is the same old posture of affairs, wherein our rulers do wrong from choice and right from necessity. They gave us the bullet to save themselves; they will yet give the ballot to save themselves. My hope of the future is founded just where it was during all the war. I always said that I had much faith in the virtue of the great North, but that I had incomparably more in the villainy of the South. The South is now on its good behavior, we are told. They have been invested with powers merely to see how they will use them. If they do certain things we are told, it will be well, but if they do certain other things—well, somebody will interfere. Very well. I expect to see the rebels consistent with their whole past. They are sworn now as at the beginning of the war, and with like results. They take the oath to support a Government they hate. They are sure to abuse the power given them, and I believe there will be virtue enough in the country, when it shall see that the loyal whites can only be saved by giving the ballot to the Negro, to do the thing now called impossible.

This Institute comes to our help. It comes at a time when hesitation to extend suffrage to the colored people finds its best apology in our alleged incapacity. I deem it fortunate that, at such a time as this, in such a city as this, so near the capital of the nation as this, there has arisen here an Institution in which we can confront ignorance and prejudice with the light and power of positive knowledge, and array against brazen falsehood the rightful influence of accomplished facts.

The very existence of this Institution, established and sustained by colored men in the city, so recently a slaveholding city—in this State, so recently a slaveholding State—in this community, among whom freedom of speech was scarcely known by even the white citizens only a few months ago—is a most striking, cheering and instructive fact. It attests the progressive spirit, the sagacity, the courage, the faith, the intelligence and manly ambition of the colored people of this city and State, and reflects credit upon the colored people of the country generally. Its effects upon those who disparage us will be good, but its effects upon ourselves will, I trust, be far better. While to them it will be a standing contradiction, to us it will be a happy concurrence with all our hopes, with all that is high, noble and desirable.

The colored boy and girl now, as they walk your streets, will hold themselves in higher estimation and assume a prouder and a more elastic step as they look up to the fine proportions of this ample and elegant building, and remember that from foundation to roof, from corner-stone to coping, in purpose and in value, in spirit and in aspiration, it is all the property of the colored citizens of Baltimore.

The establishment of this Institution may be thought by some a thing of doubtful expediency. There was a time when I should have thought it so myself. In my enthusiasm, perhaps it was my simplicity, it is not material which, I once flattered myself that the day had happily gone by when it could be necessary for colored people in this country to combine and act together as a separate class, and in any representative character whatever. I would have had them infuse themselves and their works into all the political, intellectual, artistical and mechanical activities and combinations of their white fellow countrymen. It seemed to me that colored conventions, colored exhibitions, colored associations and institutions of all kinds and descriptions had answered the ends of their existence, and might properly be abandoned; that, in short, they were hindrances rather than helps in achieving a higher and better estimation in the public mind for ourselves as a race.

I may say that I still hold this opinion in a modified degree. The latent contempt and prejudice towards our race, which recent political doctrines with reference to our future in this country have developed, the persistent determination of the present Executive of the nation, and also the apparent determination of a portion of the people to hold and treat us in a degraded relation, not only justify for the present such associate effort on our part, but make it eminently necessary.

It is the misfortune of our class that it fails to derive due advantages from the achievements of its individual members, but never fails to suffer from the ignorance or crimes of a single individual with whom the class is identified. A Benjamin Franklin could redeem, in the eyes of scientific Europe, the mental mediocrity of our young white Republic, but the genius and learning of a Benjamin Banneker of your own State of Maryland, the wisdom and heroism of Toussaint, are not permitted to do the same service for the colored race to which they belong. Wealth, learning and ability made an Irishman an Englishman. The same metamorphosing power converts a Negro into a white man in this country. When prejudice cannot deny the black man's ability, it denies his race, and claims him as a white man. It affirms that if he is not exactly white, he ought to be. If not what he ought to be in this particular, he owes whatever intelligence he possesses to the white race by contract or association. Great actions, as shown by Robert Small, the gallant captain of the Planter, and by William Tilghman, and other brave colored men, which by the war slavery has tossed to the surface, have not been sufficient to change the general estimate formed of the colored race. The eloquence and learning of Doctor Smith, Professors Vashon, Reason, Garnet, Remond, Martin, Rock, Crummell, and many others, have done us service; but they leave us yet under a cloud. The public, with the mass of ignorance—notwithstanding that ignorance has been enforced and compelled among our people, hitherto—has sternly denied the representative character of our distinguished men. They are treated as exceptions, individual cases, and the like. They contend that the race, as such, is destitute of the subjective original elemental condition of a high self-originating and self-sustaining civilization.

Such is the sweeping and damaging judgment pronounced in various high quarters against our race; and such is the current of opinion against which the colored people have to advance, if they advance at all. A few years ago, we met this unfavorable theory as best we could in three ways.[2] We pointed our assailants and traducers to the ancient civilization of Northern Africa. We traced the entangled threads of history and of civilization back to their sources in Africa. We called attention to the somewhat disagreeable fact—agreeable to us, but not so to our Teutonic brethren—that the arts, appliances and blessings of civilization flourished in the very heart of Ethiopia, at a time when all Europe floundered in the depths of ignorance and barbarism. We dwelt on the grandeur, magnificence and stupendous dimensions of Egyptian architecture, and held up the fact, now generally admitted, that that race was master of mechanical forces of which the present generations of men are ignorant.

We pointed to the nautical skill, commercial enterprise and military prowess of Carthage, and justly claimed relationship with those great nations of antiquity. We are a dark people—so were they. They stood between us and the Europeans in point of complexion, as well as in point of geography. We have contended—and not illogically—that if the fact of color was no barrier to civilization in their case, it cannot be in ours.

Our second answer has been drawn from modern examples. These have not, I confess, been very numerous or striking. but enough to demonstrate the presence of highly progressive and civilizing elements in the colored race. We find them in Africa—we find them written down in the interesting travels of Barth, Livingston and Wilson. We find them in Hayti, and we find them in our own country. Our third answer has been the unfavorable influence under which our race has been placed by Christendom during the last three centuries. Where under the whole heavens was there ever a race so blasted and withered, so shorn and bereft of all opportunities for development as ourselves? It would seem that the whole Christian world had combined for the destruction of our race, and had summoned heaven and hell, philosophy and revelation, to assist in the work. Our history has been but a track of blood. Gaunt and hungry sharks have followed us on slave ships by sea, and the hungrier and greedier slave-drivers have followed us during all these years with the bloody slave-whip on land. The question forced upon us at every moment of our generation has not been, as with other races of men, how shall we adorn, beautify, exalt and ennoble life, but how shall we retain life itself. The struggle with us was not to do, but to be. Mankind lost sight of our human nature in the idea of our being property, and the whole machinery of society was planned, directed and operated to the making us a stupid, spiritless, ignorant, besotted, brutified, and utterly degraded race of men.

Thus far we have derived little advantage from any apologies we have made or from any explanations we have patiently given. Our relationship to the ancient Egyptians has been denied; the progress made by the emancipated people of the West Indies is not believed, and men still insist that the fault of our ignorance is not in slavery, but in ourselves. So stood the question concerning us up to the second year of the fierce and sanguinary rebellion now subsiding. Since then, the colored man has come before the country in a new light. He has illustrated the highest qualities of a patriot and a soldier. He has ranged himself on the side of Government and country, and maintained both against rebels and traitors on the perilous edge of battle. They are now, many of them, sleeping side by side in bloody graves with the bravest and best of all our loyal white soldiers, and many of those who remain alive are scarred and battered veterans—mere stumps of men; armless, legless, maimed and mutilated ones are met with in the streets of every city. The veriest enemies of our race must now admit that we have at least one element of civilization. It is settled that we have manly courage, that we love our country, and that we will fight for an Idea. Both Government—the Rebel as well as the Federal—admitted the energy that slumbered in the black man's arm, and both, at the last, endeavored to render that energy useful. But the charge still remains. Now, what are those elemental and original powers of civilization about which men speak and write so earnestly, and which white men claim for themselves and deny to the Negro? I answer that they are simply consciousness of wants and ability to gratify them. Here the whole machinery of civilization, whether moral, intellectual or physical, is set in motion.

Man is distinguished from all other animals, but in nothing is he distinguished more than in this, namely, resistance, active and constant resistance, to the forces of physical nature. All other animals submit to the same conditions and limitations from generation to generation. The bear today is as he was a thousand years ago. Nature provides him with food, clothing and shelter, and he is neither wiser not better because of the experience of his bearish ancestors. Not so with man. He learns from the past, improves upon the past, looks back upon the past, and hands down his knowledge of the past to after-coming generations of men, that they may carry their achievements to a still higher point. To lack this element of progress is to resemble the lower animals, and to possess it is to be men.

The mission of this Institution and that of the colored race are identical. It is to develop manhood, to build up manly character among the colored people of this city and State. It is to teach them the true idea of manly independence and self-respect. It is to be a dispenser of knowledge, a radiator of light. In a word, we dedicate this Institution to virtue, temperance, knowledge, truth, liberty and justice:

> "In this fair hall, to Truth and Freedom given,
> Pledged to the right before all earth and heaven—
> A free arena for the strife of mind,
> No caste, or sect, or color are confined."

We who have been long debarred the privileges of culture may assemble and have our souls thrilled with heavenly music, lifted to the skies on the wings of poetry and song. Here we can assemble and have our minds enlightened upon the whole circle of social, moral, political and educational duties. Here we can come and learn true politeness and refinements. Here the loftiest and best eloquence which the country has produced, whether of Anglo-Saxon or of African descent, shall flow as a river, enriching, ennobling, strengthening and purifying all who will lave in its waters. Here may come all who have a new and unpopular truth to unfold and enforce, against which old and respectable bars and bolts are iron gates. Here, from this broad hall, shall go forth an influence which shall at last change the current of public contempt for the oppressed, and lift the race into the popular consideration which justly belongs to their manly character and achievements.

The *Liberator,* October 13, 1865

1. In the spring of 1865 an association was formed, composed of thirty or forty colored men of Baltimore, which purchased the building on Lexington Street, near Davis, formerly occupied as the Newton University, for the sum of $16,000 and organized the "Douglass Institute." The object of the Institute was "the intellectual advancement of the colored portion of the community."

2. Douglass is referring to his address before the Literary Societies of the Western Reserve College, July 12, 1854, entitled, "The Claims of the Negro Ethnologically Considered."

[In early 1866,] while in Washington, Douglass attended a convention of colored men called to express the sentiments of the Negro people on the issues of Reconstruction. Delegates from Wisconsin, Alabama, Florida, Pennsylvania, Maryland, New York, the District of Columbia, and the six New England states met in the Fifteenth Street Presbyterian Church and, with Reverend Henry Highland Garnet as presiding officer, discussed for two days the Freedmen's Bureau Bill, the Civil Rights Bill, the proposed Fourteenth amendment, and other pending legislation. The meeting went on record that while they were "unalterably opposed to foreign colonization and would resist to the utmost any attempt at compulsory emigration or removal to any place, in this country, or out of it not of our own free choice," they were prepared to support any effort of the government "to provide homes for the homeless in any portion of our country." It also urged the government, through congressional legislation, to "guarantee and secure to all loyal citizens, irrespective of race or color, equal rights before the law, including the right of impartial suffrage." Such legislation was deemed "essential to secure liberty to the freedmen and a republican form a government to the States lately in rebellion."[1]

The Convention of Colored Men appointed a delegation consisting of George T. Downing, William Whipper, John Jones, Douglass, and his son, Lewis, to visit President Johnson to get his views on the program set forth in their resolutions. On February 7, the delegation called at the White House.

After being greeted by the President, Downing, the chairman, opened with an expression of respect to "your Excellency." He told the President that the delegation had some "feeling that we are friends meeting a friend." As spokesmen for the colored people, they were here to voice dissatisfaction with the lax enforcement of the Thirteenth Amendment and to express the hope that the Negro "may be fully enfranchised, not only here in this District, but throughout the land."

Douglass followed Downing, and, in a brief statement, reminded Johnson that his "noble and humane predecessor" had called upon the Negroes to assist in saving the nation. He hoped that the President would take the next logical step, and favor the granting of the ballot to colored men "with which to save ourselves." Douglass condensed the right of the Negro to the ballot in a single sentence: "The fact that we are the subjects of the Government and subject to taxation, to volunteer in the service of the country, subject to being drafted, subject to bear the burdens of the State, makes it not improper that we should ask to share in the privileges of this condition."

In is reply Johnson stated he had "periled" everything for the colored race, and that he did not like "to be arraigned by some who can get up handsomely-rounded periods and deal in rhetoric, and talk about abstract ideas of liberty, who never periled life, liberty or property." He was willing to be the Negro's Moses "to lead him from bondage to freedom," but he was unwilling to support a policy which would result "in great injury to the white as well as to the colored man." Approaching "very near to Mr. Douglass," the President advanced the argument that the poor whites and the Negro had always been bitter enemies. If they were "thrown together at the ballot-box with this enmity and hate existing between them," a race war would begin.

When Johnson inquired if it was right to force the majority to "receive a state of things they are opposed to," Downing asked if he would apply this principle to South Carolina "where a majority of the inhabitants are colored." The President ignored this, and continued to insist that it was for the people of a state, not Congress, to determine who should vote. He closed on a mystical note. All that was necessary was to search for "a great law" controlling the proper relations between Negro and white. "All the details will then properly adjust themselves and work out well in the end."

Douglass thanked the President, but indicated a desire to differ with some of the points that had been advanced. Johnson shrugged this off with the observation that he believed that all that had been expected of him was that he set forth his views. But Douglass persisted, and declared that the enfranchisement of the Negro would prevent the very thing the President feared—"a conflict of races." To this Johnson gave the familiar argument that the problems could best be solved by the emigration of the Negroes. Douglass countered with the statement that even if the Negro wanted to leave the South he could not do so because he was "absolutely in the hands" of the master class. Johnson seized on this to advance the argument that the master would also control the Negro's vote when he was enfranchised. Douglass assured the President that once given the vote, the Negro and poor whites would unite and form a new party in the South. "There is this conflict that you speak of between the wealthy slaveholder and the poor man," he added. Irritated by the effective demolition of his main argument, Johnson charged that Douglass' statement proved that danger of a conflict existed in the South. He repeated his suggestion of emigration as the solution.

On departing, Douglass remarked to his fellow-delegates: "The President sends us to the people, and we go to the people." "Yes, sir," said Johnson; "I have great faith in the people. I believe they will do what is right."[2]

On leaving the White House, the delegates were immediately interviewed by a group of Radical Congressmen. A correspondent for the *New York Tribune* who was present reported the delegates as saying that the President had spoken to them "not without courtesy, but in a manner which indicated a subdued excitement, or 'repressed anger.' . . ." They also expressed the conviction that Johnson would oppose the extension of suffrage to Negroes.[3]

Later in the day Douglass wrote [the following] reply to the President in behalf of the entire delegation which was published in the *Washington Chronicle*. . . .

The story of the Negro delegation's interview with Johnson received wide publicity, and was used effectively in mobilizing public support for the Negro people. Republican Congressmen were quick to point out that the Negro delegates had "altogether the best of the argument," and showed "no inferiority in point of deportment either." The Abolitionists went even further. "Who that reads the speeches of the colored delegation, and the President's" wrote Elizabeth Cady Stanton, "can help seeing how much better Douglass understands the philosophy of social life and republican institutions than the President?" The *Anti-Slavery Standard* agreed: "One of the speakers in this dialogue is President of the United States, representing by his official position what there is best in the civilization of the Anglo-Saxon race. The other is Frederick Douglass, a Negro, with nothing to back him but his own manhood and talent. Yet, if we are compelled to accept Andrew Johnson as our representative, we blush for the white race. Dignity, force of speech, modesty, manliness, simple faith in justice, weight of character, are all on the side of the Negro. It would be hard to surpass the brief address of Frederick Douglass, for fitness to the occasion and point. It would be hard to find a worse speech than the diffuse, illogical, clumsy, and coarse reply of the President."[4] [IV:20–24]

REPLY OF THE COLORED DELEGATION TO THE PRESIDENT

To the Editor of the Chronicle:
  Will you do us the favor to insert in your column the following reply of the colored delegation to the President of the United States?
                                    Geo. T. Downing,
                                    In behalf of the Delegation.

Washington, February 7, 1866

Mr. President: In consideration of a delicate sense of propriety, as well as your own repeated intimations of indisposition to discuss or to listen to a reply to the views and opinions you were pleased to express to us in your elaborate speech to-day, the undersigned would respectfully take this method of replying thereto. Believing as we do that the views and opinions you expressed in that address are entirely unsound and prejudicial to the highest interest of our race as well as our country at large, we cannot do other than expose the same, and, as far as may be in our power, arrest their dangerous influence. It is not necessary at this time to call attention to more than two or three features of your remarkable address:

  1. The first point to which we feel especially bound to take exception is your attempt to found a policy opposed to our enfranchisement, upon the alleged ground of an existing hostility on the part of the former slaves toward the poor white people of the South. We admit the existence of this hostility, and hold that it is entirely reciprocal. But you obviously commit an error by drawing an argument from an incident of a state of slavery, and making it a basis for a policy adapted to a state of freedom. The hostility between the whites and blacks of the South is easily explained. It has its root and sap in the relation of slavery, and was incited on both sides by the cunning of the slave masters. Those masters secured their ascendency over both the poor whites and the blacks by putting enmity between them.

They divided both to conquer each. There was no earthly reason why the blacks should not hate and dread the poor whites when in a state of slavery, for it was from this class that their masters received their slave-catchers, slave-drivers, and overseers. They were the men called in upon all occasions by the masters when any fiendish outrage was to be committed upon the slave. Now, sir, you cannot but perceive that, the cause of this hatred removed, the effect must be removed also. Slavery is abolished. The cause of antagonism is removed, and you must see that it is altogether illogical (and "putting new wine into old bottles," "mending new garments with old cloth") to legislate from slave-holding and slave-driving premises for a people whom you have repeatedly declared your purpose to maintain in freedom.

2. Besides, even if it were true, as you allege, that the hostility of the blacks toward the poor whites must necessarily project itself into a state of freedom, and that this enmity between the two races is even more intense in a state of freedom than in a state of slavery, in the name of Heaven, we reverently ask, how can you, in view of your professed desire to promote the welfare of the black man, deprive him of all means of defence, and clothe him whom you regard as his enemy in the panoply of political power? Can it be that you would recommend a policy which would arm the strong and cast down the defenceless? Can you, by any possibility of reasoning, regard this as just, fair, or wise? Experience proves that those are oftenest abused who can be abused with the greatest impunity. Men are whipped oftenest who are whipped easiest. Peace between races is not to be secured by degrading one race and exalting another, by giving power to one race and withholding it from another; but by maintaining a state of equal justice between all classes. First pure, then peaceable.

3. On the colonization theory you were pleased to broach, very much could be said. It is impossible to suppose, in view of the usefulness of the black man in time of peace as a laborer in the South, and in time of war as a soldier at the North, and the growing respect for his rights among the people, and his increasing adaptation to a high state of civilization in this his native land, there can ever come a time when he can be removed from this country without a terrible shock to its prosperity and peace. Besides, the worst enemy of the nation could not cast upon its fair name a greater infamy than to suppose that Negroes could be tolerated among them in a state of the most degrading slavery and oppression, and must be cast away, driven into exile, for no other cause than having been freed from their chains.

George T. Downing,
John Jones,
William Whipper,
Frederick Douglass,
Lewis H. Douglass,
and others.

Edward McPherson, *The Political History of the United States During the Period of Reconstruction*, Washington, 1887, pp. 55–56

1. Washington *National Republican*, Jan. 31, 1866; George T. Downing to Douglass, Jan. 18, 1866, Frederick Douglass Papers, Frederick Douglass Memorial Home, Anacostia, D.C.

2. See Edward McPherson, *The Political History of the United States During the Period of Reconstruction*, Washington, 1887, pp. 52–55.

3. "Observer" in *New York Tribune*, Feb. 12, 1866.

4. Ibid.; *Anti-Slavery Standard*, Feb. 17, 1866.

THE FUTURE OF THE COLORED RACE

It is quite impossible, at this early date, to say with any decided emphasis what the future of the colored people will be. Speculations of that kind, thus far, have only reflected the mental bias and education of the many who have essayed to solve the problem.

We all know what the Negro has been as a slave. In this relation we have his experience of two hundred and fifty years before us, and can easily know the character and qualities he has developed and exhibited during this long and severe ordeal. In his new relation to his environment, we see him only in the twilight of twenty years of semi-freedom; for he has scarcely been free long enough to outgrow the marks of the lash on his back and the fetters on his limbs. He stands before us, to-day, physically, a maimed and mutilated man. His mother was lashed to agony before the birth of her babe, and the bitter anguish of the mother is seen in the countenance of her offspring. Slavery has twisted his limbs, shattered his feet, deformed his body and distorted his features. He remains black, but no longer comely. Sleeping on the dirt floor of the slave cabin in infancy, cold on one side and warm on the other, a forced circulation of blood on the one side and chilled and retarded circulation on the other, it has come to pass that he has not the vertical bearing of a perfect man. His lack of symmetry, caused by no fault of his own, creates a resistance to his progress which cannot well be overestimated, and should be taken into account, when measuring his speed in the new race of life upon which he has now entered. As I have often said before, we should not measure the Negro from the heights which the white race has attained, but from the depths from which he has come. You will not find Burke, Grattan, Curran and O'Connell among the oppressed and famished poor of the famine-stricken districts of Ireland. Such men come of comfortable antecedents and sound parents.

Laying aside all prejudice in favor of or against race, looking at the Negro as politically and socially related to the American people generally, and measuring the forces arrayed against him, I do not see how he can survive and flourish in this country as a distinct and separate race, nor do I see how he can be removed from the country either by annihilation or expatriation.

Sometimes I have feared that, in some wild paroxysm of rage, the white race, forgetful of the claims of humanity and the precepts of the Christian religion, will proceed to slaughter the Negro in wholesale, as some of that race have attempted to slaughter Chinamen, and as it has been done in detail in some districts of the

Southern States. The grounds of this fear, however, have in some measure decreased since the Negro has largely disappeared from the arena of Southern politics, and has betaken himself to industrial pursuits and the acquisition of wealth and education, though even here, if over-prosperous, he is likely to excite a dangerous antagonism; for the white people do not easily tolerate the presence among them of a race more prosperous than themselves. The Negro as a poor ignorant creature does not contradict the race pride of the white race. He is more a source of amusement to that race than an object of resentment. Malignant resistance is augmented as he approaches the plane occupied by the white race, and yet I think that that resistance will gradually yield to the pressure of wealth, education, and high character.

My strongest conviction as to the future of the Negro therefore is, that he will not be expatriated nor annihilated, nor will he forever remain a separate and distinct race from the people around him, but that he will be absorbed, assimilated, and will only appear finally, as the Phoenicians now appear on the shores of the Shannon, in the features of a blended race. I cannot give at length my reasons for this conclusion, and perhaps the reader may think that the wish is father to the thought, and may in his wrath denounce my conclusion as utterly impossible. To such I would say, tarry a little, and look at the facts. Two hundred years ago there were two distinct and separate streams of human life running through this country. They stood at opposite extremes of ethnological classification: all black on the one side, all white on the other. Now, between these two extremes, an intermediate race has arisen, which is neither white nor black, neither Caucasian nor Ethiopian, and this intermediate race is constantly increasing. I know it is said that marital alliance between these races is unnatural, abhorrent and impossible; but exclamations of this kind only shake the air. They prove nothing against a stubborn fact like that which confronts us daily and which is open to the observation of all. If this blending of the two races were impossible we should not have at least one-fourth of our colored population composed of persons of mixed blood, ranging all the way from a dark-brown color to the point where there is no visible admixture. Besides, it is obvious to common sense that there is no need of the passage of laws, or the adoption of other devices, to prevent what is in itself impossible.

Of course this result will not be reached by any hurried or forced process. It will not arise out of any theory of the wisdom of such blending of the two races. If it comes at all, it will come without shock or noise or violence of any kind, and only in the fullness of time, and it will be so adjusted to surrounding conditions as hardly to be observed. I would not be understood as advocating intermarriage between the two races. I am not a propagandist, but a prophet. I do not say that what I say, *should* come to pass, but what I think is likely to come to pass, and what is inevitable. While I would not be understood as advocating the desirability of such a result, I would not be understood as deprecating it. Races and varieties of the human family appear and disappear, but humanity remains and will remain forever. The American people will one day be truer to this idea than now, and will say with Scotia's inspired son:

"*A man's a man for a' that.*"

When that day shall come, they will not pervert and sin against the verity of language as they now do by calling a man of mixed blood, a Negro; they will tell the truth. It is only prejudice against the Negro which calls everyone, however nearly connected with the white race, and however remotely connected with the Negro race, a Negro. The motive is not a desire to elevate the Negro, but to humiliate and degrade those of mixed blood; not a desire to bring the Negro up, but to cast the mulatto and the quadroon down by forcing him below an arbitrary and hated color line. Men of mixed blood in this country apply the name "*Negro*" to themselves, not because it is a correct ethnological description, but to seem especially devoted to the black side of their parentage. Hence in some cases they are more noisily opposed to the conclusion to which I have come, than either the white or the honestly black race. The opposition to amalgamation, of which we hear so much on the part of colored people, is for most part the merest affectation, and will never form an impassable barrier to the union of the two varieties.

Frederick Douglass

The North American Review, May, 1866, pp. 437–440

The election of 1866 was an overwhelming victory for the Radicals. When the returns were in, they revealed that the House had a two-thirds majority that could override any Presidential veto.

Douglass had taken to the stump for the Radicals during the campaign. As Congress was about to assemble he analyzed the Republican victory in two articles in the *Atlantic Monthly,* December, 1866, and January, 1867. . . . [Congress, he wrote,] "must enfranchise the Negro, and by means of the loyal Negroes and the loyal white men of the South build up a national party there, and in time bridge the chasm between North and South, so that our country may have a common liberty and a common civilization."[1] [IV:30]

RECONSTRUCTION

The assembling of the Second Session of the Thirty-ninth Congress may very properly be made the occasion of a few earnest words on the already much-worn topic of reconstruction.

Seldom has any legislative body been the subject of a solicitude more intense, or of aspirations more sincere and ardent. There are the best of reasons for this profound interest. Questions of vast moment, left undecided by the last session of Congress, must be manfully grappled with by this. No political skirmishing will avail. The occasion demands statesmanship.

Whether the tremendous war so heroically fought and so victoriously ended shall pass into history a miserable failure, barren of permanent results,—a scandalous and shocking waste of blood and treasure,—a strife for empire, as Earl Russell characterized it, of no value to liberty or civilization,—an attempt to reestablish a Union by force, which must be the merest mockery of a Union,—an effort to bring under Federal authority States into which no loyal man from the North may safely enter, and to bring men into the national councils who deliberate with daggers and vote with revolvers, and who do not even conceal their deadly hate of the country that conquered them; or whether, on the other hand, we shall, as the rightful reward of victory over treason, have a solid nation, entirely delivered from all contradictions and social antagonisms, based upon loyalty, liberty, and equality, must be determined one way or the other by the present session of Congress. The last session really did nothing which can be considered final as to these questions. The Civil Rights Bill and the Freedmen's Bureau Bill and the proposed constitutional amendments,[2] with the amendment already adopted and recognized as the law of the land,[3] do not reach the difficulty, and cannot, unless the whole structure of the government is changed from a government by States to something like a despotic central government, with power to control even the municipal regulations of States, and to make them conform to its own despotic will. While there remains such an idea as the right of each State to control its own local affairs,—an idea, by the way, more deeply rooted in the minds of men of all sections of the country than perhaps any one other political idea,—no general assertion of human rights can be of any practical value. To change the character of the government at this point is neither possible nor desirable. All that is necessary to be done is to make the government consistent with itself, and render the rights of the States compatible with the sacred rights of human nature.

The arm of the Federal government is long, but it is far too short to protect the rights of individuals in the interior of distant States. They must have the power to protect themselves, or they will go unprotected, spite of all the laws the Federal government can put upon the national Statute-book.

Slavery, like all other great systems of wrong, founded in the depths of human selfishness, and existing for ages, has not neglected its own conservation. It has steadily exerted an influence upon all around it favorable to its own continuance. And to-day it is so strong that it could exist, not only without law, but even against law. Custom, manners, morals, religion, are all on its side everywhere in the South; and when you add the ignorance and servility of the ex-slave to the intelligence and accustomed authority of the master, you have the conditions, not out of which slavery will again grow, but under which it is impossible for the Federal government to wholly destroy it, unless the Federal government be armed with despotic power, to blot out State authority, and to station a Federal officer at every cross-road. This, of course, cannot be done, and ought not even if it could. The true way and the easiest way is to make our government entirely consistent with itself, and give to every loyal citizen the elective franchise,—a right and power which will be ever present, and will form a wall of fire for his protection.

One of the invaluable compensations of the late Rebellion is the highly instructive disclosure it made of the true source of danger to republican government. Whatever may be tolerated in monarchical and despotic governments, no republic is safe that tolerates a privileged class, or denies to any of its citizens equal rights and equal means to maintain them. What was theory before the war has been made fact by the war.

There is cause to be thankful even for rebellion. It is an impressive teacher, though a stern and terrible one. In both characters it has come to us, and it was perhaps needed in both. It is an instructor never a day before its time, for it comes only when all other means of progress and enlightenment have failed. Whether the oppressed and despairing bondman, no longer able to repress his deep yearnings for manhood, or the tyrant, in his pride and impatience, takes initiative, and strikes the blow for a firmer hold and a longer lease of oppression, the result is the same,—society is instructed, or may be.

Such are the limitations of the common mind, and so thoroughly engrossing are the cares of common life, that only the few among men can discern through the glitter and dazzle of present prosperity the dark outlines of approaching disasters, even though they may have come up to our very gates, and are already within striking distance. The yawning seam and corroded bolt conceal their defects from the mariner until the storm calls all hands to the pumps. Prophets indeed, were abundant before the war; but who cares for prophets while their predictions remain unfulfilled, and the calamities of which they tell are masked behind a blinding blaze of national prosperity?

It is asked, said Henry Clay, on a memorable occasion, Will slavery never come to an end? That question, said he, was asked fifty years ago, and it has been answered by fifty years of unprecedented prosperity. Spite of the eloquence of the earnest Abolitionists,—poured out against slavery during thirty years,—even they must confess, that, in all the probabilities of the case, that system of barbarism would have continued its horrors far beyond the limits of the nineteenth century but for the Rebellion, and perhaps only have disappeared at last in a fiery conflict, even more fierce and bloody than that which has now been suppressed.

It is no disparagement to truth, that it can only prevail where reason prevails. War begins where reason ends. The thing worse than rebellion is the thing that causes rebellion. What that thing is, we have been taught to our cost. It remains now to be seen whether we have the needed courage to have that cause entirely removed from the Republic. At any rate, to this grand work of national regeneration and entire purification Congress must now address itself, with full purpose that the work shall this time be thoroughly done. The deadly upas, root and branch, leaf and fibre, body and sap, must be utterly destroyed. The country is evidently not in a condition to listen patiently to pleas for postponement, however plausible, nor will it permit the responsibility to be shifted to other shoulders. Authority and power are here commensurate with the duty imposed. There are no cloudflung shadows to obscure the way. Truth shines with brighter light and intenser heat at every moment, and a country torn and rent and bleeding implores relief from its distress and agony.

If time was at first needed, Congress has now had time. All the requisite materials from which to form an intelligent judgment are now before it. Whether its members look at the origin, the progress, the termination of the war, or at the mockery of a peace now existing, they will find only one unbroken chain of argument in favor of a radical policy of reconstruction.[4] For the omissions of the last session, some excuses may be allowed. A treacherous President stood in the way; and it can be easily seen how reluctant good men might be to admit an apostasy which involved so much of baseness and ingratitude. It was natural that they should seek to save him by bending to him even when he leaned to the side of error. But all is changed now. Congress knows now that it must go on without his aid, and even against his machinations. The advantage of the present session over the last is immense. Where that investigated, this has the facts. Where that walked by faith, this may walk by sight. Where that halted, this must go forward, and where that failed, this must succeed, giving the country whole measures where that gave us half-measures, merely as a means of saving the elections in a few doubtful districts. That Congress saw what was right, but distrusted the enlightenment of the loyal masses; but what was forborne in distrust of the people must now be done with a full knowledge that the people expect and require it. The members go to Washington fresh from the inspiring presence of the people. In every considerable public meeting, and in almost every conceivable way, whether at court-house, school-house, or cross-roads, in doors and out, the subject has been discussed, and the people have emphatically pronounced in favor of a radical policy. Listening to the doctrines of expediency and compromise with pity, impatience, and disgust, they have everywhere broken into demonstrations of the wildest enthusiasm when a brave word has been spoken in favor of equal rights and impartial suffrage. Radicalism, so far from being odious, is now the popular passport to power. The men most bitterly charged with it go to Congress with the largest majorities, while the timid and doubtful are sent by lean majorities, or else left at home. The strange controversy between the President and Congress, at one time so threatening, is disposed of by the people. The high reconstructive powers which he so confidently, ostentatiously, and haughtily claimed, have been disallowed, denounced, and utterly repudiated; while those claimed by Congress have been confirmed.

Of the spirit and magnitude of the canvass nothing need be said. The appeal was to the people, and the verdict was worthy of the tribunal. Upon an occasion of his own selection, with the advice and approval of his astute Secretary, soon after the members of Congress had returned to their constituents, the President quitted the executive mansion, sandwiched himself between two recognized heroes,[5]—men whom the whole country delighted to honor,—and, with all the advantage which such company could give him, stumped the country from the Atlantic to the Mississippi, advocating everywhere his policy as against that of Congress. It was a strange sight, and perhaps the most disgraceful exhibition ever made by any President; but, as no evil is entirely unmixed, good has come of this, as from many others. Ambitious, unscrupulous, energetic, indefatigable, voluble, and plausible,—a political gladiator, ready for a "set-to" in any crowd,—he is beaten in his own chosen field, and stands to-day before the country as a convicted usurper, a political criminal, guilty of a bold and persistent attempt to possess himself of the legislative powers solemnly secured to Congress by the Constitution. No vindication could be more complete, no condemnation could be more absolute and humiliating. Unless reopened by the sword, as recklessly threatened in some circles, this question is now closed for all time.

Without attempting to settle here the metaphysical and somewhat theological question (about which so much has already been said and written), whether once in the Union means always in the Union,—agreeably to the formula, once in grace always in grace,—it is obvious to common sense that the rebellious States stand to-day, in point of law, precisely where they stood when, exhausted, beaten, conquered, they fell powerless at the feet of Federal authority. Their State governments were overthrown, and the lives and property of the leaders of the Rebellion were forfeited. In reconstructing the institutions of these shattered and overthrown States, Congress should begin with a clean slate, and make clean work of it. Let there be no hesitation. It would be a cowardly deference to a defeated and treacherous President, if any account were made of the illegitimate, one-sided, sham governments hurried into existence for a malign purpose in the absence of Congress. These pretended governments, which were never submitted to the people, and from participation in which four millions of the loyal people were excluded by Presidential order, should now be treated according to their true character, as shams and impositions and supplanted by true and legitimate governments, in the formation of which loyal men, black and white, shall participate.

It is not, however, within the scope of this paper to point out the precise steps to be taken, and the means to be employed. The people are less concerned about these than the grand end to be attained. They demand such a reconstruction as shall put an end to the present anarchical state of things in the late rebellious States,—where frightful murders and wholesale massacres are perpetrated in the very presence of Federal soldiers. This horrible business they require shall cease. They want a reconstruction such as will protect loyal men, black and white, in their persons and property; such a one as will cause Northern industry, Northern capital, and Northern civilization to flow into the South, and make a man from New England as much at home in Carolina as elsewhere in the Republic. No Chinese wall can now be tolerated. The South must be opened to the light of law and liberty, and this session of Congress is relied upon to accomplish this important work.

The plain, common-sense way of doing this work, as intimated at the beginning, is simply to establish in the South one law, one government, one administration of justice, one condition to the exercise of the elective franchise, for men of all races and colors alike. This great measure is sought as earnestly by loyal white men as by loyal blacks, and is needed alike by both. Let sound political prescience but take the place of an unreasoning prejudice, and this will be done.

Men denounce the Negro for his prominence in this discussion; but it is no fault of his that in peace as in war, that in conquering Rebel armies as in reconstructing the rebellious States, the right of the Negro is the true solution of our national troubles. The stern logic of events, which goes directly to the point, disdaining all concern for the color or features of men, has determined the interests of the country as identical with and inseparable from those of the Negro.

The policy that emancipated and armed the Negro—now seen to have been wise and proper by the dullest—was not certainly more sternly demanded than is now the policy of enfranchisement. If with the Negro was success in war, and without him failure, so in peace it will be found that the nation must fall or flourish with the Negro.

Fortunately, the Constitution of the United States knows no distinction between citizens on account of color. Neither does it know any difference between a citizen of a State and a citizen of the United States. Citizenship evidently includes all the rights of citizens, whether State or national. If the Constitution knows none, it is clearly no part of the duty of a Republican Congress now to institute one. The mistake of the last session was the attempt to do this very thing, by a renunciation of its power to secure political rights to any class of citizens, with the obvious purpose to allow the rebellious States to disfranchise, if they should see fit, their colored citizens. This unfortunate blunder must now be retrieved, and the emasculated citizenship given to the Negro supplanted by that contemplated in the Constitution of the United States, which declares that the citizens of each State shall enjoy all the rights and immunities of citizens of the several States,— so that a legal voter in any State shall be a legal voter in all the States.

Atlantic Monthly, December, 1866, pp. 761–765

1. Frederick Douglass, "An Appeal to Congress for Impartial Suffrage," *Atlantic Monthly,* vol. XIX, Jan. 1867.

2. The Civil Rights Bill declared that all persons born in the United States, excluding Indians not taxed, were citizens of the United States and were guaranteed "the equal protection of the law." It was passed over President Johnson's veto, and was the first important measure passed over his veto. In principle it was later incorporated in the Fourteenth Amendment.

The proposed constitutional amendment was the Fourteenth Amendment which created a Federal citizenship, and guaranteed "the equal protection of the law" to all persons born or naturalized in the United States.

3. The reference is to the Thirteenth Amendment which provided: "Neither slavery nor involuntary servitude, save as a punishment for crime . . . shall exist within the United States, nor any place subject to their jurisdiction." The amendment passed Congress in January, 1865, and secured ratification of the requisite three-fourths of the States in December, 1865.

4. Congress definitely repudiated President Johnson's policies in February and March, 1866, passing over his veto a bill extending the life of the Freedmen's Bureau and a Civil Rights Act, and declaring in a concurrent resolution that no Senator or Representative from any of the late insurrectionary States should be admitted to Congress until that body itself had declared such States entitled to representation.

In February, March, and July, 1867, the first series of Radical Reconstruction Acts was passed. They declared that no legal governments existed in the late Confederacy, and divided it into five military districts, each under a general officer of the United States Army. In the elections for delegates all Negroes over twenty-one years of age might vote, but no white who could not take a test oath. The new constitutions, when accepted by the same electorate, were to retain Negro suffrage, whereupon Congress would restore the lately rebellious States to their place in the Union as soon as they had ratified the Fourteenth Amendment.

5. The reference is to Johnson's "swing around the circle" in defense of his policies which began on August 28, 1866. He was accompanied by General Grant and Admiral Farragut who became the lions of the tour. The trip was marked by frequent altercations between Johnson and his audiences.

The summer of 1867 was an exciting period in Douglass' life. In July he met his brother Perry for the first time in forty years. When Reverend T. W. Conway met Perry in New

Orleans and learned that he was Frederick Douglass' brother, he arranged to send him and his family of six to J. J. Spellman in New York City who in turn helped them reach Rochester. Douglas returned from a visit to Virginia to find his brother and his family awaiting him. "The meeting," he wrote Spellman, ". . . is an event altogether too affecting for words to describe."[1] [IV:32–33]

TO THEODORE TILTON

[September, 1867.]

. . . I have been keeping a kind of hotel all summer! My poor brother Perry, after a bondage of fifty-six years, deeply marked by the hardships and sorrows of that hateful condition; and after a separation from me during forty years, as complete as if he had lived on another planet, came to me two months ago, with his family of six, and took up his abode with me. To him—dear old fellow!—one who has carried me on his shoulders many a time (for he is older than I, though my head seems to contradict it)—one who defended me from the assault of bigger boys when I needed defense—I have been mainly devoting myself, and gladly so.

I have now completed for him a snug little cottage on my own grounds, where my dear old slavery-scarred and long-lost brother may spend in peace, with his family, the remainder of his days. Though no longer young, he is no sluggard. Slavery got the best of his life, but he is still strong and hopeful. I wish his old master could see him now—cheerful, helpful and "taking care of himself." If slavery were not dead, and I did not in some sort wish to forget its terrible hardships, blighting curses, and shocking horrors, I would try to write a narrative of my brother Perry's bondage. But let the old system go! I would not call its guilty ghost from the depths into which its crimes have cast it. I turn gladly from the darkness of the past to the new better dispensation now dawning. . . .

The Independent, September 12, 1867

1. Douglass to J. J. Spellman, July 11, 1867, *The Independent,* July 25, 1867.

———————

During the war the country had been so engrossed in the conflict that the woman's movement could make no headway. The women had abandoned their conventions, devoting their energies to the Sanitary Commissions and the Women's Loyal Leagues.

The war over, the women revived their campaign for equality. As in the past, Douglass was ready to champion their cause. When the American Equal Rights Association was founded in May, 1866, with the aim of securing suffrage for Negro men and all women, he was chosen one of the three vice-presidents.[1]

It was at the [1866] Albany Convention of the Equal Rights Association that Douglass seriously clashed with the feminist leaders. He was concerned that Miss Anthony and Mrs. Stanton seemed more interested in the woman question than in a solution of the problems of Reconstruction, and that they were beginning to talk of opposing any extension of suffrage to male Negroes if political enfranchisement of their sex was not included. Douglass warned the Equal Rights Association that it was in danger of becoming "*merely* a woman's rights convention," and appealed that the "women must take the Negro by the hand." True, the Association had been organized to secure the suffrage for women as well as for colored men. But the question of the hour was which group should receive priority. To women the ballot was desirable, to the Negro it was a matter of life and death. Pointing to riots against Negroes in a number of cities, Douglass declared: "With us disfranchisement means New Orleans, it means Memphis, it means New York mobs."

Douglass objected to Susan B. Anthony's praise of James Brooks' championship of woman suffrage in Congress, pointing out that it was simply "the trick of the enemy to assail and endanger the right of black men." Brooks, former editor of the *New York Express,* a viciously anti-Negro, pro-slavery paper, was playing up to the leaders of the women's movement in order to secure their support in opposing Negro suffrage. Douglass warned that if the women did not see through these devices of the former slaveowners and their northern allies, "there would be trouble in our family."[2]

Despite his differences with the woman's rights leaders, Douglass still co-operated with them on certain specific issues. He joined Miss Anthony and Mrs. Stanton in petitioning the New York legislature to permit women and colored men to vote for delegates to the state constitutional convention. Along with Henry Ward Beecher and Mrs. Stanton, Douglass was appointed a representative of the Equal Rights Association to the constitutional convention to argue for the elimination of the $250 property qualification for Negro suffrage and the extension of the franchise to women.[3]

But the areas of co-operation rapidly narrowed. The women leaders were incensed at the indifference of the Republican Party to their demands, and in their anger began to echo the arguments of the most backward opponents of Negro suffrage. Women who had been active Abolitionists now argued that before the "ignorant black man" should be given the ballot, intelligent and cultured white women should be enfranchised. Some ardent feminists went as far as to appeal to southerners to support their cause on the ground that the enfranchisement of women would provide a bulwark in the South against Negro rule. Henry B. Blackwell, husband of Lucy Stone, even dispatched an open letter to southern legislatures in which he set out to prove that by granting suffrage to women the combined white vote would be increased sufficiently to defeat the combined Negro vote and thus "the Negro question would be forever removed from the political arena."[4]

Douglass was conscious of the women's bitterness that a golden opportunity was slipping through their fingers. At the second anniversary of the Equal Rights Association in May, 1868, he attempted to assuage their feelings. There had never been an hour, he told them, in which he had denied the right of women to the ballot. He shared their desire for a quick victory, but the realities of the political situation demanded that they hold off for a while. The great danger was that the linking of woman suffrage with Negro suffrage would seriously lessen the chances of securing the ballot for colored men, and to the Negro, he repeated, the ballot was "an urgent necessity." The people were ready to listen to the Negro's claims, but they still remained to be convinced of the necessity of woman suffrage. Why then jeopardize the real possibility of securing Negro suffrage by making it dependent upon the achievement of woman suffrage? In ten years, in five years, perhaps in three, it would be the woman's hour. But Gettysburg and Atlanta had not been fought on the woman question.

The women were not moved by Douglass' arguments, but they re-elected him a vice-president of the Equal Rights Association.[5]

Douglass reiterated his position later in the year at the Boston Woman's Convention, this time stressing the point that the achievement of woman suffrage "depended upon the preliminary success of Negro suffrage." The reporter for the *The Independent* noted that Douglass "shone; all the old revolutionary fire broke out" as he advanced this argument.[6]

[IV:40–43]

TO JOSEPHINE SOPHIE WHITE GRIFFING

Rochester, Sept. 27, 1868

My dear Friend:

I am impelled by no lack of generosity in refusing to come to Washington to speak in behalf of woman's suffrage. The right of woman to vote is as sacred in my judgment as that of man, and I am quite willing at anytime to hold up both my hands in favor of this right. It does not however follow that I can come to Washington or go elsewhere to deliver lectures upon this special subject. I am now devoting myself to a cause not more sacred, certainly more urgent, because it is life and death to the long-enslaved people of this country; and this is: Negro suffrage. While the Negro is mobbed, beaten, shot, stabbed, hanged, burnt, and is the target of all that is malignant in the North and all that is murderous in the South his claims may be preferred by me without exposing in any wise myself to the imputation of narrowness or meanness towards the cause of woman. As you very well know, woman has a thousand ways to attach herself to the governing power of the land and already exerts an honorable influence on the course of legislation.

She is the victim of abuses, to be sure, but it cannot be pretended I think that her cause is as urgent as that of ours. I never suspected you of sympathizing with Miss Anthony and Mrs. Stanton in this course. Their principal is: that no Negro shall be enfranchised while woman is not. Now, considering that white men have been enfranchised always, and colored men have not, the conduct of these white women, whose husbands, fathers and brothers are voters, does not seem generous.

Very truly yours,

Fred Douglass

Griffing Papers, Columbia University Library

1. *New York Tribune,* May 12, 1866. See also Benjamin Quarles, "Frederick Douglass and Woman's Rights," *Journal of Negro History,* vol. XXV, Jan. pp. 39ff.

2. *New York Tribune,* Nov. 21, 1866.

3. Susan B. Anthony to Douglass, Dec. 15, 1866; Elizabeth Cady Stanton to Douglass, Jan. 8, [1867], Frederick Douglass Papers, Douglass Memorial Home, Anacostia, D.C.; *Anti-Slavery Standard,* June 1, 1867.

4. Henry B. Blackwell, *What the South Can Do.* New York, Jan., 1867, copy in Gerrit Smith Papers, Syracuse University.

5. *The Revolution,* May 21, 1868.

6. *The Independent,* Nov. 26, 1868.

––––––––––––

Douglass' services as an agent and "forwarder" of the Underground Railroad were of great importance to the anti-slavery movement, but he was the first to recognize the superior contribution made by Harriet Tubman, the heroic woman who fearlessly "carried the war into Africa." In his [January 8, 1858] letter to the Ladies' Irish Anti-Slavery Association, Douglass [had] referred to "one coloured woman, who escaped from Slavery eight years ago, has made several returns at great risk, and has brought out, since obtaining her freedom, fifty others from the house of bondage. She has been spending a short time with us since the holidays. She possesses great courage and shrewdness, and may yet render even more important service to the Cause."[1] [II:46–47]

TO HARRIET TUBMAN

Rochester, September 29, 1868.

Dear Harriet:

I am glad to know that the story of your eventful life has been written by a kindly lady, and that the same is soon to be published.[2] You ask for what you do not need when you call upon me for a word of commendation. I need such words from you far more than you can need them from me, especially where your superior labors and devotion to the cause of the lately enslaved of our land are known as I know them. The difference between us is very marked. Most that I have done and suffered in the service of our cause has been in public, and I have received much encouragement at every step of the way. You, on the other hand, have labored in a private way. I have wrought in the day—you in the night. I have had the applause of the crowd and the satisfaction that comes of being approved by the multitude, while the most that you have done has been witnessed by a few trembling, scarred, and footsore bondmen and women, whom you have led out of the house of bondage, and whose heartfelt "*God bless you*" has been your only reward. The midnight sky and the silent stars have been the witnesses of your devotion to freedom and of your heroism. Excepting John Brown—of sacred memory—I know of no one who has willingly encountered more perils and hardships to serve our enslaved people than you have. Much that you have done would seem improbable to those who do not know you as I know you. It is to me a great pleasure and a great privilege to bear testimony to your character and your works, and to say to those to whom you may come, that I regard you in every way truthful and trustworthy.

Your friend,

Frederick Douglass

Sarah H. Bradford, *Scenes in the Life of Harriet Tubman*, Auburn, N.Y., 1869, p. 233

1. *The Anti-Slavery Reporter,* July 1, 1858, p. 168.
2. The biography referred to was Sarah H. Bradford's *Scenes in the Life of Harriet Tubman,* published in 1869 at Auburn, New York.

The story of Douglass' second newspaper venture begins before the adoption of the Fifteenth Amendment. As far back as the fall of 1866, Chief Justice Chase and Congressman John C. Underwood had urged Douglass "to establish a press on the soil of Virginia in the interests of Equal Rights." Douglass considered the proposal for several weeks and then decided against it. He explained that the proposed project would limit his work for the full freedom of his people. . . .[1]

Not until the Fifteenth Amendment had been passed by Congress and submitted to the states for ratification did Douglass feel that he could devote time to a newspaper project. In February and March, 1869, Douglass, his son Lewis, George T. Downing, and a number of other Negro leaders sent out circulars asking financial aid for the publication "of a first class weekly journal in the City of Washington, in the interest of the colored people of America; not as a separate class, but a a part of the *Whole People*. . . ." Such a paper would serve as an educator of the colored people, and would guarantee that "the growing political power in the land represented in the colored man . . . will be wielded . . . not for his special benefit alone, but for the benefit of all who with him compose this Nation."[2]

In late March, 1869, the shareholders of the proposed paper planned that Douglass become editor and J. Sella Martin associate editor. Agreeing that Douglass' work as a lecturer was of vital importance, the shareholders thought that he should continue on the platform and that Martin should serve as resident editor in Washington. Lewis Douglass was proposed as chief compositor and manager of the print shop which, it was hoped, would be manned entirely by colored people. Twenty-five hundred dollars had already been pledged by colored people in Washington, and an equal sum would soon be forthcoming from other Negroes and their white friends. The five thousand dollars would guarantee publication of the weekly for six months after which additional support could be expected, especially when it became known that Douglass was the editor-in-chief. By printing the news vitally affecting the welfare of the colored people in the South, the paper would secure a large body of southern subscribers. Given Douglass' vast experience in journalism and his "great ability and willingness" to serve his people, there was every assurance that "a well conducted weekly paper" would be the result.[3]

Douglass expected gratitude for the honor conferred upon him, but, in a letter to J. Sella Martin early in April, refused to accept the invitation to become the editor-in-chief. It was futile, he pointed out, to attempt "to venture upon this voyage of journalism upon so slender a Bark as 'five thousand dollars' as a basis. . . ." The vast majority of colored newspapers hitherto published had "died in their infancy and from starvation." Should the newspaper be discontinued after six months because of lack of funds, it "would bring more shame and mortification to our already sadly depressed people, than had not the attempt been made at all." He strongly favored the founding of a newspaper for the freedman which would speak out frankly and without fear of antagonizing anyone. But it should be a paper "which will upon first sight, go straight to his heart, raise his respect for his race, and kindle his enthusiasm. A small sheet imperfectly printed upon coarse paper—on the penny-wise principle, will not answer the purpose. Such a paper will depress rather than elevate the spirits of our people."[4]

Although deeply disappointed by Douglass' decision, the shareholders decided to proceed with the publication of the paper. Sella Martin, however, refused to accept the editorship unless Douglass agreed to serve as corresponding editor. He assured Douglass that like him he believed the paper should "reflect the sentiments and wants of the Freedmen. In other words we as Northern people should use the advantages that belong to our position in free Society to lay bare mere party machinations and so draw out the best intelligence of those to whom we speak while at the same time we should fearlessly express the peculiar grievances of those who might become the victim of even the Radicals. I insist in short upon our organ being the *Radical* of the radicals."[5]

Douglass agreed to serve as corresponding editor and the final plans to launch the weekly were drawn up. On January 13, 1870, it made its appearance in Washington as *The New Era*. Two weeks later Douglass' first article appeared under the heading, "Salutary of the Corresponding Editor." His part in the new journal would be a subordinate one, he informed the readers, but he assured them "that whatever we can do consistently with our many other studies and occupations to make *The New Era* a credit to our cause, our color and our country, shall be earnestly and faithfully done." He called upon "every intelligent and patriotic colored man in the land" to give full support to a grand national organ "through which our minutest wrongs may be exposed, our equal rights asserted, our character defended, our efforts for improvement encouraged and our whole relation to the body politic, to which we have already been virtually admitted against long continued and determined opposition, triumphantly vindicated."[6]

As Douglass had predicted, the paper encountered difficulties at once. By the summer of 1870 it was heavily in debt. The shareholders had abandoned the project, Martin had resigned as editor, the type and press were in the hands of creditors, and the paper was about to fold up. Convinced "that this was not the time to allow any proper instrumentality which could be wielded for the benefit of his people to perish," Douglass moved swiftly to prevent the journal from going out of existence. Late in August, he moved to Washington, gave up his lecturing engagements, and purchased one-half interest in both *The New Era* and the printing plant in which it was printed. On September 8, 1870, the paper carried the news that Douglass was the editor of the paper which now was to be called the *New National Era* to distinguish it from many newspapers in the country bearing the old name. . . .

On December 12, 1870, Douglass purchased the remaining one-half interest in the *New National Era* and its printing plant for $8,000. Three days later he announced that he was now the sole proprietor of the paper. Two sentences were all that Douglass required to set forth "the broad and strong platform" of the *New National Era*: "Free men, free soil, free speech, a free press, everywhere in the land. The ballot for all, education for all, fair wages for all."[7] [IV:54–57]

SALUTATORY

To the readers and friends of the *New National Era*:

May it meet your approval! To-day we enter into new, and I trust, lasting and mutually beneficial relations. According to arrangements, already made and duly announced, I have become, both in a pecuniary and a moral point of view, closely and actively connected with the *New National Era*. As editor-in-chief, and part proprietor of this journal, its character and usefulness will largely depend upon my own exertions. What I can do to make it an honor and a help to the newly enfranchised millions whose organ it will in some sense be made, shall be freely and faithfully done. Of my feelings in venturing upon this new and responsible field of labor, I need say but little. While I come to the work willingly I do so with no high confidence in my ability to discharge its duties with credit. I am encouraged, however, by the consciousness that whatever may be my deficiencies as to ability, either as respects skill or judgment, I lack neither the will nor the purpose to serve the cause of our people. To those who know of my thirty years of active service, my steadfast zeal and perseverance will be granted. It has been a cherished hope of mine, since the abolition of slavery, that out of the tumultuous waves of the grand revolution which is not yet ended, some new man (at any rate newer than myself) full of youth and vigor, thoroughly alive to the great interests of our newly enfranchised people, would arise and establish here in the Capital of the nation a large public journal, which should in some measure serve as a banner on the outer wall of our liberties. No such man having yet appeared, I have been persuaded to undertake the work. With your sympathy, aid and co-operation I believe the *New National Era* can be made such a journal as above described. But without your assistance the paper may perish as others have perished before, and its failure may be cited as another proof of the colored man's want of public spirit, enterprise and capacity. To prevent this, we have a common duty, but different offices. It is mine to make the paper worthy of support, and yours to give your good will and a reasonable effort to extend its circulation. I trust you. Do not doubt me. Let the light of the *New National Era* shine into the most distant and darkest corners of the Republic. It will cheer and gladden the masses. It will increase self-reliance, self-respect, self-help, inspire our young men with manly ambition, lift them to a higher social level, and lead our whole people onward in the pathway of civilization. But here I need not stay to say more. The aims and objects of the *New National Era* may be read elsewhere in its Prospectus.[8] They comprehend the whole circle of moral, social, political, educational and material interests of the newly enfranchised citizen. To the work of promoting these high interests, I am moved not merely by ordinary considerations. The very depths from which I have come furnish appropriate motives. I do not forget that thirty-two years ago I was a slave, within an hour's ride of this very Capital where I now am. I do not forget that on the wharves and in the ship yards of Baltimore, I studied my first lessons in spelling and took my first lessons in writing. From the time I learned to read, and learned the value of knowledge, it was among the deepest and sincerest wishes of my soul, to assist in the deliverance of my people, not only from the terrible bondage of slavery, but from the more terrible bondage of ignorance and vice.

This sentiment has lost nothing of its vigor by long years of active service. Those years of labor have only served to increase and intensify the desire to do yet more in the same cause.

In the discharge of my duty as an editor I cannot hope to meet the views and wishes of all our readers and friends. Owing to a difference of antecedents, education, local circumstances, personal perferences, and prepossessions, other differences may arise. All I ask is fair and candid consideration at points where we shall differ, and cordial support in the objects where we shall agree.

I assume, at the outset, that no man will look to this journal, so far as I am concerned, for any merely selfish utterance as to race, country, or color. To the former slave I say, I too am a former slave; to the colored man I say, I too am a colored man; and to the Indian, Mongolian, Caucasian, to the men of every nation, kindred tongue, and people of all latitudes, longitudes, and altitudes, I say, that I too am a man, and would scorn to demand for the men of my race a single right or privilege that I would not freely grant to you.

Let me also say, that no man need expect anything from my pen of a sectarian character. All who labor to lead our people out of the wilderness of social, moral, and physical evils, of whatever religious opinions, will be hailed here as "countrymen, clansmen, kinsmen, and brothers beloved." We shall deal with the known and visible interests of our people, and aim to promote them in every possible proper way. Here is ground broad enough for all reasonable men to stand upon. The ignorant, superstitious, and bigoted who lose sight of the fact that men have to live as well as to die, may quarrel with this liberal platform; but such men are exceptional, and will ultimately follow the line of progress here as elsewhere.

I have spoken thus far especially to colored men and women; but the *New National Era* must become an object of interest to our white fellow citizens. Inevitable events have linked the two races indissolubly. We are henceforth to fall or flourish together. Here is one motive for interest of all in each, and interest of each in all. But higher still: Every white man and woman who has had one pulsation of sympathy for our long oppressed and persecuted people, must wish well to our journal, and feel a desire to assist in making it efficient and successful. I have no hesitation in asking the aid and sympathy of all such. The white people of this country can never do too much for us. If they should put a schoolhouse at every crossroads of the South, supply each with a teacher, and subscribe and pay for a copy of the *New National Era* to be sent for three years to every colored voter, they would not cancel the debt contracted by the long years of slavery and suffering of this people.

The safety and prosperity of the Republic depends upon the intelligence of colored voters, and this fact will be kept in view; but let no man, however, expect to find the colored man, in the columns of the *New National Era,* treated simply as a political element, as a body of voters, which may be so manipulated as to turn the scale in favor of this or that party, or this or that partisan. Important as it may be to hold up to view and press upon the attention of the colored man the principles which should guide his political action as a voter, it is still more important to keep constantly before him those other great and vital principles of conduct which concern him at every step of his life, and which are essential to his highest social well being.

These remarks have already gone beyond their intended space, and yet, as is usual in such utterances, they are still incomplete. I will end them simply by giving you my heart and hand, in spirit at least, and by asking your hearts and hands in return. Let us stand united in the maintenance of those great rights and liberties recently acquired, but at the cost of years of effort, and through terrible loss of blood and treasure—liberties which all the experiences of the race and all history teach us can only be kept secure in presence of heroic virtue, unceasing exertion, and eternal vigilance.

Frederick Douglass

The New National Era, September 8, 1870

1. Douglass to John C. Underwood, Nov. 14, 1866, John C. Underwood Collection, Library of Congress, manuscripts division.

2. Circulars in Gerrit Smith Papers, Syracuse University. The circular also stated that the journal "will *especially advocate the policy and measures of the Republican Party,* as the most efficient, *if not the only reliable political organization,* through whose efforts Justice can be established and maintained."

3. J. Sella Martin to Douglass, Mar. 29, 1869, Frederick Douglass Papers, Douglass Memorial Home, Anacostia, D.C.

4. Douglass to Rev. J. Sella Martin, Apr. 5, 1869, Frederick Douglass *Mss.,* Douglass Memorial Home, Anacostia, D.C.

5. J. Sella Martin to Douglass, Aug. 24, 1869, Frederick Douglass Papers, Douglass Memorial Home, Anacostia, D.C.

6. *New Era,* Jan. 27, 1870. Douglass was "on the wing" and thus was unable to write anything for the first issue. (*New Era,* Jan. 13, 1870.)

7. Ibid., Dec. 15, 1870. J. H. Davis sold his interest in the paper to Douglass.

8. The "Prospectus" of the *New National Era* opened: "The *New National Era* will partake of a two-fold nature—that of an Advocate and an Educator." A good deal of space was

devoted to a reprint of sections of an address issued by the Colored National Labor Union which urged that all trades be urged be opened to Negroes and that "for every day's labor given we be paid full and fair remuneration."

SEEMING AND REAL

A fervid imagination sometimes entirely upsets and supplants the plain and obvious teachings of common sense. In the glare of enthusiasm, fiction is often mistaken for fact, and what exists, somehow or other, is confounded with what ought to be. A state of mind analogous to this, leads some of our friends to assume that all distinctions founded upon race or color have been forever abolished in the United States, and that all special efforts recognizing a different state of facts, are uncalled for, out of time, and hurtful. "There are no colored people in this country" said a highly poetic friend of ours, not long since. To his mind the fifteenth amendment[1] was not merely a law but a miracle, for nothing less than a miracle could thus so suddenly change black into white, and obliterate all traces of two hundred and fifty years of slavery, both on the part of the race enslaved and the race enslaving. This delirium of enthusiasm is very pleasant to those possessed by it, and it would seem unamiable to disturb it did it not sometimes stand directly in the way of needed effort. We would not underestimate the value of the fifteenth amendment. It has done great things for the colored man, but it has left many things undone, and this through no defect in the measure itself, but from the nature of the evil it was designed to remove. No two races of men sustaining the relations to each other that the white and colored people have sustained could have those relations instantly changed by any change in the laws however stringently worded or faithfully enforced. Slavery has left its poison behind it, both in the veins of the slave and in those of the enslaver.

There is servility in the enslaved race and haughtiness in the master race which no legislation can reach or remove. Time and endeavor must have their perfect working before we shall see the end of the effect of slavery and oppression in the United States on both races, nor should any worker in the cause of equality be in haste to abandon that work.

But the Negro now has a constitutional guarantee of equality and fair play. Very true. But law on the statute book and law in the practice of the nation are two very different things, and sometimes very opposite things. The Constitution guaranteed free speech to every American citizen in every State in the Union, but what was this guarantee worth to William Lloyd Garrison or Wendell Phillips at any time prior to the late war for the Union? The citizens of each State are guaranteed all the rights and immunities of citizens of the several States. This was a fundamental part of our United States Constitution from the beginning, but of what earthly value was it to Samuel Hoar in South Carolina, or to Mr. Hubbard in Louisiana? The declaration of independence, the oldest legal paper of the Republic, asserts the equality and liberty of man more broadly and clearly than any paper ever drawn before by human hands, and yet slavery continued in its presence nearly a hundred years.

The pen is often mightier than the sword and the settled habits of a nation mightier than a statute. It has been said that no people are better than their laws. Many have been found worse than their laws. It is no unreasonable impeachment to say that the American people, and even the American churches, are far in the rear of American law in respect to the Negro. Over the gateway of what Christian church in America is it written that no distinction shall be here made on account of color or race? And if written, who does not know that they would be mere hollow words, sound and fury, signifying nothing as to the real facts? Of what avail is it to tell the poor heathen that the Christian religion is a religion of humility and love, while the nations professing it are full of pride and hate? Of what avail is it to boast of the Bible as the book of forbearance and peace, while the nations that profess to believe in it are ever ready for battle and make haste to shed human blood? The time may come when practice and precept, life and profession will harmonize. We certainly hope that the time will come when the colored man in America shall cease to require special efforts to guard their rights and advance their interests as a class. But that time has not yet come, and is not even at the door. While the doors of nearly every workshop in the land are closed against the colored man's child; while all lucrative employments are closed to the colored race, and the highest callings opened to them are of a menial character; while a colored gentleman is compelled to walk the streets of our largest cities like New York unable to obtain admission to the public hotels; while state-rooms are refused in our steamboats, and berths are refused in our sleeping-cars, on account of color, and the Negro is a by-word and a hissing at every street corner, the Negro is not abolished as a degraded caste, nor need his friends shut up shop and cease to make his advancement in the scale of civilized life a special work. We need to-day every influence that served to put the fifteenth amendment on the national statute-book to help us put the same fully into every department of the nation's life. Especially should every colored man persevere in all the ways open to him to change the unfavorable judgment of the public concerning his race, and bring around his people more favorable conditions to improvement and elevation. Press, platform, pulpit should continue to direct their energies to the removal of the hardships and wrongs which continue to be the lot of the colored people of this country because they wear a complexion which two hundred and fifty years of slavery taught the great mass of the American people to hate, and which the fifteenth amendment has not yet taught the American people to love.

The New National Era, October 6, 1870

1. The Fifteenth Amendment, adopted in 1869, declared: "The right of citizens . . . to vote shall not be denied or abridged by the United States or by any State on account of race, color, or previous condition of servitude."

TO A. M. POWELL, ESQ.

Washington, D.C., Oct. 7, 1870

My Dear Sir:

I am just here from U. Minster, Carroll Co., Maryland, where I have been speaking on the very same subject upon which you wish to hear me in Cooper Institute. I cannot be with you on Monday night. Other duties make it impossible. The refusal of the Hotels in New York to receive and accommodate refined and wealthy colored strangers and travellers, solely because of their color, is the meanest kind of barbarism, and could happen in no other civilized country. It belongs to free, democratic America, a land of Bibles, Sabbath Schools, churches and missionary societies (perpetually boasting of liberty, manners and morals as compared with other nations) to furnish such examples of inhuman brutishness. Even a pig is willing that a fellow pig shall have shelter and food, if he can get enough for himself, but your genuine American Negro hater surpasses the pig in piggishness. He would rather have space itself entirely unoccupied than to have it occupied by one not colored like himself. The same unbrotherly and inhuman spirit of pride and hate, which excludes a respectable man and woman from the shelter of a public house in New York or elsewhere, (the only apology for the existence of which is its accommodation of strangers and travellers) would shut him out of all houses and out of the world. Neither in London, Paris, Berlin, St. Petersburgh, Rome, Vienna, nor Constantinople, could two decent persons with money in their pockets and willing to pay, be refused accommodation at any hotel on account of color. But here in the city of New York, the commercial Metropolis of the United States, sustaining relations of commerce with all nations, kindreds, tongues and peoples, men stoop to the narrowness and littleness to peep under a man's hat to find out whether he shall for his money and manhood, be accommodated with food and shelter. This inhuman treatment of men and women, for a color which they cannot alter to suit the taste of anybody, plainly enough tells the colored people, that no part of their number shall be respected as men or as gentlemen if the New York Hotels can degrade them.

After all it is not in its essence a prejudice against color, that excludes colored men from hotels or from other places. For certain purposes, the colored man is welcome anywhere. He can be employed to sweep the holy dust from the velvet of the saintly pew, in which he would not be allowed to worship God for one moment; he would be allowed to enter the most aristocratic Drawing Room car as a servant, but would be wholly unwelcome as a passenger; he would be admitted to any parlor or dining room in New York as a waiter, but never as a gentleman; as a driver he may ride with fashionable ladies and gentlemen, who seem as proud of his dark rich color, as they are of the shining carriage, prancing boys, and the gold and silver mountings of their equipage, but the skin-deep aristocracy of New York would not tolerate in such place a colored man as a gentleman—no matter how refined or how elevated in character and attainments. It is, therefore, not the Negro's color that makes him distasteful, but the assumption of equal manhood.

But after all, there is a consolation here as everywhere. If a man is determined to be a man, a good citizen, a refined, well-mannered, and cultivated gentleman, there is no power even in New York hotels to prevent him. Our hotels are powerful institutions, but they cannot long resist the enlightened and humane spirit of the age. The colored man and all other men will bye and bye be treated according to their character rather than their color.

Truly yours,
Frederick Douglass

National Standard, October 15, 1870

THE UNKNOWN LOYAL DEAD, speech delivered at Arlington National Cemetery, Virginia, on Decoration Day, May 30, 1871

Friends and Fellow Citizens:

Tarry here for a moment. My words shall be few and simple. The solemn rites of this hour and place call for no lengthened speech. There is, in the very air of this resting-ground of the unknown dead a silent, subtle and all-pervading eloquence, far more touching, impressive, and thrilling than living lips have ever uttered. Into the measureless depths of every loyal sou it is now whispering lessons of all that is precious, priceless, holiest, and most enduring in human existence.

Dark and sad will be the hour to this nation when it forgets to pay grateful homage to its greatest benefactors. The offering we bring to-day is due alike to the patriot soldiers dead and their noble comrades who still live; for, whether living or dead, whether in time or eternity, the loyal soldiers who imperiled all for country and freedom are one and inseparable.

Those unknown heroes whose whitened bones have been piously gathered here, and whose green graves we now strew with sweet and beautiful flowers, choice emblems alike of pure hearts and brave spirits, reached, in their glorious career that last highest point of nobleness beyond which human power cannot go. They died for their country.

No loftier tribute can be paid to the most illustrious of all the benefactors of mankind than we pay to these unrecognized soldiers when we write above their graves this shining epitaph.

When the dark and vengeful spirit of slavery, always ambitious, preferring to rule in hell than to serve in heaven, fired the Southern heart and stirred all the malign elements of discord, when our great Republic, the hope of freedom and self-government throughout the world, had reached the point of supreme peril, when the Union of these States was torn and rent asunder at the center, and the armies of a gigantic rebellion came forth with broad blades and bloody hands to destroy the very foundation of American society, the unknown braves who flung themselves into the yawning chasm, where cannon roared and bullets whistled, fought and fell. They died for their country.

We are sometimes asked, in the name of patriotism, to forget the merits of this fearful struggle, and to remember with equal admiration those who struck at the nation's life and those who struck to save it, those who fought for slavery and those who fought for liberty and justice.

I am no minister of malice. I would not strike the fallen. I would not repel the repentant; but may my "right hand forget her cunning and my tongue cleave to the roof of my mouth," if I forget the difference between the parties to that terrible, protracted, and bloody conflict.

If we ought to forget a war which has filled our land with widows and orphans; which has made stumps of men of the very flower of our youth; which has sent them on the journey of life armless, legless, maimed and mutilated; which has piled up a debt heavier than a mountain of gold, swept uncounted thousands of men into bloody graves and planted agony at a million hearthstones—I say, if this war is to be forgotten, I ask, in the name of all things sacred, what shall men remember?

The essence and significance of our devotions here to-day are not to be found in the fact that the men whose remains fill these graves were brave in battle. If we met simply to show our sense of bravery, we should find enough on both sides to kindle admiration. In the raging storm of fire and blood, in the fierce torrent of shot and shell, of sword and bayonet, whether on foot or on horse, unflinching courage marked the rebel not less than the loyal soldier.

But we are not here to applaud manly courage, save as it has been displayed in a noble cause. We must never forget that victory to the rebellion meant death to the republic. We must never forget that the loyal soldiers who rest beneath this sod flung themselves between the nation and the nation's destroyers. If today we have a country not boiling in an agony of blood, like France, if now we have a united country, no longer cursed by the hell-black system of human bondage, if the American name is no longer a by-word and a hissing to a mocking earth, if the star-spangled banner floats only over free American citizens in every quarter of the land, and our country has before it a long and glorious career of justice, liberty, and civilization, we are indebted to the unselfish devotion of the noble army who rest in these honored graves all around us.

Life and Times of Frederick Douglass, 1893

―――――――――

On June 2, [1872, Douglass'] house in Rochester was burned to the ground. Mrs. Douglass, her daughter and son-in-law Mr. and Mrs. Nathan Sprague, and their three children managed to escape. But the furniture and Douglass' library, including twelve volumes (1848 to 1860) of *The North Star* and *Frederick Douglass' Paper,* were destroyed.

Douglass hastened back to Rochester. He arrived at one o'clock in the morning in a drenching rain. Unaware of just where his family was staying, he decided to put up overnight at a hotel. At the Congress Hall and the Waverly House he was bluntly reminded of his color when the clerks told him that there were no empty rooms. The proprietor of the Waverly House rebuked his clerk when he discovered that Douglass was the visitor who was being turned away, and offered him accommodations. But Douglass refused to stop at a hotel which permitted only a distinguished colored man to use its facilities. . . .

All told Douglass' loss as a result of the fire amounted to about five or six thousand dollars, not counting many things to which he could "attach no money value." Rochester friends urged him to rebuild his home in the city but Douglass decided to live in the nation's capital, and moved his wife and Rosetta's family to Washington.[1] [IV:80]

LETTER FROM THE EDITOR

Dear Readers:

I am here among the ashes of my old home in Rochester, New York. As soon as I learned of the fire I hurried here from Washington, and have been here ever since. A summons home to find one's house in ashes is almost like going home to a funeral, and though only sadness greets one at the end of the journey no speed is too great to bring him there. The house destroyed had been my home during more than twenty years; and twenty years of industry and economy had there brought together many things valuable in themselves, and rendered more valuable by association. Several questions are naturally suggested by every fire; First, How did it happen? How was it extinguished? What was saved? What was lost? What was damaged? I do not mean to answer these questions in detail, nor to indulge in sentimental description. The fire was doubtless the work of an incendiary. It began in a barn well filled with hay on the south side of the house, and was first seen at midnight, when the family of my son-in-law (who occupied the dwelling) had been in bed two hours. No fire or light had been carried into the barn by any of the family for months. What could be the motive? Was it for plunder, or was it for spite, or was it mere wanton wickedness on the part of persons of the baser sort, who wander on the outskirts of cities by starlight at late hours? I do not know and I cannot guess. One thing I do know and that is, while Rochester is among the most liberal of Northern cities, and its people are among the most humane and highly civilized, it nevertheless has its full share of that Ku-Klux spirit which makes anything owned by a colored man a little less respected and secure than when owned by a white citizen. I arrived in Rochester at one o'clock in the night in thick darkness and drenching rain, and not knowing where my family might be, I applied for shelter at two of the nearest hotels and was at first refused by both, with the convenient excuse that "We are full," till it was known that my name was Frederick Douglass, when a room was readily offered me, though the house was full! I did not accept, but made my way to the police headquarters, to learn if possible where I might find the scattered members of my family. Such treatment as this does not tend to make a man secure either in his person or property. The spirit which would deny a man shelter in a public house, needs but little change to deny him shelter, even in his own house. It is the spirit of hate, the spirit of murder, the spirit which would burn a family in their beds. I may be wrong, but I fear that the sentiment which repelled me at Congress Hall burnt my house.

The fire did its work quick and with marked thoroughness and success. Scarcely a trace of the building, except brick walls and stone foundations, is left, and the trees surrounding the building, planted by my own hands and of more than twenty years' growth were not spared, but were scorched and charred beyond recovery. Much was saved in the way of furniture and much was lost, and much was damaged. Eleven thousand dollars worth of government securities (of which I have fortunately the numbers) were destroyed. Sixteen volumes of my old paper the *North Star* and *Frederick Douglass' Paper*, were destroyed;[2] a piano worth five hundred dollars was saved, but much damaged, the same with three sofas, and many mahogany chairs, and other furniture. My loss, not covered with insurance, will reach from four to five thousand dollars. Every effort possible was made by the police and fire department to save property, and the neighbors (all white) did everything in their power to afford relief to the shelterless family. Assured of the sympathy of my readers in this calamity, I have felt at liberty to make this brief statement, as an apology for absence from my post of public duty, which after all will not be long.

Frederick Douglass

The New National Era, June 13, 1872

1. Douglass to Gerrit Smith, July 1, 1872, Gerrit Smith Papers, Syracuse University. Douglass declared that he moved to Washington because his wife would feel more at home with her own people in the nation's capital.

2. The destroyed copies represented the only complete file of these papers in existence.

Usually Douglass' role in a political campaign ended on election day. But in 1872 it was different. Late in August, the Republican State Committee had assembled to select New York's Presidential electors. The delegates chose Gerrit Smith as one of the two electors-at-large. Then Thurlow Weed, the State Republican leader, arose and announced that "in his judgment the best name to be associated with G. Smith as elector-at-large, was that of Frederick Douglass." Weed's suggestion was received "with great satisfaction and was responded to by acclamation."

Two months after the election, Douglass, as official messenger, conveyed the results of the balloting in the Empire State to the president of the Senate. On the eve of the opening session in December, he issued [the following] appeal to the members of the legislative body....

But Douglass was soon to discover that there was a wide gap between the platform pledges and the Republican Party performance. He was to learn that progress for basic civil rights for all could not attained by reliance upon generalized exhortation in party platforms and in campaign speeches. [IV:85–86]

GIVE US THE FREEDOM INTENDED FOR US

We are often cautioned against demanding too much for the colored people of this country. This cautioning is invariably accompanied with a full narration of what has already been done for our people, and we are further exhorted to remember that within the past decade we were slaves without any rights entitled to respect, and that in this short space of time we have been freed and transformed into American citizens, with the right to exercise the elective franchise extended to us by amendment to the National Constitution. Having been the recipients of these very valuable gifts, it is asserted by some who have taken an active part in the giving, that we should be satisfied at least long enough to allow the nation to take breath after its strenuous exertions in the accomplishment of the results so beneficial to us. To such persons the fact that we have been oppressed, outraged, and wronged for more than two centuries seems to be no argument why the nation should hasten to undo the wrong it has sanctioned against us, now that if fully admits the evil perpetrated upon us.

The elective franchise without protection in its exercise amounts to almost nothing in the hands of a minority with a vast majority determined that no exercise of it shall be made by the minority. Freedom from the auction block and from legal claim as property is of no benefit to the colored man without the means of protecting his rights. The black man is not a free American citizen in the sense that a white man is a free American citizen; he cannot protect himself against encroachments upon the rights and privileges already allowed him in a court of justice without an impartial jury. If accused of crime, he is tried by men who have a bias against him by reason of his race, color, or previous condition of servitude. If he attempts to send his children to the nearest public school where a free white American citizen, who pays no more taxes, can have the privilege without question, he is driven away and has no redress at law. If, after purchasing tickets for a ride in a first-class railway carriage, a colored person is hustled out into a smoking car, he or she has no redress at law because a custom prevails which allows injustice in this respect to colored persons.

We claim that the thirteenth, fourteenth, and fifteenth amendments to the Constitution of the United States were intended to give full freedom to every person without regard to race or color in the United States; and, in order that this intention should be carried out and acted upon, power for that purpose was given by conferring upon Congress the right to enforce the amendments by appropriate legislation. It cannot be denied that the violent interference with the black man to prevent him from exercising the elective franchise in accordance with his own views is an abridgement of his freedom as is also the refusal of a trial by a jury of his peers; nor can it be denied that the forcing of colored men to pay for what they do not get by railroad corporations or the refusal to allow the same accommodation to them as to other citizens of the United States, is an invidious discrimination amounting to an abridgement of citizenship rights.

We cannot be asking too much when we ask this Congress to carry out the intention of this Nation as expressed in the thirteenth, fourteenth and fifteenth amendments. We are not free. We cannot be free without the appropriate legislation provided for in the above amendments. We say to those who think we are demanding too much that it is idle to point us to the amendments and ask us to be satisfied with them and wait until the nation is educated up to giving us something more. The amendments are excellent but they need to be enforced. The result intended to be reached by the nation has not been reached. Congress has neglected to do its full duty. The people one month ago reiterated in thunder tones their demand "that complete liberty and *exact equality* in the enjoyment of all civil, political, and public rights should be established and effectually maintained throughout the Union by efficient and appropriate State and Federal legislation." We join in this demand those who think we are asking too much to the contrary notwithstanding.

The people on the 5th of November last ratified the following:

"The recent amendments to the national Constitution should be cordially sustained because they are right, not merely tolerated because they are law, and should be carried out *according to their spirit* by appropriate legislation." The Liberal

Democratic platform took similar ground as follows, and all the voters in the country voted for similar principles: "We recognize the equality of all men before the law and hold that it is the duty of Government in its dealings with the people to mete out equal and exact justice to all of whatever nativity, race, color or persuasion religious or political. We pledge ourselves to maintain the Union of these States, emancipation and enfranchisement and to oppose any reopening of the questions settled by the thirteenth, fourteenth, and fifteenth amendments to the Constitution." In view of this can a Republican Congress longer refuse to enact into law such a bill as Senator Sumner brought forward in the last session of Congress and which is by far the best measure yet proposed for establishing "complete liberty and exact equality in the enjoyment of all civil, political, and public rights."

The New National Era, December 5, 1872

TO HON. GERRIT SMITH

Washington, D.C., Sept. 25, 1873.

Venerated Friend:

It did my heart good to see and read your note to me, and your printed letter to Miss Anthony.[1] They told me how grandly you yet live, think and write. General Howard gave me an interesting account of his visit to you. He was greatly pleased. He is a great and good man and is doing a great good work here. But he has too much work to do, that is, more than he can do. His presence is very much needed abroad to procure the needed support of the Institution.[2] He cannot be here and there at the same time and the trouble is to find the right man to preside over the University when he is absent as he must be for several months to come. When the question was up yesterday before [the] Board of Trustees, I ventured to say that I knew of no man who could fill General Howard's place, but Gerrit Smith. It if you could reside here for a few months and preside over this University in the absence of General Howard, it would be the crowning position of your life and the most powerful aid you could render to the Institution itself. I have faith in your presence. You would only have to visit to the different departments to diffuse your influence—the influence they so much need. Of course, in view of your age and duties at home, I cannot urge this new work upon you, but I want you to know the thought that is passing here concerning you. The suggestion was received with emphatic approval on all sides.

I am not sure that my boys will be able to continue the "*Era.*" I have put about ten thousand dollars into the concern, and have given it over entirely. They have formed a stock company and the paper is under their management.

The trouble of supporting the paper is twofold. First, the Negro is not yet a reader: Secondly he is unconscious of having an associate existence or common cause. All the social forces drive us asunder. Our confidence is in the white race. White schools, white churches, white Theology, white Legislators, white public journals, secure our highest confidence and support. Our women powder their faces and buy the hair of the white race to make themselves more acceptable or less objectionable to the white race. Nor is this strange. The honor, the power, the wisdom, wealth and glory are all with the white race. Large bodies attract small. I found myself better appreciated by the whites than by my own people at Nashville[3] and much of the attention paid me by the colored people was due to the respect paid me by the whites. It is with us as it once was with American authorship: No American writer was considered great at home till he was confessed to be great abroad. No black man is worthy of consideration in the eyes of his race, till he has gained consideration in the eyes of yours. I make no complaint. I accept the inevitable and cheerfully work on to raise my people to a higher plane of life, whether the road shall be by disintegration or combination. Pardon me for so long a note. Always yours with love and veneration.

Frederick Douglass

Gerrit Smith Papers, Syracuse University

1. The circular, dated August 15, 1873, addressed to Susan B. Anthony, was entitled: "Woman Suffrage Above Human Law." Smith argued that nobody had any right to put an interpretation on the Constitution which would deny the vote to women.

2. General Oliver O. Howard was instrumental in founding Howard University, became its president in 1869, and gave much of his time to it until 1874 when he resigned.

3. Douglass spoke in Nashville, Tennessee, on September 18, 1873, at the Third Annual Fair of the Tennessee Colored Agricultural and Mechanical Association. A copy of this speech, in pamphlet form, is in the Howard University Library.

On April 14, 1876, the anniversary of Lincoln's assassination and the emancipation of the slaves in the District of Columbia, the freedmen's memorial monument to Abraham Lincoln was . . . unveiled in Washington.[1] By a joint resolution Congress had declared the day a holiday. President Grant and his cabinet members, Supreme Court justices, and many Senators and Congressmen were seated on the platform erected for the meeting. Douglass was the "orator of the occasion."

Douglass later admitted that he did not like the statue which showed Lincoln standing erect holding the Emancipation Proclamation in his right hand while his left was poised above a kneeling slave on whose wrists were broken shackles. The statue "showed the Negro on his knees when a more manly attitude would have been indicative of freedom."[2] But the truth was that the Negro people in the South were being beaten to their knees by armed ruffians, and the Republican Party, the party of Lincoln, was doing nothing to prevent it. On the platform with Douglass was the man who had just refused to use his power as chief executive to stamp out the new terror unleashed against the Negro people and who was content simply with appealing to the southerners to stop these crimes.

Douglass' oration was impressive. Senator George S. Boutwell wrote the orator: "I can not refrain from saying after reading your oration twice, once aloud to my family, that it is the best contribution made to the department of literature in which it takes place, since the time of Mr. Webster."[3]

But in one important respect, this famous oration was disappointing. In his fourth of July oration in Rochester fourteen years before, Douglass had said: "We have to do with the past only as we can make it useful to the present and to the future."[4] Very little in his dignified address now reflected his philosophy. The bulk of the oration dealt with the past, with Lincoln's gradual acceptance of anti-slavery measures after two years of vacillation and procrastination, and his stature in the closing years of the war. But Douglass left unmentioned the fact that everything Lincoln had achieved for the Negro was being wiped out in state after state in the South. Other than the remark about "the spirit of barbarism, which still lingers to blight and destroy in some dark and distant parts of the country," there was nothing to remind the American people that Lincoln's mission had not yet been accomplished.

No other Negro had ever had so great an opportunity to reach the American people with his message. . . . Here was the place to repeat the stirring words uttered at the centennial anniversary of the Pennsylvania Anti-Slavery Society. Here, with the President of the United States and other notables listening, was the place to demand "ample protection" for the Negro people in exercising their "sacred right to vote."

Overwhelmed by the honor bestowed upon him, Douglass remained silent on the crucial issues facing his people. [IV:98–99]

ORATION IN MEMORY OF ABRAHAM LINCOLN, delivered at the unveiling of the Freedmen's Monument in Memory of Abraham Lincoln, in Lincoln Park, Washington, D.C., April 14, 1876

Friends and Fellow-citizens:

I warmly congratulate you upon the highly interesting object which has caused you to assemble in such numbers and spirit as you have today. This occasion is in some respects remarkable. Wise and thoughtful men of our race, who shall come after us, and study the lesson of our history in the United States; who shall survey the long and dreary spaces over which we have traveled; who shall count the links in the great chain of events by which we have reached our present position, will make a note of this occasion; they will think of it and speak of it with a sense of manly pride and complacency.

I congratulate you, also, upon the very favorable circumstances in which we meet today. They are high, inspiring, and uncommon. They lend grace, glory, and significance to the object for which we have met. Nowhere else in this great country, with its uncounted towns and cities, unlimited wealth, and immeasurable territory extending from sea to sea, could conditions be found more favorable to the success of this occasion than here.

We stand today at the national center to perform something like a national act—an act which is to go into history; and we are here where every pulsation of the national heart can be heard, felt, and reciprocated. A thousand wires, fed with thought and winged with lightning, put us in instantaneous communication with the loyal and true men all over this country.

Few facts could better illustrate the vast and wonderful change which has taken place in our condition as a people than the fact of our assembling here for the purpose we have today. Harmless, beautiful, proper, and praiseworthy as this demonstration is, I cannot forget that no such demonstration would have been tolerated here twenty years ago. The spirit of slavery and barbarism, which still lingers to blight and destroy in some dark and distant parts of our country, would have made our assembling here the signal and excuse for opening upon us all the flood-gates of wrath and violence. That we are here in peace today is a compliment and a credit to American civilization, and a prophecy of still greater national enlightenment and progress in the future. I refer to the past not in malice, for this is no day for malice; but simply to place more distinctly in front the gratifying and glorious change which has come both to our white fellow-citizens and ourselves, and to congratulate all upon the contrast between now and then; the new dispensation of freedom with its thousand blessings to both races, and the old dispensation of slavery with its ten thousand evils to both races—white and black. In view, then, of the past, the present, and the future, with the long and dark history of our bondage behind us, and with liberty, progress, and enlightenment before us, I again congratulate you upon this auspicious day and hour.

Friends and fellow-citizens, the story of our presence here is soon and easily told. We are here in the District of Columbia, here in the city of Washington, the most luminous point of American territory; a city recently transformed and made beautiful in its body and in its spirit; we are here in the place where the ablest and best men of the country are sent to devise the policy, enact the laws, and shape the destiny of the Republic; we are here, with the stately pillars and majestic dome of the Capitol of the nation looking down upon us; we are here, with the broad earth freshly adorned with the foliage and flowers of spring for our church, and all races, colors, and conditions of men for our congregation— in a word, we are here to express, as best we may, by appropriate forms and ceremonies, our grateful sense of the vast, high, and preëminent services rendered to ourselves, to our race, to our country, and to the whole world by Abraham Lincoln.

The sentiment that brings us here to-day is one of the noblest that can stir and thrill the human heart. It has crowned and made glorious the high places of all civilized nations with the grandest and most enduring works of art, designed to illustrate the characters and perpetuate the memories of great public men. It is the sentiment which from year to year adorns with fragrant and beautiful flowers the graves of our loyal, brave, and patriotic soldiers who fell in defence of the Union and liberty. It is the sentiment of gratitude and appreciation, which often, in the presence of many who hear me, has filled yonder heights of Arlington with the eloquence of eulogy and the sublime enthusiasm of poetry and song; a sentiment which can never die while the Republic lives.

For the first time in the history of our people, and in the history of the whole American people, we join in this high worship, and march conspicuously in the line of this time-honored custom. First things are always interesting, and this is one of our first things. It is the first time that, in this form and manner, we have sought to do honor to an American great man, however deserving and illustrious. I commend the fact to notice; let it be told in every part of the Republic; let men of all parties and opinions hear it; let those who despise us, not less than those who respect us, know that now and here, in the spirit of liberty, loyalty, and gratitude, let it be known everywhere, and by everybody who takes an interest in human progress and in the amelioration of the condition of mankind, that, in the presence and with the approval of the members of the American House of Representatives, reflecting the general sentiment of the country; that in the presence of that august body, the American Senate, representing the highest intelligence and the calmest judgment of the country; in the presence of the Supreme Court and Chief-Justice of the United States, to whose decisions we all patriotically bow; in the presence and under the steady eye of the honored and trusted President of the United States, with the members of his wise and patriotic Cabinet, we, the colored people, newly emancipated and rejoicing in our blood-bought freedom, near the close of the first century in the life of this Republic, have now and here unveiled, set apart, and dedicated a monument of enduring granite and bronze, in every line, feature, and figure of which the men of this generation may read, and those of aftercoming generations may read, something of the exalted character and great works of Abraham Lincoln, the first martyr President of the United States.

Fellow-citizens, in what we have said and done today, and in what we may say and do hereafter, we disclaim everything like arrogance and assumption. We claim for ourselves no superior devotion to the character, history, and memory of the illustrious name whose monument we have here dedicated today. We fully comprehend the relation of Abraham Lincoln both to ourselves and to the white people of the United States. Truth is proper and beautiful at all times and in all places, and it is never more proper and beautiful in any case than when speaking of a great public man whose example is likely to be commended for honor and imitation long after his departure to the solemn shades, the silent continents of eternity. It must be admitted, truth compels me to admit, even here in the presence of the monument we have erected to his memory, Abraham Lincoln was not, in the fullest sense of the word, either our man or our model. In his interests, in his associations, in his habits of thought, and in his prejudices, he was a white man.

He was preëminently the white man's President, entirely devoted to the welfare of white men. He was ready and willing at any time during the first years of his administration to deny, postpone, and sacrifice the rights of humanity in the colored people to promote the welfare of the white people of this country. In all his education and feeling he was an American of the Americans. He came into the Presidential chair upon one principle alone, namely, opposition to the extension of slavery. His arguments in furtherance of this policy had their motive and mainspring in his patriotic devotion to the interests of his own race. To protect, defend, and perpetuate slavery in the states where it existed Abraham Lincoln was not less ready than any other President to draw the sword of the nation. He was ready to execute all the supposed guarantees of the United States Constitution in favor of the slave system anywhere inside the slave states. He was willing to pursue, recapture, and send back the fugitive slave to his master, and to suppress a slave rising for liberty, though his guilty master were already in arms against the Government. The race to which we belong were not the special objects of his consideration. Knowing this, I concede to you, my white fellow-citizens, a preëminence in this worship at once full and supreme. First, midst, and last, you and yours were the objects of his deepest affection and his most earnest solicitude. You are the children of Abraham Lincoln. We are at best only his step-children; children by adoption, children by forces of circumstances and necessity. To you it especially belongs to sound his praises, to preserve and perpetuate his memory, to multiply his statues, to hang his pictures high upon your walls, and commend his example, for to you he was a great and glorious friend and benefactor. Instead of supplanting you at his altar, we would exhort you to build high his monuments; let them be of the most costly material, of the most cunning workmanship; let their forms be symmetrical, beautiful, and perfect; let their bases be upon solid rocks, and their summits lean against the unchanging blue, overhanging sky, and let them endure forever! But while in the abundance of your wealth, and in the fullness of your just and patriotic devotion, you do all this, we entreat you to despise not the humble offering we this day unveil to view; for while Abraham Lincoln saved for you a country, he delivered us from a bondage, according to Jefferson, one hour of which was worse than ages of the oppression your fathers rose in rebellion to oppose.

Fellow-citizens, ours is no new-born zeal and devotion—merely a thing of this moment. The name of Abraham Lincoln was near and dear to our hearts in the darkest and most perilous hours of the Republic. We were no more ashamed of him when shrouded in clouds of darkness, of doubt, and defeat than when we saw him crowned with victory, honor, and glory. Our faith in him was often taxed and strained to the uttermost, but it never failed. When he tarried long in the mountain; when he strangely told us that we were the cause of the war; when he still more strangely told us that we were to leave the land in which we were born; when he refused to employ our arms in defence of the Union; when, after accepting our services as colored soldiers, he refused to retaliate our murder and torture as colored prisoners; when he told us he would save the Union if he could with slavery; when he revoked the Proclamation of Emancipation of General Fremont; when he refused to remove the popular commander of the Army of the Potomac, in the days of its inaction and defeat, who was more zealous in his efforts to protect slavery than to suppress rebellion; when we saw all this, and more, we were at times grieved, stunned, and greatly bewildered; but our hearts believed while they ached and bled. Nor was this, even at that time, a blind and unreasoning superstition. Despite the mist and haze that surrounded him; despite the tumult, the hurry, and confusion of the hour, we were able to take a comprehensive view of Abraham Lincoln, and to make reasonable allowance for the circumstances of his position. We saw him, measured him, and estimated him; not by stray utterances to injudicious and tedious delegations, who often tried his patience; not by isolated facts torn from their connection; not by any partial and imperfect glimpses, caught at inopportune moments; but by a broad survey, in the light of the stern logic of great events, and in view of that divinity which shapes our ends, rough hew them how we will, we came to the conclusion that the hour and the man of our redemption had somehow met in the person of Abraham Lincoln. It mattered little to us what language he might employ on special occasions; it mattered little to us, when we fully knew him, whether he was swift or slow in his movements; it was enough for us that Abraham Lincoln was at the head of a great movement, and was in living and earnest sympathy with that movement, which, in the nature of things, must go on until slavery should be utterly and forever abolished in the United States.

When, therefore, it shall be asked what we have to do with the memory of Abraham Lincoln, or what Abraham Lincoln had to do with us, the answer is ready, full, and complete. Though he loved Caesar less than Rome, though the Union was more to him than our freedom or our future, under his wise and beneficent rule we saw ourselves gradually lifted from the depths of slavery to the heights of liberty and manhood; under his wise and beneficent rule, and by measures approved and vigorously pressed by him, we saw that the handwriting of ages, in the form of prejudice and proscription, was rapidly fading away from the face of our whole country; under his rule, and in due time, about as soon after all as the country could tolerate the strange spectacle, we saw our brave sons and brothers laying off the rags of bondage, and being clothed all over in the blue uniforms of the soldiers of the United States; under his rule we saw two hundred thousand of our dark and dusky people responding to the call of Abraham Lincoln, and with muskets on their shoulders, and eagles on their buttons, timing their high footsteps to liberty and union under the national flag; under his rule we saw the independence of the black republic of Haiti, the special object of slaveholding aversion and horror, fully recognized, and her minister, a colored gentleman, duly received here in the city of Washington; under his rule we saw the internal slave-trade, which so long disgraced the nation, abolished, and slavery abolished in the District of Columbia; under his rule we saw for the first time the law enforced against the foreign slave trade, and the first slave-trader hanged like any other pirate or murderer; under his rule, assisted by the greatest captain of our age, and his inspiration, we saw the Confederate States, based upon the idea that our race must be slaves, and slaves forever, battered to pieces and scattered to the four winds; under his rule, and in the fullness of time, we saw Abraham Lincoln, after giving the slaveholders three months' grace in which to save their hateful slave system, penning the immortal paper, which, though special in its language, was general in its principles and effect, making slavery forever impossible in the United States. Though we waited long, we saw all this and more.

Can any colored man, or any white man friendly to the freedom of all men, ever forget the night which followed the first day of January, 1863, when the world was to see if Abraham Lincoln would prove to be as good as his word? I shall never forget that memorable night, when in a distant city I waited and watched at a public meeting, with three thousand others not less anxious than myself, for the word of deliverance which we have heard read today. Nor shall I ever forget the outburst of joy and thanksgiving that rent the air when the lightning brought to us the emancipation proclamation. In that happy hour we forgot all delay, and forgot all tardiness, forgot that the President had bribed the rebels to lay down their arms by a promise to withhold the bolt which would smite the slave-system with destruction; and we were thenceforward willing to allow the President all the latitude of time, phraseology, and every honorable device that statesmanship might require for the achievement of a great and beneficent measure of liberty and progress.

Fellow-citizens, there is little necessity on this occasion to speak at length and critically of this great and good man, and of his high mission in the world. That ground has been fully occupied and completely covered both here and elsewhere. The whole field of fact and fancy has been gleaned and garnered. Any man can say things that are true of Abraham Lincoln, but no man can say anything that is new of Abraham Lincoln. His personal traits and public acts are better known to the American people than are those of any other man of his age. He was a mystery to no man who saw him and heard him. Though high in position, the humblest could approach him and feel at home in his presence. Though deep, he was transparent; though strong, he was gentle; though decided and pronounced in his convictions, he was tolerant towards those who differed from him, and patient under reproaches. Even those who only knew him through his public utterance obtained a tolerably clear idea of his character and personality. The image of the man went out with his words, and those who read them knew him.

I have said that President Lincoln was a white man, and shared the prejudices common to his countrymen towards the colored race. Looking back to his times and to the condition of his country, we are compelled to admit that this unfriendly feeling on his part may be safely set down as one element of his wonderful success in organizing the loyal American people for the tremendous conflict before them, and bringing them safely through that conflict. His great mission was to accomplish two things: first, to save his country from dismemberment and ruin; and, second, to free his country from the great crime of slavery. To do one or the other, or both, he must have the earnest sympathy and the powerful coöperation of his loyal fellow-countrymen. Without this primary and essential condition to success his efforts must have been vain and utterly fruitless. Had he put the abolition of slavery before the salvation of the Union, he would have inevitably driven from him a powerful class of the American people and rendered resistance to rebellion impossible. Viewed from the genuine abolition ground, Mr. Lincoln seemed tardy, cold, dull, and indifferent; but measuring him by the sentiment of his country, a sentiment he was bound as a statesman to consult, he was swift, zealous, radical, and determined.

Though Mr. Lincoln shared the prejudices of his white fellow-countrymen against the Negro, it is hardly necessary to say that in his heart of hearts he loathed and hated slavery. . . .* The man who could say, "Fondly do we hope, fervently do we pray, that this mighty scourge of war shall soon pass away, yet if God wills it continue till all the wealth piled by two hundred years of bondage shall have been wasted, and each drop of blood drawn by the lash shall have been paid for by one drawn by the sword, the judgments of the Lord are true and righteous altogether," gives all needed proof of his feeling on the subject of slavery. He was willing, while the South was loyal, that it should have its pound of flesh, because he thought that it was so nominated in the bond; but farther than this no earthly power could make him go.

Fellow-citizens, whatever else in this world may be partial, unjust, and uncertain, time, time! is impartial, just, and certain in its action. In the realm of mind, as well as in the realm of matter, it is a great worker, and often works wonders. The honest and comprehensive statesman, clearly discerning the needs of his country, and earnestly endeavoring to do his whole duty, though covered and

---

*"I am naturally anti-slavery. If slavery is not wrong, nothing is wrong. I cannot remember when I did not so think and feel."—*Letter of Mr. Lincoln to Mr. Hodges, of Kentucky*, April 4, 1864.

blistered with reproaches, may safely leave his course to the silent judgment of time. Few great public men have ever been the victims of fiercer denunciation than Abraham Lincoln was during his administration. He was often wounded in the house of his friends. Reproaches came thick and fast upon him from within and from without, and from opposite quarters. He was assailed by Abolitionists; he was assailed by slaveholders; he was assailed by the men who were for peace at any price; he was assailed, by those who were for a more vigorous prosecution of the war; he was assailed for not making the war an abolition war; and he was bitterly assailed for making the war an abolition war.

But now behold the change: the judgment of the present hour is, that taking him for all in all, measuring the tremendous magnitude of the work before him, considering the necessary means to ends, and surveying the end from the beginning, infinite wisdom has seldom sent any man into the world better fitted for his mission than Abraham Lincoln. His birth, his training, and his natural endowments, both mental and physical, were strongly in his favor. Born and reared among the lowly, a stranger to wealth and luxury, compelled to grapple single-handed with the flintiest hardships of life, from tender youth to sturdy manhood, he grew strong in the manly and heroic qualities demanded by the great mission to which he was called by the votes of his countrymen. The hard condition of his early life, which would have depressed and broken down weaker men, only gave greater life, vigor, and buoyancy to the heroic spirit of Abraham Lincoln. He was ready for any kind and any quality of work. What other young men dreaded in the shape of toil, he took hold of with the utmost cheerfulness.

> "A spade, a rake, a hoe,
>   A pick-axe, or a bill;
> A hook to reap, a scythe to mow,
>   A flail, or what you will."

All day long he could split heavy rails in the woods, and half the night long he could study his English Grammar by the uncertain flare and glare of the light made by a pine-knot. He was at home on the land with his axe, with his maul, with gluts, and his wedges; and he was equally at home on water, with his oars, with his poles, with his planks, and with his boat-hooks. And whether in his flat-boat on the Mississippi River, or at the fireside of his frontier cabin, he was a man of work. A son of toil himself, he was linked in brotherly sympathy with the sons of toil in every loyal part of the Republic. This very fact gave him tremendous power with the American people, and materially contributed not only to selecting him to the Presidency, but in sustaining his administration of the Government.

Upon his inauguration as President of the United States, an office, even when assumed under the most favorable conditions, fitted to tax and strain the largest abilities, Abraham Lincoln was met by a tremendous crisis. He was called upon not merely to administer the Government, but to decide, in the face of terrible odds, the fate of the Republic.

A formidable rebellion rose in his path before him; the Union was already practically dissolved; his country was torn and rent asunder at the center. Hos-

tile armies were already organized against the Republic, armed with the munitions of war which the Republic had provided for its own defence. The tremendous question for him to decide was whether his country should survive the crisis and flourish, or be dismembered and perish. His predecessor in office had
already decided the question in favor of national dismemberment, by denying
to it the right of self-defence and self-preservation—a right which belongs to the
meanest insect.

Happily for the country, happily for you and for me, the judgment of James
Buchanan, the patrician, was not the judgment of Abraham Lincoln, the ple-
beian. He brought his strong common sense, sharpened in the school of adversity, to bear upon the question. He did not hesitate, he did not doubt, he did not
falter; but at once resolved that at whatever peril, at whatever cost, the union of
the States should be preserved. A patriot himself, his faith was strong and unwavering in the patriotism of his countrymen. Timid men said before Mr. Lincoln's inauguration, that we had seen the last President of the United States. A
voice in influential quarters said, "Let the Union slide." Some said that a Union
maintained by the sword was worthless. Others said a rebellion of 8,000,000
cannot be suppressed; but in the midst of all this tumult and timidity, and against
all this, Abraham Lincoln was clear in his duty, and had an oath in heaven. He
calmly and bravely heard the voice of doubt and fear all around him; but he had
an oath in heaven, and there was not power enough on earth to make this honest boatman, backwoodsman, and broad-handed splitter of rails evade or violate
that sacred oath. He had not been schooled in the ethics of slavery; his plain life
had favored his love of truth. He had not been taught that treason and perjury
were the proof of honor and honesty. His moral training was against his saying
one thing when he meant another. The trust that Abraham Lincoln had in himself and in the people was surprising and grand, but it was also enlightened and
well founded. He knew the American people better than they knew themselves,
and his truth was based upon this knowledge.

Fellow-citizens, the fourteenth day of April, 1865, of which this is the eleventh
anniversary, is now and will ever remain a memorable day in the annals of this
Republic. It was on the evening of this day, while a fierce and sanguinary rebellion was in the last stages of its desolating power; while its armies were broken
and scattered before the invincible armies of Grant and Sherman; while a great
nation, torn and rent by war, was already beginning to raise to the skies loud anthems of joy at the dawn of peace, it was startled, amazed, and overwhelmed by
the crowning crime of slavery—the assassination of Abraham Lincoln. It was a
new crime, a pure act of malice. No purpose of the rebellion was to be served by
it. It was the simple gratification of a hell-black spirit of revenge. But it has done
good after all. It has filled the country with a deeper abhorrence of slavery and
a deeper love for the great liberator.

Had Abraham Lincoln died from any of the numerous ills to which flesh is
heir; had he reached that good old age of which his vigorous constitution and his
temperate habits gave promise; had he been permitted to see the end of his great
work; had the solemn curtain of death come down but gradually—we should still
have been smitten with a heavy grief, and treasured his name lovingly. But dying

as he did die, by the red hand of violence, killed, assassinated, taken off without warning, not because of personal hate—for no man who knew Abraham Lincoln could hate him—but because of his fidelity to union and liberty, he is doubly dear to us, and his memory will be precious forever.

Fellow-citizens, I end, as I began, with congratulations. We have done a good work for our race today. In doing honor to the memory of our friend and liberator, we have been doing highest honors to ourselves and those who come after us; we have been fastening ourselves to a name and fame imperishable and immortal; we have also been defending ourselves from a blighting scandal. When now it shall be said that the colored man is soulless, that he has no appreciation of benefits or benefactors; when the foul reproach of ingratitude is hurled at us, and it is attempted to scourge us beyond the range of human brotherhood, we may calmly point to the monument we have this day erected to the memory of Abraham Lincoln.

Inaugural Ceremonies of the Freedmen's Memorial Monument to Abraham Lincoln, Washington City, April 14, 1876, St. Louis, 1876, pp. 16–26

1. The idea of the monument originated with Charlotte Scott, an ex-slave, on the day following Lincoln's assassination. Negroes welcomed the project, and contributed $16,242 toward its completion.

The decline in interest in the anti-slavery period was also reflected in the sales of Douglass' autobiography published in 1881. On July 19, 1882, the Park Publishing Company of Hartford, Douglass' publishers, wrote: "Your book does not sell quite as well as we expected, for the simple reason that the interest in the old days of slavery is not as great as expected." (Frederick Douglass Papers, Frederick Douglass Memorial Home, Anacostia, D.C.)

2. Freeman H. M. Murray, *Emancipation and the Freed in American Sculpture,* Washington, 1916, p. 199.

3. George S. Boutwell to Douglass, Apr. 15, 1876, Frederick Douglass Papers, Frederick Douglass Memorial Home, Anacostia, D.C.

4. *Oration, Delivered in Corinthian Hall, July 5, 1852,* Rochester, 1852, p. 4.

PART EIGHT

The Post-Reconstruction Era, 1877–1895

THERE WAS A RIGHT SIDE IN THE LATE WAR, speech delivered at Union Square, New York City, on Decoration Day, May 30, 1878

Friends and fellow-citizens:

In this place, hallowed and made glorious by a statue of the best man, truest patriot, and wisest statesman of his time and country, I have been invited—I might say ordered—by Lincoln Post of the Grand Army of the Republic, to say a few words to you in appropriate celebration of this annual national memorial day. Deeply sensible of the honor thus conferred, and properly impressed with the dignity of this occasion, I accept the invitation cheerfully and gratefully; but not so much as an honor to myself, as a generous recognition of that class of our fellow-citizens to which I belong; a class hitherto excluded by popular prejudice from prominent participation in the memorial glories of our common country. Lincoln Post—most worthily named—will pardon me if I stop right here to commend it for this innovation upon an old custom; for its moral courage and soldierly independence. Abraham Lincoln was the first President of the United States brave enough to invite a colored gentleman to sit at table with him, and the post that bears his honored name is the first in this great City to invite any colored man to deliver an address on national memorial day.

But the duty you have imposed upon me is far more honorable in the distinction it confers upon me and my race, than easy of happy and successful performance. All that can be pertinently said on this occasion, has been said a thousand times before, and a thousand times better said, than anything I can now hope to say. Besides, and above all, the noble qualities and achievements to which we are here to do honor are of an order which transcends the narrow compass of speech. The eloquence of the most gifted orator of our country would fail to fitly and fully illustrate the heroic deeds and virtues of the brave men who volunteered, fought, and fell in the cause of the Union and freedom. "For greater love hath no man than this, that a man lay down his life for his friends." The topmost height of this greatness was touched by those who, in our national extremity, nobly died, that our Republic might live. We need something broader, more striking and impressive than speech, to express the thoughts and feelings proper to these memorial occasions. We need banners, badges, and battle flags; drums, fifes, and bugles; signs, sounds, and symbols; the clang of church-going bells; the heaven-shaking thunder of cannon; the steady and solemn tramp of armed men; the pomp and circumstance of glorious war; the shouts of a great nation rejoicing in its salvation, to express a proper sense of the worth of men to whose patriotic devotion and noble self-sacrifice the integrity of the nation and the existence of free institutions on this great continent are due.

For such high discourse, pageantry is better than oratory. It can be heard and seen by all. It speaks alike to the understanding and the heart. It carries us dreamily back to that dark and terrible hour of supreme peril, when the heart and the hope of a great people were smitten, stunned, and almost crushed by the stern pressure of a determined and wide-spread rebellion; when the enemies of free government all over the world watched, waited, desired, and expected the downfall of the grandest Republic in the world. It tells us of a time of trial and danger, when the boldest held their breath and the hearts of strong men failed them through fear; when the very earth seemed to crumble beneath our feet; when the sky above us was dark, and sinister whispers filled the air; when one star after another in rapid succession shot madly from the blue ground of the national flag, and this grand experiment of self-government, not yet 100 years old, torn and rent by angry passions, had fallen asunder at the centre, and our once united country was converted into two hostile camps. It is well once a year to contemplate that dismal panorama. But not alone to the gloom and disaster of rebellion and treason does this grand display recall us. It is the province of rampant evil to call out the latent good, and this day reminds us of the good as well as of the evil. It reminds us of patriotic fervor, of quenchless ardor, of heroic courage, of generous self-sacrifice, of patience, skill, and fortitude, of clearness of vision to discern the right, and invincible determination to sustain it at every cost. It brings to mind the time when each day of the week saw thousands of brave men in the full fresh bloom of youth and manly vigor, the very flower and hope of the hearths and homes of the loyal and peaceful North, deliberately sundering the ties that bound them, leaving friends and families, and periling all that was most precious to them for the sake of their country. The spectacle was solemn, sublime, and glorious, and will never be forgotten. New-York was the grand centre where these patriotic legions rallied. They arrived and departed through her hundred gates of sea and land. They came from the East, the West, and the North; from the Empire State with its millions of people; from the Old Bay State, the heart and brain of New-England, the State of Sumner, Andrew, and Wilson; from the icy slopes and beetling crags of stalwart Maine; from the beautiful lakes, winding rivers, and granite hills of New-Hampshire, where Webster was born, and the spirit of John P. Hale still lives; from the Green Mountains of Vermont, whence no slave, panting for liberty, was ever returned, to his master; from the land of Roger Williams, and the land of steady habits; from counter, farm, and factory; from schools, colleges, and courts of law they came; they came with blue coats on their backs, with eagles on their buttons and muskets on their shoulders, timing their high foot-steps to the music of the Union, and making the streets of this great Metropolis like rivers of burnished steel.

Never was there a grander call to patriotic duty, and never was there a more enthusiastic response to such a call; and both the call and the response showed that a Republic with no standing army to fight its battles, could, nevertheless, safely depend upon its patriotic citizens for defense and protection in any great emergency of peril. Brave and noble spirits! living and dead! May your memory never perish! We tender you on this memorial day the homage of the loyal nation, and the heartfelt gratitude of emancipated millions. If the great work you undertook to accomplish is still incomplete; if a lawless and revolutionary spirit is still abroad in the country; if the principles for which you bravely fought are in any way compromised or threatened; if the Constitution and the laws are in any measure dishonored and disregarded; if duty elected State Governments are in any way overthrown by violence; if the elective franchise has been overborne by intimidation and fraud; if the Southern States, under the idea of local self-government, are endeavoring to paralyze the arm and shrivel the body of the National Government so that it cannot protect the humblest citizen in his rights, the fault is not yours. You, at least, were faithful and did your whole duty.

Fellow-citizens, I am not here to fan the flame of sectional animosity, to revive old issues, or to stir up strife between races; but no candid man, looking at the political situation of the hour, can fail to see that we are still afflicted by the painful sequences both of slavery and of the late rebellion. In the spirit of the noble man whose image now looks down upon us we should have "charity toward all, and malice toward none." In the language of our greatest soldier, twice honored with the Presidency of the nation, "Let us have peace." Yes, let us have peace, but let us have liberty, law, and justice first. Let us have the Constitution, with its thirteenth, fourteenth, and fifteenth amendments, fairly interpreted, faithfully executed, and cheerfully obeyed in the fullness of their spirit and the completeness of their letter. Men can do many things in this world, some easily and some with difficulty; but there are some things which men cannot do or be. When they are here they cannot be there. When the supreme law of the land is systematically set at naught; when humanity is insulted and the rights of the weak are trampled in the dust by a lawless power; when society is divided into two classes, as oppressed and oppressor, there is no power, and there can be no power, while the instincts of manhood remain as they are, which can provide solid peace. I do not affirm that friendly feeling cannot be established between the people of the North and South. I do not say that between the white and colored people of the South, the former slaves and the former masters, friendly relations may not be established. I do not say that Hon. Rutherford B. Hayes, the lawful and rightful President of the United States, was not justified in stepping to the verge of his constitutional powers to conciliate and pacify the old master class at the South; but I do say that some steps by way of conciliation should come from the other side. The prodigal son should at least turn his back upon the field of swine, and his face toward home, before we make haste to fall upon his neck, and for him kill the fatted calf. He must not glory in his shame, and boast his non-repentance. He must not reenact at home the excesses he allowed himself to commit in the barren and desolate fields of rebellion. The last commanding utterance of Southern sentiment is from the late President of the Southern Confederacy. He says: "Let not any of the survivors [of rebellion] impugn their faith by offering the penitential plea that they believed they were right." There is reason to believe that Jefferson Davis, in this, speaks out of the fullness of the Southern heart, as well as that of his own. He says, further, that "Heroism derives its lustre from the justice of the cause in which it is displayed." And he holds, and the South holds as firmly to-day as when in rebellion, the justice of that cause, and that a just cause is never to be abandoned.

My own feeling toward the old master class of the South is well known. Though I have worn the yoke of bondage, and have no love for what are called the good old times of slavery, there is in my heart no taint of malice toward the ex-slaveholders. Many of them were not sinners above all others, but were in some sense the slaves of the slave system, for slavery was a power in the State greater than the State itself. With the aid of a few brilliant orators and plotting conspirators, it sundered the bonds of the Union and inaugurated war. Identity of interest and the sympathies created by it produced an irresistible current toward the cataract of disunion by which they were swept down. I have no denunciations for the past. The hand of friendship and affection which I recently gave my old master on his deathbed I would cordially extend to all men like him.

Speaking for my race as well as for myself, I can truthfully say that neither before the war, during the war, nor since the war have the colored people of the South shown malice or resentment toward the old slaveholding class, as a class, because of any or all the wrongs inflicted upon them during the days of their bondage. On the contrary, whenever and wherever this class has shown any disposition to respect the feelings and protect the rights of colored men, colored men have preferred to support them. No men from the East, West, North, or from any other quarter can so readily win the heart and control the political action of the colored people of the South as can the slaveholding class, if they are in the least disposed to be just to them and to faithfully carry out the provisions of the Constitution. They respect the old master class, but they hate and despise slavery.

The world has never seen a more striking example of kindness, forbearance, and fidelity than was shown by the slave population of the South during the war. To them was committed the care of the families of their masters while those masters were off fighting to make the slavery of these same slaves perpetual. The hearths and homes of those masters were left at their mercy. They could have killed, robbed, destroyed, and taken their liberty if they had chosen to do so, but they chose to remain true to the trust reposed in them, and utterly refused to take any advantage of the situation, to win liberty or destroy property. No act of violence lays to their charge. All the violence, crimes, and outrages alleged against the negro have originated since his emancipation.

Judging from the charges against him now, and assuming their truth, a sudden, startling, and most unnatural change must have been wrought in his character and composition. And, for one, I do not believe any such change has taken place. If the ex-master has lost the affection of the slave, it is his own fault. Men are not changed from lambs into tigers instantaneously, nor from tigers into lambs instantaneously. If the negro has lost confidence in the old master-class, it is due to the conduct of that class toward him since the war and since his emancipation. What has been said of the kindly temper and disposition of the colored people of the South to the old master-class, may be equally said of the feelings of the North toward the whole South. There is no malice rankling here against the South— there was none before the war, there was none during the war, and there has been none since the war. The policy of pacification of President Hayes was in the line of Northern sentiment. No American citizen is stigmatized here as a "carpetbagger," or "interloper," because of his Southern birth. He may here exercise the right of speech, the elective franchise, and all other rights of citizenship as those to the manor born. The Lamars, the Hills, the Gordons, and the Butlers of the South may stump any or all the States of New-England, and sit in safety at the hearths and homes made desolate by a causeless rebellion in which they were leaders, without once hearing an angry word, or seeing an insulting gesture.

That so much cannot be said of the South is certainly no fault of the people of the North. We have always been ready to meet rebels more than half way and to hail them as fellow-citizens, countrymen, clansmen, and brothers beloved. As against the North there is no earthly reason for the charge of persecution and punishment of the South. She has suffered to be sure, but she has been the author of her own suffering. Her sons have not been punished, but have been received back into the highest departments of the very Government they endeavored to overthrow and destroy. They now dominate the House of Representatives, and hope soon to control the United States Senate, and the most radical of the radicals of the North will bow to this control, if it shall be obtained without violence and in the legitimate exercise of constitutional rights.

Nevertheless, we must not be asked to say that the South was right in the rebellion, or to say the North was wrong. We must not be asked to put no difference between those who fought for the Union and those who fought against it, or between loyalty and treason. We must not be asked to be ashamed of our part in the war. That is much too great a strain upon Northern conscience and self-respect to be borne in silence. A certain sound was recently given to the trumpet of freedom by Gen. Grant when he told the veterans of Ohio, in a letter written from Milan, Italy, "That he trusted none of them would ever feel a disposition to apologize for the part they took in the late struggle for national existence, or for the cause for which they fought." I admit that the South believed it was right, but the nature of things is not changed by belief. The Inquisition was not less a crime against humanity because it was believed right by the Holy Fathers. The bread and wine are no less bread and wine, though to faith they are flesh and blood. I admit further, that viewed merely as a physical contest, it left very little for self-righteousness or glory on either side. Neither the victors nor the vanquished can hurl reproaches at each other, and each may well enough respect and honor the bravery and skill of the other. Each found in the other a foeman worthy of his steel. The fiery ardor and impetuosity of the one was only a little more than matched by the steady valor and patient fortitude of the other. Thus far we meet upon common ground, and strew choicest flowers upon the graves of the dead heroes of each respectively and equally. But this war will not consent to be viewed simply as a physical contest. It is not for this that the nation is in solemn procession about the graves of its patriot sons to-day. It was not a fight between rapacious birds and ferocious beasts, a mere display of brute courage and endurance, but it was a war between men, men of thought as well as action, and in dead earnest for something beyond the battlefield. It was not even a war of geography or topography or of race.

> "Lands intersected by a narrow frith
> Abhor each other.
> Mountains interposed make enemies of nations."

But the sectional character of this war was merely accidental, and its least significant feature. It was a war of ideas, a battle of principles and ideas which united one section and divided the other: a war between the old and new, slavery and freedom, barbarism and civilization; between a government based upon the broadest and grandest declaration of human rights the world ever heard or read, and another pretended government, based upon an open, bold, and shocking denial of all rights, except the right of the strongest.

Good, wise, and generous men at the North, in power and out of power, for whose good intentions and patriotism we must all have the highest respect, doubt the wisdom of observing this memorial day, and would have us forget and forgive, strew flowers alike and lovingly, on rebel and on loyal graves. This sentiment is noble and generous, worthy of all honor as such; but it is only a sentiment after all, and must submit to its own rational limitations. There was a right side and a wrong side in the late war, which no sentiment ought to cause us to forget, and while to-day we should have malice toward none, and charity toward all, it is no part of our duty to confound right with wrong, or loyalty with treason. If the observance of this memorial day has any apology, office, or significance, it is derived from the moral character of the war, from the far-reaching, unchangeable, and eternal principles in dispute, and for which our sons and brothers encountered hardship, danger, and death. Man is said to be an animal looking before and after. It is his distinction to improve the future by a wise consideration of the past. In looking back to this tremendous conflict, aftercoming generations will find much at which to marvel. They will marvel that men to whom was committed the custody of the Government, sworn to protect and defend the Constitution and the Union of the States, did not crush this rebellion in its egg; that they permitted treason to grow up under their very noses, not only without rebuke or repulse, but rather with approval, aid, and comfort—vainly thinking thus to conciliate the rebels; that they permitted the resources of the Union to be scattered, and its forts and arsenals to be taken possession of without raising a voice or lifting a finger to prevent the crime. They will marvel that the men who, with broad blades and bloody hands sought to destroy the Government were the very men who had been through all its history the most highly favored by the Government. They will marvel at this as when a child stabs the breast that nursed it into life. They will marvel still more that, after the rebellion was suppressed, and treason put down by the loss of nearly a half a million of men, and after putting on the nation's neck a debt heavier than a mountain of gold, the Government has so soon been virtually captured by the party which sought its destruction.

And what is the attitude of this same party to-day? We all know what it was in 1860. The alternative presented to the nation then was, give us the Presidency or we will plunge the country into all the horrors of a bloody revolution. The position of that party is the same to-day as then. The chosen man then was John C. Breckinridge, of Kentucky. The chosen man of that party to-day is Samuel J. Tilden. The man to be kept out of the Presidential chair by threat of revolution was Abraham Lincoln. The man to be driven from the Presidential chair by the machinery of political investigation is Rutherford B. Hayes. Now, as then, the same rebellious spirit is much disturbed by the Army and Navy. In the first instance it was the policy to scatter, now it is to starve. The plotters of mischief hate the Army. It is loyal and true to the Republic.

This is not, as I have already said, a day for speech; certainly not for long speeches. Though the portents upon our national horizon are dark and sinister; though a somewhat reckless disregard of our national obligations and national credit [is] shown in the words and votes of some of our public men; though the temper and manner of the plantation, which talk of honor and responsibility, are increasingly manifest in legislative councils of the nation; though party strife and personal ambition somewhat distract the public mind; though efforts are being made tending to embroil capital and labor, and to antagonize interests which it is for the good of each to harmonize; though freedom of speech and of the ballot have for the present fallen before the shot-guns of the South, and the party of slavery is now in the ascendant, we need bate no jot of heart or hope. The American people will, in any great emergency, be true to themselves. The heart of the nation is still sound and strong, and as in the past, so in the future, patriotic millions, with able captains to lead them, will stand as a wall of fire around the Republic, and in the end see Liberty, Equality, and Justice triumphant.

New York *Times,* May 31, 1878

JOHN BROWN, speech delivered at Storer College, Harper's Ferry, West Virginia, May 30, 1881

Not to fan the flame of sectional animosity now happily in the process of rapid and I hope permanent extinction; not to revive and keep alive a sense of shame and remorse for a great national crime, which has brought its own punishment, in loss of treasure, tears and blood; not to recount the long list of wrongs, inflicted on my race during more than two hundred years of merciless bondage; nor yet to draw, from the labyrinths of far-off centuries, incidents and achievements wherewith to rouse your passions, and enkindle your enthusiasm, but to pay a just debt long due, to vindicate in some degree a great historical character, of our own time and country, one with whom I was myself well acquainted, and whose friendship and confidence it was my good fortune to share, and to give you such recollections, impressions and facts, as I can, of a grand, brave and good old man, and especially to promote a better understanding of the raid upon Harper's Ferry of which he was the chief, is the object of this address.

In all the thirty years' conflict with slavery, if we except the late tremendous war, there is no subject which in its interest and importance will be remembered longer, or will form a more thrilling chapter in American history than this strange, wild, bloody and mournful drama. The story of it is still fresh in the minds of many who now hear me, but for the sake of those who may have forgotten its details, and in order to have our subject in its entire range more fully and clearly before us at the outset, I will briefly state the facts in that extraordinary transaction.

On the night of the 16th of October, 1859, there appeared near the confluence of the Potomac and Shenandoah rivers, a party of nineteen men—fourteen white and five colored. They were not only armed themselves, but had brought with them a large supply of arms for such persons as might join them. These men invaded Harper's Ferry, disarmed the watchman, took possession of the arsenal, rifle-factory, armory and other government property at that place, arrested and made prisoners nearly all the prominent citizens of the neighborhood, collected about fifty slaves, put bayonets into the hands of such as were able and willing to fight for their liberty, killed three men, proclaimed general emancipation, held the ground more than thirty hours, were subsequently overpowered and nearly all killed, wounded or captured, by a body of United States troops, under command of Colonel Robert E. Lee, since famous as the rebel Gen. Lee. Three out of the nineteen invaders were captured whilst fighting, and one of these was Captain John Brown, the man who originated, planned and commanded the expedition. At the time of his capture Capt. Brown was supposed to be mortally wounded, as he had several ugly gashes and bayonet wounds on his head and body; and apprehending that he might speedily die, or that he might be rescued by his friends, and thus the opportunity of making him a signal example of slave-holding vengeance would be lost, his captors hurried him to Charlestown two miles further within the border of Virginia, placed him in prison strongly guarded by troops, and before his wounds were healed, he was brought into court, subjected to a nominal trial, convicted of high treason and inciting slaves to insurrection, and was executed. His corpse was given to his woe-stricken widow, and she, assisted by Anti-slavery friends, caused it to be borne to North Elba, Essex County, N.Y., and there his dust now reposes, amid the silent, solemn and snowy grandeur of the Adirondacks.

Such is the story; with no lines softened or hardened to my inclining. It certainly is not a story to please, but to pain. It is not a story to increase our sense of social safety and security, but to fill the imagination with wild and troubled fancies of doubt and danger. It was a sudden and startling surprise to the people of Harper's Ferry, and it is not easy to conceive of a situation more abundant in all the elements of horror and consternation. They had retired as usual to rest, with no suspicion that an enemy lurked in the surrounding darkness. They had quietly and trustingly given themselves up to "tired Nature's sweet restorer, balmy sleep," and while thus all unconscious of danger, they were roused from their peaceful slumbers by the sharp crack of the invader's rifle, and felt the keen-edged sword of war at their throats, three of their number being already slain.

Every feeling of the human heart was naturally outraged at this occurrence, and hence at the moment the air was full of denunciation and execration. So intense was this feeling, that few ventured to whisper a word of apology. But happily reason has her voice as well as feeling, and though slower in deciding, her judgments are broader, deeper, clearer and more enduring. It is not easy to reconcile human feeling to the shedding of blood for any purpose, unless indeed in the excitement which the shedding of blood itself occasions. The knife is to feeling always an offence. Even when in the hands of a skillful surgeon, it refuses consent to the operation long after reason has demonstrated its necessity. It even pleads the cause of the known murderer on the day of his execution, and calls society half criminal when, in cold blood, it takes life as a protection of itself from crime. Let no word be said against this holy feeling; more than to law and government are we indebted to this tender sentiment of regard for human life for the safety with which we walk the streets by day and sleep secure in our beds at night. It is nature's grand police, vigilant and faithful, sentineled in the soul, guarding against violence to peace and life. But whilst so much is freely accorded to feeling in the economy of human welfare, something more than feeling is necessary to grapple with a fact so grim and significant as was this raid. Viewed apart and alone, as a transaction separate and distinct from its antecedents and bearings, it takes rank with the most cold-blooded and atrocious wrongs ever perpetrated; but just here is the trouble—this raid on Harper's Ferry, no more than Sherman's march to the sea can consent to be thus viewed alone.

There is, in the world's government, a force which has in all ages been recognized, sometimes as Nemesis, sometimes as the judgment of God and sometimes as retributive justice; but under whatever name, all history attests the wisdom and beneficence of its chastisements, and men become reconciled to the agents through whom it operates, and have extolled them as heroes, benefactors and demigods.

To the broad vision of a true philosophy, nothing in this world stands alone. Everything is a necessary part of everything else. The margin of chance is narrowed by every extension of reason and knowledge, and nothing comes unbidden to the feast of human experience. The universe, of which we are a part, is continually proving itself a stupendous whole, a system of law and order, eternal and perfect. Every seed bears fruit after its kind, and nothing is reaped which was not sowed. The distance between seed time and harvest, in the moral world, may not be quite so well defined or as clearly intelligible as in the physical, but there is a seed time, and there is a harvest time, and though ages may intervene, and neither he who ploughed nor he who sowed may reap in person, yet the harvest nevertheless will surely come; and as in the physical world there are century plants, so it may be in the moral world, and their fruitage is as certain in the one as in the other. The bloody harvest of Harper's Ferry was ripened by the heat and moisture of merciless bondage of more than two hundred years. That startling cry of alarm on the banks of the Potomac was but the answering back of the avenging angel to the midnight invasions of Christian slavetraders on the sleeping hamlets of Africa. The history of the African slavetrade furnishes many illustrations far more cruel and bloody.

Viewed thus broadly our subject is worthy of thoughtful and dispassionate consideration. It invites the study of the poet, scholar, philosopher and statesman. What the masters in natural science have done for man in the physical world, the masters of social science may yet do for him in the moral world. Science now tells us when storms are in the sky, and when and where their violence will be most felt. Why may we not yet know with equal certainty when storms are in the moral sky, and how to avoid their desolating force? But I can invite you to no such profound discussions. I am not the man, nor is this the occasion for such philosophical enquiry. Mine is the word of grateful memory to an old friend; to tell you what I knew of him—what I knew of his inner life—of what he did and what he attempted, and thus if possible to make the mainspring of his actions manifest and thereby give you a clearer view of his character and services.

It is said that next in value to the performance of great deeds ourselves, is the capacity to appreciate such when performed by others; to more than this I do not presume. Allow me one other personal word before I proceed. In the minds of some of the American people I was myself credited with an important agency in the John Brown raid. Governor Henry A. Wise was manifestly of that opinion. He was at the pains of having Mr. Buchanan send his Marshals to Rochester to invite me to accompany them to Virginia. Fortunately I left town several hours previous to their arrival.

What ground there was for this distinguished consideration shall duly appear in the natural course of this lecture. I wish however to say just here that there was no foundation whatever for the charge that I in any wise urged or instigated John Brown to his dangerous work. I rejoice that it is my good fortune to have seen, not only the end of slavery, but to see the day when the whole truth can be told about this matter without prejudice to either the living or the dead. I shall however allow myself little prominence in these disclosures. Your interests, like mine, are in the all-commanding figure of the story, and to him I consecrate the hour. His zeal in the cause of my race was far greater than mine—it was as the burning sun to my taper light—mine was bounded by time, his stretched away to the boundless shores of eternity. I could live for the slave, but he could die for him. The crown of martyrdom is high, far beyond the reach of ordinary mortals, and yet happily no special greatness or superior moral excellence is necessary to discern and in some measure appreciate a truly great soul. Cold, calculating and unspiritual as most of us are, we are not wholly insensible to real greatness; and when we are brought in contact with a man of commanding mold, towering high and alone above the millions, free from all conventional fetters, true to his own moral convictions, a "law unto himself," ready to suffer misconstruction, ignoring torture and death for what he believes to be right, we are compelled to do him homage.

In the stately shadow, in the sublime presence of such a soul I find myself standing to-night; and how to do it reverence, how to do it justice, how to honor the dead with due regard to the living, has been a matter of most anxious solicitude.

Much has been said of John Brown, much that is wise and beautiful, but in looking over what may be called the John Brown literature, I have been little assisted with material, and even less encouraged with any hope of success in treating the subject. Scholarship, genius and devotion have hastened with poetry and eloquence, story and song to this simple altar of human virtue, and have retired dissatisfied and distressed with the thinness and poverty of their offerings, as I shall with mine.

The difficulty in doing justice to the life and character of such a man is not altogether due to the quality of the zeal, or of the ability brought to the work, nor yet to any imperfections in the qualities of the man himself; the state of the moral atmosphere about us has much to do with it. The fault is not in our eyes, nor yet in the object, if under a murky sky we fail to discover the object. Wonderfully tenacious is the taint of a great wrong. The evil, as well as "the good that men do, lives after them." Slavery is indeed gone; but its long, black shadow yet falls broad and large over the face of the whole country. It is the old truth oft repeated, and never more fitly than now, "a prophet is without honor in his own country and among his own people." Though more than twenty years have rolled between us and the Harper's Ferry raid, though since then the armies of the nation have found it necessary to do on a large scale what John Brown attempted to do on a small one, and the great captain who fought his way through slavery has filled with honor the Presidential chair, we yet stand too near the days of slavery, and the life and times of John Brown, to see clearly the true martyr and hero that he was and rightly to estimate the value of the man and his works. Like the great and good of all ages—the men born in advance of their times, the men whose bleeding footprints attest the immense cost of reform, and show us the long and dreary spaces, between the luminous points in the progress of mankind—this our noblest American hero must wait the polishing wheels of after-coming centuries to make his glory more manifest, and his worth more generally acknowledged. Such instances are abundant and familiar. If we go back four and twenty centuries, to the stately city of Athens, and search among her architectural splendor and her miracles of art for the Socrates of today, and as he stands in history, we shall find ourselves perplexed and disappointed. In Jerusalem Jesus himself was only the "carpenter's son"—a young man wonderfully destitute of worldly prudence—a pestilent fellow, "inexcusably and perpetually interfering in the world's business,"—"upsetting the tables of the money-changers"—preaching sedition, opposing the good old religion—"making himself greater than Abraham," and at the same time "keeping company" with very low people; but behold the change! He was a great miracle-worker, in his day, but time has worked for him a greater miracle than all his miracles, for now his name stands for all that is desirable in government, noble in life, orderly and beautiful in society. That which time has done for other great men of his class, that will time certainly do for John Brown. The brightest gems shine at first with subdued light, and the strongest characters are subject to the same limitations. Under the influence of adverse education and hereditary bias, few things are more difficult than to render impartial justice. Men hold up their hands to Heaven, and swear they will do justice, but what are oaths against prejudice and against inclination! In the face of high-sounding professions and affirmations we know well how hard it is for a Turk to do justice to a Christian, or for a Christian to do justice to a Jew. How hard for an Englishman to do justice to an Irishman, for an Irishman to do justice to an Englishman, harder still for an American tainted by slavery to do justice to the Negro or the Negro's friends. "John Brown," said the late Wm. H. Seward, "was justly hanged." "John Brown," said the late John A. Andrew, "was right." It is easy to perceive the sources of these two opposite judgments: the one was the verdict of slave-holding and panic-stricken Virginia, the other was the verdict of the best heart and brain of free old Massachusetts. One was the heated judgment of the passing and passionate hour, and the other was the calm, clear, unimpeachable judgment of the broad, illimitable future.

There is, however, one aspect of the present subject quite worthy of notice, for it makes the hero of Harper's Ferry in some degree an exception to the general rules to which I have just now adverted. Despite the hold which slavery had at that time on the country, despite the popular prejudice against the Negro, despite the shock which the first alarm occasioned, almost from the first John

Brown received a large measure of sympathy and appreciation. New England recognized in him the spirit which brought the pilgrims to Plymouth rock and hailed him as a martyr and saint. True he had broken the law, true he had struck for a despised people, true he had crept upon his foe stealthily, like a wolf upon the fold, and had dealt his blow in the dark whilst his enemy slept, but with all this and more to disturb the moral sense, men discerned in him the greatest and best qualities known to human nature, and pronounced him "good." Many consented to his death, and then went home and taught their children to sing his praise as one whose "soul is marching on" through the realms of endless bliss. One element in explanation of this somewhat anomalous circumstance will probably be found in the troubled times which immediately succeeded, for "when judgments are abroad in the world, men learn righteousness."

The country had before this learned the value of Brown's heroic character. He had shown boundless courage and skill in dealing with the enemies of liberty in Kansas. With men so few, and means so small, and odds against him so great, no captain ever surpassed him in achievements, some of which seem almost beyond belief. With only eight men in that bitter war, he met, fought and captured Henry Clay Pate, with twenty-five well armed and mounted men. In this memorable encounter, he selected his ground so wisely, handled his men so skillfully, and attacked the enemy so vigorously, that they could neither run nor fight, and were therefore compelled to surrender to a force less than one-third their own. With just thirty men on another important occasion during the same border war, he met and vanquished four hundred Missourians under the command of Gen. Read. These men had come into the territory under an oath never to return to their homes till they had stamped out the last vestige of free State spirit in Kansas; but a brush with old Brown took this high conceit out of them, and they were glad to get off upon any terms, without stopping to stipulate. With less than one hundred men to defend the town of Lawrence, he offered to lead them and give battle to fourteen hundred men on the banks of the Waukerusia rivers, and was much vexed when his offer was refused by Gen. Jim Lane and others to whom the defense of the town was confided. Before leaving Kansas, he went into the border of Missouri, and liberated a dozen slaves in a single night, and, in spite of slave laws and marshals, he brought these people through a half dozen States, and landed them safely in Canada. With eighteen men this man shook the whole social fabric of Virginia. With eighteen men he overpowered a town of nearly three thousand souls. With these eighteen men he held that large community firmly in his grasp for thirty long hours. With these eighteen men he rallied in a single night fifty slaves to his standard, and made prisoners of an equal number of the slave-holding class. With these eighteen men he defied the power and bravery of a dozen of the best militia companies that Virginia could send against him. Now, when slavery struck, as it certainly did strike, at the life of the country, it was not the fault of John Brown that our rulers did not at first know how to deal with it. He had already shown us the weak side of the rebellion, had shown us where to strike and how. It was not from lack of native courage that Virginia submitted for thirty long hours and at last was relieved only by Federal troops; but because the attack was made on the side of her conscience and thus armed her against herself. She beheld at her side the sullen brow of a black Ireland. When John Brown proclaimed emancipation to the slaves of Maryland and Virginia he added to his war power the force of a moral earthquake. Virginia felt all her strong-ribbed mountains to shake under the heavy tread of armed insurgents. Of his army of nineteen her conscience made an army of nineteen hundred.

Another feature of the times, worthy of notice, was the effect of this blow upon the country at large. At the first moment we were stunned and bewildered. Slavery had so benumbed the moral sense of the nation, that it never suspected the possibility of an explosion like this, and it was difficult for Captain Brown to get himself taken for what he really was. Few could seem to comprehend that freedom to the slaves was his only object. If you will go back with me to that time you will find that the most curious and contradictory versions of the affair were industriously circulated, and those which were the least rational and true seemed to command the readiest belief. In the view of some, it assumed tremendous proportions. To such it was nothing less than a wide-sweeping rebellion to overthrow the existing government, and construct another upon its ruins, with Brown for its President and Commander-in-Chief; the proof of this was found in the old man's carpet-bag in the shape of a constitution for a new Republic, an instrument which in reality had been executed to govern the conduct of his men in the mountains. Smaller and meaner natures saw in it nothing higher than a purpose to plunder. To them John Brown and his men were a gang of desperate robbers, who had learned by some means that [the] government had sent a large sum of money to Harper's Ferry to pay off the workmen in its employ there, and they had gone thence to fill their pockets from this money. The fact is, that outside of a few friends, scattered in different parts of the country, and the slaveholders of Virginia, few persons understood the significance of the hour. That a man might do something very audacious and desperate for money, power or fame, was to the general apprehension quite possible; but, in face of plainly-written law, in face of constitutional guarantees protecting each State against domestic violence, in face of a nation of forty million of people, that nineteen men could invade a great State to liberate a despised and hated race, was to the average intellect and conscience, too monstrous for belief. In this respect the vision of Virginia was clearer than that of the nation. Conscious of her guilt and therefore full of suspicion, sleeping on pistols for pillows, startled at every unusual sound, constantly fearing and expecting a repetition of the Nat Turner insurrection, she at once understood the meaning, if not the magnitude of the affair. It was this understanding which caused her to raise the lusty and imploring cry to the Federal government for help, and it was not till he who struck the blow had fully explained his motives and object, that the incredulous nation in any wise comprehended the true spirit of the raid, or of its commander. Fortunate for his memory, fortunate for the brave men associated with him, fortunate for the truth of history, John Brown survived the saber gashes, bayonet wounds and bullet holes, and was able, though covered with blood, to tell his own story and make his own defense. Had he with all his men, as might have been the case, gone down in the shock of battle, the world would have had no true basis for its judgment, and one of the most heroic efforts ever witnessed in behalf of liberty would have been confounded with base and selfish purposes. When, like savages, the Wises, the Vallandinghams, the Washingtons, the Stuarts and others stood around the fallen and bleeding hero, and sought by torturing questions to wring from his supposed dying lips some word by which to soil the sublime undertaking, by implicating Gerrit Smith, Joshua R. Giddings, Dr. S. G. Howe, G. L. Stearns, Edwin Morton, Frank Sanborn, and other prominent Anti-slavery men, the brave old man, not only avowed his object to be the emancipation of the slaves, but serenely and proudly announced himself as solely responsible for all that had happened. Though some thought of his own life might at such a moment have seemed natural and excusable, he showed none, and scornfully rejected the idea that he acted as the agent or instrument of any man or set of men. He admitted that he had friends and sympathizers, but to his own head he invited all the bolts of slave-holding wrath and fury, and welcomed them to do their worst. His manly courage and self-forgetful nobleness were not lost upon the crowd about him, nor upon the country. They drew applause from his bitterest enemies. Said Henry A. Wise, "He is the gamest man I ever met." "He was kind and humane to his prisoners," said Col. Lewis Washington.

To the outward eye of men, John Brown was a criminal, but to their inward eye he was a just man and true. His deeds might be disowned, but the spirit which made those deeds possible was worthy highest honor. It has been often asked, why did not Virginia spare the life of this man? why did she not avail herself of this grand opportunity to add to her other glory that of a lofty magnanimity? Had they spared the good old man's life—had they said to him, "You see we have you in our power, and could easily take your life, but we have no desire to hurt you in any way; you have committed a terrible crime against society; you have invaded us at midnight and attacked a sleeping community, but we recognize you as a fanatic, and in some sense instigated by others; and on this ground and others, we release you. Go about your business, and tell those who sent you that we can afford to be magnanimous to our enemies." I say, had Virginia held some such language as this to John Brown, she would have inflicted a heavy blow on the whole Northern abolition movement, one which only the omnipotence of truth and the force of truth would have overcome. I have no doubt Gov. Wise would have done so gladly, but, alas, he was the executive of a State which thought she could not afford such magnanimity. She had that within her bosom which could more safely tolerate the presence of a criminal than a saint, a highway robber than a moral hero. All her hills and valleys were studded with material for a disastrous conflagration, and one spark of the dauntless spirit of Brown might set the whole State in flames. A sense of this appalling liability put an end to every noble consideration. His death was a foregone conclusion, and his trial was simply one of form.

Honor to the brave young Col. Hoyt who hastened from Massachusetts to defend his friend's life at the peril of his own; but there would have been no hope of success had he been allowed to plead the case. He might have surpassed Choate or Webster in power—a thousand physicians might have sworn that Capt. Brown was insane, it would have been all to no purpose; neither eloquence nor testimony could have prevailed. Slavery was the idol of Virginia, and pardon and life to Brown meant condemnation and death to slavery. He had practically illustrated a truth stranger than fiction,—a truth higher than Virginia had ever known,—a truth more noble and beautiful than Jefferson ever wrote. He had evinced a conception of the sacredness and value of liberty which transcended in sublimity that of her own Patrick Henry and made even his fire-flashing sentiment of "Liberty or Death" seem dark and tame and selfish. Henry loved liberty for himself, but this man loved liberty for all men, and for those most despised and scorned, as well as for those most esteemed and honored. Just here was the true glory of John Brown's mission. It was not for his own freedom that he was thus ready to lay down his life, for with Paul he could say, "I was born free." No chain had bound his ankle, no yoke had galled his neck. History has no better illustration of pure, disinterested benevolence. It was not Caucasian for Caucasian—white man for white man; not rich man for rich man, but Caucasian for Ethiopian—white man for black man—rich man for poor man—the man admitted and respected, for the man despised and rejected. "I want you to understand, gentlemen," he said to his persecutors, "that I respect the rights of the poorest and weakest of the colored people, oppressed by the slave system, as I do those of the most wealthy and powerful." In this we have the key to the whole life and career of the man. Than in this sentiment humanity has nothing more touching, reason nothing more noble, imagination nothing more sublime; and if we could reduce all the religions of the world to one essence we could find in it nothing more divine. It is much to be regretted that some great artist, in sympathy with the spirit of the occasion, had not been present when these and similar words were spoken. The situation was thrilling. An old man in the center of an excited and angry crowd, far away from home, in an enemy's country—with no friend near—overpowered, defeated, wounded, bleeding—covered with reproaches—his brave companions nearly all dead—his two faithful sons stark and cold by his side—reading his death-warrant in his fast-oozing blood and increasing weakness as in the faces of all around him—yet calm, collected, brave, with a heart for any fate—using his supposed dying moments to explain his course and vindicate his cause: such a subject would have been at once an inspiration and a power for one of the grandest historical pictures ever painted.

With John Brown, as with every other man fit to die for a cause, the hour of his physical weakness was the hour of his moral strength—the hour of his defeat was the hour of his triumph—the moment of his capture was the crowning victory of his life. With the Alleghany mountains for his pulpit, the country for his church and the whole civilized world for his audience, he was a thousand times more effective as a preacher than as a warrior, and the consciousness of this fact was the secret of his amazing complacency. Mighty with the sword of steel, he was mightier with the sword of the truth, and with this sword he literally swept the horizon. He was more than a match for all the Wises, Masons, Vallandinghams and Washingtons, who could rise against him. They could kill him, but they could not answer him.

In studying the character and works of a great man, it is always desirable to learn in what he is distinguished from others, and what have been the causes of this difference. Such men as he whom we are now considering, come on to the theater of life only at long intervals. It is not always easy to explain the exact and logical causes that produce them, or the subtle influences which sustain them, at the immense heights where we sometimes find them; but we know that the hour and the man are seldom far apart, and that here, as elsewhere, the demand may, in some mysterious way, regulate the supply. A great iniquity, hoary with age, proud and defiant, tainting the whole moral atmosphere of the country, subjecting both church and state to its control, demanded the startling shock which John Brown seemed especially inspired to give it.

Apart from this mission there was nothing very remarkable about him. He was a wool-dealer, and a good judge of wool, as a wool-dealer ought to be. In all visible respects he was a man like unto other men. No outward sign of Kansas or Harper's Ferry was about him. As I knew him, he was an even-tempered man, neither morose, malicious nor misanthropic, but kind, amiable, courteous, and gentle in his intercourse with men. His words were few, well chosen and forcible. He was a good business man, and a good neighbor. A good friend, a good citizen, a good husband and father: a man apparently in every way calculated to make a smooth and pleasant path for himself through the world. He loved society, he loved little children, he liked music, and was fond of animals. To no one was the world more beautiful or life more sweet. How then as I have said shall we explain his apparent indifference to life? I can find but one answer, and that is, his intense hatred to oppression. I have talked with many men, but I remember none, who seemed so deeply excited upon the subject of slavery as he. He would walk the room in agitation at mention of the word. He saw the evil through no mist or haze, but in a light of infinite brightness, which left no line of its ten thousand horrors out of sight. Law, religion, learning, were interposed in its behalf in vain. His law in regard to it was that which Lord Brougham described, as "the law above all the enactments of human codes, the same in all time, the same throughout the world—the law unchangeable and eternal—the law written by the finger of God on the human heart—that law by which property in man is, and ever must remain, a wild and guilty phantasy."

Against truth and right, legislative enactments were to his mind mere cobwebs—the pompous emptiness of human pride—the pitiful outbreathings of human nothingness. He used to say "whenever there is a right thing to be done, there is a 'thus saith the Lord' that it shall be done."

It must be admitted that Brown assumed tremendous responsibility in making war upon the peaceful people of Harper's Ferry, but it must be remembered also that in his eye a slave-holding community could not be peaceable, but was, in the nature of the case, in one incessant state of war. To him such a community was not more sacred than a band of robbers: it was the right of any one to assault it by day or night. He saw no hope that slavery would ever be abolished by moral or political means: "he knew," he said, "the proud and hard hearts of the slave-holders, and that they never would consent to give up their slaves, till they felt a big stick about their heads."

It was five years before this event at Harper's Ferry, while the conflict between freedom and slavery was waxing hotter and hotter with every hour, that the blundering statesmanship of the National Government repealed the Missouri compromise, and thus launched the territory of Kansas as a prize to be battled for between the North and the South. The remarkable part taken in this contest by Brown has been already referred to, and it doubtless helped to prepare him for the final tragedy, and though it did not by any means originate the plan, it confirmed him in it and hastened its execution.

During his four years' service in Kansas it was my good fortune to see him often. On his trips to and from the territory he sometimes stopped several days at my house, and at one time several weeks. It was on this last occasion that liberty had been victorious in Kansas, and he felt that he must hereafter devote himself to what he considered his larger work. It was the theme of all his conversation, filling his nights with dreams and his days with visions. An incident of his boyhood may explain, in some measure, the intense abhorrence he felt to slavery. He had for some reason been sent into the State of Kentucky, where he made the acquaintance of a slave boy, about his own age, of whom he became very fond. For some petty offense this boy was one day subjected to a brutal beating. The blows were dealt with an iron shovel and fell fast and furiously upon his slender body. Born in a free State and unaccustomed to such scenes of cruelty, young Brown's pure and sensitive soul revolted at the shocking spectacle and at that early age he swore eternal hatred to slavery. After years never obliterated the impression, and he found in this early experience an argument against contempt for small things. It is true that the boy is the father of the man. From the acorn comes the oak. The impression of a horse's foot in the sand suggested the art of printing. The fall of an apple intimated the law of gravitation. A word dropped in the woods of Vincennes, by royal hunters, gave Europe and the world a "William the Silent," and a thirty years' war. The beating of a Hebrew bondsman, by an Egyptian, created a Moses, and the infliction of a similar outrage on a helpless slave boy in our own land may have caused, forty years afterwards, a John Brown and a Harper's Ferry Raid.

Most of us can remember some event or incident which has at some time come to us, and made itself a permanent part of our lives. Such an incident came to me in the year 1847. I had then the honor of spending a day and a night under the roof of a man, whose character and conversation made a very deep impression on my mind and heart; and as the circumstance does not lie entirely out of the range of our present observations, you will pardon for a moment a seeming digression. The name of the person alluded to had been several times mentioned to me, in a tone that made me curious to see him and to make his acquaintance. He was a merchant, and our first meeting was at his store—a substantial brick building, giving evidence of a flourishing business. After a few minutes' detention here, long enough for me to observe the neatness and order of the place, I was conducted by him to his residence where I was kindly received by his family as an expected guest. I was a little disappointed at the appearance of this man's house, for after seeing his fine store, I was prepared to see a fine residence; but this logic was entirely contradicted by the facts. The house was a small, wooden one, on a back street in a neighborhood of laboring men and mechanics, respectable enough, but not just the spot where one would expect to find the home of a successful merchant. Plain as was the outside, the inside was plainer.

Its furniture might have pleased a Spartan. It would take longer to tell what was not in it, than what was; no sofas, no cushions, no curtains, no carpets, no easy rocking chairs inviting to enervation or rest or repose. My first meal passed under the misnomer of tea. It was none of your tea and toast sort, but potatoes and cabbage, and beef soup; such a meal as a man might relish after following the plough all day, or after performing a forced march of a dozen miles [ov]er rough ground in frosty weather. Innocent of paint, veneering, varnish or tablecloth, the table announced itself unmistakably and honestly pine and of the plainest workmanship. No hired help passed from kitchen to dining room, staring in amazement at the colored man at the white man's table. The mother, daughters and sons did the serving, and did it well. I heard no apology for doing their own work; they went through it as if used to it, untouched by any thought of degradation or impropriety. Supper over, the boys helped to clear the table and wash the dishes. This style of housekeeping struck me as a little odd. I mention it because household management is worthy of thought. A house is more than brick and mortar, wood or paint; this to me at least was. In its plainness it was a truthful reflection of its inmates; no disguises, no illusions, no make-believes here, but stem truth and solid purpose breathed in all its arrangements. I was not long in company with the master of this house before I discovered that he was indeed the master of it, and likely to become mine too, if I staid long with him. He fulfilled St. Paul's idea of the head of the family—his wife believed in him, and his children observed him with reverence. Whenever he spoke, his words commanded earnest attention. His arguments which I ventured at some points to oppose, seemed to convince all, his appeals touched all, and his will impressed all. Certainly I never felt myself in the presence of a stronger religious influence than while in this house. "God and duty, God and duty," run like a thread of gold through all his utterances, and his family supplied a ready "Amen." In person he was lean and sinewy, of the best New England mould, built for times of trouble, fitted to grapple with the flintiest hardships. Clad in plain American woolen, shod in boots of cowhide leather, and wearing a cravat of the same substantial material, under six feet high, less than one hundred and fifty lbs. in weight, aged about fifty, he presented a figure straight and symmetrical as a mountain pine. His bearing was singularly impressive. His head was not large, but compact and high. His hair was coarse, strong, slightly gray and closely trimmed and grew close to his forehead. His face was smoothly shaved and revealed a strong square mouth, supported by a broad and prominent chin. His eyes were clear and grey, and in conversation they alternated with tears and fire. When on the street, he moved with a long springing, race-horse step, absorbed by his own reflections, neither seeking nor shunning observation. Such was the man whose name I heard uttered in whispers—such was the house in which he lived—such were his family and household management—and such was Captain John Brown.

He said to me at this meeting, that he had invited me to his house for the especial purpose of laying before me his plan for the speedy emancipation of my race. He seemed to apprehend opposition on my part as he opened the subject and touched my vanity by saying, that he had observed my course at home and abroad, and wanted my co-operation. He said he had been for the last thirty years looking for colored men to whom he could safely reveal his secret, and had almost despaired, at times, of finding such, but that now he was encouraged for he saw heads rising up in all directions, to whom he thought he could with safety impart his plan. As this plan then lay in his mind it was very simple, and had much to commend it. It did not, as was supposed by many, contemplate a general rising among the slaves, and a general slaughter of the slave masters (an insurrection he thought would only defeat the object), but it did contemplate the creating of an armed force which should act in the very heart of the South. He was not averse to the shedding of blood, and thought the practice of carrying arms would be a good one for the colored people to adopt, as it would give them a sense of manhood. No people he said could have self-respect or be respected who would not fight for their freedom. He called my attention to a large map of the U. States, and pointed out to me the far-reaching Alleghanies, stretching away from the borders of New York into the Southern States. "These mountains," he said, "are the basis of my plan. God has given the strength of these hills to freedom; they were placed here to aid the emancipation of your race; they are full of natural forts, where one man for defense would be equal to a hundred for attack; they are also full of good hiding places where a large number of men could be concealed and baffle and elude pursuit for a long time. I know these mountains well and could take a body of men into them and keep them there in spite of all the efforts of Virginia to dislodge me, and drive me out. I would take at first about twenty-five picked men and begin on a small scale, supply them arms and ammunition, post them in squads of fives on a line of twenty-five miles, these squads to busy themselves for a time in gathering recruits from the surrounding farms, seeking and selecting the most restless and daring." He saw that in this part of the work the utmost care must be used to guard against treachery and disclosure; only the most conscientious and skillful should be sent on this perilous duty. With care and enterprise he thought he could soon gather a force of one hundred hardy men, men who would be content to lead the free and adventurous life to which he proposed to train them. When once properly drilled, and each had found the place for which he was best suited, they would begin work in earnest; they would run off the slaves in large numbers, retain the strong and brave ones in the mountains, and send the weak and timid ones to the North by the underground Railroad; his operations would be enlarged with increasing numbers and would not be confined to one locality. Slave-holders should in some cases be approached at midnight and told to give up their slaves and to let them have their best horses to ride away upon. Slavery was a state of war, he said, to which the slaves were unwilling parties and consequently they had a right to anything necessary to their peace and freedom. He would shed no blood and would avoid a fight except in self-defense, when he would of course do his best. He believed this movement would weaken slavery in two ways—first by making slave property insecure, it would become undesirable; and secondly it would keep the anti-slavery agitation alive and public attention fixed upon it, and thus lead to the adoption of measures to abolish the evil altogether. He held that there was need of something startling to prevent the agitation of the question from dying out; that slavery had come near being abolished in Virginia by the Nat Turner insurrection, and he thought his method would speedily put an end to it, both in Maryland and Virginia. The trouble was to get the right men to start with and money enough to equip them. He had adopted the simple and economical mode of living to which I have referred with a view to save money for this purpose. This was said in no boastful tone, for he felt that he had delayed already too long and had no room to boast either his zeal or his self-denial.

From 8 o'clock in the evening till 3 in the morning, Capt. Brown and I sat face to face, he arguing in favor of his plan, and I finding all the objections I could against it. Now mark! this meeting of ours was full twelve years before the strike at Harper's Ferry. He had been watching and waiting all that time for suitable heads to rise or "pop up" as he said among the sable millions in whom he could confide; hence forty years had passed between his thought and his act. Forty years, though not a long time in the life of a nation, is a long time in the life of a man; and here forty long years, this man was struggling with this one idea; like Moses he was forty years in the wilderness. Youth, manhood, middle age had come and gone; two marriages had been consummated, twenty children had called him father; and through all the storms and vicissitudes of busy life, this one thought, like the angel in the burning bush, had confronted him with its blazing light, bidding him on to his work. Like Moses he had made excuses, and as with Moses his excuses were overruled. Nothing should postpone further what was to him a divine command, the performance of which seemed to him his only apology for existence. He often said to me, though life was sweet to him, he would willingly lay it down for the freedom of my people; and on one occasion he added, that he had already lived about as long as most men, since he had slept less, and if he should now lay down his life the loss would not be great, for in fact he knew no better use for it. During his last visit to us in Rochester there appeared in the newspapers a touching story connected with the horrors of the Sepoy War in British India. A Scotch missionary and his family were in the hands of the enemy, and were to be massacred the next morning. During the night, when they had given up every hope of rescue, suddenly the wife insisted that relief would come. Placing her ear close to the ground she declared she heard the Slogan—the Scotch war song. For long hours in the night no member of the family could hear the advancing music but herself. "Dinna ye hear it? Dinna ye hear it?" she would say, but they could not hear it. As the morning slowly dawned a Scotch regiment was found encamped indeed about them, and they were saved from the threatened slaughter. This circumstance, coming at such a time, gave Capt. Brown a new word of cheer. He would come to the table in the morning his countenance fairly illuminated, saying that he had heard the Slogan, and he would add, "Dinna ye hear it? *Dinna* ye hear it?" Alas! like the Scotch missionary I was obliged to say "No." Two weeks prior to the meditated attack, Capt. Brown summoned me to meet him in an old stone quarry on the Conecochequi river, near the town of Chambersburgh, Penn. His arms and ammunition were stored in that town and were to be moved on to Harper's Ferry. In company with Shields Green I obeyed the summons, and prompt to the hour we met the dear old man, with Kagi, his secretary, at the appointed place. Our meeting was in some sense a council of war. We spent the Saturday and succeeding Sunday in conference on the question, whether the desperate step should then be taken, or the old plan as already described should be carried out. He was for boldly striking at Harper's Ferry at once and running the risk of getting into the mountains afterwards. I was for avoiding Harper's Ferry altogether. Shields Green and Mr. Kagi remained silent listeners throughout. It is needless to repeat here what was said, after what has happened. Suffice it, that after all I could say, I saw that my old friend had resolved on his own course and that it was idle to parley. I told him finally that it was impossible for me to join him. I could see Harper's Ferry only as a trap of steel, and ourselves in the wrong side of it. He regretted my decision and we parted.

Thus far, I have spoken exclusively of Capt. Brown. Let me say a word or two of his brave and devoted men, and first of Shields Green. He was a fugitive slave from Charleston, South Carolina, and had attested his love of liberty by escaping from slavery and making his way through many dangers to Rochester, where he had lived in my family, and where he met the man with whom he went to the scaffold. I said to him, as I was about to leave, "Now Shields, you have heard our discussion. If in view of it, you do not wish to stay, you have but to say so, and you can go back with me." He answered, "I b'l'eve I'll go down wid de old man;" and go with him he did, into the fight, and to the gallows, and bore himself as grandly as any of the number. At the moment when Capt. Brown was surrounded, and all chance of escape was cut off, Green was in the mountains and could have made his escape as Osborne Anderson did, but when asked to do so, he made the same answer he did at Chambersburg, "I b'l'eve I'll I go down wid de ole man." When in prison at Charlestown, and he was not allowed to see his old friend, his fidelity to him was in no wise weakened, and no complaint against Brown could be extorted from him by those who talked with him.

If a monument should be erected to the memory of John Brown, as there ought to be, the form and name of Shields Green should have a conspicuous place upon it. It is a remarkable fact, that in this small company of men, but one showed any sign of weakness or regret for what he did or attempted to do. Poor Cook broke down and sought to save his life by representing that he had been deceived, and allured by false promises. But Stephens, Hazlett, and Green went to their doom like the heroes they were, without a murmur, without a regret, believing alike in their captain and their cause.

For the disastrous termination of this invasion, several causes have been assigned. It has been said that Capt. Brown found it necessary to strike before he was ready; that men had promised to join him from the North who failed to arrive; that the cowardly negroes did not rally to his support as he expected, but the true cause as stated by himself, contradicts all these theories, and from his statement there is no appeal. Among the questions put to him by Mr. Vallandingham after his capture were the following: "Did you expect a general uprising of the slaves in case of your success?" To this he answered, "No, sir, nor did I wish it, I expected to gather strength from time to time and then to set them free." "Did you expect to hold possession here until then?" Answer, "Well, probably I had quite a different idea. I do not know as I ought to reveal my plans. I am here wounded and a prisoner because I foolishly permitted myself to be so. You overstate your strength when you suppose I could have been taken if I had not allowed it. I was too tardy after commencing the open attack in delaying my movements through Monday night and up to the time of the arrival of government troops. It was all because of my desire to spare the feelings of my prisoners and their families."

But the question is, Did John Brown fail? He certainly did fail to get out of Harper's Ferry before being beaten down by United States soldiers; he did fail to save his own life, and to lead a liberating army into the mountains of Virginia. But he did not go to Harper's Ferry to save his life. The true question is, Did John Brown draw his sword against slavery and thereby lose his life in vain? and to this I answer ten thousand times, No! No man fails, or can fail who so grandly gives himself and all he has to a righteous cause. No man, who in his hour of ex-tremest need, when on his way to meet an ignominious death, could so forget himself as to stop and kiss a little child, one of the hated race for whom he was about to die, could by any possibility fail. Did John Brown fail? Ask Henry A. Wise in whose house less than two years after, a school for the emancipated slaves was taught. Did John Brown fail? Ask James M. Mason, the author of the inhuman fugitive slave bill, who was cooped up in Fort Warren, as a traitor less than two years from the time that he stood over the prostrate body of John Brown. Did John Brown fail? Ask Clement C. Vallandingham, one other of the inquisitorial party; for he too went down in the tremendous whirlpool created by the powerful hand of this bold invader. If John Brown did not end the war that ended slavery, he did at least begin the war that ended slavery. If we look over the dates, places and men, for which this honor is claimed, we shall find that not Carolina, but Virginia—not Fort Sumter, but Harper's Ferry and the arse-nal—not Col. Anderson, but John Brown, began the war that ended American slavery and made this a free Republic. Until this blow was struck, the prospect for freedom was dim, shadowy and uncertain. The irrepressible conflict was one of words, votes and compromises. When John Brown stretched forth his arm the sky was cleared. The time for compromises was gone—the armed hosts of free-dom stood face to face over the chasm of a broken Union—and the clash of arms was at hand. The South staked all upon getting possession of the Federal Gov-ernment, and failing to do that, drew the sword of rebellion and thus made her own, and not Brown's, the lost cause of the century.

John Brown: An Address by Frederick Douglass at the Fourteenth Anniversary of Storer College, Harper's Ferry, West Virginia, May 30, 1881, Dover, N.H., 1881

THE COLOR LINE

Few evils are less accessible to the force of reason, or more tenacious of life and power, than a long-standing prejudice. It is a moral disorder, which creates the conditions necessary to its own existence, and fortifies itself by refusing all contradiction. It paints a hateful picture according to its own diseased imagination, and distorts the features of the fancied original to suit the portrait. As those who believe in the visibility of ghosts can easily see them, so it is always easy to see repulsive qualities in those we despise and hate.

Prejudice of race has at some time in their history afflicted all nations. "I am more holy than thou" is the boast of races, as well as that of the Pharisee. Long after the Norman invasion and the decline of Norman power, long after the sturdy Saxon had shaken off the dust of his humiliation and was grandly asserting his great qualities in all directions, the descendants of the invaders continued to regard their Saxon brothers as made of coarser clay than themselves, and were not well pleased when one of the former subject race came between the sun and their nobility. Having seen the Saxon a menial, a hostler, and a common drudge, oppressed and dejected for centuries, it was easy to invest him with all sorts of odious peculiarities, and to deny him all manly predicates. Though eight hundred years have passed away since Norman power entered England, and the Saxon has for centuries been giving his learning, his literature, his language, and his laws to the world more successfully than any other people on the globe, men in that country still boast their Norman origin and Norman perfections. This superstition of former greatness serves to fill out the shriveled sides of a meaningless race-pride which holds over after its power has vanished. With a very different lesson from the one this paper is designed to impress, the great Daniel Webster once told the people of Massachusetts (whose prejudices in the particular instance referred to were right) that they "had conquered the sea, and had conquered the land," but that "it remained for them to conquer their prejudices." At one time we are told that the people in some of the towns of Yorkshire cherished a prejudice so strong and violent against strangers and foreigners that one who ventured to pass through their streets would be pelted with stones.

Of all the races and varieties of men which have suffered from this feeling, the colored people of this country have endured most. They can resort to no disguises which will enable them to escape its deadly aim. They carry in front the evidence which marks them for persecution. They stand at the extreme point of difference from the Caucasian race, and their African origin can be instantly recognized, though they may be several removes from the typical African race. They may remonstrate like Shylock—"Hath not a Jew eyes? hath not a Jew hands, organs, dimensions, senses, affections, passions? fed with the same food, hurt with the same weapons, subject to the same diseases, healed by the same means, warmed and cooled by the same summer and winter, as a Christian is?"—but such eloquence is unavailing. They are Negroes—and that is enough, in the eye of this unreasoning prejudice, to justify indignity and violence. In nearly every department of American life they are confronted by this insidious influence. It fills the air. It meets them at the workshop and factory, when they apply for work. It meets them at the church, at the hotel, at the ballot-box, and worst of all, it meets them in the jury-box. Without crime or offense against law or gospel, the colored man is the Jean Valjean of American society. He has escaped from the galleys, and hence all presumptions are against him. The workshop denies him work, and the inn denies him shelter; the ballot-box a fair vote, and the jury-box a fair trial. He has ceased to be the slave of an individual, but has in some sense become the slave of society. He may not now be bought and sold like a beast in the market, but he is the trammeled victim of a prejudice, well calculated to repress his manly ambition, paralyze his energies, and make him a dejected and spiritless man, if not a sullen enemy to society, fit to prey upon life and property and to make trouble generally.

When this evil spirit is judge, jury, and prosecutor, nothing less than overwhelming evidence is sufficient to overcome the force of unfavorable presumptions.

Everything against the person with the hated color is promptly taken for granted; while everything in his favor is received with suspicion and doubt.

A boy of this color is found in his bed tied, mutilated, and bleeding, when forthwith all ordinary experience is set aside, and he is presumed to have been guilty of the outrage upon himself; weeks and months he is kept on trial for the offense, and every effort is made to entangle the poor fellow in the confused meshes of expert testimony (the least trustworthy of all evidence). This same spirit, which promptly assumes everything against us, just as readily denies or explains away everything in our favor. We are not, as a race, even permitted to appropriate the virtues and achievements of our individual representatives. Manliness, capacity, learning, laudable ambition, heroic service, by any of our number, are easily placed to the credit of the superior race. One drop of Teutonic blood is enough to account for all good and great qualities occasionally coupled with a colored skin; and on the other hand, one drop of negro blood, though in the veins of a man of Teutonic whiteness, is enough on which to predicate all offensive and ignoble qualities. In presence of this spirit, if a crime is committed, and the criminal is not positively known, a suspicious-looking colored man is sure to have been seen in the neighborhood. If an unarmed colored man is shot down and dies in his tracks, a jury, under the influence of this spirit, does not hesitate to find the murdered man the real criminal, and the murderer innocent.

Now let us examine this subject a little more closely. It is claimed that this wonder-working prejudice—this moral magic that can change virtue into vice, and innocence to crime; which makes the dead man the murderer, and holds the living homicide harmless—is a natural, instinctive, and invincible attribute of the white race, and one that cannot be eradicated; that even evolution itself cannot carry us beyond or above it. Alas for this poor suffering world (for four-fifths of mankind are colored), if this claim be true! In that case men are forever doomed to injustice, oppression, hate, and strife; and the religious sentiment of the world, with its grand idea of human brotherhood, its "peace on earth and good-will to men," and its golden rule, must be voted a dream, a delusion, and a snare.

But is this color prejudice the natural and inevitable thing it claims to be? If it is so, then it is utterly idle to write against it, preach, pray, or legislate against it, or pass constitutional amendments against it. Nature will have her course, and one might as well preach and pray to a horse against running, to a fish against swimming, or to a bird against flying. Fortunately, however, there is good ground for calling in question this high pretension of a vulgar and wicked prepossession.

If I could talk with all my white fellow-countrymen on this subject, I would say to them, in the language of Scripture: "Come and let us reason together." Now, without being too elementary and formal, it may be stated here that there are at least seven points which candid men will be likely to admit, but which, if admitted, will prove fatal to the popular thought and practice of the times.

First. If what we call prejudice against color be natural, *i.e.*, a part of human nature itself, it follows that it must be co-extensive with human nature, and will and must manifest itself whenever and wherever the two races are brought into contact. It would not vary with either latitude, longitude, or altitude; but like fire and gunpowder, whenever brought together, there would be an explosion of contempt, aversion, and hatred.

Second. If it can be shown that there is anywhere on the globe any considerable country where the contact of the African and the Caucasian is not distinguished by this explosion of race-wrath, there is reason to doubt that the prejudice is an ineradicable part of human nature.

Thirdly. If this so-called natural, instinctive prejudice can be satisfactorily accounted for by facts and considerations wholly apart from the color features of the respective races, thus placing it among the things subject to human volition and control, we may venture to deny the claim set up for it in the name of human nature.

Fourthly. If any considerable number of white people have overcome this prejudice in themselves, have cast it out as an unworthy sentiment, and have survived the operation, the fact shows that this prejudice is not at any rate a vital part of human nature, and may be eliminated from the race without harm.

Fifthly. If this prejudice shall, after all, prove to be, in its essence and in its natural manifestation, simply a prejudice against condition, and not against race or color, and that it disappears when this or that condition is absent, then the argument drawn from the nature of the Caucasian race falls to the ground.

Sixthly. If prejudice of race and color is only natural in the sense that ignorance, superstition, bigotry, and vice are natural, then it has no better defense than they, and should be despised and put away from human relations as an enemy to the peace, good order, and happiness of human society.

Seventhly. If, still further, this aversion to the Negro arises out of the fact that he is as we see him, poor, spiritless, ignorant, and degraded, then whatever is humane, noble, and superior, in the mind of the superior and more fortunate race, will desire that all arbitrary barriers against his manhood, intelligence, and elevation shall be removed, and a fair chance in the race of life be given him.

The first of these propositions does not require discussion. It commends itself to the understanding at once. Natural qualities are common and universal, and do not change essentially on the mountain or in the valley. I come therefore to the second point—the existence of countries where this malignant prejudice, as we know it in America, does not prevail; where character, not color, is the passport to consideration; where the right of the black man to be a man, and a man among men, is not questioned; where he may, without offense, even presume to be a gentleman. That there are such countries in the world there is ample evidence. Intelligent and observing travelers, having no theory to support, men whose testimony would be received without question in respect of any other matter, and should not be questioned in this, tell us that they find no color prejudice in Europe, except among Americans who reside there. In England and on the Continent, the colored man is no more an object of hate than any other person. He mingles with the multitude unquestioned, without offense given or received. During the two years which the writer spent abroad, though he was much in society, and was sometimes in the company of lords and ladies, he does not remember one word, look, or gesture that indicated the slightest aversion to him on account of color. His experience was not in this respect exceptional or singular. Messrs. Remond, Ward, Garnet, Brown, Pennington, Crummell, and Bruce, all of them colored, and some of them black, bear the same testimony. If what these gentlemen say (and it can be corroborated by a thousand witnesses) is true there is no prejudice against color in England, save as it is carried there by Americans—carried there as a moral disease from an infected country. It is American, not European; local, not general; limited, not universal, and must be ascribed to artificial conditions, and not to any fixed and universal law of nature.

The third point is: Can this prejudice against color, as it is called, be accounted for by circumstances outside and independent of race or color? If it can be thus explained, an incubus may be removed from the breasts of both the white and the black people of this country, as well as from that large intermediate population which has sprung up between these alleged irreconcilable extremes. It will help us to see that it is not necessary that the Ethiopian shall change his skin, nor needful that the white man shall change the essential elements of his nature, in order that mutual respect and consideration may exist between the two races.

Now it is easy to explain the conditions outside of race or color from which may spring feelings akin to those which we call prejudice. A man without the ability or the disposition to pay a just debt does not feel at ease in the presence of his creditor. He does not want to meet him on the street, or in the marketplace. Such meeting makes him uncomfortable. He would rather find fault with the bill than pay the debt, and the creditor himself will soon develop in the eyes of the debtor qualities not altogether to his taste.

Some one has well said, we may easily forgive those who injure us, but it is hard to forgive those whom we injure. The greatest injury this side of death, which one human being can inflict on another, is to enslave him, to blot out his personality, degrade his manhood, and sink him to the condition of a beast of burden; and just this has been done here during more than two centuries. No other people under heaven, of whatever type or endowments, could have been so enslaved without falling into contempt and scorn on the part of those enslaving them. Their slavery would itself stamp them with odious features, and give their oppressors arguments in favor of oppression. Besides the long years of wrong and injury inflicted upon the colored race in this country, and the effect of these wrongs upon that race, morally, intellectually, and physically, corrupting their morals, darkening their minds, and twisting their bodies and limbs out of all approach to symmetry, there has been a mountain of gold—uncounted millions of dollars—resting upon them with crushing weight. During all the years of their bondage, the slave master had a direct interest in discrediting the personality of those he held as property. Every man who had a thousand dollars so invested had a thousand reasons for painting the black man as fit only for slavery. Having made him the companion of horses and mules, he naturally sought to justify himself by assuming that the Negro was not much better than a mule. The holders of twenty hundred million dollars' worth of property in human chattels procured the means of influencing press, pulpit, and politician, and through these instrumentalities they belittled our virtues and magnified our vices, and have made us odious in the eyes of the world. Slavery had the power at one time to make and unmake Presidents, to construe the law, dictate the policy, set the fashion in national manners and customs, interpret the Bible, and control the church; and, naturally enough, the old masters set themselves up as much too high as they set the manhood of the Negro too low. Out of the depths of slavery has come this prejudice and this color line. It is broad enough and black enough to explain all the malign influences which assail the newly emancipated millions to-day. In reply to this argument it will perhaps be said that the Negro has no slavery now to contend with, and that having been free during the last sixteen years, he ought by this time to have contradicted the degrading qualities which slavery formerly ascribed to him. All very true as to the letter, but utterly false as to the spirit. Slavery is indeed gone, but its shadow still lingers over the country and poisons more or less the moral atmosphere of all sections of the republic. The money motive for assailing the negro which slavery represented is indeed absent, but love of power and dominion, strengthened by two centuries of irresponsible power, still remains.

Having now shown how slavery created and sustained this prejudice against race and color, and the powerful motive for its creation, the other four points made against it need not be discussed in detail and at length, but may only be referred to in a general way.

If what is called the instinctive aversion of the white race for the colored, when analyzed, is seen to be the same as that which men feel or have felt toward other objects wholly apart from color; if it should be the same as that sometimes exhibited by the haughty and rich to the humble and poor, the same as the Brahmin feels toward the lower caste, the same as the Norman felt toward the Saxon, the same as that cherished by the Turk against Christians, the same as Christians have felt toward the Jews, the same as that which murders a Christian in Wallachia, calls him a "dog" in Constantinople, oppresses and persecutes a Jew in Berlin, hunts down a socialist in St. Petersburg, drives a Hebrew from an hotel at Saratoga, that scorns the Irishman in London, the same as Catholics once felt for Protestants, the same as that which insults, abuses, and kills the Chinaman on the Pacific slope—then may we well enough affirm that this prejudice really has nothing whatever to do with race or color, and that it has its motive and mainspring in some other source with which the mere facts of color and race have nothing to do.

After all, some very well informed and very well meaning people will read what I have now said, and what seems to me so just and reasonable, and will still insist that the color of the Negro has something to do with the feeling entertained toward him; that the white man naturally shudders at the thought of contact with one who is black—that the impulse is one which he can neither resist nor control. Let us see if this conclusion is a sound one. An argument is unsound when it proves too little or too much, or when it proves nothing. If color is an offense, it is so, entirely apart from the manhood it envelops. There must be something in color of itself to kindle rage and inflame hate, and render the white man generally uncomfortable. If the white man were really so constituted that color were, in itself, a torment to him, this grand old earth of ours would be no place for him. Colored objects confront him here at every point of the compass. If he should shrink and shudder every time he sees anything dark, he would have little time for anything else. He would require a colorless world to live in—a world where flowers, fields, and floods should all be of snowy whiteness; where rivers, lakes, and oceans should all be white; where islands, capes, and continents should all be white; where all the men, and women, and children should be white; where all the fish of the sea, all the birds of the air, all the "cattle upon a thousand hills," should be white; where the heavens above and the earth beneath should be white, and where day and night should not be divided by light and darkness, but the world should be one eternal scene of light. In such a white world, the entrance of a black man would be hailed with joy by the inhabitants. Anybody or anything would be welcome that would break the oppressive and tormenting monotony of the all-prevailing white.

In the abstract, there is no prejudice against color. No man shrinks from another because he is clothed in a suit of black, nor offended with his boots because they are black. We are told by those who have resided there that a white man in Africa comes to think that ebony is about the proper color for man. Good old Thomas Whitson—a noble old Quaker—man of rather odd appearance—used to say that even he would be handsome if he could change public opinion.

Aside from the curious contrast to himself, the white child feels nothing on the first sight of a colored man. Curiosity is the only feeling. The office of color in the color line is a very plain and subordinate one. It simply advertises the objects of oppression, insult, and persecution. It is not the maddening liquor, but the black letters on the sign telling the world where it may be had. It is not the hated Quaker, but the broad brim and the plain coat. It is not the hateful Cain, but the mark by which he is known. The color is innocent enough, but things with which it is coupled make it hated. Slavery, ignorance, stupidity, servility, poverty, dependence, are undesirable conditions. When these shall cease to be coupled with color, there will be no color line drawn. It may help in this direction to observe a few of the inconsistencies of the color-line feeling, for it is neither uniform in its operations nor consistent in its principles. Its contradictions in the latter respect would be amusing if the feeling itself were not so deserving of unqualified abhorrence. Our Californian brothers, of Hibernian descent, hate the Chinaman, and kill him, and when asked why they do so, their answer is that a Chinaman is so industrious he will do all the work, and can live by wages upon which other people would starve. When the same people and others are asked why they hate the colored people, the answer is that they are indolent and wasteful, and cannot take care of themselves. Statesmen of the South will tell you that the Negro is too ignorant and stupid properly to exercise the elective franchise, and yet his greatest offense is that he acts with the only party intelligent enough in the eyes of the nation to legislate for the country. In one breath they tell us that the Negro is so weak in intellect, and so destitute of manhood, that he is but the echo of designing white men, and yet in another they will virtually tell you that the Negro is so clear in his moral perceptions, so firm in purpose, so steadfast in his convictions, that he cannot be persuaded by arguments or intimidated by threats, and that nothing but the shot-gun can restrain him from voting for the men and measures he approves. They shrink back in horror from contact with the Negro as a man and a gentleman, but like him very well as a barber, waiter, coachman, or cook. As a slave, he could ride anywhere, side by side with his white master, but as a freeman, he must be thrust into the smoking-car. As a slave, he could go into the first cabin; as a freeman, he was not allowed abaft the wheel. Formerly it was said he was incapable of learning, and at the same time it was a crime against the State for any man to teach him to read. To-day he is said to be originally and permanently inferior to the white race, and yet wild apprehensions are expressed lest six millions of this inferior race will somehow or other manage to rule over thirty-five millions of the superior race. If inconsistency can prove the hollowness of anything, certainly the emptiness of this pretense that color has any terrors is easily shown. The trouble is that most men, and especially mean men, want to have something under them. The rich man would have the poor man, the white would have the black, the Irish would have the Negro, and the Negro must have a dog, if he can get nothing higher in the scale of intelligence to dominate. This feeling is one of the vanities which enlightenment will dispel. A good but simple-minded Abolitionist said to me that he was not ashamed to walk with me down Broadway arm-in-arm, in open daylight, and evidently thought he was saying something that must be very pleasing to my self-importance, but it occurred to me, at the moment, this man does not dream of any reason why I might be ashamed to walk arm-in-arm with him through Broadway in open daylight. Riding in a stage-coach from Concord, New Hampshire, to Vergennes, Vermont, many years ago, I found myself on very pleasant terms with all the passengers through the night, but the morning light came to me as it comes to the stars; I was as Dr. Beecher says he was at the first fire he witnessed, when a bucket of cold water was poured down his back—"the fire was not put out, but he was." The fact is, the higher the colored man rises in the scale of society, the less prejudice does he meet.

The writer has met and mingled freely with the leading great men of his time,—at home and abroad, in public halls and private houses, on the platform and at the fireside,—and can remember no instance when among such men has he been made to feel himself an object of aversion. Men who are really great are too great to be small, This was gloriously true of the late Abraham Lincoln, William H. Seward, Salmon P. Chase, Henry Wilson, John P. Hale, Lewis Tappan, Edmund Quincy, Joshua R. Giddings, Gerrit Smith, and Charles Sumner, and many others among the dead. Good taste will not permit me now to speak of the living, except to say that the number of those who rise superior to prejudice is great and increasing. Let those who wish to see what is to be the future of America, as relates to races and race relations, attend, as I have attended, during the administration of President Hayes, the grand diplomatic reception at the executive mansion, and see there, as I have seen, in its splendid east room the wealth, culture, refinement, and beauty of the nation assembled, and with it the eminent representatives of other nations,—the swarthy Turk with his "fez," the Englishman shining with gold, the German, the Frenchman, the Spaniard, the Japanese, the Chinaman, the Caucasian, the Mongolian, the Sandwich Islander and the Negro,—all moving about freely, each respecting the rights and dignity of the other, and neither receiving nor giving offense.

> "Then let us pray that come it may,
> As come it will for a' that,
> That sense and worth, o'er a' the earth,
> May bear the gree, and a' that
>
> "That man to man, the world o'er,
> Shall brothers be, for a' that."

Frederick Douglass.

The North American Review, vol. CXXXII, June, 1881, pp. 567–577

THE UNITED STATES CANNOT REMAIN HALF-SLAVE AND HALF-FREE, speech on the occasion of the Twenty-First Anniversary of Emancipation in the District of Columbia, April 16, 1883

Friends and Fellow Citizens:

I could have wished that some one from among the younger men of Washington, some one with a mind more fruitful, with a voice more eloquent, with an oratorical ambition more lofty, more active, and more stimulating to high endeavor than mine, had been selected by your Committee of Arrangements, to give suitable utterance to the thoughts, feelings, and purposes, which this 21st anniversary of Emancipation in the District of Columbia is fitted to inspire. That such a one could have been easily found among the aspiring and promising young colored men of Washington, I am happy to know and am proud to affirm. They are the legitimate children of the great act we are met to celebrate. They have been reared in the light of its *new* born freedom, qualified by its education, and by the elevating spirit of liberty, to speak the wise and grateful words befitting the occasion. The presence of one such, as your orator to-night, would be a more brilliant illustration of the wisdom and beneficence of the act of Emancipation, than any words of mine, however well chosen and appropriate. I represent the past, they the present. I represent the downfall of slavery, they the glorious triumphs of liberty. I speak of deliverance from bondage, they speak of concessions to liberty and equality. Their mission begins where my mission ends.

Nevertheless, while I would have gladly given place to one of these rising young men, I could not well decline the duty and the honor of appearing here to-night. It may, after all, be well to have something of the past mingled with the present, well that one who has had some share in the conflict should share also in the public joy of the victory.

At the outset, as an old watchman on the walls of liberty, eagerly scanning the social and political horizon, you naturally ask me, What of the night? It is easy to break forth in joy and thanksgiving for Emancipation in the District of Columbia. It is easy to call up the noble sentiments and the startling events which made that grand measure possible. It is easy to trace the footsteps of the Negro in the past, marked as they are all the way along with blood. But the present occasion calls for something more. How stands the Negro to-day? What are the relations subsisting between him and the powerful people among whom he lives, moves, and has his being? What is the outlook, and what is his probable future?

You will readily perceive that I have raised more questions than I shall be able for the present to answer. My general response to these inquiries is a mixed one. The sky of the American Negro is dark, but not rayless; it is stormy, but not cheerless. The grand old party of liberty, union, and progress, which has been his reliance and refuge so long, though less cohesive and strong than it once was, is still a power and has a future. I give you notice, that while there is a Democratic party there will be a Republican party. As the war for the Union recedes into the misty shadows of the past, and the Negro is no longer needed to assault forts and stop rebel bullets, he is in some sense, of less importance. Peace with the old master class has been war to the Negro. As the one has risen, the other has fallen. The reaction has been sudden, marked, and violent. It has swept the Negro from all the legislative halls of the Southern States, and from those of the Congress of the United States. It has, in many cases, driven him from the ballot box and the jury box. The situation has much in it for serious thought, but nothing to cause despair. Above all the frowning clouds that lower about our horizon, there is the steady light of stars, and the thick clouds that now obscure them, will in due season pass away.

In fact, they are already passing away. Time and events which have done so much for us in the past, will, I trust, not do less for us in the future. The moral government of the universe is on our side, and cooperates, with all honest efforts, to lift up the down-trodden and oppressed in all lands, whether the oppressed be white or black.

In whatever else the Negro may have been a failure, he has, in one respect, been a marked and brilliant success. He has managed by one means or another to make himself one of the most prominent and interesting figures that now attract and hold the attention of the world.

Go where you will, you will meet with him. He is alike present in the study of the learned and thoughtful, and in the play house of the gay and thoughtless. We see him pictured at our street corners, and hear him in the songs of our market places. The low and the vulgar curse him, the snob and the flunky affect to despise him, the mean and the cowardly assault him, because they know that his friends are few, and that they can abuse him with impunity, and with the applause of the coarse and brutal crowd. But, despite of it all, the Negro remains like iron or granite, cool, strong, imperturbable and cheerful.

Men of all lands and languages make him a subject of profound thought and study. To the statesman and philosopher he is an object of intense curiosity. Men want to know more of his character, his qualities, his attainments, his mental possibilities, and his probable destiny. Notwithstanding their black faces, the Jubilee singers, with their wild and plaintive music, thrill and charm the most refined and cultivated of the white race, both here and in Europe. Generous and brave men like Andrew Jackson, Benjamin F. Butler, and General Grant, have borne ample testimony to the courage of the Negro, to his gallantry, and to his patriotism. Of the books, pamphlets, and speeches concerning him, there is literally, no end. He is the one inexhaustible topic of conversation at our firesides and in our public halls.

Great, however, as is his advantage at this point, he is not altogether fortunate after all, as to the manner in which his claims are canvassed. His misfortune is that few men are qualified to discuss him candidly and impartially. They either exalt him too high or rate him too low. Americans can consider almost any other question more calmly and fairly than this one. I know of nothing outside of religion which kindles more wrath, causes wider differences, or gives force and effect to fiercer and more irreconcilable antagonisms.

It was so in the time of slavery, and it is so now. Then, the cause was interest, now, the cause is pride and prejudice. Then, the cause was property. He was then worth twenty hundred millions to his owner. He is now worth uncounted millions to himself. While a slave there was a mountain of gold on his breast to keep him down—now that he is free there is a mountain of prejudice to hold him down.

Let any man now claim for the Negro, or worse still, let the Negro now claim for himself, any right, privilege or immunity which has hitherto been denied him by law or custom, and he will at once open a fountain of bitterness, and call forth overwhelming wrath.

It is his sad lot to live in a land where all presumptions are arrayed against him, unless we except the presumption of inferiority and worthlessness. If his course is downward, he meets very little resistance, but if upward, his way is disputed at every turn of the road. If he comes in rags and in wretchedness, he answers the public demand for a Negro, and provokes no anger, though he may provoke derision, but if he presumes to be a gentleman and a scholar, he is then entirely out of his place. He excites resentment and calls forth stern and bitter opposition. If he offers himself to a builder as a mechanic, to a client as a lawyer, to a patient as a physician, to a university as a professor, or to a department as a clerk, no matter what may be his ability or his attainments, there is a presumption based upon his color or his previous condition, of incompetency, and if he succeeds at all, he has to do so against this most discouraging presumption.

It is a real calamity, in this country, for any man, guilty or not guilty, to be accused of crime, but it is an incomparably greater calamity for any colored man to be so accused. Justice is often painted with bandaged eyes. She is described in forensic eloquence, as utterly blind to wealth or poverty, high or low, white or black, but a mask of iron, however thick, could never blind American justice, when a black man happens to be on trial. Here, even more than elsewhere, he will find all presumptions of law and evidence against him. It is not so much the business of his enemies to prove him guilty, as it is the business of himself to prove his innocence. The reasonable doubt which is usually interposed to have the life and liberty of a white man charged with crime, seldom has any force or effect when a colored man is accused of crime. Indeed, color is a far better protection to the white criminal, than anything else. In certain parts of our country, when any white man wishes to commit a heinous offence, he wisely resorts to burnt cork and blackens his face and goes forth under the similitude of a Negro. When the deed is done, a little soap and water destroys his identity, and he goes unwhipt of justice. Some Negro is at once suspected and brought before the victim of wrong for identification, and there is never much trouble here, for as in the eyes of many white people, all Negroes look alike, and as the man arrested and who sits in the dock in irons is black, he is undoubtedly the criminal.

A still greater misfortune to the Negro is that the press, that engine of omnipotent power, usually tries him in advance of the courts, and when once his case is decided in the newspapers, it is easy for the jury to bring in its verdict of "guilty as indicted."

In many parts of our common country, the action of courts and juries is entirely too slow for the impetuosity of the people's justice. When the black man is accused, the mob takes the law into its own hands, and whips, shoots, stabs, hangs or burns the accused, simply upon the allegation or suspicion of crime. Of such proceedings Southern papers are full. A crime almost unknown to the colored man in the time of slavery seems now, from report, the most common. I do not believe these reports. There are too many reasons for trumping up such charges.

Another feature of the situation is, that this mob violence is seldom rebuked by the press and the pulpit, in its immediate neighborhood. Because the public opinion which sustains and makes possible such outrages, intimidates both press and pulpit.

Besides, nobody expects that those who participate in such mob violence will ever be held answerable to the law, and punished. Of course, judges are not always unjust, nor juries always partial in cases of this class, but I affirm that I have here given you no picture of the fancy, and I have alleged no point incapable of proof, and drawn no line darker or denser than the terrible reality. The situation, my colored fellow citizens, is discouraging, but with all its hardships and horrors, I am neither desperate nor despairing as to the future.

One ground of hope is found in the fact referred to in the beginning, and that is, the discussion concerning the Negro still goes on.

The country in which we live is happily governed by ideas as well as by laws, and no black man need despair while there is an audible and earnest assertion of justice and right on his behalf. He may be riddled with bullets, or roasted over a slow fire by the mob, but his cause cannot be shot or burned or otherwise destroyed. Like the impalpable ghost of the murdered Hamlet, it is immortal. All talk of its being a dead issue is a mistake. It may for a time be buried, but it is not dead. Tariffs, free trade, civil service, and river and harbor bills, may for a time cover it, but it will rise again, and again, and again, with increased life and vigor. Every year adds to the black man's numbers. Every year adds to his wealth and to his intelligence. These will speak for him.

There is a power in numbers, wealth and intelligence, which can never be despised nor defied. All efforts thus far to diminish the Negro's importance as a man and as a member of the American body politic, have failed. We are approaching a momentous canvass. If I do not misread the signs of the times, he will play an important part in the politics of the nation during the next Presidential campaign, and will play it well.

When that crisis shall come, neither of the great political parties will fail to appreciate the influence of his voice and his vote. It would not be strange or surprising, if even the Democratic party should be seized with an appetite of unusual intensity for these colored votes. From present indications, too, I apprehend that his vote will be employed in such manner as to more fully open the gates of progress, and secure for himself a better position among his fellow countrymen than heretofore.

Without putting my head to the ground, I can even now hear the anxious inquiry as to when this discussion of the Negro will cease. When will he cease to be a bone of contention between the two great parties? Speaking for myself I can honestly say I wish it to cease. I long to see the Negro utterly out of the whirlpool of angry political debate. No one will rejoice more heartily than I shall when this consummation is reached. I want the whole American people to unite with the sentiment of their greatest captain, U. S. Grant, and say with him on this subject, "Let us have peace." I need it; you need it; the Negro needs it; and every lover of his country should endeavor to withdraw the Negro from this angry gulf. But it is idle, utterly idle to dream of peace anywhere in this world, while any part of the human family are the victims of marked injustice and oppression.

In America, no less than elsewhere, purity must go before tranquillity. Nations, no more than individuals, can reverse this fundamental and eternal order of human relations. There is no modern Joshua who can command this resplendent orb of popular discussion to stand still. As in the past, so in the future, it will go on. It may be arrested and imprisoned for a while, but no power can permanently restrain it.

If you wish to suppress it, I counsel you, my fellow citizens, to remove its cause. The voice of popular complaint, whether it is heard in this country or in other countries, does not and can not rest upon dreams, visions, or illusions of any kind. There must be solid ground for it.

The demand for Negro rights would have ceased long since but for the existence of a sufficient and substantial cause for its continuance.

Fellow citizens, the present hour is full of admonition and warning. I despise threats, and remembering as I do the depths from which I have come, and the forlorn condition of those for whom I speak, I dare not assume before the American people an air of haughtiness, but on the other hand I can not forget that the Negro is now, and of right ought to be, an American citizen in the fullest sense of the word. This high position, I take it, was not accorded him in sport, mockery or deception. I credit the American people with sincerity.

No matter what the Democratic party may say; no matter what the old master class of the South may say; no matter what the Supreme Court of the United States may say, the fact is beyond question that the loyal American people, in view of the services of the Negro in the national hour of peril, meant to make him, in good faith and according to the letter and spirit of the Constitution of the United States, a full and complete American citizen.

The amendments to the Constitution of the United States mean this, or they are a cruel, scandalous and colossal sham, and deserve to be so branded before the civilized world. What Abraham Lincoln said in respect of the United States is as true of the colored people as of the relations of those States. They can not remain half slave and half free. You must give them all or take from them all. Until this half-and-half condition is ended, there will be just ground of complaint. You will have an aggrieved class, and this discussion will go on. Until the public schools shall cease to be caste schools in every part of our country, this discussion will go on. Until the colored man's pathway to the American ballot box, North and South, shall be as smooth and as safe as the same is for the white citizen, this discussion will go on. Until the colored man's right to practice at the bar of our courts, and sit upon juries, shall be the universal law and practice of the land, this discussion will go on. Until the courts of the country shall grant the colored man a fair trial and a just verdict, this discussion will go on. Until color shall cease to be a bar to equal participation in the offices and honors of the country, this discussion will go on. Until the trades-unions and the workshops of the country shall cease to proscribe the colored man and prevent his children from learning useful trades, this discussion will go on. Until the American people shall make character, and not color, the criterion of respectability, this discussion will go on. Until men like Bishops Payne and Campbell shall cease to be driven from respectable railroad cars at the South, this discussion will go on. In a word, until truth and humanity shall cease to be living ideas, and mankind shall sink back into moral darkness, and the world shall put evil for good, bitter for sweet, and darkness for light, this discussion will go on. Until all humane ideas and civilization shall be banished from the world, this discussion will go on.

There never was a time when this great lesson could be more easily learned than now. Events are transpiring all around us that enforce consideration of the oppressed classes. In one form or another, by one means or another, the ideas of a common humanity against privileged classes, of common rights against special privileges, are now rocking the world. Explosives are heard that rival the earthquake. They are causing despots to tremble, class rule to quail, thrones to shake and oppressive associated wealth to turn pale. It is for America to be wise in time. For the present our institutions are not likely to be shaken by dynamite or daggers. We have free speech and a free press.

"Weapons of war we have cast from the battle." With us there is no apology for violence or crime. Happily we are in a position to win by peaceful means those victories more renowned than any secured by war.

The gates of reason are still open to us; and, while we may speak and vote, we need not despair.

When the nation was in peril; when the country was rent asunder at the center; when rebel armies were in the field, bold, defiant and victorious; when our recruiting sergeants were marching up and down our streets from early morn till late at night, with drum and fife, with banner and badge, footsore and weary;

when the fate of the Republic trembled in the balance, and the hearts of loyal men were failing them for fear; when nearly all hope of subduing the rebellion had vanished, Abraham Lincoln called upon the colored men of this country to reach out their iron arms and clutch with their steel fingers the faltering banner of the Republic; and they rallied, and they rallied, full two hundred thousand strong. Ah! then, my friends, the claims of the Negro found the heart of the nation a little more tender and responsive than now. But I ask Americans to remember that the arms that were needed then may be needed again; and it is best that they do not convert the cheerful and loyal brows of six millions into a black Ireland.

A nation composed of all classes should be governed by no one class exclusively. All should be included, and none excluded. Thus aggrieved classes would be rendered impossible.

The question is sometimes asked, when, where and by whom the Negro was first suspected of having any rights at all? In answer to this inquiry it has been asserted that William Lloyd Garrison originated the anti-slavery movement, that until his voice was raised against the American slave system, the whole world was silent. With all respect to those who make this claim I am compelled to dissent from it. I love and venerate the memory of William Lloyd Garrison. I knew him long and well. He was a grand man, a moral hero, a man whose acquaintance and friendship it was a great privilege to enjoy. While liberty has a friend on earth, and slavery an earnest enemy, his name and his works will be held in profound and grateful memory. To him it was given to formulate and thunder against oppression and slavery the testimonies of all ages. He revived, but did not originate.

It is no disparagement to him to affirm that he was preceded by many other good men whom it would be a pleasure to remember on occasions like this. Benjamin Lundy, an humble Quaker, though not the originator of the anti-slavery movement, was in advance of Mr. Garrison. Walker, a colored man, whose appeal against slavery startled the land like a trump of coming judgment, was before either Mr. Garrison or Mr. Lundy.[1]

Emancipation, without delay, was preached by Dr. Hopkins, of Rhode Island, long before the voice of either Garrison, Lundy or Walker was heard in the land. John Wesley, a hundred years before, had denounced slavery as the sum of all villainies. Adam Clark had done the same. The Society of Friends had abolished slavery among themselves and had borne testimony against the evil, long before the modern anti-slavery movement was inaugurated.

In fact, the rights of the Negro, as a man and a brother, began to be asserted with the earliest American Colonial history, and I derive hope from the fact, that the discussion still goes on, and the claims of the Negro rise higher and higher as the years roll by. Two hundred years of discussion has abated no jot of its power or its vitality. Behind it we have a great cloud of witnesses, going back to the beginning of our country and to the very foundation of our government. Our best men have given their voices and their votes on the right side of it, through all our generations.

It has been fashionable of late years to denounce it as a product of Northern growth, a Yankee device for disturbing and disrupting the bonds of the Union, and the like, but the facts of history are all the other way. The anti-slavery side of the discussion has a Southern rather than a Northern origin.

The first publication in assertion and vindication of any right of the Negro, of which I have any knowledge, was written more than two hundred years ago, by Rev. Morgan Godwin, a missionary of Virginia and Jamaica. This was only a plea for the right of the Negro to baptism and church membership. The last publication of any considerable note, of which I have any knowledge, is a recent article in the *Popular Science Monthly,* by Prof. Gilliam. The distance and difference between these two publications, in point of time, gives us a gauge by which we may in good degree measure the progress of the Negro. The book of Godwin was published in 1680, and the article of Gilliam was published in 1883. The space in time between the two is not greater than the space in morals and enlightenment. The ground taken in respect to the Negro, in the one, is low. The ground taken in respect to the possibilities of the Negro, in the other, is so high as to be somewhat startling, not only to the white man, but also to the black man himself.

The book of Morgan Godwin is a literary curiosity and an ethical wonder.

I deem myself fortunate in being the owner of a copy of it. I met with it while in White Haven, England, thirty-seven years ago. I was then abroad for safety rather than for health, for at that time there was no place of safety for me anywhere under the American flag or on American soil. An Irish Number 1 is safer here now, than I was then. Our Government then had no tenderness for refugees, however innocent of crime, if their skins happened to be slightly tanned or their hair a trifle woolly. But to return to Dr. Godwin and his book. He very evidently was not a Negro worshiper, nor what in our day would be called an abolitionist. He proposed no disturbance of the relation of master and slave. On the contrary, he conceded the right of the master to own and control the body of the Negro, but insisted that the soul of the Negro belonged to the Lord. His able reasoning on this point, it is true, left the Negro for himself neither soul nor body. When he claimed his body, he found that belonged to his earthly master, and when he looked around for his soul, he found that that belonged to his master in Heaven. Nevertheless the ground taken in this book by Dr. Godwin was immensely important. It was, in fact, the starting point, the foundation of all the grand concessions yet made to the claims, the character, the manhood and the dignity of the Negro. In the light of his present acknowledged position among men, here and elsewhere, a book to prove the Negro's right to baptism seems ridiculous, but so it did not seem two hundred years ago. Baptism was then a vital and commanding question, one with which the moral and intellectual giants of that day were required to grapple.

The opposition to baptizing and admitting the Negro to membership in the Christian church, was serious, determined and bitter. That ceremony was, in his case, opposed on many grounds, but especially upon three. First, the Negro's unfitness for baptism; secondly, the nature of the ordinance itself; and thirdly, because it would disturb the relation of master and slave. The wily slaveholders of that day were sharp-eyed and keen-scented, and snuffed danger from afar. They saw in this argument of Godwin the thin edge of the wedge which would sooner or later rend asunder the bonds of slavery. They therefore sought in piety to heaven security for their possessions on earth; in reverence to God contempt for man. They sought in the sacredness of baptism the salvation of slavery.

They contended that this holy ordinance could only be properly administered to free and responsible agents, men, who, in all matters of moral conduct, could exercise the sacred right of choice; and this proposition was very easily defended. For, plainly enough, the Negro did not answer that description. The laws of the land did not even know him as a person. He was simply a piece of property, an article of merchandise, marked and branded as such, and no more fitted to be admitted to the fellowship of the saints than horses, sheep or swine.

When Chief Justice Taney said that Negroes in those early days had no rights which white men felt bound to respect, he only uttered an historical truth. The trouble was that it was uttered for an evil purpose, and made to serve an evil purpose. The slave was solely answerable for his conduct to his earthly master. To thrust baptism and the church between the slave and his master was a dangerous interference with the absolute authority of the master. The slave-holders were always logical. When they assumed that slavery was right, they easily saw that everything inconsistent with slavery was wrong.

But deeper down than any modification of the master's authority, there was a more controlling motive for opposing baptism. Baptism had a legal as well as a religious significance. By the common law at that time, baptism was made a sufficient basis for a legal claim for emancipation. I am informed by Hon. A. B. Hagner, one of the Judges of the Supreme Court of this District, that there is now an old law in the State of Maryland, reversing the common law at this point.

Had I lived in Maryland before that law was enacted, I should have been baptized if I could have gotten anybody to perform the ceremony.

For in that day of Christian simplicity, honest rules of Biblical interpretation were applied. The Bible was thought to mean just what it said. When a heathen ceased to be a heathen and became a Christian, he could no longer be held as a slave. Within the meaning of the accepted word of God it was the heathen, not the Christian, who was to be bought and sold, and held as a bondman forever.

This fact stood like a roaring lion ready to tear and devour any Negro who sought the ordinance of baptism.

In the eyes of the wise and prudent of his times, Dr. Godwin was a dangerous man, a disturber of the peace of the church. Like our ever-faithful friend, Dr. Rankin, he was guilty of pressing religion into an improper interference with secular things, and making mischief generally.

In fact, when viewed relatively, low as was the ground assumed by this good man two hundred years ago, he was as far in advance of his times then as Charles Sumner was when he first took his seat in the United States Senate. What baptism and church membership were for the Negro in the days of Godwin, the ballot and civil rights were for the Negro in the days of Sumner. Though standing two centuries apart these two men are, nevertheless, conspicuous links in the great chain of causes and events which raised the Negro to his present level of freedom in this and other lands. Here, to-night on the twenty-first anniversary of Emancipation in the District of Columbia, the capital of the grandest Republic of freedom on the earth, I kneel at the grave, amid the dust and shadows of bygone centuries, and offer my gratitude, and the gratitude of six millions of my race, to Morgan Godwin, as the grand pioneer of Garrison, Lundy, Goodell, Phillips, Henry Wilson, Gerrit Smith, Joshua R. Giddings, Abraham Lincoln, Thaddeus Stevens, and the illustrious host of great men who have since risen to plead the cause of the Negro against those who would oppress him.

Fellow-citizens—In view of the history now referred to, the low point at which he started in the race of life on this continent, and the many obstacles which had to be surmounted the Negro has reasons to be proud of his progress, if not of his beginning. He is a brilliant illustration of social and anthropological revolution and evolution.

His progress has been steady, vast and wonderful. No people has ever made greater progress under similar conditions. We may trace his rise from Godwin contending for his right to baptism, to Garrison with abolitionism, and later on to Gilliam alarmed at the prospect of Negro supremacy. His progress is marked with three G's, Godwin, Garrison, Gilliam. We see him changed from a heathen to a Christian by Godwin, from a slave to a freeman by Garrison, from a serf to a sovereign by Gilliam.

I am not a disciple of Professor Gilliam, and have neither hope nor fear of black supremacy. I have very little interest in his ethics or his arithmetic. It may or it may not come to pass. Sufficient unto the day is both the evil and the good thereof. A hundred years is a little further down the steps of time than I care to look, for good or for evil.

When father Miller proved by the Bible, from whose pages so many things have been proved, that the world would come to an end in 1843,[2] and proved it so clearly that many began to make their robes in which they were to soar aloft above this burning world, he was asked by a doubting Thomas, "But father Miller, what if it does not come?" "Well," said the good old man, "then we shall wait till it does come."

The colored people of the United States imitate the wisdom of father Miller, and wait. But we should also work while we wait. For after all, our destiny is largely in our own hands. If we find, we shall have to seek. If we succeed in the race of life, it must be by our own energies, and our own exertions. Others may clear the road, but we must go forward, or be left behind in the race of life.

If we remain poor and dependent, the riches of other men will not avail us. If we are ignorant, the intelligence of other men will do but little for us. If we are foolish, the wisdom of other men will not guide us. If we are wasteful of time and money, the economy of other men will only make our destitution the more disgraceful and hurtful. If we are vicious and lawless, the virtues and good behavior of others will not save us from our vices and our crimes.

We are now free, and though we have many of the consequences of our past condition to contend against, by union, effort, co-operation, and by a wise policy in the direction and the employment of our mental, moral, industrial and political powers, it is the faith of my soul, that we can blot out the handwriting of popular prejudice, remove the stumbling blocks left in our way by slavery, rise to an honorable place in the estimation of our fellow-citizens of all classes, and make a comfortable way for ourselves in the world.

I have referred to the vast and wonderful changes which have taken place in the condition of the colored people of this country. We rejoice in those changes to-day, and we do well. We are neither wood nor stone, but men. We possess the sentiments common to right-minded men.

But do we know the history of those vast and marvellous changes and the means by which they were brought about? Do we comprehend the philosophy of our progress? Do we ever think of the time, the thought, the labor, the pain, the self-sacrifice, by which they were accomplished? Have we a just and proper conception of the noble zeal, the inflexible firmness, the heroic courage, and other grand qualities of soul, displayed by the reformers and statesmen through whose exertions these changes in our condition have been brought out and the victory won?

Mr. Williams, in his History of the Negro,[3] tells his readers that it was the dissolution of the Union that abolished slavery. He might as well have told them that Charles Sumner was a slaveholder; that Jeff Davis was an abolitionist; that Abraham Lincoln was disloyal, and that the devil founded the Christian church. Had the Union been dissolved, you and I would not be here this evening. Had the Union been dissolved, the colored people of the South would now be in the hateful chains of slavery. No, no, Mr. Williams, it was not the destruction but the salvation of the Union that saved the slave from slavery and the country to freedom, and the Negro to citizenship.

The abolition of slavery in the District of Columbia was one of the most important events connected with the prosecution of the war for the preservation of the Union, and, as such, is worthy of the marked commemoration we have given it to-day. It was not only a staggering blow to slavery throughout the country, but a killing blow to the rebellion, and was the beginning of the end to both. It placed the National dignity and the National power on the side of emancipation. It was the first step toward a redeemed and regenerated nation. It imparted a moral and human significance to what at first seemed to the outside world, only a sanguinary war for empire.

This great step in National progress, was not taken without a violent struggle in Congress. It required a large share of moral courage, large faith in the power of truth, and confidence in the enlightenment and loyalty of the people, to support this radical measure.

I need not tell you it was bitterly opposed on various grounds by the Democratic members of Congress. To them it was a measure of flagrant bad faith with the slaveholders of the district; and calculated to alienate the border States, and drive them completely into the Confederate States, and make the restoration of the Union impossible. There was much more force in such arguments then than now. The situation was critical. The rebellion was in the fullness of its strength, bold, defiant, victorious, and confident of ultimate success. The great man on horseback had not then become visible along the Western horizon. Sherman had not begun his triumphant march to the sea. But there were moral and intellectual giants in the councils of the Nation at that time. We saw in the Senate Chamber the towering form of the lamented Sumner, the earnest and practical Henry Wilson, the honest and courageous Benjamin F. Wade, the strong and fearless

Zachary Chandler—the man who took the unsuccessful General from the head of the Army of the Potomac. In the House we had an array of brilliant men such as Thaddeus Stevens, Owen Lovejoy and A. G. Riddle, the first to advocate in Congress the arming of the Negro in defence of the Union. There, too, was Thomas D. Elliot, Henry Winter Davis, William D. Kelley, Roscoe Conkling, than whom there has appeared in the Senate of the nation no patriot more pure, no orator more brilliant, no friend to liberty and progress more sincere. I speak all the more freely of him since he is now out of politics and in some sense under the shadow of defeat.[4] I cannot forget that these brave men, and others just as worthy of mention, fully comprehended the demands of the hour, and had the courage and the sagacity to meet those demands. They saw that slavery was the root, the sap, the motive, and mainspring of the rebellion, and that the way to kill the rebellion was to destroy its cause.

Among the great names which should never be forgotten on occasions like this, there is one which should never be spoken but with reverence, gratitude and affection, the one man of all the millions of our countrymen to whom we are more indebted for a United Nation and for American liberty than to any other, and that name is Abraham Lincoln, the greatest statesman that ever presided over the destinies of this Republic. The time is too short, his term of office is too recent to permit or to require extended notice of his statesmanship, or of his moral and mental qualities. We all know Abraham Lincoln by heart. In looking back to the many great men of twenty years ago, we find him the tallest figure of them all. His mission was to close up a chasm opened by an earthquake, and he did it. It was his to call back a bleeding, dying and dismembered nation to life, and he did it. It was his to free his country from the crime, curse and disgrace of slavery, and to lift millions to the plane of humanity, and he did it. Never was statesman surrounded by greater difficulties, and never were difficulties more ably, wisely and firmly met. Friends and fellow-citizens, in conclusion I return to the point from which I started, namely: What is to be the future of the colored people of this country? Some change in their condition seems to be looked for by thoughtful men everywhere; but what that change will be, no one yet has been able with certainty to predict.

Three different solutions to this difficult problem have been given and adopted by different classes of the American people. 1. Colonization in Africa; 2. Extinction through poverty, disease and death; 3. Assimilation and unification with the great body of the American people.

Plainly it is a matter about which no man can be very positive. In scanning the social sky he may fall into mistakes as great as those which vexed the souls of Wiggins and Vennor and other weather prophets. Appearances are deceptive. No man can see the end from the beginning.

It is, however, consoling to think that this limitation upon human foresight has helped us in the past and may help us in the future. Could William the Silent have foreseen the misery and ruin he would bring upon his country by taking up the sword against the Spanish Inquisition, he might have thought the sacrifice too great. Had William Lloyd Garrison foreseen that he would be hated, persecuted, mobbed, imprisoned, and drawn through the streets of his beloved Boston with a halter about his neck, even his courage might have quailed, and the native hue of his resolution been sickled o'er with the pale cast of thought. Could Abraham Lincoln have foreseen the immense cost, the terrible hardship, the awful waste of blood and treasure involved in the effort to retake and repossess the forts and arsenals and other property captured by the Confederate States; could he have foreseen the tears of the widows and orphans, and his own warm blood trickling at the bidding of an assassin's bullet, he might have thought the sacrifice too great.

In every great movement men are prepared by preceding events for those which are to come. We neither know the evil nor the good which may be in store for us. Twenty-five years ago the system of slavery seemed impregnable. Cotton was king, and the civilized world acknowledged his sway. Twenty-five years ago no man could have foreseen that in less than ten years from that time no master would wield a lash and no slave would clank a chain in the United States.

Who at that time dreamed that Negroes would ever be seen as we have seen them to-day marching through the streets of this superb city, the Capital of this great Nation, with eagles on their buttons, muskets on their shoulders and swords by their sides, timing their high footsteps to the Star Spangled Banner and the Red, White and Blue? Who at that time dreamed that colored men would ever sit in the House of Representatives and in the Senate of the United States?

With a knowledge of the events of the last score of years, with a knowledge of the sudden and startling changes which have already come to pass, I am not prepared to say what the future will be.

But I will say that I do not look for colonization either in or out of the United States. Africa is too far off, even if we desired to go there, which we do not. The navy of all the world would not be sufficient to remove our natural increase to that far off country. Removal to any of the territories is out of the question.

We have no business to put ourselves before the bayonets of the white race. We have seen the fate of the Indian. As to extinction, the prospect in that direction has been greatly clouded by the census just taken, in which it is seen that our increase is ten per cent greater than that of the white people of the South.

There is but one destiny, it seems to me, left for us, and that is to make ourselves and be made by others a part of the American people in every sense of the word. Assimilation and not isolation is our true policy and our natural destiny. Unification for us is life: separation is death. We cannot afford to set up for ourselves a separate political party, or adopt for ourselves a political creed apart from the rest of our fellow citizens. Our own interests will be subserved by a generous care for the interests of the Nation at large. All the political, social and literary forces around us tend to unification.

I am the more inclined to accept this solution because I have seen the steps already taken in that direction. The American people have their prejudices, but they have other qualities as well. They easily adapt themselves to inevitable conditions, and all their tendency is to progress, enlightenment and to the universal.

> "It's comin' yet for a' that,
> That man to man the world o'er
> Shall brothers be for a' that."

Address by Hon. Frederick Douglass, delivered in the Congregational Church, Washington, D.C., April 16, 1883, on the Twenty-First Anniversary of Emancipation in the District of Columbia, Washington, D.C., 1883

1. David Walker, a free Negro, was born in Wilmington, North Carolina, September 28, 1785. Before December, 1828, he emigrated to Boston where on September 28, 1829, he issued his revolutionary pamphlet entitled, *Walker's Appeal in Four Articles Together with a Preamble to the Colored Citizens of the World, but in Particular and Very Expressly to Those of the United States of America.* Two other editions were published the following year. Shortly after the appearance of the third edition, Walker died.

2. According to William Miller, at Christ's second coming in 1844, fire would destroy the earth. His adherents, called Adventists or Millerites, believed in Christ's personal, visible return, the necessity for repentance and faith to obtain salvation, a physical resurrection, and a millennium spanning the period between the first and second resurrections.

3. George Washington Williams, *History of the Negro Race in America from 1619 to 1880,* 2 vols., New York 1883.

4. Roscoe Conkling (1829–1888) had led the movement in the Senate to have Douglass' appointment as United States Marshal ratified. He had been a leading advocate of Radical Republican Reconstruction policies.

On May 14, 1881, as a gesture in opposition to President Garfield's appointments which threatened his control over the jobs in the New York custom-house, Conkling resigned his Senate seat, and induced his colleague, Thomas C. Platt, to resign with him. He expected to be reelected by the Albany legislature, but was turned down. For the remainder of his life, Conkling was outside politics.

As financial success came to Douglass it seemed at times that this militant champion of freedom was becoming a cautious conservative. But these were surface manifestations. Douglass understood that the future of the Negro workers was linked with the struggles of the trade unions for better conditions and with those of radical movements that advanced far-reaching changes in the economic system. Douglass repeatedly urged the rising labor movement of the 1880s to lower the barriers against Negro workers and make use of the mighty power of colored labor in its battle for the eight-hour day, higher wages, and better working conditions. Speaking at a Convention of Colored Men at Louisville, Kentucky in September, 1883, he appealed directly to the trade unions to welcome Negro workers into their ranks. [IV:111]

ADDRESS TO THE PEOPLE OF THE UNITED STATES, delivered at a Convention of Colored Men, Louisville, Kentucky, September 25, 1883.

Fellow-Citizens:

Charged with the responsibility and duty of doing what we may to advance the interest and promote the general welfare of a people lately enslaved, and who, though now free, still suffer many of the disadvantages and evils derived from their former condition, not the least among which is the low and unjust estimate entertained of their abilities and possibilities as men, and their value as citizens of the Republic; instructed by these people to make such representations and adopt such measures as in our judgment may help to bring about a better understanding and a more friendly feeling between themselves and their white fellow-citizens, recognizing the great fact as we do, that the relations of the American people and those of civilized nations generally depend more upon prevailing ideas, opinions, and long established usages for their qualities of good and evil than upon courts of law or creeds of religion. Allowing the existence of a magnanimous disposition on your part to listen candidly to an honest appeal for fair play, coming from any class of your fellow-citizens, however humble, who may have, or may think they have, rights to assert or wrongs to redress, the members of this National Convention, chosen from all parts of the United States, representing the thoughts, feelings and purposes of colored men generally, would as one means of advancing the cause committed to them, most respectfully and earnestly ask your attention and favorable consideration to the matters contained in the present paper.

At the outset we very cordially congratulate you upon the altered condition both of ourselves and our common country. Especially do we congratulate you upon the fact that a great reproach, which for two centuries rested on the good name of your country, has been blotted out; that chattel slavery is no longer the burden of the colored man's complaint, and that we now come to rattle no chains, to clank no fetters, to paint no horrors of the old plantation to shock your sensibilities, to humble your pride, excite your pity, or to kindle your indignation. We rejoice also that one of the results of this stupendous revolution in our national history, the Republic which was before divided and weakened between two hostile and irreconcilable interests, has become united and strong; risen to the possibility of the highest civilization; that this change has that from a low plain of life, which bordered upon barbarism, it has started the American Republic on a new departure, full of promise, although it has also brought you and ourselves face to face with problems novel and difficult, destined to impose upon us responsibilities and duties, which, plainly enough, will tax our highest mental and moral ability for their happy solution.

Born on American soil in common with yourselves, deriving our bodies and our minds from its dust, centuries having passed away since our ancestors were torn from the shores of Africa, we, like yourselves, hold ourselves to be in every sense Americans, and that we may, therefore, venture to speak to you in a tone not lower than that which becomes earnest men and American citizens. Having watered your soil with our tears, enriched it with our blood, performed its roughest labor in time of peace, defended it against enemies in time of war, and at all times been loyal and true to its best interests, we deem it no arrogance or presumption to manifest now a common concern with you for its welfare, prosperity, honor and glory.

If the claim thus set up by us be admitted, as we think it ought to be, it may be asked, what propriety or necessity can there be for the Convention, of which we are members? and why are we now addressing you in some sense as suppliants asking for justice and fair play? These questions are not new to us. From the day the call for this Convention went forth this seeming incongruity and contradiction has been brought to our attention. From one quarter or another, sometimes with argument and sometimes without argument, sometimes with seeming pity for our ignorance, and at other times with fierce censure for our depravity, these questions have met us. With apparent surprise, astonishment, and impatience, we have been asked: "What more can the colored people of this country want than they now have, and what more is possible to them?" It is said they were once slaves, they are now free; they were once subjects, they are now sovereigns; they were once outside of all American institutions, they are now inside of all and are a recognized part of the whole American people. Why, then, do they hold Colored National Conventions and thus insist upon keeping up the color line between, themselves and their white fellow-countrymen? We do not deny the pertinence and plausibility of these questions, nor do we shrink from a candid answer to the argument which they are supposed to contain. For we do not forget that they are not only put to us by those who have no sympathy with us, but by many who wish us well, and that in any case they deserve an answer. Before, however, we proceed to answer them, we digress here to say that there is only one element associated with them which excites the least bitterness of feeling in us, or that calls for special rebuke, and that is when they fall from the lips and pens of colored men who suffer with us and ought to know better. A few such men, well known to us and the country, happening to be more fortunate in the possession of wealth, education, and position than their humbler brethren, have found it convenient to chime in with the popular cry against our assembling, on the ground that we have no valid reason for this measure or for any other separate from the whites; that we ought to be satisfied with things as they are. With white men who thus object the case is different and less painful. For them there is a chance for charity. Educated as they are and have been for centuries, taught to look upon colored people as a lower order of humanity than themselves, and as having few rights, if any, above domestic animals, regarding them also through the medium of their beneficent religious creeds and just laws— as if law and practice were identical—some allowance can, and perhaps ought to, be made when they misapprehend our real situation and deny our wants and assume a virtue they do not possess. But no such excuse or apology can be properly framed for men who are in any way identified with us. What may be erroneous in others implies either baseness or imbecility in them. Such men, it seems to us, are either deficient in self-respect or too mean, servile and cowardly to assert the true dignity of their manhood and that of their race. To admit that there are such men among us is a disagreeable and humiliating confession. But in this respect, as in others, we are not without the consolation of company; we are neither alone nor singular in the production of just such characters. All oppressed people have been thus afflicted.

It is one of the most conspicuous evils of caste and oppression, that they inevitably tend to make cowards and serviles of their victims, men ever ready to bend the knee to pride and power that thrift may follow fawning, willing to betray the cause of the many to serve the ends of the few; men who never hesitate to sell a friend when they think they can thereby purchase an enemy. Specimens of this sort may be found everywhere and at all times. There were Northern men with Southern principles in the time of slavery, and Tories in the revolution for independence. There are betrayers and informers to-day in Ireland, ready to kiss the hand that smites them and strike down the arm reached out to save them.

Considering our long subjection to servitude and caste, and the many temptations to which we are exposed to betray our race into the hands of their enemies, the wonder is not that we have so many traitors among us as that we have so few.

The most of our people, to their honor be it said, are remarkably sound and true to each other. To those who think we have no cause to hold this convention, we freely admit that, so far as the organic law of the land is concerned, we have indeed nothing to complain of, to ask or desire. There may be need of legislation, but the organic law is sound.

Happily for us and for the honor of the Republic, the United States Constitution is just, liberal, and friendly. The amendments to that instrument, adopted in the trying times of reconstruction of the Southern States, are a credit to the courage and statesmanship of the leading men of that crisis. These amendments establish freedom and abolish all unfair and invidious discrimination against citizens on account of race and color, so far as law can do so. In their view, citizens are neither black nor white, and all are equals. With this admission and this merited reproof to trimmers and traitors, we again come to the question, Why are we here in this National Convention? To this we answer, first, because there is a power in numbers and in union; because the many are more than the few; because the voice of a whole people, oppressed by a common injustice, is far more likely to command attention and exert an influence on the public mind than the voice of single individuals and isolated organizations; because, coming together from all parts of the country, the members of a National convention have the means of a more comprehensive knowledge of the general situation, and may, therefore, fairly be presumed to conceive more clearly and express more fully and wisely the policy it may be necessary for them to pursue in the premises. Because conventions of the people are in themselves harmless, and when made the means of setting forth grievances, whether real or fancied, they are the safety-valves of the Republic, a wise and safe substitute for violence, dynamite, and all sorts of revolutionary action against the peace and good order of society. If they are held without sufficient reason, that fact will be made manifest in their proceedings, and people will only smile at their weakness and pass on to their usual business without troubling themselves about the empty noise they are able to make. But if held with good cause, and by wise, sober, and earnest men, that fact will be made apparent and the result will be salutary. That good old maxim, which has come down to us from revolutionary times, that error may be safely tolerated, while truth is left free to combat it, applies here. A bad law is all the sooner repealed by being executed, and error is sooner dispelled by exposure than by silence. So much we have deemed it fit to say of conventions generally, because our resort to this measure has been treated by many as if there were something radically wrong in the very idea of a convention. It has been treated as if it were some ghastly, secret conclave, sitting in darkness to devise strife and mischief. The fact is, the only serious feature in the argument against us is the one which respects color. We are asked not only why hold a convention, but, with emphasis, why hold a *colored* convention? Why keep up this odious distinction between citizens of a common country and thus give countenance to the color line? It is argued that, if colored men hold conventions, based upon color, white men may hold white conventions based upon color, and thus keep open the chasm between one and the other class of citizens, and keep alive a prejudice which we profess to deplore. We state the argument against us fairly and forcibly, and will answer it candidly and we hope conclusively. By that answer it will be seen that the force of the objection is, after all, more in sound than in substance. No reasonable man will ever object to white men holding conventions in their own interests, when they are once in our condition and we in theirs, when they are the oppressed and we the oppressors. In point of fact, however, white men are already in convention against us in various ways and at many important points. The practical construction of American life is a convention against us. Human law may know no distinction among men in respect of rights, but human practice may. Examples are painfully abundant.

The border men hate the Indians; the Californian, the Chinaman; the Mohammedan, the Christian, and *vice-versa*. In spite of a common nature and the equality framed into law, this hate works injustice, of which each in their own name and under their own color may justly complain. The apology for observing the color line in the composition of our State and National conventions is in its necessity and in the fact that we must do this or nothing, for if we move our color is recognized and must be. It has its foundation in the exceptional relation we sustain to the white people of the country. A simple statement of our position indicates at once our convention and our cause.

It is our lot to live among a people whose laws, traditions, and prejudices have been against us for centuries, and from these they are not yet free. To assume that they are free from these evils simply because they have changed their laws is to assume what is utterly unreasonable and contrary to facts. Large bodies move slowly. Individuals may be converted on the instant and change their whole course of life. Nations never. Time and events are required for the conversion of nations. Not even the character of a great political organization can be changed by a new platform. It will be the same old snake though in a new skin. Though we have had war, reconstruction and abolition as a nation, we still linger in the shadow and blight of an extinct institution. Though the colored man is no longer subject to be bought and sold, he is still surrounded by an adverse sentiment which fetters all his movements. In his downward course he meets with no resistance, but his course upward is resented and resisted at every step of his progress. If he comes in ignorance, rags, and wretchedness, he conforms to the popular belief of his character, and in that character he is welcome. But if he shall come as a gentleman, a scholar, and a statesman, he is hailed as a contradiction to the national faith concerning his race, and his coming is resented as impudence. In the one case he may provoke contempt and derision, but in the other he is an affront to pride, and provokes malice. Let him do what he will, there is at present, therefore, no escape for him. The color line meets him everywhere, and in a measure shuts him out from all respectable and profitable trades and callings. In spite of all your religion and laws he is a rejected man.

He is rejected by trade unions, of every trade, and refused work while he lives, and burial when he dies, and yet he is asked to forget his color, and forget that which everybody else remembers. If he offers himself to a builder as a mechanic, to a client as a lawyer, to a patient as a physician, to a college as a professor, to a firm as a clerk; to a Government Department as an agent, or an officer, he is sternly met on the color line, and his claim to consideration in some way is disputed on the ground of color.

Not even our churches, whose members profess to follow the despised Nazarene, whose home, when on earth, was among the lowly and despised, have yet conquered this feeling of color madness, and what is true of our churches is also true of our courts of law. Neither is free from this all-pervading atmosphere of color hate. The one describes the Deity as impartial, no respecter of persons, and the other the Goddess of Justice as blindfolded, with sword by her side and scales in her hand held evenly between high and low, rich and poor, white and black, but both are the images of American imagination, rather than American practices.

Taking advantage of the general disposition in this country to impute crime to color, white men *color* their faces to commit crime and wash off the hated color to escape punishment. In many places where the commission of crime is alleged against one of our color, the ordinary processes of the law are set aside as too slow for the impetuous justice of the infuriated populace. They take the law into their own bloody hands and proceed to whip, stab, shoot, hang, or burn the alleged culprit, without the intervention of courts, counsel, judges, juries, or witnesses. In such cases it is not the business of the accusers to prove guilt, but it is for the accused to prove his innocence, a thing hard for any man to do, even in a court of law, and utterly impossible for him to do in these infernal Lynch courts. A man accused, surprised, frightened and captured by a motley crowd, dragged with a rope about his neck in midnight-darkness to the nearest tree, and told in the coarsest terms of profanity to prepare for death, would be more than human if he did not, in his terror-stricken appearance, more confirm suspicion of guilt than the contrary. Worse still, in the presence of such hell-black outrages, the pulpit is usually dumb, and the press in the neighborhood is silent or openly takes side with the mob. There are occasional cases in which white men are lynched, but one sparrow does not make a summer. Every one knows that what is called Lynch law is peculiarly the law for colored people and for nobody else. If there were no other grievance than this horrible and barbarous Lynch law custom, we should be justified in assembling, as we have now done, to expose and denounce it. But this is not all. Even now, after twenty years of so-called emancipation, we are subject to lawless raids of midnight riders, who, with blackened faces, invade our homes and perpetrate the foulest of crimes upon us and our families. This condition of things is too flagrant and notorious to require specifications or proof. Thus in all the relations of life and death we are met by the color line. We cannot ignore it if we would, and ought not if we could. It hunts us at midnight, it denies us accommodation in hotels and justice in the courts; excludes our children from schools, refuses our sons the chance to learn trades, and compels us to pursue only such labor as will bring the least reward. While we recognize the color line as a hurtful force, a mountain barrier to our progress, wounding our bleeding feet with its flinty rocks at every step, we do not despair. We are a hopeful people. This convention is a proof of our faith in you, in reason, in truth and justice—our belief that prejudice, with all its malign accompaniments, may yet be removed by peaceful means; that, assisted by time and events and the growing enlightenment of both races, the color line will ultimately become harmless. When this shall come it will then only be used, as it should be, to distinguish one variety of the human family from another. It will cease to have any civil, political, or moral significance, and colored conventions will then be dispensed with as anachronisms, wholly out of place, but not till then. Do not marvel that we are discouraged. The faith within us has a rational basis, and is confirmed by facts. When we consider how deep-seated this feeling against us is; the long centuries it has been forming; the forces of avarice which have been marshaled to sustain it; how the language and literature of the country have been pervaded with it; how the church, the press, the play-house, and other influences of the country have been arrayed in its support, the progress toward its extinction must be considered vast and wonderful.

If liberty, with us, is yet but a name, our citizenship is but a sham, and our suffrage thus far only a cruel mockery, we may yet congratulate ourselves upon the fact that the laws and institutions of the country are sound, just and liberal. There is hope for a people when their laws are righteous whether for the moment they conform to their requirements or not. But until this nation shall make its practice accord with its Constitution and its righteous laws, it will not do to reproach the colored people of this country with keeping up the color line—for that people would prove themselves scarcely worthy of even theoretical freedom, to say nothing of practical freedom, if they settled down in silent, servile and cowardly submission to their wrongs, from fear of making their color visible. They are bound by every element of manhood to hold conventions in their own name and on their own behalf, to keep their grievances before the people and make every organized protest against the wrongs inflicted upon them within their power. They should scorn the counsels of cowards, and hang their banner on the outer wall. Who would be free, themselves must strike the blow. We do not believe, as we are often told, that the Negro is the ugly child of the national family, and the more he is kept out of sight the better it will be for him. You know that liberty given is never so precious as liberty sought for and fought for. The man outraged is the man to make the outcry. Depend upon it, men will not care much for a people who do not care for themselves. Our meeting here was opposed by some of our members, because it would disturb the peace of the Republican party. The suggestion came from coward lips and misapprehended the character of that party. If the Republican party cannot stand a demand for justice and fair play, it ought to go down. We were men before that party was born, and our manhood is more sacred than any party can be. Parties were made for men, not men for parties.

If the six millions of colored people of this country, armed with the Constitution of the United States, with a million votes of their own to lean upon, and millions of white men at their back, whose hearts are responsive to the claims of humanity, have not sufficient spirit and wisdom to organize and combine to defend themselves from outrage, discrimination, and oppression, it will be idle for them to expect that the Republican party or any other political party will organize and combine for them or care what becomes of them. Men may combine to prevent cruelty to animals, for they are dumb and cannot speak for themselves; but we are men and must speak for ourselves, or we shall not be spoken for at all. We have conventions in America for Ireland, but we should have none if Ireland did not speak for herself. It is because she makes a noise and keeps her cause before the people that other people go to her help. It was the sword of Washington and of Lafayette that gave us Independence. In conclusion upon this color objection, we have to say that we meet here in open daylight. There is nothing sinister about us. The eyes of the nation are upon us. Ten thousand newspapers may tell if they choose of whatever is said and done here. They may commend our wisdom or condemn our folly, precisely as we shall be wise or foolish.

We put ourselves before them as honest men, and ask their judgment upon our work.

THE LABOR QUESTION

Not the least important among the subjects to which we invite your earnest attention is the condition of the labor class at the South. Their cause is one with the labor classes all over the world. The labor unions of the country should not throw away this colored element of strength. Everywhere there is dissatisfaction with the present relation of labor and capital, and to-day no subject wears an aspect more threatening to civilization than the respective claims of capital and labor, landlords and tenants. In what we have to say for our laboring class we expect to have and ought to have the sympathy and support of laboring men everywhere and of every color.

It is a great mistake for any class of laborers to isolate itself and thus weaken the bond of brotherhood between those on whom the burden and hardships of labor fell. The fortunate ones of the earth, who are abundant in land and money and know nothing of the anxious care and pinching poverty of the laboring classes, may be indifferent to the appeal for justice at this point, but the laboring classes cannot afford to be indifferent. What labor everywhere wants, what it ought to have, and will some day demand and receive, is an honest day's pay for an honest day's work. As the laborer becomes more intelligent he will develop what capital he already possesses—that is the power to organize and combine for its own protection. Experience demonstrates that there may be a slavery of wages only a little less galling and crushing in its effects than chattel slavery, and that this slavery of wages must go down with the other.

There is nothing more common now than the remark that the physical condition of the freedmen of the South is immeasurably worse than in the time of slavery; that in respect to food, clothing and shelter they are wretched, miserable and destitute; that they are worse masters to themselves than their old masters were to them. To add insult to injury, the reproach of their condition is charged upon themselves. A grandson of John C. Calhoun, an Arkansas land-owner, testifying the other day before the Senate Committee of Labor and Education,[1] says the "Negroes are so indolent that they fail to take advantage of the opportunities offered them to procure the necessities of life; that there is danger of a war of races," etc., etc.

His testimony proclaims him the grandson of the man whose name he bears. The blame which belongs to his own class he shifts from them to the shoulders of labor. It becomes us to test the truth of that assertion by the light of reason, and by appeals to indisputable facts. Of course the land-owners of the South may be expected to view things differently from the landless. The slaveholders always did look at things a little differently from the slaves, and we therefore insist that, in order that the whole truth shall be brought out, the laborer as well as the capitalist shall be called as witnesses before the Senate Committee of Labor and Education. Experience proves that it takes more than one class of people to tell the whole truth about matters in which they are interested on opposite sides, and we protest against the allowance of only one side of the labor question to be heard by the country in this case. Meanwhile, a little reason and reflection will in some measure bring out truth! The colored people of the South are the laboring people of the South. The labor of a country is the source of its wealth; without the colored laborer to-day the South would be a howling wilderness, given up to bats, owls, wolves, and bears. He was the source of its wealth before the war, and has been the source of its prosperity since the war. He almost alone is visible in her fields, with implements of toil in his hands, and laboriously using them today.

Let us look candidly at the matter. While we see and hear that the South is more prosperous than it ever was before and rapidly recovering from the waste of war, while we read that it raises more cotton, sugar, rice, tobacco, corn, and other valuable products than it ever produced before, how happens it, we sternly ask, that the houses of its laborers are miserable huts, that their clothes are rags, and their food the coarsest and scantiest? How happens it that the land-owner is becoming richer and the laborer poorer?

The implication is irresistible—that where the landlord is prosperous the laborer ought to share his prosperity, and whenever and wherever we find this is not the case there is manifestly wrong somewhere.

This sharp contrast of wealth and poverty, as every thoughtful man knows, can exist only in one way, and from one cause, and that is by one getting more than its proper share of the reward of industry, and the other side getting less, and that in some way labor has been defrauded or otherwise denied of its due proportion, and we think the facts, as well as this philosophy, will support this view in the present case, and do so conclusively. We utterly deny that the colored people of the South are too lazy to work, or that they are indifferent to their physical wants; as already said, they are the workers of that section.

The trouble is not that the colored people of the South are indolent, but that no matter how hard or how persistent may be their industry, they get barely enough for their labor to support life at the very low point at which we find them. We therefore throw off the burden of disgrace and reproach from the laborer where Mr. Calhoun and others of his class would place it, and put it on the land-owner where it belongs. It is the old case over again. The black man does the work and the white man gets the money.

It may be said after all the colored people have themselves to blame for this state of things, because they have not intelligently taken the matter into their own hands and provided a remedy for the evil they suffer.

Some blame may attach at this point. But those who reproach us thus should remember that it is hard for labor, however fortunately and favorably surrounded, to cope with the tremendous power of capital in any contest for higher wages or improved condition. A strike for higher wages is seldom successful, and is often injurious to the strikers; the losses sustained are seldom compensated by the concessions gained. A case in point is the recent strike of the telegraph operators[2]—a more intelligent class can nowhere be found. It was a contest of brains against money, and the want of money compelled intelligence to surrender to wealth.

An empty sack is not easily made to stand upright. The man who has it in his power to say to a man, you must work the land for me for such wages as I choose to give, has a power of slavery over him as real, if not as complete, as he who compels toil under the lash. All that a man hath will he give for his life.

In contemplating the little progress made by the colored people in the acquisition of property in the South, and their present wretched condition, the circumstances of their emancipation should not be forgotten. Measurement in their case should not begin from the height yet to be attained by them, but from the depths whence they have come.

It should be remembered by our severe judges that freedom came to us not from the sober dictates of wisdom, or from any normal condition of things, not as a matter of choice on the part of the land-owners of the South, nor from moral considerations on the part of the North. It was born of battle and of blood. It came across fields of smoke and fire strewn with wounded, bleeding, and dying men. Not from the Heaven of Peace amid the morning stars, but from the hell of war—out of the tempest and whirlwind of warlike passions, mingled with deadly hate and a spirit of revenge; it came, not so much as a boon to us as a blast to the enemy. Those against whom the measure was directed were the land-owners, and they were not angels, but men, and, being men, it was to be expected they would resent the blow. They did resent it, and a part of that resentment unhappily fell upon us.

At first the land-owners drove us out of our old quarters, and told us they did not want us in their fields; that they meant to import German, Irish, and Chinese laborers. But as the passions of the war gradually subsided we were taken back to our old places; but, plainly enough, this change of front was not from choice, but necessity. Feeling themselves somehow or other entitled to our labor without the payment of wages, it was not strange that they should make the hardest bargains for our labor, and get it for as little as possible. For them the contest was easy, their tremendous power and our weakness easily gave them the victory.

Against the voice of Stevens, Sumner, and Wade, and other farseeing statesmen, the Government by whom we were emancipated left us completely in the power of our former owners. They turned us loose to the open sky and left us not a foot of ground from which to get a crust of bread.

It did not do as well by us as Russia did by her serfs, or Pharaoh did by the Hebrews. With freedom Russia gave land and Egypt loaned jewels.

It may have been best to leave us thus to make terms with those whose wrath it had kindled against us. It does not seem right that we should have been so left, but it fully explains our present poverty and wretchedness.

The marvel is not that we are poor in such circumstances, but rather that we were not exterminated. In view of the circumstances, our extermination was confidently predicted. The facts that we still live and have increased in higher ratio than the native white people of the South are proofs of our vitality, and, in some degree, of our industry.

Nor is it to be wondered at that the standard of morals is not higher among us, that respect for the rights of property is not stronger. The power of life and death held over labor which says you shall work for me on my own terms or starve, is a source of crime, as well as poverty.

Weeds do not more naturally spring out of a manure pile than crime out of enforced destitution. Out of the misery of Ireland comes murder, assassination, fire, and sword. The Irish are by nature no worse than other people, and no better. If oppression makes a wise man mad it may do the same, and worse, to a people who are not reputed wise. The woe pronounced upon those who keep back wages of the laborer by fraud is self-acting and self-executing and certain as death. The world is full of warnings.

THE ORDER SYSTEM

No more crafty and effective device for defrauding the southern laborers could be adopted than the one that substitutes orders upon shopkeepers for currency in payment of wages. It has the merit of a show of honesty, while it puts the laborer completely at the mercy of the land-owner and the shopkeeper. He is between the upper and the nether millstones, and is hence ground to dust. It gives the shopkeeper a customer who can trade with no other storekeeper, and thus leaves the latter no motive for fair dealing except his own moral sense, which is never too strong. While the laborer holding the orders is tempted by their worthlessness, as a circulating medium, to get rid of them at any sacrifice, and hence is led into extravagance and consequent destitution.

The merchant puts him off with his poorest commodities at highest prices, and can say to him take these or nothing. Worse still. By this means the laborer is brought into debt, and hence is kept always in the power of the land-owner. When this system is not pursued and land is rented to the freedman, he is charged more for the use of an acre of land for a single year than the land would bring in the market if offered for sale. On such a system of fraud and wrong one might well invoke a bolt from heaven—red with uncommon wrath.

It is said if the colored people do not like the conditions upon which their labor is demanded and secured, let them leave and go elsewhere. A more heartless suggestion never emanated from an oppressor. Having for years paid them in shop orders, utterly worthless outside the shop to which they are directed, without a dollar in their pockets, brought by this crafty process into bondage to the land-owners, who can and would arrest them if they should attempt to leave when they are told to go.

We commend the whole subject to the Senate Committee of Labor and Education, and urge upon that committee the duty to call before it not only the landowners, but the landless laborers of the South, and thus get at the whole truth concerning the labor question of that section.

EDUCATION

On the subject of equal education and educational facilities, mentioned in the call for this convention, we expect little resistance from any quarter. It is everywhere an accepted truth, that in a country governed by the people, like ours, education of the youth of all classes is vital to its welfare, prosperity, and to its existence.

In the light of this unquestioned proposition, the patriot cannot but view with a shudder the widespread and truly alarming illiteracy as revealed by the census of 1880.

The question as to how this evil is to be remedied is an important one. Certain it is that it will not do to trust to the philanthropy of wealthy individuals or benevolent societies to remove it. The states in which this illiteracy prevails either can not or will not provide adequate systems of education for their own youth. But, however this may be, the fact remains that the whole country is directly interested in the education of every child that lives within its borders. The ignorance of any part of the American people so deeply concerns all the rest that there can be no doubt of the right to pass laws compelling the attendance of every child at school. Believing that such is now required and ought to be enacted, we hereby put ourselves on record in favor of stringent laws to this end.

In the presence of this appalling picture, presented by the last census, we hold it to be the imperative duty of Congress to take hold of this important subject, and, without waiting for the States to adopt liberal school systems within their respective jurisdictions, to enter vigorously upon the work of universal education.

The National Government, with its immense resources, can carry the benefits of a sound common-school education to the door of every poor man from Maine to Texas, and to withhold this boon is to neglect the greatest assurance it has of its own perpetuity. As a part of the American people we unite most emphatically with others who have already spoken on this subject, in urging Congress to lay the foundation of a great national system of aid to education at its next session.

In this connection, and as germane to the subject of education under national auspices, we would most respectfully and earnestly request Congress to authorize the appointment of a commission of three or more persons of suitable character and qualifications to ascertain the legal claimants, as far as they can, to a large fund now in the United States treasury, appropriated for the payment of bounties of colored soldiers and sailors; and to provide by law that at the expiration of three or five years the balance remaining in the treasury be distributed among the colored colleges of the country, giving the preference as to amounts to the schools that are doing effective work in industrial branches.

FREEDMEN'S BANK

The colored people have suffered much on account of the failure of the Freedman's bank. Their loss by this institution was a peculiar hardship, coming as it did upon them in the days of their greatest weakness. It is certain that the depositors in this institution were led to believe that as Congress had chartered it and established its headquarters at the capital the government in some way was responsible for the safe keeping of their money.

Without the dissemination of this belief it would never have had the confidence of the people as it did nor have secured such an immense deposit. Nobody authorized to speak for the Government ever corrected this deception, but on the contrary, Congress continued to legislate for the bank as if all that had been claimed for it was true.

Under these circumstances, together with much more that might be said in favor of such a measure, we ask Congress to reimburse the unfortunate victims of that institution, and thus carry hope and give to many fresh encouragement in the battle of life.

BOUNTY AND PENSION LAWS

We desire, also, to call the attention of Congress and the country to the bounty and pension laws and to the filing of original claims. We ask for the passage of an act extending the time for filing original claims beyond the present limit.

This we do for the reason that many of the soldiers and sailors that served in the war of the rebellion and their heirs, and especially colored claimants living in parts of the country where they have but meagre means of information, have been, and still are, ignorant of their rights and the methods of enforcing them.

But while we urge these duties on Congress and the country, we must never forget that any race worth living will live, and whether Congress heeds our request in these and other particulars or not, we must demonstrate our capacity to live by living. We must acquire property and educate the hands and hearts and heads of our children whether we are helped or not. Races that fail to do these things die politically and socially, and are only fit to die.

One great source of independence that has been sought by multitudes of our white fellow-citizens is still open to us—we refer to the public lands in the great West. The amazing rapidity with which the public lands are being taken up warns us that we must lay hold of this opportunity soon, or it will be gone forever. The Government gives to every actual settler, under certain conditions, 160 acres of land. By addressing a letter to the United States Land Office, Washington, D.C., any person will receive full information in regard to this subject. Thousands of white men have settled on these lands with scarcely any money beyond their immediate wants, and in a few years have found themselves the lords of a 160 acre farm. Let us do likewise.

CIVIL RIGHTS

The right of every American citizen to select his own society and invite whom he will to his own parlor and table should be sacredly respected. A man's house is his castle, and he has a right to admit or refuse admission to it as he may please, and defend his house from all intruders even with force, if need be. This right belongs to the humblest not less than the highest, and the exercise of it by any of our citizens toward anybody or class who may presume to intrude, should cause no complaint, for each and all may exercise the same right toward whom he will.

When he quits his home and goes upon the public street, enters a public car or a public house, he has no exclusive right of occupancy. He is only a part of the great public, and while he has the right to walk, ride, and be accommodated with food and shelter in a public conveyance or hotel, he has no exclusive right to say that another citizen, tall or short, black or white, shall not have the same civil treatment with himself. The argument against equal rights at hotels is very improperly put upon the ground that the exercise of such rights, it is insisted, is social equality. But this ground is unreasonable. It is hard to say what social equality is, but it is certain that going into the same street car, hotel, or steamboat cabin does not make any man society for another any more than flying in the same air makes all birds of one feather.

Two men may be seated at the same table at a hotel; one may be a Webster in intellect, and the other a Guiteau[3] in feebleness of mind and morals, and, of course, socially and intellectually, they are as wide apart as are the poles of the moral universe, but their civil rights are the same. The distinction between the two sorts of equality is broad and plain to the understanding of the most limited, and yet, blinded by prejudice, men never cease to confound one with the other, and allow themselves to infringe the civil rights of their fellow-citizens as if those rights were, in some way, in violation of their social rights.

That this denial of rights to us is because of our color, only as color is a badge of condition, is manifest in the fact that no matter how decently dressed or well-behaved a colored man may be, he is denied civil treatment in the ways thus pointed out, unless he comes as a servant. His color, not his character, determines the place he shall hold and the kind of treatment he shall receive. That this is due to a prejudice and has no rational principle under it is seen in the fact that the presence of colored persons in hotels and rail cars is only offensive when they are there as guests and passengers. As servants they are welcome, but as equal citizens they are not. It is also seen in the further fact that nowhere else on the globe, except in the United States, are colored people subject to insult and outrage on account of color. The colored traveler in Europe does not meet it, and we denounce it here as a disgrace to American civilization and American religion and as a violation of the spirit and letter of the Constitution of the United States. From those courts which have solemnly sworn to support the Constitution and that yet treat this provision of it with contempt we appeal to the people, and call upon our friends to remember our civil rights at the ballot-box. On the point of the two equalities we are determined to be understood.

We leave social equality where it should be left, with each individual man and woman. No law can regulate or control it. It is a matter with which governments have nothing whatever to do. Each may choose his own friends and associates without interference or dictation of any.

POLITICAL EQUALITY

Flagrant as have been the outrages committed upon colored citizens in respect to their civil rights, more flagrant, shocking, and scandalous still have been the outrages committed upon our political rights by means of bull-dozing and Kukluxing, Mississippi plans, fraudulent counts, tissue ballots, and the like devices. Three States in which the colored people outnumber the white population are without colored representation and their political voice suppressed.[4] The colored citizens in those States are virtually disfranchised, the Constitution held in utter contempt and its provisions nullified. This has been done in the face of the Republican party and successive Republican administrations.

It was once said by the great O'Connell that the history of Ireland might be traced like a wounded man through a crowd by the blood, and the same may be truly said of the history of the colored voters of the South.

They have marched to the ballot-box in face of gleaming weapons, wounds, and death. They have been abandoned by the Government, and left to the laws of nature. So far as they are concerned, there is no Government or Constitution of the United States.

They are under control of a foul, haggard, and damning conspiracy against reason, law, and constitution. How you can be indifferent, how any leading colored men can allow themselves to be silent in presence of this state of things, we cannot see.

"Should tongues be mute while deeds are wrought which well might shame extremest hell?" And yet they are mute, and condemn our assembling here to speak out in manly tones against the continuance of this infernal reign of terror.

This is no question of party. It is a question of law and government. It is a question whether men shall be protected by law, or be left to the mercy of cyclones of anarchy and bloodshed. It is whether the Government or the mob shall rule this land; whether the promises solemnly made to us in the Constitution be manfully kept or meanly and flagrantly broken. Upon this vital point we ask the whole people of the United States to take notice that whatever of political power we have shall be exerted for no man of any party who will not, in advance of election, promise to use every power given him by the Government, State or National, to make the black man's path to the ballot-box as straight, smooth and safe as that of any other American citizen.

POLITICAL AMBITION

We are as a people often reproached with ambition for political offices and honors. We are not ashamed of this alleged ambition. Our destitution of such ambition would be our real shame. If the six millions and a half of people whom we represent could develop no aspirants to political office and honor under this Government, their mental indifference, barrenness and stolidity might well enough be taken as proof of their unfitness for American citizenship.

It is no crime to seek or hold office. If it were it would take a larger space than that of Noah's Ark to hold the white criminals.

One of the charges against this convention is that it seeks for the colored people a larger share than they now possess in the offices and emoluments of the Government.

We are now significantly reminded by even one of our own members that we are only twenty years out of slavery, and we ought therefore to be modest in our aspirations. Such leaders should remember that men will not be religious when the devil turns preacher.

The inveterate and persistent office-seeker and office-holder should be modest when he preaches that virtue to others which he does not himself practice. Wolsey could tell Cromwell to fling away ambition properly only when he had flung away his own.

We are far from affirming that there may not be too much zeal among colored men in pursuit of political preferment; but the fault is not wholly theirs. They have young men among them noble and true, who are educated and intelligent—fit to engage in enterprise of "pith and moment"—who find themselves shut out from nearly all the avenues of wealth and respectability, and hence they turn their attention to politics. They do so because they can find nothing else. The best cure for the evil is to throw open other avenues and activities to them.

We shall never cease to be a despised and persecuted class while we are known to be excluded by our color from all important positions under the Government.

While we do not make office, the one thing important, nor the one condition of our alliance with any party, and hold that the welfare, prosperity and happiness of our whole country is the true criterion of political action for ourselves and for all men, we can not disguise from ourselves the fact that our persistent exclusion from office as a class is a great wrong, fraught with injury, and ought to be resented and opposed by all reasonable and effective means in our power.

We hold it to be self-evident that no class or color should be the exclusive rulers of this country. If there is such a ruling class, there must of course be a subject class, and when this condition is once established this Government of the people, by the people, and for the people, will have perished from the earth.

Three Addresses on the Relations Subsisting Between the White and Colored People of the United States by Frederick Douglass, Washington, 1886, pp. 3–23

1. See *Report of Senate Committee on Education and Labor,* vol. II, pp. 178–79, 1885.

2. In August, 1883, twelve thousand men and women employed by the Western Union company, dominated by Jay Gould, went on strike for higher wages. In 1870 their wages had been 40 percent higher they were in 1883. The strike continued for several weeks and resulted in a defeat for the strikers.

3. On July 2, 1881, President James A. Garfield was shot by a deranged person named Guiteau who believed that he had a right to some office that had not been given to him. The President died on September 19, 1881.

4. The three states were Mississippi, South Carolina, and Louisiana. In these states registration laws were passed which disfranchised large numbers of Negroes. In South Carolina in 1876, the total vote cast for Presidential electors was 182,776; in 1888 it was only 79,561. In Mississippi it was 164,778 in 1876 and 115,807 in 1888. One student found a reduction in votes cast between 1876 and 1884 of one-half in South Carolina, of one-third in Louisiana and one-quarter in Mississippi, and concluded that by 1900 the Negro vote in the South as a whole had virtually disappeared. (See W. A. Dunning, "The Undoing of Reconstruction," *Atlantic Monthly,* vol. LXXXVIII, pp. 445–46, October, 1901.)

In 1883 . . . the Supreme Court declared unconstitutional the Civil Rights Act of 1875 which had granted equal rights to all citizens on public conveyances on land or sea, at hotels, inns, theaters, and other places of public amusement. . . .

Speaking at a mass indignation meeting at Lincoln Hall in Washington, Douglass denounced the decision as "a further illustration of the reactionary tendencies of public opinion against the black man." . . . [His] forthright address frightened some of his former associates in the anti-slavery movement. "If the colored leaders take to denouncing the Supreme Court," wrote Albert H. Walker, "they will alienate the sympathies of their best friends in the North. . . . If the colored leaders counsel a dignified submission to the inevitable, it will raise their reputation both in the North and in the South. It will show that they are above being bothered by trifles."[1] Douglass had only scorn for such timid advice. [IV:108–109]

THE CIVIL RIGHTS CASE, speech at the Civil Rights Mass-Meeting held at Lincoln Hall, Washington, D.C., October 22, 1883

> *"You take my house when you do take the prop*
> *That doth sustain my house; you take my life,*
> *When you do take the means whereby I live."*

Friends and Fellow-Citizens:

I have only a very few words to say to you this evening, and in order that those few words shall be well-chosen, and not liable to be misunderstood, distorted, or misrepresented, I have been at the pains of writing them out in full. It may be, after all, that the hour calls more loudly for silence than for speech. Later on in this discussion, when we shall have the full text of the recent decision of the Supreme Court before us, and the dissenting opinion of Judge Harlan, who must have weighty reasons for separating from all his associates, and incurring thereby, as he must, an amount of criticism from which even the bravest man might shrink, we may be in better frame of mind, better supplied with facts, and better prepared to speak calmly, correctly, and wisely, than now. The temptation at this time, is of course, to speak more from feeling than reason, more from impulse than reflection.

We have been, as a class, grievously wounded, wounded in the house of our friends, and this wound is too deep and too painful for ordinary measured speech.

> *"When a deed is done for Freedom,*
> *Through the broad earth's aching breast*
> *Runs a thrill of joy prophetic,*
> *Trembling on from east to west."*

But when a deed is done from slavery, caste and oppression, and a blow is struck at human progress, whether so intended or not, the heart of humanity sickens in sorrow and writhes in pain. It makes us feel as if some one were stamping upon the graves of our mothers, or desecrating our sacred temples of worship. Only base men and oppressors can rejoice in a triumph of injustice over the weak and defenceless, for weakness ought itself to protect from assaults of pride, prejudice and power.

The cause which has brought us here to-night is neither common nor trivial. Few events in our national history have surpassed it in magnitude, importance and significance. It has swept over the land like a moral cyclone, leaving moral desolation in its track.

We feel it, as we felt the furious attempt, years ago, to force the accursed system of slavery upon the soil of Kansas, the enactment of the Fugitive Slave Bill, the repeal of the Missouri Compromise, the Dred Scott decision. I look upon it as one more shocking development of that moral weakness in high places which has attended the conflict between the spirit of liberty and the spirit of slavery from the beginning, and I venture to predict that it will be so regarded by after-coming generations.

Far down the ages, when men shall wish to inform themselves as the real state of liberty, law, religion and civilization in the United States at this juncture of our history, they will overhaul the proceedings of the Supreme Court, and read the decision declaring the Civil Rights Bill unconstitutional and void.

From this they will learn more than from many volumes, how far we have advanced, in this year of grace, from barbarism toward civilization.

Fellow-citizens: Among the great evils which now stalk abroad in our land, the one, I think, which most threatens to undermine and destroy the foundations of our free institutions, is the great and apparently increasing want of respect entertained for those to whom are committed the responsibility and the duty of administering our government. On this point, I think all good men must agree, and against this evil I trust you feel, and we feel, the deepest repugnance, and that we will, neither here nor elsewhere, give it the least breath of sympathy or encouragement. We should never forget, that, whatever may be the incidental mistakes or misconduct of rulers, government is better than anarchy, and patient reform is better than violent revolution.

But while I would increase this feeling, and give it the emphasis of a voice from heaven, it must not be allowed to interfere with free speech, honest expression, and fair criticism. To give up this would be to give up liberty, to give up progress, and to consign the nation to moral stagnation, putrefaction, and death.

In the matter of respect for dignitaries, it should never be forgotten, however, that duties are reciprocal, and while the people should frown down every manifestation of levity and contempt for those in power, it is the duty of the possessors of power so to use it as to deserve and to insure respect and reverence.

To come a little nearer to the case now before us. The Supreme Court of the United States, in the exercise of its high and vast constitutional power, has suddenly and unexpectedly decided that the law intended to secure to colored people the civil rights guaranteed to them by the following provision of the Constitution of the United States, is unconstitutional and void. Here it is:

"No State," says the 14th Amendment, "shall make or enforce any law which shall abridge the privileges or immunities of citizens of the United States; nor shall any State deprive any person of life, liberty, or property without due process of law; nor deny any person within its jurisdiction the equal protection of the laws."

Now, when a bill has been discussed for weeks and months, and even years, in the press and on the platform, in Congress and out of Congress; when it has been calmly debated by the clearest heads, and the most skillful and learned lawyers in the land; when every argument against it has been over and over again carefully considered and fairly answered; when its constitutionality has been especially discussed, pro and con; when it has passed the United States House of Representatives, and has been solemnly enacted by the United States Senate, perhaps the most imposing legislative body in the world; when such a bill has been submitted to the Cabinet of the Nation, composed of the ablest men in the land; when it has passed under the scrutinizing eye of the Attorney-General of the United States; when the Executive of the Nation has given to it his name and formal approval; when it has taken its place upon the statute-book, and has remained there for nearly a decade, and the country has largely assented to it, you will agree with me that the reasons for declaring such a law unconstitutional and void, should be strong, irresistible and absolutely conclusive.

Inasmuch as the law in question is a law in favor of liberty and justice, it ought to have had the benefit of any doubt which could arise as to its strict constitutionality. This, I believe, will be the view taken of it, not only by laymen like myself, but by eminent lawyers as well.

All men who have given any thought to the machinery, the structure, and practical operation of our Government, must have recognized the importance of absolute harmony between its various departments of powers and duties. They must have seen clearly the mischievous tendency and danger to the body politic of any antagonisms between its various branches. To feel the force of this thought, we have only to remember the administration of President Johnson, and the conflict which then took place between the National Executive and the National Congress, when the will of the people was again and again met by the Executive veto, and when the country seemed upon the verge of another revolution. No patriot, however bold, can wish for his country a repetition of those gloomy days.

Now let me say here, before I go on a step further in this discussion, if any man has come here to-night with his breast heaving with passion, his heart flooded with acrimony, wishing and expecting to hear violent denunciation of the Supreme Court, on account of this decision, he has mistaken the object of this meeting, and the character of the men by whom it is called.

We neither come to bury Caesar, nor to praise him. The Supreme Court is the autocratic point in our National Government. No monarch in Europe has a power more absolute over the laws, lives and liberties of his people, than that Court has over our laws, lives, and liberties. Its Judges live, and ought to live, an eagle's flight beyond the reach of fear or favor, praise or blame, profit or loss. No vulgar prejudice should touch the members of that Court, anywhere. Their decisions should come down to us like the calm, clear light of Infinite justice. We should be able to think of them and to speak of them with profoundest respect for their wisdom, and deepest reverence for their virtue; for what His Holiness, the Pope, is to the Roman Catholic church, the Supreme Court is to the American State. Its members are men, to be sure, and may not claim infallibility, like the Pope, but they are the Supreme power of the Nation, and their decisions are law.

What will be said here to-night, will be spoken, I trust, more in sorrow than in anger, more in a tone of regret than of bitterness.

We cannot, however, overlook the fact that though not so intended, this decision has inflicted a heavy calamity upon seven millions of the people of this country, and left them naked and defenceless against the action of a malignant, vulgar, and pitiless prejudice.

It presents the United States before the world as a Nation utterly destitute of power to protect the rights of its own citizens upon its own soil.

It can claim service and allegiance, loyalty and life, of them, but it cannot protect them against the most palpable violation of the rights of human nature, rights to secure which, governments are established. It can tax their bread and tax their blood, but has no protecting power for their persons. Its National power extends only to the District of Columbia, and the Territories—where the people have no votes—and where the land has no people. All else is subject to the States. In the name of common sense, I ask, what right have we to call ourselves a Nation, in view of this decision, and this utter destitution of power?

In humiliating the colored people of this country, this decision has humbled the Nation. It gives to a South Carolina, or a Mississippi, Railroad Conductor, more power than it gives to the National Government. He may order the wife of the Chief Justice of the United States into a smoking-car, full of hirsute men and compel her to go and listen to the coarse jests of a vulgar crowd. It gives to a hotel-keeper who may, from a prejudice born of the rebellion, wish to turn her out at midnight into the darkness of the storm, power to compel her to go. In such a case, according to this decision of the Supreme Court, the National Government has no right to interfere. She must take her claim for protection and redress, not to the Nation, but to the State, and when the State, as I understand it, declares there is upon its Statute book, no law for her protection, the function and power of the National Government is exhausted, and she is utterly without redress.

Bad, therefore, as our case is under this decision, the evil principle affirmed by the court is not wholly confined to or spent upon persons of color. The wife of Chief Justice Waite—I speak of respectfully—is protected to-day, not by law, but solely by the accident of her color. So far as the law of the land is concerned, she is in the same condition as that of the humblest colored woman in the Republic. The difference between colored and white, here, is, that the one, by reason of color, needs legal protection, and the other, by reason of color, does not need protection. It is nevertheless true, that manhood is insulted, in both cases. No man can put a chain about the ankle of his fellow man, without at last finding the other end of it fastened about his own neck.

The lesson of all the ages on this point is, that a wrong done to one man, is a wrong done to all men. It may not be felt at the moment, and the evil day may be long delayed, but so sure as there is a moral government of the universe, so sure will the harvest of evil come.

Color prejudice is not the only prejudice against which a Republic like ours should guard. The spirit of caste is dangerous everywhere. There is the prejudice of the rich against the poor, the pride and prejudice of the idle dandy against the hard handed working man. There is, worst of all, religious prejudice; a prejudice which has stained a whole continent with blood. It is, in fact, a spirit infernal, against which every enlightened man should wage perpetual war. Perhaps no class of our fellow citizens has carried this prejudice against color to a point more extreme and dangerous than have our Catholic Irish fellow citizens, and yet no people on the fact of the earth have been more relentlessly persecuted and oppressed on account of race and religion, than the Irish people.

But in Ireland, persecution has at last reached a point where it reacts terribly upon her persecutors. England to-day is reaping the bitter consequences of her injustice and oppression. Ask any man of intelligence to-day, "What is the chief source of England's weakness?" "What has reduced her to the rank of a second-class power?" and the answer will be "*Ireland!*" Poor, ragged, hungry, starving and oppressed as she is, she is strong enough to be a standing menace to the power and glory of England.

Fellow-citizens! We want no black Ireland in America. We want no aggrieved class in America. Strong as we are without the Negro, we are stronger with him than without him. The power and friendship of seven millions of people scattered all over the country, however humble, are not to be despised.

To-day, our Republic sits as a Queen among the nations of the earth. Peace is within her walls of plenteousness within her palaces, but he is a bolder and a far more hopeful man than I am, who will affirm that this peace and prosperity will always last. History repeats itself. What has happened once may happen again.

The Negro, in the Revolution, fought for us and with us. In the war of 1812 Gen. Jackson, at New Orleans, found it necessary to call upon the colored people to assist in its defence against England. Abraham Lincoln found it necessary to call upon the Negro to defend the Union against rebellion, and the Negro responded gallantly in all cases.

Our legislators, our Presidents, and our judges should have a care, lest, by forcing these people outside of law, they destroy that love of country which is needful to the Nation's defense in the day of trouble.

I am not here, in this presence, to discuss the constitutionality or unconstitutionality of this decision of the Supreme Court. The decision may or may not be constitutional. That is a question for lawyers, and not for laymen, and there are lawyers on this platform as learned, able, and eloquent as any who have appeared in this case before the Supreme Court, or as any in the land. To these I leave the exposition of the Constitution; but I claim the right to remark upon a strange and glaring inconsistency with former decisions, in the action of the court on this Civil Rights Bill. It is a new departure, entirely out of the line of the precedents and decisions of the Supreme Court at other times and in other directions where the rights of colored men were concerned. It has utterly ignored and rejected the force and application of object and intention as a rule of interpretation. It has construed the Constitution in defiant disregard of what was the object and intention of the adoption of the Fourteenth Amendment. It has made no account whatever of the intention and purpose of Congress and the President in putting the Civil Rights Bill upon the Statute Book of the Nation. It has seen fit in this case, affecting a weak and much-persecuted people, to be guided by the narrowest and most restricted rules of legal interpretation. It has viewed both the

Constitution and the law with a strict regard to their letter, but without any generous recognition of their broad and liberal spirit. Upon those narrow principles the decision is logical and legal, of course. But what I complain of, and what every lover of liberty in the United States has a right to complain of, is this sudden and causeless reversal of all the great rules of legal interpretation by which this Court was governed in other days, in the construction of the Constitution and of laws respecting colored people.

In the dark days of slavery, this Court, on all occasions, gave the greatest importance to *intention* as a guide to interpretation. The object and *intention* of the law, it was said, must prevail. Everything in favor of slavery and against the Negro was settled by this object and *intention*. The Constitution was construed according to its *intention*. We were over and over again referred to what the framers *meant,* and plain language was sacrificed that the so affirmed *intention* of these framers might be positively asserted. When we said in behalf of the Negro that the Constitution of the United States was intended to establish justice and to secure the blessings of liberty to ourselves and our posterity, we were told that the words said so but that that was obviously not its *intention;* that it was intended to apply only to white people, and that the *intention* must govern.

When we came to that clause of the Constitution which declares that the immigration or importation of such persons as any of the States may see fit to admit shall not be prohibited, and the friends of liberty declared that that provision of the Constitution did not describe the slave-trade, they were told that while its language applied not to slaves, but to persons, still the object and *intention* of that clause of the Constitution was plainly to protect the slave-trade, and that that *intention* was the law. When we came to that clause of the Constitution which declares that "No person held to service or labor in one State, under the laws thereof, escaping into another, shall in consequence of any law or regulation therein be discharged from such service or labor, but shall be delivered up on claim of the party to whom such service or labor may be due," we insisted that it neither described nor applied to slaves; that it applied only to persons owing service and labor; that slaves did not and could not owe service and labor; that this clause of the Constitution said nothing of slaves or the masters of slaves; that it was silent as to slave States or free States; that it was simply a provision to enforce a contract; to discharge an obligation between two persons capable of making a contract, and not to force any man into slavery, for the slave could not owe service or make a contract.

We affirmed that it gave no warrant for what was called the "Fugitive Slave Bill," and we contended that that bill was therefore unconstitutional; but our arguments were laughed to scorn by that Court. We were told that the *intention* of the Constitution was to enable masters to recapture their slaves, and that the law of Ninety-three and the Fugitive Slave Law of 1850 were constitutional.

Fellow-citizens! While slavery was the base line of American society, while it ruled the church and the state, while it was the interpreter of our law and the exponent of our religion, it admitted no quibbling, no narrow rules of legal or scriptural interpretations of Bible or Constitution. It sternly demanded its pound of flesh, no matter how much blood was shed in the taking of it. It was enough for it to be able to show the *intention* to get all it asked in the Courts or out of the Courts. But now slavery is abolished. Its reign was long, dark and bloody. Liberty *now*, is the base line of the Republic. Liberty has supplanted slavery, but I fear it has not supplanted the spirit or power of slavery. Where slavery was strong, liberty is now weak.

O for a Supreme Court of the United States which shall be as true to the claims of humanity as the Supreme Court formerly was to the demands of slavery! When that day comes, as come it will, a Civil Rights Bill will not be declared unconstitutional and void, in utter and flagrant disregard of the objects and *intentions* of the National legislature by which it was enacted, and of the rights plainly secured by the Constitution.

This decision of the Supreme Court admits that the Fourteenth Amendment is a prohibition on the States. It admits that a State shall not abridge the privileges or immunities of citizens of the United States, but commits the seeming absurdity of allowing the people of a State to do what it prohibits the State itself from doing.

It used to be thought that the whole was more than a part; that the greater included the less, and that what was unconstitutional for a State to do was equally unconstitutional for an individual member of a State to do. What is a State, in the absence of the people who compose it? Land, air and water. That is all. As individuals, the people of the State of South Carolina may stamp out the rights of the Negro wherever they please, so long as they do not do so as a State. All the parts can violate the Constitution, but the whole cannot. It is not the act itself, according to this decision, that is unconstitutional. The unconstitutionality of the case depends wholly upon the party committing the act. If the State commits it, it is wrong, if the citizen of the State commits it, it is right.

O consistency, thou art indeed a jewel! What does it matter to a colored citizen that a State may not insult and outrage him, if a citizen of a State may? The effect upon him is the same, and it was just this effect that the framers of the Fourteenth Amendment plainly intended by that article to prevent.

It was the act, not the instrument, which was prohibited. It meant to protect the newly enfranchised citizen from injustice and wrong, not merely from a State, but from the individual members of a State. It meant to give him the protection to which his citizenship, his loyalty, his allegiance, and his services entitled him, and this meaning, and this purpose, and this intention, is now declared unconstitutional and void, by the Supreme Court of the United States.

I say again, fellow-citizens, O for a Supreme Court which shall be as true, as vigilant, as active, and exacting in maintaining laws enacted for the protection of human rights as in other days was that Court for the destruction of human rights!

It is said that this decision will make no difference in the treatment of colored people; that the Civil Rights Bill was a dead letter, and could not be enforced. There is some truth in all this, but it is not the whole truth. That bill, like all advance legislation, was a banner on the outer wall of American liberty, a noble moral standard, uplifted for the education of the American people. There are tongues in trees, books, in the running brooks,—sermons in stones. This law, though dead, did speak. It expressed the sentiment of justice and fair play, common to every honest heart. Its voice was against popular prejudice and meanness. It appealed to all the noble and patriotic instincts of the American people. It told the American people that they were all equal before the law; that they belonged to a common country and were equal citizens. The Supreme Court has hauled down this flag of liberty in open day, and before all the people, and has thereby given joy to the heart of every man in the land who wishes to deny to others what he claims for himself. It is a concession to race pride, selfishness and meanness, and will be received with joy by every upholder of caste in the land, and for this I deplore and denounce that decision.

It is a frequent and favorite device of an indefensible cause to misstate and pervert the views of those who advocate a good cause, and I have never seen this device more generally resorted to than in the case of the late decision on the Civil Rights Bill. When we dissent from the opinion of the Supreme Court, and give the reasons why we think that opinion unsound, we are straightway charged in the papers with denouncing the Court itself, and thus put in the attitude of bad citizens. Now, I utterly deny that there has ever been any denunciation of the Supreme Court on this platform, and I defy any man to point out one sentence or one syllable of any speech of mine in denunciation of that Court.

Another illustration of this tendency to put opponents in a false position, is seen in the persistent effort to stigmatize the "Civil Rights Bill" as a "Social Rights Bill." Now, nowhere under the whole heavens, outside of the United States, could any such perversion of truth have any chance of success. No man in Europe would ever dream that because he has a right to ride on a railway, or stop at a hotel, he therefore has the right to enter into social relations with anybody. No one has a right to speak to another without that other's permission. Social equality and civil equality rest upon an entirely different basis, and well enough the American people know it;. yet to inflame a popular prejudice, respectable papers like the New York *Times* and the Chicago *Tribune,* persist in describing the Civil Rights Bill as a Social Rights Bill.

When a colored man is in the same room or in the same carriage with white people, as a servant, there is no talk of social equality, but if he is there as a man and a gentleman, he is an offence. What makes the difference? It is not color, for his color is unchanged. The whole essence of the thing is a studied purpose to degrade and stamp out the liberties of a race. It is the old spirit of slavery, and nothing else. To say that because a man rides in the same car with another, he is therefore socially equal, is one of the wildest absurdities.

When I was in England, some years ago, I rode upon highways, byways, steamboats, stage coaches, omnibuses; I was in the House of Commons, in the House of Lords, in the British Museum, in the Coliseum, in the National Gallery, everywhere; sleeping sometimes in rooms where lords and dukes had slept; sitting at tables where lords and dukes were sitting; but I never thought that those circumstances made me socially the equal of lords and dukes. I hardly think that some of our Democratic friends would be regarded among those lords as their equals. If riding in the same car makes one equal, I think that the little poodle I saw sitting in the lap of a lady was made equal by riding in the same car. Equality, social equality, is a matter between individuals. It is a reciprocal understanding. I don't think when I ride with an educated polished rascal, that he is thereby made my equal, or when I ride with a numbskull that it makes me his equal, or makes him my equal. Social equality does not necessarily follow from civil equality, and yet for the purpose of a hell black and damning prejudice, our papers still insist that the Civil Rights Bill is a Bill to establish social equality.

If it is a Bill for social equality, so is the Declaration of Independence, which declares that all men have equal rights; so is the Sermon on the Mount, so is the Golden Rule, that commands us to do to others as we would that others should do to us; so is the Apostolic teaching, that of one blood God has made all nations to dwell on all the face of the earth; so is the Constitution of the United States, and so are the laws and customs of every civilized country in the world; for no where, outside of the United States is any man denied civil rights on account of his color.

Proceedings of the Civil Rights Mass-Meeting held at Lincoln Hall, October 22, 1883 . . ., Washington, D.C., 1883

1. Albert H. Walker to Douglass, Oct. 19, 1883, Frederick Douglass Papers, Frederick Douglass Memorial Home, Anacostia, D.C.

2. In 1883, five cases involving the constitutionality of the Civil Rights Act of 1875 were decided by the Supreme Court. Two of them concerned the rights of colored persons in inns and hotels; two, their rights in theatres; and one, in railroad cars. The Court ruled that the first and second sections of the Civil Rights Act were unconstitutional and held that the denial of privileges on public conveyances, theatres, restaurants, etc., was not an indication of slavery or involuntary servitude; that the Fourteenth Amendment applies to states, not to individuals; that no law had been made by a state abridging rights or denying equal privileges to citizens of the United States, and that the acts complained of were committed by individuals, hence the cases did not come within the meaning of the Fourteenth Amendment.

Justice John Marshall Harlan dissented strongly in the Civil Rights cases, maintaining that protection of the Negro against discrimination by individuals was intended by the framers of the Fourteenth Amendment. He argued that the majority was wrong in claiming that the laws segregating the Negro in public places did not deny him the equal protection of the law.

In January, 1884, eighteen months after Anna Douglass' death, Douglass married Helen Pitts, a college-trained white woman of forty-six who had been his secretary in the recorder's office. Her relatives opposed the marriage, but Helen was not persuaded by their arguments. "Love came to me," she said later, "and I was not afraid to marry the man I loved because of his color."[1]

Two hours after the wedding, the news of the marriage became public. Immediately a storm descended upon the happy couple. The overwhelming majority of the Negroes were bitter and felt betrayed by their leader. Some charged that Douglass had shown "contempt for the women of his own race," while others denounced him for having "married a common, poor white woman."[2]

White people responded too. The *Gazette* of Franklin, Virginia, called Douglass "a lecherous old African Solomon." A correspondent from Atlanta wrote Reverend Francis J. Grimké who had performed the marriage ceremony that he "ought to be damned out of Society." A "Little Tar and Fetters [*sic*] would be good for you," he added.[3]

But there were letters of congratulations also both from Negroes and whites. H. W. Gilbert, an old friend, expressed "great joy that you have taken for a wife a lady [of] so firm accomplishment and one who will make happy your remaining years." Elizabeth Cady Stanton denounced "the clamor" raised against the marriage. Julia Griffiths Crofts hastened to send congratulations from England and "to express the hope that the step you have now taken may tend to promote your true happiness in the evening of your days." One correspondent was convinced that though the marriage had "startled the public . . . it has set it to thinking, and a happy result of your union will do more to harmonize the 'races,' than all constitutional amendments, civil rights laws and judicial decisions."[4]

Douglass had a ready answer to the criticisms of his second marriage. He would laughingly remark that it proved that he was quite impartial—his first wife "was the color of my mother, and the second, the color of my father." In a more serious vein, he pointed out that his marriage was in keeping with his entire philosophy of life. He had always insisted that the question of color was an artificial issue raised to justify and continue the degradation of the Negro people, that men and women "no matter of what race or complexion" should "be allowed to enjoy the rights of a common nature" which included the right to obey the conviction of their own minds and hearts in marriage. He had always viewed with scorn the clamor raised against amalgamation of the races. "For 200 years and more in slavery and outside of marriage," he wrote in the 'eighties, "amalgamation went on under the fostering care of church, pulpit, press, and American statesmanship with only here and there a voice, and that a hated and despised voice, raised against it. But now that the Negro is free, and has been invested with political and civil rights, sounds of alarm reach us from all quarters." The existence of quadroons and mulattoes all over the South was sufficient proof to Douglass that the outcry against the intermarriage of Negroes and whites was pure hypocrisy.[5] [IV:115–116]

TO ELIZABETH CADY STANTON

Washington, D.C., May 30, 1884

My dear Mrs. Stanton:

I am very glad to find, as I do find by your kind good letter, that I have made no mistake in respect of your feeling concerning my marriage. I have known you and your love of liberty so long and well, that without one word from you on the subject, I had recorded your word and vote against the clamor raised against my marriage to a white woman. To those who find fault with me on this account I have no apology to make. My wife and I have simply obeyed the convictions of our own minds and hearts in a matter wherein we alone were concerned and about which nobody has any right to interfere. I could never have been at peace with my own soul or held up my head among men had I allowed the fear of popular clamor to deter me from following my convictions as to this marriage. I should have gone to my grave a self-accused and a self-convicted moral coward. Much as I respect the good opinion of my fellow men, I do not wish it at expense of my own self-respect. Circumstances have during the last forty years thrown me much more into white society than in that of colored people. While true to the rights of the colored race my nearest personal friends owing to association and common sympathy and aims have been white people and as men choose wives from friends and associates, it is not strange that I have so chosen my wife and that she has chosen me. You, Dear Mrs. Stanton, could have found a straight smooth and pleasant road through the world had you allowed the world to decide for you your sphere in life, that is had you allowed it to sink your moral and intellectual individuality into nonentity. But you have nobly asserted your own and the rights of your sex, and the world will know hereafter that you have lived and worked beneficently in the world.

You have made both Mrs. Douglass and myself very glad and happy by your letter and we both give you our warmest thanks for it. Helen is a braver woman than I am a man and bears the assaults of popular prejudice more serenely that I do. No sigh or complaint escapes her. She is steady, firm and strong and meets the gaze of the world with a tranquil heart and unruffled bow. I am amazed by her heroic bearing, and I am greatly strengthened by it. She has sometimes said she would not regret though the storm of opposition were ten times greater.

I would like to write you a long letter, but must be off to the Chicago Convention and must leave this to be folded and directed by Helen. How good it is to have a wife who can read and write, and who can as Margaret Fuller says cover one in all his range.

Very truly yours,
Frederick Douglass

Elizabeth Cady Stanton Manuscripts, Library of Congress

1. Washington *Post,* May 30, 1897. The Detroit *Free Press* of May 4, 1886, carried the following report from its Washington correspondent: "Mrs. Douglass' father has never been reconciled to her marriage, but her mother and sister who were deeply grieved at the time have recently visited her. Her uncle's family who have resided here for years have not forgiven her and hold no intercourse with her in any way."

2. Francis J. Grimké, "The Second Marriage of Frederick Douglass," *Journal of Negro History,* vol. XIX, July, 1834, p. 325.

3. Franklin, Virginia, *Gazette,* Feb. 1, 1884, scrapbook in Frederick Douglass Papers, Frederick Douglass Memorial Home, Anacostia, D.C.; Carter G. Woodson, ed., *The Works of Francis J. Grimké,* 4 vols., Washington, 1942, vol. IV, p. 1.

4. H. W. Gilbert to Douglass, June 25, 1884; Julia G. Crofts to Douglass, Feb. 11, 1884; Samuel Yorke Atlee to Douglass, Jan. 26, 1884, Frederick Douglass Papers, Frederick Douglass Memorial Home, Anacostia, D.C.
See also Cornelia D. Adams, Jan. 25; S. E. and Helen Shevitch, Jan. 25; George L. Ruffin, Jan. 26; H. B. Nordstrom, Jan. 26; John W. Ewing, Jan. 29; Elizabeth P. Peabody, Feb. 1; Mrs. W. H. Williams, March 18, 1884, Ibid.

5. Undated letter to anonymous, Frederick Douglass *Mss.,* Frederick Douglass Memorial Home, Anacostia, D. C.; *Douglass' Monthly,* September, 1862.

TO FRANCIS J. GRIMKÉ

Washington, D.C., Jan. 19, 1886.

My dear Mr. Grimké:

. . . In regard to the cause of the colored people of this country I am feeling as deeply concerned for the future as ever. Violence and crime seem to run riot, and the press here appear to delight in parading our offenses whenever committed or charged before the people of the Capital, thus strengthening opinion and sentiment against us as a class while our colored people instead of doing what they might to stem the torrents are engaged in discussing the question as to which party is likely to give the colored people the most offices and whether your humble servant should be removed from his office to be succeeded by they know not whom. Of course, I do not believe the half of all the charges brought against colored men. I do believe that many have suffered death for alleged crimes of which they are not guilty. The prevalence of Lynch Law is itself an evidence of the innocence of many of the victims, for, if the evidence were sufficient to convict, there would be no fear that alleged culprits would not be convicted and punished.

The political condition is not less deplorable than our civil conditions. With seven millions of people we ought to be able and would be able to command and compel justice from both parties. The Irish party in England[1] is just now in a position that we ought to occupy here. That party has now both the Tory and the Liberal party at its feet, not daring to touch Ireland without consulting the wishes of the Irish leaders. Alas, our leaders have no followers, and hence are in no just sense leaders. I am looking for the consolation of Israel—that some great man will arise and do for us in this new emergency what was done against our slavery. I am consoled with the thought that God reigns in eternity—and that deliverance will yet finally come. I am writing from my office or I am sure that Mrs. D. would write with me in affectionate remembrance to you and Mrs. Grimké.

Yours sincerely,
Fred'k Douglass

Carter G. Woodson, ed. *The Words of Francis J. Grimké*, Washington, 1942, vol. IV, pp. 2–3

1. In 1870 Isaac Butt founded the Irish Home League, and four years later he became the leader of a Home Rule Party in the House of Commons. In 1880 Charles Stewart Parnell became the leader of the Home Rule Party. He allied the Irish Party to neither of the great English parties but aimed at holding the balance of power between the Conservatives and the Liberals, demanding as a price for the Irish vote a pledge to introduce Home Rule. From this time on the Irish Question could no longer be treated with contempt by the leading politicians.

SOUTHERN BARBARISM, speech on the occasion of the Twenty-Fourth Anniversary of Emancipation in the District of Columbia, Washington, D.C., April 16, 1886

... Fellow-citizens, while I gratefully remember the important services of the Republican party in emancipating and enfranchising the colored people of the United States, I do not forget that the work of that party is most sadly incomplete. We are yet, as a people, only half free. The promise of liberty remains unfulfilled. We stand to-day only in the twilight of American liberty. The sunbeams of perfect day are still behind the mountains, and the mission of the Republican party will not be ended until the persons, the property, and the ballot of the colored man, shall be as well protected in every State of the American Union as are such rights in the case of the white man. The Republican party is not perfect. It is cautious even to the point of timidity; but it is, nevertheless, the best political force and friend we have.

And now I return to the point at which I commenced these remarks. I have spoken to you of the adoption of the Constitution of the United States and of the national progress and prosperity under that instrument; I have called your attention to the noble objects announced in the preamble of the Constitution. I did not stop then and there to inquire how far those objects, so solemnly proclaimed to the world, and so often sworn to, have been attained, or to point out how far they have been practically disregarded and abandoned by the Government ordained to practically carry them out. I now undertake to say that neither the Constitution of 1789, nor the Constitution as amended since the war, is the law of the land. That Constitution has been slain in the house of its friends. So far as the colored people of the country are concerned, the Constitution is but a stupendous sham, a rope of sand, a Dead Sea apple, fair without and foul within, keeping the promise to the eye and breaking it to the heart. The Federal Government, so far as we are concerned, has abdicated its functions and abandoned the objects for which the Constitution was framed and adopted, and for this I arraign it at the bar of public opinion, both of our country and that of the civilized world. I am here to tell the truth, and to tell it without fear or favor, and the truth is that neither the Republican party nor the Democratic party has yet complied with the solemn oath, taken by their respective representatives, to support the Constitution, and execute the laws enacted under its provisions. They have promised us law, and abandoned us to anarchy; they have promised protection, and given us violence; they have promised us fish, and given us a serpent. A vital and fundamental object which they have sworn to realize to the best of their ability, is the establishment of justice. This is one of the six fundamental objects for which the Constitution was ordained; but when, where, and how has any attempt been made by the Federal Government to enforce or establish justice in any one of the late slave-holding States? Has any one of our Republican Presidents, since Grant, earnestly endeavored to establish justice in the South? According to the highest legal authorities, justice is the perpetual disposition to secure to every man, by due process of law, protection to his person, his property and his political rights. "Due process of law" has a definite and legal meaning. It means the right to be tried in open court by a jury of one's peers, and before an impartial judge. It means that the accused shall be brought face to face with his accusers; that he shall be allowed to call witnesses in his defence, and that he shall have the assistance of counsel; it means that, preceding his trial, he shall be safe in the custody of the Government, and that no harm shall come to him for any alleged offence till he is fairly tried, convicted, and sentenced by the court. This protection is given to the vilest white criminal in the land. He cannot be convicted while there is even a reasonable doubt in the minds of the jury as to his guilt. But to the colored man accused of crime in the Southern States, a different rule is almost everywhere applied. With him, to be accused is to be convicted. The court in which he is tried is a lynching mob. This mob takes the place of "due process of law," of judge, jury, witness, and counsel. It does not come to ascertain the guilt or innocence of the accused, but to hang, shoot, stab, burn, or whip him to death. Neither courts, jails, nor marshals are allowed to protect him. Every day brings us tidings of these outrages. I will not stop to detail individual instances. Their name is legion. Everybody knows that what I say is true, and that no power is employed by the Government to prevent this lawless violence. Yet our chief magistrates and other officers, Democratic and Republican, continue to go through the solemn mockery, the empty form of swearing by the name of Almighty God that they will execute the laws and the Constitution; that they will establish justice, insure domestic tranquility, and secure the blessings of liberty to ourselves and to our posterity.

Only a few weeks ago, at Carrolton Court-house, Mississippi, in the absence of all political excitement, while the Government of the nation, as well as the government of the Southern States, was safely in the hands of the Democratic party; when, there was no pending election, and no pretence of a fear of possible Negro supremacy, one hundred white citizens, on horseback, armed to the teeth, deliberately assembled and in cold blood opened a deadly fire upon a party of peaceable, unarmed colored men, killing eleven of them on the spot, and mortally wounding nine others, most of whom have since died. The sad thing is that, in the average American mind, horrors of this character have become so frequent since the slaveholding rebellion that they excite neither shame nor surprise; neither pity for the slain, nor indignation for the slayers. It is the old story verified:

> "Vice is a monster of such frightful mien
> That, to be hated, needs but to be seen;
> But seen too oft, familiar with its face,
> We first endure, then pity, then embrace."

It is said that those who live on the banks of Niagara neither hear its thunder nor shudder at its overwhelming power. In any other country such a frightful crime as the Carrolton massacre—in any other country than this a scream would have gone up from all quarters of the land for the arrest and punishment of these cold-blooded murderers. But alas! nothing like this has happened here. We are used to the shedding of innocent blood, and the heart of this nation is torpid, if not dead, to the natural claims of justice and humanity where the victims are of the colored race. Where are the sworn ministers of the law? Where are the guardians of public justice?

Where are the defenders of the Constitution? What hand in House or Senate; what voice in court or Cabinet is uplifted to stay this tide of violence, blood, and barbarism? Neither governors, presidents, nor statesmen, have yet declared that these barbarities shall be stopped. On the contrary, they all confess themselves powerless to protect our class; and thus you and I and all of us are struck down, and bloody treason flourishes over us. In view of this confessed impotency of the Government and this apparent insensibility of the nation to the claims of humanity, do you ask me why I expend my time and breath in denouncing these wholesale murders when there is no seeming prospect of a favorable response? I answer in turn, how can you, how can any man with a heart in his breast do otherwise when, louder than the blood of Abel, the blood of his fellow-men cries from the ground?

> *"Shall tongues be mute when deeds are wrought*
> *Which well might shame extremest hell?*
> *Shall freeman lock the indignant thought?*
> *Shall mercy's bosom cease to swell?*
> *Shall honor bleed, shall truth succumb,*
> *Shall pen, and press, and soul be dumb?*
> *By all around, above, below,*
> *Be ours the indignant answer, No!"*

In a former address, delivered on the occasion of this anniversary, I was at the pains of showing that much of the crime attributed to colored people, and for which they were held responsible, imprisoned, and murdered, was, in fact, committed by white men disguised as Negroes. I affirm that all presumptions in courts of law and in the community were against the, Negro, and that color was the safest disguise a white man could assume in which to commit crime; that all he had to do to commit the worst crimes with impunity was to blacken his face and take on the similitude of a Negro but even this disguise sometimes fails. Only a few days ago a Mr. J. H. Justice, an eminent citizen of Granger county, Tenn., attempted under this disguise to commit a cunningly devised robbery and have his offense fixed upon a Negro. All worked well till a bullet brought him to the ground and a little soap and water was applied to his face, when he was found to be no Negro at all, but a very respectable white citizen.

Dark, desperate, and forlorn as I have described the situation, the reality exceeds the description. In most of the Gulf States, and in some parts of the border States, I have sometimes thought that we should be about as well situated for the purposes of justice if there were no Constitution of the United States at all; as well off if there were no law or law-makers, no constables, no jails, no courts of justice, and we were left entirely without the pretence of legal protection, for we are now at the mercy of midnight raiders, assassins, and murderers, and we should only be in the same condition if these pretended safeguards were abandoned. They now only mock us. Other men are presumed to be innocent until they are proved guilty. We are presumed to be guilty until we are proved to be innocent.

The charge is often made that Negroes are by nature the criminal class of America; that they furnish a larger proportion of petty thieves than any other class. I admit the charge, but deny that nature, race, or color has anything to do with the fact. Any other race with the same antecedents and the same condition would show a similar thieving propensity.

The American people have this lesson to learn: That where justice is denied, where poverty is enforced, where ignorance prevails, and where any one class is made to feel that society is an organized conspiracy to oppress, rob, and degrade them, neither persons nor property will be safe. I deny that nature has made the Negro a thief or a burglar. Look at these black criminals, as they are brought into your police courts; view and study their faces, their forms, and their features, as I have done for years as Marshal of this District, and you will see that their antecedents are written all over them. Two hundred and fifty years of grinding slavery has done its work upon them. They stand before you to-day physically and mentally maimed and mutilated men. Many of their mothers and grand-mothers were lashed to agony before their birth by cruel overseers, and the chil-dren have inherited in their faces the anguish and resentment felt by their par-ents. Many of these poor creatures have not been free long enough to outgrow the marks of the lash on their backs, and the deeper marks on their souls. No, no! It is not nature that has erred in making the Negro. That shame rests with slavery. It has twisted his limbs, deformed his body, flattened his feet, and dis-torted his features, and made him, though black, no longer comely. In infancy he slept on the cold clay floor of his cabin, with quick circulation on one side, and tardy circulation on the other. So that he has grown up unequal, unsym-metrical, and is no longer a vertical, well-rounded man, in body or in mind. Time, education, and training will restore him to natural proportions, for, though bruised and blasted, he is yet a man.

The school of the Negro since leaving slavery has not been much of an im-provement on his former condition. Individuals of the race have here and there enjoyed large benefits from emancipation, and the result is seen in their conduct, but the mass have had their liberty coupled with hardships which tend strongly to keep them a dwarfed and miserable class. A man who labors ten hours a day with pickaxe, crowbar, and shovel, and has a family to support and house rent to pay, and receives for his work but a dollar a day, and what is worse still, he is deprived of labor a large part of his time by reason of sickness and the weather, in his poverty, easily falls before the temptation to steal and rob. Hungry men will eat. Desperate men will commit crime. Outraged men will seek revenge. It is said to be hard for a rich man to enter the kingdom of heaven. I have some-times thought it harder still for a poor man to enter the kingdom of heaven. Man is so constituted that if he cannot get a living honestly, he will get it dishonestly. "Skin for skin," as the devil said of Job. "All that a man hath will he give for his life." Oppression makes even wise men mad and reckless; for illustration I pray look at East St. Louis.

In the Southern States to-day a landlord system is in operation which keeps the Negroes of that section in rags and wretchedness, almost to the point of star-vation. As a rule, this system puts it out of the power of the Negro to own land. There is, to be sure, no law forbidding the selling of land to the colored people, but there is an understanding which has the full effect of law. That understand-ing is that the land must be kept in the hands of the old master class. The col-ored people can rent land, it is true, and many of them do rent many acres, and find themselves poorer at the end of the year than at the beginning, because they are charged more a year for rent per acre than the land would bring at auction sale. The landlord and tenant system of Ireland, which has conducted that coun-try to the jaws of ruin, bad as it is, is not worse than that which prevails at this hour at the South, and yet the colored people of the South are constantly re-proached for their poverty. They are asked to make bricks without straw. Their hands are tied, and they are asked to work. They are forced to be poor, and laughed at for their destitution.

I am speaking mainly to colored men to-night, but I want my words to find their way to the eyes, ears, heads and hearts of my white fellow-countrymen, hoping that some among them may be made to think, some hearts among them will be made to feel, and some of their number will be made to act. I appeal to our white fellow-countrymen. The power to protect is in their hands. This is and must be practically the white man's government. He has the numbers and the intelligence to control and direct. To him belongs the responsibility of its honor or dishonor, its glory or its shame, its salvation or its ruin. If they can protect the rights of white men they can protect the rights of black men; if they can defend the rights of American citizens abroad they can defend them at home; if they can use the army to protect the rights of Chinamen, they can use the army to protect the rights of colored men. The only trouble is the will! the will! the will! Here, as elsewhere, "Where there is a will there is a way."

I have now said not all that could be said but enough to indicate the relations at present existing between the white and colored people of this country, especially the relations subsisting between the two classes of the late slaveholding states. Time would fail me to trace this relation in all its ramifications; but that labor is neither required by this audience nor by the country. The condition of the emancipated class is known alike to ourselves and to the Government, to pulpit and press, and to both of the great political parties. These have only to do their duty and all will be well.

One use of this annual celebration is to keep the subject of our grievances before the people and government, and to urge both to do their respective parts in the happy solution of the race problem. The weapons of our warfare for equal rights are not carnal but simple truth, addressed to the hearts and sense of justice of the American people. If this fails we are lost. We have no armies or generals, no swords or cannons to enforce our claims, and do not want any.

We are often asked with an air of reproach by white men at the North: "Why don't your people fight their way to the ballot-box?" The question adds insult to injury. Whom are are called upon to fight? They are the men who held this nation, with all its tremendous resources of men and money, at bay during four long and bloody years. Whom are we to fight? I answer, not a few midnight assassins, not the rabble mob, but trained armies, skilled generals of the Confederate army, and in the last resort we should have to meet the Federal army. Though that army cannot now be employed to defend the weak against the strong, means would certainly be found for its employment to protect the strong against the weak. In such a case insurrection would be madness.

But there is another remedy proposed. These people are advised to make an exodus to the Pacific slope. With the best intentions they are told of the fertility of the soil and salubrity of the climate. If they should tell the same as existing in the moon, the simple question, How shall they get there? would knock the life out of it at once. Without money, without friends, without knowledge, and only gaining enough by daily toil to keep them above the starvation point, where they are, how can such a people rise and cross the continent? The measure on its face is no remedy at all. Besides, who does not know that should these people ever attempt such an exodus, that they would be met with shot-guns at every cross-road. Who does not know that the white landholders of the South would never consent to let that labor which alone gives value to their land march off without opposition? Who does not know that if the Federal Government is powerless to protect these people in staying that it would be equally powerless to protect them in going *en masse?* For one, I say away with such contrivances, such lame and impotent substitutes for the justice and protection due us. The first duty that the National Government owes to its citizens is protection.

While, however, I hold now, as I held years ago, that the South is the natural home of the colored race, and that there must the destiny of that race be mainly worked out, I still believe that means can be and ought to be adopted to assist in the emigration of such of their number as may wish to change their residence to parts of the country where their civil and political rights are better protected than at present they can be at the South.

I adopt the suggestion of the *National Republican,* of this city, that *diffusion* is the true policy for the colored people of the South. All, of course, cannot leave that section, and ought not; but some can, and the condition of those who must remain will be better because of those who go. Men, like trees, may be too thickly planted to thrive. If the labor market of Mississippi were to-day not over-loaded and over supplied, the laborers would be more fully appreciated; but this work of diffusion and distribution cannot be carried on by the emancipated class alone. They need, and ought to have, the material aid of both white and colored people of the free states. A million of dollars devoted to this purpose would do more for the colored people of the South than the same amount expended in any other way. There is no degradation, no loss of self-respect, in asking this aid, considering the circumstances of these people. The white people of this nation owe them this help and a great deal more. The keynote of the future should not be concentration, but diffusion—distribution. This may not be a remedy for all evils now uncured, but it certainly will be a help in the right direction.

A word now in respect of another remedy for the black man's ills. It calls itself independent political action. This has, during the past few years, been advocated with much zeal and spirit by several of our leading colored men, and also with much ability, though I am happy to say not with much success. First, their plan, if I understand it, is to separate the colored people of the country from the Republican party. This, with them, is the primary and essential condition of making the colored vote independent. Hence all their artillery is directed to making that party odious in the eyes of the colored voters. Colored men who adhere to the Republican party are vilified as slaves, office-seekers, serviles, "knuckle-close" Republicans, as tools of white men, traitors to their race, and much more of the same sort. Perhaps no one has been a more prominent target for such denunciation than your humble speaker.

Now, the position to which these gentlemen invite us is one of neutrality between the two great political parties, and to vote with either, or against either, according to the prevailing motive when the time for action shall arrive. In the interval we are to have no standing with either party, and have no active influence in shaping the policy of either, but we are to stand alone, and hold ourselves ready to serve one or to serve the other, or both, as we may incline at the moment.

With all respect to these political doctors, I must say that their remedy is no remedy at all. No man can serve two masters in politics any more than in religion. If there is one position in life more despicable in the eyes of man, and more condemned by nature than another, it is that of neutrality. Besides, if there is one thing more impossible than another, it is a position of perfect neutrality in politics. Our friends, Fortune, Downing, and others, flatter themselves that they have reached this perfection, but they are utterly mistaken. No man can read their utterances without seeing their animus of hate to the Republican party, and their preference for the Democratic party. The fault is not so much in their intention, as in their position. They can neither act with nor against the two parties impartially. They are compelled by their position to either serve the one and oppose the other, and they cannot serve or oppose both alike. Independence, like neutrality, is also impossible. If the colored man does not depend upon the Republican party, he will depend upon the Democratic party, and if he does neither, he becomes a nonentity in American politics. But these gentlemen do, in effect, ask us to break down the power of the Republican party, when to do it is to put the Government in the hands of the Democratic party. Colored men are already in the Republican party, and to come out of it is to defeat it.

For one, I must say that the Democratic party has as yet given me no sufficient reasons for doing it any such service, nor has the Republican party sunk so low that I must abandon it for its great rival. With all its faults it is the best party now in existence. In it are the best elements of the American people, and if any good is to come to us politically it will be through that party.

I must cease to remember a great many things and must forget a great many things before I can counsel any man, colored or white, to join the Democratic party, or to occupy a position of neutrality between that party and the Republican party. Such a position of the colored people of this country will prove about as comfortable as between the upper and nether millstone. Those of our number now posing as Independents are doing better service to the Democratic party under the Independent mask than they could do if they came out honestly for the Democratic party.

I am charged with commending the inaugural address of President Cleveland. I am not ashamed of that charge. I said at the time that no better words for the colored citizen had dropped from the east portico of the Capitol since the days of Lincoln and Grant, and I say so still. I did not say, as my traducer lyingly asserts, that Mr. Cleveland said better words than Lincoln or Grant. But it would not have suited the man who left Washington with malice in his heart and falsehood in his throat to be more truthful in Petersburg than, in Washington. This malcontent accuser seeks to make the impression that those who thought and spoke well of the inaugural address did so from selfish motives, and from a desire to get or retain office. "Out of the abundance of the heart the mouth speaketh." "With what judgment ye judge, ye shall be judged, and with what measure ye mete, the same shall be measured to you again." He ought to remember, however, that a serpent without a fang, a scorpion without a sting, has no more ability to poison than a lie which has lost its ability to deceive has to injure. It so happens that we had two Presidents and one Vice-President prior to President Cleveland, and I challenge my ambitious and envious accuser to find any better word for the colored citizens of this country in the inaugural addresses of either than is found in the inaugural address of President Cleveland. I also beg my accuser to remember that I gave no pledge that Mr. Cleveland would be able to live up to the sentiments of that address, but, on the contrary, I doubted even the probability of his success in doing so. I gave him credit, however, for an honest purpose, and expressed a hope that he might be able to do as well and better than he promised. But I saw him in the rapids and predicted that they would be too strong for him. Did this look like seeking favor? He did a brave thing in removing from office an abettor of murder in Mississippi. He has expressed in a private way, to Messrs. Bruce and Lynch, his reprobation of the recent massacres at Carrollton, and for this we thank him. But he has done nothing in his position as Commander-in-chief of the army and navy to put a stop to such horrors. I am quite sure that he abhors violence and bloodshed. He has shown this in his publicly spoken words in behalf of perse-cuted and murdered Chinamen;[1] he should do the same for the persecuted and murdered black citizens of Mississippi. He could threaten the law-breakers and murderers of the West with the sword of the nation, why not the South? If it was right to protect and defend the Chinese, why not the Negro? If in the days of slav-ery the army could be used to hunt slaves, and suppress slave insurrections, why, in the days of liberty, may it not be used to enforce rights guaranteed by the Con-stitution? Alas! fellow-citizens, there is no right so neglected as the Negro's right. There is no flesh so despised as the Negro's flesh. There is no blood so cheap as the Negro's blood. I have been saying these things to the American people for nearly fifty years. In the order of nature I cannot say them much longer; but, as was said by another, "though time himself should confront me, and shake his hoary locks at any persistence, I shall not cease while life is left me, and our wrongs are unredressed, to thus cry aloud and spare not."

Fellow-citizens, I am disappointed. The accession of the Democratic party to power has not been followed by the results I expected. When the tiger has quenched his thirst in blood, and when the anaconda has swallowed his prey, they cease to pursue their trembling game and sink to rest; so I thought when the Democratic party came into power, when the solid South gave law to the land, when there could no longer be any pretence for the fear of Negro ascendency in the councils of the nation, persecution, violence, and murder would cease, and the Negro would be left in peace; but the bloody scenes at Carrollton, and the daily reports of lynch law in the South, have destroyed this cherished hope and told me that the end of our sufferings is not yet.

But, fellow-citizens, I do not despair, and no power that I know of can make me despair of the ultimate triumph of justice and liberty in this country. I have seen too many abuses outgrown, too many evils removed, too many moral and physi-cal improvements made, to doubt that the wheels of progress will still roll on. We have but to toil and trust, throw away whiskey and tobacco, improve the oppor-tunities that we have, put away all extravagance, learn to live within our means, lay up our earnings, educate our children, live industrious and virtuous lives, establish a character for sobriety, punctuality, and general uprightness, and we shall raise up powerful friends who shall stand by us in our struggle for an equal chance in the race of life. The white people of this country are asleep, but not dead. In other days we had a potent voice in the Senate which awoke the nation.

Ireland now has an advocate in the British Senate who has arrested the eye and ear of the civilized world in championing the cause of Ireland. There is to-day in the American Senate an opportunity for an American Gladstone; one whose voice shall have power to awake this nation to the stupendous wrongs inflicted upon our newly-made citizens and move the Government to a vindication of our constitutional rights. We have in other days had a Sumner, a Wilson, a Chase, a Conkling, a Thaddeus Stevens, and a Morton. These did not exhaust the justice and humanity of American statesmanship. There is heart and eloquence still left in the councils of the nation, and these will, I trust, yet make themselves potent in having both the Constitution of 1789 and the Constitution with the fourteenth and fifteenth amendments made practically the law of the land for all the people thereof.

Three Addresses on the Relations Subsisting Between the White and Colored People of the United States, by Frederick Douglass, Washington, 1886, pp. 57–68

1. The attacks on Chinese in the Territory of Washington reached such a point by the fall of 1885 that Cleveland, on November 7, 1885, issued a proclamation warning "evil disposed persons" to disperse or be met by the military power of the government.

TO W. H. THOMAS

Washington, D.C., July 16, 1886.

Dear Sir:

I am obliged by the receipt of a copy of the "Negro." Please accept my best thanks. I wish you success in your publishing enterprise. I am sorry I cannot promise to write for the "Negro." The multitude of papers showered upon me with requests for contributions from my pen and pocket stagger me. I do the best I can for all of them, and that falls far below my wishes. Of these papers, judging from the sample before me, yours promises to be among the more able and useful. But that I expect soon to leave the country I would subscribe to it at once.

To me what you call the *Negro* problem is a misnomer. It were better called a white man's problem. Here as elsewhere, the greater includes the less. The Negro problem is swallowed up in the Caucasian problem and the question is whether the white man can and will yet rise to that height of justice, humanity and Christian civilization as will permit Indians, Chinamen and Negroes to enjoy an Equal chance in the race of life among them? The Negro is few, the white man is many. The Negro is weak, the white man is strong. The few will be ruled by the many and the weak by the strong. What the future of the Negro shall be, is a problem in which the white man is the chief factor. The Negro holds only a secondary position. He is the clay, the white man is the Potter. It is for this Potter to say whether the Negro shall become a well rounded, symmetrical man, or cramped, deformed, and dwarfed. A plant deprived of moisture and sunlight will die, and a people deprived of the means of life and progress will wither and die. Give the Negro fair play and an equal chance in the race of life, and I have no doubt of a happy future for him.

The great mass of the colored people in this country are now and must continue to be in the south, and there if they are ever to rise in the scale of civilization, their persons must be protected, their rights secured, their minds enlightened, and their honest work receive honest wages. It is something to give the Negro religion. It is more to give him justice. It is something to give him the Bible, it is more to give him the ballot. It is something to tell him that there is a place for him in the Christian's heaven, it is more to let him have a place in this Christian country to live upon in peace.

Very truly yours,
Frederick Douglass

Frederick Douglass Mss., Douglass Memorial Home, Anacostia, D.C.

THE WOMAN'S SUFFRAGE MOVEMENT, address before International Council of Women, Washington, D.C, March 31, 1888

Mrs. President, Ladies and Gentlemen:

I come to this platform with unusual diffidence. Although I have long been identified with the Woman's Suffrage movement, and have often spoken in its favor, I am somewhat at a loss to know what to say on this really great and uncommon occasion, where so much has been said.

When I look around on this assembly, and see the many able and eloquent women, full of the subject, ready to speak, and who only need the opportunity to impress this audience with their views and thrill them with "thoughts that breathe and words that burn," I do not feel like taking up more than a very small space of your time and attention, and shall not. I would not, even now, presume to speak, but for the circumstance of my early connection with the cause, and of having been called upon to do so by one whose voice in this Council we all gladly obey. Men have very little business here as speakers, anyhow; and if they come here at all they should take back benches and wrap themselves in silence. For this is an International Council, not of men, but of women, and woman should have all the say in it. This is her day in court.

I do not mean to exalt the intellect of woman above man's; but I have heard many men speak on this subject, some of them the most eloquent to be found anywhere in the country; and I believe no man, however gifted with thought and speech, can voice the wrongs and present the demands of women with the skill and effect, with the power and authority of woman herself. The man struck is the man to cry out. Woman knows and feels her wrongs as man cannot know and feel them, and she also knows as well as he can know, what measures are needed to redress them. I grant all the claims at this point. She is her own best representative. We can neither speak for her, nor vote for her, nor act for her, nor be responsible for her; and the thing for men to do in the premises is just to get out of her way and give her the fullest opportunity to exercise all the powers inherent in her individual personality, and allow her to do it as she herself shall elect to exercise them. Her right to be and to do is as full, complete and perfect as the right of any man on earth. I say of her, as I say of the colored people. "Give her fair play, and hands off."

There was a time when, perhaps, we men could help a little. It was when this woman suffrage cause was in its cradle, when it was not big enough to go alone, when it had to be taken in the arms of its mother from Seneca Falls, N.Y., to Rochester, N.Y., for baptism. I then went along with it and offered my services to help it, for then it needed help; but now it can afford to dispense with me and all of my sex. Then its friends were few—now its friends are many. Then it was wrapped in obscurity—now it is lifted in sight of the whole civilized world, and people of all lands and languages give it their hearty support. Truly the change is vast and wonderful.

I thought my eye of faith was tolerably clear when I attended those meetings in Seneca Falls and Rochester, but it was far too dim to see at the end of forty years a result so imposing as this International Council, and to see yourself[1] and Miss Anthony alive and active in its proceedings. Of course, I expected to be alive myself, and am not surprised to find myself so; for such is, perhaps, the presumption and arrogance common to my sex. Nevertheless, I am very glad to see you here to-day, and to see this grand assembly of women. I am glad that you are its president. No manufactured "boom," or political contrivance, such as make presidents elsewhere, has made you president of this assembly of women in this Capital of the Nation. You hold your place by reason of eminent fitness, and I give you joy that your life and labors in the cause of woman are thus crowned with honor and glory. This I say in spite of the warning given us by Miss Anthony's friend against mutual admiration.

There may be some well-meaning people in this audience who have never attended a woman suffrage convention, never heard a woman suffrage speech, never read a woman suffrage newspaper, and they may be surprised that those who speak here do not argue the question. It may be kind to tell them that our cause has passed beyond the period of arguing. The demand of the hour is not argument, but assertion, firm and inflexible assertion, assertion which has more than the force of an argument. If there is any argument to be made, it must be made by the opponents, not by the friends of woman suffrage. Let those who want argument examine the ground upon which they base their claim to the right to vote. They will find that there is not one reason, not one consideration, which they can urge in support of man's claim to vote, which does not equally support the right of woman to vote.

There is to-day, however, a special reason for omitting argument. This is the end of the fourth decade of the woman suffrage movement, a kind of jubilee which naturally turns our minds to the past.

Ever since this Council has been in session, my thoughts have been reverting to the past. I have been thinking, more or less, of the scene, presented forty years ago in the little Methodist Church at Seneca Falls, the manger in which this organized suffrage movement was born. It was a very small thing then. It was not then big enough to be abused, or loud enough to make itself heard outside, and only a few of those who saw it had any notion that the little thing would live. I have been thinking, too, of the strong conviction, the noble courage, the sublime faith in God and man it required at that time to set this suffrage ball in motion. The history of the world has given to us many sublime undertakings, but none more sublime than this. It was a great thing for the friends of peace to organize in opposition to war; it was a great thing for the friends of temperance to organize against intemperance; it was a great thing for humane people to organize in opposition to slavery; but it was a much greater thing, in view of all the circumstances, for woman to organize herself in opposition to her exclusion from participation in government. The reason is obvious. War, intemperance and slavery are open, undisguised, palpable evils. The best feelings of human nature revolt at them. We could easily make men see the misery, the debasement, the terrible suffering caused by intemperance; we could easily make men see the desolation wrought by war and the hell-black horrors of chattel slavery; but the case was different in the movement for woman suffrage. Men took for granted all that could be said against intemperance, war and slavery. But no such advantage was found in the beginning of the cause of suffrage for women. On the contrary, everything in her condition was supposed to be lovely, just as it should be. She had no rights denied, no wrongs to redress. She herself had no suspicion but that all was going well with her. She floated along on the tide of life as her mother and grandmother had done before her, as in a dream of Paradise. Her wrongs, if she had any, were too occult to be seen, and too light to be felt. It required a daring voice and a determined hand to awake her from this delightful dream and call the nation to account for the rights and opportunities of which it was depriving her. It was well understood at the beginning that woman would not thank us for disturbing her by this call to duty, and it was known that man would denounce and scorn us for such a daring innovation upon the established order of things. But this did not appall or delay the word and work.

At this distance of time from that convention at Rochester, and in view of the present position of the question, it is hard to realize the moral courage it required to launch this unwelcome movement. Any man can be brave when the danger is over, go to the front when there is no resistance, rejoice when the battle is fought and the victory is won; but it is not so easy to venture upon a field untried with one-half the whole world against you, as these women did.

Then who were we, for I count myself in, who did this thing? We were few in numbers, moderate in resources, and very little known in the world. The most that we had to commend us was a firm conviction that we were in the right, and firm faith that the right must ultimately prevail. But the case was well considered. Let no man imagine that the step was taken recklessly and thoughtlessly. Mrs. Stanton had dwelt upon it at least six years before she declared it in the Rochester convention. Walking with her from the house of Joseph and Thankful Southwick, two of the noblest people I ever knew, Mrs. Stanton, with an earnestness that I shall never forget, unfolded her views on this woman question precisely as she has in this Council. This was six and forty years ago, and it was not until six years after, that she ventured to make her formal, pronounced and startling demand for the ballot. She had, as I have said, considered well, and knew something of what would be the cost of the reform she was inaugurating. She knew the ridicule, the rivalry, the criticism and the bitter aspersions which she and her colaborers would have to meet and to endure. But she saw more clearly than most of us that the vital point to be made prominent, and the one that included all others, was the ballot, and she bravely said the word. It was not only necessary to break the silence of woman and make her voice heard, but she must have a clear, palpable and comprehensive measure set before her, one worthy of her highest ambition and her best exertions, and hence the ballot was brought to the front.

There are few facts in my humble history to which I look back with more satisfaction than to the fact, recorded in the history of the Woman Suffrage Movement, that I was sufficiently enlightened at that early day, and when only a few years from slavery, to support your resolution for woman suffrage.[2] I have done very little in this world in which to glory except this one act—and I certainly glory in that. When I ran away from slavery, it was for myself; when I advocated emancipation, it was for my people; but when I stood up for the rights of woman, self was out of the question, and I found a little nobility in the act.

In estimating the forces with which this suffrage cause has had to contend during these forty years, the fact should be remembered that relations of long standing beget a character in the parties to them in favor of their continuance. Time itself is a conservative power—a very conservative power. One shake of his hoary locks will sometimes paralyze the hand and palsy the tongue of the reformer. The relation of man to woman has the advantage of all the ages behind it. Those who oppose a readjustment of this relation tell us that what is always was and always will be, world without end. But we have heard this old argument before, and if we live very long we shall hear it again. When any aged error shall be assailed, and any old abuse is to be removed, we shall meet this same old argument. Man has been so long the king and woman the subject—man has been so long accustomed to command and woman to obey—that both parties to the relation have been hardened into their respective places, and thus has been piled up a mountain of iron against woman's enfranchisement.

The same thing confronted us in our conflicts with slavery. Long years ago Henry Clay said, on the floor of the American Senate, "I know there is a visionary dogma that man cannot hold property in man," and, with a brow of defiance, he said, "That is property which the law makes property. Two hundred years of legislation has sanctioned and sanctified negro slaves as property." But neither the power of time nor the might of legislation has been able to keep life in that stupendous barbarism.

The universality of man's rule over woman is another factor in the resistance to the woman suffrage movement. We are pointed to the fact that men have not only always ruled over women, but that they do so rule everywhere, and they easily think that a thing that is done everywhere must be right. Though the fallacy of this reasoning is too transparent to need refutation, it still exerts a powerful influence. Even our good Brother Jasper yet believes, with the ancient church, that the sun "do move," notwithstanding all the astronomers of the world are against him. One year ago I stood on the Pincio in Rome and witnessed the unveiling of the Statue of Galileo. It was an imposing sight. At no time before had Rome been free enough to permit such a statue to be placed within her walls. It is now there, not with the approval of the Vatican. No priest took part in the ceremonies. It was all the work of laymen. One or two priests passed the statue with averted eyes, but the great truths of the solar system were not angry at the sight, and the same will be true when woman shall be clothed, as she will yet be, with all the rights of American citizenship.

All good causes are mutually helpful. The benefits accruing from this movement for the equal rights of woman are not confined or limited to woman only. They will be shared by every effort to promote the progress and welfare of mankind everywhere and in all ages. It was an example and a prophecy of what can be accomplished against strongly opposing forces, against time-hallowed abuses, against deeply intrenched error, against world-wide usage, and against the settled judgment of mankind, by a few earnest women, clad only in the panoply of truth, and determined to live and die in what they considered a righteous cause.

I do not forget the thoughtful remark of our president in the opening address to this International Council, reminding us of the incompleteness of our work. The remark was wise and timely. Nevertheless, no man can compare the present with the past, the obstacles that then opposed us, and the influences that now favor us, the meeting in the little Methodist chapel forty years ago, and the Council in this vast theatre to-day, without admitting that woman's cause is already a brilliant success. But, however this may be, and whatever the future may have in store for us, one thing is certain—this new revolution in human thought will never go backward. When a great truth once gets abroad in the world, no power on earth can imprison it, or prescribe its limits, or suppress it. It is bound to go on till it becomes the thought of the world. Such a truth is woman's right to equal liberty with man. She was born with it. It was hers before she comprehended it. It is inscribed upon all the powers and faculties of her soul, and no custom, law nor usage can ever destroy it. Now that it has got fairly fixed in the minds of the few, it is bound to become fixed in the minds of the many, and be supported at last by a great cloud of witnesses, which no man can number and no power can withstand.

The woman who have thus far carried on this agitation have already embodied and illustrated Theodore Parker's three grades of human greatness. The first is greatness in executive and administrative ability; second, greatness in the ability to organize; and, thirdly, in the ability to discover truth. Wherever these three elements of power are combined in any movement, there is a reasonable ground to believe in its final success; and these elements of power have been manifest in the women who have had the movement in hand from the beginning. They are seen in the order which has characterized the proceedings of this Council. They are seen in the depth and comprehensiveness of the discussions had upon them in this Council. They are seen in the fervid eloquence and downright earnestness with which women advocate their cause. They are seen in the profound attention with which woman is heard in her own behalf. They are seen in the steady growth and onward march of the movement, and they will be seen in the final triumph of woman's cause, not only in this country, but throughout the world.

Woman's Journal, April 14, 1888

1. The reference is to Elizabeth Cady Stanton, the pioneer woman suffrage leader and president of the Woman Suffrage Association.
2. At the first Woman's Rights Convention in the world's history held at Seneca Falls, July 19 and 20, 1848, Douglass seconded the resolution introduced by Elizabeth Cady Stanton which asserted that it was the duty of the women of this country "to secure to themselves their sacred right to the elective franchise."

In 1888 [Douglass] visited South Carolina and Georgia and realized how little he had known about the true conditions of his people in the South. On April 10, soon after his return, he wrote to one of the leaders of a movement for encouraging the emigration of southern Negroes to the northwest: "I had hoped that the relations subsisting between the former slaves and the old master class would gradually improve; but while I believed this, and still have some such weak faith, I have of late seen enough, heard enough, and learned enough of the condition of these people in South Carolina and Georgia, to make me welcome any movement which will take them out of the wretched condition in which I now know them to be. While I shall continue to labor for increased justice to those who stay in the South, I give you my hearty 'God-speed' in your emigration scheme. I believe you are doing a good work."[1]

A few days later, he spoke in Washington at the celebration of the twenty-sixth anniversary of emancipation in the District of Columbia. His address revealed how deeply he had been moved by his southern tour. His voice quivered with rage as he described how the Negro was "nominally free" but actually a slave. In earnest tones, he told the nation: "I here and now denounce his so-called emancipation as a stupendous fraud—a fraud upon him, a fraud upon the world." He drew a terrifying picture of the exploitation of the southern Negro. . . . Here was the old Douglass, the forceful anti-slavery orator who had moved audiences on two continents, the man who could bring home more vividly than any other speaker the evils of slavery and the necessity to overthrow it. Here was the tribune of the Negro people presenting the most powerful indictment of the new slavery in the new South.

Douglass' speech created a sensation. Hamilton J. Smith, who described himself as "a humbled Negro citizen of Massachusetts," hastened to thank Douglass "for the noble and manly words spoken . . . in behalf of my race." Senator George B. Edmonds called it "the greatest political speech that I have read or heard in perhaps twenty years," and believed that "it will revive fires of devotion to freedom and justice that in our boasts for past achievements had nearly died out. Your speech should be printed broadcast through our land, and similar speeches should be made in every school district in this country."

Congressman J. B. White wrote: "You spoke sorrowful facts—and such things must be stopped if this free Nation is to live." Charles N. Hunter, Negro editor of *The Progressive Educator*, official organ of the North Carolina State Teachers' Association, reported the reaction of southern Negroes to Douglass' speech. "The colored people here," he wrote from Durham, "are eagerly seeking papers containing the speech and are reading it with an interest and enthusiasm which I have not witnessed since the early days of emancipation. You should have the assurance of our people in all parts of the country that you have comprehended our situation clearly and that the noble sentiments so eloquently enunciated in your address meet a warm response form the Negro of the South. I have been longing and waiting and waiting and longing for some one of our great men to rise to the height of the occasion. I need not conceal the discouragement which your grand effort has lifted. A ray of hope pierces the gloom and I can now look hopefully forward. And is there not inspiration for us all when Douglass buckles on his armor and his gleaming cementer [*sic*] glistens in the glare of battle?"[2] [IV:109–111]

I DENOUNCE THE SO-CALLED EMANCIPATION AS A STUPENDOUS FRAUD, speech on the occasion of the Twenty-Sixth Anniversary of Emancipation in the District of Columbia, Washington, D.C., April 16, 1888

Friends and fellow citizens:

It has been my privilege to assist in several anniversary celebrations of the abolition of slavery in the District of Columbia, but I remember no occasion of this kind when I felt a deeper solicitude for the future welfare of our emancipated people than now.

The chief cause of anxiety is not in the condition of the colored people of the District of Columbia, though there is much that is wrong and unsatisfactory here, but the deplorable condition of the Negro in the Southern states. At no time since the abolition of slavery has there been more cause for alarm on this account than at this juncture in our history.

I have recently been in two of the Southern states—South Carolina and Georgia—and my impression from what I saw, heard and learned there is not favorable to my hopes for the race. I know this is a sad message to bring you on this twenty-sixth anniversary of freedom in the District of Columbia, but I know, too, that I have a duty to perform and that duty is to tell the truth, the whole truth, and nothing but the truth, and I should be unworthy to stand here, unworthy of the confidence of the colored people of this country, if I should from any considerations of policy withhold any fact or feature of the condition of the freedmen which the people of this country ought to know.

The temptation on anniversary occasions like this is to prophesy smooth things, to be joyful and glad, to indulge in the illusions of hope—to bring glad tidings on our tongues, and words of peace reveal. But while I know it is always easier to be the bearer of glad tidings than sad ones, while I know that hope is a powerful motive to exertion and high endeavor, while I know that people generally would rather look upon the bright side of their condition than to know the worst; there comes a time when it is best that the worst should be made known, and in my judgment that time, in respect to the condition of the colored people of the South, is now. There are times when neither hope nor fear should be allowed to control our speech. Cry aloud and spare not, is the word of wisdom as well as of Scripture. "Ye shall know the truth, and the truth shall make you free," applies to the body not less than the soul, to this world not less than the world to come. Outside the truth there is no solid foundation for any of us, and I assume that you who have invited me to speak, and you who have come to hear me speak, expect me to speak the truth as I understand the truth.

The truth at which we should get on this occasion respects the precise relation subsisting between the white and colored people of the South, or, in other words, between the colored people and the old master class of the South. We have need to know this and to take it to heart.

It is well said that "a people may lose its liberty in a day and not miss it in half a century," and that "the price of liberty is eternal vigilance." In my judgment, with my knowledge of what has already taken place in the South, these wise and wide-awake sentiments were never more apt and timely than now.

I have assisted in fighting one battle for the abolition of slavery, and the American people have shed their blood in defense of the Union and the Constitution, and neither I nor they should wish to fight this battle over again; and in order that we may not, we should look the facts in the face today and, if possible, nip the evil in the bud.

I have no taste for the role of an alarmist. If my wishes could be allowed to dictate my speech I would tell you something quite the reverse of what I now intend. I would tell you that everything is lovely with the Negro in the South; I would tell you that the rights of the Negro are respected, and that be has no wrongs to redress; I would tell you that he is honestly paid for his labor; that he is secure in his liberty; that he is tried by a jury of his peers when accused of crime; that he is no longer subject to lynch law; that he has freedom of speech; that the gates of knowledge are open to him; that he goes to the ballot box unmolested; that his vote is duly counted and given its proper weight in determining result; I would tell you that he is making splendid progress in the acquisition of knowledge, wealth and influence; I would tell you that his bitterest enemies have become his warmest friends; that the desire to make him a slave no longer exists anywhere in the South; that the Democratic party is a better friend to him than the Republican party, and that each party is competing with the other to see which can do the most to make his liberty a blessing to himself and to the country and the world. But in telling you all this I should be telling you what is absolutely false, and what you know to be false, and the only thing which would save such a story from being a lie would be its utter inability to deceive.

What is the condition of the Negro at the South at this moment? Let us look at it both in the light of facts and in the light of reason. To understand it we must consult nature as well as circumstances, the past as well as the present. No fact is more obvious than the fact that there is a perpetual tendency of power to encroach upon weakness, and of the crafty to take advantage of the simple. This is as natural as for smoke to ascend or water to run down. The love of power is one of the strongest traits in the Anglo-Saxon race. This love of power common to the white race has been nursed and strengthened at the South by slavery: accustomed during two hundred years to the unlimited possession and exercise of irresponsible power, the love of it has become stronger by habit. To assume that this feeling of pride and power has died out and disappeared from the South is to assume a miracle. Any man who tells you that it has died out or has ceased to be exercised and made effective, tells you that which is untrue and in the nature of things could not be true. Not only is the love of power there, but a talent for its exercise has been fully developed. This talent makes the old master class of the South not only the masters of the Negro, but the masters of Congress and, if not checked, will make them the masters of the nation.

It was something more than an empty boast in the old times, when it was said that one slave master was equal to three Northern men. Though this did not turn out to be true on the battlefield, it does seem to be true in the councils of the nation. In sight of all the nation these ambitious men of the South have dared to take possession of the government which they, with broad blades and bloody hands, sought to destroy; in sight of all the nation they have disregarded and trampled upon the Constitution, and organized parties on sectional lines. From the ramparts of the Solid South, with their 153 electoral votes in the Electoral College, they have dared to defy the nation to put a Republican in the Presidential chair for the next four years, as they once threatened the nation with civil war if it elected Abraham Lincoln. With this grip on the Presidential chair, with the House of Representatives in their hands, with the Supreme Court deciding every question in favor of the states, as against the powers of the federal government, denying to the government the right to protect the elective franchise of its own citizens, they may well feel themselves masters, not only of their former slaves, but of the whole situation. With these facts before us, tell me not that the Negro is safe in the possession of his liberty. Tell me not that power will not assert itself. Tell me not that they who despise the Constitution they have sworn to support will respect the rights of the Negro, whom they already despise. Tell me not that men who thus break faith with God will be scrupulous in keeping faith with the poor Negro laborer of the South. Tell me not that a people who have lived by the sweat of other men's faces, and thought themselves Christian gentlemen while doing it, will feel themselves bound by principles of justice to their former victims in their weakness. Such a pretense in face of facts is shameful, shocking and sickening. Yet there are men at the North who believe all this.

Well may it be said that Americans have no memories. We look over the House of Representatives and see the Solid South enthroned there. We listen with calmness to eulogies of the South and of the traitors, and forget Andersonville.[3] We look over the Senate and see the Senator from South Carolina, and we forget Hamburg. We see Robert Smalls cheated out of his seat in Congress,[4] and forget the *Planter*, and the service rendered by the colored troops in the late war for the Union.

Well, the nation may forget; it may shut its eyes to the past and frown upon any who may do otherwise, but the colored people of this country are bound to keep fresh a memory of the past till justice shall be done them in the present. When this shall be done we shall as readily as any other part of our respected citizens plead for an act of oblivion.

We are often confronted of late in the press and on the platform with the discouraging statement that the problem of the Negro as a free man and a citizen is not yet solved; that since his emancipation he has disappointed the best hopes of his friends and fulfilled the worst predictions of his enemies, and that he has shown himself unfit for the position assigned him by the mistaken statesmanship of the nation. It is said that physically, morally, socially and religiously he is in a condition vastly more deplorable than was his condition as a slave; that he has not proved himself so good a master to himself as his old master was to him; that he is gradually, but surely, sinking below the point of industry, good manners and civilization to which he attained in a state of slavery; that his industry is fitful; that his economy is wasteful; that his honesty is deceitful; that his morals are impure; that his domestic life is beastly; that his religion is fetichism, and his worship is simply emotional; and that, in a word, he is falling into a state of barbarism.

Such is the distressing description of the emancipated Negro as drawn by his enemies and as it is found reported in the journals of the South. Unhappily, however, it is a description not confined to the South. It has gone forth to the North. It has crossed the ocean; I met with it in Europe. And it has gone as far as the wings of the press and the power of speech can carry it. There is no measuring the injury inflicted upon the Negro by it. It cools our friends, heats our enemies, and turns away from us much of the sympathy and aid which we need and deserve to receive at the hands of our fellow men.

But now comes the question, Is this description of the emancipated Negro true? In answer to this question I must say, Yes and no. It is not true in all its lines and specifications and to the full extent of the ground it covers, but it certainly is true in many of its important features, and there is no race under heaven of which the same would not be equally true with the same antecedents and the same treatment which the Negro is receiving at the hands of this nation and the old master class, to which the Negro is still a subject.

I admit that the Negro, and especially the plantation Negro, the tiller of the soil, has made little progress from barbarism to civilization, and that he is in a deplorable condition since his emancipation. That he is worse off, in many respects, than when he was a slave, I am compelled to admit, but I contend that the fault is not his, but that of his heartless accusers. He is the victim of a cunningly devised swindle, one which paralyzes his energies, suppresses his ambition, and blasts all his hopes; and though he is nominally free he is actually a slave. I here and now denounce his so-called emancipation as a stupendous fraud—a fraud upon him, a fraud upon the world. It was not so meant by Abraham Lincoln; it was not so meant by the Republican party; but whether so meant or not, it is practically a lie, keeping the word of promise to the ear and breaking it to the heart.

Do you ask me why the Negro of the plantation has made so little progress, why his cupboard is empty, why he flutters in rags, why his children run naked, and why his wife hides herself behind the hut when a stranger is passing? I will tell you. It is because he is systematically and universally cheated out of his hard earnings. The same class that once extorted his labor under the lash now gets his labor by a mean, sneaking, and fraudulent device. That device is a trucking system which never permits him to see or to save a dollar of his hard earnings. The struggles and struggles, but, like a man in a morass, the more he struggles the deeper he sinks. The highest wages paid him is eight dollars a month, and this he receives only in orders on the store, which, in many cases, is owned by his employer. The scrip has purchasing power on that one store, and that one only. A blind man can see that the laborer is by this arrangement bound hand and foot, and is completely in the power of his employer. He can charge the poor fellow what he pleases and give what kind of goods he pleases, and he does both. His victim cannot go to another store and buy, and this the storekeeper knows, The only security the wretched Negro has under this arrangement is the conscience of the storekeeper—a conscience educated in the school of slavery, where the idea prevailed in theory and practice that the Negro had no rights which white men were bound to respect, an arrangement in which everything in the way of food or clothing, whether tainted meat or damaged cloth, is deemed good enough for the Negro. For these he is often made to pay a double price.

But this is not all, or the worst result of the system. It puts it out of the power of the Negro to save anything of what he earns. If a man gets an honest dollar for his day's work, he has a motive for laying it by and saving it for future emergency. It will be as good for use in the future and perhaps better a year hence than now, but this miserable scrip has in no sense the quality of a dollar. It is only good at one store and for a limited period. Thus the man who has it is tempted to get rid of it as soon as possible. It may be out of date before be knows it, or the storekeeper may move away and it may be left worthless on his hands.

But this is not the only evil involved in this satanic arrangement. It promotes dishonesty. The Negro sees himself paid but limited wages—far too limited to support himself and family, and that in worthless scrip—and he is tempted to fight the devil with fire. Finding himself systematically robbed he goes to stealing and as a result finds his liberty—such as it is—taken from him, and himself put to work for a master in a chain gang, and he comes out, if he ever gets out, a ruined man.

Every Northern man who visits the old master class, the land owners and landlords of the South, is told by the old slaveholders with a great show of virtue that they are glad that they are rid of slavery and would not have the slave system back if they could; that they are better off than they ever were before, and much more of the same tenor. Thus Northern men come home duped and go on a mission of duping others by telling the same pleasing story.

There are very good reasons why these people would not have slavery back if they could—reasons far more creditable to their cunning than to their conscience. With slavery they had some care and responsibility for the physical well-being of their slaves. Now they have as firm a grip on the freedman's labor as when he was a slave and without any burden of caring for his children or himself. The whole arrangement is stamped with fraud and is supported by hypocrisy, and I here and now, on this Emancipation Day: denounce it as a villainous swindle, and invoke the press, the pulpit and the lawmaker to assist in exposing it and blotting it out forever.

We denounce the imposition upon the working classes of England, and we do well, but in England this trucking system is abolished by law. It is a penal offense there, and it should be made so here. It should be made a crime to pay any man for his honest labor in any other than honest money. Until this is done in the Southern states the laborer of the South will be ground to the earth, and progress with him will be impossible. It is the duty of the Negro press to take up the subject. The Negro, where he may have a vote, should vote for no man who is not in favor of making this scrip and truck system unlawful.

I come now to another feature of Southern policy which bears hard and heavily on the Negro laborer and land renter. It is found in the landlord-and-tenant laws. I will read an extract to you from these laws that you may see how completely and rigidly the rights of the landlord are guarded and how entirely the tenant is in the clutches of the landlord:

REVISED CODE OF MISSISSIPPI

SEC. 1301. Every lessor of land shall have a lien on all the agricultural products of the leased premises, however and by whomsoever produced, to secure the payment of the rent and the market value of all advances made by him to his tenant for supplies for the tenant and others for whom he may contract.

SEC. 1304. When any landlord or lessor shall have just cause to suspect and shall verily believe that his tenant will remove his effects from the leased premises to any other place within or without the county before the rent or claims for supplies will fall due, so that no distress can be made, such landlord or lessor on making oath thereof, and of the amount the tenant is to pay, and at what time the same will fall due, and giving a bond as required in the preceding section, may, in like manner obtain an attachment against the goods and chattels of such tenant, and the officers making the distress shall give notice thereof and advertise the property distrained for sale, in the manner directed in the last preceding section, and if such tenant shall not, before the time appointed for such sale, give bond with sufficient security in double the amount of the rent, or other demand payable to the plaintiff, conditioned for the payment of said rent or other thing at the time it shall be due, with all cost, the goods distrained, or so much thereof as shall be necessary, shall be sold by the said officer at public sale to the highest bidder for cash, and out of the proceeds of the sale he shall pay to the plaintiff the amount due him, deducting interest for the time until the same shall become payable.

SEC. 1361. Said lien shall exist by virtue of the relation of the parties as employer and employee, and without any writing or recording.

SEC. 1362. Provides that any person who aids or assists in removing anything subject to these liens; without the consent of the landlord, shall, upon conviction, be punished by a fine of not more than $500, and be imprisoned in the county jail not more than six months, or by either such fine and imprisonment.

VOORHEE'S REVISED LAWS OF LA. 2D

SEC. 2165. Article 287 shall be so amended that a lessor may obtain a writ of pro-visional seizure even before the rent is due, and it shall be sufficient to entitle the lessor to the writ to swear to the amount which he claims, whether due or not due, and that he has good reasons to believe that the lessee will remove the furniture or property upon which he has a lien or privilege out of the premises, and that he may be, therefore, deprived of his lien.

LAWS OF FLORIDA—M'CLELLAN'S DIGEST

SEC. I, chapter 137. All claims for rent shall be a lien on agricultural products raised on the land rented, and shall be superior to all other liens and claims, though of older date, and also a superior lien on all other property of the lessee or his sub-lessee, or assigns usually kept on the premises, over any lien acquired subsequently to such property having been bought on the premises leased.

CODE OF ALABAMA

SEC. 3055, chapter 6. Lien continues and attaches to crop of succeeding years. When the tenant fails to pay any part of such rent or advances, and continues his ten-ancy under the same landlord for the next succeeding year for which the original lien for advances, if any remain unpaid, shall continue on the articles advanced or prop-erty purchased with money advanced or obtained by barter in exchange for articles advanced, and for which a lien shall also attach to the crop of such succeeding year.

You have thus seen a specimen, and a fair specimen, of the landlord-and-ten-ant laws of several of the old slave states; you have thus seen how scrupulously and rigidly the rights of the landlords are guarded and protected by these laws; you have thus seen how completely the tenant is put at the mercy of the land-lord; you have thus seen the bias, the motive, and intention of the legislators by whom these laws have been enacted, and by whom they have been administered; and now you are only to remember the sentiment in regard to the Negro, pecu-liar to the people of the South, and the character of the people against whom these laws are to be enforced, and the fact that no people are better than their laws, to have a perfectly just view of the whole situation.

To my mind these landlord-and-tenant laws are a disgrace and a scandal to American civilization. A more skillfully contrived device than these laws to crush out all aspiration, all hope of progress in the landless Negro could not well be devised. They sound to me like the grating hinges of a slave prison. They read like the inhuman bond of Shylock, stipulating for his pound of flesh. They envi-ron the helpless Negro like the devilfish of Victor Hugo, and draw the blood from every pore. He may writhe and twist, and strain every muscle, but he is held and firmly bound in a strong, remorseless and deadly grasp, a grasp from which only death can free him. Floods may rise, droughts may scorch, the elements may de-stroy his crops, famine may come, but whatever else may happen, the greedy landlord must have from his tenant the uttermost farthing. Like the den of the lion, all toes in its path turn inward.

The case is aggravated when you think of the illiteracy and ignorance of the people who sign land leases. They are ignorant of the terms of the contract, ignorant of the requirements of the law, and are thus absolutely in the power of the landholder.

You have heard much, read much, and thought much of the flagrant injustice, the monstrous cruelty and oppression inflicted on the tenant class in Ireland. I have no disposition to underrate the hardships of that class. On the contrary, I deplore them. But knowing them as I do[5] and deploring them as I do, I declare to you that the condition of the Irish tenant is merciful, tender and just, as compared with the American freedman. There are thousands in Ireland today who fix the price of their own rent, and thousands more for whom the government itself measures the amount of rent to be paid, not by the greed of the landlord, but by the actual value of the land and its productions, and by the ability of the tenant to pay.

But how is it with us? The tenant is left in the clutches of the landlord. No third party intervenes between the greed and power of one and the helplessness of the other. The landholder imposes his price, exacts his conditions, and the landless Negro must comply or starve. It is impossible to conceive of conditions more unfavorable to the welfare and prosperity of the laborer. It is often said that the law is merciful, but there is no mercy in this law.

Now let us sum up some of the points in the situation of the freedman. You will have seen how he is paid for his labor, how a full-grown man gets only eight dollars a month for his labor, out of which he has to feed, clothe and educate his children. You have seen how even this sum is reduced by the infamous truck system of payment. You have seen how easily he may be charged with one third more than the value of the goods that be buys. You have seen how easily he may be compelled to receive the poorest commodities at the highest prices. You have seen how he is never allowed to see or handle a dollar. You have seen how impossible it is for him to accumulate money or property. You have seen how completely he is chained to the locality in which he lives. You have seen, therefore, that having no money, he cannot travel or go anywhere to better his condition. You have seen by these laws that even on the premises which he rents he can own nothing, possess nothing. You have seen that he cannot sell a sheep, or a pig, or even a chicken without the consent of the landlord, whose claim to all he has is superior and paramount to all other claims whatsoever. You have seen all this and more, and I ask, in view of it all, How, in the name of human reason, could the Negro be expected to rise higher in the scale of morals, manner, religion and civilization than he has done during the twenty years of his freedom. Shame, eternal shame, on those writers and speakers who taunt, denounce and disparage the Negro because he is today found in poverty, rags and wretchedness.

But again, let us see what are the relations subsisting between the Negro and the state and national governments—what support, what assistance he has received from either of them. Take his relation to the national government and we shall find him a deserted, a defrauded, a swindled, and an outcast man—in law free, in fact a slave; in law a citizen, in fact an alien; in law a voter, in fact, a disfranchised man. In law, his color is no crime; in fact, his color exposes him to be treated as a criminal. Toward him every attribute of a just government is contradicted. For him, it is not a government of the people, by the people, and for the people. Toward him, it abandons the beneficent character of a government, and all that gives a government the right to exist. The true object for which governments are ordained among men is to protect the weak against the encroachments of the strong, to hold its strong arm of justice over all the civil relations of its citizens and to see that all have an equal chance in the race of life. Now, in the case of the Negro citizen, our national government does precisely the reverse of all this. Instead of protecting the weak against the encroachments of the strong, it tacitly protects the strong in its encroachments upon the weak. When the colored citizens of the South point to the fourteenth and fifteenth amendments of the Constitution for the protection of their civil and political rights, the Supreme Court of the United States turns them out of court and tells them they must look for justice at the hands of the states, well knowing that those states are, in effect, the very parties that deny them justice. Thus is the Negro citizen swindled. The government professes to give him citizenship and silently permits him to be divested of every attribute of citizenship. It demands allegiance, but denies protection. It taxes him as a citizen in peace, and compels him to bear arms and meet bullets in war. It imposes upon him all the burdens of citizenship and withholds from him all its benefits.

I know it is said that the general government is a government of limited powers. It was also once said that the national government could not coerce a state and it is generally said that this and that public measure is unconstitutional. But whenever an administration has had the will to do anything, it has generally found Constitutional power to do it. If the general government had the power to make black men citizens, it has the power to protect them in that citizenship. If it had the right to make them voters it has the right to protect them in the exercise of the elective franchise. If it has this right, and refuses to exercise it, it is a traitor to the citizen. If it has not this right, it is destitute of the fundamental quality of a government and ought to be hissed and hurried out of the sisterhood of government, a usurper, a sham, a delusion and a snare.

On the other hand, if the fault is not in the structure of the government, but in the treachery and indifference of those who administer it, the American people owe it to themselves, owe it to the world, and to the Negro, to sweep from place and power those who are thus derelict in the discharge of their place in the government who will not enforce the Constitutional right of every class of American citizen.

I am a Republican. I believe in the Republican party. My political hopes for the future of the colored people are enforced in the character and composition, in the wisdom and justice, in the courage and fidelity of the Republican party. I am unable to see how any honest and intelligent colored man can be a Democrat or play fast and loose between the two parties. But while I am a Republican and believe in the party, I dare to tell that party the truth. In my judgment it can no longer repose on the history of its grand and magnificent achievements. It must not only stand abreast with the times, but must create the times. Its power and greatness consisted in this at the beginning. It was in advance of the times and made the times when it abolished the slave trade between the states, when it emancipated the slaves of the District of Columbia, when it stemmed the bloody tide of disunion, when it abolished slavery in all the states, when it made the Negro a soldier and a citizen, when it conceded to him the elective franchise; and now, in my judgment, the strength, success and glory of the Republican party will be found in its holding this advanced position. It must not stand still or take any step backward. Its mission is to lead, not to follow; to make circumstances, not to be made by them. It is held and firmly bound by every sentiment of justice and honor to make a living fact out of the dead letter of the Constitutional amendments. It must make the path of the black citizen to the ballot box as safe and smooth as that of the white citizen. It must make it impossible for a man like James Russell Lowell[6] to say he sees no difference between the Democratic party and the Republican party. If it fails to do all this, I for one shall welcome the bolt which shall scatter it into a thousand fragments.

The supreme movement in the life of the Republican party is at hand. The question, to be or not to be, will be decided at Chicago, and I reverently trust in God that it may be decided rightly. If the platform it shall adopt shall be in accordance with its earlier antecedents; if the party shall have the courage in its maturity which it possessed and displayed in its infancy; if it shall express its determination to vindicate the honor and integrity of the Republic by stamping out the fraud, injustice and violence which make elections in the South a disgrace and scandal to the Republic, and place a man on that platform with a clear head, a clean hand and a heroic heart, the country will triumphantly elect him. If it, however, should fail to elect him, we shall have done our duty and shall still have under us a grand party of the future, certain of success.

I do not forget that there are other great interests beside the Negro to be thought of. The civil service is a great interest, protection to American industry is a great interest, the proper management of our finances so as to promote the business and prosperity of the country is a great interest; but the national honor—the redemption of our national pledge to the freedmen, the supremacy of the Constitution in the fullness of its spirit and in the completeness of its letter over all the states of the Union alike—is an incomparably greater interest than all others. It touches the soul of the nation, which against all things else should be preserved. Should all be lost but this, the nation would be like Chicago after the fire—more prosperous and beautiful than ever. But what I ask of the Republican party requires no sacrifice or postponement of the material interest of the country. I simply say to the Republican party: Those things ye ought to have done and not to have left the others undone, and the present is the time to enforce this lesson.

The time has come for a new departure as to the kind of man who is to be the standard-bearer of the Republican party. Events are our instructors. We have had enough of names, we now want things. We have had enough of good feeling, enough of shaking hands over the bloody chasm, enough of conciliation, enough of laudation of the bravery of our Southern brethren. We tried all that with President Hayes, of the purity of whose motives I have no shadow of doubt. His mistake was that he confided in the honor of the Confederates, who were without honor. He supposed that if left to themselves and thrown upon their honor they would obey the Constitution they had sworn to support and treat the colored citizens with justice and fairness at the ballot box.[7] Time has proved the reverse of all this, and this fact should cure the Republican party of adopting in its platform any such soft policy or any such candidate. Let us have a candidate this time of pronounced opinions and, above all, a backbone. . . .

There has been no show of federal power in the borders of the South for a dozen years. Its people have been left to themselves. Northern men have even refrained from going among them in election times to discuss the claims of public men, or the wisdom of public measures. They have had the field all to themselves, and we all now know just what has come of it, and the eyes of the leaders of the Republican party are, I trust, wide open. Mr. James G. Blaine, after, as well as before, he failed of his election,[8] pointed out the evil which now besets us as a party and a nation. Senator John Sherman[9] knows full well that the Solid South must be broken, that the colored citizen must not be cheated out of his vote any longer and that the Constitution must be obeyed in all parts of the country alike; that individual states are great, but that the United States are greater. He has said the right word, and said it calmly but firmly, in the face of the South itself, and I thank him and honor him for it. I am naming no candidate for the presidency. Any one of the dozen statesmen whose names are in the air, and many whose names are not, would suit me and gain my best word and vote. There is one who has not been named and not likely to be named, who would suit me and who would fulfill the supreme demand of the hour; and that man is a Southern man. I refer to the Honorable John M. Harlan, Justice of the Supreme Court of the United States, who, true to his convictions, stood by the plain intention of the Fourteenth Amendment of the Constitution of the United States in opposition to all his brothers on the bench.[10] The man who could do that in the circumstances in which he was placed, if made President of the United States, could be depended upon in any emergency to do the right thing.

But, as I have said, I am not naming candidates. The candidate of the Republican party will, in all the likelihoods of the case, be my candidate. I am no partisan. I have no ambition to be the first to name any man or make any man obliged to me for naming him for the high office of President. Other men may do this, and I have no disposition to find fault with them for doing it. If, however, John A. Logan were living I might name him.[11] I am sure he would not allow himself to be trifled with, or allow the Constitution to be defied or trampled in the dust. I have faith also, in Roscoe Conkling,[12] whose dangerous illness we all deplore and whose recovery we profoundly and anxiously desire. With such a man in the Presidential chair, the red shirt and rifle, horseback and tissue-ballot plan of South Carolina and the Mississippi bulldozing plan would receive no encouragement.[13]

I am, however, not here to name men. My mission now, as all along during nearly fifty years, is to plead the cause of the dumb millions of our countrymen against injustice, oppression, meanness and cruelty, and to hasten the day when the principles of liberty and humanity expressed in the Declaration of Independence and the Constitution of the United States shall be the law and the practice of every section, and of all the people of this great country without regard to race, sex, color or religion.

Washington *National Republican*, April 17, 1888

1. Frederic M. Holland, *Frederick Douglass: The Colored Orator,* New York, 1891, p. 368.

In 1892 a group of Southern Negroes called on Douglass to obtain his advice relative to an exodus of Negro people from Arkansas to Africa. Douglass suggested that they go west instead of Africa. The group formed the Washington Co-operative Improvement Society and settled in Spokane, Washington. On January 9, 1893, Chas. E. Hall, secretary of the society, wrote to Douglass: "Acting upon your suggestion and believing that America is our home and that if unable to care for ourselves here, it is almost useless to seek other climes, six of us young men have organized the above society whose purpose is clearly indicated. We propose to state facts regarding the resources of Washington, Oregon, Idaho, Montana, particularly those of Washington." The society was organized "to promote the general welfare and assist materially the condition of our fellow Afro-Americans in the pursuit of Independence and Prosperity." (Frederick Douglass Papers, Frederick Douglass Memorial Home, Anacostia, D.C.)

2. Hamilton J. Smith to Douglass, Apr. 17, 1888; Geo. B. Edmonds to Douglass, Apr. 17, 1888; J. B. White to Douglass, Apr. 17, 1888; John W. Curtis to Douglass, Apr. 18, 1888; Charles N. Hunter to Douglass, Apr. 23, 1888, Frederick Douglass Papers, Frederick Douglass Memorial Home, Anacostia, D.C.

3. Andersonville was the notorious Confederate prison in southwestern Georgia for Union prisoners, who were packed together with little food and hardly any medicine. From June to September, 1864, 8,589 prisoners died in Andersonville. [This and the following endnotes to this speech are taken from Philip S. Foner, ed., *The Voice of Black America: Major Speeches by Negroes in the United States, 1797–1971,* New York, 1972, pp. 524–536.]

4. In 1886 Robert Smalls was not seated in Congress as representative from South Carolina, even though he spoke for his right to his seat.

5. During his first trip abroad in 1845–46, Douglass toured all over Ireland and delivered more than fifty lectures there.

6. James Russell Lowell (1819–1891), poet, essayist, editor and diplomat, frequently wrote against slavery in his poetry. In his *Bigelow Papers* (1848) he had opposed the Mexican War.

7. When Rutherford B. Hayes removed the troops from Louisiana and South Carolina, he wrote in his diary that the governors and legislatures of these two states had pledged to observe the Thirteenth, Fourteenth and Fifteenth Amendments. He concluded: "I am confident this is a good work. Time will tell." Eighteen months later be was deeply shocked that Louisiana and South Carolina were not keeping their promises. Gravely, he wrote: "By State legislation, by frauds, by intimidation and by violence of the most atrocious character, colored citizens have been deprived of the right of suffrage—a right guaranteed by the Constitution, and to the protection of which the people of those States have been solemnly pledged." (T. Harry Williams, editor, *Hayes: The Diary of a President, 1875–1881,* Philadelphia, 1964, pp. 122, 196).

8. James Gillespie Blaine (1830–1893) was the Republican candidate for President in 1884 against Grover Cleveland, the victorious Democratic candidate.

9. John Sherman (1823–1900), author of the Sherman Anti-Trust Act of 1890, was a leading Republican Senator and U.S. Secretary of State (1897–98).

10. John Marshall Harlan (1833–1911), born in Kentucky, served on the U.S. Supreme Court from 1877 to 1911, during which time be consistently supported rights of black Americans. He dissented in the Civil Rights Case of 1883 and the *Plessy v. Ferguson* decision of 1896, in both cases denouncing the deprivation of the Constitutional rights of Negroes under the Fourteenth Amendment.

11. John A. Logan (1826–1886), a Union general and frequent supporter of Negro rights, was U.S. Senator from Illinois (1871–77; 1879–86).

12. Roscoe Conkling (1829–1888), leader of the Republican party in New York and Senator from that state between 1867 and 1881, was a staunch opponent of reconciliation with the South. He headed the so-called Stalwart faction in the Republican party, which stood for upholding the rights of the Negroes under the Constitutional amendments adopted during Reconstruction.

13. In states where Negroes were a majority or nearly so, virtual disfranchisement of the blacks was accomplished without legal action, after the overthrow of Reconstruction, by such

devices as the Mississippi Plan, which used violence to force Negroes to desist from political action. "Red Shirts" were armed vigilantes on horseback in South Carolina.

––––––––––

Although not a delegate, Douglass was present at the Republican National Convention in Chicago, in June [1888]. In response to a call from the convention, he delivered [this] brief address on the opening day.

Three days later, the convention adopted a platform which expressed indignation at the suppression of suffrage among the Negroes in the South, and advocated fuller control of Congressional elections by the Federal government so that the Negro should be assured of, and guaranteed, a free exercise of his rights. Benjamin Harrison, the Republican candidate for President, announced that he subscribed fully to the policy set forth in the platform.[1] [IV:128]

THE BLOODY SHIRT, speech delivered at the National Republican Convention, Chicago, June 19, 1888

I have only one word to say to this convention and it is this: I hope this convention will make such a record in its proceedings as will entirely put it out of the power of the leaders of the Democratic party and of the leaders of the Mugwump party to say that they see no difference between the position of the Republican party in respect to the class I represent and that of the Democratic party. I have a great respect for a certain quality for which the Democratic party is distinguished. That quality is fidelity to its friends, its faithfulness to those whom it has acknowledged as its masters during the last forty years. It was faithful to the slaveholding class during the existence of slavery. It was faithful to them before the war. It gave them all the encouragement that it possibly could without drawing its own neck into the halter. It was also faithful during the period of reconstruction, and it has been faithful ever since. It is to-day faithful to the solid South. I hope and believe that the great Republican party will prove itself equally faithful to its friends, those friends with black faces who during the war were eyes to your blind, shelter to your shelterless, when flying from the lines of the enemy. They are as faithful to-day as when the great Republic was in the extremest need; when its fate seemed to tremble in the balance; when the crowned heads of the Old World were gloating over our ruin, saying, "Aha! aha! the great Republican bubble is about to burst." When your army was melting away before the fire and pestilence of rebellion; when your star-spangled banner trailed in the dust or, heavy with blood, drooped at the mast head, you called upon the Negro. Yes, Abraham Lincoln called upon the Negro to reach forth with his iron arm and catch with his steel fingers your faltering flag, and he came, he came full two hundred thousand strong. Let us in the platform we are about to promulgate remember the brave black men, and let us remember that these brave black men are now stripped of their constitutional right to vote. Let this remembrance be embodied in the standard bearer whom you will present to the country. Leave these men no longer compelled to wade to the ballot-box through blood, but extend over them the protecting arm of this government, and make their pathway to the ballot-box as straight and as smooth and as safe as that of any other class of citizens. Be not deterred from this duty by the cry of the bloody shirt. Let that shirt be waved as long as there shall be a drop of innocent blood upon it. A government that can give liberty in its constitution ought to have the power in its administration to protect and defend that liberty. I will not further take up your time. I have spoken for millions, and my thought is now before you.

Life and Times of Frederick Douglass, 1893

1. James D. Richardson, *Messages and Papers of the Presidents, 1789–1897,* Washington, D.C., 1869–99, vol. IX, pp. 32–58.

————————

THE NATION'S PROBLEM, speech delivered before the Bethel Literary and Historical Society, Washington D.C., April 16, 1889

Friends and fellow citizens:

I congratulate you upon this the twenty-seventh anniversary of the abolition of slavery in the District of Columbia, and I gratefully acknowledge the compliment implied in calling upon me to assist in expressing the thoughts and sentiments natural to this and other similar occasions.

For reasons which will become apparent in the course of my address, I respond to your call with more than my usual diffidence.

One cause, like many other good causes, has its ebbs and flows, successes and failures, joyous hopes and saddening fears. I cannot forget on this occasion that Lewis Hayden, a brave and wise counseler in the cause of our people, a moral hero, has laid down his armor, filled up the measure of his days, completed his work on earth, and left a mournful void in our ranks. I am reminded, too, that John Bright, the Quaker statesman of England, the man of matchless eloquence, whose roof sheltered me when a stranger and sojourner, and whose friendship for this republic, was only equaled by his sympathy for the oppressed of all lands and nations, has passed away. The death of such a man is not a loss only to his own country and people, but to the oppressed in every quarter of the globe. We do not stand to-day where we stood one year ago, and my speech will be colored by the altered condition of our surroundings.

It has been our custom to hail the anniversary of our emancipation as a joyous event. We have observed it with every manifestation of gratitude. During the years immediately succeeding the abolition of slavery, our speeches and addresses on such occasions naturally overflowed with joy, gratitude and praise. We remembered with veneration and love the great men by whose moral testimonies, statesmanship, and philanthropy was brought about the long delayed and long prayed for deliverance of our people.

The great names of Garrison, Whittier, Sumner, Phillips, Stevens, Lincoln, and others were gratefully and lovingly repeated. We shouted the praises of these great men as God inspired benefactors. At that time, too, it was well enough and easy to blow aloud our brazen trumpets, call out the crowd, throng the streets with gay processions, and to shout aloud and make a joyful noise over the event, for since the great exodus of the Hebrews from Egyptian bondage no people had had greater cause for such joyful demonstrations. But the time for such demonstrations is over. It is not the past, but the present and the future that most concern us to-day. Our past was slavery. We cannot recur to it with any sense of complacency or composure. The history of it is a record of stripes, a revelation of agony. It is written in characters of blood. Its breath is a sigh, its voice a groan, and we turn from it with a shudder. The duty of to-day is to meet the questions that confront us with intelligence and courage.

Without the least desire to awaken undue alarm, I declare to you that, in my judgment, at no period since the abolition of slavery in the District of Columbia, have the moral, social, and political surroundings of the colored people of this country been more solemn and forboding than they are this day. If this statement is startling it is only because the facts are startling. I speak only the things I have seen. Nature has given me a buoyant disposition. I like to look upon the bright and hopeful side of affairs. No man can see the silver lining of a black cloud more joyfully than I. But he is a more hopeful man than I am who will tell you that the rights and liberties of the colored people in this country have passed beyond the danger line.

Mark, if you please, the fact, for it is a fact, an ominous fact, that at no time in the history of the conflict between slavery and freedom has the character of the Negro as a man been made the subject of a fiercer and more serious discussion in all the avenues of debate than during the past and present year. Against him have been marshalled the whole artillery of science, philosophy, and history. We are not only confronted by open foes, but we are assailed in the guise of sympathy and friendship and presented as objects of pity.

The strong point made against the Negro and his cause is the statement widely circulated and greatly relied upon that no two people so different in race and color can live together in the same country on a level of equal civil and political rights and powers; that nature herself has ordained that the relations of two such races must be that of domination and subjugation. This old slave-holding Calhoun and McDuffy doctrine, which we long ago thought dead and buried, is revived in unexpected quarters, and confronts us to-day as sternly as it did forty years ago. Then it was employed as the sure defence of slavery. Now it is employed as a justification of the fraud and violence by which colored men are divested of their citizenship, and robbed of their constitutional rights in the solid south.

To those who are hopefully assuming that there is no cause of apprehension, that we are secure in the possession of all that has been gained by the war and by reconstruction, I ask, What means the universal and palpable concern manifested through all the avenues of debate as to the future of the Negro in this country? For this question meets us now at every turn. Letters fairly pour upon me burdened with this inquiry. Whence this solicitude, or apparent solicitude? To me the question has a sinister meaning. It is prompted not so much by concern for the welfare of the Negro as by consideration of how his relation to the American government may effect the welfare and happiness of the American people. The Negro is now a member of the body politic. This talk about him implies that he is regarded as a diseased member. It is wisely said by physicians that any member of the human body is in a healthy condition when it gives no occasion to think of it. The fact that the American people of the Caucasian race are continually thinking of the Negro, and never cease to call attention to him, shows that his relation to them is felt to be abnormal and unhealthy.

I want the colored people of this country to understand the true character of the great race which rules, and must rule and determine the destiny of this republic. Justice and magnanimity are elements of American character. They may do much for us. But we are in no condition to depend upon these qualities exclusively. Depend upon it, whenever the American people shall become convinced that they have gone too far in recognizing the rights of the Negro, they will find some way to abridge those rights. The Negro is great, but the welfare of the nation will be considered greater. They will forget the Negro's service in the late war. They will forget his loyalty to the republic. They will forget the enmity of the old slaveholding class to the government. They will forget their solemn obligations of friendship to the Negro, and press to their bosoms the white enemies of the nation, while they give the cold shoulder to the black friends of the nation. Be not deceived. History repeats itself. The black man fought for American Independence. The Negro's blood mingled with the white man's blood at Bunker Hill, and in State St., Boston. But this sacrifice on his part won for him only temporary applause. He was returned to his former condition. He fought bravely with Gen. Jackson at New Orleans, but his reward was only slavery and chains. These facts speak, trumpet-tongued, of the kind of people with whom we have to deal, and through them we contemplate the sternest possibilities of the future.

I have said that at no time has the character of the Negro been so generally and seriously discussed as now. I do not regard discussion as an evil in itself. I regard it not as an enemy, but as a friend. It has served us well at other times in our history, and I hope it may serve us well at this time. Controversy, whether of words or blows, whether in the forum or on the battle field, may help us, if we but make the right use of it. We are not to be like dumb driven cattle in this discussion, in this war of words and conflicting theories. Our business is to answer back wisely, modestly, and yet grandly.

While I do not regard discussion as an enemy I cannot but deem it in this instance as out of place and unfortunate. It comes to us as a surprise and a bitter disappointment. It implies a deplorable unrest and unsoundness in the public mind. It shows that the reconstruction of our national institutions upon a basis of liberty, and equality is not yet accepted as a final and irrevocable settlement of the Negro's relation to the government, and of his membership in the body politic. There seems to be in it a lurking disposition, a looking around for some plausible excuse for dispossessing the Negro of some part of his inheritance conceded to him in the generous spirit of the new departure of our government.

Going back to the early days of the anti-slavery movement I cannot but re-mark, and I call upon you to remark, the striking contrast between the disposi-tion which then existed to utterly ignore the Negro and the present disposition to make him a topic of universal interest and deepest concern. When the Negro was a slave and stood outside the government nobody but a few so-called abo-lition fanatics thought him worthy of the smallest attention. He was almost as completely outside of the nation's thought as he was outside the nation's law and the nation's religion. But now all is changed. His freedom makes him discussed on every hand. The platform, the pulpit, the press, and the legislative hall regard him and struggle with him as a great and difficult problem, one that requires al-most divine wisdom to solve.

Now it is this gigantic representation to which I object. I deny that the Negro is correctly represented by it. The statement of it is a prejudice to the Negro's cause. It denotes the presence of the death dealing shadow of an ancient curse. We had fondly hoped, and had reason to hope, that when the Negro ceased to be a slave, when he ceased to be a thing and became a man, when he ceased to be an alien and became a citizen, when the constitution of the United States ceased to be the charter of slavery and became the charter of liberty, the Negro problem was solved and settled forever. The whole contention now raised over him is an anachronism, a misnomer, a false pretense, a delusion and a sham, a crafty substitution of a false issue for the true one.

I deny and utterly scout the idea that there is now, properly speaking, any such thing as a Negro problem now before the American people. It is not the Negro, educated or illiterate, intelligent or ignorant, who is on trial or whose qualities are giving trouble to the nation. The real problem lies in the other direction. It is not so much what the Negro is, what he has been, or what he may be that con-stitutes the problem. Here, as elsewhere, the lesser is included in the greater. The Negro's significance is dwarfed by a factor vastly larger than himself. The real question, the all-commanding question, is whether American justice, American liberty, American civilization, American law, and American Christianity can be made to include and protect alike and forever all American citizens in the rights which, in a generous moment in the nation's life, have been guaranteed to them by the organic and fundamental law of the land. It is whether this great nation shall conquer its prejudices, rise to the dignity of its professions, and proceed in the sublime course of truth and liberty marked out for itself since the late war, or swing back to its ancient moorings of slavery and barbarism. The Negro is of inferior activity and power in the solution of this problem. He is the clay, the na-tion is the potter. He is the subject, the nation is the sovereign. It is not what he shall be or do, but what the nation shall be and do, which is to solve this great national problem.

Speaking for him, I can commend him upon every ground. He is loyal and pa-triotic; service is the badge of all his tribe. He has proved it before, and he will prove it again. The country has never called upon him in vain. What he has been in the past in this respect that he will be in the future. All he asks now, all he has ever asked, all he will ever ask, is that the nation shall fulfill toward him its own recognized and self-imposed obligations. When he asks for bread he will not accept a stone. When he asks for a fish he will not accept a serpent. His protest now is against being cheated by cunningly devised judicial decisions, by frauds upon the ballot box, or by brutal violence of red-shirted rebels. He only asks the American people to adjust the practice to the justice and wisdom of their laws, and he holds that this is first, midst, and last, and the only problem to be solved.

While, however, the Negro may very properly protest against the popular statement of the question, and while he may insist that the one just stated is the proper one, and the only one; while he may hold that primarily and fundamentally it is an American problem and not a Negro problem, he may materially assist in its solution. He can assume an attitude, develop a character, improve his condition, and, in a measure, compel the respect and esteem of his fellow men.

In order to do this we have, first of all, to learn and to understand thoroughly the nature of the social, moral, and political forces that surround us, and how to shape our ends and wisely determine our destiny. We should endeavor to discover the true sources of our danger—whether they be within ourselves or in circumstances external to ourselves. If I am here for any useful purpose, it is in some measure to answer the question, "What of the night?"

For the present I have seemed to forget that this is an occasion of joy. I have thus far spoken mainly in sorrow rather than in gladness; of grief rather than in gratitude. Like the resolution of Hamlet, my outlook has been sicklied o'er with the pale cast of thought.

Now, what of the night? What of the night? Is it cheered by the beams of celestial light and hope, or is it saddened by ominous clouds, darkness, and distant thunder? You and I should be brave enough to look the facts fairly and firmly in the face.

I profoundly wish I could make a cheerful response to this inquiry. But the omens are against me. I am compelled to say that while we have no longer to contend with the physical wrongs and abominations of slavery: while we have no longer to chill the blood of our hearers by talking of whips, chains, branding irons and bloodhounds; we have, as already intimated, to contend with a foe, which though less palpable, is still a fierce and formidable foe. It is the ghost of a by-gone, dead and buried institution. It loads the very air with a malignant prejudice of race. It has poisoned the fountains of justice, and defiled the altars of religion. It acts upon the body politic as the leprous distillment acted upon the blood and body of the murdered king of Denmark. In antebellum times it was the standing defense of slavery. In our own times it is employed in defense of oppression and proscription. Until this foe is conquered and driven from the breasts of the American people, our relations will be unhappy, our progress slow, our lives embittered, our freedom a mockery, and our citizenship a delusion.

The work before us is to meet and combat this prejudice by lives and acquirements which contradict and put to shame this narrow and malignant feeling. We have errors of our own to abandon, habits to reform, manners to improve, ignorance to dispel, and character to build up. This is something which no power on earth can do for us, and which no power on earth can prevent our doing for ourselves.

In pointing out errors and mistakes common among ourselves, I shall run the risk of incurring displeasure; for no people with whom I am acquainted are less tolerant of criticism than ourselves, especially from one of our own number. We have been so long in the habit of tracing our failures and misfortunes to the views and acts of others that we seem, in some measure, to have lost the talent and disposition of seeing our own faults, or of "seeing ourselves as others see us." And yet no man can do a better service to another man than to correct his mistakes, point out his hurtful errors, show him the path of truth, duty, and safety.

One of the few errors to which we are clinging most persistently and, as I think, mischievously, has come into great prominence of late. It is the cultivation and stimulation amongst us of a sentiment which we are pleased to call race pride. I find it in all our books, papers, and speeches. For my part I see no superiority or inferiority in race or color. Neither the one nor the other is a proper source of pride or complacency. Our race and color are not of our own choosing. We have no volition in the case one way or another. The only excuse for pride in individuals or races is the fact of their own achievements. Our color is the gift of the Almighty. We should neither be proud of it nor ashamed of it. But we may well enough be proud or ashamed when we have ourselves achieved success or have failed of success. If the sun has curled our hair and tanned our skin let the sun be proud of its achievement, for we have done nothing for it one way or the other. I see no benefit to be derived from this everlasting exhortation by speakers and writers among us to the cultivation of race pride. On the contrary, I see in it a positive evil. It is building on a false foundation. Besides, what is the thing we are fighting against, and what are we fighting for in this country? What is the mountain devil, the lion in the way of our progress? What is it, but American race pride; an assumption of superiority upon the ground of race and color? Do we not know that every argument we make, and every pretension we set up in favor of race pride is giving the enemy a stick to break our own heads?

But it may be said that we shall put down race pride in the white people by cultivating race pride among ourselves. The answer to this is that devils are not cast out by Bellzebub, the prince of devils. The poorest and meanest white man when he has nothing else to commend him says: "I am a white man, I am." We can all see the low extremity reached by that sort of race pride, and yet we encourage it when we pride ourselves upon the fact of our color. Let us do away with this supercilious nonsense. If we are proud let it be because we have had some agency in producing that of which to be proud. Do not let us be proud of what we can neither help nor hinder. The Bible puts us in the condition in this respect of the leopard, and says that we can no more change our skin than the leopard his spots. If we are unfortunate in being placed among a people with whom our color is a badge of inferiority, there is no need of our making ourselves ridiculous by forever, in words, affecting to be proud of a circumstance due to no virtue in us, and over which we have no control.

You will, perhaps, think this criticism uncalled for. My answer is that truth is never uncalled for. Right thinking is essential to right acting, and I hope that we shall hereafter see the wisdom of basing our pride and complacency upon substantial results accomplished by the race.

The question here raised is not merely theoretical, but is of practical significance. In some of our colored public journals, with a view to crippling my influence with the colored race, I have seen myself charged with a lack of race pride. I am not ashamed of that charge. I have no apology or vindication to offer. If fifty years of uncompromising devotion to the cause of the colored man in this country does not vindicate me, I am content to live without vindication.

While I have no more reason to be proud of our race than another, I dare say, and I fear no contradiction, that there is no other man in the United States prouder than myself of any great achievement, mental or mechanical, of which any colored man or woman is the author. This is not because I am a colored man, but because I am a man, and because color is treated as a crime by the American people. My sentiments at this point originate not in my color, but in a sense of justice common to all right minded men. It is that which gives the sympathy of the crowd to the under dog, no matter what may be his color. When a colored man is charged with a want of race pride, he may well ask, What race? for a large percentage of the colored race are related in some degree to more than one race. But the whole assumption of race pride is ridiculous. Let us have done with complexional superiorities or inferiorities, complexional pride or shame. I want no better basis for my activities and affinities than the broad foundation laid by the Bible itself, that God has made of one blood all nations of men to dwell on all the face of the earth. This comprehends the Fatherhood of God and the brotherhood of man.

I have another criticism to make of a position which, I think, often invites unfavorable comparison and positive disparagement. It is our noisy assertion of equality with the Caucasian race. There are two kinds of equality, one potential and the other actual, one theoretical and the other practical. We should not be satisfied by merely quoting the doctrine of equality as laid down in the Declaration of Independence, but we should give it practical illustration. We have to do as well as to be. If we had built great ships, sailed around the world, taught the science of navigation, discovered far-off islands, capes, and continents, enlarged the boundaries of human knowledge, improved the conditions of man's existence, brought valuable contributions of art, science, and literature, revealed great truths, organized great states, administered great governments, defined the laws of the universe, formulated systems of mental and moral philosophy, invented railroads, steam engines, mowing machines, sewing machines, taught the sun to take pictures, the lightning to carry messages, we then might claim, not only potential and theoretical equality, but actual and practical equality. Nothing is gained to our cause by claiming for ourselves more than of right we can establish belongs to us. Manly self-assertion, I know, is a power, and I would have that power employed within the bounds of truth and sobriety. We should never forget, in our relations with our fellows, that modesty is also a power.

When it is manifested without any touch of servility it is as sure to win respect as unfounded pretension is to provoke and receive contempt. We should give our critics no advantage at this point, either by word or conduct. Our battle with popular prejudice requires on our part the utmost circumspection in word and in deed. Our men should be gentlemen and our women ladies, and we can be neither without a modest reserve in mind and in manners.

Were I not speaking to the most cultivated class of our people, for the Bethel

Literary Society comprises that class, I might hesitate to employ this course of remark. You, I am quite sure, will not misapprehend my statements or my motives.

There is one other point worthy of animadversion—it is the error that union among ourselves is an essential element of success in our relations to the white race. This, in my judgment, is a very serious mistake. I can hardly point out one more pregnant with peril. It is contended that we are now eight millions, that we hold the balance of power between the two great political parties of the country, and that, if we were only united in one body, under wise and powerful leaders, we could shape the policy of both political parties, make and unmake parties, control the destiny of the republic, and secure for ourselves a desirable and happy future. They say that in union there is strength; that united we stand and divided we fall, and much else of the same sort.

My position is the reverse of all this. I hold that our union is in weakness. In quoting these wise sayings colored men seem to forget that there are exceptions to all general rules, and that our position in this country is an exceptional position. The rule for us is the exception. There are times and places when separation and division are better than union, when to stand apart is wiser than standing together. There are buildings which will hold a few, but which will break down under the weight of a crowd; the ice of the river may be strong enough to bear a man, but would break through under the weight of an elephant. The ice under us in this country is very thin, and is made very weak by the warm fogs of prejudice. A few colored people scattered among large white communities are easily accepted by such communities, and a larger measure of liberty is accorded to the few than would be to the many. The trouble is that when we assemble in great numbers anywhere we are apt to form communities by ourselves, and our occupation of any part of a town or city, apart from the people surrounding us, brings us into separate schools, separate churches, separate benevolent and literary societies, and the result is the adoption of a scale of manners, morals, and customs peculiar to our condition and to our antecedents as an oppressed people. When we thus isolate ourselves we say to those around us, "We have nothing in common with you," and, very naturally, the reply of our neighbors is in the same tone and to the same effect; for when a people care for nobody, nobody will care for them. When we isolate ourselves we lose, in large measure, the common benefit of association with those whose advantages have been superior to ours.

The foundation upon which we stand in this country is not strong enough to make it safe to stand together. A nation within a nation is an anomaly. There can be but one American nation under the American government, and we are Americans. The constitution of the country makes us such, and our lines of activity should accord with our citizenship. Circumstances now compel us in certain directions to maintain separate neighborhoods and separate institutions. But these circumstances should only be yielded to the least practicable extent. A Negro neighborhood depreciates the market value of property. We should distribute ourselves among the people, build our houses, where if they take fire other houses will be in danger. Common dangers will create common safeguards. Our policy should be to unite with the great mass of the American people in all their activities and resolve to fall or flourish with our common country. We cannot afford to draw the color line in politics, trade, education, manners, religion, or civilization. Especially, we cannot afford to draw the color line in politics. A party acting upon that basis would be not merely a misfortune, but a dire calamity to the American peoples. The rule of the majority is the fundamental principle of the American government, and it may be safely affirmed that the American people will never permit, tolerate, or submit to the success of any political device or strategy calculated to circumvent and defeat the just application and operation of this fundamental principle of our government.

It is also fair to state that no part of the American people—Irish, Scotch, Italian, or German—could attempt any such political jugglery with less success than ourselves.

Another popular error flaunted in our faces at every turn, and for the most part by very weak and impossible editors, is the alleged duty of colored men to patronize colored newspapers, and this simply because they happen to be edited and published by colored men, and not because of their intrinsic value. Anybody who can find means to issue a paper with a patent back and hang out a colored flag at the head of its columns, demands support on the ground that it is a colored newspaper. For one I am not disposed to yield to this demand. A colored newspaper maker has no higher claim upon us for patronage than a colored carpenter, a colored shoemaker, or a colored bricklayer. Whether he should be supported should depend upon the character of the man and the quality of his work. Our people should not be required to buy an inferior article offered by a colored man, when for the same money, they can purchase a superior article from a white man. We need, and ought to have, the best supply of mental food that the American market affords.

In saying this I do not forget that an able, sound, and decent public journal, conducted in a spirit of justice and not made a vehicle of malice or personal favoritism, edited and published by colored men is a powerful lever for the elevation and advancement of the race. Such a paper has special claims upon all who desire to raise colored people in the estimation of themselves and their surroundings. But while this is true, it is also true that in the same proportion that an able and influential public journal tends to remove popular prejudice and elevate us in the judgment of those whose good opinion is worth having, a feeble, ungrammatical and wretchedly conducted public journal tends to lower us in the opinion of good men, besides having a debasing influence upon the minds of the readers. Character and quality should rule here as well as elsewhere.

But I leave this aspect of our relations and duties to make a few remarks upon the changed condition of our country.

Four years ago we assembled to celebrate the abolition of slavery in the District of Columbia. Under a dark and portentous cloud, the honorable Grover Cleveland, the approved leader and representative of the Democratic party, had, only a few weeks before, been duly inaugurated President of the United States. The fact of his election had carried alarm and consternation into every black man's cabin in the southern states. For the moment it must have seemed to them that the sun of freedom had gone down, and the night of slavery had succeeded. The terror was dismal and heartbreaking enough, and although it turned out to be groundless, it was not altogether unnatural. The Democratic party had, in its day, done much well calculated to create a dread of its return to power.

In the old time it was the ever faithful ally of the slaveholders, and the inflexible defenders of slavery. In the new time, it has been distinguished as the party of the shotgun, the cart whip, and the solid south.

While Mr. Cleveland's election brought dreadful forebodings to the cabins of the south it brought pleasing anticipations to the mansions of the south. The joy of the oppressor was the sorrow of the oppressed. It required every positive assurance from President Cleveland and his friends to allay the apprehensions of the freedmen. The impression made by the election of General Harrison was in striking contrast. It had precisely the opposite effect to that of Mr. Cleveland. The alarm was transferred from the cabin to the mansion—from the former slave to the master. In the freedmen's breasts confidence took the place of doubt, hope the place of fear, and a sense of relief the place of anxiety. Without the utterance of a single word, without the performance of a single act, the simple fact of the election of a Republican President carried with it the assurance of protection from the power of the oppressor. No higher eulogium could be bestowed upon the Republican party than this faith in the justice and beneficence by the simple, uneducated, and oppressed laborers of the south. Great, too, will be the sorrow and disappointment if some measure shall not be devised under this Republican administration to arrest the arm of lawless violence and prove to these simple people that there is a difference between the Republican party and the Democratic party.

Some of you may remember that in my celebration address four years ago I took occasion to express my satisfaction with the inaugural utterances of Hon. Grover Cleveland, and, although I have been much criticised for what I then said, I have no word of that commendation to retract or qualify. I thought well of Mr. Cleveland's words then and think well of them now. What I said was this, "No better words have dropped from the east portico of the Capitol since the days of Abraham Lincoln and Ulysses S. Grant." I did not say, as some of my critics found it necessary to allege, that Mr. Cleveland had uttered better words than either Lincoln or Grant. You will also remember that, while I commended the language of Mr. Cleveland, I strongly doubted his ability to live up to the sentiments he then and there expressed, and that doubt has been fully and sadly justified. During all the four years of his administration, after having solemnly sworn to Support and enforce the constitution of the United States, he said no word and did not act, expressed no desire to arrest the hand of violence, to stay the effusion of innocent blood, or vindicate in any manner the Negro's constitutional right to vote. He could almost hazard a war with England to protect our fishermen; he could send two ships of war to Hayti to protect an American fillibuster, but not one word or blow to protect colored citizens against southern assassins and murderers.

While I commended the words of Mr. Cleveland, I knew the party and not Mr. Cleveland would determine the character of his administration.

Well, now the American people have returned the Republican party to power, and the question is, what it will do? It has a great prestige, a glorious record. It is the party that carried on the war against treason and rebellion. It is the party that saved the Union, abolished slavery, amended the constitution, made the colored man a soldier, a citizen, and a legal voter. In view of this splendid record there ought to be no doubt or fear as to the course of this present administration. But past experience make us thoughtful. For a dozen years or more the Republican party has seemed in a measure paralyzed in the presence of high-handed fraud and brutal violence toward its newly-made citizens. The question now is, Will it regain its former health, activity and power? Will it be as true to its friends in the south as the Democratic party has been to its friends in that section, or will it sacrifice its friends to conciliate its enemies? I have seen this last alternative suggested as the possible outcome of this administration, but I stamp with unmitigated scorn and contempt all such intimations. I know General Harrison, and believe in General Harrison. I know his Cabinet and believe in its members, and no power can make me believe that this administration will not step to the verge of its constitutional power to protect the rights guaranteed by the Constitution. Not only the Negro, but all honest men, north and south, must hold the Republican party in contempt, if it fails to do its whole duty at this point. The Republican party has made the colored man free, and the Republican party must make him secure in his freedom, or abandon its pretensions.

It was once said by Abraham Lincoln that this republic, could not long endure half slave and half free, and the same may be said with even more truth of the black citizens of this country. They cannot remain half slave and half free. They must be one thing or the other.

And this brings me to consider the alternative now presented between slavery and freedom in this country. From my outlook I am free to affirm that I see nothing for the Negro of the south but a condition of absolute freedom or of absolute slavery. I see no half way place for him. One or the other of these conditions is to solve the so-called Negro problem. There are forces at work in each of these directions, and for the present, that which aims at the re-enslavement of the Negro seems to have the advantage. Let it be remembered that the labor of the Negro is his only capital. Take this from him and he dies from starvation. The present mode of obtaining his labor in the south gives his old master class a complete mastery over him. I showed this in my last annual celebration address, and I need not go into it here. The payment of the Negro by orders on stores, where the storekeeper controls price, quality, and quantity, and is subject to no competition, so that the Negro must buy there and nowhere else—an arrangement by which the Negro never has a dollar to lay by, and can be kept in debt to his employer year in and year out, puts him completely at the mercy of the master class. He who would say to the Negro, when a slave, you shall work for me or be whipped to death, can now say to him with equal emphasis, you shall work for me or I will starve you to death. This is the plain, matter-of-fact, and unexaggerated condition of the plantation Negro in the southern states today.

Why does the Negro not emigrate? I will tell you. He has not a cent of money to emigrate with, and if he had, and desired to exercise that right, he would be arrested for debt, for nonfulfillment of contract, or be shot down like a dog in his tracks. When southern senators tell you that they want to be rid of the Negro, and would be glad to have them all clear out, you know, and I know, and they know that they are speaking falsely, and simply with a view to mislead the north. Only a few days ago armed resistance was made in North Carolina to colored emigration from that state, and the first exodus to Kansas was arrested by the old master class with shotguns and Winchester rifles. The desire to get rid of the Negro is a hollow sham. His labor is wanted to-day in the south just as it was wanted in the old times when he was hunted by two-legged and four-legged bloodhounds.

Now, when a man is in one place, and held there by the force of many or few, and cannot get out of it, he is not far from a condition of slavery. But these old slave-holders have their allies, and one is strong drink. Whisky makes the Negro drunk, and drunkenness makes him a criminal as well as a pauper, and when he is made both a pauper and criminal the law steps in for satisfaction. It does not send him to prison to work for the state, but, as in the old times, puts him on the auction block and sells him to the highest bidder to work for a planter, where all the manhood he ever had is worked or whipped out of him. What is all this but slavery in another form?

I know that it will be said, that I am here exaggerating the danger that impends over the Negro. It will be said that slavery can never exist by law in the south, and that without legislation slavery cannot be revived at the south.

My answer to this argument is, that slavery can as really exist without law as with it, and in some instances more securely, because less likely to be interfered with in the absence of law than with it. No man can point to any law in the United States by which slavery was originally established. The fact of slavery always precedes enactments making it legal. Men first make slaves and then make laws affirming the right of slavery.

What they have done in the past they may also do in the future. We must not forget that there is nothing in southern morals, manners, or religion against the re-establishment of slavery. A genuine southern man looks at a Negro simply as an article of property, capable of being exchanged for rice, cotton, sugar, and tobacco.

Now, with such a conscience, armed with whisky, armed with ignorance, and the payment of labor with orders on stores, the old master class has the landless colored laborer literally by the throat, and is naturally dragging him back to the house of bondage.

Another and still more important step already taken in the direction of slavery is the precaution to deprive the Negro of all means of defense and protection. In the exercise of their power, acquired by long mastery over the Negro, they have forced him to surrender all arms and ammunition found in his log cabin. No lamb was ever more completely within the power of the wolf than the plantation Negro of to-day is in the hands of the old master class. The old masters know it, and the Negroes know it, and the fact makes the one haughty, domineering, and defiant, and the other spiritless, servile, and submissive. One is armed and the other defenceless. It is nothing against the courage of the Negro that he does not fight his way to the ballot box, instead of waiting for the government to protect him, as it is its duty to do, for even a brave man, unarmed, will stand and deliver at the mouth of a Winchester rifle or the blade of a bowie knife. To the mass of mankind life is more than liberty, for with it there ever remains the hope of liberty.

Now, when you remember that the Negro is taught to believe that the government may be against him; when it is remembered that he is denied the power to keep and bear arms; that he has not recovered from his enforced ignorance of two hundred years; that no adequate means of education has yet been provided for him; that his vote avails him nothing; that emigration is impossible; that there is neither religion nor conscience in the south to take his part, that he, of all men, is easiest convicted of crime; that he does not see or receive a dollar in payment of wages; that, labor as he will, he is brought in debt to the landed proprietor at the end of the year; that he can lay up nothing for a rainy day; that by the opinion of the Supreme Court of the United States the fourteenth amendment affords him no protection against individuals of a state—I say, when you remember all this, you may realize something of the perilous condition of the Negro citizens of the south.

Then, again, the fate of John M. Clayton and of Mr. Phillips, of Arkansas, one of them shot down while peaceably seeking proofs of his election to Congress, brutally assassinated, and the other kicked and shot to death in open daylight, and neither the murderers in the one case nor the assassinators in the other have been made to answer for their crimes, admonish us that neither the Negro nor the friends of the Negro have yet any standing before the law or in the public opinion of the old slave states.

Now I point to these facts tending toward the re-establishment of Negro slavery in the south, not because I believe slavery will finally be established there, but because they are features of the situation and should be exposed in order that the end at which they aim may not be realized—forewarned,—forearmed. The price of liberty is eternal vigilance. I bring this aspect before you upon the principle that an illustrious lawyer adopted, namely, always to try a cause first against his client.

It is easy to indulge in the illusions of hope, and to rejoice over what we have gained, and it is always more or less painful to contemplate the possibility of misfortune and disaster. But a brave man will not shrink from looking truth squarely in the face, no matter what may be the consequences, and you and I, and all of us know that if slavery is not re-established in the southern states, it will not be because there is any power inside those states, at present, to prevent this practice and return to barbarism.

From every view I have been able to take of the present situation in relation to the colored people of the United States I am forced to the conclusion that the irrepressible conflict, of which we heard so much before the war of the rebellion and during the war, is still in progress. It is still the battle between two opposite civilizations—the one created and sustained by slavery, and the other framed and fashioned in the spirit of liberty and humanity, and this conflict will not be ended until one or the other shall be completely adopted in every section of our common country. The South is still the South, and under the doctrine of local self-government it shelters the vicious idea that it can defy the constitution and the laws of the United States, especially those laws which respect the enfranchisement of colored citizens. The idea of local self-government destroyed the Freedman's bureau, drove United States soldiers out of the south, expelled northern immigrants, excluded

Negro citizens from state legislatures, and gave all power to the southern slave masters. Such is the situation to-day, and it remains to be seen whether it is to be permanent or transient. In my opinion this state of things cannot be permanent.

While revolutions may for a time seem to roll backwards; while reactionary tendencies and forces may arrest the wheels of progress, and while the colored man of the South may still have to suffer the lash and sting of a by-gone condition, there are forces and influences silently and yet powerfully working out his deliverance. The individual southern states are great, but the nation is greater. Justice, honor, liberty, and fidelity to the constitution and laws may seem to sleep, but they are not dead. They are alive and had more to do with bringing our Republican President into the presidential chair than is sometimes supposed. The red-shirted rifle companies of Carolina and Mississippi may rule for a time, but only for a time. They may rob the Negro of his vote to-day, but the Negro will have his vote tomorrow. The spirit of the age is with him. Slavery is vanishing from even the darkest corners of the earth. The schoolmaster is abroad—even in the South. The Negro of the plantation may be ignorant, but the Negro of the town and the city will be intelligent. The light of education which has illuminated the one will in time, illuminate the other.

But there is another force to be relied upon. It is the fact that the representatives of the best civilization of our times are compelled, in self-defense, to extirpate the illegal, unconstitutional barbarism of the late slave-holding states.

There is yet good reason to believe in the virtue of the loyal American people. They hate fraud, loathe rapine, and despise meanness. It was no reckless freak or madness that made them pour out their blood and their treasure in the late war, and there was a deep moral and patriotic purpose at the bottom of that sacrifice; a purpose that is not yet extinct, and will not be easily abandoned. If the Republican party shall fail to carry out this purpose, God will raise up another party which will be faithful. They resented secession, and fought to make a free, strong, and united nation. It was the aim of good men then, and it is the aim of good men now, and the effort to gain it will continue till that end shall be obtained. They may be patient and long-suffering. They have been patient and long-suffering. But patience itself will cease to be a virtue.

Do you ask me what can be done? I answer, we can at least purify the ballot box by requiring that no man shall hold a seat, in Congress, who reaches it by fraud, violence, and intimidation; by requiring that every man from the South, and from the North, and from everywhere else, shall come into that body by means uncorrupted by fraud, and unstained by blood. They will yet see to it that murder and assassination shall not be the passport to a seat in the councils of the nation. There is to-day a man in that body who holds his place because assassination has stepped between him and an honest contestant. White men may make light of the murder of a score of Negroes. They may shut their eyes and ridicule all denunciation of murder, when committed against defenceless Negroes, but they will not be deaf to the white man's blood, when it cries from the ground for vengeance. The advantage of the black man's cause is that the white man cannot help himself without helping him. Law and order for the one will ultimately be law and order for the other.

There is still another ground of hope for the freemen of the southern states. It is that the good citizens of these states cannot afford, and will not consent, to lag far behind the old free states in all the elements of civilization. They want population, capital, invention, and enterprise. They have rich resources to be developed, and they want both men and money to develop them and enhance their prosperity. The wise and loyal people in these states know very well that they can never be prosperous; that they can never have their share of immigration from at home or abroad, while they are known and distinguished for intolerance, fraud, violence, and lynch law. They know that while this character attaches to them, capital will hold aloof from them, and population shun them as it would shun a land blasted by pestilence and death. They know that their rich mines and fertile soil will fail to attract immigrants from any country unblasted by slavery. They know that industrious and enterprising men, searching for homes will turn their backs upon the South and make their way to the west and north, where they can hold and express their opinions without fear of the bowie knife and shotgun of the assassin.

Thus the self-interest of the people of these states will yet teach them justice, humanity, and civilization. For the present, the better element at the South is terror stricken and silent, but encouraged by the trend of the nation to higher and better conditions of existence, it will not always remain dumb and inactive, but will assert itself as Missouri is already doing, and as Arkansas will yet do. I was in this latter state only a few days after the assassination of John M. Clayton. I saw the wholesome horror manifested by the intelligent and worthy citizens of that state at this dastardly political murder. They were anxious for the good name of Arkansas, and asked me how the people of the north would regard them. I had to tell them in sadness that the outside world would look at them through the warm red blood of John M. Clayton and that the state of Arkansas would be held rigidly responsible till the arrest, trial, conviction, and punishment of the assassin and his instigators.

In conclusion, while I have plainly portrayed the sources of danger to our people, while I have described the reactionary forces with which we have to contend, I have no fears as to the character of the final result. The American people are governed, not only by laws and selfish interests, but by large ideas of moral and material civilization.

The spirit of justice, liberty, and fair play is abroad in the land. It is in the air. It animates men of all stations, of all professions and callings, and can neither be silenced nor extirpated. It has an agent in every bar of railroad iron, a servant in every electric wire, a missionary in every traveler. It not only tunnels the mountains, fills up the valleys, and sheds upon us the light of science, but it will ultimately destroy the unnumbered wrongs inherited by both races from the system of slavery and barbarism. In this direction is the trend of the nation. States may lag, parties may hesitate, leaders may halt, but to this complexion it must come at last. States, parties, and leaders must, and will in the end, adjust themselves to this overwhelming and irresistible tendency. It will make parties, and unmake parties, will make rulers, and unmake rulers, until it shall become the fixed, universal and irreversible law of the land. For fifty years it has made progress against all contradictions. It stemmed the current of opposition in church and state. It has removed many proscriptions. It has opened the gates of knowledge. It has abolished slavery. It has saved the Union. It has reconstructed the government upon a basis of justice and liberty, and it will see to it that the last vestige of fraud and violence on the ballot box shall disappear, and there shall be one country, one law, one liberty, for all the people of the United States.

Washington *National Leader,* April 27, 1889

INTRODUCTION TO *THE REASON WHY THE COLORED AMERICAN IS NOT IN THE WORLD'S COLUMBIAN EXPOSITION*[1]

The colored people of America are not indifferent to the good opinion of the world, and we have made every effort to improve our first years of freedom and citizenship. We earnestly desired to show some results of our first thirty years of acknowledged manhood and womanhood. Wherein we have failed, it has been not our fault but our misfortune, and it is sincerely hoped that this brief story, not only of our successes, but of trials and failures, our hopes and disappointments will relieve us of the charge of indifference and indolence. We have deemed it only a duty to ourselves, to make plain what might otherwise be misunderstood and misconstrued concerning us. To do this we must begin with slavery. The duty undertaken is far from a welcome one.

It involves the necessity of plain speaking of wrongs and outrages endured, and of rights withheld, and withheld in flagrant contradiction to boasted American Republican liberty and civilization. It is always more agreeable to speak well of one's country and its institutions than to speak otherwise; to tell of their good qualities rather than of their evil ones.

There are many good things concerning our country and countrymen of which we would be glad to tell in this pamphlet, if we could do so, and at the same time tell the truth. We would like for instance our visitors that the moral progress of the American people has kept even pace with their enterprise and their material civilization; that practice by the ruling class has gone on hand in hand with American professions; that two hundred and sixty years of progress and enlightenment have banished barbarism and race hate from the United States; that the old things of slavery have entirely passed away, and that all things pertaining to the colored people have become new; that American liberty is now the undisputed possession of all the American people; that American law is now the shield alike of black and white; that the spirit of slavery and class domination has no longer any lurking place in any part of this country; that the statement of human rights contained in its glorious Declaration of Independence, including the right to life, liberty and the pursuit of happiness is not an empty boast nor a mere rhetorical flourish, but a soberly and honestly accepted truth, to be carried out in good faith; that the American Church and clergy, as a whole, stand for the sentiment of universal human brotherhood and that its Christianity is without partiality and without hypocrisy; that the souls of Negroes are held to be as precious in the sight of God, as are the souls of white men; that duty to the heathen at home is as fully recognized and as sacredly discharged as is duty to the heathen abroad; that no man on account of his color, race or condition, is deprived of life, liberty or property without due process of law; that mobs are not allowed to supersede courts of law or usurp the place of government; that here Negroes are not tortured, shot, hanged or burned to death, merely on suspicion of crime and without ever seeing a judge, a jury or advocate; that the American Government is in reality a Government of the people, by the people and for the people, and for all the people; that the National Government is not a rope of sand, but has both the power and the disposition to protect the lives and liberties of American citizens of whatever color, at home, not less than abroad; that it will send its men-of-war to chastise the murder of its citizens in New Orleans or in any other part of the south, as readily as for the same purpose it will send them to Chile, Haiti or San Domingo; that our national sovereignty, in its rights to protect the lives of American citizens is ample and superior to any right or power possessed by the individual states; that the people of the United States are a nation in fact as well as in name; that in time of peace as in time of war, allegiance to the nation is held to be superior to any fancied allegiance to individual states; that allegiance and protection are here held to be reciprocal; that there is on the statute books of the nation no law for the protection of personal or political rights, which the nation may not or can not enforce, with or without the consent of individual states; that this World's Columbian Exposition, with its splendid display of wealth and power, its triumphs of art and its multitudinous architectural and other attractions, is a fair indication of the elevated and liberal sentiment of the American people, and that to the colored people of America, morally speaking, the World's Fair now in progress, is not a whited sepulcher.

All this, and more, we would gladly say of American laws, manners, customs and Christianity. But unhappily, nothing of all this can be said, without qualification and with flagrant disregard of the truth. The explanation is this: We have long had in this country, a system of iniquity which possessed the power of blinding the moral preception, stifling the voice of conscience, blunting all human sensibilities and perverting the plainest teaching of the religion we have here professed, a system which John Wesley truly characterized as the sum of all villainies, and one in view of which Thomas Jefferson, himself a slaveholder, said he "trembled for his country" when he reflected "that God is just and that His justice cannot sleep forever." That system was American slavery. Though it is now gone, its asserted spirit remains.

The writer of the initial chapter of this pamphlet, having himself been a slave, knows the slave system both on the inside and outside. Having studied its effects not only upon the slave and upon the master, but also upon the people and institutions by which it has been surrounded, he may therefore, without presumption, assume to bear witness to its baneful influence upon all concerned, and especially to its malign agency in explaining the present condition of the colored people of the United States, who were its victims; and to the sentiment held toward them both by the people who held them in slavery, and the people of the country who tolerated and permitted their enslavement, and the bearing it has upon the relation which we the colored people sustain to the World's Fair. What the legal and actual condition of the colored people was previous to emancipation is easily told.

It should be remembered by all who would entertain just views and arrive at a fair estimate of our character, our attainments and our worth in the scale of civilization, that prior to the slave-holder's rebellion thirty years ago, our legal condition was simply that of dumb brutes. We were classed as goods and chattels, and numbered on our master's ledgers with horses, sheep and swine. We were subject to barter and sale, and could be bequeathed and inherited by will, like real estate or any other property. In the language of the law: A slave was one in the power of his master to whom he belonged. He could acquire nothing, have nothing, own nothing that did not belong to his master. His time and talents, his mind and muscle, his body and soul, were the property of the master. He, with all that could be predicated of him as a human being, was simply the property of his master. He was a marketable commodity. His money value was regulated like any other article; it was increased or diminished according to his perfections or imperfections as a beast of burden.

Chief Justice Taney truly described the condition of our people when he said in the infamous Dred Scott decision, that they were supposed to have no rights which white men were bound to respect. White men could shoot, hang, burn, whip and starve them to death with impunity. They were made to feel themselves as outside the pale of all civil and political institutions. The master's power over them was complete and absolute. They could decide no question of pursuit or condition for themselves. Their children had no parents, their mothers had no husband and there was no marriage in a legal sense.

But I need not elaborate the legal and practical definition of slavery. What I have aimed to do, has not only been to show the moral depths, darkness and destitution from which we are still emerging, but to explain the grounds of the prejudice, hate and contempt in which we are still held by the people, who for more than two hundred years doomed us to this cruel and degrading condition. So when it is asked why we are excluded from the World's Columbian Exposition, the answer is Slavery.

Outrages upon the Negro in this country will be narrated in these pages. They will seem too shocking for belief. This doubt is creditable to human nature, and yet in view of the education and training of those who inflict the wrongs complained of, and the past condition of those upon whom they are inflicted as already described, such outrages are not only credible but entirely consistent and logical. Why should not these be inflicted?

The life of a Negro slave was never held sacred in the estimation of the people of that section of the country in the time of slavery, and the abolition of slavery against the will of the enslavers did not render a slave's life more sacred. Such a one could be branded with hot irons, loaded with chains, and whipped to death with impunity when a slave. It only needed be said that he or she was impudent or insolent to a white man, to excuse or justify the killing of him or her. The people of the south are with few exceptions but slightly improved in their sentiments towards those they once held as slaves. The mass of them are the same to-day that they were in the time of slavery, except perhaps that now they think they can murder with a decided advantage in point of economy. In the time of slavery if a Negro was killed, the owner sustained a loss of property. Now he is not restrained by any fear of such loss.

The crime of insolence for which the Negro was formerly killed and for which his killing was justified, is as easily pleaded in excuse now, as it was in the old time and what is worse, it is sufficient to make the charge of insolence to provoke the knife or bullet. This done, it is only necessary to say in the newspapers, that this dead Negro was impudent and about to raise an insurrection and kill all the white people, or that a white woman was insulted by a Negro, to lull the conscience of the north into indifference and reconcile its people to such murder. No proof of guilt is required. It is enough to accuse, to condemn and punish the accused with death. When he is dead and silent, and the murderer is alive and at large, he has it all his own way. He can tell any story he may please and will be believed. The popular ear is open to him, and his justification is sure. At the bar of public opinion in this country all presumptions are against the Negro accused of crime.

The crime to which the Negro is now said to be so generally and specially addicted, is one of which he has been heretofore, seldom accused or supposed to be guilty. The importance of this fact cannot be over estimated. He was formerly accused of petty thefts, called a chicken thief and the like, but seldom or never was he accused of the atrocious crime of feloniously assaulting white women. If we may believe his accusers this is a new development. In slaveholding times no one heard of any such crime by a Negro. During all the war, when there was the fullest and safest opportunity for such assaults, nobody ever heard of such being made by him. Thousands of white women were left for years in charge of Negroes, while their fathers, brothers and husbands were absent fighting the battles of the rebellion; yet there was no assault upon such women by Negroes, and no accusation of such assault. It is only since the Negro has become a citizen and a voter that this charge has been made. It has come along with the pretended and baseless fear of Negro supremacy. It is an effort to divest the Negro of his friends by giving him a revolting and hateful reputation. Those who do this would make the world believe that freedom has changed the whole character of the Negro, and made of him a moral monster.

This is a conclusion revolting alike to common sense and common experience. Besides there is good reason to suspect a political motive for the charge. A motive other than the one they would have the world believe. It comes in close connection with the effort now being made to disfranchise the colored man. It comes from men who regard it innocent to lie, and who are unworthy of belief where the Negro is concerned. It comes from men who count it no crime to falsify the returns of the ballot box and cheat the Negro of his lawful vote. It comes from those who would smooth the way for the Negro's disfranchisement in clear defiance of the constitution they have sworn to support—men who are perjured before God and man.

We do not deny that there are bad Negroes in this country capable of committing this, or any other crime that other men can or do commit. There are bad black men as there are bad white men, south, north and everywhere else, but when such criminals, or alleged criminals are found, we demand that their guilt shall be established by due course of law. When this will be done, the voice of the colored people everywhere will then be "Let no guilty man escape." The man in the South who says he is for Lynch Law because he honestly believes that the courts of that section are likely to be too merciful to the Negro charged with this crime, either does not know the South, or is fit for prison or an insane asylum.

Not less absurd is the pretense of these law breakers that the resort to Lynch Law is made because they do not wish the shocking details of the crime made known. Instead of a jury of twelve men to decently try the case, they assemble a mob of five hundred men and boys and circulate the story of the alleged outrage with all its concomitant, disgusting detail. If they desire to give such crimes the widest publicity they could adopt no course better calculated to secure that end than by a resort to lynch law. But this pretended delicacy is manifestly all a sham, and the members of the blood-thirsty mob bent upon murder know it to be such. It may deceive people outside of the sunny south, but not those who know as we do the bold and open defiance of every sentiment of modesty and chastity practiced for centuries on the slave plantations by this same old master class.

We know we shall be censured for the publication of this volume. The time for its publication will be thought to be ill chosen. America is just now, as never before, posing before the world as a highly liberal and civilized nation, and in many important respects she has a right to this reputation. She has brought to her shores and given welcome to a greater variety of mankind than were ever assembled in one place since the day of Pentecost. Japanese, Javanese, Soudanese, Chinese, Senegalese, Syrians, Persians, Tunisians, Algerians, Egyptians, East Indians, Laplanders, Esquimaux, and as if to shame the Negro, the Dahomians are also here to exhibit the Negro as a repulsive savage.

It must be admitted that, to outward seeming, the colored people of the United States have lost ground and have met with increased and galling resistance since the war of the rebellion. It is well to understand this phase of the situation. Considering the important services rendered by them in suppressing the late rebellion and the saving of the Union, they were for a time generally regarded with a sentiment of gratitude by their loyal white fellow citizens. This sentiment, however, very naturally became weaker as, in the course of events, those services were retired from view and the memory of them became dimmed by time and also by the restoration of friendship between the north and the south. Thus, what the colored people gained by the war they have partly lost by peace.

Military necessity had much to do with requiring their services during the war, and their ready and favorable response to that requirement was so simple, generous and patriotic, that the loyal states readily adopted important amendments to the constitution in their favor. They accorded them freedom and endowed them with citizenship and the right to vote and the right to be voted for. These rights are now a part of the organic law of the land and as such, stand today on the national statute book. But the spirit and purpose of these have been in a measure defeated by state legislation and by judicial decisions. It has nevertheless been found impossible to defeat them entirely and to relegate colored citizens to their former condition. They are still free.

The ground held by them to-day is vastly in advance of that they occupied before the war, and it may be safely predicted that they will not only hold this ground, but that they will regain in the end much of that which they seem to have lost in the reaction. As to the increased resistance met with by them of late, let us use a little philosophy. It is easy to account in a hopeful way for this reaction and even to regard it as a favorable symptom. It is a proof that the Negro is not standing still. He is not dead, but alive and active. He is not drifting with the current, but manfully resisting it and fighting his way to better conditions than those of the past, and better than those which popular opinion prescribes for him. He is not contented with his surroundings, but nobly dares to break away from them and hew out a way of safety and happiness for himself in defiance of all opposing forces.

A ship rotting at anchor meets with no resistance, but when she sets sail on the sea, she has to buffet opposing billows. The enemies of the Negro see that he is making progress and they naturally wish to stop him and keep him in just what they consider his proper place.

They have said to him "you are a poor Negro, be poor still," and "you are an ignorant Negro, be ignorant still and we will not antagonize you or hurt you." But the Negro has said a decided no to all this, and is now by industry, economy and education wisely raising himself to conditions of civilization and comparative well being beyond anything formerly thought possible for him. Hence, a new determination is born to keep him down. There is nothing strange or alarming about this. Such aspirations as his when cherished by the lowly are always resented by those who have already reached the top. They who aspire to higher grades than those fixed for them by society are scouted and scorned as upstarts for their presumptions.

In their passage from an humble to a higher position, the white man in some measure goes through the same ordeal. This is in accordance with the nature of things. It is simply an incident of a transitional condition. It is not the fault of the Negro, but the weakness, we might say the depravity, of human nature. Society resents the pretentions of those it considers upstarts. The newcomers always have to go through with this sort of resistance. The old and established are ever adverse to the new and aspiring. But the upstarts of to-day are the elite of tomorrow. There is no stopping any people from earnestly endeavoring to rise. Resistance ceases when the prosperity of the rising class becomes pronounced and permanent.

The Negro is just now under the operation of this law of society. If he were white as the driven snow, and had been enslaved as we had been, he would have to submit to this same law in his progress upward. What the Negro has to do then, is to cultivate a courageous and cheerful spirit, use philosophy and exercise patience. He must embrace every avenue open to him for the acquisition of wealth. He must educate his children and build up a character for industry, economy, intelligence and virtue. Next to victory is the glory and happiness of manfully contending for it. Therefore, contend! contend!

That we should have to contend and strive for what is freely conceded to other citizens without effort or demand may indeed be a hardship, but there is compensation here as elsewhere. Contest is itself ennobling. A life devoid of purpose and earnest effort, is a worthless life. Conflict is better than stagnation. It is bad to be a slave, but worse to be a willing and contented slave. We are men and our aim is perfect manhood, to be men among men. Our situation demands faith in ourselves, faith in the power of truth, faith in work and faith in the influence of manly character. Let the truth be told, let the light be turned on ignorance and prejudice, let lawless violence and murder be exposed.

The Americans are a great and magnanimous people and this great exposition adds greatly to their honor and renown, but in the pride of their success they have cause for repentence as well as complaisance, and for shame as well as for glory, and hence we send forth this volume to be read of all men.

Pamphlet, Chicago, 1892, pp. 2–12. Copy in Rare Book Room, Library of Congress

1. The pamphlet was published as a protest against the failure to appoint a Negro as a commissioner, or a member of an important committee, or even a guide or guard on the Exposition grounds at the Columbian World's Exposition in Chicago. It presented instances of general discrimination against the Negro in the United States and examples of lynchings. Douglass wrote the introduction.

Of all the sufferings and hardships of the Negro people during the nineties, the alarming increase in the bestial practice of lynching disturbed Douglass most deeply. Every month reports from the South told of new hangings and burnings at the stake, of Negroes taken from jails and brutally killed by white mobs, of Negroes tortured and burned to death in the sight of thousands of persons, of the savagery, brutishness, and the blood lust of white southerners. And for every Negro lynched a hundred others were in peril of their lives.

Some Negro leaders and many white friends of the Negro counseled silence. Rape, the crime of which the lynch mobs accused their victims, was too horrible to be defended. Also, by publicizing the lynchings, the position of the northern Negro would be jeopardized. The wisest thing was to say nothing.

But Douglass did not remain silent. His voice and pen were never more active. In these last years of his life he threw himself into a campaign to arouse the nation against this savage attack on his people. . . .

Accompanied by Mrs. Mary Church Terrell, Douglass went to urge President Harrison to speak out boldly against lynching in his annual message to Congress. Mrs. Terrell "listened spellbound while he [Douglass] eloquently pleaded the case for anti-lynching legislation. He implored President Harrison to act immediately against the lynching evil." Mrs. Terrill recalls that while President Harrison listened attentively, he took no action against lynching. "But Frederick Douglass," she adds, "never ceased to fight vigorously against lynching and all the wrongs of which his race was the victim."[1]

All the fire of his early years returned as Douglass struck out hard against the defenders of lynching. [IV:139–140]

LYNCH LAW IN THE SOUTH

The frequent and increasing resort to lynch law in our Southern States, in dealing with alleged offences by Negroes, marked as it is by features of cruelty which might well shock the sensibility of the most benighted savage, will not fail to attract the attention and animadversion of visitors to the World's Columbian Exposition.

Think of an American woman, in this year of grace 1892, mingling with a howling mob, and with her own hand applying the torch to the fagots around the body of a Negro condemned to death without a trial, and without judge or jury, as was done only a few weeks ago in the so-called civilized State of Arkansas.

When all lawful remedies for the prevention of crime have been employed and have failed; when criminals administer the law in the interest of crime; when the government has become a foul and damning conspiracy against the welfare of society; when men guilty of the most infamous crimes are permitted to escape with impunity; when there is no longer any reasonable ground upon which to base a hope of reformation, there is at least an apology for the application of lynch law; but, even in this extremity, it must be regarded as an effort to neutralize one poison by the employment of another. Certain it is that in no tolerable condition of society can lynch law be excused or defended. Its presence is either an evidence of governmental depravity, or of a demoralized state of society. It is generally in the hands of the worst class of men in the community, and is enacted under the most degrading and blinding influences. To break down the doors of jails, wrench off the iron bars of the cells, and in the dark hours of midnight drag out alleged criminals, and to shoot, hang, or burn them to death, requires preparation imparted by copious white, or mixed, which would in case of proof of the deed allow a guilty Negro to escape condign punishment.

Whatever may be said of their weakness when required to hold a white man or a rich man, the meshes of the law are certainly always strong enough to hold and punish a poor man or a Negro. In this case there is neither color to blind, money to corrupt, nor powerful friends to influence court or jury against the claims of justice. All the presumptions of law and society are against the Negro. In the days of slavery he was presumed to be a slave, even if free, and his word was never taken against that of a white man. To be accused was to be condemned, and the same spirit prevails to-day. This state of opinion at the South not only assures by law the punishment of black men, but enables white men to escape punishment by assuming the color of the Negro in order to commit crime. It often asserted that all Negroes look alike, and it is only necessary to bring one of the class into the presence of all accuser to have him at once identified as the criminal.

In apologizing for lynch law, Bishop Fitzgerald, of the Methodist Church South, says that the crime alleged against the Negro makes him an outlaw, and he goes on to complain of the North that it does not more fully sympathize with the South in its efforts to protect the purity of Southern women. The answer to the first proposition of the learned and pious Bishop is that no man is an outlaw unless declared to be such by some competent authority. It is not left to a lawless mob to determine whether a man is inside or outside the protection of the law. It is not for a dozen men or for a hundred men, constituting themselves a mob, to say whether or not Bishop Fitzgerald is an outlaw. We have courts, juries and governors to determine that question, and it is a shame to the South that it holds in its bosom a Bishop of the Church of Christ who could thus apologize for the subversion of all law. As to the sympathy of the North, there never was a time when it was more fully with the Southern people than now.

The distressing circumstances in this revival of lynch law in different parts of the South is, that it shows that prejudice and hatred have increased in bitterness with the increasing interval between the time of slavery and now. I have been frequently asked to explain this phase of our national problem. I explain it on the same principle by which resistance to the course of a ship is created and increased in proportion to her speed. The resistance met by the Negro is to me evidence that he is making progress. The Jew is hated in Russia, because he is thrifty. The Chinaman is hated in California because he is industrious and successful. The Negro meets no resistance when on a downward course. It is only when he rises in wealth, intelligence, and manly character that he brings upon himself the heavy hand of persecution. The men lynched at Memphis were murdered because they were prosperous. They were doing a business which a white firm desired to do,— hence the mob and hence the murder. When the Negro is degraded and ignorant he conforms to a popular standard of what a Negro should be. When he shakes off his rags and wretchedness and presumes to be a man, and a man among men, he contradicts this popular standard and becomes an offence to his surroundings. He can, at the South, ride in a first-class car as a servant, as an appendage to a white man, but is not allowed to ride in his quality of manhood alone. So extreme is the butterness of this prejudice that several States have passed laws making it a crime for a conductor to allow a colored man, however respectable, to ride in the same car with white men unless in the manner above stated.

To the question, What is to be the solution of this race hatred and persecution? I have two answers, one of hope and one of fear. There may come at the South satiety even in the appetite for blood. When a wall is raised to a height inconsistent with the law of gravitation, it will fall. The South is not all a wilderness. There are good men and good women there who will sooner or later make themselves heard and felt. No people can longer endure the shame and disgrace of lynch law. The South, which has been compelled to keep step with the music of the Union, will also be compelled to keep step with the music of the nineteenth century, which is preëminently a century of enlightenment and progress. The grand moral forces of this century no barbarism can withstand. They met serfdom in Russia, and it fell before them. They will meet our barbarism against color, and *it* will fall before them. I am the more encouraged in this belief because, in various parts of the North, and especially in the State of Massachusetts, where fifty years ago there existed the same proscription which at the present time prevails in the South, all men are now treated as equals before the law and are accorded the same civil rights.

I, however, freely confess that the present prospect has for me a gloomy side. When men sow the wind it is rational to expect that they will reap the whirlwind. It is evident to my mind that the Negro will not always rest a passive subject to the violence and bloodshed by which he is now pursued. If neither law nor public sentiment shall come to his relief, he will devise methods of his own. It should be remembered that the Negro is a man, and that in point of intelligence he is not what he was a hundred years ago. Whatever may be said of his failure to acquire wealth, it cannot be denied that he has made decided progress in the acquisition of knowledge; and he is a poor student of the natural history of civilization who does not see that the mental energies of this race, newly awakened and set in motion, must continue to advance. Character, with its moral influence; knowledge, with its power; and wealth, with its respectability, are possible to it as well as to other races of men. In arguing upon what will be the action of the Negro in case he continues to be the victim of lynch law I accept the statement often made in his disparagement, that he is an imitative being; that he will do what he sees other men do. He has already shown this facility, and he illustrates it all the way from the prize ring to the pulpit; from the plow to the professor's chair. The voice of nature, not less than the Book of books, teaches us that oppression call make even a wise man mad, and in such case the responsibility for madness will not rest upon the man but upon the oppression to which he is subjected.

How can the South hope to teach the Negro the sacredness of human life while it cheapens it and profanes it by the atrocities of mob law? The stream cannot rise higher than its source. The morality of the Negro will reach no higher point than the morality and religion that surround him. He reads of what is being done in the world in resentment of oppression and needs no teacher to make him understand what he reads. In warning the South that it may place too much reliance upon the cowardice of the Negro, I am not advocating violence by the Negro, but pointing out the dangerous tendency of his constant persecution. The Negro was not a coward at Bunker Hill; he was not a coward in Haïti; he was not a coward in the late war for the Union; he was not a coward at Harper's Ferry, with John Brown; and care should be taken against goading him to acts of desperation by continuing to punish him for heinous crimes of which he is not legally convicted.

I do not deny that the Negro may, in some instances, be guilty of the peculiar crime so often imputed to him. There are bad men among them, as there are bad men among all other varieties of the human family, but I contend that there is a good reason to question these lynch-law reports on this point. The crime imputed to the Negro is one most easily imputed and most difficult to disprove, and yet it is one that the Negro is least likely to commit. It is a crime for the commission of which opportunity is required, and no more convenient one was ever offered to any class of persons than was possessed by the Negros of the South during the War of the Rebellion.

There were then left in their custody and in their power the wives and the daughters, the mothers and the sisters of the rebels, and during all that period no instance can be cited of an outrage committed by a Negro upon the person or any white woman. The crime is a new one for the Negro, so new that a doubt may be reasonably entertained that he has learned it to any such extent as his accusers would have us believe. A nation is not born in a day. It is said that the leopard cannot change his spots nor the Ethiopian his skin, and it may be as truly said that the character of a people, established by long years of consistent life and testimony, cannot be very suddenly reversed. It is improbable that this peaceful and inoffensive class has suddenly and all at once become changed into a class of the most daring, and repulsive criminals.

Now, where rests the responsibility for the lynch law prevalent in the South?

It is evident that it is not entirely with the ignorant mob. The men who break open jails and with bloody hands destroy human life are not alone responsible. These are not the men who make public sentiment. They are simply the hangmen, not the court, judge, or jury. They simply obey the public sentiment of the South, the sentiment created by wealth and respectability, by the press and the pulpit. A change in public sentiment can be easily effected by these forces whenever they shall elect to make the effort. Let the press and the pulpit of the South unite their power against the cruelty, disgrace and shame that is settling like a mantle of fire upon these lynch-law States, and lynch law itself will soon cease to exist.

Nor is the South alone responsible for this burning shame and menace to our free institutions. Wherever contempt of race prevails, whether against African, Indian, or Mongolian, countenance and support are given to the present peculiar treatment of the Negro in the South. The finger of scorn at the North is correlated to the dagger of the assassin at the South. The sin against the Negro is both sectional and national, and until the voice of the North shall be heard in emphatic condemnation and withering reproach against these continued ruthless mob-law murders, it will remain equally involved with the South in this common crime.

Frederick Douglass

The North American Review, July, 1892, pp. 17–24

   1. Mary Church Terrell, "I Remember Frederick Douglass," *Ebony,* Sept. 12, 1953.

Douglass' attack upon the wealthy classes of the South [in "Lynch Law in the South," above] aroused a storm of protest. . . . Infuriated by these indictments of his people, Douglass answered his critics in a brilliant lecture, "The Lesson of the Hour." Beginning with the stinging sentence, "Not a breeze comes to us from the late rebellious states that is not tainted and freighted with Negro blood," it analyzed and demolished every excuse offered by the defenders of lynching and exposed the real reasons for the brutal murder of Negroes in the south. As if aware that this was the last blow he would strike for his people, Douglass poured into the address not only a most powerful indictment of lynching but a condemnation of the entire system by which the Negro people in the United States were oppressed. . . .

Excerpts from Douglass' last great address filled the columns of newspapers and magazines both in the United States and in England. And as Negroes read the burning sentences they felt a great weight being lifted from their shoulders. "As a race we can rest our cause on your argument and plea," a Negro wrote from the deep South.[1]

It is on this note that the career of Frederick Douglass draws to its close. [IV:140–143]

WHY IS THE NEGRO LYNCHED?

I. THE AFRO-AMERICAN PEOPLE INDICTED ON A NEW CHARGE. INTRODUCTORY— THE WRITER'S CLAIM TO BE HEARD.

I propose to give you a colored man's view of the so-called "Negro Problem." We have had the Southern white man's view of this subject at large in the press, in the pulpit and on the platform. He has spoken in the pride of his power and to willing ears. Colored by his peculiar environments, his version has been presented with abundant repetition, with startling emphasis, and with every advantage to his side of the question. We have also had the Northern white man's view of the subject, tempered by his distance from the scene and by his different, if not his higher, civilization.

This quality and quantity of Evidence, may be considered by some men as all sufficient upon which to found an intelligent judgment of the whole matter in controversy, and, therefore, it may be thought my testimony is not needed. But experience has taught us that it is sometimes wise and necessary to have more than two witnesses to bring out the whole truth. Especially is this the case where one of such witnesses has a powerful motive for suppressing or distorting the facts, as in this case. I therefore insist upon my right to take the witness stand and give my version of this Southern question, and though it shall widely differ from that of both the North and South, I shall submit the same to the candid judgment of all who hear me in full confidence that it will be received as true, by honest men and women of both sections of this Republic.

There is one thing, however, in which I think we must all agree at the start. It is that this so-called but mis-called Negro problem is one of the most important and urgent subjects that can now engage public attention. Its solution is, and ought to be, the serious business of the best American wisdom and statesmanship. For it involves the honour or dishonour, the glory or shame, the happiness or misery, of the whole American people. It not only touches the good name and fame of the Republic, but its highest moral welfare and its permanent safety. The evil with which it confronts us is coupled with a peril at once great and increasing, and one which should be removed, if it can be, without delay.

EPIDEMIC OF MOB-LAW

The presence of eight millions of people in any section of this country, constituting an aggrieved class, smarting under terrible wrongs, denied the exercise of the commonest rights of humanity, and regarded by the ruling class of that section as outside of the government, outside of the law, outside of society, having nothing in common with the people with whom they live, the sport of mob violence and murder, is not only a disgrace and a scandal to that particular section, but a menace to the peace and security of the whole country. There is, as we all know, a perfect epidemic of mob law and persecution now prevailing at the South, and the indications of a speedy end are not hopeful. Great and terrible as have been its ravages in the past, it now seems to be increasing, not only in the number of its victims, but in its frantic rage and savage extravagance. Lawless vengeance is beginning to be visited upon white men as well as black. Our newspapers are daily disfigured by its ghastly horrors. It is no longer local but national; no longer confined to the South but has invaded the North. The contagion is spreading, extending and overleaping geographical lines and state boundaries, and if permitted to go on, threatens to destroy all respect for law and order, not only in the South but in all parts of our common country, North as well as South. For certain it is, that crime allowed to go unpunished, unresisted and unarrested, will breed crime. When the poison of anarchy is once in the air, like the pestilence that walketh in darkness, the winds of heaven will take it up and favor its diffusion. Though it may strike down the weak to-day, it will strike down the strong to-morrow.

Not a breeze comes to us from the late rebellious states that is not tainted and freighted with Negro blood. In its thirst for blood and its rage for vengeance, the mob has blindly, boldly and defiantly supplanted sheriffs, constables and police. It has assumed all the functions of civil authority. It laughs at legal processes, courts and juries, and its red-handed murderers range abroad unchecked and unchallenged by law or by public opinion. If the mob is in pursuit of Negroes who happen to be accused of crime, innocent or guilty, prison walls and iron bars afford no protection. Jail doors are battered down in the presence of unresisting jailors, and the accused, awaiting trial in the courts of law, are dragged out and hanged, shot, stabbed or burned to death, as the blind and irresponsible mob may elect.

We claim to be a highly-civilized and Christian country. I will not stop to deny this claim, yet I fearlessly affirm that there is nothing in the history of savages to surpass the blood-chilling horrors and fiendish excesses perpetrated against the coloured people of this country, by the so-called enlightened and Christian people of the South. It is commonly thought that only the lowest and most disgusting birds and beasts, such as buzzards, vultures and hyenas, will gloat over and prey upon dead bodies; but the Southern mob, in its rage, feeds its vengeance by shooting, stabbing and burning their victims, when they are dead.

Now, what is the special charge by which this ferocity is justified, and by which mob law is excused and defended even by good men North and South? It is a charge of recent origin; a charge never brought before; a charge never heard of in the time of slavery or in any other time in our history. It is a charge of assaults by Negroes upon white women. This new charge, once fairly started on the wings of rumour, no matter by whom or in what manner originated, whether well or ill-founded, whether true or false, is certain to raise a mob and to subject the accused to immediate torture and death. It is nothing that there may be a mistake in his case as to identity. It is nothing that the victim pleads "not guilty." It is nothing that the accused is of fair reputation and his accuser is of an abandoned character. It is nothing that the majesty of the law is defied and insulted; no time is allowed for defence or explanation; he is bound with cords, hurried off amid the frantic yells and curses of the mob to the scaffold, and there, under its ghastly shadow, he is tortured, till by pain or promises, he is made to think that he can possibly gain time or save his life by confession—confesses—and then, whether guilty or innocent, he is shot, hanged, stabbed or burned to death amid the wild shouts of the mob. When the will of the mob is accomplished, when its thirst for blood has been quenched, when its victim is speechless, silent and dead, his mobocratic accusers and murderers of course have the ear of the world all to themselves, and the world, hearing only the testimony of the mob, generally approves its verdict.

Such, then, is the state of Southern law and civilization at this moment, in relation to the coloured citizens of that section of our country. Though the picture is dark and terrible, I venture to affirm that no man, North or South, can successfully deny its essential truth.

ATTITUDE OF UPPER CLASSES

Now the question arises, and it is important to know, how this state of affairs is viewed by the better classes of the Southern States. I will tell you, and I venture to say in advance, if our hearts were not already hardened by familiarity with crimes against the Negro, we should be shocked and astonished, not only by these mobocratic crimes, but by the attitude of the better classes of the Southern people and their law-makers, towards the perpetrators of them. With a few noble exceptions, just enough to prove the rule, the upper classes of the South seem to be in full sympathy with the mob and its deeds. There are but few earnest words ever uttered against either. Press, platform and pulpit are generally either silent or they openly apologize for the mob and its deeds. The mobocratic murderers are not only permitted to go free, untried and unpunished, but are lauded and applauded as honourable men and good citizens, the high-minded guardians of Southern virtue. If lynch law is in any case condemned by them, it is only condemned in one breath and excused in another.

The great trouble with the Negro in the South is that all presumptions are against him. A white man has but to blacken his face and commit a crime to have some Negro lynched in his stead. An abandoned woman has only to start a cry, true or false, that she has been insulted by a black man, to have him arrested and summarily murdered by the mob. Frightened and tortured by his captors, confused, he may be, into telling crooked stories about his whereabouts at the time when the crime is alleged to have been committed, and the death penalty is at once inflicted, though his story may be but the incoherency of ignorance or the distraction caused by terror.

In confirmation of what I have said, I have before me the utterances of some of the best people of the South, and also the testimony of one from the North, a lady of high character, from whom, considering her antecedents, we should have expected a more considerate, just and humane utterance.

In a late number of the *Forum,* Bishop Haygood, author of the "Brother in Black," says that "The most alarming fact is that execution by lynching has ceased to surprise us. The burning of a human being for any crime, it is thought, is a horror that does not occur outside of the Southern states of the American Union, yet unless assaults by Negroes come to an end, there will most probably be still further display of vengeance that will shock the world, and men who are just will consider the provocation."

In an open letter addressed to me by ex-Governor Chamberlain, of South Carolina, published in the Charleston *News and Courier,* in reply to an article of mine on the subject of lynching, published in the *North American Review,* the ex-Governor says: "Your denunciation of the South on this point is directed exclusively, or nearly so, against the application of lynch laws for the punishment of one crime; the existence, I suppose I might say the prevalence, of this crime at the South is undeniable. But I read your article in vain for any special denunciation of the crime itself. As you say, your people are lynched, tortured and burned, for assault on white women. As you value your own good fame and safety as a race, stamp out the infamous crime."

And now comes the sweet voice of a Northern woman, Miss Frances Willard, of the W.C.T.U., distinguished among her sisters for benevolence and Christian charity.[2] She speaks in the same bitter tone and hurls against us the same blasting accusation. She says in a letter now before me, "I pity the Southerners. The problem in their hands is immeasurable. The coloured race multiplies like the locusts of Egypt. The safety of women, of childhood, of the home, is menaced in a thousand localities at this moment, so that men dare not go beyond the sight of their own roof tree." Such, then, is the crushing indictment drawn up against the Southern Negroes, drawn up, too, by persons who are perhaps the fairest and most humane of the Negro's accusers. Yet even they paint him as a moral monster, ferociously invading the sacred rights of woman and endangering the home of the whites.

INCRIMINATION OF THE WHOLE RACE

Now, I hold, no less than his accusers, that the crime alleged against the Negro is the most revolting which men can commit. It is a crime that awakens the intensest abhorrence and tempts mankind to kill the criminal on first sight.

But this charge thus brought against the Negro and as constantly reiterated by his enemies, is plainly enough not merely a charge against the individual culprit, as would be the case with an individual of any other race, but it is in large measure a charge constructively against the coloured people as such. It throws over every man of colour a mantle of odium, and sets upon him a mark of popular hate, more distressing than the mark set upon the first murderer. It points the Negro out as an object of suspicion, avoidance and hate.

It is in this form of the charge that you and I and all of us are required to meet it and refute it, if that can be done. In the opinion of some of us it were well to say nothing about it, that the least said about it the better. They would have us suffer quietly under the odium in silence. In this I do not concur. Taking this charge in its broad and comprehensive sense, the sense in which it is presented and as now stated, it strikes at the whole coloured race, and, therefore, as a coloured man, I am bound to meet it. I am grateful for the opportunity now afforded me to meet it. For I believe it can be met and met successfully. I hold that a people too spiritless to defend themselves against unjust imputations, are not worth defending, and are not worthy to defend anything else.

II. THE DEFENCE—"NOT GUILTY."—CHARACTER OF THEIR ACCUSERS CHALLENGED.

Without boasting in advance, but relying upon the goodness of my cause, I will say here I am ready to confront Ex-Governor Chamberlain, Bishop Fitzgerald, Bishop Haygood and good Miss Frances Willard and all others, singly or altogether, who bring this charge against the coloured people as a class.

But I want, however, to be clearly understood at the outset. I do not pretend that Negroes are saints and angels. I do not deny that they are capable of committing the crime imputed to them, but utterly deny that they are any more addicted to the commission of that crime than is true of any other variety of the human family. In entering upon my argument, I may be allowed to say again what should be taken for granted at the start, that I am not a defender of any man guilty of this atrocious crime, but a defender of the coloured people as a class.

In answer, then, to the terrible indictment thus read, and speaking for the coloured people as a class, I venture in their name and in their stead, here and now, to plead "not guilty," and shall submit my case with confidence of acquittal by good men and women, North and South, before whom we are, as a class, now being tried. In daring to do this I know that the moral atmosphere about me is not favourable to my cause. The sentiment left by slavery is still with us, and the moral vision of the American people is still darkened by its presence.

It is the misfortune of the coloured people of this country that the sins of the few are visited more or less upon the many. In respect to the offenders, I am with General Grant and every other honest man. My motto is, "Let no guilty man escape." But while I say this, and mean to say it strongly, I am also here to say, let no guilty man be condemned and killed by the mob, or crushed under the weight of a charge of which he is not guilty.

I need not be told that the cause I have undertaken to support is not to be maintained by any mere confident assertions or general denials, however strongly worded. If I had no better ground to stand upon than this, I would at once leave the field of controversy and give up the coloured man's cause to his accusers. I am also aware that I am here to do in some measure what the masters of logic say is impossible to be done. I know that I cannot prove a negative; there is one thing that I can and will do. I will call in question the affirmative. I can and will show that there are sound reasons for doubting and denying this horrible charge of rape as the special and peculiar crime of the coloured people of the South. I doubt it, and deny it with all my soul. My doubt and denial are based upon three fundamental grounds.

The first ground is, the well-established and well-tested character of the Negro on the very point upon which he is now so violently and persistently accused. I contend that his whole history in bondage and out of bondage contradicts and gives the lie to the allegation. My second ground for doubt and denial is based upon what I know of the character and antecedents of the men and women who bring this charge against him. My third ground is the palpable unfitness of the mob to testify and which is the main witness in the case.

I therefore affirm that a fierce and frenzied mob is not and ought not to be deemed a competent witness against any man accused of any crime whatever, and especially the crime now in question. The ease with which a mob can be collected, the slight causes by which it can be set in motion, and the element of which it is composed, deprives its testimony of the qualities necessary to sound judgment and that which should inspire confidence and command belief. Blinded by its own fury, it is moved by impulses utterly unfavourable to a clear perception of facts and the ability to make an impartial statement of the simple truth. At the outset, I challenge the credibility of the mob, and as the mob is the main witness in the case against the Negro I appeal from the judgment of the mob to the judgment of law-abiding men, in support of my challenge. I lay special emphasis on the fact that it is the mob and the mob only that the country has recognised and accepted as its accredited witness against the Negro. The mob is its law, its judge, jury and executioner. I need not argue this point further. Its truth is borne upon its face.

But I go further. I dare not only to impeach the mob, I impeach and discredit the veracity of men generally, whether mobocrats or otherwise who sympathise with lynch law, whenever or wherever the acts of coloured men are in question. It seems impossible for such men to judge a coloured man fairly. I hold that men who openly and deliberately nullify the laws and violate the provisions of the Constitution of their country, which they have solemnly sworn to support and execute, are not entitled to unqualified belief in any case, and certainly not in the case of the Negro. I apply to them the legal maxim, "False in one, false in all." Especially do I apply this maxim when the conduct of the Negro is in question.

Again I question the Negro's accusers on another important ground; I have no confidence in the veracity of men who publicly justify themselves in cheating the Negro out of his constitutional right to vote. The men who do this, either by false returns, or by taking advantage of the Negro's illiteracy, or by surrounding the ballot box with obstacles and sinuosities intended to bewilder him and defeat his rightful exercise of the elective franchise, are men who should not be believed on oath. That this is done and approved in Southern States is notorious. It has been openly defended by so-called honest men inside and outside of Congress.

I met this shameless defence of crime face to face at the late Chicago Auxiliary Congress, during the World's Columbian Exposition, in a solemn paper by Prof. Weeks,[3] of North Carolina, who boldly advocated this kind of fraud as necessary and justifiable in order to secure Anglo-Saxon supremacy, and in doing so, as I believe, he voiced the moral sentiment of Southern men generally.

Now, men who openly defraud the Negro of his vote by all manner of artifice, who justify it and boast of it in the face of the world's civilization, as was done by Prof. Weeks at Chicago, I hardly need say that such men are not to be depended upon for truth in any case where the rights of the Negro are involved. Their testimony in the case of any other people than the Negro would be instantly and utterly discredited, and why not the same in this case? Every honest man will see that this point is well taken. It has for its support common sense, common honesty, and the best sentiment of mankind. On the other hand, it has nothing to oppose it but a vulgar, popular prejudice which we all know strikes men with moral blindness and renders them incapable of seeing any distinction between right and wrong where coloured people are concerned.

THE NEGRO'S CLEAN RECORD DURING WAR TIME.

But I come to a stronger position. I rest my denial not merely upon general principles but upon well-known facts. I reject the charge brought against the Negro as a class, because all through the late war, while the slave-masters of the South were absent from their homes, in the field of rebellion, with bullets in their pockets, treason in their hearts, broad blades in their bloody hands, seeking the life of the nation, with the vile purpose of perpetuating the enslavement of the Negro, their wives, their daughters, their sisters and their mothers were left in the absolute custody of these same Negroes and during all those long four years of terrible conflict, when the Negro had every opportunity to commit the abominable crime now alleged against him, there was never a single instance of such crime reported or charged against him. He was never accused of assault, insult, or an attempt to commit an assault upon any white woman in the whole South. A fact like this, though negative, speaks volumes, and ought to have some weight with the American people on the present question.

Then, again, on general principles, I do not believe the charge, because it implies an improbable change, if not an impossible change in the mental and moral character and composition of the Negro. It implies a radical change wholly inconsistent with the well-known facts of human nature. It is a contradiction to human experience. History does not present an example of a transformation in the character of any class of men so extreme, so unnatural and so complete as is implied in this charge. The change is too great and the period for it too brief. Instances may be cited where men fall like stars from heaven, but such is not the usual experience with the masses. Decline in the moral character of such is not sudden, but gradual. The downward steps are marked at first by slow degrees and by increasing momentum, going from bad to worse as they proceed. Time is an element in such changes, and I contend that the Negroes of the South have not had time to experience this great change and reach this lower depth of infamy. On the contrary, in point of fact, they have been, and still are, improving and ascending to higher and still higher levels of moral and social worth.

EXCUSES FOR LYNCHING — DELICACY OF SUBJECT; POSSIBILITY OF CRIMINAL'S ESCAPE FROM JUSTICE.

Again I utterly deny the charge on the fundamental ground that those who bring the charge do not and dare not give the Negro a chance to be heard in his own defence. He is not allowed to show the deceptive conditions out of which the charge has originated. He is not allowed to vindicate his character from blame, or to criminate the character and motives of his accusers. Even the mobocrats themselves admit that it would be fatal to their purpose to have the character of the Negro's accusers brought into court. They pretend to a delicate regard for the feelings of the parties alleged to have been assaulted. They are too modest to have them brought into court. They are, therefore, for lynching and against giving a fair trial to the accused. This excuse, it is needless to say, is contemptible and hypocritical. It is not only mock modesty, but mob modesty. Men who can collect hundreds and thousands of their kind, if we believe them, thirsting for vengeance, and can spread before them in the tempest and whirlwind of vulgar passion, the most disgusting details of crime, connecting the names of women with the same, should not be allowed to shelter themselves under any pretence of modesty. Such a pretence is absurd and shameless upon the face of it. Who does not know that the modesty of womanhood is always and in every such case an object for special protection in a court of law? On the other hand, who does not know that a lawless mob, composed in part of the basest men, can have no such respect for the modesty of women, as has a court of law. No woman need be ashamed to confront one who has insulted or assaulted her in any court of law. Besides, innocence does not hesitate to come to the rescue of justice, and need not even in this case.

Again, I do not believe it, and deny it because if the evidence were deemed sufficient to bring the accused to the scaffold by a verdict of an impartial jury, there could be and would be no objection to having the alleged offender tried in conformity to due process of law.

The only excuse for lynch law, which has a shadow of support in it is, that the criminal would probably otherwise be allowed to escape the punishment due to his crime. But this excuse is not employed by the lynchers, though it is sometimes so employed by those who apologise for the lynchers. But for it there is no foundation whatever, in a country like the South, where public opinion, the laws, the courts, the juries, the advocates, are all against the Negro, especially one alleged to be guilty of the crime now charged. That such an one would be permitted to escape condign punishment, is not only untenable but an insult to common sense. The chances are that not even an innocent Negro so charged would be allowed to escape.

III.   THE   THREE   STAGES   OF   NEGRO   PERSECUTION.   THEIR   OBJECT—HIS DISFRANCHISEMENT.

But I come to another fact, and an all important fact, bearing upon this case. You will remember that during all the first years of reconstruction, and long after the war, Negroes were slain by scores. The world was shocked by these murders, so that the Southern press and people found it necessary to invent, adopt and propagate almost every species of falsehood to create sympathy for themselves, and to formulate excuses for thus gratifying their brutal instincts against the Negro; there was never at that time a charge made against any Negro involving an assault upon any white woman or upon little white children in all the South. During all this time the white women and children were absolutely safe. During all this time there was no call for Miss Willard's pity, or for Bishop Haygood's defence of burning Negroes to death, but killing Negroes went on all the same.

You will remember also that during this time the justification for the murder of Negroes was said to be Negro conspiracies, Negro insurrections, Negro schemes to murder all the white people, Negro plots to burn the town and to commit violence generally. These were the excuses then depended upon, but never a word was then said or whispered about Negro outrages upon white women and children. So far as the history of that time is concerned, white women and children were absolutely safe, and husbands and fathers could leave their homes without the slightest anxiety for the safety of their families. But now mark the change and the reasons for the change. When events proved that no such conspiracies, no such insurrections as were then pretended to exist, and which were then paraded before the world in glaring headlines in the columns of nearly all our newspapers, had ever existed or were even meditated—when these excuses had run their course and had served their wicked purpose, when the huts of the Negroes had been searched, and searched in vain for guns and ammunition to prove these charges against the Negro, and no such proof was found, when there was no way open thereafter to prove these charges against the Negro, and no way to make the North believe in them, they did not even then bring forward the present allegation, but went on harassing and killing Negroes just the same. But this time they based their right to kill on the ground that it was necessary to check the domination and supremacy of the Negro and to secure the absolute rule of the Anglo-Saxon race.

It is important to notice and emphasize here the significant fact that there have been three distinct periods of persecutions of the Negroes in the South, and three distinct sets of excuses for their persecution. They have come along precisely in the order they were most needed. Each was made to fit its special place. First, you remember, as I have said, it was insurrection. When that wore out, Negro supremacy became the excuse. When that was worn out, then came the charge of assault upon defenceless women. I undertake to say that this orderly arrangement and periodicity of excuses are significant. They mean something, and should not be overlooked. They show design, plan, purpose and invention. And now that Negro insurrection and Negro domination are no longer defensible as an excuse for Negro persecution, there has come in due course another suited to the occasion, and that is the heart-rending cry of the white women and little white children.

Now, my friends, I ask what is the manifest meaning of this charge at this time? What is the meaning of the singular omission of this charge during the two periods preceding the present? Why was not this charge made at that time as now? The Negro was the same man then as to-day. Why, I ask again, was not this dreadful charge brought forward against the Negro in war times and in reconstruction times? Had it existed either in war times or during reconstruction, does any man doubt that it would have been added to the other charges and proclaimed upon the housetops and at the street corners as this charge is at present?

I will answer the question: or you yourselves have already given the true answer. For the plain and only rational explanation is that there was at the times specified no foundation for such a charge, or that the charge itself was either not thought of, or if thought of it was not deemed necessary to excuse the lawless violence with which the Negro was then pursued and killed. The old charges already enumerated were deemed all-sufficient.

Things have changed since then, and the old excuses are not now available. The times have changed, and the Negro's accusers have found it necessary to change with them. They have been compelled to invent a new charge to suit the times. The old charges are no longer valid. Upon them the good opinion of the North and of mankind cannot be secured. Honest men no longer believe that there is any ground to apprehend Negro supremacy. Times and events have swept away these old refuges of lies. They were once powerful. They did their work in their day and did it with terrible energy and effect, but they are now cast aside as useless. The lie has lost its ability to deceive. The altered time and circumstances have made necessary a sterner, stronger and more effective justification of Southern barbarism, and hence we have, according to my theory, to look into the face of a more shocking and blasting charge than either Negro supremacy or Negro insurrection.

I insist upon it that this new charge has come at the call of new conditions, and that nothing could have been hit upon better calculated to accomplish its brutal purpose. It clouds the character of the Negro with a crime the most shocking that men can commit, and is fitted to drive from the criminal all pity and all fair play and all mercy. It is a crime that places him outside of the pale of the law, and settles upon his shoulders a mantle of wrath and fire, that blisters and burns into his very soul.

It is for this purpose, it seems to me, that this new charge, unthought of and unknown in the times to which I have referred, has been largely invented and thundered against us. It is for the purpose that it has been constantly reiterated and adopted. It was intended to blast and ruin the Negro's character as a man and a citizen. I need not tell you how thoroughly it has already done its work. The Negro may and does feel its malign influence in the very air he breathes. He may read it in the faces of men among whom he moves. It has cooled his friends; it has heated his enemies and arrested at home and abroad, in some measure, the generous efforts that good men were wont to make for his improvement and elevation. It has deceived his friends at the North and many good friends at the South, for nearly all of them, in some measure, have accepted this charge against the Negro as true. Its perpetual reiteration in our newspapers and magazines has led men and women to regard him with averted eyes, dark suspicion and increasing hate.

Some of the Southern papers have denounced me for my unbelief in this charge and in this new crusade against the Negro, but I repeat I do not believe it, and firmly deny the grounds upon which it is based. I reject it because I see in it evidence of an invention called into being by a well-defined motive, a motive sufficient to stamp it as a gross expedient to justify murderous assault upon a long enslaved and hence a hated people.

I not only reject it because it bears upon its face the marks of being a fraud, a make-shift for a malignant purpose, but because it has sprung upon the country simultaneously, and in manifest co-operation with a declared purpose and a well-known effort, and I may say a fixed determination to degrade the Negro by judicial decisions, by legislative enactments, by repealing all laws for the protection of the ballot, by drawing the colour line in all railroad cars and stations and in all other public places in the South, thus to pave the way to a final consummation which is nothing less than the Negro's entire disenfranchisement as an American citizen. It is to this great end that all the charges and complaints against the Negro are directed and are made to converge. This is and has been from first to last the grand and all-commanding object in view. It is a part of a well-devised reactionary movement against the Negro as a citizen. The old master class are wise in their day and generation. They know if they can once divest the Negro of the elective franchise and nullify his citizenship, the partition wall between him and slavery will no longer exist, and no man can tell where the reaction will stop.

THE ATTACK LESS UPON CRIME THAN COLOUR.

Again, I do not believe it, and deny it, because the charge is not so much against the crime itself, as against the colour of the people alleged to be guilty of it. Slavery itself, you will remember, was a system of unmitigated, legalized outrage upon black women of the South, and no white man was ever shot, burned or hanged for availing himself of all the power that slavery gave him at this point.

To sum up my argument on this lynching business, it remains to be said that I have shown that the Negro's accusers in this case have violated their oaths, and have cheated the Negro out of his vote; that they have robbed and defrauded the Negro systematically and persistently, and have boasted of it. I have shown that when the Negro had every opportunity to commit the crime now charged against him, he was never accused of it by his bitterest enemies. I have shown that during all the years of reconstruction, when he was being murdered at Hamburg, Yazoo, New Orleans, Copiah and elsewhere he was never accused at that time of the crime now charged against him. I have shown that in the nature of things no such change in the character and composition of a whole people, as this implies, could have taken place within the limited period allowed for it. I have shown that those who accuse him dare not confront him in a court of law and have their witnesses subjected to proper legal inquiry. I have shown from the very constitution of a mob, the slight causes by which it may be created, and the sentiment by which it is impelled, it cannot be depended upon for either truth or justice. I have shown that its sole aim is to execute, not to find a true verdict. And showing all this and more, I have shown that they who charge the Negro with this foul crime, in such circumstances, may be justly doubted and deemed unworthy of belief.

IV. OBJECTIONS ANSWERED: PECULIARITIES OF SOUTHERN SENTIMENT. LACK OF RESPECT FOR HUMAN LIFE.

But I now come to a grave objection to my theory of this violent persecution. I shall be told by many of my Northern friends that my argument, though plausible, is not conclusive. It will be said that the charges against the Negro are specific and positive, and that there must be some foundation for them, because, as they allege, men in their normal condition do not shoot, hang and burn their fellow men who are guiltless of crime. Well! This assumption is very just and very charitable. I only wish that something like the same justice and the same charity shall be shown to the Negro. All credit is due and is accorded to our Northern friends for their humane judgment of the South. Humane themselves, they are slow to believe that the mobocrats are less humane than themselves. Their hearts are right but their heads are wrong. They apply a general rule to a special case. They forget that neither the mob nor its victims are in a normal condition. Both are exceptions to the general rule. The force of the argument against my version of the case is the assumption that the lynchers are like other men and that the Negro has the same hold on the protection of society that other men have. Neither assumption is true. The lynchers and mobocrats are not like other men, nor is the Negro hedged about by the same protection accorded other members of society.

The point I make, then, is this. That I am not, in this case, dealing with men in their natural condition. I am dealing with men brought up in the exercise of irresponsible power. I am dealing with men whose ideas, habits and customs are entirely different from those of ordinary men. It is, therefore, quite gratuitous to assume that the principles that apply to other men, apply to the lynchers and murderers of the Negro. The rules resting upon the justice and benevolence of human nature do not apply to the mobocrats, or to those who were educated in the habits and customs of a slave-holding community. What these habits are I have a right to know, both in theory and practice. Whoever has read the laws of the late slave states relating to the Negroes, will see what I mean.

I repeat, the mistake made by those who, on this ground, object to my theory of the charge against the Negro, is that they overlook the natural influence of the life education and habits of the lynchers. We must remember that these people have not now and have never had any such respect for human life as is common to other men. They have had among them for centuries a peculiar institution, and that peculiar institution has stamped them as a peculiar people. They were not before the war, they were not during the war, and have not been since the war, in their spirit or in their civilization, a people in common with the people of the North, or the civilized world. I will not here harrow up your feelings by detailing their treatment of Northern prisoners during the war. Their institutions have taught them no respect for human life, and especially the life of the Negro. It has, in fact, taught them absolute contempt for his life. The sacredness of life which ordinary men feel does not touch them anywhere. A dead Negro is with them now, as before, a common jest.

They care no more for the Negro's rights to live than they care for his rights to liberty, or his right to the ballot or any other right. Chief Justice Taney told the exact truth about these people when he said: "They did not consider that the black man had any rights which white men were bound to respect." No man of the South ever called in question that statement, and no man ever will. They could always shoot, stab, hang and burn the Negro, without any such remorse or shame as other men would feel after committing such a crime. Any Southern man, who is honest and is frank enough to talk on the subject, will tell you that he has no such idea as we have of the sacredness of human rights, and especially, as I have said, of the life of the Negro. Hence it is absurd to meet my arguments with the facts predicated of our common human nature.

I know that I shall be charged with apologising for criminals. Ex-Governor Chamberlain has already virtually done as much. But there is no foundation for such charge. I affirm that neither I nor any other coloured man of like standing with myself has ever raised a finger or uttered a word in defence of any man, black or white, known to be guilty of the dreadful crime now in question.

But what I contend for, and what every honest man, black or white, has a right to contend for, is that when any man is accused of this or any other crime, of whatever name, nature, degree or extent, he shall be confronted by his accusers; and that he shall, through proper counsel, be allowed to question his accusers in open court and in open daylight, so that his guilt or his innocence may be duly proved and established.

If this is to make me liable to the charge of apologising for crime, I am not ashamed to be so charged. I dare to contend for the coloured people of the United States that they are a law-abiding people, and I dare to insist upon it that they or any other people, black or white, accused of crime, shall have a fair trial before they are punished.

GENERAL UNFAIRNESS—THE CHICAGO EXHIBITION, ETC.

Again, I cannot dwell too much upon the fact that coloured people are much damaged by this charge. As an injured class we have a right to appeal from the judgment of the mob, to the judgment of the law and to the justice of the American people.

Full well our enemies have known where to strike and how to stab us most fatally. Owing to popular prejudice, it has become the misfortune of the coloured people of the South and of the North as well, to have, as I have said, the sins of the few visited upon the many.

When a white man steals, robs or murders, his crime is visited upon his own head alone. But not so with the black man. When he commits a crime, the whole race is made responsible. The case before us is an example. This unfairness confronts us not only here but it confronts us everywhere else.

Even when American art undertakes to picture the types of the two races, it invariably places in comparison, not the best of both races as common fairness would dictate, but it puts side by side and in glaring contrast, the lowest type of the Negro with the highest type of the white man and then calls upon the world to "look upon this picture, then upon that."

When a black man's language is quoted, in order to belittle and degrade him, his ideas are often put in the most grotesque and unreadable English, while the utterances of Negro scholars and authors are ignored. To-day, Sojourner Truth is more readily quoted than Alexander Crummell or Dr. James McCune Smith. A hundred white men will attend a concert of counterfeit Negro minstrels, with faces blackened with burnt cork, to one who will attend a lecture by an intelligent Negro.

Even the late World's Columbian Exposition was guilty of this unfairness. While I join with all other men in pronouncing the Exposition itself one of the grandest demonstrations of civilization that the world has ever seen, yet great and glorious as it was, it was made to show just this kind of injustice and discrimination against the Negro.

As nowhere in the world, it was hoped that here the idea of human brotherhood would have been grandly recognized and most gloriously illustrated. It should have been thus and would have been thus, had it been what it professed to be, a World's Exposition. It was not such, however, in its spirit at this point; it was only an American Exposition. The spirit of American caste against the educated Negro was conspicuously seen from start to finish, and to this extent the Exposition was made simply an American Exposition instead of a World's Exposition.

Since the day of Pentecost there was never assembled in any one place or on any one occasion a larger variety of peoples of all forms, features and colors and all degrees of civilization, than was assembled at this World's Exposition. It was a grand ethnological object lesson, a fine chance to study all likenesses and all differences of mankind. Here were Japanese, Soudanese, Chinese, Singalese, Syrians, Persians, Tunisians, Algerians, Egyptians, East Indians, Laplanders, Esquimaux, and, as if to shame the educated Negro of America, the Dahomeyans were there to exhibit their barbarism and increase American contempt for the Negro intellect. All classes and conditions were there save the educated American Negro. He ought to have been there, if only to show what American slavery and American freedom have done for him. The fact that all other nations were there at their best, made the Negro's exclusion the more pronounced and the more significant. People from abroad noticed the fact that while we have eight millions of colored people in the United States, many of them gentlemen and scholars, not one of them was deemed worthy to be appointed a Commissioner, or a member of an important committee, or a guide or a guard on the Exposition grounds, and this was evidently an intentional slight to the race. What a commentary is this upon the liberality of our boasted American liberty and American equality! It is a silent example, to be sure, but it is one that speaks louder than words. It says to the world that the colored people of America are not deemed by Americans as within the compass of American law, progress and civilization. It says to the lynchers and mobocrats of the South, go on in your hellish work of Negro persecution. You kill their bodies, we kill their souls.

V. NEGRO SUFFRAGE: ATTEMPT TO ABRIDGE THE RIGHT. THE LOWLY NEED ITS PROTECTION.

But now a word on the question of Negro suffrage. It has come to be fashionable of late to ascribe much of the trouble at the South to ignorant Negro suffrage. That great measure recommended by General Grant and adopted by the loyal nation, is now denounced as a blunder and a failure. The proposition now is, therefore, to find some way to abridge and limit this right by imposing upon it an educational or some other qualification. Among those who take this view of the question are Mr. John J. Ingalls and Mr. John M. Langston, one white and the other colored. They are both distinguished leaders; the one is the leader of the whites and the other is the leader of the blacks. They are both eloquent, both able, and both wrong. Though they are both Johns, neither of them is to my mind a "St. John," and not even a "John the Baptist." They have taken up an idea which they seem to think quite new, but which in reality is as old as despotism, and about as narrow and selfish as despotism. It has been heard and answered a thousand times over. It is the argument of the crowned heads and privileged classes of the world. It is as good against our Republican form of government as it is against the Negro. The wonder is that its votaries do not see its consequences. It does away with that noble and just idea of Abraham Lincoln that our government should be a government of the people, by the people and for the people and for *all* the people.

These gentlemen are very learned, very eloquent and very able, but I cannot follow them in this effort to restrict voting to the educated classes. Much learning has made them mad. Education is great but manhood is greater. The one is the principle, the other the accident. Man was not made as an attribute to education, but education as an attribute to man. I say to these gentlemen, first protect the man and you will thereby protect education. Do not make illiteracy a bar to the ballot, but make the ballot a bar to illiteracy. Take the ballot from the Negro and you take from him the means and motives that make for education. Those who are already educated and are vested with political power have thereby an advantage which they are not likely to divide with the Negro, especially when they have a fixed purpose to make this entirely a white man's government. I cannot, therefore, follow these gentlemen in a path so dangerous to the Negro. I would not make suffrage more exclusive but more inclusive. I would not have it embrace only the élite, but I would have it include the lowly. I would not only include the men, but would gladly include the women, and make our government in reality, as in name, a government by the people, of the people, and for the whole people.

But, manifestly, it is all nonsense to make suffrage to the coloured people, the cause of the failure of good government in the Southern states. On the contrary it is the lawless limitation of suffrage that makes the trouble.

Much thoughtless speech is heard about the ignorance of the Negro in the South. But plainly enough, it is not the ignorance of the Negro but the malevolence of his accusers, which is the real cause of Southern disorder. It is easy to show that the illiteracy of the Negro has no part or lot in the disturbances there. They who contend for disfranchisement on this ground, know, and know very well, that there is no truth whatever in their contention. To make out their case, they must show that some oppressive and hurtful measure has been imposed upon the country by Negro voters. But they cannot show any such thing and they know it.

The Negro has never set up a separate party, never adopted a Negro platform, never proclaimed or adopted a separate policy for himself or for the country. His assailants know this and know that he has never acted apart from the whole American people. They know that he has never sought to lead, but has always been content to follow. They know that he has not made his ignorance the rule of his political conduct, but he has been guided by the rule of white men. They know that he simply kept pace with the average intelligence of his age and country. They know that he has gone steadily along in the line of his politics with the most enlightened citizens of the country and that he has never gone faster or farther. They know that he has always voted with one or the other of the two great political parties. They know that if the votes of these parties have been guided by intelligence and patriotism, the same must be said of the vote of the Negro. Knowing all this, they ought to know also, that it is a shame and an outrage upon common sense and fair dealing to hold him or his suffrage responsible for any disorder that may reign in the Southern States. Yet while any lie may be safely told against the Negro and will be credited by popular prejudice, this lie will find eloquent tongues, bold and shameless enough to tell it.

It is true that the Negro once voted solidly for the candidates of the Republican party; but what if he did? He then only voted with John Mercer

Langston, John J. Ingalls, John Sherman, General Harrison, Senator Hoar, Henry Cabot Lodge and Governor McKinley and many of the most intelligent statesmen and noblest patriots of whom this country can boast. The charge against him at this time is, therefore, utterly groundless and is used for fraud, violence and persecution.

The proposition to disfranchise the coloured voter of the South in order to solve the race problem, I therefore denounce as a false and cowardly proposition, utterly unworthy of an honest and grateful nation. It is a proposition to sacrifice friends in order to conciliate enemies; to surrender the constitution for the lack of moral courage to execute its provisions. It is a proclamation of the helplessness of the Nation to protect its own citizens. It says to the coloured citizen, "We cannot protect you, we therefore propose to join your oppressors. Your suffrage has been rendered a failure by violence, and we now propose to make it a failure by law."

Than this, there was never a surrender more dishonorable, more ungrateful, or more cowardly. Any statesman, black or white, who dares to support such a scheme by any concession, deserves no worse punishment than to be allowed to stay at home, deprived of all legislative trusts until he repents. Even then he should only be received on probation.

DECADENCE OF THE SPIRIT OF LIBERTY.

Do not ask me what will be the final result of the so-called Negro problem. I cannot tell you. I have sometimes thought that the American people are too great to be small, too just and magnanimous to oppress the weak, too brave to yield up the right to the strong, and too grateful for public services ever to forget them or to reward them. I have fondly hoped that this estimate of American character would soon cease to be contradicted or put in doubt. But events have made me doubtful. The favour with which this proposition of disfranchisement has been received by public men, white and black, by republicans as well as democrats, has shaken my faith in the nobility of the nation. I hope and trust all will come out right in the end, but the immediate future looks dark and troubled. I cannot shut my eyes to the ugly facts before me.

Strange things have happened of late and are still happening. Some of these tend to dim the lustre of the American name, and chill the hopes once entertained for the cause of American liberty. He is a wiser man than I am who can tell how low the moral sentiment of the Republic may yet fall. When the moral sense of a nation begins to decline, and the wheels of progress to roll backward, there is no telling how low the one will fall or where the other will stop. The downward tendency, already manifest, has swept away some of the most important safeguards of justice and liberty. The Supreme Court, has, in a measure, surrendered. State sovereignty is essentially restored. The Civil Rights Bill is impaired. The Republican party is converted into a party of money, rather than a party of humanity and justice. We may well ask, what next?

The pit of hell is said to be bottomless. Principles which we all thought to have been firmly and permanently settled by the late war have been boldly assaulted and overthrown by the defeated party. Rebel rule is now nearly complete in many states, and it is gradually capturing the nation's Congress. The cause lost in the war is the cause regained in peace, and the cause gained in war is the cause lost in peace.

There was a threat made long ago by an American statesman that the whole body of legislation enacted for the protection of American liberty and to secure the results of the war for the Union, should be blotted from the national statute book. That threat is now being sternly pursued and may yet be fully realised. The repeal of the laws intended to protect the elective franchise has heightened the suspicion that Southern rule may yet become complete, though, I trust, not permanent. There is no denying that the trend is in the wrong direction at present. The late election, however, gives us hope that the loyal Republican party may yet return to its first love.

VI. DELUSIVE COLONISATION SCHEMES.

But I now come to another proposition, held up as a solution of the race problem, and this I consider equally unworthy with the one just disposed of. The two belong to the same low-bred family of ideas.

It is the proposition to colonize the coloured people of America in Africa, or somewhere else. Happily this scheme will be defeated, both by its impolicy and its impracticability. It is all nonsense to talk about the removal of eight millions of the American people from their homes in America to Africa. The expense and hardships, to say nothing of the cruelty attending such a measure, would make success impossible. The American people are wicked, but they are not fools; they will hardly be disposed to incur the expense, to say nothing of the injustice which this measure demands. Nevertheless, this colonizing scheme, unworthy as it is of American statesmanship, and American honour, and though full of mischief to the coloured people, seems to have a strong hold on the public mind, and at times has shown much life and vigor.

The bad thing about it is, that it has, of late, owing to persecution, begun to be advocated by coloured men of acknowledged ability and learning, and every little while some white statesman becomes its advocate. Those gentlemen will doubtless have their opinion of me; I certainly have mine of them. My opinion is, that if they are sensible, they are insincere; and if they are sincere, they are not sensible. They know, or they ought to know that it would take more money than the cost of the late war, to transport even one half of the coloured people of the United States to Africa. Whether intentionally or not, they are, as I think, simply trifling with an afflicted people. They urge them to look for relief where they ought to know that relief is impossible. The only excuse they can make for the measure is that there is no hope for the Negro here, and that the coloured people in America owe something to Africa.

This last sentimental idea makes colonization very fascinating to the dreamers of both colours. But there is really no foundation for it.

They tell us that we owe something to our native land. This sounds well. But when the fact is brought to view, which should never be forgotten, that a man can only have one native land and that is the land in which he is born, the bottom falls entirely out of this sentimental argument.

Africa, according to her colonization advocates, is by no means modest in her demands upon us. She calls upon us to send her only our best men. She does not want our riff-raff, but our best men. But these are just the men who are valuable and who are wanted at home. It is true that we have a few preachers and laymen with a missionary turn of mind whom we might easily spare. Some who would possibly do as much good by going there as by staying here. By this is not the colonization idea. Its advocates want not only the best, but millions of the best. Better still, they want the United States Government to vote the money to send them there. They do not seem to see that if the Government votes money to send the Negro to Africa, that the Government may employ means to complete the arrangement and compel us to go.

Now I hold that the American Negro owes no more to the Negroes in Africa than he owes to the Negroes in America. There are millions of needy people over there, but there are also millions of needy people over here as well, and the millions in America need intelligent men of their number to help them, as much as intelligent men are needed in Africa to help her people. Besides, we have a fight on our hands right here, a fight for the redemption of the whole race, and a blow struck successfully for the Negro in America, is a blow struck for the Negro in Africa. For, until the Negro is respected in America, he need not expect consideration elsewhere. All this native land talk, however, is nonsense. The native land of the American Negro is America. His bones, his muscles, his sinews, are all American. His ancestors for two hundred and seventy years have lived and laboured and died, on American soil, and millions of his posterity have inherited Caucasian blood.

It is pertinent, therefore, to ask, in view of this admixture, as well as in view of other facts, where the people of this mixed race are to go, for their ancestors are white and black, and it will be difficult to find their native land anywhere outside of the United States.

But the worst thing, perhaps, about this colonization nonsense is, that it tends to throw over the Negro a mantle of despair. It leads him to doubt the possibility of his progress as an American citizen. It also encourages popular prejudice with the hope that by persecution or by persuasion the Negro can finally be dislodged and driven from his natural home, while in the nature of the case he must stay here and will stay here, if for no other reason than because he cannot well get away.

I object to the colonization scheme, because it tends to weaken the Negro's hold on one country, while it can give him no rational hope of another. Its tendency is to make him despondent and doubtful, where he should feel assured and confident. It forces upon him the idea that he is forever doomed to be a stranger and a sojourner in the land of his birth, and that he has no permanent abiding place here.

All this is hurtful; with such ideas constantly flaunted before him, he cannot easily set himself to work to better his condition in such ways as are open to him here. It sets him to groping everlastingly after the impossible.

Every man who thinks at all, must know that home is the fountain head, the inspiration, the foundation and main support, not only of all social virtue but of all motives to human progress, and that no people can prosper, or amount to much, unless they have a home, or the hope of a home. A man who has not such an object, either in possession or in prospect, is a nobody and will never be anything else. To have a home, the Negro must have a country, and he is an enemy to the moral progress of the Negro, whether he knows it or not, who calls upon him to break up his home in this country, for an uncertain home in Africa.

But the agitation on this subject has a darker side still. It has already been given out that if we do not go of our own accord, we may be forced to go, at the point of the bayonet. I cannot say that we shall not have to face this hardship, but badly as I think of the tendency of our times, I do not think that American sentiment will ever reach a condition which will make the expulsion of the Negro from the United States by any such means, possible.

Yet, the way to make it possible is to predict it. There are people in the world who know how to bring their own prophecies to pass. The best way to get up a mob, is to say there will be one, and this is what is being done. Colonization is no solution, but an evasion. It is not repentance but putting the wronged ones out of our presence. It is not atonement, but banishment. It is not love, but hate. Its reiteration and agitation only serves to fan the flame of popular prejudice and to add insult to injury.

The righteous judgment of mankind will say if the American people could endure the Negro's presence while a slave, they certainly can and ought to endure his presence as a free man.

If they could tolerate him when he was a heathen, they might bear with him now that he is a Christian. If they could bear with him when ignorant and degraded, they should bear with him now that he is a gentleman and a scholar.

But even the Southern whites have an interest in this question. Woe to the South when it no longer has the strong arm of the Negro to till its soil, "and woe to the nation when it shall employ the sword to drive the Negro from his native land."

Such a crime against justice, such a crime against gratitude, should it ever be attempted, would certainly bring a national punishment which would cause the earth to shudder. It would bring a stain upon the nation's honor, like the blood on Lady Macbeth's hand. The waters of all the oceans would not suffice to wash out the infamy. But the nation will commit no such crime. But in regard to this point of our future, my mind is easy. We are here and are here to stay. It is well for us and well for the American people to rest upon this as final.

EMANCIPATION CRIPPLED. LANDLORD AND TENANT

Another mode of impeaching the wisdom of emancipation, and the one which seems to give special pleasure to our enemies, is, as they say, that the condition of the colored people of the South has been made worse by emancipation.

The champions of this idea are the only men who glory in the good old times when the slaves were under the lash and were bought and sold in the market with horses, sheep, and swine. It is another way of saying that slavery is better than freedom; that darkness is better than light, and that wrong is better than right; that hell is better than heaven! It is the American method of reasoning in all matters concerning the Negro. It inverts everything; turns truth upside down, and puts the case of the unfortunate Negro inside out and wrong end foremost every time. There is, however, nearly always some truth on their side of error, and it is so in this case.

When these false reasoners assert that the condition of the emancipated slave is wretched and deplorable, they partly tell the truth, and I agree with them. I even concur with them in the statement that the Negro is physically, in certain localities, in a worse condition to-day than in the time of slavery, but I part with these gentlemen when they ascribe this condition to emancipation.

To my mind the blame does not rest upon emancipation, but the defeat of emancipation. It is not the work of the spirit of liberty, but the work of the spirit of bondage. It comes of the determination of slavery to perpetuate itself, if not under one form, then under another. It is due to the folly of endeavoring to put the new wine of liberty in the old bottles of slavery. I concede the evil, but deny the alleged cause.

The landowners of the South want the labor of the Negro on the hardest terms possible. They once had it for nothing. They now want it for next to nothing. To accomplish this, they have contrived three ways. The first is, to rent their land to the Negro at an exorbitant price per annum and compel him to mortgage his crop in advance to pay this rent. The laws under which this is done are entirely in the interest of the landlord. He has a first claim upon everything produced on the land. The Negro can have nothing, can keep nothing, can sell nothing, without the consent of the landlord. As the Negro is at the start poor and empty-handed, he has had to draw on the landlord for meat and bread to feed himself and family while his crop is growing. The landlord keeps books; the Negro does not; hence, no matter how hard he may work or how hard saving he may be, he is, in most cases, brought in debt at the end of the year, and once in debt he is fastened to the land as by hooks of steel. If he attempts to leave he may be arrested under the order of the law.

Another way, which is still more effective, is the practice of paying the laborer with orders on the store instead of lawful money. By this means money is kept out of the hands of the Negro, and the Negro is kept entirely in the hands of the landlord. He cannot save money because he gets no money to save. He cannot seek a better market for his labor because he has no money with which to pay his fare, and because he is, by that vicious order system, already in debt, and therefore already in bondage. Thus he is riveted to one place, and is, in some sense, a slave; for a man to whom it can be said, "You shall work for me for what I choose to pay you, and how I shall choose to pay you," is, in fact, a slave, though he may be called a free man.

We denounce the landlord and tenant system of England, but it can be said of England as cannot be said of our free country, that by law no laborer can be paid for labor in any other than lawful money. England holds any other payment to be a penal offence and punishable by fine and imprisonment. The same should be the case in every State in the American Union.

Under the mortgage system, no matter how industrious or economical the Negro may be, he finds himself at the end of the year in debt to the landlord, and from year to year he toils on and is tempted to try again and again, but seldom with any better result.

With this power over the Negro, this possession of his labor, you may easily see why the South sometimes makes a display of its liberality and brags that it does not want slavery back. It had the Negro's labor, heretofore for nothing, and now it has it for next to nothing and at the same time is freed from the obligation to take care of the young and the aged, the sick and the decrepit. There is not much virtue in all this, yet it is the ground of loud boasting.

ATTITUDE OF WHITE RACE TOWARDS NEGROES. A NATIONAL PROBLEM

I now come to the so-called, but mis-called "Negro problem," as a characterization of the relations existing in the Southern States.

I say at once, I do not admit the justice or propriety of this formula, as applied to the question before us. Words are things. They are certainly such in this case, since they give us a misnomer that is misleading and hence mischievous. It is a formula of Southern origin and has a strong bias against the Negro. It handicaps his cause with all the prejudice known to exist and anything to which he is a party. It has been accepted by the good people of the North, as I think, without proper thought and investigation. It is a crafty invention and is in every way worthy of its inventors.

It springs out of a desire to throw off just responsibility and to evade the performance of disagreeable but manifest duty. Its natural effect and purpose is to divert attention from the true issue now before the American people. It does this by holding up and pre-occupying the public mind with an issue entirely different from the real one in question. That which is really a great national problem and which ought to be so considered by the whole American people, dwarfs into a "Negro Problem." The device is not new. It is an old trick. It has been oft repeated and with a similar purpose and effect. For truth, it gives us falsehood. For innocence, it gives us guilt. It removes the burden of proof from the old master class and imposes it upon the Negro. It puts upon the race a work which belongs to the nation. It belongs to that craftiness often displayed by disputants who aim to make the worse appear the better reason. It gives bad names to good things and good names to bad things.

The Negro has often been the victim to this kind of low cunning. You may remember that during the late war, when the South fought for the perpetuity of slavery, it usually called the slaves "domestic servants," and slavery a "domestic institution." Harmless names, indeed, but the things they stood for were far from harmless.

The South has always known how to have a dog hanged by giving him a bad name. When it prefixed "Negro" to the national problem, it knew that the device would awaken and increase a deep-seated prejudice at once and that it would repel fair and candid investigation. As it stands, it implies that the Negro is the cause of whatever trouble there is in the South. In old slave times, when a little white child lost his temper, he was given a little whip and told to go and whip "Jim" or "Sal," and he thus regained his temper. The same is true to-day on a large scale.

I repeat, and my contention is that this Negro problem formula lays the fault at the door of the Negro and removes it from the door of the white man, shields the guilty and blames the innocent, makes the Negro responsible, when it should so make the nation.

Now what the real problem is, we all ought to know. It is not a Negro problem, but in every sense a great national problem. It involves the question, whether after all our boasted civilization, our Declaration of Independence, our matchless Constitution, our sublime Christianity, our wise statesmanship, we as a people, possess virtue enough to solve this problem in accordance with wisdom and justice, and to the advantage of both races.

The marvel is that this old trick of misnaming things, so often displayed by Southern politicians, should have worked so well for the bad cause in which it is now employed; for the American people have fallen in with the bad idea that this is a Negro problem, a question of the character of the Negro and not a question of the nation. It is still more surprising that the colored press of the country, and some of our colored orators, have made the same mistake, and still insist upon calling it a "Negro problem," or a race problem, for by race they mean the Negro race. (Now, there is nothing the matter with the Negro, whatever; he is all right. Learned or ignorant, he is all right. He is neither a lyncher, a mobocrat or an anarchist. He is now what he has ever been, a loyal, law-abiding, hard working and peaceable man; so much so that men have thought him cowardly and spiritless.) Had he been a turbulent anarchist he might indeed have been a troublesome problem, but he is not. To his reproach, it is sometimes said that any other people in the world would have invented some violent way in which to resent their wrongs. If this problem depended upon the character and conduct of the Negro there would be no problem to solve; there would be no menace to the peace and order of Southern Society. He makes no unlawful fight between labor and capital. That problem, which often makes the American people thoughtful, is not of his bringing, though he may some day be compelled to talk of this tremendous problem in common with other laborers.

He has as little to do with the cause of the Southern trouble as he has with its cure. There is no reason, therefore, in the world, why his name should be given to this problem. It is false, misleading and prejudicial, and like all other falsehoods, must eventually come to naught.

I well remember, as others may remember, that this same old falsehood was employed and used against the Negro during the late war. He was then charged and stigmatized with being the cause of the war, on the principle that there would be no highway robbers if there were nobody on the road to be robbed. But as absurd as this pretence was, the color prejudice of the country was stimulated by it and joined in the accusation, and the Negro had to bear the brunt of it.

Even at the North he was hated and hunted on account of it. In the great city of New York his houses were burned, his children were hunted down like wild beasts, and his people were murdered in the streets, all because "they were the cause of the war." Even the good and noble Mr. Lincoln, one of the best and most clear-sighted men that ever lived, once told a committee of Negroes, who waited upon him at Washington, that "they were the cause of the war."

Many were the men who, in their wrath and hate, accepted this theory, and wished the Negro in Africa, or in a hotter climate, as some do now.

There is nothing to which prejudice is not equal in the way of perverting the truth and inflaming the passions of men.

But call this problem what you may or will, the all-important question is: How can it be solved? How can the peace and tranquility of the South and the country be secured and established?

There is nothing occult or mysterious about the answer to this question. Some things are to be kept in the mind when dealing with this subject and should never be forgotten. It should be remembered that, in the order of Divine Providence, the "man, who puts one end of a chain around the ankle of his fellow man, will find the other end around his own neck." And it is the same with a nation. Confirmation of this truth is as strong as proofs of holy writ. As we sow we shall reap, is a lesson that will be learned here as elsewhere. We tolerated slavery and it has cost us a million graves, and it may be that lawless murder now raging, if permitted to go on, may yet bring the red hand of vengeance, not only on the reverend head of age, and upon the heads of helpless women, but upon even the innocent babes in the cradle.

VII. HOW THE PROBLEM IS SOLVED

But how can this problem be solved? I will tell you how it cannot be solved. It cannot be solved by keeping the Negro poor, degraded, ignorant and half-starved, as I have shown is now being done in Southern States.

It cannot be solved by keeping back the wages of the laborer by fraud, as is now being done by the landlords of the South. It cannot be done by ballot-box stuffing, by falsifying election returns, or by confusing the Negro voter by cunning devices. It cannot be done by repealing all federal laws enacted to secure honest elections. It can, however, be done, and very easily done, for where there is a will there is a way.

Let the white people of the North and South conquer their prejudices.

Let the Northern press and pulpit proclaim the gospel of truth and justice against the war now being made upon the Negro.

Let the American people cultivate kindness and humanity.

Let the South abandon the system of mortgage labor and cease to make the Negro a pauper, by paying him dishonest scrip for his honest labor.

Let them give up the idea that they can be free while making the Negro a slave. Let them give up the idea that to degrade the colored man is to elevate the white man. Let them cease putting new wine into old bottles, and mending old garments with new cloth.

They are not required to do much. They are only required to undo the evil they have done, in order to solve this problem.

In old times when it was asked, "How can we abolish slavery?" the answer was "Quit stealing."

The same is the solution of the race problem to-day. The whole thing can be done simply by no longer violating the amendment of the Constitution of the United States, and no longer evading the claims of justice. If this were done, there would be no Negro problem or national problem to vex the South or to vex the nation.

Let the organic law of the land be honestly sustained and obeyed. Let the political parties cease to palter in a double sense, and live up to the noble declarations we find in their platforms. Let the statesmen of our country live up to their convictions. In the language of ex-Senator Ingalls: "Let the nation try justice and the problem will be solved."

Two hundred and twenty years ago the Negro was made a religious problem, one which gave our white forefathers about as much perplexity and annoyance as we now profess. At that time the problem was in respect of what relation a Negro sustains to the Christian Church, whether he was in fact a fit subject for baptism, and Dr. Godwin, a celebrated divine of his time, and one far in advance of his brethren, was at the pains of writing a book of two hundred pages or more, containing an elaborate argument to prove that it was not a sin in the sight of God to baptize a Negro.

His argument was very able, very learned, very long. Plain as the truth may seem, there were at that time very strong arguments against the position of the learned divine.

As usual, it was not merely the baptism of the Negro that gave trouble, but it was as to what might follow such baptism. The sprinkling him with water was a very simple thing and easily gotten along with, but the slaveholders of that day saw in the innovation something more dangerous than cold water. They said that to baptize the Negro and make him a member of the Church of Christ was to make him an important person—in fact, to make him an heir of Jesus Christ. It was to give him a place at the Lord's supper. It was to take him out of the category of heathenism and make it inconsistent to hold him a slave, for the Bible made only the heathen a proper subject for slavery.

These were formidable consequences, certainly, and it is not strange that the Christian slaveholders of that day viewed these consequences with immeasurable horror. It was something more terrible and dangerous than the Civil Rights Bill and the Fourteenth and Fifteenth Amendments to our Constitution. It was a difficult thing, therefore, at that day to get the Negro into water.

Nevertheless, our learned doctor of divinity, like many of the same class in our day, was equal to the emergency. He was able to satisfy all important parties to the problem, except the Negro, and him it did not seem necessary to satisfy.

The doctor was a skilled dialectician. He could not only divide the word with skill, but he could divide the Negro into two parts. He argued that the Negro had a soul as well as a body, and insisted that while his body rightfully belonged to his master on earth, his soul belonged to his Master in heaven. By this convenient arrangement, somewhat metaphysical, to be sure, but entirely evangelical and logical, the problem of Negro baptism was solved.

But with the Negro in the case, as I have said, the argument was not entirely satisfactory. The operation was much like that by which the white man got the turkey and the Indian got the crow. When the Negro looked for his body, that belonged to his earthly master; when he looked around for his soul, that had been appropriated by his heavenly Master; and when he looked around for something that really belonged to himself, he found nothing but his shadow, and that vanished into the air, when he might most want it.

One thing, however, is to be noticed with satisfaction; it is this: something was gained to the cause of righteousness by this argument. It was a contribution to the cause of liberty. It was largely in favour of the Negro. It was a plain recognition of his manhood, and was calculated to set men to thinking that the Negro might have some other important rights, no less than the religious right to baptism.

Thus, with all its faults we are compelled to give the pulpit the credit of furnishing the first important argument in favour of the religious character and manhood rights of the Negro.

Dr. Godwin was undoubtedly a good man. He wrote at a time of much moral darkness, and when property in man was nearly everywhere recognised as a rightful institution. He saw only a part of the truth. He saw that the Negro had a right to be baptized, but he could not all at once see that he had a primary and paramount right to himself.

But this was not the only problem slavery had in store for the Negro. Time and events brought another and it was this very important one: Can the Negro sustain the legal relation of a husband to a wife? Can he make a valid marriage contract in this Christian country?

This problem was solved by the same slaveholding authority, entirely against the Negro. Such a contract, it was argued, could only be binding upon men providentially enjoying the right to life, liberty, and the pursuit of happiness, and since the Negro is a slave and slavery a divine institution, legal marriage was wholly inconsistent with the institution of slavery.

When some of us at the North questioned the ethics of this conclusion, we were told to mind our business, and our Southern brethren asserted, as they assert now, that they alone are competent to manage this and all other questions relating to the Negro. In fact, there has been no end to the problems of some sort or other, involving the Negro in difficulty.

Can the Negro be a citizen? was the question of the Dred Scott decision. Can the Negro be educated? Can the Negro be induced to work for himself without a master? Can the Negro be a soldier? Time and events have answered these and all other like questions. We have among us Negroes who have taken the first prizes as scholars; those who have won distinction for courage and skill on the battle field; those who have taken rank as lawyers, doctors and ministers of the gospel; those who shine among men in every useful calling; and yet we are called a problem—a tremendous problem; a mountain of difficulty; a constant source of apprehension; a disturbing social force, threatening destruction to the holiest and best interests of society. I declare this statement concerning the Negro, whether by good Miss Willard, Bishop Haygood, Bishop Fitzgerald, ex-Governor

Chamberlain, or by any and all others, as false and deeply injurious to the colored citizens of the United States.

But, my friends, I must stop. Time and strength are not equal to the task before me. But could I be heard by this great nation, I would call to mind the sublime and glorious truths with which, at its birth, it saluted and started a listening world. Its voice, then, was as the trump of an archangel, summoning hoary forms of oppression and time honored tyranny, to judgment. Crowned heads heard it and shrieked. Toiling millions heard it and clapped their hands for joy. It announced the advent of a nation, based upon human brotherhood and the self-evident truths of liberty and equality. Its mission was the redemption of the world from the bondage of ages. Apply these sublime and glorious truths to the situation now before you. Put away your race prejudice. Banish the idea that one class must rule over another. Recognize the fact that the rights of the humblest citizens are as worthy of protection as are those of the highest and your problem will be solved, and—whatever may be in store for you in the future, whether prosperity or adversity, whether you have foes without or foes within, whether there shall be peace or war—based upon the eternal principles of truth, justice and humanity, with no class having cause for complaint or grievance, your Republic will stand and flourish forever.

Frederick Douglass, *The Lesson of the Hour,* pamphlet, 1894. Copy in Library of Congress

1. William V. Tunnell to Douglass, Dec. 22, 1893; H. D. Wagoner to Douglass, Mar. 15, 1894, Frederick Douglass Papers, Frederick Douglass Memorial Home, Anacostia, D.C.

2. For a study of Frances Willard, temperance leader and president of the Woman's Christian Temperance Union, see Mary Earhart, *Frances Willard: From Prayers to Politics,* Chicago, 1944.

3. See Stephen B. Weeks, *The History of Negro Suffrage in the South,* Boston, 1894.

as an anti-slavery document, 170–73,
173–74, 203–4, 265–67, 326,
352–54, 355–57, 379–90, 437, 536,
578, 672
protections for slavery, 56–57, 84–85,
109–10, 127–28, 129–33, 137–40,
203, 354–55
U.S. Supreme Court, 347–48, 353,
386–87, 500, 685–93, 720

V
"Valedictory," 543–46
Vallandigham, Clement L., 557, 647, 648
Van Buren, Martin, 122, 123, 209, 265,
409
Van Rensselaer, Thomas, 83–85
Vashon, George Boyer, 219, 271, 584
Vashon, John B., 260
Vesey, Denmark, 527
Vigilance Committee of New York, 162
Volney, Constantin de, 289, 291

W
Wade, Benjamin F., 666, 678
Wagoner, H. O., 271
Walker, Albert H., 685
Walker, David, 662
Walker, James, 379–80
Walker, Jonathan, 318
Walker, Robert John, 10
"War and How to End It, The," 486–93
"War and Slavery, The," 463–68
Ward, Samuel R., 290, 652
Warner, H. G., 134–37
Warren, E. R., 183–84
Washington, George, 193–94, 314, 356,
385
Washington, Lewis, 640
Washington, Madison, 71–72, 219–47,
367
Washington Chronicle, 586–90
Washington National Leader, 725–40
Washington National Republican,
711–24
Webb, James H., 14
Webb, Richard D., 14
Webster, Daniel, 71–72, 160, 165, 185,
302, 312, 347, 393–94, 437, 525,
615, 649
Weed, Thurlow, 612
Weeks, Stephen B., 756
Wesley, John, 311, 318, 321, 662, 741
"West India Emancipation," 358–69
West Indies
emancipation of slaves in, 93–94,

103–4, 108, 110–11, 286–87,
358–64, 368, 401–3
slavery in, 61–62
Weston, Warren and Anne Bates, 19
"What of the Night?," 97–99
"What Shall Be Done with the Slaves If
Emancipated?," 470–73
Whig Party, 183–84, 212, 254, 303
Whipper, William, 586–90
White, J. B., 712
Whitfield, James M., 219, 271, 290
Whitson, Thomas, 654
Whittier, John Greenleaf, 329, 726
"Why Is the Negro Lynched?," 750–76
"Why Should a Colored Man Enlist?,"
528–31
Wilberforce, William, 318, 368, 384, 404,
472, 480
Willard, Frances, 754
Williams, George Washington, 666
Wilson, Henry, 493, 551, 655, 665, 666,
705
Wilson, W. J., 290
Wise, Henry A., 373, 378, 459, 636, 640,
648
Witherspoon, S. F., 183–84
Woldfolk, Austin, 198
Woman's Journal, 706–11
Woman's Rights Convention, 101–3
"Woman's Suffrage Movement, The,"
706–11
women
as abolitionists, 101, 360
alleged attacks of black men on, 743,
749, 752–61
suffrage for, 101–3, 598–600,
706–11
Women's Loyal League, 553
women's rights, 323–24
and the anti-slavery movement, 323–24
first convention on, 101–3
National Negro Convention resolution
on, 117
Woodson, Carter G., 695–96
Woolman, John, 318
Words of Francis J. Grimké, The, 695–96
"Word 'White,' The," 275
"Work of the Future, The," 521–23
World's Columbian Exposition, 740–46,
756, 763–64
World Temperance Convention, 40–48,
79–81
Wright, Elizur, 318
Wright, Henry C., 26, 49–54
Wright, Silas, 393–94

The Library of Black America publishes authoritative editions of important African American writing, much of it otherwise unavailable, ranging from the earliest slave narratives to the present day. Each volume includes a selection of works either by a single author or in a single genre. The series makes accessible to all readers the impressive body of inventive, lucid, thoughtful, and passionate work that is the black contribution to American literature.